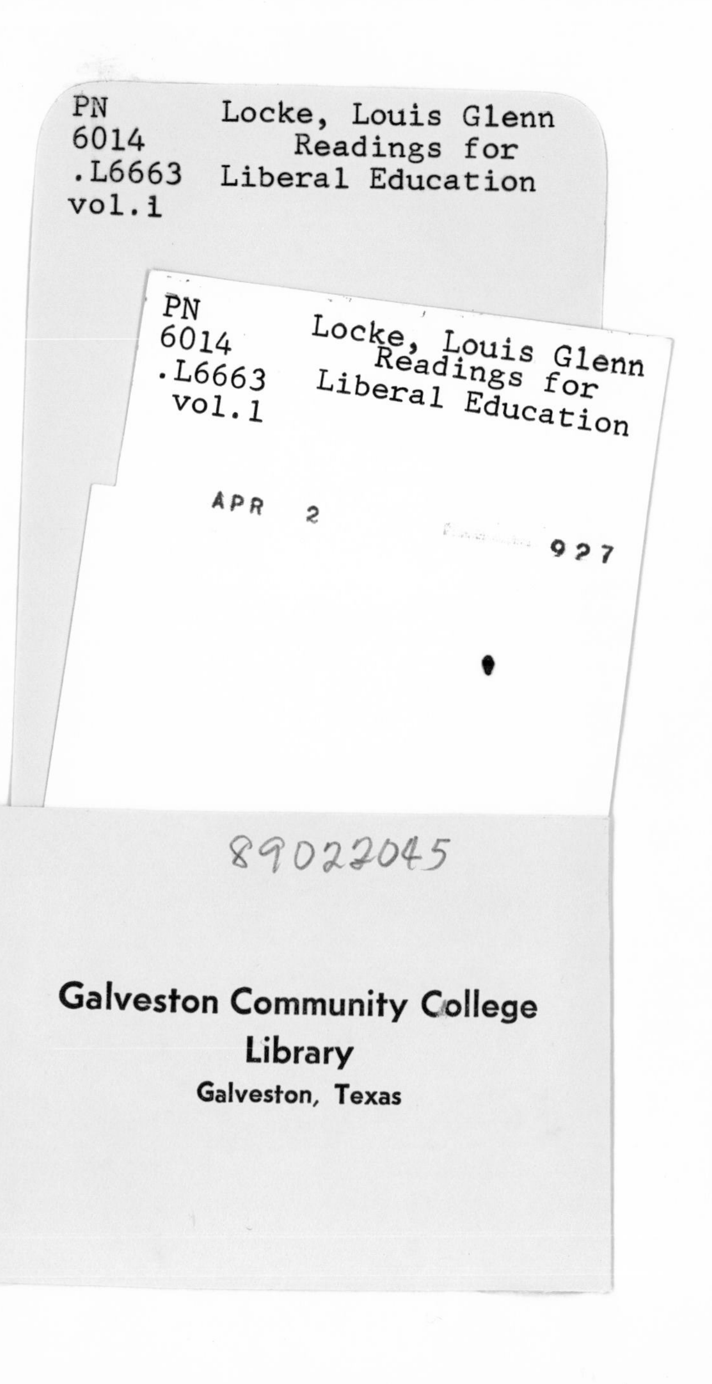
PN
6014
.L6663
vol.1
Locke, Louis Glenn
Readings for
Liberal Education
PN
6014
.L6663
vol.1
Locke, Louis Glenn
Readings for
Liberal Education
APR 2
927
89022045
Galveston Community College
Library
Galveston, Texas

TOWARD LIBERAL EDUCATION

". . . Some will then be chosen for higher privilege. The studies which they pursued without order in their early years will now be brought together, and the students will see the relationship of these studies to one another and to truth."

"Yes," he said. "That is the only kind of knowledge which takes lasting root."

PLATO, *The Republic*

READINGS FOR LIBERAL EDUCATION

I. Toward Liberal Education

II. Introduction to Literature

Edited by

LOUIS G. LOCKE

Madison College

WILLIAM M. GIBSON

New York University

GEORGE ARMS

The University of New Mexico

TOWARD LIBERAL EDUCATION

FIFTH EDITION

HOLT, RINEHART AND WINSTON

NEW YORK CHICAGO SAN FRANCISCO TORONTO

Library of Congress Catalog Card Number: 67-11844

2617058

Printed in the United States of America

PREFACE

The idea for this book began some years ago when we were thinking and reading and arguing with our colleagues about liberal education in America. Our constant purpose has been to make an anthology that would help college students understand what liberal education can mean to them.

As it seemed to us, the reading provided in most freshman courses went a good way toward realizing this purpose. But the effort was often partial and sometimes fitful. The principal differences between *Toward Liberal Education* and earlier collections of readings are those of development rather than of radical change. First, this collection points steadily in the direction indicated by its title. Without deviating into models at one time or mere entertainment at another, it seeks systematically to explore the skills and disciplines of our humanistic culture. Second, it makes this exploration by the use of writing chosen for its intrinsic worth. It does not talk down to its readers.

In this volume, *Toward Liberal Education,* the first three parts are concerned with the skills of a liberal education: learning, reading and writing, and thinking. The four parts that follow these represent the great areas of liberal learning: the arts, science, society, and philosophy and religion. The second volume, *Introduction to Literature,* turns to that discipline which is particularly cherished by teachers of English: literature of the imagination.

The development of all these parts aims at presenting the material to the student with force and meaning. In arranging the parts in their present order, we thus feel that we have provided a sound framework for a course which uses the anthology. Yet we recognize that each school and each teacher may properly wish to rearrange the order of our materials for special needs. As in earlier editions, we have provided teachers with a wide range of material with the expectation that few will want to assign everything, but with confidence that such abundance of readings provides a latitude of choice which gives individuality and richness to the course.

We have chosen writing that bears the stamp of permanent value. This standard has not meant that we stayed in the past. But it has meant the exclusion of superficial journalizing and a disregard for the timeliness of yesterday's newspaper. College students, we believe, not only are capable of hard, solid reading, but are happier when they are expected to do it. Such reading is not dull, as we hope this book demonstrates; for certainly not wisdom alone, but the sweetness and joy of wisdom as well, determines a classic.

The Fifth Edition keeps the same approach and quality of readings that have characterized the earlier editions, enhanced by the expert advice and helpful interest of the advisory editors who are named in earlier pages. In this edition we are not repeating acknowledgment to the many colleagues and friends who have helped us in previous editions, since the list has grown long. However, we recognize our indebtedness to these people, whose influence still pervades the present book.

Besides the advisory editors, for this edition we are specifically indebted to the following for help in solving special problems: Fletcher Collins, Jr., Jay L. Curtis, Mary Campbell Brill, and Elmer L. Smith; Genevieve R. Porterfield and Dorothy A. Wonsmos, librarians at the University of New Mexico; and Forest Palmer and the staff of Madison Memorial Library; Patrica Spitzer for secretarial aid; George Reinhardt III, photo laboratory technician, for assistance in securing and copying materials; and Kenney Withers, English editor, and Jane Ross, assistant to the editor, of Holt, Rinehart and Winston, who have given us invaluable help and encouragement.

L.G.L.
W.M.G.
G.A.

January 1967

CONTENTS

vii *Preface*

I. LEARNING

The Campus

1 University Days
JAMES THURBER

5 Where Is the College Generation Headed?
DAVID RIESMAN

16 Postscript, 1965
DAVID RIESMAN

19 How Agassiz Taught Shaler
NATHANIEL SOUTHGATE SHALER

22 Kittredge of Harvard
ROLLO WALTER BROWN

32 The Student Movement: Some Impressions at Berkeley
HENRY F. MAY

42 For Want of a Teacher
ART BUCHWALD

Education

44 The Marks of an Educated Man
ALAN SIMPSON

49 Trained Intelligence—The Nation's Greatest Weapon
ADLAI E. STEVENSON

56 The Meaning and Significance of Academic Freedom
ROBERT M. HUTCHINS

64 Introductory Lecture
A. E. HOUSMAN

II. READING AND WRITING

Reading

68 Of Studies
FRANCIS BACON

69 The Private World of the Man with a Book
HAROLD TAYLOR

75 Reading
HENRY DAVID THOREAU

81 Mr. K*a*p*l*a*n and Shakespeare
LEONARD Q. ROSS

86 On Misreading by the Literary
C. S. LEWIS

92 The Reading Machine
MORRIS BISHOP

Writer to Reader

95 From the *Autobiography of Benjamin Franklin*
BENJAMIN FRANKLIN

97 From "Burnt Norton"
T. S. ELIOT

98 In My Craft or Sullen Art
DYLAN THOMAS

99 From an Interview
ERNEST HEMINGWAY

Writing

100 What is Style?
F. L. LUCAS

107 Transformational Grammar
PAUL ROBERTS

113 Laments for a Dying Language
OGDEN NASH

115 The Cliché Expert Reveals Himself in His True Colors
FRANK SULLIVAN

118 The American Language
H. L. MENCKEN

125 Politics and the English Language
GEORGE ORWELL

135 The Revival of Rhetoric
WAYNE C. BOOTH

III. THINKING

144 The Emancipation of Thought from Myth
H. AND H. A. FRANKFORT

154 The Unpredictable Intellect
GILBERT HIGHET

163 Injelititis, or Palsied Paralysis
C. NORTHCOTE PARKINSON

169 That Candles May Be Brought
ROBERT M. HUTCHINS

173 Language and Thought
SUSANNE K. LANGER

177 [A Thinker: Wittgenstein]
VED MEHTA

185 Do Computers Think?
HUBERT L. DREYFUS

193 Logical Fallacies
ROBERT GORHAM DAVIS

201 Idols of the Mind
FRANCIS BACON

IV. THE ARTS

The Fine Arts

210 The Cultural Importance of the Arts
SUSANNE K. LANGER

218 The Case for Abstract Art
CLEMENT GREENBERG

225 *Et in Arcadia ego:* Poussin and the Elegiac Tradition
ERWIN PANOFSKY

243 Modern Architecture: The Cardboard House
FRANK LLOYD WRIGHT

253 How We Listen
AARON COPLAND

258 Cultural Snobbery
ARTHUR KOESTLER

Literature and Criticism

264 The Main Trends of Twentieth-Century Criticism
RENÉ WELLEK

277 The Naked Babe and the Cloak of Manliness
CLEANTH BROOKS

290 The Structure of *Macbeth*
R. S. CRANE

295 *Macbeth* as the Imitation of an Action
FRANCIS FERGUSSON

301 Aristotle
WALTER JACKSON BATE

307 Poetics
ARISTOTLE

332 Art and Neurosis
LIONEL TRILLING

346 A Lesson Read in American Books
ROBERT PENN WARREN

349 On Teaching the Appreciation of Poetry
T. S. ELIOT

V. SCIENCE

The Nature of Science

358 How to Make Our Ideas Clear
CHARLES PEIRCE

Physical Science

375 The Evolution of the Physical World
ARTHUR STANLEY EDDINGTON

378 Newton the Man
JOHN MAYNARD KEYNES

385 On Albert Einstein
ROBERT OPPENHEIMER

390 Man's Fourth Adjustment
HARLOW SHAPLEY

Biological Science

394 Of the Quantity of Blood Passing through the Heart
WILLIAM HARVEY

396 Chlorophyll: The Sun Trap
DONALD CULROSS PEATTIE

401 Carbon Monoxide Poisoning
CLAUDE BERNARD

404 The Language of Life
GEORGE AND MURIEL BEADLE

VI. SOCIETY

Sociology

419 A Changing American Character?
SEYMOUR M. LIPSET

450 The Formation of Character
DAVID RIESMAN

471 Review of Riesman's *The Lonely Crowd*
LIONEL TRILLING

476 Modernity and Mass Society
DANIEL BELL

491 The Changing Place of Women in America
CARL N. DEGLER

506 Crime in America
WILLIAM M. MC CORD

513 300,000,000 Americans Would Be Wrong
DAVID E. LILIENTHAL

519 The Two Worlds of Race
JOHN HOPE FRANKLIN

Political Philosophy

538 The American Crisis, I
THOMAS PAINE

544 Declaration of Independence
THOMAS JEFFERSON

547 The Bill of Rights

548 On the Duty of Civil Disobedience
HENRY DAVID THOREAU

564 Walden—1954
E. B. WHITE

571 A Plea for the Freedom of Dissent
LEARNED HAND

Social Analysis

576 The Anatomy of the Mental Personality
SIGMUND FREUD

591 The Apology of Socrates
PLATO

612 The Funeral Oration of Pericles
THUCYDIDES

618 A Modest Proposal
JONATHAN SWIFT

VII. PHILOSOPHY AND RELIGION

The Good Life

625 Virtue
ARISTOTLE

632 The Sermon on the Mount
ST. MATTHEW

636 The Stoic Code
MARCUS AURELIUS

640 The Sermon at Benares
GAUTAMA BUDDHA

Religion

646 The Strength and Glory of Man
PSALM 8

646 The Folly of Man
PSALM 53

647 The Providence of God
PSALM 23 AND 90

648 The Upanishads: Svetasvatara
ANONYMOUS

657 The Confessions
ST. AUGUSTINE

659 Meditation XVII
JOHN DONNE

660 In His Will Is Our Peace
JOHN WOOLMAN

661 God Is Dead
FRIEDRICH NIETZSCHE

666 God and the Spirit of Man
MARTIN BUBER

670 Confession of Faith
JACQUES MARITAIN

680 Letters from Prison
DIETRICH BONHOEFFER

688 *Pacem in Terris* (April 10, 1963)
POPE JOHN XXIII

The Nature of Reality

697 The Allegory of the Cave
PLATO

700 A Discourse on Method
RENÉ DESCARTES

707 An Essay Concerning Human Understanding
JOHN LOCKE

710 What Pragmatism Is
WILLIAM JAMES

716 Existentialism as a Symptom of Man's Contemporary Crisis
WILLIAM C. BARRETT

Can Philosophy Save Civilization?

727 The Value of Philosophy
BERTRAND RUSSELL

731 The Present Human Condition
ERICH FROMM

737 *Biographical Notes*

747 *Index*

CONTENTS

ARRANGED BY RHETORICAL TYPES

Exposition

19 How Agassiz Taught Shaler
NATHANIEL SOUTHGATE SHALER

100 What Is Style?
F. L. LUCAS

118 The American Language
H. L. MENCKEN

154 The Unpredictable Intellect
GILBERT HIGHET

173 Language and Thought
SUSANNE K. LANGER

243 Modern Architecture: The Cardboard House
FRANK LLOYD WRIGHT

349 On Teaching the Appreciation of Poetry
T. S. ELIOT

358 How to Make Our Ideas Clear
CHARLES PEIRCE

450 The Formation of Character
DAVID RIESMAN

471 Review of Riesman's *The Lonely Crowd*
LIONEL TRILLING

700 A Discourse on Method
RENÉ DESCARTES

Exposition: Meditation

636 The Stoic Code
MARCUS AURELIUS

646 The Strength and Glory of God
PSALM 8

646 The Folly of Man
PSALM 53

647 The Providence of God
PSALMS 23 and 90

657 Confessions
ST. AUGUSTINE

659 Meditation XVII
JOHN DONNE

660 In His Will Is Our Peace
JOHN WOOLMAN

680 Letters from Prison
DIETRICH BONHOEFFER

Description

68 Of Studies
FRANCIS BACON

253 How We Listen
AARON COPLAND

Process

394 Of the Quantity of Blood Passing through the Heart
WILLIAM HARVEY

396 Chlorophyll: The Sun Trap
DONALD CULROSS PEATTIE

404 The Language of Life
GEORGE AND MURIEL BEADLE

Cause and Effect

99 From An Interview
ERNEST HEMINGWAY

332 Art and Neurosis
LIONEL TRILLING

401 Carbon Monoxide Poisoning
CLAUDE BERNARD

506 Crime in America
WILLIAM M. MC CORD

707 An Essay Concerning Human Understanding
JOHN LOCKE

716 Existentialism as a Symptom of Man's Contemporary Crisis
WILLIAM BARRETT

731 The Present Human Condition
ERICH FROMM

Comparison and Contrast

218 The Case for Abstract Art
CLEMENT GREENBERG

666 God and the Spirit of Man
MARTIN BUBER

Analogy

277 The Naked Babe and The Cloak of Manliness
CLEANTH BROOKS

697 The Allegory of the Cave
PLATO

Classification

16 Postscript, 1965
DAVID RIESMAN

201 Idols of the Mind
FRANCIS BACON

264 The Main Trends of Twentieth-Century Criticism
RENÉ WELLEK

390 Man's Fourth Adjustment
HARLOW SHAPLEY

450 The Formation of Character
DAVID RIESMAN

Definition

44 The Marks of an Educated Man
ALAN SIMPSON

56 The Meaning and Significance of Academic Freedom
ROBERT M. HUTCHINS

97 From "Burnt Norton"
T. S. ELIOT

98 In My Craft or Sullen Art
DYLAN THOMAS

107 Transformational Grammar
PAUL ROBERTS

135 The Revival of Rhetoric
WAYNE C. BOOTH

185 Do Computers Think?
HUBERT L. DREYFUS

193 Logical Fallacies
ROBERT GORHAM DAVIS

301 On Aristotle
WALTER JACKSON BATE

307 Poetics
ARISTOTLE

419 A Changing American Character
SEYMOUR M. LIPSET

547 The Bill of Rights

625 Virtue
ARISTOTLE

710 What Pragmatism Is
WILLIAM JAMES

727 The Value of Philosophy
BERTRAND RUSSELL

Analysis

5 Where Is the College Generation Headed?
DAVID RIESMAN

86 On Misreading by the Literary
C. S. LEWIS

125 Politics and the English Language
GEORGE ORWELL

210 The Cultural Importance of the Arts
SUSANNE K. LANGER

258 Cultural Snobbery
ARTHUR KOESTLER

290 The Structure of *Macbeth*
R. S. CRANE

295 *Macbeth* as the Imitation of an Action
FRANCIS FERGUSSON

476 Modernity and Mass Society
DANIEL BELL

576 The Anatomy of the Mental Personality
SIGMUND FREUD

716 Existentialism as a Symptom of Man's Contemporary Crisis
WILLIAM C. BARRETT

731 The Present Human Condition
ERICH FROMM

Historical Writing

32 The Student Movement: Some Impressions at Berkeley
HENRY F. MAY

144 The Emancipation of Thought from Myth
H. AND H. A. FRANKFORT

225 *Et in Arcadia ego:* Poussin and the Elegiac Tradition
ERWIN PANOFSKY

346 A Lesson Read in American Books
ROBERT PENN WARREN

375 The Evolution of the Physical World
ARTHUR STANLEY EDDINGTON

491 The Changing Place of Women in America
CARL N. DEGLER

519 The Two Worlds of Race
JOHN HOPE FRANKLIN

Biography and Autobiography

1 University Days
JAMES THURBER

19 How Agassiz Taught Shaler
NATHANIEL SOUTHGATE SHALER

22 Kittredge of Harvard
ROLLO WALTER BROWN

95 From the *Autobiography of Benjamin Franklin*
BENJAMIN FRANKLIN

177 [A Thinker: Wittgenstein]
VED MEHTA

378 Newton the Man
JOHN MAYNARD KEYNES

385 On Albert Einstein
ROBERT OPPENHEIMER

660 In His Will Is Our Peace
JOHN WOOLMAN

670 Confession of Faith
JACQUES MARITAIN

Informal Essay

1 University Days
JAMES THURBER

69 The Private World of the Man with a Book
HAROLD TAYLOR

75 Reading
HENRY DAVID THOREAU

564 Walden—1954
E. B. WHITE

Humor and Satire

42 For Want of a Teacher
ART BUCHWALD

81 Mr. K*a*p*l*a*n and Shakespeare
LEONARD Q. ROSS

92 The Reading Machine
MORRIS BISHOP

115 The Cliché Expert Reveals Himself in His True Colors
FRANK SULLIVAN

163 Injelititis, or Palsied Paralysis
C. NORTHCOTE PARKINSON

618 A Modest Proposal
JONATHAN SWIFT

Persuasion

49 Trained Intelligence
ADLAI E. STEVENSON

169 That Candles May Be Brought
ROBERT M. HUTCHINS

513 300,000,000 Americans Would Be Wrong
DAVID E. LILIENTHAL

538 The American Crisis, I
THOMAS PAINE

548 On the Duty of Civil Disobedience
HENRY DAVID THOREAU

571 A Plea for the Freedom of Dissent
LEARNED HAND

591 The Apology of Socrates
PLATO

618 A Modest Proposal
JONATHAN SWIFT

Persuasion: Controversy

113 Laments for a Dying Language
OGDEN NASH

661 God Is Dead
FRIEDRICH NIETZSCHE

Persuasion: Sermon

632 The Sermon on the Mount
ST. MATTHEW

640 The Sermon at Benares
GAUTAMA BUDDHA

648 The Upanishads: Svetasvatara
ANONYMOUS

666 God and the Spirit of Man
MARTIN BUBER

688 *Pacem in Terris*
POPE JOHN XXIII

Persuasion: Ceremonial Essay

64 Introductory Lecture
A. E. HOUSMAN

154 The Unpredictable Intellect
GILBERT HIGHET

544 Declaration of Independence
THOMAS JEFFERSON

612 The Funeral Oration of Pericles
THUCYDIDES

TOWARD LIBERAL EDUCATION

PART I

LEARNING

The Campus

JAMES THURBER

•

University Days[1]

I passed all the other courses that I took at my University, but I could never pass botany. This was because all botany students had to spend several hours a week in a laboratory looking through a microscope at plant cells, and I could never see through a microscope. I never once saw a cell through a microscope. This used to enrage my instructor. He would wander around the laboratory pleased with the progress all the students were making in drawing the involved and, so I am told, interesting structure of flower cells, until he came to me. I would just be standing there. "I can't see anything," I would say. He would begin patiently enough, explaining how anybody can see through a microscope, but he would always end up in a fury, claiming that I could *too* see through a microscope but just pretended that I couldn't. "It takes away from the beauty of flowers anyway," I used to tell him. "We are not concerned with beauty in this course," he would say. "We are concerned solely with what I may call the *mechanics* of flars." "Well," I'd say, "I can't see anything." "Try it just once again," he'd say, and I would put my eye to the microscope and see nothing at all, except now and again, a nebulous milky substance—a phenomenon of maladjustment. You were supposed to see a vivid, restless clockwork of sharply defined plant cells. "I see what looks like a lot of milk," I would tell him. This, he claimed, was the result of my not having adjusted the microscope properly; so he would readjust it for me, or rather, for himself. And I would look again and see milk.

I finally took a deferred pass, as they called it, and waited a year and tried

[1] From *My Life and Hard Times* (New York: Harper & Row, 1933). Reprinted by permission of the author. Copyright, 1933, James Thurber. Originally published in *The New Yorker* under the title "College Days."

again. (You had to pass one of the biological sciences or you couldn't graduate.) The professor had come back from vacation brown as a berry, bright-eyed, and eager to explain cell-structure again to his classes. "Well," he said to me, cheerily, when we met in the first laboratory hour of the semester, "we're going to see cells this time, aren't we?" "Yes, sir," I said. Students to right of me and to left of me and in front of me were seeing cells; what's more, they were quietly drawing pictures of them in their notebooks. Of course, I didn't see anything.

"We'll try it," the professor said to me grimly, "with every adjustment of the microscope known to man. As God is my witness, I'll arrange this glass so that you see cells through it or I'll give up teaching. In twenty-two years of botany, I—" He cut off abruptly for he was beginning to quiver all over, like Lionel Barrymore, and he genuinely wished to hold onto his temper: his scenes with me had taken a great deal out of him.

So we tried it with every adjustment of the microscope known to man. With only one of them did I see anything but blackness or the familiar lacteal opacity, and that time I saw, to my pleasure and amazement, a variegated constellation of flecks, specks, and dots. These I hastily drew. The instructor, noting my activity, came back from an adjoining desk, a smile on his lips and his eyebrows high in hope. He looked at my cell drawing. "What's that?" he demanded, with a hint of a squeal in his voice. "That's what I saw," I said. "You didn't, you didn't, you *didn't!*" he screamed, losing control of his temper instantly, and he bent over and squinted into the microscope. His head snapped up. "That's your eye!" he shouted. "You've fixed the lens so that it reflects! You've drawn your eye!"

Another course that I didn't like, but somehow managed to pass, was economics. I went to that class straight from the botany class, which didn't help me any in understatnding either subject. I used to get them mixed up. But not as mixed up as another student in my economics class who came there direct from a physics laboratory. He was a tackle on the football team, named Bolenciecwcz. At that time Ohio State University had one of the best football teams in the country, and Bolenciecwcz was one of its outstanding stars. In order to be eligible to play it was necessary for him to keep up in his studies, a very difficult matter, for while he was not dumber than an ox he was not any smarter. Most of his professors were lenient and helped him along. None gave him more hints, in answering questions, or asked him simpler ones than the economics professor, a thin, timid man named Bassum. One day when we were on the subject of transportation and distribution, it came Bolenciecwcz's turn to answer a question. "Name one means of transportation," the professor said to him. No light came into the big tackle's eyes. "Just any means of transportation," said the professor. Bolenciecwcz sat staring at him. "That is," pursued the professor, "any medium, agency, or method of going from one place to another." Bolenciecwcz had the look of a man who is being led into a trap. "You may choose among steam, horse-drawn, or electrically propelled vehicles," said the instructor. "I might suggest the one which we commonly take in making long journeys across land." There was a profound silence in which everybody stirred uneasily, including Bolenciecwcz and Mr. Bassum. Mr. Bassum abruptly broke this silence in an amazing manner. "Choo-choo-choo," he said, in a low voice, and turned instantly scarlet. He glanced appealingly around the room. All of us, of course, shared Mr. Bassum's desire that Bolenciecwcz should stay abreast of the class in economics, for the Illinois game, one of the hardest and most important of the season, was only a week off. "Toot, toot, too-tooooooot!" some student with a deep voice moaned; and we all looked encouragingly at Bolenciecwcz. Somebody else gave a fine imitation of a locomotive letting off steam. Mr. Bassum himself rounded off the little show. "Ding, dong, ding, dong," he said, hopefully. Bolenciecwcz was staring at the floor now, trying to think, his great brow furrowed, his huge hands rubbing together, his face red.

"How did you come to college this year, Mr. Bolenciecwcz?" asked the professor. "*Chuffa* chuffa, *chuffa* chuffa."

"M'father sent me," said the football player.

"What on?" asked Bassum.

"I git an 'lowance," said the tackle, in a low, husky voice, obviously embarrassed.

"No, no," said Bassum. "Name a means of transportation. What did you *ride* here on?"

"Train," said Bolenciecwcz.

"Quite right," said the professor. "Now, Mr. Nugent, will you tell us——"

If I went through anguish in botany and economics—for different reasons—gymnasium work was even worse. I don't even like to think about it. They wouldn't let you play games or join in the exercises with your glasses on and I couldn't see with mine off. I bumped into professors, horizontal bars, agricultural students, and swinging iron rings. Not being able to see, I could take it but I couldn't dish it out. Also, in order to pass gymnasium (and you had to pass it to graduate) you had to learn to swim if you didn't know how. I didn't like the swimming pool, I didn't like swimming and I didn't like the swimming instructor, and after all these years I still don't. I never swam but I passed my gym work anyway, by having another student give my gymnasium number (978) and swim across the pool in my place. He was a quiet, amiable blond youth, number 473, and he would have seen through a microscope for me if we could have got away with it, but we couldn't get away with it. Another thing I didn't like about gymnasium work was that they made you strip the day you registered. It is impossible for me to be happy when I am stripped and being asked a lot of questions. Still, I did better than a lanky agricultural student who was cross-examined just before I was. They asked each student what college he was in—that is, whether Arts, Engineering, Commerce, or Agriculture. "What college are you in?" the instructor snapped at the youth in front of me. "Ohio State University," he said promptly.

It wasn't that agricultural student but it was another a whole lot like him who decided to take up journalism, possibly on the ground that when farming went to hell he could fall back on newspaper work. He didn't realize, of course, that that would be very much like falling back full-length on a kit of carpenter's tools. Haskins didn't seem cut out for journalism, being too embarrassed to talk to anybody and unable to use a typewriter, but the editor of the college paper assigned him to the cow barns, the sheep house, the horse pavilion, and the animal husbandry department generally. This was a genuinely big "beat," for it took up five times as much ground and got ten times as great a legislative appropriation as the College of Liberal Arts. The agricultural student knew animals, but nevertheless his stories were dull and colorlessly written. He took all afternoon on each of them, because he had to hunt for each letter on the typewriter. Once in a while he had to ask somebody to help him hunt. "C" and "L," in particular, were hard letters for him to find. His editor finally got pretty much annoyed at the farmer-journalist because his pieces were so uninteresting. "See here, Haskins," he snapped at him one day, "why is it we never have anything hot from you on the horse pavilion? Here we have two hundred head of horses on this campus—more than any other university in the Western Conference except Purdue—and yet you never get any real low-down on them. Now shoot over to the horse barns and dig up something lively." Haskins shambled out and came back in about an hour; he said he had something. "Well, start it off snappily," said the editor. "Something people will read." Haskins set to work and in a couple of hours brought a sheet of typewritten paper to the desk; it was a two-hundred word story about some disease that had broken out among the horses. Its opening sentence was simple but arresting. It read: "Who has noticed the sores on the tops of the horses in the animal husbandry building?"

Ohio State was a land grant university and therefore two years of military drill was compulsory. We drilled with old Springfield rifles and studied the tactics of the Civil War even though the World War was going on at the time. At 11 o'clock each morning thousands of freshmen and sophomores used to deploy over the campus, moodily creeping up on the old chemistry building. It was good training for the kind of warfare that was waged at Shiloh but it had no connection with what was going on in Europe. Some people used to think there was German money behind it, but they didn't dare say so or they would have been thrown in jail as German spies. It was a period of muddy thought and marked, I believe, the decline of higher education in the Middle West.

As a soldier I was never any good at all. Most of the cadets were glumly indifferent soldiers, but I was no good at all. Once General Littlefield, who was commandant of the cadet corps, popped up in front of me during regimental drill and snapped, "You are the main trouble with this university!" I think he meant that my type was the main trouble with the university but he may have meant me individually. I was mediocre at drill, certainly—that is, until my senior year. By that time I had drilled longer than anybody else in the Western Conference, having failed at military at the end of each preceding year so that I had to do it all over again. I was the only senior still in uniform. The uniform which, when new, had made me look like an interurban railway conductor, now that it had become faded and too tight made me look like Bert Williams in his bell-boy act. This had a definitely bad effect on my morale. Even so, I had become by sheer practise little short of wonderful at squad manoeuvres.

One day General Littlefield picked our company out of the whole regiment and tried to get it mixed up by putting it through one movement after another as fast as we could execute them: squads right, squads left, squads on right into line, squads right about, squads left front into line, etc. In about three minutes one hundred and nine men were marching in one direction and I was marching away from them at an angle of forty degrees, all alone. "Company, halt!" shouted General Littlefield, "That man is the only man who has it right!" I was made a corporal for my achievement.

The next day General Littlefield summoned me to his office. He was swatting flies when I went in. I was silent and he was silent too, for a long time. I don't think he remembered me or why he had sent for me, but he didn't want to admit it. He swatted some more flies, keeping his eyes on them narrowly before he let go with the swatter. "Button up your coat!" he snapped. Looking back on it now I can see that he meant me although he was looking at a fly, but I just stood there. Another fly came to rest on a paper in front of the general and began rubbing its hind legs together. The general lifted the swatter cautiously. I moved restlessly and the fly flew away. "You startled him!" remarked General Littlefield, looking at me severely. I said I was sorry. "That won't help the situation!" snapped the General, with cold military logic. I didn't see what I could do except offer to chase some more flies toward his desk, but I didn't say anything. He stared out the window at the faraway figures of co-eds crossing the campus toward the library. Finally, he told me I could go. So I went. He either didn't know which cadet I was or else he forgot what he wanted to see me about. It may have been that he wished to apologize for having called me the main trouble with the university; or maybe he had decided to compliment me on my brilliant drilling of the day before and then at the last moment decided not to. I don't know. I don't think about it much any more.

DAVID RIESMAN

•

Where Is the College Generation Headed?[1]

The conflict of the generations is neither a new nor a particularly American story, but it is perhaps exacerbated by the self-consciousness and the partial segregation of teen-age culture, to such an extent that both old and

[1] From *The Atlantic Monthly,* CCVII (April, 1961), 39-45. Reprinted by permission of the author.

young are exceptionally vulnerable to their mutual criticisms. I do not care to add to the complacency of my agemates who, from their clubs, pulpits, and other rostrums, attack the alleged "softness" of the young, whom they have themselves brought up, while failing to see the difficulties young people face today precisely because the manifest hardships with which earlier Americans coped have been, for millions, attenuated. These hardships cannot be artificially restored, at least for people over twelve; however, I believe that college students are now beginning to find new ways to become active politically, and hence responsible humanly.

It is easy to underestimate the importance of this in America, where students until recently did not play the role in politics that they do in Latin America, Turkey, Korea, or Japan. For, the cadres of the disinherited who once helped power political change in this country are diminished in numbers and even more diminished in leadership, now that nearly every bright, motivated boy gets funneled into college if he wants to go. Thus, our expanding colleges absorb increasingly large fractions of the available idealism and dynamism of our society. And at the same time, as I shall try to show, many students are not attracted by the traditional goals of commercial or professional ambition; the best of them have no love for the status quo. Rejecting careerism, they often choose familism instead. But shaken out of this, either by the open discrimination felt by Negroes or the subtler dissatisfaction with contemporary life felt by whites, they comprise a privileged minority, ignorant of its strength, yet capable of change.

College students today often act as if they believed that work in large organizations, and beyond that, work in general, could not be basically satisfying (or, at times, even honest), but is primarily a way to earn a living, to find a place in the social order, and to meet nice or not-so-nice people. This is a conclusion which is partly projected upon the occupational scene as the result of their experience with the curriculum in college and university, and also as the result of experience with college and university as organizations which are viewed as bureaucratic, monolithic, and unchangeable by many students.

I do not think it is the primary task of education to prepare students for their later occupational roles, or, indeed, any narrowly specialized roles, nor to teach them to enjoy work regardless of its quality and meaning. Rather, the relation of education to later life should be a dialectical and critical one. If, however, one result of going to college is to become alienated from work per se and defeatist about the possibility of altering one's relation to it, then it seems to me one ought to re-examine academic institutions themselves and see whether anything in them, or in one's own attitudes, or in both might be changed.

In the spring of 1955, several hundred interviews were done (at the behest of *Time* magazine) with seniors at twenty colleges throughout the country, most of them colleges of distinction. The seniors were supposed to be reasonably representative, but what this was taken to mean and how it was applied at different colleges and universities varied greatly. A good many student leaders were chosen, a good many bright people, but hardly any women were included (a questionnaire circulated by *Mademoiselle* gave me somewhat comparable data concerning college women). When I first examined the interviews, and now again when I have once more gone over them, I have been struck by what appears to be a not quite conscious ambivalence toward work in large organizations. Nevertheless, the majority are planning to enter large organizations in pursuit of their careers: big corporations, big governments, big law offices, and so on. Only a few seek independence in their work, either in terms of old-fashioned ideals of entrepreneurship or in terms of the desire to become a foreign correspondent, to enter politics, or to follow some other individualistic or exotic calling. (Moreover, hardly anyone expresses resentment against his prospective army service on the ground that the army is a large organization; there is no eagerness for service, but rather resignation to it as one of the givens of life.)

And yet, when these young people are asked about their lives outside of work, a very different picture merges. There, bigness and scale are definitely not valued. Only a tiny fraction want to head for the metropolis, even if their careers might make such a location convenient. They want the suburbs—not later, after some bachelor independence in the big city, but now, on graduation. The great majority either are already married or plan to get married soon (even if there is no special one in mind at the moment); they plan to start having children at once and to begin building a community-centered life in the suburbs. They envisage a two-car, but usually not a two-career, family, in which the prospective wife will be active in the parent-teacher association, with assistance from the husband, and in which both spouses will concern themselves with a manageable bit of real estate in a suburban neighborhood in which they can at once be active and hope to make a difference. It does not occur to them that they might be gifted and energetic enough to make a difference even in a big city. Rather, they want to be able to work through a face-to-face group—the postcollegiate fraternity of the small suburbs.

Correspondingly, the very emphasis on family life, which is one of the striking and, in so many ways, attractive qualities of young people today, is in implicit rejection of large organization. The suburban family, with its garden, its barbecue, its lack of privacy in the open-plan house, is itself a manifesto of decentralization, even though it makes use of centralized services such as television, clinics, chain stores, and *House Beautiful.* The wish to build a nest, even if a somewhat transient one, is a striking feature of the interviews, in contrast with the wish to build a fortune or a career, which might have dominated some comparable interviews a generation earlier.

This pattern—the acceptance of large organizations, combined with tacit and uncrystallized resistance to them—appears not only in the respondents' emphasis on the family but also in what they say about their plans and attitudes toward their future work. I get a sense from the the material, and from other comparable data, of a certain withdrawal of emotional adherence from work. To be sure, it has become fashionable to speak of one's work or other activities in deprecatory terms and to adopt a pose of relative indifference to the larger goals of an organization. In an era of political, economic, and cultural salesmanship, such deprecation is a way of guarding against being exploited for ends outside one's self. It is as if one had constantly to conduct psychological warfare against an outside enemy. But, as in any such process, students become to some extent the victims of their own defenses. They come to believe that work cannot really be worth doing for its own sake, whether or not it is done on behalf of a large, impersonal organization. They fear overcommitment to their work even while they are at the workplace. In the course of getting rid of earlier collegiate or rah-rah enthusiasm, these young people have come to feel that work is not worth even their part-time devotion, and perhaps that nothing, except the family, deserves their wholehearted allegiance.

We see the same attitudes, of course, among the junior echelons now engaged in work. One hears them talk of their benevolent company as "a mink-lined rat trap," or speak of "the rat race," or refer to fights over principles as "ruckuses" or "blowups"—if somebody cares, he is said to "blow his top." In a number of business novels, of which *The Man in the Gray Flannel Suit* is representative, it is taken for granted that a sensible fellow, and, indeed, an honest one, will prefer surburban domesticity and a quiet niche to ulcerous competition for large business stakes, despite the view from the top and the interesting climb.

Attitudes such as these are of course an aspect of a general cultural shift, not confined to students and not confined to those who seek employment in large organizations; similar attitudes turn up in some measure even among those who, studiously avoiding such organizations, look for a professional career in which they hope to be their own masters. Scholars, for example, are not immune to distaste for their work, nor are architects or physicians. But, while I do not intend to imply that a life without any boredom is conceivable, except for a very stupid person, still, I think we are witnessing a silent revolution against work on the part of even those relatively privileged groups who have been free to choose their work and to exercise some freedom in the doing of it. This reflects, in part, the fact that much work is meaningless per se, save as a source of income, prestige, and sociability, but it also indicates, as I have already implied, that people too readily accept their work as it comes, without the hope of making it more meaningful.

Not all large organizations are alike, despite the sorts of institutional similarities investigated by sociologists, and, of course, not all positions in them are alike. Many, although their top executives clamor for creativity and independence of mind, largely manage to process these qualities out of "their" people in the lower ranks. Others stockpile talent and expect it to keep as gold keeps at Fort Knox. Still others make products or provide services which are either antisocial or useless. But here and there one finds companies which face real and not contrived problems and apply to them an intelligence which is often remarkably disinterested and, in the best sense of the term, "academic." Young people in search of challenge and development would do well to seek out such relatively productive climates, rather than to assume offhand that these (as is true of so many brand-name products) are all alike except for the advertising and the label. And this search is necessary precisely because many of the motives which impelled work in the older generation have fortunately become attenuated, motives such as money for its own sake, power, and fame—goals, that is, whose emptiness became evident with their attainment. Our industrial and commercial plant no longer "needs" such compulsive attachments to work, which are based not on any genuine creative impulse but on the drying up of other alternatives and on the pressure of extrinsic standards of value.

There is a further issue concerning work in larger organizations where, again, differentiation is required. I refer to the conception that work in organizations requires surrender of independence of judgment, if not of intregrity. When I was in college, there was a prevalent feeling among the more sensitive that this was true only of business and commercial organizations, not of governmental or philanthropic ones, and young men debated whether they would enter Wall Street and make money, or enter government or teaching and be saved. This dichotomy has in large measure vanished, although traces of it do survive among the less cynical. For instance, I have known many graduate students in social psychology who believe that if they teach, they can be honest, but that if they work in market research, they will serve manipulation and corruption and will have no power over their own work. Such judgments oversimplify the ethical dilemmas of any calling and are, in addition, snobbish; one can find hucksterism (often hypocritically veiled) among academic people in search of reputations, grants, and promotions, as well as among market researchers and other businessmen.

Indeed, I am inclined to think that, at present, many observant young people do not need to be persuaded of this; many are actually overpersuaded to the point of believing that every occupation is a racket and that at best some of the racketeers are less pious about it than others. And this, I suspect, is one of the reasons they tend to withdraw emotional allegiance from their work—with the impression that they have no control over it anyway, that all is in the hands of the mysterious men upstairs who run the show. If there is greater wisdom in their belief that all occupations, like all forms of power, are corrupting in some degree, there is also greater resignation, greater passivity and fatalism.

Where are such attitudes learned and confirmed? Even at some of the leading colleges, the more intellectual colleges, the colleges which produce literary magazines, the relation of students to the curriculum has a certain alienated quality, in the sense that the students do not believe they have any control over their own education.

In the last few years I have visited a number of colleges of high quality, colleges which turn out eminent professional men, scholars, and scientists, and I have made it my business to talk with students informally, to read their student newspapers and, where possible, student council reports. At a number of these institutions, the livelier students complain of the educational fare they are getting, of the very little contact the curriculum makes with the problems that are meaningful to them. Sometimes they feel that opportunities for a civilized and intellectual life on campus are wanting—for example, that there are few inviting places to study or to talk, that social pressures in dormitories force any intellectual life out of the group setting, that student publications are either dominated by the school administration or devoted to campus news and trivia, that the bookstore is inadequate, or that the library is geared to meet research needs rather than to attract undergraduate browsers. They often feel that they have no access to the faculty for other than merely routine matters. Sometimes students complain about the prerequisites of a department, which serve its monopolistic aims or protect its mediocre teachers from boycott rather than serve any defensible pedagogic aims.

Yet, when I ask such students what they have done about these things, they are surprised at the very thought that they could do anything. They think I am joking when I suggest that, if things came to the worst, they could picket! They think I am wholly unrealistic when I say that many on the faculty might welcome student initiative in revising the curriculum, or that it might be possible to raise modest sums of money among alumni or others to bring visiting lecturers or poets to the campus, or to furnish commodious rooms for interest-group meetings. When I tell them that the Harvard house plan came about in considerable measure because of the report of a student council committee in 1926 which caught the attention of the philanthropist Edward Harkness, they shrug. That must have been a golden era, they say; nothing like that could happen now. Of course, as long as they think that, they will conduct themselves accordingly.

Why is it that students, often so precocious about many things—about each other, about sex, about their families, and occasionally even about national and world affairs—are comparatively inattentive to what concerns them as closely as does their curriculum?

For one thing, it seems to me that students do not want to believe that their activities might make a difference, because, in a way, they profit from their lack of commitment to what they are doing. I do not mean that they are not industrious students; they go through the required motions of working, but they seldom get really involved with the content of their courses. It is here that the better, more conscientious students sabotage their own education and restrict production; true enough, they turn out the credits and the grades, but they do not believe that it really matters in any fundamental sense what they think and feel.

When I have discussed this with students, they have often told me that it doesn't pay to be too interested in anything, because then one is tempted to spend too much time on it, at the expense of that optimal distribution of effort which will produce the best grades—and after all, they do have to get into medical school, keep their scholarship, and "please the old man." Now, I am convinced that grades contaminate education—they are a kind of currency which, like money, gets in the way of students' discovering their intellectual interests—but here, too, the students in their realism are being somewhat unrealistic. They assume, for one thing, that it is hopeless to try to alter the curriculum so that it might penalize them less for serious interest in one topic at the expense of others, or so that there might be more emphasis on reading and discussion and more opportunity for independent thinking. And here, also, the students have a distorted image of what will actually make an impression on their teachers either now or later. On this point, I have some evidence to back me up.

After I had tried in vain for some time to persuade graduate students at Chicago that they could be more independent in their course and thesis work without any heroism, any martyrdom, there was a thesis done by a student which documented my arguments. The student went around to the departments and asked them which students in recent years they had recommended for jobs or advanced training or fellowships and which they had not. Then he interviewed some of these students in various categories of faculty blessing or disapproval, looked at their grades, and so on. He concluded that those students frequently fared best who were not too obedient, who did not get an undiluted, uncomplicated, straight-A record. (The straight-A students, in fact, sometimes slipped away without anyone's noticing.)

The students who were most successful were a bit rebellious, a bit offbeat, though not entirely "goof-offs"; these were the students likely to appeal to a faculty member who had not entirely repressed a rebelliousness of his own that had led him to be a teacher in the first place, a faculty member who was looking for signs of life, even if they gave him a bit of trouble at times. To be sure, such a student had to do well in something to earn this response, but he was often better off to have written a brilliant paper or two than to have divided his time, as an investment banker his money, among a variety of subjects. Those students who were the most self-consciously opportunistic and realistic in allocating their time and emotion were in fact sacrificing themselves unprofitably, suffering not only now, during the studies which they regarded as an anteroom to life, but later on as well.

Now, not all departments at Chicago were alike in this matter; some gave more play to defiance and deviation than others. Moreover, this study encompassed only the social science departments. No doubt departments and institutions differ very much in this respect. But that is just the point I want to emphasize: by concluding prematurely that all organizations are alike, that all demand the same kinds of conformity, students not only surrender the chance to experience an atmosphere that is freer and more conducive to their own development but perpetuate a myth that then controls their passage through jobs in later life. If the University of Chicago or even one's department itself cannot be changed from below, how can one expect to change General Motors, or *Look* magazine, or the big hospitals of San Francisco? And if that is so, then why not settle for the fringe benefits, for a position of moderate respectability and adequate, if not dazzling, salary?

At work here is a characteristic social pattern in which individuals, hesitant to reveal feelings they have scarcely voiced to themselves, are misled about what in effect could be done if they expressed themselves, thereby discovering others who might share their views. (Sociologists refer to this process as "pluralistic ignorance.") Leadership, of course, whether in politics or in other affairs, often serves to help a group change its apparent mood to conform to its actual or potential but repressed views, but leadership also may, and frequently does, serve to continue enforcing the repression. Even in a large organization, radical and what were previously regarded as "impossible" changes come about almost instantaneously once people discover that views they had previously regarded as unacceptable or idiosyncratic are in fact widely shared.

The students know that there are many decisions out of their conceivable control, decisions upon which their lives and fortunes truly depend. But what I am contending is that this truth, this insight, is overgeneralized, and that, being believed, it becomes more and more "true." Not only do we fail to spot those instances in which intervention might change things quite substantially, but we fail to develop the competence and the confidence in ourselves that are necessary to any large endeavor. In that sense, despite our precociousness, we fail to grow up; we remain the children of organization, not the masters of it.

For Americans, there is something paradoxical about this development. Americans in the past have not been overimpressed by mechanical achievements. Workers in a steel mill are not awed by the giant rollers, and we take for granted that we are not awed by any large physical construction made by our hands and brains. Contrary to the prevalent impression abroad that we are slaves to our machines, we are actually relatively uninvolved with them, and we surely do not feel dominated by them. But it seems to be different with the organizational machines. These are as much the product of our thinking and our imagination as any technological feat; yet, as Erich Fromm has said, we worship like idolaters the product we have created, an image not of stone but of other images.

It is a commonplace observation that in organizational life we use arguments to convince others which we think will appeal to them, even though they do not convince us. We try to persuade people to behave justly to Negroes because "discrimination makes the United States look bad in the Cold War," as if that were why we ourselves behaved decently. Or we persuade businessmen to give money to colleges for all sorts of public relations reasons, playing on their fear of radicalism or federal control or whatnot, whereas we ourselves devote our lives to education for quite different reasons. All arguments of this nature have two qualities: they patronize the other person and they perpetuate "pluralistic ignorance." It can be contended that there may be occasions when we must appeal to others as they are, not as we should like them to be; when there is not time for idealism. But, in our realism, we often make mistakes about what others will actually respond to, and we sacrifice the integrity and clarity of our argument to our false image of what will go over. The result: we conclude that one cannot be honest while working for an organization, that one can be honest only when one is at home with one's family in the suburbs.

There is another result as well; namely, that we often end up in doubt as to what we ourselves think. We come to believe what we say to others and thus become "more sincere" in the subjective sense, but at the price of becoming still more confused as to what is actually so: we are the first victims of our own propaganda. No wonder we end up without emotional ties to what we do, for it is no longer we who do it, but some limited part of ourselves, playing a role. Not recognizing that we in some measure have done this to ourselves, we attribute to organizations the power and the primacy we have lost. And then, as I said, we strike back, not directly, but by a kind of emotional attrition in which we lend to our work willingness without enthusiasm, conscientiousness without creativity.

I am sure that many college students who are not only serious but dedicated know this as well as I do. Such students have managed to make college serve their purposes and have in this way gained some rational confidence that they will be able to do the same in the organizations they will enter later, whether these are universities, business concerns, or the many voluntary organizations through which we Americans carry out much of our communal work. What I have principally sought to do in these remarks is to encourage greater and more differentiated realism than many young people already possess, a realism which does not take for granted the social structures which seem so impressive but which looks for the points of leverage where one's own effort, joined to that of others similarly freed from mythology, might make a difference. In many situations, there is more leeway than students think, and college is a good place to find this out.

Three years later, I have naturally asked myself to what extent the foregoing remarks still strike me as true. I had in 1955 and 1957 paid very brief visits to several of the Southern Negro colleges that have since been in the forefront of sit-in demonstrations; at that time they seemed to me, as to some of their own faculty members, acquiescent and cautious, preparing students to enter the army uncomplainingly, the "Black Bourgeoisie" unthinkingly. Of course, the students were aware of the struggles over integration, but for them the issues remained somewhat abstract, particularly as many of them had chosen the shelter of a segregated college, as in their prospective occupations—teaching, the ministry, Negro business—many would choose the still segregated occupations.

As so often, appearances were deceptive; some of these students carried out the first sit-ins and refused to become daunted or disorganized when either their own pressured administrations or reactive whites sought to end the picketing and protests; a brave few, in active civil disobedience, have chosen jail rather than bail. Relatively immune to the economic boycotts that can hamstring their parents, and free, too, of the traditional Negro leadership in their communities, they have discovered their organizational powers and talents. This has been bracing and highly educative.

Meanwhile, among white students in the North, sympathetic picketing of the chain stores was rapidly organized, and many campuses had their first taste of political life in twenty years. The young people I have been describing are markedly tolerant; in the 1955 interviews, hardly any exhibited bigotry (at the Southern universities many said that once the old folks are gone, the race problem will die with them). Moreover, tolerance appears to them a virtue that is civic and personal, tied into one's own immediate human reactions and relations; to be tolerant to classmates, one does not have to fight city hall, though one may sometimes have to fight alumni guardians of the more collegiate fraternities.

Furthermore, the simplicity of the race issue, the near lack of rational or civilized defense of segregation and discrimination, allows Northern students to extrapolate public activity on the basis of private decency, without feeling themselves to be involved in "politics" or in ideology. True, the planned picketing has involved these highly individualistic students in more organization and decision making than appeals to most of them; the term "politician" is as much one of contempt on the better campuses as it is generally in American life. Even so, many students have discovered, though less dramatically than the Southern Negro students, that they are capable of action in areas outside the usual complaints about library hours, dormitory food, and parking, and that even such seemingly large outfits as Woolworth's are not invulnerable.

So, too, there have recently been some energetic student actions in the area of curriculum. In the spring of 1958, students at the University of Wisconsin submitted a petition to the administration requesting more challenge and stimulation in their courses and in their educational program generally. During the same period, undergraduates at Chicago mobilized to defend the general education program against attempts to subordinate it to the requirements of the graduate departments. A group of students at Wesleyan last year arranged a series of discussions on education, geared to the problems and opportunities faced by a liberal arts college; apparently the students helped influence curricular change. While, in some instances, students could graduate before realizing that what they did had any impact, others learned from their experiences that institutions are man-made and subject to change.

It is understandably seldom that such sporadic and ad hoc actions have been carried over into political controversies on the national scene. There have been occasional protests against compulsory ROTC, based as much on the unintellectual waste of time of the programs as on any explicit antimilitarist views. The student political party (Slate) at Berkeley was a factor in last year's protest against the Un-American Activities Committee hearings in San Francisco—a brave protest, since many students fear it will go on their records in an FBI dossier. And, increasingly, the issues of peace and disarmament have found a student audience. Students are picketing weekly on Boston Common under the auspices of the Committee for a Sane Nuclear Policy and are encountering, as they did to only a minor degree in picketing the chain stores, violent and jeering attacks as Reds or yellow appeasers. Challenge at Michigan and Yale, Concern at Ohio Wesleyan, Tocsin at Harvard are among the groups that have sprung up to discuss peace and other political questions. Only a very small minority are involved—but then only a small minority were involved in the supposedly activist 1930s. Probably some of these organizations will last only for the college lifetimes of a handful of committed students.

Indeed, the very fact that academic values have triumphed on many campuses puts heavy competition in the way of all extracurricular activity, including politics. I recall one student who recenty felt he had to choose between active participation in organizing a student chapter of SANE and writing a senior distinction thesis; he believed that if he did not do the latter, he would not get into graduate school (not an unrealistic fear) and would jeopardize his whole career (in my judgment, a less realistic fear). Perhaps more important, the professors have taught, especially the better students, that all questions are complex, all ideologies suspect, and all larger passions fanatical; the fear of being naïve prevents many young people from feeling confidence in any action or reaction. (Some of these same adults then criticize the students for apathy!) Questions of foreign policy and disarmament *are* complex—in a way that the race question is not—and students have in the past feared to take a position that expert or "classified" knowledge might explode. Once they begin, however, these same academic values lead them to a seriousness illustrated by the Tocsin students, who have organized seminars on technical problems of disarmament and, as the phrase goes, "done their homework" in Kahn, Kissinger, King-Hall, the *Bulletin of the Atomic Scientists,* and so on.

The long-buried idealism of many gifted and sensitive students has come out most strongly, however, in their response to President Kennedy's proposal of a Peace Corps. It is exciting to watch a group of them examining in detail what American students might contribute to secondary education in Nigeria and what qualities of judgment, self-reliance, pertinacity, and technique such students would need to be of real help. I have seen students who seemed, even in their own eyes, cool customers, ready to ride the organizational escalator, discover in themselves unexpected resources of dedication when beckoned by a chance to serve in an underdeveloped country. To be sure, such service appears to many students as quite unpolitical, outside the polemical orbit of American domestic struggles; and one could argue that there are escapist elements in this choice, this interpretation. But one has to start somewhere, and when one is emerging from privatism, the first movements are apt to be tentative.

We must still ask whether there will be any carry-over from these campus stirrings into the attitudes that college graduates take toward their work: will they continue to regard it as mere "bread," needful for existence, but not a locus either for defining the self or changing the world? If one is apathetic about one's work, it is hard to prevent this apathy from spreading to other areas, even to those on which one had originally thought to build one's life: domesticity, the arts, and personal relations. But, conversely, the vitality and sense for relevant accomplishment that students may gain in college should spread to their academic work and thence to their lifework. For, in the more selective colleges at present, as I have already indicated, there is very little left of the collegiate or teen-ager high jinks of the former *jeunesse dorée*; it is in the high schools now that these ersatz values reign. Thus, college is already, not always happily, an aspect of adult life, not simply a playful preparation, and experience there is no longer compartmentalized as a childish thing.

DAVID RIESMAN

•

Postscript, 1965[1]

Ten years after the interviews were done, it is striking to see what has changed in the attitudes of students in college and what has remained the same. All geologic strata survive in American cultural life, and the often cautious privatism I observed in 1955 is still a very general attitude. It has become a good deal more difficult to get into a good college than it was even a few years ago, and, at the same time, a mere college degree no longer means quite so much, so that a larger proportion of students are going on to graduate and professional work, and this future casts its shadow before, making the college experience for many a preliminary or proto-graduate one. Yet what is relatively new is the way in which students have been fighting back in many cases against the increasing pressures for academic good behavior.

In the first place, the feeling among students, at once comforting and depressing, that they cannot change their environment is no longer overpowering: there have been too many evidences of student effectiveness, whether in the sit-ins or other activities in the Deep South or in teach-ins concerning Vietnam, or in other national and international arenas where students have

[1] Written by Mr. Riesman for this book and published with his kind permission.

altered the focus of national attention. (Right Wing students in such organizations as the Young Americans for Freedom and segregationist students in the South have also had some experience of effectiveness.) Observers who once spoke of students as conformists and apathetic now are worried about them as alienated and assertively disaffected.

In the second place, the Peace Corps and many smaller private groups of similar intention at home and abroad have recruited students to work in face-to-face settings which are anything but suburban. Indeed, I was recently told that it is easier to recruit able and idealistic students for work in a slum school where real challenges and dangers may be faced, than in a well-to-do suburban school, although in my own judgment, the challenges in the latter may also be taxing. Students who have had the experience, often in the middle of their educational trajectory, of making a difference in a Latin American village or an urban slum neighborhood are more apt to return to college with the belief that they can find meaningful work than was the case when the only environment they knew before seeking a job was the academic one (with perhaps a summer's work at camp or in a supermarket or restaurant).

In the third place, there have been some highly dramatic instances of students intervening in the academic institutions themselves, of which of course the most significant has been the Free Speech Movement at Berkeley. The F.S.M. students began by protesting curbs on their political effectiveness outside the campus, but some went on from there to attack the management of the University itself, its orientation toward research as against undergraduate teaching, and its lack of a vital student voice in curricular and extra-curricular affairs. Students brought the University nearly to a halt and were responsible for ousting the Chancellor. At St. John's University in Jamaica, Long Island, run by the Vincentian Order, student protests on behalf of academic freedom also were a factor in ousting the president. College presidents throughout the country are suddenly aware of students as a political force which has to be reckoned with, and some can be found reading the mimeographed output of small student radical groups such as Students for a Democratic Society, who once would have been disregarded as fringe elements.

To be sure, the students who have done all these things are in fact a small minority. The college that has sent more students proportionately than any other into the Peace Corps, namely, Stanford, has sent three percent. At no campus, including the Southern Negro colleges that have been active in desegregation, has more than a small minority of students been politically active for any length of time. Of the two thousand colleges and universities in America, perhaps one-tenth have been influenced appreciably by student protest of any sort. But even a small proportion of the immense enrollments of American students is a substantial number of individuals, and to some extent, the activist students dramatize and represent feelings shared by many who appear to be only by-standers. Students are aware of there being more alternatives in American life than many of them thought a decade ago.

Correspondingly, students returning from teaching school in Ethiopia in the Peace Corps or community development in Venezuela under the auspices of Accion in Venezuela (a small Peace Corps-like group started by a few California students) want to make sure that their later academic work is related to the sort of experiences they have had overseas. They will demand more of the University as they will demand more of their later employers. Paradoxically, they frequently discover that it is easier to change a so-called backward country than to change America. Moreover, the anti-organizational outlook of ten years ago survives even in those who have been activist. Peace Corps Volunteers are among the first to attack the "bureaucracy" of the Peace Corps itself, often in a stereotypical way as if any group larger than three was necessarily stultifying, and often failing to realize that social inventiveness results in organizations such as the Peace Corps which give an opportunity for wider choice. In this fear of organization, there is an ironic similarity between some Left Wing and some Right Wing students, since the latter in a widespread paranoia see the federal government as the all-powerful enemy and underestimate the many competing pressures, private and public, which operate at least in domestic policy. Sometimes the wariness of the students leads them to eschew any sort of organizational work, hoping to find a way of earning a small stipend that will keep them going but not corrupt or contaminate them. But the Beat withdrawal that this implies is less common now than it was in the late Eisenhower years.

One element of my earlier account seems not to have changed, and that is cross-generational misunderstanding. The young and the old talk a different language as if they had been brought up in a different world, as, of course, they have. Many of my generation worked hard because we did not dream of doing otherwise, and because in a simple-minded way, we valued the esteem and money and feelings of virtue that hard work brought. We were often ambitious in an equally simple-minded way without awareness of what this cost to our personal relations—until perhaps we were forced to retire and suddenly found the savor of life gone. To us, the young often appear self-indulgent, querulous, and cynical. They appear cynical because they conceal their idealism even from themselves, preferring not to make claims to virtue which might seem "square" and, in any case, aware of the enormous complexity of motives and the many disguises of hypocrisy. The young I am speaking of, the college young, are better-educated than even their college-educated seniors, more tolerant, less conventionally ambitious, more aware of complex alternatives—and sometimes, therefore, more blocked in making choices. Many no longer go resignedly into Army service, particularly if they share the misgivings common on many campuses about the war in Vietnam.

Yet the experience of the last ten years makes me wary of generalizing about the future and hence about the present student temper. Some of the very colleges which in 1955 had seemed to me especially soporific are those today where an active and questioning student life goes on. As the beneficiaries, not always happily, of a greater permissiveness from parents and from society, today's college students are more plastic and often more open to new experience. Because they know that a fairly good job awaits them if they have the requisite training, they can be more experimental as well as more timid or they can alternate between bouts of activism and of acquiesence. Much has happened to shatter the pluralistic ignorances of an earlier day, but much remains opaque about the students not only to outside observers like myself, but to themselves also.

NATHANIEL SOUTHGATE SHALER

•

How Agassiz Taught Shaler[1]

At the time of my succession from the humanities, Agassiz was in Europe; he did not return, I think, until the autumn of 1859. I had, however, picked up several acquaintances among his pupils, learned what they were about, and gained some notion of his methods. After about a month he returned, and I had my first contact with the man who was to have the most influence on my life of any of the teachers to whom I am indebted. I shall never forget even the lesser incidents of this meeting, for this great master by his presence gave an importance to his surroundings, so that the room where you met him and the furniture stayed with the memory of him.

When I first met Louis Agassiz, he was still in the prime of his admirable manhood; though he was then fifty-two years old, and had passed his constructive period, he still had the look of a young man. His face was the most genial and engaging that I had ever seen, and his manner captivated me altogether. But as I had been among men who had a free swing, and for a year among people who seemed to me to be cold and super-rational, hungry as I doubtless was for human sympathy, Agassiz's welcome went to my heart—I was at once his captive. It has been my good chance to see many men of engaging presence and ways, but I have never known his equal. . . .

As my account of Agassiz's quality should rest upon my experiences with him, I shall now go on to tell how and to what effect he trained me.[2] In that day there were no written examinations on any subjects to which candidates for the Lawrence Scientific School had to pass. The professors in charge of the several departments questioned the candidates, and determined their fitness to pursue the course of study they desired to undertake. Few or none who had

[1] From *Autobiography of Nathaniel Southgate Shaler* (Boston: Houghton Mifflin Company, 1907), pp. 93-100, with omissions. Reprinted by permission of Gabriella Shaler Webb.

[2] At this time Shaler was nineteen years old.

any semblance of an education were denied admission to Agassiz's laboratory. At that time, the instructors had, in addition to their meagre salaries—his was then $2,500 per annum—the regular fees paid in by the students under his charge. So I was promptly assured that I was admitted. Be it said, however, that he did give me an effective oral examination, which, as he told me, was intended to show whether I could expect to go forward to a degree at the end of four years of study. On this matter of the degree he was obdurate, refusing to recommend some who had been with him for many years, and had succeeded in their special work, giving as reason for his denial that they were "too ignorant."

The examination Agassiz gave me was directed first to find that I knew enough Latin and Greek to make use of those languages; that I could patter a little of them evidently pleased him. He didn't care for those detestable rules for scanning. Then came German and French, which were also approved: I could read both, and spoke the former fairly well. He did not probe me in my weakest place, mathematics, for the good reason that, badly as I was off in that subject, he was in a worse plight. Then asking me concerning my reading, he found that I had read the *Essay on Classification,* and had noted in it the influence of Schelling's views. Most of his questioning related to this field, and the more than fair beginning of our relations then made was due to the fact that I had some enlargement on that side. So, too, he was pleased to find that I had managed a lot of Latin, Greek, and German poetry, and had been trained with the sword. He completed this inquiry by requiring that I bring my foils and masks for a bout. In this test he did not fare well, for, though not untrained, he evidently knew more of the *Schläger* than of the rapier. He was heavy-handed, and lacked finesse. This, with my previous experience, led me to the conclusion that I had struck upon a kind of tutor in Cambridge not known in Kentucky.

While Agassiz questioned me carefully as to what I had read and what I had seen, he seemed in this preliminary going over in no wise concerned to find what I knew about fossils, rocks, animals, and plants; he put aside the offerings of my scanty lore. This offended me a bit, as I recall, for the reason that I thought I knew, and for a self-taught lad really did know, a good deal about such matters, especially as to the habits of insects, particularly spiders. It seemed hard to be denied the chance to make my parade; but I afterward saw what this meant—that he did not intend to let me begin my tasks by posing as a naturalist. The beginning was indeed quite different, and, as will be seen, in a manner that quickly evaporated my conceit. It was made and continued in a way I will now recount.

Agassiz's laboratory was then in a rather small two-storied building, looking much like a square dwelling-house, which stood where the College Gymnasium now stands . . . Agassiz had recently moved into it from a shed on the marsh near Brighton bridge, the original tenants, the engineers, having come to riches in the shape of the brick structure now known as the Lawrence Building. In this primitive establishment Agassiz's laboratory, as distinguished from the storerooms where the collections were crammed, occupied one room about thirty feet long and fifteen feet wide—what is now the west room on the lower floor of the edifice. In this place, already packed, I had assigned to me a small pine table with a rusty tin pan upon it. . . .

When I sat me down before my tin pan, Agassiz brought me a small fish, placing it before me with the rather stern requirement that I should study it, but should on no account talk to any one concerning it, nor read anything relating to fishes, until I had his permission so to do. To my inquiry, "What shall I do?" he said in effect: "Find out what you can without damaging the specimen; when I think that you have done the work I will question you." In the course of an hour I thought I had compassed that fish; it was rather an unsavory object, giving forth the stench of old alcohol, then loathsome to me, though in time I came to like it. Many of the scales were loosened so that they fell off. It appeared to me to be a case for a summary report, which I was anxious to make and get on to the next stage of the business. But Agassiz, though always within call, concerned himself no further with me that day, nor the next, nor for a week. At first, this neglect was distressing; but I saw that it was a game, for he was, as I discerned rather than saw, covertly watching me. So I set my wits to work upon the thing, and in the course of a hundred hours or so thought I had done much—a hundred times as much as seemed possible at the start. I got interested in finding out how the scales went in series, their shape, the form and placement of the teeth, etc. Finally, I felt full of the subject, and probably expressed it in my bearing; as for words about it then, there were none from my master except his cheery "Good morning." At length, on the seventh day, came the question, "Well?" and my disgorge of learning to him as he sat on the edge of my table puffing his cigar. At the end of the hour's telling, he swung off and away, saying: "That is not right." Here I began to think that, after all, perhaps the rules for scanning Latin verse were not the worst infliction in the world. Moreover, it was clear that he was playing a game with me to find if I were capable of doing hard, continuous work without the support of a teacher, and this stimulated me to labor. I went at the task anew, discarded my first notes, and in another week of ten hours a day labor I had results which astonished myself and satisfied him. Still there was no trace of praise in words or manner. He signified that it would do by placing before me about a half a peck of bones, telling me to see what I could make of them, with no further directions to guide me. I soon found that they were the skeletons of half a dozen fishes of different species; the jaws told me so much at a first inspection. The task evidently was to fit the separate bones together in their proper order. Two months or more went to this task with no other help than an occasional looking over my grouping with the stereotyped remark: "That is not right." Finally, the task was done, and I was again set upon alcoholic specimens—this time a remarkable lot of specimens representing, perhaps, twenty species of the side-swimmers or Pleuronectidae.

I shall never forget the sense of power in dealing with things which I felt in beginning the more extended work on a group of animals. I had learned the art of comparing objects, which is the basis of the naturalist's work. At this stage I was allowed to read, and to discuss my work with others about me. I did both eagerly, and acquired a considerable knowledge of the literature of ichthyology, becoming especially interested in the system of classification, then most imperfect. I tried to follow Agassiz's scheme of division into the order of ctenoids and ganoids, with the result that I found one of my species of side-swimmers had cycloid scales on one side and ctenoid on the other. This not only shocked my sense of the value of classification in a way that permitted of no full recovery of my original respect for the process, but for a time shook my confidence in my master's knowledge. At the same time I had a malicious pleasure in exhibiting my "find" to him, expecting to repay in part the humiliation which he had evidently tried to inflict on my conceit. To my question as to how the nondescript should be classified he said: "My boy, there are now two of us who know that."

This incident of the fish made an end of my novitiate. After that, with a suddenness of transition which puzzled me, Agassiz became very communicative; we passed indeed into the relation of friends of like age and purpose, and he actually consulted me as to what I should like to take up as a field of study. Finding that I wished to devote myself to geology, he set me to work on the Brachiopoda as the best group of fossils to serve as data in determining the Palaeozoic horizons. So far as his rather limited knowledge of the matter went, he guided me in the field about Cambridge, in my reading, and to acquaintances of his who were concerned with earth structures. I came thus to know Charles T. Jackson, Jules Marcou, and, later, the brothers Rogers, Henry and James. At the same time I kept up the study of zoology, undertaking to make myself acquainted with living organic forms as a basis for a knowledge of fossils.

ROLLO WALTER BROWN

•

Kittredge of Harvard[1]

There could be no doubt about the matter: George Lyman Kittredge consisted of more than one man. Just how many men were required to constitute him, nobody seemed able to say. But that he was not less than two, everybody who knew him was ready to admit.

The first of these two—the one he was most widely thought of as being—

[1] From *Harvard Yard in the Golden Age,* by Rollo Walter Brown. Copyright, 1948, by permission of Current Books, Inc., A. A. Wyn. Publisher, New York.

was the "Kitty" of Harvard Hall. Undergraduates with vivid imaginations made sketches of the old building on the point of blowing up, with zigzag electric fragments of Shakespeare shooting from windows and roof, whenever "Kitty" held forth. To many of them for a lifetime the total meaning of Harvard Hall was "Kitty."

The sight of him as he came to the ten-o'clock class was in itself something that had to be recognized as dramatic. In the pleasant autumn or spring, men stood high on the steps or out on the turf in front and watched in the direction of Christ Church to see who could catch the first glimpse of him.

"There he comes!" somebody called, and then everybody who was in a position to see watched him as he hurried breezily along—a graceful, tallish man in very light gray suit and gray fedora hat, with a full square beard at least as white as his suit, who moved with energy, and smoked passionately at a big cigar. Students used to say that he smoked an entire cigar while he walked the short distance along the iron fence of the old burying ground and across the street to Johnston Gate. But as he came through the gate he tossed the remnant of his cigar into the shrubbery with a bit of a flourish, and the students still outside hurried in and scrambled up the long stairway in order to be in their places—as he liked—before he himself entered. If any of them were still on the stairway when he came in at the outer door like a gust, they gave way and he pushed up past them, and into the good-sized room and down the aisle to the front, threw his hat on the table in the corner, mounted the two steps to the platform, looked about with a commanding eye, and there was sudden silence and unrestrained expectancy.

"Any questions?" he asked—meaning questions about matters considered at the last meeting of the course. After five minutes of these questions, he was ready to begin.

The play under consideration was *Macbeth*—let us say; and he was ready to take up Act III. Always his method was a meticulously careful examination of every line, every significant word, with a running commentary on problems of drama and theatre. At the end of the year we were supposed to know five plays—sometimes a sixth—so thoroughly that in the final examination we could spot any line or piece of line that he quoted (usually about sixty), tell what came just before and after, tell who said the words and to whom, and be able to comment on whatever was significant in the passage. Then there were somewhat more than six hundred lines of memory passages. And there were books of assigned reading. Even the least wise in the course filled the margins of his copy of the text, and pages of gummed interleaving paper, with notes against an oncoming evil day.

"Now," he said, after he had read and commented upon Banquo's opening speech, and had reminded us once more that *Macbeth* is a swift-moving play, "there are three very important questions on this next page. They are neatly imbedded, yet for the purposes of the play, they stand out in red ink. What are they?"—and he glanced up and down the class list—"Mr. Howard."

Mr. Howard—it might have been Cabot or Flynn or Jones—did not seem to be present.

"Mr. Howard?" "Kitty" repeated, with the slightest trace of irritation in his voice.

When there was still no response he suddenly exploded. "The college office had two ghost men on my list for two or three weeks before I could get them off! Is this Mr. Howard another?"

There was no response.

"Is there anybody in this room who knows anything about this spook Mr. Howard?"

There was not a murmur, seemingly not even a breath, among the hundred or more students.

He slapped the book down on his desk so sharply that some of the men in the front row jumped. "By heavens, this is not to be endured! I asked a perfectly decent question, and I am going to have an answer if I have to take a poll of the entire class!"

A man in the middle of the room hesitantly lifted a hand. "I am Mr. Howard."

"Then why didn't you answer?"

"I was not prepared."

"Kitty" flew into so vast a rage that even the top of his head was ruddy. "Well, couldn't you at least have identified yourself? Stand up, Mr. Howard" —and he made a movement as if to step down off the platform—"so that this class can see who you are. And"—after Mr. Howard had very promptly stood up—"you are to come over to Sever 3 at twelve o'clock and expostulate with me—in the Elizabethan sense."

He picked up the book and in a twinkling went on, quite as if nothing unusual had happened, to point out that the three questions down the page were the ones that Macbeth asked Banquo:

Ride you this afternoon?
Is't far you ride?
Goes Fleance with you?

And then in an engaging smoothness of temper and in flowing brilliance he commented on one passage after another, made compact explanation of linguistic details, reminded us that it was not the words that had become obsolete that made the most trouble for us in understanding Shakespeare, but the words that had not become obsolete, and otherwise rounded out the whole scene until we felt as if we must be knowing the play somewhat as the audience knew it when it was originally produced.

He came to a very brief stage direction. "Note that Shakespeare is usually brief. If Mr. George Bernard Shaw had been writing that stage direction, he would have filled a page, at least."

There was a flutter of mirthfulness. It was the style then to laugh at any mention of this new playwright, as though of course he could not be much.

"Incidentally," he said, as he paced the platform, "there are other differences between William Shakespeare and Mr. Shaw."

There was greater mirthfulness still; and time flowed on harmoniously.

Some professor of economics had great charts and maps on rollers all over the front of the room, and there were two or three long, gracefully sloping pointers at hand. "Kitty" picked up one of these and used it as a stafflike cane as he paced back and forth and commented. He was magnificent. He was an Anglo-Saxon king speaking to his people.

Once in his march as he socked the royal staff down, it came in two where there was a knot in the wood, and he made a somewhat unkingly lurch. A few students snickered very cautiously.

He glowered upon them. "You have a fine sense of humor!" Then without taking his eyes off the humbled faces, he drew his arm back as if he were hurling a javelin, and drove the long remnant of the pointer into the corner of the room. "Now laugh!" he dared them.

When "Kitty" was having a run of bad days, an hour might be highly electric from beginning to end.

One wintry morning when he was late and the legitimate seven minutes of grace had ticked away, somebody called bravely, "All out!" There was much shuffiing of feet and there were echoing cries all over the room, "Time up!" "Let's go!" But nobody moved. Finally one man arose and marched defiantly toward the door, to the accompaniment of whoops and cheers.

Soon there was a solid procession pushing out through the doorway. Just when the Arnolds and Bonbrights from down in front were approaching the door and the room suddenly looked deserted, somebody called from downstairs: "Here he is!"

There was a mad scramble to get back into the room. But he was moving faster than any crowd could move. On the long semicircular stairway he pushed through with his green bookbag and smart gray hat held high, and let everyone give way in the manner possible. He was in the front of the room, and had his hat and overcoat and bookbag on the table, and was mounting the platform all in readiness to begin before the last of the returning students were in their chairs.

He waited for a moment of silence before he spoke—with something of scorn in his voice. "When I was an undergraduate in this college, by thunder we never went back for a professor."

Then for an hour he treated us as if we were a bunch of softies. He commented on words, on lines, on entire speeches with lightning speed. He assumed vast historical and linguistic knowledge on our part which we did not possess. He fired questions in every direction. One of these he addressed to a thirty-eight-year-old graduate student—a professor on leave from a well-known institution—and gave him such a cross-examination that he never came back to the course.

And then, just before bell time when even the laziest student in the course had been stimulated by the charged atmosphere to make notes and otherwise try to keep up, "Kitty" broke off in the middle of a sentence with a terrifying shout that was also a roar, slapped his copy of the play down on the desk, hurried toward the door, nervously pushing his hand back through his white hair, and disappeared into the hallway.

A moment later he reappeared at the door, bowing a man in with extraordinary graciousness. The man was frightened almost beyond speech.

"I b-beg your pardon," he stammered, "I am not a member of the course; I am a visitor."

"That does not excuse you from the rules of courtesy. You were disrespectful to me and to the young gentlemen of the class. Nobody leaves this room till the bell rings."

By the time he was back at his desk and had found the interrupted sentence in the play, the bell was ringing and he made a gesture of dismissal. As the men crowded toward the door they somehow felt sheepish, like schoolboys.

It was always a double experience. "Kitty" might suddenly step out of the Elizabethan world and pounce upon some man and scare him until he was unable to define the diaphragm—it once happened—and require him to come to the next meeting "prepared to discuss the diaphragm" as a preliminary to an hour of *King Lear*. No man might feel altogether sure that he would escape. Once "Kitty" read with such a poetic impression of reality that a man who was later to be widely known as a magazine editor sat lost in rapturous enjoyment. Suddenly "Kitty" stopped. "Now what is the commanding word in that passage"—and he picked up the printed class list and let his eye run down over the names—"Mr. . . . Smith?" Mr. Smith had been so rapturously lost that he did not even know where the passage was. A neighbor whispered the number of the line to him and he answered correctly: "Why—'God.' " "Don't you 'Why—God' me!" "Kitty" stormed back at him, and then gave him such a dressing down for using the unnecessary word as he had never known, so that he always had that to carry along with his memory of the perfect reading. On another occasion "Kitty" picked up the class list, started on the *R*'s, became interested in one man's brilliant answers to his rapid-fire cross-examination, and left the rest of the *R*'s dangling in suspense throughout the three remaining months of the year.

Men knew that he was a miracle man, and thought it worth accepting all hazards in order to possess some part of his basic richness of life. They completed the year, grumbled a little about the marks he gave them—there were few *A*'s—and very probably came back the next year to study the alternating group of plays. In that case they had the thorough knowledge of ten or eleven plays, instead of five or six; they knew eleven or twelve hundred lines of good passages by heart; they had vast information about drama and theatre and sources and language and Elizabethan life, and they had interesting fragments of such a store of miscellaneous knowledge and wisdom as they had not supposed until last year could be the possession of any one human being.

That was one of the men in the total George Lyman Kittredge. That part of him could not be brushed aside as if it were not an essential part. It was. But it was the more external part. Many of the men in the course in Shakespeare knew this well enough. They saw that it was their irresponsibility, or laziness, or grotesque ignorance, that touched him off into his tantrums. His disgust and amazement and scorn were release for a sensitive mind—usually in need of sleep—whose everyday high level made it impossible for him not to suffer in the presence of unlimited imperfections. And his graduate students who had never taken the course in Shakespeare found it difficult to believe the wild stories about him. For to them he was a courteous gentleman who begged them to smoke some of his good cigars and know that they were potential scholars about to be admitted to the most honorable company of men on earth.

His courtesy did not prevent him from exercising the dominant mind. When a student explained somewhat fearfully that he had noticed in the dictionary that a certain word was accented on the second syllable, "Kitty" said, as he put the word down on the back of an envelope, "That's wrong; I'll see that that is changed." Through generations of Shakespeare students—and his place on the board of editors of one dictionary—he caused a shift in preference to the pronunciation of "Elizabethan" with an accented long *e*. But he could never establish "Shakspere" as a preferred spelling. Sometimes, too, his overpositiveness came back upon him in ironic ways. He insisted on withholding a degree from a man for insufficient acquaintance with the drama who later became a national figure in play-writing. He once prevented a man from receiving honors in English with whom ten years later he marched down the aisle at a university commencement where both received honorary degrees—the young author and the white-haired professor.

Men who were chiefly concerned with the literature of the eighteenth and nineteenth centuries very justly felt that he placed heavy emphasis on the early centuries. But he insisted that the early centuries were of the utmost importance, and that they were full of interest. The age of Chaucer, he contended, was closer to us than the age of Pope. Always there were students who had looked upon Chaucer as some vague accident back there on the edge of the pure night of the Dark Ages, and for a time they sat skeptical, although they assumed that Chaucer was somebody about whom they should know a little.

But when they listened to Professor Kittredge—or "Mr. Kittredge"—they saw the age of Chaucer coming to such vividness of view that they had to admit that it outshone the nearer centuries in brightness. He invited them to see that

> the spirit of radicalism was abroad in the land. To describe as an era of dumb submissiveness the age of Wyclif, and John Huss, and the Great Schism, of the Jacquerie in France and Tyler and Ball in England, is to read both literature and history with one's eyes shut. . . . It was a scrambling and unquiet time when nobody was at rest but the dead. In a word, it was a good age to live in, and so Chaucer found it.[2]

And so they found it—and the heroic world of Beowulf, and the world of English and Scottish popular ballads, and all the other less familiar worlds to which he introduced them. Something of his own vividness had gone into his original exploring, and now something of it went into the revelation of what he had discovered.

But whatever the area in which he for the moment was occupied, he was engaged in perhaps the most difficult—and most desperately needed—of all educational endeavors in the United States; that is, in having pure scholarship recognized as a source of life for all men. Scholarship is the final high honesty. Men worked with Professor Kittredge—always the least bit awesomely—and came to feel how great was the disgrace of a human mind that let itself be content with anything short of the completest disinterested understanding.

From his fortunate position he all the while was sending out great numbers of men to important college and university posts. They were such men as John M. Manly, of the University of Chicago, one of his earliest students; Walter Morris Hart, of the University of California; John Samuel Kenyon, of Hiram College; Karl Young, of Yale; Carleton Brown, chiefly of Bryn Mawr; John A. Lomax, of the field of American ballads and folk songs; John Livingston Lowes, who came back from Washington University to teach in the Yard for the rest of his active life—and write *The Road to Xanadu*.

At times the objection made its way back to Cambridge that some of his disciples were not important men of this kind, but only "little Kittredges." And sometimes the reports were true. If men are basically small they are sure to adopt the accessible mannerisms of anyone whose superior qualities are out of reach. But Professor Kittredge's distinguished former students constituted a great company. In Texas, in Iowa, in Pennsylvania, in California, men accustomed to the ax-to-grind sort of thinking in what they called the practical world looked upon these honest scholars as an ultimate standard of excellence to be applied in matters of every perplexing sort.

And in Professor Kittredge it was more than honesty; it was high faith in honesty. His former students often traveled a thousand miles—sometimes farther—to have his counsel when they were in doubt. A young professor in a Midwestern college had confided in an older man in one of the chief universities of America about an original project that he had in mind for the next year, and then found that the older man had immediately hurried off a young colleague to work at the idea and be first in the field. Sleepless, the young professor went to consult someone who was wise.

[2] *Chaucer and His Poetry*. 1915. Harvard University Press. By permission.

Professor Kittredge sat erect and smoked at a great fragrant cigar and listened in silence until the man was through. Then he said without a moment's hesitation: "Don't let the matter trouble you for one minute. And don't modify your plans—not by as much as a hair. Scurvy business of that kind doesn't work out—in the end. It is not the other man's idea; he is working at it because his chief suggested it to him. He will make little of it. The idea is yours, from the inside of you, and consequently you will be aware of all sorts of possibilities in it that the other man, whoever he is, will never see." And when it turned out precisely so, Professor Kittredge said with a trace of a smile round his eyes and down into his white beard, "We have to count on its being like that."

He gave his complete self to the world of the teacher. He required nothing else. In it he had labor and recreation and profound joy—without end. For forty-eight years (1888-1936) he taught at Harvard. He never took a year of leave, nor a half year. He did not like to have breaks in his work. He did not like to go off to other universities to lecture in term time. He made a number of trips to Europe, but with one exception he made them in the summer-vacation period. England was his great fascination east of the Atlantic. When he was made an honorary fellow of Jesus College, Cambridge, he was delighted and proud. When Oxford wished to confer on him an honorary degree he felt highly honored, of course. But the great joy of work was at home.

In this world of the teacher to which he was devoted, he carried on endless research. When he was confronted by the teacher's much-discussed choice between teaching and research, he said: "Thank you, I'll take both."

In his own explorations the range that he covered was so wide that some persons actually believed that there were at least two persons named G. L. Kittredge writing at the time. He was interested in such matters as Increase Mather's views on smallpox, the ballads of Kentucky, the vocabulary of the Australasians, the history of witchcraft, the history of words for popular reading, cowboy songs, the early Teutonic notions of immortality, the toad in folklore, Chaucer on marriage, the history of religion, and scores of subjects thought of as more strictly within the field of language and literature. And his books ranged from *Chaucer and His Poetry* to *The Old Farmer and His Almanack*—and manuals of grammar and composition for high school.

It was at Barnstable, down on the Cape, that he was able to do much of his own work. For there he had long summer weeks that were little interrupted. If one chanced to be at the house on Hilliard Street in Cambridge just when he was about to go away for the summer, one might well decide that he was leaving for all time, so completely did he seem to be transferring his scholarly effects. Eventually he built a study a little away from the house in Barnstable so that he might work in entire seclusion, with only the cheerful voices of his children and their friends on the tennis court to remind him pleasantly—if he heard them at all—that he was not completely isolated in time and space.

On the Cape, too, he could be elementally refreshed. On the Cape, he was happy to say, he—or his son—had come upon the perfect pessimist, a native who grew chickens. When it was suggested that a few chicks just outside a coop were sturdy youngsters, the native replied, "Yes, but the trouble is, the old hen hatched out six, and by God all of them have died on me but five."

The Cape was heaven for work; yet back in Cambridge in the autumn he carried his own work right along with his teaching—and thereby constantly gave his teaching enrichment. He moved briskly from his classroom to Gore Hall, and very quickly disappeared. Then one came upon him somewhere deep in the stacks, lost to the immediate world over a puzzling text or fat galleys of proofs. The library was nothing musty and dead for him. It was man recorded. When the great new Widener Memorial Library was spoken of as an elephant among the other buildings in the Yard, he asked, "What if it is? You could destroy all the other Harvard buildings to the northward, and with Widener left standing, still have a university."

If days were not long enough, always there were nights. Like Charles Péguy, he considered night as the part of existence that holds everything together that is sacred to man, "wherein he accomplishes his being." But for Professor Kittredge this was not to be done through sleep; it was to be done through work.

For many years one of his intimate friends walked from Boston to Cambridge on Sunday afternoon, had supper with the Kittredges, and then the two read Greek together till eleven o'clock—as relaxation. But that still left the body of the night ahead. So, too, was it when his "ballad course" met at his house in the evening, and some of the most enthusiastic lingered a little in the big study. It was when his own house had become quiet, and the lights in houses everywhere were beginning to disappear, and the roar of the city had lost its nearness, and the world was otherwise losing the last signs of its daytime confusion, that he knew freedom. In the enveloping quiet he could give himself to work without fear of distraction. If he felt the need of diversion, he could read one more detective story.

When Mrs. Kittredge chanced to know at two or two-thirty or three in the morning that he was still at work, she would slip down and remind him that it was time for him to be getting some sleep. Very obediently he would go off to bed for the rest of the night. In the course of years, Mrs. Kittredge wearied a little of making the trip downstairs and had an electric bell installed with a button by her bed. But he did not like it. In the perfect quiet of night it made him jump. Sometimes nobody reminded him that he ought to be in bed, and he did not think of the matter himself; and when Thomas the chore man slipped into the study at six in the morning to build a new fire, there sat Professor Kittredge peacefully asleep in his comfortable chair before the empty fireplace, with one hand clutching a book on the arm of the chair as firmly as if he were awake. On such a night he did not get to bed at all.

When a vivid man does a sufficient number of things that are unfailingly characteristic, legend begins to attach itself to his name. And when he lives on and on through one college generation after another until men who were in his classes almost a half century before come back to visit their grandsons in the freshman class and find him still teaching with the same old fire, the contributions of legendary instance mount till the constitute a kind of running supplemental biography.

Men argued over the original color of his hair and beard, for he was gray—or white—so early that nobody could quite remember him when he was not gray or white. They liked to speak, too, of the fact that "Kitty" never bothered with any degree except an A.B. They laughed over the gushing woman who asked in disappointment why he had never taken a Ph.D. and his supposed reply: "Who would have examined me?" Or they repeated the story of the famous woman college president who wished a Harvard man as an instructor in English, but said she could not consider anyone who lacked a Ph.D., and of Charles Townsend Copeland's stentorian reply to her: "Thank God, then we'll not lose Kittredge!"

Legend was helped, too, by the fact that in his highly charged life there was always unpredictable heartening for the less positive, the less courageous. When a frightened young candidate for honors in English had to say in reply to a question: "I'm afraid I can't answer; I have not read all of Wordsworth," Professor Kittredge brought him quickly to life and confidence by replying: "Neither have I! I couldn't be hired to!" When the efficiency experts were rising up everywhere in institutions, and one of them asked Professor Kittredge just how many hours and minutes it took him to prepare one of his "lectures" on Shakespeare, he replied: "I refuse to answer. It's one of my trade secrets." Then he relented and said, "Just a lifetime—can't you see that?" When graduate students in the field of English made their way to Professor K. G. T. Webster's house at Gerry's Landing for a relaxing great dinner and then a joyous session on the third floor in a room that some of the guests thought of as an Anglo-Saxon mead hall, Professor Kittredge was always so full of wit and generosity of spirit that the guests were stirred to believe they could face anything.

So there he was, about to be seventy-five, full of fiery power, and seemingly without a thought that he had already taught ten years past the usual retiring age. He walked energetically through the traffic of Harvard Square and the policeman said bravely but so that Professor Kittredge would be sure not to hear, "Be a little careful there, Santa Claus!" In the Yard the general assumption seemed to be that nobody quite dared to tell him that he must retire.

On his seventy-fifth birthday, when he went to his class at Radcliffe the girls had put seventy-five magnificent crimson roses on his desk.

What was this they had done? Often enough he had scolded them. Sometimes he had walked out on them when they did not come up to his expectations in brilliance. And now they had remembered him in this fashion. They had almost taken an unfair advantage of him—so startling was it all. He told them—and suddenly he was deeply touched—that he found it difficult to express his great appreciation. "If it would help, I'd declare a holiday. And I do hereby declare a holiday." Then quite as suddenly he recovered his usual manner, looked up, and said with a self-defiant kind of smile: "Now if only some of you will tell me how to get them home without looking like a bridegroom!"

At home he admitted modestly to his wife that not every man received that many roses from his girl students on his seventy-fifth birthday. In the afternoon when one of his former students and his wife dropped in to offer best wishes, he was in the happiest of moods. He told them how near he had come to being born on the twenty-ninth of February. He admitted in great joviality that undergraduates had at times led him to make "characteristic remarks" and do "characteristic things," and he drew out of the past a few instances himself. Yes, he supposed he would be giving up teaching sooner or later, for he had in mind finishing that annotated edition of such plays of Shakespeare as had interested him most, and that would keep him busy for a number of years ahead.

And so it did.

HENRY F. MAY

•

The Student Movement
Some Impressions at Berkeley[1]

This is not a historical survey of the Free Speech Crisis at Berkeley. The events of the fall of 1964 have been well and repeatedly summarized. Here in Berkeley these events—the sudden suspension of certain student political privileges, the defiance and violations, the attempted arrests and the blocking of the police car, the agreements and negotiations which always broke down, the concessions which came too late, the final student occupation of Sproul Hall, the resultant mass arrests and the ensuing strike—all these have become as familiar as the events that led up to the French and the Russian Revolutions. And like the events of these big revolutions, the events of our

[1] Reprinted from *The American Scholar,* XXXIV, 3, Summer, 1965. Copyright © 1965 by the United Chapters of Phi Beta Kappa. By permission of the publishers.

little one sound distressingly different in the versions given by equally honest men of differing political emotions.

Another thing this is not is an attempt to assess the blame for our conflict. The ineptness of the administration and the unwieldiness of our huge institution, both major causes of the trouble, have been dealt with again and again. Here, my sole concern is with the students. They were, as I saw it, the actors: faculty and administration merely reactors. They won major victories, they have great power here, and they are being watched—with anticipation or foreboding—on other campuses of the nation.

My approach toward the Free Speech Movement and its constituency is necessarily that of an outsider, although I have talked to members and sympathizers a good deal and attended a good many of the open rallies. To supplement what immediate knowledge I have, I must rely on two kinds of analogy. First, in the mid-thirties I was a student at Berkeley and cannot help comparing this generation of students to my own. Second, I am by profession a student and teacher of American intellectual history, and I cannot talk or think about any popular movement without other movements coming to my mind.

In some ways students in Berkeley have changed a lot since the thirties. They are more intelligent now. The University is harder to get into, and many enter from "enriched" high school courses. Telegraph Avenue, the "Left Bank" area near the campus, now offers an intellectual bill-of-fare of almost indigestible richness. It is easier to find Italian, French or Japanese movies than Hollywood products near the University. Bookstores offer everywhere overwhelming displays of the latest paperbacks in philosophy, religion and pornography. A wide range of magazines and newspapers of dissent, displayed everywhere around the campus, plead all possible and impossible causes.

Many students are nourished and stimulated by this fare. It is not surprising to find sophomores who read Sartre and Camus in the time they can spare from their assignments. Yet now, even more than in the thirties, range and excitement are commoner than intellectual discipline. Languages, including English, are seldom a bright student's strongest point. History, particularly European history, attracts great numbers, but this does not indicate that students are at all traditionalist. Institutions of the past make few claims on people who have not yet managed to feel any great identity with institutions in the present. Formal systems of thought—abandoned anyway in philosophy departments—attract no allegiance; the students are likely to be eclectic and experimental. The more rigid simplifications, including Marxist ones, fall apart under their uncommitted scrutiny.

The best quality of Berkeley students is their uncompromising effort to be honest with themselves and others. The defensive, pseudosophisticated pursuit of intellectual fashion that plagues some colleges is the last thing one need worry about here. Whether one talks to our students about politics, religion or art, one feels that as they listen they are trying to decide, somewhat warily, what they believe and like—not what is In or Out. Despite all that has been said, justly but too simply, about the University's concentration on research, despite the heartbreaking problems of teaching undergraduates in such numbers, I know some faculty members who refuse high salaries elsewhere and stay in Berkeley not for prestige, libraries or climate, but for Berkeley's undergraduate students.

The nature of the student body in general has much to do with the shape of the radical movement that has grown up here. In the thirties, notoriously and also in actuality, the student movement was ranged in concentric circles around a Communist core. The Communists, open or secret—and there were both kinds—repelled most students by their pomposity of manner and language. Yet the causes of Communists espoused in those days of the "United Front" were everybody's causes: liberal unemployment relief, racial equality, and particularly international peace. In the late thirties, among "student leaders," it actually became fashionable and respectable to dabble a little in the movement. Thus there was a fairly clear series of stages or levels of radicalism, from fellow travelers to on-and-off sympathizers and beyond them to respectable but worried liberals. Beyond all these, of course, was a very large group—larger then than now—of students who were interested in dates and athletics and not at all in politics.

Today, a free-form figure, or even a mobile, has to be used instead of a system of concentric circles to symbolize the political makeup of the Berkeley campus. At the center there is still a group of dedicated, more or less full-time radical leaders. At the edge of the picture a large semistudent fringe fades by imperceptible shadings into the immediate background. And in between is a large and rapidly shifting mass of students, sometimes indifferent, but occasionally, in particular crises that involve their strong feelings, suddenly moved to dramatic action in thousands. Each of these three parts of our picture, the radical leadership, the semistudent fringe, and the shifting, potentially active mass needs separate definition before a pattern can even begin to emerge.

In discussing the full-time leadership, one is led, regrettably but inevitably, to the Communist question. In discussions of the F.S.M., as of other American radical movements, Communist influence has been both irresponsibly exaggerated and uncritically denied, and probably given too much importance in both cases. Grizzled and battle-scarred Stalinist veterans of the thirties are certainly on hand in Berkeley, as are shrill young devotees of Mao and Castro. A few of the leaders of the Free Speech Movement have themselves linked the student struggle with the Cuban Revolution and the supermilitant tactics of the Progressive Labor Movement. Yet insiders report that the orthodox Marxist minority in the movement has often opposed the direct-action tactics—to them unrealistic—that have proved so successful. It may be worth noting that demonstrations against American policy in Vietnam draw only a few hundred, whereas Free Speech demonstrations sometimes draw thousands. In the leadership, Communism exists but is probably unimportant. Various kinds of socialism, unaffiliated radicalism, and above all ultramilitant devotion to the Civil Rights movement are inextricably mixed together.

The relation between radical leadership of any kind and large-scale student support is very tenuous. It has been demonstrated that the thousand who occupied Sproul Hall were mostly without political affiliation or experience, and this is doubtless true also of the thousands more who supported the student strike. Yet it is not irrelevant that an experienced radical leadership has existed in Berkeley since long before the administrative mistakes that immediately produced the current crisis. At least since the so-called "San Francisco riots" of 1960 (the much misinterpreted protest against the House Un-American Activities Committee) Berkeley has been something of a radical Mecca. Some administrative quarters, here and elsewhere, have claimed that Berkeley is the first target of a deliberate nationwide drive which will later hit all major campuses. I have no knowledge whatever that this is (or is not) so, but more than one graduate student has told me frankly that he chose Berkeley partly because of the movement. Some former undergraduate leaders stay around and lend a hand.

Since 1960, the student movement has carried on guerrilla war with the Kerr administration over a set of presidential directives that then attempted, plausibly but unrealistically, to define the rights and duties of several distinct and complicated categories of undergraduate organizations. Since then, important concessions have been made and student victories won. By this fall, it was nonsense to talk about a "climate of oppression" in Berkeley. Students, by observing certain forms and rules, could *say* (although in theory they could not *do*) what they wanted. The climate was rather one of bureaucracy. It is particularly hard to explain to our students why a given kind of organization can have open meetings but not membership meetings on the campus, why Communism or free love may be advocated here but not there, as long as one has an associate or full professor—but not an assistant professor—as chairman. All these rules had their historical *raisons d'être,* but this kind of history is not a favorite subject here.

Last year, the movement's center of attention shifted with new intensity to the compelling cause of Civil Rights. Berkeley contributed a few students to Mississippi and many to militant demonstrations in the Bay Region. And finally, at the beginning of the fall term of 1964, before administration errors revived the question of campus political action, a publication of the left student organization called Slate seemed to suggest another major shift of emphasis, this time to the alleged outrages of the academic "system" itself. A Slate pamphlet called for "AN OPEN, FIERCE, AND THOROUGHGOING REBELLION ON THIS CAMPUS," demanding that grades be eliminated in the social sciences and humanities, rules be abolished in university housing units, and negotiations undertaken about the question of examinations. Ways suggested to achieve these dazzling goals included civil disobedience at university public ceremonies and maybe "a mass student strike . . . something which seems unthinkable at present."

Thus, before the outbreak of the recent controversy and the formation of the Free Speech Movement, an experienced, tough, continuing radical leadership existed. The leadership of the new movement consisted partly of old-timers, partly of newcomers.

In one unpleasant way the Free Speech Movement seems more reminiscent of the Communist-led "United Front" movements of the thirties than it really is. These always started with lists of respectable constituent organizations and impeccable liberal objectives. The key posts, however, were always filled by the tried and true, who somehow ended in firm control. The F.S.M., formed this October to protest new political regulations, originally included representatives of radical, liberal and even conservative student groups, and also of student religious organizations. Before long, however, the moderate groups fell away, and it became obvious that the movement was dominated by militants. The process in the two instances was different. In the thirties, radical caucuses consciously arranged to run the "United Fronts." In the F.S.M., extreme tactics, derived from the Civil Rights movement, were, I believe, invoked without much planning in response to administration blunders. These tactics alienated moderates but drew sudden waves of student mass support which far outran, for short periods, the expectations of the most radical leaders.

Much has been said about the nonstudents, radical or Bohemian, who surround our campus in considerable numbers. Tourist buses stop near Telegraph Avenue, so that sightseers can goggle at the "beatniks," with their bare feet, beards and long dirty hair. With luck, they may even hear a speech, by a well-known nonstudent character, in favor of marijuana.

Nothing irritates the F.S.M. more than the newspaper charge that it is made up of a bunch of beatniks. During the height of the crisis some sitters-in and other protesters wrote to the local newspapers insisting angrily on their own high grades, clean clothes and bourgeois habits. Yet to some, beards and sandals do represent part of a general protest against confining restrictions. And people who *look* like extreme caricatures of nineteenth-century Bohemians appear at all demonstrations. The F.S.M. is indeed not Beat, but Beats favor, and perhaps slightly affect, the F.S.M.

Real Beats are usually nonstudents. Semistudents, a group more important here, may or may not be unconventional in behavior and dress. Many bright, attractive and serious young people, often from bourgeois families, cannot bring themselves to accept for long either the discipline of grades and requirements, or the professional goals these sometimes imply. Disaffected by the campus program but fascinated by campus life, many are in and out of the university.

Among those who are in, out and halfway, some students here and elsewhere suffer deeply, like many young people everywhere, from various kinds of psychic malaise. Resort to psychotherapy is almost as commonplace as getting treatment for mononucleosis. Student worries and even student neuroses are not peculiar to Berkeley or America. To some extent—I suspect a slight one—their immediate cause may indeed lie in the system of grades and examinations the student movement is always condemning. Students here take, as they took in the thirties, five courses at a time. Ambitious and even devoted professors have sometimes raised the requirements of individual courses to quite unrealistic levels. Thus students are harassed by too many examinations and papers—a fault that the crisis has brought to the university's attention and one that will be corrected. But it is hardly necessary to point out that student malaise comes from a whole range of causes, individual and cultural, which lie far beyond the power of the university to deal with.

The relation of psychic disorder to political unrest is complex. But I suspect that it is important, for the understanding of the Berkeley crisis, to remember that a considerable minority of young people here has withdrawn, in whole or in part, from conventional competition. These are, admirably in their way, impossible to deter by appeals for individual prudence. Fear of the security check and the police record has declined together with career ambition. For secession, some have paid a heavy price. Others are willing to pay it, and many more contemplate joining the seceders but keep one foot in respectability.

The main body of students who have supported the F.S.M. in action belongs neither to the radical core nor to any kind of semistudent fringe. Many are apparently well adjusted and highly successful students even in the most conventional terms of grades. Yet even among these, even among those least identifiable with any obvious source of unrest, many are asking ultimate questions in immediate and personal terms.

The most striking fact about the present generation, to me, is that large groups are both more idealistic and more alienated than any but a handful in the radical thirties. Not only is this student generation critical of the parents and the parental social order; it is often trained to be critical by the parents, themselves perplexed and somewhat guilty in their attitude toward their own times. Exposed early to a quite unprecedented range of ideas and committed to none, they will follow no leader consistently. But for the kind of immediate cause that stirs them, they will follow any leader who is going their way, and going fast enough.

The alienation of our students is social rather than political, and it is to this alienation that Mario Savio, far the most effective of the F.S.M. leaders, is best able to speak. Always extreme but never sectarian, at times Messianic and—to adult ears, often skirting the edges of the ridiculous—Savio is the only leader who seems to represent a new genre, as different from the Slate leaders of 1960 as from the Marxists of the thirties. Many students, he says, find "that for them to become part of society, to become lawyers, ministers, business men, people in government, very often they must compromise those principles which were most dear to them, they must suppress the most creative impulses that they have; this is a prior condition for being part of the system." In the thirties most students, and particularly the Marxists, took the "system" more for granted than this.

The sort of potential radicalism I am describing finds few easy outlets. Normally, I believe, our students are not much stirred by politics. They will turn out to work against laws that interfere with free speech or menace racial integration, and the Peace Corps offers one real outlet for their zeal for personal, concrete involvement with the problems of the world. President Johnson's profound political practicality fails to attract them; still less are most of them drawn toward the disciplined ruthlessness of the Communist world. I cannot imagine that sexual freedom presents, today, much of a fighting cause; the question now is more what to do with it than how to get it. Thus the Civil Rights movement is the one organized effort that can claim their complete allegiance; it is personal, immediate and revolutionary. The local sit-ins, shop-ins and the like roused much white resentment, but scored some undeniable successes in forcing the employment of Negroes. The high purpose of these efforts, their achievements, and also the courage they demanded gave them unrivaled prestige.

From Civil Rights to Free Speech proved to be an easy road. One participant in the Sproul Hall F.S.M. sit-in told me that he had long felt guilty about not participating in Civil Rights civil disobedience. Perhaps, he thought, because of his conventional upbringing he had never been able to persuade himself that real integration could be brought about in this manner. The Sproul Hall sit-in, on the other hand, took place in the name of Free Speech—a cause he had been taught to consider an absolute, and this gave him a chance to prove his courage. This honest self-analysis may well be representative. Many argue plausibly that the relation between the two causes is a more concrete one, that the restrictions on campus political action were tightened because of outside resentment at Civil Rights demonstrations. Some students devoutly believe that the efforts to suspend leaders of the demonstrations were intended to cripple the Civil Rights cause.

In my opinion the links between the movements should not be allowed to obscure the differences. Surely it is not the same thing to stay in a restaurant for the purpose of insisting on one's moral and even legal rights and to occupy a university building for the stated purpose of obtaining a "capitulation" on matters of university regulations. Defying a dean, or even risking academic units, does not call for the same kind of heroism—or the same degree of anger—as defying an Alabama sheriff and risking one's life.

No cause other than these two could have made so many students follow the F.S.M. leaders into the startling actions of this fall. And nothing but the cause of Free Speech—not even Civil Rights—could have drawn together the amorphous and shifting mass, together with some of the disaffected fringe, behind the experienced leadership. No other cause could have combined so many resentments, dispelled so many misgivings, and brought to the surface so much frustrated idealism.

If one looks, as I cannot help looking, to analogies in other times, one passes fairly quickly by the various forms of American proletarian radicalism. The I.W.W., with its free speech fights and its insistent toughness of language and manner, is closer than any kind of Marxism. But at its most effective, the F.S.M. speaks a language very different from the studied truculence of syndicalist revolt. Like other movements of youthful rebellion in America, the F.S.M. is far more deeply rooted in the national tradition than it seems, or than its members always realize.

In the person of Savio, the movement speaks with a voice that has been heard in America since the beginning, the voice of an exalted, quasi-religious romantic anarchism. For all of their toughness, some of the F.S.M. are crypto-transcendentalists and neo-antinomians. It is interesting that the movement has been patronized by some, although not all, of the Christian chaplains that surround our nonreligious campus like holy wolves, waiting to pick off anyone who strays away from the secularist campfire. One of the most eloquent and penetrating early appraisals of the movement came from a Methodist minister who could not but approve moral outrage in the face of depersonalization. Despite the F.S.M.'s frequent ugliness of speech and action, this observer found to his own surprise "a remarkable gentleness and sweetness of spirit which comes out here and there as the life of the movement goes on."

In terms of standard American transcendentalism, Emerson is obviously too decorous and optimistic to furnish much support. The American ancestor most nearly admitted is Thoreau. In his wake Tolstoi and Gandhi, with their methods of passive resistance and their hatred of the machine, obviously provide some precedent for the sit-ins and also for the continual F.S.M. denunciations of I.B.M. cards and factory methods. One of the few relieving light moments in the tense day when students lay down around the police car, and hundreds of police waited around the corner for the word of attack, occurred in the name of the Indian saint. The harsh and unpleasantly professional exhortations coming from the improvised speakers' stand on top of the car were interrupted by an announcement that it was Gandhi's birthday and the crowd, lying and standing, responded by singing "Happy Birthday to You." Actually the intensely individualistic discipline of Thoreau contrasts sharply with the F.S.M.'s dependence on crowd emotion. And Gandhi's insistence that in an unjust society one must remain in jail is sharply different from the F.S.M.'s confusing insistence that court punishment of demonstrators is an outrage and a grievance.

In terms of religious and quasi-religious precedent, modern existentialism seems closer than Tolstoyan nonviolence. What Savio was demanding, when he urged in a peak of passion that students throw their bodies on the administrative machine and bring it to a grinding halt, was something like an existentialist *acte gratuit,* a gesture of self-identification.

Radical democracy, with its love of liberty and its dangers of tyranny, its trust in the mass and its contempt for institutions, seems to me to pervade the movement as it has many American movements. At times Whitman, that protean patron of American cranks and prophets, democrats and loners, furnishes texts that might well be used by the F.S.M.:

> I hear it was charged against me that I sought to destroy institutions
> But really I am neither for nor against institutions,
> (What indeed have I in common with them? Or what with the
> destruction of them?)
> Only I will establish . . .
> Without edifices or rules or trustees or any argument,
> The institution of the dear love of comrades.

The F.S.M. would agree with Walt about rules and trustees, and also about love, a word it often invokes. Joan Baez, the F.S.M.'s Maid in Armor, urged them to go into Sproul Hall with love in their hearts. And several of their leaflets have talked about the need for a "loving university," instead of a brutal and bureaucratic one.

Knowing that the movement proceeds partly from alienation, one is tempted to look to the 1920's for precedents. The literary rebels of that period interest our students, but they were very different. Sometimes frivolous, but often as serious as Savio, the writers of the twenties were more interested in literature than politics, sometimes inclined to dabble in Menckenian elitism, and concerned about Negroes mainly in terms of art and music. Perhaps significantly, the less completely alienated rebels of 1912 seem to offer a closer parallel. Their mixture of socialism and anarchism has its similarities to the present mood, especially when, as in the case of Randolph Bourne, it developed tragic implications.

One contemporary analogy that has often occurred to me I hesitate to bring up, because it is partly—only partly—misleading. This is the analogy to the Goldwater movement. When I hesitantly suggested this to a pro-F.S.M. graduate student of my acquaintance, he surprised me by saying that the same analogy had haunted his own dreams. The resemblance does not rest on the actual temporary cooperation between the Goldwaterites and leftists in the earliest days of the movement, when in protest against prohibition of certain kinds of political activities, students sang "Left and Right together, we shall Overcome." The relation I am speaking of is less direct and more lasting. Both the so-called conservative political movement and the radical student movement are protests against bigness, bureaucracy and official liberalism. Clark Kerr is actually a rather better symbol of the Liberal Establishment than is Lyndon Johnson, who has his archaic side. Both protest movements express vague wishes for immediate and simple solutions to complex problems. No statement could better summarize the whole F.S.M. defense of its methods than "In Defense of Liberty Extremism is No Vice." And both movements appeal to the heart—by implication, sometimes, against the head.

So far I much prefer the anarchism of the left to that of the right. On the whole, the causes in which laws have been violated by the Bay Area Movement or the F.S.M. are to me noble causes, although I think their tactics have distorted these causes. And even discounting its disastrous "Southern" strategy, the Goldwater movement had far more hate and less love than the F.S.M., although skeptics have to expect harsh treatment from both.

All these analogies seem to me to help, and none to explain fully, the student movement that came of age in Berkeley. To go further one must, in the first place, keep in mind the place and time, the American mass university in a time both of quickening intellectual life and collapsing patterns. And finally, one must admit that one never understands a new generation, although one deals with it every day.

Not understanding entirely, one may either accept or oppose the student movement. Perhaps one can defend certain boundaries against it. What one cannot do—and this one faculty group after another has learned with considerable cost—is to bargain or compromise. Essentially, the movement is absolutist. It is therefore very hard to fit into the habits or structure of our campus institutions, based, like all our institutions, on consensus or compromise.

What remains in doubt is not the existence of the student movement, although it will continue to have its ups and downs, or its militance, although this too will wax and wane. It is rather its direction. Having won nearly everything it could ask in terms of campus free speech, will the movement turn its energies once more completely outward into Civil Rights or some other major cause, or inward into further university revolt? Some leaders call for the "Free University," a new kind of academic community without grades and rules, in which students share in all academic decisions. In Berkeley, moreover, faculty and administration have been so shaken that it is not clear that either has the moral authority or the will to draw clear lines and defend them if necessary. Like modern parents, deans and professors find it easy to sympathize with revolt, very hard to act their traditional roles.

Even if the program of the Free University collapses, as it may, for lack of support, and even if no further "internal" causes emerge, a student body so deeply committed to off-campus causes presents many subtle problems. In the midst of conflict, with slogans screaming from the placards and blaring from the loudspeakers on the edge of the campus, can the faculty insist on the values, never the easiest to defend in America, of precision and complexity and patience, even of humility before one's subject? How great will be the continuing appeal of subjects that have—at least on the surface—little to do with current controversy? American education has long been plagued by utilitarianism, and there is a utilitarianism of the left as well as of the Dewey-to-Kerr center.

A few years ago many professors, I among them, were deploring the passivity and complacency of American students and of American life, and wishing for a revival of campus radicalism. Somewhat wryly, we are forced to realize that radicalism never comes in the shape or size one has asked for. It is the breath of life, and it is full of danger. Our campus now is lively and dangerous. Divided between hope and anxiety, I can look for comfort only to the very considerable reserves, in Berkeley and elsewhere, of intelligence and honesty.

ART BUCHWALD

•

For Want of a Teacher[1]

There has been a great deal of discussion about campus revolts spreading across the Nation. It is obvious the students are restless and it's making our educators very nervous.

The question is why, and I think I've got the answer. The reason the college students are doing so much demonstrating is that there is no one in class to teach them any more and the students have nothing else to do.

Almost every full professor is either writing a book, guest lecturing at another university, or taking a year off to write a report for President Johnson.

Therefore, he has turned over his course to a graduate instructor who is either working on his Ph.D., traveling on a Fulbright Scholarship, or picketing in Montgomery, Ala. So he in turn has turned the class over to one of the brighter students who is never there because he works on the college newspaper, is a member of the student senate, or is a delegate to his national fraternity.

When the students arrive at class there is no one in front of the room, so usually a Socialist student takes over the class and tells the students it's about time they revolted against the system.

The students pour out on campus heading for the administration building to protest to the chancellor of the university who, unfortunately, is away trying to raise money for a new business administration building.

The vice chancellor is at the state capital testifying on a new education bill and the dean of men is at a convention in Phoenix, Arizona.

The dean of women is addressing a garden club in the next state, and the only one left in the administration building is the chief of campus police who isn't quite sure what the students are yelling about.

So he arrests the ringleaders of the group (those standing in front) and this plays right into the students' hands because now with the arrests they have something to demonstrate about.

In the meantime the chancellor flies home to see if he can settle the matter.

[1] Reprinted with permission from Publishers Newspaper Syndicate.

The students present him with a petition demanding the release of the arrested demonstrators. He is about to do this when the Board of Regents holds an emergency meeting and votes to back the chancellor in meting out punishment to the "ringleaders."

The faculty, made up of visiting professors from other schools, votes to support the students and the Chancellor finds himself in an impossible position.

He therefore resigns and accepts a grant from the Ford Foundation to make a study of higher education.

The state politicians call for an investigation of the student demonstrations to discover if they were Communist-inspired.

Finally, the Governor makes a statement pledging full support for law and order, whatever that means.

By this time the demonstrations start petering out.

The students begin wandering back to class hoping there will be someone to teach them something. But even the Socialist student who started the demonstrations is not there. He's been booked on a lecture tour to talk about free speech at other universities.

So everyone decides to go to Washington and picket the White House over its policy on Viet-Nam.

Education

ALAN SIMPSON

•

The Marks of an Educated Man[1]

Any education that matters is *liberal.* All the saving truths and healing graces that distinguish a good education from a bad one or a full education from a half-empty one are contained in that word. Whatever ups and downs the term "liberal" suffers in the political vocabulary, it soars above all controversy in the educational world. In the blackest pits of pedagogy the squirming victim has only to ask, "What's liberal about this?" to shame his persecutors. In times past a liberal education set off a free man from a slave or a gentleman from laborers and artisans. It now distinguishes whatever nourishes the mind and spirit from the training which is merely practical or professional or from the trivialities which are no training at all. Such an education involves a combination of knowledge, skills, and standards.

So far as knowledge is concerned, the record is ambiguous. It is sufficiently confused for the fact-filled freak who excels in quiz shows to have passed himself off in some company as an educated man. More respectable is the notion that there are some things which every educated man ought to know; but many highly educated men would cheerfully admit to a vast ignorance, and the framers of curriculums have differed greatly in the knowledge they prescribe. If there have been times when all the students at school or college studied the same things, as if it were obvious that without exposure to a common body of knowledge they would not be educated at all, there have been other times when specialization ran so wild that it might almost seem as if educated men had abandoned the thought of ever talking to each other once their education was completed.

If knowledge is one of our marks, we can hardly be dogmatic about the kind or the amount. A single fertile field tilled with care and imagination can probably develop all the instincts of an educated man. However, if the framer of a curriculum wants to minimize his risks, he can invoke an ancient doctrine which holds that an educated man ought to know a little about everything and a lot about something.

The "little about everything" is best interpreted these days by those who have given most thought to the sort of general education an informed in-

[1] From *Context,* I, No. 1 (Spring, 1961), pp. 4–7. Copyright by Alan Simpson, 1961, and reprinted with his permission.

dividual ought to have. More is required than a sampling of the introductory courses which specialists offer in their own disciplines. Courses are needed in each of the major divisions of knowledge—the humanities, the natural sciences, and social sciences—which are organized with the breadth of view and the imaginative power of competent staffs who understand the needs of interested amateurs. But, over and above this exciting smattering of knowledge, students should bite deeply into at least one subject and taste its full flavor. It is not enough to be dilettantes in everything without striving also to be craftsmen in something.

If there is some ambiguity about the knowledge an educated man should have, there is none at all about the skills. The first is simply the training of the mind in the capacity to think clearly. This has always been the business of education, but the way it is done varies enormously. Marshalling the notes of a lecture is one experience; the opportunity to argue with a teacher is another. Thinking within an accepted tradition is one thing; to challenge the tradition itself is another. The best results are achieved when the idea of the examined life is held firmly before the mind and when the examination is conducted with the zest, rigor, and freedom which really stretches everyone's capacities.

The vital aid to clear thought is the habit of approaching everything we hear and everything we are taught to believe with a certain skepticism. The method of using doubt as an examiner is a familiar one among scholars and scientists, but it is also the best protection which a citizen has against the cant and humbug that surround us.

To be able to listen to a phony argument and to see its dishonesty is surely one of the marks of an educated man. We may not need to be educated to possess some of this quality. A shrewd peasant was always well enough protected against impostors in the market place, and we have all sorts of businessmen who have made themselves excellent judges of phoniness without the benefit of a high-school diploma; but this kind of shrewdness goes along with a great deal of credulity. Outside the limited field within which experience has taught the peasant or the illiterate businessman his lessons, he is often hopelessly gullible. The educated man, by contrast, has tried to develop a critical faculty for general use, and he likes to think that he is fortified against imposture in all its forms.

It does not matter for our purposes whether the impostor is a deliberate liar or not. Some are, but the commonest enemies of mankind are the unconscious frauds. Most salesmen under the intoxication of their own exuberance seem to believe in what they say. Most experts whose *expertise* is only a pretentious sham behave as if they had been solemnly inducted into some kind of priesthood. Very few demagogues are so cynical as to remain undeceived by their own rhetoric, and some of the worst tyrants in history have been fatally sincere. We can leave the disentanglement of motives to the students of fraud and error, but we cannot afford to be taken in by the shams.

We are, of course, surrounded by shams. Until recently the schools were full of them—the notion that education can be had without tears, that puffed rice is a better intellectual diet than oatmeal, that adjustment to the group is more important than knowing where the group is going, and that democracy has made it a sin to separate the sheep from the goats. Mercifully, these are much less evident now than they were before Sputnik startled us into our wits.

In front of the professor are the shams of the learned fraternity. There is the sham science of the social scientist who first invented a speech for fuddling thought and then proceeded to tell us in his lockjawed way what we already knew. There is the sham humanism of the humanist who wonders why civilization that once feasted at his table is repelled by the shredded and desiccated dishes that often lie on it today. There is the sham message of the physical scientist who feels that his mastery of nature has made him an expert in politics and morals, and there are all the other brands of hokum which have furnished material for satire since the first quacks established themselves in the first cloisters.

If this is true of universities with their solemn vows and limited temptations, how much truer is it of the naughty world outside, where the prizes are far more dazzling and the only protection against humbug is the skepticism of the ordinary voter, customer, reader, listener, and viewer? Of course, the follies of human nature are not going to be exorcised by anything that the educator can do, and I am not sure that he would want to exorcise them if he could. There is something irresistibly funny about the old Adam, and life would be duller without his antics. But they ought to be kept within bounds. We are none the better for not recognizing a clown when we see one.

The other basic skill is simply the art of self-expression in speech and on paper. A man is uneducated who has not mastered the elements of clean forcible prose and picked up some relish for style.

It is a curious fact that we style everything in this country—our cars, our homes, our clothes—except our minds. They still chug along like a Model T—rugged, persevering, but far from graceful.

No doubt this appeal for style, like the appeal for clear thinking, can be carried too far. There was once an American who said that the only important thing in life was "to set a chime of words ringing in a few fastidious minds." As far as can be learned, he left this country in a huff to tinkle his little bell in a foreign land. Most of us would think that he lacked a sense of proportion. After all, the political history of this country is full of good judgment expressed in bad prose, and the business history has smashed through to some of its grandest triumphs across acres of broken syntax. But we can discard some of these frontier manners without becoming absurdly precious.

The road ahead bristles with obstacles. There is the reluctance of many people to use one word where they can get away with a half-dozen or a word of one syllable if they can find a longer one. No one has ever told them about the first rule in English composition: every slaughtered syllable is a good deed. The most persuasive teachers of this maxim are undoubtedly the commercial firms that offer a thousand dollars for the completion of a slogan in twenty-five words. They are the only people who are putting a handsome premium on economy of statement.

There is the decay of the habit of memorizing good prose and good poetry in the years when tastes are being formed. It is very difficult to write a bad sentence if the Bible has been a steady companion and very easy to imagine a well-turned phrase if the ear has been tuned on enough poetry.

There is the monstrous proliferation of gobbledy-gook in government, business, and the professions. Take this horrible example of verbal smog.

> It is inherent to motivational phenomena that there is a drive for more gratification than is realistically possible, on any level or in any type of personality organization. Likewise it is inherent to the world of objects that not all potentially desirable opportunities can be realized within a human life span. Therefore, any personality must involve an organization that allocates opportunities for gratifications, that systematizes precedence relative to the limited possibilities. The possibilities of gratification, simultaneously or sequentially, of all need-dispositions are severely limited by the structure of the object system and by the intra-systemic incompatibility of the consequences of gratifying them all.

What this smothered soul is trying to say is simply, "We must pick and choose, because we cannot have everything we want."

Finally, there is the universal employment of the objective test as part of the price which has to be paid for mass education. Nothing but the difficulty of finding enough readers to mark essays can condone a system which reduces a literate student to the ignoble necessity of "blackening the answer space" when he might be giving his mind and pen free play. Though we have managed to get some benefits from these examinations, the simple fact remains that the shapely prose of the Declaration of Independence or the "Gettysburg Address" was never learned under an educational system which employed objective tests. It was mastered by people who took writing seriously, who had good models in front of them, good critics to judge them, and an endless capacity for taking pains. Without that sort of discipline, the arts of self-expression will remain as mutilated as they are now.

The standards which mark an educated man can be expressed in terms of three tests.

The first is a matter of sophistication. Emerson put it nicely when he talked about getting rid of "the nonsense of our wigwams." The wigwam may be an uncultivated home, a suburban conformity, a crass patriotism, or a cramped dogma. Some of this nonsense withers in the classroom. More of it rubs off by simply mixing with people, provided they are drawn from a wide range of backgrounds and exposed within a good college to a civilized tradition. An educated man can be judged by the quality of his prejudices. There is a refined nonsense which survives the raw nonsense which Emerson was talking about.

The second test is a matter of moral values. Though we all know individuals who have contrived to be both highly educated and highly immoral, and though we have all heard of periods in history when the subtlest resources of wit and sophistication were employed to make a mockery of simple values, we do not really believe that a college is doing its job when it is simply multiplying the number of educated scoundrels, hucksters, and triflers.

The health of society depends on simple virtues like honesty, decency, courage, and public spirit. There are forces in human nature which constantly tend to corrupt them, and every age has its own vices. The worst features of ours is probably the obsession with violence. Up to some such time as 1914, it was possible to believe in a kind of moral progress. The quality which distinguished the Victorian from the Elizabethan was a sensitivity to suffering and a revulsion from cruelty which greatly enlarged the idea of human dignity. Since 1914 we have steadily brutalized ourselves. The horrors of modern war, the bestialities of modern political creeds, the uncontrollable vices of modern cities, the favorite themes of modern novelists—all have conspired to degrade us. Some of the corruption is blatant. The authors of the best sellers, after exhausting all the possibilities of sex in its normal and abnormal forms and all the variations of alcoholism and drug addiction, are about to invade the recesses of the hospitals. A clinical study of a hero undergoing the irrigation of his colon is about all there is left to gratify a morbid appetite.

Some of the corruption is insidious. A national columnist recently wrote an article in praise of cockfighting. He had visited a cockfight in the company of Ernest Hemingway. After pointing out that Hemingway had made bullfighting respectable, he proceeded to describe the terrible beauty of fierce indomitable birds trained to kill each other for the excitement of the spectators. Needless to say, there used to be a terrible beauty about Christians defending themselves against lions or about heretics being burned at the stake, and there are still parts of the world where a public execution is regarded as a richly satisfying feast. But for three or four centuries the West taught itself to resist these excitements in the interest of a moral idea.

Educators are needlessly squeamish about their duty to uphold moral values and needlessly perplexed about how to implant them. The corruptions of our times are a sufficient warning that we cannot afford to abandon the duty to the homes and the churches, and the capacity which many institutions have shown to do their duty in a liberal spirit is a sufficient guaranty against bigotry.

Finally, there is the test imposed by the unique challenge of our own times. We are not unique in suffering from moral confusion—these crises are a familiar story—but we are unique in the tremendous acceleration of the rate of social change and in the tremendous risk of a catastrophic end to all our hopes. We cannot afford educated men who have every grace except the gift for survival. An indispensable mark of the modern educated man is the kind of versatile, flexible mind that can deal with new and explosive conditions.

With this reserve, there is little in this profile which has not been familiar for centuries. Unfortunately, the description which once sufficed to suggest its personality has been debased in journalistic currency. The "well-rounded man" has become the organization man, or the man who is so well rounded that he rolls wherever he is pushed. The humanists who invented the idea and preached it for centuries would recoil in contempt from any such notion. They understood the possibilities of the whole man and wanted an educational system which would give the many sides of his nature some chance to develop in harmony. They thought it a good idea to mix the wisdom of the world with the learning of the cloister, to develop the body as well as the mind, to pay a great deal of attention to character, and to neglect no art which could add to the enjoyment of living. It was a spacious idea which offered every hospitality to creative energy. Anyone who is seriously interested in a liberal education must begin by rediscovering it.

ADLAI E. STEVENSON

•

Trained Intelligence—The Nation's Greatest Weapon[1]

The World Must Be Made Safe and Fit for People

Nietzsche said that women were God's second mistake. And I say that Radcliffe is my third mistake. I made a commencement address at Vassar College one time, and wisely concluded that I would never make that mistake again. But I did. The next time it was Smith; and once more I wisely concluded never to face all those disconcerting, lovely young faces again. And here I am, as uncomfortable as I look, making the same mistake for a third time—and of all places at Radcliffe which is such a luminous and pretty part of the boundless intellectual galaxy of Harvard.

I've been wondering *why* I make this foolhardy mistake again and again. Perhaps, like the ancient Greeks, I am so desperate for learning that I even turn to lecturing to acquire it. Or is it, as Dr. Johnson wrote, that one of the last things we men are willing to give up, even in advanced age, is the supposi-

[1] *Vital Speeches of the Day,* July 15, 1963, pp. 581-84. (City News Publ. Co., Pelham, N.Y. delivered at Radcliffe College, Cambridge, Massachusetts, June 12, 1963.)

tion that we have something to say of interest to the opposite sex? But, of course, it's neither. I'm just an old man who can't say no—to President Bunting and certain charming young ladies of my acquaintance.

Do you, by the way, know the difference between a beautiful woman and a charming one? A beauty is a woman you notice; a charmer is one who notices *you!*

I hope you are all going to be charming today, because my assignment is to talk to you for awhile, and yours is to listen to me. I trust we will both finish our work at the same time.

In previous appearances at women's colleges, my solemn remarks were addressed to women specifically—about the place of educated women in our society; about bringing up children in a neurotic world; about the conflict between the office desk and the kitchen sink. After listening to my highly instructive addresses I came to the enlightened conclusion that women would not be truly emancipated until commencement speakers ignored the fact that they were women, and directed their remarks to graduating students who happened to be women and not to women who happened to be graduating.

So, like most of my decisions, I shall of course ignore it and talk to you as women.

I proceed at once, then, to the central question. The question is whether the wonderfully diverse and gifted assemblage of humans on this earth really know how to operate a civilization. Survival is still an open question—not because of environmental hazards, but because of the workings of the human mind. And day by day the problem grows more complex.

However, there is something even more difficult—something even more essential—than comprehending the great complexities. And that is comprehending the great simplicities.

Let me mention only a few. The first is that human ingenuity has shot far ahead of human responsibility. The destructive intelligence has far outstripped the moral imagination. We have created the engines of world annihilation long before we have given sustained thought to the mechanisms of control, let alone mastered them.

Another simplicity is that this world exists for people before it exists for anything else—whether we are talking about ideologies or politics or economics. It exists for people ahead of nations, notions, machines, schemes, or systems.

Therefore, this world must be made safe for people. And it must be made fit for people.

And a third great simplicity is that each of us is born with a capacity for growth—not just physical growth but growth of the ability to think, to create works of beauty, to live freely and wondrously, and to add to the lives of others.

And that is where you come in. For nowadays trained intelligence is the nation's greatest weapon in the battle for a world fit for people and safe for people. We can no longer be content—in the old Ivy League-Oxbridge tradition—to educate a few supremely well. We have to educate every citizen capable of intellectual development. We have to cherish and expand every "erg" of brain power our society can uncover. Our gravest social evils now spring from the neglect of training and opportunity. One thinks of the immature adolescents in our big cities, often from colored families, who are flung skill-less on a labor market which is hungry only for skills. Our greatest social opportunities—in every field of research and discovery—spring, on the contrary, from the scale of the investment we are prepared to make in minds. Some economists are ready to argue that perhaps 60 per cent of our gains in output and productivity over the last fifty years can be traced back not to physical capital—in plant and tools—but to mental investment in quick brains and visionary imagination.

But I believe the need for trained minds extends far beyond the limits of economic life. The forces of science and technology have made the world one, abolished space, given us instant communication, brought the world's leaders into our homes and showed us all the cultures of our shrinking globe co-existing with our own in a familiarity we might not have felt for even the next county a hundred years back.

In such a transformed environment, we cannot rely on tradition or habit or what has been called the "conventional wisdom." We can rely on only the rational response of trained minds—minds that can discern facts and judge outcomes, minds sufficiently informed of the lessons of the past to know when, say, an analogy from Thucydides makes sense in the modern context and when it does not, minds disinterested enough to distinguish between a prejudice and a principle, minds steady enough to weigh risks and imaginative enough to take them. Genius consists in anticipating events and knowing how to accelerate or prevent them.

At any time of great social upheaval—and no age has undergone such changes as our own—profound emotions, above all the emotion of fear, are unleashed. There always seems to be so much to lose when changes are proposed—even though more will be lost if the changes are not accomplished.

In the summer before the French Revolution, all of France was, it seems, gripped by a deep malaise, an underlying panic to which contemporaries gave the name of *la grande Peur*—the great Fear. In our own country, where vast social transformations, especially in the relations between the races, have to be achieved, you will find, too, a fringe of hate and fear mongers who appeal to panic, ignorance and suspicion.

Again, I ask, with what can we combat these panic reactions except with steady intelligence in command of the facts, with the moderation that comes from knowledge, with the freedom that springs from objectivity? Today, as always, it is the truth that makes us free. But how, in this confused and confusing world, can we recognize the truth and ahere to it unless we have the tools for truth-seeking—a critical faculty, a certain humility in face of the facts, the coolness and disinterest which comes from habits of study, concentration and judgment? A mind clear of cant, a mind that "is not passion's slave," is *not* the natural state of our grasping egos; it is something we have to achieve, and it is something which it is the proudest aim of education to produce.

So, I repeat, for all who love the human city and wish to see its commerce proceed in dignity and peace, commencement day is or should be a day of rejoicing. And indeed, as I look about, I do rejoice. For Radcliffe is about to launch another task force of intelligent and disciplined good will. And we can take comfort from the fact that one of the truly revolutionary consequences of modern science is that the great majority of you here today will be alive and effective some fifty years hence—yielding a steady return in terms of good sense, good work and calm and rational influence.

When, on Commencement Day, a man looks forward to his unfolding future, he is unlikely to see, as it were built into it, any marked discontinuity. He will change jobs and places, no doubt, but probably remain broadly within his chosen calling, advancing in it with what skill and industry he has, establishing his family and his reputation, and hopefully ending as Chairman of the Board. Of course, there are exceptions. I, for one, can guarantee that there are few discontinuities as marked as those of politics and public affairs.

But for most women there is a large and obvious "discontinuity" to be faced —by most of you, I suspect, fairly soon—and that is to be married and raise a family. Then—in our servantless society—will follow some years in which the life of the mind will co-exist, with some difficulty, with the life of the diaper and the kitchen sink. From the kind of work pursued in the Greek ideal of the academy, you proceed to the work which in the Greek definition is the work of the slave. For the Greeks, the servile quality of domestic work lay precisely in its recurrent rhythm—meal after meal, bed-making after bed-making, washing day after washing day.

Is this, then, the parabola of your future—from scholar to slave? The contrast is too savage, no doubt, but the dilemma is one on which we must reflect.

Let us put into the balance first all the obvious, unquestionable joys and rewards of family life—love, companionship, the excitement of unfolding young minds, the satisfactions of dreary work well done. And in our democratic society where politics are in large measure a "do-it-yourself" job, much community action depends upon voluntary work and many housewives will be able to make their contribution as educated citizens, too.

So, I do not suggest in our free, open society that woman's home is her prison. On the contrary, it will be for many of you the proud center of a rich and satisfying life.

And yet my doubts persist. It is partly a social concern. Fifty per cent of our brains are locked up on the female side. (Perhaps your estimate is even higher!) Can we afford to waste a large percentage of this intellectual power? Can we afford not to use it in the sciences, in the professions?

It is also an individual problem. Many women *are* content with the domestic role. But some are not. And since, with women as with men, brain power comes not as an evenly distributed mental quota but often in large patchy concentrations, it is often where the talents are highest that the frustration is greatest, too. Social and individual waste reach a peak when the young woman who has it in her to be, say, a brilliant atomic physicist, or a pioneering sociologist, or an historian of formidable insight finds herself in front of the dishes and the diapers. The case may be exceptional. But surely in a free society we must never let the tyranny of the normal trample down the supreme contribution of the unique.

Another problem, as I have said, is that today a woman of forty is still young. She has thirty years or more of active life ahead of her. Is there not here again a factor of waste if, after ten or twenty years of housework, re-entry into active professional, civic or academic life is not available?

Marietta Tree describes it as

> the dilemma in which the woman of the West frequently finds herself; her children grown, her life span longer, her tastes whetted by her education—unhappiness and dissatisfaction are all too often her lot at a time when the challenges and the achievements of the 20th Century should occupy her interest and her being.

In a world still very largely run by men, you will not find many ready-made answers to these questions—even though they are urgent for you and should be urgent for all of us. Men, clearly, have had some difficulty in making up their minds about women and their role: Freud remarked that after 30 years of research into the feminine soul, he still could not answer the great question: What do women want? Some philosophers dismiss you as a "second sex," inferior, says Schopenhauer, in every respect to the first. Lord Chesterfield was not alone in thinking women "only children of a larger growth" and relegated these creatures without "solid reasoning or good sense" to the kitchen or the boudoir. And we all know the restricted sphere of influence Bismark allotted you in children, kitchen and church. But I like best Maeterlinck's observation—that woman is mysterious—like everyone else!

You have, of course, had noble defenders too—Plato, John Stuart Mill, Erasmus, Darwin, Shelley. One of the most unequivocal recent statements in favor of removing all irrational restraints upon your capacities came from that remarkable man, Pope John XXIII.

Certainly our Western tradition has never denied you souls—as did the ancient world—or made your total segregation an essential foundation of the social order. But contemporary reactions to the role of women in our society remain ambiguous, and, as a result, women often lack a clear, confident picture of their status and even their identity, and for some this uncertainty reaches a tragic pitch of frustration.

Nor do some of the impersonal forces in our society help to clarify the issue.

When were women so bombarded with the suggestion that their success depends upon the right mascara on the eyelash and the right beguiling whiff of irresistible perfume? The aspect of glamor, of allure, of conquest screams at you from a million color ads and television screens. Influenced by these hosts of persuaders, you could come to believe that your rating as a woman, as a wife, as a mother depended on the sheen of your hair, the softness of your hands, your ability to do fifty hot, vexing, repetitive jobs, and emerge looking like Jackie Kennedy or Princess Grace.

I remember one of those masterly Thurber drawings portraying his furiously funny view of the war between the sexes. A shapeless Thurber male leans aggressively over the back of a sofa at a startled and equally shapeless Thurber female. "Where," he hisses at her, "where did you get those great brown eyes and that tiny mind?" Can you have such perpetual insistence upon those aspects of women which are determined by her sex, and not diminish in some degree her other attributes—intellectual power, executive ability, common sense, mature wisdom?

Her image can be moulded in other ways, too. "A woman preaching," said the great Johnson, "is like a dog on its hind legs. It is not that she does it well. The remarkable thing is that she does it at all." It is frustrating, it is humiliating, it can be destructive of ease and confidence if women have to feel like dogs on their hind legs whenever they leave the domestic haven to which so much of the folk thought of our society assigns them.

None of all this should, however, discourage you. Many great social transformations have occurred *against* the grain of accepted thought and practice, and if society is slow to realize how much it loses by this potential stifling and inhibiting of half its brain power, there is a good deal that can be done to speed up the recognition. Radcliffe is the sponsor of one such approach in your Institute for Independent Study, at which women receive fellowships to enable them to carry on their scholastic and professional interests part-time to prepare themselves for greater participation in the post-domestic years.

I would hope to see every university in America provided with similar institutes, so that no woman graduate need be out of reach of what, I imagine, she chiefly needs—a center for continuing work, for encouragement, for contact, for the exchange of ideas, for guidance and stimulus and, where feasible, for assistance, at the right stage, in making her return or her entry to professional and academic life.

In devising institutes for retraining, in fashioning tax patterns which encourage both continuous and post-domestic professional life, in reconsidering problems of responsibility and promotion, we have to use genuine social inventiveness, and with institutes such as yours—and with others of similar intent—an initiative of first class importance has been taken.

Society could help more than it does to give its women citizens the fullest sense of participation. Yet I believe that for men and women alike the fundamental liberations, the genuine experiences of equality, depend not only upon the opportunities—or disabilities—society offers, but also on the reactions and beliefs of the human beings involved. Confusion of roles, problems of identity have their origins in divided and uncertain minds, and there are ways, I think, in which all of us, as members of this strange, varied, immensely talented yet sometimes delinquent human family, can confront the future with some hope of making better sense of the years ahead.

In what I have to say now—do not be perturbed, this *is* the peroration—I confess that I have been profoundly influenced by a great and noble woman whose friendship was one of the exhilarating rewards of a political career in which the rewards were not, shall we say, the most notable feature. Since Eleanor Roosevelt's death last year, I have reflected often on what made up the peculiar quality of her greatness. And I can only conclude that it was the absolute quality of her disinterestedness. She did everything because it was worth doing. She did nothing because it would help to enhance her own role. Of that she seemed simply to be unconscious. Work was there. Work had to be done. And it would require all the energy and concentration of which she was capable. But the fact that Eleanor Roosevelt was doing it interested her not at all.

I have never known her equal for objectivity, for unbiased judgment, for a sort of divine fairness and simplicity which sprang from the fact that she never felt her own interests or status or reputation to be involved in her activities. And perhaps for all of us who aspire to that most satisfactory form of equality—parity of esteem, equality of respect—the lesson of Eleanor Roosevelt's greatness was her lack of personal, prideful involvement in the work which came her way.

I recall the beguiling statement of an 18th century lady, who remarked that she did not find the Doge's garden so remarkable as the fact that *she* was sitting in it. For Eleanor Roosevelt, what *she* did, what *her* role might be, how people thought of *her, her* image, *her* repute—all this meant nothing. The work to be done meant all.

So this is the thought that I would leave with you as you start to play all the various parts which life will bring you—do them all if you can for the sake of the work, do them as little as possible for the sake of yourself. Resist those obsessive commercial voices. Be indifferent—if possible—to any limited view of your part in society. See your life as a whole, with times, no doubt, of concentrated domesticity, with times beyond when you will have leisure and energy and experience for work in the human city.

All these forms of work and dedication will be fruitful, will support your self-respect and give you tranquility, if they are done with self-forgetfulness because they are good in themselves. None of them, on the contrary, will release you if you are imprisoned in a narrow, inward-looking self and see them as means of *self* expression, *self* fulfillment, and heaven knows what other confusions of purpose and integrity.

That this mood of detachment is more difficult for women than for men in our society, I do not doubt. If people constantly exclaim that you as a woman are doing this or that, your role, not the work in hand, can appear the main objective. But never doubt one thing. The more the work is done for its own sake, the more it imposes its own respect. The more objective and disinterested your efforts, the more rapidly shall we all—men and women alike—reach that condition for which a famous English woman pleaded so eloquently when she wrote:

> Let us consider women in the grand light of human creatures, who in common with men are placed on earth to unfold their faculties.

May every one of you stand beside us males, not as the classical helpmeet one step behind, but shoulder to shoulder, "in the grand light of human creatures."

ROBERT M. HUTCHINS

•

The Meaning and Significance of Academic Freedom[1]

The arguments for academic freedom are the same as those for freedom of speech, and they rest on the same foundation. Here are the familiar words of John Stuart Mill:

> If all mankind minus one were of one opinion, and only one person were of the contrary opinion, mankind would be no more justified in silencing that one person, than he, if he had the power, would be justified in silencing mankind. . . . the peculiar evil of silencing the expression of an opinion is, that it is robbing the human race; posterity as well as the existing generation; those who dissent from the opinion, still more than those who hold it. If the opinion is right, they are deprived of the opportunity of exchanging error for truth: if wrong, they lose, what is almost as great a benefit, the clearer perception and livelier impression of truth, produced by its collision with error.

Man is a learning animal. The state is an association the primary aim of which is the virtue and intelligence of the people. Men learn by discussion, through the clash of opinion. The best and most progressive society is that in which expression is freest. Mill said, "There ought to exist the fullest liberty

[1] From *The Annals of the American Academy of Political and Social Science,* XXX (July, 1955), 72-78. Copyright, 1955, The American Academy of Political and Social Science.

of professing and discussing, as a matter of ethical conviction, any doctrine, however immoral it may be considered." The civilization we seek is the civilization of the dialogue, the civilization of the logos.

In such a society the intelligent man and the good citizen are identical. The educational system does not aim at indoctrination in accepted values but at the improvement of society through the production of the intelligent man and the good citizen. Education necessarily involves the critical examination of conflicting points of view; it cannot flourish in the absence of free inquiry and discussion.

In a democracy what the public needs to know about the teachers in the educational system is that they are competent. The competent teacher knows the subject he is teaching and how to communicate it to his pupils. Unlike the teacher in a totalitarian state, he is not supposed to purvey the prevailing dogma. He is supposed to encourage his students to use their own intelligence and to reach their own conclusions.

The definition of competence does not shift with every wind of prejudice, religious, political, racial, or economic. If competence had been the issue at Brown University during the free silver controversy, the President would not have been asked to resign because of his premature distaste for the Gold Standard. The modern note was struck there. What was requested of the President was "not a renunciation of his views, but a forbearance to promulgate them." And the reason was that these views were "injurious to the pecuniary interests of the University." On the other hand, the standard of competence did protect a professor at the University of Chicago who was a leading critic of Samuel Insull and the other local oligarchs of the time. He was doubtless injurious to the pecuniary interests of the university, but he and it lived through it, and he is today the senior Senator from Illinois.

WRONG QUESTIONS

We have been stifling education in this country because we have been asking the wrong questions. If you are asking the right questions, you ask about a subject of discussion whether it is important. You do not forbid students to discuss a subject, like the entry of Red China into the United Nations, on the ground that it is too important. The right question about a subject of research and the methods of investigation is whether competent scholars believe that the subject should be investigated and that this is the way to investigate it. You do not permit the Post Office Department to protect the Johns Hopkins School of Advanced International Studies from *Izvestia* and *Pravda*. The right question about a textbook is whether competent people think it can make a contribution to education. You do not ask whether incompetent people are going to be offended by passages taken out of context. The right question about a research man on unclassified work is whether he is competent to do it. You do not act like the United States Public Health Service and weaken the country by withdrawing contracts from research workers on unstated grounds that can only be grounds of loyalty.

As I have said, the right question about a teacher is whether he is competent. If we had been asking about competence we should have had quite a different atmosphere in the case of teachers who were Communists or ex-Communists, who refused to testify about themselves, or who declined to discuss the political affiliations of others. We have been so busy being sophisticated anti-Communists, detecting the shifts and devices of Communist infiltration, that we have failed to observe that our educational responsibility is to have a good educational system. We do not discharge that responsibility by invading civil liberties, reducing the number of qualified teachers available, eliminating good textbooks, and intimidating the teaching staff. The standard of competence means that there must be some relation between the charges against a teacher and the quality of his teaching. The standard of competence would have protected us against teachers following a party line or conducting propaganda. If a teacher sought to indoctrinate his pupils, which is the only circumstance under which he could be dangerous as a teacher, he would be incompetent, and should be removed as such. The standard of competence would have saved us from the excesses of the silly season, such as the refusal of the University of Washington to let Professor Oppenheimer lecture there on physics, and from the consequences of concentrating on the negative task of preventing one particular unpopular variety of infiltration. If we had used the standard of competence we should have been free to fix our minds on the positive responsibility of building an educational system, and with half the energy we have put into being scared to death we might have built a great one.

Since our guilty conscience tells us that there ought to be some connection between what a man does and the punishment visited upon him, we often try to pretend that this is the rule we are following. The Attorney General of the United States, speaking in New York three weeks ago, said that schools should not be sanctuaries or proving grounds "for subversives shaping the minds of innocent children."

This picture of subversives shaping the minds of innocent children has nothing to do with the case. The teachers who have lost their jobs in the campaign against subversives have not been charged with doing anything to the minds of any children. The case of Goldie Watson here in Philadelphia is typical: testimony about the good she had done the minds of the children in her classes was rejected as impertinent. The only evidence allowed was as to whether she had declined to answer questions about her political affiliations. She had, and she was fired. The same procedure seems to be followed everywhere, even at Harvard. When a professor there is called on the carpet, the issue is whether he is a member of something or other, or whether he has lied or refused to answer questions about such membership. The matter of his competence in his field or what he has done to the innocent minds of the Harvard students is never referred to.

FEAR OF IDEAS

We are getting so afraid of ideas that we are afraid of people who associate with people who are said to have ideas, even if they themselves have not expressed them. The State Curriculum Commission of California is now studying investigators' reports on the authors of twenty-three textbooks. Dr. C. C. Trillingham, Los Angeles County Superintendent of Schools and a member of the commission, said, "If an author is aligned with the Communists, we don't want his textbook, even if there is no Red propaganda in it."

We regard what a man says as irrelevant in determining whether we will listen to him. What a man does in his job is irrelevant in determining whether he should continue in it. This amounts to a decision that people whose ideas or whose associates' ideas we regard as dangerous cannot be permitted to earn a living or make a contribution in any capacity to the well-being of the community. The Supreme Court of California has just taken this logical next step: it has held, in effect, that a Communist can have no contractual rights that the rest of us are bound to respect.

Not long ago at a dinner of the senior members of the faculty of the University of Birmingham in England, I sat across the table from a professor who is a member of the executive committee of the Communist party of Great Britain. The British appear to be getting value out of a scholar whom none of the great American universities could appoint.

FIFTH AMENDMENT

One of the more important advances in law and government effected by the struggles of our ancestors is that proclaimed by the Fifth Amendment. Why should the government demand that a man convict himself out of his own mouth instead of requiring prosecution to make the effort to establish the charges that it has brought against him? All the Fifth Amendment means is: prove it. Injury is added to insult if there is no pretence that the questions asked must be relevant or proper. In some public school systems refusal to answer any questions by the Board of Education or any other public body is insubordination; insubordination justifies dismissal.

Surely the issue is whether the questions are legitimate. It cannot be insubordination to refuse to answer illegitimate questions. We have gone very far under the influence of one of the rollicking dicta of Mr. Justice Holmes, that there is no constitutional right to be a policeman; but not so far that public employment can be denied on a ground that has nothing to do with the duties to be performed. If the President were to refuse to employ baldheaded men in the federal establishment, the Supreme Court would find, I believe, that the bald had been deprived of their constitutional rights.

IS IT TOO LATE?

You may say that the issue I am discussing is academic in every sense: there is no use now in talking about the right of Communists, ex-Communists, or persons who decline to answer questions about their political affiliations to teach in the United States. Milton Mayer in his forthcoming book, *They Thought They Were Free*, tells the story of the way history passed Martin Niemoeller by. When the Nazis attacked the Communists, he was a little uneasy, but he was not a Communist, and he did nothing. When they attacked the Socialists, he was uneasy, but he was not a Socialist, and he did nothing. They went after the schools, the press, and the Jews, but he was not directly affected, and he did nothing. Then they attacked the Church. Pastor Niemoeller was a churchman. He tried to do something, but it was too late.

I hope it is not too late to point out where our preoccupation with public relations and our failure of courage and intelligence may take us. The New York *Times* on March 17 and the New York *Herald Tribune* on March 19 published editorials on the question whether teachers who decline to testify about others should be dismissed. The significant thing about the editorials is this: they both, perhaps unconsciously, extend the limits of the prevailing boycott. The *Times* condemns "adherence to Communist doctrine," thus adding theoretical Marxists to those automatically disqualified. The *Herald Tribune* comes out against Communists "or any other brands of subversives," thus opening vast new unmapped areas of investigation, recrimination, and confusion.

REECE COMMITTEE

These two newspapers bitterly attacked the Reece committee, appointed in the House to investigate foundations; but they appear to have succumbed to its influence, which is another evidence that if you say something outrageous authoritatively, loudly, and often enough you will eventually find yourself quoted in the most respectable places. The Reece committee includes among the subversives almost anybody who differs with the two members of the committee who constitute the majority. Zechariah Chafee, Jr., said at the University of Oregon last October, "The word 'subsersive' has no precise definition in American law. It is as vague as 'heretical' was in the medieval trials which sent men to the stake." Leading the list of Reece committee subversives are those who do not share its philosophical prejudices. The committee condemned a philosophical doctrine, empiricism, and those who hold it as the fountainhead of the subversive tendencies now engulfing the country. If a philosophical position can be treasonable, particularly one as harmless as a preference for fact over theory, and if two politicians can make it treasonable, freedom of thought, discussion, and teaching may not be with us long.

By repetition the Reece committee is obtaining unconscious acceptance of another proposition, which, coupled with the proposition that politicians may declare a doctrine and its adherents subversive, still further imperils freedom of teaching and inquiry. This is the proposition that tax-exempt money is public money and that a tax-exempt institution is therefore subject to a special variety of public surveillance. An extension of this proposition is found in the California statute requiring all claimants of tax exemption to take a nondisloyalty oath. If carried to the logical limits hinted at in the Reece Report, this notion of the public control of private, tax-exempt corporations could deprive the independent educational institutions of this country of their autonomy, that characteristic which has given them their value in the development of the American educational system.

Tax exemption is conferred for the purpose of facilitating the performance of a public task by a private agency. A corporation that carries on education and research to that extent relieves the taxpayers of their obligation to finance such work in state-supported institutions. Tax exemption imposes no duty on colleges and universities except that of conducting teaching and research according to their best judgment of what good teaching and research are. It does not impose the duty of making sure that the teaching and research conform to the views of the majority of a legislative committee.

CALIFORNIA SENATE COMMITTEE ON UN-AMERICAN ACTIVITIES

Consider what those views might be. Richard E. Combs, Chief Counsel for the California Senate Committee on Un-American Activities, testified two years ago before a subcommittee of the United States Senate. He gave an account of how Communists reorient courses of instruction. He thought it worth while to report that the name of a course at a California university had been changed from public speaking to speech, and the books had been changed from Robert Louis Stevenson, Masefield, and Kipling to John Stuart Mill. The subversive nature of these changes may not be clear to you, but it was clear to Mr. Combs and, from all that appears, to the California committee that employs him and the committee of the United States Senate before which he testified. The appraisal of courses of study or of the performance of teachers is a professional job, not to be undertaken by the naïve and unskilled.

Consider the role of the California Senate Committee on Un-American Activities in the administration of California institutions of higher learning. The committee claims that a chain of security officers on campuses has been welded by its efforts. If its claims are correct—and they have been disputed—professors and students at eleven institutions are being continuously spied upon for the benefit of a legislative committee. The committee has an arrangement whereby it passes on the qualifications of members and prospective members of the faculties from the standpoint of their Americanism. The reason for this is said to be that the colleges and universities are not competent to assess the Americanism of their teachers, and the committee is. According to the committee at least a hundred members of these faculties have been forced to resign and at least one hundred prospective members have failed of appointment because of the committe's work. It is too bad that the committee has not disclosed the information that led to the interdiction of its victims. One shudders to think that it may have been enough to have been heard quoting John Stuart Mill.

BEHIND ACADEMIC FREEDOM

But the issue of legal control is not basic. Academic freedom comes and goes because of some conviction about the purpose of education on the part of those who make the decisions in society. The Kaiser gave professors freedom of research because he believed that this was one way to make Germany strong and prosperous. This freedom did not extend to professors who wanted to engage actively in politics on the wrong side, the side of the Social Democratic party. The Kaiser did not set a high value on independent criticism.

In a democratic community the question is what do the people think education is and what do they think it is for? I once asked a former Minister of Education of the Netherlands what would have happened if he had exercised his undoubted legal authority and appointed professors of whom the faculties of the Dutch universities did not approve. He said, "My government would have fallen." He meant that the people of Holland would not tolerate political interference with the universities: they understood the universities well enough to recognize interference when they saw it and felt strongly enough about it to make their wishes effective.

The public officers and businessmen who are the trustees of the provincial universities in the United Kingdom have legal control over them, but would never think of exercising it in any matter affecting education and research. They limit themselves to business. The taxpayers now meet more than half the cost of Oxford and Cambridge, but no Englishman supposes that this entitles the government to exert any influence in their academic affairs.

If the people believe that independent thought and criticism are essential to the progress of society, if they think that universities are centers of such criticism and that the rest of the educational system is intended primarily to prepare the citizen to think for himself, then academic freedom will not be a problem, it will be a fact. Under these circumstances teachers would not be second-class citizens, subject to limitations of expression and behavior that show the public thinks the teacher of today is the nursemaid of yesterday. A teacher would be appointed because he was capable of independent thought and criticism and because he could help the rising generation learn to think for itself. He would be removed only if those who appointed him proved to be mistaken in these matters. The proof of their error would have to be made to persons who could understand the issue—an out-of-hand administrative removal approved by a board of laymen without participation by academic experts is a denial of academic freedom.

ACADEMIC RESPONSIBILITY

The people of this country think that education is a perfectly splendid thing and have not the faintest idea of what it is about. The reason that they are in this condition is that educators have had no time and little inclination to explain. After all, the great desideratum of American education in the last thirty-five years has been money. If you want money, you do not talk about independent thought and criticism; you do not engage in it too obtrusively; you may even suppress it if it becomes too flagrant. To get money you must be popular. "He thinks too much" is a classical reference to an unpopular man. Or as a great industralist once remarked to a friend of mine, "You are either a Communist or a thinker."

I have no doubt that much of the trouble of recent years about academic freedom has been the result of the cold war and our panic about it. As Professor Chafee has said, "Freedom of speech belongs to a people which is free from fear." But the basic issue is public understanding. If public understanding had been serious and complete, the cold war could not have thrown us off our balance.

I do not deny that many eloquent statements of the purpose of American education have been made. They cannot offset the impression created by the official propaganda of educational institutions, by their fatuous efforts to please everybody, and by their emphasis on the nonintellectual and even anti-intellectual activities associated with education in this country. Freedom of teaching and research will not survive unless the people understand why it should. They will not understand if there is no relation between the freedom that is claimed and the purpose it is supposed to serve. If the teacher of today is the nursemaid of yesterday, he does not need academic freedom—at least the nursemaid never did.

Academic freedom is indispensable to the high calling of the academic profession. If the profession is true to the calling, it will deserve the freedom, and it will get it.

A. E. HOUSMAN

•

Introductory Lecture[1]

The acquisition of knowledge needs no formal justification: its true sanction is a much simpler affair, and inherent in itself. People are too prone to torment themselves with devising far-fetched reasons: they cannot be content with the simple truth asserted by Aristotle: "all men possess by nature a craving for knowledge." πάντες ἄνθρωποι τοῦ εἰδέναι ὀρέγονται φύσει. This is no rare endowment scattered sparingly from heaven that falls on a few heads and passes others by: curiosity, the desire to know things as they are, is a craving no less native to the being of man, no less universal through mankind, than the craving for food and drink. And do you suppose that such a desire means nothing? The very definition of the good, says Aristotle again, is that which all desire. Whatever is pleasant is good, unless it can be shewn that in the long run it is harmful, or, in other words, not pleasant but unpleasant. Mr. Spencer himself on another subject speaks thus: "So profound an ignorance is there of the laws of life, that men do not even know that their sensations are their natural guides, and (when not rendered morbid by long continued disobedience) their trustworthy guides." The desire of knowledge does not need, nor could it possibly possess, any higher or more authentic sanction than the happiness which attends its gratification.

Perhaps it will be objected that we see, every day of our lives, plenty of people who exhibit no pleasure in learning and experience no desire to know; people, as Plato agreeably puts it, who wallow in ignorance with the complacency of a brutal hog. We do; and here is the reason. If the cravings of hunger and thirst are denied satisfaction, if a man is kept from food and drink, the man starves to death, and there is an end of him. This is a result which arrests the attention of even the least observant mind; so it is generally recognised that hunger and thirst cannot be neglected with impunity, that a man ought to eat and drink. But if the craving for knowledge is denied satisfaction, the result which follows is not so striking to the eye. The man, worse luck, does not starve to death. He still preserves the aspect and motions of a living human being; so people think that the hunger and thirst for knowledge can be neglected with impunity. And yet, though the man does not die altogether, part of him dies, part of him starves to death: as Plato says, he never attains completeness and health, but walks lame to the end of his life and returns imperfect and good for nothing to the world below.

But the desire of knowledge, stifle it though you may, is none the less originally born with every man; and nature does not implant desires in us for nothing, nor endow us with faculties in vain. "Sure," says Hamlet,

[1] From A. E. Housman, *Introductory Lecture, Delivered . . . October 3, 1892* (1937), pp. 26-36. By permission of Cambridge University Press.

> Sure, He that made us with such large discourse,
> Looking before and after, gave us not
> That capability and godlike reason
> To fust in us unused.

The faculty of learning is ours that we may find in its exercise that delight which arises from the unimpeded activity of any energy in the groove nature meant it to run in. Let a man acquire knowledge not for this or that external and incidental good which may chance to result from it, but for itself; not because it is useful or ornamental, but because it is knowledge, and therefore good for man to acquire. "Brothers," says Ulysses in Dante, when with his old and tardy companions he had left Seville on the right hand and Ceuta on the other, and was come to that narrow pass where Hercules assigned his landmarks to hinder man from venturing farther: "Brothers, who through a hundred thousand dangers have reached the West, deny not, to this brief vigil of your senses that remains, experience of the unpeopled world behind the sunset. Consider of what seed ye are sprung: ye were not formed to live like brutes, but to follow virtue and knowledge." For knowledge resembles virtue in this, and differs in this from other possessions, that it is not merely a means of procuring good, but is good in itself simply: it is not a coin which we pay down to purchase happiness, but has happiness indissolubly bound up with it. Fortitude and continence and honesty are not commended to us on the ground that they conduce, as on the whole they do conduce, to material success, nor yet on the ground that they will be rewarded hereafter: those whose office it is to exhort mankind to virtue are ashamed to degrade the cause they plead by proffering such lures as these. And let us too disdain to take lower ground in commending knowledge: let us insist that the pursuit of knowledge, like the pursuit of righteousness, is part of man's duty to himself, and remember the Scripture where it is written: "He that refuseth instruction despiseth his own soul."

I will not say, as Prof. Tyndall has somewhere said, that all happiness belongs to him who can say from his heart "I covet truth." Entire happiness is not attainable either by this or by any other method. Nay it may be urged on the contrary that the pursuit of truth in some directions is even injurious to happiness, because it compels us to take leave of delusions which were pleasant while they lasted. It may be urged that the light shed on the origin and destiny of man by the pursuit of truth in some directions is not altogether a cheerful light. It may be urged that man stands to-day in the position of one who has been reared from his cradle as the child of a noble race and the heir to great possessions, and who finds at his coming of age that he has been deceived alike as to his origin and his expectations, that he neither springs of the high lineage he fancied, nor will inherit the vast estate he looked for, but must put off his towering pride, and contract his boundless hopes, and begin the world anew from a lower level: and this, it may be urged, comes of pursuing knowledge. But even conceding this, I suppose the answer to be that knowledge, and especially disagreeable knowledge, cannot by any art be totally excluded even from those who do not seek it. Wisdom, said Aeschylus long ago, comes to men whether they will or no. The house of delusions is cheap to build, but draughty to live in, and ready at any instant to fall; and it is surely truer prudence to move our furniture betimes into the open air than to stay indoors until our tenement tumbles about our ears. It is and it must in the long run be better for a man to see things as they are than to be ignorant of them; just as there is less fear of stumbling or of striking against corners in the daylight than in the dark.

Nor again will I pretend that, as Bacon asserts, "the pleasure and delight of knowledge and learning far surpasseth all other in nature." This is too much the language of a salesman crying his own wares. The pleasures of the intellect are notoriously less vivid than either the pleasures of sense or the pleasures of the affections, and therefore, especially in the season of youth, the pursuit of knowledge is likely enough to be neglected and lightly esteemed in comparison with other pursuits offering much stronger immediate attractions. But the pleasure of learning and knowing, though not the keenest, is yet the least perishable of pleasures; the least subject to external things, and the play of chance, and the wear of time. And as a prudent man puts money by to serve as a provision for the material wants of his old age, so too he needs to lay up against the end of his days provision for the intellect. As the years go by, comparative values are found to alter: Time, says Sophocles, takes many things which once were pleasures and brings them nearer to pain. In the day when the strong men shall bow themselves, and desire shall fail, it will be a matter of yet more concern than now, whether one can say "my mind to me a kingdom is"; and whether the windows of the soul look out upon a broad and delightful landscape, or face nothing but a brick wall.

Well then, once we have recognised that knowledge in itself is good for man, we shall need to invent no pretexts for studying this subject or that; we shall import no extraneous considerations of use or ornament to justify us in learning one thing rather than another. If a certain department of knowledge specially attracts a man, let him study that, and study it because it attracts him; and let him not fabricate excuses for that which requires no excuse, but rest assured that the reason why it most attracts him is that it is best for him. The majority of mankind, as is only natural, will be most attracted by those sciences which most nearly concern human life; those sciences which, in Bacon's phrase, are drenched in flesh and blood, or, in the more elegant language of the *Daily Telegraph,* palpitate with actuality. The men who are attracted to the drier and the less palpitating sciences, say logic or pure mathematics or textual criticism, are likely to be fewer in number; but they are not to suppose that the comparative unpopularity of such learning renders it any the less worthy of pursuit. Nay they may if they like console themselves with Bacon's observation that "this same *lumen siccum* doth parch and offend most men's watery and soft natures," and infer, if it pleases them, that their natures are less soft and watery than other men's. But be that as it may, we can all dwell together in unity without crying up our own pursuits or depreciating the pursuits of others on factitious grounds. We are not like the Ottoman sultans of old time, who thought they could never enjoy a moment's security till they had murdered all their brothers. There is no rivalry between the studies of Arts and Laws and Science but the rivalry of fellow-soldiers in striving which can most victoriously achieve the common end of all, to set back the frontier of darkness.

It is the glory of God, says Solomon, to conceal a thing: but the honour of kings is to search out a matter. Kings have long abdicated that province; and we students are come into their inheritance: it is our honour to search out the things which God has concealed. In Germany at Easter time they hide coloured eggs about the house and the garden that the children may amuse themselves in hunting after them and finding them. It is to some such game of hide-and-seek that we are invited by that power which planted in us the desire to find out what is concealed, and stored the universe with hidden things that we might delight ourselves in discovering them. And the pleasure of discovery differs from other pleasures in this, that it is shadowed by no fear of satiety on the one hand or of frustration on the other. Other desires perish in their gratification, but the desire of knowledge never: the eye is not satisfied with seeing nor the ear filled with hearing. Other desires become the occasion of pain through dearth of the material to gratify them, but not the desire of knowledge: the sum of things to be known is inexhaustible, and however long we read we shall never come to the end of our story-book. So long as the mind of man is what it is, it will continue to exult in advancing on the unknown throughout the infinite field of the universe; and the tree of knowledge will remain for ever, as it was in the beginning, a tree to be desired to make one wise.

PART II

READING AND WRITING

Reading

FRANCIS BACON

•

Of Studies[1]

Studies serve for delight, for ornament, and for ability. Their chief use for delight is in privateness and retiring; for ornament, is in discourse; and for ability, is in the judgment and disposition of business; for expert men can execute, and perhaps judge of particulars, one by one; but the general counsels, and the plots and marshaling of affairs come best from those that are learned. To spend too much time in studies is sloth; to use them too much for ornament is affectation; to make judgment wholly by their rules is the humor of a scholar. They perfect nature, and are perfected by experience; for natural abilities are like natural plants, that need pruning by study; and studies themselves do give forth directions too much at large, except they be bounded in by experience. Crafty men contemn studies, simple men admire them, and wise men use them; for they teach not their own use; but that is a wisdom without them and above them, won by observation. Read not to contradict and confute, nor to believe and take for granted, nor to find talk and discourse, but to weigh and consider. Some books are to be tasted, others to be swallowed, and some few to be chewed and digested; that is, some books are to be read only in parts; others to be read but not curiously, and some few to be read wholly, and with diligence and attention. Some books also may be read by deputy, and

[1] From *The Essayes or Counsels, Civill and Morall* (enlarged ed., London, 1625), No. 50. The text has been somewhat modernized.

extracts made of them by others; but that would be only in the less important arguments and the meaner sort of books; else distilled books are, like common distilled waters, flashy things. Reading maketh a full man; conference a ready man; and writing an exact man. And, therefore, if a man write little, he had need have a great memory; if he confer little, he had need have a present wit; and if he read little, he had need have much cunning, to seem to know that he doth not. Histories make men wise; poets, witty; the mathematics, subtle; natural philosophy, deep; moral, grave; logic and rhetoric, able to contend; *Abeunt studia in mores.*[2] Nay, there is no stand or impediment in the wit but may be wrought out by fit studies; like as diseases of the body may have appropriate exercises. Bowling is good for the stone and reins, shooting for the lungs and breast, gentle walking for the stomach, riding for the head and the like. So if a man's wit be wandering, let him study the mathematics; for in demonstrations, if his wit be called away never so little, he must begin again. If his wit be not apt to distinguish or find differences, let him study the schoolmen; for they are *cymini sectores.*[3] If he be not apt to beat over matters, and to call up one thing to prove and illustrate another, let him study the lawyers' cases; so every defect of the mind may have a special receipt.

[2] Studies form manners.
[3] Dividers of cuminseed, i.e., hairsplitters.

HAROLD TAYLOR

•

The Private World of the Man with a Book[1]

The temptation of the educator is to explain and describe, to organize a body of knowledge for the student, leaving the student with nothing to do. I have never been able to understand why educators do this so often, especially where books are concerned. Much of the time they force their students to read the wrong books at the wrong time, and insist that they read them in the wrong way. That is, they lecture to the students about what is in the books, reduce the content to a series of points that can be remembered, and, if there are discussions, arrange them to deal with the points.

Schools and colleges thus empty books of their true meaning, and addict their students to habits of thought that often last for the rest of their lives. Everything must be reduced to a summary, ideas are topic sentences, to read is to prepare for a distant test. This is why so many people do not know how to read. They have been taught to turn books into abstractions.

[1] From *Saturday Review,* XLIV (January 7, 1961), 17-19. Reprinted by permission of the author and of *Saturday Review.*

This goes against everything we know about what it means to read a book in real life, life, that is to say, which is uncorrupted by educational purpose. There is only one way to read a book, to give yourself up to it, alone, without instruction as to what you should be finding in it, without the necessity of making it into a series of points, but enjoying it, coming to know in personal terms what is in the mind of the writer. Only after that should there be discussion, criticism, comment by the educators. Otherwise education becomes too much like another kind of real life, the kind in which nobody reads the book, everyone reads the reviews, and everyone talks as if he knew the book.

The difficulty is that something happens to educators, and to other people, when they think or talk about education. They draw themselves to their full height and make large statements. They seem not to think that what applies to human experience in general may also apply to experience in schools and colleges. They assume that there is something peculiar about education which demands that unless a book is read out of a sense of duty, as a piece of "material" to be "covered," in order for the reader to become "educated," it is not serving the cause of education.

Yet most of the most important experiences that truly educate cannot be arranged ahead of time with any precision. All the educator can do is to surround the student with a rich variety of intellectual and personal experience chosen with a view to quickening his mind and emotions into action. The ends are achieved by indirect means—something said in private conversation one day in the street, a remark by a teacher in the middle of a discussion, a book picked up in someone's room. When George Saintsbury was once asked how to interest the young in good literature, he replied, "Leave books around."

I grew up in a city that was culturally sterile, in a college whose curriculum lacked intellectual vitality. There were no little magazines, no experimental theatres, no dance groups, no philosophical movements, no strong views held, no centers of new effort. Those of us who were happy to know about Auden, Spender, MacNeice, Isherwood, Malraux, Faulkner, Hemingway, Melville, James, Dostoevsky, Tolstoy, Dewey, or Marx were quite rare, and we pursued our illicit reading without benefit of curriculum or librarians.

We read and talked in our rooms, in the newspaper office, in drugstores, and found the writers who meant most to us in little bookstores and reading rooms, where one person speaks of a book to another, where the books have been left around. In this way we learned what it was like to become so involved with an idea that sleep was impossible, or, to put it more broadly, to possess an intellectual life of our own. We did the educational things required of us, because that was what the educators wanted. We did them well, won prizes for them. But our real lives were elsewhere.

From that day to this I have never been able to understand why educators do not seize upon this truth and make it the center of their educational plans, make one life of the double lives which students lead. The heart of education, where books are concerned, is to get the student alone with a book, in a right state of mind.

Students are made to read more than they can ever enjoy, too little of too many things, in a way calculated to destroy personal involvement with the writer. The brighter the student, the more he is asked to read, until he develops prodigious skill in reading quickly and cleverly, for purposes of taking examinations and talking in discussions. Students are always reading to deadlines, in order to return books to the library, in order to answer questions and prove only that they have covered the ground. The educational system thus becomes a barrier to the creation by the student of a body of knowledge of his own.

True learning is not a matter of the formal organization of knowledge of books. It is a series of personal experiences. The written word makes public a state of mind; it transfers from private to public expression a set of ideas and facts that might otherwise remain unknown. For the writer, it is more than communication. It is the revelation, to oneself as writer, of things that have been hidden, now forced into expression.

On the other side, the side of the reader, it is the revelation of one person to another, a personal communication in an impersonal world. The reader in his true role is a private person, learning what another private person has to tell him. He may be seated in a library with a thousand others, but his way of knowing is by taking to himself the writer whose book he is reading. The teacher exists to get his students ready to read for and by themselves.

I would mark down as one of the physical barriers to the free flow of knowledge in the university and the American community, the absence of a sufficient number of intimate little bookshops and reading rooms where the librarian or the owner who loves books and knows what is in them has assembled a spread of inviting titles to capture the affection and involvement of the reader who comes as a welcome guest.

We will not have the atmosphere for learning or the true content of learning until we have teachers who themselves haunt the bookshops and who think of librarians as friends and companions in the pursuit of ideas rather than as clerks and custodians of book collections. Nor will we have the atmosphere for learning in our colleges and in our libraries unless we have librarians who work directly with teachers and students because they want to, and because they too are involved in the intellectual life of their own time.

My plea is for the restoration of the personal element in modern life and in modern education at a time when everything is pushing us into collective states of mind, when intellectuals huddle together in committees that issue reports in anonymous prose, when so many people are willing to strip themselves of their personal qualities in order to become clusters of approved characteristics.

It is a time when everybody talks and nobody listens. Instead, people exchange statements which each thinks will raise himself in the estimate of the other. Had we in the United States in recent months been listening to intelligent private persons in Cuba, Japan, Korea, Turkey, and elsewhere in Asian countries, we would have known that their best thinking and their deepest motivations were not of a kind that could respond to the policies which our government had designed for them and so innocently applied.

Most communications to the world by governments are calculated efforts at raising the level of impersonality and at concealment of the reality with which they are concerned. This habit of concealment in public speech has crept into private discourse and is seen, for example, in the loss of the old-fashioned habit of writing personal letters which are so honestly personal that they are not intended for eventual publication.

At another level, it has meant no longer asking our students for private essays each week which can give their teachers an understanding of who the student is and what are his honest thoughts, what are his weaknesses and inadequacies, what are his strengths, his needs, his hopes. Instead we seek for ways in which he can provide answers to questions he would never dream of asking, answers that merely reflect the demands we make upon him for information on topics of our choosing.

In the United States we justify our impersonality and lack of sensitivity to students by referring to the growing size of the student body, the excess of numbers of students who thus cannot be dealt with in personal ways, and we turn to technology for more devices to do the teaching for us. This is surely sensible where mechanical tasks, like keeping records, can be done mechanically, where films and television can bring the immediacy of the outside world into the school and college, or in cases where information is to be conveyed quickly and effectively.

But as far as the deeper aims of education are concerned, the problem is not how to distribute more information to larger numbers of students. That, as we have seen, is fairly easy to solve. You put more students into the same classes and pump the material in.

The question is: What intellectual, personal, and moral qualities are we developing in our students? What are they learning to care about? What are they doing with their lives?

It is as if we were deliberately turning back from the real problems, and keeping ourselves busy while we hope they will go away. We are asking not to know our students by what they say in writing or in speech, but to know whether or not they possess correct information as revealed in mechanical tests that can be graded like eggs, by nonhuman means.

What has happened is that many of the concepts of an American public-relations culture and the mass media have been transferred from the realm of business and industry into education, and the university has been organized not as a place where student talent is nurtured but as a bureaucracy for the dissemination of information. It has its own organization man, its own managerial class, its own habits of the market place by which the man with the largest amount of published academic prose commands the highest salary and receives the ultimate reward of the university—not to have to teach. With the combination of speeded-up sabbaticals, foundation grants, and continuous leaves of absence, the criterion of highest prestige for the university scholar will soon be that he is excused even from residence at the university and will be paid simply for the privilege of listing his name in the faculty roster. In the meantime, there are students.

We must teach these students and citizens the necessity of withdrawal into their own thoughts as a preparation for independent thinking and independent action. They must learn to feel their own emotions, not those that are considered culturally appropriate by the educational authorities or politically correct by their government. This is why the question of what books should be in the curriculum is one that should be decided, not by committees, but by teachers who themselves can enter into the experience of the young and feel with them the impulses of their own time, by teachers who know the responses the young are making to their own society.

Each generation has its own truth, its own private world, its own way of knowing, and we who are educators would be wise to listen to them for the knowledge they can bring. The young have the supreme advantage of not having been here before; they are not yet settled, they have almost no history and they can consider the world freshly (that is, they can and do when they talk to each other), and they test and retest the ideas that are old and known and reputable. They reject some, they revive and re-create others.

The comradeship of the young both sustains them in their own image of themselves and gives them the emotional sustenance they need for the independence of their lives. They live apart from us, they hold themselves back, and from the untouchable center of their personal lives they look distantly at our existence and our knowledge as items possessed by beings on a different planet. They are not what they seem to the professor who merely looks at the faces before him. He cannot be certain even of their attention, since they have learned how to occupy a classroom and look attentive while they take their minds elsewhere. He cannot be sure of their respect, since they have learned how to be quiet and how to act respectfully. The silence of the present generation has been in many ways deceptive, and it is false to assume that the silence has meant either consent or lack of creative and critical thought. They have played the system but have not been convinced of its claim to be believed in.

They are not to be presented with the familiar lists of the Great Books with an air of authority vested in the educators and the curriculum-makers. The students must be asked to determine for themselves which books are great, which ideas are viable, which values are compelling. To do otherwise is to use the familiar brand-name approach as a form of intellectual propaganda, like saluting the flag or bowing to royalty. It is to take the young through an educational tour of the museums of literature, to inspire a dutiful and pious attitude to authors rather than an attitude of expectancy and involvement.

If our aim is to create a vivid sense of awareness of the joy in learning and the satisfaction of intellectual mastery, we must trust the student to come away from his experience with the authors we ask him to read with ideas and convictions of his own. From the point of view of the student, every idea is inert until it comes alive in his consciousness. But first he must learn to read in personal terms, to invest himself in the reading, to bring something of his own to the book. If the books in his education are ill-chosen, or chosen chiefly on the basis of scholarly correctness, the student can bring almost nothing of himself to the enterprise, because what the author is saying corresponds to nothing in his lived experience. In order to learn how to expand that experience in imagination, to make links to the past and to cultures alien to his own, he must first learn how to come close to books and ideas themselves, he must have an experience with the immediacy of ideas. This involves a different way of choosing books for his education, and usually a sequence different from conventional chronology or historical periods.

If he reads, for example, in order to be able to tell an eighteenth-century rationalist from a nineteenth-century romantic, he may very well not be able to tell more than this, nor be able to enter into the experience of the writer whose work he is studying. Or he may simply be able to say to himself that he has read the best representatives of all the great periods in cultural history.

Whenever we take a writer out of his natural element, that is, treat him as other than a human being who is writing what he knows, we run the risk of destroying his value to the reader by making him represent a category of thought to which he has been assigned after the fact, usually after his death. In graduate schools, this unnatural treatment of writers leads to the continual preoccupation with tracing influences, classifying authors into categories, and otherwise drawing attention away from the writer himself. The writer must be allowed to stand on his own feet. Indeed, his greatness is established by the fact that he continues to stand on his own feet from generation to generation, and that he is perpetually rediscovered for himself and for what he has to say.

The student who is being educated is in fact discovering his own self and learning how to relate it to other selves. At its best, education is a series of private conversations in which all sham, pretense, and intellectual hypocrisy or name-dropping is stripped away and the student is free to respond with honesty to the intellectual and personal situation in which he finds himself. This is why it is so important to keep the student's situation as free of educational formalities as possible, to insist upon some version of the tutorial system, to resist all effort to build an impersonal administrative machine in place of a fascinating intellectual community, to assure that the student and the teacher are known to each other and that the student may thus benefit by the fact that his individuality is known, recognized, and respected.

For it is finally in the individual response of one person to another—whether through books or in person—that the heart of the matter rests.

HENRY DAVID THOREAU

•

Reading[1]

With a little more deliberation in the choice of their pursuits, all men would perhaps become essentially students and observers, for certainly their nature and destiny are interesting to all alike. In accumulating property for ourselves or our posterity, in founding a family or a state, or acquiring fame even, we are mortal; but in dealing with truth we are immortal, and need fear no change nor accident. The oldest Egyptian or Hindoo philosopher raised a corner of the veil from the statue of the divinity; and still the trembling robe remains raised, and I gaze upon as fresh a glory as he did, since it was I in him that was then so bold, and it is he in me that now reviews the vision. No dust has settled on that robe; no time has elapsed since that divinity was revealed. That time which we really improve, or which is improbable, is neither past, present, nor future.

My residence was more favorable, not only to thought, but to serious reading, than a university; and though I was beyond the range of the ordinary circulating library, I had more than ever come within the influence of those books which circulate round the world, whose sentences were first written on bark, and are now merely copied from time to time onto linen paper. Says the poet Mîr Camar Uddîn Mast, "Being seated, to run through the region of the spiritual world; I have had this advantage in books. To be intoxicated by a single glass of wine; I have experienced this pleasure when I have drunk the liquor of the esoteric doctrines." I kept Homer's Iliad on my table through the summer, though I looked at his page only now and then. Incessant labor with my hands, at first, for I had my house to finish and my beans to hoe at the same time, made more study impossible. Yet I sustained myself by the prospect of such reading in future. I read one or two shallow books of travel in the intervals of my work, till that employment made me ashamed of myself, and I asked where it was then that *I* lived.

The student may read Homer or Æschylus in the Greek without danger of dissipation or luxuriousness, for it implies that he in some measure emulate their heroes, and consecrate morning hours to their pages. The heroic books, even if printed in the character of our mother tongue, will always be in a lan-

[1] From *Walden,* ed. by Norman Holmes Pearson, "Rinehart Editions" (New York: Holt, Rinehart and Winston, Inc., 1948), pp. 81-90. First printed in 1854.

guage dead to degenerate times; and we must laboriously seek the meaning of each word and line, conjecturing a larger sense than common use permits out of what wisdom and valor and generosity we have. The modern cheap and fertile press, with all its translations, has done little to bring us nearer to the heroic writers of antiquity. They seem as solitary, and the letter in which they are printed as rare and curious, as ever. It is worth the expense of youthful days and costly hours, if you learn only some words of an ancient language, which are raised out of the trivialness of the street, to be perpetual suggestions and provocations. It is not in vain that the farmer remembers and repeats the few Latin words which he has heard. Men sometimes speak as if the study of the classics would at length make way for more modern and practical studies; but the adventurous student will always study classics, in whatever language they may be written and however ancient they may be. For what are the classics but the noblest recorded thoughts of man? They are the only oracles which are not decayed, and there are such answers to the most modern inquiry in them as Delphi and Dodona never gave. We might as well omit to study Nature because she is old. To read well, that is, to read true books in a true spirit, is a noble exercise, and one that will task the reader more than any exercise which the customs of the day esteem. It requires a training such as the athletes underwent, the steady intention almost of the whole life to this object. Books must be read as deliberately and reservedly as they were written. It is not enough even to be able to speak the language of that nation by which they were written, for there is a memorable interval between the spoken and the written language, the language heard and the language read. The one is commonly transitory, a sound, a tongue, a dialect merely, almost brutish, and we learn it unconsciously, like the brutes, of our mothers. The other is the maturity and experience of that; if that is our mother tongue, this is our father tongue, a reserved and select expression, too significant to be heard by the ear, which we must be born again in order to speak. The crowds of men who merely *spoke* the Greek and Latin tongues in the Middle Ages were not entitled by the accident of birth to *read* the works of genius written in those languages; for these were not written in that Greek or Latin which they knew, but in the select language of literature. They had not learned the nobler dialects of Greece and Rome, but the very materials on which they were written were waste paper to them, and they prized instead a cheap contemporary literature. But when the several nations of Europe had acquired distinct though rude written languages of their own, sufficient for the purposes of their rising literatures, then first learning revived, and scholars were enabled to discern from that remoteness the treasures of antiquity. What the Roman and Grecian multitude could not *hear,* after the lapse of ages a few scholars *read,* and a few scholars only are still reading it.

However much we may admire the orator's occasional bursts of eloquence, the noblest written words are commonly as far behind or above the fleeting spoken language as the firmament with its stars is behind the clouds. *There* are the stars, and they who can may read them. The astronomers forever comment on and observe them. They are not exhalations like our daily colloquies and vaporous breath. What is called eloquence in the forum is commonly found to be rhetoric in the study. The orator yields to the inspiration of a transient occasion, and speaks to the mob before him, to those who can *hear* him; but the writer, whose more equable life is his occasion, and who would be distracted by the event and the crowd which inspire the orator, speaks to the intellect and heart of mankind, to all in any age who can *understand* him.

No wonder that Alexander carried the Iliad with him on his expeditions in a precious casket. A written word is the choicest of relics. It is something at once more intimate with us and more universal than any other work of art. It is the work of art nearest to life itself. It may be translated into every language, and not only be read but actually breathed from all human lips;—not be represented on canvas or in marble only, but be carved out of the breath of life itself. The symbol of an ancient man's thought becomes a modern man's speech. Two thousand summers have imparted to the monuments of Grecian literature, as to her marbles, only a maturer golden and autumnal tint, for they have carried their own serene and celestial atmosphere into all lands to protect them against the corrosion of time. Books are the treasured wealth of the world and the fit inheritance of generations and nations. Books, the oldest and the best, stand naturally and rightfully on the shelves of every cottage. They have no cause of their own to plead, but while they enlighten and sustain the reader his common sense will not refuse them. Their authors are a natural and irresistible aristocracy in every society, and, more than kings or emperors, exert an influence on mankind. When the illiterate and perhaps scornful trader has earned by enterprise and industry his coveted leisure and independence, and is admitted to the circles of wealth and fashion, he turns inevitably at last to those still higher but yet inaccessible circles of intellect and genius, and is sensible only of the imperfection of his culture and the vanity and insufficiency of all his riches, and further proves his good sense by the pains which he takes to secure for his children that intellectual culture whose want he so keenly feels; and thus it is that he becomes the founder of a family.

Those who have not learned to read the ancient classics in the language in which they were written must have a very imperfect knowledge of the history of the human race; for it is remarkable that no transcript of them has ever been made into any modern tongue, unless our civilization itself may be regarded as such a transcript. Homer has never yet been printed in English, nor Æschylus, nor Virgil even,—works as refined, as solidly done, and as beautiful almost as the morning itself; for later writers, say what we will of their genius, have rarely, if ever, equalled the elaborate beauty and finish and the lifelong and heroic literary labors of the ancients. They only talk of forgetting them who never knew them. It will be soon enough to forget them when we have the learning and the genius which will enable us to attend to and appreciate them. That age will be rich indeed when those relics which we call Classics, and the still older and more than classic but even less known Scriptures of the nations, shall have still further accumulated, when the Vaticans shall be filled with Vedas and Zendavestas and Bibles, with Homers and Dantes and Shakespeares, and all the centuries to come shall have successively deposited their trophies in the forum of the world. By such a pile we may hope to scale heaven at last.

The works of the great poets have never yet been read by mankind, for only great poets can read them. They have only been read as the multitude read the stars, at most astrologically, not astronomically. Most men have learned to read to serve a paltry convenience, as they have learned to cipher in order to keep accounts and not be cheated in trade; but of reading as a noble intellectual exercise they know little or nothing; yet this only is reading, in a high sense, not that which lulls us as a luxury and suffers the nobler faculties to sleep the while, but what we have to stand on tip-toe to read and devote our most alert and wakeful hours to.

I think that having learned our letters we should read the best that is in literature, and not be forever repeating our a-b-abs, and words of one syllable, in the fourth or fifth classes, sitting on the lowest and foremost form all our lives. Most men are satisfied if they read or hear read, and perchance have been convicted by the wisdom of one good book, the Bible, and for the rest of their lives vegetate and dissipate their faculties in what is called easy reading. There is a work in several volumes in our Circulating Library entitled "Little Reading," which I thought referred to a town of that name which I had not been to. There are those who, like cormorants and ostriches, can digest all sorts of this, even after the fullest dinner of meats and vegetables, for they suffer nothing to be wasted. If others are the machines to provide this provender, they are the machines to read it. They read the nine thousandth tale about Zebulon and Sophronia, and how they loved as none had ever loved before, and neither did the course of their true love run smooth,—at any rate, how it did run and stumble, and get up again and go on! how some poor unfortunate got up on to a steeple, who had better never have gone up as far as the belfry; and then having needlessly got him up there, the happy novelist rings the bell for all the world to come together and hear, O dear! how he did get down again! For my part, I think that they had better metamorphose all such aspiring heroes of universal noveldom into man weather-cocks, as they used to put heroes among the constellations, and let them swing round there till they are rusty, and not come down at all to bother honest men with their pranks. The next time the novelist rings the bell I will not stir though the meeting-house burn down. "The Skip of the Tip-Toe-Hop, a Romance of the Middle Ages, by the celebrated author of 'Tittle-Tol-Tan,' to appear in monthly parts; a great rush; don't all come together." All this they read with saucer eyes, and erect and primitive curiosity, and with unwearied gizzard, whose corrugations even yet need no sharpening, just as some little four-year-old bencher his two-cent gilt-covered edition of Cinderella,—without any improvement, that I can see, in the pronunciation, or accent, or emphasis, or any more skill in extracting or inserting the moral. The result is dulness of sight, stagnation of the vital circulations, and a general deliquium and sloughing off of all the intellectual faculties. This sort of gingerbread is baked daily and more sedulously than pure wheat or rye-and-Indian in almost every oven, and finds a surer market.

The best books are not read even by those who are called good readers. What does our Concord culture amount to? There is in this town, with a very few exceptions, no taste for the best or for very good books even in English literature, whose words all can read and spell. Even the college-bred and so-called liberally educated men here and elsewhere have really little or no acquaintance with the English classics; and as for the recorded wisdom of mankind, the ancient classics and Bibles, which are accessible to all who will know of them, there are the feeblest efforts anywhere made to become acquainted with them. I know a woodchopper, of middle age, who takes a French paper, not for news as he says, for he is above that, but to "keep himself in practice," he being a Canadian by birth; and when I ask him what he considers the best thing he can do in this world, he says, beside this, to keep up and add to his English. This is about as much as the college-bred generally do or aspire to do, and they take an English paper for the purpose. One who has just come from reading perhaps one of the best English books will find how many with whom he can converse about it? Or suppose he comes from reading a Greek or Latin classic in the original, whose praises are familiar even to the so-called illiterate; he will find nobody at all to speak to, but must keep silence about it. Indeed, there is hardly the professor in our colleges, who, if he has mastered the difficulties of the language, has proportionally mastered the difficulties of the wit and poetry of a Greek poet, and has any sympathy to impart to the alert and heroic reader; and as for the sacred Scriptures, or Bibles of mankind, who in this town can tell me even their titles? Most men do not know that any nation but the Hebrews have had a scripture. A man, any man, will go considerably out of his way to pick up a silver dollar; but here are golden words, which the wisest men of antiquity have uttered, and whose worth the wise of every succeeding age have assured us of;—and yet we learn to read only as far as Easy Reading, the primers and class-books, and when we leave school, the "Little Reading," and story-books, which are for boys and beginners; and our reading, our conversation and thinking, are all on a very low level, worthy only of pygmies and manikins.

I aspire to be acquainted with wiser men than this our Concord soil has produced, whose names are hardly known here. Or shall I hear the name of Plato and never read his book? As if Plato were my townsman and I never saw him,—my next neighbor and I never heard him speak or attended to the wisdom of his words. But how actually is it? His Dialogues, which contain what was immortal in him, lie on the next shelf, and yet I never read them. We are underbred and low-lived and illiterate; and in this respect I confess I do not make any very broad distinction between the illiterateness of my townsman who cannot read at all and the illiterateness of him who has learned to read only what is for children and feeble intellects. We should be as good as the worthies of antiquity, but partly by first knowing how good they were. We are a race of titmen, and soar but little higher in our intellectual flights than the columns of the daily paper.

It is not all books that are as dull as their readers. There are probably words addressed to our condition exactly, which, if we could really hear and understand, would be more salutary than the morning of the spring to our lives and possibly put a new aspect on the face of things for us. How many a man has dated a new era in his life from the reading of a book! The book exists for us, perchance, which will explain our miracles and reveal new ones. The at present unutterable things we may find somewhere uttered. These same questions that disturb and puzzle and confound us have in their turn occurred to all the wise men; not one has been omitted; and each has answered them, according to his ability, by his words and his life. Moreover, with wisdom we shall learn liberality. The solitary hired man on a farm in the outskirts of Concord, who has had his second birth and peculiar religious experience, and is driven as he believes into silent gravity and exclusiveness by his faith, may think it is not true; but Zoroaster, thousands of years ago, travelled the same road and had the same experience; but he, being wise, knew it to be universal, and treated his neighbors accordingly, and is even said to have invented and established worship among men. Let him humbly commune with Zoroaster then, and through the liberalizing influence of all the worthies, with Jesus Christ himself, and let "our church" go by the board.

We boast that we belong to the Nineteenth Century and are making the most rapid strides of any nation. But consider how little this village does for its own culture. I do not wish to flatter my townsmen, nor to be flattered by them, for that will not advance either of us. We need to be provoked,—goaded like oxen, as we are, into a trot. We have a comparatively decent system of common schools, schools for infants only; but excepting the half-starved Lyceum in the winter, and latterly the puny beginning of a library suggested by the State, no school for ourselves. We spend more on almost any article of bodily aliment or ailment than on our mental aliment. It is time that we had uncommon schools, that we did not leave off our education when we begin to be men and women. It is time that villages were universities, and their elder inhabitants the fellows of universities, with leisure—if they are, indeed, so well off—to pursue liberal studies the rest of their lives. Shall the world be confined to one Paris or one Oxford forever? Cannot students be boarded here and get a liberal education under the skies of Concord? Can we not hire some Abélard to lecture to us? Alas! what with foddering the cattle and tending the store, we are kept from school too long, and our education is sadly neglected. In this country, the village should in some respect take the place of the nobleman of Europe. It should be the patron of the fine arts. It is rich enough. It wants only the magnanimity and refinement. It can spend money enough on such things as farmers and traders value, but it is thought Utopian to propose spending money for things which more intelligent men know to be of far more worth. This town has spent seventeen thousand dollars on a town-house, thank fortune or politics, but probably it will not spend so much on living wit, the true meat to put into that shell, in a hundred years. The one hundred and twenty-five dollars annually subscribed for a Lyceum in the winter is better spent than any other equal sum raised in the town. If we live in the Nineteenth Century, why should we not enjoy the advantages which the Nineteenth Century offers? Why should our life be in any respect provincial? If we will read newspapers, why not skip the gossip of Boston and take the best newspaper in the world at once?—not be sucking the pap of "neutral family" papers, or browsing "Olive-Branches" here in New England. Let the reports of all the learned societies come to us, and we will see if they know anything. Why should we leave it to Harper & Brothers and Redding Co. to select our reading? As the nobleman of cultivated tastes surrounds himself with whatever conduces to his culture,—genius—learning—wit—books—paintings—statuary—music—philosophical instruments, and the like; so let the village do,—not stop short at a pedagogue, a parson, a sexton, a parish library, and three selectmen, because our Pilgrim forefathers got through a cold winter once on a bleak rock with these. To act collectively is according to the spirit of our institutions; and I am confident that, as our circumstances are more flourishing, our means are greater than the nobleman's. New England can hire all the wise men in the world to come and teach her, and board them round the while, and not be provincial at all. That is the *uncommon* school we want. Instead of noblemen, let us have noble villages of men. If it is necessary, omit one bridge over the river, go round a little there, and throw one arch at least over the darker gulf of ignorance which surrounds us.

LEONARD Q. ROSS

•

*Mr. K*a*p*l*a*n and Shakespeare*[1]

It was Miss Higby's idea in the first place. She had suggested to Mr. Parkhill that the students came to her class unaware of the *finer* side of English,

[1] From *The Education of Hyman Kaplan,* by Leonard Q. Ross, pp. 129-140. Copyright, 1937, by Harcourt, Brace & World, Inc.; copyright, 1965, by Leo Rosten. Reprinted by permission of the publisher.

of its beauty and, as she put it, "the glorious heritage of our literature." She suggested that perhaps poetry might be worked into the exercises of Mr. Parkhill's class. The beginner's grade had, after all, been subjected to almost a year of English and might be presumed to have achieved some linguistic sophistication. Poetry would make the students conscious of precise enunciation; it would make them read with greater care and an ear for sounds. Miss Higby, who had once begun a master's thesis on Coventry Patmore, *loved* poetry. And, it should be said in all justice, she argued her cause with considerable logic. Poetry *would* be excellent for the enunciation of the students, thought Mr. Parkhill.

So it was that when he faced the class the following Tuesday night, Mr. Parkhill had a volume of Shakespeare on his desk, and an eager, almost an expectant, look in his eye. The love that Miss Higby bore for poetry in general was as nothing compared to the love that Mr. Parkhill bore for Shakespeare in particular. To Mr. Parkhill, poetry meant Shakespeare. Many years ago he had played Polonius in his senior class play.

"Tonight, class," said Mr. Parkhill, "I am going to try an experiment."

The class looked up dutifully. They had come to regard Mr. Parkhill's pedagogical innovations as part of the natural order.

"I am going to introduce you to poetry—great poetry. You see—" Mr. Parkhill delivered a modest lecture on the beauty of poetry, its expression of the loftier thoughts of men, its economy of statement. He hoped it would be a relief from spelling and composition exercises to use poetry as the subject matter of the regular Recitation and Speech period. "I shall write a passage on the board and read it for you. Then, for Recitation and Speech, you will give short addresses, using the passage as the general topic, telling us what it has brought to your minds, what thoughts and ideas."

The class seemed quite pleased by the announcement. Miss Mitnick blushed happily. (This blush was different from most of Miss Mitnick's blushes; there was aspiration and idealism in it.) Mr. Norman Bloom sighed with a businesslike air: you could tell that for him poetry was merely another assignment, like a speech on "What I Like to Eat Best" or a composition on "A Day at a Picnic." Mrs. Moskowitz, to whom any public performance was unpleasant, tried to look enthusiastic, without much success. And Mr. Hyman Kaplan, the heroic smile on his face as indelibly as ever, looked at Mr. Parkhill with admiration and whispered to himself: "Poyetry! Now is poyetry! My! Mus' be progriss ve makink awreddy!"

"The passage will be from Shakespeare," Mr. Parkhill announced, opening the volume.

An excited buzz ran through the class as the magic of that name fell upon them.

"Imachine!" murmured Mr. Kaplan. "Jakesbeer!"

"*Shakes*peare, Mr. Kaplan!"

Mr. Parkhill took a piece of chalk and, with care and evident love, wrote the following passage on the board in large, clear letters:

> Tomorrow, and tomorrow, and tomorrow
> Creeps in this petty pace from day to day,
> To the last syllable of recorded time;
> And all our yesterdays have lighted fools
> The way to dusty death. Out, out, brief candle!
> Life's but a walking shadow, a poor player
> That struts and frets his hour upon the stage,
> And then is heard no more; it is a tale
> Told by an idiot, full of sound and fury,
> Signifying nothing.

A reverent hush filled the classroom, as eyes gazed with wonder on this passage from the Bard. Mr. Parkhill was pleased at this.

"I shall read the passage first," he said. "Listen carefully to my enunciation—and—er—let Shakespeare's thoughts sink into your minds."

Mr. Parkhill read: " 'Tomorrow, and tomorrow, and tomorrow . . .' " Mr. Parkhill read very well and this night, as if some special fire burned in him, he read with rare eloquence. "Out, out, brief candle!" In Miss Mitnick's eyes there was inspiration and wonder. "Life's but a walking shadow . . ." Mrs. Moskowitz sat with a heavy frown, indicating cerebration. "It is a tale told by an idiot . . ." Mr. Kaplan's smile had taken on something luminous; but his eyes were closed: it was not clear whether Mr. Kaplan had surrendered to the spell of the Immortal Bard or to that of Morpheus.

"I shall—er—read the passage again," said Mr. Parkhill, clearing his throat vociferously until he saw Mr. Kaplan's eyes open. " 'Tomorrow, and tomorrow, and tomorrow. . . .' "

When Mr. Parkhill had read the passage for the second time, he said: "That should be quite clear now. Are there any questions?"

There were a few questions. Mr. Scymzak wanted to know whether "frets" was "a little kind excitement." Miss Schneiderman asked about "struts." Mr. Kaplan wasn't sure about "cripps." Mr. Parkhill explained the words carefully, and several illustrative uses of each word. "No more questions? Well, I shall allow a few minutes for you all to—er—think over the meaning of the passage. Then we shall begin Recitation and Speech."

Mr. Kaplan promptly closed his eyes again, his smile beatific. The students sank into that revery miscalled thought, searching their souls for the symbols evoked by Shakespeare's immortal words.

"Miss Caravello, will you begin?" asked Mr. Parkhill at last.

Miss Caravello went to the front of the room. "Da poem isa gooda," she said slowly. "Itsa have—"

"It *has*."

"It hasa beautiful wordsa. Itsa lak Dante, Italian poet—"

"Ha!" cried Mr. Kaplan scornfully. "Shaksbeer you metchink mit Tante? *Shaksbeer?* Mein Gott!"

It was obvious that Mr. Kaplan had identified himself with Shakespeare and would tolerate no disparagement of his *alter ego*.

"Miss Caravello is merely expressing her own ideas," said Mr. Parkhill pacifically. (Actually, he felt completely sympathetic to Mr. Kaplan's point of view.)

"Hau Kay," agreed Mr. Kaplan, with a generous wave of the hand. "But to me is no comparink a high-cless man like Shaksbeer mit a Tante, dat's all."

Miss Caravello, her poise shattered, said a few more words and sat down.

Mrs. Yampolsky's contribution was brief. "This is full deep meanings," she said, her eyes on the floor. "Is hard for a person not so good in English to unnistand. But I like."

" '*Like!*' " cried Mr. Kaplan with a fine impatience. " '*Like?*' Batter *love*, Yampolsky. Mit Shaksbeer mus' be *love!*"

Mr. Parkhill had to suggest that Mr. Kaplan control his aesthetic passions. He did understand how Mr. Kaplan felt, however, and sensed a new bond between them. Mrs. Yampolsky staggered through several more nervous comments and retired.

Mr. Bloom was next. He gave a long declamation, ending: "So is passimistic ideas in the poem, and I am optimist. Life should be happy—so we should remember this is only a poem. Maybe is Shakespeare too passimistic."

"You wronk, Bloom!" cried Mr. Kaplan with prompt indignation. "Shaksbeer is passimist because is de *life* passimist also!"

Mr. Parkhill, impressed by this philosophical stroke, realized that Mr. Kaplan, afire with the glory of the Swan of Avon, could not be suppressed. Mr. Kaplan was the kind of man who brooked no criticism of his gods. The only solution was to call on Mr. Kaplan for his recitation at once. Mr. Parkhill was, indeed, curious about what fresh thoughts Mr. Kaplan would utter after his passionate defences of the Bard. When Mr. Parkhill had corrected certain parts of Mr. Bloom's speech, emphasizing Mr. Bloom's failure to use the indefinite article, he said: "Mr. Kaplan, will *you* speak next?"

Mr. Kaplan's face broke into a glow; his smile was like a rainbow. "Soitinly," he said, walking to the front of the room. Never had he seemed so dignified, so eager, so conscious of a great destiny.

"Er—Mr. Kaplan," added Mr. Parkhill, suddenly aware of the possibilities which the situation (Kaplan on Shakespeare) involved: "Speak *carefully*."

"*Spacially* careful vill I be," Mr. Kaplan reassured him. He cleared his throat, adjusted his tie, and began: "Ladies an' gantleman, you hoid all kinds minninks abot dis piece poyetry, an'—"

"*Po*etry."

"—abot dis piece *po*etry. But to me is a difference minnink altogadder. Ve mus' tink abot Julius Scissor an' how *he* falt!"

Mr. Parkhill moved nervously, puzzled.

"In dese exact voids is Julius Scissor sayink—"

"Er—Mr. Kaplan," said Mr. Parkhill once he grasped the full import of Mr. Kaplan's error. "The passage is from 'Macbeth.' "

Mr. Kaplan looked at Mr. Parkhill with injured surprise. "*Not* fromm 'Julius Scissor'?" There was pain in his voice.

"No. And it's—er—'Julius *Cae*sar.' "

Mr. Kaplan waited until the last echo of the name had permeated his soul. "Podden me, Mr. Pockheel. Isn't '*see*zor' vat you cottink somting op mit?"

"That," said Mr. Parkhill quickly, "is 'scissor.' You have used 'Caesar' for 'scissor' and 'scissor' for 'Caesar.' "

Mr. Kaplan nodded, marveling at his own virtuosity.

"But go on with your speech, please." Mr. Parkhill, to tell the truth, felt a little guilty that he had not announced at the very beginning that the passage was from "Macbeth." "Tell us *why* you thought the lines were from 'Julius Caesar.' "

"Vell," said Mr. Kaplan to the class, his smile assuming its normal serenity. "I vas positif, becawss I can *see* de whole ting." He paused, debating how to explain this cryptic remark. Then his eyes filled with a strange enchantment. "I see de whole scinn. It's in a tant, on de night bafore dey makink Julius de Kink fromm Rome. Se he is axcited an' ken't slip. He is layink in bed, tinking: 'Tomorrow an' tomorrow an' tomorrow. How slow dey movink! Almost cripps! Soch a pity de pace!' "

Before Mr. Parkhill could explain that "petty pace" did not mean "Soch a pity de pace!" Mr. Kaplan had soared on.

"De days go slow, fromm day to day, like leetle tsyllables on phonograph racords fromm time."

Anxiety and bewilderment invaded Mr. Parkhill's eyes.

" 'An' vat abot yestidday?' tinks Julius Scissor. Ha! 'All our yestiddays are only makink a good light for fools to die in de dost!' "

" 'Dusty death' doesn't mean—" There was no interrupting Mr. Kaplan.

"An' Julius Scissor is so tired, an' he vants to fallink aslip. So he hollers, mit fillink, 'Go ot! Go ot! Short candle!' So it goes ot."

Mr. Kaplan's voice dropped to a whisper. "But he ken't slip. Now is bodderink him de idea fromm life. 'Vat is de life altogether?' tinks Julius Scissor. An' he gives enswer, de pot I like de bast. 'Life is like a bum actor, strottink an' hollerink arond de stage for only vun hour bafore he's kicked ot. Life is a tale told by idjots, dat's all, full of fonny sonds an' phooey!' "

Mr. Parkhill could be silent no longer. " 'Full of sound and fury!' " he cried desperately. But inspiration, like an irresistible force, swept Mr. Kaplan on.

" 'Life is monkey business! It don' minn a ting. It signifies nottink!' An' den Julius Scissor closes his ice fest—" Mr. Kaplan demonstrated the Consul's exact ocular process in closing his "ice"—"an' falls dad!"

The class was hushed as Mr. Kaplan stopped. In the silence, a tribute to the fertility of Mr. Kaplan's imagination and the power of his oratory, Mr. Kaplan went to his seat. But just before he sat down, as if adding a postscript, he sighed: "Dat vas mine idea. But ufcawss is all wronk, becawss Mr. Pockheel said de voids ain't abot Julius Scissor altogadder. It's all abot an Irishman by de name Macbat."

Then Mr. Kaplan sat down.

It was some time before Mr. Parkhill could bring himself to criticize Mr. Kaplan's pronunciation, enunciation, diction, grammar, idiom, and sentence structure. For Mr. Parkhill discovered that he could not easily return to the world of reality. He was still trying to tear himself away from that tent outside Rome, where "Julius Scissor," cursed with insomnia, had thought of time and life—and philosophized himself to a strange and sudden death.

Mr. Parkhill was distinctly annoyed with Miss Higby.

C. S. LEWIS

•

On Misreading By the Literary[1]

We must now return to the point which I postponed in the last chapter. We have to consider a fault in reading which cuts right across our distinction between the literary and the unliterary. Some of the former are guilty of it and some of the latter are not.

Essentially, it involves a confusion between life and art, even a failure to allow for the existence of art at all. Its crudest form is pilloried in the old story of the backwoodsman in the gallery who shot the 'villain' on the stage. We see it also in the lowest type of reader who wants sensational narrative but will not accept it unless it is offered him as "news." On a higher level it appears as the belief that all good books are good primarily because they give us knowledge, teach us "truths" about "life." Dramatists and novelists are praised as if they were doing, essentially, what used to be expected of theologians and philosophers, and the qualities which belong to their works as inventions and as designs are neglected. They are reverenced as teachers and insufficiently appreciated as artists. In a word, De Quincey's "literature of power" is treated as a species within his "literature of knowledge."

We may begin by ruling out of consideration one way of treating fictions as sources of knowledge which, though not strictly literary, is pardonable

[1] From *An Experiment in Criticism,* C. S. Lewis (Cambridge, England: University Press, 1961), pp. 74-88. Reprinted by permission of Cambridge University Press.

at a certain age and usually transient. Between the ages of twelve and twenty nearly all of us acquired from novels, along with plenty of misinformation, a great deal of information about the world we live in: about the food, clothes, customs and climates of various countries, the working of various professions, about methods of travel, manners, law, and political machinery. We were getting not a philosophy of life but what is called "general knowledge." In a particular case a fiction may serve this purpose for even an adult reader. An inhabitant of the cruel countries might come to grasp our principle that a man is innocent till he is proved guilty from reading our detective stories (in that sense such stories are a great proof of real civilisation). But in general this use of fiction is abandoned as we grow older. The curiosities it used to satisfy have been satisfied or simply died away, or, if they survive, would now seek information from more reliable sources. That is one reason why we have less inclination to take up a new novel than we had in our youth.

Having got this special case out of the way, we may now return to the real subject.

It is obvious that some of the unliterary mistake art for an account of real life. As we have seen, those whose reading is conducted, egoistic castle-building will inevitably do so. They wish to be deceived; they want to feel that though these beautiful things have not really happened to them, yet they might. ("He might take a fancy to me like that Duke did to that factory girl in the story.") But it is equally obvious that a great many of the unliterary are not in this state at all—are indeed almost safer from it than anyone else. Try the experiment on your grocer or gardener. You cannot often try it about a book, for he has read few, but a film will do just as well for our purpose. If you complain to him about the gross improbability of its happy ending, he will very probably reply "Ah. I reckon they just put that in to wind it up like." If you complain about the dull and perfunctory love-interest which has been thrust into a story of masculine adventure, he will say "Oh well, you know, they usually got to put in a bit of that. The women like it." He knows perfectly well that the film is art, not knowledge. In a sense his very unliterariness saves him from confusing the two. He never expected the film to be anything but transitory, and not very important, entertainment; he never dreamed that any art could provide more than this. He goes to the pictures not to learn but to relax. The idea that any of his opinions about the real world could be modified by what he saw there would seem to him preposterous. Do you take him for a fool? Turn the conversation from art to life—gossip with him, bargain with him—and you will find he is as shrewd and realistic as you can wish.

Contrariwise, we find the error, in a subtle and especially insidious form, among the literary. When my pupils have talked to me about Tragedy (they have talked much less often, uncompelled, about tragedies), I have sometimes discovered a belief that it is valuable, is worth witnessing or reading, chiefly because it communicates something called the tragic "view" or "sense" or "philosophy" of "life." This content is variously described, but in the most widely diffused version it seems to consist of two propositions: (1) That great miseries result from a flaw in the principal sufferer. (2) That these miseries, pushed to the extreme, reveal to us a certain splendour in man, or even in the universe. Though the anguish is great, it is at least not sordid, meaningless, or merely depressing.

No one denies that miseries with such a cause and such a close can occur in real life. But if tragedy is taken as a comment on life in the sense that we are meant to conclude from it "This is the typical or usual, or ultimate, form of human misery," then tragedy becomes wishful moonshine. Flaws in character do cause suffering; but bombs and bayonets, cancer and polio, dictators and road-hogs, fluctuations in the value of money or in employment, and mere meaningless coincidence, cause a great deal more. Tribulation falls on the integrated and well adjusted and prudent as readily as on anyone else. Nor do real miseries often end with a curtain and a roll of drums "in calm of mind, all passion spent." The dying seldom make magnificent last speeches. And we who watch them die do not, I think, behave very like the minor characters in a tragic death-scene. For unfortunately the play is not over. We have no *exeunt omnes*. The real story does not end: it proceeds to ringing up undertakers, paying bills, getting death certificates, finding and proving a will, answering letters of condolence. There is no grandeur and no finality. Real sorrow ends neither with a bang nor a whimper. Sometimes, after a spiritual journey like Dante's, down to the centre and and then, terrace by terrace, up the mountain of accepted pain, it may rise into peace—but a peace hardly less severe than itself. Sometimes it remains for life, a puddle in the mind which grows always wider, shallower, and more unwholesome. Sometimes it just peters out, as other moods do. One of these alternatives has grandeur, but not tragic grandeur. The other two—ugly, slow, bathetic, unimpressive—would be of no use at all to a dramatist. The tragedian dare not present the totality of suffering as it usually is in its uncouth mixture of agony with littleness, all the indignities and (save for pity) the uninterestingness, of grief. It would ruin his play. It would be merely dull and depressing. He selects from the reality just what his art needs; and what it needs is the exceptional. Conversely, to approach anyone in real sorrow with these ideas about tragic grandeur, to insinuate that he is now assuming that "sceptred pall," would be worse than imbecile: it would be odious.

Next to a world in which there were no sorrows we should like one where sorrows were always significant and sublime. But if we allow the "tragic view of life" to make us believe that we live in such a world, we shall be deceived. Our very eyes teach us better. Where in all nature is there anything uglier and more undignified than an adult male face blubbered and distorted with weeping? And what's behind it is not much prettier. There is no sceptre and no pall.

It seems to me undeniable, that tragedy, taken as a philosophy of life, is the most obstinate and best camouflaged of all wish-fulfilments, just because its pretensions are so apparently realistic. The claim is that it has faced the worst. The conclusion that, despite the worst, some sublimity and significance remains, is therefore as convincing as the testimony of a witness who appears to speak against his will. But the claim that it has faced the worst—at any rate the commonest sort of "worst"—is in my opinion simply false.

It is not the fault of the tragedians that this claim deceives certain readers, for the tragedians never made it. It is critics who make it. The tragedians chose for their themes stories (often grounded in the mythical and impossible) suitable to the art they practised. Almost by definition, such stories would be atypical, striking, and in various other ways adapted to the purpose. Stories with a sublime and satisfying *finale* were chosen not because such a *finale* is characteristic of human misery, but because it is necessary to good drama.

It is probably from this view of tragedy that many young people derive the belief that tragedy is essentially "truer to life" than comedy. This seems to me wholly unfounded. Each of these forms chooses out of real life just those sorts of events it needs. The raw materials are all around us, mixed anyhow. It is selection, isolation, and patterning, not a philosophy, that makes the two sorts of play. The two products do not contradict one another any more than two nosegays plucked out of the same garden. Contradiction comes in only when we (not the dramatists) turn them into propositions such as "This is what human life is like."

It may seem odd that the same people who think comedy less true than tragedy often regard broad farce as realistic. I have often met the opinion that in turning from the *Troilus* to his *fabliaux* Chaucer was drawing nearer to reality. I think this arises from a failure to distinguish between realism of presentation and realism of content. Chaucer's farce is rich in realism of presentation; not in that of content. Criseyde and Alisoun are equally probable women, but what happens in the *Troilus* is very much more probable than what happens in the *Miller's Tale*. The world of farce is hardly less ideal than that of pastoral. It is a paradise of jokes where the wildest coincidences are accepted and where all works together to produce laughter. Real life seldom succeeds in being, and never remains for more than a few minutes, nearly as funny as a well-invented farce. That is why the people feel that they cannot acknowledge the comicality of a real situation more emphatically than by saying "It's as good as a play."

All three forms of art make the abstractions proper to them. Tragedies omit the clumsy and apparently meaningless bludgeoning of much real misfortune and the prosaic littlenesses which usually rob real sorrows of their dignity. Comedies ignore the possibility that the marriage of lovers does not always lead to permanent, nor ever to perfect, happiness. Farce excludes pity for its butts in situations where, if they were real, they would deserve it. None of the three kinds is making a statement about life in general. They are all constructions: things made *out* of the stuff of real life; additions to life rather than comments on it.

At this point I must take pains not to be misunderstood. The great artist—or at all events the great literary artist—cannot be a man shallow either in his thoughts or his feelings. However improbable and abnormal a story he has chosen, it will, as we say, "come to life" in his hands. The life to which it comes will be impregnated with all the wisdom, knowledge and experience the author has; and even more by something which I can only vaguely describe as the flavour or "feel" that actual life has for him. It is this omnipresent flavour or feel that makes bad inventions so mawkish and suffocating, and good ones so tonic. The good ones allow us temporarily to share a sort of passionate sanity. And we may also—which is less important—expect to find in them many psychological truths and profound, at least profoundly felt, reflections. But all this comes to us, and was very possibly called out of the poet, as the "spirit" (using that word in a quasi-chemical sense) of a work of art, a play. To formulate it as a philosophy, even if it were a rational philosophy, and regard the actual play as primarily a vehicle for that philosophy, is an outrage to the thing the poet has made for us.

I use the words *thing* and *made* advisedly. We have already mentioned, but not answered, the question whether a poem "should not mean but be." What guards the good reader from treating a tragedy—he will not talk much about an abstraction like "Tragedy"—as a mere vehicle for truth is his continual awareness that it not only means, but is. It is not merely *logos* (something said) but *poiema* (something made). The same is true of a novel or narrative poem. They are complex and carefully made objects. Attention to the very objects they are is our first step. To value them chiefly for reflections which they may suggest to us or morals we may draw from them, is a flagrant instance of "using" instead of "receiving."

What I mean by "objects" need not remain mysterious. One of the prime achievements in every good fiction has nothing to do with truth or philosophy or a *Weltanschauung* at all. It is the triumphant adjustment of two different kinds of order. On the one hand, the events (the mere plot) have their chronological and causal order, that which they would have in real life. On the other, all the scenes or other divisions of the work must be related to each other according to principles of design, like the masses in a picture or the passages in a symphony. Our feelings and imaginations must be led through "taste after taste, upheld with kindliest change." Contrasts (but also premonitions and echoes) between the darker and the lighter, the swifter and the slower, the simpler and the more sophisticated, must have something like a balance, but never a too perfect symmetry, so that the shape of the whole work will be felt as inevitable and satisfying. Yet this second order must never confuse the first. The transition from the "platform" to the court scene at the beginning of *Hamlet,* the placing of Aeneas' narrative in *Aeneid* II and III, or the darkness in the first two books of *Paradise Lost* leading to the ascent in the third, are simple illustrations. But there is yet another requisite. As little as possible must exist solely for the sake of other things. Every episode, explanation, description, dialogue—ideally every sentence—must be pleasureable and interesting for its own sake. (A fault in Conrad's *Nostromo* is that we have to read so much pseudo-history before we get to the central matter, for which alone this history exists.)

Some will discount this as "mere technique." We must certainly agree that these orderings, apart from that which they order, are worse than "mere"; they are nonentities, as shape is a nonentity apart from the body whose shape it is. But an "appreciation" of sculpture which ignored the statue's shape in favour of the sculptor's "view of life" would be self-deception. It is by the shape that it is a statue. Only because it is a statue do we come to be mentioning the sculptor's view of life at all.

It is very natural that when we have gone through the ordered movements which a great play or narrative excites in us—when we have danced that dance or enacted that ritual or submitted to that pattern—it should suggest to us many interesting reflections. We have "put on mental muscle" as a result of this activity. We may thank Shakespeare or Dante for that muscle, but we had better not father on them the philosophical or ethical use we make of it. For one thing, this use is unlikely to rise very much—it may rise a little—above our own ordinary level. Many of the comments on life which people get out of Shakespeare could have been reached by very moderate talents without his assistance. For another, it may well impede future receptions of the work itself. We may go back to it chiefly to find further confirmation for our belief that it teaches this or that, rather than for a fresh immersion in what it is. We shall be like a man poking his fire, not to boil the kettle or warm the room, but in the hope of seeing in it the same pictures he saw yesterday. And since a text is "but a cheverel glove" to a determined critic—since everything can be a symbol, or an irony, or an ambiguity—we shall easily find what we want. The supreme objection to this is that which lies against the popular use of all the arts. We are so busy doing things with the work that we give it too little chance to work on us. Thus increasingly we meet only ourselves.

But one of the chief operations of art is to remove our gaze from that mirrored face, to deliver us from that solitude. When we read the "literature of knowledge" we hope, as a result, to think more correctly and clearly. In reading imaginative work, I suggest, we should be much less concerned with altering our own opinions—though this of course is sometimes their effect—than with entering fully into the opinions, and therefore also the attitudes, feelings and total experience, of other men. Who in his ordinary senses would try to decide between the claims of materialism and theism by reading Lucretius and Dante? But who in his literary senses would not delightedly learn from them a great deal about what it is like to be a materialist or a theist?

In good reading there ought to be no "problem of belief." I read Lucretius and Dante at a time when (by and large) I agreed with Lucretius. I have read them since I came (by and large) to agree with Dante. I cannot find that this has much altered my experience, or at all altered my evaluation, of either. A true lover of literature should be in one way like an honest examiner, who is prepared to give the highest marks to the telling, felicitous and well-documented exposition of views he dissents from or even abominates.

The sort of misreading I here protest against is unfortunately encouraged by the increasing importance of "English Literature" as an academic discipline. This directs to the study of literature a great many talented, ingenious, and diligent people whose real interests are not specifically literary at all. Forced to talk incessantly about books, what can they do but try to make books into the sort of things they can talk about? Hence literature becomes for them a religion, a philosophy, a school of ethics, a psychotherapy, a sociology—anything rather than a collection of works of art. Lighter works—*divertissements*—are either disparaged or misrepresented as being really far more serious than they look. But to a real lover of literature an exquisitely made *divertissement* is a very much more respectable thing than some of the "philosophies of life" which are foisted upon the great poets. For one thing, it is a good deal harder to make.

This is not to say that all critics who extract such a philosophy from their favourite novelists or poets produce work without value. Each attributes to his chosen author what he believes to be wisdom; and the sort of thing that seems to him wise will of course be determined by his own calibre. If he is a fool he will find and admire foolishness, if he is a mediocrity, platitude, in all his favourites. But if he is a profound thinker himself, what he acclaims and expounds as his author's philosophy may be well worth reading, even if it is in reality his own. We may compare him to the long succession of divines who have based edifying and eloquent sermons on some straining of their texts. The sermon, though bad exegesis, was often good homiletics in its own right.

MORRIS BISHOP

•

The Reading Machine[1]

"I have invented a reading machine," said Professor Entwhistle, a strident energumen whose violent enthusiasms are apt to infect his colleagues with nausea or hot flashes before the eyes.

Every head in the smoking room of the Faculty Club bowed over a magazine, in an attitude of prayer. The prayer was unanswered, as usual.

[1] Reprinted by permission of the author. Copyright, 1947, The New Yorker Magazine, Inc. (Formerly The F-R. Publishing Corp.)

"It is obvious," said Professor Entwhistle, "that the greatest waste of our civilization is the time spent in reading. We have been able to speed up practically everything to fit the modern tempo—communication, transportation, calculation. But today a man takes just as long to read a book as Dante did, or—"

"Great Caesar!" said the Professor of Amphibology, shutting his magazine with a spank.

"Or great Caesar," continued Professor Entwhistle. "So I have invented a machine. It operates by a simple arrangement of photoelectric cells, which scan a line of type at lightning speed. The operation of the photoelectric cells is synchronized with a mechanical device for turning the pages—rather ingenious. I figure that my machine can read a book of three hundred pages in ten minutes."

"Can it read French?" said the Professor of Bio-Economics, without looking up.

"It can read any language that is printed in Roman type. And by an alteration of the master pattern on which the photoelectric cells operate, it can be fitted to read Russian, or Bulgarian, or any language printed in the Cyrillic alphabet. In fact, it will do more. By simply throwing a switch, you can adapt it to read Hebrew, or Arabic, or any language that is written from right to left instead of from left to right."

"Chinese?" said the Professor of Amphibology, throwing himself into the arena. The others still studied their magazines.

"Not Chinese, as yet," said Professor Entwhistle. "Though by inserting the pages sidewise . . . Yes, I think it could be done."

"Yes, but when you say this contrivance reads, exactly what do you mean? It seems to me—"

"The light waves registered by the photoelectric cells are first converted into sound waves."

"So you can listen in to the reading of the text?"

"Not at all. The sound waves alter so fast that you hear nothing but a continuous hum. If you hear them at all. You can't, in fact, because they are on a wave length inaudible to the human ear."

"Well, it seems to me—"

"Think of the efficiency of the thing!" Professor Entwhistle was really warming up. "Think of the time saved! You assign a student a bibliography of fifty books. He runs them through the machine comfortably in a weekend. And on Monday morning he turns in a certificate from the machine. Everything has been conscientiously read!"

"Yes, but the student won't remember what he has read!"

"He doesn't remember what he reads now."

"Well, you have me there," said the Professor of Amphibology. "I confess you have me there. But it seems to me we would have to pass the machine and fail the student."

"Not at all," said Professor Entwhistle. "An accountant today does not think of doing his work by multiplication and division. Often he is unable to multiply and divide. He confides his problem to a business machine and the machine does his work for him. All the accountant has to know is how to run the machine. That is efficiency."

"Still, it seems to me that what we want to do is to transfer the contents of the book to the student's mind."

"In the mechanized age? My dear fellow! What we want is to train the student to run machines. An airplane pilot doesn't need to know the history of aerodynamics. He needs to know how to run his machine. A lawyer doesn't want to know the development of theories of Roman law. He wants to win cases, if possible by getting the right answers to logical problems. That is largely a mechanical process. It might well be possible to construct a machine. It could begin by solving simple syllogisms, you know—drawing a conclusion from a major premise and a minor premise—"

"Here, let's not get distracted. This reading machine of yours, it must *do* something, it must make some kind of record. What happens after you get the sound waves?"

"That's the beauty of it," said Professor Entwhistle. "The sound waves are converted into light waves, of a different character from the original light waves, and these are communicated to an automatic typewriter, working at inconceivable speed. This transforms the light impulses into legible typescript, in folders of a hundred pages each. It tosses them out the way a combine tosses out sacked wheat. Thus, everything the machine reads is preserved entire, in durable form. The only thing that remains is to file it somewhere, and for this you would need only the services of a capable filing clerk."

"Or you could read it?" persisted the Professor of Amphibology.

"Why, yes, if you wanted to, you could read it," said Professor Entwhistle.

An indigestible silence hung over the Faculty Club.

"I see where the Athletic Association has bought a pitching machine," said the Assistant Professor of Business Psychology (Retail). "Damn thing throws any curve desired, with a maximum margin of error of three centimetres over the plate. What'll they be thinking of next?"

"A batting machine, obviously," said Professor Entwhistle.

Writer to Reader

BENJAMIN FRANKLIN

•

From the *Autobiography of Benjamin Franklin*[1]

From my infancy I was passionately fond of reading, and all the little money that came into my hands was laid out in the purchasing of books. I was very fond of voyages. My first acquisition was Bunyan's works in separate little volumes. I afterwards sold them to enable me to buy R. Burton's historical collections; they were small chapmen's books[2] and cheap, forty or fifty in all. My father's little library consisted chiefly of books in polemic divinity, most of which I read. I have since often regretted that at a time when I had such a thirst for knowledge, more proper books had not fallen in my way, since it was now resolved I should not be bred to divinity. There was among them Plutarch's *Lives,* in which I read abundantly, and I still think that time spent to great advantage. There was also a book of Defoe's called an *Essay on Projects* and another of Dr. Mather's called *Essays to do Good,*[3] which perhaps gave me a turn of thinking that had an influence on some of the principal future events of my life.

This bookish inclination at length determined my father to make me a printer, though he had already one son (James) of that profession. In 1717 my brother, James, returned from England with a press and letters to set up his business in Boston. I liked it much better than that of my father, but still had a hankering for the sea. To prevent the apprehended effect of such an inclination, my father was impatient to have me bound[4] to my brother. I stood out some time, but at last was persuaded and signed the indenture, when I was yet but twelve years old. I was to serve as apprentice till I was twenty-one years of age, only I was to be allowed journeyman's wages during the last year. In a little time I made a great progress in the business and became a useful hand to my brother. I now had access to better books. An acquaintance with the apprentices of booksellers enabled me sometimes to borrow a small one, which I was careful to return soon and clean. Often I sat up in my room read-

[1] From Max Farrand, ed., *Autobiography of Benjamin Franklin* University of California Press and the Huntington Library (Riverside edition) 1949, pp. 28-38.

[2] Paper books sold by street peddlers.

[3] Daniel Defoe's *Essay on Projects* appeared in 1697, the Reverend Cotton Mather's *Essays to do Good* in 1710.

[4] Apprenticed.

ing the greatest part of the night, when the book was borrowed in the evening and to be returned early in the morning, lest it should be found missing or wanted.

After some time a merchant, an ingenious, sensible man, Mr. Matthew Adams, who had a pretty collection of books and who frequented our printing house, took notice of me, invited me to see his library, and very kindly proposed to lend me such books as I chose to read. I now took a fancy to poetry and made some little pieces. My brother, supposing it might turn to account, encouraged me and induced me to compose two occasional ballads. One was called the "Lighthouse Tragedy," and contained an account of the shipwreck of Capt. Worthilake with his two daughters; the other was a "Sailor's Song on the Taking of the Famous *Teach,* or Blackbeard, the Pirate." They were wretched stuff, in street ballad style; and when they were printed, he sent me about the town to sell them. The first sold prodigiously, the event being recent and having made a great noise. This success flattered my vanity, but my father discouraged me by ridiculing my performances and telling me verse-makers were generally beggars. Thus I escaped being a poet and probably a very bad one. But as prose writing has been of great use to me in the course of my life and was a principal means of my advancement, I shall tell you how in such a situation I acquired what little ability I may be supposed to have in that way.

There was another bookish lad in the town, John Collins by name, with whom I was intimately acquainted. We sometimes disputed, and very fond we were of argument, and very desirous of confuting one another—which disputatious turn, by the way, is apt to become a very bad habit, making people often extremely disagreeable in company, by the contradiction that is necessary to bring it into practice; and thence besides souring and spoiling the conversation, it is productive of disgusts and perhaps enmities where you may have occasion for friendship. I had caught it by reading my father's books of dispute on religion. Persons of good sense, I have since observed, seldom fall into it, except lawyers, university men, and men of all sorts who have been bred at Edinburgh. A question was once somehow or other started between Collins and me on the propriety of educating the female sex in learning and their abilities for study. He was of opinion that it was improper and that they were naturally unequal to it. I took the contrary side, perhaps a little for dispute sake. He was naturally more eloquent, having a greater plenty of words, and sometimes, as I thought, I was vanquished more by his fluency than by the strength of his reasons. As we parted without settling the point and were not to see one another again for some time, I sat down to put my arguments in writing, which I copied fair and sent to him. He answered and I replied. Three or four letters on a side had passed, when my father happened to find my papers and read them. Without entering into the subject in dispute, he took occasion to talk with me about my manner of writing, observed that though I had the advantage of my antagonist in correct spelling and pointing[5] (which

[5] Punctuation.

I owed to the printing house) I fell far short in elegance of expression, in method, and in perspicuity—of which he convinced me by several instances. I saw the justice of his remarks and thence grew more attentive to my manner of writing, and determined to endeavour to improve my style.

About this time I met with an odd volume of the *Spectator*.[6] It was the third. I had never before seen any of them. I bought it, read it over and over, and was much delighted with it. I thought the writing excellent and wished if possible to imitate it. With that view, I took some of the papers, and making short hints of the sentiment in each sentence, laid them by a few days, and then without looking at the book, tried to complete the papers again by expressing each hinted sentiment at length and as fully as it had been expressed before, in any suitable words that should occur to me. Then I compared my *Spectator* with the original, discovered some of my faults, and corrected them. But I found I wanted a stock of words or a readiness in recollecting and using them, which I thought I should have acquired before that time if I had gone on making verses; since the continual search for words of the same import but of different length to suit the measure, or of different sound for the rhyme would have laid me under a constant necessity of searching for variety, and also have tended to fix that variety in my mind, and make me master of it. Therefore I took some of the tales in the *Spectator* and turned them into verse, and after a time, when I had pretty well forgotten the prose, turned them back again. I also sometimes jumbled my collections of hints into confusion, and after some weeks endeavoured to reduce them into the best order before I began to form the full sentences and complete the paper. This was to teach me method in the arrangement of the thoughts. By comparing my work afterwards with the original, I discovered many faults and corrected them; but I sometimes had the pleasure of fancying that in certain particulars of small import I had been lucky enough to improve the method or the language, and this encouraged me to think that I might possibly in time come to be a tolerable English writer, of which I was extremely ambitious.

[6] Joseph Addison's and Richard Steele's celebrated London periodical, published 1711-1712.

T. S. ELIOT

•

From "Burnt Norton"[1]

V

Words move, music moves
Only in time; but that which is only living
Can only die. Words, after speech, reach
Into the silence. Only by the form, the pattern,

[1] From *Four Quartets,* copyright, 1943, by T. S. Eliot. Reprinted by permission of Harcourt, Brace & World, Inc.

Can words or music reach
The stillness, as a Chinese jar still
Moves perpetually in its stillness.
Not the stillness of the violin, while the note lasts,
Not that only, but the co-existence,
Or say that the end precedes the beginning,
And the end and the beginning were always there
Before the beginning and after the end.
And all is always now. Words strain,
Crack and sometimes break, under the burden,
Under the tension, slip, slide, perish,
Decay with imprecision, will not stay in place,
Will not stay still. Shrieking voices
Scolding, mocking, or merely chattering,
Always assail them. The Word in the desert
Is most attacked by voices of temptation,
The crying shadow in the funeral dance,
The loud lament of the disconsolate chimera.

DYLAN THOMAS

•

In My Craft or Sullen Art[1]

In my craft or sullen art
Exercised in the still night
When only the moon rages
And the lovers lie abed
With all their griefs in their arms,
I labour by singing light
Not for ambition or bread
Or the strut and trade of charms
On the ivory stages
But for the common wages
Of their most secret heart.

Not for the proud man apart
From the raging moon I write
On these spindrift pages
Nor for the towering dead
With their nightingales and psalms

[1] *The Collected Poems of Dylan Thomas*, copyright 1953 by Dylan Thomas, © 1957 by New Directions. Reprinted by permission of the publisher, New Directions Publishing Corporation.

But for the lovers, their arms
Round the griefs of the ages,
Who pay no praise or wages
Nor heed my craft or art.

ERNEST HEMINGWAY

•

From an Interview[1]

INTERVIEWER A fundamental question: namely, as a creative writer what do you think is the function of your art? Why a representation of fact, rather than fact itself.

HEMINGWAY Why be puzzled by that? From things that have happened and from things as they exist and from all things that you know and all those you cannot know, you make something through your invention that is not a representation but a whole new thing truer than anything true and alive, and you make it alive, and if you make it well enough, you give it immortality. That is why you write and for no other reason that you know of. But what about all the reasons that no one knows?

[1] George Plimpton, "The Art of Fiction XXI," *The Paris Review*, #18 (Spring, 1958). Reprinted by permission of George Plimpton.

Writing

F. L. LUCAS

•

What Is Style?[1]

When it was suggested to Walt Whitman that one of his works should be bound in vellum, he was outraged—"Pshaw!" he snorted, "—hangings, curtains, finger bowls, chinaware, Matthew Arnold!" And he might have been equally irritated by talk of style; for he boasted of "my barbaric yawp"—he would *not* be literary; his readers should touch not a book but a man. Yet Whitman took the pains to rewrite *Leaves of Grass* four times, and his style is unmistakable. Samuel Butler maintained that writers who bothered about their style became unreadable but he bothered about his own. "Style" has got a bad name by growing associated with precious and superior persons who, like Oscar Wilde, spend a morning putting in a comma, and the afternoon (so he said) taking it out again. But such abuse of "style" is misuse of English. For the word means merely "a way of expressing oneself, in language, manner, or appearance"; or, secondly, "a *good* way of so expressing oneself"—as when one says, "Her behavior never lacked style."

Now there is no crime in expressing oneself (though to try to *im*press oneself on others easily grows revolting or ridiculous). Indeed one cannot help expressing oneself, unless one passes one's life in a cupboard. Even the most rigid Communist, or Organization-man, is compelled by Nature to have a unique voice, unique fingerprints, unique handwriting. Even the signatures of the letters on your breakfast table may reveal more than their writers guess. There are blustering signatures that swish across the page like cornstalks bowed before a tempest. There are cryptic signatures, like a scrabble of lightning across a cloud, suggesting that behind is a lofty divinity whom all must know, or an aloof divinity whom none is worthy to know (though, as this might be highly inconvenient, a docile typist sometimes interprets the mystery in a bracket underneath). There are impetuous squiggles implying that the author is a sort of strenuous Sputnik streaking round the globe every eighty minutes. There are florid signatures, all curlicues and danglements and flamboyance, like the youthful Disraeli (though these seem rather out of fashion). There are humble, humdrum signatures. And there are also, sometimes, signa-

[1] From *Holiday*, XXVII (March, 1960), 11 *et passim*. Reprinted by permission of the author.

tures that are courteously clear, yet mindful of a certain simple grace and artistic economy—in short, of style.

Since, then, not one of us can put pen to paper, or even open his mouth, without giving something of himself away to shrewd observers, it seems mere common sense to give the matter a little thought. Yet it does not seem very common. Ladies may take infinite pains about having style in their clothes, but many of us remain curiously indifferent about having it in our words. How many women would dream of polishing not only their nails but also their tongues? They may play freely on that perilous little organ, but they cannot often be bothered to tune it. And how many men think of improving their talk as well as their golf handicap?

No doubt strong silent men, speaking only in gruff monosyllables, may despise "mere words." No doubt the world does suffer from an endemic plague of verbal dysentery. But that, precisely, is bad style. And consider the amazing power of mere words. Adolf Hitler was a bad artist, bad statesman, bad general, and bad man. But largely because he could tune his rant, with psychological nicety, to the exact wave length of his audiences and make millions quarrelsome-drunk all at the same time by his command of windy nonsense, skilled statesmen, soldiers, scientists were blown away like chaff, and he came near to rule the world. If Sir Winston Churchill had been a mere speechifier, we might well have lost the war; yet his speeches did quite a lot to win it.

No man was less of a literary aesthete than Benjamin Franklin; yet this tallow-chandler's son, who changed world history, regarded as "a principal means of my advancement" that pungent style which he acquired partly by working in youth over old *Spectators*; but mainly by being Benjamin Franklin. The squinting demagogue, John Wilkes, as ugly as his many sins, had yet a tongue so winning that he asked only half an hour's start (to counteract his face) against any rival for a woman's favor. "Vote for you!" growled a surly elector in his constituency. "I'd sooner vote for the devil!" "But in case your friend should not stand . . . ?" Cleopatra, that ensnarer of world conquerors, owed less to the shape of her nose than to the charm of her tongue. Shakespeare himself has often poor plots and thin ideas; even his mastery of character has been questioned; what does remain unchallenged is his verbal magic. Men are often taken, like rabbits, by the ears. And though the tongue has no bones, it can sometimes break millions of them.

"But," the reader may grumble, "I am neither Hitler, Cleopatra, nor Shakespeare. What is all this to me?" Yet we all talk—often too much; we all have to write letters—often too many. We live not by bread alone but also by words. And not always with remarkable efficiency. Strikes, lawsuits, divorces, all sorts of public nuisance and private misery, often come just from the gaggling incompetence with which we express ourselves. Americans and British get at cross-purposes because they use the same words with different meanings. Men have been hanged on a comma in a statute. And in the valley of Balaclava a mere verbal ambiguity, about *which* guns were to be captured, sent the whole Light Brigade to futile annihilation.

Words can be more powerful, and more treacherous, than we sometimes suspect; communication more difficult than we may think. We are all serving life sentences of solitary confinement within our own bodies; like prisoners, we have, as it were, to tap in awkward code to our fellow men in their neighboring cells. Further, when A and B converse, there take part in their dialogue not two characters, as they suppose, but six. For there is A's real self—call it A_1; there is also A's picture of himself—A_2; there is also B's picture of A—A_3. And there are three corresponding personalities of B. With six characters involved even in a simple tête-à-tête, no wonder we fall into muddles and misunderstandings.

Perhaps, then, there are five main reasons for trying to gain some mastery of language:

We have no other way of understanding, informing, misinforming, or persuading one another.

Even alone, we think mainly in words; if our language is muddy, so will our thinking be.

By our handling of words we are often revealed and judged. "Has he written anything?" said Napoleon of a candidate for an appointment. "Let me see his *style*."

Without a feeling for language one remains half-blind and deaf to literature.

Our mother tongue is bettered or worsened by the way each generation uses it. Languages evolve like species. They can degenerate; just as oysters and barnacles have lost their heads. Compare ancient Greek with modern. A heavy responsibility, though often forgotten.

Why and how did I become interested in style? The main answer, I suppose, is that I was born that way. Then I was, till ten, an only child running loose in a house packed with books, and in a world (thank goodness) still undistracted by radio and television. So at three I groaned to my mother, "Oh, I *wish* I could read," and at four I read. Now travel among books is the best travel of all, and the easiest, and the cheapest. (Not that I belittle ordinary travel—which I regard as one of the three main pleasures in life.) One learns to write by reading good books, as one learns to talk by hearing good talkers. And if I have learned anything of writing, it is largely from writers like Montaigne, Dorothy Osborne, Horace Walpole, Johnson, Goldsmith, Montesquieu, Voltaire, Flaubert and Anatole France. Again, I was reared on Greek and Latin, and one can learn much from translating Homer or the Greek Anthology, Horace or Tacitus, if one is thrilled by the originals and tries, however vainly, to recapture some of that thrill in English.

But at Rugby I could *not* write English essays. I believe it stupid to torment boys to write on topics that they know and care nothing about. I used to rush to the school library and cram the subject, like a python swallowing rabbits;

then, still replete as a postprandial python, I would tie myself in clumsy knots to embrace those accursed themes. Bacon was wise in saying that reading makes a full man; talking, a ready one; writing, an exact one. But writing from an empty head is futile anguish.

At Cambridge, my head having grown a little fuller, I suddenly found I *could* write—not with enjoyment (it is always tearing oneself in pieces)—but fairly fluently. Then came the War of 1914–18; and though soldiers have other things than pens to handle, they learn painfully to be clear and brief. Then the late Sir Desmond MacCarthy invited me to review for the *New Statesman;* it was a useful apprenticeship, and he was delightful to work for. But I think it was well after a few years to stop; reviewers remain essential, but there are too many books one *cannot* praise, and only the pugnacious enjoy amassing enemies. By then I was an ink-addict—not because writing is much pleasure, but because not to write is pain; just as some smokers do not so much enjoy tobacco as suffer without it. The positive happiness of writing comes, I think, from work when done—decently, one hopes, and not without use—and from the letters of readers which help to reassure, or delude, one that so it is.

But one of my most vivid lessons came, I think, from service in a war department during the Second War. Then, if the matter one sent out was too wordy, the communication channels might choke; yet if it was not absolutely clear, the results might be serious. So I emerged, after six years of it, with more passion than ever for clarity and brevity, more loathing than ever for the obscure and the verbose.

For forty years at Cambridge I have tried to teach young men to write well, and have come to think it impossible. To write really well is a gift inborn; those who have it teach themselves; one can only try to help and hasten the process. After all, the uneducated sometimes express themselves far better than their "betters." In language, as in life, it is possible to be perfectly correct—and yet perfectly tedious, or odious. The illiterate last letter of the doomed Vanzetti was more moving than most professional orators; 18th Century ladies, who should have been spanked for their spelling, could yet write far better letters than most professors of English; and the talk of Synge's Irish peasants seems to me vastly more vivid than the later style of Henry James. Yet Synge averred that his characters owed far less of their eloquence to what he invented for them than to what he had overheard in the cottages of Wicklow and Kerry:

"*Christy.* 'It's little you'll think if my love's a poacher's, or an earl's itself, when you'll feel my two hands stretched around you, and I squeezing kisses on your puckered lips, till I'd feel a kind of pity for the Lord God is all ages sitting lonesome in His golden chair.'

"*Pegeen.* 'That'll be right fun, Christy Mahon, and any girl would walk her heart out before she'd meet a young man was your like for eloquence, or talk at all.' "

Well she might! It's not like that they talk in universities—more's the pity.

But though one cannot teach people to write well, one can sometimes teach them to write rather better. One can give a certain number of hints, which often seem boringly obvious—only experience shows they are not.

One can say: Beware of pronouns—they are devils. Look at even Addison, describing the type of pedant who chatters of style without having any: "Upon enquiry I found my learned friend had dined that day with Mr. Swan, the famous punster; and desiring *him* to give me some account of Mr. Swan's conversation, *he* told me that *he* generally talked in the Paronomasia, that *he* sometimes gave in to the Plocé, but that in *his* humble opinion *he* shone most in the Antanaclasis." What a sluttish muddle of *he* and *him* and *his!* It all needs rewording. Far better repeat a noun, or a name, than puzzle the reader, even for a moment, with ambiguous pronouns. Thou shalt not puzzle thy reader.

Or one can say: Avoid jingles. The B.B.C. news bulletins seem compiled by earless persons, capable of crying round the globe: "The enemy is re*port*ed to have seized this im*port*ant *port,* and reinforcements are hurrying up in sup*port*." Any fool, once told, can hear such things to be insupportable.

Or one can say: Be sparing with relative clauses. Don't string them together like sausages, or jam them inside one another like Chinese boxes or the receptacles of Buddhas' tooth. Or one can say: Don't flaunt jargon, like Addison's Mr. Swan, or the type of modern critic who gurgles more technical terms in a page than Johnson used in all his *Lives* or Sainte-Beuve in thirty volumes. But dozens of such snippety precepts, though they may sometimes save people from writing badly, will help them little toward writing well. Are there no general rules of a more positive kind, and of more positive use?

Perhaps. There *are* certain basic principles which seem to me observed by many authors I admire, which I think have served me and which may serve others. I am not talking of geniuses, who are a law to themselves (and do not always write a very good style, either); nor of poetry, which has different laws from prose; nor of poetic prose, like Sir Thomas Browne's or De Quincey's, which is often more akin to poetry; but of the plain prose of ordinary books and documents, letters and talk.

The writer should respect truth and himself; therefore honesty. He should respect his readers; therefore courtesy. These are two of the cornerstones of style. Confucius saw it, twenty-five centuries ago: "The Master said, The gentleman is courteous, but not pliable: common men are pliable, but not courteous."

First, honesty. In literature, as in life, one of the fundamentals is to find, and be, one's true self. One's true self may indeed be unpleasant (though one can try to better it); but a false self, sooner or later, becomes disgusting—just as a nice plain woman, painted to the eyebrows, can become horrid. In writing, in the long run, pretense does not work. As the police put it, anything you say may be used as evidence against you. If handwriting reveals character, writing reveals it still more. You cannot fool *all* your judges *all* the time.

Most style is not honest enough. Easy to say, but hard to practice. A writer may take to long words, as young men to beards—to impress. But long words, like long beards, are often the badge of charlatans. Or a writer may cultivate the obscure, to seem profound. But even carefully muddied puddles are soon fathomed. Or he may cultivate eccentricity, to seem original. But really original people do not have to think about being original—they can no more help it than they can help breathing. They do not need to dye their hair green. The fame of Meredith, Wilde or Bernard Shaw might now shine brighter, had they struggled less to be brilliant; whereas Johnson remains great, not merely because his gifts were formidable but also because, with all his prejudice and passion, he fought no less passionately to "clear his mind of cant."

Secondly, courtesy—respect for the reader. From this follow several other basic principles of style. Clarity is one. For it is boorish to make your reader rack his brains to understand. One should aim at being impossible to misunderstand—though men's capacity for misunderstanding approaches infinity. Hence Molière and Po Chu-i tried their work on their cooks; and Swift his on his men-servants—"which, if they did not comprehend, he would alter and amend, until they understood it perfectly." Our bureaucrats and pundits, unfortunately, are less considerate.

Brevity is another basic principle. For it is boorish, also, to waste your reader's time. People who would not dream of stealing a penny of one's money turn not a hair at stealing hours of one's life. But that does not make them less exasperating. Therefore there is no excuse for the sort of writer who takes as long as a marching army corps to pass a given point. Besides, brevity is often more effective; the half can say more than the whole, and to imply things may strike far deeper than to state them at length. And because one is particularly apt to waste words on preambles before coming to the substance, there was sense in the Scots professor who always asked his pupils—"Did ye remember to tear up that fir-r-st page?"

Here are some instances that would only lose by lengthening:

> It is useless to go to bed to save the light, if the result is twins. (Chinese proverb.)
>
> My barn is burnt down—
> Nothing hides the moon. (Complete Japanese poem.)
>
> Je me regrette. (Dying words of the gay Vicomtesse d'Houdetot.)
>
> I have seen their backs before. (Wellington, when French marshals turned their backs on him at a reception.)
>
> Continue until the tanks stop, then get out and walk. (Patton to the Twelfth Corps, halted for fuel supplies at St. Dizier, 8/30/44.)

Or there is the most laconic diplomatic note on record: when Philip of Macedon wrote to the Spartans that, if he came within their borders, he would leave not one stone of their city, they wrote back the one word—"If."

Clarity comes before even brevity. But it is a fallacy that wordiness is necessarily clearer. Metternich when he thought something he had written was obscure would simply go through it crossing out everything irrelevant. What remained, he found, often became clear. Wellington, asked to recommend three names for the post of Commander-in-Chief, India, took a piece of paper and wrote three times—"Napier." Pages could not have been clearer—or as forcible. On the other hand the lectures, and the sentences, of Coleridge became at times bewildering because his mind was often "wiggle-waggle"; just as he could not even walk straight on a path.

But clarity and brevity, though a good beginning, are only a beginning. By themselves, they may remain bare and bleak. When Calvin Coolidge, asked by his wife what the preacher had preached on, replied "Sin," and, asked what the preacher had said, replied, "He was against it," he was brief enough. But one hardly envies Mrs. Coolidge.

An attractive style requires, of course, all kinds of further gifts—such as variety, good humor, good sense, vitality, imagination. Variety means avoiding monotony of rhythm, of language, of mood. One needs to vary one's sentence length (this present article has too many short sentences; but so vast a subject grows here as cramped as a djin in a bottle); to amplify one's vocabulary; to diversify one's tone. There are books that petrify one throughout, with the rigidly pompous solemnity of an owl perched on a leafless tree. But ceaseless facetiousness can be as bad; or perpetual irony. Even the smile of Voltaire can seem at times a fixed grin, a disagreeable wrinkle. Constant peevishness is far worse, as often in Swift; even on the stage too much irritable dialogue may irritate an audience, without its knowing why.

Still more are vitality, energy, imagination gifts that must be inborn before they can be cultivated. But under the head of imagination two common devices may be mentioned that have been the making of many a style—metaphor and simile. Why such magic power should reside in simply saying, or implying, that A is like B remains a little mysterious. But even our unconscious seems to love symbols; again, language often tends to lose itself in clouds of vaporous abstraction, and simile or metaphor can bring it back to concrete solidity; and, again, such imagery can gild the gray flats of prose with sudden sun-glints of poetry.

If a foreigner may for a moment be impertinent, I admire the native gift of Americans for imagery as much as I wince at their fondness for slang. (Slang seems to me a kind of linguistic fungus; as poisonous, and as short-lived, as toadstools.) When Matthew Arnold lectured in the United States, he was likened by one newspaper to "an elderly macaw pecking at a trellis of grapes"; he observed, very justly, "How lively journalistic fancy is among the Americans!" General Grant, again, unable to hear him, remarked: "Well, wife, we've paid to see the British lion, but as we can't hear him roar, we'd better go home." By simile and metaphor, these two quotations bring before us the slightly pompous, fastidious, inaudible Arnold as no direct description could have done.

Or consider how language comes alive in the Chinese saying that lending to the feckless is "like pelting a stray dog with dumplings," or in the Arab proverb: "They came to shoe the pasha's horse, and the beetle stretched forth his leg"; in the Greek phrase for a perilous cape—"stepmother of ships"; or the Hebrew adage that "as the climbing up a sandy way is to the feet of the aged, so is a wife full of words to a quiet man"; in Shakespeare's phrase for a little England lost in the world's vastness—"in a great Poole, a Swan's-nest"; or Fuller's libel on tall men—"Ofttimes such who are built four stories high are observed to have little in their cockloft"; in Chateaubriand's "I go yawning my life"; or in Jules Renard's portrait of a cat, "well buttoned in her fur." Or, to take a modern instance, there is Churchill on dealings with Russia: "Trying to maintain good relations with a Communist is like wooing a crocodile. You do not know whether to tickle it under the chin or beat it over the head. When it opens its mouth, you cannot tell whether it is trying to smile or preparing to eat you up." What a miracle human speech can be, and how dull is most that one hears! Would one hold one's hearers, it is far less help, I suspect, to read manuals on style than to cultivate one's own imagination and imagery.

I will end with two remarks by two wise old women of the civilized 18th Century.

The first is from the blind Mme. du Deffand (the friend of Horace Walpole) to that Mlle. de Lespinasse with whom, alas, she was to quarrel so unwisely: "You must make up your mind, my queen, to live with me in the greatest truth and sincerity. You will be charming so long as you let yourself be natural, and remain without pretension and without artifice." The second is from Mme. de Charrière, the Zélide whom Boswell had once loved at Utrecht in vain, to a Swiss girl friend: "Lucinde, my clever Lucinde, while you wait for the Romeos to arrive, you have nothing better to do than become perfect. Have ideas that are clear, and expressions that are simple." ("*Ayez des idées nettes et des expressions simples.*") More than half the bad writing in the world, I believe, comes from neglecting those two very simple pieces of advice.

In many ways, no doubt, our world grows more and more complex; sputniks cannot be simple; yet how many of our complexities remain futile, how many of our artificialities false. Simplicity too can be subtle—as the straight lines of a Greek temple, like the Parthenon at Athens, are delicately curved, in order to look straighter still.

PAUL ROBERTS

•

Transformational Grammar[1]

. . . Immediate-constituent grammar was a product of linguistics—largely American linguistics—of the 1930's and 40's. It was most available to the

[1] From *English Sentences, Teacher's Manual,* by Paul Roberts, © 1962 by Harcourt, Brace & World, Inc., and reprinted with their permission.

general reader in a book called *The Structure of English* by Charles Carpenter Fries of the University of Michigan, published in 1952. The grammar was characterized by certain fundamental tenets which still characterize work in linguistics and presumably always will:

(1) *That language is primarily speech and only secondarily writing.* This is not to degrade writing or to say that it is not properly the central concern of the school system. It is only to indicate the actual relationship of writing and speech. Writing is a symbolization of speech and not vice versa. We approach writing and its problems more easily if we understand what it is.

(2) *That word classes (parts of speech and their subgroups) can be identified only by their distribution, their formal characteristics, and the like that they share.* Efforts to define them on the basis of meaning are doomed to failure. Such definitions turn out always to be either false or circular.

(3) *That correctness in language is a relative matter, not an absolute one.* There are no *linguistic* considerations for preferring one variety of English to another, but only sociological ones. In the sight of both God and logic, "He brung it" is no better and no worse than "He flung it," But to say that correctness is a sociological matter is not to say that it is unimportant. Obviously children being educated must learn that "He brung it" is not what educated people say. . . .

IMMEDIATE-CONSTITUENT GRAMMAR

Immediate-constituent analysis makes the basic assumption that sentences can be viewed as being made up of two-part constructions on a series of levels. A sentence consists of two main parts (two immediate constituents); each of those parts consists of two parts; each of those of two parts, until one gets down to the ultimate constituents, the smallest meaningful units in the sentence—i.e., words or morphemes. For many sentences this structure can be shown very easily:

The little girls walked to the store.
The little girls / walked to the store.
The / little girls walked / to the store.
The little / girls walk / ed to / the store.
The little girl / s walk ed to the / store.

Not only did this analysis provide interesting insights into the nature of the sentence, but it proved to have various useful practical applications in solving problems of modification and the like.

However, there were certain types of constructions to which immediate-constituent analysis proved difficult to apply. What are the immediate constituents, for example, of "Did the little girls walk to the store?" If it consists of two parts, what are they? The further one tried to push the concept of immediate constituents, the more one confronted problems to which only uncertain or arbitrary answers could be given.

This difficulty, along with many others that had troubled linguistics, was surmounted by the development of transformational analysis, which was certainly the most interesting advance of linguistic science in the 1950's. . . .

TRANSFORMATIONAL GRAMMAR

Transformational analysis begins with the assumption that the sentences of English or of any language are of two basic types: *kernel sentences* and *transformed sentences*. The heart of the grammar is a relatively small set of kernel or basic-sentence types. These are basic in the sense that they cannot be derived from any sentences or sentence types underlying them. They are the foundation on which all else is built. All the rest of the language can be most economically described as a series of changes rung on the kernel sentences, as transformations of them.

Thus, for example, the sentence "John saw Bill" is a kernel sentence. The following are all transformations of it:

Did John see Bill?	Who saw Bill?
John didn't see Bill.	Whom did John see?
John did see Bill.	Where did John see Bill?
John saw Bill, didn't he?	John's seeing Bill
Bill was seen by John.	that John saw Bill
Bill wasn't seen by John.	for John to see Bill

And so on.

. . . What we might try to do in this place is to see some of the more general consequences of transformational analysis and some of its relationship both to immediate-constituent grammar and to prescientific grammar.

One thing that transformational analysis demonstrates is that immediate-constituent analysis applies wholly and simply *only to kernel sentences.* Indeed, transformational analysis provides, for the kernel, a much more powerful proof of immediate-constituent theory than was ever possible before. It is quite easy to show that any kernel sentence can be evolved by a simple forking process, each higher or more general unit splitting into two lower or more particular units until actual words are reached:

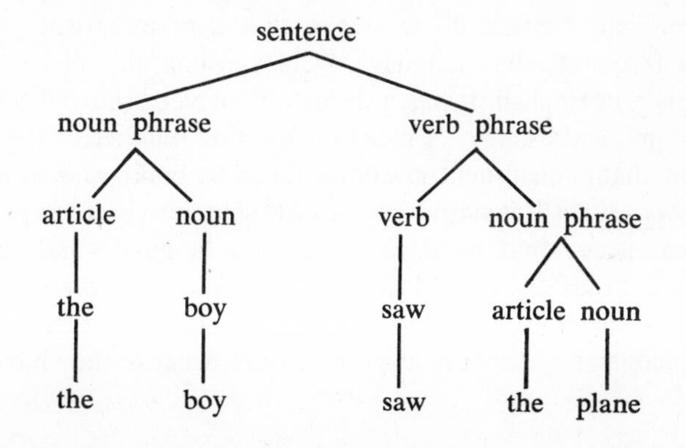

This process, refined to take into account the various types of predicates possible in English and to indicate the grammatical agreements necessary and the compatibility of various word groups, can display the whole kernel of English in a relatively small space. The entire kernel is produced by simple forking into immediate constituents.

But this system will not work to produce all of English sentences. One cannot produce "Did the boy see the plane?" for example, in this fashion. The easiest way to arrive at "Did the boy see the plane?" is to describe the changes made in the statement to produce the question. "Did the boy see the plane?" is a transformation of "The boy saw the plane." Like all transformations, it involves additions, the switching around of things, and the like. Its production requires rules or directions of a fundamentally different sort than the rules and directions which produce kernel sentences. Because it cannot be reached by a simple forking process, immediate-constituent analysis does not apply to it, or at least does not apply in the same simple way that it applies to the kernel.

It must be emphasized that transformational analysis is much more than simply a neater or more defensible way of describing language. It goes a long way to describe how languages are learned in the first place. It explains something of how virtually all human beings, even the dullest, manage to grasp and use at least one language. Language appears as a finite and comprehensible system. We somehow, as children, learn the kernel plus the rules for transforming the kernel into the various structures permitted by the language. This makes the possibilities infinite, and makes it possible for us to produce sentences which are completely grammatical but which we have never specifically learned. Given the kernel sentence "The boy saw the plane" and knowledge of how to make that kind of statement into a yes/no question, we can produce "Did the boy see the plane?" without ever having heard the question previously. Thus grasp of a finite system permits us to produce infinitely many grammatical sentences.

We are led from here to a much better understanding of the complex question of grammaticality. What do we mean when we say a sentence is or is not grammatical? We obviously can't mean that it makes sense. The sentence "Chicago is a dish of fried sofas" makes no sense, but we accept it as wholly grammatical. Neither do we mean that a grammatical sentence is one that occurs frequently in a language. "Chicago is a dish of fried sofas" has a zero frequency in English. It has, presumably, never occurred before. Yet it is quite as grammatical as, say, "Chicago is the hog butcher of the world."

Immediate-constituent grammar tends to make and describe an inventory. In theory, at least, it simply records the sentences—more precisely, a sample of the sentences—that have occurred in a language and then describes their features. Transformational analysis goes much further than this. It seeks to figure out the grammatical system of a language and then project it. Thus it not only recognizes sentences as grammatical because they have occurred but also undertakes to predict what sentences will be grammatical when and if they occur in the future.

WORD CLASSES

The problem of grammaticality is closely connected with the problem of definition of word classes, something that has plagued students and teachers of grammar since at least the time of Aristotle. Grammars previous to transformational analysis have tended to begin with the smallest units and work up to the sentence unit. One begins by describing the sounds, then shows how these go together to make morphemes, how these make words, how the words are arranged in word classes, and how the word classes go together to form sentences. In this process, definition is crucial. One had to find some way of identifying each class and fencing it off from its neighbors. Both scientific and prescientific grammars spent much time in this pursuit with no really satisfactory conclusion. Thus we find in grammars of one sort or another the following definitions of *adjective:*

(1) A word that modifies a noun. (Absurd. This would put *bad* and *bank* in the same class: "a bad robber," "a bank robber.")
(2) A word that indicates a quality. (Absurd. This puts *courageous* and *courage* in the same class: "He's courageous," "He has courage.")
(3) A word that patterns with *very*. (Absurd. This puts *old* and *much* in the same class: "very old," "very much.")
(4) A word that takes the endings /ər/ and /əst/ (*-er*, *-est*). (Absurd. This puts *fine* and *tear* in the same class: *fine, finer, finest*— /fayn/, /faynər/, /faynəst/; *tear, terror, terraced*— /ter/, /terər/, /terəst/.)[2]

Thus, though some of the definitions proposed work pretty well in a general sort of way, all of them encounter absurdity when pushed to conclusion. Transformational analysis does not solve the problem by providing better definitions in the same sense of *definition*. Rather it avoids the problem altogether by beginning with the largest, most abstract level—sentence—and working down to the concrete items. Every higher-level concept is automatically defined by indicating what it consists of on the next level down. There is never any need to frame a definition of *sentence*, because the whole grammar is a definition of sentence. The whole grammar is a level-to-level description of the make-up of sentences in some particular language. . . .

We start with some such rule as this:

$$S \rightarrow NP + VP$$

S stands for *sentence*. The arrow means "rewrite as." Formulas of this type define the term to the left of the arrow by the terms given to the right of the arrow. The formula $S \rightarrow NP + VP$ means that any sentence consists of an

[2] Chomsky's example.

NP and a *VP*, whatever they are. (*NP* stands for *noun phrase*, and *VP* for *verb phrase*, but the terms and symbols are arbitrary; we could just as well write $S \rightarrow X + Y$; the meaning of *NP* and *VP*, or *X* and *Y*, will be indicated in successive rules below.)

$$NP \rightarrow T + N$$
$$T \rightarrow \text{the, a}$$
$$N \rightarrow \text{man, boy, table} \ldots$$

Thus an *NP* is shown to consist of a *T* and an *N*, and *T* and *N* are defined, as we arrive at the concrete level, by showing the words, or examples of the words, that occur in these classes—articles and nouns. We would come at adjective in the *VP:*

$$VP \rightarrow Aux + V$$
$$V \rightarrow \begin{Bmatrix} Vi \\ Vt + NP \\ Vs + Adj \end{Bmatrix}$$
$$Vi \rightarrow \text{occur, arrive} \ldots$$
$$Vt \rightarrow \text{see, find} \ldots$$
$$Vs \rightarrow \text{seem, appear} \ldots$$
$$Adj \rightarrow \text{old, fine} \ldots$$

The class *adjective*, when it appears, appears as a set of words. But it is a set of words in a complex, a piece in the pattern that goes to make up grammatical English sentences. Classroom experience shows that when word classes are approached in this direction, the problem of definition largely vanishes. It just isn't there any more. Teacher and student are relieved of the burden and enabled to proceed to examination of the actual characteristics of the sentences of English.[3]

A transformational grammar is intended to produce all grammatical sentences of a language and only those. That is, if you follow out all the possibilities given in the rules, you eventually can construct all the grammatical sentence types, but you will not produce any sentences that are not grammatical. This clearly necessitates the subdivision of word classes. If, for example, we have a sentence type "noun-verb-noun" and if the verb class contains all verbs with no differentiation, we would be able to derive not only the grammatical "The boy saw the table" but also "The boy occurred the table," which is not grammatical. So we must subdivide verb into transitive, intransitive, and various other subclasses, as traditional grammar has done, too.

We come eventually, however, to a point at which grammatical subclassifica-

[3] These examples are not intended to display the actual content of a transformational grammar, either a scholarly or a textbook one. A full grammar would have to be considerably more elaborate in the area shown and would proceed differently in respect to some particulars. . . .

tion stops. This is the point where grammar leaves off and semantics begins. For example, there is no *grammatical* way to rule out the sentence "Chicago is a dish of fried sofas." There is no grammatical way to classify the words *Chicago, dish, fried,* and *sofa* to keep them from coming together in this order, though semantic groupings might be possible. This is why we say that the sentence, though semantically absurd, is perfectly grammatical. . . .

It would be a mistake to make too much of the newness of transformational analysis or to suggest that it is a rejection of the work in linguistics of the past or is unrelated to that work. Much of transformational analysis is implicit in immediate-constituent grammars—in such books as Fries's *The Structure of English* or Francis's *Structure of American English* or Lloyd and Warfel's *American English in Its Cultural Setting.* In all these works we find descriptions of basic-sentence types (something that looks very much like the kernel) and descriptions of the mechanism for expanding the basic sentences (something that looks very much like transformation). All these books share with transformational analysis the same kind of interest in speech, in form and function, in language as a signaling system. All look at the same language in the same objective way, working from the same data to very similar conclusions. . . .

Transformational analysis is more truly conceived as a going-on, as a building on earlier work. Penetrating more profoundly into very general questions concerning the nature of language, of grammar, of linguistics, it gains a vantage point from which to discern more promising new routes to the solution of old problems. It explains conclusions which before were only intuited. Often, in working with immediate-constituent grammar, one felt that beyond certain points progress became steeply difficult. The description was right as far as it went, but one couldn't take it farther. In transformational analysis one doesn't have this sense of a blocking-off. One feels that the way is open from a rough and general sketch to a complete and satisfying description of English. If this also is illusory, the illusion is at least not easily dispelled. . . .

OGDEN NASH

•

Laments for a Dying Language[1]

What's the monster of this week?
"Mystique"—
A noun that in its current arcane use leaves me frigid,
Since it is not to be found in either the O.E.D. or Webster's Unabridgèd.

[1] Reprinted by permission of Curtis Brown, Ltd. Copyright © 1960 by Ogden Nash. This poem was originally published in The New Yorker Magazine.

It is primarily the invention of the mystagogues of esoteric criticism, so it means whatever they choose,
But I will give you an example of what I think they think it means, only from the domain of a different muse.
I recently heard on the air a song in which the lover states that the loved one is his idea
Of a band of angels singing "Ave Maria."
This is not only a metaphor unique,
It is also an example of the songwriter's mystique at its peak.

II

Someone comes up with a linguistic gimmick,
And thousands flock to mimic.
This noisy age, when big loud bangs give way to bangs louder and bigger still,
And admirals, congressmen, and minor government officials pop off at will,
Gives us two gimmicks that reflect our minds' corrosion:
"Crash program" and "explosion."
See here the population explosion, the freedom explosion, the Broadway and off-Broadway incest-theme explosion, the explosion of British secretaries in offices of grandiose pretensions,
And there the crash program for defense, for space exploration, for a third major league, for nominating the candidates previous to the conventions.
With each successive bang my hopes grow limper
That the world's end will be a simple whimper.

III

In the nice-minded Department of Prunes and Prisms,
It's I for you
And euphemisms.
Hence the phrase I would eagerly jettison:
"Senior citizen."
Let us, then, retranslate
Joel, 2, 28.
To the sociologist squeamish
The words "Your old men shall dream dreams" are less than beamish,
So "Your senior citizens shall dream dreams" it shall henceforth be,
Along with Hemingway's "The Senior Citizen and the Sea"
I, though no Joel, prophesy that someday while the senior citizens are projecting the image of an age-adjusted social group,
The old men will rise up and knock them for a loop.

IV

Those authors I can never love
Who write, "It fit him like a glove."
Though baseballs may be hit, not "hitted,"
The past of "fit" is always "fitted."
The sole exception worth a *haricot*
Is "Joshua fit de battle ob "Jericho."

V

Coin brassy words at will, debase the coinage;
We're in an if-you-cannot-lick-them-join age,
A slovenliness-provides-its-own-excuse age,
Where usage overnight condones misusage.
Farewell, farewell to my beloved language,
Once English, now a vile orangutanguage.

FRANK SULLIVAN

•

The Cliché Expert Reveals Himself in His True Colors[1]

Q Mr. Arbuthnot, would you mind telling us today how you happened to become a cliché expert? Was it easy?

A Easy! Don't make me laugh, Mr. Crouse. It was an uphill climb. A cliché novitiate is no bed of roses, and if anyone ever tells you it is, do you know how I want you take his statement?

Q How?

A With a grain of salt. I shall tell you about my career, since you insist, and as a special treat, I shall describe it to you entirely in terms of the seesaw cliché.

Q The seesaw cliché?

A You'll see what I mean. Before I made my mark as a cliché expert, I had my ups and downs. Sometimes, when everything was at sixes and sevens, it almost seemed as though my dearest ambitions were going to wrack and ruin. I had moments when I was almost tempted to believe that everything was a snare and a delusion. Even my own flesh and blood discouraged me, in spite of the fact that I was their pride and joy . . . You aren't listening, Mr. Crouse.

Q Yes I am. I just closed my eyes because the light hurt. You were saying that your own kith and kin discouraged you.

A I didn't say kith and kin, but it doesn't matter. For a considerable period of time it was nip and tuck whether I would sink or swim. If I had not been hale and hearty, and well equipped for a rough-and-tumble struggle, I wouldn't have come through. But I kept at it, hammer and tongs. I gave 'em tit for tat . . . Mr. Crouse, you *are* asleep.

Q No, I'm not, Mr. Arbuthnot. You were saying you went after your goal hard and fast.

A I did. I eschewed wine, woman, and song—

Q Ah, but wine, woman, and song is not a seesaw cliché, Mr. Arbuthnot.

A Yes it is, too. Woman is standing in the middle, balancing. I worked morn-

[1] From *A Pearl in Every Oyster* (Boston: Little, Brown and Company, 1938), pp. 284-290. Reprinted by permission of the author.

ing, noon, and night, and kept to the straight and narrow. The consequence was that in the due course of time—

Q And tide?

A Please! In the due course of time things began to come my way by fits and starts, and a little later by leaps and bounds. Now, I'm fine and dandy.

Q High, wide, and handsome, eh?

A I wish I had said that, Mr. Crouse.

Q You—

A Will, Oscar. Had you there, Mr. Crouse, didn't I, ha ha! When I started I was free, white, and twenty-one. Now I'm fat, fair, and forty, and I venture to predict that no man, without regard to race, creed, or color, is a better master of the cliché than your servant—your *humble* servant—Magnus Arbuthnot. So much for my life story in terms of the seesaw cliché.

Q It certainly is an interesting story, Mr. Arbuthnot—by and large.

A Well, in all due modesty, I suppose it is, although sometimes, to tell you the truth, I think there is neither rhyme nor reason to it.

Q Where were you born, Mr. Arbuthnot?

A In the altogether.

Q I see. How?

A On the impulse of the moment.

Q And when?

A In the nick of time.

Q It is agreeable to find a man so frank about himself, Mr. Arbuthnot.

A Why not? You asked me a question. You know what kind of question it was?

Q Impertinent?

A Oh, my dear man, no.

Q Personal?

A Civil. You asked me a civil question. I answered you by telling you the truth. I gave it to you, if I may be permitted to say so, straight from the shoulder. I revealed myself to you in my—

Q True colors?

A Ah, someone told you. Rather, someone *went* and told you.

Q Were you ever in love, Mr. Arbuthnot, or am I out of order in asking that?

A Not at all. I have had my romances.

Q How nice.

A Ah, you wouldn't say so if you knew what kind of romances they were.

Q What kind were they?

A Blighted romances, all of 'em. I kept trying to combine single blessedness with wedded bliss. It didn't work. I had a sweetheart in every port, and I worshiped the ground they walked on, each and every one of them. This ground amounts to a matter of 18,467 acres, as of my latest blighted romance.

Q Hm! You must have been quite a pedestrian.

A Well, those are the figures when the tide was out; only 16,468 acres at the neap. I was land-poor at the end. And you take the advice of a sadder—

Q And a wiser man.

A That's what I was going to say. And never trust the weaker sex, or you'll have an awakening. You seem to be so smart, interrupting me all the while, maybe you can tell me what kind of awakening.

Q Awakening? Awakening? I'm afraid you have me.

A Rude awakening.

Q Oh, of course. Now, I don't think your story would be complete, Mr. Arbuthnot, without some statement from you regarding your material circumstances. Are you well-to-do, or are you—

A Hard pressed for cash? No, I'm solvent. I'm well paid.

Q You mean you get a handsome salary?

A I prefer to call it a princely stipend. You know what kind of coin I'm paid in?

Q No. What?

A Coin of the realm. Not that I give a hoot for money. You know how I refer to money?

Q As the root of all evil?

A No, but you have a talking point there. I call it lucre—filthy lucre.

Q On the whole, you seem to have a pretty good time, Mr. Arbuthnot.

A Oh, I'm not complaining. I'm as snug as a bug in a rug. I'm clear as crystal —when I'm not dull as dishwater. I'm cool as a cucumber, quick as a flash, fresh as a daisy, pleased as Punch, good as my word, regular as clockwork, and I suppose at the end of my declining years, when I'm gathered to my ancestors, I'll be dead as a doornail.

Q *Eh bien! C'est la vie!*

A *Mais oui, mon vieux.* I manage. I'm the glass of fashion and the mold of form. I have a finger in every pie, all except this finger. I use it for pointing with scorn. When I go in for malice, it is always malice aforethought. My nods are significant. My offers are standing. I am at cross-purposes and in dire straits. My motives are ulterior, my circles are vicious, my retainers are faithful, and my hopefuls are young. My suspicions are sneaking, my glee is fiendish, my stories are likely. I am drunk.

Q Drunk?

A Yes, with power. You know where?

Q Where?

A Behind the throne. I am emotional. My mercies are tender, and when I cry, I cry quits. I am lost in thought and up in arms. I am a square shooter with my trusty revolver. My courage is vaunted and my shame is crying, but I don't care —a rap. I have been in the depths of despair, when a watery grave in the briny deep seemed attractive. Eventually I want to marry and settle down, but the woman I marry must be clever.

Q Clever?

A With the needle.

Q Well, I'd certainly call you a man who had led a full life, Mr. Arbuthnot, and a likable chap, too.

A Yes, I'm a peach of a fellow. I'm a diamond in the rough, all wool and a yard wide. I'm too funny for words and too full for utterance. I'm a gay dog, and I like to trip the light fantastic and burn the candle at both ends with motley throngs of boon companions. I may be foolish but my folly is at least sheer.

Q I think you certainly have run—

A I certainly have. The entire gamut of human emotions. I know the facts of life. I'm afraid I've got to go now, Mr. Crouse. I'm due back at my abode. Do you know what kind of abode I live in?

Q Humble, Mr. Arbuthnot?

A Certainly not. Palatial! Goodbye, my little periwinkle!

H. L. MENCKEN

•

The American Language[1]

The first Englishman to notice an Americanism sneered at it aloofly, thus setting a fashion that many of his countrymen have been following ever since. He was one Francis Moore, a ruffian who came out to Georgia with Oglethorpe in 1735, and the word that upset him was *bluff,* in the sense of "a cliff or headland with a broad precipitous face." He did not deign to argue against it; he simply dismissed it as "barbarous," apparently assuming that all Englishmen of decent instincts would agree with him. For nearly a century they seem to have done so, and *bluff* lingered sadly below the salt. When it was printed at all in Great Britain it was set off by sanitary quotation marks, or accompanied by other hints of deprecation, as *rubberneck, hot spot* and *nerts* are accompanied today. But then, in 1830, the eminent Sir Charles Lyell used it shamelessly in the first volume of his monumental "Principles of Geology," and from that day to this it has been a perfectly respectable if somewhat unfamiliar word in England, with a place in every dictionary.

Its history is the history of almost countless other Americanisms. They have been edging their way into English since early colonial times, and, for more than a century past, in constantly increasing volume, but I can't recall one that didn't have to run a gauntlet of opposition in the motherland, at times verging upon the frantic. After the Revolution, that opposition took on the proportions of a holy war. Never an American book came out that the English reviewers did not belabor its vocabulary violently. The brunt of the attack, of course, had to be borne by the poetasters of the era—for example, Joel Barlow, whose "Columbiad" (1807) loosed a really terrifying geyser of abuse. But even the most serious writers got their share—among them, Jefferson, John Marshall, Noah Webster, and John Quincy Adams. Jefferson's crime was that he had invented the verb to *belittle.* It was, one may argue plausibly, a very logical, useful, and perhaps even nifty word, and seventy-five years later the prissy Anthony Trollope was employing it without apology. But when Jefferson ventured to use it in his "Notes on Virginia" (1787) "The London Review" tossed and raged in a manner befitting the discovery of a brace of duelling pistols

[1] From *The Yale Review,* XXV (March, 1936), 538-552, with omissions. Copyright Yale University Press.

beneath the cope of the Archbishop of Canterbury, and for several years following its dudgeon was supported virtuously by most of the other reviews. "What an expression!" roared the "London." "It may be an elegant one in Virginia, but for our part, all we can do is to *guess* at its meaning. For shame, Mr. Jefferson! Freely, good sir, will we forgive all your attacks, impotent as they are illiberal, upon our national character: but for the future spare—O spare, we beseech you, our mother-tongue!"

The underscoring of *guess* was a fling in passing at another foul Americanism. It was the belief of most Englishmen then, as it is today, that the use of the verb in the sense of *to suppose* or *assume* originated in this country. It is actually to be found, in that meaning precisely, in "Measure for Measure" and "Henry VI"; nay, in Chaucer, Wycliffe, and Gower. But such historical considerations have never daunted the more ardent preservers of the King's English. When a word acquires an American flavor it becomes anathema to them, even though it may go back to Boadicea. To *advocate* offers an instructive example. It appeared in English in the dark backward and abysm of time, but during the eighteenth century it seems to have dropped out of general use, though Burke used it. Towards the end of the century it came into vogue in this country and soon it made its way back to the land of its birth. It was received with all the honors proper to an invasion of Asiatic cholera. The reviews denounced it as loutish, "Gothic," and against God, and lumped it with *to compromit* and *to happify* as proof that civilization was impossible in America, and would be so forevermore. Even Benjamin Franklin, returning from England in 1789, was alarmed into begging Noah Webster to "reprobate" it, along with *to notice, to progress,* and *to oppose*. There is no record of Noah's reply, but it is most unlikely that he did any reprobating, for when he began to make dictionaries he included all four verbs, and they have been listed in every considerable dictionary published since, whether in this country or in England.

The leader of the heroic struggle to keep Americanisms out of Britain, in its early stages, was the celebrated William Gifford, editor of "The Quarterly Review." Gifford was a killer in general practice, and his savage assaults on Wordsworth, Shelley, and Keats are still unpleasantly remembered. He was the first magazine editor in history to make the trade pay, and when he died in 1828 he left £25,000 and was buried in Westminster Abbey. One of his major specialties was the villainousness of everything American, from politics to table manners and from theology to speechways. Among the allegations that he either made himself or permitted his contributors to make were these: (*a*) that the Americans employed naked colored women to wait upon them at table, (*b*) that they kidnapped Scotsmen, Irishmen, Hollanders, and Welshmen and sold them into slavery, and (*c*) that they were planning to repudiate the English language altogether, and adopt Hebrew in its place. This last charge, as it flew from tongue to tongue, acquired variorum readings. One of them made the new American language an Indian dialect, another made it Greek, and a third was to the effect that the people of Britain would be forced to acquire Greek, thus leaving English to the wicked will of the barbaric Yankees. It all sounds idiotic today, but in 1814 it was taken quite seriously by many Englishmen. Gifford was a tyrannical editor and so vastly enjoyed slashing his contributors' copy that Southey once denounced him as "a butcherly review-gelder." But anything that was against the damyankee passed his eye unscathed, and he piled up accusations in a manner so shameless that "The North American Review" was moved to protest that if the tirade went on it would "turn into bitterness the last drops of good-will towards England that exist in the United States."

In the early Twenties of that century there was some amelioration, and when Gifford retired from the "Quarterly" in 1824, voices that were almost conciliatory began to be heard. They heaped praises on Niagara Falls, found something to commend in Cooper's "Spy," and even had kind words for the speed and luxuriousness of American canalboats. But my most diligent researches have failed to unearth anything complimentary to the American language. It continued to be treated as a grotesque and immoral gibberish, full of uncouth terms and at war with all the canons of English. Every British traveller who came to these shores between the War of 1812 and the Civil War had something to say about the neologisms his ears and eyes encountered on his tour, and nearly all were constrained to deplore them. Captain Basil Hall, who was here in 1827 and 1828, went about in a palpitating daze, confounded and outraged by the signs on American places of business. *Clothing Store* he interpreted after long thought, and *Flour and Feed Store* after prayer and soul-searching, but what on earth was a *Leather and Finding Store?* Captain Thomas Hamilton, who followed five years later, found it impossible to penetrate to "the precise import" of *Dry-Goods Store,* and when he encountered an established offering *Hollow Ware, Spiders, and Fire-Dogs* he gave up in despair.

Hall was not one to take it lying down. He decided to call upon Noah Webster, whose American Dictionary of the English Language had just come out, to find out what the Yankees meant by using the mother tongue so cruelly. Webster shocked him by arguing stoutly that "his countrymen had not only a right to adopt new words, but were obliged to modify the language to suit the novelty of the circumstances, geographical and political, in which they were placed." The great lexicographer "who taught millions to spell but not one to sin" went on to observe judicially that it was "quite impossible to stop the progress of language—it is like the course of the Mississippi, the motion of which, at times, is scarcely perceptible; yet even then it possesses a momentum quite irresistible. Words and expressions will be forced into use in spite of all the exertions of all the writers in the world."

"But surely," persisted Hall, "such innovations are to be deprecated?"

"I don't think that," replied old Noah. "If a word becomes universally current in America, where English is spoken, why should it not take its station in the language.

"Because," declared Hall with magnificent pertinacity, "there are words enough already."

This heroic dogma is still heard in England, where even native novelties are commonly opposed violently, and not infrequently strangled at birth. There seems to be, in the modern Englishman, very little of that ecstasy in word-making which so prodigiously engrossed his Elizabethan forebears. Shakespeare alone probably put more new words into circulation than all the English writers since Carlyle, and they were much better ones. The ideal over there today is not picturesque and exhilarating utterance, but correct and reassuring utterance, and one of its inevitable fruits is that bow-wow jargon which Sir Arthur Quiller-Couch describes in "On the Art of Writing" as "the medium through which boards of government, county councils, syndicates, committees, commercial firms, express the processes as well as the conclusions of their thought, and so voice the reason of their being." It is, at its worst, at least in accord with what are taken to be the principles of English grammar, and at its best it shows excellent manners and even a kind of mellifluous elegance; indeed, the English, taking one with another, may be said to write much better than we do—at all events by the standards of the schoolmaster. But what they write is seldom animated by anything properly describable as bounce. It lacks novelty, variety, audacity. There is little juice in it. The reader confronted by it is treated politely and lulled pleasantly, but he seldom enjoys the enchantment of surprise. That diligent search for new and racy locutions which occupied so much of the work day of Walt Whitman and William Dean Howells alike, and is practised so assiduously by scores of saucy Andersons and Hemingways, Sandburgs and Saroyans today, is carried on across the ocean by only a few extravagant eccentrics, virtually all of whom—for example, James Joyce and Ezra Pound—are non- and even anti-Englishmen. The hundred-per-cent English writers, save when they stoop to conscious wickedness, seldom depart very far from the jargon of Quiller-Couch. It is by no means a monopoly of the classes he named, nor is it reserved for solemn occasions. I find it also in my favorite English weekly, the "News of the World," which is devoted principally to sports, the theatres, and the more scabrous varieties of crime, and is probably a far better mirror of England than the "Times." When the "News of the World" reports the downfall of a rural dean or a raid on a Mayfair night club, the thing is done in a style so tight and brittle that nothing to match it is discoverable in this country, at least outside the pages of "The Homiletic Review." "When we want to freshen our speech," Mrs. Virginia Woolf was lately saying, "we borrow from American—*poppycock, rambunctious, flip-flop, booster, good mixer*. All the expressive, ugly, vigorous slang which creeps into use among us, first in talk, later in writing, comes from across the Atlantic." . . .

Whenever an Americanism comes publicly into question in England, there are efforts to track down its etymology, and sometimes the theories offered are extremely bizarre. In January, 1935, for example, the London "Morning Post" opened its columns to a furious and fantastic discussion of the verb-phrase, *to get his goat*. I content myself with one of the explanations: "Among the Negroes in Harlem it is the custom for each household to keep a goat to act as general scavenger. Occasionally one man will steal another's goat, and the household débris then accumulates to the general annoyance." The truth is that *to get his goat* seems to be of French origin, and in the form of *prendre sa chèvre* philological genealogists have traced it back to the year 1585. But whatever is strange and upsetting is put down, in England, to the hellish ingenuity of Americans—save, of course, when genuine Americanisms are claimed as really English. This last happens often enough to give what may be called a cockeyed aspect to the perennial pother. In 1934 even the learned Dr. C. T. Onions, one of the editors of the great Oxford Dictionary, succumbed to the madness by offering to find in the dictionary any alleged Americanism that a reporter for the London "Evening News" could name. The reporter began discreetly with *fresh* (in the sense of *saucy*), *to figure* (in the sense of *to believe* or *conclude*), and to *grill* (in the sense of *to question*), and Dr. Onions duly found them all. But when the reporter proceeded to *bunkum,* the learned editor had to forget conveniently that its progenitor was the thoroughly American *buncombe*, when *rake-off* followed he had to admit that the earliest example in the dictionary was from an American work, and when *baloney* and *nerts* were hurled at him he blew up with a bang.

Here, of course, Dr. Onions and his interlocutor ended on the level of slang, but there is no telling where they would be if they could be translated to the year 2036. *Baloney,* like *to belittle,* has the imprimatur of an eminent tribune of the people, and is quite as respectable, philologically speaking, as *buncombe, gerrymander, pork barrel, filibuster, carpetbagger, gag rule,* or *on the fence.* All these came into American from the argot of politics, and got only frowns from the schoolmarm, but they are all quite sound American today, and most of them have gone into English. As for *nerts,* it seems to be but one more member of an endless dynasty of euphemisms, beginning with *zounds* and coming down to *son-of-a-gun*, *gee* and *darn*. *Darn*, like *nerts*, is an Americanism, and Dr. Louise Pound has demonstrated that it descends from *eternal,* which first turned into *tarnal* and then lost its tail and borrowed the head of *damn*. I have heard a bishop use it freely in private discourse, with a waggish sprinkling of actual *damns*. *Son-of-a-gun* is now so feeble and harmless that the Italians in America use it as a satirical designation for native Americans, who seem to them to fall far behind the Italian talent for profanity and objurgation. It is, I believe, a just criticism. Some time ago I was engaged by a magazine to do an article on American and English swearwords. After two or three attempts I had to give it up, for I found that neither branch of our ancient Frisian tongue could show anything worthy of serious consideration. The antinomians of England stick to two or three banal obscenities, one of which, *bloody,* is obscene only formally, and we Americans seldom get beyond variations of *hell* and *damn.* A single Neapolitan boatman could swear down the whole population of Anglo-Saxondom.

Bloody is perfectly innocuous in the United States, and it may be innocuous in England also on some near tomorrow—or even more disreputable than it is today. There is no predicting the social career of words. Dr. Leonard Bloomfield says that even "our word *whore,* cognate with the Latin *carus* (dear), must have been at one time a polite substitute for some term now lost." Prophecy fails just as dismally when propriety does not come into question. Shakespeare's numerous attempts to introduce new words, some of them his own inventions and others borrowed from the slang of the Bankside, failed almost as often as they succeeded. He found ready takers for *courtship, lonely, sportive, multitudinous, hubbub* and *bump,* but his audiences would have none of *definement,* in the sense of description, or of *citizen* as an adjective, and both seem strange and uncouth to us today, though all the others are as familiar and as decorous as *cat* or *rat.* When John Marston used *strenuous* in 1599 it was attacked by Ben Jonson as barbarous, but a dozen years later it had got into Chapman's Homer, and by 1670 it was being used by Milton. It remained perfectly respectable until 1900, when Theodore Roosevelt announced the Strenuous Life. Both the idea and the term struck the American fancy, and in a little while the latter passed into slang, and was worn so threadbare that all persons of careful speech sickened of it. To this day it carries a faintly ridiculous connotation, and is seldom used seriously. But by 1975 it may be restored to the dignity of *psychopath* or *homoousian.* No one can say yes with any confidence, and no one can say no. "Even the greatest purist," observes Robert Lynd, "does not object to the inclusion of *bogus* in a literary English vocabulary, though a hundred years ago it was an American slang word meaning an apparatus for coining false money. *Carpetbagger* and *bunkum* are other American slang words that have naturalized themselves in English speech, and *mob* is an example of English slang that was once as vulgar as *photo.*" . . .

One finds in current American all the characters and tendencies that marked the rich English of Shakespeare's time—an eager borrowing of neologisms from other languages, bold and often very ingenious use of metaphor, and a fine disdain of the barricades separating the parts of speech. The making of new words is not carried on only, or even principally, to fill gaps in the vocabulary; indeed, one may well agree with Captain Hall that "there are words enough already." It is carried on because there survives in the American something that seems to have faded out of the Englishman: an innocent joy in word-making for its own sake, a voluptuous delight in the vigor and elasticity of the language. The search for the *mot juste* is an enterprise that is altogether too pedantic for him; he much prefers to solve his problem by non-Euclidian devices. *Hoosegow* was certainly not necessary when it appeared, for we already had a large repertory of synonyms for *jail*. But when the word precipitated itself from the Spanish *juzgado* somewhere along the Rio Grande it won quick currency, and in a little while it was on the march through the country, and soon or late, I suppose, It will produce its inevitable clipped forms, *hoose* and *gow,* and its attendant adjective and verb. *Corral,* which entered by the same route in the Forties of the last century, had hatched a verb before the Civil War, and that verb, according to Webster's New International (1934), now has four separate and distinct meanings. *Bummer,* coming in from the German, is now clipped to *bum,* and is not only noun, verb, and adjective but also adverb. *Buncombe,* borrowed by the English as *bunkum,* has bred *bunco* and *bunk* at home, both of which rove the parts of speech in a loose and easy way, and the last of which has issue in the harsh verb *to debunk,* still under heavy fire in England.

The impact of such lawless novelties upon the more staid English of the motherland is terrific. The more they are denounced as heathen and outlandish, the quicker they get into circulation. Nor do they prosper only on the level of the vulgate, and among careless speakers. There are constant complaints in the English newspapers about their appearance in the parliamentary debates, and even in discourses from the sacred desk, and they begin to show themselves also in *belles-lettres*, despite the English dislike of new ways of writing. Their progress, in fact, is so widespread and so insidious that they often pop up in the diatribes that revile them; the Englishman, conquered at last, can no longer protest against Americanisms without using them. Moreover, they are now supported actively by a definitely pro-American party of writers and scholars, and though it is still small in numbers, at least compared to the patriot band, it shows some distinguished names. The late Robert Bridges, Poet Laureate, was an active member of it, and among its other adherents are Wyndham Lewis, Edward Shanks, Richard Adington, and Sir John Foster Fraser. Sir William Craigie, perhaps the first living lexicographer, is so greatly interested in the American form of English that he has spent the years since 1925 in a scientific examination of it, and will presently begin the publication of an elaborate dictionary. If only because of the greater weight of the population behind it, it seems destined to usurp the natural leadership of British English, and to determine the general course of the language hereafter. But its chief advantage in this struggle is really not the numerical one, but the fact that its daring experiments and iconoclasms lie in the grand tradition of English, and are signs of its incurable normalcy and abounding vigor.

How far it will move away from the theorizing of grammarians and the policing of schoolmarms remains to be seen. They will make valiant efforts to curb its wayward spirit, but with gradually diminishing success. When, a few years ago, the late Sterling A. Leonard of the University of Wisconsin submitted a long series of their admonitions to a committee of educated Americans, including many philologians, he found that opinion was against them on that high level almost as decidedly as it was on lower ones. His judges favored scores of forms that the school grammars and popular handbooks of usage still condemn. Since then a more direct attack upon the conservative position has been made by Dr. Robert C. Pooley of the same university. He shows that some of the rules laid down with most assurance by pedants have no support in either history or logic, and are constantly violated by writers of unquestionable authority. There have even been rumblings of revolt in the conservative camp. The late George Philip Krapp of Columbia, who was surely anything but a radical, was of the opinion that English would undergo profound changes in the United States, and that many of them would be of such a character that its very grammatical structure would be shaken. Dr. George O. Curme of Northwestern University is another eminent grammarian who warns his colleagues that the rules they cherish have no genuine authority, and must be overhauled from time to time. Once they steel themselves to that sacrifice of their professional dignity, he says, "it will give a thrill to English-speaking students to discover that the English language does not belong to the schoolteacher but belongs to them, and that its future destiny will soon rest entirely in their hands."

Dr. Curme is always careful to think and speak of American as no more than a variation of English. But it must be obvious that, in late years, the tail has begun a vigorous wagging of the dog. "The facts that we ought to realize," says Edward Shanks to his fellow Britons, "and that we ignore when we talk loftily about Americanisms, are that America is making a formidable contribution to the development of our language, and that all our attempts to reject that contribution will in the long run be vain."

GEORGE ORWELL

•

Politics and the English Language[1]

Most people who bother with the matter at all would admit that the English language is in a bad way, but it is generally assumed that we cannot by conscious action do anything about it. Our civilization is decadent, and our language—so the argument runs—must inevitably share in the general collapse. It follows that any struggle against the abuse of language is a sentimental archaism, like preferring candles to electric light or hansom cabs to aeroplanes. Underneath this lies the half-conscious belief that language is a natural growth and not an instrument which we shape for our own purposes.

[1] From *Shooting An Elephant and Other Essays* by George Orwell, copyright, 1945, 1946, 1949, 1950, by Sonia Brownell Orwell. Reprinted by permission of Harcourt, Brace & World, Inc., and Martin Secker & Warburg, Ltd.

Now, it is clear that the decline of a language must ultimately have political and economic causes: it is not due simply to the bad influence of this or that individual writer. But an effect can become a cause, reinforcing the original cause and producing the same effect in an intensified form, and so on indefinitely. A man may take to drink because he feels himself to be a failure, and then fail all the more completely because he drinks. It is rather the same thing that is happening to the English language. It becomes ugly and inaccurate because our thoughts are foolish, but the slovenliness of our language makes it easier for us to have foolish thoughts. The point is that the process is reversible. Modern English, especially written English, is full of bad habits which spread by imitation and which can be avoided if one is willing to take the necessary trouble. If one gets rid of these habits one can think more clearly, and to think clearly is a necessary first step towards political regeneration: so that the fight against bad English is not frivolous and is not the exclusive concern of professional writers. I will come back to this presently, and I hope that by that time the meaning of what I have said here will have become clearer. Meanwhile, here are five specimens of the English language as it is now habitually written.

These five passages have not been picked out because they are especially bad—I could have quoted far worse if I had chosen—but because they illustrate various of the mental vices from which we now suffer. They are a little below the average, but are fairly representative samples. I number them so that I can refer back to them when necessary:

> (1) I am not, indeed, sure whether it is not true to say that the Milton who once seemed not unlike a seventeenth-century Shelley had not become, out of an experience ever more bitter in each year, more alien (*sic*) to the founder of that Jesuit sect which nothing could induce him to tolerate.
>
> Professor Harold Laski (Essay in *Freedom of Expression*)

> (2) Above all, we cannot play ducks and drakes with a native battery of idioms which prescribes such egregious collocations of vocables as the Basic *put up with* for *tolerate* or *put at a loss* for *bewilder*.
>
> Professor Lancelot Hogben (*Interglossa*)

> (3) On the one side we have the free personality; by definition it is not neurotic, for it has neither conflict nor dream. Its desires, such as they are, are transparent, for they are just what institutional approval keeps in the forefront of consciousness; another institutional pattern would alter their number and intensity; there is little in them that is natural, irreducible, or culturally dangerous. But *on the other side*, the social bond itself is nothing but the mutual reflection of these self-secure integrities. Recall the definition of love. Is not this the very picture of a small academic? Where is there a place in this hall of mirrors for either personality or fraternity?
>
> Essay on psychology in *Politics* (*New York*)

> (4) All the "best people" from the gentlemen's clubs, and all the frantic fascist captains, united in common hatred of Socialism and bestial horror of the rising tide of the mass revolutionary movement, have turned to acts of provocation, to foul incendiarism, to medieval legends of poisoned wells, to legalize their own destruction of proletarian organizations, and rouse the

agitated petty-bourgeoisie to chauvinistic fervor on behalf of the fight against the revolutionary way out of the crisis. Communist pamphlet

(5) If a new spirit *is* to be infused into this old country, there is one thorny and contentious reform which must be tackled, and that is the humanization and galvanization of the B.B.C. Timidity here will bespeak canker and atrophy of the soul. The heart of Britain may be sound and of strong beat, for instance, but the British lion's roar at present is like that of Bottom in Shakespeare's *Midsummer Night's Dream*—as gentle as any sucking dove. A virile new Britain cannot continue indefinitely to be traduced in the eyes, or rather ears, of the world by the effete languors of Langham Place, brazenly masquerading as "standard English." When the Voice of Britain is heard at nine o'clock, better far and infinitely less ludicrous to hear aitches honestly dropped than the present priggish, inflated, inhibited, school-ma'amish arch braying of blameless bashful mewing maidens.

Letter in *Tribune*

Each of these passages has faults of its own, but quite apart from avoidable ugliness, two qualities are common to all of them. The first is staleness of imagery; the other is lack of precision. The writer either has a meaning and cannot express it, or he inadvertently says something else, or he is almost indifferent as to whether his words mean anything or not. This mixture of vagueness and sheer incompetence is the most marked characteristic of modern English prose, and especially of any kind of political writing. As soon as certain topics are raised, the concrete melts into the abstract and no one seems able to think of turns of speech that are not hackneyed: prose consists less and less of *words* chosen for the sake of their meaning, and more and more of *phrases* tacked together like the sections of a prefabricated hen-house. I list below, with notes and examples, various of the tricks by means of which the work of prose-construction is habitually dodged:

Dying metaphors. A newly-invented metaphor assists thought by evoking a visual image, while on the other hand a metaphor which is technically "dead" (e.g., *iron resolution*) has in effect reverted to being an ordinary word and can generally be used without loss of vividness. But in between these two classes there is a huge dump of worn-out metaphors which have lost all evocative power and are merely used because they save people the trouble of inventing phrases for themselves. Examples are: *Ring the changes on, take up the cudgels for, toe the line, ride roughshod over, stand shoulder to shoulder with, play into the hands of, an axe to grind, grist to the mill, fishing in troubled waters, on the order of the day, Achilles' heel, swan song, hotbed.* Many of these are used without knowledge of their meaning (what is a "rift," for instance?), and incompatible metaphors are frequently mixed, a sure sign that the writer is not interested in what he is saying. Some metaphors now current have been twisted out of their original meaning without those who use them even being aware of the fact. For example, *toe the line* is sometimes written *tow the line.* Another example is *the hammer and the anvil,* now always used with the implication that the anvil gets the worst of it. In real life it is always the anvil that breaks the hammer, never the other way about: a writer who stopped to think what he was saying would be aware of this, and would avoid perverting the original phrase.

Operators, or *verbal false limbs.* These save the trouble of picking out appropriate verbs and nouns, and at the same time pad each sentence with extra syllables which give it an appearance of symmetry. Characteristic phrases are: *render inoperative, militate against, prove unacceptable, make contact with, be subjected to, give rise to, give grounds for, have the effect of, play a leading part* (role) *in, making itself felt, take effect, exhibit a tendency to, serve the purpose of, etc., etc.* The keynote is the elimination of simple verbs. Instead of being a single word, such as *break, stop, spoil, mend, kill,* a verb becomes a phrase, made up of a noun or adjective tacked on to some general-purposes verb such as *prove, serve, form, play, render.* In addition, the passive voice is wherever possible used in preference to the active, and noun constructions are used instead of gerunds (*by examination of* instead of *by examining*). The range of verbs is further cut down by means of the *-ize* and *de-* formations, and banal statements are given an appearance of profundity by means of the *not un-* formation. Simple conjunctions and prepositions are replaced by such phrases as *with respect to, having regard to, the fact that, by dint of, in view of, in the interests of, on the hypothesis that;* and the ends of sentences are saved from anti-climax by such resounding commonplaces as *greatly to be desired, cannot be left out of account, a development to be expected in the near future, deserving of serious consideration, brought to a satisfactory conclusion,* and so on and so forth.

Pretentious diction. Words like *phenomenon, element, individual* (as noun), *objective, categorical, effective, virtual, basis, primary, promote, constitute, exhibit, exploit, utilize, eliminate, liquidate,* are used to dress up simple statements and give an air of scientific impartiality to biased judgments. Adjectives like *epoch-making, epic, historic, unforgettable, triumphant, age-old, inevitable, inexorable, veritable,* are used to dignify the sordid processes of international politics, while writing that aims at glorifying war usually takes on an archaic color, its characteristic words being: *realm, throne, chariot, mailed fist, trident, sword, shield, buckler, banner, jackboot, clarion.* Foreign words and expressions such as *cul de sac, ancien régime, deus ex machina, mutatis mutandis, status quo, gleichschaltung, weltanschauung,* are used to give an air of culture and elegance. Except for the useful abbreviations *i.e., e.g.,* and *etc.,* there is no real need for any of the hundreds of foreign phrases now current in English. Bad writers, and especially scientific, political and sociological writers, are nearly always haunted by the notion that Latin or Greek words are grander than Saxon ones, and unnecessary words like *expedite, ameliorate, predict, extraneous, deracinated, clandestine, subaqueous* and hundreds of others constantly gain ground from their Anglo-Saxon opposite numbers.[2] The jargon peculiar to Marxist writing (*hyena, hangman, cannibal, petty bourgeois, these gentry, lackey, flunkey, mad dog, White Guard, etc.*) consists largely of words and phrases translated from Russian, German or French; but the normal way of coining a new word is to use a Latin or Greek root with the appropriate affix and, where necessary, the *-ize* formation. It is often easier to make up words of this kind (*deregionalize, impermissible, extramarital, non-fragmentary* and so forth) than to think up the English words that will cover

[2] An interesting illustration of this is the way in which the English flower names which were in use till very recently are being ousted by Greek ones, *snap-dragon* becoming *antirrhinum, forget-me-not* becoming *myosotis,* etc. It is hard to see any practical reason for this change of fashion: it is probably due to an instinctive turning-away from the more homely word and a vague feeling that the Greek word is scientific.

one's meaning. The result, in general, is an increase in slovenliness and vagueness.

Meaningless words. In certain kinds of writing, particularly in art criticism and literary criticism, it is normal to come across long passages which are almost completely lacking in meaning.[3] Words like *romantic, plastic, values, human, dead, sentimental, natural, vitality,* as used in art criticism, are strictly meaningless, in the sense that they not only do not point to any discoverable object, but are hardly even expected to do so by the reader. When one critic writes, "The outstanding feature of Mr. X's work is its living quality," while another writes, "The immediately striking thing about Mr. X's work is its peculiar deadness," the reader accepts this as a simple difference of opinion. If words like *black* and *white* were involved, instead of the jargon words *dead* and *living,* he would see at once that language was being used in an improper way. Many political words are similarly abused. The word *Fascism* has now no meaning except in so far as it signifies "something not desirable." The words *democracy, socialism, freedom, patriotic, realistic, justice,* have each of them several different meanings which cannot be reconciled with one another. In the case of a word like *democracy,* not only is there no agreed definition, but the attempt to make one is resisted from all sides. It is almost universally felt that when we call a country democratic we are praising it: consequently the defenders of every kind of régime claim that it is a democracy, and fear that they might have to stop using the word if it were tied down to any one meaning. Words of this kind are often used in a consciously dishonest way. That is, the person who uses them has his own private definition, but allows his hearer to think he means something quite different. Statements like *Marshal Pétain was a true patriot, The Soviet Press is the freest in the world, The Catholic Church is opposed to persecution,* are almost always made with intent to deceive. Other words used in variable meanings, in most cases more or less dishonestly, are: *class, totalitarian, science, progressive, reactionary, bourgeois, equality.*

Now that I have made this catalogue of swindles and perversions, let me give another example of the kind of writing that they lead to. This time it must of its nature be an imaginary one. I am going to translate a passage of good English into modern English of the worst sort. Here is a well-known verse from *Ecclesiastes:*

> I returned, and saw under the sun, that the race is not to the swift, nor the battle to the strong, neither yet bread to the wise, nor yet riches to men of understanding, nor yet favor to men of skill; but time and chance happeneth to them all.

Here it is in modern English:

> Objective consideration of contemporary phenomena compels the conclusion that success or failure in competitive activities exhibits no tendency to

[3] Example: "Comfort's catholicity of perception and image, strangely Whitmanesque in range, almost the exact opposite in aesthetic compulsion, continues to evoke that trembling atmospheric accumulative hinting at a cruel, an inexorably serene timelessness . . . Wrey Gardiner scores by aiming at simple bullseyes with precision. Only they are not so simple, and through this contented sadness runs more than the surface bittersweet of resignation." (*Poetry Quarterly.*)

> be commensurate with innate capacity, but that a considerable element of the unpredictable must invariably be taken into account.

This is a parody, but not a very gross one. Exhibit (3), above, for instance, contains several patches of the same kind of English. It will be seen that I have not made a full translation. The beginning and ending of the sentence follow the original meaning fairly closely, but in the middle the concrete illustrations—race, battle, bread—dissolve into the vague phrase "success or failure in competitive activities." This had to be so, because no modern writer of the kind I am discussing—no one capable of using phrases like "objective consideration of contemporary phenomena"—would ever tabulate his thoughts in that precise and detailed way. The whole tendency of modern prose is away from concreteness. Now analyze these two sentences a little more closely. The first contains 49 words but only 60 syllables, and all its words are those of everyday life. The second contains 38 words of 90 syllables: 18 of its words are from Latin roots, and one from Greek. The first sentence contains six vivid images, and only one phrase ("time and chance") that could be called vague. The second contains not a single fresh, arresting phrase, and in spite of its 90 syllables it gives only a shortened version of the meaning contained in the first. Yet without a doubt it is the second kind of sentence that is gaining ground in modern English. I do not want to exaggerate. This kind of writing is not yet universal, and outcrops of simplicity will occur here and there in the worst-written page. Still, if you or I were told to write a few lines on the uncertainty of human fortunes, we should probably come much nearer to my imaginary sentence than to the one from *Ecclesiastes.*

As I have tried to show, modern writing at its worst does not consist in picking out words for the sake of their meaning and inventing images in order to make the meaning clearer. It consists in gumming together long strips of words which have already been set in order by some else, and making the results presentable by sheer humbug. The attraction of this way of writing is that it is easy. It is easier—even quicker, once you have the habit—to say *In my opinion it is a not unjustifiable assumption that* than to say *I think.* If you use ready-made phrases, you not only don't have to hunt about for words; you also don't have to bother with the rhythms of your sentences, since these phrases are generally so arranged as to be more or less euphonious. When you are composing in a hurry—when you are dictating to a stenographer, for instance, or making a public speech—it is natural to fall into a pretentious, Latinized style. Tags like *a consideration which we should do well to bear in mind* or *a conclusion to which all of us would readily assent* will save many a sentence from coming down with a bump. By using stale metaphors, similes and idioms, you save much mental effort at the cost of leaving your meaning vague, not only for your reader but for yourself. This is the significance of mixed metaphors. The sole aim of a metaphor is to call up a visual image. When these images clash—as in *The Fascist octopus has sung its swan song, the jackboot is thrown into the melting pot*—it can be taken as certain that the writer is not seeing a mental image of the objects he is naming; in other words he is not really thinking. Look again at the examples I gave at the beginning of this essay. Professor Laski (1) uses five negatives in 53 words. One of these is superfluous, making nonsense of the whole passage, and in addition there is the slip *alien* for akin, making further nonsense, and several avoidable pieces of clumsiness which increase the general vagueness. Professor Hogben (2) plays ducks and drakes with a battery which is able to write prescriptions, and, while disapproving of the everyday phrase *put up with,* is unwilling to look *egregious* up in the dictionary and see what it means. (3), if one takes an uncharitable attitude towards it, is simply meaningless: probably one could work out its intended meaning by reading the whole of the article in which it occurs. In (4), the writer knows more or less what he wants to say, but an accumulation of stale phrases chokes him like tea leaves blocking a sink. In (5), words and meaning have almost parted company. People who write in this manner usually have a general emotional meaning—they dislike one thing and want to express solidarity with another—but they are not interested in the detail of what they are saying. A scrupulous writer, in every sentence that he writes, will ask himself at least four questions, thus: What am I trying to say? What words will express it? What image or idiom will make it clearer? Is this image fresh enough to have an effect? And he will probably ask himself two more: Could I put it more shortly? Have I said anything that is avoidably ugly? But you are not obliged to go to all this trouble. You can shirk it by simply throwing your mind open and letting the ready-made phrases come crowding in. They will construct your sentences for you—even think your thoughts for you, to a certain extent—and at need they will perform the important service of partially concealing your meaning even from yourself. It is at this point that the special connection between politics and the debasement of language becomes clear.

In our time it is broadly true that political writing is bad writing. Where it is not true, it will generally be found that the writer is some kind of rebel, expressing his private opinions and not a "party line." Orthodoxy, of whatever color, seems to demand a lifeless, imitative style. The political dialects to be found in pamphlets, leading articles, manifestoes, White Papers and the speeches of under-secretaries do, of course, vary from party to party, but they are all alike in that one almost never finds in them a fresh, vivid, home-made turn of speech. When one watches some tired hack on the platform mechanically repeating the familiar phrases—*bestial atrocities, iron heel, bloodstained tyranny, free peoples of the world, stand shoulder to shoulder*—one often has a curious feeling that one is not watching a live human being but some kind of dummy: a feeling which suddenly becomes stronger at moments when the light catches the speaker's spectacles and turns them into blank discs which seem to have no eyes behind them. And this is not altogether fanciful. A speaker who uses that kind of phraseology has gone some distance towards turning himself into a machine. The appropriate noises are coming out of his larynx, but his brain is not involved as it would be if he were choosing his words for himself. If the speech he is making is one that he is accustomed to make over and over again, he may be almost unconscious of what he is saying, as one is when one utters the responses in church. And this reduced state of consciousness, if not indispensable, is at any rate favorable to political conformity.

In our time, political speech and writing are largely the defense of the indefensible. Things like the continuance of British rule in India, the Russian purges and deportations, the dropping of the atom bombs on Japan, can indeed be defended, but only by arguments which are too brutal for most people to face, and which do not square with the professed aims of political parties. Thus political language has to consist largely of euphemism, question-begging and sheer cloudy vagueness. Defenseless villages are bombarded from the air, the inhabitants driven out into the countryside, the cattle machine-gunned, the huts set on fire with incendiary bullets: this is called *pacification*. Millions of peasants are robbed of their farms and sent trudging along the roads with no more than they can carry: this is called *transfer of population* or *rectification of frontiers*. People are imprisoned for years without trial, or shot in the back of the neck or sent to die of scurvy in Arctic lumber camps: this is called *elimination of unreliable elements*. Such phraseology is needed if one wants to name things without calling up mental pictures of them. Consider for instance some comfortable English professor defending Russian totalitarianism. He cannot say outright, "I believe in killing off your opponents when you can get good results by doing so." Probably, therefore, he will say something like this:

> While freely conceding that the Soviet régime exhibits certain features which the humanitarian may be inclined to deplore, we must, I think, agree that a certain curtailment of the right to political opposition is an unavoidable concomitant of transitional periods, and that the rigors which the Russian people have been called upon to undergo have been amply justified in the sphere of concrete achievement.

The inflated style is itself a kind of euphemism. A mass of Latin words falls upon the facts like soft snow, blurring the outlines and covering up all the details. The great enemy of clear language is insincerity. When there is a gap between one's real and one's declared aims, one turns, as it were instinctively, to long words and exhausted idioms, like a cuttlefish squirting out ink. In our age there is no such thing as "keeping out of politics." All issues are political issues, and politics itself is a mass of lies, evasions, folly, hatred and schizophrenia. When the general atmosphere is bad, language must suffer. I should expect to find—this is a guess which I have not sufficient knowledge to verify—that the German, Russian and Italian languages have all deteriorated in the last ten or fifteen years as a result of dictatorship.

But if thought corrupts language, language can also corrupt thought. A bad usage can spread by tradition and imitation, even among people who should and do know better. The debased language that I have been discussing is in some ways very convenient. Phrases like *a not unjustifiable assumption, leaves much to be desired, would serve no good purpose, a consideration which we should do well to bear in mind,* are a continuous temptation, a packet of aspirins always at one's elbow. Look back through this essay, and for certain you will find that I have again and again committed the very faults I am protesting against. By this morning's post I have received a pamphlet dealing with conditions in Germany. The author tells me that he "felt impelled" to write it. I open it at random, and here is almost the first sentence that I see: "[The Allies] have an opportunity not only of achieving a radical transformation of Germany's social and political structure in such a way as to avoid a nationalistic reaction in Germany itself, but at the same time of laying the foundations of a cooperative and unified Europe." You see, he "feels impelled" to write—feels, presumably, that he has something new to say—and yet his words, like cavalry horses answering the bugle, group themselves automatically into the familiar dreary pattern. This invasion of one's mind by ready-made phrases (*lay the foundations, achieve a radical transformation*) can only be prevented if one is constantly on guard against them, and every such phrase anesthetizes a portion of one's brain.

I said earlier that the decadence of our language is probably curable. Those who deny this would argue, if they produced an argument at all, that language merely reflects existing social conditions, and that we cannot influence its development by any direct tinkering with words and constructions. So far as the general tone or spirit of a language goes, this may be true, but it is not true in detail. Silly words and expressions have often disappeared, not through any evolutionary process but owing to the conscious action of a minority. Two recent examples were *explore every avenue* and *leave no stone unturned,* which were killed by the jeers of a few journalists. There is a long list of flyblown metaphors which could similarly be got rid of if enough people would interest themselves in the job; and it should also be possible to laugh the *not un-* formation out of existence,[4] to reduce the amount of Latin and Greek in the average sentence, to drive out foreign phrases and strayed scientific words, and, in general, to make pretentiousness unfashionable. But all these are minor points. The defense of the English language implies more than this, and perhaps it is best to start by saying what it does *not* imply.

To begin with, it has nothing to do with archaism, with the salvaging of obsolete words and turns of speech, or with the setting-up of a "standard English" which must never be departed from. On the contrary, it is especially concerned with the scrapping of every word or idiom which has outworn its usefulness. It has nothing to do with correct grammar and syntax, which are

[4] One can cure oneself of the *not un-* formation by memorizing this sentence: *A not unblack dog was chasing a not unsmall rabbit across a not ungreen field.*

of no importance so long as one makes one's meaning clear, or with the avoidance of Americanisms, or with having what is called a "good prose style." On the other hand it is not concerned with fake simplicity and the attempt to make written English colloquial. Nor does it even imply in every case preferring the Saxon word to the Latin one, though it does imply using the fewest and shortest words that will cover one's meaning. What is above all needed is to let the meaning choose the word, and not the other way about. In prose, the worst thing one can do with words is to surrender to them. When you think of a concrete object, you think wordlessly, and then, if you want to describe the thing you have been visualizing, you probably hunt about till you find the exact words that seem to fit it. When you think of something abstract you are more inclined to use words from the start, and unless you make a conscious effort to prevent it, the existing dialect will come rushing in and do the job for you, at the expense of blurring or even changing your meaning. Probably it is better to put off using words as long as possible and get one's meaning as clear as one can through pictures or sensations. Afterwards one can choose —not simply *accept*—the phrases that will best cover the meaning, and then switch round and decide what impressions one's words are likely to make on another person. This last effort of the mind cuts out all stale or mixed images, all prefabricated phrases, needless repetitions, and humbug and vagueness generally. But one can often be in doubt about the effect of a word or a phrase, and one needs rules that one can rely on when instinct fails. I think the following rules will cover most cases:

(i) Never use a metaphor, simile or other figure of speech which you are used to seeing in print.

(ii) Never use a long word where a short one will do.

(iii) If it is possible to cut a word out, always cut it out.

(iv) Never use the passive where you can use the active.

(v) Never use a foreign phrase, a scientific word or a jargon word if you can think of an everyday English equivalent.

(vi) Break any of these rules sooner than say anything barbarous.

These rules sound elementary, and so they are, but they demand a deep change of attitude in anyone who has grown used to writing in the style now fashionable. One could keep all of them and still write bad English, but one could not write the kind of stuff that I quoted in these five specimens at the beginning of this article.

I have not here been considering the literary use of language, but merely language as an instrument for expressing and not for concealing or preventing thought. Stuart Chase and others have come near to claiming that all abstract words are meaningless, and have used this as a pretext for advocating a kind of political quietism. Since you don't know what Fascism is, how can you struggle against Fascism? One need not swallow such absurdities as this, but one ought to recognize that the present political chaos is connected with the decay of language, and that one can probably bring about some improvement by starting at the verbal end. If you simplify your English, you are freed from the worst follies of orthodoxy. You cannot speak any of the necessary dialects, and when you make a stupid remark its stupidity will be obvious, even to yourself. Political language—and with variations this is true of all political parties, from Conservatives to Anarchists—is designed to make lies sound truthful and murder respectable, and to give an appearance of solidity to pure wind. One cannot change this all in a moment, but one can at least change one's habits, and from time to time one can even, if one jeers loudly enough, send some worn-out and useless phrase—some *jackboot, Achilles' heel, hot-bed, melting pot, acid test, veritable inferno* or other lump of verbal refuse—into the dustbin where it belongs.

WAYNE C. BOOTH

•

The Revival of Rhetoric[1]

Every year just after Christmas we English teachers—several thousand of us who belong to the Modern Language Association—gather in Chicago or New York to talk about the fruits of our literary scholarship. At other times of the year, even more thousands—those of us who belong either to the National Council of Teachers of English or the Conference on College Composition and Communication—gather in a more exotic place like Miami or Los Angeles to talk about the teaching of "English," defined as "language, literature, and composition."

There is of course no inherent conflict between literary scholarship and the effort to improve the teaching of English. But until recently the MLA meetings have been conducted as if the scholars who attended them were not also teachers of literature and composition. For good or ill, such purity is now being lost. As one of my colleagues complained, commenting on the speech reprinted below, "You can't tell by reading it whether it was designed for the CCCC, the NCTE, or the MLA!"

Now we are confusing things further by pretending that the speech might be profitably overheard by college students. Even if we are wrong about the profit, it should prove amusing to eavesdrop on a professor of rhetoric trying to use rhetoric on a group of rhetoricians, in favor of rhetorical studies.

W.C.B.

As teachers of language and literature, you have all noticed that my title is even more ambiguous than most. Those of you who are amiably disposed may even have called it general, in the old style, rather than ambiguous, in the new.

[1] Reprinted by permission of the Modern Language Association from *PMLA,* LXXX (May 1965), 8-12. (An address given at the General Meeting on English in New York, December 29, 1964.)

The word "rhetoric" has for a long time served for both the study of the art of persuasion and for the art itself; Aristotle's *Rhetoric,* upper-case, is still unsurpassed, but take away the capital letter and Aristotle's rhetoric is often very bad indeed, at least as we view it. In the second sense rhetoric has never had a real quantitative revival because it has always thrived; but in the first sense we seem to be in the midst of a revival of rhetoric unmatched in the twentieth century. Unfortunately, in spite of some very good work, there are signs that it may prove a very shoddy revival indeed, with no more lasting effect than the rhetorically-oriented "communications" movement of a decade ago, unless we take thought about what we are doing. Judging from some of the recent freshman texts I have seen, I would not be surprised to find in my box tomorrow when I return a new work entitled *A Speller's Rhetoric.*

What, exactly, are we reviving? As applied to art, the term is today given every conceivable degree of narrowness and generality, meaning anything from mere ornamental figures that can be tacked on a discourse or subtracted at will to the whole range of all possible forms of discourse; as systematic study, rhetoric may be anything from a classification of ornamental figures to the theory of man as a logos-possessing animal. What is worse, one cannot even now, after nearly a decade of revived popularity, predict whether the term will be used to refer to something good or something bad. In publications for freshmen it has recently been an O.K.-term. Yet it is still used in ways that might well deter us from calling ourselves "Professors of Rhetoric." Listen to Malcolm Muggeridge, in a recent *Esquire* article: "Like a man in a dark place without a lantern, Churchill in his war memoirs has to fall back on shouting—that is, rhetoric, which is a factor of power rather than of understanding. If the Sermon on the Mount had been expressed rhetorically it would have made little impact, and that only at the moment of delivery. . . . Churchill's rhetoric, like Henry V's in Shakespeare's play, was essential for war purposes, but proves increasingly disastrous as a literary style."

Here, as in much of current usage, rhetoric is still bombast, mere propaganda, perhaps necessary for the affairs of men but necessarily tainted, anti-literary. Now obviously I did not come here to plead for a revival of such stuff. But I might well have come to describe how it feels to live in an age dominated by it. A case could be made for the claim that we live in the most rhetorical age of all time, if by rhetoric we mean whatever men do to change each other's minds without giving good reasons for change. I have in mind not only our fantabulous annual expenditures on advertising and public relations and political campaigns, though these alone might brand us, quantitatively, as the most rhetorical age of all time. I am thinking even more about how image building and propaganda have come to dominate fields where traditionally one could expect to find not blandishment or trickery but either solid action or genuine argument. The hand that used to guide the plow now pens the Agricultural Association Press Release. The warrior's sword is now either literally a typewriter or, if still in fact a destructive weapon, one that is wielded not so much to win battles as to change men's minds. The whole affair in South Viet Nam, as President Johnson has said, is carried on in order to prevent Peking and Hanoi "from *thinking* that their current policy of military force will pay dividends" [my italics]. Our nuclear deterrent power is not discussed much any more in terms of its superior strength—nobody doubts that—but in terms of its "credibility." But surely credibility is a rhetorical term. We ask not whether our weapons will destroy you but whether you *believe* that they will destroy you.

I could go on through almost every part of our lives and show a similar reliance on suasion rather than substance. In journalism we find traditional notions of news accuracy replaced more and more, especially in the news magazines, by standards of rhetorical effectiveness; in place of the facts we are titillated and aroused by weekly collections of little short stories, rhetorically organized to sell an editorial point of view. Or again, our notions of personal worth, once decided by such hard substantive matters as moral virtue, or family history, or money in the bank, are now settled rhetorically. The new annual publication, *Celebrity Register,* as Daniel Boorstin has pointed out, says of itself: "We think we have a better yardstick than the *Social Register,* or *Who's Who*, or any such book. . . . It's impossible to list accurately the success or value of men; but you *can* judge a man as a celebrity—all you have to do is weigh his press clippings." But of course *Who's Who* is not much different. Its criterion is announced under the exalted phrase, "subjectivity of reference," which, after long puzzlement, I take to mean simply the number of times people are likely to want to look you up.

More significant to us here, perhaps, is the transformation of intellectual disciplines to mere rhetorical uses—to continue to think of rhetoric as divorced from genuine argument. I have a strong conviction, difficult to prove, that standards of controversy in history, philosophy, and literary criticism—to name only three—have become less and less substantive throughout this century; irrelevant blandishment, name-calling, sheer one-upmanship have increased, while solid argument has diminished—sometimes to the point of disappearing altogether.[2] There are, of course, splendid exceptions in all disci-

[2] Critical comments by two of my friends have made me think that this claim is not only difficult to prove but quite probably mistaken. Mr. Ronald Crane suggests that it reflects plain ignorance of just how low controversy sank in previous centuries. "Have you read the attacks on Bentley?" Mr. Laurence Lerner reminds me of the standards, if they can be called that, of political controversy in the seventeenth century. And I remind myself, now, of what public debate could be like in nineteenth-century England and America.

Clearly the sweeping historical claims that run throughout this first section of my talk are in no way demonstrated by my examples. They might, in fact, be taken as illustrations of the very thing I am claiming to oppose: the use of mere assertion (the more extreme the better) in place of careful argument. Fortunately my argument that we need more and better rhetorical theorizing does not depend on the extreme claim that we are the *most* rhetorical age: it is enough that our lives are permeated by rhetoric, good or bad, and nobody doubts that.

plines; if there were not, the disciplines would themselves disappear. But I invite you to examine your favorite journal—even if it is one of those few that have tried to maintain serious standards—and count the number of solid reasons offered for conclusions as compared with irrelevant ploys like guilt-by-association, old-hatism, and so's-your-old-thesis-chairman. Wherever one looks one is likely to find, in place of a coherent effort to move from evidence to conclusions, an outpouring of what one of my colleagues calls a mere rhetoric of conclusions. Controversy is conducted as if all strong effects were equally valuable; to shock or simply to win are more important than the discovery of truth. I announce no secrets here, of course; many of our most prominent controversialists have explicitly repudiated reason in the name of rhetorical effects like shock or outrage.

In short, it is not difficult to find signs that we are a rhetorical age, if we mean by that—once again—an age in which men try to change each other's minds without giving good reasons for change. I know of no past culture where power was so persistently thought of as power to manipulate men's minds; where beauty was so persistently tested by mere popularity or saleability; where the truth of propositions was so persistently judged by whether this or that group accepts them; where notions of human greatness were so persistently reduced to the question of fame or "national luminosity"; where, finally, educational goals and methods were so persistently reduced to the notion of conditioning or imposition of already formed ideas or practices upon an infinitely malleable material.

I might very well, then, have come to plead for a further revival of rhetorical studies in order to protect ourselves and our students from rhetoric as a bad thing. Many popular prophets have in fact, like David Riesman in his portrayal of the other-directed man, implored us to find a mode of guidance for our lives somewhat more substantive than a perpetually operating radar set turned to receive rhetorical directions from other members of the lonely crowd.

But I have played too long with a definition that I don't believe in. Rhetoric can mean good things, too. All of the critics who have taken part in the revival of rhetorical studies that began in the mid-fifties have defined the term in ways that would require us to speak of "*bad* rhetoric" when we refer to the perversions I have just described. The definition of *good* rhetoric, or of rhetoric in general, good *and* bad, varies from critic to critic. But beneath the differences there is general agreement that to engage with one's fellow men in acts of mutual persuasion, that is, of mutual inquiry, is potentially a noble thing. In-

---

I still suspect, *pace* Mr. Crane, that we are *quantitatively* the most rhetorical age in history—and not only in the undeniable sense that more men are living by rhetoric than ever before. Surely the *proportion* of rhetorical activities to non-rhetorical (like plowing, shearing, or building) is higher now than ever before. But this modified claim, a radical retreat from my original assertions, may be unimportant, and it is certainly one that would be hard to prove (Crane: "Can you think of any previous age with as much pure science or pure music? These two areas are *less* rhetorical than ever before").

deed, none of the corruptions found in our rhetorical time would even be possible in a society which had not also laid itself open to the great virtues of moral and intellectual suasion when properly used. Consider once again, for example, my summary description of our rhetorical age. One can easily translate it, proposition by proposition, into a description of a kind of utopia. Supposing I could say of our society the following: I can think of no previous society in which questions of political power were so persistently referred to the people for consultation and decision; where questions of beauty were so often decided not by arbitrary rules imposed by an elite but by reference to a genuine capacity of art works to please those who experience them; where questions of truth were so often tested by debate rather than settled by decree; where notions of human greatness were so consistently determined not by fiat of an hereditary aristocracy or plutocracy but by reference to standards testable on the popular pulse; where, finally, educational goals and methods were tested so constantly against practical experience, and where it was unfailingly assumed that, since all men are educable—that is, subject to good rhetoric—there is no limit to the good that can be done through improving the rhetoric of education. Would not such a society—fully as rhetorical as the earlier one—be a noble thing indeed? All of the evils of a rhetorical age are thus corruptions of tendencies that might be ennobling, or at least liberating. Or, to put it again in terms of Riesman's radar set owned by the other-directed man, everything depends on how the radar set is aimed and on the quality of the messages received. An other-directed society would be an ideal society if the "others" were in fact bearers of truth, goodness, and beauty.

Why is it, then, that so much of what we see about us, so much that is done in the name of advertising, of news reporting, of political campaigning, of education, is so cheap, so obviously aimed at persuasion without justification? If I thought I could get away with it here, I might intone an answer something like this: the bad rhetoric of our rhetorical time can be blamed on our almost total failure to develop good rhetorical theory adequate to our needs. I could not get away with such oversimplification, because you are all aware of how little can be changed, directly, by *any* theory, good or bad. But perhaps I *can* get away with a statement only slightly less forceful: of all the causes of our rhetorical shoddiness, the only one that you and I have much chance of doing anything about is our shoddy rhetorical theory and our shoddier teaching thereof. To our non-majors we have offered a collection of high school and freshman textbooks that, with a few exceptions, are as shameful as any of the ills they purport to cure. To our majors, graduate and undergraduate, we have offered even less: at most universities still a student cannot undertake serious rhetorical study even if he wants to, for lack of teachers, courses, or library facilities.

Finally, what have we offered to the public? That the American public wants rhetorical assistance in an age of rhetoric is shown by the almost incredible success of a popular rhetorician like Rudolf Flesch. Flesch's sophistries about achieving an interesting style by using short words, short sentences, and a personal tone are dangerous, but it is hard to think of what guide to recommend to a literate adult in their place. If someone asks me for works that will help him in reading poetry, I can suggest dozens of respectable works, some of them very good indeed. But if I am asked for guidance in distinguishing good controversial argument from bad, or in constructing a really powerful argument on one's own, or even in constructing an effective—not just a passable—staff report, what do I say? Where, in all of our textbooks about how to write, do we send an intelligent adult for guidance in the true arts of transferring ideas, motives, intentions from his mind to other men's minds?

Please don't try to fob me off with the title of your favorite freshman text. There are some good ones, but we must be quite clear about what is needed, and it is not to be found in works designed, for the most part, for semi-literates. What is needed can be seen clearly if we ask where I might turn, in the available rhetorics, for help in improving this talk. I can get help in improving my diction and sentence structure, help of a general kind, from most freshman texts. But where is the theory, where are the practical rules for ensuring that this talk will not only grab you, as the Madison Avenue rhetoricians say, but keep you grabbed and send you away determined to behave differently?

Most of the rhetorical advice I find, even in texts that go beyond simple formulae for correctness, is entirely general. Be brief. Be clear. Be forceful. Revise carefully. Use short words. Such advice is not plainly wrong. It can even be useful. But since it is general, it gives me no help in deciding what arguments might appeal to you, sitting out there in all your particularity on a particular occasion. What appeals are available to me? What order should I give them? Brevity, clarity, unity, coherence, emphasis—none of these will be worth a brass farthing with you unless somehow I have managed to invent an organized chain of arguments about *this* subject for *this* audience that will bridge the gap between what you believed when you came and what I want you to believe when you depart. But you will look a long while in the available modern rhetorics before you will find much that could possibly help me in this central task.

I do find considerable help about such matters in Aristotle and the many traditional rhetorics fathered by him. They all tell me to look to my arguments and to make sure that there is at least a semblance of genuine connection between them and my conclusions. They all tell me, more importantly, that what will *be* a semblance of sound connection can be decided only by considering my audience, and they all give me, by implication, some notion of what a large gathering of more-or-less-middle-aged and thoroughly fatigued teachers of language and literature will demand or allow, as a ratio of real proof to other, incidental appeals. They all suggest ways of handling emotional appeals and those essential, disguised claims that I am a citizen of good standing in the world of letters. I find it interesting, incidentally, that with all our modern passion for inventing new studies with proper labels we do not even have words in our language for the sciences of invention and arrangement or for the study of emotional and ethical appeal. With all our new grammars and new stylistics, with our proxemics and tagmemics, surely it is time for someone to make himself a professor of inventionics or arrangementistics.

The traditional rhetorics had terms for such matters, and they can still give us more help than most of us suspect. We would be in much better condition if everyone now reviving rhetoric took at least the trouble to learn one traditional rhetoric thoroughly.

But it would be naive to think that reviving Aristotle or Quintilian or Campbell or Whately could solve our problems if we only studied them carefully. For one thing, the age of rhetoric has invented forms of persuasion that earlier ages knew not of. Much, perhaps most, of our rhetoric occurs in informal situations; we need a rhetoric of the symposium, of the conference room—I would hope somewhat more respectable intellectually than what is now offered the public under terms like "group dynamics" and "conference techniques."

Perhaps more important, we cannot take for granted, as most traditional rhetoricians felt that *they* could, a systematic coverage under other categories of such matters as logic and dialectic. Our students are not trained, as they could assume of their students, in the analysis of serious argument. Whether we choose to extend the term rhetoric to include the whole art of meaningful discourse or confine it to non-belletristic, obviously persuasive forms, or confine it even further to the paralogical elements in such persuasive forms, we must find some place in our revived rhetorical studies for training in how to build arguments that coerce, by their cogency, the agreement of all who will attend to them. Traditional logics and grammars will help us here, but I suspect that modern logics and semantics and grammars will prove indispensable. The revival, here again, must do more than echo the past.

But this leads to a final reason for rejecting the notion that the revival of rhetoric can mean only the revival of earlier rhetorics. It is simply that none of them can possibly give us the comprehensive rhetorical theory we seek. Living in a new kind of rhetorical age, surrounded by, indeed practicing daily, forms of persuasion their authors never dreamed of, we inevitably hunger for a theory that will do justice to *our* manifold rhetorical experiences, and we do not find that the categories used by earlier theorists quite do the job. I can illustrate this point by asking if you have not felt impatient, so far in my talk, by my omission of the rhetoric of literature. I have talked as if the whole problem were that of finding a theory of rhetoric for the teaching of composition. But you and I are groping for much more than that, as we work at reviving this old, magical term. Why have some of the greatest theorists of our time —men like Richard McKeon and Kenneth Burke—found themselves trying to construct unified rhetorical views of all the verbal arts? Obviously I cannot answer this rhetorical question about rhetoric in our time, but I can suggest an answer by asking another: Why do we find ourselves gathered here engaged in rhetoric about rhetoric and literature? Whatever answer we give must include,

I think, a recognition that we are a rhetorical age in a sense far more profound than the one I began with. We believe in mutual persuasion as a way of life; we live from conference to conference. More significantly, the intellectual inquiries of our time, even at their most responsible level, have tended to be inquiries that can best be called rhetorical. In philosophy we do not begin with metaphysical questions and pursue *being* and *substance* to the bitter end; rather, we begin with existentialist commitment, induced by rhetorical works in philosophical garb, or we analyze the uses of language. We *do* philosophy on each other, as it were, rather than pursue truth as if it were a thing to be obtained. In literary criticism, similarly, we have constructed innumerable semantics and rhetorics and stylistics and linguistics. Even our histories tend to be histories of linguistic or rhetorical fashion. New sciences like cybernetics are invented to unite all human inquiry under one science of information. Even the so-called hard sciences are discussed in terms of information theory. Last month a new interdepartmental committee was formed at Chicago, to supervise information studies—I assume that they will be studying the rhetoric of genes, atoms, and computers.

To try to deal with such a profusion of sciences of communication with traditional theories would be folly. We hunger, or at least I hunger, for a comprehensive view of the arts and sciences of man, a view at least as comprehensive, say, as the two radically different but equally thoroughgoing views of Plato and Aristotle. What we have instead is a logomachy, a rhetorical babel about forms of rhetoric. And the warring factions wage their battles without generals and without having had their basic infantry training.

It is time now for me to come out from behind that feeble metaphor and make my main plea quite openly. My rhetorical point to a group of rhetoricians is twofold: first, that in a rhetorical age rhetorical studies should have a major, respected place in the training of all teachers at all levels; and secondly, that in such an age, specialization in rhetorical studies of all kinds, narrow and broad, should carry at least as much professional respectability as literary history or as literary criticism in non-rhetoric modes. Whether we restore the old chairs of rhetoric by name or not, chairs like my own Pullman Professorship ought to exist in every department, to provide visible proof that to dirty one's hands in rhetorical studies is not a sure way to professional oblivion.

If I had made such a plea for a genuine revival of advanced rhetorical studies ten years ago, I would have had to base my appeal almost entirely on your sense of duty: "the condition of our writing courses demands that we sacrifice ourselves by doing the unpopular thing." But in 1964 one can indulge in that appeal dear to the hearts of all rhetoricians, namely: "Here for once duty and profit and pleasure are reconciled." The fashionable demand for rhetorical studies is such that even the worst textbook profits from the word rhetoric in the title. (I speak from experience: whatever the faults or merits of *The Rhetoric of Fiction*, it has profited factitiously from my having used a fad term, quite unwittingly, in the title. I learned last month of a teacher who had ordered it as the basic text for his freshman composition course.) If, as I am assuming, you want to do serious intellectual work without undue penalties from society, and if—like most of us—you want your work to have some relevance to the real needs of society, you need neither to blush nor to tighten your belt when your turn from *belles lettres* to rhetoric.

To those of you who feel that your present research is trivial though respected, I would say: drop that study of Phineas Fletcher or of Suckling's imitators and take up the great rhetorical theorists and the great rhetoricians who helped to mold our age. Those of you, on the other hand, who are doing seemingly non-rhetorical literary study that you know to be not in the least trivial can find both fun and profit in discovering what happens if you grasp your subject by a rhetorician's handle. Best of all, you might in the process even discover how to make literary studies genuinely relevant to the literate and semi-literate public of a rhetorical age.

PART III

THINKING

H. AND H. A. FRANKFORT

•

The Emancipation of Thought from Myth[1]

When we read in Psalm xix that "the heavens declare the glory of God; and the firmament sheweth his handiwork," we hear a voice which mocks the beliefs of Egyptians and Babylonians. The heavens, which were to the psalmist but a witness of God's greatness, were to the Mesopotamians the very majesty of godhead, the highest ruler, Anu. To the Egyptians the heavens signified the mystery of the divine mother through whom man was reborn. In Egypt and Mesopotamia the divine was comprehended as immanent: the gods were in nature. The Egyptians saw in the sun all that a man may know of the Creator; the Mesopotamians viewed the sun as the god Shamash, the guarantor of justice. But to the psalmist the sun was God's devoted servant who "is as a bridegroom coming out of his chamber, and rejoiceth as a strong man to run a race." The God of the psalmists and the prophets was not in nature. He transcended nature—and transcended, likewise, the realm of mythopoeic thought. It would seem that the Hebrews, no less than the Greeks, broke with the mode of speculation which had prevailed up to their time. . . .

The Hebrews arrived late upon the scene and settled in a country pervaded by influences from the two superior adjacent cultures. One would expect the newcomers to have assimilated alien modes of thought, since these were supported by such vast prestige. Untold immigrants from deserts and mountains had done so in the past; and many individual Hebrews did, in fact, conform to the ways of the Gentiles. But assimilation was not characteristic for Hebrew thought. On the contrary, it held out with a peculiar stubbornness and insolence against the wisdom of Israel's neighbours. It is possible to detect the reflection of Egyptian and Mesopotamian beliefs in many episodes of the Old Testament; but the overwhelming impression left by that document is one, not of derivation, but of originality.

[1] Chapter VIII, reprinted from *The Intellectual Adventure of Ancient Man,* by H. and H. A. Frankfort, by permission of The University of Chicago Press and of the authors. Copyright 1946 by The University of Chicago.

The dominant tenet of Hebrew thought is the absolute transcendence of God. Yahweh is not in nature. Neither earth nor sun nor heaven is divine; even the most potent natural phenomena are but reflections of God's greatness. It is not even possible properly to name God:

> And Moses said unto God, Behold, when I come unto the children of Israel and shall say unto them, The God of your fathers hath sent me unto you; and they shall say to me: What is his name? what shall I say unto them?
> And God said unto Moses: I AM THAT I AM: and he said, Thus shalt thou say unto the children of Israel, I AM hath sent me unto you (Exod. iii, 13–14).

The God of the Hebrews is pure being, unqualified, ineffable. He is *holy*. That means that he is *sui generis*. It does not mean that he is taboo or that he is power. It means that all values are ultimately attributes of God alone. Hence, all concrete phenomena are devaluated. It may be true that in Hebrew thought man and nature are not necessarily corrupt; but both are necessarily *valueless* before God. As Eliphaz said to Job (and we use the Chicago translation):

> Can a mortal be righteous before God
> Or a man be pure before his Maker?
> Even in his servants he does not trust,
> And his angels he charges with error.
> How much less them that dwell in houses of clay,
> Whose foundation is in the dust . . . (Job iv, 17–19*a*).

A similar meaning lies in the words of Deutero-Isaiah (lxiv, 6*a*): "We are all as an unclean thing, and all our righteousnesses are as filthy rags." Even man's righteousness, his highest virtue, is devaluated by the comparison with the absolute.

In the field of material culture such a conception of God leads to iconoclasm; and it needs an effort of the imagination to realize the shattering boldness of a contempt for imagery at the time, and in the particular historical setting, of the Hebrews. Everywhere religious fervour not only inspired verse and rite but also sought plastic and pictorial expression. The Hebrews, however, denied the relevancy of the "graven image"; the boundless could not be given form, the unqualified could but be offended by a representation, whatever the skill and the devotion that went into its making. Every finite reality shrivelled to nothingness before the absolute value which was God.

The abysmal difference between the Hebrew and the normal Near Eastern viewpoints can best be illustrated by the manner in which an identical theme, the instability of the social order, is treated. We have a number of Egyptian texts which deal with the period of social upheaval which followed the great era of the pyramid builders. The disturbance of the established order was viewed with horror. Neferrohu said:

> I show thee the land in lamentation and distress. The man with a weak arm (now) has (a strong) arm. . . . I show thee how the undermost is turned to uppermost. . . . The poor man will acquire riches.[2]

The most famous of the sages, Ipuwer, is even more explicit. For instance, he condemns as a disastrous parody of order the fact that

> gold and lapis lazuli are hung about the necks of slave girls. But noble ladies walk through the land and mistresses of houses say: "Would that we had something to eat. . . . Behold they that possessed beds now lie upon the ground. He that slept with dirt upon him now stuffeth for himself a cushion."

The upshot is unmitigated misery for all: "Nay, but great and small say: I wish I were dead."[3]

In the Old Testament we meet the same theme—the reversal of established social conditions. When Hannah, after years of barrenness, had prayed for a son, and Samuel was born, she praised God:

> There is none holy as the Lord: for there is none beside thee: neither is there any rock like our God. . . . The bows of the mighty men are broken, and they that stumbled are girded with strength. They that were full have hired out themselves for bread; and they that were hungry ceased. . . . The Lord maketh poor and maketh rich: he bringeth low, and lifteth up. He raiseth up the poor out of the dust, and lifteth up the beggar from the dunghill, to set them among princes, and to make them inherit the throne of glory: for the pillars of the earth are the Lord's and he hath set the world upon them (I Sam. ii, 2–8).

Notice that the last verses state explicitly that God created the existing social order; but, quite characteristically, this order did not derive any sacredness, any value, from its divine origin. The sacredness and value remain attributes of God alone, and the violent changes of fortune observed in social life are but signs of God's omnipotence. Nowhere else do we meet this fanatical devaluation of the phenomena of nature and the achievements of man: art, virtue, social order—in view of the unique significance of the divine. It has been rightly pointed out that the monotheism of the Hebrews is a correlate of their insistence on the unconditioned nature of God.[4] Only a God who transcends every phenomenon, who is not conditioned by any mode of manifestation—only an unqualified God can be the one and only ground of *all* existence.

This conception of God represents so high a degree of abstraction that, in reaching it, the Hebrews seem to have left the realm of mythopoeic thought.

[2] Blackman's translation of Erman, *Literature of the Egyptians,* p. 115.
[3] After Blackman, *ibid.,* pp. 94 ff.
[4] Johannes Hehn, *Die biblische und die bablylonische Gottes Idee* (1913), p. 284.

The impression that they did so is strengthened when we observe that the Old Testament is remarkably poor in mythology of the type we have encountered in Egypt and Mesopotamia. But this impression requires correction. The processes of mythopoeic thought are decisive for many sections of the Old Testament. For instance, the magnificent verses from the Book of Proverbs (viii, 22–31) describe the Wisdom of God, personified and substantialized in the same manner in which the corresponding concept of *ma'at* is treated by the Egyptians. Even the great conception of an only and transcendent God was not entirely free from myth, for it was not the fruit of detached speculation but of a passionate and dynamic experience. Hebrew thought did not entirely overcome mythopoeic thought. It created, in fact, a new myth—the myth of the Will of God.

Although the great "Thou" which confronted the Hebrews transcended nature, it stood in a specific relationship to the people. For when they were freed from bondage and roamed in "a desert land . . . the waste howling wilderness . . . the Lord alone did lead (them) and there was no strange god with (them)" (Deut. xxxii, 10–12). And God had said:

> But thou, Israel, art my servant, Jacob whom I have chosen, the seed of Abraham my friend. Thou whom I have taken from the ends of the earth, and called thee from the chief men thereof, and said unto thee, Thou art my servant; I have chosen thee, and not cast thee away (Isa. xli, 8–9).

Thus God's will was felt to be focused on one particular and concrete group of human beings; it was asserted to have manifested itself at one decisive moment in their history and ceaselessly and relentlessly to have urged, rewarded, or chastised the people of its choice. For in Sinai, God had said, "Ye shall be unto me a kingdom of priests and an holy nation" (Exod. xix, 6).

It is a poignant myth, this Hebrew myth of a chosen people, of a divine promise made, of a terrifying moral burden imposed—a prelude to the later myth of the Kingdom of God, that more remote and more spiritual "promised land." For in the myth of the chosen people the ineffable majesty of God and the worthlessness of man are correlated in a dramatic situation that is to unfold in time and is moving toward a future where the distant yet related parallels of human and divine existence are to meet in infinity. . . .

All this may help to explain the strange poignancy of single individuals in the Old Testament. Nowhere in the literature of Egypt or Babylonia do we meet the loneliness of the biblical figures, astonishingly real in their mixture of ugliness and beauty, pride and contrition, achievement and failure. There is the tragic figure of Saul, the problematical David; there are countless others. We find single men in terrible isolation facing a transcendent God: Abraham trudging to the place of sacrifice with his son, Jacob in his struggle, and Moses and the prophets. In Egypt and Mesopotamia man was dominated, but also supported, by the great rhythm of nature. If in his dark moments he felt himself caught and held in the net of unfathomable decisions, his involvement in nature had, on the whole, a soothing character. He was gently carried along on the perennial cosmic tides of the seasons. The depth and intimacy of man's relationship with nature found expression in the ancient symbol of the mother-goddess. But Hebrew thought ignored this image entirely. It only recognized the stern Father, of whom it was said: "he led him (Jacob, the people) about, he instructed him, he kept him as the apple of his eye," (Deut. xxxii, 10*b*).

The bond between Yahweh and his chosen people had been finally established during the Exodus. The Hebrews considered the forty years in the desert the decisive phase in their development. And we, too, may understand the originality and the coherence of their speculations if we relate them to their experience in the desert.

Preceding chapters took great care to describe the Egyptian and Mesopotamian landscapes. In doing so, the authors did not succumb to an unwarranted naturalism; they did not claim that cultural phenomena could be derived from physiographical causes. They merely suggested that a relation between land and culture may exist, a suggestion we can accept the more readily since we have seen that the surrounding world confronted early man as a "Thou." We may ask, then, what was the natural setting which determined the Hebrew's experience of the world around him. Now, the Hebrews, whatever their ancestry and historical antecedents, were tribal nomads. And since they were nomads in the Near East, they must have lived, not in boundless steppes, but between the desert and the sown, between the most fertile of lands and the total negation of life, which, in this remarkable corner of the earth, lie cheek by jowl. They must, therefore, have known through experience both the reward and the cost of existence in either.

The Hebrews craved to settle for good in the fertile plains. But characteristically they dreamed of lands overflowing with milk and honey, not lands of super-abundant crops like those the Egyptians imagined for their hereafter. It seems that the deserts as a metaphysical experience loomed very large for the Hebrews and coloured all their valuations. It is, perhaps, the tension between two valuations—between a desire and a contempt for what is desired—that may explain some of the paradoxes of ancient Hebrew beliefs.

The organized states of the ancient Near East were agricultural; but the values of an agricultural community are the opposites of those of the nomadic tribe, especially of the extreme type of nomads of the desert. The settled peasant's reverence for impersonal authority, and the bondage, the constraint which the organized state imposes, mean an intolerable lack of personal freedom for the tribesman. The farmer's everlasting preoccupation with phenomena of growth and his total dependence on these phenomena appear to the nomad a form of slavery. Moreover, to him the desert is clean, but the scene of life, which is also the scene of decay, is sordid.

On the other hand, nomadic freedom can be bought only at a price; for whoever rejects the complexities and mutual dependencies of agricultural society not only gains freedom but also loses the bond with the phenomenal world; in fact, he gains his freedom at the cost of significant form. For, wherever we find reverence for the phenomena of life and growth, we find preoccupation with the immanence of the divine and with the *form* of its manifestation. But in the stark solitude of the desert, where nothing changes, nothing moves (except man at his own free will), where features in the landscape are only pointers, landmarks, without significance in themselves—there we may expect the image of God to transcend concrete phenomena altogether. Man confronting God will not contemplate him but will hear his voice and command, as Moses did, and the prophets, and Mohammed.

When we compared the lands of origin of Egyptians, and Mesopotamians, we were concerned, not with the relation between group psychology and habitat, but with profound differences in pristine religious experience. The peculiar experience which we have just described seems characteristic for all the most significant figures of the Old Testament. It is important to realize this, not because it enables us to understand them better as individuals, but because we then recognize what coloured and integrated their thought. They propounded, not speculative theory, but revolutionary and dynamic teaching. The doctrine of a single, unconditioned, transcendent God rejected time-honoured values, proclaimed new ones, and postulated a metaphysical significance for history and for man's actions. With infinite *moral* courage the Hebrews worshipped an absolute God and accepted as the correlate of their faith the sacrifice of an harmonious existence. In transcending the Near Eastern myths of immanent godhead, they created, as we have seen, the new myth of the will of God. It remained for the Greeks, with their peculiar *intellectual* courage, to discover a form of speculative thought in which myth was entirely overcome.

In the sixth century B.C. the Greeks, in their great cities on the coast of Asia Minor, were in touch with all the leading centres of the civilized world: Egypt and Phoenicia; Lydia, Persia, and Babylon. There can be no doubt that this contact played some part in the meteoric development of Greek culture. But it is impossible to estimate the Greek indebtedness to the ancient Near East. As is usual when cultural contact is truly fruitful, simple derivations are rare. What the Greeks borrowed, they transmuted.

In the Greek mystery religions we meet well-known oriental themes. Demeter was the sorrowing mother-goddess searching for her child; Dionysus died a violent death but was resurrected. In some of the rites the participants experienced an immediate relationship with the divine in nature; and in this respect there is similarity with the ancient Near East. But it would be hard to find antecedents for the individual salvation vouchsafed to the initiates. A possible parallel would be the Osiris cult; but, as far as we know, the Egyptian did not undergo an initiation or share the god's fate during his lifetime. In any case, the Greek mysteries show several features which were without precedent. These generally amount to a diminished distance between men and gods. The initiate of the Orphic mysteries, for instance, not only hoped to be liberated from the "wheel of births" but actually emerged as a god from his union with the mother-goddess, "queen of the dead." The Orphic myths contain speculations about the nature of man which are characteristically Greek in their tenor. It was said that the Titans had devoured Dionysus-Zagreus and were therefore destroyed by the lightning of Zeus, who made man from their ashes. Man, in so far as he consists of the substance of the Titans, is evil and ephemeral; but since the Titans had partaken of a god's body, man contains a divine and immortal spark. Such dualism and the recognition of an immortal part in man are unknown in the ancient Near East outside Persia. . . .

Hesiod starts his account [of the universe, in his Theogony, written about 700 B.C.] with Chaos and proclaims Sky and Earth the parents of gods and men. He introduces numerous personifications which recall Egyptian *ma'at* or the "Wisdom of God" in the Book of Proverbs. ". . . Next he (Zeus) wedded bright Themis who bare the Horai, even Eunomia (Good Government) and Dike (Justice) and blooming Eirene (Peace) who care for the works of mortal man," (ll. 901–3).[5]

Associations and "participations" typical of mythopoeic thought appear often. A particularly clear example is: "And Night bare hateful Doom; and black Fate and Death and Sleep she bare, and she bare the tribe of dreams; all these did dark Night bear, albeit mated unto none," (ll. 211 ff.). The natural process of procreation thus supplied Hesiod with a scheme which allowed him to connect the phenomena and to arrange them in a comprehensible system. The Babylonian Epic of Creation and the An-Anum list use the same device; and we meet it in Egypt when Atum is said to have begotten Shū and Tefnūt (Air and Moisture), who, in their turn, brought forth Geb and Nūt (Earth and Sky).

And yet Hesiod is without oriental precedent in one respect: the gods and the universe were described by him as a matter of private interest. Such freedom was unheard of in the Near East, except among the Hebrews, where Amos, for instance, was a herdsman. In Egypt and Mesopotamia religious subjects were treated by members of the established hierarchy. But Hesiod was a Boeotian farmer called by the Muses, "which time he tended his flocks under holy Helicon." He says: "(The Muses) breathed in me a voice divine that I might celebrate the things that shall be and the things that were aforetime. They bade me sing the race of the Blessed Ones that are forever" (ll. 29 ff.). Thus a Greek layman recognized his vocation and became a singer who took the gods and nature as his theme, although he continued to use the traditional forms of epic poetry.

The same freedom, the same unconcern as regards special function and hierarchy, is characteristic for the Ionian philosophers who lived a century or more after Hesiod. Thales seems to have been an engineer and statesman; Anaximander, a map-maker. Cicero stated: "Almost all those whom the

[5] F. M. Cornford, *From Religion to Philosophy* (London, 1912), 119-20.

Greeks called the Seven Sages, you will see to have been engaged in public life," (*De Rep.* i. 7). These men, then, in contrast to the priests of the Near East, were not charged by their communities to concern themselves with spiritual matters. They were moved by their own desire for an understanding of nature; and they did not hesitate to publish their findings, although they were not professional seers. Their curiosity was as lively as it was unhampered by dogma. Like Hesiod, the Ionian philosophers gave their attention to the problem of origins; but for them it assumed an entirely new character. The origin, the ἀρχή, which they sought was not understood in the terms of myth. They did not describe an ancestral divinity or a progenitor. They did not even look for an 'origin' in the sense of an initial condition which was superseded by subsequent states of being. The Ionians asked for an immanent and *lasting* ground of existence. 'Αρχή means "origin," not as "beginning," but as "sustaining principle" or "first cause."

This change of viewpoint is breath-taking. It transfers the problems of man in nature from the realm of faith and poetic intuition to the intellectual sphere. A critical appraisal of each theory, and hence a continuous inquiry into the nature of reality, became possible. A cosmogonic myth is beyond discussion. It describes a sequence of sacred events, which one can either accept or reject. But no cosmogony can become part of a progressive and cumulative increase of knowledge. As we said in our first chapter, myth claims recognition by the faithful, not justification before the critical. But a sustaining principle or first cause must be comprehensible, even if it was first discovered in a flash of insight. It does not pose the alternative of acceptance or rejection. It may be analysed, modified, or corrected. In short, it is subject to intellectual judgment.

Yet the doctrines of the early Greek philosophers are not couched in the language of detached and systematic reflection. Their sayings sound rather like inspired oracles. And no wonder, for these men proceeded, with preposterous boldness, on an entirely unproved assumption. They held that the universe is an intelligible whole. In other words, they presumed that a single order underlies the chaos of our perceptions and, furthermore, that we are able to comprehend that order.

The speculative courage of the Ionians is often overlooked. Their teachings were, in fact, predestined to be misunderstood by modern—or rather, nineteenth-century—scholars. When Thales proclaims water to be the first cause, or Anaximenes air; when Anaximander speaks of the "Boundless," and Heraclitus of fire; when, moreover, Democritus' theory of atoms can be considered the outcome of these earlier speculations; then we need not be astonished that commentators in a positivistic age unwittingly read familiar connotations into the quasi-materialist doctrines of the Ionians and regarded these earliest philosophers as the first scientists. No bias could more insidiously disfigure the greatness of the Ionian achievement. The materialist interpretation of their teachings takes for granted what was to be discovered only as a result of the labours of these ancient thinkers—the distinction between the objective and the subjective. And only on the basis of this distinction is scientific thought possible. . . .

Early Greek philosophy showed a twofold originality. In the first place (in Cornford's words) it "ignored with astonishing boldness the prescriptive sanctities of religious representation."[6] Its second characteristic is a passionate consistency. Once a theory is adopted, it is followed up to its ultimate conclusion irrespective of conflicts with observed facts or probabilities. Both of these characteristics indicate an implicit recognition of the autonomy of thought; they also emphasize the intermediate position of early Greek philosophy. The absence of personification, of gods, sets it apart from mythopoeic thought. Its disregard for the data of experience in its pursuit of consistency distinguishes it from later thought. Its hypotheses were not induced from systematic observations but were much more in the nature of inspired conjectures or divinations by which it was attempted to reach a vantage point where the phenomena would reveal their hidden coherence. It was the unshakable conviction of the Ionians, Pythagoreans, and early Eleatics that such a vantage point existed; and they searched for the road towards it, not in the manner of scientists, but in that of conquistadors. . . .

With Heraclitus of Ephesus philosophy found its *locus standi.* "Wisdom is one thing. It is to know the *thought* by which all things are steered through all things."[7] Here, for the first time, attention is centred, not on the thing known, but on the knowing of it. Thought, γνώμη (which may also be translated "judgment," or "understanding"), controls the phenomena as it constitutes the thinker. The problem of understanding nature is moved once more to a new plane. In the ancient Near East it had remained within the sphere of myth. The Milesian school of philosophers had moved it to the realm of the intellect in that they claimed the universe to be an *intelligible* whole. The manifold was to be understood as deriving from a sustaining principle or first cause, but this was to be looked for in the phenomena. The question of how we can know what is outside us was not raised. Heraclitus asserted that the universe was intelligible because it was ruled by "thought" or "judgment," and that the same principle, therefore, governed both existence and knowledge. He was conscious that this wisdom surpassed even the loftiest conception of Greek mythopoeic thought: "The wise is one only. It is unwilling and willing to be called by the name of Zeus."[8]

Heraclitus calls this wisdom *Logos,* a term so heavily laden with associations as to be an embarrassment whether we translate it or not. "Reason" is perhaps the least objectionable rendering. "It is wise to hearken, not to me, but to the Logos and to confess that all things are one."[9] All things are one. Things that are distinct from one another, or qualities that are each

[6] *Iliad* xiv, 201, 241.
[7] This and the following quotations are taken from A. W. Mair, *Hesiod, the Poems and Fragments* (Oxford: Clarendon Press, 1908).
[8] This and the following quotations are taken from J. Burnet, *Early Greek Philosophy* (4th ed.; London, 1930).
[9] *Cambridge Ancient History,* IV, 532.

other's opposites, have no permanent existence. They are but transitory stages in a perpetual flux. No static description of the universe is true. "Being" is but "becoming." The cosmos is but the dynamics of existence. The opposites which Anaximander saw "separating out" from the "Boundless" are for Heraclitus united by a tension which causes each of them ultimately to change into its opposite. "Men do not know how what is at variance agrees with itself. It is an attunement (ἁρμονιή) of opposite tensions, like that of the bow and the lyre."[10]

But if the universe changes continually according to the tensions between opposites, it is senseless to ask for its origin in the manner of myth. There is no beginning and no end; there is only existence. Heraclitus states magnificently; "This world (κόσμος) which is the same for all, no one of the gods or men has made; but it was ever, is now, and ever shall be an ever-living fire, with measures of it kindling, and measures going out."[11] Fire is the symbol for a universe in flux between tensional opposites. As Burnet says: "The quantity of fire in a flame burning steadily appears to remain the same, the flame seems to be what we call a 'thing.' And yet the substance of it is continually changing. It is always passing away in smoke, and its place is always taken by fresh matter from the fuel that feeds it."[12]

Heraclitus takes pains to stress that it is only the total process that is lasting and, hence, significant: "The way up and the way down is one and the same,"[13] or "it rests by changing,"[14] or, more metaphorically, 'fire is want *and* surfeit,'[15] or one 'cannot step twice in the same river, for fresh waters are forever flowing in upon you. . . ."[16]

With conviction the Greek thinkers of the sixth and fifth centuries B.C. propounded theories which resulted from intuitive insight and which were elaborated by deductive reasoning. Each system was based upon an assumption held to be true and made to bear a structure erected without further reference to empirical data. Consistency was valued more highly than probability. This fact in itself shows that throughout early Greek philosophy *reason* is acknowledged as the highest arbiter, even though the Logos is not mentioned before Heraclitus and Parmenides. It is this tacit or outspoken appeal to reason, no less than the independence from "the prescriptive sanctities of religion," which places early Greek philosophy in the sharpest contrast with the thought of the ancient Near East.

As we have said before, the cosmologies of mythopoeic thought are basically revelations received in a confrontation with a cosmic "Thou." And one cannot argue about a revelation; it transcends reason. But in the systems

[10] Burnet, *op. cit.,* p. 52.
[11] Burnet, Frag. 29.
[12] Burnet, Frag. 65. This statement gains in pregnancy if we remember that Heraclitus was a contemporary of Aeschylus.
[13] Burnet, Frag. 1. Burnet translates "my word."
[14] Burnet, Frag. 45.
[15] Burnet, Frag. 20.
[16] *Op. cit.,* p. 145.

of the Greeks the human mind recognizes its own. It may take back what it created or change or develop it. This is true even of the Milesian philosophies, although they have not entirely shed the concrescence of myth. It is patently true of the doctrine of Heraclitus, which established the sovereignty of thought, rejected Anaximander and Pythagoras, and proclaimed an absolute *becoming*. It is equally true of the teaching of Parmenides, who confounded Heraclitus and proclaimed an absolute *being*.

One question remains to be answered. If mythopoeic thought took shape in an undissolved relationship between man and nature, what became of that relationship when thought was emancipated? We may answer this question with a quotation to balance the one with which we began this chapter. We saw that in Psalm xix nature appears bereaved of divinity before an absolute God: "The heavens declare the glory of God and the firmament sheweth his handiwork." And we read in Plato's *Timaeus,* in Jowett's translation (47*c*):

> . . . had we never seen the stars, and the sun, and the heaven, none of the words which we have spoken about the universe would ever have been uttered. But now the sight of day and night, and the months and the revolutions of the years, have created number, and have given us a conception of time; and the power of enquiring about the nature of the universe; and from this source we have derived philosophy, than which no greater good ever was or will be given by the gods to mortal man.

SUGGESTED READINGS

Burnet, John. *Early Greek Philosophy*. London, 1930.

Cassirer, Ernst. 'Die Philosophie der Griechen von den Anfängen bis Platon,' in Max Dessoir, *Handbuch der Philosophie,* I, 7–140. Berlin, 1925.

Cornford, F. M. *From Religion to Philosophy*. London, 1912.

Joël, Karl. *Geschichte der antiken Philosophie,* Vol. I. Tübingen 1921.

Myers, J. L. 'The Background of Greek Science,' *University of California Chronicle,* Vol. XIV, No. 4.

GILBERT HIGHET

•

The Unpredictable Intellect[1]

Yet we cannot foresee the stages of this war in which we are all engaged—the war for the enslavement or liberation of the mind of humanity. The movement of the human intellect is impossible to prophesy: difficult even

[1] From *Man's Unconquerable Mind* (New York: Columbia University Press, 1954), pp. 29-45. Copyright, 1954, Columbia University Press.

to record and analyze. Whether we shall ever be able to write a systematic history of thought, explaining the laws that govern its growth and movement, I know not; but at present those who have studied the migration of ideas find it far beyond their powers. Historians such as Sorokin and Toynbee and anthropologists such as Kroeber and Linton have found it hard enough to describe the manifold, the illimitably various stimuli that awaken the sleeping reason and the multiple channels through which thought flows from one mind to another, from one region to another. So far, scholars have able to establish only the broadest and vaguest rules to assist us in understanding these processes. They are wonders. They are mysteries.

It is difficult, for instance, to see why a single nation should be able in one century to produce a thousand inventors, philosophers, poets, and statesmen, and then, within a few generations, become speechless and apparently thoughtless. Why should one country seethe with intellectual energy as long as it is poor and danger-ridden, only to fall into indolent stupor when it gets wealth and security, while its neighbor, long silent during centuries of poverty and humiliation, finds its voice only after acquiring power and riches? How is it that, within the same country at different times, scientists are now admired and now neglected, poets are sometimes blessed as benefactors and sometimes despised as eccentrics? We know well how often two men, or two groups in different parts of the world, will make the same discovery or think similar thoughts without knowing each other; and that is strange; but it is stranger still to roam through the history of genius, and watch, and see how often mighty minds have appeared in lonely lands and savage tribes and eras full of repression and of hateful violence.

LONELY GENIUS

Sometimes, climbing among the western mountains, one crosses a long wind-lashed and snow-beaten shoulder of harsh broken rocks; and in a tiny hollow halfway across it, see, there is a tuft of bright flowers. Sometimes, from higher up, one looks down into a barren canyon, whose stony walls echo with the dull roar of the torrent below and with the crash of crumbling slabs and pinnacles above: there is not a patch of green, not a visible handful of nourishing earth; but halfway down those precipitous walls, raising its gallant head and spreading its hopeful arms, there grows a pine tree rooted in an invisible notch, and the birds flicker around it.

No less delightful and wonderful is it to read the history of some bloody epoch, crusted with murder and torture, resounding with dull groans, choked hymns, and shouts of senseless violence, and in the midst of it to meet a serene and gracious mind, studying nature and making poetry; or to discover, among lazy bourgeois or glum earthbound peasants, a powerful intellect grappling with abstractions of number, producing unique inventions, or building a systematic interpretation of the universe.

Such was the Buddha. Such was Sequoyah, the Cherokee Indian who, alone, created a written language for his people. Such was the greatest philosopher of the Dark Ages, Johannes Scotus Eriugena—John the Celt from Ireland, as he emphatically called himself—who, almost alone in western Europe at that time, contrived to learn Greek, and created a vast philosophical vision of the spiritual world such as no thinker today could equal. Such was Gregor Mendel, the quiet monk who worked and thought patiently in his garden until he had discovered some of the fundamental laws of heredity. And such were many artists who lived obscurely and whose personalities are all but forgotten, but who made masterpieces of beauty. We may know the name of Aleijadinho, that pathetic figure who became the finest sculptor of Latin America; but the carvers of Chartres are known only by their work, and we cannot even guess the race of the artist who made the exquisite bronze heads from Benin in west Africa.

NEW SYNTHESIS

Yet even apart from such lonely geniuses there are other surprises in the history of thought, phenomena almost as unexpected and almost as inexplicable. There are men who express the age and the milieu in which they were educated, but who, by the intensity of their imagination, the sweep of their knowledge, and their astounding versatility, rise high above their era and their neighbors, so that they inhabit both time and eternity at once. When we analyze their minds we can identify nearly all the component elements, tracing this to family and that to school and the other to social climate, and yet the compound is far more than the sum of all these elements: richer, intenser, different in quality as a diamond is different from carbon. Shallow thinkers often fail to understand that this qualitative difference occurs again and again in the realm of the intellect. That is what leads some critics to deny that Shakespeare could have written those plays because he was only a middle-class provincial youth who went from a small-town school to become an actor: they expect the real author to be someone calculable, like the university-trained lawyer and statesman Bacon, or a witty and graceful young nobleman with the learning and worldly experience of the Renaissance in his very blood. But they are wrong. They are making the elementary error of believing that, in the world of the mind, two and two make four.

Such people can never have taught. One of the few but great rewards of teaching is to see, not once but again and again, how one boy indistinguishable from the others in an average group, will, stimulated by a single remark of the teacher or excited by exploring a new subject, suddenly begin to change. He grows in wisdom; he throws out original ideas of his own; his very speech and handwriting become more mature; he lives on a new time-scale; he changes so rapidly that he distances all his friends and cannot remember or recognize his twelve-months-younger self. Somehow, some happy chance or providential effort has—what can we say? there are no images to describe the event, which is as mysterious as all vital processes—something has caused the energies of his mind, hitherto dissonant or unused, and the emotions with which he once played, or which played with him, to combine into a new, living, active, creative synthesis. This boy astonishes his friends and his parents: usually not himself, for he feels he is simply learning to use powers which are already his own; and never the teacher, who knows the almost limitless treasures of ability and creativity that every pupil carries about in the locked safe of his mind, and who always hopes and strives to unlock it.

And further, those who believe that forces and results in the field of the intellect are always calculable—those who think Bacon or Oxford ought to have written the Shakespearean dramas because that would be easier to understand—must know very little of the personal history of genius. In a touchingly awkward poem representing the shy self-encouragement of a lonely young man in a far country, John Masefield writes

> I have seen flowers come in stony places;
> And kindness done by men with ugly faces;
> And the gold cup won by the worst horse at the races;
> So I trust, too.

And one certain truth about the great works of the mind—inventions, philosophical systems, poems and plays, pictures and music, scientific discoveries and political institutions—is that many of them were made by men who started life in ordinary, even in unfavorable, situations and then far outsoared their origins.

Isaac Newton was the son of a Lincolnshire farmer: unlike some mathematicians, he was not even bright in boyhood; he was a mediocre student when he went to Cambridge; and then within a few years, the spark descended. Gauss, one of the supreme geniuses of mathematics and electromagnetism, was a village boy like a million others. The founder of modern art-history, Winckelmann, was miserably poor and started as a hack schoolmaster, taking classes all day, sleeping in his schoolhouse, staying awake half the night to teach himself Latin and Greek in preparation for the magnificent career he could only dimly foresee. The by-blow of an Italian gentleman and a country girl was apprenticed to the trade of painting, like many thousands before and after him: but this one was Leonardo da Vinci. Such handicaps hamper but do not crush the growth of the mind: they may even stimulate it. Even the general enemy, ordinariness and routine, cannot always spoil the seed. Loyola, founder of the Jesuits, was a brave ignorant soldier in an age full of stupid men with swords. Luther and Rabelais were monks indistinguishable from myriads of other monks in other lands and times. Socrates was a stonemason in a city crowded with builders. No, the whole history of human thought is as various, as marvelous, as unexpected, and as inexplicable as other mysteries of this universe. Science, with its search for laws, always oversimplifies. But the wise scientist always makes his way through the realm of law into the region of wonder. In a few years he can master the principles of plant and animal life, reproduction, and distribution—and then, for ever thereafter, he remains astounded by the incalculable multiplicity of animal forms, the unthinkable subtlety of plants, knowing that when new varieties are discovered they may contain something as unpredictable as a new divine creation. The complexities of human language, the intricate life of microorganisms, the invisible radiations that fill the universe, the power of mutation in living forms—all these can be faintly or crudely grasped, but never fully understood. One of the truest sayings of the medieval thinkers was OMNIA EXEVNT IN MYSTERIVM, *All things pass into mystery*. We are not intended only to diagnose and calculate, but also to wonder, to admire; to expect the unexpected.

THE MIND A MYSTERY

Yes, the outer world—both visible and invisible—is ultimately a mystery. So too is the other world we inhabit—the inner world, the world of the mind. Not one of us knows what his own mind contains. Not one of us knows what his own mind can do, or will produce.

Some of the busy and complex activity of the mind is permanently hidden. We can scarcely ever see its vaguest outlines, except now and then in dreams or apparently purposeless actions. Priests at confession, psychoanalysts listening and probing, lawyers and judges analyzing acts of cunning and violence, ethnologists examining myths, and critics penetrating poems, yes, all of us when we listen to music, that wordless language of the soul, experience something of that powerful and terrible world, but can never know it fully. It means to hide itself. The pupils of Freud have sometimes made the problem too simple, saying that the inner activity of the mind was a ferment of "immoral" or rejected, censored, and repressed material—a living skeleton chained in our cupboard. But the true picture is far more complex. Much of our hidden life literally cannot be dominated, directly helped or impeded, or ever understood by our reasoning mind. The instincts, memory, invention, imagination—these and other activities lie largely outside the range of consciousness. The reason can observe them at work, occasionally intervene, and with constant and difficult effort learn to influence them; but their origins, their full power, their methods, all remain beyond its scope. Jesus once asked "Which of you, by thinking about it, can add a foot to his height?" But we might also ask ourselves whether any of us can forecast what ideas will be put up by his mind a year from now; a week from now; tomorrow; within the next hour.

We are all cave men. The cave we inhabit is our own mind; and consciousness is like a tiny torch, flickering and flaring, which can at best show us only a few outlines of the cave wall that stands nearest, or reflect a dangerous underground river flowing noiselessly at our feet, so that we start back in horror before we are engulfed; as we explore, we come often on shapes of beauty, glittering stalactites, jewel-encrusted pillars, delicate and trusting animals which befriend and follow us; sometimes we even find relics of an earlier time, a primitive statue with flowers still fresh at its feet, or shapes of beasts painted on the wall with bloody handprints beside them; now and then we stumble over a heap that crackles and mutters and moves, but we turn our light away and hurry on; the path we follow sometimes seems to trace an elaborate pattern, although our little flame shows us only a few lines, converging and then curving off into darkness; often its rays die down, threatening to go out altogether and leave us in the resounding gloom; at least thrice in our journey we must crouch down because the cave roof sinks low above us, so that we can go forward only on our knees; when we emerge, it is into another cavern larger than the last but more awesome, where we hear the beat of unseen wings above our head; there are side openings into which our light shines only faintly, to reveal glowing eyes and fearful teeth far in their recesses; the worst of all our trials is that when we venture to speak, the vast invisible walls and roof distort our words into formidable echoes, dying away in superhuman whispers or hateful growls; and, after many a year of wandering, when our torch gleams upon a silent pool and we bend over its calm surface, we do not recognize the face that stares up into our anxious and astonished eyes.

The self is hidden. We do not know ourselves, our brothers and sisters, husbands or wives or children. No friend knows his friend.

Yet all this mystery holds greatness as well as darkness. The cavern is dim, somber, unexplored; but it contains treasures. Every human brain is filled with unused power. Out of all the billions of men and women who have lived, only a few hundred thousand have been able to employ so much of that power as to change the world. The rest have been dutiful or lazy, good or bad, sensuous or self-denying, thrifty or wasteful, cowardly or brave. Those few hundred thousand, perhaps only a score of thousands in all, are the minds that have made our world. Scientists, strategists, industrialists, aesthetes, explorers, inventors, organizers, authors, musicians, philosophers, doctors and teachers, lawyers and statesmen, several thousand in each class, these are the minds who have given the rest of mankind incalculable benefits, or done it immeasurable damage. They are responsible for much of human history.

Consider the world, apart from mankind. It is either static or else changing in a gradual and apparently automatic rhythm. The planet swings around the sun, steadily slowing down. The tides flow back and forward with the retreating and returning moon. Weather wears the rocks, the sea eats at the shores, the polar ice advances and recedes. The air and land and water are filled with living things—but they scarcely ever change, or if they do, it is over vast spaces of time. Ferns grow and fish swim and micro-organisms vibrate in our world just as they did long before men walked upon the earth; the industrious ants continue with their routine of self-preservation and self-perpetuation as they did when the dinosaurs ruled. But man, in his brief history, has transformed both the world and himself. His specific quality is purposeful change through thought. He is most truly alive when he thinks.

There are only three secular explanations of history. One is that it is made by groups of people acting together. The second is that historical change is produced by blind impersonal "forces." The third is that it is decided and led by powerful individuals. Of course all these theories are true to some extent; and none is true exclusively. Climatic shifts and epidemic diseases move or destroy populations. Social, economic, religious, aesthetic patterns are worked out by successive generations; vast migrations occur without a single leader. Heroes and villains and geniuses preach, rebel, invent, govern. Yet in man's more recent history many of the most powerful and vital changes have been initiated by strong individuals. Not all of these were thinkers. Some were driven by passions of love or hatred or violence or pride. But the work of the thinking man has been more lasting.

Since it is all a mystery, we can never tell how great thinkers emerge. There are very few rules for producing them. They do not grow like trees; they cannot be bred like selected animals. People are not born thoughtless or thoughtful. Probably the surest way to grow up stupid is to be part of a large static population doing manual labor and living just on the level of subsistence; and the next best is to be born in a nice family with inherited wealth, brought up in an assured social position, and sent to a quiet and correct school. The young ploughboy and the young marquis are both in a mental prison, one following the furrow, the other set in his comfortable rut.

TRAINING THE THINKER

No, we can never tell how great minds arise, and it is very hard to tell how to detect and encourage them when they do appear. But we do know two methods of feeding them as they grow.

One is to give them constant challenge and stimulus. Put problems before them. Make things difficult for them. They need to think. Produce things for them to think about and question their thinking at every stage. They are inventive and original. Propose experiments to them. Tell them to discover what is hidden.

The second method is to bring them into contact with other eminent minds. It is not enough, not nearly enough, for a clever boy or girl to meet his fellows and his teachers and his parents. He (or she) must meet men and women of real and undeniable distinction. That is, he must meet the immortals. That brilliant and pessimistic scoundrel Plato died just over 2,300 years ago, but through his books he is still talking and thinking and leading others to think; and there is no better way, none, for a young man to start thinking about any kind of philosophical problem—human conduct, political action, logical analysis, metaphysics, aesthetics—than by reading Plato and trying to answer his arguments, detect his sophisms, resist his skillful persuasions, and become both his pupil and his critic. No one can learn to write music better than by studying *The Well-tempered Clavier* of Bach and the symphonies of Beethoven. A young composer who does so will not, if he is any good, write music like Bach and Beethoven. He will write music more like the music that he wanted to write. A man may become a routine diplomat by following the rule book and solving every problem as it comes up, but if he is to grow into a statesman he must read his Machiavelli and consider the lives of Bismarck and Lincoln and Disraeli. The best way toward greatness is to mix with the great.

Challenge and experiment; association with immortal minds: these are the two sure ways of rearing intelligent men and women. And these two opportunities for greatness are, or ought to be, provided by schools and colleges and universities. "But," you will ask, "do schools exist only to train genuises?" No, but they do not exist only to train the average and to neglect or benumb the talented. They exist to make the best of both. One of the heaviest responsibilities in education is to do justice to exceptional minds, remembering that they may emerge in any place, at any time, and in any body—even a clumsy and misshapen frame may hold a brilliant mind. It must be a strange experience to teach in a little country school, the same subjects year after year to the same families, and then to find a gifted young engineer or a born dramatist among one's pupils. Disconcerting. Difficult. Difficult to know how to encourage without patronizing; difficult not to be a little jealous. Yet the history of knowledge is filled with true stories of teachers who recognized outstanding gifts in a pupil and gave him all he needed to set him on his way to eminence: touching and encouraging, these tales. Such is the story of the Spanish peasant boy who was drawing with charcoal on a plank when a teacher saw him, started training him, and helped to make the artist Goya. Such is the tale of the thin sensitive undersized London schoolboy whose schoolmaster's son gave him the run of his private library: it was among those shelves and as a result of that kindness that the youngster wrote a poem called "On First Looking into Chapman's Homer." Behind almost every great man there stands either a good parent or a good teacher.

Education in America and in the other countries of the West is an inspiriting achievement: all those light, healthy schools, those myriad colleges, so many youngsters having a fine time and not working too hard. Yet it has a couple of weaknesses. One is that education has become almost too easy to get. It is accepted like a supply of pure water: no one expects to get much stimulus or nourishment from it, but it is used to keep the tissues well filled and the outer surface clean. The other is that it does not often carry over into mature life. The average American would rather be driving a car along a crowded highway than reading a book and thinking. The average Frenchman would rather be drinking an extra bottle of wine than watching a play by Racine. The average

Britisher would rather fill up a football-pool form than listen to Elgar's *Enigma*. Why this should be so, I cannot tell. It must be something wrong with education. Probably it is the cult of the average: the idea that schools exist in order to make everyone pretty much the same, and that happiness consists in sharing a group life, sweet, humming, undifferentiated, and crowded like bees in a hive.

Schools do exist for the average. They also exist to serve the distinguished. America was built both by a multitude of common men and women and also by a few eccentrics, heroes, and giants, those whom Stephen Spender exalts when he writes

> I think continually of those who were truly great.
> Who, from the womb, remembered the soul's history
> Through corridors of light where the hours are suns
> Endless and singing. Whose lovely ambition
> Was that their lips, still touched with fire,
> Should tell of the spirit clothed from head to foot in song.
>
> . . . .
>
> Born of the sun they travelled a short while towards the sun
> And left the vivid air signed with their honour.

The life of every teacher is partly dedicated to discovering and encouraging those few powerful minds who will influence our future, and the secret of education is never to forget the possibility of greatness.

We owe them reverence, the great minds of the past and present and future. It is inspiring and delightful even to scan their names. One shines on another, receiving light in return. It is like looking at the stars, when the eye travels from the Bear to Orion, from Aldebaran to Sirius and Vega, from glory to glory.

When we think of the most majestic mind of the Middle Ages, of Dante, our thought soon travels to his master and companion Vergil, who guided him through Hell and Purgatory until he attained the vision of the beloved; from Dante to the prose counterpart of his poem, the *Summa* of St. Thomas Aquinas; and back from St. Thomas to his master Aristotle. If we read an essay by Francis Bacon, we soon remember the earlier, kinder essayist Montaigne; and then, recalling that Bacon was a scientific thinker, we turn to Descartes, and from him to a kindred mind, Leibnitz, and so from greatness to greatness. Descartes and Newton both interpreted the universe: from Newton it is inevitable to travel back to Kepler and Brahe, forward to Laplace. Sometimes, again, great minds recall each other because, although they were strangers and worked in different media, they saw similar aspects of the universe. It is difficult to play certain fugues by Bach (such as the E flat minor in Book II, full of cold harmonies, meditative rhythms, and somber melancholy) without thinking of the wise old men with unsmiling wrinkled faces and deep eyes, who watch us from the shadows of Rembrandt's last pictures. It is difficult to look at Dürer's mystical etchings without thinking of Goethe's *Faust*.

Such men were not—as shallow historians try to tell us—creatures of their time and place. Often they were eccentrics who ignored or preceded their epoch; nearly always they were largely self-made; by giving their age a voice and by teaching it, they helped to form it, to dominate it. To read the life of even one such thinker is to renew one's faith in humanity, one's sense of duty to the world. To move freely among the captain minds of any one great age—say the seventeenth century, or the century that produced Cicero, Lucretius, Vergil, Horace, and Livy, or the nineteenth century—is to be perpetually astounded at the depth unplumbable, the infinite variety of the human mind, and to repeat the words of the Greek tragedian:

> Wonders are many, but none,
> none is more wondrous than man.

C. NORTHCOTE PARKINSON

•

Injelititis, or Palsied Paralysis[1]

We find everywhere a type of organization (administrative, commercial, or academic) in which the higher officials are plodding and dull, those less senior are active only in intrigue against each other, and the junior men are frustrated or frivolous. Little is being attempted. Nothing is being achieved. And in contemplating this sorry picture, we conclude that those in control have done their best, struggled against adversity, and have finally admitted defeat. It now appears from the results of recent investigation, that no such failure need be assumed. In a high percentage of the moribund institutions so far examined the final state of coma is something gained of set purpose and after prolonged effort. It is the result, admittedly, of a disease, but of a disease that is largely self-induced. From the first signs of the condition, the progress of the disease has been encouraged, the causes aggravated, and the symptoms welcomed. It is the disease of induced inferiority, called Injelititis. It is a commoner ailment than is often supposed, and the diagnosis is far easier than the cure.

Our study of this organizational paralysis begins, logically, with a description of the course of the disease from the first signs to the final coma. The

[1] From *Parkinson's Law and Other Studies in Administration,* C. Northcote Parkinson (Boston: Houghton Mifflin Company, 1957), pp. 78-90. Copyright, 1957, by C. Northcote Parkinson. Reprinted by permission of Houghton Mifflin Company and John Murray, Ltd.

second stage of our inquiry concerns symptoms and diagnosis. The third stage should properly include some reference to treatment, but little is known about this. Nor is much likely to be discovered in the immediate future, for the tradition of British medical research is entirely opposed to any emphasis on this part of the subject. British medical specialists are usually quite content to trace the symptoms and define the cause. It is the French, by contrast, who begin by describing the treatment and discuss the diagnosis later, if at all. We feel bound to adhere in this to the British method, which may not help the patient but which is unquestionably more scientific. To travel hopefully is better than to arrive.

The first sign of danger is represented by the appearance in the organization's hierarchy of an individual who combines in himself a high concentration of incompetence and jealousy. Neither quality is significant in itself and most people have a certain proportion of each. But when these two qualities reach a certain concentration—represented at present by the formula I^3J^5—there is a chemical reaction. The two elements fuse, producing a new substance that we have termed "injelitance." The presence of this substance can be safely inferred from the actions of any individual who, having failed to make anything of his own department, tries constantly to interfere with other departments and gain control of the central administration. The specialist who observes this particular mixture of failure and ambition will at once shake his head and murmur, "Primary or idiopathic injelitance." The symptoms, as we shall see, are quite unmistakable.

The next or secondary stage in the progress of the disease is reached when the infected individual gains complete or partial control of the central organization. In many instances this stage is reached without any period of primary infection, the individual having actually entered the organization at that level. The injelitant individual is easily recognizable at this stage from the persistence with which he struggles to eject all those abler than himself, as also from his resistance to the appointment or promotion of anyone who might prove abler in course of time. He dare not say, "Mr. Asterisk is too able," so he says, "Asterisk? Clever perhaps—but is he sound? I incline to prefer Mr. Cypher." He dare not say, "Mr. Asterisk makes me feel small," so he says, "Mr. Cypher appears to me to have the better judgment." Judgment is an interesting word that signifies in this context the opposite of intelligence; it means, in fact, doing what was done last time. So Mr. Cypher is promoted and Mr. Asterisk goes elsewhere. The central administration gradually fills up with people stupider than the chairman, director, or manager. If the head of the organization is second-rate, he will see to it that his immediate staff are all third-rate; and they will, in turn, see to it that their subordinates are fourth-rate. There will soon be an actual competition in stupidity, people pretending to be even more brainless than they are.

The next or tertiary stage in the onset of this disease is reached when there is no spark of intelligence left in the whole organization from top to bottom.

This is the state of coma we described in our first paragraph. When that stage has been reached the institution is, for all practical purposes, dead. It may remain in a coma for twenty years. It may quietly disintegrate. It may even, finally, recover. Cases of recovery are rare. It may be thought odd that recovery without treatment should be possible. The process is quite natural, nevertheless, and closely resembles the process by which various living organisms develop a resistance to poisons that are at first encounter fatal. It is as if the whole institution had been sprayed with a DDT solution guaranteed to eliminate all ability found in its way. For a period of years this practice achieves the desired result. Eventually, however, individuals develop an immunity. They conceal their ability under a mask of imbecile good humor. The result is that the operatives assigned to the task of ability-elimination fail (through stupidity) to recognize ability when they see it. An individual of merit penetrates the outer defenses and begins to make his way toward the top. He wanders on, babbling about golf and giggling feebly, losing documents and forgetting names, and looking just like everyone else. Only when he has reached high rank does he suddenly throw off the mask and appear like the demon king among a crowd of pantomine fairies. With shrill screams of dismay the high executives find ability right there in the midst of them. It is too late by then to do anything about it. The damage has been done, the disease is in retreat, and full recovery is possible over the next ten years. But these instances of natural cure are extremely rare. In the more usual course of events, the disease passes through the recognized stages and becomes, as it would seem, incurable.

We have seen what the disease is. It now remains to show by what symptoms its presence can be detected. It is one thing to detail the spread of the infection in an imaginary case, classified from the start. It is quite a different thing to enter a factory, barracks, office, or college and recognize the symptoms at a glance. We all know how an estate agent will wander round a vacant house when acting for the purchaser. It is only a question of time before he throws open a cupboard or kicks a baseboard and exclaims, "Dry rot!" (acting for the vendor, he would lose the key of the cupboard while drawing attention to the view from the window). In the same way a political scientist can recognize the symptoms of Injelititis even in its primary stage. He will pause, sniff, and nod wisely, and it should be obvious at once that he knows. But how does he know? How can he tell that injelitance has set in? If the original source of the infection were present, the diagnosis would be easier, but it is still quite possible when the germ of the disease is on holiday. His influence can be detected in the atmosphere. It can be detected, above all, in certain remarks that will be made by others, as thus: "It would be a mistake for us to attempt too much. We cannot compete with Toprank. Here in Lowgrade we do useful work, meeting the needs of the country. Let us be content with that." Or again, "We do not pretend to be in the first flight. It is absurd the way these people at Much-Striving talk of their work, just as if they were in the Toprank class." Or finally, "Some of our younger men have transferred to Toprank—one or two even to Much-Striving. It is probably their wisest plan. We are quite happy to let them succeed in that way. An exchange of ideas and personnel is a good thing—although, to be sure, the few men we have had from Toprank have been rather disappointing. We can only expect the people they have thrown out. Ah well, we must not grumble. We always avoid friction when we can. And, in our humble way we can claim to be doing a good job."

What do these remarks suggest? They suggest—or, rather, they clearly indicate—that the standard of achievement has been set too low. Only a low standard is desired and one still lower is acceptable. The directives issuing from a second-rate chief and addressed to his third-rate executives speak only of minimum aims and ineffectual means. A higher standard of competence is not desired, for an efficient organization would be beyond the chief's power to control. The motto, "Ever third-rate" has been inscribed over the main entrance in letters of gold. Third-rateness has become a principle of policy. It will be observed, however, that the existence of higher standards is still recognized. There remains at this primary stage a hint of apology, a feeling of uneasiness when Toprank is mentioned. Neither this apology nor unease lasts for long. The second stage of the disease comes on quickly and it is this we must now describe.

The secondary stage is recognized by its chief symptom, which is Smugness. The aims have been set low and have therefore been largely achieved. The target has been set up within ten yards of the firing point and the scoring has therefore been high. The directors have done what they set out to do. This soon fills them with self-satisfaction. They set out to do something and they have done it. They soon forget that it was a small effort to gain a small result. They observe only that they have succeeded—unlike those people at Much-Striving. They become increasingly smug and their smugness reveals itself in remarks such as this: "The chief is a sound man and very clever when you get to know him. He never says much—that is not his way—but he seldom makes a mistake." (These last words can be said with justice of someone who never does anything at all.) Or this: "We rather distrust brilliance here. These clever people can be a dreadful nuisance, upsetting established routine and proposing all sorts of schemes that we have never seen tried. We obtain splendid results by simple common sense and teamwork." And finally this: "Our canteen is something we are really rather proud of. We don't know how the caterer can produce so good a lunch at the price. We are lucky to have him!" This last remark is made as we sit at a table covered with dirty oilcloth, facing an uneatable, nameless mess on a plate and shuddering at the sight and smell of what passes for coffee. In point of fact, the canteen reveals more than the office. Just as for a quick verdict we judge a private house by inspection of the WC (to find whether there is a spare toilet roll), just as we judge a hotel by the state of the cruet, so we judge a larger institution by the appearance of the canteen. If the decoration is in dark brown and pale green; if the curtains are purple (or absent); if there are no flowers in sight; if there is barley in the soup (with or without a dead fly); if the menu is one of hash and mold; and if the executives are still delighted with everything—why, then the institution is in a pretty bad way. For self-satisfaction, in such a case, has reached the point at which those responsible cannot tell the difference between food and filth. This is smugness made absolute.

The tertiary and last stage of the disease is one in which apathy has taken the place of smugness. The executives no longer boast of their efficiency as compared with some other institution. They have forgotten that any other institution exists. They have ceased to eat in the canteen, preferring now to bring sandwiches and scatter their desks with the crumbs. The bulletin boards carry notices about the concert that took place four years ago; Mr. Brown's office has a nameplate saying, "Mr. Smith." Mr. Smith's door is marked, "Mr. Robinson," in faded ink on an adhesive luggage label. The broken windows have been repaired with odd bits of cardboard. The electric light switches give a slight but painful shock when touched. The whitewash is flaking off the ceiling and the paint is blotchy on the walls. The elevator is out of order and the cloakroom tap cannot be turned off. Water from the broken skylight drips wide of the bucket placed to catch it, and from somewhere in the basement comes the wail of a hungry cat. The last stage of the disease has brought the whole organization to the point of collapse. The symptoms of the disease in this acute form are so numerous and evident that a trained investigator can often detect them over the telephone without visiting the place at all. When a weary voice answers "Ullo!" (that most unhelpful of replies), the expert has often heard enough. He shakes his head sadly as he replaces the receiver. "Well on in the tertiary phase," he will mutter to himself, "and almost certainly inoperable." It is too late to attempt any sort of treatment. The institution is practically dead.

We have now described this disease as seen from within and then again from outside. We know now the origin, the progress, and the outcome of the infection, as also the symptoms by which its presence is detected. British medical skill seldom goes beyond that point in its research. Once a disease has been identified, named, described, and accounted for, the British are usually quite satisfied and ready to investigate the next problem that presents itself. If asked about treatment they look surprised and suggest the use of penicillin preceded or followed by the extraction of all the patient's teeth. It becomes clear at once that this is not an aspect of the subject that interests them. Should our attitude be the same? Or should we as political scientists consider what, if anything, can be done about it? It would be premature, no doubt, to discuss any possible treatment in detail, but it might be useful to indicate very generally the lines along which a solution might be attempted. Certain principles, at least, might be laid down. Of such principles, the first would have to be this: a diseased institution cannot reform itself. There are instances, we know, of a disease vanishing without treatment, just as it appeared without warning; but these cases are rare and regarded by the specialist as irregular and undesirable. The cure, whatever its nature, must come from outside. For a patient to remove his own appendix under a local anaesthetic may be physically possible, but the practice is regarded with disfavor and is open to many objections. Other operations lend themselves still less to the patient's own dexterity. The first principle we can safely enunciate is that the patient and the surgeon should not be the same person. When an institution is in an advanced state of disease, the services of a specialist are required and even, in some instances, the services of the greatest living authority: Parkinson himself. The fees payable may be very heavy indeed, but in a case of this sort, expense is clearly no object. It is a matter, after all, of life and death.

The second principle we might lay down is this, that the primary stage of the disease can be treated by a simple injection, that the secondary stage can be cured in some instances by surgery, and that the tertiary stage must be regarded at present as incurable. There was a time when physicians used to babble about bottles and pills, but this is mainly out of date. There was another period when they talked more vaguely about psychology; but that too is out of date, most of the psychoanalysts having since been certified as insane. The present age is one of injections and incisions and it behooves the political scientists to keep in step with the Faculty. Confronted by a case of primary infection, we prepare a syringe automatically and only hesitate as to what, besides water, it should contain. In principle, the injection should contain some active substance—but from which group should it be selected? A kill-or-cure injection would contain a high proportion of Intolerance, but this drug is difficult to procure and sometimes too powerful to use. Intolerance is obtainable from the bloodstream of regimental sergeant majors and is found to comprise two chemical elements, namely: (a) the best is scarcely good enough (GG^{nth}) and (b) there is no excuse for anything (NE^{nth}). Injected into a diseased institution, the intolerant individual has a tonic effect and may cause the organism to turn against the original source of infection. While this treatment may well do good, it is by no means certain that the cure will be permanent. It is doubtful, that is to say, whether the infected substance will be actually expelled from the system. Such information as we have rather leads us to suppose that this treatment is merely palliative in the first instance, the disease remaining latent though inactive. Some authorities believe that repeated injections would result in a complete cure, but others fear that repetition of the treatment would set up a fresh irritation, only slightly less dangerous than the original disease. Intolerance is a drug to be used, therefore, with caution.

There exists a rather milder drug called Ridicule, but its operation is uncertain, its character unstable, and its effects too little known. There is little reason to fear that any damage could result from an injection of ridicule, but neither is it evident that a cure would result. It is generally agreed that the injelitant individual will have developed a thick protective skin, insensitive to ridicule. It may well be that ridicule may tend to isolate the infection, but that is as much as could be expected and more indeed than has been claimed.

We may note, finally, that Castigation, which is easily obtainable, has been tried in cases of this sort and not wholly without effect. Here again, however, there are difficulties. This drug is an immediate stimulus but can produce a result the exact opposite of what the specialist intends. After a momentary spasm of activity, the injelitant individual will often prove more supine than before and just as harmful as a source of infection. If any use can be made of castigation it will almost certainly be as one element in a preparation composed otherwise of intolerance and ridicule, with perhaps other drugs as yet untried. It only remains to point out that this preparation does not as yet exist.

The secondary stage of the disease we believe to be operable. Professional readers will all have heard of the Nuciform Sack and of the work generally associated with the name of Cutler Walpole. The operation first performed by that great surgeon involves, simply, the removal of the infected parts and the simultaneous introduction of new blood drawn from a similar organism. This operation has sometimes succeeded. It is only fair to add that it has also sometimes failed. The shock to the system can be too great. The new blood may be unobtainable and may fail, even when procured, to mingle with the blood previously in circulation. On the other hand, this drastic method offers, beyond question, the best chance of a complete cure.

The tertiary stage presents us with no opportunity to do anything. This institution is for all practical purposes dead. It can be founded afresh but only with a change of name, a change of site, and an entirely different staff. The temptation, for the economically minded, is to tranfer some portion of the original staff to the new institution—in the name, for example, of continuity. Such a transfusion would certainly be fatal, and continuity is the very thing to avoid. No portion of the old and diseased foundation can be regarded as free from infection. No staff, no equipment, no tradition must be removed from the original site. Strict quarantine should be followed by complete disinfection. Infected personnel should be dispatched with a warm testimonial to such rival institutions as are regarded with particular hostility. All equipment and files should be destroyed without hesitation. As for the buildings, the best plan is to insure them heavily and then set them alight. Only when the site is a blackened ruin can we feel certain that the germs of the disease are dead.

ROBERT M. HUTCHINS

•

That Candles May Be Brought[1]

My father came home from India about thirty years ago with the story of a British woman who was plagued to death by the questions of her Indian ser-

[1] From *Recall,* I (November-December, 1959), 5-10. Reprinted by permission of the author.

vant. Finally she said to him, "Why don't you use your common sense?" He replied, "Lady, common sense is the gift of God; I have only a technical education."

In college students learn to think. The question is whether they continue to do so upon graduation. We know that whereas a great deal of thinking is required to get through college, none is necessary to get through life. By definition a moron is a person who cannot think, and one of the benefits conferred upon us by the Industrial Revolution is that it has made it possible for morons to be successful. In 1948, Dr. Ruby Jo Reeves Kennedy, sociologist at the Connecticut College for Women, reported to the American Association on Mental Deficiency that the typical male moron earned as much as $3.50 a week more than the average industrial wage and that the female moron uniformly made more money than the normal industrial worker.

These figures should not surprise us, for it is obvious that the aim of mechanization is to get the operation simplified to the point where only his presence, and very little of that, is demanded of the operator. A capacity to think, and still worse, an insistence on doing so, may in such operations be a positive handicap.

We here begin to discern one of the reasons for the prevailing anti-intellectualism in this country. People who think do not fit in easily. The trouble with thinking is that it leads to criticism. A person who thinks is one who dislikes falsehood. And since it is impossible to dislike it and never say anything about it, it is impossible to think and never say anything controversial.

The unpopularity of thinking has a good deal to do with bringing about the alteration in the aims of education that has taken place in the thirty-five years and more that I have been employed by educational institutions. We exhibit a certain shyness now when we talk about those aims, intellectual training and intellectual activity, which were accepted as a matter of course in my youth. The current doctrine is that the aim of education is to adjust the young to the group. Not long ago a young woman at a co-educational college in Oklahoma was asked why she was depressed. She replied, "I come here to be went with and I ain't." The failure of education to perform its proper function in her case justified her disappointment with it.

Thinking is painful, unnecessary, and unpopular. The din of public and private propaganda in which we live, the pressure exerted by the institutions in which we work and have our being, and the tyranny of our neighbor's lifted eyebrow are making thinking next to impossible. Under these circumstances the habit of not thinking, of not caring, or not protesting is the easiest in the world to acquire. The most common statement you can hear today is, "I don't want to get involved."

Thinking proceeds in the effort to raise and answer questions. The Socratic dialogue is the model of civilized society. Certain technical and economic changes have placed the present generation at a disadvantage. The forum and the general store, which used to be the centers of discussion in this country, are being driven out of business by television and the supermarket. There can't be much conversation when you are watching that little screen or pushing your cart down those unending corridors of cans.

Far more serious are the fashions of silence with which we are afflicted. Only the other day the commandants of the Military and Naval Academies thought it dangerous to have their young gentlemen on either side of the question whether Red China should be admitted to the United Nations. Nobody would care to ask today whether our conviction that we need to spend twice or twenty times the amount of money on education that we now devote to it is justified by the quality of education that our children are now receiving or precisely how the quality of education is to be improved by the expenditures proposed. It is now tacitly understood that American education needs nothing but money, that all teachers, all subjects, and all schools and colleges need more money, and it would be rude to ask whether it is absolutely certain that they all deserve it.

If it is possible to ask a question, it may not be possible to get an intelligible answer. The world is hidden from us by the cliché curtain. Just as the question of the actual danger from the Communist Party in America can't be raised because the Party is a treasonable conspiracy, and the question of educational expenditures can't be raised because education is a good thing, so the question of Strontium 90 is disposed of by saying that if leukemia doesn't get us the Russians will, desegregation in the South by saying that everything takes time, inflation by saying that we must reduce Federal expenditures, and the problems of labor organization by referring to the right to work.

According to the law of contradiction, it is impossible to say that the same statement is at the same time in the same respect both true and false. One reason why the Civilization of the Dialogue is so hard to attain is that constant efforts are made to repeal this law. So the great historian of freedom, Lord Acton, had no difficulty in concluding that slavery was necessary to democracy, because, he said, the lower elements in the population would degrade it if they were allowed membership in the political society. According to Acton, slavery is essential if a democratic state is to be free. So, in spite of the fact that Christian love would seem to require that distinctions based on color should never appear in Christian congregations, it has been said that segregation reaches its peak in this country at 11 o'clock on Sunday mornings.

Consider the possibilities in a local wit's report that the cigarette companies are about to embark on a national advertising campaign with the slogan, "Cancer is good for you." The more one ponders this suggestion the more probable it sounds. If the cigarette companies did enter upon this campaign, who can doubt that it would succeed? The genius and the devices at the disposal of private and public propaganda have made smooth the pathway to 1984, where slavery is freedom, war is peace, hate is love, and disease is health. We are so used to violations of the law of contradiction that we are startled when the Supreme Court upholds it and rules in civil liberties cases that the Constitution means what it says.

If thinking is painful, unnecessary, unpopular, and, under present circumstances, next to impossible, why should you do it? Consider what our problems are. They are how to make democracy work, how to survive in the nuclear age, and what to do with ourslves if we do survive.

The first of these questions is how to make democracy work. It is basically the question of how we get the information and intelligence to cope with the totally new economic, social and political situation in which we find ourselves. When it appears likely that $175,000,000 was spent in the last national election, when fewer and fewer voices can be heard through the media of mass communications, when those media are chiefly devoted to mass entertainment, and when the educational system is dedicated largely to adjusting the young to the group, we see that discussion has been replaced by private and public propaganda and that the kind of education we are offering is unlikely to provide a defense against it.

Nor can we suppose that without thought we can survive in the nuclear age. Since we know that the simultaneous explosion of a finite number of bombs can make the world uninhabitable, we must recognize that in two hundred years we have moved from polite wars for limited aims fought without disturbing most of the population to the point where we can all go up in one big megabang. To suppose that we can avoid this fate by preparing to make the bang bigger or by talking about the reduction of one or two kinds of forces in one or two kinds of places is as absurd as it was to imagine that the last wars could be avoided by an armament race or by endless conferences about whether the armor plate permitted on a battleship should be reduced by one-quarter or one-eighth of an inch.

And what shall we do with ourselves if we do survive? We have almost reached the 36-hour week, and as automation and atomic energy are brought into industrial use the proportion of our time that we shall have to devote to earning a living will decline still further. In my lifetime the hours of labor have been cut by a third. We don't know what to do with ourselves now. Some think that there is no limit to the capacity and willingness of people to seek and enjoy entertainment, relaxation, and recreation. I do not believe it. It is more likely that the alternatives presented by modern technology are either that we shall all be killed or we shall all be bored to death.

There are two ways to get through life that the educated person cannot permit himself, and they are to fill the time with aimless, and hence thoughtless activity, or to sink into a vegetable torpor. The reasons why these pastimes fail is that neither one is human. Every human being sooner or later has to feel that there is some meaning to his life. He must have a purpose.

You must think for your own sake, and also for your country's. We can be contented with nothing less for this nation than that it should cherish the best things there are. It seems altogether likely that these are art and education, freedom and justice, courage and compassion—the things the ancients summed up under the three heads of truth, beauty, and goodness. And what are these but the fullest development of man's highest powers in their individual and social aspects?

Let us remember that there have been dark days in the past. There was a famous one in New England in 1780 when the sun scarcely appeared at all. Thousands of people took it for the end of the world. Among them were many in the Connecticut Assembly, in which Colonel Abraham Davenport was sitting. It was proposed that the Assembly adjourn. Colonel Davenport said, "The Day of Judgment is either approaching or it is not. If it is not, there is no cause for adjournment. If it is, I choose to be found doing my duty. I wish therefore that candles may be brought."

SUSANNE K. LANGER

•

Language and Thought[1]

A symbol is not the same thing as a sign; that is a fact that psychologists and philosophers often overlook. All intelligent animals use signs; so do we. To them as well as to us sounds and smells and motions are signs of food, danger, the presence of other beings, or of rain or storm. Furthermore, some animals not only attend to signs but produce them for the benefit of others. Dogs bark at the door to be let in; rabbits thump to call each other; the cooing of doves and the growl of a wolf defending his kill are unequivocal signs of feelings and intentions to be reckoned with by other creatures.

We use signs just as animals do, though with considerably more elaboration. We stop at red lights and go on green; we answer calls and bells, watch the sky for coming storms, read trouble or promise or anger in each other's eyes. That is animal intelligence raised to the human level. Those of us who are dog lovers can probably all tell wonderful stories of how high our dogs have sometimes risen in the scale of clever sign interpretation and sign using.

A sign is anything that announces the existence or the imminence of some event, the presence of a thing or a person, or a change in a state of affairs. There are signs of the weather, signs of danger, signs of future good or evil, signs of what the past has been. In every case a sign is closely bound up with something to be noted or expected in experience. It is always a part of the situation to which it refers, though the reference may be remote in space and time. In so far as we are led to note or expect the signified event we are making correct use of a sign. This is the essence of rational behavior, which animals show in varying degrees. It is entirely realistic, being closely bound up with the actual objective course of history—learned by experience, and cashed in or voided by further experience.

[1] From Susanne K. Langer, "The Lord of Creation." Reprinted from the January 1944 issue of *Fortune* Magazine by special permission of the Editors. Copyright, 1944, Time, Inc.

If man had kept to the straight and narrow path of sign using, he would be like the other animals, though perhaps a little brighter. He would not talk, but grunt and gesticulate and point. He would make his wishes known, give warnings, perhaps develop a social system like that of bees and ants, with such a wonderful efficiency of communal enterprise that all men would have plenty to eat, warm apartments—all exactly alike and perfectly convenient—to live in, and everybody could and would sit in the sun or by the fire, as the climate demanded, not talking but just basking, with every want satisfied, most of his life. The young would romp and make love, the old would sleep, the middle-aged would do the routine work almost unconsciously and eat a great deal. But that would be the life of a social, superintelligent, purely sign-using animal.

To us who are human, it does not sound very glorious. We want to go places and do things, own all sorts of gadgets that we do not absolutely need, and when we sit down to take it easy we want to talk. Rights and property, social position, special talents and virtues, and above all our ideas, are what we live for. We have gone off on a tangent that takes us far away from the mere biological cycle that animal generations accomplish; and that is because we can use not only signs but symbols.

A symbol differs from a sign in that it does not announce the presence of the object, the being, condition, or whatnot, which is its meaning, but merely *brings this thing to mind*. It is not a mere "substitute sign" to which we react as though it were the object itself. The fact is that our reaction to hearing a person's name is quite different from our reaction to the person himself. There are certain rare cases where a symbol stands directly for its meaning: in religious experience, for instance, the Host is not only a symbol but a Presence. But symbols in the ordinary sense are not mystic. They are the same sort of thing that ordinary signs are; only they do not call our attention to something necessarily present or to be physically dealt with—they call up merely a conception of the thing they "mean."

The difference between a sign and a symbol is, in brief, that a sign causes us to think or act *in face of* the thing signified, whereas a symbol causes us to think *about* the thing symbolized. Therein lies the great importance of symbolism for human life, its power to make this life so different from any other animal biography that generations of men have found it incredible to suppose that they were of purely zoological origin. A sign is always embedded in reality, in a present that emerges from the actual past and stretches to the future; but a symbol may be divorced from reality altogether. It may refer to what is *not* the case, to a mere idea, a figment, a dream. It serves, therefore, to liberate thought from the immediate stimuli of a physically present world; and that liberation marks the essential difference between human and nonhuman mentality. Animals think, but they think *of* and *at* things; men think primarily *about* things. Words, pictures, and memory images are symbols that may be combined and varied in a thousand ways. The result is a symbolic structure whose meaning is a complex of all their respective meanings, and this kaleidoscope of *ideas* is the typical product of the human brain that we call the "stream of thought."

The process of transforming all direct experience into imagery or into that supreme mode of symbolic expression, language, has so completely taken possession of the human mind that it is not only a special talent but a dominant, organic need. All our sense impressions leave their traces in our memory not only as signs disposing our practical reactions in the future but also as symbols, images representing our *ideas* of things; and the tendency to manipulate ideas, to combine and abstract, mix and extend them by playing with symbols, is man's outstanding characteristic. It seems to be what his brain most naturally and spontaneously does. Therefore his primitive mental function is not judging reality, but *dreaming his desires.*

Dreaming is apparently a basic function of human brains, for it is free and unexhausting like our metabolism, heartbeat, and breath. It is easier to dream than not to dream, as it is easier to breathe than to refrain from breathing. The symbolic character of dreams is fairly well established. Symbol mongering, on this ineffectual, uncritical level, seems to be instinctive, the fulfillment of an elementary need rather than the purposeful exercise of a high and difficult talent.

The special power of man's mind rests on the evolution of this special activity, not on any transcendently high development of animal intelligence. We are not immeasurably higher than other animals; we are different. We have a biological need and with it a biological gift that they do not share.

Because man has not only the ability but the constant need of *conceiving* what has happened to him, what surrounds him, what is demanded of him—in short, of symbolizing nature, himself, and his hopes and fears—he has a constant and crying need of *expression.* What he cannot express, he cannot conceive; what he cannot conceive is chaos, and fills him with terror.

If we bear in mind this all-important craving for expression we get a new picture of man's behavior; for from this trait spring his powers and his weaknesses. The process of symbolic transformation that all our experiences undergo is nothing more nor less than the process of *conception,* which underlies the human faculties of abstraction and imagination.

When we are faced with a strange or difficult situation, we cannot react directly, as other creatures do, with flight, aggression, or any such simple instinctive pattern. Our whole reaction depends on how we manage to conceive the situation—whether we cast it in a definite dramatic form, whether we see it as a disaster, a challenge, a fulfillment of doom, or a fiat of the Divine Will. In words or dreamlike images, in artistic or religious or even in cynical form, we must *construe* the events of life. There is great virtue in the figure of speech, "I can *make* nothing of it," to express a failure to understand something. Thought and memory are processes of *making* the thought content and the memory image; the pattern of our ideas is given by the symbols through which we express them. And in the course of manipulating those symbols we inevitably distort the original experience, as we abstract certain features of it, embroider and reinforce those features with other ideas, until the conception we project on the screen of memory is quite different from anything in our real history.

Conception is a necessary and elementary process; what we do with our conceptions is another story. That is the entire history of human culture—of intelligence and morality, folly and superstition, ritual, language, and the arts—all the phenomena that set man apart from, and above, the rest of the animal kingdom. As the religious mind has to make all human history a drama of sin and salvation in order to define its own moral attitudes, so a scientist wrestles with the mere presentation of "the facts" before he can reason about them. The process of *envisaging* facts, values, hopes, and fears underlies our whole behavior pattern; and this process is reflected in the evolution of an extraordinary phenomenon found always, and only, in human societies—the phenomenon of language.

Language is the highest and most amazing achievement of the symbolistic human mind. The power it bestows is almost inestimable, for without it anything properly called "thought" is impossible. The birth of language is the dawn of humanity. The line between man and beast—between the highest ape and the lowest savage—is the language line. Whether the primitive Neanderthal man was anthropoid or human depends less on his cranial capacity, his upright posture, or even his use of tools and fire, than on one issue we shall probably never be able to settle—whether or not he spoke.

In all physical traits and practical responses, such as skills and visual judgments, we can find a certain continuity between animal and human mentality. Sign using is an ever evolving, ever improving function throughout the whole animal kingdom, from the lowly worm that shrinks into his hole at the sound of an approaching foot, to the dog obeying his master's command, and even to the learned scientist who watches the movements of an index needle.

This continuity of the sign-using talent has led psychologists to the belief that language is evolved from the vocal expressions, grunts and coos and cries, whereby animals vent their feelings or signal their fellows; that man has elaborated this sort of communion to the point where it makes a perfect exchange of ideas possible.

I do not believe that this doctrine of the origin of language is correct. The essence of language is symbolic, not signific; we use it first and most vitally to formulate and hold ideas in our own minds. Conception, not social control, is its first and foremost benefit.

Watch a young child that is just learning to speak play with a toy; he says the name of the object, e.g.: "Horsey! horsey! horsey!" over and over again, looks at the object, moves it, always saying the name to himself or to the world at large. It's quite a time before he talks to anyone in particular; he talks first of all to himself. This is his way of forming and fixing the *conception* of the object in his mind, and around this conception all his knowledge of it grows. *Names* are the essence of language; for the *name* is what abstracts the conception of the horse from the horse itself, and lets the mere idea recur at the speaking of the name. This permits the conception gathered from one horse experience to be exemplified again by another instance of a horse, so that the notion embodied in the name is a general notion.

To this end, the baby uses a word long before he *asks* for the object; when he wants his horsey he is likely to cry and fret, because he is reacting to an actual environment, not forming ideas. He uses the animal language of *signs* for his wants; talking is still a purely symbolic process—its practical value has not really impressed him yet.

Language need not be vocal; it may be purely visual, like written language, or even tactual, like the deaf-mute system of speech; but it *must be denotative*. The sounds, intended or unintended, whereby animals communicate do not constitute a language, because they are signs, not names. They never fall into an organic pattern, a meaningful syntax of even the most rudimentary sort, as all language seems to do with a sort of driving necessity. That is because signs refer to actual situations, in which things have obvious relations to each other that require only to be noted; but symbols refer to ideas, which are not physically there for inspection, so their connections and features have to be represented. This gives all true language a natural tendency toward growth and development, which seems almost like a life of its own. Languages are not invented; they grow with our need for expression.

In contrast, animal "speech" never has a structure. It is merely an emotional response. Apes may greet their ration of yams with a shout of "Nga!" But they do not say "Nga" between meals. If they could *talk about* their yams instead of just saluting them, they would be the most primitive men instead of the most anthropoid of beasts. They would have ideas, and tell each other things true or false, rational or irrational; they would make plans and invent laws and sing their own praises, as men do.

VED MEHTA

•

[A Thinker: Wittgenstein][1]

After saying goodbye to Hampshire, I returned to John's rooms and took from the shelf "Ludwig Wittgenstein: A Memoir," by Norman Malcolm, with a prefatory biographical sketch by Professor Georg Henrik von Wright, of the University of Helsinki. Because each meeting with a philosopher had

[1] From *Fly and the Fly-Bottle,* by Ved Mehta, by permission of Atlantic-Little, Brown and Co. The material in this book originated, in 1961 and 1962, in *The New Yorker.*

made me more curious about Wittgenstein, I set myself the task of finding out more about him.

Ludwig Josef Johann Wittgenstein was born in 1889. His parents were Saxon, but at the time of his birth they were living in Vienna. His paternal grandfather was a convert from Judaism to Protestantism; his mother, however, was a Catholic, and the child was baptized in her faith. His father was an engineer, whose remarkable intelligence and will power had raised him to a leading position in the steel-and-iron industry of the Austro-Hungarian Empire. Ludwig was one of eight children. Both of his parents were extremely musical, and their home was a center of artistic activity. He received his early education at home, learning mathematics and the clarinet, and acquiring a burning boyhood wish to become a conductor. At fourteen, he was sent to a school in Linz, and after three years there he was ready for the engineering course at the Technische Hochschule in Berlin. He completed his Berlin course in two years and went to England, where he registered at the University of Manchester as a research student. His first step on the path of philosophy was the reading of Bertrand Russell's "Principles of Mathematics," published in 1903, to which he turned when he wished to plumb the foundations of mathematics. After Russell, he read Gottlob Frege, the German mathematician, thus coming face to face with the two most brilliant exponents of the "new" logic. He sought out Frege in Jena, only to be directed by him to go back to England and study with Russell. By 1912, he was housed in Trinity College, Cambridge, whose walls also enclosed Bertrand Russell, G. E. Moore, and John Maynard Keynes. Young Wittgenstein was immediately befriended by them, and he found himself part of the golden years of Cambridge. He was there for eighteen months, and in addition to his other work, did some psychological experiments in rhythm and music. Even though he was on intimate terms with the leading minds of England, he did not take to the relaxed atmosphere of Cambridge life. In the autumn of 1913, he visited Norway, and he returned there later that same year in a sort of intellectual huff, to live in seclusion near Skjolden; he soon became fluent in Norwegian. His father had died in 1912, and his stay at Manchester and Cambridge had simply driven him deeper into a depression whose history was as long as his life. "It is probably true that he lived on the border of mental illness," Professor von Wright says at the opening of his sketch. "A fear of being driven across it followed him throughout his life." The outbreak of the First World War found him a volunteer in the Austrian Army, and he eventually fought on both the eastern and southern fronts. For Wittgenstein, war was a time of personal crisis and of the birth of great ideas. At one moment he was calmed by Leo Tolstoy's ethical writings—which led him to the warm light of the Synoptic Gospels—and at the next he was excited by his own revolutionary views.

Wittgenstein's earthquake hit the philosophers of the twentieth century as hard as David Hume's cyclone—which swept away cause and effect from the human experience—had hit their eighteenth-century predecessors. The new philosophical shudder started at the Austrian front. One day in the middle of the war, while Wittgenstein was reading a newspaper in a trench, he was arrested by a sketch of a possible sequence of events in a car accident. As he studied it, he became aware that the diagram of the accident stood for a possible pattern of occurrences in reality; there was a correspondence between the parts of the drawing and certain things in the world. He noticed a similar correspondence between the parts of a sentence and elements of the world, and he developed the analogy, coming to regard a proposition as a kind of picture. The structure of a proposition—that is, the way in which the parts of a statement were combined—depicted a possible combination of elements in reality. Thus he hit upon the central idea of his "Tractatus": Language was the picture of the world. The "Tractatus" and the Wittgenstein revolution in philosophy were under way.

When Wittgenstein was captured by the Italians, in 1918, he had the manuscript of his first great philosophical work in his rucksack, and he was able to bring it through the war intact. He thought his masterpiece had solved all philosophical problems, and when the work was published (first in Germany, in 1921, and then in England, the following year), some leading minds agreed, with him, that philosophy had come to the end of its road. Wittgenstein, on the other hand, was at the beginning of his. Both his livelihood and his reputation were assured. He had inherited a large fortune from his father, his genius was proclaimed to the world, and he was free to live in leisure and intellectual preëminence. But such safe ways were not those of Ludwig Wittgenstein. In the first year after the war, he renounced his fortune, became indifferent to the success of the "Tractatus," and enrolled in a teachers' college in Vienna. When he had completed his education course, he taught in schools in Lower Austria for six years, wandering from one remote village to another. Being a schoolmaster enabled him to lead a life of simplicity and seclusion, but Wittgenstein was not at peace with himself or the world. He gave up the profession and for a time became a gardener, working mostly at monasteries, and, as he had done in the past, considered joining a religious order. Once more, however, the monastic life did not seem to be the answer. Terminating his restless wanderings, he returned to Vienna, and spent two solid years designing and constructing a mansion for one of his sisters. A modern building of concrete, steel, and glass, it provided an outlet for his particular architectural genius, and according to Professor von Wright, "Its beauty is of the same simple and static kind that belongs to the sentences of the 'Tractatus.' " But architecture could not contain Wittgenstein's soaring genius, and he spent some time sculpturing at a friend's studio. Again according to Professor von Wright, his sculpture of an elf has a perfection of symmetry that recalls the Greeks. Wittgenstein's period of withdrawal from philosophy was now nearing an end. In Vienna, he heard a philosophical lecture and decided that perhaps philosophy did have a little way to go, so he allowed his old friend Keynes to raise some money for his return to Cambridge. He arrived at his college in 1929, and presented his "Tractatus" as a dissertation for a Doctorate of Philosophy—a degree that was a negligible accolade to a philosopher with a worldwide reputation. A year later, at the age of forty-one, he was elected a Fellow of Trinity College, Cambridge.

As suddenly as a sketch of a car accident had inspired the ideas in "Tractatus," so a gesture of an Italian friend destroyed them. The gesture that divided Wittgenstein I from Wittgenstein II was made sometime in the year 1933. "Wittgenstein and P. Sraffa, a lecturer in economics at Cambridge, argued together a great deal over the ideas of the 'Tractatus,'" Professor Malcolm records. "One day (they were riding, I think, on a train), when Wittgenstein was insisting that a proposition and that which it describes must have the same 'logical form,' the same 'logical multiplicity,' Sraffa made a gesture, familiar to Neapolitans as meaning something like disgust or contempt, of brushing the underneath of his chin with an outward sweep of the fingertips of one hand. And he asked: 'What is the logical form of that?' Sraffa's example produced in Wittgenstein the feeling that there was an absurdity in the insistence that a proposition and what it describes must have the same 'form.' This broke the hold on him of the conception that a proposition must literally be a 'picture' of the reality it describes." It was many years before Wittgenstein II worked out his new ideas, but the old views, which at one time had finished philosophy forever, were discarded in the train.

Wittgenstein II, though he spent thirteen years at Cambridge, did not surround himself with any of the atmosphere of an English college. The stark simplicity of his way of living would have put any undergraduate to shame. His two rooms in Whewell's Court were like barracks; he did not have a single book, painting, photograph, or reading lamp. He sat on a wooden chair and did his writing at a card table. These two objects, with two canvas chairs, a fireproof safe for his manuscripts, and a few empty flowerpots, constituted the total furnishings of the room that served him as both study and classroom. His other concession to life was a cot, in the second room.

His classes were held late in the afternoon, and his pupils arrived carrying chairs from the landing. They always found the philosopher standing in the middle of the room, by his wooden chair. He was slender, of medium height, and simply dressed, habitually wearing a flannel shirt, flannel trousers, a leather jacket, and no tie. Unlike the other Fellows, he did not have any notes or set procedure for his lectures; he just sat on his wooden chair and, according to Malcolm, "carried on a visible struggle with his thoughts." His lectures were simply a continuation of his other waking hours; as always, he thought about problems and tried to find new solutions. The principal difference between his lonely hours and the lecture time was the difference between a monologue and a dialogue. He would direct questions to the members of the class and let himself be drawn into discussions, but whenever he sensed that he was standing on the edge of a difficult problem or a new thought, his hand would silence his interlocutor with a peremptory motion. If he reached an impasse or felt confused, he would say, "I'm just too stupid today," or "You have a dreadful teacher," or "I'm a fool." He worried about the possibility that his teaching might stop the growth of independent minds, and he was also besieged by a fear that he would not be able to last the period, but somehow he always managed to go on.

The years of the Second World War found Wittgenstein working as an orderly, first at Guy's Hospital, in London, and then in an infirmary at Newcastle-upon-Tyne. Toward the close of the war, he returned to Cambridge to take up the Chair of Philosophy. When Malcolm returned there to study with him, in 1946, he found Wittgenstein trying, with strenuous work, to dam the depression that always threatened to flood him. Wittgenstein was composing his "Philosophical Investigations" (which he kept on revising for the rest of his life). "One day," Malcolm recounts, "when Wittgenstein was passing a field where a football game was in progress, the thought first struck him that in language we play *games* with *words*. A central idea of his philosophy [in 'Investigations"], the notion of a 'language game,' apparently had its genesis in this incident." At this time, most of his day was spent in teaching, talking, and writing the "Investigations." His only relief from the constant motion of his thoughts was an occasional film or an American detective magazine. But this was no opiate, and he ultimately felt compelled to tender his resignation to the Vice-Chancellor of the university. Late in 1947, when the decision was taken, he wrote to Malcolm, "I shall cease to be professor on Dec. 31st at 12 P.M." He did. Now began the loneliest period of his never convivial life. He first moved to a guesthouse a couple of hours' bus ride from Dublin, where he lived friendless and in a state of nervous instability. He tired easily, and his work on "Investigations" went slowly and painfully. He wrote to Malcolm that he did not miss conversation but wished for "someone to smile at occasionally." After five months at the guesthouse, he migrated to the west coast of Ireland, where he became a legend among the primitive fishermen for his power to tame birds. But there was no rest for him. He went to Vienna, visited Cambridge, returned to Dublin, rushed again to Vienna, where a sister was now dangerously ill, proceeded from there to America to see the Malcolms, and was forced back to England and Cambridge by an undiagnosed illness. He was eventually found to have cancer. His father had been destroyed by this disease, and his sister was even then dying of it. He left for Austria and his family, but some months later he returned to England—this time to Oxford, which he quickly came to dislike. He called it "the influenza area" and "a philosophical desert." After spending some time at Miss Anscombe's house in Oxford, he visited Norway, only to return to Cambridge and live with his doctor. Never a happy man, he became convinced during the last two years of his life that he had lost his philosophical talent; he was also haunted by the suicides of three of his brothers. He died in April, 1951.

I read the last paragraph of Malcolm's memoir: "When I think of his profound pessimism, the intensity of his mental and moral suffering, the relentless way in which he drove his intellect, his need for love together with the harshness that repelled love, I am inclined to believe that his life was fiercely unhappy. Yet at the end he himself exclaimed that it had been 'wonderful!' To me this seems a mysterious and strangely moving utterance."

When John returned, he found me in a sombre mood.

"Yes," he said. "Wittgenstein was a tortured genius. He could have been a first-class conductor, mathematician, architect, or sculptor, but he chose to be a philosopher." He started leafing through "A Memoir," and read aloud: " 'A person caught in a philosophical confusion is like a man in a room who wants to get out but doesn't know how. He tries the window but it is too high. He tries the chimmey but it is too narrow. And if he would only *turn around,* he would see that the door has been open all the time!' "

To both of us, this particular passage seemed to stand as an epitaph for Ludwig Wittgenstein.

Next morning, I rolled out of my makeshift bed and, with the help of my jottings, started writing furiously the conclusions of my researches. To my great surprise, complicated sentences streamed out of my typewriter and I discovered that I had a philosophical voice keyed somehow to the right pitch.

"Modern philosophy," I wrote, "has had two great pushes, one from Russell and one from Wittgenstein, and we're now waiting for another one. Like all philosophies, its claim to be heard rests on two assumptions: first, that what it says is true and lucid; second, that these particular truths are more satisfying than any alternative answers to the inquiring and reflective mind. Naturally, not all reflective minds will be better satisfied at Oxford than, say, in Paris, Moscow, New Delhi, or New York, but some clearly are. Oxford philosophers do not claim to be sages. In few cases, indeed, would the claim be credited if it should be made. By their own admission, they are not wiser than other men. They often assert that their researches do not lead to wisdom but only relieve certain feelings of puzzlement (which you are bound to have if you ask their questions). Once they have found answers to their questions, they go on living just as before, and, unlike their French contemporaries, many remain *dégagé;* they lead dons' comfortable lives in north Oxford (though even so a few manage to be evangelists, Socialists, or great eccentrics). This had led Gellner to ask what the point of their activities can be, since they seem to cure only a disease they have induced in themselves and, in many cases, in their students. Why should one pay philosophers, he asks, if philosophy really, as Wittgenstein said, 'leaves the world as it is'? Gellner's is a mistaken objection.

Certainly many philosophers are unadventurous, prosaic, and boring, but there are also Strawsons and Ayers and plenty of others who are not. Whatever they may do in their private lives, it cannot correctly be said that in their work they 'leave the world as it is.' If one man begins to see more clearly how the *rest* of the world is, then the world is not as it was. One man sees more truth than was seen in the past; the more widely this truth is disseminated, the more the world is changed. Indeed, once one considers this, Gellner's criticism seems absurd. For philosophy has never changed the world except by bringing to consciousness in the minds that engage in it certain truths that they did not know (or did not know clearly) before. Oxford philosophers are fond of quoting a remark of Wittgenstein's to the effect that there need be nothing in common among all the members of a class of things called by the same name. If we must generalize about the Oxford philosophers and their subject, their philosophy is essentially agnostic, not in respect to the question of God's existence but in relation to many of the great problems whose definitive solution has in the past been taken as the aim of philosophy: questions like whether life is meaningful, whether history has a purpose, whether human nature is good—in fact, all the questions that have to be asked when a man reflectively considers the question 'How should I live?' It is true that most Oxford philosophers are not agnostic in religion; on the contrary, several are Catholic or Protestant communicants. But they regard these matters as being outside their philosophy. As men, they decide to answer these questions in one way; as philosophers, they teach and develop techniques that are neutral in respect to the different answers to them.

"Oxford philosophers tend to talk chiefly to each other—and, in cases like Wittgenstein's, to themselves. These practitioners are highly technical (even if they claim they make a 'technique of being non-technical'). There are exceptions: Ayer is one; another is Hampshire, who on some subjects—especially literary subjects, as opposed to philosophical ones—succeeds in being illuminating to the simple. Still, most of the philosophers go on thinking that technical philosophy is a good thing, necessary in order to keep the subject from 'popularization,' which they interpret as oversimplification or quackery. The pity is that their insistence on professionalism means that 'ordinary men' are left not without any philosophy at all but with old, dead, or quack varieties of it. Oxford philosophy, by comparison with the past, is non-systematic. Where traditional practitioners thought it right to deal with questions like 'What is Truth?' Oxford philosophers are liable to say, following the later Wittgenstein, 'Look at all the different ways the word "true" is used in ordinary speech.' (They refuse to look into the uses of words in extraordinary speech, like poetry because English philosophy has been dominated since Hume by a prosaic contempt for the imagination.) When you have considered all the ways 'true' is used in ordinary speech, they say, you have understood the concept of 'Truth.' If there is a further question lingering at the back of your mind ('But all the same, what *is* Truth?'), this is the result of a mistake—a hangover from reading earlier philosophers. This approach—philosophy as the study of language rather than as the means of answering the big questions about life and the universe—which is basically that of the later Wittgenstein, has given Oxford philosophy a tendency to formlessness. Until recently, the body of philosophical thought has existed mainly in a vast number of small articles minutely considering a few uses of some single concept. Only the aesthetic sense of some of its practitioners—Wittgenstein I, Ayer, Hampshire, Strawson, and a few others—has kept it from overwhelming diffuseness.

"Now there is a change coming. The Oxford school is breaking up; all the signs are that there isn't going to be an orthodoxy much longer—that things are going to get eccentric again. Austin is no more, and at the moment Ryle is not producing. Strawson is going in for talking about metaphysics in the old vein, and there is every indication that the Wittgenstein wave is petering out rather rapidly. In the ten years since Ryle tried to solve the mind-body problem by a vast number of small chapters on different psychological concepts in 'The Concept of Mind,' Oxford philosophy has begun to develop its own system builders. Probably the strict discipline of the late Austin helped induce guilt about the looseness and untidiness that these uncoördinated researches—each one precise and tidy—were creating in the subject as a whole. Two recent books, Hampshire's 'Thought and Action' and Strawson's 'Individuals,' offer quite systematic approaches to some of the most puzzling traditional problems in philosophy: the value of freedom of thought and the relation of intelligence to morality, in the first; the problem of sense data and the mind-body puzzle, in the second. The new systematic quality comes from a recent insight: that while linguistic philosophy is the study of language, certain wider truths *can* be deduced from the conditions that must be presupposed if there is to be language at all—or language of the kind we have. On propositions deduced from the statement of such conditions, necessary truths (like the relation between the mind and the body) can be built systematically. The non-systematic decades may have been an aberration—partly, no doubt, owing to the tendency of philosophers to imitate Wittgenstein II and his stylistic lapses from the poetic and architectural sensibility he displayed in the 'Tractatus.' As Shakespeare said of the pedants in 'Love's Labour's Lost,' 'They have been at a great feast of languages, and stolen the scraps. O! they have lived long on the alms-basket of words.' But then, as the proverb, more than two thousand years old, has it, 'Those that study particular sciences and neglect philosophy'—however defined and however studied—'are like Penelope's wooers, who made love to the waiting-women.' "

These sentences were no sooner out of my typewriter than they seemed to have been written by a stranger. Reading them over, I couldn't shake loose the feeling that they were one more walker on the common street where on a morning stroll I'd first met Lord Russell.

HUBERT L. DREYFUS

•

Do Computers Think?[1]

It is fitting to begin with a statement made in 1957 by H. A. Simon, one of the originators of the field of artificial intelligence:

> It is not my aim to surprise or shock you. . . . But the simplest way I can summarize is to say that there are now in the world machines that think, that learn and that create. Moreover, their ability to do these things is going to increase rapidly until—in a visible future—the range of problems they can handle will be coextensive with the range to which the human mind has been applied.

The speaker predicts:

1) That within ten years a digital computer will be the world's chess champion.
2) That within ten years a digital computer will discover and prove an important mathematical theorem.

We do not have time to go into the deliberate confusions surrounding the supposed proof of an important theorem. Suffice it to say that to date no important or even original theorem has been proved. We will, however, follow the chess-playing story in some detail since it might well serve as a model for the production of intellectual smog in this area. In 1958, a year after his prediction, Simon presented an elaborate chess-playing program. As described in his classic paper, "Chess Playing and the Problem of Complexity," his program was "not yet fully debugged," so that one "cannot say very much about the behavior of the program." Still, it is clearly "good in the opening." This is the last detailed published report on the program. In the same year, however, Simon announced: "We have written a program that plays chess."

In fact, in its few recorded games, the Simon program played poor but legal chess, and in its last bout (October, 1960) was beaten in 35 moves by a ten-year-old novice. Fact, however, had ceased to be relevant. Simon's claims concerning his still bugged program had launched the chess machine into the

[1] Copyright 1967 by Hubert L. Dreyfus. Reprinted from the Proceedings of the Society for Phenomenology and Existential Philosophy, Quadrangle Press, 1967. Delivered under the title, "Phenomenology and Artificial Intelligence," at the Fourth Annual Meeting of the Society for Phenomenology and Existential Philosophy. Research for this paper was sponsored by the Rand Corp. and a more detailed analysis of the philosophical problems raised by artificial intelligence appears as Rand Paper P-3244.

realm of scientific mythology. In 1959, Norbert Weiner, whose optimism was strengthened by the claim that the program was "good in the opening," informed the N.Y.U. Institute of Philosophy that "chess-playing machines as of now will counter the moves of a master game with the moves recognized as right in the textbooks, up to some point in the middle game." In the same symposium, Michael Scriven moved from the ambiguous claim that machines play chess to the claim that "machines are already capable of a good game."

While his program was losing its five or six poor games—and the myth he had engendered was holding its own against masters in the middle game—Simon kept silent. When he speaks again, three years later, he does not report his difficulties and disappointments; rather, as if to take up where the myth had left off, Simon published an article in *Behavioral Science* announcing a program which will play "highly creative" chess end games involving "combinations as difficult as any that have been recorded in chess history." That the program restricts these end games to dependence on continuing checks, so that the number of relevant moves is greatly reduced, is mentioned but not emphasized. On the contrary, it is misleadingly implied that similar simple procedures would account for master play even in the middle game.

Thus, the article gives the impression that the chess prediction is almost realized, and indeed, with such progress, the chess championship may be *claimed* at any moment. This output of confusion makes one think of a French mythical beast which is supposed to secrete the fog necessary for its own respiration.

Equally unjustified claims have been made in the areas of problem solving and pattern recognition, but we do not have time to examine them here. For our discussion it will be more instructive to concentrate on the area that had the earliest success, the most publicity, the most extensive and expensive research, and the most unequivocal failure: the field of language translation.

It was clear from the start that a mechanical dictionary could easily be constructed in which linguistic items, whether they be parts of words, whole words, or groups of words, could be processed independently and converted one after another into corresponding items in another language. This initial success and the subsequent disillusionment provides a sort of paradigm for the field. It is aptly described by Bar-Hillel in his report on "The Present Status of Automatic Translation of Languages."

> During the first year of the research in machine translation, a considerable amount of progress was made. . . . It created among many of the workers actively engaged in this field the strong feeling that a working system was just around the corner. Though it is understandable that such an illusion should have been formed at the time, it was an illusion. It was created . . . by the fact that a large number of problems were rather readily solved. . . . It was not sufficiently realized that the gap between such output . . . and high quality translation proper was still enormous, and that the problems solved until then were indeed many but just the simplest ones whereas the "few" remaining problems were the harder ones—very hard indeed.

During the ten years since the development of a mechanical dictionary, five government agencies have spent about 16 million dollars on mechanical translation research. In spite of journalistic claims at various moments that machine translation was at last operational, this research produced primarily a much deeper knowledge of the unsuspected complexity of syntax and semantics. As Anthony Oettinger of the Harvard Computation Laboratory remarks, "the major problem of selecting an appropriate target correspondent for a source word on the basis of context remains unsolved, as does the related one of establishing a unique syntactic structure for a sentence that human readers find unambiguous." Oettinger concludes: "The outlook is grim for those who still cherish hopes for fully automatic high-quality mechanical translation."

Once we cease to be intimidated by false claims of computer progress, we can recover some of our common sense skepticism and our philosophical doubts. We can even begin to see the early success and later failures characteristic of work in the field of artificial intelligence as just what phenomenologists and existentialists might have expected. We will now consider in more detail the ease and the difficulties encountered in trying to develop chess-playing and language-translating programs, and draw out their psychological and metaphysical implications. . . .

It is necessary first to say a word about computers. I am not trying to argue in this paper that *no* computer could engender intelligent behavior. It seems obvious to common sense that at least one computer, viz. the brain, does engender such behavior. What I am trying to argue here is that such behavior cannot be exhibited by a certain kind of computer: the digital computer which is the only high-speed, all-purpose, information-processing device which we know how to design at present, and therefore the device on which all work in artificial intelligence has been and must be done. The fundamental characteristic of the digital computer which concerns us here is that all information with which it operates must be represented in binary bits, i.e., in terms of a series of yeses or noes, of switches being open or closed. The significance of this condition will become apparent in the following.

I. The Chess Program: Horizonal Consciousness vs. Heuristically Guided Search

It is common knowledge that a certain class of games is decidable on present-day computers with present-day techniques—games like nim and tic-tac-toe can be programmed so that the machine will win or draw every time. Other games, however, cannot be decided in this way on present-day computers, and yet have been successfully programmed. In checkers, for example, because only two kinds of moves are possible, the captures forced, and pieces block each other, one can explore all possibilities to a depth of as many as twenty moves, which proves sufficient for playing a good game.

Chess, too, is in principle decidable, but chess presents the problem inevitably connected with very large choice mazes: exponential growth. We cannot run through all the branching possibilities far enough even to form a reliable judgment as to whether a given branch is sufficiently promising to merit further exploration. The right heuristics are supposed to limit the number of branches explored while retaining the more promising alternatives. However, no such heuristics have as yet been found. All current heuristics either exclude some possibly good moves or leave open the risk of exponential growth.

Simon is nonetheless convinced that minds work like digital computers, and since people find chess moves in reasonably short times they must be using heuristics. He is confident that if we listen to the reports of chess masters, follow their eye movements, perhaps question them under bright lights, we will eventually be able to discover these heuristics and build them into our program —thereby pruning the exponential tree. But let us examine more closely the evidence that chess playing is governed by the use of heuristics.

Consider the following report quoted by Simon, noting especially how it begins rather than how it ends. The player says, "Again I notice that one of his pieces is not defended, the Rook, and there must be ways of taking advantage of this. Suppose now, if I push the pawn up at Bishop four, if the Bishop retreats I have a Queen check and I can pick up the Rook. If, etc., etc." At the end we have an example of what I shall call "counting out"—thinking through the various possibilities by brute-force enumeration. We have all engaged in this process, which, guided by suitable heuristics, is supposed to account for the performances of chess masters. But how did our subject notice the opponent's Rook was undefended? Did he examine each of his opponent's pieces and their possible defenders sequentially (or simultaneously) until he stumbled on the vulnerable Rook?

We need not appeal to introspection to discover what a player in fact does before he begins to count out; the report itself indicates it: the subject "zeroes in" on the promising situation. Only *after* the player has zeroed in on an area does he begin to count out, to test, what he can do from there.

The player need not be aware of having explicitly considered or explicitly excluded from consideration any of the hundreds of possibilities that would have had to be enumerated in order to have arrived at this particular area by counting out. Still, the specific portion of the board which finally attracts the subject's attention depends on the overall configuration. . . . Such a phenomenon has been systematically studied by Husserl in his account of perceptual horizons. Polanyi aptly describes this horizon:

> Seen thus from the corner of our eyes, or remembered at the back of our mind, this area compellingly affects the way we see the object on which we are focusing. We may indeed go so far as to say that we are aware of this subsidiarily noticed area mainly in the appearance of the object to which we are attending.

If information, rather than being explicitly considered, can remain on the fringes of consciousness and be implicitly taken into account through its effect on the appearance of the objects on which our attention is focused, then there is no reason to suppose that, in order to discover an undefended Rook, our subject must have counted out rapidly and unconsciously until he arrived at the area in which he began consciously counting out. Moreover, there are good reasons to reject this assumption, since it raises more problems than it resolves.

If the subject has been unconsciously counting out thousands of alternatives with brilliant heuristics to get to the point where he focuses on that Rook, why doesn't he carry on with that unconscious process all the way to the end, until the best move just pops into his consciousness? Why, if the *unconscious* counting is rapid and accurate, does he resort at the particular point where he spots the Rook to a cumbersome method of slowly, awkwardly, and consciously counting things out? Or if, on the other hand, the unconscious counting is *inadequate,* what is the advantage of switching to a conscious version of the same process?

Moreover, even if he does unconsciously count out, using unconscious heuristics—which there is no reason to suppose and good reason to doubt—what kind of program could convert this unconscious counting into the kind of fringe-influenced awareness of the centers of interest, which is the way zeroing-in presents itself in our experience? It seems that "unconsciously" he is engaged in a sort of information processing which differs from counting out and that conscious counting begins when he has to refine this global process in order to deal with details.

This distinction between zeroing-in and counting-out clarifies the early success and the later failure of work in artificial intelligence. In all game-playing programs, early success is attained by working on those games or parts of games in which counting-out is feasible; failure occurs when global awareness is necessary to avoid exponential growth.

The failure of all heuristic chess programs suggests that even when experience is as formalized as a chess game, an associationist model of mental processes is unable to cope with it. The difficulties of artificial intelligence thus call our attention to the necessity for a non-associationist function of consciousness—what workers in artificial intelligence would have to call a non-digital form of information processing—precisely the global awareness which phenomenologists and gestalt psychologists have shown to be characteristic of human consciousness. The working model of associationist psychology turns out not to work at all.

II. Language Translation: Open-Texture vs. Formalization

Thus far we have restricted ourselves to the implications of work in artificial intelligence for the philosophy of mind. We have considered a case where the information to be given to the computer is of the discrete and determinate kind that can be punched on cards and stored in computer memories, and have concentrated on the computer's inability to process such information.

But in order to count as humanly intelligent, computers would not only have to play chess but also be able to deal with situations in the world in which we ordinarily perceive and live. Here the ambition of the workers in artificial intelligence takes on ontological or metaphysical dimensions, for such a claim not only asserts that the *way* we process information can be formalized and presented in a series of discrete steps so as to be simulated on a digital computer, but further that the *information itself* can be made exhaustively explicit and determinate so that it can be fed into a digital machine. . . .

We have seen that Bar-Hillel and Oettinger, two of the most respected and most informed workers in the field of automatic language translation, have each been led to pessimistic conclusions concerning the possibility of further progress in the field. They have each realized that, in order to translate a natural language, more is needed than a mechanical dictionary, no matter how complete, and a set of rules of grammar, no matter how sophisticated. The order of the words in a sentence does not provide enough information to enable a machine to determine which of several possible parsings is the appropriate one, nor does the context of a word indicate which of several possible readings is the one the author had in mind.

As Oettinger puts it:

> [Work] to date has revealed a far higher degree of legitimate *syntactic* ambiguity in English and in Russian than has been anticipated. This, and a related fuzziness of the boundary between the grammatical and the non-grammatical, raises serious questions about the possibility of effective fully automatic manipulation of English or Russian for any purposes of translation or information retrieval.

Instead of claiming, on the basis of his early partial successes with a mechanical dictionary, that, in spite of a few exceptions and difficulties, the mystery surrounding human understanding is beginning to dissolve—a frequent Simon claim—Oettinger draws attention to the "very mysterious semantic processes that enable most reasonable people to interpret most reasonable sentences univocally most of the time. . . ."

Here is another example of the fringe effect. Obviously, the user of a natural language is not aware of many of the cues he responds to in determining the intended syntax and meaning. But here the fundamental difficulty is not that machines, lacking fringe consciousness, cannot deal with formal complexities, but rather that what has to be dealt with cannot be formalized. The cues in question are not the sort which *could be* taken up and considered by a sequential or even parallel list-searching program.

Thus, even if a manageable number of relevant cues existed, they would not help us. In order to use a computer to interpret these cues, we would have to formulate syntactic and semantic criteria in terms of strict rules; and our use of language, while precise, is not strictly rule-like. Pascal, the first to invent a calculator and the second to see its limitations, noted that the *esprit de finesse* functions "tacitly, naturally, and without technical rules." Wittgenstein has spelled out this insight in the case of language.

A natural language is used by people involved *in situations* in which they are pursuing certain goals. These extra-linguistic goals, which need not themselves be precisely stated or statable, provide the cues which reduce the ambiguity of expressions as much as is necessary for the task at hand. The practical context, or more broadly the world, which enables us to use language precisely and yet in a non-rule-like way, is not a determinate object or set of objects which can be handled by information theory.

But to refute the metaphysical assumption that all ambiguity can be overcome in advance, that, in the case of language, the rules governing the use of words can be completely formalized, it is not sufficient to point out that thus far no adequate language translation system has been developed, or that our language is used in flexible and apparently non-rule-like ways. The formalizer can always retort that our inability to feed information describing the *Lebenswelt* to a digital computer shows only that we have not fully understood (analyzed) the use of a natural language.

This might at first sight seem to be similar to the heuristic programmer's claim that he will someday find the heuristics which will enable a machine to play chess, even if he has not yet found them. But there is an important difference. The heuristic programmer's confidence is based on a misconception of the way the mind processes information, while the formalist's claim is based on a correct understanding of the nature of scientific explanation. To the extent that we have not specified our behavior in terms of unique and precisely-definable reactions to precisely-definable situations, we have not understood that behavior in the only sense of "understanding" appropriate to science.

We must be more specific in our critique of the metaphysical presupposition of artificial intelligence in order to show in what sense the attempt to formalize is illegitimate. A machine can always revise its program each time it makes a mistake, but it would have to fail first and then revise its rules to take account of the new case. Humans, however, are able to adapt as they go along and then reflect on and formalize the revision they have already made. In trying to program a computer to use natural language, any specific uses of words, once they have occurred, can be added to the rules, even if the rules become more and more complicated. What cannot be accounted for, however, is the open texture of language, our ability to use these words in ever new ways, and still be understood.

This is not a problem for science since science is always done from the point of view of an objective observer and, as Kierkegaard pointed out in the *Postscript,* the objective thinker treats all experience as if it were already in the past. The originality, the importance, and the misery of artificial intelligence is that it tries to push this metaphysical attitude one step further and to use its formalization to cope with real life situations *as they occur*. Thus the formalist is not laboring under a misconception of the way consciousness functions, but a misconception of the relation between theoretical and practical understanding. He supposes that we can understand the practical and perceptual world in the same terms as we must try to understand the conceptual universe of science, and this is just another way of saying that the champion of artificial intelligence is the ultimate metaphysician, and his failure is the failure of metaphysics.

Descartes, the first to have conceived the possibility of robots, was also the first to grasp the essential inadequacy of digital computers. He remarks in the *Discourse* that:

> . . . although such machines could do many things as well as, or perhaps even better than, men, they would infallibly fail in certain others . . . . For while reason is a universal instrument which can be used in all sorts of situations, the organs of a machine have to be arranged in a particular way for each particular action. From this it follows that it is morally impossible that there should be enough different devices in a machine to make it behave in all the occurrences of life as our reason makes us behave. (LLA, p. 36)

Thus, although not aware of the difference between the world and things in the world, Descartes already saw that the mind can cope with an indefinite number of acts or situations, whereas a machine has only a limited number of on/off states and so will eventually reveal itself by its failure to respond appropriately. This intrinsic limitation of mechanism, Descartes claims, shows the necessity of presupposing an immaterial soul.

Of all the workers in artificial intelligence, only Shannon, the inventor of information theory, seems to be aware of this important incapacity of the digital computer. In a discussion of "What Computers Should Be Doing," he observes that:

> . . . Efficient machines for such problems as pattern recognition, language translation, and so on, may require a different type of computer than any we have today. It is my feeling that this will be a computer whose natural operation is in terms of patterns, concepts, and vague similarities, rather than sequential operations on ten-digit numbers.

Such a brain-like machine would not be mechanical in Descartes' narrow and precise sense, and, not being limited to a definite number of states, might be able to respond to an indefinite number of specific situations. It would thus, on Descartes' view, be indistinguishable from a human, destroying his argument that intelligent behavior is possible only if the mechanism behaving is somehow attached to a non-material soul. But one can raise a new objection, in some ways the exact opposite of Descartes', to this robot. If the arguments developed by S. J. Todes are correct, a brain in a bottle or a non-digital computer would still not be able to respond to new sorts of situations because our ability to cope with the open texture of the *Lebenswelt* depends not just on the flexibility of our nervous system but rather upon our ability to engage in practical activity. If such a Shannon-type computer is ever built, it might become apparent that what distinguishes persons from machines, no matter how cleverly constructed, is not a universal immaterial soul, but a self-moving material body. . . .

ROBERT GORHAM DAVIS

•

Logical Fallacies[1]

UNDEFINED TERMS

The first requirement for logical discourse is knowing what the words you use actually mean. Words are not like paper money or counters in a game. Except for technical terms in some of the sciences, they do not have a fixed face value. Their meanings are fluid and changing, influenced by many considerations of context and reference, circumstance and association. This is just as true of common words such as *fast* as it is of literary terms such as *romantic*. Moreover, if there is to be communication, words must have approximately the same meaning for the reader that they have for the writer. A speech in an unknown language means nothing to the hearer. When an adult speaks to a small child or an expert to a layman, communication may be seriously limited by lack of a mature vocabulary or ignorance of technical terms. Many arguments are meaningless because the speakers are using important words in quite different senses.

Because we learn most words—or guess at them—from the contexts in which we first encounter them, our sense of them is often incomplete or wrong. Readers sometimes visualize the Assyrian who comes down like the wolf on fold as an enormous man dressed in cohorts (some kind of fancy armor, possibly) gleaming in purple and gold. "A rift in the lute" suggests vaguely a cracked mandolin. Failure to ascertain the literal meaning of figurative language is a frequent reason for mixed metaphors. We are surprised to find that the "devil" in "the devil to pay" and "the devil and the deep blue sea" is not Old Nick, but part of a ship. Unless terms mean the same thing to both writer and reader, proper understanding is impossible.

[1] From *Handbook for English A* (Cambridge, Mass.: Harvard University, 1941), pp. 58-66. Reprinted by permission of Theodore Morrison and Robert Gorham Davis.

ABSTRACTIONS

The most serious logical difficulties occur with abstract terms. An abstraction is a word which stands for a quality found in a number of different objects or events from which it has been "abstracted" or taken away. We may, for instance, talk of the "whiteness" of paper or cotton or snow without considering qualities of cold or inflammability or usefulness which these materials happen also to possess. Usually, however, our minds carry over other qualities by association. See, for instance, the chapter called "The Whiteness of the Whale" in *Moby-Dick*.

In much theoretic discussion the process of abstraction is carried so far that although vague associations and connotations persist, the original objects or events from which the qualities have been abstracted are lost sight of completely. Instead of thinking of words like *sincerity* and *Americanism* as symbols standing for qualities that have to be abstracted with great care from examples and test cases, we come to think of them as real things in themselves. We assume that Americanism is Americanism just as a bicycle is a bicycle, and that everyone knows what it means. We forget that before the question, "Is Father Coughlin sincere?" can mean anything, we have to agree on the criteria of sincerity.

When we try to define such words and find examples, we discover that almost no one agrees on their meaning. The word *church* may refer to anything from a building on the corner of Spring Street to the whole tradition of institutionalized Christianity. *Germany* may mean a geographical section of Europe, a people, a governing group, a cultural tradition, or a military power. Abstractions such as *freedom, courage, race, beauty, truth, justice, nature, honor, humanism, democracy,* should never be used in a theme unless their meaning is defined or indicated clearly by the context. Freedom for whom? To do what? Under what circumstances? Abstract terms have merely emotional value unless they are strictly defined by asking questions of this kind. The study of a word such as *nature* in a good unabridged dictionary will show that even the dictionary, indispensable though it is, cannot determine for us the sense in which a word is being used in any given instance. Once the student understands the importance of definition, he will no longer be betrayed into fruitless arguments over such questions as whether free verse is "poetry" or whether you can change "human nature."

NAME-CALLING

It is a common unfairness in controversy to place what the writer dislikes or opposes in a generally odious category. The humanist dismisses what he dislikes by calling it *romantic;* the liberal, by calling it *fascist;* the conservative, by calling it *communistic*. These terms tell the reader nothing. What is *piety* to some will be *bigotry* to others. *Non-Catholics* would rather be called

Protestants than *heretics*. What is *right-thinking* except a designation for those who agree with the writer? Labor leaders become *outside agitators;* industrial organizations, *forces of reaction;* the Child Labor Amendment, the *youth control bill;* prison reform, *coddling;* progressive education, *fads and frills*. Such terms are intended to block thought by an appeal to prejudice and associative habits. Three steps are necessary before such epithets have real meaning. First, they must be defined; second, it must be shown that the object to which they are applied actually possesses these qualities; third, it must be shown that the possession of such qualities in this particular situation is necessarily undesirable. Unless a person is alert and critical both in choosing and in interpreting words, he may be alienated from ideas with which he would be in sympathy if he had not been frightened by a mere name.

GENERALIZATION

Similar to the abuse of abstract terms and epithets is the habit of presenting personal opinions in the guise of universal laws. The student often seems to feel that the broader the terms in which he states an opinion, the more effective he will be. Ordinarily the reverse is true. An enthusiasm for Thomas Wolfe should lead to a specific critical analysis of Wolfe's novels that will enable the writer to explain his enthusiasm to others; it should not be turned into the argument that Wolfe is "the greatest American novelist," particularly if the writer's knowledge of American novelists is somewhat limited. The same questions of *who* and *when* and *why* and under what *circumstances* which are used to check abstract terms should be applied to generalizations. Consider how contradictory proverbial wisdom is when detached from particular circumstances. "Look before you leap," but "he who hesitates is lost."

Superlatives and the words *right* and *wrong, true* and *untrue, never* and *always* must be used with caution in matters of opinion. When a student says flatly that X is true, he often is really saying that he or his family or the author of a book he has just been reading, persons of certain tastes and background and experience, *think* that X is true. Unless these people are identified and their reasons for thinking so explained, the assertion is worthless. Because many freshmen are taking survey courses in which they read a single work by an author or see an historical event through the eyes of a single historian whose bias they may not be able to measure, they must guard against this error.

SAMPLING

Assertions of a general nature are frequently open to question because they are based on insufficient evidence. Some persons are quite ready, after meeting one Armenian or reading one medieval romance, to generalize about Armenians and medieval romances. One ought, of course, to examine objectively as many examples as possible before making a generalization, but the number is less important than the representativeness of the examples chosen. The Literary Digest Presidential Poll, sent to hundreds of thousands of people selected from telephone directories, was far less accurate than the Gallup Poll which questioned far fewer voters, but selected them carefully and proportionately from all different social groups. The "typical" college student, as portrayed by moving pictures and cartoons, is very different from the "representative" college student as determined statistically. We cannot let uncontrolled experience do our sampling for us; instances and examples which impress themselves upon our minds do so usually because they are exceptional. In propaganda and arguments extreme cases are customarily treated as if they were characteristic.

If one is permitted arbitrarily to select some examples and ignore others, it is possible to find convincing evidence for almost any theory, no matter how fantastic. The fact that the mind tends naturally to remember those instances which confirm its opinions imposes a duty upon the writer, unless he wishes to encourage prejudice and superstition, to look carefully for exceptions to all generalizations which he is tempted to make. We forget the premonitions which are not followed by disaster and the times when our hunches failed to select the winner in a race. Patent medicine advertisements print the letters of those who survived their cure, and not of those who died during it. All Americans did not gamble on the stock exchange in the twenties, and all Vermonters are not thin-lipped and shrewd. Of course the search for negative examples can be carried too far. Outside of mathematics or the laboratory, few generalizations can be made airtight, and most are not intended to be. But quibbling is so easy that resort to it is very common, and the knowledge that people can and will quibble over generalizations is another reason for making assertions as limited and explicitly conditional as possible.

FALSE ANALOGY

Illustration, comparison, analogy are most valuable in making an essay clear and interesting. It must not be supposed, however, that they prove anything or have much argumentative weight. The rule that what is true of one thing in one set of circumstances is not necessarily true of another thing in another set of circumstances seems almost too obvious to need stating. Yet constantly nations and businesses are discussed as if they were human beings with human habits and feelings; human bodies are discussed as if they were machines; the universe, as if it were a clock. It is assumed that what held true for seventeenth century New England or the thirteen Atlantic colonies also holds true for an industrial nation of 130,000,000 people. Carlyle dismissed the arguments for representative democracy by saying that if a captain had to take a vote among his crew every time he wanted to do something, he would never get around Cape Horn. This analogy calmly ignores the distinction between the lawmaking and the executive branches of constitutional democracies. Moreover, voters may be considered much more like the stockholders of a merchant line than its hired sailors. Such arguments introduce assumptions in a metaphorical guise in which they are not readily detected or easily criticized. In place of analysis they attempt to identify their position with some familiar symbol which will evoke a predictable, emotional response in the reader. The revival during the 1932 presidential campaign of Lincoln's remark, "Don't swap horses in the middle of the stream," was not merely a picturesque way of saying keep Hoover in the White House. It made a number of assumptions about the nature of depressions and the function of government. This propagandist technique can be seen most clearly in political cartoons.

DEGREE

Often differences in degree are more important than differences in kind. By legal and social standards there is more difference between an habitual drunkard and a man who drinks temperately, than between a temperate drinker and a total abstainer. In fact differences of degree produce what are regarded as differences of kind. At known temperatures ice turns to water and water boils. At an indeterminate point affection becomes love and a man who needs a shave becomes a man with a beard. The fact that no men or systems are perfect make rejoinders and counter-accusations very easy if differences in degree are ignored. Newspapers in totalitarian states, answering American accusations of brutality and suppression, refer to lynchings and gangsterism here. Before a disinterested judge could evaluate these mutual accusations, he would have to settle the question of the degree to which violent suppression and lynching are respectively prevalent in the countries under consideration. On the other hand, differences in degree may be merely apparent. Lincoln Steffens pointed out that newspapers can create a "crime wave" any time they wish, simply by emphasizing all the minor assaults and thefts commonly ignored or given an inch or two on a back page. The great reported increases in insanity may be due to the fact that in a more urban and institutionalized society cases of insanity more frequently come to the attention of authorities and hence are recorded in statistics.

CAUSATION

The most common way of deciding that one thing causes another thing is the simple principle: *post hoc, ergo propter hoc*, "After this, therefore because of this." Rome fell after the introduction of Christianity; therefore Christianity was responsible for the fall of Rome. Such reasoning illustrates another kind of faulty generalization. But even if one could find ten cases in which a nation "fell" after the introduction of Christianity, it still would not be at all certain that Christianity caused the fall. Day, it has frequently been pointed out, follows night in every observable instance, and yet night cannot be called the cause of day. Usually a combination of causes produces a result. Sitting in a draught may cause a cold, but only given a certain physical condition in the person sitting there. In such instances one may distinguish between necessary and sufficient conditions. Air is a necessary condition for the maintenance of plant life, but air alone is not sufficient to produce plant life. And often different causes at different times may produce the same result. This relation is known as plurality of causes. If, after sitting in a stuffy theatre on Monday, and then again after eating in a stuffy restaurant on Thursday, a man suffered from headaches, he might say, generalizing, that bad air gave him headaches. But actually the headache on Monday may have been caused by eye-strain and on Thursday by indigestion. To isolate the causative factor it is necessary that all other conditions be precisely the same. Such isolation is possible, except in very simple instances, only in the laboratory or with scientific methods. If a picture falls from the wall every time a truck passes, we can quite certainly say that the truck's passing is the cause. But with anything as complex and conditional as a nation's economy or human character, the determination of cause is not easy or certain. A psychiatrist often sees a patient for an hour daily for a year or more before he feels that he understands his psychosis.

Ordinarily when we speak of cause we mean the proximate or immediate cause. The plants were killed by frost; we had indigestion from eating lobster salad. But any single cause is one in an unbroken series. When a man is murdered, is his death caused by the loss of blood from the wound, or by the firing of the pistol, or by the malice aforethought of the murderer? Was the World War "caused" by the assassination at Sarajevo? Were the Navigation Acts or the ideas of John Locke more important in "causing" the American Revolution? A complete statement of cause would comprise the sum total of the conditions which preceded an event, conditions stretching back indefinitely into the past. Historical events are so interrelated that the isolation of a causative sequence is dependent chiefly on the particular preoccupations of the historian. An economic determinist can "explain" history entirely in terms of economic developments; an idealist, entirely in terms of the development of ideas.

SYLLOGISTIC REASONING

The formal syllogism of the type,

All men are mortal
John is a man
Therefore John is mortal,

is not so highly regarded today as in some earlier periods. It merely fixes an individual as a member of a class, and then assumes that the individual has the given characteristics of the class. Once we have decided who John is, and what "man" and "mortal" mean, and have canvassed all men, including John, to make sure that they are mortal, the conclusion naturally follows. It can be seen that the chief difficulties arise in trying to establish acceptable premises. Faults in the premises are known as "material" fallacies, and are usually more serious than the "formal" fallacies, which are logical defects in drawing a conclusion from the premises. But although directly syllogistic reasoning is not much practiced, buried syllogisms can be found in all argument, and it is often a useful clarification to outline your own or another writer's essay in syllogistic form. The two most frequent defects in the syllogism itself are the undistributed and the ambiguous middle. The middle term is the one that appears in each of the premises and not in the conclusion. In the syllogism,

All good citizens vote
John votes
Therefore John is a good citizen,

the middle term is not "good citizens," but "votes." Even though it were true that all good citizens vote, nothing prevents bad citizens from voting also, and John may be one of the bad citizens. To distribute the middle term "votes" one might say (but only if that is what one meant),

All voters are good citizens
John is a voter
Therefore John is a good citizen.

The ambiguous middle term is even more common. It represents a problem in definition, while the undistributed middle is a problem in generalization. All acts which benefit others are virtuous, losing money at poker benefits others, therefore losing at poker is a virtuous act. Here the middle term "act which benefits others" is obviously used very loosely and ambiguously.

NON-SEQUITUR

This phrase, meaning "it does not follow," is used to characterize the kind of humor found in pictures in which the Marx Brothers perform. It is an amusing illogicality because it usually expresses, beneath its apparent incongruity, an imaginative, associative, or personal truth. "My ancestors came over on the *Mayflower*; therefore I am naturally opposed to labor unions." It is not logically necessary that those whose ancestors came over on the *Mayflower* should be opposed to unions; but it may happen to be true as a personal fact in a given case. Contemporary psychologists have effectively shown us that there is often such a wide difference between the true and the purported reasons for an attitude that, in rationalizing our behavior, we are often quite unconscious of the motives that actually influence us. A fanatical antivivisectionist, for instance, may have temperamental impulses toward cruelty which he is suppressing and compensating for by a reasoned opposition to any kind of permitted suffering. We may expect, then, to come upon many conclusions which are psychologically interesting in themselves, but have nothing to do with the given premises.

IGNORATIO ELENCHI

This means, in idiomatic English, "arguing off the point," or ignoring the question at issue. A man trying to show that monarchy is the best form of government for the British Empire may devote most of his attention to the character of George V and the affection his people felt for him. In ordinary conversational argument it is almost impossible for disputants to keep to the point. Constantly turning up are tempting side-issues through which one can discomfit an opponent or force him to irrelevant admissions that seem to weaken his case.

BEGGING THE QUESTION; ARGUING IN A CIRCLE

The first of these terms means to assume in the premises what you are pretending to prove in the course of your argument. The function of logic is to demonstrate that because one thing or group of things is true, another must be true as a consequence. But in begging the question you simply say in varying language that what is assumed to be true is assumed to be true. An argument which asserts that we shall enjoy immortality because we have souls which are immaterial and indestructible establishes nothing, because the idea of immortality is already contained in the assumption about the soul. It is the premise which needs to be demonstrated, not the conclusion. Arguing in a circle is another form of this fallacy. It proves the premise by the conclusion and the conclusion by the premise. The conscience forbids an act because it is wrong; the act is wrong because the conscience forbids it.

ARGUMENTS AD HOMINEM AND AD POPULUM

It is very difficult for men to be persuaded by reason when their interest or prestige is at stake. If one wishes to preach the significance of physiognomy, it is well to choose a hearer with a high forehead and a determined jaw. The arguments in favor of repealing the protective tariff on corn or wheat in England were more readily entertained by manufacturers than by landowners. The cotton manufacturers in New England who were doing a profitable trade with the South were the last to be moved by descriptions of the evils of slavery. Because interest and desire are so deeply seated in human nature, arguments are frequently mingled with attempts to appeal to emotion, arouse fear, play upon pride, attack the characters of proponents of an opposite view, show that their practice is inconsistent with their principles; all matters which have, strictly speaking, nothing to do with the truth or falsity, the general desirability or undesirability, of some particular measure. If men are desperate enough they will listen to arguments proper only to an insane asylum but which seem to promise them relief.

After reading these suggestions, which are largely negative, the student may feel that any original assertion he can make will probably contain one or several logical faults. This assumption is not true. Even if it were, we know from reading newspapers and magazines that worldly fame is not dimmed by the constant and, one suspects, conscious practice of illogicality. But generalizations are not made only by charlatans and sophists. Intelligent and scrupulous writers also have a great many fresh and provocative observations and conclusions to express and are expressing them influentially. What is intelligence but the ability to see the connection between things, to discern causes, to relate the particular to the general, to define and discriminate and compare? Any man who thinks and feels and observes closely will not want for something to express.

And in his expression a proponent will find that a due regard for logic does not limit but rather increases the force of his argument. When statements are not trite, they are usually controversial. Men arrive at truth dialectically; error is weeded out in the course of discussion, argument, attack, and counter-attack. Not only can a writer who understands logic show the weaknesses of arguments he disagrees with, but also, by anticipating the kind of attack likely to be made on his own ideas, he can so arrange them, properly modified with qualifications and exceptions, that the anticipated attack is made much less effective. Thus, fortunately, we do not have to depend on the spirit of fairness and love of truth to lead men to logic; it has the strong support of argumentative necessity and of the universal desire to make ideas prevail.

FRANCIS BACON

•

Idols of the Mind[1]

XXXVIII

The idols and false notions which are now in possession of the human understanding, and have taken deep root therein, not only so beset men's minds that truth can hardly find entrance, but even after entrance obtained, they will again in the very instauration of the sciences meet and trouble us, unless men being forewarned of the danger fortify themselves as far as may be against their assaults.

[1] From *The Works of Francis Bacon,* ed. by James Spedding, Robert Ellis, and Douglas Heath (New York: Hurd and Houghon, 1869), VIII, 76-90. The *Novum Organum* was first printed in 1620.

XXXIX

There are four classes of Idols which beset men's minds. To these for distinction's sake I have assigned names—calling the first class *Idols of the Tribe*; the second, *Idols of the Cave*; the third, *Idols of the Marketplace*; the fourth, *Idols of the Theatre*.

XL

The formation of ideas and axioms by true induction is no doubt the proper remedy to be applied for the keeping off and clearing away of idols. To point them out, however, is of great use; for the doctrine of Idols is to the Interpretation of Nature what the doctrine of the refutation of Sophisms is to common Logic.

XLI

The Idols of the Tribe have their foundation in human nature itself, and in the tribe or race of men. For it is a false assertion that the sense of man is the measure of things. On the contrary, all perceptions as well of the sense as of the mind are according to the measure of the individual and not according to the measure of the universe. And the human understanding is like a false mirror, which, receiving rays irregularly, distorts and discolours the nature of things by mingling its own nature with it.

XLII

The Idols of the Cave are the idols of the individual man. For everyone (besides the errors common to human nature in general) has a cave or den of his own, which refracts and discolours the light of nature; owing either to his own proper and peculiar nature; or to his education and conversation with others; or to the reading of books, and the authority of those whom he esteems and admires; or to the differences of impressions, accordingly as they take place in a mind preoccupied and predisposed or in a mind indifferent and settled; or the like: So that the spirit of man (according as it is meted out to different individuals) is in fact a thing variable and full of perturbation, and governed as it were by chance. Whence it was well observed by Heraclitus that men look for sciences in their own lesser worlds, and not in the greater or common world.

XLIII

There are also Idols formed by the intercourse and association of men with each other, which I call Idols of the Marketplace, on account of the commerce and consort of men there. For it is by discourse that men associate; and words are imposed according to the apprehension of the vulgar. And therefore the ill and unfit choice of words wonderfully obstructs the understanding. Nor do the definitions or explanations wherewith in some things learned men are wont to guard and defend themselves, by any means set the matter right. But words plainly force and overrule the understanding, and throw all into confusion, and lead men away into numberless empty controversies and idle fancies.

XLIV

Lastly, there are Idols which have immigrated into men's minds from the various dogmas of philosophies, and also from wrong laws of demonstration. These I call Idols of the Theatre; because in my judgment all the received systems are but so many stage-plays, representing worlds of their own creation after an unreal and scenic fashion. Nor is it only of the systems now in vogue, or only of the ancient sects and philosophies, that I speak; for many more plays of the same kind may yet be composed and in like artificial manner set forth; seeing that errors the most widely different have nevertheless causes for the most part alike. Neither again do I mean this only of entire systems, but also of many principles and axioms in science, which by tradition, credulity, and negligence have come to be received.

But of these several kinds of Idols I must speak more largely and exactly, that the understanding may be duly cautioned.

XLV

The human understanding is of its own nature prone to suppose the existence of more order and regularity in the world than it finds. And though there be many things in nature which are singular and unmatched, yet it devises for them parallels and conjugates and relatives which do not exist. Hence the fiction that all celestial bodies move in perfect circles; spirals and dragons being (except in name) utterly rejected. Hence too the element of Fire with its orb is brought in, to make up the square with the other three which the sense perceives. Hence also the ratio of density of the so-called elements is arbitrarily fixed at ten to one. And so on of other dreams. And these fancies affect not dogmas only, but simple notions also.

XLVI

The human understanding when it has once adopted an opinion (either as being the received opinion or as being agreeable to itself) draws all things else to support and agree with it. And though there be a greater number and weight of instances to be found on the other side, yet these it either neglects and despises, or else by some distinction sets aside and rejects; in order that by this great and pernicious predetermination the authority of its former conclusions may remain inviolate. And therefore it was a good answer that was made by one who when they showed him hanging in a temple a picture of those who had paid their vows as having escaped shipwreck, and would have him say whether he did not now acknowledge the power of the gods—— "Aye," asked he again, "but where are they painted that were drowned after their vows?" And such is the way of all superstition, whether in astrology, dreams, omens, divine judgments, or the like; wherein men, having a delight in such vanities, mark the events where they are fulfilled, but where they fail, though this happen much oftener, neglect and pass them by. But with far more subtlety does this mischief insinuate itself into philosophy and the sciences; in which the first conclusion colours and brings into conformity with itself all that come after, though far sounder and better. Besides, independently of that delight and vanity which I have described, it is the peculiar and perpetual error of the human intellect to be more moved and excited by affirmatives than by negatives; whereas it ought properly to hold itself indifferently disposed towards both alike. Indeed in the establishment of any true axiom, the negative instance is the more forcible of the two.

XLVII

The human understanding is moved by those things most which strike and enter the mind simultaneously and suddenly, and so fill the imagination; and then it feigns and supposes all other things to be somehow, though it cannot see how, similar to those few things by which it is surrounded. But for that going to and fro to remote and heterogeneous instances, by which axioms are tried as in the fire, the intellect is altogether slow and unfit, unless it be forced thereto by severe laws and overruling authority.

XLVIII

The human understanding is unquiet; it cannot stop or rest, and still presses onward, but in vain. Therefore it is that we cannot conceive of any end or limit to the world; but always as of necessity it occurs to us that there is something beyond. Neither again can it be conceived how eternity has flowed down to the present day; for that distinction which is commonly received of infinity in time past and in time to come can by no means hold; for it would thence follow that one infinity is greater than another, and that infinity is wasting away and tending to become finite. The like subtlety arises touching the infinite divisibility of lines, from the same inability of thought to stop. But this inability interferes more mischievously in the discovery of causes; for although the most general principles in nature ought to be held merely positive, as they are discovered, and cannot with truth be referred to a cause; nevertheless the human understanding being unable to rest still seeks something prior in the order of nature. And then it is that in struggling towards that which is further off it falls back upon that which is more nigh at hand; namely, on final causes: which have relation clearly to the nature of man rather than to the nature of the universe; and from this source have strangely defiled philosophy. But he is no less an unskilled and shallow philosopher who seeks causes of that which is most general, than he who in things subordinate and subaltern omits to do so.

XLIX

The human understanding is no dry light, but receives an infusion from the will and affections; whence proceed sciences which may be called "sciences as one would." For what a man had rather were true he more readily believes. Therefore he rejects difficult things from impatience of research; sober things, because they narrow hope; the deeper things of nature, from superstition; the light of experience, from arrogance and pride, lest his mind should seem to be occupied with things mean and transitory; things not commonly believed, out of deference to the opinion of the vulgar. Numberless in short are the ways, and sometimes imperceptible, in which the affections colour and infect the understanding.

L

But by far the greatest hindrance and aberration of the human understanding proceeds from the dullness, incompetency, and deceptions of the senses; in that things which strike the sense outweigh things which do not immediately strike it, though they be more important. Hence it is that speculation commonly ceases where sight ceases; insomuch that of things invisible there is little or no observation. Hence all the working of the spirits inclosed in tangible bodies lies hid and unobserved of men. So also all the more subtle changes of form in the parts of coarser substances (which they commonly call alteration, though it is in truth local motion through exceedingly small spaces) is in like manner unobserved. And yet unless these two things just mentioned be searched out and brought to light, nothing great can be achieved in nature, as far as the production of works is concerned. So again the essential nature of our common air, and of all bodies less dense than air (which are very many), is almost unknown. For the sense by itself is a thing infirm and erring; neither can instruments for enlarging or sharpening the senses do much; but all the truer kind of interpretation of nature is effected by instances and experiments fit and apposite; wherein the sense decides touching the experiment only, and the experiment touching the point in nature and the thing itself.

LI

The human understanding is of its own nature prone to abstractions and gives a substance and reality to things which are fleeting. But to resolve nature into abstractions is less to our purpose than to dissect her into parts; as did the school of Democritus, which went further into nature than the rest. Matter rather than forms should be the object of our attention, its configurations and changes of configuration, and simple action, and law of action or motion; for forms are figments of the human mind, unless you will call those laws of action forms.

LII

Such then are the idols which I call *Idols of the Tribe;* and which take their rise either from the homogeneity of the substance of the human spirit, or from its preoccupation, or from its narrowness, or from its restless motion, or from an infusion of the affections, or from the incompetency of the senses, or from the mode of impression.

LIII

The *Idols of the Cave* take their rise in the peculiar constitution, mental or bodily, of each individual; and also in education, habit, and accident. Of this kind there is a great number and variety; but I will instance those the pointing out of which contains the most important caution, and which have most effect in disturbing the clearness of the understanding.

LIV

Men become attached to certain particular sciences and speculations, either because they fancy themselves the authors and inventors thereof, or because they have bestowed the greatest pains upon them and become most habituated to them. But men of this kind, if they betake themselves to philosophy and contemplations of a general character, distort and colour them in obedience to their former fancies; a thing especially to be noticed in Aristotle, who made his natural philosophy a mere bond-servant to his logic, thereby rendering it contentious and well nigh useless. The race of chemists again out of a few experiments of the furnace have built up a fantastic philosophy, framed with reference to a few things; and Gilbert also, after he had employed himself most laboriously in the study and observation of the loadstone, proceeded at once to construct an entire system in accordance with his favourite subject.

LV

There is one principal and as it were radical distinction between different minds, in respect of philosophy and the sciences; which is this: that some minds are stronger and apter to mark the differences of things, others to mark their resemblances. The steady and acute mind can fix its contemplations and dwell and fasten on the subtlest distinctions: the lofty and discursive mind recognises and puts together the finest and most general resemblances. Both kinds however easily err in excess, by catching the one at gradations, the other at shadows.

LVI

There are found some minds given to an extreme admiration of antiquity, others to an extreme love and appetite for novelty; but few so duly tempered that they can hold the mean, neither carping at what has been well laid down by the ancients, nor despising what is well introduced by the moderns. This however turns to the great injury of the sciences and philosophy; since these affectations of antiquity and novelty are the humours of partisans rather than judgments; and truth is to be sought for not in the felicity of any age, which is an unstable thing, but in the light of nature and experience, which is eternal. These factions therefore must be abjured, and care must be taken that the intellect be not hurried by them into assent.

LVII

Contemplations of nature and of bodies in their simple form break up and distract the understanding, while contemplations of nature and bodies in their composition and configuration overpower and dissolve the understanding: a distinction well seen in the school of Leucippus and Democritus as compared with the other philosophies. For that school is so busied with the particles that it hardly attends to the structure; while the others are so lost in admiration of the structure that they do not penetrate to the simplicity of nature. These kinds of contemplation should therefore be alternated and taken by turns; that so the understanding may be rendered at once penetrating and comprehensive, and the inconveniences above mentioned, with the idols which proceed from them, may be avoided.

LVIII

Let such then be our provision and contemplative prudence for keeping off and dislodging the *Idols of the Cave*, which grow for the most part either out of the predominance of a favourite subject, or out of an excessive tendency to compare or to distinguish, or out of partiality for particular ages, or out of the largeness or minuteness of the objects contemplated. And generally let every student of nature take this as a rule—that whatever his mind seizes and dwells upon with peculiar satisfaction is to be held in suspicion, and that so much the more care is to be taken in dealing with such questions to keep the understanding even and clear.

LIX

But the *Idols of the Marketplace* are the most troublesome of all: idols which have crept into the understanding through the alliances of words and names. For men believe that their reason governs words; but it is also true that words react on the understanding; and this it is that has rendered philosophy and the sciences sophistical and inactive. Now words, being commonly framed and applied according to the capacity of the vulgar, follow those lines of division which are most obvious to the vulgar understanding. And whenever an understanding of greater acuteness or a more diligent observation would alter those lines to suit the true divisions of nature, words stand in the way and resist the change. Whence it comes to pass that the high and formal discussions of learned men end oftentimes in disputes about words and names; with which (according to the use and wisdom of the mathematicians) it would be more prudent to begin, and so by means of definitions reduce them to order. Yet even definitions cannot cure this evil in dealing with natural and material things; since the definitions themselves consist of words, and those words beget others: so that it is necessary to recur to individual instances, and those in due series and order; as I shall say presently when I come to the method and scheme for the formation of notions and axioms.

LX

The idols imposed by words on the understanding are of two kinds. They are either names of things which do not exist (for as there are things left unnamed through lack of observation, so likewise are there names which result from fantastic suppositions and to which nothing in reality corresponds), or they are names of things which exist, but yet confused and ill-defined, and hastily and irregularly derived from realities. Of the former kind are Fortune, the Prime Mover, Planetary Orbits, Element of Fire, and like fictions which owe their origin to false and idle theories. And this class of idols is more easily expelled, because to get rid of them it is only necessary that all theories should be steadily rejected and dismissed as obsolete.

But the other class, which springs out of a faulty and unskillful abstraction, is intricate and deeply rooted. Let us take for example such a word as *humid*; and see how far the several things which the word is used to signify agree with each other; and we shall find the word *humid* to be nothing else than a mark loosely and confusedly applied to denote a variety of actions which will not bear to be reduced to any constant meaning. For it both signifies that which easily spreads itself round any other body; and that which in itself is undeterminate and cannot solidise; and that which readily yields in every direction; and that which easily divides and scatters itself; and that which easily unites and collects itself; and that which readily flows and is put in motion; and that which readily clings to another body and wets it; and that which is easily reduced to a liquid, or being solid easily melts. Accordingly when you come to apply the word—if you take it in one sense, flame is humid; if in another, air is not humid; if in another, fine dust is humid; if in another, glass is humid. So that it is easy to see that the notion is taken by abstraction only from water and common and ordinary liquids, without any due verification.

There are however in words certain degrees of distortion and error. One of the least faulty kinds is that of names of substances, especially of lowest species and well-deduced (for the notion of *chalk* and of *mud* is good, of *earth* bad); a more faulty kind is that of actions, as *to generate, to corrupt, to alter;* the most faulty is of qualities (except such as are the immediate objects of the sense) as *heavy, light, rare, dense,* and the like. Yet in all these cases some notions are of necessity a little better than others, in proportion to the greater variety of subjects that fall within the range of the human sense.

LXI

But the *Idols of the Theatre* are not innate, nor do they steal into the understanding secretly, but are plainly impressed and received into the mind from the play-books of philosophical systems and the perverted rules of demonstration. To attempt refutations in this case would be merely inconsistent with what I have already said: for since we agree neither upon principles nor upon demonstrations there is no place for argument. And this is so far well, inasmuch as it leaves the honour of the ancients untouched. For they are no wise disparaged—the question between them and me being only as to the way. For as the saying is, the lame man who keeps the right road outstrips the runner who takes a wrong one. Nay it is obvious that when a man runs the wrong way, the more active and swift he is the further he will go astray.

But the course I propose for the discovery of sciences is such as leaves but little to the acuteness and strength of wits, but places all wits and understandings nearly on a level. For as in the drawing of a straight line or a perfect circle, much depends on the steadiness and practice of the hand, if it be done by aim of hand only, but if with the aid of rule or compass, little or nothing: so is it exactly with my plan. But though particular confutations would be of no avail, yet touching the sects and general divisions of such systems I must say something; something also touching the external signs which show that they are unsound; and finally something touching the causes of such great infelicity and of such lasting and general agreement in error; that so the access to truth may be made less difficult, and the human understanding may the more willingly submit to its purgation and dismiss its idols.

PART IV

THE ARTS

The Fine Arts

SUSANNE K. LANGER

•

The Cultural Importance of the Arts[1]

Every culture develops some kind of art as surely as it develops language. Some primitive cultures have no real mythology or religion, but all have some art—dance, song, design (sometimes only on tools or on the human body). Above all, dances; that seems to be the oldest elaborated art.

The ancient ubiquitous character of art contrasts sharply with the prevalent idea that art is a luxury product of civilization, a cultural frill, a piece of social veneer.

It fits better with the conviction held by most artists, that art is the epitome of human life, the truest record of insight and feeling, and that the strongest military or economic society without art is poor in comparison with the most primitive tribe of savage painters, dancers, or idol-carvers. Wherever a society has really achieved culture (in the ethnological, not the popular sense of social form) it has begotten art, not late in its career, but at the very inception of it.

Art is, indeed, the spearhead of human development, social and individual. The vulgarization of art is the surest symptom of ethnic decline. The growth of a new art or even a great and radically new style always bespeaks a young and vigorous mind, whether collective or single.

What sort of thing is art, that it should play such a leading role in human development? It is not an intellectual pursuit, but is necessary to intellectual life; it is not religion, but grows up with religion, serves it and in large measure determines it (as Herodotus said, "Homer made the gods," and

[1] From *Problems of Art: Ten Philosophical Lectures,* by Susanne Langer, published by Charles Scribner's Sons. Copyright 1957 by, and used by permission of, Susanne Langer.

surely the Egyptian deities grew under the chisels of sculptors in strangely solemn forms).

We cannot enter here on a long discussion of what has been claimed as the essence of art, the true nature of art, or its defining function; in a single lecture dealing with one aspect of art, namely its cultural influence, I can only give you by way of preamble my own definition of art, with categorical brevity. That does not mean that I set up this definition in a categorical spirit, but only that we have no time to debate it, so you are asked to accept it as an assumption underlying these reflections.

Art, in the sense here intended—that is, the generic term subsuming painting, sculpture, architecture, music, dance, literature and drama—may be defined as the practice of creating perceptible forms expressive of human feeling. I say "perceptible" rather than "sensuous" forms because some works of art are given to imagination rather than to the outward senses. A novel, for instance, usually is read silently with the eye, but is not made for vision, as a painting is; and though sound plays a vital part in poetry, words even in poetry are not essentially sonorous structures like music. Dance requires to be seen, but its appeal is to deeper centers of sensation. The difference between dance and mobile sculpture makes this immediately apparent. But all works of art are purely perceptible forms that seem to embody some sort of feeling.

"Feeling" as I am using it here covers much more than it does in the technical vocabulary of psychology, where it denotes only pleasure and pain, or even in the shifting limits of ordinary discourse, where it sometimes means sensation (as when one says a paralyzed limb has no feeling in it), sometimes sensibility (as we speak of hurting someone's feelings), sometimes emotion (e.g., as a situation is said to harrow your feeling, or to evoke tender feeling), or a directed emotional attitude (we say we feel strongly *about* something), or even our general mental or physical condition, feeling well or ill, blue, or a bit above ourselves. As I use the word, in defining art as the creation of perceptible forms expressive of human feeling, it takes in all those meanings; it applies to *everything that may be felt.*

Another word in the definition that might be questioned is "creation." I think it is justified, not pretentious, as perhaps it sounds; but that issue is slightly beside the point here, so let us shelve it. If anyone prefers to speak of the "making" or "construction" of expressive forms that will do here just as well.

What does have to be understood is the meaning of "form," and more particularly "expressive form"; for that involves the very nature of art and therefore the question of its cultural importance.

The word "form" has several current uses; most of them have some relation to the sense in which I am using it here, though a few, such as: "a *form* to be filled in for tax purposes," or "a mere matter of form," are fairly remote, being quite specialized. Since we are speaking of art, it might be good to point out that the meaning of *stylistic patter*—"the sonata form," "the sonnet form"—is not the one I am assuming here. I am using the word in a simpler sense, which it has when you say, on a foggy night, that you see dimly moving forms in the mist; one of them emerges clearly, and is the form of a man. The trees are gigantic forms; the rills of rain trace sinuous forms on the window pane. The rills are not fixed things; they are forms of motion. When you watch gnats weaving in the air, or flocks of birds wheeling overhead, you see dynamic forms—forms made by motion.

It is in this sense of an apparition given to our perception, that a work of art is a form. It may be a permanent form like a building or a vase or a picture, or a transient, dynamic form like a melody or a dance, or even a form given to imagination, like the passage of purely imaginary, apparent events that constitutes a literary work. But it is always a perceptible, self-identical whole; like a natural being, it has a character of organic unity, self-sufficiency, individual reality. And it is thus, as an appearance, that a work of art is good or bad or perhaps only rather poor; as an appearance, not as a comment on things beyond it in the world, nor as a reminder of them.

This, then, is what I mean by "form"; but what is meant by calling such forms "expressive of human feeling"? How do apparitions "express" anything—feeling, or anything else? First of all, let us ask just what is meant here by "express"; what sort of "expression" we are talking about.

Most people believe that music and poetry are expressions of emotion, and will further agree that a picture is a glimpse of reality seen through a temperament. Even a Gothic cathedral is supposed to express the religious emotions of its countless, anonymous builders. Its age makes the process indistinct enough to put it beyond very searching question. But it is harder to imagine how a modern office building or a fine flung-out overpass across a highway—an architectural work of art, as many of our offices and ramps and bridges are—could be, in any essential way, an expression of its designer's emotion or state of mind. To treat it just like a lyric or an easel picture seems a bit silly.

The incongruity, however, points to a misunderstanding that becomes apparent only when we try to conceive the skyscraper as an emotional exhibition, but that really confuses our judgment of the lyric and the picture as well. It is a misconception of what is meant by "expression" in art.

The word "expression" has two principal meanings: in one sense it means *self*-expression—giving vent to our feelings. In this sense it refers to a *symptom* of what we feel. Self-expression is a spontaneous reaction to a situation an event, the company we are in, things people say, or what the weather does to us; it bespeaks the physical and mental state we are in and the emotions that stir us. In another sense, however, "expression" means the presentation of an idea, usually by the proper and apt use of words. But a device for the presentation of an idea is what we call a *symbol,* not a symptom. Thus a *word* is a symbol, and so is a meaningful combination of words. A common word, such as "horse," conveys an idea even when no one is exclaiming over the presence of a horse, or offering his kingdom for one—for instance, in the phrase "White Horse Whiskey," or in the dictionary, somewhere between "horror" and "horticulture."

A sentence, which is a special combination of words, expresses the idea of some state of affairs, real or imagined. Sentences are complicated symbols—so complicated, sometimes, that we have to consider them word by word and analyze the way they are put together to understand the meanings they convey. And sometimes the meaning is an idea we never had before, or concerns something we have never seen—a new animal, a foreign place, or what not. Language will formulate new ideas as well as communicate old ones, so that all people know a lot of things that they have merely heard or read about. Symbolic expression, therefore, extends our knowledge beyond the scope of our actual experience.

If an idea is clearly conveyed by means of symbols we say it is *well expressed*. A person may work for a long time to give his statement the best possible form, to find the exact words for what he means to say and to carry his account or his argument most directly from one point to another. But a discourse so worked out is certainly not a spontaneous reaction. Giving expression to an idea is obviously a different thing from giving expression to feelings by laughing, crying, blushing, or quivering. You do not say of a man in a rage that his anger is well expressed; you either try to calm him down, or you rage back at him, but in either case you understand quite well that he is furious. The symptoms just are what they are, there is no critical standard for symptoms. If, on the other hand, the angry man tries to tell you what he is fuming about, he will have to collect himself, curtail his emotional expression, and find words to express his ideas. For to tell a story coherently involves "expression" in quite a different sense: this sort of expression is not "self-expression," but may be called "conceptual expression."

Language, of course, is our prime instrument of conceptual expression. The things we can say are in effect the things we can think. Words are the terms of our thinking as well as the terms in which we present our thoughts, because they present the objects of thought to the thinker himself. Before language communicates ideas, it gives them form, makes them clear, and in fact makes them what they are. Whatever has a name is an object for thought. Without words, sense experience is only a flow of impressions, as subjective as our feelings; words make it objective, and carve it up into *things* and *facts* that we can note, remember, and think about. Language gives outward experience its form, and makes it definite and clear.

There is, however, an important part of reality that is quite inaccessible to the formative influence of language: that is the realm of so-called "inner experience," the life of feeling and emotion. The reason why language is so powerless here is not, as many people suppose, that feeling and emotion are irrational; on the contrary, they seem irrational because language does not help to make them conceivable, and most people cannot conceive anything without the logical scaffolding of words. The unfitness of language to convey subjective experience is a somewhat technical subject, easier for logicians to understand than for artists; but the gist of it is that the form of language does not reflect the natural form of feeling, so we cannot shape any concepts of feeling with the help of ordinary, discursive language. Therefore the words whereby we refer to feeling only name very general kinds of inner experience —excitement, calm, joy, sorrow, love, hate, etc. But there is no language to describe just how one joy differs so radically from another, or what the experience of hate is really like, how it can interplay with feelings usually called love, how it burns and then goes cold in almost the same moment. The real nature of feeling is something language as such—as discursive symbolism—cannot render.

For this reason, the phenomena of feeling and emotion are usually treated by philosophers as irrational. The only pattern discursive thought can find in them is the pattern of outward events that occasion them. There are different degrees of fear, but they are thought of as so many degrees of the same simple feeling.

But human feeling is a fabric, not a vague mass. It has an intricate dynamic pattern, possible combinations and new emergent phenomena. It is a pattern of organically interdependent and interdetermined tensions and resolutions; a pattern of almost infinitely complex activation and cadence. To it belongs the whole gamut of our sensibility, the sense of straining thought, all mental attitude and motor set. Those are the deeper reaches that underlie the surface waves of our emotion, and make human life a *life of feeling* instead of an unconscious metabolic existence interrupted by feelings.

It is, I think, this dynamic pattern that finds its formal expression in the arts. The expressiveness of art is like that of a symbol, not that of an emotional symptom; it is as a formulation of feeling for our conception that a work of art is properly said to be expressive. It may serve somebody's need of self-expression besides; but that is not what makes it good or bad art. In a special sense one may call a work of art a symbol of feeling, for, like a symbol, it formulates our ideas of inward experience, as discourse formulates our ideas of things and facts in the outside world. A work of art differs from a genuine symbol—that is, a symbol in the full and usual sense—in that it does not point beyond itself to something else. The word "symbol" does not originally connote any representative function, or reference to something beyond itself; it means "thrown together"—συμβαλλειν. But in English usage it has come to mean a sign that stands for something else to which it directs our attention. This is something a work of art does not do. Its relation to feeling is a rather special one that we cannot undertake to analyze here; in effect, the feeling it expresses appears to be directly given with it, as the sense of a true metaphor, or the value of a religious myth, is not separable from its expression. We speak of the feeling *of,* or the feeling *in,* a work of art, not the feeling it means. And we speak truly; a work of art presents something like a direct vision of vitality, emotion, subjective reality.

The primary function of art is to objectify feeling so we can contemplate and understand it. It is the formulation of so-called "inward experience," the "inner life," that is impossible to achieve by discursive thought, because its forms are incommensurable with the forms of language and all its derivatives (e.g. mathematics, symbolic logic). Art objectifies the sentience and desire, self-consciousness and world-consciousness, emotions and moods that are generally regarded as irrational because words cannot give us clear ideas of them. But the premise tacitly assumed in such a judgment—namely, that anything language cannot express is formless and irrational—seems to me to be an error. I believe the life of feeling is not irrational; its logical forms are merely very different from the structures of discourse. But they are so much like the dynamic forms of art that art is their natural symbol. Through plastic works, music, fiction, dance, or dramatic forms we can conceive what vitality and emotion feel like.

All this time I have been expounding, word by word, what I mean by the definition of art proposed at the beginning of this lecture: Art is the practice of creating perceptible forms expressive of human feeling. We have dwelt on the exact sense of "form," and "expressive," and "feeling." Form in this context means a configuration, something seen or heard or imaginatively grasped as an entity, an integral whole given to perception like an apparition. Every work of art is a form in this sense. It may be a solid form, or a dynamic form like a whirl or a stream, or it may be a sounding form like a melody, or even the image of events known as a story, that, like dreams or memory, presents its form to imagination alone. "Expression" is here taken to mean articulation, not *self*-expression or venting of one's feeling. And "feeling," finally, is used in the broadest sense, denoting anything that can or could be felt—sensation, emotion, every tension in a sentient organism, from the feeling of vitality itself to the highest development of personal or even transcendent consciousness. The reason why works of art can express the nature of feeling, which language cannot present, is that artistic forms and the forms of feeling, or subjective reality, are logically similar, so that our directly felt life is reflected, symbolically articulated, and objectively presented to our understanding in works of art.

This brings us, at last, to the question of the cultural importance of the arts. Why is it so apt to be the vanguard of cultural advance, as it was in Egypt, in Greece, in Christian Europe (think of Gregorian music and Gothic architecture), in Renaissance Italy—not to speculate about ancient cavemen, whose art is all that we know of them? One thinks of culture as economic increase, social organization, the gradual ascendancy of rational thinking and scientific control of nature over superstitious imagination and magical practices. But art is not practical; it is neither philosophy nor science; it is not religion, morality, nor even social comment (as many drama critics take comedy to be). What does it contribute to culture that could be of major importance?

It merely presents forms—sometimes intangible forms—to imagination. Its direct appeal is to that faculty, or function, that Lord Bacon considered the chief stumbling block in the way of reason, that enlightened writers like Stuart Chase never tire of condemning as the source of all nonsense and bizarre erroneous beliefs. And so it is; but it is also the source of all insight and true beliefs. Imagination is probably the oldest mental trait that is typically human—older than discursive reason; it is probably the common source of dream, reason, religion, and all true general observation. It is this primitive human power—imagination—that engenders the arts and is in turn directly affected by their products.

Somewhere at the animalian starting line of human evolution lie the beginnings of that supreme instrument of the mind, language. We think of it as a device for communication among the members of a society. But communication is only one, and perhaps not even the first, of its functions. The first thing it does is to break up what William James called the "blooming, buzzing confusion" of sense perception into units and groups, events and chains of events—things and relations, causes and effects. All these patterns are imposed on our experience by language. We think, as we speak, in terms of objects and their relations.

But the process of breaking up our sense experience in this way, making reality conceivable, memorable, sometimes even predictable, is a process of imagination. Primitive conception is imagination. Language and imagination grow up together in a reciprocal tutelage.

What discursive symbolism—language in its literal use—does for our awareness of things about us and our own relation to them, the arts do for our awareness of subjective reality, feeling and emotion; they give inward experiences form and thus make them conceivable. The only way we can really envisage vital movement, the stirring and growth and passage of emotion, and ultimately the whole direct sense of human life, is in artistic terms. A musical person thinks of emotions musically. They cannot be discursively talked about above a very general level. But they may none the less be known —objectively set forth, publicly known—and there is nothing necessarily confused or formless about emotions.

As soon as the natural forms of subjective experience are abstracted to the point of symbolic presentation, we can use those forms to *imagine* feeling and understand its nature. Self-knowledge, insight into all phases of life and mind, springs from artistic imagination. That is the cognitive value of the arts.

But their influence on human life goes deeper than the intellectual level. As language actually gives form to our sense-experience, grouping our impressions around those things which have names, and fitting sensations to the qualities that have adjectival names, and so on, the arts we live with—our picture books and stories and the music we hear—actually form our emotive experience. Every generation has its styles of feeling. One age shudders and blushes and faints, another swaggers, still another is godlike in a universal indifference. These styles in actual emotion are not insincere. They are largely unconscious—determined by many social causes, but *shaped* by artists, usually popular artists of the screen, the juke-box, the shop window and the picture magazine. (That, rather than incitement to crime, is my objection to the comics.) Irwin Edman remarks in one of his books that our emotions are largely Shakespeare's poetry.

This influence of art on life gives us an indication why a period of efflorescence in the arts is apt to lead a cultural advance: it formulates a new way of feeling, and that is the beginning of a cultural age. It suggests another matter for reflection, too: that a wide neglect of artistic education is a neglect in the education of feeling. Most people are so imbued with the idea that feeling is a formless total organic excitement in humans as in animals, that the idea of educating feeling, developing its scope and quality, seems odd to them, if not absurd. It is really, I think, at the very heart of personal education.

There is one other function of the arts that benefits not so much the advance of culture as its stabilization; an influence on individual lives. This function is the converse and complement of the objectification of feeling, the driving force of creation in art: it is the education of vision that we receive in seeing, hearing, reading works of art—the development of the artist's eye, that assimilates ordinary sights (or sounds, motions, or events) to inward vision, and lends expressiveness and emotional import to the world. Wherever art takes a motif from actuality—a flowering branch, a bit of landscape, a historic event or a personal memory, any model or theme from life—it transforms it into a piece of imagination, and imbues its image with artistic vitality. The result is an impregnation of ordinary reality with the significance of created form. This is the *subjectification of nature,* that makes reality itself a symbol of life and feeling.

I cannot say much about this last point because I am just working with the idea myself. One of my students gave it to me, in a criticism of my own theory. But it seems to me to be of great significance.

Let us sum up briefly, then, why the arts, which many people regard as a cultural frill, are actually never a late addition to civilized life, an ornament gracing society like tea ceremonies or etiquette, but are born during the rise and the primitive phases of cultures, and often outrun all other developments in achieving mature character and technical competence. Cultures begin with the development of personal and social and religious feeling. The great instrument of this development is art. For, (1) art makes feeling apparent, objectively given so we may reflect on it and understand it; (2) the practice and familiar knowledge of any art provides forms for actual feeling to take, as language provides forms for sensory experience and factual observation; and (3) art is the education of the senses to see nature in expressive form. Thereby the actual world becomes in some measure symbolic of feeling (without being "anthropomorphized," supposed to *have* feelings) and personally significant.

The arts objectify subjective reality, and subjectify outward experience of nature. Art education is the education of feeling, and a society that neglects it gives itself up to formless emotion. Bad art is corruption of feeling. This is a large factor in the irrationalism which dictators and demagogues exploit.

CLEMENT GREENBERG

•

The Case for Abstract Art[1]

Many people say that the kind of art our age produces is one of the major symptoms of what's wrong with the age. The disintegration and, finally, the disappearance of recognizable images in painting and sculpture, like the obscurity in advanced literature, are supposed to reflect a disintegration of values in society itself. Some people go further and say that abstract, non-representational art is pathological art, crazy art, and that those who practice it and those who admire and buy it are either sick or silly. The kindest critics are those who say it's all a joke, a hoax, and a fad, and that modernist art in general, or abstract art in particular, will soon pass. This sort of thing is heard or read pretty constantly, but in some years more often than others.

There seems to be a certain rhythm in the advance in popularity of modernist art, and a certain rhythm in the counter-attacks which try to stem it. More or less the same words or arguments are used in all the polemics, but the targets usually change. Once it was the impressionists who were a scandal, next it was Van Gogh and Cézanne, then it was Matisse, then it was cubism and Picasso, after that Mondrian, and now it is Jackson Pollock. The fact that Pollock was an American shows, in a backhanded way, how important American art has lately become.

Some of the same people who attack modernist art in general, or abstract art in particular, happen also to complain that our age has lost those habits of disinterested contemplation, and that capacity for enjoying things as ends in themselves and for their own sake, which former ages are supposed to have cultivated. This idea has been advanced often enough to convert it into a cliché. I hate to give assent to a cliché, for it is almost always an over-simplification, but I have to make an exception in this case. While I strongly doubt that disinterested comtemplation was as unalloyed or as popular in ages

[1] From *Adventures of the Mind,* ed. Richard Thruelsen and John Kobler (New York: Vintage Books, 1960), pp. 270-280. Copyright 1958, 1959, The Curtis Publishing Company. Reprinted by permission of Clement Greenberg.

past as is supposed, I do tend to agree that we could do with more of it in this time, and especially in this country.

I think a poor life is lived by anyone who doesn't regularly take time out to stand and gaze, or sit and listen, or touch, or smell, or brood, without any further end in mind, simply for the satisfaction gotten from that which is gazed at, listened to, touched, smelled or brooded upon. We all know, however, that the climate of Western life, and particularly of American life, is not conducive to this kind of thing; we are all too busy making a living. This is another cliché, of course. And still a third cliché says that we should learn from Oriental society how to give more of ourselves to the life of the spirit, to contemplation and meditation, and to the appreciation of what is satisfying or beautiful in its own sole right. This last is not only a cliché, but a fallacy, since most Orientals are even more preoccupied than we are with making a living. I hope that I myself am not making a gross and reductive simplification when I say that so much of Oriental contemplative and aesthetic discipline strikes me as a technique for keeping one's eyes averted from ugliness and misery.

Every civilization and every tradition of culture seem to possess capacities for self-cure and self-correction that go into operation automatically, unbidden. If the given tradition goes too far in one direction it will usually try to right itself by going equally far in the opposite one. There is no question but that our Western civilization, especially in its American variant, devotes more mental energy than any other to the production of material things and services; and that, more than any other, it puts stress on interested, purposeful activity in general. This is reflected in our art, which, as has been frequently observed, puts such great emphasis on movement and development and resolution, on beginnings, middles, and endings—that is, on dynamics. Compare Western music with any other kind, or look at Western literature, for that matter, with its relatively great concern with plot and over-all structure and its relatively small concern with tropes and figures and ornamental elaborations; think of how slow-moving Chinese and Japanese poetry is by comparison with ours, and how much it delights in static situations; and how uncertain the narrational logic of non-Western fiction tends to be. Think of how encrusted and convoluted Arabic poetry is by contrast even with our most euphuistic lyrical verse. And as for non-Western music, does it not almost always, and literally, strike us as more monotonous than ours?

Well, how does Western art compensate for, correct, or at least qualify its emphasis on the dynamic—an emphasis that may or may not be excessive? And how does Western life itself compensate for, correct, or at least qualify its obsession with material production and purposeful activity? I shall not here attempt to answer the latter question. But in the realm of art an answer is beginning to emerge of its own accord, and the shape of part of that answer is abstract art.

Abstract decoration is almost universal, and Chinese and Japanese calligraphy is quasi-abstract—abstract to the extent that few occidentals can read the characters of Chinese or Japanese writing. But only in the West, and only in the last fifty years, have such things as abstract pictures and free-standing pieces of abstract sculpture appeared. What makes the big difference between these and abstract decoration is that they are, exactly, pictures and free-standing sculpture—solo works of art meant to be looked at for their own sake and with full attention, and not as the adjuncts, incidental aspects, or settings of things other than themselves. These abstract pictures and pieces of sculpture challenge our capacity for disinterested contemplation in a way that is more concentrated and, I daresay, more conscious than anything else I know of in art. Music is an essentially abstract art, but even at its most rarefied and abstract, and whether it's Bach's or the middle-period Schoenberg's music, it does not offer this challenge in quite the same way or degree. Music tends from a beginning through a middle toward an ending. We wait to see how it "comes out"—which is what we also do with literature. Of course, the *total* experience of literature and music is completely disinterested, but it becomes that only at a further remove. While undergoing the experience we are caught up and expectant as well as detached—disinterested and at the same time interested in a way resembling that in which we are interested in how things turn out in real life. I exaggerate to make my point—aesthetic experience *has* to be disinterested, and when it is genuine it always is, even when bad works of art are involved—but the distinctions I've made and those I've still to make are valid nevertheless.

With representational painting it is something like what it is with literature. This has been said before, many times before, but usually in order to criticize representational painting in what I think is a wrong-headed when not downright silly way. What I mean when I say, in this context, that representational painting is like literature, is that it tends to involve us in the interested as well as the disinterested by presenting us with the images of things that are inconceivable outside time and action. This goes even for landscapes and flower pieces and still lifes. It is not simply that we sometimes tend to confuse the attractiveness of the things represented in a picture with the quality of the picture itself. And it is not only that attractiveness as such has nothing to do with the abiding success of a work of art. What is more fundamental is that the meaning—as distinct from the attractiveness—of what is represented becomes truly inseparable from the representation itself. That Rembrandt confined impasto—thick paint, that is—to his highlights, and that in his later portraits especially these coincide with the ridges of the noses of his subjects is important to the artistic effect of these portraits. And that the effectiveness of the impasto, as impasto—as an abstract element of technique—coincides with its effectiveness as a means of showing just how a nose looks under a certain kind of light is also genuinely important. And that the lifelike delineation of the nose contributes to the evocation of the personality of the individual to whom the nose belongs is likewise important. And the manner and degree of insight into that individual's personality which Rembrandt exhibits in his portrait is important too. None of these factors can be, or ought to be, separated from the legitimate effect of the portrait as a picture pure and simple.

But once we have to do with personalities and lifelikeness we have to do with things from which we cannot keep as secure a distance for the sake of disinterestedness as we can, say, from abstract decoration. As it happens, the whole tendency of our Western painting, up until the later stages of impressionism, was to make distance and detachment on the part of the spectator as insecure as possible. It laid more of a stress than any other tradition on creating a sculpture-like, or photographic, illusion of the third dimension, on thrusting images at the eye with a lifelikeness that brought them as close as possible to their originals. Because of their sculptural vividness, Western paintings tend to be far less quiet, far more agitated and active—in short, far more explicitly dynamic—than most non-Western paintings do. And they involve the spectator to a much greater extent in the practical and actual aspects of the things they depict and represent.

We begin to wonder what we think of the people shown in Rembrandt's portraits, *as* people; whether or not we would like to walk through the terrain shown in a Corot landscape; about the life stories of the burghers we see in a Steen painting; we react in a less than disinterested way to the attractiveness of the models, real or ideal, of the personages in a Renaissance painting. And once we begin to do this we begin to participate in the work of art in a so-to-speak practical way. In itself this participation may not be improper, but it does become so when it begins to shut out all other factors. This it has done and does, all too often. Even though the connoisseurs have usually been able in the long run to prefer the picture of a dwarf by Velasquez to that of a pretty girl by Howard Chandler Christy, the enjoyment of pictorial and sculptural art in our society has tended, on every other level than that of professional connoisseurship, to be excessively "literary," and to center too much on merely technical feats of copying.

But, as I've said, every tradition of culture tends to try to correct one extreme by going to its opposite. And when our Western tradition of painting came up at last with reservations about its forthright naturalism, these quickly took the form of an equally forthright antinaturalism. These reservations started with late impressionism, and have now culminated in abstract art. I don't at all wish to be understood as saying that it all happened because some artist or artists decided it was time to curb the excesses of realistic painting, and that the main historical significance of abstract art lies in its function as an antidote to these. Nor do I wish to be understood as assuming that realistic or naturalistic art inherently needs, or ever needed, such a thing as an antidote. The motivations, conscious and unconscious, of the first modernist artists, and of present modernists as well, were and are quite different.

Impressionism itself started as an effort to push naturalism further than ever before. And all through the history of art—not only in recent times—consequences have escaped intentions.

It is on a different, and more impersonal and far more general level of meaning and history that our culture has generated abstract art as an antidote. On that level this seemingly new kind of art has emerged as an epitome of almost everything that disinterested contemplation requires, and as both a challenge and a reproof to a society that exaggerates, not the necessity, but the intrinsic value of purposeful and interested activity. Abstract art comes, on this level, as a relief, an archexample of something that does not have to mean, or be useful for, anything other than itself. And it seems fitting, too, that abstract art should at present flourish most in this country. If American society is indeed given over as no other society has been to purposeful activity and material production, then it is right that it should be reminded, in extreme terms, of the essential nature of disinterested activity.

Abstract art does this in very literal and also in very imaginative ways. First, it does not exhibit the illusion or semblance of things we are already familiar with in real life; it gives us no imaginary space through which to walk with the mind's eye; no imaginary objects to desire or not desire; no imaginary people to like or dislike. We are left alone with shapes and colors. These may or may not remind us of real things; but if they do, they usually do so incidentally or accidentally—on our own responsibility as it were; and the genuine enjoyment of an abstract picture does not ordinarily depend on such resemblances.

Second, pictorial art in its highest definition is static; it tries to overcome movement in space or time. This is not to say that the eye does not wander over a painted surface, and thus travel in both space and time. When a picture presents us with an illusion of real space, there is all the more inducement for the eye to do such wandering. But ideally the whole of a picture should be taken in at a glance; its unity should be immediately evident, and the supreme quality of a picture, the highest measure of its power to move and control the visual imagination, should reside in its unity. And this is something to be grasped only in an indivisible instant of time. No expectancy is involved in the true and pertinent experience of a painting; a picture, I repeat, does not "come out" the way a story, or a poem, or a piece of music does. It's all there at once, like a sudden revelation. This "at-onceness" an abstract picture usually drives home to us with greater singleness and clarity than a representational painting does. And to apprehend this "at-onceness" demands a freedom of mind and untrammeledness of eye that constitute "at-onceness" in their own right. Those who have grown capable of experiencing this know what I mean. You are summoned and gathered into one point in the continuum of duration. The picture does this to you, willy-nilly, regardless of whatever else is on your mind: a mere glance at it creates the attitude required for its appreciation, like a stimulus that elicits an automatic response. You become all attention, which means that you become, for the moment, selfless and in a sense entirely identified with the object of your attention.

The "at-onceness" which a picture or a piece of sculpture enforces on you is not, however, single or isolated. It can be repeated in a succession of instants, in each one remaining an "at-onceness," an instant all by itself. For the cultivated eye, the picture repeats its instantaneous unity like a mouth repeating a single word.

This pinpointing of the attention, this complete liberation and concentration of it, offers what is largely a new experience to most people in our sort of society. And it is, I think, a hunger for this particular kind of experience that helps account for the growing popularity of abstract art in this country: for the way it is taking over in the art schools, the galleries, and the museums. The fact that fad and fashion are also involved does not invalidate what I say. I know that abstract art of the latest variety—that originating with painters like Pollock and Georges Mathieu—has gotten associated with progressive jazz and its cultists; but what of it? That Wagner's music became associated with German ultranationalism, and that Wagner was Hitler's favorite composer, still doesn't detract from its sheer quality as music. That the present vogue for folk music started, back in the 1930's, among the Communists doesn't make our liking for it any the less genuine, or take anything away from folk music itself. Nor does the fact that so much gibberish gets talked and written about abstract art compromise it, just as the gibberish in which art criticism in general abounds, and abounds increasingly, doesn't compromise art in general.

One point, however, I want to make glaringly clear. Abstract art is not a special kind of art; no hard-and-fast line separates it from representational art; it is only the latest phase in the development of Western art as a whole, and almost every "technical" device of abstract painting is already to be found in the realistic painting that preceded it. Nor is it a superior kind of art. I still know of nothing in abstract painting, aside perhaps from some of the near-abstract cubist works that Picasso, Braque and Léger executed between 1910 and 1914, which matches the highest achievements of the old masters. Abstract painting may be a purer, more quintessential form of pictorial art than the representational kind, but this does not of itself confer quality upon an abstract picture. The ratio of bad abstract painting to good is actually much greater than the ratio of bad to good representational painting. Nonetheless, the very best painting, the major painting, of our age is almost exclusively abstract. Only on the middle and lower levels of quality, on the levels below the first-rate—which is, of course, where most of the art that gets produced places itself—only there is the better painting preponderantly representational.

On the plane of culture in general, the special, unique value of abstract art, I repeat, lies in the high degree of detached contemplativeness that its appreciation requires. Contemplativeness is demanded in greater or lesser degree for the appreciation of every kind of art, but abstract art tends to present this requirement in quintessential form, at its purest, least diluted, most immediate. If abstract art—as does happen nowadays—should chance to be the first kind of pictorial art we learn to appreciate, the chances are that when we go to other kinds of pictorial art—to the old masters, say, and I hope we all do go to the old masters eventually—we shall find ourselves all the better able to enjoy them. That is, we shall be able to experience them with less intrusion of irrelevancies, therefore more fully and more intensely.

The old masters stand or fall, their pictures succeed or fail, on the same ultimate basis as do those of Mondrian or any other abstract artist. The abstract formal unity of a picture by Titian is more important to its quality than what that picture images. To return to what I said about Rembrandt's portraits, the whatness of what is imaged is not unimportant—far from it—and cannot be separated, really, from the formal qualities that result from the way it is imaged. But it is a fact, in my experience, that representational paintings are essentially and most fully appreciated when the identities of what they represent are only secondarily present to our consciousness. Baudelaire said he could grasp the quality of a painting by Delacroix when he was still too far away from it to make out the images it contained, when it was still only a blur of colors. I think it was really on this kind of evidence that critics and connoisseurs, though they were almost always unaware of it, discriminated between the good and the bad in the past. Put to it, they more or less unconsciously dismissed from their minds the connotations of Rubens' nudes when assessing and experiencing the final worth of his art. They may have remained aware of the pinkness as a *nude* pinkness, but it was a pinkness and a nudity devoid of most of their usual associations.

Abstract paintings do not confront us with such problems. Or at least the frequenting of abstract art can train us to relegate them automatically to their proper place; and in doing this we refine our eyes for the appreciation of non-abstract art. That has been my own experience. That it is still relatively rare can be explained perhaps by the fact that most people continue to come to painting through academic art—the kind of art they see in ads and in magazines—and when and if they discover abstract art it comes as such an overwhelming experience that they tend to forget everything produced before. This is to be deplored, but it does not negate the value, actual or potential, of abstract art as an introduction to the fine arts in general, and as an introduction, too, to habits of disinterested contemplation. In this respect, the value of abstract art will, I hope, prove far greater in the future than it has yet. Not only can it confirm instead of subverting tradition; it can teach us, by example, how valuable so much in life can be made without being invested with ulterior meanings. How many people I know who have hung abstract pictures on their walls and found themselves gazing at them endlessly, and then exclaiming, "I don't know what there is in that painting, but I can't take my eyes off it." This kind of bewilderment is salutary. It does us good not to be able to explain, either to ourselves or to others, what we enjoy or love; it expands our capacity for experience.

ERWIN PANOFSKY

•

Et in Arcadia ego: Poussin and The Elegiac Tradition[1]

In 1769 Sir Joshua Reynolds showed to his friend Dr. Johnson his latest picture: the double portrait of Mrs. Bouverie and Mrs. Crewe, still to be seen in Crewe Hall in England.[2] It shows the two lovely ladies seated before a tombstone and sentimentalizing over its inscription: one points out the text to the other, who meditates thereon in the then fashionable pose of Tragic Muses and Melancholias.[3] The text of the inscription reads: *"Et in Arcadia ego."*

"What can this mean?" exclaimed Dr. Johnson. "It seems very nonsensical —I am in Arcadia." "The King could have told you," replied Sir Joshua. "He saw it yesterday and said at once: 'Oh, there is a tombstone in the background: Ay, ay, death is even in Arcadia.' "[4]

To the modern reader the angry discomfiture of Dr. Johnson is very puzzling. But no less puzzling is the quick understanding of George III, who instantly grasped the purport of the Latin phrase but interpreted it in a manner dissimilar to that which seems self-evident to most of us. In contrast to Dr. Johnson, we are no longer stumped by the phrase *Et in Arcadia ego.* But in contrast to George III, we are accustomed to reading a very different meaning into it. For us, the formula *Et in Arcadia ego* has come to be synonymous with such paraphrases as "Et tu in Arcadia vixisti," "I, too, was born in Arcadia," "Ego fui in Arcadia,"[5] "Auch ich war in Arkadien geboren,"[6]

[1]From *Meaning in the Visual Arts* (Garden City, N.Y.: Doubleday & Company, Inc., 1955), pp. 295–320. Reprinted by permission of the author.

[2] C. R. Leslie and Tom Taylor, *Life and Times of Sir Joshua Reynolds,* London, 1865, I, p. 325.

[3] See E. Wind, "Humanitätsidee und heroisiertes Porträt in der englischen Kultur des 18. Jahrhunderts," *Vorträge der Bibliothek Warburg,* 1930–1931, p. 156 ff., especially p. 222 ff.

[4] Leslie and Taylor, *loc. cit.*

[5] This form of the phrase is found in Richard Wilson's picture (in the collection of the Earl of Strafford), cited below, p. 241.

[6] This is the beginning of Friedrich Schiller's famous poem *Resignation* (quoted, for example, in Büchmann, *Geflügelte Worte,* 27th ed., p. 441 f., with many other instances from German literature), where the frustrated hero has renounced Pleasure and Beauty in favor of Hope and Truth and unsuccessfully requests

"Moi aussi je fus pasteur en Arcadie"[7]; and all these and many similar versions amount to what Mrs. Felicia Hemans expressed in the immortal words: "I, too, shepherds, in Arcadia dwelt."[8] They conjure up the retrospective vision of an unsurpassable happiness, enjoyed in the past, unattainable ever after, yet enduringly alive in the memory: a bygone happiness ended by death; and not, as George III's paraphrase implies, a present happiness menaced by death.

I shall try to show that this royal rendering—"Death is even in Arcadia"—represents a grammatically correct, in fact, the only grammatically correct, interpretation of the Latin phrase *Et in Arcadia ego,* and that our modern reading of its message—"I, too, was born, or lived, in Arcady"—is in reality a mistranslation. Then I shall try to show that this mistranslation, indefensible though it is from a philological point of view, yet did not come about by "pure ignorance" but, on the contrary, expressed and sanctioned, at the expense of grammar but in the interest of truth, a basic change in interpretation. Finally, I shall try to fix the ultimate responsibility for this change, which was of paramount importance for modern literature, not on a man of letters but on a great painter.

Before attempting all this, however, we have to ask ourselves a preliminary question: how is it that that particular, not overly opulent, region of central Greece, Arcady, came to be universally accepted as an ideal realm of perfect bliss and beauty, a dream incarnate of ineffable happiness, surrounded nevertheless with a halo of "sweetly sad" melancholy?

There had been, from the beginning of classical speculation, two contrasting opinions about the natural state of man, each of them, of course, a "Gegen-Konstruktion" to the conditions under which it was formed. One view, termed "soft" primitivism in an illuminating book by Lovejoy and Boas,[9] conceives of primitive life as a golden age of plenty, innocence and happiness—in other words, as civilized life purged of its vices. The other, "hard" form of primitivism conceives of primitive life as an almost subhuman existence full of terrible hardships and devoid of all comforts—in other words, as civilized life stripped of its virtues.

Arcady, as we encounter it in all modern literature, and as we refer to it

---

compensation. In English dictionaries of quotations, the passage is often erroneously ascribed to Goethe (by way of confusion with the motto superscribed on his *Italienische Reise,* for which see below, p. 319); cf., e.g., Burt Stevenson, *The Home Book of Quotations,* New York, 1937, p. 94; *A New Dictionary of Quotations,* H. L. Mencken, ed., New York, 1942, p. 53 (here with the equally erroneous assertion that "the phrase begins to appear on paintings in the XVI century"); Bartlett's *Familiar Quotations,* Boston, 1947, p. 1043.

[7] Jacques Delille, *Les Jardins,* 1782, quoted, e.g., in Büchmann, *loc. cit.,* and Stevenson, *loc. cit.*

[8] *The Poetical Works of Mrs. Felicia Hemans,* Philadelphia, 1847, p. 398. See also below, Note 50.

[9] A. O. Lovejoy and G. Boas, *Primitivism and Related Ideas in Antiquity,* Baltimore, I, 1935.

in our daily speech, falls under the heading of "soft" or golden-age primitivism. But of Arcady as it existed in actuality, and as it is described to us by the Greek writers, almost the opposite is true.

To be sure, this real Arcady was the domain of Pan, who could be heard playing the syrinx on Mount Maenalus,[10] and its inhabitants were famous for their musical accomplishments as well as for their ancient lineage, rugged virtue, and rustic hospitality; but they were also famous for their utter ignorance and low standards of living. As the earlier Samuel Butler was to summarize it in his well-known satire against ancestral pride:

> The old Arcadians that could trace
> Their pedigree from race to race
> Before the moon, were once reputed
> Of all the Grecians the most stupid,
> Whom nothing in the world could bring
> To civil life but fiddleing.[11]

And from a purely physical point of view their country lacked most of the charms which we are wont to associate with a land of ideal pastoral bliss. Polybius, Arcady's most famous son, while doing justice to his homeland's simple piety and love of music, describes it otherwise as a poor, bare, rocky, chilly country, devoid of all the amenities of life and scarcely affording food for a few meager goats.[12]

Small wonder, then, that the Greek poets refrained from staging their pastorals in Arcady. The scene of the most famous of them, the *Idylls* of Theocritus, is laid in Sicily, then so richly endowed with all those flowery meadows, shadowy groves and mild breezes which the "desert ways" (William Lithgow) of the actual Arcady conspicuously lacked. Pan himself has to

[10] Pausanius, *Periegesis,* VIII, 36, 8: "Mount Maenalus is particularly sacred to Pan so that people assert that Pan could be heard there playing the syrinx."

[11] Samuel Butler, *Satires and Miscellaneous Poetry and Prose,* R. Lamar, ed., Cambridge, 1929, p. 470.

[12] Polybius, *Historiae,* IV, 20. For further authors emphasizing the negative aspects of primordial simplicity, see, for example, Juvenal, who characterized a peculiarly boring orator as an "Arcadian youth" (*Saturae,* VII, 160) and Philostratus, *Vita Apollonii,* VIII, 7, who calls the Arcadians "acorn-eating swine." Even their musical achievements were disparaged by Fulgentius, *Expositio Virgilianae continentiae,* 748, 19 (R. Helm, ed., Leipzig, 1898, p. 90), who by *Arcadicae aures* (the reading *Arcadicis auribus* is better documented than, and preferable to, *arcaicis auribus*) meant "ears not susceptible to real beauty." The much discussed question as to whether there had existed in Arcady a genuine pastoral or bucolic poetry preceding Theocritus' *Idylls* now seems to have been decided in the negative. In addition to the literature adduced in E. Panofsky, "Et in Arcadia Ego; On the Conception of Transcience in Poussin and Watteau," *Philosophy and History, Essays Presented to Ernst Cassirer,* R. Klibansky and H. J. Paton, eds., Oxford, 1936, p. 223 ff., see now B. Snell, "Arkadien, die Entstehung einer geistigen Landschaft," *Antike und Abendland,* I, 1944, p. 26 ff. An article by M. Petriconi, "Das neue Arkadien," *ibidem,* III, 1948, p. 187 ff., does not contribute much to the problem discussed in this essay.

journey from Arcady to Sicily when Theocritus' dying Daphnis wishes to return his shepherd's flute to the god.[13]

It was in Latin, not in Greek, poetry that the great shift took place and that Arcady entered upon the stage of world literature. But even here we can still distinguish between two opposite manners of approach, one represented by Ovid, the other by Virgil. Both of them based their conception of Arcady to some extent on Polybius; but they used him in diametrically opposed ways. Ovid describes the Arcadians as primeval savages, still representing that period "prior to the birth of Jupiter and the creation of the moon," to which Samuel Butler alludes:

> Ante Jovem genitum terras habuisse feruntur
> Arcades, et Luna gens prior illa fuit.
> Vita ferae similis, nullos agitata per usus;
> Artis adhuc expers et rude volgus erat.[14]

"The Arcadians are said to have inhabited the earth before the birth of Jupiter; their tribe was older than the moon. Not as yet enhanced by discipline and manners, their life was similar to that of beasts; they were an uncouth lot, still ignorant of art." Very consistently, Ovid makes no mention of their one redeeming feature, their musicality: he made Polybius' Arcady even worse than it was.

Virgil, on the other hand, idealized it: not only did he emphasize the virtues that the real Arcady had (including the all-pervading sound of song and flutes not mentioned by Ovid); he also added charms which the real Arcady had never possessed: luxuriant vegetation, eternal spring, and inexhaustible leisure for love. In short, he transplanted the bucolics of Theocritus to what he decided to call Arcadia, so that Arethusa, the fountain nymph of Syracuse, must come to his assistance in Arcady,[15] whereas Theocritus' Pan, as mentioned before, had been implored to travel in the opposite direction.

In so doing, Virgil accomplished infinitely more than a mere synthesis of "hard" and "soft" primitivism, of the wild Arcadian pine trees with the Sicilian groves and meadows, of Arcadian virtue and piety with Sicilian sweetness and sensuousness: he transformed two realities into one Utopia, a realm sufficiently remote from Roman everyday life to defy realistic interpretation (the very names of the characters as well as of the plants and animals suggest an unreal, far-off atmosphere when the Greek words occur in the context of Latin verse), yet sufficiently saturated with visual concreteness to make a direct appeal to the inner experience of every reader.

It was, then, in the imagination of Virgil, and of Virgil alone, that the concept of Arcady, as we know it, was born—that a bleak and chilly district

[13] Theocritus, *Idylls,* I, 123 ff.
[14] Ovid, *Fasti,* II, 289 ff.
[15] Virgil, *Eclogues,* X, 4–6.

of Greece came to be transfigured into an imaginary realm of perfect bliss. But no sooner had this new, Utopian Arcady come into being than a discrepancy was felt between the supernatural perfection of an imaginary environment and the natural limitations of human life as it is. True enough, the two fundamental tragedies of human existence, frustrated love and death, are by no means absent from Theocritus' *Idylls.* On the contrary, they are strongly accentuated and depicted with haunting intensity. No reader of Theocritus will ever forget the desperate, monotonous invocations of the abandoned Simaetha, who, in the dead of night, spins her magic wheel in order to regain her lover;[16] or the end of Daphnis, destroyed by Aphrodite because he has dared challenge the power of love.[17] But with Theocritus these human tragedies are real—just as real as the Sicilian scenery—and they are things of the present. We actually witness the despair of the beautiful sorceress; we actually hear the dying words of Daphnis even though they form part of a "pastoral song." In Theocritus' real Sicily, the joys and sorrows of the human heart complement each other as naturally and inevitably as do rain and shine, day and night, in the life of nature.

In Virgil's ideal Arcady human suffering and superhumanly perfect surroundings create a dissonance. This dissonance, once felt, had to be resolved, and it was resolved in that vespertinal mixture of sadness and tranquillity which is perhaps Virgil's most personal contribution to poetry. With only slight exaggeration one might say that he "discovered" the evening. When Theocritus' shepherds conclude their melodious converse at nightfall, they like to part with a little joke about the behavior of nannies and billy goats.[18] At the end of Virgil's *Eclogues* we feel evening silently settle over the world: "Ite domum saturae, venit Hesperus, ite, capellae";[19] or: "Majoresque cadunt altis de montibus umbrae."[20]

Virgil does not exclude frustrated love and death; but he deprives them, as it were, of their factuality. He projects tragedy either into the future or, preferably, into the past, and he thereby transforms mythical truth into elegiac sentiment. It is this discovery of the elegiac, opening up the dimension of the

16 Theocritus, *Idylls,* II.

17 Theocritus, *Idylls,* I.

18 Theocritus, *Idylls,* I, 151 f.; V, 147 ff.

19 Virgil, *Eclogues,* X, 77: "Come home, you've had your fill; the evening star is here; come home, my goats." Cf. also *Eclogues,* VI, 84 ff.:

> Ille canit (pulsae referunt ad sidera valles),
> Cogere donec ovis stabulis numerumque referre
> Iussit et invito processit Vesper Olympo.

"[Silenus] sings, the echoing valleys wafting the sound to the stars, until Hesperus has ordered the flocks to be stabled and counted and, against Olympus' wishes, has pursued his course." The *invito Olympo* ("Olympus" here used for "the Olympians" as we use "the Kremlin" for the Russian government) has to be construed as an ablative absolute: the gods regret that the relentless progress of the evening star puts an end to the song of Silenus.

20 Virgil, *Eclogues,* I, 83: "And longer fall the shadows from the mountains high."

past and thus inaugurating that long line of poetry that was to culminate in Thomas Gray, which makes Virgil's bucolics, in spite of their close dependence on Greek models, a work of original and immortal genius. The Daphnis motif, for instance, was used by Virgil in two of his *Eclogues,* the Tenth and the Fifth. But in both cases, tragedy no longer faces us as stark reality but is seen through the soft, colored haze of sentiment either anticipatory or retrospective.

In the Tenth *Eclogue,* the dying Daphnis is boldly—and, it would seem, not without humor—transformed into a real person, Virgil's friend and fellow poet, Gallus. And while Theocritus' Daphnis is really dying because he has refused to love, Virgil's Gallus announces to a group of sympathizing shepherds and sylvan divinities that he is going to die because his mistress, Lycoris, has left him for a rival: she dwells in the dreary North but she is happy in the arms of her handsome soldier, Antony; he, Gallus, is surrounded by all the beauties of Utopia but wastes away with grief, comforted only by the thought that his sufferings and ultimate demise will be the subject of an Arcadian dirge.

In the Fifth *Eclogue,* Daphnis has retained his identity; but—and this is the novelty—his tragedy is presented to us only through the elegiac reminiscences of his survivors, who are preparing a memorial ceremony and are about to raise a tombstone for him:

> A lasting monument to Daphnis raise
> With this inscription to record his praise:
> "Daphnis, the fields' delight, the shepherds' love,
> Renown'd on earth and deifi'd above;
> Whose flocks excelled the fairest on the plains,
> But less than he himself surpassed the swains."[21]

Here, then, is the first appearance of the "Tomb in Arcadia," that almost indispensable feature of Arcady in later poetry and art. But after Virgil's passing, this tomb, and with it Virgil's Arcady as a whole, was to sink into oblivion for many centuries. During the Middle Ages, when bliss was sought in the beyond and not in any region of the earth, however perfect, pastoral poetry assumed a realistic, moralizing and distinctly non-Utopian character.[22] The *dramatis personae* were "Robin" and "Marion" instead of "Daphnis" and "Chloe," and the scene of Boccaccio's *Ameto,* where more than thirteen hundred years after Virgil at least the name of Arcadia reappears, is laid near Cortona in Tuscany. Arcadia is represented only by an emissary, so to speak, and this emissary—a shepherd named Alcesto di Arcadia—limits himself to defending, after the fashion of the conventional "debates" (*concertationes* or

[21] Virgil, *Eclogues,* V, 42 ff., here quoted from Dryden's translation.
[22] For a brief summary of the development, see L. Levraut, *Le Genre pastoral,* Paris, 1914.

Nicolas Poussin *"Et in Arcadia ego,"* Paris, Louvre (Scala, Florence)

Giovanni Francesco Guercino *"Et in Arcadia ego,"* Rome, Galleria Corsini (Scala, Florence)

Nicolas Poussin *"Et in Arcadia ego,"* Devonshire Collection, Chatsworth. Reproduced by permission of the Trustees of the Chatsworth Settlement. (Zoltan Wegner, London)

Jackson Pollock *Number 5*. 1950. Collection, The Museum of Modern Art, New York. Gift of Mr. and Mrs. Walter Bareiss

Unity Church, Oak Park, Illinois; architect, Frank Lloyd Wright. Courtesy, The Museum of Modern Art, New York

Robie House, Chicago; architect, Frank Lloyd Wright. Courtesy, The Museum of Modern Art, New York

conflictus), the Polybian and Ovidian ideal of rough and healthy frugality against the charms of wealth and comfort extolled by his rival, Achaten di Achademia from Sicily.[23]

In the Renaissance, however, Virgil's—not Ovid's and Polybius'—Arcady emerged from the past like an enchanting vision. Only, for the modern mind, this Arcady was not so much a Utopia of bliss and beauty distant in space as a Utopia of bliss and beauty distant in time. Like the whole classical sphere, of which it had become an integral part, Arcady became an object of that nostalgia which distinguishes the real Renaissance from all those pseudo- or proto-Renaissances that had taken place during the Middle Ages:[24] it developed into a haven, not only from a faulty reality but also, and even more so, from a questionable present. At the height of the Quattrocento an attempt was made to bridge the gap between the present and the past by means of an allegorical fiction. Lorenzo the Magnificent and Politian metaphorically identified the Medici villa at Fiesole with Arcady and their own circle with the Arcadian shepherds; and it is this alluring fiction which underlies Signorelli's famous picture—now, unhappily, destroyed—which used to be admired as the *Realm of Pan*.[25]

Soon, however, the visionary kingdom of Arcady was reestablished as a sovereign domain. In Boccaccio's *Ameto* it had figured only as a distant home of rustic simplicity, and the Medicean poets had used it only as a classical disguise for their own country life. In Jacopo Sannazaro's *Arcadia*[26] of 1502 Arcady itself is the scene of the action and is glorified for its own sake; it is revived as an emotional experience *sui generis* and *sui juris* instead of serving as a classical pseudonym for the poet's and his patrons' own surroundings. Sannazaro's Arcady is, like Virgil's, a Utopian realm. But in addition it is a realm irretrievably lost, seen through a veil of reminiscent melancholy: "La musa vera del Sannazaro è la malinconia," as an Italian scholar puts it.[27] Reflecting the feeling of a period that, for the first time, had realized that Pan was dead, Sannazaro wallows in those funeral hymns and ceremonies,

[23] Boccaccio, *Ameto,* V (Florence edition of 1529, p. 23 ff.).

[24] Cf. E. Panofsky, "Renaissance and Renascences," *Kenyon Review,* VI, 1944, p. 201 ff.

[25] For an analysis of Signorelli's painting, see F. Saxl, *Antike Götter in der Spätrenaissance, Studien der Bibliothek Warburg,* VIII, Leipzig and Berlin, 1927, p. 22 ff.

[26] For Jacopo Sannazaro's *Arcadia,* see M. Scherillo's illuminating introduction to his edition of 1888. Sannazaro's poem—first published at Venice in 1502—is based on both Italian and classical sources (Petrarch and Boccaccio on the one hand, Virgil, Polybius, Catullus, Longus, Nemesius, etc., on the other), thereby resuscitating the Virgilian conception of Arcadia within the limits of a modern, more subjective *Weltanschauung.* Sannazaro's is the first postclassical pastoral actually staged *in* Arcadia, and it is a significant fact that the few allusions to the contemporary scene, the court of Naples, were added, or at least made explicit, only in the second edition of 1504.

[27] A. Sainati, *La lirica latina del Rinascimento,* Pisa, 1919, I, p. 184, quoted by Saxl, *ibidem.*

yearning love songs and melancholy memories which occur in Virgil only occasionally; and his very predilection for triple rhymes, technically known as *drucciolo* (a few lines of this kind will be quoted later), endows his verses with a sweet, lingering plaintiveness. It was through him that the elegiac feeling—present but, as it were, peripheral in Virgil's *Eclogues*—became the central quality of the Arcadian sphere. One more step and this nostalgic but as yet impersonal longing for the unbroken peace and innocence of an ideal past was sharpened into a bitter, personal accusation against the real present. The famous "O bell'età de l'oro" in Torquato Tasso's *Aminta* (1573) is not so much a eulogy of Arcady as an invective against the constrained and conscience-ridden spirit of Tasso's own period, the age of the Counter-Reformation. Flowing hair and nude bodies are bound and concealed, deportment and carriage have lost touch with nature; the very spring of pleasure is polluted, the very gift of Love perverted into theft.[28] Here is the outburst of an actor stepping before the footlights and in the presence of all contrasting the misery of his real existence with the splendor of his role.

Almost exactly half a century later, Giovanni Francesco Guercino—not Bartolommeo Schidone, as stated in all "Dictionaries of Familiar Quotations"—produced the first pictorial rendering of the Death in Arcady theme; and it is in this picture, painted at Rome between 1621 and 1623 and now preserved in the Galleria Corsini, that we first encounter the phrase *Et in Arcadia ego.*[29] There are reasons to believe that the subject was of special interest to Giulio Rospigliosi (later Pope Clement IX), whose family palace, which housed Guido Reni's *Aurora,* must have been frequently visited by Guercino when he composed his own, more modern *Aurora* in the Casino Ludovisi; and Giulio Rospigliosi—a humanist, a lover of the arts, and a poet of no mean merits—may even be the inventor of the famous phrase, which is not classical and does not seem to occur in literature before it made its appearance in Guercino's picture.[30] What, then, is the literal sense of this phrase?

[28] Tasso, *Aminta,* I, 2 (E. Grillo, ed., London and Toronto, 1924, p. 90 ff.).

[29] Guercino's picture is referred to as Schidone's in, for example, Büchmann, *loc. cit.*, Bartlett, *loc. cit.* (where, in addition, the inscription on Poussin's Louvre painting is misquoted as *Et ego in Arcadia vixi*) and Hoyt's *New Cyclopedia of Poetical Quotations* (which has the text right but translates it as: "I, too, was in Arcadia"). For the correct attribution of the painting, see H. Voss, "Kritische Bemerkungen zu Seicentisten in den römischen Galerien," *Repertorium für Kunstwissenschaft,* XXXIV, 1911, p. 119 ff. (p. 121).

[30] For Giulio Rospigliosi, see L. von Pastor, *The History of the Popes,* E. Graf, tr. XXXI, London, 1940, p. 319 ff.; for his poetical works, G. Cavenazzi, *Papa Clemente IX Poeta,* Modena, 1900. He was born in 1600 at Pistoia but educated at the Jesuits' College at Rome, subsequently studied at the University of Pisa, and taught philosophy there from 1623 to 1625 (which, of course, did not prevent him from visiting Rome at intervals). Soon after, he seems to have settled in Rome (in 1629 he composed poems on a Barberini-Colonna wedding) and obtained high offices at the Curia in 1632. After nine years as papal nuncio in Spain (1644–1653), he became governor of Rome (1655), was created cardinal in 1657, elected pope in 1667, and died in 1669. That this cultured and

As was mentioned at the beginning, we are now inclined to translate it as "I, too, was born, or lived, in Arcady." That is to say, we assume that the *et* means "too" and refers to *ego,* and we further assume that the unexpressed verb stands in the past tense; we thus attribute the whole phrase to a defunct inhabitant of Arcady. All these assumptions are incompatible with the rules of Latin grammar. The phrase *Et in Arcadia ego* is one of those elliptical sentences like *Summum jus summa iniuria, E pluribus unum, Nequid nimis* or *Sic semper tyrannis,* in which the verb has to be supplied by the reader. This unexpressed verb must therefore be unequivocally suggested by the words given, and this means that it can never be a preterite. It is possible to suggest a subjunctive as in *Nequid nimis* ("Let there never be done too much") or *Sic semper tyrannis* ("May this be the fate of all tyrants"); it is also possible, though fairly unusual, to suggest a future as in Neptune's famous *Quos ego* ("These I shall deal with"); but it is not possible to suggest a past tense. Even more important: the adverbial *et* invariably refers to the noun or pronoun directly following it (as in *Et tu, Brute*), and this means that it belongs, in our case, not to *ego* but to *Arcadia;* it is amusing to observe that some modern writers accustomed to the now familiar interpretation but blessed with an inbred feeling for good Latin—for instance, Balzac,[31] the

---

unselfish prince of the Church—who patronized the first "Exhibition of Old Masters," organized by his brother, in the last year of his papacy (Pastor, p. 331)—was in some way involved with the *Et in Arcadia* subject is suggested by a passage in G. P. Bellori, *Le vite de' pittori, scultori, et architetti moderni,* Rome, 1672, p. 447 f. After having described Poussin's *"Ballo della vita humana,"* now in the Wallace Collection at London, Bellori informs us that the subject of this *morale poesia* had been "suggested by Pope Clement IX, when still a prelate," and goes on to say that the painter did full justice to the *sublimità dell' Autore che aggiunse le due seguenti invenzioni,* to wit, *"La verità scoperta del Tempo"* (probably not identical with the painting now in the Louvre but with another version, transmitted through the engravings listed in A. Andresen, *Nicolaus Poussin; Verzeichnis der nach seinen Gemälden gefertigten Kupferstiche,* Leipzig, 1863, Nos. 407 and 408, the latter dedicated to Clement IX) and *"La Felicità soggetta a la Morte,"* that is to say, the *Et in Arcadia ego* composition. Barring a typographical error (omission of a *si* before *che aggiunse*), the "exalted" *Autore* can only be Giulio Rospigliosi (for Poussin is referred to, at the beginning of the same sentence, as *Niccolo*): according to Bellori it was he, Rospigliosi, who "added the two following inventions," that is to say, in addition to the *Ballo della vita humana,* the *Verità scoperta del Tempo* and the Arcadia subject.

The difficulty is that—as we know while Bellori probably did not—this subject had already been treated by Guercino between 1621 and 1623 while he was engaged upon his Aurora fresco in the Casino Ludovisi. Bellori's brief account may have simplified a situation which might be tentatively reconstructed as follows: Bellori knew from Poussin that Giulio Rospigliosi had ordered the Louvre version of the *Et in Arcadia ego* and had informed Poussin that he, Rospigliosi, was the actual inventor of the subject. Bellori took this to mean that Rospligiosi had "invented" the subject when ordering the Louvre picture; but what Rospigliosi had really claimed was that he had suggested it to Guercino (doubtless a frequent visitor to Guido Reni's *Aurora*) and, subsequently, asked Poussin to repeat it in an improved redaction.

[31] Balzac, *Madame Firmiani:* "J'ai aussi aimé, *et ego in Arcadia.*"

German Romanticist C. J. Weber,[32] and the excellent Miss Dorothy Sayers[33] —instinctively misquote the *Et in Arcadia ego* into *Et ego in Arcadia.* The correct translation of the phrase in its orthodox form is, therefore, not "I, too, was born, or lived, in Arcady," but: "Even in Arcady there am I," from which we must conclude that the speaker is not a deceased Arcadian shepherd or shepherdess but Death in person. In short, King George III's interpretation is, grammatically, absolutely right. And with reference to Guercino's painting, it is also absolutely right from a visual point of view.

In this painting two Arcadian shepherds are checked in their wanderings by the sudden sight, not of a funerary monument but of a huge human skull that lies on a moldering piece of masonry and receives the attentions of a fly and a mouse, popular symbols of decay and all-devouring time.[34] Incised on the masonry are the words *Et in Arcadia ego,* and it is unquestionably by the skull that they are supposed to be pronounced; an old description of the picture mistakenly but understandably even places them on a scroll issuing from the skull's mouth.[35] The skull, now, was and is the accepted symbol

[32] C. J. Weber, *Demokritos oder hinterlassene Papiere eines lachenden Philosophen,* n. d., XII, 20, p. 253 ff.: "Gräber und Urnen in englischen Gärten verbreiten die nämliche sanfte Wehmut wie ein Gottesacker oder ein 'Et ego in Arcadia,' in einer Landschaft von Poussin," and the same erroneous reading, now fairly well explained, occurs in the earlier editions of Büchmann's *Geflügelte Worte* (in the 16th edition, for instance, on p. 582).

[33] Dorothy Sayers, "The Bone of Contention," *Lord Peter Views the Body* (Harcourt Brace and Co., N. Y.), p. 139. This feeling for Latin grammar seems to be widespread among British mystery-story writers. In Nicholas Blake's *Thou Shell of Death,* XII (Continental Albatross Edition, 1937), p. 219, an elderly nobleman says: "*Et ego,* Superintendent, *in Arcadia vixi*—what?"

[34] The significance of the mouse as a symbol of all-devouring time is already pointed out in Horapollo's *Hieroglyphica* I, 50 (now easily accessible in G. Boas, *The Hieroglyphics of Horapollo* [Bollingen Series, XXIII], New York, 1950, p. 80) and remained well known throughout the centuries (cf. the mediaeval allegory of human life known as "The Tree of Barlaam"; according to Condivi, *Vita di Michelangelo,* cap. xlv, even Michelangelo is said to have planned the inclusion of a mouse in the iconography of the Medici Chapel). Viewed through the medium of "Romantic irony" the motive of the Guercino picture looks as follows: "Ein gar herrliches 'Memento mori' ist . . . ein hübscher gebleichter *Menschenschädel* auf der Toilette. So ein leerer Hirnkasten . . . müsste Wunder tun, wenn die Macht der Gewohnheit nicht noch stärker wäre. . . . Man würde zuletzt das Dasein des Totenschädels ganz vergessen. wenn nicht schon zu Zeiten *eine Maus* ihn wieder lebendig gemacht . . . hätte" (C. J. Weber, *loc. cit.*).

[35] Leslie and Taylor, *loc. cit.,* with reference to Reynolds' portrait of Mrs. Bouverie and Mrs. Crewe: "The thought is borrowed from Guercino where the gay frolickers stumble over a death's-head with a scroll proceeding from his mouth inscribed *Et in Arcadia ego.*" The "scroll" allegedly proceeding from the mouth of the skull is obviously due to a misinterpretation of the mouse's tail. Only, as I don't know the Reynolds sketch (unfortunately the "Roman Sketchbook," formerly belonging to R. Gwatkin, cf. Leslie and Taylor, *op. cit.,* I, p. 51, could not be located), I cannot tell whether Reynolds misinterpreted the picture or Tom Taylor misinterpreted the sketch. In any case this very misinterpretation shows that even at a comparatively recent period an unbiased observer of the Guercino composition naturally assumed that the words *Et in Arcadia ego* were voiced by the skull.

of Death personified, as is borne out by the very fact that the English language refers to it, not as a "dead man's head," but as a "death's-head." The speaking death's-head was thus a common feature in sixteenth- and seventeenth-century art and literature[36] and is even alluded to by Falstaff (*Henry IV,* second part, ii, 4) when he answers Doll Tearsheet's well-intentioned warnings as to his conduct: "Peace, good Doll, do not speak like a death's-head; do not bid me remember mine end."

This "remember mine end" is precisely the message of Guercino's painting. It conveys a warning rather than sweet, sad memories. There is little or nothing elegiac about it, and when we try to trace the iconographic antecedents of the composition, we find them in such moralistic representations as the renderings of the Legend of the Three Quick and the Three Dead (known to all from the Camposanto at Pisa), where three young knights, setting out for a hunt, come upon three corpses that rise from their coffins and warn the elegant young men against their thoughtless enjoyment of life. As these mediaeval dandies are stopped by the coffins, so are Guercino's Arcadians stopped by the skull; the old description just mentioned even speaks of them as "gay frolickers *stumbling over* a death's-head."[37] In both cases Death catches youth by the throat, so to speak, and "bids it remember the end." In short, Guercino's picture turns out to be a mediaeval *memento*

[36] As to the significance of skulls and skeletons in connection with the general conception of life and destiny, cf. R. Zahn, *81. Berliner Winckelmanns-Programm,* 1923; T. Creizenach, "Gaudeamus igitur," *Verhandlungen der 28. Versammlung Deutscher Philologen und Schulmänner.* Leipzig, 1872; C. H. Becker, "Ubi sunt qui ante nos in mundo fuere?," *Aufsätze zur Kultur- und Sprachgeschichte, vornehmlich des Islam,* Ernst Kuhn zum 70. Geburtstage gewidmet, 1916, pp. 87 ff. It appears that the original significance of those morbid symbols, occurring on goblets and table decorations before they appeared on sepulchral monuments, was a purely hedonistic one, viz., an invitation to enjoy the pleasures of life as long as it lasts, and only subsequently was turned into a moralistic sermon of resignation and penitence. This development took place in ancient Egypt as well as in the civilizations deriving from classical antiquity, both occidental and oriental. In them, the inversion of the original idea was chiefly due to patristic writing. In point of fact, the *Vita brevis* idea is characterized by an intrinsic ambivalence implying both the Horatian *Carpe diem* and the Christian *surge, surge, vigila, semper esto paratus* (refrain of a song of 1267). From the later phase of the Middle Ages the "speaking" skulls and skeletons became so common a symbol of the *memento mori* idea (in the Camaldulensian sense of this formula) that these motifs invaded almost every sphere of everyday life. Innumerable instances are not only to be found in sepulchral art (mostly with such inscriptions as *Vixi ut vivis, moriers ut sum mortuus* or *Tales vos eritis, fueram quandoque quod estis*), but also in portraits, on clocks, on medals, and, most especially, on finger rings (many instances adduced in the London Shakespeare edition of 1785 with reference to the notorious dialogue between Falstaff and Doll Tearsheet). On the other hand, the menace of a "speaking skull" could also be interpreted as a hopeful prospect for the afterlife, as is the case in a short stanza by the German seventeenth-century poet D. C. von Lohenstein, in which the *Redender Todtenkopff des Herrn Matthäus Machners* says: *Ja/ wenn der Höchste wird vom Kirch-Hof erndten ein/ So werd ich Todten-Kopff ein Englisch Antlitz seyn* (quoted in W. Benjamin, *Ursprung des deutschen Trauerspiels,* 1928, p. 215).

[37] See the passage quoted in Note 35.

mori in humanistic disguise—a favorite concept of Christian moral theology shifted to the ideal milieu of classical and classicizing pastorals.

We happen to know that Sir Joshua Reynolds not only knew but even sketched Guercino's painting (ascribing it, incidentally, to its true author instead of to Bartolommeo Schidone).[38] It is a fair assumption that he remembered this very painting when he included the *Et in Arcadia ego* motif in his portrait of Mrs. Crewe and Mrs. Bouverie; and this firsthand connection with the very source of the phrase may account for the fact that its grammatically correct interpretation (as "Even in Arcadia, I, Death, hold sway"), while long forgotten on the Continent, remained familiar to the circle of Reynolds and, later on, became part of what may be termed a specifically English or "insular" tradition—a tradition which tended to retain the idea of a *memento mori.* We have seen that Reynolds himself adhered to the correct interpretation of the Latin phrase and that George III understood it at once. In addition, we have an *Et in Arcadia ego* composition by Giovanni Battista Cipriani, born in Florence but active in England from the end of his apprenticeship up to his death in 1785,[39] which shows the coat-of-arms of Death, the skull and bones, surmounted by the inscription *"Ancora in Arcadia morte,"* which means: "Even in Arcady there is Death," precisely as King George had translated it. Even the ironic iconoclasm of our own century still draws, in England, from this original, sinister conception of the *Et in Arcadia* theme. Augustus John, who likes to designate portraits of Negro girls with such Arcadian names as "Daphne," "Phyllis," or even "Aminta," has affixed the title *Atque in Arcadia ego* (the unorthodox *atque* expressing the "even" still more emphatically than does the orthodox *et*) to a morbid, morning-after scene where Death has assumed the guise of a ghastly guitar player;[40] and in Evelyn Waugh's *Brideshead Revisited* the narrator, while a sophisticated undergraduate at Oxford, adorns his rooms at college with a "human skull lately purchased from the School of Medicine which, resting on a bowl of roses, formed at the moment the chief decoration of my table. It bore the motto *Et in Arcadia ego* inscribed on its forehead."

However, Cipriani, while faithful to the "insular" tradition in the translation of the Latin phrase, drew from another source for his pictorial com-

[38] See Leslie and Taylor, *op. cit.,* p. 260: "I find a sketch of Guercino's picture in Reynolds' Roman notebook." It was obviously from this sketch, probably bearing the usual explanatory note, that Tom Taylor learned about the Corsini picture and its author, and so surprising was this knowledge that a later biographer of Reynolds, ignorant as he was of the Guercino painting, ventured to state that Reynolds had been inspired by Poussin (W. Armstrong, *Joshua Reynolds,* übersetzt von E. von Kraatz, n.d., p. 89).

[39] Cipriani produced, among other things, the illustrations of the famous Ariosto edition brought out by the Baskerville Press at Birmingham in 1773.

[40] J. Rothenstein, *Augustus John,* Oxford, n.d., Fig. 71. The Negro portraits referred to are illustrated there in Figs. 66, 67, 69. According to a letter from Sir John Rothenstein, the titles given to Augustus John's works in his book were furnished orally by the artist.

position. A thoroughgoing eclectic, he expanded the landscape and added sheep, dogs, and fragments of classical buildings; he increased the personnel by seven figures of a, generally speaking, Raphaelesque character (five of them women); and he replaced Guercino's artless masonry and actual death's-head by an elaborately classicizing tomb, with the skull and bones carved upon it in relief.

In doing all this, this rather indifferent artist shows himself familiar with the innovations of that one man whose pictures mark the turning point in the history of the *Et in Arcadia ego* theme: the great French painter Nicolas Poussin.

Poussin had come to Rome in 1624 or 1625, one or two years after Guercino had left it. And a few years later (presumably about 1630) he produced the earlier of his two *Et in Arcadia ego* compositions, now in the Devonshire Collection at Chatsworth. Being a Classicist (though in a very special sense), and probably conversant with Virgil, Poussin revised Guercino's composition by adding the Arcadian river god Alpheus and by transforming the decaying masonry into a classical sarcophagus inscribed with the *Et in Arcadia ego;* moreover, he emphasized the amorous implications of the Arcadian milieu by the addition of a shepherdess to Guercino's two shepherds. But in spite of these improvements, Poussin's picture does not conceal its derivation from Guercino's. In the first place, it retains to some extent the element of drama and surprise: the shepherds approach as a group from the left and are unexpectedly stopped by the tomb. In the second place, there is still the actual skull, placed upon the sarcophagus above the word *Arcadia,* though it has become quite small and inconspicuous and fails to attract the attention of the shepherds who—a telling symptom of Poussin's intellectualistic inclinations—seem to be more intensely fascinated by the inscription than they are shocked by the death's-head. In the third place, the picture still conveys, though far less obtrusively than Guercino's, a moral or admonitory message. It formed, orginally, the counterpart of a *Midas Washing His Face in the River Pactolus* (now in the Metropolitan Museum at New York), the iconographically essential figure of the river god Pactolus accounting for the inclusion of its counterpart, the less necessary river god Alpheus, in the Arcadia picture.[41]

In conjunction, the two compositions thus teach a twofold lesson, one warning against a mad desire for riches at the expense of the more real values of life, the other against a thoughtless enjoyment of pleasures soon to be ended. The phrase *Et in Arcadia ego* can still be understood to be voiced by

[41] The connection between Poussin's earlier *Et in Arcadia* composition, viz., the painting owned by the Duke of Devonshire, and the New York Midas picture was recognized and completely analyzed by A. Blunt, "Poussin's Et in Arcadia ego," *Art Bulletin,* XX, 1938, p. 96 ff. Blunt dates the Duke of Devonshire version about 1630, with which I am now inclined to agree.

Death personified, and can still be translated as "Even in Arcady I, Death, hold sway," without being out of harmony with what is visible in the painting itself.

After another five or six years, however, Poussin produced a second and final version of the *Et in Arcadia ego* theme, the famous picture in the Louvre. And in this painting—no longer a *memento mori* in classical garb paired with a *cave avaritiam* in classical garb, but standing by itself—we can observe a radical break with the mediaeval, moralizing tradition. The element of drama and surprise has disappeared. Instead of two or three Arcadians approaching from the left in a group, we have four, symmetrically arranged on either side of a sepulchral monument. Instead of being checked in their progress by an unexpected and terrifying phenomenon, they are absorbed in calm discussion and pensive contemplation. One of the shepherds kneels on the ground as though rereading the inscription for himself. The second seems to discuss it with a lovely girl who thinks about it in a quiet, thoughtful attitude. The third seems trajected into a sympathetic, brooding melancholy. The form of the tomb is simplified into a plain rectangular block, no longer foreshortened but placed parallel to the picture plane, and the death's-head is eliminated altogether.

Here, then, we have a basic change in interpretation. The Arcadians are not so much warned of an implacable future as they are immersed in mellow meditation on a beautiful past. They seem to think less of themselves than of the human being buried in the tomb—a human being that once enjoyed the pleasures which they now enjoy, and whose monument "bids them remember their end" only in so far as it evokes the memory of one who had been what they are. In short, Poussin's Louvre picture no longer shows a dramatic encounter with Death but a contemplative absorption in the idea of mortality. We are confronted with a change from thinly veiled moralism to undisguised elegiac sentiment.

This general change in content—brought about by all those individual changes in form and motifs that have been mentioned, and too basic to be accounted for by Poussin's normal habit of stabilizing and in some measure tranquillizing the second version of an earlier picture dealing with the same subject[42]—can be explained by a variety of reasons. It is consistent with the more relaxed and less fearful spirit of a period that had triumphantly emerged from the spasms of the Counter-Reformation. It is in harmony with the principles of Classicist art theory, which rejected "les objets bizarres," especially such gruesome objects as a death's-head.[43] And it was facilitated, if not caused, by Poussin's familiarity with Arcadian literature, already evident in

[42] The importance of this habit is, in my opinion, somewhat overestimated in J. Klein, "An Analysis of Poussin's 'Et in Arcadia ego,'" *Art Bulletin,* XIX, 1937, p. 314 ff.

[43] See, for example, H. Jouin, *Conférences de l'Académie Royale de Peinture et de Sculpture,* Paris, 1883, p. 94.

the Chatsworth picture, where the substitution of a classical sarcophagus for Guercino's shapeless piece of masonry may well have been suggested by the tomb of Daphnis in Virgil's Fifth *Eclogue*. But the reverent and melancholy mood of the Louvre picture, and even a detail such as the simple, rectangular shape of the tomb, would seem to reveal a fresh contact with Sannazaro. His description of the "Tomb in Arcadia"—characteristically no longer enclosing the reluctant shepherd Daphnis but a no less reluctant shepherdess named Phyllis—actually foreshadows the situation visualized in Poussin's later composition:

> . . . . farò fra questi rustici
> La sepoltura tua famosa e celebre.
> Et da' monti Thoscani et da' Ligustici
> Verran pastori ad venerar questo angulo
> Sol per cagion che alcuna volta fustici.
> Et leggeran nel bel sasso quadrangulo
> Il titol che ad tutt'hore il cor m'infrigida,
> Per cui tanto dolor nel petto strangulo:
> "Quella che ad Meliseo si altera et rigida
> Si mostrò sempre, hor mansueta et humile
> Si sta sepolta in questa pietra frigida."[44]

"I will make thy tomb famous and renowned among these rustic folk. Shepherds shall come from the hills of Tuscany and Liguria to worship this corner of the world solely because thou hast dwelt here once. And they shall read on the beautiful square monument the inscription that chills my heart at all hours, that makes me strangle so much sorrow in my breast: 'She who always showed herself so haughty and rigid to Meliseo now lies entombed, meek and humble, in this cold stone.' "

These verses not only anticipate the simple, rectangular shape of the tomb in Poussin's Louvre picture which strikes us as a direct illustration of Sannazaro's *bel sasso quadrangulo;* they also conform in an amazing degree to the picture's strange, ambiguous mood—to that hushed brooding over the silent message of a former fellow being: "I, too, lived in Arcady where you now live; I, too, enjoyed the pleasures which you now enjoy; I, too, was hard-hearted where I should have been compassionate. And now I am dead and buried." In thus paraphrasing, according to Sannazaro, the meaning of the *Et in Arcadia ego* as it appears in Poussin's Louvre painting, I have done what nearly all the Continental interpreters did: I have distorted the original meaning of the inscription in order to adapt it to the new appearance and content of the picture. For there is no doubt that this inscription, translated correctly, no longer harmonizes with what we see with our eyes.

[44] Sannazaro, *Arcadia* (Scherillo, ed.), p. 306, lines 257–67. Further tombs occur in Sannazaro's poem on p. 70, line 49 ff., and p. 145, line 246 ff. (a literal translation of Virgil, *Eclogues,* X, 31 ff.).

When read according to the rules of Latin grammar ("Even in Arcady, there am I"), the phrase had been consistent and easily intelligible as long as the words could be attributed to a death's-head and as long as the shepherds were suddenly and frighteningly interrupted in their walk. This is manifestly true of Guercino's painting, where the death's-head is the most prominent feature of the composition and where its psychological impact is not as yet weakened by the competition of a beautiful sarcophagus or tomb. But it is also true, if in a considerably lesser degree, of Poussin's earlier picture, where the skull, though smaller and already subordinated to the newly introduced sarcophagus, is still in evidence, and where the idea of sudden interruption is retained.

When facing the Louvre painting, however, the beholder finds it difficult to accept the inscription in its literal, grammatically correct, significance. In the absence of a death's-head, the *ego* in the phrase *Et in Arcadia ego* must now be taken to refer to the tomb itself. And though a "speaking tomb" was not unheard of in the funerary poetry of the time, this conceit was so unusual that Michelangelo, who used it in three of his fifty epitaphs on a handsome boy, thought it necessary to enlighten the reader by an explanatory remark to the effect that here it is, exceptionally, "the tomb which addresses him who reads these verses."[45] It is infinitely more natural to ascribe the words, not to the tomb but to the person buried therein. Such is the case with ninety-nine per cent of all epitaphs, including the inscriptions of the tomb of Daphnis in Virgil and the tomb of Phyllis in Sannazaro; and Poussin's Louvre picture suggests this familiar interpretation—which, as it were, projects the message of the Latin phrase from the present into the past—all the more forcibly as the behavior of the figures no longer expresses surprise and dismay but quiet, reminiscent meditation.

Thus Poussin himself, while making no verbal change in the inscription, invites, almost compels, the beholder to mistranslate it by relating the *ego* to a dead person instead of to the tomb, by connecting the *et* with *ego* instead of with *Arcadia,* and by supplying the missing verb in the form of a *vixi* or *fui* instead of a *sum*. The development of his pictorial vision had outgrown the significance of the literary formula, and we may say that those who, under the impact of the Louvre picture, decided to render the phrase *Et in Arcadia ego* as "I, too, lived in Arcady," rather than as "Even in Arcady, there am I," did violence to Latin grammar but justice to the new meaning of Poussin's composition.

This *felix culpa* can, in fact, be shown to have been committed in Poussin's

[45] See the discussion between W. Weisbach, "Et in Arcadia ego," *Gazette des Beaux-Arts,* ser. 6, XVIII, 1937, p. 287 ff., and this writer, " 'Et in Arcadia ego' et le tombeau parlant," *ibidem,* ser. 6, XIX, 1938, p. 305 f. For Michelangelo's three epitaphs in which the tomb itself addresses the beholder ("La sepoltura parla a chi legge questi versi"), see K. Frey, *Die Dichtungen des Michelagniolo Buonaroti,* Berlin, 1897, No. LXXVII, 34, 38, 40.

own circle. His friend and first biographer, Giovanni Pietro Bellori, had given, in 1672, a perfectly correct and exact interpretation of the inscription when he wrote: *"Et in Arcadia ego,* cioè, che *il sepolcro si trova ancora* in Arcadia, e la Morte a luogo in mezzo le felicità"[46] (*"Et in Arcadia ego,* which means that the *grave is to be found* [present tense!] *even* in Arcady and that death occurs in the very midst of delight"). But only a few years later (1685) Poussin's second biographer, André Félibien, also acquainted with him, took the first and decisive step on the road to bad Latinity and good artistic analysis: "Par cette inscription," he says, "on a voulu marquer que *celui qui est dans cette sépoulture a vécu* en Arcadie et que la mort se rencontre parmi les plus grandes félicitez"[47] ("This inscription emphasizes the fact that the *person buried in this tomb has lived* [past tense!] in Arcady"). Here, then, we have the occupant of the tomb substituted for the tomb itself, and the whole phrase projected into the past: what had been a menace has become a remembrance. From then on the development proceeded to its logical conclusion. Félibien had not bothered about the *et;* he had simply left it out, and this abbreviated version, quaintly retranslated into Latin, survives in the inscription of a picture by Richard Wilson, painted at Rome in 1755: "Ego fui in Arcadia." Some thirty years after Félibien (1719), the Abbé du Bos rendered the *et* by an adverbial "cependant"; "Je vivais cependant en Arcadie,"[48] which is in English: "And yet I lived in Arcady." The final touch, it seems, was put by the great Diderot, who, in 1758, firmly attached the *et* to the *ego* and rendered it by *aussi:* "Je vivais aussi dans la délicieuse Arcadie,"[49] "I,

[46] G. P. Bellori, *loc. cit.*

[47] A. Félibien, *Entretiens sur les vies et les ouvrages des peintres,* Paris, 1666–1685 (in the edition of 1705, IV, p. 71); cf. also the inscription of Bernard Picart's engraving after Poussin's Louvre picture as quoted by Andresen, *op. cit.,* No. 417.

[48] Abbé du Bos, *Réflexions critiques sur la poésie et sur la peinture* (first published in 1719), I, section VI; in the Dresden edition of 1760, p. 48 ff.

[49] Diderot, "De la poésie dramatique," *Oeuvres complétes,* J. Assézat, ed., Paris, 1875–1877, VII, p. 353. Diderot's description of the painting itself is significantly inaccurate: "Il y a un paysage de Poussin où l'on voit de jeunes bergères qui dansent au son du chalumeau [!]; et à l'écart, un tombeau avec cette inscription *'Je vivais aussi dans a délicieuse Arcadie.'* Le prestige de style dont il s'agit, tient quelquefois à un mot qui detourne ma vue du sujet principal, et qui me montre de côte, comme dans le paysage du Poussin, l'espace, le temps, la vie, la mort ou quelque autre idée grande et mélancolique jetée toute au travers des images de la gaieté" (cf. also another reference to the Poussin picture in Diderot's "Salon de 1767," *Oeuvres,* XI, p. 161; later on the misplaced *aussi* became as much a matter of course in French literature as the misplaced *Auch* in Germany, as illustrated by Delille's *Et moi aussi, je fus pasteur dans l'Arcadie*). The picture described by Diderot seemed to bear out his well-known theory of the *contrastes dramatiques,* because he imagined that it showed the shepherds dancing to the sound of a flute. This error is due either to a confusion with other pictures by Poussin, such, for example, as the *Bacchanal* in the London National Gallery or the *Feast of Pan* in the Cook Collection at Richmond, or to the impression of some later picture dealing with the same subject. Angelica Kauffmann, for instance, in 1766 exhibited a picture described as follows: "a shepherd and shepherdess of Arcadia moralizing at the side of a sepulchre,

too, lived in delightful Arcady." His translation must thus be considered as the literary source of all the later variations now in use, down to Jacques Delille, Johann Georg Jacobi, Goethe, Schiller, and Mrs. Felicia Hemans."[50]

Thus, while—as we have seen—the original meaning of *Et in Arcadia ego* precariously survived in the British Isles, the general development outside England resulted in the nearly universal acceptance of what may be called the elegiac interpretation ushered in by Poussin's Louvre picture. And in Poussin's own homeland, France, the humanistic tradition had so much decayed in the nineteenth century that Gustave Flaubert, the great contemporary of the early Impressionists, no longer understood the famous phrase at all. In his beautiful description of the Bois de la Garenne—"parc très beau malgré ces beautés factices"—he mentions, together with a Temple of Vesta, a Temple of Friendship, and a great number of artificial ruins: "sur une pierre taillée en forme de tombe, *In Arcardia ego,* non-sens dont je n'ai pu découvrir l'intention,"[51] "on a stone cut in the shape of a tomb one reads *In Arcadia ego,* a piece of nonsense the meaning of which I have been unable to discover."

We can easily see that the new conception of the Tomb in Arcady initiated by Poussin's Louvre picture, and sanctioned by the mistranslation of its inscription, could lead to reflections of almost opposite nature, depressing and melancholy on the one hand, comforting and assuaging on the other; and, more often than not, to a truly "Romantic" fusion of both. In Richard Wilson's painting, just mentioned, the shepherds and the funerary monument —here a slightly mutilated *stele*—are reduced to a *staffage* accentuating the muted serenity of the Roman Campagna at sundown. In Johann Georg Jacobi's *Winterreise* of 1769—containing what seems to be the earliest "Tomb in Arcady" in German literature—we read: "Whenever, in a beautiful landscape, I encounter a tomb with the inscription *Auch ich war in Arkadien,* I point it out to my friends; we stop a moment, press each other's hands, and

while others are dancing at a distance" (cf. Lady Victoria Manners and Dr. W. C. Williamson, *Angelica Kauffmann,* London, 1924, p. 239; also Leslie and Taylor, *op. cit.,* I, p. 260).

[50] For Jacques Delille, Goethe and Schiller, see above, Notes 6, 7. As to Mrs. Felicia Hemans (cf. Note 8), the motto superscribed on her poem appears to confuse Poussin's Louvre picture with one or more of its later variations: "A celebrated picture of Poussin represents a band of shepherd youths and maidens suddenly checked in their wanderings and affected with various emotions by the sight of a tomb which bears the inscription 'Et in Arcadia ego.'" In the poem itself Mrs. Hemans follows in the footsteps of Sannazaro and Diderot in assuming that the occupant of the tomb is a young girl:

> Was some gentle kindred maid
> In that grave with dirges laid?
> Some fair creature, with the tone
> Of whose voice a joy is gone?

[51] Gustave Flaubert, "Par les champs et par les grèves." *Oeuvres complètes,* Paris, 1910, p. 70; the passage was kindly brought to my attention by Georg Swarzenski.

proceed."[52] And in a strangely attractive engraving by a German Romanticist named Carl Wilhelm Kolbe, who had a trick of constructing wondrous jungles and forests by magnifying grass, herbs or cabbage leaves to the size of bushes and trees, the tomb and its inscription (here, correctly, *Et in Arcadia ego* although the legend of the engraving consists of the erroneous "Auch ich war in Arkadien") serve only to emphasize the gentle absorption of two lovers in one another. In Goethe's use of the phrase *Et in Arcadia ego,* finally, the idea of death has been entirely eliminated.[53] He uses it, in an abbreviated version ("Auch ich in Arkadien") as a motto for his famous account of his blissful journey to Italy, so that it merely means: "I, too, was in the land of joy and beauty."

Fragonard, on the other hand, retained the idea of death; but he reversed the original moral. He depicted two cupids, probably spirits of departed lovers, clasped in an embrace within a broken sarcophagus while other, smaller cupids flutter about and a friendly genius illumines the scene with the light of a nuptial torch. Here the development has run full cycle. To Guercino's "Even in Arcady, there is death" Fragonard's drawing replies: "Even in death, there may be Arcady."

[52] See Büchmann, *loc. cit.*

[53] Cf. also Goethe's *Faust,* iii, 3:

> Gelockt, auf sel'gem Grund zu wohnen,
> Du flüchtetest ins heiterste Geschick!
> Zur Laube wandeln sich die Thronen,
> Arcadisch frei sei unser Glück!

In later German literature this purely hedonistic interpretation of Arcadian happiness was to degenerate into the trivial conception of "having a good time." In the German translation of Offenbach's *Orphée aux Enfers* the hero therefore sings "Als ich noch Pinz war von *Arkadien*" instead of "Quand j'étais prince de *Béotie*."

FRANK LLOYD WRIGHT

•

Modern Architecture: The Cardboard House[1]

Let us take for text on this, our fourth afternoon, the greatest of all references to simplicity, the inspired admonition: *"Consider the lilies of the field—they toil not, neither do they spin, yet verily I say unto thee—Solomon in all his glory was not arrayed like one of these."* An inspired saying—

[1] Reprinted by permission of the publishers, Horizon Press, from *The Future of Architecture* by Frank Lloyd Wright. Copyright 1953.

attributed to an humble Architect in ancient times, called Carpenter, who gave up Architecture nearly two thousand years ago to go to work upon its Source.

And if the text should seem to you too far away from our subject this afternoon—

"The Cardboard House"

—consider that for that very reason the text has been chosen. The cardboard house needs an antidote. The antidote is far more important than the house. As antidote—and as practical example, too, of the working out of an ideal of organic simplicity that has taken place here on American soil, step by step, under conditions that are your own—could I do better than to take apart for your benefit the buildings I have tried to build, to show you how they were, long ago, dedicated to the Ideal of Organic Simplicity? It seems to me that while another might do better than that, I certainly could not—for that is, truest and best, what I know about the Subject. What a man *does, that* he has.

When, "in the cause of Architecture," in 1893, I first began to build the houses, sometimes referred to by the thoughtless as "The New School of the Middle West" (some advertiser's slogan comes along to label everything in this our busy woman's country), the only way to simplify the awful building in vogue at the time was to conceive a finer entity—a better building—and get it built. The buildings standing then were all tall and all tight. Chimneys were lean and taller still, sooty fingers threatening the sky. And beside them, sticking up by way of dormers through the cruelly sharp, saw-tooth roofs, were the attics for "help" to swelter in. Dormers were elaborate devices, cunning little buildings complete in themselves, stuck to the main roof slopes to let "help" poke heads out of the attic for air.

Invariably the damp sticky clay of the prairie was dug out for a basement under the whole house, and the rubblestone walls of this dank basement always stuck up above the ground a foot or more and blinked, with half-windows. So the universal "cellar" showed itself as a bank of some kind of masonry running around the whole house, for the house to sit up on—like a chair. The lean, upper house-walls of the usual two floors above this stone or brick basement were wood, set on top of this masonry-chair, clapboarded and painted, or else shingled and stained, preferably shingled and mixed, up and down, all together with mouldings crosswise. These overdressed wood house-walls had, cut in them—or cut out of them, to be precise—big holes for the big cat and little holes for the little cat to get in and out or for ulterior purposes of light and air. The house-walls were be-corniced or bracketed up at the top into the tall, purposely profusely complicated roof, dormers plus. The whole roof, as well as the roof as a whole, was scalloped and ridged and tipped and swanked and gabled to madness before they would allow it to be either shingled or slated. The whole exterior was be-deviled—that is to say, mixed to puzzle-pieces, with corner boards, panel-boards, window-frames, corner-blocks, plinth-blocks, rosettes, fantails, ingenious and jigger work in general. This was the only way they seemed to have, then, of "putting on style." The scroll-saw and turning-lathe were at the moment the honest means of this fashionable mongering by the wood-butcher and to this entirely "moral" end. Unless the householder of the period were poor indeed, usually an ingenious corner-tower on his house eventuated into a candle-snuffer dome, a spire, an inverted rutabaga or radish or onion or—what is your favorite vegetable? Always elaborate bay-windows and fancy porches played "ring around a rosy" on this "imaginative" corner feature. And all this the building of the period could do equally well in brick or stone. It was an impartial society. All material looked pretty much alike in that day.

Simplicity was as far from all this scrap-pile as the pandemonium of the barn-yard is far from music. But it was easy for the Architect. All he had to do was to call: "Boy, take down No. 37, and put a bay-window on it for the lady!"

So—the first thing to do was to get rid of the attic and, therefore, of the dormer and of the useless "heights" below it. And next, get rid of the unwholesome basement, entirely—yes, absolutely—in any house built on the prairie. Instead of lean, brick chimneys, bristling up from steep roofs to hint at "judgment" everywhere, I could see necessity for one only, a broad generous one, or at most, for two, these kept low down on gently sloping roofs or perhaps flat roofs. The big fireplace below, inside, became now a place for a real fire, justified the great size of this chimney outside. A real fireplace at that time was extraordinary. There were then "mantels" instead. A mantel was a marble frame for a few coals, or a piece of wooden furniture with tiles stuck in it and a "grate," the whole set slam up against the wall. The "mantel" was an insult to comfort, but the *integral* fireplace became an important part of the building itself in the houses I was allowed to build out there on the prairie. It refreshed me to see the fire burning deep in the masonry of the house itself.

Taking a human being for my scale, I brought the whole house down in height to fit a normal man; believing in no other scale, I broadened the mass out, all I possibly could, as I brought it down into spaciousness. It has been said that were I three inches taller (I am 5 feet 8½ inches tall), all my houses would have been quite different in proportion. Perhaps.

House-walls were now to be started at the ground on a cement or stone water-table that looked like a low platform under the building, which it usually was, but the house-walls were stopped at the second story window-sill level, to let the rooms above come through in a continuous window-series, under the broad eaves of a gently sloping, overhanging roof. This made enclosing screens out of the lower walls as well as light screens out of the second story walls. Here was true *enclosure of interior space*. A new sense of building, it seems.

The climate, being what it was, a matter of violent extremes of heat and cold, damp and dry, dark and bright, I gave broad protecting roof-shelter to the whole, getting back to the original purpose of the "Cornice." The undersides of the roof projections were flat and light in color to create a glow of reflected light that made the upper rooms not dark, but delightful. The overhangs had double value, shelter and preservation for the walls of the house as well as diffusion of reflected light for the upper story, through the "light screens" that took the place of the walls and were the windows.

At this time, a house to me was obvious primarily as interior space under fine shelter. I liked the sense of *shelter*. I liked the sense of shelter in the "look of the building." I achieved it, I believe. I then went after the variegated bands of material in the old walls to eliminate odds and ends in favor of one material and a single surface from grade to eaves, or grade to second story sill-cope, treated as simple enclosing screens,—or else made a plain screen band around the second story above the window-sills, turned up over on to the ceiling beneath the eaves. This screen band was of the same material as the under side of the eaves themselves, or what architects call the "soffit." The planes of the building parallel to the ground were all stressed, to grip the whole to earth. Sometimes it was possible to make the enclosing wall below this upper band of the second story, from the second story window-sill clear down to the ground, a heavy "wainscot" of fine masonry material resting on the cement or stone platform laid on the foundation. I liked that wainscot to be of masonry material when my clients felt they could afford it.

As a matter of form, too, I liked to see the projecting base, or water-table, set out over the foundation walls themselves—as a substantial preparation for the building. This was managed by setting the studs of the walls to the inside of the foundation walls, instead of to the outside. All door and window tops were now brought into line with each other with only comfortable head-clearance for the average human being. Eliminating the sufferers from the "attic" enabled the roofs to lie low. The house began to associate with the ground and become natural to its prairie site. And would the young man in architecture ever believe that this was all "new" then? Not only new, but destructive heresy—or ridiculous eccentricity. So New that what little prospect I had of ever earning a livelihood by making houses was nearly wrecked. At first, "they" called the houses "dress-reform" houses, because Society was just then excited about that particular "reform." This simplification looked like some kind of "reform" to them. Oh, they called them all sorts of names that cannot be repeated, but "they" never found a better term for the work unless it was "Horizontal Gothic," "Temperance Architecture" (with a sneer), etc., etc. I don't know how I escaped the accusation of another "Renaissance."

What I have just described was all on the *outside* of the house and was there chiefly because of what had happened *inside*. Dwellings of that period were "cut-up," advisedly and completely, with the grim determination that should go with any cutting process. The "interiors" consisted of boxes beside or inside other boxes, called *rooms.* All boxes inside a complicated boxing. Each domestic "function" was properly box to box. I could see little sense in this inhibition, this cellular sequestration that implied ancestors familiar with the cells of penal institutions, except for the privacy of bed-rooms on the upper floor. They were perhaps all right as "sleeping boxes." So I declared the whole lower floor as one room, cutting off the kitchen as a laboratory, putting servants' sleeping and living quarters next to it, semi-detached, on the ground floor, screening various portions in the big room, for certain domestic purposes—like dining or reading, or receiving a formal caller. There were no plans like these in existence at the time and my clients were pushed toward these ideas as helpful to a solution of the vexed servant-problem. Scores of doors disappeared and no end of partition. They liked it, both clients and servants. The house became more free as "space" and more liveable, too. Interior spaciousness began to dawn.

Having got what windows and doors that were left lined up and lowered to convenient human height, the ceilings of the rooms, too, could be brought over on to the walls, by way of the horizontal, broad bands of plaster on the walls above the windows, the plaster colored the same as the room ceilings. This would bring the ceiling-surface down to the very window tops. The ceilings thus expanded, by extending them downward as the wall band above the windows, gave a generous overhead to even small rooms. The sense of the whole was broadened and made plastic, too, by this expedient. The enclosing walls and ceilings were thus made to flow together.

Here entered the important element of Plasticity—indispensable to successful use of the Machine, for true expression of Modernity. The outswinging windows were fought for because the casement window associated the house with out-of-doors—gave free openings, outward. In other words the so-called "casement" was simple and more human. In use and effect, more natural. If it had not existed I should have invented it. It was not used at that time in America, so I lost many clients because I insisted upon it when they wanted the "guillotine" or "double-hung" window then in use. The Guillotine was not simple nor human. It was only expedient. I used it once in the Winslow House—my first house—and rejected it thereafter—forever. Nor at that time did I entirely eliminate the wooden trim. I did make it "plastic," that is, light and continuously flowing instead of the heavy "cut and butt" of the usual carpenter work. No longer did the "trim," so-called, look like carpenter work. The machine could do it perfectly well as I laid it out. It was all after "quiet." This plastic trim, too, with its running "back-hand" enabled poor workmanship to be concealed. It was necessary with the field resources at hand at that time to conceal much. Machinery versus the union had already demoralized the workmen. The Machine resources were so little understood that extensive drawings had to be made merely to show the "mill-man" what to leave off. But the "trim" finally became only a single, flat, narrow, horizontal wood-band running around the room, one at the top of the windows and doors and another next to the floors, both connected with narrow, vertical, thin wood-bands that were used to divide the wall-surfaces of the whole room smoothly and flatly into folded color planes. The trim merely completed the window and door openings in this same plastic sense. When the interior had thus become wholly plastic, instead of structural, a New element, as I have said, had entered Architecture. Strangely enough an element that had not existed in Architectural History before. Not alone in the trim, but in numerous ways too tedious to describe in words, this revolutionary sense of the plastic whole, an instinct with me at first, began to work more and more intelligently and have fascinating, unforeseen consequences. Here was something that began to organize itself. When several houses had been finished and compared with the house of the period, there was very little of that house left standing. Nearly every one had stood the house of the period as long as he could stand it, judging by appreciation of the change. Now all this probably tedious description is intended to indicate directly in bare outline how thus early there *was* an ideal of organic simplicity put to work, with historical consequences, here in your own country. The main motives and indications were (and I enjoyed them all):

First—To reduce the number of necessary parts of the house and the separate rooms to a minimum, and make all come together as enclosed space—so divided that light, air and vista permeated the whole with a sense of unity.

Second—To associate the building as a whole with its site by extension and emphasis of the planes parallel to the ground, but keeping the floors off the best part of the site, thus leaving that better part for use in connection with the life of the house. Extended level planes were found useful in this connection.

Third—To eliminate the room as a box and the house as another by making all walls enclosing screens—the ceilings and floors and enclosing screens to flow into each other as one large enclosure of space, with minor subdivisions only.

Make all house proportions more liberally human, with less wasted space in structure, and structure more appropriate to material, and so the whole more liveable. *Liberal* is the best word. Extended straight lines or streamlines were useful in this.

Fourth—To get the unwholesome basement up out of the ground, entirely above it, as a low pedestal for the living-portion of the home, making the foundation itself visible as a low masonry platform, on which the building should stand.

Fifth—To harmonize all necessary openings to "outside" or to "inside" with good human proportions and make them occur naturally—singly or as a series in the scheme of the whole building. Usually they appeared as "light-screens" instead of walls, because all the "Architecture" of the house was chiefly the way these openings came in such walls as were grouped about the rooms as enclosing screens. The *room* as such was now the essential architectural expression, and there were to be no holes cut in the walls as holes are cut in a box, because this was not in keeping with the ideal of "plastic." Cutting holes was violent.

Sixth—To eliminate combinations of different materials in favor of mono-material so far as possible; to use no ornament that did not come out of the nature of materials to make the whole building clearer and more expressive as a place to live in, and give the conception of the building appropriate revealing emphasis. Geometrical or straight lines were natural to the machinery at work in the building trades then, so the interiors took on this character naturally.

Seventh—To incorporate all heating, lighting, plumbing so that these systems became constituent parts of the building itself. These service features became architectural and in this attempt the ideal of an organic architecture was at work.

Eighth—To incorporate as organic Architecture—so far as possible—furnishings, making them all one with the building and designing them in simple terms for machine work. Again straight lines and rectilinear forms.

Ninth—Eliminate the Decorator. He was all curves and all efflorescence, if not all "period."

This was all rational enough so far as the thought of an organic architecture went. The particular form this thought took in the feeling of it all could only be personal. There was nothing whatever at this time to help make them what they were. All seemed to be the most natural thing in the world and grew up out of the circumstances of the moment. Whatever they may be worth in the long run is all they are worth.

Now *simplicity* being the point in question in this early constructive effort, organic simplicity I soon found to be a matter of true coordination. And Beauty I soon felt to be a matter of the sympathy with which such coordination was affected. Plainness was not necessarily simplicity. Crude furniture of the Roycroft-Stickley-Mission Style, which came along later, was offensively plain, plain as a barn door—but never was simple in any true sense. Nor, I found, were merely machine-made things in themselves simple. To think "in simple," is to deal in simples, and that means with an eye single to the altogether. This, I believe, is the secret of simplicity. Perhaps we may truly regard nothing at all as simple in itself. I believe that no one thing in itself is ever so, but must achieve simplicity (as an Artist should use the term) as a perfectly realized part of some organic whole. Only as a feature or any part becomes an harmonious element in the harmonious whole does it arrive at the estate of simplicity. Any wild flower is truly simple, but double the same wild flower by cultivation, it ceases to be so. The *scheme* of the original is no longer clear. Clarity of design and perfect significance both are first essentials of the spontaneously born simplicity of the lilies of the field who neither toil nor spin, as contrasted with Solomon who had "toiled and spun"—that is to say, no doubt had put on himself and had put on his temple, properly "composed," everything in the category of good things but the cook-stove.

Five lines where three are enough is stupidity. Nine pounds where three are sufficient is stupidity. But to eliminate expressive words that intensify or vivify meaning in speaking or writing is not simplicity; nor is similar elimination in Architecture simplicity—it, too, may be stupidity. In Architecture, expressive changes of surface, emphasis of line and especially textures of material, may go to make facts eloquent, forms more significant. Elimination, therefore, may be just as meaningless as elaboration, perhaps more often so. I offer any fool, for an example.

To know what to leave out and what to put in, just where and just how—Ah, *that* is to have been educated in knowledge of SIMPLICITY.

As for Objects of Art in the house even in that early day they were the "bête noir" of the new simplicity. If well chosen, well enough in the house, but only if each was properly digested by the whole. Antique or modern sculpture, paintings, pottery, might become objectives in the Architectural scheme and I accepted them, aimed at them, and assimilated them. Such things may take their places as elements in the design of any house. They are then precious things, gracious and good to live with. But it is difficult to do this well. Better, if it may be done, to design all features together. At that time, too, I tried to make my clients see that furniture and furnishings, not built in as integral features of the building, should be designed as attributes of whatever furniture was built in and should be seen as minor parts of the building itself, even if detached or kept aside to be employed on occasion. But when the building itself was finished, the old furniture the clients already possessed went in with them to await the time when the interior might be completed. Very few of the houses were, therefore, anything but painful to me after the clients moved in and, helplessly, dragged the horrors of the old order along after them.

But I soon found it difficult, anyway, to make some of the furniture in the "abstract"; that is, to design it as architecture and make it "human" at the same time—fit for human use. I have been black and blue in some spot, somewhere, almost all my life from too intimate contacts with my own furniture. Human beings must group, sit or recline—confound them—and they must dine, but dining is much easier to manage and always was a great artistic opportunity. Arrangements for the informality of sitting comfortably, singly or in groups, where it is desirable or natural to sit, and still to belong in disarray to the scheme as a whole—that is a matter difficult to accomplish. But it can be done now, and should be done, because only those attributes of human comfort and convenience, made to belong in this digested or integrated sense to the architecture of the home as a whole, should be there at all, in Modern Architecture. For that matter about four-fifths of the contents of nearly every home could be given away with good effect to that home. But the things given away might go on to poison some other home. So why not at once destroy undesirable things . . . make an end of them?

Here then, in foregoing outline, is the gist of America's contribution to Modern American Architecture as it was already under way in 1893. But the gospel of elimination is one never preached enough. No matter how much preached, Simplicity is a spiritual ideal seldom organically reached. Nevertheless, by assuming the virtue by imitation—or by increasing structural makeshifts to get superficial simplicity—the effects may cultivate a taste that will demand the reality in course of time, but it may also destroy all hope of the real thing.

Standing here, with the perspective of long persistent effort in the direction of an organic Architecture in view, I can again assure you out of this initial experience that Repose is the reward of true simplicity and that organic simplicity is sure of Repose. Repose is the highest quality in the Art of Architecture, next to integrity, and a reward for integrity. Simplicity may well be held to the fore as a spiritual ideal, but when actually achieved, as in the "lilies of the field," it is something that comes of itself, something spontaneously born out of the nature of the doing whatever it is that is to be done. Simplicity, too, is a reward for fine feeling and straight thinking in working a principle, well in hand, to a consistent end. Solomon knew nothing about it, for he was only wise. And this, I think, is what Jesus meant by the text we have chosen for this discourse—"Consider the lilies of the field," as contrasted, for beauty, with Solomon.

Now, a chair *is* a machine to sit in.

A home *is* a machine to live in.

The human body *is* a machine to be worked by will.

A tree *is* a machine to bear fruit.

A plant *is* a machine to bear flowers and seeds.

And, as I've admitted before somewhere, a heart *is* a suction-pump. Does that idea thrill you?

Trite as it is, it may be as well to think it over because the *least* any of these things may be, *is* just that. All of them are that before they are anything else. And to violate that mechanical requirement in any of them is to finish before anything of higher purpose can happen. To ignore the fact is either sentimentality or the prevalent insanity. Let us acknowledge in this respect, that this matter of mechanics is just as true of the work of Art as it is true of anything else. But, were we to stop with that trite acknowledgment, we should only be living in a low, rudimentary sense. This skeleton rudiment accepted, *understood,* is the first condition of any fruit or flower we may hope to get from ourselves. Let us continue to call this flower and fruit of ourselves, even in this Machine Age, ART. Some Architects, as we may see, now consciously acknowledge this "Machine" rudiment. Some will eventually get to it by circuitous mental labor. Some *are* the thing itself without question and already in need of "treatment." But "Americans" (I prefer to be more specific and say "Usonians") have been educated "blind" to the higher human uses of it all—while actually in sight of this higher human use all the while.

Therefore, now let the declaration that "all is machinery" stand nobly forth for what it is worth. But why not more profoundly declare that "Form follows Function" and let it go at that? Saying, "Form follows Function," is not only deeper, it is clearer, and it goes further in a more comprehensive way to say the thing to be said, because the implication of this saying includes the heart of the whole matter. It may be that Function follows Form, as, or if, you prefer, but it is easier thinking with the first proposition just as it is easier to stand on your feet and nod your head than it would be to stand on your head and nod your feet. Let us not forget that Simplicity of the Universe is very different from the Simplicity of a Machine.

New significance in Architecture implies new materials qualifying form and textures, requires fresh feeling, which will eventually qualify both as "ornament." But "Decoration" must be sent on its way or now be given the meaning that it has lost, if it is to stay. Since "Decoration" became acknowledged as such, and ambitiously set up for itself as Decoration, it has been a makeshift, in the light of this ideal of Organic Architecture. Any House Decoration, as such, is an architectural makeshift, however well it may be done, unless the decoration, so called, is part of the Architect's design in both concept and execution.

Since Architecture in the old sense died and Decoration has had to shift for itself more and more, all so-called Decoration has become *ornamental,* therefore no longer *integral.* There can be no true simplicity in either Architecture or Decoration under any such condition. Let Decoration, therefore, die for Architecture, and the Decorator become an Architect, but not an "Interior Architect."

Ornament can never be applied to Architecture any more than Architecture should ever be applied to Decoration. All ornament, if not developed within the nature of Architecture and as organic part of such expression, vitiates the whole fabric no matter how clever or beautiful it may be as something in itself.

Yes—for a century or more Decoration has been setting up for itself, and in our prosperous country has come pretty near to doing very well, thank you. I think we may say that it is pretty much all we have now to show as Domestic Architecture, as Domestic Architecture still goes with us at the present time. But we may as well face it. The Interior Decorator thrives with us because we have no Architecture. Any Decorator is the natural enemy of organic simplicity in Architecture. He, persuasive Doctor-of-Appearances that he *must* be when he becomes Architectural substitute, will give you an imitation of anything, even an imitation of imitative simplicity. Just at the moment, May 1930, he is expert in this imitation. France, the born Decorator, is now engaged with "Madame," owing to the good fortune of the French market, in selling us this ready-made or made-to-order simplicity. Yes, Imitation Simplicity is the latest addition to imported "stock." The Decorators of America are now equipped to furnish *especially* this. Observe. And how very charming the suggestions conveyed by these imitations sometimes are!

Would you have again the general principles of the spiritual-ideal of organic simplicity at work in our Culture? If so, then let us reiterate: First, Simplicity is Constitutional Order. And it is worthy of note in this connection that 9 times 9 equals 81 is just as simple as 2 plus 2 equals 4. Nor is the obvious more simple necessarily than the occult. The obvious is obvious simply because it falls within our special horizon, is therefore easier for us to *see;* that is all. Yet all simplicity near or far has a countenance, a visage, that is characteristic. But this countenance is visible only to those who can grasp the whole and enjoy the significance of the minor part, as such, in relation to the whole when in flower. This is for the critics.

This characteristic visage may be simulated—the real complication glossed over, the internal conflict hidden by surface and belied by mass. The internal complication may be and usually is increased to create the semblance of and get credit for—simplicity. This is the Simplicity-lie usually achieved by most of the "surface and mass" architects. This is for the young architect.

Truly ordered simplicity in the hands of the great artist may flower into a bewildering profusion, exquisitely exuberant, and render all more clear than ever. Good William Blake says exuberance is *beauty,* meaning that it is so in this very sense. This is for the Modern Artist with the Machine in his hands. False Simplicity—Simplicity as an affectation, that is Simplicity constructed as a Decorator's outside put upon a complicated, wasteful engineer's or carpenter's "Structure," outside or inside—is not good enough Simplicity. It cannot be simple at all. But that is what passes for Simplicity, now that startling Simplicity-effects are becoming the *fashion.* That kind of Simplicity is *violent.* This is for "Art and Decoration."

Soon we shall want Simplicity inviolate. There is one way to get that Simplicity. My guess is, there is *only* one way really to get it. And that way is, on principle, by way of *Construction* developed as Architecture. That is for us, one and all.

AARON COPLAND

•

How We Listen[1]

We all listen to music according to our separate capacities. But, for the sake of analysis, the whole listening process may become clearer if we break it up into its component parts, so to speak. In a certain sense we all listen to music on three separate planes. For lack of a better terminology, one might name

[1] From *What to Listen for in Music,* by Aaron Copland. Revised Edition. Copyright © 1957 by McGraw-Hill, Inc. Used by permission of the McGraw-Hill Book Company.

these: (1) the sensuous plane, (2) the expressive plane, (3) the sheerly musical plane. The only advantage to be gained from mechanically splitting up the listening process into these hypothetical planes is the clearer view to be had of the way in which we listen.

The simplest way of listening to music is to listen for the sheer pleasure of the musical sound itself. That is the sensuous plane. It is the plane on which we hear music without thinking, without considering it in any way. One turns on the radio while doing something else and absent-mindedly bathes in the sound. A kind of brainless but attractive state of mind is engendered by the mere sound appeal of the music.

You may be sitting in a room reading this book. Imagine one note struck on the piano. Immediately that one note is enough to change the atmosphere of the room—proving that the sound element in music is a powerful and mysterious agent, which it would be foolish to deride or belittle.

The surprising thing is that many people who consider themselves qualified music lovers abuse that plane in listening. They go to concerts in order to lose themselves. They use music as a consolation or an escape. They enter an ideal world where one doesn't have to think of the realities of everyday life. Of course they aren't thinking about the music either. Music allows them to leave it, and they go off to a place to dream, dreaming because of and apropos of the music yet never quite listening to it.

Yes, the sound appeal of music is a potent and primitive force, but you must not allow it to usurp a disproportionate share of your interest. The sensuous plane is an important one in music, a very important one, but it does not constitute the whole story.

There is no need to digress further on the sensuous plane. Its appeal to every normal human being is self-evident. There is, however, such a thing as becoming more sensitive to the different kinds of sound stuff as used by various composers. For all composers do not use that sound stuff in the same way. Don't get the idea that the value of music is commensurate with its sensuous appeal or that the loveliest sounding music is made by the greatest composer. If that were so, Ravel would be a greater creator than Beethoven. The point is that the sound element varies with each composer, that his usage of sound forms an integral part of his style and must be taken into account when listening. The reader can see, therefore, that a more conscious approach is valuable even on this primary plane of music listening.

The second plane on which music exists is what I have called the expressive one. Here, immediately, we tread on controversial ground. Composers have a way of shying away from any discussion of music's expressive side. Did not Stravinsky himself proclaim that his music was an "object," a "thing," with a life of its own, and with no other meaning than its own purely musical existence? This intransigent attitude of Stravinsky's may be due to the fact that so many people have tried to read different meanings into so many pieces. Heaven knows it is difficult enough to say precisely what it is that a piece of music means, to say it definitely, to say it finally so that everyone is satisfied with your explanation. But that should not lead one to the other extreme of denying to music the right to be "expressive."

My own belief is that all music has an expressive power, some more and some less, but that all music has a certain meaning behind the notes and that that meaning behind the notes constitutes, after all, what the piece is saying, what the piece is about. This whole problem can be stated quite simply by asking, "Is there a meaning to music?" My answer to that would be, "Yes." And "Can you state in so many words what the meaning is?" My answer to that would be, "No." Therein lies the difficulty.

Simple-minded souls will never be satisfied with the answer to the second of these questions. They always want music to have a meaning, and the more concrete it is the better they like it. The more the music reminds them of a train, a storm, a funeral, or any other familiar conception the more expressive it appears to be to them. This popular idea of music's meaning—stimulated and abetted by the usual run of musical commentator—should be discouraged wherever and whenever it is met. One timid lady once confessed to me that she suspected something seriously lacking in her appreciation of music because of her inability to connect it with anything definite. That is getting the whole thing backward, of course.

Still, the question remains, How close should the intelligent music lover wish to come to pinning a definite meaning to any particular work? No closer than a general concept, I should say. Music expresses, at different moments, serenity or exuberance, regret or triumph, fury or delight. It expresses each of these moods, and many others, in a numberless variety of subtle shadings and differences. It may even express a state of meaning for which there exists no adequate word in any language. In that case, musicians often like to say that it has only a purely musical meaning. They sometimes go farther and say that *all* music has only a purely musical meaning. What they really mean is that no appropriate word can be found to express the music's meaning and that, even if it could, they do not feel the need of finding it.

But whatever the professional musician may hold, most musical novices still search for specific words with which to pin down their musical reactions. That is why they always find Tschaikovsky easier to "understand" than Beethoven. In the first place, it is easier to pin a meaning-word on a Tschaikovsky piece than on a Beethoven one. Much easier. Moreover, with the Russian composer, every time you come back to a piece of his it almost always says the same thing to you, whereas with Beethoven it is often quite difficult to put your finger right on what he is saying. And any musician will tell you that that is why Beethoven is the greater composer. Because music which always says the same thing to you will necessarily soon become dull music, but music whose meaning is slightly different with each hearing has a greater chance of remaining alive.

Listen, if you can, to the forty-eight fugue themes of Bach's *Well Tempered*

Clavichord. Listen to each theme, one after another. You will soon realize that each theme mirrors a different world of feeling. You will also soon realize that the more beautiful a theme seems to you the harder it is to find any word that will describe it to your complete satisfaction. Yes, you will certainly know whether it is a gay theme or a sad one. You will be able, in other words, in your own mind, to draw a frame of emotional feeling around your theme. Now study the sad one a little closer. Try to pin down the exact quality of its sadness. Is it pessimistically sad or resignedly sad; is it fatefully sad or smilingly sad?

Let us suppose that you are fortunate and can describe to your own satisfaction in so many words the exact meaning of your chosen theme. There is still no guarantee that anyone else will be satisfied. Nor need they be. The important thing is that each one feel for himself the specific expressive quality of a theme or, similarly, an entire piece of music. And if it is a great work of art, don't expect it to mean exactly the same thing to you each time you return to it.

Themes or pieces need not express only one emotion, of course. Take such a theme as the first main one of the *Ninth Symphony*, for example. It is clearly made up of different elements. It does not say only one thing. Yet anyone hearing it immediately gets a feeling of strength, a feeling of power. It isn't a power that comes simply because the theme is played loudly. It is a power inherent in the theme itself. The extraordinary strength and vigor of the theme results in the listener's receiving an impression that a forceful statement has been made. But one should never try to boil it down to "the fateful hammer of life," etc. That is where the trouble begins. The musician, in his exasperation, says it means nothing but the notes themselves, whereas the nonprofessional is only too anxious to hang on to any explanation that gives him the illusion of getting closer to the music's meaning.

Now, perhaps the reader will know better what I mean when I say that music does have an expressive meaning but that we cannot say in so many words what that meaning is.

The third plane on which music exists is the sheerly musical plane. Besides the pleasurable sound of music and the expressive feeling that it gives off, music does exist in terms of the notes themselves and of their manipulation. Most listeners are not sufficiently conscious of this third plane. It will be largely the business of this book to make them more aware of music on this plane.

Professional musicians, on the other hand, are, if anything, too conscious of the mere notes themselves. They often fall into the error of becoming so engrossed with their arpeggios and staccatos that they forget the deeper aspects of the music they are performing. But from the layman's standpoint, it is not so much a matter of getting over bad habits on the sheerly musical plane as of increasing one's awareness of what is going on, in so far as the notes are concerned.

When the man in the street listens to the "notes themselves" with any degree of concentration, he is most likely to make some mention of the melody. Either he hears a pretty melody or he does not, and he generally lets it go at that. Rhythm is likely to gain his attention next, particularly if it seems exciting. But harmony and tone color are generally taken for granted, if they are thought of consciously at all. As for music's having a definite form of some kind, that idea seems never to have occurred to him.

It is very important for all of us to become more alive to music on its sheerly musical plane. After all, an actual musical material is being used. The intelligent listener must be prepared to increase his awareness of the musical material and what happens to it. He must hear the melodies, the rhythms, the harmonies, the tone colors in a more conscious fashion. But above all he must, in order to follow the line of the composer's thought, know something of the principles of musical form. Listening to all of these elements is listening on the sheerly musical plane.

Let me repeat that I have split up mechanically the three separate planes on which we listen merely for the sake of greater clarity. Actually, we never listen on one or the other of these planes. What we do is to correlate them—listening in all three ways at the same time. It takes no mental effort, for we do it instinctively.

Perhaps an analogy with what happens to us when we visit the theater will make this instinctive correlation clearer. In the theater, you are aware of the actors and actresses, costumes and sets, sounds and movements. All these give one the sense that the theater is a pleasant place to be in. They constitute the sensuous plane in our theatrical reactions.

The expressive plane in the theater would be derived from the feeling that you get from what is happening on the stage. You are moved to pity, excitement, or gayety. It is this general feeling, generated aside from the particular words being spoken, a certain emotional something which exists on the stage, that is analogous to the expressive quality in music.

The plot and plot development is equivalent to our sheerly musical plane. The playwright creates and develops a character in just the same way that a composer creates and develops a theme. According to the degree of your awareness of the way in which the artist in either field handles his material will you become a more intelligent listener.

It is easy enough to see that the theatergoer never is conscious of any of these elements separately. He is aware of them all at the same time. The same is true of music listening. We simultaneously and without thinking listen on all three planes.

In a sense, the ideal listener is both inside and outside the music at the same moment, judging it and enjoying it, wishing it would go one way and watching it go another—almost like the composer at the moment he composes it; because in order to write his music, the composer must also be inside and outside his music, carried away by it and yet coldly critical of it. A subjective and objective attitude is implied in both creating and listening to music.

What the reader should strive for, then, is a more *active* kind of listening. Whether you listen to Mozart or Duke Ellington, you can deepen your understanding of music only by being a more conscious and aware listener—not someone who is just listening, but someone who is listening *for* something.

ARTHUR KOESTLER

•

Cultural Snobbery[1]

A friend of mine, whom I shall call Brenda, was given for her birthday by one of her admirers a Picasso line drawing in a simple modern frame. It was an admirable and typical sample of Picasso's "classical" period: a Greek youth carrying a girl in his arms, the contours of the two figures somehow mixed up and partly indistinguishable like those of Siamese twins with shared limbs, yet adding up to a charming and harmonious total effect. It looked like a lithograph, but it bore no serial number, so Brenda took it to be a reproduction and hung it, somewhat disappointed with the gift, over her staircase. On my next visit, several weeks later, it was hanging over her drawing room mantelpiece. "I see the Picasso reproduction has been promoted," I said. *"Reproduction!"* she cried indignantly. "It turned out it's an *original!* Isn't it lovely? Look at that line along the girl's hip . . . ," etc.

As a matter of fact, it *was* an original—a shyly understated gift of the mumbling and devoted admirer. But as it was a line drawing consisting of nothing but black contour on white paper, it needed an expert, or at least a good magnifying lens, to decide whether it was an original, a lithograph, or a reproduction. Neither Brenda nor any of her vistiors could tell the difference. But they took it for granted, as we all do, that an original deserves a proud display, whereas a reproduction belongs, at best, over the staircase.

I shall now try to analyze, in a pedantic way, the reason for this apparently so natural attitude. The original is of course many times more expensive than a reproduction; but we would indignantly reject the idea of displaying a picture simply because it is expensive; we pretend to be guided in these matters by purely aesthetic considerations. Next, one might surmise that our contempt for reproductions originates in the poor quality and even poorer choice of subjects of the Victorian print. But modern printing techniques have achieved miracles, and some Ganymede reproductions are almost indistinguishable from the original. In the extreme case of the line drawing, we have complete aesthetic equivalence between original and reproduction.

And yet there is something revolting in this equivalence. It even takes a cer-

[1] From *The Anchor Review Number One,* ed. Melvin J. Lasky (Garden City, N.Y.: Doubleday Anchor Books, 1955), pp. 3–14. Reprinted by permission of A. D. Peters.

tain courage to admit to oneself that the aesthetic effect of a copy might be indistinguishable from that of the original. We live in an age of stereotyped mass production; and after mass-produced furniture, mass-produced and prefabricated houses, the idea of mass-produced Piero della Francescas is indeed revolting. But then, we have no similar objection to mass-produced gramophone records. Nor to mass-produced books, and yet they too fall into the category of "reproductions." Why then do you prefer, according to your income, a more or less second-rate original picture on the wall to a first-rate reproduction of a masterpiece? Would you rather read a mediocre young poet in manuscript than Shakespeare in a paper-cover edition?

Our argument seems to have become bogged down. Let us find out what Brenda herself has to say to explain her behavior, in a dialogue with the writer:

BRENDA "I simply can't understand what all this fuss and talk is about. But *of course* my attitude to the drawing has changed since I know that Picasso himself did it. That's nothing to do with snobbery—it's just that I wasn't told before."

K "Your attitude has changed—but has that thing on the wall changed?"

B "Of course it hasn't, but now I *see* it differently!"

K "I would like to understand what it is that determines your attitude to a picture in general."

B "Its quality, of course."

K "And what determines its quality?"

B "Oh, don't be such a pedant. Color, composition, balance, harmony, power, what have you."

K "So, in looking at a picture, you are guided by purely aesthetic value judgments, depending on the qualities you mentioned?"

B "Of course I am."

K "Now, as that picture hasn't changed, and its qualities haven't changed, how can your attitude have changed?"

B "But I have told you before, you idiot. Of course my attitude to it is now different, since I know it isn't one reproduction in a million, but done by Picasso himself. Can't you see?"

K "No, I can't; you are contradicting yourself. The rarity of the object, and your knowledge of the manner in which it came into being, do not alter the qualities of that object, and accordingly should not alter your judgment of it, if it were really based on purely aesthetic criteria—as you believe it to be. But it isn't. Your judgment is not based on what you *see,* but on a purely accidental bit of information, which might be right or wrong and is entirely extraneous to the issue."

B "Wrong? How *dare* you insinuate that my Picasso isn't an original? And how *dare* you say that the question whether he drew it himself is 'extraneous' to the issue?"

And so it will go on indefinitely. Yet Brenda is not stupid; she is merely confused in believing that her attitude to an object of art is determined by purely aesthetic considerations, whereas in fact it is decisively influenced by factors of a quite different order. She is unable to see her picture isolated from the context of her knowledge of its origin. For, in our minds, the question of origin, authorship, or authenticity, *though in itself extraneous to aesthetic value,* is so intimately and indistinguishably fused with our attitude to the object that we find it well-nigh impossible to isolate the two. Thus, Brenda unconsciously projects one scale of values onto a system of quite different values.

Is Brenda, then, a snob? It depends on the definition of snobbery at which we hope to arrive at the end. But as a working hypothesis, I would like to suggest that this process of unconsciously applying to any given field a judgment derived from an alien system of values constitutes the essence of the phenomenon of snobbery. By these standards Brenda would *not* be a snob if she had said: "The reproduction in this case is just as beautiful as the original. But one gives me a greater thrill than the other for reasons which have nothing to do with beauty." She is an unconscious snob because she is unable to distinguish between the two elements of her experience, unable to name the extraneous cause of her biased aesthetic judgment, or to see that it is biased.

I am aware of pedantically laboring an apparently obvious point. But it will become at once less obvious if we turn to a different yet related problem.

In 1948, a German art restorer named Dietrich Fey, engaged in reconstruction work on Lübeck's ancient St. Marien Church, stated that his workmen had discovered traces of old Gothic wall paintings dating back to the thirteenth century, under a coating of chalk on the church walls. The restoration of the paintings was entrusted to Fey's assistant, Lothar Malskat, who finished the job two years later. In 1950, Chancellor Adenauer presided over the ceremonies marking the completion of the restoration work in the presence of art experts from all parts of Europe. Their unanimous opinion, voiced by Chancellor Adenauer, was that the twenty-one thirteenth-century Gothic saints on the church walls were "a valuable treasure and a fabulous discovery of lost masterpieces."

None of the experts on that or any later occasion expressed doubt as to the authenticity of the frescoes. It was Herr Malskat himself who, two years later, disclosed the fraud. He presented himself on his own initiative at Lübeck police headquarters, where he stated that the frescoes were entirely his own work, undertaken by order from his boss, Herr Fey, and asked to be tried for forgery. The leading German art experts, however, stuck to their opinion: the frescoes, they said, were no doubt genuine, and Herr Malskat was merely seeking cheap publicity. An official Board of Investigation was appointed which came to the conclusion that the restoration of the wall paintings was a hoax—but only after Herr Malskat had confessed that he had also manufactured hundreds of Rembrandts, Watteaus, Toulouse-Lautrecs, Picassos, Henri Rousseaus, Corots, Chagalls, Vlamincks, and other masters, and sold them as originals—some of which were actually found by the police in Herr Fey's house. Without this evidence, it is doubtful whether the German experts would ever have admitted having been fooled.

My point is not the fallibility of the experts. Herr Malskat's exploit is merely the most recent of a number of similarly successful hoaxes and forgeries—of which the most fabulous were probably van Megeeren's false Vermeers. The disturbing question which they raise is whether the Lübeck saints are less beautiful, and have ceased to be "a valuable treasure of masterpieces," simply because they had been painted by Herr Malskat and not by somebody else?

There are several answers to this line of argument, but before going into them I want to continue in the part of *advocatus diaboli* by considering an example of a forgery in a different field: Macpherson's *Ossian*. The case is so notorious that the facts need only be briefly mentioned. James Macpherson (1736-96), a Scottish poet and adventurer, alleged that in the course of his wanderings in the Highlands he had discovered some ancient Gaelic manuscripts. Enthusiastic Scottish littérateurs put up a subscription to enable Macpherson to pursue his researches, and in 1761 he published *Fingal, an Ancient Epic Poem in Six Books, together with Several Other Poems composed by Ossian, the Son of Fingal*. Ossian is the legendary third-century hero and bard of Celtic literature. *Fingal* was soon followed by the publication of a still larger Ossianic epic called *Temora,* and this by a collected edition, *The Works of Ossian*. The authenticity of Macpherson's text was at once questioned in England, particularly by Dr. Johnson (whom Macpherson answered by sending him a challenge to a duel), and to his death Macpherson refused, under various unconvincing pretexts, to publish his alleged Gaelic originals. By the turn of the century the controversy was settled and it was established that, while Macpherson had used fragments of ancient Celtic lore, most of the "Ossianic" texts were of his own making.

Yet here again the question arises whether the poetic quality of the work itself is altered by the fact that it was written not by Ossian, the son of Fingal, but by James Macpherson? The "Ossianic" texts were translated into many languages, and had a considerable influence on the literature and cultural climate of Europe at the late eighteenth and early nineteenth centuries. This is how the *Encyclopedia Britannica* sums up its evaluation of Macpherson:

> The varied sources of his work and its worthlessness as a transcript of actual Celtic poems do not alter the fact that he produced a work of art which . . . did more than any single work to bring about the romantic movement in European, and especially in German, literature. . . . Herder and Goethe . . . were among its profound admirers.

These examples could be continued indefinitely. Antique furniture, Roman statuary, Greek tanagra figures, and Italian madonnas are being forged, copied, counterfeited all the time, and the value we set on them is not determined by aesthetic appreciation and pleasure to the eye, but by the precarious and often uncertain judgment of experts. A mediocre but authenticated picture by a known master is held in higher esteem than an artistically superior work of his unknown pupil or "school"—not only by art dealers guided by "investment," but by all of us, including this writer. Are we, then, all snobs to whom a signature, an expert testimonial, or the postmark of a given period is more important than the intrinsic beauty of the object itself?

I now propose to present the case for the defense. It can be summed up in a single sentence: our appraisal of any work of literature or art is never a unitary act, but the result of two independent and simultaneous processes which tend to distort each other.

When we look at an Egyptian fresco, we do not enjoy the painting at its face value, but by means of an unconscious reattunement of the mind to the values of the period. We know, for instance, that the Egyptians had not discovered the technique of perspective in depth. We know that on certain Egyptian murals the size of the figures is determined by their relative social rank. Similarly, we look at every picture through a double frame: the solid frame which isolates it from its surroundings and creates for it a hole in space, as it were; and the unconscious frame of reference in our minds which creates for it a hole in time and locates it in its period and cultural climate. Every time we think that we are making a purely aesthetic judgment based on pure sensory perception, we are in fact judging relative to this second frame or context or mental field.

Any work of art, or literature, or music, can only be appreciated against the background of its period, and that is what we unconsciously do: when we naïvely believe that we are applying absolute criteria, we are in fact applying relative ones. When we contemplate the false Vermeer the first time believing it to be authentic and the second time knowing that it is a fake, our aesthetic experience will indeed completely change, though the picture has remained the same. For it is now seen in a different frame of reference and therefore, in fact, differently. The same considerations apply to the perpetrator of the fake. He may be able to imitate the technique of the seventeenth-century Dutch School, but he could not spontaneously start painting like Vermeer—because his visual organization is different, his perception of reality is different, and because he cannot, except by an artificial effort, erase from his mind the accumulated experience of everything that happened in painting since Vermeer. And if, by a tour de force, a contemporary artist succeeded in reconditioning his own vision to that of the Dutch seventeenth century or the Italian *quattrocento,* he would have to use mass hypnosis to recondition the vision of his customers in a similar manner.

We can add to our knowledge and experience, but we cannot subtract from it. When Picasso decides to disregard the laws of perspective, that means that he has passed through and beyond a certain technique—unlike the Egyptian painter, who has never acquired it. Evolution is an irreversible process; the culture of a period might apparently point into the same direction as an earlier one, but it does so from a different turn of the spiral. A modern primitive is different from a primitive primitive; contemporary classicism is different from any classical classicism; only the mentally insane are able to amputate part of their past.

And yet when we contemplate works of the past, we must perform just such a process of mental subtraction, by attuning our minds to the climate and experience of the period. In order to appreciate them, we must enter into their spirit, by forgetting our modern experience and all that we have learnt since that Homeric epic or Byzantine mosaic was created. We must descend into the past, making our mind a blank; and as we do so, we unconsciously condescend. We close our eyes to crudities of technique, naïveties of perception, prevailing superstitions, limitations of knowledge, factual errors. We make allowances. A little honest introspection will always reveal the element of condescension contained in our admiration for the classics; and part of our enjoyment when listening to the voices of the past is derived from this half-consciously patronizing attitude—"how clever of them to know that at their age." We feel that we have descended a turn of the spiral; we are looking up in awe and wonder at Dante's dreadful Paradise, but at the same time we seem to be bending down, with a tender antiquarian stoop.

This legitimate kind of aesthetic double-think degenerates into snobbery at the point where the frame of reference becomes more important than the picture, when the thrill derived from the gesture of bending over the past dominates the aesthetic experience. The result is a widespread confusion of critical judgment—overestimation of the dead and belittlement of the living, indiscriminate reverence for anything that is "classical," "antique," "primitive," or simply old. In its extreme form this tendency prompts people to have their wall brackets and picture frames artificially dirtied to lend them the patina of age; so let us call it the "patina snobbery."

The process that leads to these distortions of judgment is basically the same as outlined before: the projection of one scale of values to a psychologically related but objectively alien field of experience. The essence of snobbery is to assess value according to a wrong type of scale; the snob is always trying to measure beauty with a thermometer or weight with a clock.

The thirteen-year-old daughter of a friend was recently taken to the Greenwich Museum. When she was asked which was the most beautiful thing she had seen in the Museum, she said unhesitatingly: "Nelson's shirt." When asked what was so beautiful about it, she explained: "That shirt with the blood on it was jolly nice. Fancy real blood on a real shirt, which belonged to somebody really historic!"

The child's thrill is obviously derived from the same source as the magic that emanates from Napoleon's inkpot, the lock of hair on the Egyptian mummy's head, the relic of the saint carried in annual procession, the strand of the rope by which a famous murderer was hanged, and from Tolstoi's laundry bill. In the mentality of the primitive, an object which had been in contact with a person is not merely a souvenir: it becomes magically imbued with the substance of that personality and in turn magically emanates something of that substance.

"There is, I am sure, for most of us, a special pleasure in sinking your teeth into a peach produced on the estate of an earl who is related to the Royal Family," a London columnist wrote recently in the *Daily Express*.

Primitive magic survives in the subconscious; the strand of hair carried in the locket, grandmother's wedding dress, the faded fan of the first ball, the regimental badge, all have a half-conscious fetish character. The bobby-soxers who tear shreds off the crooner's garb are the vulgarized twentieth-century version of the worshipers cherishing a splinter from a saint's bone. The value that we set on original manuscripts, on "signed" pieces of furniture, on Dickens' quill and Kepler's telescope, are more dignified manifestations of the same unconscious tendency. It is, as the child said, "jolly nice" to behold a fragment of a marble by Praxiteles—even if it is battered out of human shape, with a leper's nose and broken ears. The contact with the master's hand has imbued it with a magic quality which has lingered on and radiates at us, conveying the same thrill as "the real blood on Nelson's real shirt."

The change in our attitude—and in the art dealer's price—when it is learned that a cracked and blackened piece of canvas is an "authenticated" work by X has nothing to do with beauty, aesthetics, or what have you—it is the working of sympathetic magic in us. (See Brenda and her Picasso drawing.) The inordinate importance that we attribute to the original, the authenticated, in those borderline cases where only the expert could tell the difference, is a derivative from primitive fetishism. And as every honest art dealer will admit, these borderline cases are so frequent as to be almost the rule. Moreover, it was a general practice in the past for the master to let his pupils assist in the execution of larger undertakings. It is not the eye that guides the average museum visitor, but the magic of names and the magic of age. The bedevilment of aesthetic experience by unconscious fetish worship and patina snobbery is so general that it has become a major factor in our attitude to the art of past epochs—an attitude as remote from spontaneous appreciation as the "Emperor's Clothes" fallacy regarding hyper-modern art forms.

Literature and Criticism

RENÉ WELLEK

•

The Main Trends of Twentieth-Century Criticism[1]

Both the eighteenth and the nineteenth centuries have been called "the age of criticism": surely the twentieth century deserves this title with a

[1] From *The Yale Review,* copyright 1961, Yale University Press.

vengeance. Not only has a veritable spate of criticism descended upon us, but criticism has achieved a new self-consciousness, a much greater public status, and has developed, in recent decades, new methods and new evaluations. Criticism, which even in the later nineteenth century was of no more than local significance outside of France and England, has made itself heard in countries that before seemed on the periphery of critical thought: in Italy since Croce, in Russia, in Spain, and, last but not least, in the United States. Any survey of twentieth-century criticism must take account of this geographical expansion and of the simultaneous revolution of methods. We need some principles of selection among the mountains of printed matter that confront us.

Obviously even today much criticism is being written that is not new: we are surrounded by survivals, leftovers, throwbacks to older stages in the history of criticism. Ordinary book reviewing still mediates between the author and the general public by the old methods of impressionistic description and arbitrary pronouncements of taste. Historical scholarship continues to be of great importance for criticism. There will always be a place for a simple comparison between literature and life: for the judging of current novels by standards of probability and accuracy of the social situations reflected in them. In all countries there are writers, and often good writers, who practice these methods marked out by nineteenth-century criticism: impressionistic appreciation, historical explanation, and realistic comparison. Let us recall the charming evocative essays of Virginia Woolf or the nostalgic vignettes of the American past by Van Wyck Brooks or the mass of social criticism of the recent American novel and allude to the contribution which historical scholarship has been making to a better understanding of almost all periods and authors of literary history. But at the risk of some injustice I shall try to sketch out what seem to me the new trends in twentieth-century criticism.

First of all, one is struck by the fact that there are certain international movements in criticism which have transcended the boundaries of any one nation, even though they may have originated in a single nation; one is struck by the fact that from a very wide perspective a large part of twentieth-century criticism shows a remarkable resemblance of aim and method, even where there are no direct historical relationships. At the same time, one cannot help observing how ingrained and almost unsurmountable national characteristics seem to be: how within this very wide range of Western thought with cross-currents from Russia to the Americas, from Spain to Scandinavia, the individual nations still tenaciously preserve their own traditions in criticism.

The new trends of criticism, of course, have also roots in the past, are not without antecedents, and are not absolutely original. Still, one can distinguish at least six general trends which are new in this last half-century: (1) Marxist criticism, (2) psychoanalytic criticism, (3) linguistic and stylistic criticism, (4) a new organistic formalism, (5) myth criticism appealing to the results of cultural anthropology and the speculations of Carl Jung, and (6) what amounts to a new philosophical criticism inspired by existentialism and kindred world views, I shall take up these trends in the order I have mentioned them, which is roughly chronological.

In taste and in theory Marxist criticism grows out of the realistic criticism of the nineteenth century. It appeals to a few pronouncements made by Marx and Engels, but as a systematic doctrine it cannot be found before the last decade of the nineteenth century. In Germany Franz Mehring (1846–1916) and in Russia Georgi Plekhanov (1856–1918) were the first practitioners of Marxist criticism, but they were very unorthodox from the point of view of later Soviet dogma. Both Mehring and Plekhanov recognize a certain autonomy of art and think of Marxist criticism rather as an objective science of the social determinants of a literary work than as a doctrine which decides aesthetic questions and prescribes subject matter and style to authors.

Prescriptive Marxism is the result of much later developments in Soviet Russia. In the twenties there was still possible in Russia a considerable debate between different doctrines. Only about 1932 was devised and imposed the uniform doctrine which goes under the name of "socialist realism." The term covers a theory which asks the writer, on the one hand, to reproduce reality accurately, to be a realist in the sense of depicting contemporary society with an insight into its structure, and, on the other hand, asks the writer to be a socialist realist, which in practice means that he is *not* to reproduce reality objectively but must use his art to spread socialism: that is, communism, the party spirit, and the party line. Soviet literature, the authoritative theoretician declared, must be "instrumental in the ideological molding of the working masses in the spirit of socialism"—a command which fits Stalin's saying that writers are "engineers of the human soul." Literature is thus frankly didactic and even idealizing in the sense that it shows us life not as it is but as it ought to be according to Marxist doctrine. Good Marxist critics understand that art operates with characters and images, actions and feelings. The focus on the concept of "type" is the bridge between realism and idealism. Type does not mean simply the average or the representative, but rather the ideal type, the model or simply the hero which the reader is to imitate in actual life. Georgi Malenkov—briefly the great expert on aesthetics—proclaimed the typical to be "the basic sphere of the manifestation of party spirit in art. The problem of the type is always a political problem." Criticism in Russia is almost entirely criticism of characters and types: authors are taken to task for not depicting reality correctly, that is, for not assigning sufficient weight to the role of the party, or for not depicting certain characters favorably enough. Soviet criticism, especially since the second World War, is in addition highly nationalistic and provincial: no suggestion of foreign influences is tolerated and comparative literature is a subject on the blacklist. Criticism has become an organ of party discipline, not only in Russia and its many satellites but apparently also in China. Even the genuine insights of Marxism into social processes and economic motivations are hardly used today.

Marxism spread abroad, especially in the twenties, and found adherents and followers in most nations. In the United States there was a short-lived Marxist movement in the early thirties. Its best-known proponent, Granville Hicks, gave a remarkably innocuous reinterpretation of American literature; Bernard Smith's *Forces in American Criticism* (1939) is a bolder attempt to write a history of American criticism from a social point of view. But the influence of Marxist criticism extends far beyond the strict adherents of the doctrine. It is visible in certain stages of the development of Edmund Wilson and Kenneth Burke. In England Christopher Caudwell (1907–37) was the outstanding Marxist critic. His main book, *Illusion and Reality* (1937), is actually a weird mixture of Marxism, anthropology, and psychoanalysis, a diatribe against individualistic civilization and false "bourgeois" freedom. But by far the most outstanding Marxist critic today is Georg Lukács (born 1885), a Hungarian who writes mostly in German. He combines a thorough grasp of dialectical materialism and its sources in Hegel with a real knowledge of German literature. His many books, among them brilliant studies of *Goethe and His Age* (1947) and of the *Historical Novel* (1955), reinterpret the course of nineteenth-century literature in terms of realism, with emphasis on the social and political implications but not without sensitivity to literary values.

Marxism is at its best when it serves as a device to expose the latent social and ideological implications of a work of literature. The second of the six critical trends listed above, psychoanalysis, although with very different assumptions, serves the same general purpose: a reading of literature behind its ostensive surface, i.e., an unmasking. Freud himself suggested the leading *motifs* of psychoanalytical criticism. The artist is a neurotic who by his creative process keeps himself from a crack-up but also from any real cure. The poet is a daydreamer who publishes his phantasies and is thus strangely socially validated. These phantasies, we all know today, are based on childhood experiences and complexes and can be found symbolized also in dreams, in myths and fairy tales, and even in smoking-car jokes. Literature thus contains a rich storehouse of evidence for man's subconscious life. Freud drew the name of the Oedipus complex from a play by Sophocles and interpreted *Hamlet* and *The Brothers Karamazov* as allegories of incestuous love and hatred. But Freud had only slight literary interests and always recognized that psychoanalysis did not solve the question of art. His followers have applied his methods systematically to an interpretation of literature: *Imago* (1912–38) was a German magazine devoted to these problems, and many of Freud's close followers have studied the subconscious meanings of works of art, the subconscious drives of fictional figures, and the subconscious intentions of authors.

Freudian psychoanalysis spread slowly around the world. Dr. Ernest Jones, an English physician who spent many years at Toronto, wrote as early as 1910 an article on "The Oedipus Complex as an Explanation of Hamlet's Mystery"; and in this country in 1912 Frederic Clark Prescott expounded the relation of "Poetry and Dreams" in psychoanalytical terms. Orthodox Freudian literary criticism usually indulges in a tiresome search for sexual symbols and very frequently violates the meaning and integrity of a work of art; but again, as with Marxism, the methods of psychoanalysis have contributed to the tools of many modern critics who cannot be simply called Freudians. Thus Edmund Wilson, in *The Wound and the Bow,* has skillfully used the Freudian method for a psychological interpretation of Dickens and Kipling, and in England Herbert Read has defended Shelley and interpreted Wordsworth with the insights of the same school.

A third trend of twentieth-century criticism could be called linguistic. It takes seriously the famous saying of Mallarmé that "poetry is not written with ideas but with words." But one must distinguish between several approaches in different countries. In Russia, during the first World War, a "Society for the Study of Poetic Language" (OPOJAZ) was organized which became the nucleus of the Russian formalist movement. In its early stages this group was primarily interested in the problem of poetic language, which the members conceived as a special language characterized by a purposeful "deformation" of ordinary speech by "organized violence" committed against it. They studied mainly the sound stratum of language—vowel harmonies, consonant clusters, rhyme, prose rhythm, and meter—and leaned heavily on the concept of the phoneme, developed at first by De Saussure and the Geneva school, and then by Russian linguists such as Trubetskoy. They devised many technical (even statistical) methods for the study of a work of literature, which they conceived, often mechanically, as a sum of its devices. They were positivists with a scientific ideal of literary scholarship.

In Germany, after the first World War, very different linguistic concepts were applied to the study of literature, mainly by a group of Romance scholars. In many finely analytical books, ranging widely from Dante to Racine and the Spanish poetry of solitude, Karl Vossler (1872–1949) drew on Croce's identification of language and art in order to study syntax and style as individual creation. Leo Spitzer (1887–1960) developed his method of interpreting style at first under the stimulus of Freud. The observation of a stylistic trait allowed him to infer the "biography of a soul"; but later Spitzer himself repudiated his earlier method and turned to a structural interpretation of literary works in which style is seen as the surface which, properly observed, leads the student to the discovery of a central motive, a basic attitude or way of viewing the world which is not necessarily subconscious or personal. Spitzer analyzed hundreds of passages of works of literature using grammatical, stylistic, and historical categories, with unparalleled ingenuity. Most of Spitzer's work concerns French, Spanish, and Italian literature, but during his later years, spent in the United States, he also interpreted poems by Donne, Marvell, Keats, and Whitman, and other English texts. Spitzer worked usually on a small scale, concentrating almost micrologically on specific passages. Erich Auerbach (1892–1957) used essentially the same method. His *Mimesis* (1946) is a history of realism from Homer to Proust which always starts with individual passages analyzed stylistically in order to reflect on literary, social, and intellectual history. Auerbach's concept of realism is very special and possibly contradictory: it means to him both a concrete insight into social and political reality, and a sense of existence, understood tragically, as man in solitude facing moral decisions.

The German type of stylistics has had astonishing success in the Spanish-speaking world. Dámaso Alonso (born 1898) is the most distinguished practitioner who identifies literary criticism with stylistics and who has revalued Spanish poetry with a new taste for the Baroque, for Góngora and St. John of the Cross. Unfortunately Alonso often abandons linguistic and stylistic methods for gestures toward some ultimate ineffable mystical insight.

In the Anglo-Saxon world, surprisingly enough, no such linguistic and stylistic criticism took hold. Here the gulf between linguistics and literary criticism has widened deplorably. The critics are more and more ignorant of philology; and the linguists, especially the Yale school headed by the late Leonard Bloomfield, have expressly proclaimed their lack of interest in questions of style and poetic language. Interest in "language" is, however, prominent among English and American critics: but it is rather in "semantics," in the analysis of the role of "emotive" language contrasted with intellectual, scientific language. It is at the basis of the theories propounded by I. A. Richards.

I. A. Richards (born 1893) developed a theory of meaning which distinguishes among sense, tone, feeling, and intention, and emphasizes, in poetry, the ambiguities of language. In his *Practical Criticism* (1928) Richards analyzed, with great pedagogical skill, the various sources of our misunderstanding of poetry by using the papers of his students written on anonymous poems. But, unfortunately to my mind, the finely analytical work of Richards is overlaid by a theory of the psychic effect of poetry which seems to me not only erroneous but detrimental to literary study. Richards does not recognize a world of aesthetic values. Rather the only value of art is in the psychic organization it imposes on us: what Richards calls the "patterning of impulses," the equilibrium of attitudes that art induces. The artist is conceived almost as a mental healer and art as a therapy or a tonic for our nerves. Richards has not been able to describe this effect of art concretely, though he claims that art (in his sense) will replace religion as a social force. He has finally to admit that the desired balanced pose can be given by "a carpet, or a pot, by a gesture as well as by the Parthenon." It does not matter whether we like good or bad poetry as long as we order our minds. Thus Richards' theory—which is scientific in its pretensions and often appeals to future advances of neurology—ends in critical paralysis. It leads to a complete divorce between the poem as an objective structure and the reader's mind. Poetry is deliberately cut off from all knowledge and even reference to reality. Poetry, at most, elaborates the myths by which men live, even though these myths may be untrue, may be mere "psuedo-statements" in the light of science.

Richards' dissolution of poetry into an occasion for the ordering of our impulses, as a means toward mental hygiene seems to me a blind alley of literary theory. But Richards had the real merit of turning attention to the language of poetry. When his central psychological teaching was ignored, his method of analysis could be made to yield concrete results. This is precisely what William Empson (born 1906) did. Ignoring and later rejecting altogether Richards' emotive theory, he developed Richards' concept of the flexibility and ambiguity of poetic language by a technique of multiple definitions. *Seven Types of Ambiguity* (1930) pursues to the farthest ends the implications, poetic and social, of difficult, witty, metaphorical poetry by a method of verbal analysis which often loses all contact with the text and indulges in private associations. In his later books Empson combined this semantic analysis with ideas drawn from psychoanalysis and Marxism, and recently he has practically left the realm of literary criticism for a special kind of linguistic analysis which is often only a pretext for the fireworks of his wit and recondite ingenuity.

The Richardsian semantic analysis has had an important influence on several American critics who are usually called New Critics. Kenneth Burke (born 1897) combines the methods of Marxism, psychoanalysis, and anthropology with semantics in order to devise a system of human behavior and motivation which uses literature only as a document or illustration. The early Burke was a good literary critic, but his work in recent decades must rather be described as aiming at a philosophy of meaning, human behavior, and action whose center is not in literature at all. All distinctions between life and literature, language and action disappear in Burke's theory.

In Burke the expansion of criticism has reached its extreme limits. On the opposite pole is Cleanth Brooks (born 1906). He also starts with Richards but arrives at very different conclusions. He takes Richards' terminology, deprives it of its psychologistic assumptions, and transforms it into an instrument of analysis. This allows Brooks, while still talking of attitudes, to analyze poems concretely as structures of tensions: in practice, as structures of paradoxes and ironies. Brooks uses these terms very broadly. Irony indicates the recognition of incongruities, the ambiguity, the reconciliation of opposites which Brooks finds in all good, that is, complex poetry. Poetry must be ironic in the sense of being able to withstand ironic contemplation. The method, no doubt, works best when applied to Donne or Shakespeare, Eliot or Yeats, but in *The Well Wrought Urn* (1947) Brooks has shown that even Wordsworth and Tennyson, Gray and Pope yield to this kind of analysis. The theory emphasizes the contextual meaning of the poem, its wholeness, its organicity, and thus draws significantly on the central insight of what I called the fourth type of twentieth-century criticism: the new organistic and symbolistic formalism.

This organistic formalism has many antecedents: it started in Germany late in the eighteenth century and came to England with Coleridge. Through devious channels many of its ideas entered the theories of French symbolism late in the ninteenth century and, more directly, from Hegel and De Sanctis this organistic formalism found an impressive formulation in the aesthetics of Benedetto Croce. Coleridge, Croce, and French symbolism are the immediate antecedents of modern English and American so-called New Criticism, though strangely and surprisingly this tradition—idealistic in its philosophical assumptions—combined here with the positivistic psychology and utilitarian semantics of I. A. Richards.

Benedetto Croce (1866–1952) has completely dominated Italian criticism and scholarship for the last fifty years, but outside of Italy his theories have had only a negative influence. Even his propagandist in this country, the fine historian of Renaissance criticism, Joel E. Spingarn, hardly understood Croce's peculiar doctrines. *Estetica* (1902) propounds a theory of art as intuition which is at the same time expression. Art for Croce is not a physical fact, but purely a matter of the mind; it is not pleasure, it is not morality, it is not science and not philosophy. There is no distinction between form and content. The common view that Croce is a "formalist" or a defender of "art for art's sake" is mistaken. Art does play a role in society and can even be controlled by it. In his criticism Croce pays little attention to form in the ordinary sense but rather to what he calls the "leading sentiment." In Croce's radical monism there is no place for rhetorical categories, for style, for symbol, for genres, even for distinctions among the arts, because every work of art is a unique intuition-expression. For Croce, the creator, the work, and the reader are identified. Criticism can do little more than remove the obstacles to this identification, and pronounce whether a work is poetry or nonpoetry. Croce's position hangs together remarkably well and is not open to objections which neglect its basis in an idealistic metaphysics. If we demur that Croce neglects the medium or technique of art, he answers that "what is external is no longer a work of art." Literary history, psychology and biography, sociology, philosophical interpretation, stylistics, genre criticism—all are ruled out from Croce's scheme. We arrive at an intuitionism which, in Croce's critical practice, is hard to distinguish from impressionism. It isolates appealing passages or anthologizes arbitrarily from unargued pronouncements of judgment. Mainly due to the influence of Croce, Italian criticism today presents a situation very different from that in other countries. There is erudition, there is taste, there is judgment, but on the other hand there is no systematic analysis of texts, no intellectual history, no stylistics, except among a small group which is definitely anti-Crocean in outlook (Giuseppe de Robertis, Gianfranco Contini) and leans instead towards stylistics.

In Germany an organistic, symbolist concept of poetry revived as a consequence of French influence within the circle around the poet Stefan George. George's disciples elaborated the hints and sayings of the master into a body of criticism which, for the first time after a long period of philological factualism, asserted a critical creed with definite standards. Unfortunately the genuine insights of the school into the nature of poetry were marred by the doctrinaire tone of delivery, the aristocratic pretensions, and the often comically high-pitched, almost oracular solemnity of their pronouncements. By far the best of George's disciples was Friedrich Gundolf (1880–1931), who studied the influence of Shakespeare on German literature and wrote a large book on Goethe (1916). He tried to construe Goethe's "figure" as a unity of life and work, in terms of a scheme which allows a grading of his writings in three main categories: lyrical, symbolic, and allegorical. The book, though finely written and well composed, fails to convince. It transforms the eminently humane and even bourgeois figure of Goethe into a superhuman creator for creation's sake. But in the writings of Gundolf, in those of the sensitive and elegant Hugo von Hofmannsthal, and the violent, passionate Rudolf Borchardt (1871–1945), Germany has found its way back to the great tradition and a restatement of the age-old view of poetry as symbolism.

In France formalist criticism found its most impressive restatement in the writings of Paul Valéry (1871–1945). Valéry, in contrast to Croce, asserts the discontinuity of author, work, and reader. He stresses the importance of form divorced from emotion and takes poetry completely out of history into the realm of the absolute. For Valéry there is a deep gulf between creative process and work. At times it seems as if Valéry were hardly interested in the work but only in the process of creation. He seems to have been content to analyze creativity in general. Poetry is not inspiration, not dream, but making. It must be impersonal to be perfect. Emotional art seems to him always inferior. A poem should aim to be "pure," absolute poetry, free from factual, personal, and emotional admixtures. It cannot be paraphrased, it cannot be translated. It is a tight universe of sound and meaning, so closely interlocked that we cannot distinguish content and form. Poetry exploits the resources of language to the utmost, removing itself from ordinary speech by sound and meters and all the devices of imagery. Poetic language is a language within the language, language completely formalized. To Valéry poetry is both a calculus, an exercise, even a game, and a song, a chant, an enchantment, a charm. It is figurative and incantatory: a compromise between sound and meaning which, with its own conventions, even arbitrary conventions, achieves the ideal work of art, unified, beyond time, absolute. The novel, with its plot complications and irrelevances, and tragedy with its appeal to violent emotions, seem to Valéry inferior genres—not quite properly art. Valéry defends a position which seems extreme in its austerity and vulnerable for its discontinuities. But it has been fruitful in asserting a central concern of modern poetics: the discovery of pure representation, of the "unmediated vision" for which two other great poets of the century, Eliot and Rilke, were also searching.

The affinity with Eliot is obvious. In Eliot we find the English version of the formalist, symbolist theories. Eliot defined the enormous change of poetic taste in our time and asserted a return to a tradition which he calls "classical." Eliot's theory of poetry starts with a psychology of poetic creation. Poetry is not "the spontaneous overflow of powerful feelings," not the expression of personality, but is an impersonal organization of feelings which demands a "unified sensibility," a collaboration of intellect and feeling in order to find the precise "objective correlative," the symbolic structure of the work. In Eliot there is a certain conflict between an ideological classicism and his own spontaneous taste, which could be described as baroque and symbolist; and Eliot's increasing preoccupation with orthodoxy has led him to the mistaken introduction of a double standard in criticism: aesthetic and religious. He dissolves again the unity of the work of art that had been the basic insight of formalist aesthetics.

The impulses from Eliot and Richards were most effectively combined in England, at least, in the work of Frank Raymond Leavis (born 1895) and his disciples grouped around the magazine *Scrutiny* (1932–53). Leavis is a man of strong convictions and harsh polemical manners. He has in recent years sharply underlined his disagreements with the later development of Eliot and Richards. But his starting point is there: in Eliot's taste and Richards' technique of analysis. He differs from them mainly by a strong Arnoldian concern for a moralistic humanism. Leavis practices close reading, a training of sensibility, which has little use for literary theory or history. But "sensibility" with Leavis means also a sense of tradition, a concern for local culture, the organic community of the old English countryside. He has criticized the commercialization of English literary life and has defended the need of a social code and order, "maturity," "sanity," and "discipline." But these terms are purely secular and include the ideals of D. H. Lawrence. Leavis' concern with the text is often deceptive: he quickly leaves the verbal surface in order to define the peculiar emotions which an author conveys. He becomes a social and moral critic who, however, insists on the continuity of language and ethics, on the morality of form.

The so-called Southern critics share Leavis' general position between Eliot and Richards and share his concern with the evils of urbanization and commercialization, the need of a healthy society which alone can produce a vital literature. The Southern critics—John Crowe Ransom, Allen Tate, Cleanth Brooks, and R. P. Warren—differ from Eliot, however, by rejecting his emotionalism. They recognize that poetry is not merely emotive language but a particular kind of presentational knowledge. John Crowe Ransom (born 1888), in *The World's Body* (1938), argued that poetry conveys a sense of the particularity of the world. "As science more and more completely reduces the world to its types and forms, art, replying, must invest it again with a body." True poetry is metaphysical poetry, a new awareness of the "thinginess" of the world conveyed mainly by extended metaphor and pervasive symbolism. Ransom emphasizes the "texture" of poetry, its seemingly irrelevant detail, so strongly that he runs into the danger of a new split, within the work of art, between "structure" and "texture." Allen Tate (born 1899) is like Ransom preoccupied with the defense of poetry against science. Science gives us abstraction, poetry concreteness; science partial knowledge, poetry complete knowledge. Abstraction violates art. Good art proceeds from a union of intellect and feeling, or rather from a "tension" between abstraction and sensation.

There are other critics who cannot be discussed here at length who share, in general, this organistic symbolistic outlook: R. P. Blackmur (born 1904) who, however subtle a reader of poetry, seems in recent years more and more entangled in a private web of terms and elusive feelings; W. K. Wimsatt (born 1907) whose *Verbal Icon* (1954) is an attempt at a consolidation of the teachings of the New Criticism; and Yvor Winters (born 1900) who is much more rationalistic and moralistic than the other American critics but still shares their general taste and methods of analysis.

The New Criticism—whose basic insights seem to me valid for poetic theory—has, no doubt, reached a point of exhaustion. In some points the movement has not been able to go beyond its initial restricted sphere: its selection of European writers is oddly narrow. The historical perspective remains very short. Literary history is neglected. The relations to modern linguistics are left unexplored with the result that the study of style, diction, and meter remains often dilettantish. The basic aesthetics seems often without a sure philosophical foundation. Still the movement has immeasurably raised the level of awareness and sophistication in American criticism. It has developed ingenious methods for the analysis of imagery and symbol. It has defined a new taste averse to the romantic tradition. It has supplied an important apology for poetry in a world dominated by science. But it has not been able to avoid the dangers of ossification and mechanical imitation. There seems time for a change.

A polemical movement still within the limits of formalism, Chicago Aristotelianism has recently challenged the concern of the New Criticism with poetic language and symbolism. The Chicago school emphasizes plot, composition, and genre. The group has scored a good many points against the hunters of paradoxes, symbols, ambiguities, and myths. But neither R. S. Crane nor Elder Olson is able to offer any positive solutions beyond arid classifications of hero types, plot structures, and genres. The armature of scholarship hides an insensitivity to aesthetic values. It seems an ultra-academic exercise destined to wither on the vine.

Much more vital is the fifth trend on our list, myth criticism. It developed from cultural anthropology and the Jungian version of the subconscious as collective reservoir for the "archetypal patterns," and primordial images of mankind. Jung himself was cautious in applying his philosophy to literature, but in England and in the United States his caution was thrown to the winds and whole groups of critics have tried to discover the original myths of mankind behind all literature: the divine father, the descent into hell, the sacrificial death of the god, etc. In England Maud Bodkin, in *Archetypal Patterns in Poetry* (1934), studied, for instance, the "Ancient Mariner" and the *Waste Land* as poems of the rebirth pattern. In the United States myth criticism can be described as the most successful attempt to replace the New Criticism. It allows, to put it bluntly, the discussion of subject matter, of folklore, of themes and content that were slighted by the New Critics. The dangers of the method are obvious: the boundary lines between art and myth and even art and religion are obliterated. An irrationalistic mysticism reduces all poetry to a conveyor of a few myths: rebirth and purification. After decoding each work of art in these terms, one is left with a feeling of futility and monotony. Many of the writings of Wilson Knight, which extract an esoteric wisdom from Shakespeare, Milton, Pope, Wordsworth, and even Byron, are open to such objections. The best practitioners manage to combine the insights of myth criticism with a grasp on the nature of art. Thus Francis Fergusson, in his *Idea of a Theater* (1949), keeps his own version of Aristotelianism, and Philip Wheelwright, in *The Burning Fountain* (1954), his own insight into the semantics of poetry. Northrop Frye began with an excellent interpretation of the private mythology of Blake in his *Fearful Symmetry* (1947), and in his *Anatomy of Criticism* (1957) combines myth criticism with motifs from the New Criticism. The *Anatomy* aims at an all-embracing theory of literature of the most grandiose pretensions. A more modest view of the function of criticism seems to me wiser.

The other recent vital trend is existentialism, our sixth and last trend in twentieth-century criticism. Existentialism dominated the French and German intellectual scene after the second World War and is only now slowly receding. If we interpret it as a philosophy of despair, of "fear and trembling," of man's exposure to a hostile universe, the reasons for its spread are not far to seek. But the main work of Martin Heidegger (born 1889), *Sein und Zeit,* dates from 1927, and existentialist ideas have been familiar in Germany since the early twenties when Kierkegaard was in fashion. Heidegger's version of existentialism is a kind of new humanism, profoundly different from the far more gloomy French school with its dominant concept of "the absurd." Heidegger's influence on literary criticism is due rather to his vocabulary and his preoccupation with the concept of time than to his own eccentric interpretations of poems by Hölderlin and Rilke. In Germany existentialism in literary criticism has meant a turning to the text, to the object of literature: a rejection of the psychology and biography, the sociology and intellectual history with which German literary scholarship had been almost exclusively concerned. Max Kommerell (1902–44), for instance, in his many close readings of poems studied poetry as self-knowledge, and Emil Staiger (born 1908) has interpreted time as a form of poetic imagination and has devised a scheme of poetics in which the main kinds, or rather modes—the lyric, the epic and tragic—are aligned with the three dimensions of the time concept. The lyric is associated with the present, the epic with the past, and the drama, strangely enough, with the future.

In France, Jean-Paul Sartre is the main expounder of existentialism, though most of us will remember him as a defender of art committed to its social responsibility. But Sartre's *Qu'est-ce que la littérature?* (1948) is an impassioned plea for a metaphysical conception of art. The right of pure poetry is recognized. The final goal of art is not very different from Schiller's aesthetic education: "to recover the world by making us see it not as it is, but as if it had its source in human freedom." Still, the imagination is suspect in Sartre: it creates a shadow-world of distortion, unreality, and illusion, shattered at the first contact with the absurdity and horror of actual existence.

Genuine existentialist criticism has been developed rather apart from Sartre, though often in combination with motifs derived from symbolism, surrealism, and Thomism. Marcel Raymond's *De Baudelaire au surréalisme* (1935) is the fountainhead of a conception of criticism which aims less at an analysis of a work of art than at the discovery of the particular "consciousness" and the existential feelings of the poets. Raymond traced here the myth of modern poetry to its source in Baudelaire. Albert Béguin (1901–57), in *L'Ame romantique et le rêve* (1939), went back to the dream world of the German romantics and in his later writings to the visionary Balzac, to Nerval and Lautréamont, more and more accepting a Catholic mysticism. Georges Poulet, in his *Études sur le temps humain* (1950), has analyzed the time concepts and feelings of French writers from Montaigne to Proust with dazzling ingenuity. Somewhat apart stands Maurice Blanchot who, acutely aware of the shortcomings of language, can ask such questions as "whether literature is possible," and meditate on essential solitude and the "space of death," using Mallarmé, Kafka, Rilke, and Hölderlin for his texts. Ideas from existentialist criticism have begun to filter into American critical writings. Geoffrey Hartman's subtle readings of Wordsworth, Hopkins, Valéry, and Rilke in *The Unmediated Vision* (1954) culminate in a concept of poetry as an understanding of existence in its immediacy; and J. Hillis Miller has applied Poulet's method to the study of time and space in the novels of Dickens (1959).

But while I sympathize with many insights of myth criticism and existentialism into the human soul and condition and admire some of the recent critics of these persuasions, I do not think that either myth criticism or existentialism offers a solution of the problems of literary theory. With mythology and existentialism we are back again at an identification of art with philosophy, or art with truth. The work of art as an aesthetic entity is broken up or ignored in favor of a study of attitudes, feelings, concepts, and philosophies of the poets. The act of creation and the poet rather than the work become the centers of interest. It still seems to me that formalistic, organistic, symbolistic aesthetics, rooted as it is in the great tradition of German aesthetics from Kant to Hegel, restated and justified in French symbolism, in

De Sanctis and Croce, has a firmer grasp on the nature of poetry and art. Today it would need a closer collaboration with linguistics and stylistics, a clear analysis of the stratification of the work of poetry to become a coherent literary theory capable of further development and refinement, but it would hardly need a radical revision.

This survey of the main trends of twentieth-century criticism is necessarily something like a Cook's tour, or possibly like an airplane trip: only the main features of the landscape stand out and the selection of names is often arbitrary. I can plead only that its shortcomings are due to its very brevity and to the novelty of my task. I am not acquainted with any attempt, however brief, to survey the present scene on an international scale. But today more than ever this international perspective is needed in criticism.

CLEANTH BROOKS

•

The Naked Babe and the Cloak of Manliness[1]

With Donne, of course, the chains of imagery, "always vivid" and "often minute," are perfectly evident. For many readers they are all too evident. The difficulty is not to prove that they exist, but that, on occasion, they may subserve a more imaginative unity. With Shakespeare, the difficulty may well be to prove that the chains exist at all. In general, we may say, Shakespeare has made it relatively easy for his admirers to choose what they like and neglect what they like. What he gives on one or another level is usually so magnificent that the reader finds it easy to ignore other levels.

Yet there are passages not easy to ignore and on which even critics with the conventional interests have been forced to comment. One of these passages occurs in *Macbeth,* Act I, Scene vii, where Macbeth compares the pity for his victim-to-be, Duncan, to

> a naked new-born babe,
> Striding the blast, or heaven's cherubim, hors'd
> Upon the sightless couriers of the air . . . .

The comparison is odd, to say the least. Is the babe natural or supernatural—an ordinary, helpless baby, who, as newborn, could not, of course, even toddle, much less stride the blast? Or is it some infant Hercules, quite capable

[1] From *The Well Wrought Urn,* copyright 1947 by Cleanth Brooks. Reprinted by permission of Harcourt, Brace & World, Inc. The first six pages of the chapter have been omitted by the editors.

of striding the blast, but, since it is powerful and not helpless, hardly the typical pitiable object?

Shakespeare seems bent upon having it both ways—and, if we read on through the passage—bent upon having the best of both worlds; for he proceeds to give us the option: pity is like the babe "or heaven's cherubim" who quite appropriately, of course, do ride the blast. Yet, even if we waive the question of the legitimacy of the alternative (of which Shakespeare so promptly avails himself), is the cherubim comparison really any more successful than is the babe comparison? Would not one of the great warrior archangels be more appropriate to the scene than the cherub? Does Shakespeare mean for pity or for fear of retribution to be dominant in Macbeth's mind?

Or is it possible that Shakespeare could not make up his own mind? Was he merely writing hastily and loosely, letting the word "pity" suggest the typically pitiable object, the babe naked in the blast, and then, stirred by the vague notion that some threat to Macbeth should be hinted, using "heaven's cherubim"—already suggested by "babe"—to convey the hint? Is the passage vague or precise? Loosely or tightly organized? Comments upon the passage have ranged all the way from one critic's calling it "pure rant, and intended to be so" to another's laudation: "Either like a mortal babe, terrible in helplessness; or like heaven's angel-children, mighty in love and compassion. This magnificent passage . . . ."

An even more interesting, and perhaps more disturbing passage in the play is that in which Macbeth describes his discovery of the murder:

> Here lay Duncan,
> His silver skin lac'd with his golden blood;
> And his gash'd stabs look'd like a breach in nature
> For ruin's wasteful entrance: there, the murderers,
> Steep'd in the colours of their trade, their daggers
> Unmannerly breech'd with gore. . . .

It is amusing to watch the textual critics, particularly those of the eighteenth century, fight a stubborn rear-guard action against the acceptance of "breech'd." Warburton emended "breech'd" to "reech'd"; Johnson, to "drench'd"; Seward, to "hatch'd." Other critics argued that the *breeches* implied were really the handles of the daggers, and that, accordingly, "breech'd" actually here meant "sheathed." The Variorum page witnesses the desperate character of the defense, but the position has had to be yielded, after all. *The Shakespeare Glossary* defines "breech'd" as meaning "covered as with breeches," and thus leaves the poet committed to a reading which must still shock the average reader as much as it shocked that nineteenth-century critic who pronounced upon it as follows: "A metaphor must not be far-fetched nor dwell upon the details of a disgusting picture, as in these lines. There is little, and that far-fetched, similarity between *gold lace* and *blood,* or between *bloody daggers* and *breech'd legs*. The slightness of the similarity, recalling the greatness of the dissimilarity, disgusts us with the attempted comparison."

The two passages are not of the utmost importance, I dare say, though the speeches (of which each is a part) are put in Macbeth's mouth and come at moments of great dramatic tension in the play. Yet, in neither case is there any warrant for thinking that Shakespeare was not trying to write as well as he could. Moreover, whether we like it or not, the imagery is fairly typical of Shakespeare's mature style. Either passage ought to raise some qualms among those who retreat to Shakespeare's authority when they seek to urge the claims of "noble simplicity." They are hardly simple. Yet it is possible that such passages as these may illustrate another poetic resource, another type of imagery which, even in spite of its apparent violence and complication, Shakespeare could absorb into the total structure of his work.

Shakespeare, I repeat, is not Donne—is a much greater poet than Donne; yet the example of his typical handling of imagery will scarcely render support to the usual attacks on Donne's imagery—for, with regard to the two passages in question, the second one, at any rate, is about as strained as Donne is at his most extreme pitch.

Yet I think that Shakespeare's daggers attired in their bloody breeches can be defended as poetry, and as characteristically Shakespearean poetry. Furthermore, both this passage and that about the newborn babe, it seems to me, are far more than excrescences, mere extravagances of detail: each, it seems to me, contains a central symbol of the play, and symbols which we must understand if we are to understand either the detailed passage or the play as a whole.

If this be true, then more is at stake than the merit of the quoted lines taken as lines. (The lines as constituting mere details of a larger structure could, of course, be omitted in the acting of the play without seriously damaging the total effect of the tragedy—though this argument obviously cuts two ways. Whole scenes, and admittedly fine scenes, might also be omitted—have in fact *been* omitted—without quite destroying the massive structure of the tragedy.) What is at stake is the whole matter of the relation of Shakespeare's imagery to the total structures of the plays themselves.

I should like to use the passages as convenient points of entry into the larger symbols which dominate the play. They *are* convenient because, even if we judge them to be faulty, they demonstrate how obsessive for Shakespeare the symbols were—they demonstrate how far the conscious (or unconscious) symbolism could take him.

If we see how the passages are related to these symbols, and they to the tragedy as a whole, the main matter is achieved; and having seen this, if we still prefer "to wish the lines away," that, of course, is our privilege. In the meantime, we may have learned something about Shakespeare's methods—not merely of building metaphors—but of encompassing his larger meanings.

One of the most startling things which has come out of Miss Spurgeon's book on Shakespeare's imagery is her discovery of the "old clothes" imagery in *Macbeth.* As she points out: "The idea constantly recurs that Macbeth's new honours sit ill upon him, like a loose and badly fitting garment, belonging to someone else." And she goes on to quote passage after passage in which the idea is expressed. But, though we are all in Miss Spurgeon's debt for having pointed this out, one has to observe that Miss Spurgeon has hardly explored the full implications of her discovery. Perhaps her interest in classifying and cataloguing the imagery of the plays has obscured for her some of the larger and more important relationships. At any rate, for reasons to be given below, she has realized only a part of the potentialities of her discovery.

Her comment on the clothes imagery reaches its climax with the following paragraphs:

> And, at the end, when the tyrant is at bay at Dunsinane, and the English troops are advancing, the Scottish lords still have this image in their minds. Caithness sees him as a man vainly trying to fasten a large garment on him with too small a belt:
>
> He cannot buckle his distemper'd cause
> Within the belt of rule;
>
> while Angus, in a similar image, vividly sums up the essence of what they all have been thinking ever since Macbeth's accession to power:
>
> now does he feel his title
> Hang loose about him, like a giant's robe
> Upon a dwarfish thief.
>
> This imaginative picture of a small, ignoble man encumbered and degraded by garments unsuited to him, should be put against the view emphasized by some critics (notably Coleridge and Bradley) of the likeness between Macbeth and Milton's Satan in grandeur and sublimity.
>
> Undoubtedly Macbeth . . . is great, magnificently great. . . . But he could never be put beside, say, Hamlet or Othello, in nobility of nature; and there *is* an aspect in which he is but a poor, vain, cruel, treacherous creature, snatching ruthlessly over the dead bodies of kinsman and friend at place and power he is utterly unfitted to possess. It is worth remembering that it is thus that Shakespeare, with his unshrinking clarity of vision, repeatedly *sees* him.

But this is to make primary what is only one aspect of the old-clothes imagery! And there is no warrant for interpreting the garment imagery as used by Macbeth's enemies, Caithness and Angus, to mean that Shakespeare sees Macbeth as a poor and somewhat comic figure.

The crucial point of the comparison, it seems to me, lies not in the smallness of the man and the largeness of the robes, but rather in the fact that—whether the man be large or small—these are not *his* garments; in Macbeth's case they are actually stolen garments. Macbeth is uncomfortable in them because he is continually conscious of the fact that they do not belong to him. There is a further point, and it is one of the utmost importance; the oldest symbol for the hypocrite is that of the man who cloaks his true nature under a disguise. Macbeth loathes playing the part of the hypocrite—and actually does not play it too well. If we keep this in mind as we look back at the instances of the garment images which Miss Spurgeon has collected for us, we shall see that the pattern of imagery becomes very rich indeed. Macbeth says in Act I:

> The Thane of Cawdor lives: why do you dress me
> In borrow'd robes?

Macbeth at this point wants no honors that are not honestly his. Banquo says in Act I:

> New honours come upon him,
> Like our strange garments, cleave not to their mould,
> But with the aid of use.

But Banquo's remark, one must observe, is not censorious. It is indeed a compliment to say of one that he wears new honors with some awkwardness. The observation becomes ironical only in terms of what is to occur later.

Macbeth says in Act I:

> He hath honour'd me of late; and I have bought
> Golden opinions from all sorts of people,
> Which would be worn now in their newest gloss,
> Not cast aside so soon.

Macbeth here is proud of his new clothes: he is happy to wear what he has truly earned. It is the part of simple good husbandry not to throw aside these new garments and replace them with robes stolen from Duncan.

But Macbeth has already been wearing Duncan's garments in anticipation, as his wife implies in the metaphor with which she answers him:

> Was the hope drunk,
> Wherein you dress'd yourself?

(The metaphor may seem hopelessly mixed, and a full and accurate analysis of such mixed metaphors in terms of the premises of Shakepeare's style waits upon some critic who will have to consider not only this passage but many more like it in Shakespeare.) For our purposes here, however, one may observe that the psychological line, the line of the basic symbolism, runs on unbroken. A man dressed in a drunken hope is garbed in strange attire indeed —a ridiculous dress which accords thoroughly with the contemptuous picture that Lady Macbeth wishes to evoke. Macbeth's earlier dream of glory has been a drunken fantasy merely, if he flinches from action now.

But the series of garment metaphors which run through the play is paralleled by a series of masking or cloaking images which—if we free ourselves of Miss Spurgeon's rather mechanical scheme of classification—show themselves to be merely variants of the garments which hide none too well his disgraceful self. He is consciously hiding that self throughout the play.

"False face must hide what the false heart doth know," he counsels Lady Macbeth before the murder of Duncan; and later, just before the murder of Banquo, he invokes night to "Scarf up the eye of pitiful day."

One of the most powerful of these cloaking images is given to Lady Macbeth in the famous speech in Act I:

> Come, thick night,
> And pall thee in the dunnest smoke of hell,
> That my keen knife see not the wound it makes,
> Nor heaven peep through the blanket of the dark,
> To cry, "Hold, Hold!"

I suppose that it is natural to conceive the "keen knife" here as held in her own hand. Lady Macbeth is capable of wielding it. And in this interpretation, the imagery is thoroughly significant. Night is to be doubly black so that not even her knife may see the wound it makes. But I think that there is good warrant for regarding her "keen knife" as Macbeth himself. She has just, a few lines above, given her analysis of Macbeth's character as one who would "not play false,/ And yet [would] wrongly win." To bring him to the point of action, she will have to "chastise [him] with the valour of [her] tongue." There is good reason, then, for her to invoke night to become blacker still—to pall itself in the "dunnest smoke of hell." For night must not only screen the deed from the eye of heaven—conceal it at least until it is too late for heaven to call out to Macbeth "Hold, Hold!" Lady Macbeth would have night blanket the deed from the hesitant doer. The imagery thus repeats and reinforces the substance of Macbeth's anguished aside uttered in the preceding scene:

> Let not light see my black and deep desires;
> The eye wink at the hand; yet let that be
> Which the eye fears, when it is done, to see.

I do not know whether "blanket" and "pall" qualify as garment metaphors in Miss Spurgeon's classification: yet one is the clothing of sleep, and the other, the clothing of death—they are the appropriate garments of night; and they carry on an important aspect of the general clothes imagery. It is not necessary to attempt to give here an exhaustive list of instances of the garment metaphor; but one should say a word about the remarkable passage in II, iii.

Here, after the discovery of Duncan's murder, Banquo says

> And when we have our naked frailties hid,
> That suffer in exposure, let us meet,
> And question this most bloody piece of work—

that is, "When we have clothed ourselves against the chill morning air, let us meet to discuss this bloody piece of work." Macbeth answers, as if his subconscious mind were already taking Banquo's innocent phrase, "naked frailties," in a deeper, ironic sense:

> Let's briefly put on manly readiness. . . .

It is ironic; for the "manly readiness" which he urges the other lords to put on, is, in his own case, a hypocrite's garment: he can only pretend to be the loyal, grief-stricken liege who is almost unstrung by the horror of Duncan's murder.

But the word "manly" carries still a further ironic implication: earlier, Macbeth had told Lady Macbeth that he dared

> do all that may become a man;
> Who dares do more is none.

Under the weight of her reproaches of cowardice, however, he *has* dared do more, and has become less than a man, a beast. He has already laid aside, therefore, one kind of "manly readiness" and has assumed another: he has garbed himself in a sterner composure than that which he counsels to his fellows—the hard and inhuman "manly readiness" of the resolved murderer.

The clothes imagery, used sometimes with emphasis on one aspect of it, sometimes, on another, does pervade the play. And it should be evident that the daggers "breech'd with gore"—though Miss Spurgeon does not include the passage in her examples of clothes imagery—represent one more variant of this general symbol. Consider the passage once more:

> Here lay Duncan,
> His silver skin lac'd with his golden blood;
> And his gash'd stabs look'd like a breach in nature
> For ruin's wasteful entrance: there, the murderers,
> Steep'd in the colours of their trade, their daggers
> Unmannerly breech'd with gore. . . .

The clothes imagery runs throughout the passage; the body of the king is dressed in the most precious of garments, the blood royal itself; and the daggers too are dressed—in the same garment. The daggers, "naked" except for their lower parts which are reddened with blood, are like men in "unmannerly" dress—men, naked except for their red breeches, lying beside the red-handed grooms. The figure, though vivid, is fantastic; granted. But the basis for the comparison is *not* slight and adventitious. The metaphor fits the real situation on the deepest levels. As Macbeth and Lennox burst into the room, they find the daggers wearing, as Macbeth knows all too well, a horrible masquerade. They have been carefully "clothed" to play a part. They are not honest daggers, honorably naked in readiness to guard the king, or, "mannerly" clothed in their own sheaths. Yet the disguise which they wear will enable Macbeth to assume the robes of Duncan—robes to which he is no more entitled than are the daggers to the royal garments which they now wear, grotesquely.

The reader will, of course, make up his own mind as to the value of the passage. But the metaphor in question, in the light of the other garment imagery, cannot be dismissed as merely a strained ingenuity, irrelevant to the play. And the reader who *does* accept it as poetry will probably be that reader who knows the play best, not the reader who knows it slightly and regards Shakespeare's poetry as a rhetoric more or less loosely draped over the "content" of the play.

And now what can be said of pity, the "naked new-born babe"? Though Miss Spurgeon does not note it (since the governing scheme of her book would have hardly allowed her to see it), there are, by the way, a great many references to babes in this play—references which occur on a number of levels. The babe appears sometimes as a character, such as Macduff's child; sometimes as a symbol, like the crowned babe and the bloody babe which are raised by the witches on the occasion of Macbeth's visit to them; sometimes, in a metaphor, as in the passage under discussion. The number of such references can hardly be accidental; and the babe turns out to be, as a matter of fact, perhaps the most powerful symbol in the tragedy.

But to see this fully, it will be necessary to review the motivation of the play. The stimulus to Duncan's murder, as we know, was the prophecy of the Weird Sisters. But Macbeth's subsequent career of bloodshed stems from the same prophecy. Macbeth was to have the crown, but the crown was to pass to Banquo's children. The second part of the prophecy troubles Macbeth from the start. It does not oppress him, however, until the crown has been won. But from this point on, the effect of the prophecy is to hurry Macbeth into action and more action until he is finally precipitated into ruin.

We need not spend much time in speculating on whether Macbeth, had he been content with Duncan's murder, had he tempted fate no further, had he been willing to court the favor of his nobles, might not have died peaceably in bed. We are dealing, not with history, but with a play. Yet, even in history the usurper sometimes succeeds; and he sometimes succeeds on the stage. Shakespeare himself knew of, and wrote plays about, usurpers who successfully maintained possession of the crown. But, in any case, this much is plain: the train of murders into which Macbeth launches aggravates suspicions of his guilt and alienates the nobles.

Yet, a Macbeth who could act once, and then settle down to enjoy the fruits of this one attempt to meddle with the future would, of course, not be Macbeth. For it is not merely his great imagination and his warrior courage in defeat which redeem him for tragedy and place him beside the other great tragic protagonists: rather, it is his attempt to conquer the future, an attempt involving him, like Oedipus, in a desperate struggle with fate itself. It is this which holds our imaginative sympathy, even after he has degenerated into a bloody tyrant and has become the slayer of Macduff's wife and children.

To sum up, there can be no question that Macbeth stands at the height of his power after his murder of Duncan, and that the plan—as outlined by Lady Macbeth—has been relatively successful. The road turns toward disaster only when Macbeth decides to murder Banquo. Why does he make this decision? Shakespeare has pointed up the basic motivation very carefully:

> Then prophet-like,
> They hail'd him father to a line of kings.
> Upon my head they plac'd a fruitless crown,
> And put a barren sceptre in my gripe,
> Thence to be wrench'd with a unlineal hand,
> No son of mine succeeding. If't be so,
> For Banquo's issue have I fil'd my mind;
> For them the gracious Duncan have I murder'd;
> Put rancours in the vessel of my peace
> Only for them; and mine eternal jewel
> Given to the common enemy of man,
> To make them kings, the seed of Banquo kings!

Presumably, Macbeth had entered upon his course from sheer personal ambition. Ironically, it is the more human part of Macbeth—his desire to have more than a limited personal satisfaction, his desire to found a line, his wish to pass something on to later generations—which prompts him to dispose of Banquo. There is, of course, a resentment against Banquo, but that resentment is itself closely related to Macbeth's desire to found a dynasty. Banquo, who has risked nothing, who has remained upright, who has not defiled himself, will have kings for children; Macbeth, none. Again, ironically, the Weird Sisters who have given Macbeth, so he has thought, the priceless gift of knowledge of the future, have given the real future to Banquo.

So Banquo's murder is decided upon, and accomplished. But Banquo's son escapes, and once more, the future has eluded Macbeth. The murder of Banquo thus becomes almost meaningless. This general point may be obvious enough, but we shall do well to note some of the further ways in which Shakespeare has pointed up the significance of Macbeth's war with the future.

When Macbeth, at the beginning of Scene vii, Act I, contemplates Duncan's murder, it is the future over which he agonizes:

> If it were done, when 'tis done, then 'twere well
> It were done quickly; if the assassination
> Could trammel up the consequence, and catch
> With his surcease success; that but this blow
> Might be the be-all and the end-all here. . . .

But the continuum of time cannot be partitioned off; the future is implicit in the present. There is no net strong enough to trammel up the consequence—not even in this world.

Lady Macbeth, of course, has fewer qualms. When Macbeth hesitates to repudiate the duties which he owes Duncan—duties which, by some accident of imagery perhaps—I hesitate to press the significance—he has earlier actually called "children"—Lady Macbeth cries out that she is willing to crush her own child in order to gain the crown:

> I have given suck, and know
> How tender 'tis to love the babe that milks me;
> I would, while it was smiling in my face,
> Have pluck'd my nipple from his boneless gums
> And dash'd the brains out, had I so sworn as you
> Have done to this.

Robert Penn Warren has made the penetrating observation that all of Shakespeare's villains are rationalists. Lady Macbeth is certainly of their company. She knows what she wants; and she is ruthless in her consideration of means. She will always "catch the nearest way." This is not to say that she ignores the problem of scruples, or that she is ready to oversimplify psychological complexities. But scruples are to be used to entangle one's enemies. One is not to become tangled in the mesh of scruples himself. Even though she loves her husband and though her ambition for herself is a part of her ambition for him, still she seems willing to consider even Macbeth at times as pure instrument, playing upon his hopes and fears and pride.

Her rationalism is quite sincere. She is apparently thoroughly honest in declaring that

> The sleeping and the dead
> Are but as pictures; 'tis the eye of childhood
> That fears a painted devil. If he do bleed,
> I'll gild the faces of the grooms withal,
> For it must seem their guilt.

For her, there is no moral order: *guilt* is something like *gilt*—one can wash it off or paint it on. Her pun is not frivolous and it is deeply expressive.

Lady Macbeth abjures all pity; she is willing to unsex herself; and her continual taunt to Macbeth, when he falters, is that he is acting like a baby—not like a man. This "manhood" Macbeth tries to learn. He is a dogged pupil. For that reason he is almost pathetic when the shallow rationalism which his wife urges upon him fails. His tone is almost one of puzzled bewilderment at nature's unfairness in failing to play the game according to the rules—the rules which have applied to other murders:

> the time has been,
> That, when the brains were out, the man would die,
> And there an end; but now they rise again. . . .

Yet, after the harrowing scene, Macbeth can say, with a sort of dogged weariness:

> Come, we'll to sleep. My strange and self-abuse
> Is the initiate fear that wants hard use:
> We are yet but young in deed.

Ironically, Macbeth is still echoing the dominant metaphor of Lady Macbeth's reproach. He has not yet attained to "manhood"; that *must* be the explanation. He has not yet succeeded in hardening himself into something inhuman.

Tempted by the Weird Sisters and urged on by his wife, Macbeth is thus caught between the irrational and the rational. There is a sense, of course, in which every man is caught between them. Man must try to predict and plan and control his destiny. That is man's fate; and the struggle, if he is to realize himself as a man, cannot be avoided. The question, of course, which has always interested the tragic dramatist involves the terms on which the struggle is accepted and the protagonist's attitude toward fate and toward himself. Macbeth in his general concern for the future is typical—is Every Man. He becomes the typical tragic protagonist when he yields to pride and *hybris*. The occasion for temptation is offered by the prophecy of the Weird Sisters. They offer him knowledge which cannot be arrived at rationally. They offer a key—if only a partial key—to what is otherwise unpredictable. Lady Macbeth, on the other hand, by employing a ruthless clarity of perception, by discounting all emotional claims, offers him the promise of bringing about the course of events which he desires.

Now, in the middle of the play, though he has not lost confidence and though, as he himself says, there can be no turning back, doubts have begun to arise; and he returns to the Weird Sisters to secure unambiguous answers to his fears. But, pathetically and ironically for Macbeth, in returning to the Weird Sisters, he is really trying to impose rationality on what sets itself forth plainly as irrational: that is, Macbeth would force a rigid control on a future which, by definition—by the very fact that the Weird Sisters already know it—stands beyond his manipulation.

It is because of his hopes for his own children and his fears of Banquo's that he has returned to the witches for counsel. It is altogether appropriate, therefore, that two of the apparitions by which their counsel is revealed should be babes, the crowned babe and the bloody babe.

For the babe signifies the future which Macbeth would control and cannot control. It is the unpredictable thing itself—as Yeats has put it magnificently, "The uncontrollable mystery on the bestial floor." It is the one thing that can justify, even in Macbeth's mind, the murders which he has committed. Earlier in the play, Macbeth had declared that if the deed could "trammel up the consequence," he would be willing to "jump the life to come." But he cannot jump the life to come. In his own terms he is betrayed. For it is idle to speak of jumping the life to come if one yearns to found a line of kings. It is the babe that betrays Macbeth—his own babes, most of all.

The logic of Macbeth's distraught mind, thus, forces him to make war on children, a war which in itself reflects his desperation and is a confession of weakness. Macbeth's ruffians, for example, break into Macduff's castle and kill his wife and children. The scene in which the innocent child prattles with his mother about his absent father, and then is murdered, is typical Shakespearean "fourth act" pathos. But the pathos is not adventitious; the scene ties into the inner symbolism of the play. For the child, in its helplessness, defies the murderers. Its defiance testifies to the force which threatens Macbeth and which Macbeth cannot destroy.

But we are not, of course, to placard the child as The Future in a rather stiff and mechanical allegory. *Macbeth* is no such allegory. Shakespeare's symbols are richer and more flexible than that. The babe signifies not only the future; it symbolizes all those enlarging purposes which make life meaningful, and it symbolizes, furthermore, all those emotional and—to Lady Macbeth—irrational ties which make man more than a machine—which render him human. It signifies pre-eminently the pity which Macbeth, under Lady Macbeth's tutelage, would wean himself of as something "unmanly." Lady Macbeth's great speeches early in the play become brilliantly ironical when we realize that Shakespeare is using the same symbol for the unpredictable future that he uses for human compassion. Lady Macbeth is willing to go to any length to grasp the future: she would willingly dash out the brains of her own child if it stood in her way to that future. But this is to repudiate the future, for the child is its symbol.

Shakespeare does not, of course, limit himself to the symbolism of the child: he makes use of other symbols of growth and development, notably that of the plant. And this plant symbolism patterns itself to reflect the development of the play. For example, Banquo says to the Weird Sisters, early in the play:

> If you can look into the seeds of time,
> And say which grain will grow and which will not,
> Speak then to me. . . .

A little later, on welcoming Macbeth, Duncan says to him:

> I have begun to plant thee, and will labour
> To make thee full of growing.

After the murder of Duncan, Macbeth falls into the same metaphor when he comes to resolve on Banquo's death. The Weird Sisters, he reflects, had hailed Banquo as

> . . . father to a line of kings.
> Upon my head they placed a fruitless crown,
> And put a barren sceptre in my gripe. . . .

Late in the play, Macbeth sees himself as the winter-stricken tree:

> I have liv'd long enough: my way of life
> Is fall'n into the sear, the yellow leaf. . . .

The plant symbolism, then, supplements the child symbolism. At points it merges with it, as when Macbeth ponders bitterly that he has damned himself

> To make them kings, the seed of Banquo kings!

And, in at least one brilliant example, the plant symbolism unites with the clothes symbolism. It is a crowning irony that one of the Weird Sisters' prophecies on which Macbeth has staked his hopes is fulfilled when Birnam Wood comes to Dunsinane. For, in a sense, Macbeth is here hoist on his own petard. Macbeth, who has invoked night to "Scarf up the tender eye of pitiful day," and who has, again and again, used the "false face" to "hide what the false heart doth know," here has the trick turned against him. But the garment which cloaks the avengers is the living green of nature itself, and nature seems, to the startled eyes of his sentinels, to be rising up against him.

But it is the babe, the child, that dominates the symbolism. Most fittingly, the last of the prophecies in which Macbeth has placed his confidence, concerns the child: and Macbeth comes to know the final worst when Macduff declares to him that he was not "born of woman" but was from his "mother's womb/ Untimely ripp'd." The babe here has defied even the thing which one feels may reasonably be predicted of him—his time of birth. With Macduff's pronouncement, the unpredictable has broken through the last shred of the net of calculation. The future cannot be trammelled up. The naked babe confronts Macbeth to pronounce his doom.

The passage with which we began this essay, then, is an integral part of a larger context, and of a very rich context:

> And pity, like a naked new-born babe,
> Striding the blast, or heaven's cherubim, hors'd
> Upon the sightless couriers of the air,
> Shall blow the horrid deed in every eye,
> That tears shall drown the wind.

Pity is like the naked babe, the most sensitive and helpless thing; yet, almost as soon as the comparison is announced, the symbol of weakness begins to turn into a symbol of strength; for the babe, though newborn, is pictured as "Striding the blast" like an elemental force—like "heaven's cherubim, hors'd/ Upon the sightless couriers of the air." We can give an answer to the question put earlier: is Pity like the human and helpless babe, or powerful as the angel that rides the winds? It is both; and it is strong because of its very weakness. The paradox is inherent in the situation itself; and it is the paradox that will destroy the overbrittle rationalism on which Macbeth founds his career.

For what will it avail Macbeth to cover the deed with the blanket of the dark if the elemental forces that ride the winds will blow the horrid deed in every eye? And what will it avail Macbeth to clothe himself in "manliness"—to become bloody, bold, and resolute,—if he is to find himself again and again, viewing his bloody work through the "eye of childhood/ That fears a painted devil"? Certainly, the final and climactic appearance of the babe symbol merges all the contradictory elements of the symbol. For, with Macduff's statement about his birth, the naked babe rises before Macbeth as not only the future that eludes calculation but as avenging angel as well.

The clothed daggers and the naked babe—mechanism and life—instrument and end—death and birth—that which should be left bare and clean and that which should be clothed and warmed—these are facets of two of the great symbols which run throughout the play. They are not the only symbols, to be sure; they are not the most obvious symbols: darkness and blood appear more often. But with a flexibility which must amaze the reader, the image of the garment and the image of the babe are so used as to encompass an astonishingly large area of the total situation. And between them—the naked babe, essential humanity, humanity stripped down to the naked thing itself, and yet as various as the future—and the various garbs which humanity assumes, the robes of honor, the hypocrite's disguise, the inhuman "manliness" with which Macbeth endeavors to cover up his essential humanity—between them, they furnish Shakespeare with his most subtle and ironically telling instruments.

R. S. CRANE

•

The Structure of Macbeth[1]

We must also distinguish between critical hypotheses in the strict sense and interpretative hypotheses concerning the details of literary works in their

[1] Reprinted from *The Language of Criticism and the Structure of Poetry* by R. S. Crane with the permission of the University of Toronto Press. Parts of the chapter have been omitted by the editors.

material aspects. It is not one of our presuppositions that "form" in poetry is "meaning"; we should hold, rather, that meaning is something involved in poems as a necessary, but not sufficient, condition of the existence in them of poetic form, and hence that the recovery of meaning is an essential prerequisite to the discovery of form though not in itself such a discovery. Before we can understand a poem as an artistic structure we must understand it as a grammatical structure made up of successive words, sentences, paragraphs, and speeches which give us both meanings in the ordinary sense of that term and signs from which we may infer what the speakers, whether characters or narrators, are like and what they are thinking, feeling, or doing. The great temptation for critics who are not trained and practising scholars is to take this understanding for granted or to think that it may easily be obtained at second hand by consulting the works of scholars. This is an illusion, just as it is an illusion in scholars to suppose that they can see, without training in criticism, all the problems which their distinctive methods are fitted to solve. The ideal would be that all critics should be scholars and all scholars critics; but, although there ought to be the closest correlation of the two functions in practice, they are nevertheless distinct in nature and in the kinds of hypotheses to which they lead. The hypotheses of interpretation are concerned with the meanings and implications in texts that result from their writers' expressive intentions in setting down particular words and constructions and arranging these in particular sequences. Such meanings and implications, indeed, are forms, of which words and sentences are the matter; but they are forms of a kind that can appear in any sort of discourse, however unpoetic. They are to be interpreted by resolving the forms into the elements which poems share with the common speech or writing and the common thought and experience of the times when they were written; and this requires the use of techniques and principles quite different from any that poetic theory can afford: the techniques and principles of historical grammar, of the analysis and history of ideas, of the history of literary conventions, manners, and so on, and the still more general techniques and principles, seldom methodized, by which we construe characters and actions in everyday life.

The hypotheses of criticism, on the contrary, are concerned with the shaping principles, peculiar to the poetic arts, which account in any work for the power of its grammatical materials, in the particular ordering given to these, to move our opinions and feelings in such-and-such a way. They will be of two sorts according as the questions to which they are answers relate to the principles by which poetic works have been constructed as wholes of certain definite kinds or to the reasons which connect a particular part of a given work, directly or indirectly, with such a principle by way of the poetic problems it set for the writer at this point. And there can be no good practical criticism in this mode in which both sorts are not present; for although the primary business of the critic is with the particulars of any work he studies down to its minuter details of diction and rhythm, he can never exhibit the artistic problems involved in these or find other than extra-poetic reasons for their solutions without the guidance of an explicit definition of the formal whole which they have made possible.

A single work will suffice to illustrate both kinds of critical hypotheses as well as the relation between them, and I will begin by considering what idea of the governing form of *Macbeth* appears to accord best with the facts of that play and the sequence of emotions it arouses in us. I need not say again why it seems to me futile to look for an adequate structural formula for *Macbeth* in any of the more "imaginative" directions commonly taken by recent criticism; I shall assume, therefore, without argument, that we have to do, not with a lyric "statement of evil" or an allegory of the workings of sin in the soul and the state or a metaphysical myth of destruction followed by recreation or a morality play with individualized characters rather than types, but simply with an imitative tragic drama based on historical materials. To call it an imitative tragic drama, however, does not carry us very far; it merely limits roughly the range of possible forms we have to consider. Among these are the contrasting plot-forms embodied respectively in *Othello* and in *Richard III*: the first a tragic plot-form in the classic sense of Aristotle's analysis in *Poetics* 13; the second a plot-form which Aristotle rejected as non-tragic but which appealed strongly to tragic poets in the Renaissance—a form of serious action designed to arouse moral indignation for the deliberately unjust and seemingly prospering acts of the protagonist and moral satisfaction at his subsequent ruin. The plot-form of *Macbeth* clearly involves elements which assimilate it now to the one and now to the other of both these kinds. The action of the play is twofold, and one of its aspects is the punitive action of Malcolm, Macduff, and their friends which in the end brings about the protagonist's downfall and death. The characters here are all good men, whom Macbeth has unforgivably wronged, and their cause is the unqualifiedly just cause of freeing Scotland from a bloody tyrant and restoring the rightful line of kings. All this is made clear in the representation not only directly through the speeches and acts of the avengers but indirectly by those wonderfully vivid devices of imagery and general thought in which modern critics have found the central value and meaning of the play as a whole; and our responses, when this part of the action is before us, are such as are clearly dictated by the immediate events and the poetic commentary: we desire, that is, the complete success of the counter-action and this as speedily as possible before Macbeth can commit further horrors. We desire this, however—and that is what at once takes the plot-form out of the merely retributive class—not only for the sake of humanity and Scotland but also for the sake of Macbeth himself. For what most sharply distinguishes our view of Macbeth from that of his victims and enemies is that, whereas they see him from the outside only, we see him also, throughout the other action of the play—the major action—from the inside, as he sees himself; and what we see thus is a moral spectacle the emotional quality of which, for the impartial observer, is not too far removed from the tragic *dynamis* specified in the *Poetics*. This is not to say that the main action of *Macbeth* is not significantly different, in several respects, from the kind of tragic action which Aristotle envisages. The change is not merely from good to bad fortune, but from a good state of character to a state in which the hero is almost, but not quite, transformed into a monster; and the tragic act which initiates the change, and still more the subsequent unjust acts which this entails, are acts done—unlike Othello's killing of Desdemona—in full knowledge of their moral character. We cannot, therefore, state the form of this action in strictly Aristotelian terms, but the form is none the less one that involves, like tragedy in Aristotle's sense, the arousal and catharsis of painful emotions for, and not merely with respect to, the protagonist—emotions for which the terms pity and fear are not entirely inapplicable.

Any adequate hypothesis about the structure of *Macbeth,* then, would have to take both of these sets of facts into account. For both of the views we are given of the hero are true: he is in fact, in terms of the nature and objective consequences of his deeds, what Macduff and Malcolm say he is throughout Acts IV and V, but he is also—and the form of the play is really the interaction of the two views in our opinions and emotions—what we ourselves see him to be as we witness the workings of his mind before the murder of Duncan, then after the murder, and finally when, at the end, all his illusions and hopes gone, he faces Macduff. He is one who commits monstrous deeds without becoming wholly a monster, since his knowledge of the right principle is never altogether obscured, though it is almost so in Act IV. We can understand such a person and hence feel fear and pity of a kind for him because he is only doing upon a grander scale and with deeper guilt and more terrifying consequences for himself and others what we can, without too much difficulty, imagine ourselves doing, however less extremely, in circumstances generally similar. For the essential story of *Macbeth* is that of a man, not naturally depraved, who has fallen under the compulsive power of an imagined better state for himself which he can attain only by acting contrary to his normal habits and feelings; who attains this state and then finds that he must continue to act thus, and even worse, in order to hold on to what he has got; who persists and becomes progressively hardened morally in the process; and who then, ultimately, when the once alluring good is about to be taken away from him, faces the loss in terms of what is left of his original character. It is something like this moral universal that underlies, I think, and gives emotional form to the main action of *Macbeth*. It is a form that turns upon the difference between what seemingly advantageous crime appears to be in advance to a basically good but incontinent man and what its moral consequences for such a man inevitably are; and the catharsis is effected not merely by the man's deserved overthrow but by his own inner suffering and by his discovery, before it is too late, of what he had not known before he began to act. If we are normal human beings we must abhor his crimes; yet we cannot completely abhor but must rather pity the man himself, and even when he seems most the monster (as Macbeth does in Act IV) we must still wish for such an outcome as will be best, under the circumstances, not merely for Scotland but for him.

But if this, or something close to it, is indeed the complex emotional structure intended in *Macbeth,* then we have a basis for defining with some precision the various problems of incident, character, thought, imagery, diction, and representation which confronted Shakespeare in writing the play, and hence a starting-point for discussing, in detail, the rationale of its parts. Consider—to take only one instance—the final scene. In the light of the obvious consequences of the form I have attributed to the play as a whole, it is not difficult to state what the main problems at this point are. If the catharsis of the tragedy is to be complete, we must be made to feel both that Macbeth is being killed in a just cause and that his state of mind and the circumstances of his death are such as befit a man who, for all his crimes, has not altogether lost our pity and goodwill. We are of course prepared for this double response by all that has gone before, and, most immediately, in the earlier scenes of Act V, by the fresh glimpses we are given of the motivation of the avengers and by Macbeth's soliloquies. But it will clearly be better if the dual effect can be sustained until the very end; and this requires, on the one hand, that we should be vividly reminded once more of Macbeth's crimes and the justified hatred they have caused and of the prospect of a new and better time which his death holds out for Scotland, and, on the other hand, that we should be allowed to take satisfaction, at last, in the manner in which Macbeth himself behaves. The artistic triumph of the scene lies in the completeness with which both problems are solved: the first in the words and actions of Macduff, the speeches about young Siward, and Malcolm's closing address; the second by a variety of devices, both of invention and of representation, the appropriateness of which to the needed effect can be seen if we ask what we would not want Macbeth to do at this moment. We want him to be killed, as I have said, for his sake no less than that of Scotland; but we would not want him either to seek out Macduff or to flee the encounter when it comes or to "play the Roman fool"; we would not want him to show no recognition of the wrongs he has done Macduff or, when his last trust in the witches has gone, to continue to show fear or to yield or to fight with savage animosity; and he is made to do none of these things, but rather the contraries of all of them, so that he acts in the end as the Macbeth whose praises we have heard in the second scene of the play. And I would suggest that the cathartic effect of these words and acts is reinforced indirectly, in the representation, by the analogy we can hardly help drawing between his conduct now and the earlier conduct of young Siward, for of Macbeth too it can be said that "he parted well and paid his score"; the implication of this analogy is surely one of the functions, though not the only one, which the lines about Siward are intended to serve.

FRANCIS FERGUSSON

•

Macbeth *as the Imitation of an Action*[1]

I propose to attempt to illustrate the view that *Macbeth* may be understood as "the imitation of an action," in approximately Aristotle's sense of this phrase.

The word "action"—*praxis*—as Aristotle uses it in the *Poetics,* does not mean outward deeds or events, but something much more like "purpose" or "aim." Perhaps our word "motive" suggests most of its meaning. Dante (who in this respect is a sophisticated Aristotelian) uses the phrase *moto spirital,* spiritual movement, to indicate *praxis.* In Aristotle's own writings *praxis* is usually rational, a movement of the will in the light of the mind. But Dante's *moto spirital* refers to all modes of the spirit's life, all of its directions, or focuses, or motives, including those of childhood, dream, drunkenness, or passion, which are hardly rationalized at all. When using Aristotle's definition for the analysis of modern drama it is necessary to generalize his notion of action in this way, to include movements of the spirit in response to sensuous or emotionally charged images, as well as consciously willed purpose. But this seems to me a legitimate extension of the basic concept; and I do not think it does real violence to Aristotle's meaning.

Aristotle, in his *Psychology* and his *Ethics,* as well as in the *Poetics,* and Dante in the *Divine Comedy,* seem to imagine the psyche much as an amoeba looks under the microscope: moving toward what attracts it, continually changing direction or aim, and taking its shape and color from the object to which it is attached at the moment. This movement is "action"; and so we see that while the psyche is alive it always has action; and that this changing action in pursuit of real or imagined objects defines its mode of being moment by moment.

When Aristotle says that a tragedy is the imitation of an action, he is thinking of an action, or motive, which governs the psyche's life for a considerable length of time. Such an action is the quest for Laius's slayer in *Oedipus Rex,* which persists through the changing circumstances of the play. In this period of time, it has a beginning, a middle, and an end, which comes when the slayer is at last identified.

I remarked that action is not outward deeds or events; but on the other hand, there can be no action without resulting deeds. We guess at a man's action by way of what he does, his outward and visible deeds. We are aware that our own action, or motive, produces deeds of some sort as soon as it

[1] From *English Institute Essays 1951* (New York: Columbia University Press, 1952), pp. 31–43. Also printed in Francis Fergusson, *The Human Image in Dramatic Literature* (Garden City, N.Y.: Doubleday & Co., 1957), pp. 115–125.

exists. Now the plot of a play is the arrangement of outward deeds or incidents, and the dramatist uses it, as Aristotle tells us, as the first means of imitating the action. He arranges a set of incidents which point to the action or motive from which they spring. You may say that the action is the spiritual content of the tragedy—the playwright's inspiration—and the plot defines its existence as an intelligible *play*. Thus, you can never have a play without both plot and action; yet the distinction between plot and action is as fundamental as that between form and matter. The action is the matter; the plot is the "first form," or, as Aristotle puts it, the "soul" of the tragedy.

The dramatist imitates the action he has in mind, first by means of the plot, then in the characters, and finally in the media of language, music, and spectacle. In a well-written play, if we understood it thoroughly, we should perceive that plot, character, diction, and the rest spring from the same source, or, in other words, realize the same action or motive in the forms appropriate to their various media.

You will notice that this is a diagrammatic description of the perfect play, perfectly understood. Therefore one cannot hope to illustrate it perfectly, even in the case of a play like *Macbeth. Macbeth,* however, does impress most of its readers as having a powerful and unmistakable unity of this kind: the plot, characters, and imagery all seem to spring from the one inspiration. It is that strong and immediately felt unity which I rely on—and upon your familiarity with the play. Not that I am so foolish as to suppose I grasp the play completely or that I could persuade you of my view of it in these few minutes. All I can attempt is to suggest the single action which seems to me to be the spiritual content of the play, and illustrate it, in only a few of its metaphors, plot devices, and characterizations.

The action of the play as a whole is best expressed in a phrase which Macbeth himself uses in Act II, scene 3, the aftermath of the murder. Macbeth is trying to appear innocent, but everything he says betrays his clear sense of his own evil motivation, or action. Trying to excuse his murder of Duncan's grooms, he says,

> The expedition of my violent love [for Duncan, he means]
> Outran the pauser, reason.

It is the phrase "to outrun the pauser, reason," which seems to me to describe the action, or motive, of the play as a whole. Macbeth, of course, literally means that his love for Duncan was so strong and swift that it got ahead of his reason, which would have counseled a pause. But in the same way we have seen his greed and ambition outrun his reason when he committed the murder; and in the same way all of the characters, in the irrational darkness of Scotland's evil hour, are compelled in their action to strive beyond what they can see by reason alone. Even Malcolm and Macduff, as we shall see, are compelled to go beyond reason in the action which destroys Macbeth and ends the play.

But let me consider the phrase itself for a moment. To "outrun" reason suggests an impossible stunt, like lifting oneself by one's own bootstraps. It also suggests a competition or race, like those of nightmare, which cannot be won. As for the word "reason," Shakespeare associates it with nature and nature's order, in the individual soul, in society, and in the cosmos. To outrun reason is thus to violate nature itself, to lose the bearings of common sense and of custom, and to move into a spiritual realm bounded by the irrational darkness of hell one way, and the superrational grace of faith the other way. As the play develops before us, all the modes of this absurd, or evil, or supernatural action are attempted, the last being Malcolm's and Macduff's acts of faith.

In the first part of the play Shakespeare, as is his custom, gives us the intimate feel of this paradoxical striving beyond reason in a series of echoing tropes and images. I remind you of some of them, as follows.

From the first Witches' scene:

> When the battle's lost and won.
>
> Fair is foul and foul is fair.

From the "bleeding-sergeant" scene:

> Doubtful it stood;
> As two spent swimmers that do cling together
> And choke their art. . . .
> So from that spring whence comfort seem'd to come
> Discomfort swells.
>
> Confronted him with self-comparisons
> Point against point, rebellious arm 'gainst arm.
> What he hath lost noble Macbeth hath won.

From the second Witches' scene:

> So fair and foul a day.
>
> Lesser than Macbeth, and greater.
>
> His wonders and his praises do contend
> Which should be thine or his.
>
> This supernatural soliciting
> Cannot be ill, cannot be good.
>
> Nothing is, but what is not.

These are only a few of the figures which suggest the desperate and paradoxical struggle. They are, of course, not identical with each other or with outrunning reason, which seems to me the most general of all. But they all point to the "action" I mean, and I present them as examples of the imitation of action by means of the arts of language.

But notice that though these images themselves suggest the action, they also confirm the actions of the characters as these are shown in the story. The bleeding sergeant, for instance, is striving beyond reason and nature in his effort to report the battle—itself a bewildering mixture of victory and defeat—in spite of his wounds. Even the old King Duncan, mild though he is, is caught in the race and sees his relation to Macbeth competitively. "Thou art so far before," he tells Macbeth in the next scene, "That swiftest wing of recompense is slow To overtake thee." He then races Macbeth to his castle, whither the Messenger has outrun them both; and when he arrives, he is at once involved in a hollow competition with Lady Macbeth, to outdo her in ceremony.

I do not need to remind you of the great scenes preceding the murder, in which Macbeth and his Lady pull themselves together for their desperate effort. If you think over these scenes, you will notice that the Macbeths understand the action which begins here as a competition and a stunt, against reason and nature. Lady Macbeth fears her husband's human nature, as well as her own female nature, and therefore she fears the light of reason and the common daylight world. As for Macbeth, he knows from the first and he is engaged in an irrational stunt: "I have no spur To prick the sides of my intent, but only Vaulting ambition, which o'erleaps itself And falls on the other." In this sequence there is also the theme of outwitting or transcending time, an aspect of nature's order as we know it: catching-up the consequences, jumping the life to come, and the like. But this must suffice to remind you of the Macbeths' actions, which they paradoxically understand so well.

The Porter scene has been less thoroughly studied as a variation on the play's main action. But it is, in fact, a farcical and terrible version of "outrunning reason," a witty and very concentrated epitome of this absurd movement of spirit. The Porter first teases the knockers at the gate with a set of paradoxes, all of which present attempts to outrun reason; and he sees them all as ways into Hell. Henry N. Paul[2] has explained the contemporary references: the farmer who hanged himself on the expectation of plenty, the equivocator who swore both ways to commit treason for God's sake. When the Porter has admitted the knockers he ironically offers them lewd physical analogies for outrunning reason: drink as tempting lechery into a hopeless action; himself as wrestling with drink. The relation of the Porter to the knockers is like that of the Witches to Macbeth—he tempts them into Hell with ambiguities. And the inebriation of drink and lust, lewd and laughable as it is, is closely analogous to the more terrible and spiritual intoxication of the Macbeths.

Thus, in the first part of the play both the imagery and the actions of the various characters indicate or "imitate" the main action. Aristotle says the characters are imitated "with a view to the action"—and the Porter, who has little importance in the story—is presented to reveal the action of the play as a whole in the unexpected light of farcical analogies, contemporary or lewd and physical.

[2] See *The Royal Play of Macbeth,* New York, 1950.

Before I leave this part of the play I wish to point out that the plot itself—"the arrangement or synthesis of the incidents"—also imitates a desperate race. This is partly a matter of the speed with which the main facts are presented, partly the effect of simultaneous movements like those of a race: Lady Macbeth is reading the letter at the same moment that her husband and Duncan are rushing toward her. And the facts in this part of the play are ambiguous in meaning and even as facts.

These few illustrations must serve to indicate how I understand the imitation of action in language, character, and plot in the first two acts of the play. Macbeth and his Lady are embarked on a race against reason itself; and all Scotland, the "many" whose lives depend upon the monarch, is precipitated into the same darkness and desperate strife. Shakespeare's monarchs do usually color the spiritual life of their realms. And we, who remember Hitlerite Germany, can understand that, I think. Even Hitler's exiles, like the refugees from Russian or Spanish tyranny, brought the shadow to this country with them.

I now wish to consider the action of the play at a later stage, in Act IV, scene 3. This is the moment which I mentioned before, the beginning of Malcolm's and Macduff's act of faith which will constitute the final variation on "outrunning reason." The scene is laid in England, whither Malcolm and Macduff have fled, and it immediately follows the murder of Macduff's wife and child. Like the exiles we have known in this country, Macduff and Malcolm, though in England, have brought Scotland's darkness with them. They have lost all faith in reason, human nature, and common sense, and can therefore trust neither themselves nor each other. They are met in the hope of forming an alliance, in order to get rid of Macbeth; and yet under his shadow everything they do seems unreasonable, paradoxical, improbable.

In the first part of the scene, you remember, Malcolm and Macduff fail to find any basis for mutual trust. Malcolm mistrusts Macduff because he has left his wife and child behind; Macduff quickly learns to mistrust Malcolm, because he first protests that he is unworthy of the crown, to test Macduff, and then suddenly reverses himself. The whole exchange is a tissue of falsity and paradox, and it ends in a sort of nightmarish paralysis.

At this point there is the brief interlude with the Doctor. The King's Evil and its cure and the graces which hang about the English throne are briefly described. Paul points out that this interlude may have been introduced to flatter James I; but however that may be, it is appropriate in the build of the scene as a whole. It marks the turning point, and it introduces the notion of the appeal by faith to Divine Grace which will reverse the evil course of the action when Malcolm and Macduff learn to outrun reason in that way, instead of by responding to the Witches' supernatural solicitations as Macbeth has done. Moreover, the Doctor in this scene, in whom religious and medical healing are associated, foreshadows the Doctor who will note Lady Macbeth's sleepwalking and describe it as a perturbation in nature which requires a cure beyond nature.

But to return to the scene. After the Doctor's interlude, Ross joins Malcolm and Macduff, bringing the latest news from Scotland. To greet him, Malcolm clearly states the action, or motive, of the scene as a whole: "Good God, betimes remove The means that make us strangers!" he says. Ross's chief news is, of course, Lady Macduff's murder. When he has gradually revealed that, and Macduff and Malcolm have taken it in, accepting some of the guilt, they find that the means that made them strangers has in fact been removed. They recognize themselves and each other once more, in a sober, but not nightmarish light. And at once they join in faith in their cause and prepare to hazard all upon the ordeal of battle, itself an appeal beyond reason. The scene, which in its opening sections moved very slowly, reflecting the demoralization of Malcolm and Macduff, ends hopefully, with brisk rhythms of speech which prepare the marching scenes to follow.

> This tune goes manly. . . .
>
> Receive what hope you may:
> The night is long that never finds the day.

The whole scene is often omitted or drastically cut in production, and many critics have objected to it. They complain of its slowness, of the baroque overelaboration of Malcolm's protests, and of the fact that it is too long for what it tells us about the story. All we learn is that Malcolm and Macduff are joining the English army to attack Macbeth, and this information could have been conveyed much more quickly. In the first part of the play, and again after this scene, everything moves with the speed of a race; and one is tempted to say, at first, that in this scene Shakespeare lost the rhythm of his own play.

Now, one of the reasons I chose this scene to discuss is that it shows, as does the Porter scene, the necessity of distinguishing between plot and action. One cannot understand the function of the scene in the whole plot unless one remembers that the plot itself is there to imitate the action. It is then clear that this scene is the peripeteia, which is brought about by a series of recognitions. It starts with Malcolm and Macduff blind and impotent in Macbeth's shadow and ends when they have gradually learned to recognize themselves and each other even in that situation. "Outrunning reason" looks purely evil in the beginning, and at the end we see how it may be good, an act of faith beyond reason. The scene moves slowly at first because Shakespeare is imitating the action of groping in an atmosphere of the false and unnatural; yet we are aware all the while of continuing speed offstage, where

> each new morn
> New widows howl, new orphans cry, new sorrows
> Strike heaven on the face.

The scene is thus (within the rhythmic scheme of the whole play) like a slow eddy on the edge of a swift current. After this turning, or peripeteia, the actions of Malcolm and Macduff join the rush of the main race, to win. I admit that these effects might be hard to achieve in production, but I believe that good actors could do it.

Shakespeare's tragedies usually have a peripeteia in the fourth act, with scenes of suffering and prophetic or symbolic recognitions and epiphanies. In the fourth act of *Macbeth* the Witches' scene reveals the coming end of the action in symbolic shows; and this scene also, in another way, foretells the end. The last act, then, merely presents the literal facts, the wind-up of the plot, long felt as inevitable in principle. The fifth act of *Macbeth* shows the expected triumph of Malcolm's and Macduff's superrational faith. The wood does move; Macbeth does meet a man unborn of woman; and the paradoxical race against reason reaches its paradoxical end. The nightmare of Macbeth's evil version of the action is dissolved, and we are free to return to the familiar world, where reason, nature, and common sense still have their validity.

To sum up: my thesis is that *Macbeth* is the imitation of an action (or motive) which may be indicated by the phrase "to outrun the pauser, reason." I have tried to suggest how this action is presented in the metaphors, characters, and plot of the first two acts; and also in the peripeteia, with pathos and recognitions, the great scene between Malcolm, Macduff, and Ross.

I am painfully aware that these few illustrations are not enough to establish my thesis. Only a detailed analysis of the whole play might do that—and such an analysis would take hours of reading and discussion. But I think it would show that Aristotle was essentially right. He had never read *Macbeth,* and I suppose if he could he would find Shakespeare's Christian, or post-Christian, vision of evil hard to understand. But he saw that the art of drama is the art of imitating action; and this insight, confirmed and deepened by some of Aristotle's heirs, can still show us how to seek the unity of a play, even one which shows modes of the spirit's life undreamed of by Aristotle himself.

WALTER JACKSON BATE

•

Aristotle[1]

I

Aristotle's *Poetics* is not only the most important critical work of classical antiquity. It is also perhaps the most influential work in the entire history of criticism. The unique value of the *Poetics* may be expressed in at least three ways, not to mention others. (1) It marks the beginning of literary criticism.

[1] From *Criticism: The Major Texts,* by Walter J. Bate, copyright, 1952, by Harcourt, Brace & World, Inc. and reprinted with their permission.

The beginning of critical analysis and the discovery of principles by which analysis can proceed are obviously larger and more essential steps than any one later elaboration or development of these principles. (2) Throughout some periods, particularly the Renaissance and the early eighteenth century, the *Poetics* served as a starting point and sometimes a guide for literary criticism. Even those critics whose works have appeared since the decline of neoclassicism have revealed their awareness of it as a document which is very much to be reckoned with. (3) The *Poetics* is the best key to the temper and aims of Greek art generally. Aristotle, as we have said, did not try to deduce a theory of literature from an abstract theory of esthetics. He looked at literature directly, almost as a naturalist would regard it. He scrutinized it as a province of knowledge with a concrete body of material of its own; and this body of material was Greek literature itself. He not only described the technical characteristics of Greek literature, drawing from it general aims and principles. In answering Plato's suspicions about the moral effect of art, he also stressed, as we have indicated earlier, the healthful and formative effect of art on the mind; and, in doing so, he was quite in accord with the general Greek confidence in the power of art as *psychagogia,* the leading out of the soul, and as a molder and developer of human character. More than any other critical statement of antiquity, the *Poetics* offers, however briefly and incompletely, the approach to literature of one of the most gifted peoples in history—a people, indeed, which virtually created the premises and values of Western civilization. It thus has more than the ordinary importance of a critical work that mirrors a particular, local background. Many of the issues it raises have a perennial importance—an importance that results from the range and penetration of Aristotle's own mind, and also from the remarkable success and fertile creativity of the Greek approach to art upon which the *Poetics* rests.

II

In so far as it is an answer to Plato, Aristotle's *Poetics* justifies poetry on two grounds: the truth and validity, first of all, of poetry as an *imitation* of nature—or as a form of knowledge—and, secondly, the morally desirable effect of this awareness upon the human mind. Both of these justifications Plato had seriously questioned. Whereas Plato regarded ultimate reality as consisting of pure "Ideas," divorced from the concrete, material world, Aristotle conceived of reality or nature as a process of becoming or developing: a process in which form manifests itself through concrete material and in which the concrete takes on form and meaning, working in accordance with persisting, ordered principles. Now art, as Aristotle said in the *Physics*, has this characteristic in common with nature. For art, too, employs materials—concrete images, human actions, and sounds—and it deals with these materials as form of meaning emerges or dawns through them.

Poetry, then, although it imitates concrete nature, as Plato charged, does not imitate *just* the concrete. In fact, its focal point of interest—the process of which it is trying to offer a duplicate or counterpart—is form shaping, guiding, and developing the concrete into a unified meaning and completeness. The word "form" here should be interpreted broadly, and not as a synonym for mere "technique" in art. It applies to the *direction* which something would take if it were permitted to carry itself out to its final culmination. It thus applies to what is distinctive, significant, or true about that person, object, or event, if *accidental* elements are not allowed to intervene or obstruct its fulfillment. Thus, classical sculpture concerns itself not with individual features, expressions, or isolated acts, but with the total capacity of the figure carried out to the fulfillment which it would attain if it were permitted to do so. Or again, in a drama, the plot does not include every incident that might happen to us in ordinary life. For any number of casual incidents occur that are irrelevant to certain other events that interlock with each other and lead to a conclusion; and it is this chain of events interlocked through cause and effect upon which the dramatist concentrates, the form and meaning of which he is attempting to disclose. Hence Aristotle's remark that poetry can be "a more philosophical and higher thing than history: for poetry tends to express the *universal,* history the *particular.*" That is, history concentrates on specific details as they happened, regardless of the ultimate form (the "universal") that things would take if they were allowed to carry themselves out to their logical conclusion. The dramatist, however, is selective: he omits the irrelevant, and draws out the potential form or pattern of an event as a complete unit.

III

The term "form" also applies to the *value* of that object or event—to its full meaning and character, and hence to its worth and importance. Accordingly, the object or event must have, said Aristotle, "a certain magnitude," if the development of it is to have a significance worth the disclosing. This ordered carrying out of an object to an unobstructed and completed fulfillment is also what is meant by the classical conception of the "ideal" or what "ought to be": not something subjectively "idealized," not something as it "ought to be" in the way that one might, for any private feeling, wish it to be, but rather the way things would be, to use Aristotle's own phrase, "according to the law of probability or necessity," if they were to fulfill their total end and complete their potential form. Aristotle applied this principle not only to *what* poetry should seek to disclose or "imitate," but also to the *way* (the *harmonia*) in which this imitation is made and presented as a unified thing in itself. For this reason his emphasis was on plot rather than particular characters; indeed, for Aristotle, the plot was the "soul" or proper form of the drama. The drama imitates *actions;* otherwise it is not a drama, but something else. In imitating actions, therefore, the drama should appropriately be an activity itself; and this activity is the plot; hence Aristotle's emphasis on unity or interconnection and on a rounded completeness in this activity that comprises the plot. The plot must contain *within itself* the conditions that lead to its culmination rather than rely on mere chance or some external *deus ex machina* who suddenly resolves all the difficulties artificially. And if tragedy occupied most of Aristotle's attention, it is because, more than any other genre or type, it can best fulfill the general aim of poetry: to present a heightened and harmonious imitation of nature, and, in particular, those aspects of nature that touch most closely upon human life. Because it is itself an activity, and because of its necessary brevity, tragedy can offer a more packed, vivid, and closely unified imitation of events than narrative verse offers.

There must, in short, be probability. For "probability," as Aristotle used the term, does not mean a narrow, realistic verisimilitude, nor does it mean "ordinary"; great events and remarkable persons, such as tragedy deals with, may both be rare. "Probability" applies to the inner coherence and structure, the ordered interconnection and working out of a plot. As opposed to mere chance—however "possible" that chance may be—"probability" implies that the culmination of what happens arises naturally and inevitably, by causal interrelation, out of what precedes it. The plot, in other words, must possess what Aristotle called a "unity of action." It must have "a beginning, middle, and end." Nothing in our experience, of course, is really a beginning or an end: related events or causes always exist before any one point, and further results always follow. What *is* meant is simply a beginning that does not need preceding action on the stage in order to explain it; a development (or "middle"); and an end that generally concludes this development so that more action is not needed to complete the total sequence. Except for a descriptive remark about the amount of time covered in most Greek tragedies, Aristotle did not insist on the other two unities—those of "time" and "place"—which Renaissance critics were to formulate into rules.

Aristotle's emphasis on probability of dramatic structure, and on the ordered self-sufficiency of the plot, also led him to suggest another desirable principle: that the main character in a tragedy should have a "tragic flaw." To allow the character to be simply the victim of unpredictable and undeserved calamities would violate the complete, self-contained unity of action. But there are also psychological justifications for selecting, as the central character, a man of some stature "brought from prosperity to adversity" as a result "of some great error or frailty." For if the character is superhumanly good, it is difficult to identify oneself with him sympathetically; he appears almost an abstraction. Moreover, if the calamity that befalls a virtuous man is completely undeserved, our sense of shock may be so violent that it prevents or obstructs other emotional reactions: the emotional and imaginative elevation, for example, that comes in witnessing the working out of a pattern of events to their culmination, and seeing the total significance emerge into universal applicability. On the other hand, the character should have standing and capacity; he must certainly be above average, whether in rank, mind, or capacity to feel. For, unless the character is too far removed above us, admiration stimulates sympathetic identification; we all like to regard ourselves as at least somewhat better than we are, and are more likely to surrender our identification to someone we consider worthy of it. Moreover, the tragic fall is much greater to the degree that the character has more "multiplicity of consciousness," in Samuel Johnson's phrase, and to the degree that he himself is aware, therefore, of what is happening. Again, the tragic character must have a place from which to fall. And the loftier his position is, the more disastrous the fall. Needless to say, "the downfall of the utter villain," as Aristotle stated, is not tragic; it "would, doubtless, satisfy the moral sense, but it would inspire neither pity nor fear; for pity is aroused by unmerited misfortune, fear by the misfortune of a man like ourselves." The "tragic flaw," it should be added, is not stated to be *necessary* for a tragedy. It is regarded as desirable in an ideal or "perfect tragedy . . . arranged not on the simple but complex plan": a tragedy in which the calamity does not simply descend from above, but emerges as a closely interconnected series of incidents which arise from various sources including qualities in the character himself.

IV

Aristotle's belief in the formative and morally desirable effect of art is implicit in many of his writings. This attitude is quite in accord with Greek thought generally; and it was Plato who took a novel and atypical position by voicing the misgivings he did. One must not, therefore, expect to find a real defense of art in Aristotle. He would doubtless have regarded a detailed defense as unnecessary. He did state, however, more or less in answer to Plato, that tragedy produces a healthful effect on the human character through what he called a *katharsis,* "through pity and fear effecting a proper purgation of these emotions." A successful tragedy, then, exploits and appeals at the start to two basic emotions. One is "fear"—the painful sense, as Aristotle elsewhere describes it, "of impending evil which is destructive. . . ." Tragedy, in other words, deals with the element of evil, with what we least want and most fear to face, with what is destructive to human life and values; it is this concern that makes the theme of the play *tragic.* In addition, tragedy exploits our sense of "pity": it draws out our ability to sympathize with others, so that, in our identification with the tragic character, we ourselves feel something of the impact and extent of the evil befalling him. But tragedy does more than simply *arouse* sympathetic identification and a vivid sense of tragic evil or destructiveness. It offers a *katharsis,* a "proper purgation" of "pity and terror."

It is plain that the subject of *katharsis* had an important place in Aristotle's conception of poetry. For he used the term in discussing music in the *Politics,* and mentioned that a fuller account was to be found in the *Poetics.* The reference may well have been to an entire chapter now missing. The term has consequently caused as much discussion as any in the history of criticism.

However one may interpret it, at least a few general implications may be borne in mind. To begin with, the *katharsis* that tragedy offers is not merely an outlet or escape for emotion. The point is not that the sight of a dramatic tragedy every once in a while serves as a safety valve, so to speak, by which we can let off steam. Rather, tragedy first of all deliberately *excites* in the spectator the emotions of pity and fear which are then to undergo the "proper purgation." The tragic *katharsis* operates by a process which first excites and then tranquillizes emotion; and it does the first in order to accomplish the second. It is, in short, a controlling and directing of emotion. Whereas Plato, in the *Republic,* had adversely criticized poetry because it "feeds and waters the passions instead of starving them," Aristotle—both psychologically more sophisticated and also more typically Greek—took for granted that it is undesirable to "starve" the emotions, and assumed feeling—though he believed it should be directed and controlled by intelligence—to be a necessary aspect of human life.

Katharsis, as Aristotle employed the term, may be described as the use, control, and *purification* of emotion. In the medical language of the school of Hippocrates, as S. H. Butcher points out, the Greek word "strictly denotes the removal of a painful or disturbing element . . . and hence the purifying of what remains." Something desirable, in other words, happens to emotion when it is aroused and managed by poetic tragedy: the personally disturbing and morbid is purged or shed, and the emotion, after undergoing this "purgation," has been purified and lifted, as it were, to a harmonious serenity.

Now from what we know of the direction of Aristotle's thought as a whole, and from what we know of his conception of the mind in particular, we can generalize even further. The morbid element purged from the emotion is the subjective, the purely personal and egoistic element. Our emotion is caught up, as it were, by sympathetic identification with the tragic character and the tragic situation. It is extended *outward,* that is, away from self-centered absorption. This enlarging of the soul through sympathy, this lifting of one above the egocentric, is itself desirable and operates to the advantage of one's psychological and moral health: it joins emotion to awareness, directing it outward to what is being conceived. But in addition to this, there is a further effect on the emotion of the observer. Tragic drama not only arouses our sympathetic identification through presenting an "imitation" of human actions; but, by appealing to our instinct for *harmonia* as well as for mimesis (imitation), it also presents an ordered and proportioned regularity of structure, interrelated through "the law of probability and necessity." And to the degree that the tragedy has been successful in offering, in its own completed and harmonious form, a truthful duplication of the forms of events significant in human life, it rises into universality. The meaning of what has occurred—its inevitability, the various respects in which it is applicable to human life and destiny—is caught with a full and vivid awareness. Moreover, it is reduced to a clarity of outline, and transmuted—purified and heightened—into a harmonious form created through the medium of poetic language. Accordingly, the emotion of the spectator, after being drawn out and identified with the "imitation" before him, is then carried along and made a part of the harmonious development and working out of the particular drama. And the intellectual realization of what has happened, emerging through the ordered structure and body of the drama, is therefore also emerging through the spectator's *own* feelings. In so emerging, the intellectual realization lifts our feelings to a state of harmonized serenity and tranquillity. It has "purged" them of the subjective and self-centered. It has enlarged and extended them through sympathy. Above all, it has joined feeling to insight, conditioning our habitual emotion to that awareness of the essential import of human actions which poetry, through "imitation," is capable of offering. For beneath the theory of *katharsis* lies the general Greek premise that art, in presenting a heightened and harmonious "imitation" of reality, is formative; that, in enlarging, exercising, and refining one's feelings, and in leading them outward, art possesses a unique power to form the "total man," in whom emotion may become reconciled to intelligence and harmoniously integrated with it.

ARISTOTLE

•

Poetics[1]

A Translation by Ingram Bywater

1

Our subject being Poetry, I propose to speak not only of the art in general but also of its species and their respective capacities; of the structure of plot required for a good poem; of the number and nature of the constituent parts of a poem; and likewise of any other matters in the same line of inquiry. Let us follow the natural order and begin with the primary facts.

Epic poetry and Tragedy, as also Comedy, Dithyrambic poetry, and most flute-playing and lyre-playing, are all, viewed as a whole, modes of imitation. But at the same time they differ from one another in three ways, either by a difference of kind in their means, or by differences in the objects, or in the manner of their imitations.

Just as colour and form are used as means by some, who (whether by art or constant practice) imitate and portray many things by their aid, and the voice

[1] From Richard McKeon, ed., *The Basic Works of Aristotle* (New York: Random House, 1941), pp. 1455–1487 with omissions.

is used by others; so also in the above-mentioned group of arts, the means with them as a whole are rhythm, language, and harmony—used, however, either singly or in certain combinations. A combination of harmony and rhythm alone is the means in flute-playing and lyre-playing, and any other arts there may be of the same description, e.g. imitative piping. Rhythm alone, without harmony, is the means in the dancer's imitations; for even he, by the rhythms of his attitudes, may represent men's characters, as well as what they do and suffer. There is further an art which imitates by language alone, without harmony, in prose or in verse, and if in verse, either in some one or in a plurality of metres. This form of imitation is to this day without a name. We have no common name for a mime of Sophron or Xenarchus and a Socratic Conversation; and we should still be without one even if the imitation in the two instances were in trimeters or elegiacs or some other kind of verse—though it is the way with people to tack on 'poet' to the name of a metre, and talk of elegiac-poets and epic-poets, thinking that they call them poets not by reason of the imitative nature of their work, but indiscriminately by reason of the metre they write in. Even if a theory of medicine or physical philosophy be put forth in a metrical form, it is usual to describe the writer in this way; Homer and Empedocles, however, have really nothing in common apart from their metre; so that, if the one is to be called a poet, the other should be termed a physicist rather than a poet. We should be in the same position also, if the imitation in these instances were in all the meters, like the *Centaur* (a rhapsody in a medley of all metres) of Chaeremon; and Chaeremon one has to recognize as a poet. So much, then, as to these arts. There are, lastly, certain other arts, which combine all the means enumerated, rhythm, melody, and verse, e.g. Dithyrambic and Nomic poetry, Tragedy and Comedy; with this difference, however, that the three kinds of means are in some of them all employed together, and in others brought in separately, one after the other. These elements of difference in the above arts I term the means of their imitation.

2

The objects the imitator represents are actions, with agents who are necessarily either good men or bad—the diversities of human character being nearly always derivative from this primary distinction, since the line between virtue and vice is one dividing the whole of mankind. It follows, therefore, that the agents represented must be either above our own level of goodness, or beneath it, or just such as we are; in the same way as, with the painters, the personages of Polygnotus are better than we are, those of Pauson worse, and those of Dionysius just like ourselves. It is clear that each of the above-mentioned arts will admit of these differences, and that it will become a separate art by representing objects with this point of difference. Even in dancing, flute-playing, and lyre-playing such diversities are possible; and they are also possible in the nameless art that uses language, prose or verse without harmony, as its means; Homer's personages, for instance, are better than we are; Cleophon's are on our own level; and those of Hegemon of Thasos, the first writer of parodies, and Nicochares, the author of the *Diliad*, are beneath it. The same is true of the Dithyramb and the Nome: the personages may be presented in them with the difference exemplified in the . . . of . . . and Argas, and in the Cyclopses of Timotheus and Philoxenus. This difference it is that distinguishes Tragedy and Comedy also; the one would make its personages worse, and the other better, than the men of the present day.

3

A third difference in these arts is in the manner in which each kind of object is represented. Given both the same means and the same kind of object for imitation, one may either (1) speak at one moment in narrative and at another in an assumed character, as Homer does; or (2) one may remain the same throughout, without any such change; or (3) the imitators may represent the whole story dramatically, as though they were actually doing the things described.

As we said at the beginning, therefore, the differences in the imitation of these arts come under three heads, their means, their objects, and their manner.

So that as an imitator Sophocles will be on one side akin to Homer, both portraying good men; and on another to Aristophanes, since both present their personages as acting and doing. This in fact, according to some, is the reason for plays being termed dramas, because in a play the personages act the story. Hence too both Tragedy and Comedy are claimed by the Dorians as their discoveries; Comedy by the Megarians—by those in Greece as having arisen when Megara became a democracy, and by the Sicilian Megarians on the ground that the poet Epicharmus was of their country, and a good deal earlier than Chionides and Magnes; even Tragedy also is claimed by certain of the Peloponnesian Dorians. In support of this claim they point to the words 'comedy' and 'drama.' Their word for the outlying hamlets, they say, is *comae,* whereas Athenians call them *demes*—thus assuming that comedians got the name not from their *comoe* or revels, but from their strolling from hamlet to hamlet, lack of appreciation keeping them out of the city. Their word also for 'to act', they say, is *dran,* whereas Athenians use *prattein.*

So much, then, as to the number and nature of the points of difference in the imitation of these arts.

4

It is clear that the general origin of poetry was due to two causes, each of them part of human nature. Imitation is natural to man from childhood, one of his advantages over the lower animals being this, that he is the most imitative creature in the world, and learns at first by imitation. And it is also natural for all to delight in works of imitation. The truth of this second point is shown by experience: though the objects themselves may be painful to see, we delight to view the most realistic representations of them in art, the forms for example of the lowest animals and of dead bodies. The explanation is to be found in a further fact: to be learning something is the greatest of pleasures not only to the philosopher but also to the rest of mankind, however small their capacity for it; the reason of the delight in seeing the picture is that one is at the same time learning—gathering the meaning of things, e.g. that the man there is so-and-so; for if one has not seen the thing before, one's pleasure will not be in the picture as an imitation of it, but will be due to the execution or colouring or some similar cause. Imitation, then, being natural to us—as also the sense of harmony and rhythm, the meters being obviously species of rhythms—it was through their original aptitude, and by a series of improvements for the most part gradual on their first efforts, that they created poetry out of their improvisations.

Poetry, however, soon broke up into two kinds according to the differences of character in the individual poets; for the graver among them would represent noble actions, and those of noble personages; and the meaner sort the actions of the ignoble. The latter class produced invectives at first, just as others did hymns and panegyrics. We know of no such poem by any of the pre-Homeric poets, though there were probably many such writers among them; instances, however, may be found from Homer downwards, e.g. his *Margites*, and the similar poems of others. In this poetry of invective its natural fitness brought an iambic metre into use; hence our present term 'iambic', because it was the metre of their 'iambs' or invectives against one another. The result was that the old poets became some of them writers of heroic and others of iambic verse. Homer's position, however, is peculiar: just as he was in the serious style the poet of poets, standing alone not only through the literary excellence, but also through the dramatic character of his imitations, so too he was the first to outline for us the general forms of Comedy by producing not a dramatic invective, but a dramatic picture of the Ridiculous; his *Margites* in fact stands in the same relation to our comedies as the *Iliad* and *Odyssey* to our tragedies. As soon, however, as Tragedy and Comedy appeared in the field, those naturally drawn to the one line of poetry became writers of comedies instead of iambs, and those naturally drawn to the other, writers of tragedies instead of epics, because these new modes of art were grander and of more esteem than the old.

If it be asked whether Tragedy is now all that it need be in its formative elements, to consider that, and decide it theoretically and in relation to the theatres, is a matter for another inquiry.

It certainly began in improvisations—as did also Comedy; the one originating with the authors of the Dithyramb, the other with those of the phallic songs, which still survive as institutions in many of our cities. And its advance after that was little by little, through their improving on whatever they had before them at each stage. It was in fact only after a long series of changes that the movement of Tragedy stopped on its attaining to its natural form. (1)

The number of actors was first increased to two by Aeschylus, who curtailed the business of the Chorus, and made the dialogue, or spoken portion, take the leading part in the play. (2) A third actor and scenery were due to Sophocles. (3) Tragedy acquired also its magnitude. Discarding short stories and a ludicrous diction, through its passing out of its satyric stage, it assumed, though only at a late point in its progress, a tone of dignity; and its metre changed then from trochaic to iambic. The reason for their original use of the trochaic tetrameter was that their poetry was satyric and more connected with dancing than it now is. As soon, however, as a spoken part came in, nature herself found the appropriate metre. The iambic, we know, is the most speakable of metres, as is shown by the fact that we very often fall into it in conversation, whereas we rarely talk hexameters, and only when we depart from the speaking tone of voice. (4) Another change was a plurality of episodes or acts. As for the remaining matters, the superadded embellishments and the account of their introduction, these must be taken as said, as it would probably be a long piece of work to go through the details.

5

As for Comedy, it is (as has been observed) an imitation of men worse than the average; worse, however, not as regards any and every sort of fault, but only as regards one particular kind, the Ridiculous, which is a species of the Ugly. The Ridiculous may be defined as a mistake or deformity not productive of pain or harm to others; the mask, for instance, that excites laughter, is something ugly and distorted without causing pain.

Though the successive changes in Tragedy and their authors are not unknown, we cannot say the same of Comedy; its early stages passed unnoticed, because it was not as yet taken up in a serious way. It was only at a late point in its progress that a chorus of comedians was officially granted by the archon; they used to be mere volunteers. It had also already certain definite forms at the time when the record of those termed comic poets begins. Who it was who supplied it with masks, or prologues, or a plurality of actors and the like, has remained unknown. The invented Fable, or Plot, however, originated in Sicily with Epicharmus and Phormis; of Athenian poets Crates was the first to drop the Comedy of invective and frame stories of a general and non-personal nature, in other words, Fables or Plots.

Epic poetry, then, has been seen to agree with Tragedy to this extent, that of being an imitation of serious subjects in a grand kind of verse. It differs from it, however, (1) in that it is in one kind of verse and in narrative form; and (2) in its length—which is due to its action having no fixed limit of time, whereas Tragedy endeavours to keep as far as possible within a single circuit of the sun, or something near that. This, I say, is another point of difference between them, though at first the practice in this respect was just the same in tragedies as in epic poems. They differ also (3) in their constituents, some being common to both and others peculiar to Tragedy—hence a judge of good and bad in Tragedy is a judge of that in epic poetry also. All the parts of an epic are included in Tragedy; but those of Tragedy are not all of them to be found in the Epic.

6

Reserving hexameter poetry and Comedy for consideration hereafter,[2] let us proceed now to the discussion of Tragedy; before doing so, however, we must gather up the definition resulting from what has been said. A tragedy, then, is the imitation of an action that is serious and also, as having magnitude, complete in itself; in language with pleasurable accessories, each kind brought in separately in the parts of the work; in a dramatic, not in a narrative form; with incidents arousing pity and fear, wherewith to accomplish its catharsis of such emotions. Here by 'language with pleasurable accessories' I mean that with rhythm and harmony or song superadded; and by 'the kinds separately' I mean that some portions are worked out with verse only, and others in turn with song.

I. As they act the stories, it follows that in the first place the Spectacle (or stage-appearance of the actors) must be some part of the whole; and in the second Melody and Diction, these two being the means of their imitation. Here by 'Diction' I mean merely this, the composition of the verses; and by 'Melody', what is too completely understood to require explanation. But further: the subject represented also is an action; and the action involves agents, who must necessarily have their distinctive qualities both of character and thought, since it is from these that we ascribe certain qualities to their actions. There are in the natural order of things, therefore, two causes, Thought and Character, of their actions, and consequently of their success or failure in their lives. Now the action (that which was done) is represented in the play by the Fable or Plot. The Fable, in our present sense of the term, is simply this, the combination of the incidents, or things done in the story; whereas Character is what makes us ascribe certain moral qualities to the agents; and Thought is shown in all they say when proving a particular point or, it may be, enunciating a general truth. There are six parts consequently of every tragedy, as a whole (that is) of such or such quality, viz. a Fable or Plot, Characters, Diction, Thought, Spectacle, and Melody; two of them arising from the means, one from the manner, and three from the objects of the dramatic imitation; and there is nothing else besides these six. Of these, its formative elements, then, not a few of the dramatists have made due use, as every play, one may say, admits of Spectacle, Character, Fable, Diction, Melody and Thought.

II. The most important of the six is the combination of the incidents of the story. Tragedy is essentially an imitation not of persons but of action and

[2] For hexameter poetry cf. Chap. 23 f.; comedy was treated of in the lost Second Book.

life, of happiness and misery. All human happiness or misery takes the form of action; the end for which we live is a certain kind of activity, not a quality. Character gives us qualities, but it is in our actions—what we do—that we are happy or the reverse. In a play accordingly they do not act in order to portray the Characters; they include the Characters for the sake of the action. So that it is the action in it, i.e. its Fable or Plot, that is the end and purpose of the tradgedy; and the end is everywhere the chief thing. Besides this, a tragedy is impossible without action, but there may be one without Character. The tragedies of most of the moderns are characterless—a defect common among poets of all kinds, and with its counterpart in painting in Zeuxis as compared with Polygnotus; for whereas the latter is strong in character, the work of Zeuxis is devoid of it. And again: one may string together a series of characteristic speeches of the utmost finish as regards Diction and Thought, and yet fail to produce the true tragic effect; but one will have much better success with a tragedy which, however inferior in these respects, has a Plot, a combination of incidents, in it. And again: the most powerful elements of attraction in Tragedy, the Peripeties and Discoveries, are parts of the Plot. A further proof is in the fact that beginners succeed earlier with the Diction and Characters than with the construction of a story; and the same may be said of nearly all the early dramatists. We maintain, therefore, that the first essential, the life and soul, so to speak, of Tragedy is the Plot; and that the Characters come second—compare the parallel in painting, where the most beautiful colours laid on without order will not give one the same pleasure as a simple black-and-white sketch of a portrait. We maintain that Tragedy is primarily an imitation of action, and that it is mainly for the sake of the action that it imitates the personal agents. Third comes the element of Thought, i.e. the power of saying whatever can be said, or what is appropriate to the occasion. This is what, in the speeches in Tragedy, falls under the arts of Politics and Rhetoric; for the older poets make their personages discourse like statesmen, and the modern like rhetoricians. One must not confuse it with Character. Character in a play is that which reveals the moral purpose of the agents, i.e. the sort of thing they seek or avoid, where that is not obvious—hence there is no room for Character in a speech on a purely indifferent subject. Thought, on the other hand, is shown in all they say when proving or disproving some particular point, or enunciating some universal proposition. Fourth among the literary elements is the Diction of the personages, i.e., as before explained, the expression of their thoughts in words, which is practically the same thing with verse as with prose. As for the two remaining parts, the Melody is the greatest of the pleasurable accessories of Tragedy. The Spectacle, though an attraction, is the least artistic of all the parts, and has least to do with the art of poetry. The tragic effect is quite possible without a public performance and actors; and besides, the getting-up of the Spectacle is more a matter for the costumier than the poet.

7

Having thus distinguished the parts, let us now consider the proper construction of the Fable or Plot, as that is at once the first and the most important thing in Tragedy. We have laid it down that a tragedy is an imitation of an action that is complete in itself, as a whole of some magnitude; for a whole may be of no magnitude to speak of. Now a whole is that which has beginning, middle, and end. A beginning is that which is not itself necessarily after anything else, and which has naturally something else after it; an end is that which is naturally after something itself, either as its necessary or usual consequent, and with nothing else after it; and a middle, that which is by nature after one thing and has also another after it. A well-constructed Plot, therefore, cannot either begin or end at any point one likes; beginning and end in it must be of the forms just described. Again: to be beautiful, a living creature, and every whole made up of parts, must not only present a certain order in its arrangement of parts, but also be of a certain definite magnitude. Beauty is a matter of size and order, and therefore impossible either (1) in a very minute creature, since our perception becomes indistinct as it approaches instantaneity; or (2) in a creature of vast size—one, say, 1,000 miles long—as in that case, instead of the object being seen all at once, the unity and wholeness of it is lost to the beholder.

Just in the same way, then, as a beautiful whole made up of parts, or a beautiful living creature, must be of some size, but a size to be taken in by the eye, so a story or Plot must be of some length, but of a length to be taken in by the memory. As for the limit of its length, so far as that is relative to public performances and spectators, it does not fall within the theory of poetry. If they had to perform a hundred tragedies, they would be timed by water-clocks, as they are said to have been at one period. The limit, however, set by the actual nature of the thing is this: the longer the story, consistently with its being comprehensible as a whole, the finer it is by reason of its magnitude. As a rough general formula, 'a length which allows of the hero passing by a series of probable or necessary stages from misfortune to happiness, or from happiness to misfortune', may suffice as a limit for the magnitude of the story.

8

The Unity of a Plot does not consist, as some suppose, in its having one man as its subject. An infinity of things befall that one man, some of which it is impossible to reduce to unity; and in like manner there are many actions of one man which cannot be made to form one action. One sees, therefore, the mistake of all the poets who have written a *Heracleid,* a *Theseid,* or similar poems; they suppose that, because Heracles was one man, the story also of Heracles must be one story. Homer, however, evidently understood this point quite well, whether by art or instinct, just in the same way as he excels the rest in every other respect. In writing an *Odyssey,* he did not make the poem cover all that ever befell his hero—it befell him, for instance, to get wounded on Parnassus and also to feign madness at the time of the call to arms, but the two incidents had no necessary or probable connexion with one another—instead of doing that, he took as the subject of the *Odyssey,* as also of the *Iliad,* an action with a Unity of the kind we are describing. The truth is that, just as in the other imitative arts one imitation is always of one thing, so in poetry the story, as an imitation of action, must represent one action, a complete whole, with its several incidents so closely connected that the transposal or withdrawal of any one of them will disjoin and dislocate the whole. For that which makes no perceptible difference by its presence or absence is no real part of the whole.

9

From what we have said it will be seen that the poet's function is to describe, not the thing that has happened, but a kind of thing that might happen, i.e. what is possible as being probable or necessary. The distinction between historian and poet is not in the one writing prose and the other verse—you might put the work of Herodotus into verse, and it would still be a species of history; it consists really in this, that the one describes the thing that has been, and the other a kind of thing that might be. Hence poetry is something more philosophic and of graver import than history, since its statements are of the nature rather of universals, whereas those of history are singulars. By a universal statement I mean one as to what such or such a kind of man will probably or necessarily say or do—which is the aim of poetry, though it affixes proper names to the characters; by a singular statement, one as to what, say, Alcibiades did or had done to him. In Comedy this has become clear by this time; it is only when their plot is already made up of probable incidents that they give it a basis of proper names, choosing for the purpose any names that may occur to them, instead of writing like the old iambic poets about particular persons. In Tragedy, however, they still adhere to the historic names; and for this reason: what convinces is the possible; now whereas we are not yet sure as to the possibility of that which has not happened, that which has happened is manifestly possible, else it would not have come to pass. Nevertheless even in Tragedy there are some plays with but one or two known names in them, the rest being inventions; and there are some without a single known name, e.g. Agathon's *Antheus,* in which both incidents and names are of the poet's invention; and it is no less delightful on that account. So that one must not aim at a rigid adherence to the traditional stories on which tragedies are based. It would be absurd, in fact, to do so, as even the known stories are only known to a few, though they are a delight none the less to all.

It is evident from the above that the poet must be more the poet of his stories or Plots than of his verses, inasmuch as he is a poet by virtue of the imitative element in his work, and it is actions that he imitates. And if he should come to take a subject from actual history, he is none the less a poet for that; since some historic occurrences may very well be in the probable and possible order of things; and it is in that aspect of them that he is their poet.

Of simple Plots and actions the episodic are the worst. I call a Plot episodic when there is neither probability nor necessity in the sequence of its episodes. Actions of this sort bad poets construct through their own fault, and good ones on account of the players. His work being for public performance, a good poet often stretches out a Plot beyond its capabilities, and is thus obliged to twist the sequence of incident.

Tragedy, however, is an imitation not only of a complete action, but also of incidents arousing pity and fear. Such incidents have the very greatest effect on the mind when they occur unexpectedly and at the same time in consequence of one another; there is more of the marvellous in them than if they happened of themselves or by mere chance. Even matters of chance seem most marvellous if there is an appearance of design as it were in them; as for instance the statue of Mitys at Argos killed the author of Mitys' death by falling down on him when a looker-on at a public spectacle; for incidents like that we think to be not without a meaniing. A Plot, therefore, of this sort is necessarily finer than others.

10

Plots are either simple or complex, since the actions they represent are naturally of this twofold description. The action, proceeding in the way defined, as one continuous whole, I call simple, when the change in the hero's fortunes takes place without Peripety or Discovery; and complex, when it involves one or the other, or both. These should each of them arise out of the structure of the Plot itself, so as to be the consequence, necessary or probable, of the antecedents. There is a great difference between a thing happening *propter hoc* and *post hoc*.

11

A Peripety is the change of the kind described from one state of things within the play to its opposite, and that too in the way we are saying, in the probable or necessary sequence of events; as it is for instance in *Oedipus:* here the opposite state of things is produced by the Messenger, who, coming to gladden Oedipus and to remove his fears as to his mother, reveals the secret of his birth. And in *Lynceus:* just as he is being led off for execution, with Danaus at his side to put him to death, the incidents preceding this bring it about that he is saved and Danaus put to death. A Discovery is, as the very word implies, a change from ignorance to knowledge, and thus to either love or hate, in the personages marked for good or evil fortune. The finest form of Discovery is one attended by Peripeties, like that which goes with the Discovery in *Oedipus*. There are no doubt other forms of it; what we have said may happen in a way in reference to inanimate things, even things of a very casual kind; and it is also possible to discover whether some one has done or not done something. But the form most directly connected with the Plot and the action of the piece is the first-mentioned. This, with a Peripety, will arouse either pity or fear—actions of that nature being what Tragedy is assumed to represent; and it will also serve to bring about the happy or unhappy ending. The Discovery, then, being of persons, it may be that of one party only to the other, the latter being already known; or both the parties may have to discover themselves. Iphigenia, for instance, was discovered to Orestes by sending the letter; and another Discovery was required to reveal him to Iphigenia.

Two parts of the Plot, then, Peripety and Discovery, are on matters of this sort. A third part is Suffering; which we may define as an action of a destructive or painful nature, such as murders on the stage, tortures, woundings, and the like. The other two have been already explained.

12

The parts of Tragedy to be treated as formative elements in the whole were mentioned in a previous Chapter.[3]

From the point of view, however, of its quantity, i.e. the separate sections into which it is divided, a tragedy has the following parts: Prologue, Episode, Exode, and a choral portion, distinguished into Parode and Stasimon; these two are common to all tragedies, whereas songs from the stage and *Commoe* are only found in some. The Prologue is all that precedes the Parode of the chorus; an Episode all that comes in between two whole choral songs; the Exode all that follows after the last choral song. In the choral portion the Parode is the whole first statement of the chorus; a Stasimon, a song of the chorus without anapaests or trochees; a *Commos,* a lamentation sung by chorus and actor in concert. The parts of Tragedy to be used as formative elements in the whole we have already mentioned; the above are its parts from the point of view of its quantity, or the separate sections into which it is divided.

13

The next points after what we have said above will be these: (1) What is the poet to aim at, and what is he to avoid, in constructing his Plots? and (2) What are the conditions on which the tragic effect depends?

We assume that, for the finest form of Tragedy, the Plot must be not simple but complex; and further, that it must imitate actions arousing fear and pity, since that is the distinctive function of this kind of imitation. It follows, therefore, that there are three forms of Plot to be avoided. (1) A

[3] Ch. 6.

good man must not be seen passing from happiness to misery, or (2) a bad man from misery to happiness. The first situation is not fear-inspiring or piteous, but simply odious to us. The second is the most untragic that can be; it has no one of the requisites of Tragedy; it does not appeal either to the human feeling in us, or to our pity, or to our fears. Nor, on the other hand, should (3) an extremely bad man be seen falling from happiness into misery. Such a story may arouse the human feeling in us, but it will not move us to either pity or fear; pity is occasioned by undeserved misfortune, and fear by that of one like ourselves; so that there will be nothing either piteous or fear-inspiring in the situation. There remains, then, the intermediate kind of personage, a man not preeminently virtuous and just, whose misfortune, however, is brought upon him not by vice and depravity but by some error of judgment, of the number of those in the enjoyment of great reputation and prosperity; e.g. Oedipus, Thyestes, and the men of note of similar families. The perfect Plot, accordingly, must have a single, and not (as some tell us) a double issue; the change in the hero's fortunes must be not from misery to happiness, but on the contrary from happiness to misery; and the cause of it must lie not in any depravity, but in some great error on his part; the man himself being either such as we have described, or better, not worse, than that. Fact also confirms our theory. Though the poets began by accepting any tragic story that came to hand, in these days the finest tragedies are always on the story of some few houses, on that of Alcmeon, Oedipus, Orestes, Meleager, Thyestes, Telephus, or any others that may have been involved, as either agents or sufferers, in some deed of horror. The theoretically best tragedy, then, has a Plot of this description. The critics, therefore, are wrong who blame Euripides for taking this line in his tragedies, and giving many of them an unhappy ending. It is, as we have said, the right line to take. The best proof is this: on the stage, and in the public performances, such plays, properly worked out, are seen to be the most truly tragic; and Euripides, even if his execution be faulty in every other point, is seen to be nevertheless the most tragic certainly of the dramatists. After this comes the construction of Plot which some rank first, one with a double story (like the *Odyssey*) and an opposite issue for the good and the bad personages. It is ranked as first only through the weakness of the audiences; the poets merely follow their public, writing as its wishes dictate. But the pleasure here is not that of Tragedy. It belongs rather to Comedy, where the bitterest enemies in the piece (e.g. Orestes and Aegisthus) walk off good friends at the end, with no slaying of any one by any one.

14

The tragic fear and pity may be aroused by the Spectacle; but they may also be aroused by the very structure and incidents of the play—which is the better way and shows the better poet. The Plot in fact should be so framed that, even without seeing the things take place, he who simply hears the account of them shall be filled with horror and pity at the incidents; which is just the effect that the mere recital of the story in *Oedipus* would have on one. To produce this same effect by means of the Spectacle is less artistic, and requires extraneous aid. Those, however, who make use of the Spectacle to put before us that which is merely monstrous and not productive of fear, are wholly out of touch with Tragedy; and not every kind of pleasure should be required of a tragedy, but only its own proper pleasure.

The tragic pleasure is that of pity and fear, and the poet has to produce it by a work of imitation; it is clear, therefore, that the causes should be included in the incidents of his story. Let us see, then, what kinds of incident strike one as horrible, or rather as piteous. In a deed of this description the parties must necessarily be either friends, or enemies, or indifferent to one another. Now when enemy does it on enemy, there is nothing to move us to pity either in his doing or in his meditating the deed, except so far as the actual pain of the sufferer is concerned; and the same is true when the parties are indifferent to one another. Whenever the tragic deed, however, is done within the family—when murder or the like is done or meditated by brother on brother, by son on father, by mother on son, or son on mother—these are the situations the poet should seek after. The traditional stories, accordingly, must be kept as they are, e.g. the murder of Clytaemnestra by Orestes and of Eriphyle by Alcmeon. At the same time even with these there is something left to the poet himself; it is for him to devise the right way of treating them. Let us explain more clearly what we mean by 'the right way'. The deed of horror may be done by the doer knowingly and consciously, as in the old poets, and in Medea's murder of her children in Euripides. Or he may do it, but in ignorance of his relationship, and discover that afterwards, as does the Oedipus in Sophocles. Here the deed is outside the play; but it may be within it, like the act of the Alcmeon in Astydamas, or that of the Telegonus in *Ulysses Wounded*. A third possibility is for one meditating some deadly injury to another, in ignorance of his relationship, to make the discovery in time to draw back. These exhaust the possibilities, since the deed must necessarily be either done or not done, and either knowingly or unknowingly.

The worst situation is when the personage is with full knowledge on the point of doing the deed, and leaves it undone. It is odious and also (through the absence of suffering) untragic; hence it is that no one is made to act thus except in some few instances, e.g. Haemon and Creon in *Antigone*. Next after this comes the actual perpetration of the deed meditated. A better situation than that, however, is for the deed to be done in ignorance, and the relationship discovered afterwards, since there is nothing odious in it, and the Discovery will serve to astound us. But the best of all is the last; what we have in *Cresphontes*,[4] for example, where Merope, on the point of slaying her

[4] By Euripides.

son, recognizes him in time; in *Iphigenia,* where sister and brother are in a like position; and in *Helle,*[5] where the son recognizes his mother, when on the point of giving her up to her enemy.

This will explain why our tragedies are restricted (as we said just now) to such a small number of families. It was accident rather than art that led the poets in quest of subjects to embody this kind of incident in their Plots. They are still obliged, accordingly, to have recourse to the families in which such horrors have occurred.

On the construction of the Plot, and the kind of Plot required for Tragedy, enough has now been said.

15

In the Characters there are four points to aim at. First and foremost, that they shall be good. There will be an element of character in the play, if (as has been observed) what a personage says or does reveals a certain moral purpose; and a good element of character, if the purpose so revealed is good. Such goodness is possible in every type of personage, even in a woman or a slave, though the one is perhaps an inferior, and the other a wholly worthless being. The second point is to make them appropriate. The Character before us may be, say, manly; but it is not appropriate in a female Character to be manly, or clever. The third is to make them like the reality, which is not the same as their being good and appropriate, in our sense of the term. The fourth is to make them consistent and the same throughout; even if inconsistency be part of the man before one for imitation as presenting that form of character, he should still be consistently inconsistent. We have an instance of baseness of character, not required for the story, in the Menelaus in *Orestes;* of the incongruous and unbefitting in the lamentation of Ulysses in *Scylla,*[6] and in the (clever) speech of Melanippe,[7] and of inconsistency in *Iphigenia at Aulis,* where Iphigenia the suppliant is utterly unlike the later Iphigenia. The right thing, however, is in the Characters just as in the incidents of the play to endeavour always after the necessary or the probable; so that whenever such-and-such a personage says or does such-and-such a thing, it shall be the necessary or probable outcome of his character; and whenever this incident follows on that, it shall be either the necessary or the probable consequence of it. From this one sees (to digress for a moment) that the Dénouement also should arise out of the plot itself, and not depend on a stage-artifice, as in *Medea,* or in the story of the (arrested) departure of the Greeks in the *Iliad.* The artifice must be reserved for matters outside the play—for past events beyond human knowledge, or events yet to come, which require to be foretold or announced; since it is the privilege of the Gods to know everything. There should be nothing improbable among the ac-

[5] Authorship unknown.
[6] A dithyramb by Timotheus.
[7] (Euripides.)

tual incidents. If it be unavoidable, however, it should be outside the tragedy, like the improbability in the *Oedipus* of Sophocles. But to return to the Characters. As Tragedy is an imitation of personages better than the ordinary man, we in our way should follow the example of good portrait-painters, who reproduce the distinctive features of a man, and at the same time, without losing the likeness, make him handsomer than he is. The poet in like manner, in portraying men quick or slow to anger, or with similar infirmities of character, must know how to represent them as such, and at the same time as good men, as Agathon and Homer have represented Achilles.

All these rules one must keep in mind throughout, and, further, those also for such points of stage-effect as directly depend on the art of the poet, since in these too one may often make mistakes. Enough, however, has been said on the subject in one of our published writings.[8]

16

Discovery in general has been explained already. As for the species of Discovery, the first to be noted is (1) the least artistic form of it, of which the poets make most use through mere lack of invention, Discovery by signs or marks. Of these signs some are congenital, like the 'lance-head which the Earth-born have on them,'[9] or 'stars,' such as Carcinus brings in his Thyestes; others acquired after birth—these latter being either marks on the body, e.g. scars, or external tokens, like necklaces, or (to take another sort of instance) the ark in the *Discovery of Tyro*.[10] Even in these, however, admit of two uses, a better and a worse; the scar of Ulysses is an instance; the Discovery of him through it is made in one way by the nurse[11] and in another by the swineherds.[12] A Discovery using signs as a means of assurance is less artistic, as indeed are all such as imply reflection; whereas one bringing them in all of a sudden, as in the *Bath-story*,[13] is of a better order. Next after these are (2) Discoveries made directly by the poet; which are inartistic for that very reason; e.g. Orestes' Discovery of himself in *Iphigenia:* whereas his sister reveals who she is by the letter,[14] Orestes is made to say himself what the poet rather than the story demands.[15] This, therefore, is not far removed from the first-mentioned fault, since he might have presented certain tokens as well. Another instance is the 'shuttle's voice' in the *Tereus* of Sophocles. (3) A third species is Discovery through memory, from a man's consciousness being awakened by something seen. Thus in *The Cyprioe of Dicaeogenes,* the sight

[8] In the lost dialogue *On Poets.*
[9] Authorship unknown.
[10] By Euripides
[11] *Od.* xix. 386–475.
[12] *Od.* xxi. 205–25.
[13] *Od.* xix. 392.
[14] *Iph. Taur.* 727 ff.
[15] Ib., 800 ff.

of the picture makes the man burst into tears; and in the *Tale of Alcinous,*[16] hearing the harper Ulysses is reminded of the past and weeps; the Discovery of them being the result. (4) A fourth kind is Discovery through reasoning; e.g. in *The Choephoroe,*[17] 'One like me is here; there is no one like me but Orestes; he, therefore, must be here.' Or that which Polyidus the Sophist suggested for *Iphigenia;* since it was natural for Orestes to reflect; 'My sister was sacrificed, and I am to be sacrificed like her.' Or that in the *Tydeus* of Theodectes: 'I came to find a son, and am to die myself.' Or that in *The Phinidae:* on seeing the place the women inferred their fate, that they were to die there, since they had also been exposed there. (5) There is, too, a composite Discovery arising from bad reasoning on the side of the other party. An instance of it is in *Ulysses the False Messenger:*[18] he said he should know the bow—which he had not seen; but to suppose from that that he would know it again (as though he had once seen it) was bad reasoning. (6) The best of all Discoveries, however, is that arising from the incidents themselves, when the great surprise comes about through a probable incident, like that in the *Oedipus* of Sophocles; and also in *Iphigenia*;[19] for it was not improbable that she should wish to have a letter taken home. These last are the only Discoveries independent of the artifice of signs and necklaces. Next after them come Discoveries through reasoning.

17

At the time when he is constructing his Plots, and engaged on the Diction in which they are worked out, the poet should remember (1) to put the actual scenes as far as possible before his eyes. In this way, seeing everything with the vividness of an eye-witness as it were, he will devise what is appropriate, and be least likely to overlook incongruities. This is shown by what was censured in Carcinus, the return of Amphiaraus from the sanctuary; it would have passed unnoticed, if it had not been actually seen by the audience; but on the stage his play failed, the incongruity of the incident offending the spectators. (2) As far as may be, too, the poet should even act his story with the very gestures of his personages. Given the same natural qualifications, he who feels the emotions to be described will be the most convincing; distress and danger, for instance, are portrayed most truthfully by one who is feeling them at the moment. Hence it is that poetry demands a man with a special gift for it, or else one with a touch of madness in him; the former can easily assume the required mood, and the latter may be actually beside himself with emotion. (3) His story, again, whether already made or of his own making, he should first simplify and reduce to a universal form, before proceeding to lengthen it out by the insertion of episodes. The follow-

[16] *Od.* viii, 521 ff. (Cf. viii, 83 ff.)
[17] 11. 168–234.
[18] Authorship unknown.
[19] *Iph. Taur.* 582.

ing will show how the universal element in *Iphigenia,* for instance, may be viewed: A certain maiden having been offered in sacrifice, and spirited away from her sacrificers into another land, where the custom was to sacrifice all strangers to the Goddess, she was made there the priestess of this rite. Long after that the brother of the priestess happened to come; the fact, however, of the oracle having for a certain reason bidden him go thither, and his object in going, are outside the Plot of the play. On his coming he was arrested, and about to be sacrificed, when he revealed who he was—either as Euripides puts it, or (as suggested by Polyidus) by the not improbable exclamation, 'So I too am doomed to be sacrified, as my sister was'; and the disclosure led to his salvation. This done, the next thing, after the proper names have been fixed as a basis for the story, is to work in episodes or accessory incidents. One must mind, however, that the episodes are appropriate, like the fit of madness[20] in Orestes, which led to his arrest, and the purifying,[21] which brought about his salvation. In plays, then, the episodes are short; in epic poetry they serve to lengthen out the poem. The argument of the *Odyssey* is not a long one. A certain man has been abroad many years; Poseidon is ever on the watch for him, and he is all alone. Matters at home too have come to this, that his substance is being wasted and his son's death plotted by suitors to his wife. Then he arrives there himself after his grievous sufferings; reveals himself, and falls on his enemies; and the end is his salvation and their death. This being all that is proper to the *Odyssey,* everything else in it is episode.

18

(4) There is a further point to be borne in mind. Every tragedy is in part Complication and in part Dénouement; the incidents before the opening scene, and often certain also of those within the play, forming the Complication; and the rest the Dénouement. By Complication I mean all from the beginning of the story to the point just before the change in the hero's fortunes; by Dénouement, all from the beginning of the change to the end. In the *Lynceus* of Theodectes, for instance, the Complication includes, together with the presupposed incidents, the seizure of the child and that in turn of the parents; and the Dénouement all from the indictment for the murder to the end. Now it is right, when one speaks of a tragedy as the same or not the same as another, to do so on the ground before all else of their Plot, i.e. as having the same or not the same Complication and Dénouement. Yet there are many dramatists who, after a good Complication, fail in the Dénouement. But it is necessary for both points of construction to be always duly mastered. (5) There are four distinct species of Tragedy—that being the number of the constituents also that have been mentioned:[22] first, the complex Tragedy,

[20] *Iph. Taur.* 281 ff.
[21] Ib., 1163 ff.
[22] This does not agree with anything actually said before.

which is all Peripety and Discovery; second, the Tragedy of suffering, e.g. the *Ajaxes* and *Ixions;* third, the Tragedy of character, e.g. *The Phthiotides*[23] and *Peleus*.[24] The fourth constituent is that of "Spectacle," exemplified in *The Phorcides,*[25] in *Prometheus,*[26] and in all plays with the scene laid in the nether world. The poet's aim, then, should be to combine every element of interest, if possible, or else the more important and the major part of them. This is now especially necessary owing to the unfair criticism to which the poet is subjected in these days. Just because there have been poets before him strong in the several species of tragedy, the critics now expect the one man to surpass that which was the strong point of each one of his predecessors. (6) One should also remember what has been said more than once, and not write a tragedy on an epic body of incident (i.e one with a plurality of stories in it), by attempting to dramatize, for instance, the entire story of the *Iliad.* In the epic owing to its scale every part is treated at proper length; with a drama, however, on the same story the result is very disappointing. This is shown by the fact that all who have dramatized the fall of Ilium in its entirety, and not part by part, like Euripides, of the whole of the Niobe story, instead of a portion, like Aeschylus, either fail utterly or have but ill success on the stage; for that and that alone was enough to ruin even a play by Agathon. Yet in their Peripeties, as also in their simple plots, the poets I mean show wonderful skill in aiming at the kind of effect they desire—a tragic situation that arouses the human feeling in one, like the clever villain (e.g. Sisyphus) deceived, or the brave wrongdoer worsted. This is probable, however, only in Agathon's sense, when he speaks of the probability of even improbabilities coming to pass. (7) The Chorus too should be regarded as one of the actors; it should be an integral part of the whole, and take a share in the action—that which it has in Sophocles, rather than in Euripides. With the later poets, however, the songs in a play of theirs have no more to do with the Plot of that than of any other tragedy. Hence it is that they are now singing intercalary pieces, a practice first introduced by Agathon. And yet what real difference is there between singing such intercalary pieces, and attempting to fit in a speech, or even a whole act, from one play into another?

19

The Plot and Characters having been discussed, it remains to consider the Diction and Thought. As for the Thought, we may assume what is said of it in our Art of Rhetoric, as it belongs more properly to that department of inquiry. The Thought of the personages is shown in everything to be effected by their langauge—in every effort to prove or disprove, to arouse emotion (pity, fear, anger, and the like), or to maximize or minimize things. It is clear, also, that their mental procedure must be on the same lines in their

[23] By Sophocles.
[24] Probably Sophocles' *Peleus* is incorrect.
[25] By Aeschylus.
[26] Probably a satyric drama by Aeschylus.

actions likewise, whenever they wish them to arouse pity or horror, or to have a look of importance or probability. The only difference is that with the act the impression has to be made without explanation; whereas with the spoken word it has to be produced by the speaker, and result from his language. What, indeed, would be the good of the speaker, if things appeared in the required light even apart from anything he says? . . .

21

. . . Metaphor consists in giving the thing a name that belongs to something else; the transference being either from genus to species, or from species to genus, or from species to species, or on the grounds of analogy. That from genus to species is exemplified in 'Here stands my ship'; for lying at anchor is the 'standing' of a particular kind of thing. That from species to genus in 'Truly ten thousand good deeds has Ulysses wrought,' where 'ten thousand,' which is a particular large number, is put in place of the generic 'a large number.' That from species to species in 'Drawing the life with the bronze,' and in 'Severing with the enduring bronze'; where the poet uses 'draw' in the sense of 'sever' and 'sever' in that of 'draw,' both words meaning to 'take away' something. That from analogy is possible whenever there are four terms so related that the second (B) is to the first (A), as the fourth (D) to the third (C); for one may then metaphorically put D in lieu of B, and B in lieu of D. Now and then, too, they qualify the metaphor by adding on to it that to which the word it supplants is relative. Thus a cup (B) is in relation to Dionysus (A) what a shield (D) is to Ares (C). The cup accordingly will be metaphorically described as the 'shield of *Dionysus*' (D+A), and the shield as the 'cup of *Ares*' (B+C). Or to take another instance: As old age (D) is to life (C), so is evening (B) to day (A). One will accordingly describe evening (B) as the 'old age *of the day*' (D+A)—or by the Empedoclean equivalent; and old age (D) as the 'evening' or 'sunset *of life*' (B+C). It may be that some of the terms thus related have no special name of their own, but for all that they will be metaphorically described in just the same way. Thus to cast forth seed-corn is called 'sowing'; but to cast forth its flame, as said of the sun, has no special name. This nameless act (B), however, stands in just the same relation to its object, sunlight (A), as sowing (D) to the seed-corn (C). Hence the expression in the poet, 'sowing around a god-created *flame*' (D+A). There is also another form of qualified metaphor. Having given the thing the alien name, one may by a negative addition deny of it one of the attributes naturally associated with its new name. An instance of this would be to call the shield not the 'cup *of Ares,*' as in the former case, but a 'cup *that holds no wine*' . . . .

22

The perfection of Diction is for it to be at once clear and not mean. The clearest indeed is that made up of the ordinary words for things, but it is mean, as is shown by the poetry of Cleophon and Sthenelus. On the other hand the Diction becomes distinguished and non-prosaic by the use of unfamiliar terms, i.e. strange words, metaphors, lengthened forms, and everything that deviates from the ordinary modes of speech.—But a whole statement in such terms will be either a riddle or a barbarism, a riddle, if made up of metaphors, a barbarism, if made up of strange words. . . . It is a great thing, indeed, to make a proper use of these poetical forms, as also of compounds and strange words. But the greatest thing by far is to be a master of metaphor. It is the one thing that cannot be learnt from others; and it is also a sign of genius, since a good metaphor implies an intuitive perception of the similarity in dissimilars. . . .

Let this, then, suffice as an account of Tragedy, the art imitating by means of action on the stage.

23

As for the poetry which merely narrates, or imitates by means of versified language (without action), it is evident that it has several points in common with Tragedy.

I. The construction of its stories should clearly be like that in a drama; they should be based on a single action, one that is a complete whole in itself, with a beginning, middle, and end, so as to enable the work to produce its own proper pleasure with all the organic unity of a living creature. Nor should one suppose that there is anything like them in our usual histories. A history has to deal not with one action, but with one period and all that happened in that to one or more persons, however disconnected the several events may have been. Just as two events may take place at the same time, e.g. the sea-fight off Salamis and the battle with the Carthaginians in Sicily, without converging to the same end, so too of two consecutive events one may sometimes come after the other with no one end as their common issue. Nevertheless most of our epic poets, one may say, ignore the distinction.

Herein, then, to repeat what we have said before, we have a further proof of Homer's marvellous superiority to the rest. He did not attempt to deal with the Trojan war in its entirety, though it was a whole with a definite beginning and end—through a feeling apparently that it was too long a story to be taken in in one view, or if not that, too complicated from the variety of incident in it. As it is, he has singled out one section of the whole; many of the other incidents, however, he brings in as episodes, using the Catalogue of the Ships, for instance, and other episodes to relieve the uniformity of his narrative. As for the other epic poets, they treat of one man, or one period; or else of an action which, although one, has a multiplicity of parts in it. This last is what the authors of the *Cypria*[27] and *Little Iliad*[27] have done. And the result is that, whereas the *Iliad* or *Odyssey* supplies materials for only one, or at most two tragedies, the *Cypria* does that for several and the *Little*

[27] Authorship unknown.

Iliad for more than eight: for an *Adjudgment of Arms,* a *Philoctetes,* a *Neoptolemus,* a *Eurypylus,* a *Ulysses as Beggar,* a *Laconian Women,* a *Fall of Ilium,* and a *Departure of the Fleet;* as also a *Sinon,* and a *Women of Troy.*

24

II. Besides this, Epic poetry must divide into the same species as Tragedy; it must be either simple or complex, a story of character or one of suffering. Its parts, too, with the exception of Song and Spectacle, must be the same, as it requires Peripeties, Discoveries, and scenes of suffering just like Tragedy. Lastly, the Thought and Diction in it must be good in their way. All these elements appear in Homer first; and he has made due use of them. His two poems are each examples of construction, the *Iliad* simple and a story of suffering, the *Odyssey* complex (there is Discovery throughout it) and a story of character. And they are more than this, since in Diction and Thought too they surpass all other poems.

There is, however, a difference in the Epic as compared with Tragedy, (1) in its length, and (2) in its metre. (1) As to its length, the limit already suggested will suffice: it must be possible for the beginning and end of the work to be taken in in one view—a condition which will be fulfilled if the poem be shorter than the old epics, and about as long as the series of tragedies offered for one hearing. For the extension of its length epic poetry has a special advantage, of which it makes large use. In a play one cannot represent an action with a number of parts going on simultaneously; one is limited to the part on the stage and connected with the actors. Whereas in epic poetry the narrative form makes it possible for one to describe a number of simultaneous incidents; and these, if germane to the subject, increase the body of the poem. This then is a gain to the Epic, tending to give it grandeur, and also variety of interest and room for episodes of diverse kinds. Uniformity of incident by the satiety it soon creates is apt to ruin tragedies on the stage. (2) As for its metre, the heroic has been assigned it from experience; were any one to attempt a narrative poem in some one, or in several, of the other metres, the incongruity of the thing would be apparent. The heroic in fact is the gravest and weightiest of metres—which is what makes it more tolerant than the rest of strange words and metaphors, that also being a point in which the narrative form of poetry goes beyond all others. The iambic and trochaic, on the other hand, are metres of movement, the one representing that of life and action, the other that of the dance. Still more unnatural would it appear, if one were to write an epic in a medley of metres, as Chaeremon did.[28] Hence it is that no one has ever written a long story in any but heroic verse; nature herself, as we have said, teaches us to select the metre appropriate to such a story.

Homer, admirable as he is in every other respect, is especially so in this,

[28] *Centaur.*

that he alone among epic poets is not unaware of the part to be played by the poet himself in the poem. The poet should say very little *in propria persona,* as he is no imitator when doing that. Whereas the other poets are perpetually coming forward in person, and say but little, and that only here and there, as imitators, Homer after a brief preface brings in forthwith a man, a woman, or some other Character—no one of them characterless, but each with distinctive characteristics.

The marvellous is certainly required in Tragedy. The Epic, however, affords more opening for the improbable, the chief factor in the marvellous, because in it the agents are not visibly before one. The scene of the pursuit of Hector would be ridiculous on the stage—the Greeks halting instead of pursuing him, and Achilles shaking his head to stop them;[29] but in the poem the absurdity is overlooked. The marvellous, however, is a cause of pleasure, as is shown by the fact that we all tell a story with additions, in the belief that we are doing our hearers a pleasure.

Homer more than any other has taught the rest of us the art of framing lies in the right way. I mean the use of paralogism. Whenever, if A is or happens, a consequent, B, is or happens, men's notion is that, if the B is, the A also is—but that is a false conclusion. Accordingly, if A is untrue, but there is something else, B, that on the assumption of its truth follows as its consequent, the right thing then is to add on the B. Just because we know the truth of the consequent, we are in our own minds led on to the erroneous inference of the truth of the antecedent. Here is an instance, from the *Bath-story* in the *Odyssey.*[30]

A likely impossibility is always preferable to an unconvincing possibility. The story should never be made up of improbable incidents; there should be nothing of the sort in it. If, however, such incidents are unavoidable, they should be outside the piece, like the hero's ignorance in *Oedipus* of the circumstances of Laius' death; not within it, like the report of the Pythian games in *Electra,*[31] or the man's having come to Mysia from Tegea without uttering a word on the way, in *The Mysians.*[32] So that it is ridiculous to say that one's Plot would have been spoilt without them, since it is fundamentally wrong to make up such Plots. If the poet has taken such a Plot, however, and one sees that he might have put it in a more probable form, he is guilty of absurdity as well as a fault of art. Even in the *Odyssey* the improbabilities in the setting-ashore of Ulysses[33] would be clearly intolerable in the hands of an inferior poet. As it is, the poet conceals them, his other excellences veiling their absurdity. Elaborate Diction, however, is required only in places where there is no action, and no Character or Thought to be revealed. Where

[29] *Il.* xxii. 205.
[30] xix. 164–260.
[31] Soph. *El.* 660 ff.
[32] Probably by Aeschylus.
[33] xiii. 116 ff.

there is Character or Thought, on the other hand, an over-ornate Diction tends to obscure them.

25

As regards Problems and their Solutions, one may see the number and nature of the assumptions on which they proceed by viewing the matter in the following way. (1) The poet being an imitator just like the painter or other maker of likenesses, he must necessarily in all instances represent things in one or other of three aspects, either as they were or are, or as they are said or thought to be or to have been, or as they ought to be. (2) All this he does in language, with an admixture, it may be, of strange words and metaphors, as also of the various modified forms of words, since the use of these is conceded in poetry. (3) It is to be remembered, too, that there is not the same kind of correctness in poetry as in politics, or indeed any other art. There is, however, within the limits of poetry itself a possibility of two kinds of error, the one directly, the other only accidentally connected with the art. If the poet meant to describe the thing correctly, and failed through lack of power of expression, his art itself is at fault. But if it was through his having meant to describe it in some incorrect way (e.g. to make the horse in movement have both legs thrown forward) that the technical error (one in a matter of, say, medicine or some other special science), or impossibilities of whatever kind they may be, have got into his description, his error in that case is not in the essentials of the poetic art. These, therefore, must be the premises of the Solutions in answer to the criticisms involved in the Problems.

I. As to the criticisms relating to the poet's art itself. Any impossibilities there may be in his descriptions of things are faults. But from another point of view they are justifiable, if they serve the end of poetry itself—if (to assume what we have said of that end) they make the effect of either that very portion of the work or some other portion more astounding. The Pursuit of Hector is an instance in point. If, however, the poetic end might have been as well or better attained without sacrifice of technical correctness in such matters, the impossibility is not to be justified, since the description should be, if it can, entirely free from error. One may ask, too, whether the error is in a matter directly or only accidentally connected with the poetic art; since it is a lesser error in an artist not to know, for instance, that the hind has no horns, than to produce an unrecognizable picture of one.

II. If the poet's description be criticized as not true to fact, one may urge perhaps that the object ought to be as described—an answer like that of Sophocles, who said that he drew men as they ought to be, and Euripides as they were. If the description, however, be neither true nor of the thing as it ought to be, the answer must be then, that it is in accordance with opinion. The tales about Gods, for instance, may be as wrong as Xenophanes thinks, neither true nor the better thing to say; but they are certainly in accordance with opinion. Of other statements in poetry one may perhaps say, not that they are better than the truth, but that the fact was so at the time; e.g. the description of the arms: 'their spears stood upright, butt-end upon the ground';[34] for that was the usual way of fixing them then, as it is still with the Illyrians. As for the question whether something said or done in a poem is morally right or not, in dealing with that one should consider not only the intrinsic quality of the actual word or deed, but also the person who says or does it, the person to whom he says or does it, the time, the means, and the motive of the agent—whether he does it to attain a greater good, or to avoid a greater evil.

III. . . . Speaking generally, one has to justify (1) the Impossible by reference to the requirements of poetry, or to the better, or to opinion. For the purposes of poetry a convincing impossibility is preferable to an unconvincing possibility; and if men such as Zeuxis depicted be impossible, the answer is that it is better they should be like that, as the artist ought to improve on his model. (2) The Improbable one has to justify either by showing it to be in accordance with opinion, or by urging that at times it is not improbable; for there is a probability of things happening also against probability. (3) The contradictions found in the poet's language one should first test as one does an opponent's confutation in a dialectical argument, so as to see whether he means the same thing, in the same relation, and in the same sense, before admitting that he has contradicted either something he has said himself or what a man of sound sense assumes as true. But there is no possible apology for improbability of Plot or depravity of character, when they are not necessary and no use is made of them, like the improbability in the appearance of Aegeus in *Medea*[35] and the baseness of Menelaus in *Orestes*.

The objections, then, of critics start with faults of five kinds: the allegation is always that something is either (1) impossible, (2) improbable, (3) corrupting, (4) contradictory, or (5) against technical correctness. The answers to these objections must be sought under one or other of the above-mentioned heads, which are twelve in number.

26

The question may be raised whether the epic or the tragic is the higher form of imitation. It may be argued that, if the less vulgar is the higher, and the less vulgar is always that which addresses the better public, an art addressing any and every one is of a very vulgar order. It is a belief that their public cannot see the meaning, unless they add something themselves, that causes the perpetual movements of the performers—bad flute-players, for instance, rolling about, if quoit-throwing is to be represented, and pulling at the conductor, if Scylla is the subject of the piece. Tragedy, then, is said to be an art

[34] *Il.* x. 152.
[35] 1. 663.

of this order—to be in fact just what the later actors were in the eyes of their predecessors; for Mynniscus used to call Callippides 'the ape,' because he thought he so overacted his parts; and a similar view was taken of Pindarus also. All Tragedy, however, is said to stand to the Epic as the newer to the older school of actors. The one, accordingly, is said to address a cultivated audience, which does not need the accompaniment of gesture; the other, an uncultivated one. If, therefore, Tragedy is a vulgar art, it must clearly be lower than the Epic.

The answer to this is twofold. In the first place, one may urge (1) that the censure does not touch the art of the dramatic poet, but only that of his interpreter; for it is quite possible to overdo the gesturing even in an epic recital, as did Socistratus, and in a singing contest, as did Mnasitheus of Opus. (2) That one should not condemn all movement, unless one means to condemn even the dance, but only that of ignoble people—which is the point of the criticism passed on Callippides and in the present day on others, that their women are not like gentlewomen. (3) That Tragedy may produce its effect even without movement or action in just the same way as Epic poetry; for from the mere reading of a play its quality may be seen. So that, if it be superior in all other respects, this element of inferiority is no necessary part of it.

In the second place, one must remember (1) that Tragedy has everything that the Epic has (even the epic metre being admissible), together with a not inconsiderable addition in the shape of the Music (a very real factor in the pleasure of the drama) and the Spectacle. (2) That its reality of presentation is felt in the play as read, as well as in the play as acted. (3) That the tragic imitation requires less space for the attainment of its end; which is a great advantage, since the more concentrated effect is more pleasurable than one with a large admixture of time to dilute it—consider the *Oedipus* of Sophocles, for instance, and the effect of expanding it into the number of lines of the *Iliad*. (4) That there is less unity in the imitation of the epic poets, as is proved by the fact that any one work of theirs supplies matter for several tragedies; the result being that, if they take what is really a single story, it seems curt when briefly told, and thin and waterish when on the scale of length usual with their verse. In saying that there is less unity in an epic, I mean an epic made up of a plurality of actions, in the same way as the *Iliad* and *Odyssey* have many such parts, each one of them in itself of some magnitude; yet the structure of the two Homeric poems is as perfect as can be, and the action in them is as nearly as possible one action. If, then, Tragedy is superior in these respects, and also, besides these, in its poetic effect (since the two forms of poetry should give us, not any or every pleasure, but the very special kind we have mentioned), it is clear that, as attaining the poetic effect better than the Epic, it will be the higher form of art.

So much for Tragedy and Epic poetry—for these two arts in general and their species; the number and nature of their constituent parts; the causes of success and failure in them; the Objections of the critics, and the Solutions in answer to them.

LIONEL TRILLING

•

Art and Neurosis[1]

The question of the mental health of the artist has engaged the attention of our culture since the beginning of the Romantic Movement. Before that time it was commonly said that the poet was "mad," but this was only a manner of speaking, a way of saying that the mind of the poet worked in different fashion from the mind of the philosopher; it had no real reference to the mental hygiene of the man who was the poet. But in the early nineteenth century, with the development of a more elaborate psychology and a stricter and more literal view of mental and emotional normality, the statement was more strictly and literally intended. So much so, indeed, that Charles Lamb, who knew something about madness at close quarters and a great deal about art, undertook to refute in his brilliant essay, "On the Sanity of True Genius," the idea that the exercise of the imagination was a kind of insanity. And some eighty years later, the idea having yet further entrenched itself, Bernard Shaw felt called upon to argue the sanity of art, but his cogency was of no more avail than Lamb's. In recent years the connection between art and mental illness has been formulated not only by those who are openly or covertly hostile to art, but also and more significantly by those who are most intensely partisan to it. The latter willingly and even eagerly accept the idea that the artist is mentally ill and go on to make his illness a condition of his power to tell the truth.

This conception of artistic genius is indeed one of the characteristic notions of our culture. I should like to bring it into question. To do so is to bring also into question certain early ideas of Freud's and certain conclusions which literary laymen have drawn from the whole tendency of the Freudian psychology. From the very start it was recognized that psychoanalysis was likely to have important things to say about art and artists. Freud himself thought so, yet when he first addressed himself to the subject he said many clumsy and misleading things. I have elsewhere and at length tried to separate the useful from the useless and even dangerous statements about art that Freud has made.[2] To put it briefly here, Freud had some illuminating and

[1] From *The Liberal Imagination,* by Lionel Trilling. Copyright 1945, 1947 by Lionel Trilling. Reprinted by permission of The Viking Press, Inc.

[2] See "Freud and Literature."

even beautiful insights into certain particular works of art which made complex use of the element of myth. Then, without specifically undertaking to do so, his "Beyond the Pleasure Principle" offers a brilliant and comprehensive explanation of our interest in tragedy. And what is of course, most important of all—it is a point to which I shall return—Freud, by the whole tendency of his psychology, establishes the *naturalness* of artistic thought. Indeed, it is possible to say of Freud that he ultimately did more for our understanding of art than any other writer since Aristotle; and this being so, it can only be surprising that in his early work he should have made the error of treating the artist as a neurotic who escapes from reality by means of "substitute gratifications."

As Freud went forward he insisted less on this simple formulation. Certainly it did not have its original force with him when, at his seventieth birthday celebration, he disclaimed the right to be called the discoverer of the unconscious, saying that whatever he may have done for the systematic understanding of the unconscious, the credit for its discovery properly belonged to the literary masters. And psychoanalysis has inherited from him a tenderness for art which is real although sometimes clumsy, and nowadays most psychoanalysts of any personal sensitivity are embarrassed by occasions which seem to lead them to reduce art to a formula of mental illness. Nevertheless Freud's early belief in the essential neuroticism of the artist found an all too fertile ground—found, we might say, the very ground from which it first sprang, for, when he spoke of the artist as a neurotic, Freud was adopting one of the popular beliefs of his age. Most readers will see this belief as the expression of the industrial rationalization and the bourgeois philistinism of the nineteenth century. In this they are partly right. The nineteenth century established the basic virtue of "getting up at eight, shaving close at a quarter-past, breakfasting at nine, going to the City at ten, coming home at half-past five, and dining at seven." The Messrs. Podsnap who instituted this scheduled morality inevitably decreed that the arts must celebrate it and nothing else. "Nothing else to be permitted to these . . . vagrants the Arts, on pain of excommunication. Nothing else To Be—anywhere!" We observe that the virtuous day ends with dinner—bed and sleep are naturally not part of the Reality that Is, and nothing must be set forth which will, as Mr. Podsnap put it, bring a Blush to the Cheek of a Young Person.

The excommunication of the arts, when it was found necessary, took the form of pronouncing the artist mentally degenerate, a device which eventually found its theorist in Max Nordau. In the history of the arts this is new. The poet was always known to belong to a touchy tribe—*genus irritabile* was a tag anyone would know—and ever since Plato the process of the inspired imagination, as we have said, was thought to be a special one of some interest, which the similitude of madness made somewhat intelligible. But this is not quite to say that the poet was the victim of actual mental aberration. The eighteenth century did not find the poet to be less than other men, and certainly the Renaissance did not. If he was a professional, there might be condescension to his social status, but in a time which deplored all professionalism whatever, this was simply a way of asserting the high value of poetry, which ought not to be compromised by trade. And a certain good nature marked even the snubbing of the professional. At any rate, no one was likely to identify the poet with the weakling. Indeed, the Renaissance ideal held poetry to be, like arms or music, one of the signs of manly competence.

The change from this view of things cannot be blamed wholly on the bourgeois or philistine public. Some of the "blame" must rest with the poets themselves. The Romantic poets were as proud of their art as the vaunting poets of the sixteenth century, but one of them talked with an angel in a tree and insisted that Hell was better than Heaven and sexuality holier than chastity; another told the world that he wanted to lie down like a tired child and weep away this life of care; another asked so foolish a question as "Why did I laugh tonight?"; and yet another explained that he had written one of his best poems in a drugged sleep. The public took them all at their word—they were not as other men. Zola, in the interests of science, submitted himself to examination by fifteen psychiatrists and agreed with their conclusion that his genius had its source in the neurotic elements of his temperament. Baudelaire, Rimbaud, Verlaine found virtue and strength in their physical and mental illness and pain. W. H. Auden addresses his "wound" in the cherishing language of a lover, thanking it for the gift of insight it has bestowed. "Knowing you," he says, "has made me understand." And Edmund Wilson in his striking phrase, "the wound and the bow," has formulated for our time the idea of the characteristic sickness of the artist, which he represents by the figure of Philoctetes, the Greek warrior who was forced to live in isolation because of the disgusting odor of a suppurating wound and who yet had to be sought out by his countrymen because they had need of the magically unerring bow he possessed.

The myth of the sick artist, we may suppose, has established itself because it is of advantage to the various groups who have one or another relation with art. To the artist himself the myth gives some of the ancient powers and privileges of the idiot and the fool, half-prophetic creatures, or of the mutilated priest. That the artist's neurosis may be but a mask is suggested by Thomas Mann's pleasure in representing his untried youth as "sick" but his successful maturity as senatorially robust. By means of his belief in his own sickness, the artist may the more easily fulfill his chosen, and assigned, function of putting himself into connection with the forces of spirituality and morality; the artist sees as insane the "normal" and "healthy" ways of established society, while aberration and illness appear as spiritual and moral health if only because they controvert the ways of respectable society.

Then too, the myth has its advantage for the philistine—a double advantage. On the one hand, the belief in the artist's neuroticism allows the philistine to shut his ears to what the artist says. But on the other hand it allows him to listen. For we must not make the common mistake—the contemporary philistine does want to listen, at the same time that he wants to shut his ears. By supposing that the artist has an interesting but not always reliable relation to reality, he is able to contain (in the military sense) what the artist tells him. If he did not want to listen at all, he would say "insane"; with "neurotic," which hedges, he listens when he chooses.

And in addition to its advantage to the artist and to the philistine, we must take into account the usefulness of the myth to a third group, the group of "sensitive" people, who, although not artists, are not philistines either. These people form a group by virtue of their passive impatience with philistinism, and also by virtue of their awareness of their own emotional pain and uncertainty. To these people the myth of the sick artist is the institutional sanction of their situation; they seek to approximate or acquire the character of the artist, sometimes by planning to work or even attempting to work as the artist does, always by making a connection between their own powers of mind and their consciousness of "difference" and neurotic illness.

The early attempts of psychoanalysis to deal with art went on the assumption that, because the artist was neurotic, the content of his work was also neurotic, which is to say that it did not stand in a correct relation to reality. But nowadays, as I have said, psychoanalysis is not likely to be so simple in its transactions with art. A good example of the psychoanalytical development in this respect is Dr. Saul Rosenzweig's well-known essay, "The Ghost of Henry James."[3] This is an admirable piece of work, marked by accuracy in the reporting of the literary fact and by respect for the value of the literary object. Although Dr. Rosenzweig explores the element of neurosis in James's life and work, he nowhere suggests that this element in any way lessens James's value as an artist or moralist. In effect he says that neurosis is a way of dealing with reality which, in real life, is uncomfortable and uneconomical, but that this judgment of neurosis in life cannot mechanically be transferred to works of art upon which neurosis has had its influence. He nowhere implies that a work of art in whose genesis a neurotic element may be found is for that reason irrelevant or in any way diminished in value. Indeed, the manner of his treatment suggests, what is of course the case, that every neurosis deals with a real emotional situation of the most intensely meaningful kind.

Yet as Dr. Rosenzweig brings his essay to its close, he makes use of the current assumption about the causal connection between the psychic illness of the artist and his power. His investigation of James, he says, "reveals the aptness of the Philoctetes pattern." He accepts the idea of "the sacrificial roots of literary power" and speaks of "the unhappy sources of James's genius." "The broader application of the inherent pattern," he says, "is familiar to readers of Edmund Wilson's recent volume *The Wound and the*

[3] First published in *Character and Personality,* December 1943, and reprinted in *Partisan Review,* Fall, 1944.

Bow. . . . Reviewing the experience and work of several well-known literary masters, Wilson discloses the sacrificial roots of their power on the model of the Greek legend. In the case of Henry James, the present account . . . provides a similar insight into the unhappy sources of his genius. . . ."

This comes as a surprise. Nothing in Dr. Rosenzweig's theory requires it. For his theory asserts no more than that Henry James, predisposed by temperament and family situation to certain mental and emotional qualities, was in his youth injured in a way which he believed to be sexual; that he unconsciously invited the injury in the wish to identfy himself with his father, who himself had been similarly injured—"castrated": a leg had been amputated—and under strikingly similar circumstances; this resulted for the younger Henry James in a certain pattern of life and in a preoccupation in his work with certain themes which more or less obscurely symbolize his sexual situation. For this I think Dr. Rosenzweig makes a sound case. Yet I submit that this is not the same thing as disclosing the roots of James's power or discovering the sources of his genius. The essay which gives Edmund Wilson's book its title and cohering principle does not explicitly say that the roots of power are sacrificial and that the source of genius is unhappy. Where it is explicit, it states only that "genius and disease, like strength and mutilation, may be inextricably bound up together," which of course, on its face, says no more than that personality is integral and not made up of detachable parts; and from this there is no doubt to be drawn the important practical and moral implication that we cannot judge or dismiss a man's genius and strength because of our awareness of his disease or mutilation. The Philoctetes legend in itself does not suggest anything beyond this. It does not suggest that the wound is the price of the bow, or that without the wound the bow may not be possessed or drawn. Yet Dr. Rosenzweig has accurately summarized the force and, I think, the intention of Mr. Wilson's whole book; its several studies do seem to say that effectiveness in the arts does depend on sickness.

An examination of this prevalent idea might well begin with the observation of how pervasive and deeply rooted is the notion that power may be gained by suffering. Even at relatively high stages of culture the mind seems to take easily to the primitive belief that pain and sacrifice are connected with strength. Primitive beliefs must be treated with respectful alertness to their possible truth and also with the suspicion of their being magical and irrational, and it is worth noting on both sides of the question, and in the light of what we have said about the ambiguous relation of the neurosis to reality, that the whole economy of the neurosis is based exactly on this idea of the *quid pro quo* of sacrificial pain: the neurotic person unconsciously subscribes to a system whereby he gives up some pleasure or power, or inflicts pain on himself in order to secure some other power or some other pleasure.

In the ingrained popular conception of the relation between suffering and power there are actually two distinct although related ideas. One is that there exists in the individual a fund of power which has outlets through various organs or faculties, and that if its outlet through one organ or faculty be prevented, it will flow to increase the force or sensitivity of another. Thus it is popularly believed that the sense of touch is intensified in the blind not so much by the will of the blind person to adapt himself to the necessities of his situation as, rather, by a sort of mechanical redistribution of power. And this idea would seem to explain, if not the origin of the ancient mutilation of priests, then at least a common understanding of their sexual sacrifice.

The other idea is that a person may be taught by, or proved by, the endurance of pain. There will easily come to mind the ritual suffering that is inflicted at the tribal initiation of youths into full manhood or at the admission of the apprentice into the company of journeyman adepts. This idea in sophisticated form found its way into high religion at least as early as Aeschylus, who held that man achieves knowledge of God through suffering, and it was from the beginning an important element of Christian thought. In the nineteenth century the Christianized notion of the didactic suffering of the artist went along with the idea of his mental degeneration and even served as a sort of countermyth to it. Its doctrine was that the artist, a man of strength and health, experienced and suffered, and thus learned both the facts of life and his artistic craft. "I am the man, I suffered, I was there," ran his boast, and he derived his authority from the knowledge gained through suffering.

There can be no doubt that both these ideas represent a measure of truth about mental and emotional power. The idea of didactic suffering expresses a valuation of experience and of steadfastness. The idea of natural compensation for the sacrifice of some faculty also says something that can be rationally defended: one cannot be and do everything and the wholehearted absorption in any enterprise, art for example, means that we must give up other possibilities, even parts of ourselves. And there is even a certain validity to the belief that the individual has a fund of undifferentiated energy which presses the harder upon what outlets are available to it when it has been deprived of the normal number.

Then, in further defense of the belief that artistic power is connected with neurosis, we can say that there is no doubt that what we call mental illness may be the source of psychic knowledge. Some neurotic people, because they are more apprehensive than normal people, are able to see more of certain parts of reality and to see them with more intensity. And many neurotic or psychotic patients are in certain respects in closer touch with the actualities of the unconscious than are normal people. Further, the expression of a neurotic or psychotic conception of reality is likely to be more intense than a normal one.

Yet when we have said all this, it is still wrong, I believe, to find the root of the artist's power and the source of his genius in neurosis. To the idea that literary power and genius spring from pain and neurotic sacrifice there are two major objections. The first has to do with the assumed uniqueness of the artist as a subject of psychoanalytical explanation. The second has to do with the true meaning of power and genius.

One reason why writers are considered to be more available than other people to psychoanalytical explanation is that they tell us what is going on inside them. Even when they do not make an actual diagnosis of their malaises or describe "symptoms," we must bear it in mind that it is their profession to deal with fantasy in some form or other. It is in the nature of the writer's job that he exhibit his unconscious. He may disguise it in various ways, but disguise is not concealment. Indeed, it may be said that the more a writer takes pains with his work to remove it from the personal and subjective, the more—and not the less—he will express his true unconscious, although not what passes with most for the unconscious.

Further, the writer is likely to be a great hand at personal letters, diaries, and autobiographies: indeed, almost the only good autobiographies are those of writers. The writer is more aware of what happens to him or goes on in him and often finds it necessary or useful to be articulate about his inner states, and prides himself on telling the truth. Thus, only a man as devoted to the truth of the emotions as Henry James was would have informed the world, despite his characteristic reticence, of an accident so intimate as his. We must not of course suppose that a writer's statements about his intimate life are equivalent to true statements about his unconscious, which, by definition, he doesn't consciously know; but they may be useful clues to the nature of an entity about which we can make statements of more or less cogency, although never statements of certainty; or they at least give us what is surely related to a knowledge of his unconscious—that is, an insight into is personality.[4]

But while the validity of dealing with the writer's intellectual life in psychoanalytical terms is taken for granted, the psychoanalytical explanation of the intellectual life of scientists is generally speaking not countenanced. The old myth of the mad scientist, with the exception of an occasional mad psychiatrist, no longer exists. The social position of science requires that it should cease, which leads us to remark that those partisans of art who insist on explaining artistic genius by means of psychic imbalance are in effect capitulating to the dominant mores which hold that the members of the respectable professions are, however dull they may be, free from neurosis.

[4] I am by no means in agreement with the statements of Dr. Edmund Bergler about "the" psychology of the writer, but I think that Dr. Bergler has done good service in warning us against taking at their face value a writer's statements about himself, the more especially when they are "frank." Thus, to take Dr. Bergler's notable example, it is usual for biographers to accept Stendhal's statements about his open sexual feelings for his mother when he was a little boy, feelings which went with an intense hatred of his father. But Dr. Bergler believes that Stendhal unconsciously used his consciousness of his love of his mother and of his hatred of his father to mask an unconscious love of his father, which frightened him. ("Psychoanalysis of Writers and of Literary Productivity" in *Psychoanalysis and the Social Sciences,* vol. I.)

Scientists, to continue with them as the best example of the respectable professions, do not usually give us the clues to their personalities which writers habitually give. But no one who has ever lived observantly among scientists will claim that they are without an unconscious or even that they are free from neurosis. How often, indeed, it is apparent that the devotion to science, if it cannot be called a neurotic manifestation, at least can be understood as going very cozily with neurotic elements in the temperament, such as, for example, a marked compulsiveness. Of scientists as a group we can say that they are less concerned with the manifestations of personality, their own or others', than are writers as a group. But this relative indifference is scarcely a sign of normality—indeed, if we choose to regard it with the same sort of eye with which the characteristics of writers are regarded, we might say the indifference to matters of personality is in itself a suspicious evasion.

It is the basic assumption of psychoanalysis that the acts of *every* person are influenced by the forces of the unconscious. Scientists, bankers, lawyers, or surgeons, by reason of the traditions of their professions, practice concealment and conformity; but it is difficult to believe that an investigation according to psychoanalytical principles would fail to show that the strains and imbalances of their psyches are not of the same frequency as those of writers, and of similar kind. I do not mean that everybody has the same troubles and identical psyches, but only that there is no special category for writers.[5]

If this is so, and if we still want to relate the writer's power to his neurosis, we must be willing to relate all intellectual power to neurosis. We must find the roots of Newton's power in his emotional extravagances, and the roots of Darwin's power in his sorely neurotic temperament, and the roots of Pascal's mathematical genius in the impulses which drove him to extreme religious masochism—I choose but the classic examples. If we make the neurosis-power equivalence at all, we must make it in every field of endeavor. Logician, economist, botanist, physicist, theologian—no profession may be so respectable or so remote or so rational as to be exempt from the psychological interpretation.[6]

[5] Dr. Bergler believes that there is a particular neurosis of writers, based on an oral masochism which makes them the enemy of the respectable world, courting poverty and persecution. But a later development of Dr. Bergler's theory of oral masochism makes it *the* basic neurosis, not only of writers but of everyone who is neurotic.

[6] In his interesting essay, "Writers and Madness" (*Partisan Review,* January–February 1947), William Barrett has taken issue with this point and has insisted that a clear distinction is to be made between the relation that exists between the scientist and his work and the relation that exists between the artist and his work. The difference, as I understand it, is in the claims of the ego. The artist's ego makes a claim upon the world which is personal in a way that the scientist's is not, for the scientist, although he does indeed want prestige and thus "responds to one of the deepest urges of his ego, it is only that his prestige may come to attend his person through the public world of other men; and it is not in the end his own being that is exhibited or his own voice that is heard in the learned report to the Academy." Actually, however, as is sug-

Further, not only power but also failure or limitation must be accounted for by the theory of neurosis, and not merely failure or limitation in life but even failure or limitation in art. Thus it is often said that the warp of Dostoevski's mind accounts for the brilliance of his psychological insights. But it is never said that the same warp of Dostoevski's mind also accounted for his deficiency in insight. Freud, who greatly admired Dostoevski, although he did not like him, observed that "his insight was entirely restricted to the workings of the abnormal psyche. Consider his astounding helplessness before the phenomenon of love; he really only understands either crude, instinctive desire or masochistic submission or love from pity."[7] This, we must note, is not merely Freud's comment on the extent of the province which Dostoevski chose for his own, but on his failure to understand what, given the province of his choice, he might be expected to understand.

And since neurosis can account not only for intellectual success and for failure or limitation but also for mediocrity, we have most of society involved in neurosis. To this I have no objection—I think most of society is indeed involved in neurosis. But with neurosis accounting for so much, it cannot be made exclusively to account for one man's literary power.

We have now to consider what is meant by genius when its source is identified as the sacrifice and pain of neurosis.

In the case of Henry James, the reference to the neurosis of his personal life does indeed tell us something about the latent intention of his work and thus about the reason for some large part of its interest for us. But if genius and its source are what we are dealing with, we must observe that the reference to neurosis tells us nothing about James's passion, energy, and devotion,

---

gested by the sense which mathematicians have of the *style* of mathematical thought, the creation of the abstract thinker is as deeply involved as the artist's—see *An Essay on the Psychology of Invention in the Mathematical Field* by Jacques Hadamard, Princeton University Press, 1945—and he quite as much as the artist seeks to impose *himself,* to *express* himself. I am of course not maintaining that the processes of scientific thought are the same as those of artistic thought, or even that the scientist's creation is involved with his total personality *in the same way* that the artist's is—I am maintaining only that the scientist's creation is as *deeply* implicated with his total personality as is the artist's.

This point of view seems to be supported by Freud's monograph on Leonardo. One of the problems that Freud sets himself is to discover why an artist of the highest endowment should have devoted himself more and more to scientific investigation, with the result that he was unable to complete his artistic enterprises. The particular reasons for this that Freud assigns need not be gone into here; all that I wish to suggest is that Freud understands these reasons to be the working out of an inner conflict, the attempt to deal with the difficulties that have their roots in the most primitive situations. Leonardo's scientific investigations were as necessary and "compelled" and they constituted as much of a claim on the whole personality as anything the artist undertakes; and so far from being carried out for the sake of public prestige, they were largely private and personal, and were thought by the public of his time to be something very like insanity.

[7] From a letter quoted in Theodor Reik's *From Thirty Years With Freud,* p. 175.

nothing about his architectonic skill, nothing about the other themes that were important to him which are not connected with his unconscious concern with castration. We cannot, that is, make the writer's inner life exactly equivalent to his power of expressing it. Let us grant for the sake of argument that the literary genius, as distinguished from other men, is the victim of a "mutilation" and that his fantasies are neurotic.[8] It does not then follow as the inevitable next step that his ability to express these fantasies and to impress us with them is neurotic, for that ability is what we mean by his genius. Anyone might be injured as Henry James was, and even respond within himself to the injury as James is said to have done, and yet not have his literary power.

The reference to the artist's neurosis tells us something about the material on which the artist exercises his powers, and even something about his reasons for bringing his powers into play, but it does not tell us anything about the source of his power, it makes no causal connection between them and the neurosis. And if we look into the matter, we see that there is in fact no causal connection between them. For, still granting that the poet is uniquely neurotic, what is surely not neurotic, what indeed suggests nothing but health, is his power of using his neuroticism. He shapes his fantasies, he gives them social form and reference. Charles Lamb's way of putting this cannot be improved. Lamb is denying that genius is allied to insanity; for "insanity" the modern reader may substitute "neurosis." "The ground of the mistake," he says, "is, that men, finding in the raptures of the higher poetry a condition of exaltation, to which they have no parallel in their own experience, besides the spurious resemblance of it in dreams and fevers, impute a state of dreaminess and fever to the poet. But the true poet dreams being awake. He is not possessed by his subject but has dominion over it. . . . Where he seems most to recede from humanity, he will be found the truest to it. From beyond the scope of nature if he summon possible existences, he subjugates them to the law of her consistency. He is beautifully loyal to that sovereign directress, when he appears most to betray and desert her. . . . Herein the great and the little wits are differenced; that if the latter wander ever so little from nature or natural existence, they lose themselves and their readers. . . . They do not create, which implies shaping and consistency. Their imaginations are not active—for to be active is to call something into act and form—but passive as men in sick dreams."

The activity of the artist, we must remember, may be approximated by many who are themselves not artists. Thus, the expressions of many schizophrenic people have the intense appearance of creativity and an inescapable

[8] I am using the word *fantasy,* unless modified, in a neutral sense. A fantasy, in this sense, may be distinguished from the representation of something that actually exists, but it is not opposed to "reality" and not an "escape" from reality. Thus the idea of a rational society, or the image of a good house to be built, as well as the story of something that could never really happen, is a fantasy. There may be neurotic or non-neurotic fantasies.

interest and significance. But they are not works of art, and although Van Gogh may have been schizophrenic he was in addition an artist. Again, as I have already suggested, it is not uncommon in our society for certain kinds of neurotic people to imitate the artist in his life and even in his ideals and ambitions. They follow the artist in everything except successful performance. It was, I think, Otto Rank who called such people half-artists and confirmed the diagnosis of their neuroticism at the same time that he differentiated them from true artists.

Nothing is so characteristic of the artist as his power of shaping his work, of subjugating his raw material, however aberrant it be from what we call normality, to the consistency of nature. It would be impossible to deny that whatever disease or mutilation the artist may suffer is an element of his production which has its effect on every part of it, but disease and mutilation are available to us all—life provides them with prodigal generosity. What marks the artist is his power to shape the material of pain we all have.

At this point, with our recognition of life's abundant provision of pain, we are at the very heart of our matter, which is the meaning we may assign to neurosis and the relation we are to suppose it to have with normality. Here Freud himself can be of help, although it must be admitted that what he tells us may at first seem somewhat contradictory and confusing.

Freud's study of Leonardo da Vinci is an attempt to understand why Leonardo was unable to pursue his artistic enterprises, feeling compelled instead to advance his scientific investigations. The cause of this Freud traces back to certain childhood experiences not different in kind from the experiences which Dr. Rosenzweig adduces to account for certain elements in the work of Henry James. And when he has completed his study Freud makes this *caveat:* "Let us expressly emphasize that we have never considered Leonardo as a neurotic. . . . We no longer believe that health and disease, normal and nervous, are sharply distinguished from each other. We know today that neurotic symptoms are substitutive formations for certain repressive acts which must result in the course of our development from the child to the cultural man, that we all produce such substitutive formations, and that only the amount, intensity, and distribution of these substitutive formations justify the practical conception of illness. . . ." The statement becomes the more striking when we remember that in the course of his study Freud has had occasion to observe that Leonardo was both homosexual and sexually inactive. I am not sure that the statement that Leonardo was not a neurotic is one that Freud would have made at every point in the later development of psychoanalysis, yet it is in conformity with his continuing notion of the genesis of culture. And the *practical,* the quantitative or economic, conception of illness he insists on in a passage in the *Introductory Lectures*. "The neurotic symptoms," he says, ". . . are activities which are detrimental, or at least useless, to life as a whole; the person concerned frequently complains of them as obnoxious to him or they involve suffering and distress for him. The principal injury they inflict lies in the expense of energy they entail, and, besides this, in the energy needed to combat them. Where the symptoms are extensively developed, these two kinds of effort may exact such a price that the person suffers a very serious impoverishment in available mental energy which consequently disables him for all the important tasks of life. This result depends principally upon the amount of energy taken up in this way; therefore you will see that 'illness' is essentially a practical conception. But if you look at the matter from a theoretical point of view and ignore this question of degree, you can very well see that we are all ill, i.e., neurotic; for the conditions required for symptom-formation are demonstrable also in normal persons."

We are all ill: the statement is grandiose, and its implications—the implications, that is, of understanding the totality of human nature in the terms of disease—are vast. These implications have never been properly met (although I believe that a few theologians have responded to them), but this is not the place to attempt to meet them. I have brought forward Freud's statement of the essential sickness of the psyche only because it stands as the refutation of what is implied by the literary use of the theory of neurosis to account for genius. For if we are all ill, and if, as I have said, neurosis can account for everything, for failure and mediocrity—"a very serious impoverishment of available mental energy"—as well as for genius, it cannot uniquely account for genius.

This, however, is not to say that there is no connection between neurosis and genius, which would be tantamount, as we see, to saying that there is no connection between human nature and genius. But the connection lies wholly in a particular and special relation which the artist has to neurosis.

In order to understand what this particular and special connection is we must have clearly in mind what neurosis is. The current literary conception of neurosis as a *wound* is quite misleading. It inevitably suggests passivity, whereas, if we follow Freud, we must understand a neurosis to be an *activity,* an activity with a purpose, and a particular kind of activity, a *conflict.* This is not to say that there are no abnormal mental states which are not conflicts. There are; the struggle between elements of the unconscious may never be instituted in the first place, or it may be called off. As Freud says in a passage which follows close upon the one I last quoted, "If regressions do not call forth a prohibition on the part of the ego, no neurosis results; the libido succeeds in obtaining a real, although not a normal, satisfaction. But if the ego . . . is not in agreement with these regressions, conflict ensues." And in his essay on Dostoevski Freud says that "there are no neurotic complete masochists," by which he means that the ego which gives way completely to masochism (or to any other pathological excess) has passed beyond neurosis; the conflict has ceased, but at the cost of the defeat of the ego, and now some other name than that of neurosis must be given to the condition of the person who thus takes himself beyond the pain of the neurotic conflict. To understand this is to become aware of the curious complacency with which literary men regard mental disease. The psyche of the neurotic is not equally complacent; it regards with the greatest fear the chaotic and destructive forces it contains, and it struggles fiercely to keep them at bay.[9]

We come then to a remarkable paradox: we are all ill, but we are ill in the service of health, or ill in the service of life, or, at the very least, ill in the service of life-in-culture. The form of the mind's dynamics is that of the neurosis, which is to be understood as the ego's struggle against being overcome by the forces with which it coexists, and the strategy of this conflict requires that the ego shall incur pain and make sacrifices of itself, at the same time seeing to it that its pain and sacrifice be as small as they may.

But this is characteristic of all minds: no mind is exempt except those which refuse the conflict or withdraw from it; and we ask wherein the mind of the artist is unique. If he is not unique in neurosis, is he then unique in the significance and intensity of his neurosis? I do not believe that we shall go more than a little way toward a definition of artistic genius by answering this question affirmatively. A neurotic conflict cannot ever be either meaningless or merely personal; it must be understood as exemplifying cultural forces of great moment, and this is true of any neurotic conflict at all. To be sure, some neuroses may be more interesting than others, perhaps because they are fiercer or more inclusive; and no doubt the writer who makes a claim upon our interest is a man who by reason of the energy and significance of the forces in struggle within him provides us with the largest representation of the culture in which we, with him, are involved; his neurosis may thus be thought of as having a connection of concomitance with his literary powers. As Freud says in the Dostoevski essay, "the neurosis . . . comes into being all the more readily the richer the complexity which has to be controlled by his ego." Yet even the rich complexity which his ego is doomed to control is not the definition of the artist's genius, for we can by no means say that the artist is preeminent in the rich complexity of elements in conflict within him. The slightest acquaintance with the clinical literature of psychoanalysis will suggest that a rich complexity of struggling elements is no uncommon possession. And that

[9] In the article to which I refer in the note on page 339, William Barrett says that he prefers the old-fashioned term "madness" to "neurosis." But it is not quite for him to choose—the words do not differ in fashion but in meaning. Most literary people, when they speak of mental illness, refer to neurosis. Perhaps one reason for this is that the neurosis is the most benign of the mental ills. Another reason is surely that psychoanalytical literature deals chiefly with the neurosis, and its symptomatology and therapy have become familiar; psychoanalysis has far less to say about psychosis, for which it can offer far less therapeutic hope. Further, the neurosis is easily put into a causal connection with the social maladjustments of our time. Other forms of mental illness of a more severe and degenerative kind are not so widely recognized by the literary person and are often assimilated to neurosis with a resulting confusion. In the present essay I deal only with the conception of neurosis, but this should not be taken to imply that I believe that other pathological mental conditions, including actual madness, do not have relevance to the general matter of the discussion.

same literature will also make it abundantly clear that the devices of art—the most extreme devices of poetry, for example—are not particular to the mind of the artist but are characteristic of mind itself.

But the artist is indeed unique in one respect, in the respect of his relation to his neurosis. He is what he is by virtue of his successful objectification of his neurosis, by his shaping it and making it available to others in a way which has its effect upon their own egos in struggle. His genius, that is, may be defined in terms of his faculties of perception, representation, and realization, and in these terms alone. It can no more be defined in terms of neurosis than can his power of walking and talking, or his sexuality. The use to which he puts his power, or the manner and style of his power, may be discussed with reference to his particular neurosis, and so may such matters as the untimely diminution or cessation of its exercise. But its essence is irreducible. It is, as we say, a gift.

We are all ill: but even a universal sickness implies an idea of health. Of the artist we must say that whatever elements of neurosis he has in common with his fellow mortals, the one part of him that is healthy, by any conceivable definition of health, is that which gives him the power to conceive, to plan, to work, and to bring his work to a conclusion. And if we are all ill, we are ill by a universal accident, not by a universal necessity, by a fault in the economy of our powers, not by the nature of the powers themselves. The Philoctetes myth, when it is used to imply a causal connection between the fantasy of castration and artistic power, tells us no more about the source of artistic power than we learn about the source of sexuality when the fantasy of castration is adduced, for the fear of castration may explain why a man is moved to extravagant exploits of sexuality, but we do not say that his sexual power itself derives from his fear of castration; and further the same fantasy may also explain impotence or homosexuality. The Philoctetes story, which has so established itself among us as explaining the source of the artist's power, is not really an explanatory myth at all; it is a moral myth having reference to our proper behavior in the circumstances of the universal accident. In its juxtaposition of the wound and the bow, it tells us that we must be aware that weakness does not preclude strength nor strength weakness. It is therefore not irrelevant to the artist, but when we use it we will do well to keep in mind the other myths of the arts, recalling what Pan and Dionysius suggest of the relation of art to physiology and superabundance, remembering that to Apollo were attributed the bow and the lyre, two strengths together, and that he was given the lyre by its inventor, the baby Hermes—that miraculous infant who, the day he was born, left his cradle to do mischief: and the first thing he met with was a tortoise, which he greeted politely before scooping it from its shell, and, thought and deed being one with him, he contrived the instrument to which he sang "the glorious tale of his own begetting." These were gods, and very early ones, but their myths tell us something about the nature and source of art even in our grim, late human present.

ROBERT PENN WARREN

•

A Lesson Read in American Books[1]

Once upon a time there was a nation, which we shall call X. At the time of which we write this nation stood at a moment of great power and great promise. A few generations earlier it had concluded a long and bloody civil war to achieve unity. More recently, in that unity, it had won a crashing victory over foreign foes. It had undergone, and was undergoing, a social revolution; there was unparalleled prosperity, a relaxing of old sanctions and prejudices, a widening of opportunity for all classes, great rewards for energy and intelligence. Its flag was on strange seas; its power was felt in the world. It was, even, producing a famous literature.

But—and here is the strange thing in that moment of energy and optimism—a large part, the most famous part, of that literature exhibited violence, degradation and despair as part of the human condition: tales of the old time of the civil war, tales of lust and horror, brother pimping for sister, father lusting for daughter, a head of the state doting on a fair youth, an old man's eyes plucked out, another old man killed in his sleep, friendship betrayed, obligations foregone, good men cursing the gods, and the whole scene drenched in blood. Foreigners encountering this literature might well conclude that the Land of X was peopled by degenerates sadly lacking in taste, manners and principle.

This is England, Elizabethan England, that we are talking about, and not the United States in this year of Our Lord and the Great Prosperity. But *mutatis mutandis,* and with proper recognition of the fact that we can scarcely claim a William Shakespeare, only John Fords and John Websters, we can talk about the United States in this connection, and join in conversation with Father Bruckberger, who has lately appeared in these pages, and with the editorial writer of *Life* magazine for Sept. 12.

These writers are concerned, as we must all be concerned, with America's image in the eyes of the world. "Is it right," asks Father Bruckberger, a sympathetic Frenchman visiting our shores, "that the great *flowering* of the American novel should hamper . . . America's leadership of the free world?" And the editorial writer in *Life:* "Europeans are already prejudiced against America by savage animadversions in their own classics against our 'vulgar' democracy. . . . Small wonder that our own self-depreciation helps them enlarge the evil image. . . ."

These two quotations raise a question, vexed and vexing, a question already old, no doubt, when the Greeks worried about it: how should esthetic value be related to prudential considerations? Presumably some of our literature has

[1] From *The New York Times Book Review,* December 11, 1955. Reprinted by permission of the author and *The New York Times Book Review.*

esthetic value (Father Bruckberger handsomely calls it a "flowering"), but it confirms some Europeans in their inherited low opinion of America, the country of "the almighty dollar," and of "respect to ordinary artisans," as Stendhal puts it, and the "land of money and selfishness, where souls are cold," as Balzac puts it. What do we do, then, when esthetic value is in conflict, or in apparent conflict, with political values?

Father Bruckberger does not undertake to answer this for us. On the one hand, he says that the "honor" of a literature is that it creates and sustains "a great quarrel within the national consciousness." But on the other hand, he bewails the effect abroad of this very quarrel within our national consciousness. Certainly, he is too informed to attempt to resolve the difficulty along the lines laid down by the editorial writer in *Life,* who, with certain ritualistic reservations, says that because America is now enjoying a boom, our literature should be optimistic, and applauds the current success of *The Man in the Gray Flannel Suit* because, though "flimsy art," it is "at least affirmative."

In fact, the editorial writer of *Life* takes as his golden text a quotation from Sloan Wilson, the author of *The Man in the Gray Flannel Suit:* "The world's treated me awfully well, and I guess it's crept into my work. . . . These are, we forget, pretty good times. Yet too many novelists are still writing as if we were back in the Depression years."

Though I have not yet read *The Man in the Gray Flannel Suit,* I should venture to doubt that the world is going to treat its author quite as well as it has treated Ernest Hemingway, William Faulkner, Theodore Dreiser, Sinclair Lewis, T. S. Eliot, Robert Frost, and quite a few other American writers who never found such a ready equation between bank balance and philosophy. What is really at stake in this is a question of freedom. If the creative act is of any value it is, in its special way, an act of freedom. It is, of course, conditioned by a thousand factors, but study of its conditions—economic, biologic, or whatever—has yet to reveal the secret of how that new intuition, the truly created object whose *newness* is the mark of freedom, comes to be. But Mr. Wilson, and presumably the approving editorial writer in *Life,* would deny this freedom, would, in fact, go even farther than Karl Marx in asserting the economic determinism of literature. If you are not making dough, you will not be a booster. Literature is a reflex of the stock market.

The philosophers of the Age of Conformism grant, however, that criticism was once all right, long back. As the *Life* editorial puts it: "*The Great Gatsby* still speaks eloquently of Prohibition's frauds and deceits, *Main Street* of the high tide of provincial self-satisfaction, *The Grapes of Wrath* with a just anger for the unnecessary humiliations of Depression. . . ." But criticism isn't all right in this day and time, for there is nothing really wrong now to be criticized, and anybody who is critical, who isn't "affirmative," is a fool or knave, a traitor or a sexual deviant, or a failure. May we not, however, in some chill hour between dark and dawn, have the thought that our own age may—just possibly—have its own frauds and deceits, deeper and more ambiguous than those anatomized in *The Great Gatsby,* that though this is not the age of provincial self-satisfaction, it may be the age of national self-righteousness and require a sharper scalpel than even *Main Street,* and that Divine Providence has given no written guarantee that It will not rebuke the smuggery of the Great Boom?

I do not think that the novel has yet been written to anatomize adequately this moment of our history, and I share the distaste of the editorial writer in *Life* for some of the works he alludes to, but the "American novel" which we should call for would not be less, but more, critical than those now current. At the same time I should hope that the literature to come will be more "affirmative," to use the word of the editorial. But the paradox here is that the literature that is most truly and profoundly critical is always the most profoundly affirmative.

In so far as a literature struggles to engage the deep, inner issues of life, the more will that literature be critical—the more, that is, will it engender impatience with the compromises, the ennui, the materialism, the self-deception, the complacency, and the secret, unnamable despairs that mark so much of ordinary life. Such a critical literature is at the same time affirmative because it affirms the will and courage to engage life at fundamental levels: the rock, if struck hard enough, will give forth the living waters.

The editorial writer in *Life* would not, I suppose, find these kinds of affirmation significant. He is concerned with doctrine, more or less explicitly put. But sometimes, even when doctrine is explicitly put, he has not, cannot, or does not, read it. Faulkner, he says, "for all his enormous gifts, can be searched in vain for that quality of redemption, through love and brotherhood, which always shines amid Dostoevsky's horrors." That very redemption, and its cost, is a recurrent theme of Faulkner's work. There is, for example, *The Bear,* with old Ike's vision of man's place in creation: God created man to hold suzerainty over the earth in His name, "not to hold for himself and his descendants' inviolable title forever, generation after generation, to the oblongs and squares of the earth, but to hold the earth mutual and intact in the communal anonymity of brotherhood, and all the fee He asked was pity and humility and sufferance and endurance and the sweat of his face for bread."

But let us go back where we started: the bad political impression which some of our literature presumably gives abroad. What are we to do? If we can't get writers to write the kind of literature we think useful for foreign consumption—if there really isn't such a thing as literature to specification—what then?

The answer is, I think, simple—and appalling. We must trust in our humility, and in our strength.

We must trust in our humility, because only by humility, the recognition that we have not fulfilled our best possibilities, can we hope to fulfill those possibilities. Some day, far-called, our navies may melt away, and on that day we may need the wisdom of ultimate humility. Meanwhile, in our moment of strength we hope that our strength is more than a historical accident, an index of the weakness of others. We hope that it has a moral grounding. But if that hope is to be more than a hope, it must be subjected to the test of conscience, and literature is one of the voices of our national conscience, however faltering and defective that voice may sometimes be. We must rebuke our *hubris,* not out of fear, but from love of a truth that we hope is within us.

We must trust in our strength, because only the strong can afford the luxury of radical self-criticism. Only if we believe in our strength can we take the risks of our full political and cultural development, with all the disintegrative and paradoxical possibilities in that dialectic. We should trust our strength, because America has a secret weapon, if we choose to use it: the weapon of not having a secret. It is the weapon of radical self-criticism—*radical* in the non-political and literal sense of the word. There was an old name for this, a name not often now used in this connection. That name was *democracy.*

So much for ourselves. But what of those poor foreigners who are so readily deceived by our literature? Are they, in the long run, quite so trapped in their prejudice, quite so incapable of the imaginative act, as Father Bruckberger seems to think? If so, why do they find our literature so fascinating, and why do they honor it? Can it be that, in a measure, they find in it a vital image of man, and some comment on his condition? Do they find in it, in the very fact of its existence, some mark of freedom?

I shall tell a story. A little while after the war in Europe I became acquainted with a young Italian who, in the first year of the war, as an officer in the Fascist Army, had deserted and taken to the mountains, to fight on our side. I once asked him what led him to this drastic step. He replied that American novelists had converted him. How, I asked. "Well," he said, "the Fascists used to let us read American fiction because it gave, they thought, a picture of a decadent America. They thought it was good propaganda for fascism to let us read Dreiser, Faulkner, Sinclair Lewis. But you know, it suddenly occurred to me that if democracy could allow that kind of criticism of itself, it must be very strong and good. So I took to the mountains."

T. S. ELIOT

•

On Teaching the Appreciation of Poetry[1]

I hold no diploma, certificate, or other academic document to show that I am qualified to discuss this subject. I have never taught anybody of any age how to enjoy, understand, appreciate poetry, or how to speak it. I have known

[1] From *The Critic,* XVIII (1960). By permission of the editor and Mr. Eliot.

a great many poets, and innumerable people who wanted to be told that they were poets. I have done some teaching, but I have never "taught poetry." My excuse for taking up this subject is of wholly different origin. I know that not only young people in colleges and universities, but secondary school children also, have to study, or at least acquaint themselves with, poems by living poets; and I know that my poems are among those studied, by two kinds of evidence. My play *Murder in the Cathedral* is a set book in some schools: there is an edition of the English text published in Germany with notes in German, and an edition published in Canada with notes in English. The fact that this play, and some of my other poems, are used in schools brings some welcome supplement to my income; and it also brings an increase in my correspondence, which is more or less welcome, though not all the letters get answered. These are letters from the children themselves, or more precisely, the teenagers. They live mostly in Britain, the United States, and Germany, with a sprinkling from the nations of Asia. It is in a spirit of curiosity, therefore, that I approach the subject of the teaching of poetry: I should like to know more about these young people and about their teachers and the methods of teaching.

For some of my young correspondents seem to be misguided. Sometimes I have been assigned to them as a "project," more often they have made the choice themselves—it is not always clear why. (There was one case, that of an Egyptian boy, who wanted to write a thesis about my work, and as none of my work was locally available and as he wanted to read it, asked me to send him all my books. That was very exceptional, however.) Very often the writers ask for information about myself, sometimes in the form of a questionnaire. I remember being asked by one child whether it was true that I only cared to associate with lords and bishops. Sometimes a photograph is asked for. Some young persons seem to want me to provide them with all the material for a potted biography, including mention of my interests, tastes, and ways of amusing myself. Are these children studying poetry, or merely studying poets? Very often they want explanations, either of a whole poem ("what does it mean") or of a particular line or phrase; and the kind of question they ask often suggests that their approach to that poem has been wrong, for they want the wrong kind of explanation, or ask questions which are simply unanswerable. Sometimes, but more rarely, they are avid for literary sources, which would seem to indicate that they have started too early on the road to Xanadu.

THE OLDER PATTERN

Now, when I was young, this sort of thing did not happen. I did study English at school, beginning, thank God, with grammar, and going on to "rhetoric"—for which also I am grateful. And we had to read a number of set books of prose and verse—mostly in school editions which made them look peculiarly unappetizing. But we never were made to read any literature which could be called contemporary: Tennyson could hardly be called "contemporary" by the time I had to study some of the *Idylls of the King*. I must admit that at the turn of the twentieth century there were precious few great poets about, and still fewer poets whom the authorities would have considered suitable for our perusal. Swinburne would hardly have done in those days; I don't know whether he has reached the school curriculum today. Yeats was still a minor poet of the 'Nineties. But even if Trumbull Stickney and George Cabot Lodge, two poets of whose work I remain ignorant to this day, had been famous instead of merely respectable, I doubt if my school authorities would have set any of their poetry for us.

No. Not only were we not encouraged to take an interest in the poetry actually being written, but even had we been, I doubt whether we should have thought of entering into correspondence with the authors. Some of the juvenile correspondence I receive seems to be instigated by the teachers, but the greater part does not. Indeed, some of my letters, I suspect, are inspired by a desire to score off teacher in the hope of getting some statement from the horse's mouth which will be a direct contradiction of what has been taught. (I confess that this last type of letter is one which I sometimes take pleasure in answering—when teacher seems to me to have been wrong.) But my point is that this pressure upon the poet from young people who have been compelled to read his work is a modern phenomenon. I don't believe that Tennyson and Browning, Longfellow and Whittier (to say nothing of Poe and Whitman, poets whose works we did not study) were embarrassed by juvenile correspondence choking up their letter boxes. The teaching of the contemporary literature, the introduction of the young to poetry by living poets, is something that came about in my time without my being aware of what was happening. I have had other surprises of this kind. When I returned to give a course of lectures at Harvard in 1932, after seventeen years' absence from America, I looked out of my window and saw a bird which arrested my attention because it looked like a starling. As a boy I had been an eager bird-watcher, and I knew most of the resident and migratory birds of New England, but I knew no bird with that peculiar stumpy tail. On inquiry, I found that it *was* a starling: that bird had arrived and multiplied in America while I wasn't looking. The starling has come to stay, and so, I think, has the academic study of the work of living authors.

I do not wish to suggest that I deplore the introduction of the young, as a part of their education, to the work of living authors—to the work of *some* living authors. Nor am I suggesting that I think that the methods of teaching are altogether wrong. All I aim to indicate is that the teaching of contemporary poetry is a difficult task, and that contemporary poetry cannot be taught by exactly the same methods as are suitable for poetry of the past. And I mean by "poetry of the past" the poetry of any period as soon as that period has become a part of history. The teacher who aims at teaching pupils to appreciate contemporary poetry, to distinguish between the good and the bad, the genuine and the spurious, the original and the imitative, to enjoy the best and only the best, needs himself to have both enthusiasm and discrimination. He needs to be as well educated, as scholarly in his knowledge of the literature of the past, as the teacher who confines his tuition to the literature of the past; and he needs independent good taste.

POETRY AS HISTORY

I am not suggesting that to teach the curriculum as it was taught when I was a boy, we can dispense with enthusiasm and good taste. But that curriculum was limited to authors whose place had been pretty well fixed by the judgment of time. It included a couple of plays of Shakespeare, several of Milton's minor poems, and selections from standard English and American authors down to the latter part of the nineteenth century. These were authors of whose works, it could be assumed, no educated man should be wholly ignorant. And here, as I have already asserted, is the important difference: the poetry of the past is already a part of history. No man can be called educated if ignorant of the history of his own country, or his own race, or his own language: indeed we should know something of the history of civilization, of the struggle of man to raise himself from savagery to the condition of the highest triumphs of the arts and sciences, of religion and morals. And our historical knowledge of any past age is incomplete unless we know something of the literature of that age. To enter imaginatively into the life of men in a past age we need everything we can learn from their literature, and particularly from their poetry, of the way they thought and felt. Thus, the teacher of the literature of the past may find his task to be primarily that of an historian, though he should also be a lover of that literature and have the capacity to communicate his feeling for it to his pupils. But the poetry of the present, the best of which *will become* a part of history, cannot be studied in exactly the same way as the poetry which is already history.

Let me at this point consider first the drawbacks to that school study of the poetry of the past which ignores the fact that poetry is something which *goes on being written,* which is being written now while the pupils are sitting at their desks construing *L'Allegro* or *Il Penseroso,* and that the poet hopes that people will read it for enjoyment. And then let me consider the disadvantages of over-emphasis upon actuality which ignores the fact that much of the poetry written in the same language in the past is as good as, and that some of it is better than, what is being written now.

The great weakness of the method by which I was introduced—academically introduced, I mean—to English poetry was that it did not help me to enjoy it. I think that many people have suffered in the same way from their introduction to the plays of Shakespeare: I took a dislike to *Julius Caesar* which lasted, I am sorry to say, until I saw the film of Marlon Brando and John Gielgud, and a dislike to *The Merchant of Venice* which persists to this day. Perhaps the fact that I had to memorize and declaim, in front of the class, Antony's oration and Portia's quality of mercy, and that I was a very poor declaimer, may have had something to do with it. But I also disliked *L'Allegro* and *Il Penseroso*. I am thankful that I did not have to study *Lycidas* in the same way. Coleridge's *Ancient Mariner* barely survived. I have no fault to find with our teacher. We had examinations to pass; and it was his business to see that we should be able to answer the questions.

I do not know that there is any better way of studying English literature at that stage; and it may be that a few plays and poems must be sacrificed in order that we may learn that English literature exists, and that an orderly historical acquaintance with it is desirable. We also, I remember, had a history book of English literature to study, and we had to learn something about the great writers of every period from the Age of Shakespeare to the end of the nineteenth century. The knowledge that we acquired served a purpose; and I do not believe it would have served that purpose so well if the emphasis had been on appreciation instead of on an orderly outline of literature and some information about the chief historical reputations. After all, how many boys and girls of thirteen or fourteen can appreciate Shakespeare or Milton? I didn't.

THE DISCOVERY OF POETRY

I think I have mentioned somewhere among my essays that my first experience of intense excitement from poetry came when I was fourteen, and came, not from anything put in my way by my work at school, but by happening to pick up at home a copy of FitzGerald's *Omar Khayyám*. And, at the risk of repeating myself, I will suggest that it is at or on the approach of puberty that a boy or girl may suddenly discover that poetry is capable of giving a kind of delight hitherto wholly unsuspected. Very likely this illumination will come as the sudden shock of a particular poem: a poem discovered by oneself or presented by an older person or by one's teacher. But it will probably not be one of the poems that one has had to study in a school text supported by notes (and for passing examinations the notes may be more important than the text!). I am not sorry that I was made to study certain things of Shakespeare and Milton in the way I have described. But the discovery of poetry is a different experience altogether, and the discovery may be more important than the poem through which we make the discovery. Our first "discovery" of poetry—say at fourteen or fifteen or sixteen—may be through a poem of which, after our acquaintance is wider and our taste more developed, we cease to think very highly.

There are, in fact, some poems and some poets whose function seems to be to awaken our capacity for enjoyment, to retire later on to a lower (but still, most often, honorable) place. The earlier poems of Byron, for instance; *The Shropshire Lad* of A. E. Housman; the poems of Rupert Brooke. The greatest poets are those whom we have to grow up to and whose work we appreciate more fully as we mature. At sixteen I discovered (by reading a section of our history of English literature which we were *not* required to read) Thomson's *The City of Dreadful Night* and the poems of Ernest Dowson. Each was a new and vivid experience. But *The City of Dreadful Night* or Dowson's *Impenitentia Ultima* would hardly, even today, be considered suitable for academic study at the age I have in mind. It is in fact *necessary* to choose works by the greatest writers for us to study at an age which we are not yet mature enough to enjoy them.

THE TRAINING OF TASTE

Let me now consider the situation when our emphasis, in teaching children of the same ages, is on enjoyment rather than on information, and upon contemporary poets rather than upon a selection of the great classics. This offers the teacher greater liberty, but prepares for him greater pitfalls. That rough and ready valuation, ordinarily called "the verdict of history," has not yet been passed, and the teacher must follow his own judgment as to what poets, and what poems, he should choose for initiating his pupils into the delights of poetry. There is plenty of contemporary poetry to serve the purpose. But opinion about the relative importance of living poets can vary widely, even among persons of taste, apart from the permanent chasm between those who lean towards what is called "traditional" verse and those who prefer the "experimental." And the successful teacher, who teaches the poetry of his choice with enthusiasm, will be in danger of implanting his own personal tastes in the minds of his pupils, or (what is worse) teaching them to parrot opinions which they are too passive to share. But even if we postulate an ideal teacher of impeccable taste—and I have never known anyone incapable of going wrong at one time or another about living authors, and I include myself in this universal fallibility—that teacher could rouse enthusiasm but could do little to train taste and understanding. For without some knowledge of the poetry of the past and enjoyment of what we know, we cannot really appreciate the poetry of the present.

The dangers of a concentration of interest upon contemporary poetry appears most clearly and painfully when the reader aspires to write poetry himself, or herself. I have never judged a poetry competition, but I have known those who have. One friend who had on one occasion undertaken to read a great number of such contributions was appalled by the evidence of the meagerness of the contestants' knowledge of poetry of the past. Most aspirants had some acquaintance with the poetry of John Donne; a good many had read poems by Blake; and coming down to recent times, they were familiar with the work of Gerard Manley Hopkins and William Butler Yeats. There are would-be poets who write regular verse with, at best, dull metronomic accuracy: modern poetry is unknown to them. There are others who write "free verse" with an ear untrained by the practice of regular verse: they have probably dieted solely on contemporary verse.

PAST AND PRESENT

It is not, however, for students who aspire to write poetry, but simply with those capable of becoming intelligent and sensitive readers, that I am chiefly concerned. I maintain that no one can go very far in the discerning enjoyment of poetry who is incapable of enjoying any poetry other than that of his own place and time. It is in fact a part of the function of education to help us to escape—not from our own time, for we are all bound by that—but from the intellectual and emotional limitations of our own time. It is a commonplace that we appreciate our home all the more fully and consciously after foreign travel; it is not such a commonplace to assert that we can appreciate the poetry of our own time better for knowing and enjoying the best poetry of previous ages. We understand and appreciate our own language the better for having some command of a foreign language. Those whose knowledge of poetry in the English language extends no further than to the immediate precursors of the poetry of our time, such as Hopkins and Yeats, or whose knowledge of the past is limited to the poetry extolled by some persuasive critic of the day (like myself), are limited in their understanding of the poetry that they do know. If, as I believe, poetry plays an important part in the process of education, then these readers are uneducated.

You may think at this point that I have reached an *impasse*. On the one hand, the historical approach to English and American literature, with obligatory reading, of a selection of classics, seems unlikely to awaken any appetite or curiosity that would lead to independent reading; nor does it present poetry and prose as living arts. On the other hand, the study of contemporary poetry, while it may be an immediate stimulant, may encourage a provincialism of taste—for provincialism in *time* is as deplorable as provincialism in *place*—which is the opposite of educative.

To me it seems that the two ways of approach to poetry should be combined, so that young people might be brought to see literature—and poetry especially—both in its historical aspect and in its actuality as a permanent heritage and as something which is still going on, as a necessary part of knowledge and as something to be enjoyed. Here are involved two different, though related meanings of the word *understanding*. In the teaching of the great literature of the past, *understanding* is primarily what ensues from a knowledge of historical and biographical facts, the conditions under which a masterpiece was written, the peculiarities of idiom and vocabulary which mark it as of a different age from ours, etc. In approaching a contemporary work, a poem by a living poet, our understanding is primarily a matter of insight. I know of one teacher who, without any preliminary explanation, played to her pupils a gramophone record of a poem by a living poet. She played it twice and then told her girls to write down their feelings and impressions, to put in words as well as they could what this poem had meant to them. And I know that for one of her pupils at least—they were girls of fourteen—the impression that this poem made upon her opened the path to understanding not only of other poems of the same poet, but to poetry of earlier times, indeed to all poetry. And the teacher had not told the class that they were to admire this poem, still less what they were to admire about it; least of all had she given any hint as to what it was about or what it meant. She had chosen wisely and with taste, but had left the poem to do its own work.

This incident seems to me to suggest that at that age—from fourteen to sixteen I should say—when the sensibility begins, if ever, to respond passionately to poetry, the poetry of our own age may be able to make a more immediate impact than that of earlier generations. It is not merely that there are no difficulties of style and idiom; not merely that there is less oppression by the mass of critical opinion. There is more than enough of the latter: and may I suggest in passing that the young should be encouraged to read poetry by living poets rather than books about contemporary poetry—that they should know and love certain poetry before they read *about* that poetry. I think that young people often recognize obscurely that the poet speaking to them is of their own time and that his sensibility and theirs have something in common.

THE IDEAL TEACHER

I do not believe that the work of living poets should be taught formally. I do not believe that youngsters should take examinations in it. I think that the choice of poems to present to a class should represent the taste of the teacher, not be set by a board. Unless the teacher is a person who reads poetry for enjoyment, he or she cannot stimulate pupils to enjoy it. Nor should the young have a great deal of contemporary verse forced upon them; at this stage we are not concerned to equip young people with a familiarity with the names of all the living poets of reputation, but with starting them on the way to enjoying poetry.

I am assuming, of course, that the teacher who introduces them to modern poetry will be the same teacher who takes them through their annotated textbooks of the classics and who wants them to pass their examination on these texts with credit. Perhaps I am merely clamouring for the Ideal Teacher. But don't "educationists" sometimes forget, in their teaching about teaching, that the one essential for good teaching is the good teacher? The good teacher then will instruct his or her pupils well in the historical understanding of literature, and at the same time will lead those of them who have the capacity to see that the literature of the past, about which the educated person must be informed as a part of history, is also literature to be enjoyed, and that without enjoyment it is meaningless. The good teacher will make pupils aware that literature is a continuous activity, and that more literature is being made even while they are busy with that of the past. In introducing the pupils to modern poetry that the teacher likes, he will be reminding them of the essential part of enjoyment. For it doesn't matter so much, in my opinion, that the teacher's enthusiasm should be aroused by the very best contemporary poetry —in other words, the poetry of which I myself approve—as that the enthusiasm should be infectious. The pupils capable of developing good taste will eventually discover for themselves the better poetry, and as for the others it is probably better that they should like the second rate, the unoriginal, than that they should not like any poetry at all.

My Ideal Teacher, accordingly, will teach the prescribed classics of literature as history, as a part of history which every educated person should know something about whether he likes it or not; and then he should lead some of the pupils to enjoyment and the rest at least to the point of recognizing that there are other persons who do enjoy it. And he will introduce the pupils to contemporary poetry by exciting enjoyment: enjoyment first and understanding second. It may be only by reading such poetry to them as an extracurricular activity, or it may be by a reading or a gramophone record, and then asking the class to set down impressions and reactions. I think that such an introduction to poetry is justifiable even for those pupils who never come to show any love for poetry or any intelligent and sensitive appreciation of it. And the pupils who have some aptitude for enjoyment and understanding of what is good in literature (and as this is a question of degree, there can be no clear division between the sheep and the goats) will find that their knowledge of the great poetry which has had the approval of successive generations will sharpen their discrimination and refine their enjoyment of the poetry which is being written in their own time, and their enjoyment of the poetry written in their own time will help them towards enjoyment of the classics of literature. For our own poetry of today and that of our forefathers, the foundations upon which we build and without which our poetry would not be what it is, will eventually be seen as forming one harmonious whole.

PART V

SCIENCE

The Nature of Science

CHARLES PEIRCE

•

How to Make Our Ideas Clear[1]

[This second paper was originally written in French for the *Revue Philosophique* in 1877, and appeared with a translation of the first paper in Volumes 6 and 7 (December 1878 and January 1879) of that French periodical. Perhaps no earlier and clearer presentation of the "operationalist" theory of meaning can be found in American philosophy, and no bolder claim to improve upon Descartes' method of *a priori* appeal to self-evidence and Leibniz's method of abstract definition. These first two levels of clarity are limited by the fact that what is evident to one mind may not be so to another, and by the fact that "nothing new can ever be learned by analyzing definitions." Peirce's third and highest level of clarification appears in his maxim that the whole meaning of any idea is to be found in considering what effects that "might conceivably have practical bearings, we conceive the object of our conception to have." This operational and pragmatic maxim renders meaningless any notion that there is something more to the meaning of electricity than the sum total of its possible effects on observable objects like magnetized wires or ionized substances or a shocked animal. Any hypothesis about electricity is meaningful to the extent that it specifies what we must do to observe certain effects predesignated by the hypothesis. So also, a personality, dead or alive, has his meaning preserved in his effects on other living persons and in the changes he has wrought in his environment. Consider Emerson's notion that an institution is the shadow of a great man, and Peirce's theory can be seen to have its illustrations in the human as well as in the physical domain from which he

[1] From Wiener, Philip P. (ed.), *Values in a Universe of Chance: Selected Writings of C. S. Peirce.* (Stanford University Press, Stanford, California, 1958), pp. 114–136. Reprinted as *Charles S. Peirce: Selected Writings* edited by Philip P. Wiener by Dover Publications, Inc., New York, 1966.

draws his illustrations (hardness, force, reality). "Truth" means that opinion which investigators are bound to come to in the long run, and the object of their convergent opinion would be the meaning of "reality."]

I

Whoever has looked into a modern treatise on logic of the common sort, will doubtless remember the two distinctions between *clear* and *obscure* conceptions, and between *distinct* and *confused* conceptions. They have lain in the books now for nigh two centuries, unimproved and unmodified, and are generally reckoned by logicians as among the gems of their doctrine.

A clear idea is defined as one which is so apprehended that it will be recognized wherever it is met with, and so that no other will be mistaken for it. If it fails of this clearness, it is said to be obscure.

This is rather a neat bit of philosophical terminology; yet, since it is clearness that they were defining, I wish the logicians had made their definition a little more plain. Never to fail to recognize an idea, and under no circumstances to mistake another for it, let it come in how recondite a form it may, would indeed imply such prodigious force and clearness of intellect as is seldom met with in this world. On the other hand, merely to have such an acquaintance with the idea as to have become familiar with it, and to have lost all hesitancy in recognizing it in ordinary cases, hardly seems to deserve the name of clearness of apprehension, since after all it only amounts to a subjective feeling of mastery which may be entirely mistaken. I take it, however, that when the logicians speak of "clearness," they mean nothing more than such a familiarity with an idea, since they regard the quality as but a small merit, which needs to be supplemented by another, which they call *distinctness*.

A distinct idea is defined as one which contains nothing which is not clear. This is technical language; by the *contents* of an idea logicians understand whatever is contained in its definition. So that an idea is *distinctly* apprehended, according to them, when we can give a precise definition of it, in abstract terms. Here the professional logicians leave the subject; and I would not have troubled the reader with what they have to say if it were not such a striking example of how they have been slumbering through ages of intellectual activity, listlessly disregarding the enginery of modern thought, and never dreaming of applying its lessons to the improvement of logic. It is easy to show that the doctrine that familiar use and abstract distinctness make the perfection of apprehension, has its only true place in philosophies which have long been extinct; and it is now time to formulate the method of attaining to a more perfect clearness of thought, such as we see and admire in the thinkers of our own time.

When Descartes set about the reconstruction of philosophy, his first step was to (theoretically) permit skepticism and to discard the practice of the schoolmen of looking to authority as the ultimate source of truth. That done, he sought a more natural fountain of true principles, and professed to find it in the human mind; thus passing, in the directest way, from the method of authority to that of apriority, as described in my first paper. Self-consciousness was to furnish us with our fundamental truths, and to decide what was agreeable to reason. But since, evidently, not all ideas are true, he was led to note, as the first condition of infallibility, that they must be clear. The distinction between an idea *seeming* clear and really being so, never occurred to him. Trusting to introspection, as he did, even for a knowledge of external things, why should he question its testimony in respect to the contents of our own minds? But then, I suppose, seeing men, who seemed to be quite clear and positive, holding opposite opinions upon fundamental principles, he was further led to say that clearness of ideas is not sufficient, but that they need also to be distinct, i.e., to have nothing unclear about them. What he probably meant by this (for he did not explain himself with precision) was that they must sustain the test of dialectical examination; that they must not only seem clear at the outset, but that discussion must never be able to bring to light points of obscurity connected with them.

Such was the distinction of Descartes, and one sees that it was precisely on the level of his philosophy. It was somewhat developed by Leibniz. This great and singular genius was as remarkable for what he failed to see as for what he saw. That a piece of mechanism could not do work perpetually without being fed with power in some form, was a thing perfectly apparent to him; yet he did not understand that the machinery of the mind can only transform knowledge, but never originate it, unless it be fed with facts of observation. He thus missed the most essential point of the Cartesian philosophy, which is, that to accept propositions which seem perfectly evident to us is a thing which, whether it be logical or illogical, we cannot help doing. Instead of regarding the matter in this way, he sought to reduce the first principles of science to formulas which cannot be denied without self-contradiction, and was apparently unaware of the great difference between his position and that of Descartes.[2] So he reverted to the old formalities of logic, and, above all, abstract definitions played a great part in his philosophy. It was quite natural, therefore, that on observing that the method of Descartes labored under the difficulty that we may seem to ourselves to have clear apprehensions of ideas which in truth are very hazy, no better remedy occurred to him than to require an abstract definition of every important term. Accordingly, in adopting the distinction of *clear* and *distinct* notions, he described the latter quality as the clear apprehension of everything contained in the definition; and the books have ever since copied his words. There is no danger that his chimerical scheme will ever again be overvalued. Nothing new can ever be learned by analyzing definitions. Nevertheless, our existing beliefs can be set in order by this process, and

[2] He was, however, above all, one of the minds that grow; while at first he was an extreme nominalist, like Hobbes, and dabbled in the nonsensical and impotent *Ars Magna* of Raymond Lully, he subsequently embraced the law of continuity and other doctrines opposed to nominalism. I speak here of his early views.—1903.

order is an essential element of intellectual economy, as of every other. It may be acknowledged, therefore, that the books are right in making familiarity with a notion the first step toward clearness of apprehension, and the defining of it the second. But in omitting all mention of any higher perspicuity of thought, they simply mirror a philosophy which was exploded a hundred years ago. That much-admired "ornament of logic"—the doctrine of clearness and distinctness—may be pretty enough, but it is high time to relegate to our cabinet of curiosities the antique *bijou*, and to wear about us something better adapted to modern uses.

The very first lesson that we have a right to demand that logic shall teach us is how to make our ideas clear; and a most important one it is, depreciated only by minds who stand in need of it. To know what we think, to be masters of our own meaning, will make a solid foundation for great and weighty thought. It is most easily learned by those whose ideas are meagre and restricted; and far happier they than such as wallow helplessly in a rich mud of conceptions. A nation, it is true, may, in the course of generations, overcome the disadvantage of an excessive wealth of language and its natural concomitant, a vast, unfathomable deep of ideas. We may see it in history, slowly perfecting its literary forms, sloughing at length its metaphysics, and, by virtue of the untirable patience which is often a compensation, attaining great excellence in every branch of mental acquirement. The page of history is not yet unrolled which is to tell us whether such a people will or will not in the long run prevail over one whose ideas (like the words of their language) are few, but which possesses a wonderful mastery over those which it has. For an individual, however, there can be no question that a few clear ideas are worth more than many confused ones. A young man would hardly be persuaded to sacrifice the greater part of his thoughts to save the rest; and the muddled head is the least apt to see the necessity of such a sacrifice. Him we can usually only commiserate, as a person with a congenital defect. Time will help him, but intellectual maturity with regard to clearness comes rather late, an unfortunate arrangement of nature, inasmuch as clearness is of less use to a man settled in life, whose errors have in great measure had their effect, than it would be to one whose path lies before him. It is terrible to see how a single unclear idea, a single formula without meaning, lurking in a young man's head, will sometimes act like an obstruction of inert matter in an artery, hindering the nutrition of the brain, and condemning its victim to pine away in the fullness of his intellectual vigor and in the midst of intellectual plenty. Many a man has cherished for years as his hobby some vague shadow of an idea, too meaningless to be positively false; he has, nevertheless, passionately loved it, has made it his companion by day and by night, and has given to it his strength and his life, leaving all other occupations for its sake, and in short has lived with it and for it, until it has become, as it were, flesh of his flesh and bone of his bone; and then he has waked up some bright morning to find it gone, clean vanished away like the beautiful Melusina of the fable, and the essence of his life gone with it. I have myself known such a man; and who can tell how many histories of circle-squarers, metaphysicians, astrologers, and what not, may not be told in the old German story?

II

The principles set forth in the first of these papers lead, at once, to a method of reaching a clearness of thought of a far higher grade than the "distinctness" of the logicians. We have there found that the action of thought is excited by the irritation of doubt, and ceases when belief is attained; so that the production of belief is the sole function of thought. All these words, however, are too strong for my purpose. It is as if I had described the phenomena as they appear under a mental microscope. Doubt and Belief, as the words are commonly employed, relate to religious or other grave discussions. But here I use them to designate the starting of any question, no matter how small or how great, and the resolution of it. If, for instance, in a horsecar, I pull out my purse and find a five-cent nickel and five coppers, I decide, while my hand is going to the purse, in which way I will pay my fare. To call such a question Doubt, and my decision Belief, is certainly to use words very disproportionate to the occasion. To speak of such a doubt as causing an irritation which needs to be appeased, suggests a temper which is uncomfortable to the verge of insanity. Yet, looking at the matter minutely, it must be admitted that, if there is the least hesitation as to whether I shall pay the five coppers or the nickel (as there will be sure to be, unless I act from some previously contracted habit in the matter), though irritation is too strong a word, yet I am excited to such small mental activity as may be necessary to deciding how I shall act. Most frequently doubts arise from some indecision, however momentary, in our action. Sometimes it is not so. I have, for example, to wait in a railway-station, and to pass the time I read the advertisements on the walls, I compare the advantages of different trains and different routes which I never expect to take, merely fancying myself to be in a state of hesitancy, because I am bored with having nothing to trouble me. Feigned hesitancy, whether feigned for mere amusement or with a lofty purpose, plays a great part in the production of scientific inquiry. However the doubt may originate, it stimulates the mind to an activity which may be slight or energetic, calm or turbulent. Images pass rapidly through consciousness, one incessantly melting into another, until at last, when all is over—it may be in a fraction of a second, in an hour, or after long years—we find ourselves decided as to how we should act under such circumstances as those which occasioned our hesitation. In other words, we have attained belief.

In this process we observe two sorts of elements of consciousness, the distinction between which may best be made clear by means of an illustration. In a piece of music there are the separate notes, and there is the air. A single tone may be prolonged for an hour or a day, and it exists as perfectly in each second of that time as in the whole taken together; so that, as long as it is sounding, it might be present to a sense from which everything in the past was as completely absent as the future itself. But it is different with the air, the performance of which occupies a certain time, during the portions of which only portions of it are played. It consists in an orderliness in the succession of sounds which strike the ear at different times; and to perceive it there must be some continuity of consciousness which makes the events of a lapse of time present to us. We certainly only perceive the air by hearing the separate notes; yet we cannot be said to directly hear it, for we hear only what is present at the instant, and an orderliness of succession cannot exist in an instant. These two sorts of objects, what we are *immediately* conscious of and what we are *mediately* conscious of, are found in all consciousness. Some elements (the sensations) are completely present at every instant so long as they last, while others (like thought) are actions having beginning, middle, and end, and consist in a congruence in the succession of sensations which flow through the mind. They cannot be immediately present to us, but must cover some portion of the past or future. Thought is a thread of melody running through the succession of our sensations.

We may add that just as a piece of music may be written in parts, each part having its own air, so various systems of relationship of succession subsist together between the same sensations. These different systems are distinguished by having different motives, ideas, or functions. Thought is only one such system; for its sole motive, idea, and function is to produce belief, and whatever does not concern that purpose belongs to some other system of relations. The action of thinking may incidentally have other results. It may serve to amuse us, for example, and among *dilettanti* it is not rare to find those who have so perverted thought to the purposes of pleasure that it seems to vex them to think that the questions upon which they delight to exercise it may ever get finally settled; and a positive discovery which takes a favorite subject out of the arena of literary debate is met with ill-concealed dislike. This disposition is the very debauchery of thought. But the soul and meaning of thought, abstracted from the other elements which accompany it, though it may be voluntarily thwarted, can never be made to direct itself toward anything but the production of belief. Thought in action has for its only possible motive the attainment of thought at rest; and whatever does not refer to belief is no part of the thought itself.

And what, then, is belief? It is the demi-cadence which closes a musical phrase in the symphony of our intellectual life. We have seen that it has just three properties: first, it is something that we are aware of; second, it appeases the irritation of doubt; and, third, it involves the establishment in our nature of a rule of action, or, say for short, a *habit*. As it appeases the irritation of doubt, which is the motive for thinking, thought relaxes, and comes to rest for a moment when belief is reached. But, since belief is a rule for action, the application of which involves further doubt and further thought, at the same time that it is a stopping-place, it is also a new starting-place for thought. That is why I have permitted myself to call it thought at rest, although thought is essentially an action. The *final* upshot of thinking is the exercise of volition, and of this thought no longer forms a part; but belief is only a stadium of mental action, an effect upon our nature due to thought, which will influence future thinking.

The essence of belief is the establishment of a habit, and different beliefs are distinguished by the different modes of action to which they give rise. If beliefs do not differ in this respect, if they appease the same doubt by producing the same rule of action, then no mere differences in the manner of consciousness of them can make them different beliefs, any more than playing a tune in different keys is playing different tunes. Imaginary distinctions are often drawn between beliefs which differ only in their mode of expression—the wrangling which ensues is real enough, however. To believe that any objects are arranged among themselves as in Fig. 1, and to believe that they are arranged as in Fig. 2, are one and the same belief; yet it is conceivable that a man should assert

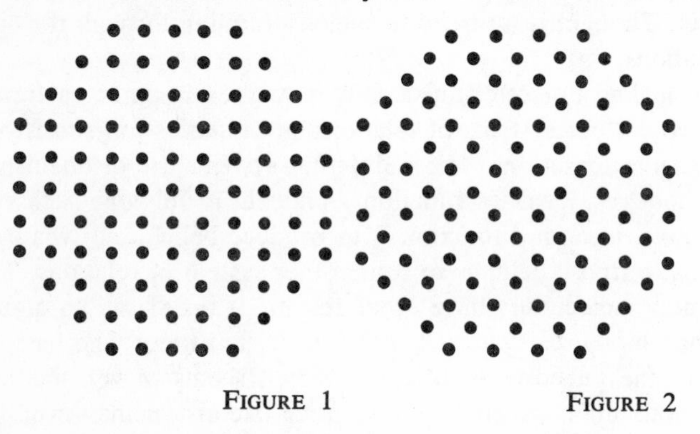

FIGURE 1 FIGURE 2

one proposition and deny the other. Such false distinctions do as much harm as the confusion of beliefs really different, and are among the pitfalls of which we ought constantly to beware, especially when we are upon metaphysical ground. One singular deception of this sort, which often occurs, is to mistake the sensation produced by our own unclearness of thought for a character of the object we are thinking. Instead of perceiving that the obscurity is purely subjective, we fancy that we contemplate a quality of the object which is essentially mysterious; and if our conception be afterward presented to us in a clear form we do not recognize it as the same, owing to the absence of the feeling of unintelligibility. So long as this deception lasts, it obviously puts an impassable barrier in the way of perspicuous thinking; so that it equally interests the opponents of rational thought to perpetuate it, and its adherents to guard against it.

Another such deception is to mistake a mere difference in the grammatical construction of two words for a distinction between the ideas they express. In this pedantic age, when the general mob of writers attend so much more to words than to things, this error is common enough. When I just said that thought is an *action*, and that it consists in a *relation*, although a person performs an action but not a relation, which can only be the result of an action, yet there was no inconsistency in what I said, but only a grammatical vagueness.

From all these sophisms we shall be perfectly safe so long as we reflect that the whole function of thought is to produce habits of action; and that whatever there is connected with a thought, but irrelevant to its purpose, is an accretion to it, but no part of it. If there be a unity among our sensations which has no reference to how we shall act on a given occasion, as when we listen to a piece of music, why, we do not call that thinking. To develop its meaning, we have, therefore, simply to determine what habits it produces, for what a thing means is simply what habits it involves. Now, the identity of a habit depends on how it might lead us to act, not merely under such circumstances as are likely to arise, but under such as might possibly occur, no matter how improbable they may be. What the habit is depends on *when* and *how* it causes us to act. As for the *when*, every stimulus to action is derived from perception; as for the *how*, every purpose of action is to produce some sensible result. Thus, we come down to what is tangible and practical as the root of every real distinction of thought, no matter how subtile it may be; and there is no distinction of meaning so fine as to consist in anything but a possible difference of practice.

To see what this principle leads to, consider in the light of it such a doctrine as that of transubstantiation. The Protestant churches generally hold that the elements of the sacrament are flesh and blood only in a tropical sense; they nourish our souls as meat and the juice of it would our bodies. But the Catholics maintain that they are literally just that, meat and blood; although they possess all the sensible qualities of wafer-cakes and diluted wine. But we can have no conception of wine except what may enter into a belief, either—

1. That this, that, or the other, is wine; or,
2. That wine possesses certain properties.

Such beliefs are nothing but self-notifications that we should, upon occasion, act in regard to such things as we believe to be wine according to the qualities which we believe wine to possess. The occasion of such action would be some sensible perception, the motive of it to produce some sensible result. Thus our action has exclusive reference to what affects the senses, our habit has the same bearing as our action, our belief the same as our habit, our conception the same as our belief; and we can consequently mean nothing by wine but what has certain effects, direct or indirect, upon our senses; and to talk of something as having all the sensible characters of wine, yet being in reality blood, is senseless jargon. Now, it is not my object to pursue the theological question; and having used it as a logical example I drop it, without caring to anticipate the theologian's reply. I only desire to point out how impossible it is that we should have an idea in our minds which relates to anything but conceived sensible effects of things. Our idea of anything *is* our idea of its sensible effects; and if we fancy that we have any other we deceive ourselves, and mistake a mere sensation accompanying the thought for a part of the thought itself. It is absurd to say that thought has any meaning unrelated to its only function. It is foolish for Catholics and Protestants to fancy themselves in disagreement about the elements of the sacrament, if they agree in regard to all their sensible effects, here or hereafter.

It appears, then, that the rule for attaining the third grade of clearness of apprehension is as follows: consider what effects, which might conceivably have practical bearings, we conceive the object of our conception to have. Then, our conception of these effects is the whole of our conception of the object.

III

Let us illustrate this rule by some examples; and, to begin with the simplest one possible, let us ask what we mean by calling a thing *hard*. Evidently that it will not be scratched by many other substances. The whole conception of this quality, as of every other, lies in its conceived effects. There is absolutely no difference between a hard thing and a soft thing so long as they are not brought to the test. Suppose, then, that a diamond could be crystallized in the midst of a cushion of soft cotton, and should remain there until it was finally burned up. Would it be false to say that that diamond was soft? This seems a foolish question, and would be so, in fact, except in the realm of logic. There such questions are often of the greatest utility as serving to bring logical principles into sharper relief than real discussions ever could. In studying logic we must not put them aside with hasty answers, but must consider them with attentive care, in order to make out the principles involved. We may, in the present case, modify our question, and ask what prevents us from saying that all hard bodies remain perfectly soft until they are touched, when their hardness increases with the pressure until they are scratched. Reflection will show that the reply is this: there would be no *falsity* in such modes of speech. They would involve a modification of our present usage of speech with regard to the words "hard" and "soft," but not of their meanings. For they represent no fact to be different from what it is; only they involve arrangements of facts which would be exceedingly maladroit. This leads us to remark that the question of what would occur under circumstances which do not actually arise is not a question of fact, but only of the most perspicuous arrangement of them. For example, the question of free-will and fate in its simplest form, stripped of verbiage, is something like this: I have done something of which I am ashamed; could I, by an effort of the will, have resisted the temptation, and done otherwise? The philosophical reply is that this is not a question of fact, but only of the [possible] arrangement of facts. Arranging them so as to exhibit what is particularly pertinent to my question—namely, that I ought to blame myself for having done wrong—it is perfectly true to say that, if I had willed to do otherwise than I did, I should have done otherwise. On the other hand, arranging the facts so as to exhibit another important consideration, it is equally true that when a temptation has once been allowed to work, it will, if it has a certain force, produce its effect, let me struggle how I may. There is no objection to a contradiction in what would result from a false supposition. The *reductio ad absurdum* consists in showing that contradictory results would follow from a hypothesis which is consequently judged to be false. Many questions are involved in the free-will discussion, and I am far from desiring to say that both sides are equally right. On the contrary, I am of opinion that one side [determinism] denies important facts, and that the other does not. But what I do say is that the above single question was the origin of the whole doubt; that, had it not been for this question, the controversy would never have arisen; and that this question is perfectly solved in the manner which I have indicated.

Let us next seek a clear idea of Weight. This is another very easy case. To say that a body is heavy means simply that, in the absence of opposing force, it will fall. This (neglecting certain specifications of how it will fall, etc., which exist in the mind of the physicist who uses the word) is evidently the whole conception of weight. It is a fair question whether some particular facts may not *account* for gravity; but what we mean by the force itself is completely involved in its effects.

This leads us to undertake an account of the idea of Force in general. This is the great conception which, developed in the early part of the seventeenth century from the rude idea of a cause, and, constantly improved upon since, has shown us how to explain all the changes of motion which bodies experience, and how to think about all physical phenomena; which has given birth to modern science, and changed the face of the globe; and which, aside from its more special uses, has played a principal part in directing the course of modern thought, and in furthering modern social development. It is, therefore, worth some pains to comprehend it. According to our rule, we must begin by asking what is the immediate use of thinking about force; and the answer is that we thus account for changes of motion. If bodies were left to themselves, without the intervention of forces, every motion would continue unchanged both in velocity and in direction. Furthermore, change of motion never takes place abruptly; if its direction is changed, it is always through a curve without angles; if its velocity alters, it is by degrees. The gradual changes which are constantly taking place are conceived by geometers to be compounded together according to the rules of the parallelogram of forces. If the reader does not already know what this is, he will find it, I hope, to his advantage to endeavor to follow the following explanation; but if mathematics are insupportable to him, pray let him skip three paragraphs rather than that we should part company here.

A *path* is a line whose beginning and end are distinguished. Two paths are considered to be equivalent, which, beginning at the same point, lead to the same point. Thus the two paths, *A B C D E* and *A F G H E* (Fig. 3), are equivalent. Paths which do *not* begin at the same point are considered to be equivalent, provided that, on moving either of them without turning it, but keeping it always parallel to its original position, [so that] when its beginning coincides with that of the other path, the ends also coincide. Paths are considered as geometrically added together, when one begins where the other ends; thus the path *A E* is conceived to be a sum of *A B, B C, C D,* and *D E.* In the parallelogram of Fig. 4 the diagonal *A C* is the sum of *A B* and *B C;* or, since *A D* is geometrically equivalent to *B C, A C* is the geometrical sum of *A B* and *A D.*

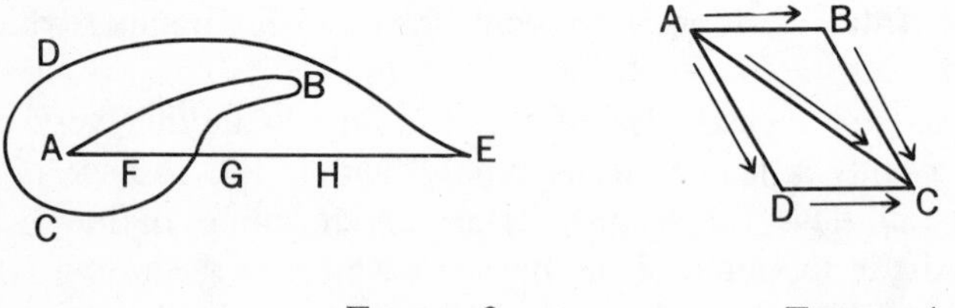

FIGURE 3 FIGURE 4

All this is purely conventional. It simply amounts to this: that we choose to call paths having the relations I have described equal or added. But, though it is a convention, it is a convention with a good reason. The rule for geometrical addition may be applied not only to paths, but to any other things which can be represented by paths. Now, as a path is determined by the varying direction and distance of the point which moves over it from the starting-point, it follows that anything which from its beginning to its end is determined by a varying direction and a varying magnitude is capable of being represented by a line. Accordingly, *velocities* may be represented by lines, for they have only directions and rates. The same thing is true of *accelerations,* or changes of velocities. This is evident enough in the case of velocities; and it becomes evident for accelerations if we consider that precisely what velocities are to positions—namely, states of change of them—that accelerations are to velocities.

The so-called "parallelogram of forces" is simply a rule for compounding accelerations. The rule is, to represent the accelerations by paths, and then to geometrically add the paths. The geometers, however, not only use the "parallelogram of forces" to compound different accelerations, but also to resolve one acceleration into a sum of several. Let *A B* (Fig. 5) be the path which represents a certain accleration—say, such a change in the motion of a body that at the end of one second the body will, under the influence of that change, be in a position different from what it would have had if its motion had continued unchanged, such that a path equivalent to *A B* would lead from the latter position to the former. This acceleration may be considered as the sum of the accelerations represented by *A C* and *C B*. It may also be considered as the sum of the very different accelerations represented by *A D* and *D B*, where *A D* is almost the opposite of *A C*. And it is clear that there is an immense variety of ways in which *A B* might be resolved into the sum of two accelerations.

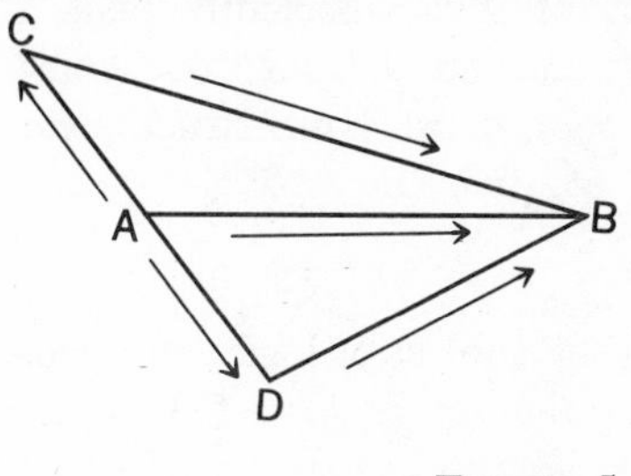

FIGURE 5

After this tedious explanation, which I hope, in view of the extraordinary interest of the conception of force, may not have exhausted the reader's patience, we are prepared at last to state the grand fact which this conception embodies. This fact is that if the actual changes of motion which the different particles of bodies experience are each resolved in its appropriate way, each component acceleration is precisely such as is prescribed by a certain law of Nature, according to which bodies in the relative positions which the bodies in question actually have at the moment,[3] always receive certain accelerations, which, being compounded by geometrical addition, give the acceleration which the body actually experiences.

This is the only fact which the idea of force represents, and whoever will take the trouble clearly to apprehend what this fact is perfectly comprehends what force is. Whether we ought to say that a force *is* an acceleration, or that it *causes* an acceleration, is a mere question of propriety of language, which has no more to do with our real meaning than the difference between the French idiom *"Il fait froid"* and its English equivalent *"It is cold."* Yet it is surprising to see how this simple affair has muddled men's minds. In how many profound treatises is not force spoken of as a "mysterious entity," which seems to be only a way of confessing that the author despairs of ever getting a clear notion of what the word means! In a recent, admired work on *Analytic Mechanics* [by Kirchhoff] it is stated that we understand precisely the effect of force, but what force itself is we do not understand! This is simply a self-contradiction. The idea which the word "force" excites

[3] Possibly the velocities also have to be taken into account.

in our minds has no other function than to affect our actions, and these actions can have no reference to force otherwise than through its effects. Consequently, if we know what the effects of force are, we are acquainted with every fact which is implied in saying that a force exists, and there is nothing more to know. The truth is, there is some vague notion afloat that a question may mean something which the mind cannot conceive; and when some hair-splitting philosophers have been confronted with the absurdity of such a view, they have invented an empty distinction between positive and negative conceptions, in the attempt to give their non-idea a form not obviously nonsensical. The nullity of it is sufficiently plain from the considerations given a few pages back; and, apart from those considerations, the quibbling character of the distinction must have struck every mind accustomed to real thinking.

IV

Let us now approach the subject of logic, and consider a conception which particularly concerns it, that of *reality*. Taking clearness in the sense of familiarity, no idea could be clearer than this. Every child uses it with perfect confidence, never dreaming that he does not understand it. As for clearness in its second grade, however, it would probably puzzle most men, even among those of a reflective turn of mind, to give an abstract definition of the real. Yet such a definition may perhaps be reached by considering the points of difference between reality and its opposite, fiction. A figment is a product of somebody's imagination; it has such characters as his thought impresses upon it. That those characters are independent of how you or I think is an external reality. There are, however, phenomena within our own minds, dependent upon our thought, which are at the same time real in the sense that we really think them. But though their characters depend on how we think, they do not depend on what we think those characters to be. Thus, a dream has a real existence as a mental phenomenon, if somebody has really dreamt it; that he dreamt so and so, does not depend on what anybody thinks was dreamt, but is completely independent of all opinion on the subject. On the other hand, considering, not the fact of dreaming, but the thing dreamt, it retains its peculiarities by virtue of no other fact than that it was dreamt to possess them. Thus we may define the real as that whose characters are independent of what anybody may think them to be.

But, however satisfactory such a definition may be found, it would be a great mistake to suppose that it makes the idea of reality perfectly clear. Here, then, let us apply our rules. According to them, reality, like every other quality, consists in the peculiar, sensible effects which things partaking of it produce. The only effect which real things have is to cause belief, for all the sensations which they excite emerge into consciousness in the form of beliefs. The question, therefore, is, how is true belief (or belief in the real) distinguished from false belief (or belief in fiction). Now, as we have seen in the former paper, the ideas of truth and falsehood, in their full development, appertain exclusively to the scientific method of settling opinion. A person who arbitrarily chooses the propositions which he will adopt can use the word truth only to emphasize the expression of his determination to hold on to his choice. Of course, the method of tenacity never prevailed exclusively; reason is too natural to men for that. But in the literature of the Dark Ages we find some fine examples of it. When Scotus Erigena is commenting upon a poetical passage in which hellebore is spoken of as having caused the death of Socrates, he does not hesitate to inform the inquiring reader that Helleborus and Socrates were two eminent Greek philosophers, and that the latter having been overcome in argument by the former took the matter to heart and died of it! What sort of an idea of truth could a man have who could adopt and teach, without the qualification of a "perhaps," an opinion taken so entirely at random? The real spirit of Socrates, who I hope would have been delighted to have been "overcome in argument," because he would have learned something by it, is in curious contrast with the naïve idea of the glossist, for whom (as for the "born missionary" of today) discussion would seem to have been simply a struggle. When philosophy began to awake from its long slumber, and before theology completely dominated it, the practice seems to have been for each professor to seize upon any philosophical position he found unoccupied and which seemed a strong one, to intrench himself in it, and to sally forth from time to time to give battle to the others. Thus, even the scanty records we possess of those disputes enable us to make out a dozen or more opinions held by different teachers at one time concerning the question of nominalism and realism. Read the opening part of the *Historia Calamitatum* of Abélard, who was certainly as philosophical as any of his contemporaries, and see the spirit of combat which it breathes. For him, the truth is simply his particular stronghold. When the method of authority prevailed, the truth meant little more than the Catholic faith. All the efforts of scholastic doctors are directed toward harmonizing their faith in Aristotle and their faith in the Church, and one may search their ponderous folios through without finding an argument which goes any further. It is noticeable that where different faiths flourish side by side, renegades are looked upon with contempt even by the party whose belief they adopt; so completely has the idea of loyalty replaced that of truth-seeking. Since the time of Descartes, the defect in the conception of truth has been less apparent. Still, it will sometimes strike a scientific man that the philosophers have been less intent on finding out what the facts are than on inquiring what belief is most in harmony with their system. It is hard to convince a follower of the *a priori* method by adducing facts; but show him that an opinion he is defending is inconsistent with what he has laid down elsewhere, and he will be very apt to retract it. These minds do not seem to believe that disputation is ever to cease; they seem to think that the opinion which is natural for one man is not so for another, and that belief will, consequently, never be settled. In contenting themselves with fixing their own opinions by a method which would lead another man to a different result, they betray their feeble hold of the conception of what truth is.

On the other hand, all the followers of science are fully persuaded that the processes of investigation, if only pushed far enough, will give one certain solution to each question to which they can be applied. One man may investigate the velocity of light by studying the transits of Venus and the aberration of the stars; another by the oppositions of Mars and the eclipses of Jupiter's satellites; a third by the method of Fitzeau; a fourth by that of Foucault; a fifth by the motions of the curves of Lissajous; a sixth, a seventh, an eighth, and a ninth, may follow the different methods of comparing the measures of statical and dynamical electricity. They may at first obtain different results, but, as each perfects his method and his processes, the results will move steadily together toward a destined center. So with all scientific research. Different minds may set out with the most antagonistic views, but the progress of investigation carries them by a force outside of themselves to one and the same conclusion. This activity of thought by which we are carried, not where we wish, but to a foreordained goal, is like the operation of destiny. No modification of the point of view taken, no selection of other facts for study, no natural bent of mind even, can enable a man to escape the predestinate opinion. This great law is embodied in the conception of truth and reality. The opinion which is fated[4] to be ultimately agreed to by all who investigate is what we mean by the truth, and the object represented in this opinion is the real. That is the way I would explain reality.

But it may be said that this view is directly opposed to the abstract definition which we have given of reality, inasmuch as it makes the characters of the real depend on what is ultimately thought about them. But the answer to this is that, on the one hand, reality is independent, not necessarily of thought in general, but only of what you or I or any finite number of men may think about it; and that, on the other hand, though the object of the final opinion depends on what that opinion is, yet what the opinion is does not depend on what you or I or any man thinks. Our perversity and that of others may indefinitely postpone the settlement of opinion; it might even conceivably cause an arbitrary proposition to be universally accepted as long as the human race should last. Yet even that would not change the nature of the belief, which alone could be the result of investigation carried sufficiently far; and if, after the extinction of our race, another should arise with faculties and disposition for investigation, that true opinion must be the one which they would ultimately come to. "Truth crushed to earth shall

[4] Fate means merely that which is sure to come true, and can nohow be avoided. It is a superstition to suppose that a certain sort of events are ever fated, and it is another to suppose that the word "fate" can never be freed from its superstitious taint. We are all fated to die.

rise again," and the opinion which would finally result from investigation does not depend on how anybody may actually think. But the reality of that which is real does[5] depend on the real fact that investigation is destined to lead, at last, if continued long enough, to a belief in it.

But I may be asked what I have to say to all the minute facts of history, forgotten never to be recovered, to the lost books of the ancients, to the buried secrets.

> "Full many a gem of purest ray serene
> The dark, unfathomed caves of ocean bear;
> Full many a flower is born to blush unseen,
> And waste its sweetness on the desert air."

Do these things not really exist because they are hopelessly beyond the reach of our knowledge? And then, after the universe is dead (according to the prediction of some scientists), and all life has ceased forever, will not the shock of atoms continue though there will be no mind to know it? To this I reply that, though in no possible state of knowledge can any number be great enough to express the relation between the amount of what rests unknown to the amount of the known, yet it is unphilosophical to suppose that, with regard to any given question (which has any clear meaning), investigation would not bring forth a solution of it, if it were carried far enough. Who would have said, a few years ago, that we could ever know of what substances stars are made whose light may have been longer in reaching us than the human race has existed? Who can be sure of what we shall not know in a few hundred years? Who can guess what would be the result of continuing the pursuit of science for ten thousand years, with the activity of the last hundred? And if it were to go on for a million, or a billion, or any number of years you please, how is it possible to say that there is any question which might not ultimately he solved?

But it may be objected, "Why make so much of these remote considerations, especially when it is your principle that only practical distinctions have a meaning?" Well, I must confess that it makes very little difference whether we say that a stone on the bottom of the ocean, in complete darkness, is brilliant or not—that is to say, that it *probably* makes no difference, remembering always that that stone *may* be fished up tomorrow. But that there are gems at the bottom of the sea, flowers in the untraveled desert, etc., are propositions which, like that about a diamond being hard when it is not pressed, concern much more the arrangement of our language than they do the meaning of our ideas.

It seems to me, however, that we have, by the application of our rule, reached so clear an apprehension of what we mean by reality, and of the

[5] In the French version, of which this essay is a translation, "does not depend" (*ne dépend pas*); cf. *Revue Philosophique,* "Comment rendre nos idées claires" (Jan. 1879), p. 56.—Editor's note.

fact which the idea rests on, that we should not, perhaps, be making a pretension so presumptuous as it would be singular, if we were to offer a metaphysical theory of existence for universal acceptance among those who employ the scientific method of fixing belief. However, as metaphysics is a subject much more curious than useful, the knowledge of which, like that of a sunken reef, serves chiefly to enable us to keep clear of it, I will not trouble the reader with any more Ontology at this moment.[6] I have already been led much further into that path than I should have desired; and I have given the reader such a dose of mathematics, psychology, and all that is most abstruse, that I fear he may already have left me, and that what I am now writing is for the compositor and proofreader exclusively. I trusted to the importance of the subject. There is no royal road to logic, and really valuable ideas can only be had at the price of close attention. But I know that in the matter of ideas the public prefer the cheap and nasty; and in my next paper I am going to return to the easily intelligible, and not wander from it again. The reader who has been at the pains of wading through this paper shall be rewarded in the next one by seeing how beautifully what has been developed in this tedious way can be applied to the ascertainment of the rules of scientific reasoning.

We have, hitherto, not crossed the threshold of scientific logic. It is certainly important to know how to make our ideas clear, but they may be ever so clear without being true. How to make them so, we have next to study. How to give birth to those vital and procreative ideas which multiply into a thousand forms and diffuse themselves everywhere, advancing civilization and making the dignity of man, is an art not yet reduced to rules, but of the secret of which the history of science affords some hints.

[6] The French version ends here.—Editor's note.

Physical Science

ARTHUR STANLEY EDDINGTON

•

The Evolution of the Physical World[1]

Looking back through the long past we picture the beginning of the world —a primeval chaos which time has fashioned into the universe that we know. Its vastness appalls the mind; space boundless though not infinite, according to the strange doctrine of science. The world was without form and almost void. But at the earliest stage we can contemplate the void is sparsely broken by tiny electric particles, the germs of the things that are to be; positive and negative they wander aimlessly in solitude, rarely coming near enough to seek or shun one another. They range everywhere so that all space is filled, and yet so empty that in comparison the most highly exhausted vacuum on earth is a jostling throng. In the beginning was vastness, solitude and the deepest night. Darkness was upon the face of the deep, for as yet there was no light.

The years rolled by, million after million. Slight aggregations occurring casually in one place and another drew to themselves more and more particles. They warred for sovereignty, won and lost their spoil, until the matter was collected round centers of condensation leaving vast empty spaces from which it had ebbed away. Thus gravitation slowly parted the primeval chaos. These first divisions were not the stars but what we should call "island universes" each ultimately to be a system of some thousands of millions of stars. From our own island universe we can discern the other islands as spiral nebulae lying one beyond another as far as the telescope can fathom. The nearest of them is such that light takes 900,000 years to cross the gulf between us. They acquired rotation (we do not yet understand how) which bulged them into flattened form and made them wreathe themselves in spirals. Their forms, diverse, yet with underlying regularity, make a fascinating spectacle for telescopic study.

As it had divided the original chaos, so gravitation subdivided the island universes. First the star clusters, then the stars themselves were separated. And with the stars came light, born of the fiercer turmoil which ensued when the electrical particles were drawn from their solitude into dense throngs. A star is not just a lump of matter casually thrown together in the general confusion; it is of nicely graded size. There is relatively not much more diversity in the

[1] From Arthur Stanley Eddington, *Science and the Unseen World,* 1930, pp. 11–21. Copyright, 1930, by The Macmillan Company. By permission of The Macmillan Company, publishers, and of George Allen & Unwin Ltd., London.

masses of new-born stars than in the masses of new-born babies. Aggregations rather greater than our Sun have a strong tendency to subdivide, but when the mass is reduced a little the danger quickly passes and the impulse to subdivision is satisfied. Here it would seem the work of creation might cease. Having carved chaos into stars, the first evolutionary impulse has reached its goal. For many billions of years the stars may continue to shed their light and heat through the world, feeding on their own matter which disappears bit by bit into aetherial waves.

Not infrequently a star, spinning too fast or strained by the radiant heat imprisoned within it, may divide into two nearly equal stars, which remain yoked together as a double star; apart from this no regular plan of further development is known. For what might be called the second day of creation we turn from the general rule to the exceptions. Amid so many myriads there will be a few which by some rare accident have a fate unlike the rest. In the vast expanse of the heavens the traffic is so thin that a star may reasonably count on travelling for the whole of its long life without serious risk of collision. The risk is negligible for any individual star, but ten thousand million stars in our own system and more in the systems beyond afford a wide playground for chance. If the risk is one in a hundred millions some unlucky victims are doomed to play the role of "one." This rare accident must have happened to our Sun—an accident to the Sun, but to us the cause of our being here. A star journeying through space casually overtook the Sun, not indeed colliding with it, but approaching so close as to raise a great tidal wave. By this disturbance jets of matter spurted out of the Sun; being carried round by their angular momentum they did not fall back again but condensed into small globes—the planets.

By this and similar events there appeared here and there in the universe something outside Nature's regular plan, namely a lump of matter small enough and dense enough to be cool. A temperature of ten million degrees or more prevails through the greater part of the interior of a star; it cannot be otherwise so long as matter remains heaped in immense masses. Thus the design of the first stage of evolution seems to have been that matter should ordinarily be endowed with intense heat. Cool matter appears as an afterthought. It is unlikely that the Sun is the only one of the starry host to possess a system of planets, but it is believed that such development is very rare. In these exceptional formations Nature has tried the experiment of finding what strange effects may ensue if matter is released from its usual temperature of millions of degrees and permitted to be cool.

Out of the electric charges dispersed in the primitive chaos ninety-two different kinds of matter—ninety-two chemical elements—have been built. This building is also a work of evolution, but little or nothing is known as to its history. In the matter which we handle daily we find the original bricks fitted together and cannot but infer that somewhere and somewhen a process of matter-building has occurred. At high temperature this diversity of matter remains as it were latent; little of consequence results from it. But in the cool experimental stations of the universe the differences assert themselves. At root the diversity of the ninety-two elements reflects the diversity of the integers from one to ninety-two; because the chemical characteristics of element No. 11 (sodium) arise from the fact that it has the power at low temperatures of gathering round it eleven negative electric particles; those of No. 12 (magnesium) from its power of gathering twelve particles; and so on.

It is tempting to linger over the development out of this fundamental beginning of the wonders studied in chemistry and physics, but we must hurry on. The provision of certain cool planetary globes was the second impulse of evolution, and it has exhausted itself in the formation of inorganic rocks and ores and other materials. We must look to a new exception or abnormality if anything further is to be achieved. We can scarcely call it an accident that among the integers there should happen to be the number 6; but I do not know how otherwise to express the fact that organic life would not have begun if Nature's arithmetic had overlooked the number 6. The general plan of ninety-two elements, each embodying in its structural pattern one of the first ninety-two numbers, contemplates a material world of considerable but limited diversity; but the element carbon, embodying the number 6, and because of the peculiarity of the number 6, rebels against limits. The carbon atoms love to string themselves in long chains such as those which give toughness to a soap-film. Whilst other atoms organise themselves in twos and threes or it may be in tens, carbon atoms organise themselves in hundreds and thousands. From this potentiality of carbon to form more and more elaborate structures, a third impulse of evolution arises.

I cannot profess to say whether anything more than this prolific structure-building power of carbon is involved in the beginning of life. The story of evolution here passes into the domain of the biological sciences for which I cannot speak, and I am not ready to take sides in the controversy between the Mechanists and the Vitalists. So far as the earth is concerned the history of development of living forms extending over nearly a thousand million years is recorded (though with many breaks) in fossil remains. Looking back over the geological record it would seem that Nature made nearly every possible mistake before she reached her greatest achievement Man—or perhaps some would say her worst mistake of all. At one time she put her trust in armaments and gigantic size. Frozen in the rock is the evidence of her failures to provide a form fitted to endure and dominate—failures which we are only too ready to imitate. At last she tried a being of no great size, almost defenceless, defective in at least one of the more important sense-organs; one gift she bestowed to save him from threatened extinction—a certain stirring, a restlessness, in the organ called the brain.

And so we come to Man.

JOHN MAYNARD KEYNES

•

Newton the Man[1]

It is with some diffidence that I try to speak to you in his own home of Newton *as he was himself*. I have long been a student of the records and had the intention to put my impressions into writing to be ready for Christmas Day 1942, the tercentenary of his birth. The war has deprived me both of leisure to treat adequately so great a theme and of opportunity to consult my library and my papers and to verify my impressions. So if the brief study which I shall lay before you to-day is more perfunctory than it should be, I hope you will excuse me.

One other preliminary matter. I believe that Newton was different from the conventional picture of him. But I do not believe he was less great. He was less ordinary, more extraordinary, than the nineteenth century cared to make him out. Geniuses *are* very peculiar. Let no one here suppose that my object to-day is to lessen, by describing, Cambridge's greatest son. I am trying rather to see him as his own friends and contemporaries saw him. And they without exception regarded him as one of the greatest of men.

In the eighteenth century and since, Newton came to be thought of as the first and greatest of the modern age of scientists, a rationalist, one who taught us to think on the lines of cold and untinctured reason.

I do not see him in this light. I do not think that any one who has pored over the contents of that box which he packed up when he finally left Cambridge in 1696 and which, though partly dispersed, have come down to us, can see him like that. Newton was not the first of the age of reason. He was the last of the magicians, the last of the Babylonians and Sumerians, the last great mind which looked out on the visible and intellectual world with the same eyes as those who began to build our intellectual inheritance rather less than 10,000 years ago. Isaac Newton, a posthumous child born with no father on Christmas Day, 1642, was the last wonder-child to whom the Magi could do sincere and appropriate homage.

Had there been time, I should have liked to read to you the contemporary record of the child Newton. For, though it is well known to his biographers, it has never been published *in extenso*, without comment, just as it stands. Here, indeed, is the makings of a legend of the young magician, a most joyous picture of the opening mind of genius free from the uneasiness, the melancholy and nervous agitation of the young man and student.

[1] Reprinted by permission of the publisher, Horizon Press, from *Essays In Biography* by John Maynard Keynes. Copyright 1951, Horizon Press, Inc. [Address] read by Mr. Geoffrey Keynes at the Newton Tercentenary Celebrations at Trinity College, Cambridge, on 17 July 1946, and therefore not revised by the author who had written it some years earlier.

For in vulgar modern terms Newton was profoundly neurotic of a not unfamiliar type, but—I should say from the records—a most extreme example. His deepest instincts were occult, esoteric, semantic—with profound shrinking from the world, a paralyzing fear of exposing his thoughts, his beliefs, his discoveries in all nakedness to the inspection and criticism of the world. "Of the most fearful, cautious and suspicious temper that I ever knew," said Whiston, his successor in the Lucasian Chair. The too well-known conflicts and ignoble quarrels with Hooke, Flamsteed, Leibnitz are only too clear an evidence of this. Like all his type he was wholly aloof from women. He parted with and published nothing except under the extreme pressure of friends. Until the second phase of his life, he was a wrapt, consecrated solitary, pursuing his studies by intense introspection with a mental endurance perhaps never equalled.

I believe that the clue to his mind is to be found in his unusual powers of continuous concentrated introspection. A case can be made out, as it also can with Descartes, for regarding him as an accomplished experimentalist. Nothing can be more charming than the tales of his mechanical contrivances when he was a boy. There are his telescopes and his optical experiments. These were essential accomplishments, part of his unequalled all-round technique, but not, I am sure, his *peculiar* gift, especially amongst his contemporaries. His peculiar gift was the power of holding continuously in his mind a purely mental problem until he had seen straight through it. I fancy his pre-eminence is due to his muscles of intuition being the strongest and most enduring with which a man has ever been gifted. Anyone who has ever attempted pure scientific or philosophical thought knows how one can hold a problem momentarily in one's mind and apply all one's powers of concentration to piercing through it, and how it will dissolve and escape and you find that what you are surveying is a blank. I believe that Newton could hold a problem in his mind for hours and days and weeks until it surrendered to him its secret. Then being a supreme mathematical technician he could dress it up, how you will, for purposes of exposition, but it was his intuition which was pre-eminently extraordinary—"so happy in his conjectures," said de Morgan, "as to seem to know more than he could possibly have any means of proving." The proofs, for what they are worth, were, as I have said, dressed up afterwards—they were not the instrument of discovery.

There is the story of how he informed Halley of one of his most fundamental discoveries of planetary motion. "Yes," replied Halley, "but how do you know that? Have you proved it?" Newton was taken aback—"Why, I've known it for years," he replied. "If you'll give me a few days, I'll certainly find you a proof of it"—as in due course he did.

Again, there is some evidence that Newton in preparing the *Principia* was held up almost to the last moment by lack of proof that you could treat a solid sphere as though all its mass was concentrated at the centre, and only hit on the proof a year before publication. But this was a truth which he had known for certain and had always assumed for many years.

Certainly there can be no doubt that the peculiar geometrical form in which the exposition of the *Principia* is dressed up bears no resemblance at all to the mental processes by which Newton actually arrived at his conclusions.

His experiments were always, I suspect, a means, not of discovery, but always of verifying what he knew already.

Why do I call him a magician? Because he looked on the whole universe and all that is in it *as á riddle*, as a secret which could be read by applying pure thought to certain evidence, certain mystic clues which God had laid about the world to allow a sort of philosopher's treasure hunt to the esoteric brotherhood. He believed that these clues were to be found partly in the evidence of the heavens and in the constitution of elements (and that is what gives the false suggestion of his being an experimental natural philosopher), but also partly in certain papers and traditions handed down by the brethren in an unbroken chain back to the original cryptic revelation in Babylonia. He regarded the universe as a cryptogram set by the Almighty—just as he himself wrapt the discovery of the calculus in a cryptogram when he communicated with Leibnitz. By pure thought, by concentration of mind, the riddle, he believed, would be revealed to the initiate.

He *did* read the riddle of the heavens. And he believed that by the same powers of his introspective imagination he would read the riddle of the Godhead, the riddle of past and future events divinely foreordained, the riddle of the elements and their constitution from an original undifferentiated first matter, the riddle of health and of immortality. All would be revealed to him if only he could persevere to the end, uninterrupted, by himself, no one coming into the room, reading, copying, testing—all by himself, no interruption for God's sake, no disclosure, no discordant breakings in or criticism, with fear and shrinking as he assailed these half-ordained, half-forbidden things, creeping back into the bosom of the Godhead as into his mother's womb. "Voyaging through strange seas of thought *alone*," not as Charles Lamb "a fellow who believed nothing unless it was as clear as the three sides of a triangle."

And so he continued for some twenty-five years. In 1687, when he was forty-five years old, the *Principia* was published.

Here in Trinity it is right that I should give you an account of how he lived amongst you during these years of his greatest achievement. The east end of the Chapel projects farther eastwards than the Great Gate. In the second half of the seventeenth century there was a walled garden in the free space between Trinity Street and the building which joins the Great Gate to the Chapel. The south wall ran out from the turret of the Gate to a distance overlapping the Chapel by at least the width of the present pavement. Thus the garden was of modest but reasonable size, as is well shown in Loggan's print of the College in 1690. This was Newton's garden. He had the Fellow's set of rooms between the Porter's Lodge and the Chapel—that, I suppose, now occupied by Professor Broad. The garden was reached by a stairway which was attached to a veranda raised on wooden pillars projecting into the garden from the range of buildings. At the top of this stairway stood his telescope—not to be confused with the observatory erected on the top of the Great Gate during Newton's lifetime (but after he had left Cambridge) for the use of Roger Cotes and Newton's successor, Whiston. This wooden erection was, I think, demolished by Whewell in 1856 and replaced by the stone bay of Professor Broad's bedroom. At the Chapel end of the garden was a small two-storied building, also of wood, which was his laboratory. When he decided to prepare the *Principia* for publication he engaged a young kinsman, Humphrey Newton, to act as his amanuensis (the MS. of the *Principia*, as it went to the press, is clearly in the hand of Humphrey). Humphrey remained with him for five years—from 1684 to 1689. When Newton died his nephew-in-law Conduitt wrote to Humphrey for his reminiscences, and among the papers I have is Humphrey's reply.

During these twenty-five years of intense study mathematics and astronomy were only a part, and perhaps not the most absorbing, of his occupations. Our record of these is almost wholly confined to the papers which he kept and put in his box when he left Trinity for London.

Let me give some brief indications of their subject. They are enormously voluminous—I should say that upwards of 1,000,000 words in his handwriting still survive. They have, beyond doubt, no substantial value whatever except as a fascinating sidelight on the mind of our greatest genius.

Let me not exaggerate through reaction against the other Newton myth which has been so sedulously created for the last two hundred years. There was extreme method in his madness. All his unpublished works on esoteric and theological matters are marked by careful learning, accurate method and extreme sobriety of statement. They are just as *sane* as the *Principia,* if their whole matter and purpose were not magical. They were nearly all composed during the same twenty-five years of his mathematical studies. They fall into several groups.

Very early in life Newton abandoned orthodox belief in the Trinity. At this time the Socinians were an important Arian sect amongst intellectual circles. It may be that Newton fell under Socinian influences, but I think not. He was rather a Judaic monotheist of the school of Maimonides. He arrived at this conclusion not on so-to-speak rational or sceptical grounds, but entirely on the interpretation of ancient authority. He was persuaded that the revealed documents give no support to the Trinitarian doctrines which were due to late falsifications. The revealed God was one God.

But this was a dreadful secret which Newton was at desperate pains to conceal all his life. It was the reason why he refused Holy Orders, and therefore had to obtain a special dispensation to hold his Fellowship and Lucasian Chair and could not be Master of Trinity. Even the Toleration Act of 1689 excepted anti-Trinitarians. Some rumours there were, but not at the dangerous dates when he was a young Fellow of Trinity. In the main the secret died with him. But it was revealed in many writings in his big box. After his death Bishop Horsley was asked to inspect the box with a view to publication. He saw the contents with horror and slammed the lid. A hundred years later Sir David Brewster looked into the box. He covered up the traces with carefully selected extracts and some straight fibbing. His latest biographer, Mr. More, has been more candid. Newton's extensive anti-Trinitarian pamphlets are, in my judgement, the most interesting of his unpublished papers. Apart from his more serious affirmation of belief, I have a completed pamphlet showing up what Newton thought of the extreme dishonesty and falsification of records for which St. Athanasius was responsible, in particular for his putting about the false calumny that Arius died in a privy. The victory of the Trinitarians in England in the latter half of the seventeenth century was not only as complete, but also as extraordinary, as St. Athanasius's original triumph. There is good reason for thinking that Locke was a Unitarian. I have seen it argued that Milton was. It is a blot on Newton's record that he did not murmur a word when Whiston, his successor in the Lucasian Chair, was thrown out of his professorship and out of the University for publicly avowing opinions which Newton himself had secretly held for upwards of fifty years past.

That he held this heresy was a further aggravation of his silence and secrecy and inwardness of disposition.

Another large section is concerned with all branches of apocalyptic writings from which he sought to deduce the secret truths of the Universe—the measurements of Solomon's Temple, the Book of Daniel, the Book of Revelations, an enormous volume of work of which some part was published in his later days. Along with this are hundreds of pages of Church History and the like, designed to discover the truth of tradition.

A large section, judging by the handwriting amongst the earliest, relates to alchemy—transmutation, the philosopher's stone, the elixir of life. The scope and character of these papers have been hushed up, or at least minimized, by nearly all those who have inspected them. About 1650 there was a considerable group in London, round the publisher Cooper, who during the next twenty years revived interest not only in the English alchemists of the fifteenth century, but also in translations of the medieval and post-medieval alchemists.

There is an unusual number of manuscripts of the early English alchemists in the libraries of Cambridge. It may be that there was some continuous esoteric tradition within the University which sprang into activity again in the twenty years from 1650 to 1670. At any rate, Newton was clearly an unbridled addict. It is this with which he was occupied "about 6 weeks at spring and 6 at the fall when the fire in the elaboratory scarcely went out" at the very years when he was composing the *Principia*—and about this he told Humphrey Newton not a word. Moreover, he was almost entirely concerned, not in serious experiment, but in trying to read the riddle of tradition, to find meaning in cryptic verses, to imitate the alleged but largely imaginary experiments of the initiates of past centuries. Newton has left behind him a vast mass of records of these studies. I believe that the greater part are translations and copies made by him of existing books and manuscripts. But there are also extensive records of experiments. I have glanced through a great quantity of this—at least 100,000 words, I should say. It is utterly impossible to deny that it is wholly magical and wholly devoid of scientific value; and also impossible not to admit that Newton devoted years of work to it. Some time it might be interesting, but not useful, for some student better equipped and more idle than I to work out Newton's exact relationship to the tradition and MSS. of his time.

In these mixed and extraordinary studies, with one foot in the Middle Ages and one foot treading a path for modern science, Newton spent the first phase of his life, the period of life in Trinity when he did all his real work. Now let me pass to the second phase.

After the publication of the *Principia* there is a complete change in his habit and way of life. I believe that his friends, above all Halifax, came to the conclusion that he must be rooted out of the life he was leading at Trinity which must soon lead to decay of mind and health. Broadly speaking, of his own motion or under persuasion, he abandons his studies. He takes up University business, represents the University in Parliament; his friends are busy trying to get a dignified and remunerative job for him—the Provostship of King's, the Mastership of Charterhouse, the Controllership of the Mint.

Newton could not be Master of Trinity because he was a Unitarian and so not in Holy Orders. He was rejected as Provost of King's for the more prosaic reason that he was not an Etonian. Newton took this rejection very ill and prepared a long legalistic brief which I possess, giving reasons why it was not unlawful for him to be accepted as Provost. But, as ill-luck had it, Newton's nomination for the Provostship came at the moment when King's had decided to fight against the right of Crown nomination, a struggle in which the College was successful.

Newton was well qualified for any of these offices. It must not be inferred from his introspection, his absent-mindedness, his secrecy and his solitude that he lacked aptitude for affairs when he chose to exercise it. There are many records to prove his very great capacity. Read, for example, his correspondence with Dr. Covell, the Vice-Chancellor, when, as the University's representative in Parliament, he had to deal with the delicate question of the oaths after the revolution of 1688. With Pepys and Lowndes he became one of the greatest and most efficient of our civil servants. He was a very successful investor of funds, surmounting the crisis of the South Sea Bubble, and died a rich man. He possessed in exceptional degree almost every kind of intellectual aptitude—lawyer, historian, theologian, not less than mathematician, physicist, astronomer.

And when the turn of his life came and he put his books of magic back into the box, it was easy for him to drop the seventeenth century behind him and to evolve into the eighteenth-century figure which is the traditional Newton.

Nevertheless, the move on the part of his friends to change his life came almost too late. In 1689 his mother, to whom he was deeply attached, died. Somewhere about his fiftieth birthday on Christmas Day, 1692, he suffered what we should now term a severe nervous breakdown. Melancholia, sleeplessness, fears of persecution—he writes to Pepys and to Locke and no doubt to others letters which lead them to think that his mind is deranged. He lost, in his own words, the "former consistency of his mind." He never again concentrated after the old fashion or did any fresh work. The breakdown probably lasted nearly two years, and from it emerged, slightly "gaga," but still, no doubt, with one of the most powerful minds of England, the Sir Isaac Newton of tradition.

In 1696 his friends were finally successful in digging him out of Cambridge, and for more than another twenty years he reigned in London as the most famous man of his age, of Europe, and—as his powers gradually waned and his affability increased—perhaps of all time, so it seemed to his contemporaries.

He set up house with his niece Catharine Barton, who was beyond reasonable doubt the mistress of his old and loyal friend Charles Montague, Earl of Halifax and Chancellor of the Exchequer, who had been one of Newton's intimate friends when he was an undergraduate at Trinity. Catharine was reputed to be one of the most brilliant and charming women in the London of Congreve, Swift and Pope. She is celebrated not least for the broadness of her stories, in Swift's *Journal to Stella.* Newton puts on rather too much weight for his moderate height. "When he rode in his coach one arm would be out of his coach on one side and the other on the other." His pink face, beneath a mass of snow-white hair, which "when his peruke was off was a venerable sight," is increasingly both benevolent and majestic. One night in Trinity after Hall he is knighted by Queen Anne. For nearly twenty-four years he reigns as President of the Royal Society. He becomes one of the principal sights of London for all visiting intellectual foreigners, whom he entertains handsomely. He liked to have clever young men about him to edit new editions of the *Principia*—and sometimes merely plausible ones as in the case of Fatio de Duillier.

Magic was quite forgotten. He has become the Sage and Monarch of the Age of Reason. The Sir Isaac Newton of orthodox tradition—the eighteenth-century Sir Isaac, so remote from the child magician born in the first half of the seventeeth century—was being built up. Voltaire returning from his trip to London was able to report of Sir Isaac—" 'twas his peculiar felicity, not only to be born in a country of liberty, but in an Age when all scholastic impertinences were banished from the World. Reason alone was cultivated and Mankind cou'd only be his Pupil, not his Enemy." Newton, whose secret heresies and scholastic superstitions it had been the study of a lifetime to conceal!

But he never concentrated, never recovered "the former consistency of his mind." "He spoke very little in company." "He had something rather languid in his look and manner."

And he looked very seldom, I expect, into the chest where, when he left Cambridge, he had packed all the evidences of what had occupied and so absorbed his intense and flaming spirit in his rooms and his garden and his elaboratory between the Great Gate and Chapel.

But he did not destory them. They remained in the box to shock profoundly any eighteenth- or nineteeth-century prying eyes. They became the possession of Catharine Barton and then of her daughter, Lady Lymington. So Newton's chest, with many hundreds of thousands of words of his unpublished writings, came to contain the "Portsmouth Papers."

In 1888 the mathematical portion was given to the University Library at Cambridge. They have been indexed, but they have never been edited. The rest, a very large collection, were dispersed in the auction room in 1936 by Catharine Barton's descendant, the present Lord Lymington. Disturbed by this impiety, I managed gradually to reassemble about half of them, including nearly the whole of the biographical portion, that is, the "Conduitt Papers," in order to bring them to Cambridge which I hope they will never leave. The greater part of the rest were snatched out of my reach by a syndicate which hoped to sell them at a high price, probably in America, on the occasion of the recent tercentenary.

As one broods over these queer collections, it seems easier to understand—with an understanding which is not, I hope, distorted in the other direction—this strange spirit, who was tempted by the Devil to believe, at the time when within these walls he was solving so much, that he could reach *all* the secrets of God and Nature by the pure power of mind—Copernicus and Faustus in one.

ROBERT OPPENHEIMER

•

On Albert Einstein[1]

Though I knew Einstein for two or three decades, it was only in the last decade of his life that we were close colleagues and something of friends. But I thought that it might be useful, because I am sure that it is not too soon—and for our generation perhaps almost too late—to start to dispel

[1] Reprinted from *The New York Review of Books.* Copyright © 1966, The New York Review. Reprinted by permission of Professor Robert Oppenheimer. (This was a lecture delivered at UNESCO House in Paris on December 13, 1965.)

the clouds of myth and to see the great mountain peak that these clouds hide. As always, the myth has its charms; but the truth is far more beautiful.

Late in his life, in connection with his despair over weapons and wars, Einstein said that if he had to live it over again he would be a plumber. This was a balance of seriousness and jest that no one should now attempt to disturb. Believe me, he had no idea of what it was to be a plumber; least of all in the United States, where we have a joke that the typical behavior of this specialist is that he never brings his tools to the scene of the crisis. Einstein brought his tools to his crises; Einstein was a physicist, a natural philosopher, the greatest of our time.

What we have heard, what you all know, what is the true part of the myth is his extraordinary originality. The discovery of quanta would surely have come one way or another, but he discovered them. Deep understanding of what it means that no signal could travel faster than light would surely have come; the formal equations were already known; but this simple, brilliant understanding of the physics could well have been slow in coming, and blurred, had he not done it for us. The general theory of relativity which, even today, is not well proved experimentally, no one but he would have done for a long, long time. It is in fact only in the last decade, the last years, that one has seen how a pedestrian and hard-working physicist, or many of them, might reach that theory and understand this singular union of geometry and gravitation; and we can do even that today only because some of the *a priori* open possibilities are limited by the confirmation of Einstein's discovery that light would be deflected by gravity.

Yet there is another side besides the originality. Einstein brought to the work of originality deep elements of tradition. It is only possible to discover in part how he came by it, by following his reading, his friendships, the meager record that we have. But of these deep-seated elements of tradition —I will not try to enumerate them all; I do not know them all—at least three were indispensable and stayed with him.

The first is from the rather beautiful but recondite part of physics that is the explanation of the laws of thermodynamics in terms of the mechanics of large numbers of particles, statistical mechanics. This was with Einstein all the time. It was what enabled him from Planck's discovery of the law of black body radiation to conclude that light was not only waves but particles, particles with an energy proportional to their frequency and momentum determined by their wave-number, the famous relations that de Broglie was to extend to all matter, to electrons first and then clearly to all matter.

It was this statistical tradition that led Einstein to the laws governing the emission and absorption of light by atomic systems. It was this that enabled him to see the connection between de Broglie's waves and the statistics of light-quanta proposed by Bose. It was this that kept him an active proponent and discoverer of the new phenomena of quantum physics up to 1925.

The second and equally deep strand—and here I think we do know where it came from—was his total love of the idea of a field: the following of physical phenomena in minute and infinitely subdividable detail in space and in time. This gave him his first great drama of trying to see how Maxwell's equations could be true. They were the first field equations of physics; they are still true today with only very minor and well-understood modifications. It is this tradition which made him know that there had to be a field theory of gravitation, long before the clues to that theory were securely in his hand.

The third tradition was less one of physics than of philosophy. It is a form of the principle of sufficient reason. It was Einstein who asked what do we mean, what can we measure, what elements in physics are conventional? He insisted that those elements that were conventional could have no part in the real predictions of physics. This also had roots: for one the mathematical invention of Riemann, who saw how very limited the geometry of the Greeks had been, how unreasonably limited. But in a more important sense, it followed from the long tradition of European philosophy, you may say starting with Descartes—if you wish you can start it in the Thirteenth Century, because in fact it did start then—and leading through the British empiricists, and very clearly formulated, though probably without influence in Europe, by Charles Peirce: One had to ask how do we do it, what do we mean, is this just something that we can use to help ourselves in calculating, or is it something that we can actually study in nature by physical means? For the point here is that the laws of nature not only describe the results of observations, but the laws of nature delimit the scope of observations. That was the point of Einstein's understanding of the limiting character of the velocity of light; it also was the nature of the resolution in quantum theory, where the quantum of action, Planck's constant, was recognized as limiting the fineness of the transaction between the system studied and the machinery used to study it, limiting this fineness in a form of atomicity quite different from and quite more radical than any that the Greeks had imagined or than was familiar from the atomic theory of chemistry.

In the last years of Einstein's life, the last twenty-five years, his tradition in a certain sense failed him. They were the years he spent at Princeton and this, though a source of sorrow, should not be concealed. He had a right to that failure. He spent those years first in trying to prove that the quantum theory had inconsistencies in it. No one could have been more ingenious in thinking up unexpected and clever examples; but it turned out that the inconsistencies were not there; and often their resolution could be found in earlier work of Einstein himself. When that did not work, after repeated efforts, Einstein had simply to say that he did not like the theory. He did not like the elements of indeterminacy. He did not like the abandonment of continuity or of causality. These were things that he had grown up with, saved by him, and enormously enlarged; and to see them lost, even though he had put the dagger in the hand of their assassin by his own work, was very hard on him. He fought with Bohr in a noble and furious way, and he fought with the theory which he had fathered but which he hated. It was not the first time that this has happened in science.

He also worked with a very ambitious program, to combine the understanding of electricity and gravitation in such a way as to explain what he regarded as the semblance—the illusion—of discreteness, of particles in nature. I think that it was clear then, and believe it to be obviously clear today, that the things that this theory worked with were too meager, left out too much that was known to physicists but had not been known much in Einstein's student days. Thus it looked like a hopelessly limited and historically rather accidentally conditioned approach. Although Einstein commanded the affection, or, more rightly, the love of everyone for his determination to see through his program, he lost most contact with the profession of physics, because there were things that had been learned which came too late in life for him to concern himself with them.

Einstein was indeed one of the friendliest of men. I had the impression that he was also, in an important sense, alone. Many very great men are lonely; yet I had the impression that although he was a deep and loyal friend, the stronger human affections played a not very deep or very central part in his life taken as a whole. He had of course incredibly many disciples, in the sense of people who, reading his work or hearing it taught by him, learned from him and had a new view of physics, of the philosophy of physics, of the nature of the world that we live in. But he did not have, in the technical jargon, a school. He did not have very many students who were his concern as apprentices and disciples. And there was an element of the lone worker in him, in sharp contrast to the teams we see today, and in sharp contrast to the highly cooperative way in which some other parts of science have developed. In later years, he had people working with him. They were typically called assistants and they had a wonderful life. Just being with him was wonderful. His secretary had a wonderful life. The sense of grandeur never left him for a minute, nor his sense of humor. The assistants did one thing which he lacked in his young days. His early papers are paralyzingly beautiful, but there are many errata. Later there were none. I had the impression that, along with its miseries, his fame gave him some pleasures, not only the human pleasure of meeting people but the extreme pleasure of music played not only with Elizabeth of Belgium but more with Adolf Busch, for he was not that good a violinist. He loved the sea and he loved sailing and was always grateful for a ship. I remember walking home with him on his seventy-first birthday. He said, "You know, when it's once been given to a man to do something sensible, afterward life is a little strange."

Einstein is also, and I think rightly, known as a man of very great good will and humanity. Indeed, if I had to think of a single word for his attitude towards human problems, I would pick the Sanskrit word *Ahinsa,* not to hurt, harmlessness. He had a deep distrust of power; he did not have that convenient and natural converse with statesmen and men of power that was quite appropriate to Rutherford and to Bohr, perhaps the two physicists of this century who most nearly rivaled him in eminence. In 1915, as he made the general theory of relativity, Europe was tearing itself to pieces and half losing its past. He was always a pacifist. Only as the Nazis came into power in Germany did he have some doubts, as his famous and rather deep exchange of letters with Freud showed, and began to understand with melancholy and without true acceptance that, in addition to understanding, man sometimes has a duty to act.

After what you have heard, I need not say how luminous was his intelligence. He was almost wholly without sophistication and wholly without worldliness. I think that in England people would have said that he did not have much "background," and in America that he lacked "education." This may throw some light on how these words are used. I think that this simplicity, this lack of clutter and this lack of cant, had a lot to do with his preservation throughout of a certain pure, rather Spinoza-like, philosophical monism, which of course is hard to maintain if you have been "educated" and have a "background." There was always with him a wonderful purity at once childlike and profoundly stubborn.

Einstein is often blamed or praised or credited with these miserable bombs. It is not in my opinion true. The special theory of relativity might not have been beautiful without Einstein; but it would have been a tool for physicists, and by 1932 the experimental evidence for the inter-convertibility of matter and energy which he had predicted was overwhelming. The feasibility of doing anything with this in such a massive way was not clear until seven years later, and then almost by accident. This was not what Einstein really was after. His part was that of creating an intellectual revolution, and discovering more than any scientist of our time how profound were the errors made by men before then. He did write a letter to Roosevelt about atomic energy. I think this was in part his agony at the evil of the Nazis, in part not wanting to harm any one in any way; but I ought to report that that letter had very little effect, and that Einstein himself is really not answerable for all that came later. I believe he so understood it himself.

His was a voice raised with very great weight against violence and cruelty wherever he saw them and, after the war, he spoke with deep emotion and I believe with great weight about the supreme violence of these atomic weapons. He said at once with great simplicity: Now we must make a world government. It was very forthright, it was very abrupt, it was no doubt "uneducated," no doubt without "background"; still all of us in some thoughtful measure must recognize that he was right.

Without power, without calculation, with none of the profoundly political humor that characterized Gandhi, he nevertheless did move the political world. In almost the last act of his life, he joined with Lord Russell in suggesting that men of science get together and see if they could not understand one another and avert the disaster which he foresaw from the arms race. The so-called Pugwash movement, which has a longer name now, was the direct result of this appeal. I know it to be true that it had an essential part to play in the Treaty of Moscow, the limited test-ban treaty, which is a tentative, but to me very precious, declaration that reason might still prevail.

In his last years, as I knew him, Einstein was a twentieth-century Ecclesiastes, saying with unrelenting and indomitable cheerfulness, "Vanity of vanities, all is vanity."

HARLOW SHAPLEY

•

Man's Fourth Adjustment[1]

The scattering of galaxies, the habits of macromolecules, and the astounding abundance of stars are forcing those who ponder such matters to a further adjustment of their concept of the place and functioning of man in the material universe.

In the history of the evolving human mind, with its increasing knowledge of the surrounding world, there must have been a time when the philosophers of the early tribes began to realize that the world was not simply anthropocentric—centered on man himself. The geocentric concept became common doctrine. It accepted a universe centered on the earth. This first adjustment was only mildly deflationary to the human ego, for man appeared to surpass all other living forms.

The second adjustment in the relation of man to the physical universe, that is, the abandoment of the earth-center theory, was not generally acceptable until the sixteenth-century Copernican revolution soundly established the heliocentric concept—the theory of a universe centered on the sun. Man is a stubborn adherent to official dogma. Eventually, however, he accepted the sun as the center not only of the local family of planets, but also of the total sidereal assemblage, and long held that view.

He had slowly given up the earth-center. But why, in spite of increasing evidence, did he then hold so persistently to the heliocentric view? Was it only because of vanity—his feeling, nourished by the unscientific dogmatists, that he is of paramount significance in the world? There were several better reasons

[1] From *The American Scholar,* XXV (Autumn, 1956), 453–457. Copyright by Harlow Shapley, 1956. Reprinted by permission of the author.

for his second delusion. For example, the Milky Way is a great circle, a band of starlight that divides the sky into two nearly equal parts. It is of about the same brightness in all its parts. By implication, therefore, the sun and earth are centrally located. Also, the numbers of stars seemed to the early census-takers to fall off with distance from the sun as though it were central, and such a position for his star among the stellar millions brought to man a dignity of position not at all disagreeable.

The shift from the geocentric to the heliocentric concept doubtless had some philosophical impact in the sixteenth century, but not much. After all, the hot, turbulent, gaseous sun is no place for the delicate biology in which man finds himself at or near the top. Earth-center or sun-center seemed to make little difference to cosmic thinking during the past four centuries. But then, less than forty years ago, came the inescapable need for a third adjustment—one that should have deeply affected and to some extent has disturbed man's thoughts about his place, his career and his cosmic importance.

This shift has dug deeply into man's pride and self-assurance, for it has carried with it the knowledge of the appalling number of galaxies. He could accept rather cheerfully the Darwinian evidence of his animal origin, for that still left him at the summit of all terrestrial organisms. But the abandonment of the heliocentric universe on the authority of the astronomical evidence was certainly deflationary, from the standpoint of man's position in the material world, however flattering it was to the human mind.

The "galactocentric universe" suddenly puts the earth and its life near the edge of one great galaxy in a universe of millions of galaxies. Man becomes peripheral among the billions of stars of his own Milky Way; and, according to the revelations of paleontology and geochemistry, he is recent and apparently ephemeral in the unrolling of cosmic time. And here is a somber or happy thought, whichever mood you prefer. There is no retreat! The inquiring human has passed the point of no return. We cannot restore geocentrism or heliocentrism. The apes, eagles and honeybees may be wholly content to be peripheral ephemerals, and thus miss the great vision that opens before us. For them, egocentrism and lococentrism may suffice; for us, no! And since we cannot go back to the cramped but comfortable past (without sacrificing completely our cultures and civilizations), we go forward and find there is more to the story.

The downgrading of the earth and sun, and the elevation of the galaxies, is not the end of this progress of scientific pilgrims through philosophic fields. The need for a further jolting adjustment now appears—not wholly unexpected by workers in science, nor wholly the result of one or two scientific revelations.

Our new problem concerns the spread of life throughout the universe. As unsolicited spokesmen for all the earthly organisms of land, sea and air, we ask the piquant question: Are we alone?

From among the many measures and thoughts that promote this fourth adjustment of *Homo sapiens sapiens* in the galaxy of galaxies (the metagalaxy), I select three phenomena as most demanding of our consideration. The first refers to the number of stars, the second to catastrophes of ancient days, and the third to the origin of self-duplicating molecules.

To the ancients, only a few thousand stars were known; to the early telescopes, however, it was a million; and that astounding number has increased spectacularly with every telescopic advance. Finally, with the discovery that the "extragalactic nebulae" are in reality galaxies, each with its hundreds or thousands of millions of stars, and with our inability to "touch metagalactic bottom" with the greatest telescopes, we are led to accept the existence of more than 10^{20} stars in our explorable universe, perhaps many more.

The significance of this discovery, or rather of this uncovering, is that we have at hand—that is, the universe contains—more than one hundred million million million sources of light and warmth for whatever planets accompany these radiant stars.

The second phenomenon, the expanding metagalaxy, bears on the question: Do planets accompany at least some of the stars that pour forth energy suitable for the complex biological activity that we call life?

We now accept the observational evidence for an expanding universe of galaxies. The rapid expansion of the measurable part of the metagalaxy implies an increasingly greater concentration of these cosmic units (galaxies) as we go back in time. A few thousand million years ago, the average density of matter in space was so great that collisions, near encounters, and gravitational disruptions were of necessity frequent. The crust of the earth, radioactively measured, is also a few thousand million years old, and therefore the earth and the other planets of our sun's system were "born" in those days of turbulence. At that time countless millions of other planetary systems must have developed, for our sun is of a very common stellar variety. (Miss Cannon's catalogue of spectra reports forty thousand sun-like stars in our immediate neighborhood.)

Other ways in which planets may form—other than this primitive process of the early days—are recognized. The contraction of protostars out of the hypothetical primeval gas, giving birth on the way to protoplanets, is an evolutionary process now widely favored. It would imply the existence of countless planets.

The head-on-collision theory of planetary origin has also been considered. But the stars are now so widely dispersed that collisions must be exceedingly rare—so very unlikely, in fact, that we might claim uniqueness for our planetary system and for ourselves if planet birth depended only on such procedure. The expanding universe discovery, however, has shown the crowded conditions when our earth was born.

Passing over details, we state the relevant conclusion: *Millions of planetary systems must exist.* Whatever the method of origin, planets may be the common heritage of all stars except those so situated that planetary materials would be swallowed or cast off through gravitational action. In passing we note that astrophysicists have shown that our kinds of chemistry and physics prevail throughout the explorable universe. There is nothing uncommon here or now.

Remembering our 10^{20} stars and the high probability of millions of planets with suitable chemistry, dimensions and distance from their nutrient stars, we are ready for the question: On some of these planets is there actually life; or is that biochemical operation strangely limited to our planet, No. 3 in the family of the sun, which is a run-of-the-mill star located in the outer part of a galaxy that contains a hundred thousand million other stars—and this galaxy but one of millions already on the records?

Is life thus restricted? Of course not. We are not alone. And we can accept life's wide dispersion still more confidently when our third argument is indicated.

To put it briefly: biochemistry and microbiology, with the assistance of geophysics, astronomy and other sciences, have gone so far in bridging the gap between the inanimate and the living that we can no longer doubt but that whenever the physics, chemistry and climates are right on a planet's surface, life will emerge and persist.

This consequence has long been suspected by scientists, but the many researches of the past few years in the field of macromolecules have made it unnecessary any longer to postulate miracles and the supernatural for the origin of life.

The astronomical demonstration of the great number of stars, and therefore the abundance of life opportunities, naturally leads to the belief that countless planets have had long and varied experience with biochemical evolution. Thousands of kinds of terrestrial animals are known to develop neurotic complexes, that is "intelligence." It comes naturally. No higher animal is without it in high degree. Could it be otherwise on another life-bearing planet?

And here we must end with the simple but weighty proposal: There is no reason in the world to believe that our own mental stature has not been excelled by that of sentient beings elsewhere. I am not suggesting, however, that *Homo* is repeated. There are a million variations on the animal theme.

In conclusion, I need not emphasize the possible relevance to philosophy and perhaps to religion of this fourth adjustment in man's view of himself in the material universe.

Biological Science

WILLIAM HARVEY

•

Of the Quantity of Blood Passing through the Heart[1]

Thus far I have spoken of the passage of the blood from the veins into the arteries, and of the manner in which it is transmitted and distributed by the action of the heart; points to which some, moved either by the authority of Galen or Columbus, or the reasonings of others, will give in their adhesion. But what remains to be said upon the quantity and source of the blood which thus passes, is of so novel and unheard-of character, that I not only fear injury to myself from the envy of a few, but I tremble lest I have mankind at large for my enemies, so much doth wont and custom, that become as another nature, and doctrine once sown and that hath struck deep root, and respect for antiquity influence all men: Still the die is cast, and my trust is in my love of truth, and the candour that inheres in cultivated minds. And sooth to say, when I surveyed my mass of evidence, whether derived from vivisections, and my various reflections on them, or from the ventricles of the heart and the vessels that enter into and issue from them, the symmetry and size of these conduits—for nature doing nothing in vain, would never have given them so large a relative size without a purpose—or from the arrangement and intimate structure of the valves in particular, and of the other parts of the heart in general, with many things besides, I frequently and seriously be-thought me, and long revolved in my mind, what might be the quantity of blood which was transmitted, in how short a time its passage might be effected, and the like; and not finding it possible that this could be supplied by the juices of the ingested aliment without the veins on the one hand becoming drained, and the arteries on the other getting ruptured through the excessive charge of blood, unless the blood should somehow find its way from the arteries into the veins, and so return to the right side of the heart; I began to think whether there might not be a MOTION, AS IT WERE, IN A CIRCLE. Now this I afterwards found to be true; and I finally saw that the blood, forced by the action of the left ventricle

[1] From William Harvey, *On the Motion of the Heart and Blood in Animals,* Robert Willis trans., revised by Alexander Bowie in *Scientific Papers, Physiology, Medicine, Surgery, Geology* (New York: P. F. Collier & Son Corporation, 1910), p. 382. Reprinted by permission of the publishers. First published, 1628.

into the arteries, was distributed to the body at large, and its several parts, in the same manner as it is sent through the lungs, impelled by the right ventricle into the pulmonary artery, and that it then passed through the veins and along the vena cava, and so round to the left ventricle in the manner already indicated. Which motion we may be allowed to call circular, in the same way as Aristotle says that the air and the rain emulate the circular motion of the superior bodies; for the moist earth, warmed by the sun, evaporates; the vapours drawn upwards are condensed, and descending in the form of rain, moisten the earth again; and by this arrangement are generations of living things produced; and in like manner too are tempests and meteors engendered by the circular motion, and by the approach and recession of the sun.

And so, in all likelihood, does it come to pass in the body, through the motion of the blood; the various parts are nourished, cherished, quickened by the warmer, more perfect, vaporous, spirituous, and, as I may say, alimentive blood; which, on the contrary, in contact with these parts becomes cooled, coagulated, and, so to speak, effete; whence it returns to its sovereign the heart, as if to its source, or to the inmost home of the body, there to recover its state of excellence or perfection. Here it resumes its due fluidity and receives an infusion of natural heat—powerful, fervid, a kind of treasury of life, and is impregnated with spirits, and it might be said with balsam; and thence it is again dispersed; and all this depends on the motion and action of the heart.

The heart, consequently, is the beginning of life; the sun of the microcosm, even as the sun in his turn might well be designated the heart of the world; for it is the heart by whose virtue and pulse the blood is moved, perfected, made apt to nourish, and is preserved from corruption and coagulation; it is the household divinity which, discharging its function, nourishes, cherishes, quickens the whole body, and is indeed the foundation of life, the source of all action. But of these things we shall speak more opportunely when we come to speculate upon the final cause of this motion of the heart.

Hence, since the veins are the conduits and vessels that transport the blood, they are of two kinds, the cava and the aorta; and this not by reason of there being two sides of the body, as Aristotle has it, but because of the difference of office; nor yet, as is commonly said, in consequence of any diversity of structure, for in many animals, as I have said, the vein does not differ from the artery in the thickness of its tunics, but solely in virtue of their several destinies and uses. A vein and an artery, both styled vein by the ancients, and that not undeservedly, as Galen has remarked, because the one, the artery to wit, is the vessel which carries the blood from the heart to the body at large, the other or vein of the present day bringing it back from the general system to the heart; the former is the conduit from, the latter the channel to, the heart; the latter contains the cruder, effete, blood, rendered unfit for nutrition; the former transmits the digested, perfect, peculiarly nutritive fluid.

DONALD CULROSS PEATTIE

•

Chlorophyll: The Sun Trap[1]

What we love, when on a summer day we step into the coolness of a wood, is that its boughs close up behind us. We are escaped, into another room of life. The wood does not live as we live, restless and running, panting after flesh, and even in sleep tossing with fears. It is aloof from thoughts and instincts; it responds, but only to the sun and wind, the rock and the stream—never, though you shout yourself hoarse, to propaganda, temptation, reproach, or promises. You cannot mount a rock and preach to a tree how it shall attain the kingdom of heaven. It is already closer to it, up there, than you will grow to be. And you cannot make it see the light since in the tree's sense you are blind. You have nothing to bring it, for all the forest is self-sufficient; if you burn it, cut, hack through it with a blade, it angrily repairs the swathe with thorns and weeds and fierce suckers. Later there are good green leaves again, toiling, adjusting, breathing—forgetting you.

For this green living is the world's primal industry; yet it makes no roar. Waving its banners, it marches across the earth and the ages, without dust around its columns. I do not hold that all of that life is pretty; it is not, in purpose, sprung for us, and moves under no compulsion to please. If ever you fought with thistles, or tried to pull up a cattail's matted root-stocks, you will know how plants cling to their own lives and defy you. The pond-scums gather in the cistern, frothing and buoyed with their own gases; the storm waves fling at your feet upon the beach the limp sea-lettuce wrenched from its submarine hold—reminder that there too, where the light is filtered and refracted, there is life still to intercept and net and by it proliferate. Inland from the shore I look and see the coastal ranges clothed in chaparral—dense shrubbery and scrubbery, close-fisted, intricately branched, suffocating the rash rambler in the noon heat with its pungency. Beyond, on the deserts, under a fierce sky, between the harsh lunar ranges of unweathered rock, life still, somehow, fights its way through the year, with thorn and succulent cell and indomitable root.

Between such embattled life and the Forest of Arden, with its ancient beeches and enchanter's nightshade, there is no great biologic difference. Each lives by the cool and cleanly and most commendable virtue of being green. And though that is not biological language, it is the whole story in two words. So that we ought not to speak of getting at the root of a matter, but of going back to the leaf of things. The orator who knows the way to the country's salvation and does not know that the breath of life he draws was blown into his nostrils by green leaves, had better spare his breath. And before anyone

[1] From *Flowering Earth,* by Donald Culross Peattie. Reprinted by permission of The Author's Estate and its Agent, James Brown Associates, Inc.

builds a new state upon the industrial proletariat, he will be wisely cautioned to discover that the source of all wealth is the peasantry of grass.

The reason for these assertions—which I do not make for metaphorical effect but maintain quite literally—is that the green leaf pigment, called chlorophyll, is the one link between the sun and life; it is the conduit of perpetual energy to our own frail organisms.

For inert and inorganic elements—water and carbon dioxide of the air, the same that we breathe out as a waste—chlorophyll can synthesize with the energy of sunlight. Every day, every hour of all the ages, as each continent and, equally important, each ocean rolls into sunlight, chlorophyll ceaselessly creates. Not figuratively, but literally, in the grand First Chapter Genesis style. One instant there are a gas and water, as lifeless as the core of earth or the chill of space; and the next they are become living tissue—mortal yet genitive, progenitive, resilient with all the dewy adaptability of flesh, ever changing in order to stabilize some unchanging ideal of form. Life, in short, synthesized, plant-synthesized, light-synthesized. Botanists say photosynthesized. So that the post-Biblical synthesis of life is already a fact. Only when man has done as much, may he call himself the equal of a weed.

Plant life sustains the living world; more precisely, chlorophyll does so, and where, in the vegetable kingdom, there is not chlorophyll or something closely like it, then that plant or cell is a parasite—no better, in vital economy, than a mere animal or man. Blood, bone and sinew, all flesh is grass. Grass to mutton, mutton to wool, wool to the coat on my back—it runs like one of these cumulative nursery rhymes, the wealth and diversity of our material life accumulating from the primal fact of chlorophyll's activity. The roof of my house, the snapping logs upon the hearth, the desk where I write, are my imports from the plant kingdom. But the whole of modern civilization is based upon a whirlwind spending of the plant wealth long ago and very slowly accumulated. For, fundamentally, and away back, coal and oil, gasoline and illuminating gas had green origins too. With the exception of a small amount of water power, a still smaller of wind and tidal mills, the vast machinery of our complex living is driven only by these stores of plant energy.

We, then, the animals, consume those stores in our restless living. Serenely the plants amass them. They turn light's active energy to food, which is potential energy stored for their own benefit. Only if the daisy is browsed by the cow, the maple leaf sucked of its juices by an insect, will that green leaf become of our kind. So we get the song of a bird at dawn, the speed in the hoofs of the fleeing deer, the noble thought in the philosopher's mind. So Plato's Republic was builded on leeks and cabbages.

Animal life lives always in the red; the favorable balance is written on the other side of life's page, and it is written in chlorophyll. All else obeys the thermodynamic law that energy forever runs down hill, is lost and degraded. In economic language, this is the law of diminishing returns, and it is obeyed by the cooling stars as by man and all the animals. They float down its Lethe stream. Only chlorophyll fights up against the current. It is the stuff in life that rebels at death, that has never surrendered to entropy, final icy stagnation. It is the mere cobweb on which we are all suspended over the abyss.

And what then is this substance which is not itself alive but is made by life and makes life, and is never found apart from life?

I remember the first time I ever held it, in the historic dimness of the old Agassiz laboratories, pure, in my hands. My teacher was an owl-eyed master, with a chuckling sense of humor, who had been trained in the greatest laboratory in Germany, and he believed in doing the great things first. So on the first day of his course he set us to extracting chlorophyll, and I remember that his eyes blinked amusement behind his glasses, because when he told us all to go and collect green leaves and most went all the way to the Yard for grass, I opened the window and stole from a vine upon the wall a handful of Harvard's sacred ivy.

We worked in pairs, and my fellow student was a great-grand-nephew or something of the sort, of Elias Fries, the founder of the study of fungi. Together we boiled the ivy leaves, then thrust them in alcohol. After a while it was the leaves which were colorless while the alcohol had become green. We had to dilute this extract with water, and then we added benzol, because this will take the chlorophyll away from the alcohol which, for its part, very conveniently retains the yellow pigments also found in leaves. This left us with a now yellowsih alcohol and, floating on top of it, a thick green benzol; you could simply decant the latter carefully off into a test tube, and there you had chlorophyll extract, opaque, trembling, heavy, a little viscous and oily, and smelling, but much too rankly, like a lawn-mower's blades after a battle with rainy grass.

Then, in a darkened room where beams from a spectroscope escaped in painful darts of light as from the cracks in an old-fashioned magic lantern, we peered at our extracted chlorophyll through prisms. Just as in a crystal chandelier the sunlight is shattered to a rainbow, so in the spectroscope light is spread out in colored bands—a long narrow ribbon, sorting the white light by wave lengths into its elemental parts. And the widths, the presence or the absence, of each cross-band on the ribbon, tell the tale of a chemical element present in the spectrum, much as the bands on a soldier's insignia ribbon show service in Asia, in the tropics, on the border, in what wars. When the astronomer has fixed spectroscope instead of telescope upon a distant star, he reads off the color bands as easily as one soldier reads another's, and will tell you whether sodium or oxygen, helium or iron is present.

Just so our chlorophyll revealed its secrets. The violet and blue end of the spectrum was almost completely blacked out. And that meant that chlorophyll absorbed and used these high-frequency waves. So, too, the red and orange were largely obliterated, over at the right hand side of our tell-tale bar. It was the green that came through clearly. So we call plants green because they use that color least. It is what they reject as fast as it smites the upper cells; it is what they turn back, reflect, flash into our grateful retinas.

It was only routine in a young botanist's training to make an extraction and spectrum analysis of chlorophyll. My student friends over in the chemistry laboratories were more excited than I about it. They were working under Conant, before he became president of Harvard and had to sneak into his old laboratory at night with a key he still keeps. For chlorophyll was Conant's own problem. His diagram of its structure, displayed to me by his students, was closely worked over with symbols and signs, unfolded to something like the dimensions of a blue print of Boulder Dam, and made clear—to anyone who could understand it!—how the atoms are arranged and deployed and linked in such a tremendous molecule as $MgN_4C_{55}H_{72}O_5$.

To Otto and Alfred and Mort every jot and joint in the vast Rube Goldberg machinery of that structural formula had meaning, and more than meaning—the geometrical beauty of the one right, inevitable position for every atom. To me, a botanist's apprentice, a future naturalist, there was just one fact to quicken the pulse. That fact is the close similarity between chlorophyll and hemoglobin, the essence of our blood.

So that you may lay your hand upon the smooth flank of a beech and say, "We be of one blood, brother, thou and I."

The one significant difference in the two structural formulas is this: that the hub of every hemoglobin molecule is one atom of iron, while in chlorophyll it is one atom of magnesium.

Iron is strong and heavy, clamorous when struck, avid of oxygen and capable of corruption. It does not surprise us by its presence in our blood stream. Magnesium is a light, silvery, unresonant metal; its density is only one seventh that of iron, it has half of iron's molecular weight, and melts at half the temperature. It is rustless, ductile and pliant; it burns with a brilliant white light rich in actinic rays, and is widely distributed through the upper soil, but only, save at mineral springs, in dainty quantities. Yet the plant succeeds always in finding that mere trace that it needs, even when a chemist might fail to detect it.

How does the chlorophyll, green old alchemist that it is, transmute the dross of earth into living tissue? Its hand is swifter than the chemist's most sensitive analyses. In theory, the step from water and carbon dioxide to the formation of sugar (the first result readily discerned) must involve several syntheses; yet it goes on in a split hundredth of a second. One sunlight particle or photon strikes the chlorophyll, and instantaneously the terribly tenacious molecule of water, which we break down into its units of hydrogen and oxygen only with difficulty and expense, is torn apart; so too is the carbon dioxide molecule. Building blocks of the three elements, carbon, hydrogen and oxygen, are then whipped at lightning speed into carbonic acid; this is instantly changed over into formic acid—the same that smarts so in our nerve endings when an ant stings us. No sooner formed than formic acid becomes formaldehyde and hydrogen peroxide. This last is poisonous, but a ready enzyme in the plant probably splits it as fast as it is born into harmless water and oxygen, while the formaldehyde is knocked at top speed into a new pattern—and is grape sugar, glucose. And all before you can say Albert Einstein. Indeed, by the time you have said Theophrastus Bombastus Aureolus Paracelsus von Hohenheim, the sugar may have lost a modicum of water—and turned into starch, the first product of photosynthesis that could be detected by the methods of fifty years ago.

At this very instant, with the sun delivering to its child the earth, in the bludgeoning language of mathematics, 215×10^{15} calories per second, photosynthesis is racing along wherever the leaf can reach the light. (All else goes to waste.) True, its efficiency is very low—averaging no better than one per cent, while our machines are delivering up to twenty-five per cent of the fuel they combust. But that which they burn—coal and gas, oils and wood—was made, once, by leaves in ancient geologic times. The store of such energy is strictly finite. Chlorophyll alone is hitched to what is, for earthly purposes, the infinite.

Light, in the latest theory, is not waves in a sea of ether, or a jet from a nozzle; it could be compared rather to machine gun fire, every photo-electric bullet of energy traveling in regular rhythm, at a speed that bridges the astronomical gap in eight minutes. As each bullet hits an electron of chlorophyll it sets it to vibrating, at its own rate, just as one tuning fork, when struck, will cause another to hum in the same pitch. A bullet strikes—and one electron is knocked galley west into a dervish dance like the madness of the atoms in the sun. The energy splits open chlorophyll molecules, recombines their atoms, and lies there, dormant, in foods.

The process seems miraculously adjusted. And yet, like most living processes it is not perfect. The reaction time of chlorophyll is not geared as high as the arrival of the light-bullets. Light comes too fast; plants, which are the very children of light, can get too much of it. Exposure to the sunlight on the Mojave desert is something that not a plant in my garden, no, nor even the wiry brush in the chaparral, could endure. Lids against the light plants do not have; but by torsions of the stalk some leaves may turn their blades edge-on to dazzling radiation, and present them again broadside in failing light. Within others the chlorophyll granules too, bun or pellet-shaped as they are, can roll for a side or frontal exposure toward the light. In others they can crowd to the top of a cell and catch faint rays, or sink or flee to the sides to escape a searing blast. . . .

When I began to write these pages, before breakfast, the little fig tree outside my window was rejoicing in the early morning light. It is a special familiar of my work, a young tree that has never yet borne fruit. It is but a little taller than I, has only two main branches and forty-three twigs, and the brave if not impressive sum of two hundred and sixteen leaves—I have touched every one with a counting finger. Though sparse, they are large, mitten-shaped, richly green with chlorophyll. I compute, by measuring the leaf and counting both sides, that my little tree has a leaf surface of about eighty-four square feet. This sun-trap was at work today long before I.

Those uplifted hand-like leaves caught the first sky light. It was poor for the fig's purpose, but plant work begins from a nocturnal zero. When I came to my desk the sun was full upon those leaves—and it is a wondrous thing how they are disposed so that they do not shade each other. By the blazing California noon, labor in the leaves must have faltered from very excess of light; all the still golden afternoon it went on; now as the sun sets behind a sea fog the little fig slackens peacefully at its task.

Yet in the course of a day it has made sugar for immediate burning and energy release, put by a store of starch for future use; with the addition of nitrogen and other salts brought up in water from the roots it has built proteins too—the very bricks and mortar of the living protoplasm, and the perdurable stuff of permanent tissue. The annual growth ring in the wood of stem and twigs has widened an infinitesimal but a real degree. The fig is one day nearer to its coming of age, to flowering and fruiting. Then, still leafing out each spring, still toiling in the sunlight that I shall not be here to see, it may go on a century and more, growing eccentric, solidifying whimsies, becoming a friend to generations. It will be "the old fig" then. And at last it may give up the very exertion of bearing. It will lean tough elbows in the garden walks, and gardeners yet unborn will scold it and put up with it. But still it will leaf out till it dies.

Dusk is here now. So I switch on the lamp beside my desk. The powerhouse burns its hoarded tons of coal a week, and gives us this instant and most marvelous current. But that light is not new. It was hurled out of the sun two hundred million years ago, and was captured by the leaves of the Carboniferous tree-fern forests, fell with the falling plant, was buried, fossilized, dug up and resurrected. It is the same light. And, in my little fig tree as in the ancient ferns, it is the same unchanging green stuff from age to age, passed without perceptible improvement from evolving plant to plant. What it is and does, so complex upon examination, lies about us tranquil and simple, with the simplicity of a miracle.

CLAUDE BERNARD

•

Carbon Monoxide Poisoning[1]

About 1846, I wished to make experiments on the cause of poisoning with carbon monoxide. I knew that this gas had been described as toxic, but I knew

1 From Claude Bernard, *An Introduction to the Study of Experimental Medicine*, translated by Henry Copley Greene (New York: The Macmillan Company, 1927), pp. 159–161. Reprinted by permission of the General Education Board.

literally nothing about the mechanism of its poisoning; I therefore could not have a preconceived opinion. What, then, was to be done? I must bring to birth an idea by making a fact appear, i.e., make another experiment to see. In fact I poisoned a dog by making him breathe carbon monoxide and after death I at once opened his body. I looked at the state of the organs and fluids. What caught my attention at once was that its blood was scarlet in all the vessels, in the veins as well as the arteries, in the right heart as well as in the left. I repeated the experiment on rabbits, birds and frogs, and everywhere I found the same scarlet coloring of the blood. But I was diverted from continuing this investigation, and I kept this observation a long time unused except for quoting it in my course *a propos* of the coloring of blood.

In 1856, no one had carried the experimental question further, and in my course at the Collège de France on toxic and medicinal substances, I again took up the study of poisoning by carbon monoxide which I had begun in 1846. I found myself then in a confused situation, for at this time I already knew that poisoning with carbon monoxide makes the blood scarlet in the whole circulatory system. I had to make hypotheses, and establish a preconceived idea about my first observation, so as to go ahead. Now, reflecting on the fact of scarlet blood, I tried to interpret it by my earlier knowledge as to the cause of the color of blood. Whereupon all the following reflections presented themselves to my mind. The scarlet color, said I, is peculiar to arterial blood and connected with the presence of a large proportion of oxygen, while dark coloring belongs with absence of oxygen and presence of a larger proportion of carbonic acid; so the idea occurred to me that carbon monoxide, by keeping venous blood scarlet, might perhaps have prevented the oxygen from changing into carbonic acid in the capillaries. Yet it seemed hard to understand how that could be the cause of death. But still keeping on with my inner preconceived reasoning, I added: If that is true, blood taken from the veins of animals poisoned with carbon monoxide should be like arterial blood in containing oxygen; we must see if that is the fact.

Following this reasoning, based on interpretation of my observation, I tried an experiment to verify my hypothesis as to the persistence of oxygen in the venous blood. I passed a current of hydrogen through scarlet venous blood taken from an animal poisoned with carbon monoxide, but I could not liberate the oxygen as usual. I tried to do the same with arterial blood; I had no greater success. My preconceived idea was therefore false. But the impossibility of getting oxygen from the blood of a dog poisoned with carbon monoxide was a second observation which suggested a fresh hypothesis. What could have become of the oxygen in the blood? It had not changed with carbonic acid, because I had not set free large quantities of that gas in passing a current of hydrogen through the blood of the poisoned animals. Moreover, that hypothesis was contrary to the color of the blood. I exhausted myself in conjectures about how carbon monoxide could cause the oxygen to disappear from the blood; and as gases displace one another I naturally thought that the carbon monoxide might have displaced the oxygen and driven it out of the blood. To learn this, I decided to vary my experimentation by putting the blood in artificial conditions that would allow me to recover the displaced oxygen. So I studied the action of carbon monoxide on blood experimentally. For this purpose I took a certain amount of arterial blood from a healthy animal; I put this blood on the mercury in an inverted test tube containing carbon monoxide; I then shook the whole thing so as to poison the blood sheltered from contact with the outer air. Then, after an interval, I examined whether the air in the test tube in contact with the poisoned blood had been changed, and I noted that the air thus in contact with the blood had been remarkably enriched with oxygen, while the proportion of carbon monoxide was lessened. Repeated in the same conditions, these experiments taught me that what had occurred was an exchange, volume by volume, between the carbon monoxide and the oxygen of the blood. But the carbon monoxide, in displacing the oxygen that it had expelled from the blood, remained chemically combined in the blood and could no longer be displaced either by oxygen or by other gases. So that death came through death of the molecules of blood, or in other words by stopping their exercises of a physiological property essential to life.

This last example, which I have very briefly described, is complete; it shows from one end to the other, how we proceed with the experimental method and succeed in learning the immediate cause of phenomena. To begin with I knew literally nothing about the mechanism of the phenomenon of poisoning with carbon monoxide. I undertook an experiment to see, i,e., to observe. I made a preliminary observation of a special change in the coloring of blood. I interpreted this observation, and I made an hypothesis which proved false. But the experiment provided me with a second observation about which I reasoned anew, using it as a starting point for making a new hypothesis as to the mechanism, by which the oxygen in the blood was removed. By building up hypotheses, one by one, about the facts as I observed them, I finally succeeded in showing that carbon monoxide replaces oxygen in a molecule of blood, by combining with the substance of the molecule. Experimental analysis, here, has reached its goal. This is one of the cases, rare in physiology, which I am happy to be able to quote. Here the immediate cause of the phenomenon of poisoning is found and is translated into a theory which accounts for all the facts and at the same time includes all the observations and experiments. Formulated as follows, the theory posits the main facts from which all the rest are deducted: Carbon monoxide combines more intimately than oxygen with the hemoglobin in a molecule of blood. It has quite recently been proved that carbon monoxide forms a definite combination with hemoglobin. So that the molecule of blood, as if petrified by the stability of the combination, loses its vital properties. Hence everything is logically deduced: because of its property of more intimate combination, carbon monoxide drives out of the blood the oxygen essential to life; the molecules of blood become inert, and the animal dies, with symptoms of hemorrhage, from true paralysis of the molecules.

GEORGE AND MURIEL BEADLE

•

The Language of Life: The Structure of DNA[1]

THEORY

Just before the American chemist Linus Pauling went to Sweden to accept the Nobel prize for his work on the atomic structure of protein, his colleagues at Caltech staged a lighthearted musical revue in his honor. A show-stopper entitled "Crystal Crackin' Papa" (which was sung, more or less, to the tune of "Pistol Packin' Mama") included these words:

> Peptide bonds and side groups,
> He put them all in place;
> It sure was plain
> They formed a chain
> And had such helical grace . . .

"Helical" is the adjectival form of helix, which is a figure in three-dimensional space patterned like the threads of a screw or a spiral staircase. The interior of the Guggenheim Museum in New York City, its ramps rising as they turn, is a helix.

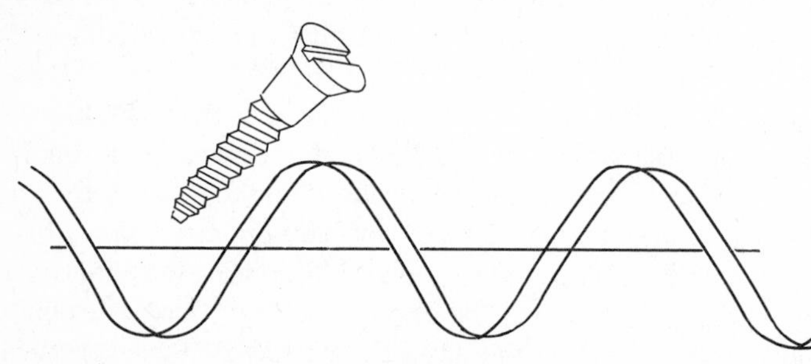

FIGURE 1

What Pauling had shown, in 1950, was that a protein's component chains of amino acids (which are called peptides) are neatly arranged in the twisting turns of a helix and are held in that configuration by hydrogen bonds between successive turns of the helix. Research occurring at the same time, in various labs—notably by a group led by Maurice Wilkins of King's College, London—indicated that DNA molecules were likewise disposed in a helix. Scientists began to struggle in earnest with the *how* of DNA's structure.

[1] From *The Language of Life* by George and Muriel Beadle. Copyright © 1966 by George W. Beadle and Muriel Beadle. Reprinted by permission of Doubleday & Company, Inc. (New York: Doubleday & Company, Inc.), pp. 162–180.
[Note: Figures have been renumbered for this text.—Eds.]

Since the units that we are now talking about—atoms—are almost too small to comprehend, and are completely invisible, perhaps this is a good place to pause and look briefly at modern methods of investigation. How do scientists go about discovering the atomic structure of anything?

They begin with a chemical analysis. For example, it was found early in the nineteenth century that water can be decomposed electrolytically (between two oppositely charged plates) into hydrogen and oxygen, always in constant proportions of two-to-one. Later, when atomic weights could be assigned to the elements, it was discovered that this two-to-one relationship corresponded to two atoms of hydrogen to one atom of oxygen; and the chemical formula of water could be written as H_2O. Similarly, common table salt was found to consist of sodium and chlorine atoms in equal numbers (NaCl).

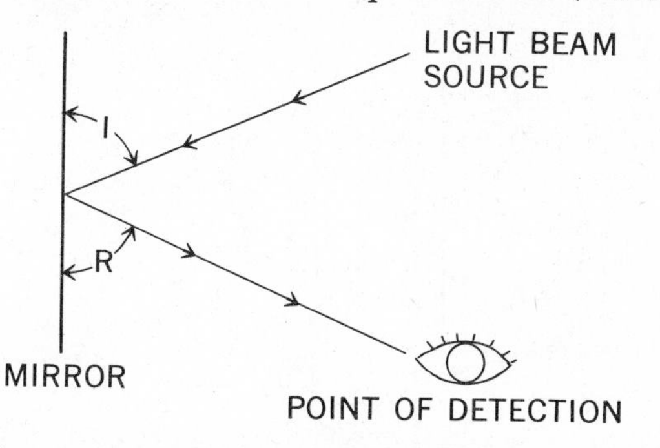

FIGURE 2

For complex molecules such as the amino acids or the nucleotides, more steps are involved. First one determines the kinds of atoms present, and their proportions. Then you go after the molecular subgroupings. In an amino acid, for example, the amino group (NH_2) has certain chemical properties, and so does the hydroxyl (OH). Once the various subgroupings are identified, the chemical formula can be written. To a chemist, $CH_2(NH_2)COOH$ says "glycine" as clearly as the word itself.

As physicists have come to understand more about the nature of light and as technology has improved, it has become possible to analyze substances on the basis of how they respond to light. In the last chapter, for example, we mentioned Caspersson's photography of chromosomes under ultraviolet light. The bases within nucleotides absorb different wave lengths of visible, infrared, or ultraviolet light. The characteristic absorption patterns of these and other molecules, which can be measured with instruments called spectrophotometers, help determine a substance's chemical composition.

But what about its physical structure—the spatial arrangements of the atoms within a molecule? How does one find out how far apart the atoms are, or the angles and lengths of the chemical bonds that hold them together?

One powerful and widely used tool for getting answers to such questions is X-ray diffraction. In practice, this procedure is complex; but in principle it is simple. (See Figure 2.) A beam of light impinging on a flat mirror is reflected at an angle (R) exactly equal to the angle of incidence (I). You can check this yourself with a light source and a mirror. If one knows the position of the light source and the point of detection of the reflected light, the plane of the mirror can easily be determined—for the angles R and I must be equal, and only one position of the mirror will make them so.

Now in crystals, say of salt (shown in Figure 3), the atoms are arranged in a regular pattern from which an incident beam of X-rays will be reflected as if the planes of atoms were mirrors. The X-rays register a pattern on a photographic plate that corresponds to the structural pattern of the crystal. It was by this X-ray diffraction technique that investigators "cracked" the structure of such simple crystals as those of salt and ice. Thus the positions of their atoms became known, and the distances between them.[2]

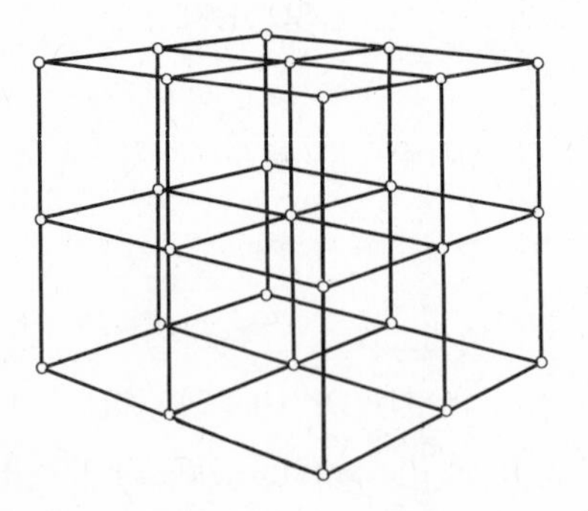

FIGURE 3

With considerable difficulty, the methods of X-ray diffraction have been extended to such complex organic molecules as the proteins and nucleic acids. But these are giant molecules with a great many subgroupings, and X-rays bounce off so many planes that it is sometimes difficult to read the photographic record. This is the point at which model-building becomes useful.

Pauling and his collaborator Robert Corey worked out the so-called alpha helix configuration of protein molecules in this way. (At Caltech, their models were called their "Tinker Toys.") Once a model is constructed that is consistent with available information on interatomic distances, bond angles, X-ray diffraction patterns, and so on, predictions can be made regarding additional X-ray diffraction patterns that should exist. If these are then confirmed, the evidence of the correctness of the structure is greatly strengthened.

In the same year that the structure of protein was discovered—1950—the University of Indiana awarded a Ph.D. degree to a rugged individualist named

[2] Incidentally, when science began to probe the atom, a new micromeasure was needed. You will remember that things the size of viruses are measured in millimicrons, which are roughly 1/25,000,000th of an inch. Atoms, of course, are much smaller than viruses; hence, atomic measurements are expressed in Ångstrom units, after the Swedish astronomer who suggested them. An Ångstrom ("Å") unit is 1/10th of a millimicron in size; that is, 1/250,000,000th of an inch.

James Dewey Watson. His doctoral research had centered on details of radiation effects on bacterial viruses; to pursue it further, he was awarded a fellowship by the National Research Council and went to the University of Copenhagen.

A year later he informed the fellowship committee that he had changed horses. He'd decided, he told them, that the most important problem in genetics was to determine the structure of DNA; therefore, that's what he wanted to work on. To do so he went to Cambridge University to collaborate with the British chemist Francis Crick.

The committee was not enthusiastic. There was the matter of setting a precedent for midstream changes. There was Watson's own capability to consider. He was not yet twenty-five years old; how likely was it that he could solve a problem that was stumping older and wiser men? Permission was therefore at first refused.

Watson stubbornly said he was going to work at Cambridge anyway, and he did. Although the fellowship committe later invited him to reapply for a portion of this original grant, he had meanwhile obtained support from the National Foundation for Infantile Paralysis. When the Watson-Crick collaboration produced a theory that many scientists consider the most momentous since Mendel's, the original committee, one suspects, may have experienced anguish somewhat akin to that of a bettor who has thrown away his ticket on the longshot winner of a Kentucky Derby.

What the American biochemist and the English chemist did was to fit the known chemical facts about DNA into a proposed molecular structure that explains how DNA makes copies of itself. In so doing, they also enabled science to discover how genetic directions are "written," how they are translated into orders which the cells obey, and how they are modified by mutation. Finally, they enabled chemists, physicists, and biologists to discuss the structure and behavior of living organisms—for the first time in the history of science—in a common language, the language of molecular structure.

Watson and Crick did no research—as laymen understand the word. They reread all the literature about DNA; they covered paper and blackboards with formulas and equations; they snipped "nucleotides" from thin metal sheets and used them for model-making. But mostly they just *thought.*

Their object was to put together the following pieces of an atomic jigsaw puzzle:

1. It was known from X-ray diffraction studies that the bases, sugars, and phosphates in each nucleotide are joined in the pattern shown in Figure 4 in a strand at least 200,000 such units long per molecule.

2. In addition to the dots and splashes spaced to correspond to the phosphate-sugar-base relationship shown below, the X-ray plates also showed another wider-spaced set of markings that almost certainly reflected the turns of a helix. The diameter of this helix was known: it is of uniform width, about 20 Å across.

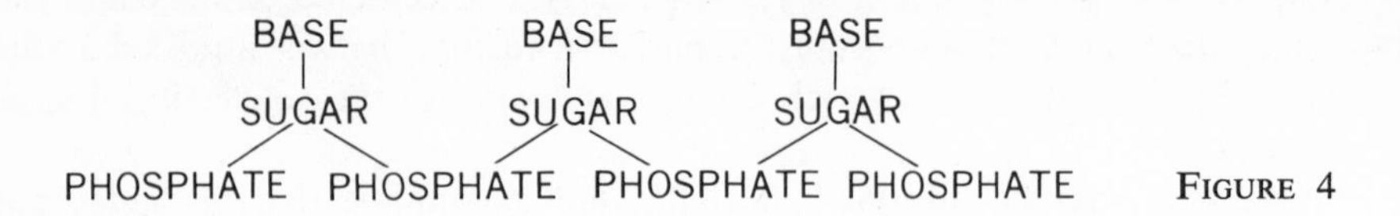

FIGURE 4

3. Whether the sugars and phosphates are on the "outside" and the bases closer to the axis of the helix, or vice versa, was not known. Nor was it known whether all three components of a nucleotide are oriented alike, as at left in Figure 5 (using drinking glasses as an example) or whether the bases are

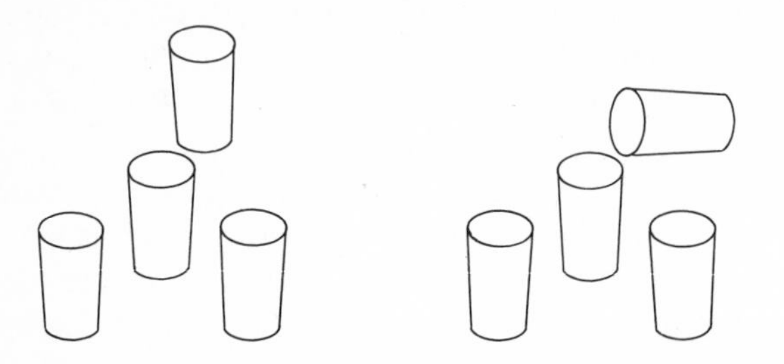

FIGURE 5

turned at right angles to the sugars and phosphates, as at right in Figure 5. There was some evidence indicating the right-angled orientation, so Watson and Crick provisionally opted for that belief.

4. Quantitative analysis by various chemists had shown that in all organisms the sugars and phosphates are in the same proportion, thus confirming the regularity of sequence shown by X-ray diffraction studies.

5. But different organisms vary greatly in total amounts of adenine, guanine, cytosine, and thymine. One organism can have twice as many thymine-containing nucleotides as another organism, for example. This could only mean that there is no particular regularity of sequence governing the order of bases.

6. Offsetting this apparent complete variability was a curious fact that had been turned up by the American biochemist Erwin Chargaff. Within the DNA of any particular organism, the ratio of nucleotides containing adenine to those containing thymine is one-to-one, and so is that of nucleotides containing guanine to those containing cytosine.

In other words, your cells and the cells of a rabbit may have different total amounts of the four bases, but in both you and the rabbit the amount of adenine equals the amount of thymine, and the guanine equals the cytosine.

This latter point was really the key to the structure that Watson and Crick finally proposed, because it suggested, first, that adenine and thymine are paired and so are guanine and cytosine; and, second, that a pairing of bases within nucleotides requires the DNA strands of which they are a part to be paired, too. In other words, the DNA helix must be a *double* strand.

A chemical condition would have to be met, however, before one could postulate such pairing. The bases in the two strands would have to come together in such a way that hydrogen bonds would form. Assuming that the bases are right-angled relative to the sugars and phosphates, such bonds will form only at points indicated in the formulas in Figure 6.

If the bases are bonded in this fashion, the sugars and phosphates become positioned on the outside of each strand of DNA as shown in Figure 7.

In three dimensions, the assembly would appear as in Figure 8.

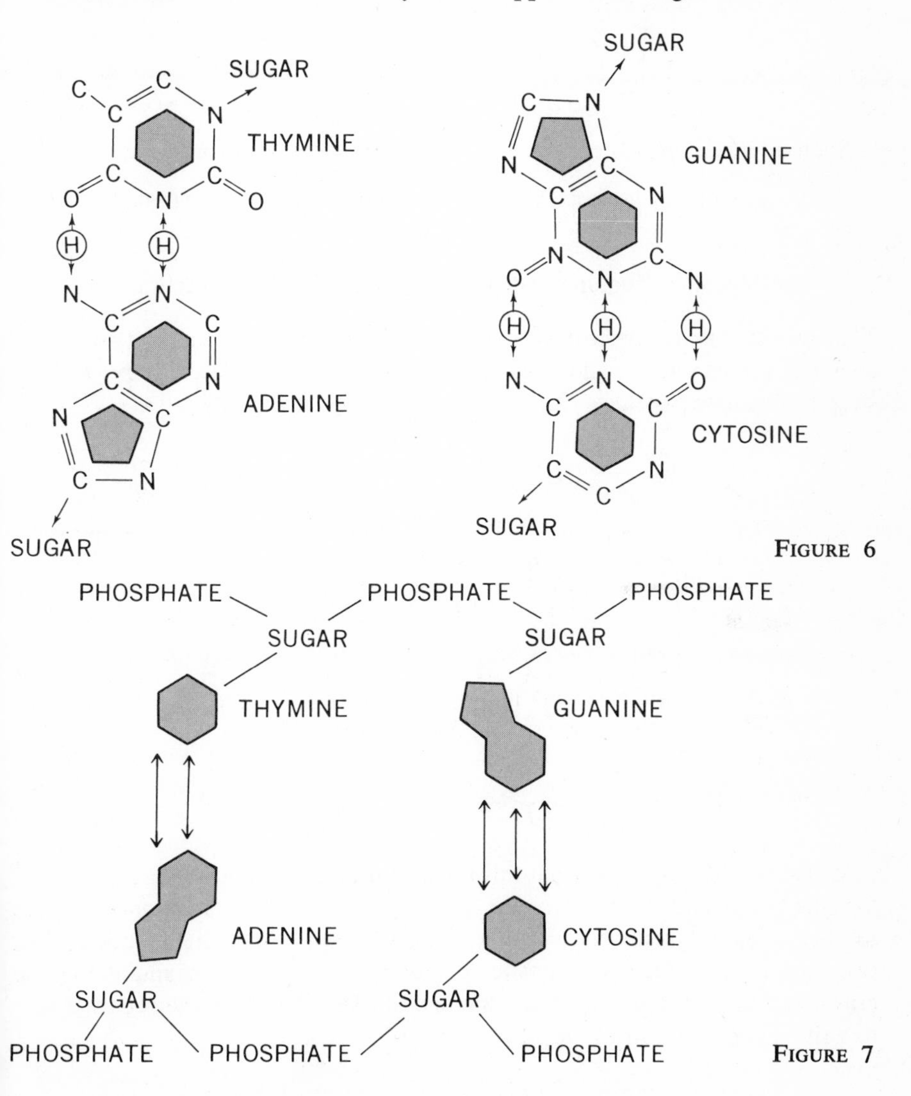

FIGURE 6

FIGURE 7

And flattened out into a diagrammatic representation, it would look like Figure 9.

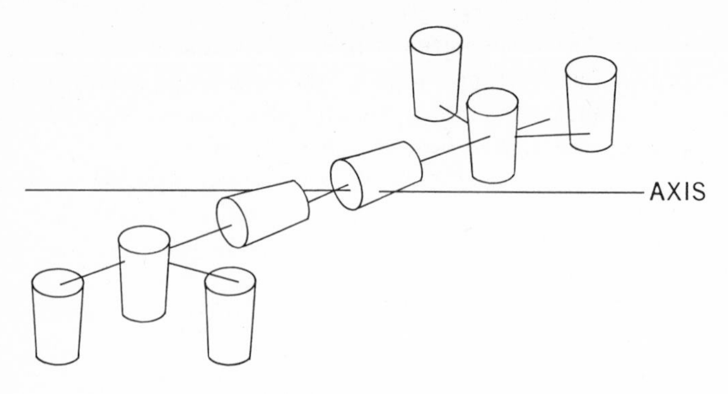

FIGURE 8

Such an assembly, except for one fact, could be written thus:

Adenine Cytosine Thymine Adenine Cytosine Thymine

| | | | | |

Thymine Guanine Adenine Thymine Guanine Adenine

That one fact is apparent if you study the bases in the top strand—take an adenine, for example—and compare it with the same base in the bottom strand. You'll soon realize that each is a reversal of the other.

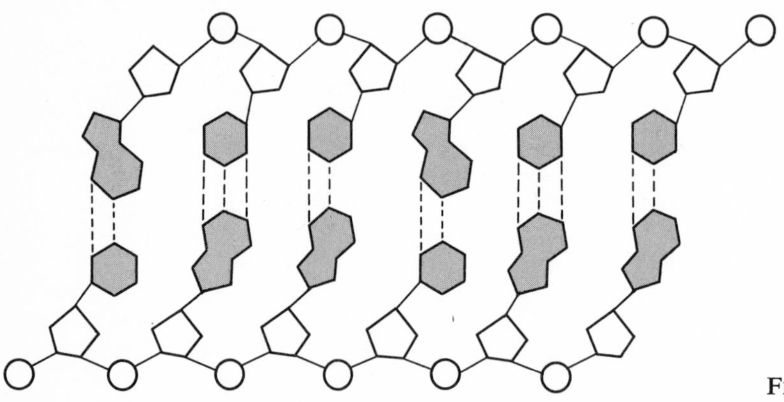

FIGURE 9

Watson and Crick knew what this reversal means: the nucleotides and therefore the two strands of the helix are "anti-parallel"—that is, positioned relative to each other (to resurrect a figure of speech used earlier in this book) like two swimmers headed in opposite directions, one face-down and doing the crawl, the other face-up and doing the backstroke. Therefore, the accurate way to write a series of pairings as above is:

Adenine Cytosine Thymine Adenine Cytosine Thymine

| | | | | |

Thymine Guanine Adenine Thymine Guanine Adenine

And a good way to identify the bases on a diagram is:

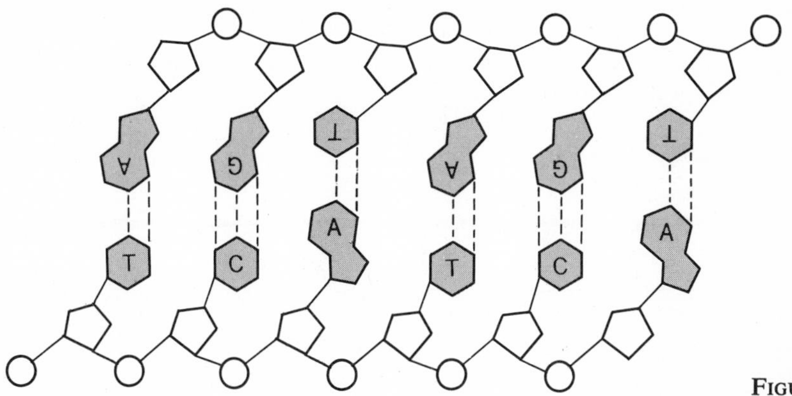

FIGURE 10

Now, by turning Figure 10 into a helix, one gets Figure 11. The sugars and phosphates on the outside of each strand would be held in steady alignment because the paired bases would serve as "connecting rods." A fact that fitted here was that X-ray diffraction studies showed the DNA molecule to be of uniform diameter. The pairing of a double-ring with a single-ring base in each case would add up to the same over-all width for each pair.

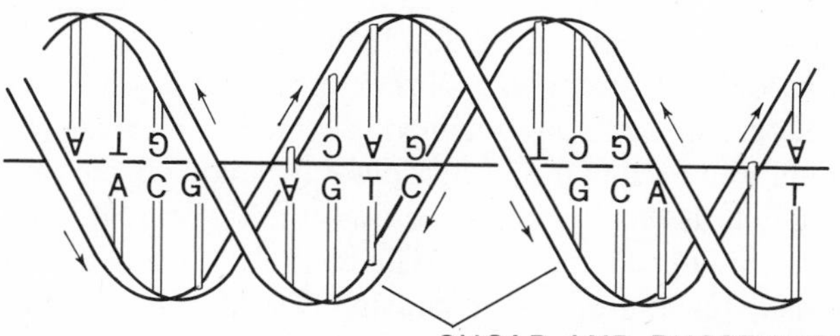

FIGURE 11

In sum, everything about this possible structure corresponded to what was known about the physical nature of DNA. But the most exciting aspect of Watson and Crick's emerging solution for their atomic jigsaw puzzle was that molecules of this design could make copies of themselves—which DNA was, of course, known to do.

If the hydrogen bonds between the two strands were to break (see Figure 12), the two strands were to unwind, and the bases in each strand were to pick up (from raw materials in the cell) their proper partners (see Figure 13), each double-stranded DNA molecule would have made a copy of itself!

It must have required almost superhuman restraint for Watson and Crick to write in their published account, "It has not escaped our notice that the

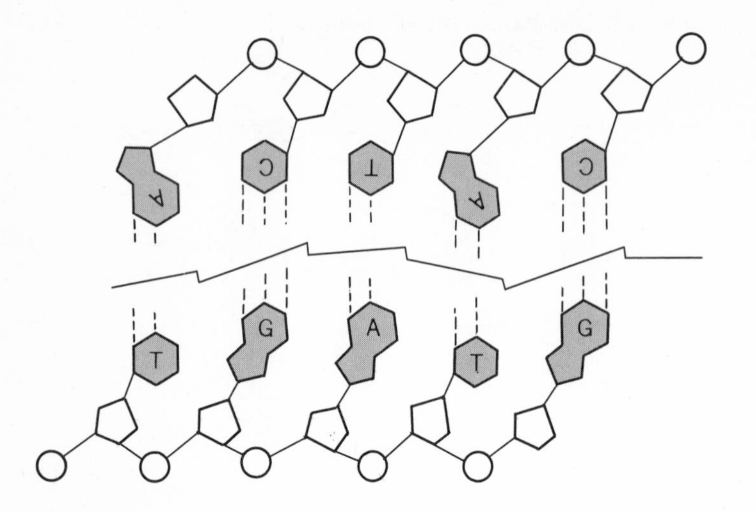

FIGURE 12

specific pairing we have postulated immediately suggests a possible copying mechanism for the genetic material."

The two men also realized that so long as A in one chain paired with T in the other chain, and C in one chain with G in the other, the over-all sequence could be infinitely varied.

If *any* sequence of the four pairs—A-T, T-A, C-G, and G-C—is possible (and chemists' quantitative analysis, remember, had found widely differing amounts of the bases in different organisms), the possible variations are astronomical. Just four pairs seem a small and limiting number only up to the point where you envision them strung in chains of approximately 200,000, the number of nucleotides estimated to be contained in some DNA molecules. Yes, such a structure would well explain the endless diversity among living things.

It was a wonderfully neat theory. In fact, it was almost *too* neat.

Watson and Crick had talked to Maurice Wilkins at King's College. He and his colleagues had made much progress in studying DNA by X-ray diffraction techniques, and the scientific grapevine was buzzing with news about what they were finding. It confirmed what Watson and Crick had deduced (and vice versa): that the DNA molecule is a double helix, anti-parallel in structure, the sugar-phosphates on the outside being linked by the bases.

Therefore, in 1953, publication was joint—Watson and Crick emphasizing the specific pairing of nucleotides that was their unique contribution, Wilkins emphasizing the structural details as revealed by X-ray diffraction. The complementarity of the data provided by the two sets of investigators strengthened their case.

Nevertheless, a sizable number of scientists couldn't accept it. Some objected for a wholly subjective and non-scientific reason: the great mystery of life couldn't, at its base, be that simple. Others criticized details. How could a

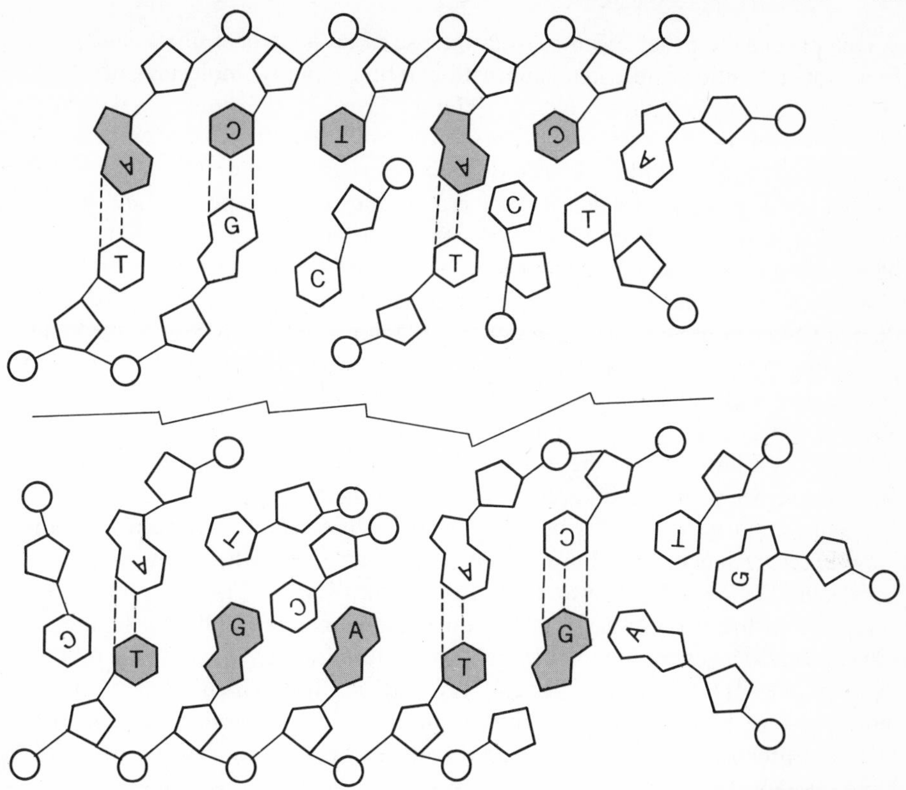

FIGURE 13

chain of 200,000 or more nucleotides unwind and rewind within minutes? By what stretch of the imagination could one assume that 200,000 additional nucleotides of exactly the right kind would be floating around in the cell at just the right moment? Let alone the several *billion* that would be needed when a human cell, its forty-six chromosomes each containing far more than 200,000 nucleotides per chromosome, replicated. Finally, what possible device could the cell possess for getting the correct partners together? To do all these things, they said, would require a degree of precision, speed, and coordination that was inconceivable. And in this assessment they were quite right: the cellular processes that are triggered by DNA *are* almost inconceivably precise, swift, and well-coordinated. But the inconceivable is not necessarily impossible, nor was it in this case.

PROOF

Proof that the Watson-Crick structure was essentially correct came fast; and when it came, was almost as elegant as the initial hypothesis.

One part of the proof resulted from the use of an analytical ultracentrifuge. In a proper solution and when spun with extreme rapidity, molecules of varying densities suspend themselves at different levels in the liquid—a kind of invisible layering, but one which can be read by chemists as successfully as geologists read the visible evidence of rock layers in a gorge. The position of a given band indicates the density of the molecules that compose it; and if the molecules in that band are DNA you can check how much DNA is present by exposing it to ultraviolet light and measuring the amount of UV absorption.

Knowing this, Matthew Meselson, Frank Stahl, and Jerome Vinograd (all then at Caltech) grew several generations of colon bacilli on a culture medium containing N^{15}, a heavy stable isotope of nitrogen—a procedure which increases the molecular weight and density of the DNA in those bacteria by about 1 per cent over those that contain only the normal N^{14} isotope. DNA from bacteria nurtured on these two different culture mediums will "band" in an ultracentrifuge at two different levels, as in Figure 14.

Having bred bacteria with built-in "heavy" DNA, the three chemists then grew a generation on a culture medium containing only the "light"—N^{14}—hydrogen. Their reasoning was a follows: If the Watson-Crick hypothesis is correct, and the two chains of DNA *do* make complete duplicates of themselves, the first generation of bacteria (as determined by a doubling of the number of cells) should have one heavy and one light chain in each DNA molecule (see Figure 15). And those molecules should form a band in the ultracentrifuge exactly intermediate in density between N^{15} heavy and N^{14} light DNA. Which is exactly what happened when the experiment was done.

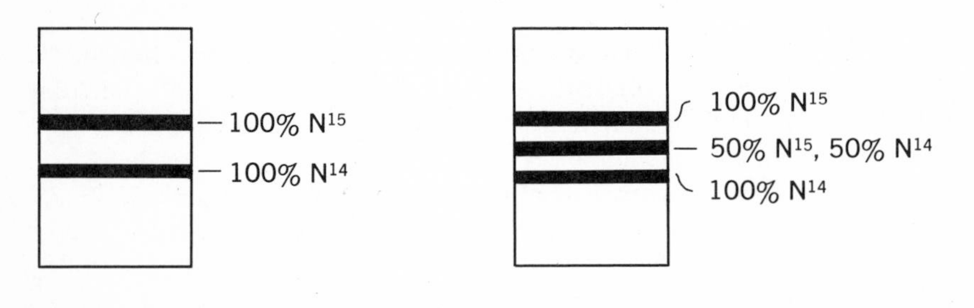

FIGURE 14

FIGURE 15

Then Meselson and his colleagues grew a second generation determining two generations when each original cell had increased to four, again on a medium containing light hydrogen. This time, according to theory, half the DNA molecules should be composed of one chain containing N^{15} and one chain containing N^{14}, whereas the other half of DNA molecules should have N^{14} in both chains. DNA in the centrifuge should band equally in two positions, light and intermediate (see Figure 16). Which is also what happened.

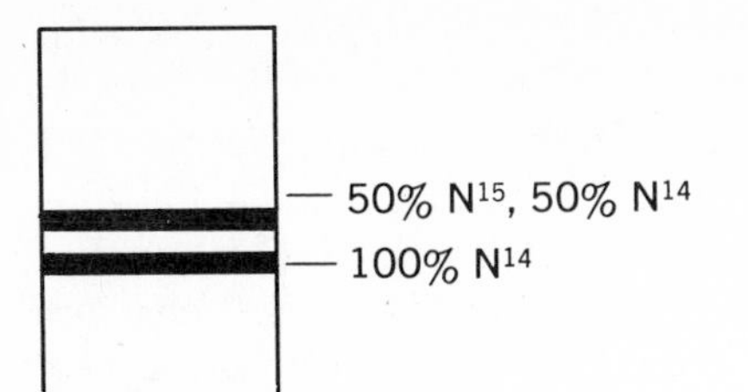

FIGURE 16

Another version of the same approach was the labeling of DNA in bean plant chromosomes with tritium (radioactive hydrogen-3) by the American cytologist J. Herbert Taylor and his associates.

If you dope broad bean root cells with colchicine (it's a gout remedy for humans, too), cell division will cease but the chromosomes inside those cells will continue to replicate. Taylor therefore fed the bean cells thymine which had been exposed to tritium. This put a radioactive raw material, whose presence could later be detected on film, into the environment in which the chromosomes would be duplicating. Then an application of colchicine stopped cell division. This enabled investigators, after counting the number of chromosomes in a given cell, to determine how many chromosome replications had occurred within a given period.

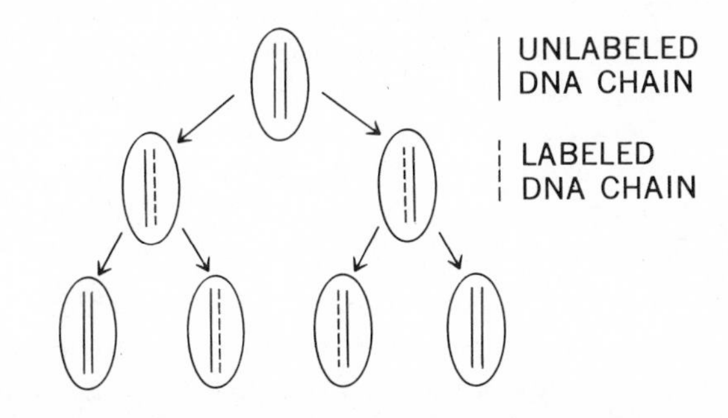

FIGURE 17

If the Watson-Crick theory was right, as the strands of DNA separated for the first chromosome replication and each strand picked up a new partner strand, the thymine-containing nucleotides in the new molecule would be radioactive. Therefore all chromosomes of that "generation" would contain one labeled and one unlabeled strand as in Figure 17. On the *next* replication—the cell nutrients in this case being unlabeled—one would expect (again if the Watson-Crick theory is correct) to find that half the daughter chromosomes are radioactive and the other half are not.

And that too is what happened when the experiment was made.[3] The tri-

[3] It should be mentioned that chromosomes do not contain just one longitudinal double DNA molecule the same length as the chromosome. In fact, DNA is coiled into the chromosomes so compactly that it may be a thousand times longer than the chromosome. But the point of Taylor's experiment was that the chromosome segments behaved *as if* they contained single double strands of DNA. Clearly the individual molecules of DNA replicated with each chromosome duplication in a manner consistent with the Watson-Crick hypothesis.

tium-labeling of DNA in whole chromosomes gave a result which agreed with the nitrogen labeling experiments of Meselson.

Still more evidence that the Watson-Crick hypothesis is correct came from the synthesis of DNA, in 1956, by Arthur Kornberg (then at Washington University, St. Louis). This achievement caused newspapers to break out in a rash of headlines predicting that living things will be created in a test tube any day now. Happily or alas, according to one's point of view, the brave new world is not yet at hand; nevertheless, Kornberg's achievement was a great one. He proved that the nucleotide bases in DNA *do* replicate by finding their complements.

It is necessary to interrupt at this point to remind you that all chemical reactions in a cell are engineered by enzymes. DNA is like a plant manager. Enzymes are its section foremen. The cytoplasm of the cell is a stock room full of necessary raw materials, including the high-energy phosphates which supply the "push" required to join groups of atoms into molecules. Whenever DNA says the word, the enzymes see to it that whatever materials have to be collected *are* collected and whatever energy has to be supplied *is* supplied.

Returning to Kornberg's experiment: First, he mixed together in a test tube the raw materials that DNA would need to duplicate itself: the four nucleotides (with two extra phosphate groups on each), inorganic salts, magnesium, and an enzyme required for DNA construction. Then he popped in a bit of natural DNA from a colon bacillus. Using the materials in its artificial environment, it made copies of itself. Furthermore, these copies made copies of *themselves.*

Some time later, an even more astounding event occurred.

We have not said much, so far, about the necessity of establishing "controls" —but when doing an experiment one must always try a variety of methods in order to check the nature and authenticity of a reaction. With regard to Kornberg's experiment just described, for example, one would assume that all four nucleotides must be present in the vessel in order for DNA synthesis to take place; but the only way to *know* whether this is the case is to set up a battery of test tubes, omit one or more nucleotides from each, and observe what happens. This is what Kornberg and his associates did. They discovered that the logical assumption *is* correct: for a bit of natural DNA to copy itself in an artificial environment such as they had created, all four nucleotides are necessary.

In doing this experiment, Kornberg had incubated his mixes for two to three hours, then had used optical and chemical methods for measuring the increase in DNA. In 1957, however, he and his colleagues decided to try a new measurement technique. Would the increase in DNA correlate with an increase in the viscosity of the solution in which the DNA was replicating? Again, they set up the same controls that had been used previously; but this time, in addition, they took measurements for longer than the two to three hours that had been the cut-off point before.

The investigators were happy to discover that viscosity *did* correlate with increase in DNA. They had indeed found a useful new method of measurement. But they found something else, too—something much more important. In one of the control test tubes, a solution from which guanine nucleotide had been omitted—and in which, therefore, no natural DNA could have been synthesized—an investigator noted, at the fourth hour, that a very rapid increase in viscosity was taking place. This continued until the sixth hour. If increase in viscosity correlated with the formation of DNA, DNA must have formed in that test tube—but how could it have, without one of the nucleotides?

That evening, Kornberg and his associates considered their several possible sources of error. Perhaps someone had mistakenly put into the mix the guanine that should have been omitted. Perhaps the control test tube had been contaminated by bacteria. Perhaps there was something wrong with the equipment that measured viscosity. Therefore, they reran the experiment the next day, being sure to eliminate each possible source of error. The same rapid increase in viscosity, at the same time interval after incubation, again occurred.

Controls were again set up, each omitting various of the ingredients known to be essential for laboratory synthesis of DNA. It was found that, given enough time, rapid increase in viscosity occurred even in the test tube from which natural DNA—the model, or "primer," in previous experiments—had been omitted. This particular vessel produced an unusual kind of DNA, with the following sequence:

∀ ⊥ ∀ ⊥ ∀ ⊥ ∀ ⊥ ∀ ⊥
· · · · · · · · · ·
T A T A T A T A T A

Subsequently, another experimental mix produced another unusual DNA. It had this sequence:

Ɔ Ɔ Ɔ Ɔ Ɔ Ɔ Ɔ Ɔ Ɔ
· · · · · · · · ·
G G G G G G G G G

Both types, once made, produced copies of themselves—and without the four-to-six-hour lag period.

Note that Kornberg's original intention was not to find out whether DNA synthesis would take place without a bit of natural DNA as the model; he and his colleagues were simply running a routine check on the raw-material requirements of natural DNA when replicating in an artificial environment. What they found is a scientific example of serendipity.

Here, then, at a more advanced level of life, was reinforcement for the findings of experiments that had re-created a supposed primeval atmosphere and had made in it organic molecules from non-organic raw materials. Stanley Miller, in 1952, had gone back four or five billion years in his laboratory; Kornberg, in 1957, perhaps three billion.

It is amusing to note that when Kornberg undertook these experiments he was repeatedly warned by friends and colleagues that he didn't have a chance of success, and why go knowingly into a dead-end street? But he decided to risk a big failure, knowing that the opposite side of the same coin was a big success—and he proved that the process of replication isn't as complex as most people imagined.

In so doing, he did something even more important: he knocked the final prop from under the comfortable assumption of mankind that "life" is inherently different from "non-life."

PART VI

SOCIETY

Sociology

SEYMOUR M. LIPSET

•

A Changing American Character?[1]

Two themes, equality and achievement, emerged from the interplay between the Puritan tradition and the Revolutionary ethos in the early formation of America's institutions. In this section the thesis is advanced that the dynamic interaction of these two predominant values has been a constant element in determining American institutions and behavior. As we have seen, equalitarianism was an explicit part of the revolt against the traditions of the Old World, while an emphasis upon success and hard work had long been a part of the Protestant ethic. In addition, the need to maximize talent in the new nation's search to "overtake" the Old World placed an added premium on an individual's achievement, regardless of his social station. The relatively few changes that Andrew Jackson made in the civil service, despite his aggressive equalitarian ethos, and the fact that his appointments were well-trained, highly educated men, show that ability was valued along with equality in the young republic.[2]

[1] From *The First New Nation.* © 1963 by Seymour Martin Lipset (New York: Basic Books, Inc., 1963), pp. 101–139.

[2] See Erik M. Erikkson, "The Federal Civil Service Under President Jackson," *Mississippi Valley Historical Review,* 13 (1927), pp. 517–540. Erikkson demonstrates convincingly that Jackson did not inaugurate a spoils system, that relatively few civil servants were fired after he took office. His conclusions have been reiterated recently in a detailed analysis of the backgrounds of the upper echelons of government under Jackson. Sidney Aronson agrees with Erikkson that there was little turnover when Jackson took office. Both men point to the fact that the changes introduced by Jefferson were about as great as by Jackson. Aronson also demonstrates that Jackson's appointees were highly qualified men, that most of them were college graduates in an age when the total number of such graduates was insignificant. See Sidney Aronson, *Status and Kinship in the Higher Civil*

The relationship between these themes of equality and success has been complex. On the one hand, the ideal of equal opportunity institutionalized the notion that success should be the goal of *all,* without reference to accidents of birth or class or color. On the other hand, in actual operation these two dominant values resulted in considerable conflict. While everyone was supposed to succeed, obviously certain persons were able to achieve greater success than others. The wealth of the nation was never distributed as equally as the political franchise. The tendency for the ideal of achievement to undermine the fact of equality, and to bring about a society with a distinct class character, has been checked by the recurrent victories of the forces of equality in the political order. Much of our political history, as Tocqueville noted, can be interpreted in terms of a struggle between proponents of democratic equality and would-be aristocracies of birth or wealth.[3]

In recent years, many social analysts have sought to show how the increasing industrialization, urbanization, and bureaucratization of American society have modified the values of equality and achievement. In both the 1930's and the 1950's American social scientists were certain that the country was undergoing major structural changes. In the 1930's they were sure that these changes were making status lines more rigid, that there was a movement away from achieved status back to ascribed status, and that the equalitarian ethic was threatened as a consequence.[4] Such typical writers of the 1950's as David Riesman and William H. Whyte contend that it is the achievement motive and the Protestant ethic of hard work that are dying: they think that the new society prefers security, emotional stability, and "getting along with others." Riesman posits a transformation of the American character structure from "inner direction" (i.e., responding to a fixed internal code of morality) to "other direction" (i.e., responding to demands of others in complex situations).[5] Whyte believes that values themselves have changed. He argues that the old value system of the Protestant ethic, which he defines as the "pursuit of individual salvation through hard work, thrift, and competitive struggle," is being replaced by the "social ethic," whose basic tenets are a "belief in the group as the source of creativity; a belief in "belongingness' as the ultimate need of the individual; and a belief in the application of science to achieve the belongingness."[6]

If the changes suggested by the critics of the 1930's or the 1950's were

---

Service: The Administrations of John Adams, Thomas Jefferson and Andrew Jackson (doctoral dissertation, Columbia University Department of Sociology, 1961).

[3] Alexis de Tocqueville, *Democracy in America* (New York: Vintage Books, 1955), Vol. I, pp. 185–186.

[4] These studies of the 1930's are discussed at the end of this chapter in more detail.

[5] David Riesman, *The Lonely Crowd* (New Haven, Conn.: Yale University Press, 1950).

[6] William H. Whyte, *The Organization Man* (New York: Simon & Schuster, 1956).

occurring in the drastic form indicated in their books, then America no longer could be said to possess the traits formed as a consequence of its origin as a new nation with a Protestant culture. As I read the historical record, however, it suggests that there is more continuity than change with respect to the main elements in the national value system. This does not mean that our society is basically static. Clearly, there have been great secular changes—industrialization, bureaucratization, and urbanization are real enough—and they have profoundly affected other aspects of the social structure. Many American sociologists have documented changes in work habits, leisure, personality, family patterns, and so forth. But this very concentration on the obvious social changes in a society that has spanned a continent in a century, that has moved from a predominantly rural culture as recently as 1870 to a metropolitan culture in the 1950's, has introduced a fundamental bias against looking at what has been relatively constant and unchanging.

Basic alterations of social character or values are rarely produced by change in the means of production, distribution, and exchange alone. Rather, as a society becomes more complex, its institutional arrangements make adjustments to new conditions within the framework of a dominant value system. In turn, the new institutional patterns may affect the socialization process which, from infancy upward, instills fundamental character traits. Through such a process, changes in the dominant value system develop slowly—or not at all. There are constant efforts to fit the "new" technological world into the social patterns of the old, familiar world.

In this section I examine the thesis that a fundamental change has occurred in American society by treating three topics, each of which has been widely discussed as reflecting important modifications in the basic value system. This chapter deals with the arguments and evidence of changes in the basic predominant character traits of Americans as suggested by men like David Riesman and William Whyte. The following chapter, 4, examines the evidence of major changes in religious participation and belief, since many have argued that American religion, the institution most closely identified with values, is much different from what it was in the nineteenth century. And the last chapter of the section, 5, analyzes an institution which has become significant only in in this century, and especially in the past three decades: the trade union. Trade unions are given special treatment because the growth of these "class" organizations has suggested to some that the United States is finally entering the era of working-class consciousness as a result of the hardening of class lines, and that we are witnessing the end of the emphases on achievement and equality.

In brief, I attempt in this section to present some of the evidence for my thesis that it is the basic value system, as solidified in the early days of the new nation, which can account for the kinds of changes that have taken place in the American character and in American institutions as these faced the need to adjust to the requirements of an urban, industrial, and bureaucratic society.

Marcus Cunliffe has remarked on the American tendency to assert that a wondrous opportunity has been ruined, "that a golden age has been tarnished, that the old ways have disappeared, or that they offer no useful guide to a newer generation."[7] He points out that, American belief to the contrary, there has been surprising continuity in American history as compared with the histories of European nations. This American propensity to feel that the country is going through a major change at any "present time" is related to an almost "inherent American tendency to believe that one has been cut off decisively from the past as if by a physical barrier." Cunliffe attributes this tendency to three main elements:

> First it is a consequence of the undeniable fact of continuous and rapid social change since the origins of settlement. This process has, understandably, revealed itself in regrets and neuroses as well as in pride and exuberance. Second, the tendency is rooted in the constant American determination to repudiate Europe—Europe equated with the Past, in contrast with America as the Future—and so to lose the Past altogether. Third, the tendency is a consequence of the American sense of a society which is uniquely free to choose its own destiny. The sense of mission, of dedication and of infinite possibility, in part a fact and in part an article of faith, has led to acute if temporary despairs, to suspicions of betrayal and the like, as well as to more positive and flamboyant results.[8]

In a sense, Cunliffe's analysis shows how some of the values we have seen arising from America's revolutionary origins continue to be a part of its image of itself. And perhaps more important, his observation that there has been more continuity in American history than in European history suggests that the values around which American institutions are built have not changed abruptly. Others have pointed out that America is an example of a country where social change does not have to destroy the fabric of society, precisely because it is based upon an ideological commitment to change.[9]

The thesis that the same basic values which arose in the American Revolution have shaped the society under changing geographical and economic conditions, has also been advanced by many historians. Thus Henry Nash Smith has sought to show how the rural frontier settlements established in the West on the Great Plains reflected not only the physical environment but also "the assumptions and aspirations of a whole society."[10] He has argued that revisions in the Homestead Act, which would have permitted large farms and a more economical use of arid land, were opposed by the new settlers

[7] Marcus Cunliffe, "American Watersheds," *American Quarterly,* 13 (1961), pp. 479–494.

[8] *Ibid.,* pp. 489–490.

[9] Daniel Bell, "The Theory of Mass Society," *Commentary,* 22 (1956), pp. 75–83.

[10] Henry Nash Smith, *Virgin Land: The American West as Symbol and Myth* (Cambridge, Mass.: Harvard University Press, 1950), p. 124; for a similar point see George W. Pierson, "The Frontier and American Institutions," *New England Quarterly,* 15 (1942), p. 253.

because they believed in the ideal of the family farm. Walt Rostow suggests there is a "classic American style [which] . . . emerged distinctively toward the end of the seventeenth century as the imperatives and opportunities of a wild but ample land began to assert themselves over various transplanted autocratic attitudes and institutions which proved inappropriate to the colonial scene . . . [and] came fully to life . . . after the War of 1812." And he further contends that this style has not changed basically, since "the cast of American values and institutions and the tendency to adapt them by cumulative experiment rather than to change them radically has been progressively strengthened by the image of the gathering success of the American adventure."[11] Commager, writing of America in general, has said: "Circumstances change profoundly, but the character of the American people has not changed greatly or the nature of the principles of conduct, public and private, to which they subscribe."[12] Three books dealing with American values, by Daniel Boorstin, Louis Hartz, and Ralph Gabriel, have each, in a different way, argued the effective continuity of the fundamental ideals of the society.[13]

The conclusions of these historians are affirmed also in a "lexicographic analysis of alleged American characteristics, ideals, and principles" reported in a myriad of books and articles dealing with "the American way." American history was divided for the purposes of the study into four periods, "Pre-Civil War (to 1865), Civil War to World War (1866–1917), World War to Depression (1918–1929), and Depression to present (1930–1940)." For each period a list of traits alleged by observers was recorded, and "when the lists for each of the four time periods were compared, no important difference between the traits mentioned by modern observers and those writing in the earlier periods of American history was discovered." Among the traits mentioned in all four periods were: "Belief in equality of all as a fact and as a right" and "uniformity and conformity."[14]

[11] W. W. Rostow, "The National Style," in Elting E. Morison, ed., *The American Style: Essays in Value and Performance* (New York: Harper & Row, 1958), pp. 247, 259.
[12] Henry Steele Commager, *Living Ideas in America* (New York: Harper & Row, 1951), p. xviii. In the introduction to a collection of the writings of foreign observers, Commager reported also that "a real unity emerges from these heterogeneous selections . . . implicit in the material itself. . . . To the visitors of the seventeen-seventies and the nineteen-forties, America *meant* much the same thing. *America in Perspective* (New York: Random House, 1947), p. xvi. (Emphasis in original.)
[13] See Daniel Boorstin, *The Genius of American Politics* (Chicago: University of Chicago Press, 1953), and his *The Lost World of Thomas Jefferson* (New York: Holt, Rinehart and Winston, 1948); Louis M. Hartz, *The Liberal Tradition in America: An Interpretation of American Political Thought since the Revolution* (New York: Harcourt, Brace & World, 1955); and Ralph H. Gabriel, *The Course of American Democratic Thought* (New York: Ronald Press, 1956). Boorstin sees these values or basic premises as "naturalism." Hartz calls his version "liberalism," while Gabriel speaks of a "democratic faith" with three aspects.
[14] Lee Coleman, "What is America? A Study of Alleged American Traits," *Social Forces,* 19 (1941), pp. 492–499.

The Unchanging American Character

Foreign travelers' accounts of American life, manners, and character traits constitute a body of evidence with which to test the thesis that the American character has been transformed during the past century and a half. Their observations provide us with a kind of comparative mirror in which we can look at ourselves over time. It is important to note, therefore, that the type of behavior which Riesman and Whyte regard as distinctly modern, as reflecting the decline of the Protestant Ethic, was repeatedly reported by many of the nineteenth-century travelers as a peculiarly American trait in their day. Thus the English writer Harriet Martineau at times might be paraphrasing *The Lonely Crowd* in her description of the American of the 1830's:

> [Americans] may travel over the world, and find no society but their own which will submit to the restraint of perpetual caution, and reference to the opinions of others. They may travel over the whole world, and find no country but their own where the very children beware of getting into scrapes, and talk of the effect of actions upon people's minds; where the youth of society determine in silence what opinions they shall bring forward, and what avow only in the family circle; where women write miserable letters, almost universally, because it is a settled matter that it is unsafe to commit oneself on paper; and where elderly people seem to lack almost universally that faith in principles which inspires a free expression of them at any time, and under all circumstances. . . .
>
> There is fear of vulgarity, fear of responsibility; and above all, fear of singularity. . . . There is something little short of disgusting to the stranger who has been unused to witness such want of social confidence, in the caution which presents probably the strongest aspect of selfishness that he has ever seen. The Americans of the northern states are, from education and habit, as accustomed to the caution of which I speak, as to be unaware of its extent and singularity. . . .
>
> Few persons [Americans] really doubt this when the plain case is set down before them. They agree to it in church on Sundays, and in conversation by the fireside: and the reason why they are so backward as they are to act upon it in the world, is that habit and education are too strong for them. They have worn their chains so long that they feel them less than might be supposed.[15]

Harriet Martineau is only one observer of early American life, and not necessarily more reliable than others. But it is significant that her comments on American "other-directedness" and conformism do not flow, as do those of other nineteenth-century visitors who made comparable observations, from fear or dislike of democracy. Many upper-class visitors, such as Tocqueville or Ostrogorski, saw here a threat to genuine individuality and creativity in po-

[15] Harriet Martineau, *Society in America* (New York: Saunders and Otlay, 1837), Vol. III, pp. 14–15, 17.

litical and intellectual life, in that democracy and equalitarianism give the masses access to elites, so that the latter must be slaves to public opinion in order to survive. Harriet Martineau, as a left-wing English liberal, did not come to America with such fears or beliefs. She remained an ardent admirer of American democracy, even though she ultimately decided that "the worship of Opinion is, at this day, the established religion of the United States."[16]

The most celebrated post-Civil War nineteenth-century English visitor to America, James Bryce, saw inherent in American society "self-distrust, a despondency, a disposition to fall into line, to acquiesce in the dominant opinion. . . ." This "tendency to acquiescence and submission" is not to be "confounded with the tyranny of the majority. . . . [It] does not imply any compulsion exerted by the majority," in the sense discussed by Tocqueville. Rather Bryce, like Harriet Martineau fifty years earlier, described what he felt to be a basic psychological trait of Americans, their "fatalism," which involved a "loss of resisting power, a diminished sense of personal responsibility, and of the duty to battle for one's own opinions. . . ."[17]

Although Harriet Martineau and James Bryce stand out among nineteenth-century visitors in specifying that these other-directed traits were deeply rooted in the *personalities* of many Americans, the general *behaviors* that they and Tocqueville reported were mentioned by many other foreign travelers. For example, a summary of the writings of English travelers from 1785 to 1835 states that one important characteristic mentioned in a number of books "was the acute sensitiveness to opinion that the average American revealed."[18] A German aristocrat, who became a devotee of American democracy and a citizen of the country, stated in the 1830's that "nothing can excite the contempt of an educated European more than the continual fears and apprehensions in which even the 'most enlightened citizens' of the United States seem to live with regard to their next neighbors, lest their actions, principles, opinions and beliefs should be condemned by their fellow creatures."[19] An interpreter of nineteenth-century foreign opinion, John Graham Brooks, mentions various other writers who noted the unwillingness of Americans to be critical of each other. He quotes James Muirhead, the English editor of the *Baedeker* guide to the United States, as saying: "Americans invented the slang word 'kicker,' but so far as I could see their vocabulary is here miles ahead of their practice; they dream noble deeds, but do not do them; Englishmen 'kick' much better without having a name for it." Brooks suggested that it was the American "hesitation to face unpleasant facts rather than be

[16] *Ibid.*, p. 7.

[17] James Bryce, *The American Commonwealth* (New York: Crowell-Collier and Macmillan, 1912), Vol. II, pp. 351–352.

[18] Jane L. Mesick, *The English Traveller in America 1785–1835* (New York: Columbia University Press, 1922), p. 301.

[19] Francis J. Grund, *Aristocracy in America* (New York: Harper Torchbooks, 1959), p. 162; see also pp. 52 and 157 for further comments.

disagreeable and pugnacious about them, after the genius of our English cousins, that calls out the criticism."[20]

The observation that the early Americans were cautious and sensitive has been made not only by foreign visitors but also, at different times, by Americans—as in fact many of the foreign authors report. In 1898, the American writer John Jay Chapman echoed Tocqueville's dictum of seventy years before, that he knew "of no country in which there is so little independence of mind and real freedom of discussion as in America." Chapman saw the general caution and desire to please as the source of many of the ills of his day:

> "Live and let live," says our genial prudence. Well enough, but mark the event. No one ever lost his social standing merely because of his offenses, but because of the talk about them. As free speech goes out the rascals come in.
>
> Speech is a great part of social life, but not the whole of it. Dress, bearing, expression, betray a man, customs show character, all these various utterances mingle and merge into the general tone which is the voice of a national temperament; private motive is lost in it.
>
> This tone penetrates and envelops everything in America. It is impossible to condemn it altogether. This desire to please, which has so much of the shopman's smile in it, graduates at one end of the scale into a general kindliness, into public benefactions, hospitals, and college foundations; at the other end it is seen melting into a desire to efface one's self rather than give offense, to hide rather than be noticed.
>
> In Europe, the men in the pit at the theatre stand up between the acts, face the house, and examine the audience at leisure. The American dares not do this. He cannot stand the isolation, nor the publicity. The American in a horse car can give his seat to a lady, but dares not raise his voice while the conductor tramps over his toes.[21]

Although these accounts by travelers and American essayists cannot be taken as conclusive proof of an unchanging American character, they do suggest that the hypothesis which sees the American character changing with respect to the traits "inner-" and "other-directedness" may be incorrect.

The Unchanging American Values and Their Connection with American Character

The foreign travelers were also impressed by the American insistence on equality in social relations, and on achievement in one's career. Indeed, many perceived an intimate connection between the other-directed behavior they witnessed and the prevalence of these values, such that the behavior could not be understood without reference to them. An analysis of the writings of hundreds of British travelers in America before the Civil

[20] J. G. Brooks, *As Others See Us* (New York: Crowell-Collier and Macmillan, 1908), p. 95.

[21] *The Selected Writings of John Jay Chapman,* Jacques Barzun, ed. (New York: Doubleday Anchor, 1959), p. 278.

War reports: "Most prominent of the many impressions that Britons took back with them [between 1836 and 1860] was the aggressive egalitarianism of the people."[22] If one studies the writings of such celebrated European visitors as Harriet Martineau, the Trollopes (both mother and son), Tocqueville, or James Bryce, it is easy to find many observations documenting this point.[23]

Baedeker's advice to any European planning to visit the United States in the late nineteenth or early twentieth century was that he "should, from the outset, reconcile himself to the absence of deference, or servility, on the part of those he considers his social inferiors."[24] A detailed examination of the comments of European visitors from 1890 to 1910 reports general agreement concerning the depth and character of American equalitarianism:

> Whether they liked what they saw or not, most foreign observers did not doubt that America was a democratic society. . . . Different occupations of course, brought differences in prestige, but neither the occupation nor the prestige implied any fundamental difference in the value of individuals. . . . The similarity of conclusions based on diverse observations was simply another indication of the absence of sharp class differences. Even hostile visitors confirmed this judgment. . . . Some foreign observers found the arrogance of American workers intolerable.[25]

Even today this contrast between Europe and America with respect to patterns of equality in interpersonal relations among men of different social positions is striking. A comparison of writings of European visitors at the turn of this century with those made by British groups visiting here to study American industrial methods since World War II states that "the foreign

[22] Max Berger, *The British Traveller in America, 1836–1860* (New York: Columbia University Press, 1943), pp. 54–55.

[23] For some detailed citations and references see S. M. Lipset, "Stability in the Midst of Change," *The Social Welfare Forum, 1959* (New York: Columbia University Press, 1959), pp. 16–18. See also Commager, *America in Perspective,* pp. xvi–xvii.

[24] Quoted by Philip Burne-Jones, *Dollars and Democracy* (London: Sidney Appleton, 1904), p. 69. Burne-Jones agrees with Baedeker and tells his English readers to follow his good advice, because he who "doesn't do so . . . will probably live in a perpetual state of indignation and annoyance . . . [since Americans at every social level think] that they are really every bit as good as you are, in a country where all social distinctions are supposed to be non-existent."

[25] Robert W. Smuts, *European Impressions of the American Worker* (New York: King's Crown Press, 1953), pp. 3–7. It is interesting to note the similarity between the complaints of presumably conservative upper-class Europeans of the 1890's who found "the arrogance of American workers intolerable" and the complaint of Frances Trollope in 1830 concerning that "coarse familiarity, untempered by any shadow of respect, which is assumed by the grossest and lowest in their intercourse with the highest and most refined," or that of her son Anthony who visited America in 1860 and objected that "the man to whose service one is entitled answers one with determined insolence." See Frances Trollope, *Domestic Manners of the Americans* (London: Whittaker, Treacher, 1832), p. 109, and Anthony Trollope, *North America* (New York: Alfred A. Knopf, 1951), p. 77.

descriptions of . . . America in 1890 and 1950 are remarkably similar. . . . The British teams [in the 1950's reported] . . . the same values . . . which impressed visitors a half century ago. Like them they found the American worker is more nearly the equal of other members of society than the European, with respect not only to his material prosperity, but also to . . . the attitudes of others toward him."[26] And this attitude is apparent at other levels of American society as well. As one commentator put it when describing the high-status Europeans who have come to America in recent years as political refugees from Nazism and Communism:

> With his deep sense of class and status, integration in American society is not easy for the émigré. The skilled engineer or physician who . . . finally establishes himself in his profession, discovers that he does not enjoy the same exalted status that he would have had in the old country. I met several young Croatian doctors in the Los Angeles area who were earning $25,000 to $35,000 a year, but still felt declassed.[27]

American emphasis on equalitarianism as a dominant value is significant in determining what to many of the Europeans were three closely related processes: competition, status uncertainty, and conformity. Tocqueville, for example, argued that equalitarianism maximizes competition among the members of a society.[28] But if equalitarianism fosters competition for status, the combination of the two values of equality and achievement results, according to many of the travelers, in an amorphous social structure in which individuals are uncertain about their social position. In fact, those travelers who were so impressed with the pervasive equalitarianism of American society also suggested that, *precisely as a result of the emphasis on equality and opportunity,* Americans were *more* status-conscious than those who lived in the more aristocratic societies of Europe. They believed, for example, that it was easier for the *nouveaux riches* to be accepted in European high society than in American. British travelers before the Civil War noted that Americans seemed to love titles more than Englishmen. European observers, from Harriet Martineau and Frances Trollope in the 1830's to James Bryce in the 1880's[29] and Denis Brogan in recent years, have pointed out that the actual strength of equality as a dominant American value—with the consequent lack of any well-defined deference structure linked to a legitimate aristocratic tradition where the propriety of social rankings is unquestioned—forces Americans to *emphasize* status background and symbolism.[30] As Brogan has remarked,

[26] Smuts, *European Impressions of the American Worker,* p. 54.

[27] Bogden Raditsa, "Clash of Two Immigrant Generations," *Commentary,* 25 (1958), p. 12.

[28] Tocqueville, *Democracy in America,* Vol. II, p. 146. See also Smuts, *European Impressions of the American Worker,* p. 13.

[29] For citations and references in the foreign travel literature, see Lipset, "Stability in the Midst of Change," *op. cit.,* pp. 32–35.

[30] "It is only an apparent contradiction in terms to assert that the fundamental

the American value system has formed "a society which, despite all efforts of school, advertising, clubs and the rest, makes the creation of effective social barriers difficult and their maintenance a perpetually repeated task. American social fences have to be continually repaired; in England they are like wild hedges, they grow if left alone."[31]

Status-striving and the resultant conformism have not been limited solely, or even primarily, to the more well-to-do classes in American society. Many of the early nineteenth-century travelers commented on the extent to which workers attempted to imitate middle-class styles of life. Smuts notes that visitors at the turn of this century were struck by "what they regarded as the spend-thrift pattern of the American worker's life"; Paul Bourget, a French observer, interpreted this behavior as reflecting "the profound feeling of equality [in America which] urges them to make a show." As Werner Sombart, the German sociologist and economist, put it, "since all are seeking success . . . everyone is forced into a struggle to beat every other individual; and a steeple-chase begins . . . that differs from all other races in that the goal is not fixed

---

democratic and egalitarian character of American life is demonstrated by the ingenuity and persistence shown in inventing marks of difference and symbols of superiority. In a truly class-conscious and caste-dominated society, the marks of difference are universally recognized even if resented. In America they must be stressed, or they might easily be forgotten, and they must be added to, as the old standards of distinction cease to serve their purpose. Apart from the simple economic criterion of conspicuous display, there are no generally accepted marks of social difference in America. And modern salesmanship makes clothes, cars, and personal adornment far more alike than was possible in the old days of belated styles and the Model T Ford. It is worth noting that the main stress of American class distinction is put on 'exclusiveness.' In a society without formal public recognition of difference in rank, with a poor and diminishing stock of reverence for hereditary eminence, and with a constant rise to the top of the economic system of new men amply provided with the only substitute for hereditary eminence, wealth, it becomes extremely difficult to make 'society' anything but the spare-time activities of the rich. It is characteristic that it is in cities whose days of economic advance are over, in Boston, Philadelphia, Charleston, that it has proved easiest to keep out the newcomers." Denis W. Brogan, *U. S. A.: An Outline of the Country, Its People and Institutions* (New York: Oxford University Press, 1941), pp. 116–117.

[31]Denis W. Brogan, *The English People* (London: Hamish Hamilton, 1943), p. 99. Gabriel Almond has commented in the same vein. "*In a sense America is a nation of parvenus.* A historically unique rate of immigration, social and geographic mobility has produced a people which has not had an opportunity to 'set,' to acquire the security and stability which come from familiar ties, associations, rights, and obligations. . . . In more stably stratified societies the individual tends to have a greater sense of 'location,' a broader and deeper identification with his social surroundings. [The American pattern, consequently,] leaves the individual somewhat doubtful as to his social legitimacy. . . ." *The American People and Foreign Policy* (New York: Harcourt, Brace & World, 1950), pp. 63–64. (Emphasis mine.)

An American historian, Rowland Berthoff, has also noted recently: "The evidence is already becoming plain that status striving is no latter-day degeneracy of Americans: rather . . . such insecurity was a by-product of excessive mobility." "The American Social Order: A Conservative Hypothesis," *American Historical Review,* 65 (1960), p. 512.

but constantly moves even further away from the runners." And in an equalitarian democracy "the universal striving for success [becomes a major cause of] . . . the worker's extravagance, for, as Münsterberg [a German psychologist] pointed out, the ability to spend was the only public sign of success at earning."[32] And lest it be thought that such concerns with conspicuous consumption emerged only in the Gilded Age of the 1890's as analyzed by Veblen, sixty years earlier a medical study of the "Influence of Trades, Professions, and Occupations, in the United States, in the Production of Disease," described and analyzed behavior in much the same terms:

> The population of the United States is beyond that of other countries an anxious one. All classes are either striving after wealth, or endeavoring to keep up its appearance. From the principle of imitation which is implanted in all of us, sharpened perhaps by the existing equality of conditions, the poor follow as closely as they are able the habits and manner of living of the rich. . . . From these causes, and perhaps from the nature of our political institutions, and the effects arising from them, we are an anxious, care-worn people.[33]

While some Europeans explained American behavior that they found strange—the sensitivity, kindliness, concern for others' feelings, and moral meekness—by reference to the nature of political democracy or the overbearing desire to make money, others saw these traits as consequences of the extreme emphasis on equality of opportunity, the basic American value which they properly regarded as unique. Many argued that this very emphasis on equality, and the constant challenging of any pretensions to permanent

[32] Smuts, *European Impressions of the American Worker,* p. 13.

[33] Benjamin McCready, "On the Influence of Trades, Professions, and Occupations in the United States, in the Production of Disease," *Transactions of the Medical Society of the State of New York* (1836–1837), III, pp. 146–147. It is interesting to note the congruence between this report and Tocqueville's comments about the same period. He noted: "In America I saw the freest and most enlightened men placed in the happiest circumstances that the world affords; [yet] it seemed to me as if a cloud hung upon their brow, and I thought them serious and almost sad, even in their pleasures.

"The chief reason for this contrast is that the former [the peasants in Europe] do not think of the ills they endure, while the latter [the Americans] are forever brooding over advantages they do not possess. It is strange to see with what feverish ardor the Americans pursue their own welfare, and to watch the vague dread that constantly torments them lest they should not have chosen the shortest path that leads to it." Tocqueville, *Democracy in America,* Vol. II, p. 144.

Riesman apparently overlooked this observation of Tocqueville's, since he suggests that things have changed "since Tocqueville wrote . . . [in] that the sphere of pleasure has itself become a sphere of cares." *The Lonely Crowd,* p. 148.

Herbert Spencer and Matthew Arnold made similar observations about work and play in post-Civil War America. Gabriel Almond cites Spencer as reporting that in America, "Exclusive devotion to work has the result that amusements cease to please; and when relaxation becomes imperative, life becomes dreary from lack of its sole interest—the interest in business," and states that Arnold felt that Americans "were extremely nervous because of excessive worry and overwork." Almond, *The American People and Foreign Policy,* pp. 34–35.

high status, has made Americans in all social positions extremely sensitive to the opinions of others, and causes status aspirants greater anxiety about the behavior and characteristics indicative of rank than is the case with their counterparts in more aristocratic societies. Discussing the writings of various travelers, John Graham Brooks states:

> One deeper reason why the English are blunt and abrupt about their rights . . . is because class lines are more sharply drawn there. Within these limits, one is likely to develop the habit of demanding his dues. He insists on his prerogatives all the more because they are narrowly defined. When an English writer (Jowett) says, "We are not nearly so much afraid of one another as you are in the States," he expressed this truth. In a democracy every one at least hopes to get on and up. This ascent depends not upon the favor of a class, but upon the good-will of the whole. This social whole has to be conciliated. It must be conciliated in both directions—at the top and at the bottom. To make one's self conspicuous and disagreeable, is to arouse enmities that block one's way.[34]

One may find an elaboration of this causal analysis among many writers at different periods. Thus Max Weber, after a visit to America in the early 1900's, noted the high degree of "submission to fashion in America, to a degree unknown in Germany" and explained it in terms of the lack of inherited class status.[35] Seven decades earlier another German, Francis Grund, who saw in American equality and democracy the hope of the world, nevertheless also believed that the ambiguous class structure made status-striving tantamount to conformity. He presents both sides of the picture in the following items:

> Society in America . . . is characterized by a spirit of exclusiveness and persecution unknown in any other country. Its gradations not being regulated according to rank and title, selfishness and conceit are its principal elements . . . What man is there in this city [New York] that dares to be independent, at the risk of being considered bad company? And who can venture to infringe upon a single rule of society?
>
> This habit of conforming to each other's opinions, and the penalty set upon every transgression of that kind, are sufficient to prevent a man from wearing a coat cut in a different fashion, or a shirt collar no longer *à la mode*, or, in fact, to do, say, or appear anything which could render him unpopular among a certain set. In no other place, I believe, is there such a stress laid upon "saving appearances."[36]

[34] Brooks, *As Others See Us*, p. 97.
[35] H. H. Gerth and C. Wright Mills, eds., *From Max Weber: Essays in Sociology* (New York: Oxford University Press, 1946), p. 188.
[36] Grund, *Aristocracy in America*, pp. 52, 157. In describing the emerging America of pre-Civil War days, Dixon Wecter reports that "already in the making was that peculiarly American psychology—symbolized in the great caravans moving westward—of keeping up with one's neighbors, of regarding solitude and independence as a little eccentric, if not dangerous. In business and mechanics the most daring of innovators, the American was already developing that social and

James Bryce, a half-century later, also linked conformity to the ambiguity of the status system, particularly as it affected the wealthy classes. He pointed out that it was precisely the emphasis on equality, and the absence of well-defined rules of deference, which made Americans so concerned with the behavior of others and seemingly more, rather than less, snobbish toward each other than were comparably placed Englishmen.

> It may seem a paradox to observe that a millionaire has a better and easier social career open to him in England, than in America. . . . In America, if his private character be bad, if he be mean or openly immoral, or personally vulgar, or dishonest, the best society may keep its doors closed against him. In England great wealth, skillfully employed, will more readily force these doors to open. . . . The existence of a system of artificial rank enables a stamp to be given to base metal in Europe which cannot be given in a thoroughly republican country.[37]

In comparing the reactions of Englishmen and Americans to criticism, James Muirhead (the editor of the American *Baedeker*) stated that "the Briton's indifference to criticism is linked to the fact of caste, that it frankly and even brutally asserts the essential inequality of man. . . . Social adaptability is not his [the Briton's] foible. He accepts the conventionality of his class and wears it as an impenetrable armor."[38]

A number of the foreign travelers, particularly those who visited America after the 1880's, were startled to find overt signs of anti-Semitism, such as placards barring Jews from upper-class resorts and social clubs which denied them membership.[39] But this, too, could be perceived as a consequence of the fact that "the very absence of titular distinction often causes the lines to be more clearly drawn; as Mr. Charles Dudley Warner says: 'Popular commingling in pleasure resorts is safe enough in aristocratic countries, but it will not answer in a republic.' "[40] The most recent effort by a sociologist, Howard Brotz, to account for the greater concern about close contact with Jews in

---

personal timidity, that love of conformity, which is the hallmark of the *parvenu.*" *The Saga of American Society* (New York: Scribner's, 1937), p. 103; see also his comments on p. 314.

In an essay concerning early Kansas, written in 1910, the historian Carl Becker pointed to the interrelationship of intolerance, individualism, and equalitarianism in American behavior. He asserted that intolerance has been fundamental in the American character. American individualistic values, according to Becker, stress personal achievement, rather than eccentricity; conformity has always been a prerequisite to success. And he notes, as did many of the nineteenth-century foreign travelers, that Americans have tolerated different religions, but have been intolerant of irreligion. See Carl L. Becker, "Kansas," in his *Everyman His Own Historian* (New York: Appleton-Century-Crofts, 1935), pp. 1–28.

[37] James Bryce, *The American Commonwealth,* Vol. II, p. 815.

[38] James Fullerton Muirhead, *America, the Land of Contrasts: A Briton's View of His American Kin* (London: Lemson, Wolffe, 1898), p. 91.

[39] Andrew J. Torrielli, *Italian Opinion on America as Revealed by Italian Travelers, 1850–1900* (Cambridge, Mass.: Harvard University Press, 1941), p. 99.

[40] Muirhead, *America, the Land of Contrasts,* p. 27.

America than in England, also suggests that "in a democracy snobbishness can be far more vicious than in an aristocracy.

> Lacking that natural confirmation of superiority which political authority alone can give, the rich and particularly the new rich, feel threatened by mere contact with their inferiors. . . . Nothing could be more fantastic than this to an English lord living in the country in the midst, not of other peers, but of his tenants. His position is such that he is at ease in the presence of members of the lower classes and in associating with them in recreation. . . . It is this "democratic" attitude which, in the first instance, makes for an openness to social relations with Jews. One cannot be declassed, so to speak, by play activities.[41]

The intimate connection between other-directedness and equalitarian values perceived by these observers recalls the same connection noted by Plato in his theoretical analysis of democracy. In *The Republic* we find these words:

> [In a democracy, the father] accustoms himself to become like his child and to fear his sons. . . Metic [resident alien] is like citizen and citizen like metic, and stranger like both. . . . The schoolmaster fears and flatters his pupils. . . . The young act like their seniors, and compete with them in speech and action, while the old men condescend to the young and become triumphs of versatility and wit, imitating their juniors in order to avoid the appearance of being sour or despotic. . . . And the wonderful equality of law and . . . liberty prevails in the mutual relations of men and women . . . the main result of all these things, taken together, is that it makes the souls of the citizens so sensitive that they take offense and will not put up with the faintest suspicion of slavery [strong authority] that anyone may introduce.[42]

Plato's analysis points up the main question to which this chapter is addressed: Are the conformity and the sensitivity to others—"other directedness"—observed in the contemporary American character solely a function of the technology and social structure of a bureaucratic, industrialized, urban society, as Riesman and Whyte imply, or are they also to some considerable degree an expected consequence of a social system founded upon the values of equality and achievement? It seems that sociological theory, especially as expounded by Max Weber and Talcott Parsons, and much historical and

[41] Howard Brotz, "The Position of the Jews in English Society," *Jewish Journal of Sociology,* 1 (1959), p. 97. Writing twenty years earlier Dixon Wecter also suggested that "the present anti-Semitism of Society—as expressed in visiting lists, club memberships, and personal attitudes is markedly keener in the United States than in England or France, where Rothschilds, for example, seem to find virtually no doors barred against them. It is probably an aspect of that insecurity, that timidity and conventionalism which looms so large in our social picture." *The Saga of American Society,* p. 152.

[42] Plato, *The Republic,* Ernest Rhys, ed. (London: J. M. Dent, 1935), pp. 200–226.

comparative evidence, lend credence to the belief that the basic value system is at least a major, if not the pre-eminent, source of these traits.

As Plato noted, and as the foreign travelers testify, democratic man is deeply imbued with the desire to accommodate to others, which results in kindness and generosity in personal relations, and in a reluctance to offend. All books that are published are "exalted to the skies," teachers "admire their pupils," and flattery is general.[43] The travelers also bear out Plato's remarks about the socialization of children in a democracy. It appears that equalitarian principles were applied to child-rearing early in the history of the republic. Early British opinions of American children have a modern flavor:

> The independence and maturity of American children furnished another surprise for the British visitor. Children ripened early. . . . But such precosity, some visitors feared, was too often achieved at the loss of parental control. Combe claimed that discipline was lacking in the home, and children did what they pleased. Marryat corroborated this. . . . Children were not whipped here [as in England], but treated like rational beings.[44]

Harriet Martineau's description of child-rearing in the America of Andrew Jackson sounds like a commentary on the progressive other-directed parent of the mid-twentieth century:

> My [parent] friend observed that the only thing to be done [in child-rearing] is to avoid to the utmost the exercise of authority, and to make children friends from the very beginning. . . . They [the parents] do not lay aside their democratic principles in this relation, more than in others. . . . They watch and guard: they remove stumbling blocks: they manifest approbation and disapprobation: they express wishes, but, at the same time, study the wishes of their little people: they leave as much as possible to natural retribution: they impose no opinions, and quarrel with none: in short, they exercise the tenderest friendship without presuming upon it. . . . the children of Americans have the advantage of the best possible early discipline; that of activity and self-dependence.[45]

[43] Martineau, *Society in America,* Vol. III, pp. 63–64.

[44] Berger, *The British Traveller in America,* pp. 83–84. Dixon Wecter, who relied more on the French foreign visitors, detailed similar comments and reached the same conclusions: "Indeed without some mention of the dictatorship of the young, any chapter on American manners would be incomplete. No other country in the world has made so much of its children, or given them so free a hand in shaping its customs. . . . As early as Revolutionary times, French visitors in the more aristocratic households like the Schuylers', for example, reported that children were 'spoiled' and 'self willed.' Yet social precosity was one evident result of the attention paid them: Bayard describes the master of a country house near Winchester, Virginia, where, 'dinner hour having sounded, we sat down at a round table, his daughter, nine years old, doing the honors very gracefully in the absence of her mother.' " And Wecter goes on to report that throughout the nineteenth and twentieth centuries, "the surprise of visitors from abroad over the autocracy of our youth has never ceased." *The Saga of American Society,* pp. 191–192.

[45] Martineau, *Society in America,* pp. 168, 177. See also Arthur W. Calhoun, *A Social History of the American Family from Colonial Times to the Present*

What struck the democratic Miss Martineau as progressive was interpreted quite differently by Anthony Trollope, who visited this country in 1860: "I must protest that American babies are an unhappy race. They eat and drink as they please; they are never punished; they are never banished, snubbed, and kept in the background as children are kept with us."[46] And forty years later, another English visitor, typical of the many who described American child-parent relations during a century and a half, tells us that nowhere else, as in America, "is the child so constantly in evidence; nowhere are his wishes so carefully consulted; nowhere is he allowed to make his mark so strongly on society. . . . The theory of the equality of man is rampant in the nursery. . . . You will actually hear an American mother say of a child of two or three years of age: 'I can't *induce* him to do this. . . .' "[47]

If these reports from the middle and late nineteenth century are reminiscent of contemporary views, it is still more amazing to find, in a systematic summary of English travelers' opinion *in the last part of the eighteenth and early years of the nineteenth centuries,* that the emphasis on equality and democracy had *already* created the distinctive American child-oriented family which astonished the later visitors:

> A close connection was made by the stranger between the republican form of government and the unlimited liberty which was allowed the younger generation. . . . They were rarely punished at home, and strict discipline was not tolerated in the schools. . . . It was feared that respect for elders or for any other form of authority would soon be eliminated from American life. . . . As he could not be punished in the school, he learned to regard his teacher as an inferior and to disregard all law and order.[48]

Equality was thus perceived by many of the foreign travelers as affecting the socialization of the child not only within the family but in the school as well. The German psychologist Hugo Münsterberg joins the late-eighteenth-century visitors in complaining, over a century later in 1900, that "the feeling of equality will crop up where nature designed none, as for instance between

---

(Cleveland: The Arthur H. Clark Co., 1918), Vol. II, pp. 63–64. For a thorough documentation of child-centeredness in the nineteenth-century American family, see Anne L. Kuhn, *The Mother's Role in Childhood Education: New England Concepts, 1830–1860* (New Haven, Conn.: Yale University Press, 1947).

[46] Anthony Trollope, *North America,* p. 142; for similar comments see also J. S. Buckingham, *America: Historical, Statistic, and Descriptive* (New York: Harper & Row, 1841), pp. 362–363; J. Boardman, *America and the Americans* (London: Longman, Rees, Orme, Brown, Green and Longman, 1833), p. 156; Brooks, *As Others See Us,* pp. 48–50.

[47] Muirhead, *America, The Land of Contrasts,* pp. 67–68. (Emphasis in original.)

[48] Mesick, *The English Traveller in America,* pp. 83–84. A detailed summary of the opinion of foreign travelers concerning the indulgent, child-centered, pre-Civil War family may be found in "The Emancipation of Childhood," in Calhoun, *A Social History of the American Family,* Vol. II, pp. 50–77. Calhoun also tells us that the freedom of children was "attributed . . . to the spirit of republicanism. . . . All men are sovereigns. Personality is exalted; and the political status overflows and democratizes family institutions." *Ibid.,* p. 53.

youth and mature years. . . . Parents even make it a principle to implore and persuade their children, holding it to be a mistake to compel or punish them; and they believe that the schools should be conducted in the same spirit."[49] Various visitors were struck by the extent to which the schools did carry out this objective. The following description by an Englishman of schools in the New York area in 1833 sounds particularly modern:

> The pupils are entirely independent of their teacher. No correction, no coercion, no manner of restraint is permitted to be used. . . . Parents also have as little control over their offspring at home, as the master has at school. . . . Corporal punishment has almost disappeared from American day-schools; and a teacher, who should now give recourse at such means of enforcing instruction, would meet with reprehension from the parents and perhaps retaliation from his scholars.[50]

Tocqueville also found examples of the American's mistrust of authority "even in the schools," where he marveled that "the children in their games are wont to submit to rules which they have themselves established."[51]

The educational policies which have become linked with the name of John Dewey and labeled "progressive education" actually began in a number of school systems around the country long before Dewey wrote on the subject: "To name but one example, the lower schools of St. Louis had adopted a system intended to develop spontaneously the inventive and intellectual faculties of the children by the use of games and with no formal teaching of ideas, no matter how practical."[52]

The Inadequacy of a Materialistic Interpretation of Change

Many of the foreign observers referred to above explained the other-directedness and status-seeking of Americans by the prevalence of the twin values of equality and achievement. Character and behavior were thus explained by values. They pointed out that the ethic of equality not only pervaded status relations but that it influenced the principal spheres of socialization, the family, and the school, as well.

Both Whyte's and Riesman's arguments, in contrast, explain character and values by reference to the supposed demands of a certain type of economy and its unique organization. The economy, in order to be productive, requires certain types of individuals, and requires that they hold certain values. In the final analysis, theirs is a purely materialistic interpretation of social phenom-

[49] Hugo Münsterberg, *The Americans* (New York: McClure, Phillips, 1904), p. 28.

[50] Isaac Fidler, *Observations in Professions, Literature, Manners and Emigration, in the United States and Canada, Made During a Residence There in 1832* (New York: J. and J. Harper, 1833), pp. 40–41.

[51] Tocqueville, *Democracy in America,* Vol. I, p. 198.

[52] Torrielli, *Italian Opinion on America,* p. 115.

ena and is open to the criticisms to which such interpretations are susceptible.

The inadequacy of such an explanation of change in values and social character is best demonstrated by comparative analysis. British and Swedish societies, for example, have for many decades possessed occupational structures similar to that of America. Britain, in fact, reached the stage of an advanced industrial society, thoroughly urbanized, where the majority of the population worked for big business or government, long before any other nation. The occupational profiles of Sweden, Germany, and the United States have been similar for decades. If the causal connection between technology and social character were direct, then the patterns described as typical of "other-direction" or "the organization man" should have occurred in Great Britain prior to their occurrence in the United States, and should now be found to predominate in other European nations. Yet "other-direction" and the "social ethic" appear to be pre-eminently American traits. In Europe, one sees the continued, even though declining, strength of deferential norms, enjoining conformity to class standards of behavior.

Thus, comparative analysis strikingly suggests that the derivation of social character almost exclusively from the traits associated with occupational or population profiles is invalid. So important an element in a social system as social character must be deeply affected by the dominant value system. For the value system is perhaps the most enduring part of what we think of as society, or a social system. Comparative history shows that nations may still present striking differences, even when their technological, demographic, or political patterns are similar. Thus it is necessary to work out the implications of the value system within a given material setting—while always observing, of course, the gradual, cumulative effect that technological change has upon values.

In attempting to determine how American values have been intertwined with the profound changes that have taken place in American society, it is not sufficient to point out that American values are peculiarly congenial to change. Although equality and achievement have reinforced each other over the course of American history, they have never been entirely compatible either. Many of the changes that have taken place in family structure, education, religion, and "culture," as America has become a "modern" society, have manifested themselves in a constant conflict between the democratic equalitarianism, proclaimed as a national ideal in the basic documents of the American Revolution, and the strong emphasis on competition, success, and the acquisition of status—the achievement orientation—which is also deeply embedded in our national value system.

Richard Hofstadter has urged the recurring pattern of value *conflict* and *continuity* in commenting on papers presented at a conference on changes in American society:

> Culturally and anthropologically, human societies are cast in a great variety of molds, but once a society has been cast in its mold—Mr. Rostow is right

> that our mold as a nation was established by the early nineteenth century—the number of ways in which, short of dire calamity, it will alter its pattern are rather limited. I find it helpful also to point to another principle upon which Mr. Rostow has remarked—the frequency with which commentators find societies having certain paradox polarities in them. . . . We may find in this something functional; that is, *Societies have a need to find ways of checking their own tendencies. In these polarities there may be something of a clue to social systems.* . . .
>
> Mr. Kluckhohn's report contains some evidence that we have already passed the peak of this shift about which I have been speaking. I find some additional evidence myself in the growing revolt of middle-class parents against those practices in our education that seem to sacrifice individualism and creativity for adjustment and group values. Granted the initial polarities of the success ethic, which is one of the molds in which our society is cast, this ethic must in some way give rise, sooner or later, to a reaction. . . . I do not think that we must be persuaded that our system of values has ceased to operate.[53]

The analyses of American history and culture in the nineteenth and twentieth centuries, by both foreign and native interpreters, often differ according to whether they stress democracy and equality, or capitalism and achievement. Generally, conservatives have found fault with the decline of individuality and the pampering of children, and have seen both as manifestations of democracy and equality; while liberals have noted, with dismay, tendencies toward inequality and aristocracy, and have blamed them upon the growth of big business. These contrary political philosophies have also characterized the interpretation of American culture that predominates at any given period. Arthur Schlesinger, Sr., has even tried to measure the systematic characteristic duration of the "epochs of radicalism and conservatism [that] have followed each other in alternating order" in American history.[54]

A cursory examination of the numerous differences between the conclusions of American social scientists in the 1930's and in the 1950's shows the way in which interpretations of American culture vary with social conditions. Writers of the 1930's amassed evidence of the decline of equalitarianism and the effect of this on a variety of institutions. Karen Horney in *The Neurotic Personality of Our Time,* for example, named anxiety over chances of economic success as the curse of what she, with many of her contemporaries, regarded as a completely pecuniary, achievement-oriented culture dominated by the giant corporations. Such analysts as Robert S. Lynd and W. L. Warner all agreed that the egalitarian emphasis in American democracy was declining sharply under the growth of the large-scale corporation, monopoly capitalism,

[53] Richard Hofstadter, "Commentary: Have There Been Discernible Shifts in Values During the Past Generation?" in Elting E. Morison, ed., *The American Style: Essays in Value and Performance* (New York: Harper & Row, 1958), p. 357. (Emphasis mine.)

[54] Arthur M. Schlesinger, Sr., *New Viewpoints in American History* (New York: Crowell-Collier and Macmillan, 1922), p. 123.

and economic competition.[55] They asserted categorically that mobility had decreased, and Warner predicted the development of rigid status lines based on family background.

Twenty years later, these interpretations are almost unanimously rejected. Warner himself in one of his most recent works shows that chances of rising into the top echelons of the largest corporations are *greater* than they were in the 1920's.[56] As indicated earlier in this chapter, typical writers of the 1950's are concerned that the emphasis on achievement in American society may be dying out.

In large measure, the difference between writers of the two decades reflects the contrast between the economic circumstances of the times. The depression of the 1930's inclined intellectuals toward an equalitarian radicalism, which condemned capitalism and achievement orientation as the source of evils. Even a conservative like Warner was led to emphasize the growth of inequality and the restriction of opportunity. The prosperity of the 1950's, however, renewed the legitimacy of many conservative institutions and values, and discredited some of the innovations of the previous decades. The social analyses of the 1950's, even those written by men who still considered themselves liberals or socialists, involved at least a critique of the radical excesses of the former period, if not a critique of equalitarian values themselves. Perhaps the similarity in attitudes between the analysts of the 1950's and many of the foreign travelers of the last century is due to the fact that most of the European visitors have been conservatives, or members of the elite of much more aristocratic societies, and the modern Americans reflect the post-war revival of conservative values.

While Riesman and Whyte would deny that their works contain conservative value preferences, and insist that they are simply analyzing changes, it seems fairly evident that like the more elitist travelers of the nineteenth century, they deplore many of the dominant trends. They point to the spread of progressive education, with its disbelief in rewards for hard work, as illustrating the decay of the Protestant ethic, and they assume, as a result of this, a decline in the opportunity for developing creativity. Whyte points to the shift in scientific research from individual to group projects, which in his opinion are less creative. Neither Riesman nor Whyte explicitly asserts that there is more conformity now than in the past, for the reason that men have always conformed to the values of the day; but both argue that contemporary values and personality traits emphasize accommodation to others, while the declining Protestant ethic and the inner-directed character structure stressed

[55] Robert S. Lynd, *Knowledge for What?* (Princeton, N.J.: Princeton University Press; 1940), p. 75; Harold Laski, *The American Democracy* (New York: Viking Press, 1948); W. L. Warner and Paul S. Lunt, *The Social Life of a Modern Community* (New Haven, Conn.: Yale University Press, 1941).

[56] W. L. Warner and J. C. Abegglen, *Occupational Mobility in American Business and Industry* (Minneapolis: University of Minnesota Press, 1953).

conformity to a fixed rule of conduct rather than to the fluctuating actions and moods of others.[57]

This reaction against the apparent decline of the Protestant ethic of achievement and hard work, which has become a dominant theme among the intellectual middle class of the 1950's and early 1960's, should be viewed as the counterpart of the concern with the seeming breakdown of equality which moved comparable groups in the 1930's. The differences in the concerns of the two periods illustrate the important point that although the equalitarian ethos of the American Revolution and the achievement orientation of the Protestant ethic are mutually supporting, they also involve normative conflict. Complete commitment to equality involves rejecting some of the implications of valuing achievement; and the opposite is also true. Thus, when the equalitarianism of left or liberal politics is dominant, there is a reaction against achievement, and when the values of achievement prevail in a conservative political and economic atmosphere, men tend to depreciate some of the consequences of equality, such as the influence of popular taste on culture.

The supremacy of equalitarian values and liberal politics in the 1930's was reflected in the school system in the triumph of progressive education, a cause always associated with left-of-center leaders and ideologies; in industry, by the introduction of the human relations approach as an attempt to "keep the worker happy"; and in the society at large by efforts toward a general redistribution of goods and services. Social scientists and others interested in family structure criticized the supposedly typical middle-class family as too authoritarian and rigid in its treatment of children, suggesting that, in contrast to the more democratic and affectionate working-class family, it bred "authoritarian" and "neurotic" personalities. Popular psychology saw the "compet-

[57] It is ironic to note that most contemporary discussions which employ Weber's concept of the Protestant ethic to typify a certain type of behavior, which is then contrasted with other-directed behavior, ignore the fact that, to Weber, one of the significant components distinguishing ascetic Protestantism, and particularly Calvinism, from other religious ethics was precisely its use of the need to conform to the judgment of others as a means of enforcing discipline: "The member of the sect (or conventicle) had to have qualities of a certain kind in order to enter the community circle. . . . In order to hold his own in this circle, the member had to *prove* repeatedly that he was endowed with these qualities. . . . According to all experience there is no stronger means of breeding traits than through the necessity of holding one's own in the circle of one's associates. . . . The Puritan sects put the most powerful individual interest of social self-esteem in the service of this breeding of traits . . . to repeat, it is not the ethical *doctrine* of a religion, but that form of ethical conduct upon which *premiums* are placed that matters. . . . The premiums were placed upon 'proving' oneself before God in the sense of attaining salvation—which is found in *all* Puritan denominations—and 'proving' oneself before men in the sense of socially holding one's own within the Puritan sects." A key difference between the Puritans and the Lutherans and Catholics, in Weber's judgment, lies in this extensive use of an appeal to "social self-esteem" or the power of group opinion by the former, and imposing religious discipline "through authoritarian means" and punishing or placing premiums on "concrete individual acts," by the latter. Gerth and Mills, eds., *From Max Weber,* pp. 320–321.

itive personality" of our time as the source of many personal and social evils. Historians pictured the creators of American industry as "robber barons" and as irresponsible exploiters of American resources.

This equalitarian liberalism was perhaps strongest in the school system, where educators carried the ideal of equal treatment to a point where even intellectual differences were ignored. Special encouragement of the gifted child was regarded as an unfair privilege that inflicted psychic punishment on the less gifted: personality adjustment for *all* became the objective. In New York City, Fiorello La Guardia, the militant progressive mayor, abolished Townsend Harris High School—a special school for gifted boys in which four years of work was completed in three—on the grounds that the very existence of such a school was undemocratic, because it conferred special privileges on a minority.

In the prosperous 1950's and 1960's, these tendencies have been almost completely reversed. Big business and business careers once more have become legitimate. The Republicans held office in the 1950's, and centrists rather than liberals dominate the revived Democratic Party of the 1960's. Although Keynesian economics has remained official government policy, and is still supported by most economists, some leading members of that profession have emerged who oppose almost all government intervention.[58] Studies of the social structure of the family have reversed the findings of the 1930's, suggesting that it is the working-class family that is more likely to be a source of "authoritarian" personality traits. Vulgarizations of the theses of Riesman and Whyte have been published in many magazines and are cited at P.T.A. meetings all over the country, where outraged middle-class parents demand a return to "old-fashioned" methods of teaching, in which hard work is rewarded and the gifted receive special attention.[59] Many middle-class parents have placed their children in private schools. While the rapid growth of private schools in large part stems from the increasing prosperity of the country, it also reflects the desire of middle-class parents that their children receive an elite education.

The political battle between the reactions stemming from the pre-war depression and those reflecting the post-war prosperity, between equality and achievement, has been most conspicuously joined today in the debate over schools. As the "progressive educationalists" begin to counterattack, they appeal specifically to the values of equality and democracy. A speech by Pro-

[58] For example, Milton Friedman of the University of Chicago even advocates that the entire educational system from elementary school on up be placed under private ownership, since only through economic competition can we be assured of securing the best system.

[59] It should be noted again that the available evidence does not confirm the assumptions that educational standards have declined, as judged by the records and abilities of entering college freshmen over a thirty-year period. In addition, more teenagers are learning Greek and Latin and foreign languages now than in 1900, largely as a result of the great spread of educational facilities, though it is true that the *proportion* of students studying classical tongues has declined greatly.

fessor A. Harry Passow of Columbia University Teachers' College attacked a proposal to create twenty-five elite high schools for gifted children in the following terms: "It is a perversion of democracy to set aside certain youngsters and give them privileges which automatically set them apart as an elite group of society. It goes against the basic idea of American education, which is to give all children an equal opportunity for the best possible education."[60]

A leading expert, who has testified before Congressional committees for the past twenty years or more concerning the need for educational research, once reported that when a committee was discussing research on underprivileged or mentally deficient children, the Democrats on the committee would exhibit great interest; but when the committee turned to the question of the gifted child, the Republicans perked up and the Democrats sat back. The two parties did not, of course, oppose each other formally on these questions, since both favored research on all questions; but Republicans were simply more interested in *achievement,* or the problem of the gifted child, while Democrats were more interested in *equality,* or the problem of the underprivileged.

To stress the coincidence of these differing interpretations of American social trends with the political and economic cycle is not to suggest that they are simply ideological reflections of material conditions or of the climate of opinion. Most of them have pointed out genuine aspects of the culture, and in so doing have improved our understanding of the functions of different institutions and values. Both strands, the equalitarian and the achievement-oriented, remain strong, but changing conditions sometimes fortify one at the expense of the other, or alter the internal content of each. Thus opportunity, as measured by the chances of success in building up a major enterprise of one's own, has given way to opportunity measured by advancement in the bureaucratic elites.[61] The politics of liberalism and equality have fostered institutional changes, such as the constant spread of public education and of training facilities within corporations, which have increased opportunities for advancement.

CONCLUSION

This chapter essentially has urged that a materialistic interpretation of American society sharply underestimates the extent to which basic national values, once institutionalized, give shape to the consequences of technological

[60] See "Plan of Schools for 'Elite' Scored," *The New York Times,* March 25, 1958, p. 25.

[61] It should be noted, however, that the desire and the number of attempts to start one's own small business certainly do not seem to have abated in this country, unless past rates were fantastically high. Survey studies indicate that the majority of American workers have thought of going into business, and that a fifth of them actually have once owned a small business. Conversely, of those in small businesses, 20 per cent have previously been manual workers. S. M. Lipset and R. Bendix, *Social Mobility in Industrial Society* (Berkeley: University of California Press, 1959), p. 102.

and economic change.[62] Clearly, many nations may be described as urbanized, industrialized, and capitalist, but they vary considerably in their status systems, their political institutions, parent-child relations, and so forth. The absence of a feudal past, with a concomitant emphasis on equality of manners and of opportunity, has played a major role in differentiating American behavior from that of other nations.

On the other hand, it may be argued that the entire Western world has been moving in the American direction in their patterns of class relationships, family structure, and "other-directedness," and that America, which was democratic and equalitarian before industrialization, has merely led the way in these patterns. Thus, at any given time, the differences between America and much of Europe may have remained constant, but this difference might have represented little more than a time lag.

If one compares the America of the 1960's with the America of the 1880's or the 1830's one would undoubtedly note changes in the direction suggested by Riesman. The vast majority of early- and mid-nineteenth-century Americans were self-employed and lived on farms or in small towns, while today most people are employees and live in cities. This change alone has many consequences along the lines suggested by *The Lonely Crowd:*

> We can contrast the small grocer who must please his individual patrons, perhaps by a "counter-side manner," with the chain-store employee who must please both the patrons and his co-workers. . . . The colleague, like the peer-grouper, is the very person with whom one engages in competition for the *scarce commodity of approval* and the very person to whom one looks for guidance as to what is desirable.[63]

The entrepreneur becomes an "other-directed person [who] gives up the one-face policy of the inner-directed man for a multiface policy that he sets in

[62] In this discussion I have not been concerned with the truth of Riesman's description of the changes in technology and in the nature of the economy. One must be warned, however, against overestimating the drastic and far-reaching nature of these changes. For example, the common image of professional occupations is that they are increasingly embedded in bureaucratic structures, while they were formerly free of such structures. While this may be true of some professions, it is not true of others. Daniel Calhoun, in his recent study of American civil engineers, argues: "When a twentieth-century writer describes the earlier engineer as 'free and named on his own shingle,' he was slipping into a romantic notion of nineteenth-century society. This notion applies not to the typical nineteenth-century engineer, but to the exceptional or cantankerous individual. Almost as soon as American internal improvements became extensive enough to give the civil engineer much employment, the engineer became an organization man, a respectable member of a bureaucracy." See Daniel Calhoun, *The American Civil Engineer: Origins and Conflict* (Cambridge, Mass.: Technology Press, 1960), pp. 194–195. Calhoun's reference is to C. Wright Mills' description of the engineer in *White Collar.* But when Riesman speaks of the inner-directed man as "wanting to build a bridge, to run a railroad," (*The Lonely Crowd,* p. 120), he presumably has the image of the engineer in the back of his mind.

[63] P. 140. (Emphasis mine.)

secrecy and varies with each set of encounters."[64] An employee has less freedom and motivation to be individualistic than does the self-employed. Farm and small-town dwellers know each other as total human beings rather than as actors in specific relations, and are presumably less motivated to exhibit status-seeking or to seek the good opinion of those whom they have known all their lives and who are "significant others" in a variety of limited contexts.[65] Residents of small communities are judged by their total background and personal history and by any specific set of acts. As many sociological studies of such communities have revealed, they tend to have a relatively static status system, permitting much less social mobility than that occurring in large cities. Consequently, the resident of the small town tends to be somewhat like the citizens of more rigidly stratified European states. The awareness of the relative permanence of status position reduces the anxiety to win the good opinion of others that exists where status is less stable.

There can be little question that Riesman and Whyte are right also in showing how bureaucratization and urbanization *reinforce* those social mechanisms which breed other-directedness. Success in a bureaucracy, and in the proliferating service occupations of modern society, depends primarily on the ability to get along well with others.

But it cannot be stressed too often that these mechanisms operate within the context of an historic American value-system and status structure that had also generated such traits in a non-bureaucratic and non-urban society. Other-direction, or, to put it less dramatically, sensitivity to the judgments of others,

[64] *Ibid.*, p. 147.

[65] However, it should be noted that an early history of the state of Illinois, written by a man who pioneered in the state, reports that the desire to be admired by others at the major social event of the week, Sunday church services, played an important role in stimulating general ambition: "For this advancement in civilization, the young people were much indebted to their practice of attending church on Sundays. Here they were regularly brought together at stated times; and their meeting, if it affected no better end, at least accustomed them to admire and wish to be admired. Each one wanted to make as good a figure as he could; and to that end came to meeting well-dressed and clean. . . . With pride of dress came ambition, industry, the desire of knowledge, and a love of decency. It has been said that civilization is a forced state of mind, to which [man] is stimulated by a desire to gratify artificial wants. . . ." Thomas Ford, *History of Illinois* (Chicago: S. C. Griggs, 1854), pp. 95–96.

In contrast, Albert Blumenthal emphasized that "putting on a front" in order to lay claim to a higher social status than one is entitled to is usually unsuccessful in a small town. He stated, "He who would indulge in pretense in Mineville must be very cautious lest he be wasting his time or be making himself a target for scorn, ridicule, or amusement. To be sure, a certain amount of bluffing can be done since, after all, persons have some privacy, even in Mineville. But this bluffing must not be of a sort that easily can be uncovered, for the people have little patience with pretenders. Persons long in the community know that there is scant use for them to 'put on front' of the more obvious sort such as by the wearing of fine clothes or the purchasing of a costly automobile. . . . By a ferreting-out process the people soon discover whether or not a newcomer 'has anything to be stuck up about.'" *Small-Town Stuff* (Chicago: University of Chicago Press, 1932), pp. 104–105.

is an epiphenomenon of the American equalitarian ethos, of the opportunities for rapid status mobility, *and* of the general growth of an urban, bureaucratic society.[66] The increasing complexity introduced by industrialization and urbanization makes adherence to a rigid normative code obsolete, because such a code cannot be used as a guide to the great variety of situations confronting modern, bureaucratic man. This Riesman and Whyte have well noted. However, the greater flexibility and need to adapt to others that are demanded by urban and bureaucratic life add to an already existing disposition to be concerned with the opinions of others, a disposition caused by equalitarianism and by the emphasis placed on social mobility.

Even despite the changes brought about by urbanization and bureaucratization, Americans still appear to be quite achievement oriented when compared to persons from more status-bound nations. Foreign travelers are still struck by the individual American's striving to get ahead.[67] Indeed, there is some evidence that the higher valuation placed on social skills in present American socialization practices is precisely oriented toward upward social mobility in contemporary society. A study comparing British and American beliefs about socialization points out that while it places "getting along with others" as the most important aim of socialization, the American pattern differs from the British in that it aims "at a smoothly functioning individual, equipped for getting ahead with a varied armament of social skills."[68]

Some evidence that achievement still ranks high in the United States as

[66] In commenting on the analyses of various, more psychologically oriented, writers who preceded Riesman in describing "other-directed" character traits (which, however, they tended to explain psychologically rather than sociologically, that is, by the patterns of child-rearing in the modern American family rather than by the structural changes that seemingly underlie these changes in child-rearing), Gabriel Almond also points up the dual causal pattern. "De Tocqueville attributed it [American conformism] to competitiveness and the equality of conditions of the American people. It is, of course, both factors taken together. What Horney, Fromm and Mead have done is to trace this and other tendencies from aspects of the culture, to patterns of child rearing in the family, to adult behavior." Almond, *The American People and Foreign Policy,* p. 43.

[67] Arvid Brodersen comments in this way on the beliefs of prominent foreign visitors about the typical value orientations of the American people: "[They] repeated the pattern of positive-negative reciprocity stressing notions such as 'hard-working,' 'active,' and 'energetic' as well as 'materialistic,' 'ambitious,' 'rush all the time.' " Arvid Brodersen, "Themes in the Interpretation of America by Prominent Visitors from Abroad," *The Annals of the American Academy of Political and Social Science,* 295 (1954), pp. 21–32. Comments by Indian students in America reflect the same traits. "They are constantly in a hurry to get done whatever they are doing and give very little thought to the meaning of what they are doing. They see only the material values in life—get more money, get more luxuries. . . . Most [Indian students] are captivated by the opportunities for an open class system with its ample chances to climb on the basis of ability and work with the widespread sharing of a high standard of living." Ruth Hill Useem and John Useem, "Images of the United States and Britain Held by Foreign Educated Indians," *The Annals of the American Academy of Political and Social Studies,* 295 (1954), pp 73–82.

[68] Maurice L. Farber, "English and American Values in the Socialization Process," *Journal of Psychology,* 36 (1953), pp. 243–250.

compared to other nations may be seen in the data from a comparative study of the attitudes of school youth in five countries—the United States, Norway, West Germany, England, and France. Surprisingly, at least so far as concerns the expectations of the researchers, American children were less "other-directed" than those in the European countries, except Norway, as judged by their responses to the question: "Would you rather be the most popular person in your class or the one who gets the highest grades?" Among both ten-year-olds and fourteen-year-olds, Americans were more likely to prefer high grades to popularity than were German, English, and French youth.

Another indicator of the relatively high level of concern for academic achievement may be seen in the response to a question concerning anxiety

TABLE I PREFERENCE FOR HIGHEST GRADES RATHER THAN POPULARITY AMONG STUDENTS IN FIVE NATIONS

	Per Cent Preferring Highest Grades		
Nation	*10 year olds*	*14 year olds*	*combined ages*
Norway	86%	83%	85%
United States	82	63	73
West Germany	62	50	56
England	63	45	54
France	53	30	42

Source: George Gallup and Evan Hill, "Is European Education Better than Ours?" *The Saturday Evening Post,* 233 (Dec. 24, 1960), p. 70.

over school examinations. American and French youth led in the proportion who reported worrying about exams (63 per cent); Norwegians were slightly less anxious as a group (60 per cent), while English and German students showed considerably less concern (48 and 28 per cent).[69]

Comparative evidence that achievement orientation and other-directedness may, in fact, be mutually reinforcing has been presented by David McClelland as a conclusion of his extensive comparative studies of the psychological processes which are related to economic development. He suggests that " 'other-directedness' is an essential feature of rapid economic development even in its early stages, rather than a special feature of advanced urban culture in the United States as Riesman suggests."[70] As he puts it:

> [W]hat a modern society needs for successful development is flexibility in a man's role relationships. His entire network of relations to others should not be traditionally determined by his caste or even his occupational

[69] George Gallup and Evan Hill, "Is European Education Better than Ours?" *The Saturday Evening Post,* 233 (Dec. 24, 1960), p. 73.
[70] David C. McClelland, *The Achieving Society* (Princeton, N.J.: Van Nostrand, 1961), p. 192.

> status. . . . The transition to the new order is certainly likely to be helped if people can learn to listen to what "other people" say is the right thing to do.[71]

An increase in other-directedness helps facilitate economic development by making individuals more receptive to "the opinion of the 'generalized other.' " It creates greater willingness to accept new norms or techniques, and it helps reduce particularistic ties, thus facilitating the operation of pure market criteria.

To test the hypothesis of the interrelationship of other-directedness and achievement orientation, McClelland analyzed children's readers from over thirty countries in 1925 and 1950 by coding the themes of the stories in terms of measures of other-directedness and achievement motivation. Countries were then classified as above or below the median score for other-directedness and achievement motivation in each period. Nations could be categorized as high on both dimensions, low on both, or high on one and low on the other. Looking then at the various countries and the extent to which they grew economically during the succeeding years (as indicated by growth in electric power), McClelland found that nations which were high on both factors greatly outperformed countries which were low on both, "whereas those that were high on one and low on the other showed an average gain somewhere in between."[72]

> It may come as something of a shock to realize that more could have been learned about the rate of future economic growth of a number of these countries in 1925 or 1950 by reading elementary school books than by studying such presumably more relevant matters as power politics, wars and depressions, economic statistics, or government policies governing international trade, taxation, or public finance. The reason apparently lies in the fact that the readers reflect sufficiently accurately the motives and values of key groups of men in a country which *in the long run* determine the general drift of economic and political decisions and their effect on productivity. Economic and political policies are of course the means by which economic change is brought about, but whether policies will be implemented, or even decided on in the first place, appears to depend ultimately on the motives and values of men as we have succeeded in detecting them in the stories which they think it is right for their children to read.[73]

The two orientations of other-directedness and achievement motivation, therefore, may be viewed as mutually supportive, rather than, as Riesman and Whyte suggest, mutually contradictory.

The concern with specifying how various structural changes have weakened the Protestant ethic or inner-directed traits in American life has led Riesman and others sometimes to ignore the beneficial consequences of these changes.

[71] *Ibid.*, p. 194.
[72] *Ibid.*, pp. 201–202.
[73] *Ibid.*, p. 202.

Thus, I have pointed out elsewhere that while bureaucratization results in a heightened need to make personality adjustments to win the esteem of colleagues and supervisors, it also sets bounds to arbitrary power. By establishing rules of fair treatment, and by reducing the area of personal discretion in personnel policy, bureaucracy can reduce the fear of the employer or of the supervisor.[74] Trade unions, found most commonly under conditions of large industry, accurately reflect their member's desires when their policies involve more, rather than less, bureaucratization of factory life. (As an example of this, unions have sought seniority rules in hiring, firing, and promoting, which increase bureaucratization and reduce arbitrary power.)

Similarly, it may be urged that some of the consequences of bureaucratization reinforce, rather than weaken, strong work and achievement orientations, particularly—but not exclusively[75]—in the upper echelons of white-collar and executive life. The shift from the family-owned company to the management-run corporation, as Whyte pointed out, has made group activities and adjustment to group norms seem more important than before. But whatever else group dynamics in industry may be concerned with, it certainly provides an excellent way of getting men to work hard for the company. Traditionally, it has been a postulate of business management, and an empirical finding of industrial sociology, that men do not work as hard as they are able when the rewards of their work seem to be going to others. Holding other factors constant, no one works so hard as the head of an organization, or the self-employed or the creative professional who is directly rewarded for his labors. By extending the control of work to committees at different levels in the corporation, contemporary American business has found a means of inculcating into a large number of people a sense of responsibility for the whole organization. "Non-owners" now feel individually responsible, and the number of hard-working executives who never watch the clock, and who take work home with them, has been enormously enlarged. Thus, while other-direction may have increased, the motivation for competition and hard work remains, because the best are chosen to move up the bureaucratic hierarchy.

It is a peculiar paradox that the same structural processes may account for diverse and even sharply conflicting tendencies. Many analyses of American society have stressed the fact that individualism *and* conformism, cre-

[74] S. M. Lipset, *Political Man: The Social Bases of Politics* (Garden City, N.Y.: Doubleday, 1960), p. 414.

[75] In the midst of the greatest prosperity in history, the U.S. Census reported that in the summer of 1957, three and a half million workers had two jobs, with the second job averaging twelve hours per week. In Akron, Ohio, where many rubber workers were on a six-hour day and a five-day week, at relatively high pay, and where a sizable proportion of wives were employed, it was estimated that among the men "from one in seven down to one in five rubber workers holds a second full-time job. . . . In addition, something like 40 per cent engage in some sort of part-time outside work . . . the shorter day even with a higher pay scale, increases the number of men who obtain second jobs . . ." August Heckscher, "Time, Work and Leisure," *Political Research: Organization and Design* (PROD), 1 (1958), p. 156.

ative innovation *and* dominance by low-level mass taste, are outgrowths of identical forces. For example, the pronounced spread of higher education and a high standard of living have caused an unprecedented increase in both the proportion of the population involved in genuinely creative, intellectual activities, and the influence by the populace on the major expressions of art, literature, and drama.[76] Alexis de Tocqueville was fully aware of these dual tendencies when he pointed out that "the same equality that renders him [The American] independent of each of his fellow citizens, taken severally, exposes him alone and unprotected to the influence of the greater number. . . . I very clearly discern two tendencies; one leading the mind of every man to untried thoughts, the other prohibiting him from thinking at all."[77]

Today, too, there are many trends making for an increase in autonomous behavior, in free choice. Various social scientists have recently begun to document these countervailing tendencies, a phenomenon that may reflect the ever-present cyclical pattern of social analysis. Rowland Berthoff points to the seeming "gradual decline since 1920 of those makeshift communities, the fraternal lodges," which were part of the associational pattern that impressed Tocqueville, and suggests that "the psychic energy that Americans formerly expended on maintaining the jerry-built framework of such 'institutions' as these has in our more assured institutional structure of recent years been freed, at least potentially, for the creation of more valuable kinds of 'culture.' " He also infers that "the recent popular success of books deploring the unworthiness of status striving indicates that Americans are throwing off this obsession and making it, as in other societies, including preindustrial America, merely one concern among many."[78] Robert Wood suggests, in the same vein, that "the pattern of inconspicuous consumption, the web of friendship, and the outgoing life that Whyte describes also have something of the flavor of a renaissance. Although 'keeping down with the Joneses' may indicate group tyranny, it is still better than keeping up with them. At least it displays disapproval of overt snobbishness. . . . While Whyte finds pressures for benevolent conformity, he also discovers brotherhood."[79] Daniel Bell has argued

[76] Daniel Miller and Guy Swanson state, in their detailed study of changes in the American family: "[W]e wish to urge that serious consideration be given to the possibility advanced here that bureaucratization has begun to provide a new level of security and comfort for Americans and a new sense of participation in a responsible moral community. As a consequence, we are less disposed than some commentators to see the growth of 'do-it-yourself' projects and of adult education and the apparent increase of interest in morality and religion as symptoms of a population withdrawing from a complicated and confusing world. Instead, we suggest that these may well signify the seizing of newly available opportunities for self-expression in the fine and practical arts, for the development of sophistication about leisure, and for a confronting of the problems of the relations of man to his fellows and to history." Daniel R. Miller and Guy E. Swanson, *The Changing American Parent* (New York: John Wiley, 1958), p. 212.

[77] Tocqueville, *Democracy in America,* Vol. I, p. 12.

[78] Berthoff, *op. cit.,* p. 512.

[79] Robert Wood, *Suburbia: Its People and Their Politics* (Boston: Houghton Mifflin, 1959), p. 15.

that the growth in education, among other factors, has reduced conformity. He comments that "one would be hard put to find today the 'conformity' *Main Street* exacted of Carol Kennicott thirty years ago. With rising educational levels, more individuals are able to indulge a wider variety of interests," such as serious music, good books, high-level FM radio, and the like.[80]

It may be fitting to conclude this chapter with the paradox formulated by Clyde Kluckhohn, who has suggested:

> Today's kind of "conformity" may actually be a step toward more genuine individuality in the United States. "Conformity" is less of a personal and psychological problem—less tinged with anxiety and guilt. . . . If someone accepts outwardly the conventions of one's group, one may have greater psychic energy to develop and fulfill one's private potentialities as a unique person. I have encountered no substantial evidence that this "conformity" is thoroughgoingly "inward."[81]

As status-seeking is the by-product of strong equalitarianism, so conformity and other-directedness may permit, or even demand, inner autonomy.

The institution most intimately connected with the value system is, of course, religion. And many have suggested that developments within the American church establishment have reflected the increase in "other-directed" traits. For example, the American's greater propensity to conform is alleged to explain why church membership is at an all-time high point; men increasingly join churches because it is the expected thing to do. I would question the extent to which change has occurred in American religious participation and belief. The next chapter, therefore, turns to an examination of the evidence supporting the assumptions that such major modifications have occurred, and seeks to account for some of the persistent traits in American religion by relating them to continuities in the essential values of the society.

DAVID RIESMAN

•

The Formation of Character[1]

Q. Do you think the teachers should punish the children for using make-up?

[80] Bell, "The Theory of Mass Society," *op. cit.*, p. 82.

[81] Clyde Kluckhohn, "Have There Been Discernible Shifts in American Values during the Past Generation?" in Elting E. Morison, ed., *The American Style: Essays in Value and Performance*, p. 187. This article is the best single summary and reference guide to the various empirical studies of changes in values in America.

[1] From *The Lonely Crowd* by David Riesman, with Nathan Glazer and Reuel Denney (New York: Doubleday & Co., 1955), Chapter II: "From Morality To Morale: Changes in the Agents of Character Formation" (title changed by the

A. Yes, I think they should punish them, but understand, I'm a modern mother and while I'm strict with my daughters, I am still modern. You know you can't punish your children too much or they begin to think you are mean and other children tell them you are mean.

From an interview

Population curves and economic structures are only a part of the ecology of character formation. Interposed between them and the resultant social character are the human agents of character formation: the parents, the teachers, the members of the peer-group, and the storytellers. These are the transmitters of the social heritage, and they wield great influence over the lives of children and hence on the whole society. For children live at the wave front of the successive population phases and are the partially plastic receivers of the social character of the future. In this chapter we consider the changing role of parents and teachers in socializing the young in each of the three population phases. Chapter III considers the socializing function of the peer-group. Chapter IV treats of the changes in the role of the storytellers, or, as they are now called, the mass media of communication.

We shall concentrate here on the shift from inner-direction to other-direction as the principal mode of insuring conformity in the urban American middle class. Perspective, however, requires a glance at societies in which tradition-direction is the principal mode of insuring conformity; and since the tradition-directed types have played a very minor role in America, we will take examples from primitive and medieval society. As we compare methods of socialization we shall see what is new about the newer types—and particularly what is new about other-direction.

I. CHANGES IN THE ROLE OF THE PARENTS

There has been a tendency in current social research, influenced as it is by psychoanalysis, to overemphasize and overgeneralize the importance of very early childhood in character formation. Even within this early period an almost technological attention has sometimes been focused on what might be called the tricks of the child-rearing trade: feeding and toilet-training schedules. The view implicit in this emphasis happens to be both a counsel of optimism and of despair. It is an optimistic view because it seems to say that facile mechanical changes in what the parent does will profoundly alter the character of the progeny. It is pessimistic because it assumes that once the child has reached, say, the weaning stage its character structure is so formed that, barring intensive psychiatric intervention, not much that happens afterward will do more than bring out tendencies already set.

Increasingly it is recognized, however, that character may change greatly after this early period and that cultural agents other than the parents may play important roles. Cultures differ widely not only in their timing of the various

---

steps in character formation but also in the agents they rely on at each step. Each new historical phase on the curve of population is marked by an increase in the length of life and in the period of socialization—that is, the period before full entry into one's adult social and ecomonic role. At the same time there is an increase in the responsibility placed on character-forming agents outside the home, the clan, or the village.

Parental Role in the Stage of Tradition-Direction

In societies depending on tradition-direction children can be "finished off" at an early point to assume an adult role. Adult roles are almost unchanging from generation to generation, and apart from training toward technical and manual skill, which may often be intensive, grown-up life demands little in the way of complex and literate instruction. Children begin very early to learn how to act like adults simply by watching adults around them. In the population phase of high growth potential there are many children to imitate a comparatively small number of adult models. The children live, ordinarily, in a large family setting. What the adults do is simple enough for children to grasp, so simple that children can often understand and imitate it before they have the physical skills to take a full part. Social maturity waits on biological maturity. Yet the biological roles of adult life are, in many cases, not themselves remote, for since there is little inhibition of childhood play and curiosity, children know what there is to know about sex and other adult functions—even though certain ceremonial mysteries may remain to testify to adult power and child helplessness.

Physical living patterns are an important factor in this setting. Houses consist typically of one room, without walls to separate the age groups and their varied functions. The households are often also economic units; the man does not go off to office or factory—and he does not go far. People are not yet so worried about saving time that they feel children are a nuisance; indeed, they may not feel themselves to be so very different from children anyway.

Furthermore, societies in the phase of high growth potential are characterized by a very low degree of social mobility. The parents train the child to succeed *them*, rather than to "succeed" by rising in the social system. Within any given social class society is age ranked, so that a person rises as a cork does in water: it is simply a matter of time, and little *in him* needs to change.

The upper social groups in such a society mature almost as quickly as the lower ones; the roles to be learned by children in both ranks of society differ only slightly in complexity. Even so, it is likely that a greater degree of individualization occurs at an earlier historical point in the upper strata than in the lower—as seems to have been the case in the Middle Ages when nobles, wandering artists, and priests were often closer to inner-direction than to the peasant's type of tradition-direction. Yet while the training of the leaders is of course somewhat more prolonged and their characters are more individuated, the young at all social levels take their places quickly in work, ceremony, and sexual role.

In summary: the major agency of character formation in societies dependent on tradition-direction is the extended family and its environing clan or group. Models for imitation are apt to be generalized in terms of the adult group as a whole rather than confined to the parents. What is imitated is behavior and specific traits such as bravery or cunning. The growing child does not confront problems of choice very different from those he watched his elders face; and his growth is conceived as a process of becoming an older, and therefore wiser, interpreter of tradition.

Parental Role In the Stage of Inner-Direction

Character and social mobility. With the onset of the transitional-growth phase of the population curve, opportunities open for a good deal of social and geographical mobility. People begin to pioneer on new frontiers: frontiers of production, of colonization, of intellectual discovery. Although this affects only a few directly, society as mediated by the primary group no longer proclaims unequivocally what one must do in order to conform. Rather, the growing child soon becomes aware of competing sets of customs—competing paths of life—from among which he is, in principle, free to choose. And while parentage and social origins are still all but determinative for most people, the wider horizon of possibilities and of wants requires a character which can adhere to rather generalized and more abstractly defined goals. Such a character must produce under its own motive power the appropriate specific means to gain these general ends.

To be sure, the goals and ideals that are held up to children and exemplified for them by their parents' own goals and ideals differ between, on the one hand, the confident, secular man of the Renaissance, glorying in his individuality and freedom from old restraints, and, on the other hand, the God-fearing puritan, driven by conscience and anxious about his salvation.[2] Yet both types are very much individuals, both are internally driven, and both are capable of pioneering. Finally, a society in which many people are internally driven—and are driven toward values, such as wealth and power, which are by their nature limited—contains in itself a dynamic of change by the very competitive forces it sets up. Even those who do not care to compete for higher places must do so in order not to descend in the social system, which has become a more open and less age-graded and birth-graded one.

All these tendencies are reinforced when roles become more complicated

[2] Margaret Mead, whose contribution to this whole field has been tremendously stimulating, has pointed out how the Protestant parent passed on to the child the legacy of his own unfulfilled strivings to live up to an ideal and how this drive spurred progress and change even though the statement of the ideal as such did not change. See, e.g., "Social Change and Cultural Surrogates," *Journal of Educational Sociology,* 14 (1940), 92; reprinted in *Personality in Nature, Society, and Culture,* ed. Kluckhohn and Murray, p. 511, and especially pp. 520–521.

as the division of labor progresses. The acceleration of the division of labor means that increasing numbers of children can no longer take their parents' roles as models. This is especially true on the male side; characterological change in the west seems to occur first with men. Mothers and grandmothers could until very recent times train daughters for the feminine role on the basis of tradition alone. Thus in the recent movie, *House of Strangers,* the Italian-born banker who, like Giannini or Ponzi, rises out of an immigrant setting and departs from his own father's pattern, sets for himself ambitious goals of power and money such as he believes to be characteristic of a true-born American, while his wife is a stereotype of the woman who clings to the tradition-directed ways of her early background.

Yet, while parents in the stage of transitional growth of population cannot be sure of what the adult working role and mode of life of their children will be, neither can conformity to that role be left to chance and behavioral opportunism. To possess the drive that is required to fulfill demanding and ever more demanding roles calls for greater attention to formal character training. Especially in the Protestant countries character training becomes an important part of education, though of course this does not mean that most parents consciously undertake to produce children to meet new social specifications.

The new situation created by increased social mobility implies that children must frequently be socialized in such a way as to be unfitted for their parents' roles, while being fitted for roles not as yet fully determined. Homing pigeons can be taught to fly home, but the inner-directed child must be taught to fly a straight course away from home, with destination unknown; naturally many meet the fate of Icarus. Nevertheless, the drive instilled in the child is to *live up to ideals* and to test his ability to be on his own by continuous experiments in self-mastery—instead of by following tradition.

Character training as a conscious parental task. In a society depending on tradition-direction to insure conformity, much of the parent's effort is directed toward keeping the child from being a nuisance to the adult world; and this task is regularly delegated to older brothers or sisters or to other adults. The child soon learns that behavioral conformity is the price of peace, and he learns to propitiate—or at least not to annoy—those around him. The inner-directed parent, on the other hand, asks more of his child, just as he asks more of himself. He can do this because, with the passing of the extended kinship family, the parent has his children much more under his own undivided and intensive scrutiny and control. Not satisfied with mere behavioral conformity, such a parent demands conformity of a more subtle sort, conformity as evidence of characterological fitness and self-discipline. The Puritan, especially, relentlessly scrutinizes his children as well as himself for the signs of election, that is, of salvation by the predestining God. And with secularization these signs are translated into signs predicting social mobility—signs that indicate a future facility in "passing," not from hell to heaven, but in the status hierarchy. On the one hand the parent looks for signs of potential failure—this search arises in part from guilty and anxious preoccupation about himself. On the other hand he looks for signs of talent—this must not be wasted.

In this way begins the process we see in extravagant form in the forced-draft childhood of John Stuart Mill, who studied the classics and wrote long essays under the zealous eye of his father before he was ten. Even when parents are less self-consciously pedagogical than James Mill, they may unconsciously impose their demands on children merely by being forceful, tense, and highly charged themselves. Indeed, the inner-directed man is frequently quite incapable of casual relationships. For one thing, he is preoccupied with his own concerns and therefore worried about wasting time; conversely, by not wasting time he avoids anxious self-preoccupation. For another thing, his relation to people, his children included, is mediated by his continuing, character-conditioned need to test and discipline himself.

This process, in the Renaissance-Reformation character which we term inner-directed, is less tense in the Latin countries than in the Protestant or Jansenist north, and in the north less tense in Lutheran or Anglican communicants than in the Calvinistic and Pietistic sects. Wherever inner-direction has attained relatively undisputed sway in a significantly large middle class, however, the production of the character structures of the coming generation becomes increasingly rationalized, just as is production in the non-household economy. In both cases the responsibility for production is no longer left to an external group sanction or situational pressure but is installed as a drive in the individual, and tremendous energies are unleashed toward the alteration of the material, social, and intellectual environment and toward the alteration of the self.

The social and spatial arrangements of middle-class life make it hard for the child to see through, let alone evade, the pressures put upon him to become inner-directed. As compared with the one-room house of the peasant or the "long house" of many primitive tribes, he grows up within walls that are physical symbols of the privacy of parental dominance. Walls separate parents from children, office from home, and make it hard if not impossible for the children to criticize the parents' injunctions by an "undress" view of the parents or of other parents. What the parents say becomes more real in many cases than what they do—significant training for a society in which words become increasingly important as a means of exchange, direction, and control. The conversation between parents and children, interrupted by the social distance that separates them, is continued by the child with himself in private.

The very pressure applied to the process of socialization by strict child rearing prolongs, as compared with the earlier era, the period in which socialization takes place. Freud has described this situation wonderfully in his concept of the watchful superego as a socializing agency incorporated into the child and accompanying him throughout life with ever renewed injunctions. This concept, while less fruitful in application to other societies, does seem to fit the middle class during the heyday of inner-direction in the west. One might even say that the character structure of the inner-directed person consists of the tension between superego, ego, and id. In a current cliché children are "brought up" rather than, as some would have it, "loved up"; and even when they have left home they continue to bring themselves up. They tend to feel throughout life that their characters are something to be worked on. The diary-keeping that is so significant a symptom of the new type of character may be viewed as a kind of inner time-and-motion study by which the individual records and judges his output day by day. It is evidence of the separation between the behaving and the scrutinizing self.

Passage from home. As the growing child takes over from his parents the duty of self-observation and character training, he becomes prepared to face and meet situations that are novel. Indeed, if he rises in the occupational hierarchy that becomes increasingly elaborated in the phase of transitional growth or if he moves toward the various opening frontiers, he finds that he can flexibly adapt his behavior precisely because he need not change his character. He can separate the two by virtue of the fact that he is an *individual* with a historically new level of self-awareness.

This awareness of the self is cause and consequence of the fact that choice is no longer automatically provided—or, rather, excluded—by the social setting of the primary group. Under the new conditions the individual must decide what to do—and therefore what to do with himself. This feeling of personal responsibility, this feeling that he matters as an individual, apart from his family or clan, makes him sensitive to the signals emanating from his internalized ideal. If the ideal, as in the puritan, is to be "good" or, as in the child of the Renaissance, to be "great," what must he do to fulfill the injunction? And how does he know that he has fulfilled these difficult self-demands? As Max Weber and R. H. Tawney saw very clearly in their portraits of the puritan, little rest is available to those who ask themselves such questions.

The relative uncomfortableness of the more powerfully inner-directed homes—the lack of indulgence and casualness in dealing with children—prepares the child for the loneliness and psychic uncomfortableness of such questions and of the social situations that he may confront. Or, more exactly, the child's character is such that he feels comfortable in an environment which, like his home, is demanding and which he struggles to master.

We may say, then, that parents who are themselves inner-directed install a psychological gyroscope in their child and set it going; it is built to their own and other authoritative specifications; if the child has good luck, the governor will spin neither too fast, with the danger of hysteric outcomes, nor too slow, with the danger of social failure.

Parental Role In the Stage of Other-Direction

Character and social mobility. In the phase of incipient population decline, the conditions for advancement alter significantly.

The inner-directed person is able to see industrial and commercial possibilities and to work with the zeal and ruthlessness required by expanding frontiers in the phase of transitional growth of population. Societies in the phase of incipient population decline, on the other hand, need neither such zeal nor such independence. Business, government, the professions, become heavily bureaucratized, as we see most strikingly, for instance, in France. Such societies increasingly turn to the remaining refractory components of the industrial process: the men who run the machines. Social mobility under these conditions continues to exist. But it depends less on what one is and what one does than on what others think of one—and how competent one is in manipulating others and being oneself manipulated. To look at it from another point of view, when the basic physical plant of a society is felt to be built, or rather when the building can be routinized by management planning, there begins to be room at the top for the other-directed person who can see the subtle opportunities given in the human setting.[3] Though material abundance becomes technologically possible, people continue to work—and do make-work—at a pace more in keeping with the earlier era of transitional growth: mobility drives are still imbedded in their character. *But the product now in demand is neither a staple nor a machine; it is a personality.*

To bring the other-directed personality type and his typical economic framework together it might be observed that there exists in the production of personality the same sort of "product differentiation" that is characteristic of monopolistic competition generally. The economists apply the term "product differentiation" to a firm's effort to distinguish products not by price but by small differences, sufficient, however, in connection with advertising, to take the product out of direct price competition with otherwise similar competing products. Thus one cigarette is made slightly longer, another nearly oval, while still another is given a cork tip or a green box. *Time* and *Newsweek* engage in product differentiation. So do the makers of automobiles, streamliners, and toothpastes, and the operators of hotels and universities. So, too, people who are competing for jobs in the hierarchies of business, government, and professional life try to differentiate their personalities (as contrasted with their actual technical skills)—without getting as far out of line, let us say, as a 1934 prematurely streamlined Chrysler. In this study, the social aspect of this competitive procedure, since it will be extended to cover persons and services as well as commodities, will be termed "marginal differentiation," and thus distinguished from the related concept used by the economists.

Freud coined the phrase "narcissism with respect to minor differences" for the pride which individuals, groups, and nations manifest about small insignia

[3] Of course there is no law that societies in the stage of incipient population decline have to become top-heavy and bureaucratic. It is conceivable that even more mobility could be opened up by shifting population and other resources rapidly into tertiary services, by greatly expanding leisure and the industries catering to leisure. We shall return to these matters in Part III.

which distinguish them from other individuals, groups, and nations. Marginal differentiation sometimes does have this quality of pride or of what Veblen called "invidious distinction." But the phenomenon I have in mind is one of anxiety rather than pride, of veiled competition rather than openly rivalrous display; the narcissism is muted or, as we shall see, alloyed with other, stronger elements.

In these circumstances parents who try, in inner-directed fashion, to compel the internalization of disciplined pursuit of clear goals run the risk of having their children styled clear out of the personality market. Gyroscopic direction is just not flexible enough for the rapid adaptations of personality that are required, precisely because there will be other competitors who do not have gyroscopes. Inhibited from presenting their children with sharply silhouetted images of self and society, parents in our era can only equip the child to do his best, whatever that may turn out to be. What is best is not in their control but in the hands of the school and peer-group that will help locate the child eventually in the hierarchy. But even these authorities speak vaguely; the clear principles of selection that once guided people of inner-directed character no longer apply. For example, social climbing itself may be called into public question at the same time that it is no longer so unequivocally desirable in terms of private wish. As some *Fortune* surveys indicate, a safe and secure job may be preferred to a risky one involving high stakes. What is more, it is no longer clear which way *is* up even if one wants to rise, for with the growth of the new middle class the older, hierarchical patterns disintegrate, and it is not easy to compare ranks among the several sets of hierarchies that do exist. Does an army colonel "rank" the head of an international union? A physics professor, a bank vice-president? A commentator, the head of an oil company?

Increasingly in doubt as to how to bring up their children, parents turn to other contemporaries for advice; they also look to the mass media; and like the mother quoted at the outset of this chapter they turn, in effect, to the children themselves. They may, nevertheless, fasten on some inflexible scheme of child rearing and follow that. Yet they cannot help but show their children, by their own anxiety, how little they depend on themselves and how much on others. Whatever they may seem to be teaching the child in terms of content, they are passing on to him their own contagious, highly diffuse anxiety. They reinforce this teaching by giving the child approval—and approving themselves because of the child—when he makes good.

To be sure, inner-directed parents also often were able to "love" only those children who made good in the outer world. But at least the canons of success were reasonably clear. The other-directed child, however, faces not only the requirement that he make good but also the problem of defining what making good means. He finds that both the definition and the evaluation of himself depend on the company he keeps: first, on his schoolmates and teachers; later, on peers and superiors. But perhaps the company one keeps is itself at fault? One can then shop for other preferred companies in the mass circulation media.

Approval itself, irrespective of content, becomes almost the only unequivocal good in this situation: one makes good when one is approved of. Thus all power, not merely some power, is in the hands of the actual or imaginary approving group, and the child learns from his parents' reactions to him that nothing in his character, no possession he owns, no inheritance of name or talent, no work he has done is valued for itself but only for its effect on others. Making good becomes almost equivalent to making friends, or at any rate the right kind of friends. "To him that hath approval, shall be given more approval."

From bringing up children to "Bringing up Father." The typical other-directed child grows up in a small family, in close urban quarters, or in a suburb. Even more than in the earlier epoch the father leaves home to go to work, and he goes too far to return for lunch. Home, moreover, is no longer an area of solid privacy. As the size and living space of the family diminish and as the pattern of living with older relatives declines, the child must directly face the emotional tensions of his parents. There is a heightening of awareness of the self in relation to others under these conditions, especially since the parents, too, are increasingly self-conscious.

Under the new social and economic conditions, the position of children rises. They are not subjected to a period of deprivation and hardship which leads to compensatory dreams of a life of ease and pleasure. Girls are not, as they were in some earlier societies, drudges at home until, at puberty, they were suddenly given the only "capital" they were ever likely to find—that of their bodies—to live on as income, or exhaust as principal. Even boys from comfortable homes were expected until recently to hit the sunrise trail with paper routes or other economically profitable and "character-building" chores.

The parents lack not only the self-assurance that successful inner-direction brings but also the strategy of withdrawal available to many unsuccessful inner-directed types. The loss of old certainties in the spheres of work and social relations is accompanied by doubt as to how to bring up children. Moreover, the parents no longer feel themselves superior to the children. While children no longer have immediate economic value, they are less numerous, "scarcer" in relation to the number of adults: the effort is made, and it is objectively possible, to want all children who are conceived and to raise very nearly all children who are born. More is staked on every single child than in the earlier epoch when many children were not raised to maturity. In addition, apart from the fact that the children may be better Americans than the parents, in ethnic or social terms—as Jiggs's daughter is more up to date than he—there are undoubtedly other solid reasons (which I shall not go into) for the general emphasis on youth which runs through all forms of popular culture.[4]

[4] This, too, is a development whose importance Margaret Mead has stressed. See *And Keep Your Powder Dry* (New York, William Morrow, 1942).

Historical changes in the lives of adolescents can be seen most clearly, perhaps, if one looks back to those *Bildungsromane* of the nineteenth century that described the misunderstood youth who struggled against the harsh or hypocritical tyranny of his parents, particularly if one compares one of the best of such novels, Samuel Butler's *The Way of All Flesh,* with one of the best of our contemporary examples, for instance Lionel Trilling's short story, "The Other Margaret."[5] In Trilling's story we have a picture of a precocious young girl in the intellectual, urban, upper middle class. Margaret, who goes to a progressive school, believes that Negroes are exploited, and she resents the inferior position in the home of "the other Margaret," a Negro domestic. It is the daughter Margaret who is self-righteous, not the parents.

In the face of her criticism, buttressed as it is by the authority of the school, the parents, themselves progressive, are on the defensive. They are tense and very much concerned with what their daughter thinks—and thinks of them. Eventually, all three adults manage to destroy Margaret's illusion of the virtues of the other Margaret—the parents by reasoning; the other Margaret by bad behavior. But in the end the parents are anxious about their victory, lest it harm their sensitive child. They possess little of the certainty and security of Theobald's parents in *The Way of All Flesh.*

In this change of parental attitude the mass media of communication play a dual role. From the mass media—radio, movies, comics—as well as from their own peers, children can easily learn what the norm of parental behavior is, and hold it over their parents' heads. Thus a kind of realism is restored to the child which was his property much more simply in the societies depending on tradition-direction: the other-directed child is often more knowing than his parents—like the proverbial Harvard man, there is little they can tell *him.*[6]

As already noted, the parents also have their sources of direction in the mass media. For in their uneasiness as to how to bring up children they turn increasingly to books, magazines, government pamphlets, and radio programs. These tell the already anxious mother to accept her children. She learns that

[5] *Partisan Review,* XII (1945), 381.

[6] Yet the knowingness, particularly in the middle class, has limits that were less important in the tradition-directed family. There the child, knowledgeable for example about sex, could see reflections of it in the daily adult life around him. He would know that if his uncle was particularly gay or particularly cross at work this was connected with what happened in the village the night before. As against this, the other-directed child knows about sex only, so to speak, in the abstract. He cannot reasonably connect the night life he knows exists with the seriousness of the adult world that faces him at school, at the store, or at home. While he has doffed the myths of sex that Freud found among the young of his day, he still finds passion playing a greater role in the comics and the movies than in the life he is able to observe—the latter being a life in which people are trained to hide their passions and to act generally in a disembodied way. Perhaps this is one reason why sex often remains an exciting mystery for the other-directed adult—as we shall see in Chap. VII—despite all his learning, all his disenchantment, and even all his experience of it. And, in general, the other-directed child's realism about the adult world is hampered not so much by Victorian inhibitions as by the far subtler partitions of adult life itself, such as the shadowy partitions between work and play to be discussed later.

there are no problem children, only problem parents; and she learns to look into her own psyche whenever she is moved to deny the children anything, including an uninterrupted flow of affection. If the children are cross then the mother must be withholding something. And while these tutors also tell the mother to "relax" and to "enjoy her children," even this becomes an addition injunction to be anxiously followed.

It may be that children today do not gain the strength that adults—no longer inner-directed—have lost. To be sure, this was often a factitious strength, as Samuel Butler saw; but it was usually sufficient both to crush the child's spontaneity and anesthetize his diffuse anxiety. "Shades of the prison-house begin to close upon the growing boy"—and the prisoner might feel oppressed, even guilty, but not too anxious behind his bars. In contrast, what the other-directed child does "learn" from his parents is anxiety—the emotional tuning appropriate to his other-directed adjustment.

The rule of "reason." Despite the diminution of their authority, the parents still try to control matters; but with the loss of self-assurance their techniques change. They can neither hold themselves up as exemplars—when both they and the child know better—nor resort, in good conscience, to severe corporal punishment and deprivations. At most there are token spankings, with open physical warfare confined to the lower classes.

The parents' recourse, especially in the upper middle class, is to "personnel" methods—to manipulation in the form of reasoning, or, more accurately, of rationalizing. The child responds in the same manner. One might summarize the historical sequence by saying that the tradition-directed child propitiates his parents; the inner-directed child fights or succumbs to them; the other-directed child manipulates them and is in turn manipulated.

A movie of several years ago, *The Curse of the Cat People,* while it testified to American preoccupation with certain child-rearing themes which do not directly concern us here, also provides an interesting example of these manipulative relations between parent and child. A little girl lives in a suburban, middle-class home with its typical neatness, garden, and Negro servant. As in "The Other Margaret," there is a terrific pressure of adult emotion focused around this one child from the parents and servant. The child is supposed to invite the other children in the neighborhood for her birthday party; but believing her father's joke that the big tree in the yard is a mailbox, she puts the invitations there and they never go out. When her birthday arrives, the other children whom she had said she would invite tease her and refuse to play with her. Her father scolds her for taking him seriously, and she is also in difficulties for not getting along better with the other children. But the parents (plus servant) decide to go ahead with the party anyway, "as if." There follows a "party" which tries to persuade the child that there has been no tragedy, that this party is just as good as the one which failed.

The parents insist that the child somehow know, without a formal etiquette, when things are supposed to be "real" and when "pretend." The tree as the mailbox is pretend; the party real. Feeling misunderstood and alone, the little girl discovers a real friend in a strange woman who lives almost as a recluse in a great house. The parents frown upon this "friend" and her gift of a ring to the child. The little girl then discovers an imaginary friend at the bottom of the yard, a beautiful older woman with whom she talks. The father cannot see, that is to say "see," this latter friend and punishes the child for lying.

Notice this fictional family's lack of privacy for the child. The discovery of the gift of the ring seems to be typical of the fact that few of her excitements escape parental scrutiny. Moreover, the very fact that the father suggests to the daughter the secret about the make-believe "mailbox tree" is symbolic of the intrusion of his knowledge: the daughter is not allowed her own make-believe but must share it with him, subject to his determination of when it applies. That the daughter and father finally come into open conflict over the little girl's fantasy friend is only to be expected; the girl cannot put a lock on the door of her room or the door of her mind. (In a lower-class home there would be, spatially at least, even less privacy; but there might be more psychic privacy because the parents would often be less interested in the child.)

Notice, in the second place, the "reasonable" but subtly manipulative tone of parent-child relations. This is evidenced by the parental planning of the party for the daughter and her peers and by the parental irritation when the plan miscarries. Still more significant is the way in which the family meets the crisis of blocked peer-group communication symbolized by the nonoperative mailbox—a failure that is itself occasioned by a blockage of understanding about the real and the unreal between daughter and parents.

The fiasco is, obviously enough, a matter that requires immediate corrective action; parents in this pass, it seems, should *do* something. The parents of the child in this movie do nothing; they prefer to talk away the situation, to manipulate the child into the acceptance of a formal illusion of party making. The result is to produce a sort of exaggeration and burlesque of the way in which other-directed persons, in parent-child as in all other relations, constantly resort to manipulation and countermanipulation.

As contrasted with all this, the inner-directed parent is not particularly worried by his child's resentment or hostility. Nor is he as apt to be as aware of it. He and the child are both protected by the gap that separates them. The other-directed parent, however, has to win not only his child's good behavior but also his child's good will. Therefore, he is tempted to use his superior dialectic skill to "reason" with the child. And when the child learns—this is part of his sensitive radar equipment—how to argue too, the parent is torn between giving in and falling uneasily back on the sterner methods of *his* inner-directed parents. The father in *The Curse of the Cat People,* after trying to reason away the little girl's belief in her fantasy friend, finally spanks her. But such scenes are always succeeded by parental efforts at reconciliation, turning the spanking itself into a step in the manipulative chain.

Finally, we must observe the change in the content of the issues at stake between parent and child. The more driving and tense inner-directed parents compel their children to work, to save, to clean house, sometimes to study, and sometimes to pray. Other less puritanical types of inner-directed parent want their boys to be manly, their girls to be feminine and chaste. Such demands make either economic or ideological sense in the population phase of transitional growth. The large home could absorb enormous amounts of labor; even today those who putter in small house and small garden can still find lots to do. The parents themselves often set the example, in which they are supported by the school, of work and study: these are believed to be the paths of upward mobility both in this world and in the next.

In the other-directed home, on the other hand, the issues between parent and child concern the nonwork side of life. For in the phase of incipient population decline—most markedly, of course, in America but elsewhere too—there is no work for children to do inside the urban home, and little outside. They need not brush and clean (except themselves)—they are less efficient than a vacuum cleaner. Nor is there an array of younger brothers and sisters to be taken care of. The American mother, educated, healthy, and efficient, has high standards for care of the apartment or small home and would, where she is not working, often feel quite out of a job if the children took over the housework. Fortunately released from the quandary of the old woman who lived in a shoe, she faces—just, as we shall see, as her husband does—the problem of leisure; care for the house and children is frequently her self-justification and escape.

So parents and children debate over eating and sleeping time as later they will debate over use of the family car. And they argue tensely, as in *The Curse of the Cat People,* about the contacts of the child with the "others" and about the emotional hue of the argument itself. But by the nature of these discussions the parents have a less easy victory. In the population phase of transitional growth they can point to self-evident tasks that need doing—self-evident at least according to accepted standards that have survived from the still earlier epoch. In the phase of incipient decline, however, the consumption or leisure issues are no longer self-evident; to decide them, if they are to be decided, one has to resort to models outside the particular home—in search of the ever changing norms of the group in which the parents happen to live. And indeed the radio and print bring the models into the home, like a trial record from which the child and parent legalists prepare briefs.[7]

[7] Morris Janowitz has suggested that if one wanted to get a very rough index of homes in which other-direction was being transmitted, as against those in which inner-direction prevailed, one might separate the homes which took only such magazines as *Life, Look,* the comics, or movie journals from those which took such periodicals as the *Saturday Evening Post* or *Collier*'s. The former group is for the whole family, interpreted as easily or more easily by children than by adults. The latter group is mainly for the grownups and not shared with the children.

To sum up: parents in the groups depending on other-direction install in their children something like a psychological radar set—a device not tuned to control movement in any particular direction while guiding and steadying the person from within but rather tuned to detect the action, and especially the symbolic action, of others. Thereafter, the parents influence the children's character only insofar as (a) their own signals mingle with others over the radar, (b) they can locate children in a certain social environment in order to alter to a very limited degree what signals they will receive, (c) they take the risks of a very partial and precarious censorship of incoming messages. Thus the parental role diminishes in importance as compared with the same role among the inner-directed.

II. CHANGES IN THE ROLE OF THE TEACHER

Much could be said about the changing configuration of adult authorities, other than the parents, as society moves from dependence on inner-direction to dependence on other-direction. Largely for economic reasons the governess, mammy, or hired tutor, for instance, virtually disappears from middle- and upper middle-class homes. One significant consequence is that children are no longer raised by people who hold up to them the standard of a family or class. Such a standard is good training in inner-direction—in the acquisition of generalized goals; it is at the same time a partial buffer against the indiscriminate influence of the peer-group. But there is another more subtle consequence. The child who has been raised by a governess and educated by a tutor gains a very keen sense for the disparities of power in the home and in the society. When he goes off to boarding school or college he is likely to remain unimpressed by his teachers—like the upper-class mother who told the school headmaster: "I don't see why the masters can't get along with Johnny; all the other servants do." Such a child is not going to be interested in allowing his teachers to counsel him in his peer-group relations or emotional life.

Furthermore, the presence of these adults in the home—somewhat like the extended family in earlier eras—helps reduce the emotional intensity of parent-child relations. Though the child knows who is boss in the home, he can still play these other "officials" off against parental authority. And, indeed, the inner-directed parents, frequently not overeager for warmth from the child, are quite willing to have the child's experience of affection associated with persons of lower status. The inner-directed young man raised under these conditions learns to find emotional release with prostitutes and others of low status. He becomes capable of impersonal relations with people and sometimes incapable of any other kind. This is one of the prices he pays for his relative impermeability to the needs and wishes of his peers, and helps account for his ability, when in pursuit of some end he values, to steel himself against their indifference or hostility.

Grandmothers as authorities are almost as obsolete as governesses. There is no room for them in the modern apartment, nor can they, any more than the children themselves, find a useful economic role. Nevertheless they endure, concomitant with the increased longevity of the later population phases. The increased personalization of relationships that other-direction brings means that "strangers" in the home are less and less endurable: the in-law problem, a standard joke in many cultures over many centuries, takes on new meaning where sensitive, highly individuated people live without characterological defenses against each other.

The elimination of the grandmother from a central role in the home is, moreover, symbolic of the rapidity of the changes we are discussing. She is two generations removed from current practices on the "frontier of consumption." While the parents try to keep up with their children, both as a means of staying young and as a means of staying influential, this is seldom possible for the grandparents. Hence their role in the formation of the other-directed character is negligible. Far from presenting the child with a relatively consistent "family portrait," standing in back of the parents and strengthening them, grandparents stand as emblems of how little one can learn from one's elders about the things that matter.

A parallel development removes another set of parent surrogates who played an important role in earlier periods: the older brothers or sisters who, like sophomores, hazed the younger in subjecting them to the family pattern of discipline. Today the older children—if there are any—are frequently more willing to earn cash as baby sitters than to supervise the training of their own younger brothers and sisters. The lure of a job may get children to work outside their homes; that still makes sense to them. But within their own home they are the privileged guests in a rather second-rate hotel, a hotel whose harassed but smiling managers they put under constant pressure for renovation.

The Teacher's Role In the Stage of Inner-Direction

One important authority, however, remains: a proxy parent whose power has probably increased as a consequence of the shift to other-direction. This is the schoolteacher, and we turn now to a fuller exploration of the change in her role.

In the period when inner-direction insures middle-class conformity, school starts relatively late—there are few nursery schools. The teacher's task is largely to train the children in decorum and in intellectual matters. The decorum may be the minimum of discipline needed to keep order in the classroom or the maximum of polish needed to decorate girls of the upper social strata. As schools become more plentiful and more readily accessible and "democratic," the obligation to train the child in middle-class speech and manners—that he may be aided in his rise above his parents' rank—falls upon the teacher. But the teacher does not work close to the child's emotional level. And the teacher regards her job as a limited one, sharply demarcated from the equally rigorous task of the home.

The physical setting in school reflects this situation. Seating is formal—all face front—and often alphabetical. The walls are decorated with the ruins of Pompeii and the bust of Caesar. For all but the few exceptional children who can transcend the dead forms of their classical education and make the ancient world come alive, these etchings and statues signify the irrelevance of the school to the emotional problems of the child.

The teacher herself has neither understanding of nor time for these emotional problems, and the child's relation to other children enters her purview only in disciplinary cases. Often she has simply no authority: she is a common scold with too large a brood. Or she manages to maintain discipline by strictures and punishments. But these absorb the emotional attention of the children, often uniting them in opposition to authority.

In the recent Swedish movie *Torment* we see this pattern still at work in the near-contemporary scene. Teachers and parents share the task of instilling inner-directed values. The villain is a harsh and overbearing, neurotic prep-school teacher. All the boys hate him; some fear him; no self-respecting boy would dream—despite the teacher's groping efforts—of being his friend. The hero is a boy who rebels, not so much because he wants to but rather because he is forced to by his teacher. He and his friends suffer, but their parents and teachers do not invade their lives, and they have privacy with each other and with girls, so long as no serious breach of decorum is evident. This rebellion itself—its success is not the issue—is part of the process of developing an inner-directed character.

An equally moving portrait is Antonia White's novel of a girl's convent school, *Frost in May*. Though the nuns at the school go quite far in "molding character" and viciously cut down signs of spontaneity and open-mindedness in the gifted heroine, they have back of them only the old-fashioned sanctions of penance and salvation. Their charges break or bend or run away or join the church—they do not open up to the nuns as friends. The universal uniforms, as in a military school, symbolize the barriers of rank and restraint that separate the authorities from the children.

We may sum all this up by saying that the school of this period is concerned largely with impersonal matters. The sexes are segregated. The focus is on an intellectual content that for most children has little emotional bite. Elocution, like female accomplishment, is impersonal, too; the child is not asked to "be himself"—nor does the school aim to be like "real life." Teachers, whether spinsterly or motherly types, do not know enough, even if they had the time and energy, to take an active hand in the socialization of tastes or of peer-group relations. While parents may permit the teachers to enforce certain rules of morality directly related to school, such as modesty of dress and honesty in examinations, and to inculcate certain rules of manners directly related to social ascent, they hardly allow interference with play groups, even in the interests of enforcing ethnic or economic democracy. The teacher is supposed to see that the children learn a curriculum, not that they enjoy it or learn group cooperation. The present practice of progressive grammar schools which decide whether or not to take a child by putting him in his putative group and seeing how he fits in would hardly have been conceivable.

Nevertheless, despite the social distance between teacher and child, the school's unquestioning emphasis on intellectual ability is profoundly important in shaping the inner-directed character. It affirms to the child that what matters is what he can *accomplish,* not how nice is his smile or how cooperative his attitude. And while the objectivity of the criteria for judging these skills and competences is rightfully called into question today—when we can see very clearly, for instance, the class bias in intelligence tests and written examinations—the inner-directed school is not aware of such biases, and hence its standards can appear unequivocal and unalterable. For this reason these standards can be internalized both by those who succeed and by those who fail. They are felt as real and given, not as somebody's whim. Thus the school reinforces the home in setting for the child goals that are clear to all and that give direction and meaning to life thereafter.

Whatever the security children gain from knowing where they stand—a security they no longer have in the other-directed progressive school—we must not forget how harshly this system bears on those who cannot make the grade: they are often broken; there is little mercy for them on psychological grounds. Brains, status, perhaps also docility, win the teacher, rather than "personality" or "problems." Some of the failures rebel. But these, too, are hammered into shape by the school—bad shape. Occasionally the frontier and other opportunities for mobility provide an exit for the academically outclassed; and, still more occasionally, the rebel returns, like a mythical hero, having lived his troubles down, to alleviate the guilt of other misfits and give them hope for their own future. By and large, however, the very unequivocality of the school's standards that gives the children a certain security also means that the standards will be internalized even by those who fail. They will carry with them the aftereffects of emotional shock whose violence lies beyond criticism—sometimes even beyond recall.

The Teacher's Role in the Stage of Other-Direction

Progressive education began as a movement to liberate children from the crushing of talent and breaking of will that was the fate of many, even of those whose inner-direction might have seemed to them and to the observer stable and sound enough. Its aim, and to a very considerable degree, its achievement, was to develop the individuality of the child; and its method was to focus the teacher's attention on more facets of the child than his intellectual abilities. Today, however, progressive education is often no longer progressive; as people have become more other-directed, educational methods that were once liberating may even tend to thwart individuality rather than advance and protect it. The story can be quickly told.

Progressive schools have helped lower the age of school entry; the two- to five-year-old groups learn to associate school not with forbidding adults and dreary subjects but with play and understanding adults. The latter are, increasingly, young college graduates who have been taught to be more concerned with the child's social and psychological adjustment than with his academic progress—indeed, to scan the intellectual performance for signs of social maladjustment. These new teachers are more specialized. They don't claim to "understand children" but to have studied Gesell on the "fives" or the "nines"; and this greater knowledge not only prevents the children from uniting in a wall of distrust or conspiracy against the school but also permits the teacher to take a greater hand in the socialization of spheres—consumption, friendship, fantasy—which the older-type teacher, whatever her personal desires, could not touch. Our wealthier society can afford this amount of individuation and "unnecessary" schooling.

Physical arrangements, too—in seating, age-grading, decoration—symbolize the changes in the teacher's function. The sexes are mixed. Seating is arranged "informally." That is, *alphabetic* forms disappear, often to be replaced by *sociometric* forms that bring together compeers. This often means that where to sit becomes problematical—a clue to one's location on the friendship chart. Gesell grading is as severe as intellectual grading was in the earlier era; whatever their intellectual gifts, children stay with their presumed social peers.[8] The desks change their form, too; they are more apt to be movable tables with open shelves than places where one may hide things. The

[8] Howard C. Becker ("Role and Career Problems of the Chicago Public School Teacher," unpublished Ph.D. dissertation, University of Chicago, 1951) has been observing the classroom consequences of the decline of the practice both of skipping grades and of holding children back who must repeat the grade. The teachers, faced with a group of identical age but vastly different capacities and willingnesses, meet the situation by dividing the class into two or three like-minded groups. Mobility between groups is discouraged, and children are encouraged to imitate their groupmates. The teacher herself, in the public schools, is probably inner-directed, but she is forced by her situation to promote other-direction among her charges.

The following quotation from Mr. Becker's interviews is a poignant example of how a teacher will promote other-direction in her efforts to get the children to have more interesting weekends: "Every class I have I start out the year by making a survey. I have each child get up and tell what he did over the weekend. These last few years I've noticed that more and more children get up and say, 'Saturday I went to the show, Sunday I went to the show' . . . I've been teaching twenty-five years, and it never used to be like that. Children used to do more interesting things, they would go places instead of 'Saturday I went to the show, Sunday I went to the show' . . . What I do is to give a talk on all the interesting things that could be done—like going to museums and things like that. And also things like playing baseball and going on bike rides. By the end of the term a child is ashamed if he has to get up and say, 'Saturday I went to the show, Sunday I went to the show.' All the rest of the children laugh at him. So they really try to do some interesting things."

teacher no longer sits on a dais or struts before a blackboard but joins the family circle.

Above all, the walls change their look. The walls of the modern grade school are decorated with the paintings of the children or their montages from the class in social studies. Thus the competitive and contemporary problems of the children look down on them from walls which, like the teacher herself, are no longer impersonal. This looks progressive, looks like a salute to creativeness and individuality; but again we meet paradox. While the school de-emphasizes grades and report cards, the displays seem almost to ask the children: "Mirror, mirror on the wall, who is fairest of us all?"[9]

While the children's paintings and montages show considerable imaginative gift in the pre-adolescent period, the school itself is nevertheless still one of the agencies for the destruction of fantasy, as it was in the preceding era. Imagination withers in most of the children by adolescence. What survives is neither artistic craft nor artistic fantasy but the socialization of taste and interest that can already be seen in process in the stylization of perception in the children's paintings and stories. The stories of the later progressive grades are apt to be characterized by "realism." This realism is subtly influenced by the ideals of the progressive movement. Caesar and Pompeii are replaced by visits to stores and dairies, by maps from *Life,* and by *The Weekly Reader;* and fairy tales are replaced by stories about trains, telephones, and grocery stores, and, later, by material on race relations or the United Nations or "our Latin American neighbors."

These changes in arrangement and topic assist the breakdown of walls between teacher and pupil; and this in turn helps to break down walls between student and student, permitting that rapid circulation of tastes which is a prelude to other-directed socialization. Whereas the inner-directed school child might well have hidden his stories and paintings under his bed—like the adult who, as we saw, often kept a diary—the other-directed child reads his stories to the group and puts his paintings on the wall. Play, which in the earlier epoch is often an extracurricular and private hobby, shared at most with a small group, now becomes part of the school enterprise itself, serving a "realistic" purpose.

The teacher's role in this situation is often that of opinion leader. She is the one who spreads the messages concerning taste that come from the progressive urban centers. She conveys to the children that what matters is not

[9] Still more paradoxically, it often happens that those schools that insist most strongly that the child be original and creative by this very demand make it difficult for him to be so. He dare not imitate an established master nor, in some cases, even imitate his own earlier work. Though the introduction of the arts into the school opens up the whole art world to many children, who would have no time or stimulation outside, other children are forced to socialize performances that would earlier have gone unnoticed by peers and adults.

their industry or learning as such but their adjustment in the group, their cooperation, their (carefully stylized and limited) initiative and leadership.

Especially important is the fact that the cooperation and leadership that are inculcated in and expected of the children are frequently contentless. In nursery school it is not important whether Johnny plays with a truck or in the sandbox, but it matters very much whether he involves himself with Bill—via any object at all. To be sure, there are a few, a very few, truly progressive schools where the children operating on the Dalton plan and similar plans exercise genuine choice of their program, move at their own pace, and use the teacher as a friendly reference library; here cooperation is necessary and meaningful in actual work on serious projects. Far more frequently, however, the teacher continues to hold the reins of authority in her hands, hiding her authority, like her compeer, the other-directed parent, under the cloak of "reasoning" and manipulation. She determines the program and its pace—indeed, often holding the children back because she fails to realize that children, left to themselves, are capable of curiosity about highly abstract matters. She may delay them by making arithmetic "realistic" and languages fun—as well as by substituting social studies for history. In extreme forms of this situation there is nothing on which the children have to cooperate in order to get it done. The teacher will do it for them anyway. Hence when she asks that they be cooperative she is really asking simply that they be nice.

However, though the request seems simple, it is not casually made: the teacher is very tense about it. Deprived of older methods of discipline, she is, if anything, even more helpless than the parents who can always fall back on those methods in a pinch, though guiltily and rather ineffectively. The teacher neither dares to nor cares to; she has been taught that bad behavior on the children's part implies poor management on her part. Moreover, she herself is not interested in the intellectual content of what is taught, nor is this content apt to come up in a staff meeting or PTA discussion. These adult groups are often concerned with teaching tolerance, both ethnic and economic; and the emphasis on social studies that results means that intellectual content and skill become still more attenuated. Consequently, the teacher's emotional energies are channeled into the area of group relations. Her social skills develop; she may be sensitive to cliques based on "mere friendship" and seek to break them up lest any be left out. Correspondingly, her love for certain specific children may be trained out of her. All the more, she needs the general cooperation of all the children to assure herself that she is doing her job. Her surface amiability and friendliness, coupled with this underlying anxiety concerning the children's response, must be very confusing to the children, who will probably conclude that to be uncooperative is about the worst thing one can be.

Of course the teacher will see to it that the children practice cooperation in small matters: in deciding whether to study the Peruvians or the Columbians, in nominating class officers for early practice in the great contemporary rituals of electioneering and parliamenteering, and in organizing contributions for the Red Cross or a Tag Day. Thus the children are supposed to learn democracy by underplaying the skills of intellect and overplaying the skills of gregariousness and amiability—skill democracy, in fact, based on respect for ability to *do* something, tends to survive only in athletics.

There is, therefore, a curious resemblance between the role of the teacher in the small-class modern school—a role that has spread from the progressive private schools to a good number of the public schools—and the role of the industrial relations department in a modern factory. The latter is also increasingly concerned with cooperation between men and men and between men and management, as technical skill becomes less and less of a major concern. In a few of the more advanced plants there is even a pattern of democratic decision on moot matters—occasionally important because it affects piecework rates and seniority rules, but usually as trivial as the similar decisions of grammar-school government. Thus the other-directed child is taught at school to take his place in a society where the concern of the group is less with what it produces than with its internal group relations, its morale.

LIONEL TRILLING | Review of Riesman's *The Lonely Crowd*[1]

David Riesman's *The Lonely Crowd* seems to me one of the most important books about America to have been published in recent times. And quite apart from the particularity of its subject, it is one of the most interesting books I have ever read.

This is very large praise, and as I write it I find myself wondering whether I may not be overstating the case for this sociological study in order to counteract the antagonisms to the social sciences which I know to be pretty common among people who like literature very much. But I do not think I am saying more than I mean. My opinion was formed before I ever thought of writing about Mr. Riesman's book and I have tested it by more than one reading.

Yet since I have raised the question of the literary suspiciousness of the social sciences, especially sociology, it might be well to take it specifically into account in connection with *The Lonely Crowd*.

One reason for this suspiciousness is that sociology tends to use a kind of language which must arouse antagonism in people who are at all sensitive to language. This is not because the language of sociology is scientific but because

[1] From *A Gathering of Fugitives* by Lionel Trilling (Boston: The Beacon Press, 1956), pp. 107–112. Copyright © 1952, 1956, by Lionel Trilling. Reprinted by permission of the Beacon Press and of Martin Secker & Warburg, Limited.

it is often pseudo-scientific and jargonistic and has the effect of giving a false value to ideas that are simple and platitudinous. To any such charge *The Lonely Crowd* is certainly not liable. Mr. Riesman uses two terms that some might boggle at—he speaks of people as being "inner-directed" and "other-directed." But I do not know how else he could denominate the two categories of character that are essential to his thought. In general the book is precisely a work of literature in the old comprehensive sense of the word according to which Hume's essays are literature, or Gibbon's history, or Tocqueville's *Democracy in America.*

Another objection is that sociology is likely to be tendentious without admitting it is, and that it proceeds on unexamined assumptions while insisting that it is wholly objective. But we can count on Mr. Riesman's objectivity because he admits his subjectivity and the hypothetical nature of his enterprise. He is under no illusion of scientific neutrality. He admires certain human qualities and makes no bones about wanting them to be influential in our national life.

Then it is said, and with justice, that sociology often gives the appearance of denying personal autonomy. What is more, much sociological investigation has for its avowed aim the discovery of how to manipulate human behavior in clandestine ways. But Mr. Riesman's book is as far as it can be from denying the possibility of autonomy without denying the inescapable limits of civilized society. Its whole effort, indeed, is directed toward the affirmation of the possibility of autonomy.

People of literary inclinations, I believe, have a natural jealousy of sociology because it seems to be in process of taking over from literature one of literature's most characteristic functions, the investigation and criticism of morals and manners. Yet it is but fair to remark that sociology has preempted only what literature has voluntarily surrendered. Twenty years ago, when the Lynds produced their famous study, *Middletown,* it was possible to say that with all their staff and paraphernalia they had not really told us more about American life than we had learned from a solitary insightful observer, which is what some sociologists call a novelist—they had done no more than confirm *Babbitt* by statistics. Since that time, however, few novelists have added anything genuinely new to our knowledge of American life. But the sociologists have, and Mr. Riesman, writing with a sense of social actuality which Scott Fitzgerald might have envied, does literature a service by suggesting to the novelists that there are new and wonderfully arable social fields for them to till.

The research from which *The Lonely Crowd* developed began as an investigation of the social causes of political attitudes, specifically that of apathy to politics. The book does not consist of conclusions drawn from this research but was written in the course of the still continuing enterprise as the hypothesis on which the research might proceed. In its simplest form this hypothesis consists of the statement that there has been a change in the character of the American people, that where once men whose character was "inner-directed" were dominant in our culture, the tendency is now toward the dominance of men of "other-directed" character. Inner-directed persons are those who internalize adult authority, most notably the ideals and demands of their parents. Other-directed persons are those whose character is formed chiefly by their contemporaries and peers, the formation beginning as soon as they enter social life in play or at school.

Something of the nature of the inner-directed man may be understood from the phrase which, in the nineteenth century, he so often made his motto—*"Ad astra per aspera,"* through difficulties to the seemingly unattainable heights. The old tag might also be translated, "To the heights by means of asperity," for a kind of asperity marks the dealings of the inner-directed man with the world, his fellow-men, and himself. The man of business as well as the scientific or artistic genius, or the religious leader, or the philosopher, were all at one in their submission to inner-direction. The belief that energy, self-control, and self-reverence would achieve miracles was held not only by the dullest spirits of the age but also by the noblest. We must think of the Alger books as being the expression not merely of a strenuous philistinism but of a general culture in which strenuousness was valued in all walks of life. There was a connection between the passions of a Bounderby and a Beethoven.

In America, even as far back as Tocqueville's visit, there was always a tendency for inner-direction to be modified by what Tocqueville regarded as an extravagant awareness of the opinion of others. Emerson believed that this tendency constituted a prime threat to the American spirit and he never wearied of warning his countrymen that Self Reliance—his name for inner-direction—was sadly on the wane. Yet in nineteenth century America the "hardness of the material" still called for a large measure of inner-direction—there were still frontiers to be conquered, social forms to be imposed or broken, technology to be established. It was still useful to idealize "faith," the belief that one's personal vision was right no matter how the world mocked it. School children were assiduously taught in their readers that the heroic man was one who followed his gleam, and that society as a whole was likely to be stupid, retrograde, and cowardly, as witness its treatment of Columbus. And in the poem that every child learned, it was right of Columbus, and not arrogant or undemocratic of him, to say, "Sail on! Sail on!" when his men begged him to turn back. To be "misunderstood," to be alone with one's rightness and virtue, was the stuff of the dreams of youth.

But in the early years of the twentieth century—around 1920, Mr. Riesman believes—the inner-directed character began to lose its ascendancy. The hard, resistant materiality of the world no longer supplied the goal and validated the hard, strenuous will of inner-directed people. Children were less impelled to establish the old parental authority within themselves—parents were less certain of how to establish it in their children and of whether it ought to be established at all. It was by no means clear that the old standards applied to the new kind of work. For in the degree that work had less to do with *things,* it had more to do with *people.* In Mr. Riesman's phrase, the interest shifted from the hardness of the material to the softness of the personnel, and the arts of personality, by which one could manipulate one's fellows or win valuable approval from them, because more important to more people than the direct force of the will exerted upon material difficulties. And children increasingly formed their characters according to the demands of their playmates and schoolmates, equipping themselves with a quick, unconscious sensitivity to the judgment of others—they became increasingly other-directed.

The evidence of this new means of character-formation is manifest in every discussion of juvenile or adolescent social behavior, in which it is always taken for granted that parents are virtually helpless before the power of the child-society. And indeed this power is supported and rationalized by the family and the school, which, on theories of normality and adjustment, second the anxious antagonism which the child-society directs upon any show of difference. For the group life of contemporary children achieves its particular kind of democracy by suppressing special interests and abilities (except in athletics) and by prohibiting the display of vanity or ambition. Even before the child is ready for sociability, his life in literature has prepared him for social adjustment and conformity. *Scuffy the Tugboat* instructs him in the dangers of the Columbus principle, while *Tootle the Engine* leads him to believe that he must not fail to be like all the other little engines and never leave the track to stray into green fields, like a horse.

The ideal of behavior which is indigenous to the social life of the modern child is the model and perhaps the mold of the ideal of adults, at least of the middle class. We are coming to be a civilization in which overt ambition, aggression, and competition are at a discount. Not, of course, that the sources of natural aggression are drying up or that people no longer seek prestige. But self-aggrandizement takes new forms as the ideals of other-direction become increasingly compelling. Overt ambition gives way to what Mr. Riesman calls antagonistic co-operation, which implies affability, blandness, a lively sensitivity to the opinion of the group, the suppression of asperity. Social differences must be minimized as far as possible. Wealth must depreciate itself, and must seek to express itself not in symbols of power but in fineness of taste. Food is ordered less for the old-fashioned virtues of substantiality and abundance, than for the new charms of elegance and artistry—but in this limited space it is impossible to follow Mr. Riesman in the fascinating detail of his description of the cultural changes which other-direction is instituting.

The general opinion is not likely to be in accord with Mr. Riesman—the general opinion is that our culture is marked by an especially fierce and open competitiveness, an unmasked aggressiveness, a crude assertiveness. This is the received idea of a great deal of our literature and of our progressive social thought. It is the pious certainty of Europe, constituting, one sometimes feels, the larger part of the European social and political thought of the moment.

And Mr. Riesman's students at the University of Chicago tell him that American life resembles the grim, paranoid Dobu culture or the competitive conspicuously-consuming Kwakiutl culture—none ever finds any resemblance to the peaceable, co-operative Pueblo Indians, although *all* of them wish they could.

I am sure that it is Mr. Riesman who is in the right of the matter. My own experience in teaching confirms his, one incident in particular. For some time I had been increasingly aware that my students had no very great admiration for Stendhal's *The Red and the Black,* gave it nothing like the response that it had had from my college generation. Then one day a whole class, almost all its members gifted men, agreed in saying that they were bored by Julien Sorel and didn't like him. Bored by Julien Sorel! But didn't he, I asked, represent their own desires for preeminence, their own natural young ambition? They snubbed me with their answer and fixed between themselves and me the great gulf of the generations: they did not, they said, understand ambition of Julien's self-referring kind; what they wanted was a decent, socially useful co-operative work to do. I felt like an aging Machiavelli among the massed secretariat of the U.N.

Young men of this kind certainly do not represent anything like the full development of the other-directed character which Mr. Riesman describes. It is even possible that their rejection of the extreme inner-direction of Julien Sorel is not so much in favor of other-direction as of the "autonomous" character which Mr. Riesman proposes as the possible optimum of our culture. More likely, however, they represent a compromise between inner-direction and other-direction. As such they make a spectacle which in many ways is very attractive.

But the tendency of other-direction does not stop with the character of these young men. And the consequences of its fuller development are disquieting. Mr. Riesman remarks that he has found it almost impossible to make a comparison of the two forms of character-direction without making inner-direction seem the more attractive of the two. I don't agree with Mr. Riesman that the preference is a mere prejudice which we must guard against. Granting all that is to be said against the tendency of inner-direction to cut itself off from what is warm and personal, granting too all that may be said for what other-direction does to refine leisure and consumption, it is still inner-direction that must seem the more fully human, even in its excess. Mr. Riesman himself seems to be saying something of this sort when, in speaking of the autonomous character, he remarks that the inner-directed character more closely resembles it than does the other-directed, and that, indeed, it is easier for inner-directed people to approach actual autonomy.

It is in any case true, on Mr. Riesman's showing, that the political life is far more likely to be healthy in a culture in which inner-direction is dominant. The exacerbated sense of others, of oneself in relation to others, does not, it seems, make for the sense of the polity. On the contrary—other-direction is concomitant with a sense of powerlessness in political matters, and this impotence masks itself in many ways, often as hatred or of contempt for politics. This in turn is easily rationalized into a desire for metapolitics, for a perfect and absolute form of government which shall make impossible the conflict of wills of actual politics.

And the apathy which marks our political life lies as a threat beneath all the life of other-direction. Social approval and the desire for it are not love, nor even friendship, nor even community. The life of leisure, of fun, of narcissism, of right choice among the articles of consumption, of sex as the "last frontier" of adventure, of bland adjustment—this life is at every moment suceptible to the cankering boredom which lies beneath its surface.

This is not, I must make clear, the note on which Mr. Riesman ends. It is one of his decisive intellectual virtues that he has no love for the opiate of pessimism. He is not charmed by apocalyptic visions. It is not the end of a culture that he has undertaken to describe but a moment in its history.

DANIEL BELL

•

Modernity and Mass Society: On the Varieties of Cultural Experience[1]

I. THE GREAT SOCIETY

WHO KNOWS WHOM

In 1789, when George Washington was inaugurated as the first President of the United States, there were less than four million persons in all thirteen states of the Union, of whom 750,000 were Negro. It was a young population—the median age was sixteen, and there were only 816,000 males older than that. Few persons lived in cities. New York, then the capital of the country, had a population of 33,000. In all, 200,000 individuals lived in what were defined as "urban areas"—meaning, at that time, places with more than 2,500 inhabitants. Because it was a small country, members of the American political elite knew each other well, as did the thin stratum of leading families. But most people lived in small communities or in sparsely in-

[1] Reprinted from *Studies in Public Communication,* No. 4, Autumn 1962, "Modernity and Mass Society: On the Varieties of Cultural Experience" by Daniel Bell by permission of The University of Chicago Press and Daniel Bell. Copyright 1962 by the University of Chicago. This selection is a shortened version of the original essay as it appears in *Paths of American Thought,* edited by Arthur M. Schlesinger and Morton White (Boston: Houghton Mifflin Company, 1963), pp. 411–431.

habited areas, rarely traveled great distances, and considered a visitor from afar a rarity. News meant local gossip, and the few news sheets concentrated on parochial events. The ordinary citizen's image of the world and its politics was exceedingly circumscribed.

Today the United States numbers over 180,000,000 persons. The median age is over thirty, and 130,000,000 persons are over fourteen years of age. About forty million people live in rural areas, but only half of these live on farms. More than a hundred million Americans live in metropolitan areas (i.e., within a county that contains at least one city with 50,000 residents). If one thinks today of the number of persons each of us *knows,* and, even more striking, of the number of persons one *knows of*, the change in dimensions becomes extraordinary. With multiplication of contacts, increased geographical and social mobility, and distintegration of folk and regional patterns, America in recent years has become, perhaps for the first time, truly a national society.

But only in a most tenuous way have there been truly *national institutions,* other than the specifically political ones. A hundred years after Henry James complained of the thinness of American culture, institutional ties are still vague and fitful. There is no established church, no legal or military caste, no Society. There is a national party system, but few commanding national figures. There is a burgeoning intellectual class, tied together by the major large universities; a managerial elite, yet one that recognizes itself more through formal ideology than personal ties or acquaintance; and national groups of scientists, military figures, and journalists. Yet these do not provide American society with a clearly identifiable Establishment.

Rather the emergent national society has been pulled together primarily by popular culture. With the rise of movies, radio, and television, and with the simultaneous printing in different cities of the weekly magazines, to provide uniform national distribution on the same day, for the first time in American history there exists a common set of images, ideas, and entertainments, presented simultaneously to a national audience. American society is woven together precisely through the mass media.

The Mass as Equal

This distinctive character of the times is best conveyed by the phrase *mass society*. Although the term has been used variously and has become entangled with an assortment of judgments and feelings about modern society, it does help one communicate the fact that modern society differs from all previous societies—call them folk, traditional, aristocratic, hierarchical, or organic. And just as the word *culture* has been redefined in our time, so that what once signified refinement of a moral and intellectual nature and the cultivation of the arts, has been expanded to include the total codes of conduct of a group or a people, so, too, the idea of *society,* which once meant a group of genteel people of refined manner, has been broadened to include all the individuals who form a particular social unit. The theme of equality—the fight for political, economic, and social rights, symbolized most strongly in the nineteenth century by the demand for political suffrage and equality of opportunity—the fact that the masses will no longer permit their "exclusion" from society, becomes one of the distinguishing characteristics of the mass society. The style of life, the rights, the norms and values, the desires, the access to privilege, the culture that was once the exclusive property of an elite, are now extended to everyone. In a *democratic* mass society, to belong *in* society means other things as well—not only to share the fruits of society but to have the right—and the chance—to choose: to choose lawmakers, to choose an occupation or profession, to choose where one lives, to choose one's friends, to choose what to buy; in short, to have the right to make and pass judgments in all areas of life, from politics to the arts.

All of this has been made possible by the rise of mass production and mass consumption, and the consequent leveling of distinctive class styles of life. Since 1920, the distinctions between rich and poor have been either modified or glossed over. The great estates have shrunk, and society has been replaced by celebrity. Distinctive modes of dress and travel have been in large part erased. Differences remain, but they are more a matter of degree than of kind, of multitude rather than quality.

Many of the changes that lie behind the rise of a national society and the creation of a mass culture have been due in great measure to the structural transformation of the country's labor force: the change-over from an agrarian to an industrialized urban population, and the end, with the spread of cheap auto transport and radio, of rural isolation; the transformation of the industrial working class from a predominantly immigrant group, speaking languages and leading lives unrelated to American culture, to one largely native-born, speaking English and possessing at least a grade-school education; the entry of women into the labor force, creating vastly different kinds of markets; and, finally, the growing *embourgeoisement* of the work force, with the spread of white-collar jobs. Hand in hand with all this has gone both a reduction of hours worked and a rise in the number of years spent in school by the population as a whole.

With this rapid process of "upgrading," there arises the problem of who becomes the arbiter of taste, the guide to "culture." A society undergoing rapid change inevitably spawns confusion about appropriate modes of behavior, taste, and dress. Victorian and post-Victorian society assumed the task of initiating a rising commercial class into "good manners," through its books on etiquette. Today, this function is performed by the mass media—the guides to behavior are the movies, television, and advertising. In this respect, the mass media do not, like advertising, merely stimulate wants; they play a more subtle role in the changing of habits. The mass media "upgrade" taste, and then a whole series of specialized agencies begins to take over for the new culture-hungry public. The new "tastemakers"—the women's magazines, house-and-home journals, sophisticated periodicals like *The New Yorker* or *Esquire,* prestige institutions like the Museum of Modern Art—teach people style in clothes, home furnishings, standards of design, taste in art, the right wines to stock, the cheeses to buy; in short, the style of life appropriate to the new-found status.

Though these changes initially influence the surface of life—manners, dress, tastes, food habits, and standards of entertainment—sooner or later the metamorphosis affects more basic patterns as well: the structure of authority in the family, and the values of the society as a whole. Where culture was once the "superstructure" of society, shaped by patterns of work and family and religious life, the greed for culture now becomes the foundation; its drives and modes shape the other patterns of life. All of this should add up to a glowingly positive achievement. And yet this new culture has more detractors than defenders. In the very years of this new culture's boom its critics have become increasingly vocal. What is the nature of their indictment?

II. THE IMPEACHMENT OF THE MASS

From Politics to Culture

The preoccupation with the effects of mass culture was one of the distinctive features of the cultural scene in the 1950's. There were many reasons for this. One was the extraordinarily rapid spread of television—the true *mass* medium and the most potent agency available for reaching the largest number of persons simultaneously. And the fact that so much television time was consumed by witless comedy and stereotyped stories of violence, either cowboy-western or big-city gangster, led to concern that the national taste was being debauched.

A second reason for anxiety about mass culture, more diffuse in its effects but sociologically more potent, was America's altered relationship with the rest of the world, particularly Europe, following the Second World War. For the first time, America was claiming, albeit awkwardly and self-consciously, the moral leadership of the world. This evoked an increasing fear, particularly among the European intelligentsia, of an "Americanization of Europe" and a breakdown of cultural standards and of cultural homogeneity. Americans' self-consciousness about their own past and present, and European intellectuals' scrutiny of the key features in contemporary American life, focused most intensely on the nature of mass culture.

Extraordinary social changes became manifest after the war—the cultural absorption into American life of the children of the immigrant generation; the *embourgeoisement* of the working class; the spread of suburbia; the increase of income—involving, in turn, a growing desire on the part of the lower middle class to live conspicuously well; the new affluence, symbolized by the acquisition of television sets, dishwashers, automobiles, even by a taste for "gourmet" foods; the rising curve of higher education, which was given a strong push by the G. I. Bill of Rights for veterans of the Second World War. Yet the self-consciousness generated by these changes, the uncertainties about taste and behavior, created an anxiety about "self" and a concern about "identity" unique in sociocultural history. The very titles of such best sellers as *The Lonely Crowd, The Organization Man, The Status Seekers*—each of which sold over 200,000 copies in paperback editions—underline the preoccupation with popular sociology. And these self-examinations about the validity of American life focused upon mass culture as the inescapable product and symbol of the new age.

Finally, in seeking to account for the nervous preoccupation with mass culture in this decade, one must also take into account the changes in the character of political liberalism, and particularly of political radicalism. The number of political radicals in the United States has never been very large, but radical critics have always had an influence far beyond their numbers. For one thing, the charges they made—about poverty, unequal opportunity, injustice, corruption—found their mark; and these charges were, to a considerable extent, accepted by the society. For another, American intellectual culture, particularly in the last thirty years, has been predominantly liberal, and radical critics have formed a large proportion of the intellectual community as a whole—the large universities, the publishing houses, the "small" magazines. In the 1930's, the major radical criticism of American life centered on economic and social injustice. But in the succeeding decades, which saw the rise of the welfare state and the disenchantment with Communism, radical criticism lost much of its impulse and impact. By the 1950's, political criticism had turned to cultural criticism. In part this was a carry-over of the critical stance in general. Having defined a role for himself as critic, the radical intellectual, once the most extreme economic ills had been meliorated, turned his attention to the quality of American life.

At the same time, the mass media themselves were reaching out for the avant-garde intellectual. In 1959, the *Saturday Evening Post,* for example, began running a feature series entitled "Adventures of the Mind," composed of articles by, among others, the poet Randall Jarrell, the art critic Clement Greenberg, and the novelist C. P. Snow. A magazine like *The New Yorker,* which in the forties was attacked by *Partisan Review* as being too slick, now regularly printed *Partisan Review* writers such as Edmund Wilson, Dwight Macdonald, and Mary McCarthy. The terms "highbrow" and "lowbrow"—which had been coined in 1915 by Van Wyck Brooks, in his famous essay *America's Coming of Age,* to distinguish between the intellectual ("who . . . in his isolation was out of the stream") and the philistine businessman ("who knew nothing but acquisition")—were now resurrected, and in between the high and the low brow was added the new category "middlebrow." Cultural criticism had become a game, and the game caught on.

But even though cultural criticism became a game, it was also a serious problem for the intellectual, who now found himself invited to play some role, albeit an ambiguous one, in a culture he had always spurned. Many of the radical critics felt that the purpose of their being invited into the mass media was to provide "window-dressing," or a spurious prestige, for the mass magazines and television, or because the ideas and themes of serious writing would now be exploited for their "shock value." An even more sinister motive was suspected—the blunting of radical criticism altogether. The relationship of the serious critic and intellectual to the burgeoning mass culture of the fifties became an anxiety in itself, and the source of many a solemn essay and symposium.

High-Low-Middle

The multifarious critique of American mass culture may be divided into four kinds of charges. The first is that genuinely creative work is insufficiently encouraged. Various reasons are cited: that there does not exist an audience to support new and experimental work; that since popular art pays better than serious art, the creative artist is diverted from his true task of producing high culture; and that since the market is the arbiter of taste, large-scale production—whether in the theater, television, movies, or the world of music—has to be diluted to please the lowest common denominator, which means that serious work cannot find a producer or sponsor on its own terms.

The second charge is that serious work, particularly of the past (the so-called high culture), has been debased by being made glibly popular and too readily accessible—as when *Life* or *Look,* for example, prints a reproduction of a serious painting alongside a flashy photograph of a Hollywood starlet. Thus T. W. Adorno has argued that, although radio and hi-fi have permitted people to listen to more records of Beethoven than ever before, they listen to them in order to hum or whistle a melody, and not to appreciate the complex structure of the symphony itself. The mass audience, by accepting slick over-simplifications as serious art, has cheapened our most precious cultural legacy.

The third argument, reversing the second, is that mediocre and middlebrow works become acclaimed as serious art because in purpose, theme, or even in style they seem difficult—though in fact they are not. Dwight Macdonald, for example, singles out Hemingway's *The Old Man and the Sea,* Thornton Wilder's *Our Town,* and Archibald MacLeish's *J.B.* as such speciously serious writing. "Technically, they are advanced enough to impress the middlebrows without worrying them. In content, they are 'central' and 'universal,' in that line of hollowly portentous art which the French call *pompier*, after the glittering golden beplumed helmets of their firemen." The "real" enemy is therefore not the vast sea of self-evident trash but meretricious middlebrow culture—or, as Macdonald labels it, "midcult." In "Masscult," Macdonald writes, "the trick is plain—to please the crowd by any means. But Midcult has it both ways: it pretends to respect the standards of High Culture while in fact it waters them down and vulgarizes them." To critics like Mr. Macdonald, the special danger of "midcult" is that in the upgrading of American taste and standards, the lines between high culture and midcult have been blurred, and midcult standards, precisely because they seem to advance culture, now predominate.

And, finally, there is the argument that most of the run-of-the-mill material that fills up the main bulk of television and the mass magazines is cheap, vulgar, titillating, inciting to violence, prurient and debasing. The material aimed at the mass audience directly, with no pretensions to seriousness, is thus corrupting in itself.

THE ROOT CRITICISMS OF MASS CULTURE

If these complaints reached the heart of the matter, one might deal with the problem by taking several remedial steps: by greater encouragement of serious work by foundations, such as the Ford Foundation program to provide support for novelists, dramatists, painters, and other artists who have already demonstrated their talent; by strengthening the Federal Communications Commission rules toward giving more network time to public-service programs; and by more intensive scrutiny of critical standards and of cultural products by detached agencies such as universities.

But beyond criticism such as Mr. Macdonald's lies an analysis that challenges the possibility of any improvement at all, and denies the possibility of serious culture in a mass society. Such a viewpoint is the basic source of much of the attack on mass culture.

Perhaps the most sweeping indictment of mass culture comes from Ortega y Gasset's *The Revolt of the Masses,* a book written by a Spaniard in 1930, at once humane and aristocratic, culminating a century of Continental thought, fearful since the French Revolution of the impact of the masses on traditional society. For Ortega, mass society meant that the qualified members of society lost authority. Ortega equated culture with classical studies; in his view only the humanist was cultivated. Specialization became the main "enemy" and science was believed to have undermined the authority of the humanities. This defense of classicism as the heart of the traditionalist position, is also to be found in the work of the Catholic theologian Josef Pieper and the Anglican T. S. Eliot. In the United States it has been most strongly echoed in the quondam school of Southern Agrarians, especially in the work of its historical spokesman, Donald Davidson, and sporadically of its literary spokesmen, such as John Crowe Ransom and Allen Tate.

Hannah Arendt, a thoughtful and disquieting social critic, takes this argument one step further and blends it with a historical-Marxist analysis. She argues that "society"—that relatively homogeneous unity of educated and cultivated persons—had always treated culture as a commodity, and had gained snob value from its production and dissemination. But, she continues, there are two crucial differences between the past and the present. First of all, in the past individualism was made possible through an escape *from* society into rebel or bohemian worlds. But in mass society these avenues of escape are closed because such a society incorporates all the strata of the population. Secondly, although society in the past coveted culture largely for its snob appeal, it did not corrupt culture, even if it abused or devaluated it. But mass society does not want culture, it wants entertainment, hence the wares offered by the entertainment industry are consumed by society just as are any other consumer goods.

This charge that mass culture is a form of distraction, and therefore a surrender of standards, is as old as Juvenal's despairing cry that the once proud Roman race now "limits its anxious longings to two things only—bread and the games of the circus." The argument that the mass media simply reformulate the reactionary strategy of social restraint was given its most elegant modern statement by Thorstein Veblen. *Panem et circenses*—"the formula for the politicians of Imperial Rome on which they relied to keep the underlying population from imagining vain remedies for their own hard case"—Veblen rendered as "The Breadline and the Movies." But Veblen pointed out sardonically that modern industry as a form of commercial exploitation is superior to the old Roman imperium. Whereas "the Roman *circenses* appear to have cut somewhat wastefully into the ordinary 'earnings' of those vested interests for whose benefit the Roman imperium was administered . . . the movies of the twentieth century are a business proposition in their own right." And if the manufacture of "pomp and circumstance" and the "rant and swagger" is expensive, since the function of such display is to relieve the common man "of afterthought," it is "only reasonable that the common man should pay the cost."

But contemporary mass culture, the French sociologist Edgar Morin has argued, goes beyond the age-old purpose of social control. Its essential function is "mythic"—to provide, since religion no longer can do so, a giant stage on which the new heroes and gods can be deployed. The authentic mythological hero, M. Morin claims, is the movie actor James Dean. In his brief explosive life, Dean fulfilled the classic requirements. He was an orphan, he ran away, he sought many different experiences ("labors"), and he became, at last, "what in the modern world incarnates the myth of a total life, a film star." Seeking the "absolute," unable to realize this in a woman's love, he found it instead in the ersatz absolute of "speed," and finally, meeting death in an auto crash, he gained immortality. On the first anniversary of his death, three thousand people visited his grave, and for almost a year after his death, two thousand letters a week were written to him in the belief, apparently, that secretly he was still alive, or that somewhere his spirit was accessible.

The distinctive feature of modern society, Morin argues, is that it has invented a new age of man—adolescence. In archaic societies, a boy was often violently initiated into manhood. In modern societies, youth refuses to be absorbed, and seeks, either through nihilism, delinquency, or beatnikism, to drop out of society. Rimbaud pointed the way, with his nostalgia for childhood, his refusal to be "corrupted" by the adult world, by his desire "to live." In contemporary society, adolescents form their own world and elect their own heroes. With its "insatiable demand for personalities," mass culture today feeds upon this youth culture, Morin argues, and in doing so it has made heroes out of adolescent stars. "Anti-culture," he writes, "is not the 'massification' of culture, nor even its vulgarization—on the contrary, anti-culture is the metaphysic of success. . . . Of course, mass culture welcomes the damned, such as Rimbaud and Lawrence, but only to confer posthumous success upon them."

III. MODERNITY AND HIGH CULTURE

The Varieties of Cultural Experience

The difficulty in dealing with such "root" criticism of mass culture is that its spokesmen formulate the problems in all-or-nothing terms. They seek to penetrate to the Platonic essence of modern society, to discover some transcendent principle—the "judgment of the unqualified" or "culture is being destroyed to yield entertainment"—which singularly defines and annihilates the character of mass society. While some specific observations, notably Miss Arendt's and M. Morin's, are dazzlingly brilliant, the question nevertheless arises whether mass society can be defined by any single formula. For the most striking aspect of mass society is that, while it incorporates the broad mass into society, it creates diversity and variety and sharpens hunger for experience, as more and more aspects of the world—geographical, political, and cultural—come within the purview of ordinary men.

At the heart of the problem is the meaning of culture. When one speaks of a "classical culture" or a "Catholic culture" one thinks of a long-linked set of beliefs, traditions, rituals, and injunctions, which in the course of its history has achieved something of a homogeneous style. But modernity is, distinctively, a break with the past *as past,* catapulting it into the present. Mass society contains "the tradition of the new," in Harold Rosenberg's phrase. Under such conditions, not even an avant-garde is possible, for it is by its very nature a rejection of a specific tradition. The characteristic avant-garde tactic is scandal. In modern culture, scandal is eagerly pursued only as still another sensation. Modernity castrates an avant-garde by quickly accepting it, just as it accepts, with equal flexibility, elements from the Western past, the Byzantine past, the Oriental past (and present) in its omnium-gatherum of cultures. The old concept of culture is based on continuity, the modern on variety; the old valued tradition, the contemporary ideal is syncretism.

Little more than a hundred years ago, the Anglo-American world of cultivated discourse was bounded by the classical writers, Latin poets, Greek and Renaissance art, the French *philosophes,* and some German literature introduced mostly through the translations of Carlyle. Today the boundaries of the world, geographically speaking, have been broken, and the range of the arts, both within the traditional frames of literature, painting, sculpture, and music, and outside those frames, is almost limitless. It is not only that the art market has become international, so that Polish painters show in Paris and American painting is bought in England, or that the theater now ignores national frontiers, so that Chekhov, Strindberg, Brecht, O'Neill, Tennessee Williams, Miller, Giradoux, Anouilh, Ionesco, Genet, Beckett, and Osborne are performed simultaneously in Paris, London, New York, Berlin, Frankfurt, Stockholm, Warsaw, and a hundred other cities on several continents. Even more, the range of culture is so diffuse, the "topics" of interest so proliferated, that it is almost impossible to find a center of gravity that can truly define the contemporary "cultivated" man.

The Lack of a Center

It is not only the bewildering variety of cultural demesnes and the vast multiplication of practitioners—serious, semiskilled, or amateur—that create a sense of diffuseness. There is also, in America, the lack of a *center,* spiritual or geographical, which can provide both authority and a place where the leading painters, musicians, and novelists might meet and get to know one another. In the past almost all societies with a "high culture" had some center —the agora, piazza, marketplace, or club located in a national capital—where, in the concentration, exchange, competition, and jousting, each stimulated the other, creating and deriving a sense of vitality from the interchange. Paris, in the early decades of the twentieth century ("the banquet years," as Roger Shattuck has called them) and later, in the 1920's, was such a center. A ballet by Fokine might have decor by Chagall or Picasso and music by Stravinsky or Satie. Through its public schools and the tight triangle of Oxford, Cambridge, and London, England has had an elite whose members could count on direct literary and social acquaintance with each other.

The United States has lacked such a center. In the second quarter of the nineteenth century, Boston provided a unifying ground and, through the mingling of church, wealth, and culture, created a style of sorts. But its very unity was self-defeating in that it was a New England style, and could never dominate the country as a whole. Toward the end of the century, New York became a center for aspiring and parvenu Society, and to some extent a cultural center as well, but it could never quite encompass the different American regional cultures—the Midwest, the Border States, the South, and the Southwest—that had begun to manifest themselves distinctly. Even with the burgeoning of Greenwich Village as topography and symbol, in the years shortly before the First World War and after, New York caught but one element of American culture, the avant-garde, and that only for a while, since it turned out to serve mostly as a way station on the road to Paris.

Given the sheer size of the country, the heterogeneity of ethnic and religious groups, American intellectuals, as Irving Kristol has put it, "meet one another in the dark, so to speak." The United States is probably the only major country in the world (with the exception of Germany) that lacks a national center where the various elites can mingle. The men who edit the large magazines usually lack the opportunity to meet anyone of distinction in politics, drama, or music. The political people are in Washington, the publishing and theater people in New York, the movie people in Los Angeles, and the professoriat is scattered across the country in the large universities. The universities have become the dominant force in the American cultural world today: many novelists, composers, painters, and critics find their haven in the far-flung universities, and many of the major literary and cultural quarterlies are edited there.

Even when, as in New York, there does exist an acknowledged, large center for publishing, theater, music, and painting, the enormous numbers who congregate there, plus the great stress on professionalism, make for a compartmentalization that isolates serious artists from one another. Few painters know theater people or musicians or writers. Composers talk to composers, painters to painters, writers to writers. And where the audience resists compartmentalization, it does so at the expense of the distinctive qualities of the separate arts. A voracious audience of sophisticates quickly snaps up and adopts any avant-garde before it even has a chance to proclaim its rebellion, and the increasingly technical nature of experimentation in the arts, whether it be serial composition in music or *Tachisme* in painting, seems to deny the possibility of a common aesthetic.

The Visual Culture

But the most important way in which modernity confronts high culture is in its denial of the unity of culture. Traditional culture made the distinction between the creative and utilitarian arts. Literature and music, as the contemplative arts, stood at the highest rungs of culture. The status of painting, or sculpture or architecture, because they involved artisan skills, was more ambiguous. Modernity refuses to create any hierarchies. If anything, the "dominant outlook" is visual. It is "sight and sound," and particularly sight, which organize the aesthetic and command the audience. It almost could not be otherwise in a mass society. Mass entertainments (circuses, spectacles, theaters) have always been visual, but today two distinct facts about contemporary life necessarily place the visual element in the forefront: first, that the modern world is an urban world, providing a preponderance of occasions for people to *see* and *want to see* (rather than read and hear) things; the other, that the modern temper, with its hunger for action (as against contemplation), its search for novelty, and its lust for sensation, invites the visual element in the arts as the means of appeasing these compulsions.

The cityscape, man-made, is etched in its architecture and its bridges. The key materials of an industrial civilization, steel and concrete, find their distinctive use in these structures. The use of steel, replacing masonry, allowed architects to erect a simple frame on which to "drape" a building, and to push that frame high into the sky. The use of reinforced concrete allowed the architect to create "sculptured" shapes that have a free-flowing life of their own. In these new forms, one finds a powerful new comprehension and organization of space.

There is an inherent "eclipse of distance" in modern life. Not only is physical distance compressed by modern modes of transportation, but the very techniques of the new arts, principally cinema and modern painting, eclipse the psychic and aesthetic distance between the viewer and the visual experience. The emphases in cubism on "simultaneity" and in abstract expressionism on "impact" are efforts to intensify the immediacy of the emotion, to pull the spectator into the action, rather than allow him to contemplate the experience. Such is the underlying principle, as well, of the cinema, which, in its use of montage, goes the farthest of any of the contemporary arts in this direction of the "regulation" of emotion: to select the images, the angles of vision, the length of time in viewing a single scene, and the "synapse" of composition. This central aspect of modernity—the organization of social and aesthetic responses in terms of novelty, sensation, simultaneity, and impact—finds its major expression in the visual arts.

IV. THE MARKET AND MASS CULTURE

AUDIENCES: THE ONE AND THE MANY

Today, the "mass" is part of society, and constitutes the largest audience for culture known in history. But reaching such an audience—or audiences—is a costly affair, and in a society that expects culture to pay its own way, rather than be subsidized, the problem of marketing becomes crucial.

A mass society, however, implies not only the great audience—the largest in human history—but equally, the growth of many, differentiated audiences, of varying tastes and interests; and the problem of how to reach such audiences is also one of marketing. In a crucial sense, television has pre-empted the mass market, and in so doing has changed the pattern of magazine audiences and of movie-making in America. As a result of television, the large "general circulation" magazines in the country are losing out. Advertisers are not interested in the sheer size of the magazine audience, since on this count, television can always do better. Despite its four million circulation, *Collier's* folded because it could not attract sufficient advertising, and *Coronet,* despite a record circulation of more than three million, suspended publication because it could not keep up with rising production costs.

But the magazines based on specialized markets do very well indeed. *The New Yorker* has become the national arbiter of sophisticated reading taste. *Esquire,* with Dwight Macdonald as its film critic, and novelists like Norman

Mailer and Saul Bellow as contributors, has established itself as the highbrow magazine of the new junior-executive sophisticates. Magazines such as *Harper's* and *Atlantic,* which seek to discuss socio-political issues, have been growing. And, with less fanfare, the range and varieties of new cultural experience are strongly reflected in smaller, specialized magazines that catch the enthusiasms of their special audiences—in painting, in music, the dance, jazz, photography, cinema, and criticism—and in little magazines as well.

As in the theater, the problems of costs are particularly crucial for the large commercial endeavors that, as on Broadway, depend on large audiences. For Broadway, the high rentals in the midtown areas, the high salaries of the stars, and the make-work practices of the unions all combine to kite the costs of production. But the influx of a new, younger generation of theater entrepreneurs, along with the emergence of an audience for experimental plays, has spurred the extraordinary phenomenon of the off-Broadway theater—usually small out-of-the-way lofts or converted neighborhood movie houses—where Beckett, Genet, Ionesco, Brecht, as well as Tennessee Williams, Edward Albee, and younger playwrights are produced. It takes between $50,000 and $125,000 to mount a Broadway play (triple that cost for a musical), while the average off-Broadway show costs, on the average, $5,000 to $12,000.

In the cinema, which, before television, had been the prime mass medium, the competition of home-viewing has produced a similar transmutation. On the one hand, Hollywood has sought to produce huge "spectaculars" (*Spartacus, Exodus, Ben-Hur*), exhibited on a road-show basis of two-a-day screenings at high prices; on the other hand, the breakup of the old studios has released a host of independent movie-makers who produce films aimed at particular audiences. The growth of "art houses" (the movie trade's name for small cinemas that show only "serious" or "foreign" films) from twelve to over six hundred since the end of the Second World War, according to *Variety,* has encouraged the production of semidocumentary and experimental films, such as Morris Engel's *The Little Fugitive,* John Cassavetes' *Shadows,* Sidney Meyer's *The Savage Eye,* and Jack Kerouac's beatnik joke, *Pull My Daisy.* Just as off-Broadway has become a permanent fact of the New York theater, so, too, off-Hollywood cinema promises to become a new dimension of cinema life.

Nowhere has the conquest of new audiences been as dramatic as in publishing. The so-called paperback revolution has been primarily a revolution in marketing. Until fairly recently publishing in the United States followed the nineteenth-century practice of selling books through bookstores. In a country as "small" as England, bookstores have concentrated markets. But in the United States, except for a few major cities and university towns, bookstores have been an inadequate means of reaching mass audiences. The marketing revolution consisted mainly in finding thousands of additional outlets—in bus and air terminals, cigar and candy stores, supermarkets, and the like—for the sale of paperbacks. As against the few thousand bookstores that sold books, there are today over thirty thousand outlets for paperbacks. Sales of paperbacks have risen from about six million copies in 1940 to an estimated five hundred million in 1960. Not only have sales of individual volumes been astounding but the variety of books brought back into print now makes it possible for nearly everyone to build a serious library.

Not only has the range of the arts and culture been widely extended, but in the last forty years there has been an extraordinary multiplication in the number of persons trying to make a living as painters, writers, actors, or holding jobs (e.g., in colleges) that allow them to produce novels, poetry, critical essays and books, or paint, sculpt, compose music, or put on experimental drama. In New York, for example, the Telephone Directory now lists about 400 art galleries, and the critics regularly cover about 250 of these. If one assumes that each gallery has between fifteen and twenty shows a season, and that a good many of these are group shows, then it is reasonable to assume that the work of about three thousand painters is displayed each year in New Yok. It is extraordinarily difficult to pin down, statistically, any comparative figures, but the very increase in population, the rise of an urban audience, the change-over in the labor force, and, most particularly, the spread of education would allow one to say that more persons are now engaged in producing and consuming cultural works than at any other time in world history.

STANDARDS AND SUBSIDIES

The problem of numbers—either of producers of culture, or of audience—brings one back to the debate about standards: the arguments that mass culture is necessarily a debauched one; that, as Nietzsche once put it, popular art "counterfeits" the serious arts and lowers standards of excellence.

The arguments drawn from history are inconclusive; we know little about the way the masses spent their time a hundred years ago. From novels and from travelers' accounts, we know, for example, that the popular entertainments in England, as late as the early nineteenth century, consisted of cockfighting, bear-baiting, and attending the public hangings of criminals. How does one compare the effects of the direct viewing of violence and bloodletting with the vicarious viewing of such events today? "The major error of the analysts of popular culture," writes Edward Shils, "is their belief that it has succeeded to something which was intrinsically worthy, that man has sunk into a hitherto unknown mire because of it, and that it is a necessary prelude to the further degradation and perhaps ultimate extinction of high culture. . . . It would be far more correct to assume that mass culture is now less damaging to the lower classes than the dismal and harsh existence of earlier centuries had ever been. The reading of good books, the enjoyment of superior music and painting, although perhaps meager, is certainly more widespread than in previous centuries, and there is no reason to believe that it is less profound and less genuine."

In the curious dialectic of the debate, popular sociology—the analysis of mass culture—has tried to replace literary criticism as the arbiter of taste. Popular sociology establishes categories like highbrow, middlebrow, and lowbrow, or masscult and midcult—based either on audience reaction or the presumed intention of the cultural work—and then judges by these categories, rather than by explicit literary or aesthetic standards. But this usurpation of function can help neither sociology nor literary criticism. In critical terms, a work is either good or bad, whatever audience it is aimed at. Many highbrow works are pretentious and empty, and many items of mass appeal, particularly in the movies, are skilled works of art. The judgment belongs to the critic and the creators, and their peers.

It is curious, too, that in a whole decade of writing about the vacuities of mass culture and the problem of maintaining standards of serious culture, almost no attention has been paid to concrete matters of public policy: to what can be done to eliminate some of the overwhelming vulgarity, particularly on television, what can be done to raise public taste and, through public subsidy, support composers, painters, writers, the opera, or serious dramatic productions. As Arthur Schlesinger, Jr., has pointed out, the machinery for regulating television does exist. A television channel is a quasi-public utility; the number of wave lengths is limited, and a television license is a lucrative thing. The Federal Communications Commission does have the power, which until recently it has rarely exercised, to encourage better programs, to limit advertising, to increase the time for public-service presentations and the like. Whether the specific proposals Schlesinger makes are valid or not is less relevant than the fact that the problem remains singularly unexplored. One clear reason for this, as has been pointed out earlier, is that critics of mass culture, as part of their general political stance, prefer to be critics rather than doers.

If, however, one wishes to do something, one must distinguish the modest problem of improving the mass media from the more difficult and complex problem of how an age comes to create great art at all. The solution of the first depends in great measure on the willingness of the institutions of the community—universities, foundations, community groups, and government—to produce a competent audience and to channel moneys into the support of the arts. But the second is of a different magnitude and is not—and here is where I feel the critics of mass culture have gone awry—dependent on audience at all. The great art of any time is an act of decisive and solitary affirmation. It arises when, in the uneven development of styles, specific arts break the bounds of convention and develop new modes of expression, and this is as much an *immanent* problem in the nature of an art form as it is a response to social environment. The great art of the twentieth century—the modern movement—arose out of the hatred of bourgeois conventions (and, in part, was also a masked pastoral protest against the requirements of an industrial society). That art did not depend on a large audience, or even on a cultivated one, as much as it did on a community of its own, and on an attendant circle of sympathetic critics. As in many instances of the past, that defiant model—the artist as rebel, as alienated figure, as avant-garde—became the image that a later society has accepted almost as valid.

Modernity, however, has in this respect run its course. The old rebellious styles have become the new academicism, and the artists have been absorbed and defeated by the audience.

As to the future of "mass culture" in America? The greatness of America has been its openness. Few Americans have "inherited" a culture or a style of life through the thread of tradition or family. In culture, as in politics, they have had to "make" their own way. Neither the immigrant boy from the New York slum nor the farm boy from the midwest prairie who sought art as an experience or as life, has been barred because of caste or class, though other difficulties—notably the scorn for the aesthetic or the emphasis on the practical—have stood in his way. Today, the paths are wider than ever before. The varieties of cultural experience are being matched by the diversities of audience. The philistinism of the past has been replaced by a hunger for culture; every critic can find his forum, and the American is anxious to say his *mea culpa.* The period of modernity, from 1910 on, has already provided an enormous capital for the future—in painting, architecture, and literature. Whether it is squandered or not depends upon the imagination and will of those who make public policy and on the audiences' concern, as shaped by the colleges and universities of the land.

CARL N. DEGLER

•

The Changing Place of Women in America[1]

If feminism is defined as the belief that women are human beings and entitled to the same opportunities for self-expression as men, then America has harbored a feminist bias from the beginning. In both the eighteenth and nineteenth centuries foreign travelers remarked on the freedom for women in America. "A paradise for women," one eighteenth-century German called America, and toward the close of the nineteenth century Lord Bryce wrote that in the United States "it is easier for women to find a career, to obtain work of an intellectual as of a commercial kind, than in any part of Europe."

[1] Reprinted by permission from *Daedalus,* published by the American Academy of Arts and Sciences, Boston, Massachusetts. Vol. 93, No. 2, *The Woman in America.*

Certainly the long history of a frontier in America helps to account for this feminist bias. In a society being carved out of a wilderness, women were active and important contributors to the process of settlement and civilization. Moreover, because women have been scarce in America they have been highly valued. During almost the whole of the colonial period men outnumbered women, and even in the nineteenth century women remained scarce in the West. As late as 1865, for example, there were three men for each woman in California; in Colorado the ratio was as high as 20 to 1. Such disparities in the sex ratio undoubtedly account for the West's favorable attitude toward women as in an Oregon law of 1850 that granted land to single women and, even more significant for the time, to married women; or in the willingness of western territories like Wyoming (1869) and Utah (1870) to grant the suffrage to women long before other regions where the sex ratio was more nearly equal.

Another measure of women's high esteem in American society was the rapidity with which the doors of higher education opened to women. Even without counting forerunners like Oberlin College, which admitted women in 1837, the bars against women came down faster and earlier in America than anywhere. The breakthrough came during the Civil War era, when women's colleges like Elmira, Vassar and Smith were founded, and universities like Michigan and Cornell became coeducational. The process was later and slower in Europe. Girton College, Cambridge, for example, which opened in 1869, was the sole English institution of higher education available to women until London University accorded women full privileges in 1879. Heidelberg, which was the first German university to accept women, did not do so until 1900. More striking was the fact that at its opening Girton provided six places for young women; Vassar alone, when it opened in 1865, counted some 350 students in residence. Another indication of the American feminist bias was that at the end of the century girls outnumbered boys among high school graduates.

But if the frontier experience of America helped to create a vague feminist bias that accorded women more privileges than in settled Europe, the really potent force changing women's place had little to do with the frontier or the newness of the country. It was the industrial revolution that provided the impetus to women's aspirations for equality of opportunity; it was the industrial revolution that carried through the first stage in the changing position of women—the removal of legal and customary barriers to women's full participation in the activities of the world.

Today it is axiomatic that men work outside the home. But before the industrial revolution of the nineteenth century, the great majority of men and women were co-workers on the land and in the home. Women worked in the fields when the chores of the home and child-rearing permitted, so that there was not only close association between work and home for both sexes, but even a certain amount of overlap in the sexual division of labor. The coming of machine production changed all that. For a time, it is true, many unmarried women and children—the surplus labor of the day—were the mainstay of the new factory system, but that was only temporary. By the middle of the nineteenth century the bulk of industrial labor was male. The coming of the factory and the city thus wholly changed the nature of men's work. For the first time in history, work for most men was something done outside the family, psychologically as well as physically separated from the home.

The same industrial process that separated work and home also provided the opportunities for women to follow men out of the home. For that reason the feminist movement, both socially and intellectually, was a direct consequence of the industrial changes of the nineteenth century. Furthermore, just as the new industrial system was reshaping the rural men who came under its influence, so it reshaped the nature of women.

The process began with the home, which, in the early years of industrialization, was still the site of most women's work. Because of high land values, the city home was smaller than the farm house, and with less work for children, the size of the urban family was smaller than the rural. Moreover, in the city work in the home changed. Machines in factories now performed many of the tasks that had long been women's. In truth, the feminist movement began not when women felt a desire for men's jobs, but when men in factories began to take away women's traditional work. Factory-produced clothing, commercial laundries, prepared foods (e.g. prepared cereals, canned vegetables, condensed milk, bakery bread) were already available in the years after the Civil War. Toward the end of the century an advanced feminist like Charlotte Perkins Gilman, impressed by the accelerating exodus of women's chores from the middle-class home, predicted that the whole kitchen would soon be gone. She was wrong there, but even today the flight continues with precooked and frozen foods, TV dinners, cake mixes, special packaging for easy disposal, diaper services and the like.

Middle-class women were the main beneficiaries of the lightening of the chores of the home; few working-class or immigrant women could as yet take advantage of the new services and products. These middle-class women became the bone and sinew of the feminist movement, which was almost entirely an urban affair. They joined the women's clubs, organized the temperance crusades and marched in the suffrage parades. With an increasing amount of time available to them in the city, and imbued with the historic American value of work, they sought to do good. And there was much to be done in the raw, sometimes savage, urban environment of the late nineteenth century. For example, public playgrounds in the United States began in Boston only in the 1880's, when two public-spirited middle-class women caused a cartload of sand to be piled on an empty lot and set the neighborhood children loose upon it. Many a city and small town at the turn of the century owed its public library or its park to the dedicated work of women's clubs. The venerable giant redwood trees of northern California survive today because clubwomen of San Francisco and nearby towns successfully campaigned in 1900 to save them from being cut down for lumber. The saloon and prostitution were two other prevalent urban blights that prompted study and action by women's organizations.

More important than women's opposition to social evils was the widening of women's knowledge and concerns that inevitably accompanied it. What began as a simple effort to rid the community of a threat to its purity often turned into a discovery of the economic exploitation that drove young working girls into brothels and harried working men into saloons. Frances Willard for example, while head of the Women's Christian Temperance Union, broadened the WCTU's reform interests far beyond the liquor question, causing it to advocate protective legislation for working women, kindergartens and training programs for young working girls. Jane Addams, at Hull-House in Chicago's slums, quickly learned what historians have only recently discovered, that it was the urban boss's undeniable services to the immigrants that were the true sources of his great political power and the real secret of his successful survival of municipal reform campaigns.

The most direct way in which industrialization altered the social function of women was by providing work for women outside the home. Production by machine, of course, widened enormously the uses to which women's labor could be put once physical strength was no longer a consideration. And toward the end of the century, as business enterprises grew and record-keeping, communications and public relations expanded, new opportunities for women opened up in business offices. The telephone operator, the typist, the clerical worker and the stenographer now took places beside the seamstress, the cotton mill operator and the teacher.

As workers outside the home, women buried the Victorian stereotype of the lady under a mountain of reality. After all, it was difficult to argue that women as a sex were weak, timid, incompetent, fragile vessels of spirituality when thousands of them could be seen trudging to work in the early hours of the day in any city of the nation. Nor could a girl who worked in a factory or office help but become more worldly. A young woman new to a shop might have been embarrassed to ask a male foreman for the ladies' room, as some working girls' autobiographies report, but such maidenly reticence could hardly survive very long. Even gentle, naïve farm girls soon found out how to handle the inevitable, improper advances of foremen. They also learned the discipline of the clock, the managing of their own money, the excitement of life outside the home, the exhilaration of financial independence along with the drudgery of machine labor. Having learned something of the ways of the world, women could not be treated then, nor later in marriage, as the hopeless dependents Victorian ideals prescribed.

In time work transformed the outer woman, too. First to go were the hobbling, trailing skirts, which in a factory were a hazard and a nuisance.

Even before the Civil War, Amelia Bloomer and other feminists had pointed out that women, if they were to work in the world as human beings, needed looser and lighter garments than those then in fashion. Until working women were numbered in the millions, no change took place. After 1890 women's skirts gradually crept up from the floor, and the neat and simple shirtwaist became the uniform of the working girl. A costume very like the original bloomer was widely worn by women factory workers during the First World War. Later the overall and the coverall continued the adaptation of women's clothes to the machine.

The most dramatic alteration in the image of woman came after the First World War, when there was a new upsurge in women's employment. The twenties witnessed the emergence of the white-collar class, and women were a large part of it. Over twice as many women entered the labor force that decade as in the previous one; the number of typists alone in 1930 was three-quarters of a million, a tenfold increase since 1900. And woman's appearance reflected the requirements of work. Except for some of the extreme flapper fashions, which were transient, the contemporary woman still dresses much as the woman of the 1920's did. In the 1920's women threw out the corset and the numerous petticoats in favor of light undergarments, a single slip, silk or rayon stockings, short skirts and bobbed hair. So rapid and widespread was the change that an investigation in the 1920's revealed that even most working-class girls no longer wore corsets, and the new interest in bobbed hair resulted between 1920 and 1930 in an increase of 400 per cent in the number of women hair dressers.

The physical freedom of dress that women acquired during the 1920's was but the superficial mark of a new social equality. The social forces behind this new equality are several. Some of these forces, like the growing number of college-trained women and the increasing number of women in the working force, go back far into the past; others, like the impact of the war and the arduous campaign for women's suffrage, were more recent. But whatever the causes, the consequences were obvious. Indeed, what is generally spoken of as the revolution in morals of the 1920's is more accurately a revolution in the position of women. Within a few short years a spectrum of taboos was shed. For the first time women began to smoke and drink in public; cigarette manufacturers discovered and exploited in advertising a virtually untouched market. As recently as 1918 it was considered daring for a New York hotel to permit women to sit at a bar. In the twenties, despite prohibition, both sexes drank in public.

Perhaps most significant, as well as symbolic, of the new stage in the position of women was their new sexual freedom. The twenties have long been associated with the discovery of Freud and a fresh, publicly acknowledged interest in sex. But insofar as these attitudes were new they represented changes in women, particularly those of the middle and upper classes. Premarital and extramarital sexuality by men had never been severely criticized, and discussion of sexual matters was commonplace wherever men gathered. Now, though, middle-class women also enjoyed that freedom. For the first time, it has been said, middle-class men carried on their extramarital affairs with women of their own social class instead of with cooks, maids and prostitutes.

An easier sexuality outside of marriage was only the most sensational side of the revolution in morals; more important, if only because more broadly based, was a new, informal, equal relationship between the sexes, culminating in a new conception of marriage. The day was long since past when Jennie June Croly could be barred, as she was in 1868, from a dinner in honor of Charles Dickens at a men's club even though her husband was a member and she was a professional writer. (Indeed, so thoroughly has such separation of the sexes been abandoned that the new Princeton Club in New York City has closed all but one of its public rooms to any man who is not accompanied by a woman!) And at least in the gatherings of the educated middle class, talk between the sexes was often free, frank and wide-ranging. The same mutual acceptance of the sexes was visible in the prevalent talk about the "new marriage," in which the woman was a partner and a companion, not simply a mother, a social convenience and a housekeeper.

The reality of the new conception of marriage was reflected in the sharp increase in the divorce rate. Because marriage, legally as well as socially, in the nineteenth century was more confining for women than for men, the early feminists had often advocated more liberal divorce laws. And even though divorce in the nineteenth century was more common in the United States than in any European country, the divorce rate in the 1920's shot up 50 per cent over what it had been only ten years before. One sign that women in the 1920's were seeking freedom from marriage if they could not secure equality in marriage was that two thirds of the divorces in that decade were instituted by women.

By the close of the twenties the ordinary woman in America was closer to a man in the social behavior expected of her, in the economic opportunities open to her and in the intellectual freedom enjoyed by her than at any time in history. To be sure there still was a double standard, but now its existence was neither taken for granted nor confidently asserted by men.

In truth, the years since the twenties have witnessed few alterations in the position of women that were not first evident in that crucial decade. The changes have penetrated more deeply and spread more widely through the social structure, but their central tendency was then already spelled out. Even the upsurge in women's employment, which was so striking in the twenties, continued in subsequent years. Each decade thereafter has counted a larger number of working women than the previous one. During the depression decade of the 1930's, even, half a million more women entered the labor force than in the prosperous twenties. By 1960 some 38 per cent of all women of working age—almost two out of five women—were employed outside the home.

The movement of women out of the home into remunerative work, however, has been neither steady nor unopposed. Undoubtedly one of the underlying conditions is an expanding economy's need for labor. But something more than that is needed to break society's traditional habits of mind about the proper work for women. Certainly here the feminist demands for equality for women played a part. But a social factor of equal importance was war. By their very disruption of the steady pulse of everyday living, wars break the cake of custom, shake up society and compel people to look afresh at old habits and attitudes. It is not accidental, for instance, that women's suffrage in England, Russia and Germany, as well as the United States, was achieved immediately after the First World War and in France and Italy after the Second.

At the very least, by making large and new demands upon the established work force, war draws hitherto unused labor into the economic process. During the Civil War, for example, young women assumed new roles in the economy as workers in metal and munitions factories, as clerks in the expanded bureaucracy in Washington and as nurses in war hospitals. Moreover, when the war was over women had permanently replaced men as the dominant sex in the teaching profession. Furthermore, since many women found a new usefulness in the Sanitary Fairs and other volunteer work, the end of hostilities left many women unwilling to slip back into the seclusion of the Victorian home. It is not simply coincidental that the women's club movement began very soon after the war.

When the First World War came to the United States, feminist leaders, perhaps recalling the gains of the Civil War, anticipated new and broad advances for their sex. And the demand for labor, especially after the United States entered the war, did open many jobs to women, just as it was doing in contemporary Great Britain and Germany. All over the United States during the war customary and legal restrictions on the employment of women fell away. Women could be seen doing everything from laying railroad ties to working in airplane factories. The war also brought to a successful climax the struggle for the suffrage. Pointedly women had argued that a war for democracy abroad should at least remedy the deficiencies of democracy at home.

If politically the war was a boon to women, economically it failed to live up to feminist anticipations. The First World War, unlike the Civil War, did not result in a large permanent increase in the number of working women. Indeed, by 1920 there were only 800,000 more women working than in 1910. But as a result of wartime demands, women did get permanent places in new job categories, like elevator operators and theater ushers. (But women street car conductors disappeared soon after the armistice.) Certain traditional professions for women, like music teaching, lost members between 1910 and 1920, while professions that required more training and provided steadier income, like library and social work and college teaching, doubled or tripled their numbers in the same period.

The Second World War, with its even more massive demands for labor and skills, brought almost four million new women workers into the nation's factories and offices. Once again jobs usually not filled by women were opened to them. For example, the number of women bank officers rose 40 per cent during the four years of the war and the number of women employees in finance has continued to rise ever since. Furthermore, unlike the situation after the First World War, the female work force after 1945 not only stayed up but then went higher.

Measured in the number of women working, the changes in the economic position of women add up to a feminist success. Twenty-four million working women cannot be ignored. But weighed in the scales of quality instead of quantity, the change in women's economic status is not so striking. It is true that women now work in virtually every job listed by the Bureau of the Census. Moreover, the popular press repeatedly tells of the inroads women are making into what used to be thought of as men's jobs. Three years ago, for example, a woman won a prize as the mutual fund salesman of the year. Women are widely represented in advertising and in real estate, and even women taxicab drivers are no longer rare. Yet the fact remains that the occupations in which the vast majority of women actually engage are remarkably similar to those historically held by women. In 1950 almost three quarters of all employed women fell into twenty occupational categories, of which the largest was stenographers, typists and secretaries—a category that first became prominent as a woman's occupation over a half century ago. Other occupations which have traditionally been women's, like domestic service, teaching, clerical work, nursing and telephone service, are also conspicuous among the twenty categories. Further than that, the great majority of women are employed in occupations in which they predominate. This sexual division of labor is clearly evident in the professions, even though women are only a small proportion of total professional workers. Two thirds of all professional women are either nurses or teachers; and even in teaching there is a division between the sexes. Most women teach in the primary grades; most men teach in high school. Women are notoriously underrepresented in the top professions like law, medicine, engineering and scientific research. No more than 7 per cent of all professional women in 1950 were in the four of these categories together. Only 6 per cent of medical doctors and 4 per cent of lawyers and judges were women. In contrast, almost three quarters of medical doctors are women in the Soviet Union; in England the figure is 16 per cent. In both France and Sweden women make up a high proportion of pharmacists and dentists; neither of those professions attracts many women in the United States.

One consequence as well as manifestation of the sexual division of labor in the United States has been the differences in pay for men and women. That difference has been a historical complaint of feminist leaders. In 1900 one study found women's wages to be, on the average, only 53 per cent of men's.

The reason was, of course, that women were concentrated in the poorer paying jobs and industries of the economy. The disparity in pay between the sexes has been somewhat reduced today, but not very much. In 1955 among full-time women workers of all types the median wage was about two thirds of that for men. In short, women are still supplying the low-paid labor in the economy just as they were in the last century. (In substance, women workers and Negroes of both sexes perform a similar function in the economy.) The willingness of women to supply cheap labor may well account for their getting the large number of jobs they do; men often will not work for the wages that women will accept.

Today, there does not seem to be very much disparity between men's and women's wages for the same work, though the sexual division of labor is so nearly complete that it is difficult to find comparable jobs of the two sexes to make a definitive study.

There has been no improvement in women's position in higher education; indeed, it can be argued that women have failed to maintain the place reached much earlier. As we have seen, the United States led the world in opening higher education to women. This country also led in broadening the social base of education for women. No other country educated such a large proportion of women in its universities and colleges as did the United States. At the close of the nineteenth century, one third of American college students were women; by 1937 women made up almost 40 per cent of the students in American institutions of higher learning. In Germany, just before Hitler took power, no more than one out of ten university students was a woman; in Swedish universities in 1937 only 17 per cent of the students were women; in British universities the ratio was 22 per cent.

But since the Second World War the gap between American and European proportions of women in higher education has narrowed considerably. In 1952–1953 women constituted only 35 per cent of the American college population, while France counted women as 36 per cent of its university students and Sweden 26 per cent. The *number* of women in American colleges, of course, is considerably greater than it was in the 1920's and 1930's, but in proportion to men, women have lost ground in America while gaining it in Europe.

A further sign of the regression in the educational position of women in the United States is that in the early 1950's women earned about 10 per cent of the doctoral degrees in this country as compared with almost 15 per cent in the 1920's.

How is one to explain this uneven, almost contradictory record of women in America? How does it happen that a country with a kind of built-in feminism from the frontier falls behind more traditional countries in its training of college women; that a country with one of the highest proportions of working women in the world ends up with such a small proportion of its women in medicine, in law and in the sciences? Perhaps the correct answer is that the question should not be asked—at least not by Americans. For like so much else in American society, such contradictions are a manifestation of the national avoidance of any ideological principle, whether it be in feminist reform or in anything else. To be sure there has been no lack of feminist argument or rationale for women's work outside the home, for women's education and for other activities by women. But American women, like American society in general, have been more concerned with individual practice than with a consistent feminist ideology. If women have entered the labor force or taken jobs during a war they have done so for reasons related to the immediate individual or social circumstances and not for reasons of feminist ideology. The women who have been concerned about showing that women's capabilities can match men's have been the exception. As the limited, and low-paying, kinds of jobs women occupy demonstrate, there is not now and never has been any strong feminist push behind the massive and continuing movement of women into jobs. Most American women have been interested in jobs, not careers. To say, as many feminists have, that men have opposed and resisted the opening of opportunities to women is to utter only a half truth. The whole truth is that American society in general, which includes women, shuns like a disease any feminist ideology.

Another way of showing that the historical changes in the status of women in America bear little relation to a feminist ideology is to examine one of those rare instances when women did effect a social improvement through an appeal to ideology, for instance, the struggle for the suffrage. By the early twentieth century the feminist demand for the vote overrode every other feminist goal. Once women achieved the vote, it was argued, the evils of society would be routed, for women, because of their peculiar attributes, would bring a fresh, needed and wholesome element into political life. In form, and in the minds of many women leaders, the arguments for the suffrage came close to being a full-blown ideology of feminism.

In point of fact, of course, the Nineteenth Amendment ushered in no millennium. But that fact is of less importance than the reason why it did not. When American women obtained the vote they simply did not use it ideologically; they voted not as women but as individuals. Evidence of this was the failure of many women to vote at all. At the end of the first decade of national suffrage women still did not exercise the franchise to the extent that men did. Nor did many women run for or hold political offices. The first woman to serve in Congress was elected in 1916; in 1920, the first year of national women's suffrage, four women were elected to Congress, but until 1940 no more than nine women served at one time in the House of Representatives and the Senate together. That we are here observing an American and not simply a sexual phenomenon is shown by a comparison with European countries. In nonfeminist Germany, where the ballot came to women at about the same time as in the United States, the first Reichstag after suffrage counted forty-one women as members. In 1951 seventeen women sat in the British

House of Commons as compared with ten in the United States House of Representatives. Twice the number of women have served as cabinet ministers in Britain between 1928 and 1951 as have served in the United States down to the present.

Another instance in which social change was effected by feminist ideology was prohibition. The achievement of national prohibition ran second only to the suffrage movement as a prime goal of the organized women's movement; the Eighteenth Amendment was as much a product of feminist ideology as the Nineteenth. Yet like the suffrage movement, prohibition, despite its feminist backing, failed to receive the support of women. It was *after* prohibition was enacted, after all, that women drank in public.

In the cases of both suffrage and prohibition, women acted as individuals, not as members of a sex. And so they have continued to act. It is not without relevance that the women's political organization that is most respected—the League of Women Voters—is not only nonpartisan but studiously avoids questions pertaining only to women. To do otherwise would be feminist and therefore ideological.

One further conclusion might be drawn from this examination of the non-ideological character of American women. That the changes that have come to the position of women have been devoid of ideological intent may well explain why there has been so little opposition to them. The most successful of American reforms have always been those of an impromptu and practical nature. The great revolution of the New Deal is a classic example. The American people, like F. D. R. himself, simply tried one thing after another, looking for something—anything—that would get the nation out of the depression. If lasting reforms took place too, so much the better. On the other hand, reforms that have been justified by an elaborate rationale or ideology, like abolition, have aroused strong and long-drawn-out opposition. By the same token, when women became ideological in support of suffrage and prohibition, they faced their greatest opposition and scored their most disappointing triumphs.

The achievement of the suffrage in 1920 is a convenient date for marking the end of the first phase in the changing position of women, for by then women were accorded virtually the same rights as men even if they did not always exercise them. The second phase began at about the same time. It was the participation of married women in the work force. During the nineteenth century few married women worked; when they did it was because they were childless or because their husbands were inadequate providers. Even among the poor, married women normally did not work. A survey of the slum districts in five large cities in 1893 revealed that no more than 5 per cent of the wives were employed. Only Negro wives in the South and immigrant wives in big northern cities provided any significant exceptions to this generalization.

Before the First World War, the movement of wives into the working force was barely noticeable. During the 1920's there was an acceleration, but as late as 1940 less than 17 per cent of all married women were working. Among working women in 1940, 48 per cent were single and only 31 per cent were married. The Second World War dramatically reversed these proportions—another instance of the influence of war on the position of women. By 1950 the proportion of married women living with their husbands had risen to 48 per cent of all working women while that of single women had fallen to 32 per cent. In 1960 the Census reported that almost 32 per cent of all married women were employed outside the home and that they comprised 54 per cent of all working women. No industrial country of Europe, with the exception of the Soviet Union, counted such a high proportion. Today, married women are the greatest source of new labor in the American economy. Between 1949 and 1959, for example, over four million married women entered the labor force, some 60 per cent of *all* additions, male and female.

Such a massive movement of married women out of the home was a development few of the early feminists could have anticipated. That it has taken place is at once a sign and a yardstick of the enormous change in women's position in society and in the family. In the nineteenth century work outside the home was unthinkable for the married woman. Not only were there children to care for, but there were objections from husbands and society to consider. That is why the convinced feminist of the nineteenth century often spurned marriage. Indeed, it is often forgotten that the feminist movement was a form of revolt against marriage. For it was through marriage, with the legal and social dominance of the husband, that women were most obviously denied opportunities for self-expression. Even after the legal superiority of the husband had been largely eliminated from the law, middle-class social conventions could still scarcely accommodate the working wife. To the woman interested in realizing her human capabilities, marriage in the nineteenth century was not an opportunity but a dead end. And it was indeed a minor scandal of the time that many of the "new women" did in fact reject marriage. The tendency was most pronounced, as was to be expected, among highly educated women, many of whom felt strongly their obligation to serve society through careers. Around 1900 more than one fourth of women who graduated from college never married; more than half of the women medical doctors in 1890 were single.

Like other changes in the position of women, the movement of married women into the work force—the reconciliation of marriage and work—must be related to the social changes of the last three decades. One of these social changes was the increase in contraceptive knowledge, for until married women could limit their families they could not become steady and reliable industrial workers. Information about contraceptive techniques which had been known for a generation or more to educated middle-class women did not seep down to the working class until the years of the Great Depression. In 1931, for instance, there were only 81 clinics disseminating birth control information in the United States; in 1943 there were 549, of which 166 were under public auspices. As the number of public clinics suggest, by the end of the 1930's birth control was both socially and religiously acceptable, at least among Protestants. And a method was also available then to Roman Catholics, since it was in the same decade that the rhythm method, the only one acceptable to the Roman Catholic Church, was first brought to popular attention with the approval of ecclesiastical authorities.

Another social force underlying the movement of wives and mothers in the work force was the growing affluence of an industrial society, especially after 1940. Higher health standards, enlarged incomes of husbands and a better standard of living in general permitted a marked alteration in the temporal cycle of women's lives. Women now lived longer, stayed in school later and married earlier. In 1890 half the girls left school at 14 or before—that is, when they finished grammar school; in 1957 the median age was 18—after graduation from high school. The girl of 1890, typically, did not marry until she was 22; the age of her counterpart in 1957 was 20, leaving no more than two years for work between the end of school and marriage. Among other things this fact explains the fall in the proportion of single women in the work force in the United States as compared with other industrial societies. Few other countries have such an early median age of marriage for girls.

Early marriages for women produce another effect. With knowledge of contraceptive techniques providing a measure of control over child-bearing, women are now having their children early and rapidly. When this tendency is combined with a younger age of marriage, the result is an early end to child-bearing. In 1890 the median age of a mother when her last child was born was 32; in 1957 it was 26. A modern mother thus has her children off to school by the time she is in her middle thirties, leaving her as much as thirty-five years free for work outside the home. And the fact is that almost half of working women today are over forty years of age. Put another way, 34 per cent of married women between the ages of thirty-five and forty-four years are gainfully employed.

Unquestionably, as the practical character of the woman's movement would lead us to expect, an important force behind the influx of married women into the work force is economic need. But simple poverty is not the only force. Several studies, for example, have documented the conclusion that many women who work are married to men who earn salaries in the upper income brackets, suggesting that poverty is not the controlling factor in the wife's decision to work. A similar conclusion is to be drawn from the positive correlation between education and work for married women. The more education a wife has (and therefore the better salary her husband is likely to earn) the more likely she is to be working herself. Many of these women work undoubtedly in order to raise an adequate standard of living to a comfortable one. Many others work probably because they want to realize their potentialities in the world. But that women are so poorly represented in the professions and other careers suggests that most married women who work are realizing their full capabilities neither for themselves nor for society.

Over sixty years ago, in *Women and Economics,* the feminist Charlotte Perkins Gilman cogently traced the connection between work and the fulfillment of women as human beings. In subsequent writings she grappled with the problem of how this aim might be realized for married women. As a mother herself, raising a child under the trying circumstances of divorce, Gilman knew first hand that work outside the home and child-rearing constituted *two* full-time jobs. No man, she knew, was expected or required to shoulder such a double burden. Gilman's remedies of professional domestic service and kitchenless apartments never received much of a hearing, and considering the utopian if not bizarre character of her solutions, that is not surprising. Yet the problem she raised remained without any solution other than the eminently individualistic and inadequate one of permitting a woman to assume the double burden if she was so minded. Meanwhile, as the economy has grown, the problem has entered the lives of an ever increasing number of women. Unlike most of her feminist contemporaries, who were mainly concerned with the suffrage and the final elimination of legal and customary barriers to women's opportunities, Gilman recognized that the logic of feminism led unavoidably to the working mother as the typical woman. For if women were to be free to express themselves, then they should be able to marry as well as to work. Women should not have to make a choice any more than men. To make that possible, though, would require that some way be found to mitigate the double burden which biology and society had combined to place only on women.

As women moved into the second stage of their development—the reconciliation of work and marriage—the problem which Gilman saw so early was increasingly recognized as the central issue. Virginia Collier, for example, in a book *Marriage and Careers,* published in 1926, wrote that since so many married women were working, "The question therefore is no longer should women combine marriage with careers, but how do they manage it and how does it work." Interestingly enough, her study shows that what today Betty Friedan, in *The Feminine Mystique,* has called the "problem that has no name," was already apparent in the 1920's. One working wife explained her reasons for taking a job in these words, "I am burning up with energy and it is rather hard on the family to use it up in angry frustration." Another said, "I had done everything for Polly for six years. Suddenly she was in school all day and I had nothing to do. My engine was running just as hard as ever, but my car was standing still." A year after Collier's book appeared, President William A. Neilson of Smith College observed "that the outstanding problem confronting women is how to reconcile a normal life of marriage and motherhood with intellectual activity such as her college education has fitted her for." That the issue was taken seriously is attested by an action of the Board of

Trustees of Barnard College in 1932. The board voted to grant six months' maternity leave with pay to members of the staff and faculty. In announcing the decision, Dean Virginia Gildersleeve clearly voiced its import. "Neither the men nor the women of our staff," she said, "should be forced into celibacy, and cut off from that great source of experience, of joy, sorrow and wisdom which marriage and parenthood offer."

With one out of three married women working today, the problem of reconciling marriage and work for women is of a social dimension considerably larger than in the days of Charlotte Gilman or even in the 1930's. But the fundamental issue is still the same: how to make it possible, as Dean Gildersleeve said, to pursue a career or hold a job while enjoying the "experience . . . joy, sorrow and wisdom" of marriage and parenthood. The practical solutions to this central problem of the second stage in the changing position of women seem mainly collective or governmental, not individual. Child-care centers, efficient and readily available house-keeping services, and emergency child-care service such as the Swedes have instituted are obviously a minimal requirement if women are to have the double burdens of homemaking and employment lightened. The individual working woman cannot be expected to compensate for the temporary disabilities consequent upon her role as mother any more than the individual farmer or industrial worker can be expected single-handedly to overcome the imbalance between himself and the market. Today both farmers and workers have government and their own organizations to assist them in righting the balance.

But as the history of farmers and industrial labor makes evident, to enact legislation or to change mores requires persuasion of those who do not appreciate the necessity for change. Those who would do so must organize the like-minded and mobilize power, which is to say they need a rationale, an ideology. And here is the rub; in pragmatic America, as we have seen, any ideology must leap high hurdles. And one in support of working wives is additionally handicapped because women themselves, despite the profound changes in their status in the last century, do not acknowledge such an ideology. Most American women simply do not want work outside the home to be justified as a normal activity for married women. Despite the counter-argument of overwhelming numbers of working wives, they like to think of it as special and exceptional. And so long as they do not advance such an ideology, American society surely will not do so, though other societies, like Israel's and the Soviet Union's, which are more ideological than ours, obviously have.

Perhaps the kind of gradual, piecemeal advance toward a feminist ideology that Mrs. Rossi proposes in other pages of this issue may contain the seeds of change. But a reading of the past reminds us forcefully that in America the soil is thin and the climate uncongenial for the growth of any seedlings of ideology.

WILLIAM M. McCORD

•

Crime in America[1]

America is by far the most criminal nation in the world. On a per capita basis, Americans commit about twice as many assaults as Frenchmen, triple the number of rapes as Italians, and five times as many murders as Englishmen. From the price manipulations of Westinghouse-General Electric and the mass violence of Los Angeles down to the subway muggings and the petty thievery of juvenile gangs, it is apparent, in James Truslow Adams's words, that "lawlessness has been and is one of the most distinctive American traits."

Yet we are at the same time one of the most puritanical of peoples, forever searching for some means to cure, suppress or punish wicked tendencies. This urge to reform has produced that recurring phenomenon in American life, the investigating commission, of which the latest example is the National Crime Commission appointed by President Johnson. Unfortunately, however, he has asked this newest blue-ribbon panel to answer the wrong questions and it may well end its investigations without adding much to what we already know.

Why is drug addiction increasing among young people? This is probably the most sensitive of the five questions the Commission will consider. In posing it, the President's advisers—perhaps responding to the public's appetite for sensation—have misled the commission. Any reasonable discussion of juvenile drug addiction (which, in America, means primarily addiction to heroin) should start by clearing up several prevalent misconceptions.

Drug addiction is *not* increasing; in all probability it has declined since the turn of the century. In 1915 (the year after the Harrison Act declared opiate addiction illegal), responsible scientists estimated that 215,000 Americans were addicts; by 1922, the number dropped to 110,000 (undoubtedly, most of those who gave up the habit were not true addicts); by 1960, the Federal Bureau of Narcotics reported only 45,391 known addicts in America—a figure that, however open to criticism, is the best available and shows a declining rate of addiction. The average age of drug addicts has not changed.

Secondly, drug addiction does *not* cause crime; it may in fact decrease it.

Many juvenile addicts are, of course, criminal. The "junkie" is likely to rob or shoplift or burglarize. But the best study of the subject (Isidor Chein's "The Road to H") shows that drug addiction tends to redirect the potential

[1] From *The New York Times Magazine,* November 21, 1965. The original title "We Ask the Wrong Questions about Crime" has been changed by the editors.

delinquent from more serious crimes toward those that will bring him the money to buy drugs. In all probability, drug addicts are less prone to commit really violent crimes like rape, assault or murder. The "flattening" effect of heroin often causes sexual desire to disappear and also reduces aggressiveness. In some recorded cases, addiction has actually eliminated vicious criminal tendencies.

Thirdly, drug addiction per se does not seriously injure mind or body, as do barbiturates, alcohol or tobacco. Even after 50 years of addiction in some cases, no discernible physical or mental harm has been traced to the use of narcotics. Further, the habit can be cured. Although hospital treatment has been discouraging (about 90 per cent failure among adult addicts), Synanon, a group similar to Alcoholics Anonymous, has reported a high degree of success and Chein's research shows that 26 per cent of teen-age addicts spontaneously cure themselves. Cured or not, however, many addicts continue to work—indeed, some deteriorate only when taken off the drug.

The average juvenile drug addict is admittedly an unhappy person, plagued by a sense of futility and aimlessness. Typically, he comes from a deprived ethnic group (97 per cent of youthful addicts come from families affected by divorce, desertion or open hostility between their members). He tries narcotics at an early age, usually by 15. Normally, he takes his first dose at the encouragement of a friend rather than as a result of a "pusher's" influence. For such young people—passive, dependent, loveless—the drug serves to reduce intolerable anxiety.

Should we deny them this satisfaction? For most addicts, drugs are an indispensable psychological crutch, as important to them as insulin is for the diabetic. To declare narcotics illegal may change the ways in which disordered people control their anxiety but it does nothing to cure the underlying condition; the *form* of misbehavior changes, but the causes stay the same.

In fact, the evidence suggests that juvenile drug addiction should not be considered a major social problem at all. The most civilized approach for the President's commission would be to examine ways of legalizing the dispensation of drugs under medical advice and prescription. England has long ago removed the problem from police jurisdiction. As a result, some authorities claim, the nation has only 700 known addicts. Others take issue with this figure and a few believe that drug addiction is on the rise. But Britain has apparently eliminated illegal traffic in drugs and, what is most important, stopped much of the criminal behavior which, in America, is inevitably associated with addiction.

A balanced appraisal of the English solution, rather than the study of even more intensive attempts to curb the supposed terrors of addiction, would thus seem to be the most fruitful avenue of investigation for the commission. The legalization of drug-taking (under medical supervision) might result in a slight increase in addiction but I do not find this possibility frightening since: (1) addiction in itself does not appear physically harmful; (2) crimes prompted by the present necessity for purchasing drugs illegally would possibly decrease.

The second crucial question the commission has been asked to consider is, Why does organized crime continue to expand?

Whether the ranks of organized crime *have* actually expanded remains a subject of debate. Certain facts are apparent: mobs of strike-breakers no longer find lucrative employment; gangland killings, like the St. Valentine's Day massacre, have become a rarity. And contemporary racketeers can seldom boast, like Al Capone, that "the biggest bankers and businessmen and politicians and professional men are looking to me to keep the system going."

Certainly, organized crime—labor racketeering, Mafia operations in gambling and vice, underworld penetration of sports and business—is still an important part of American life. Admittedly, the "invisible government" of the Mafia is highly institutionalized and its power affects police and politicians in many American cities. And clearly, as the Kefauver investigation hinted, gangsters have also, from time to time, found a receptive attitude in such respectable organizations as Western Union, major telephone companies and Wall Street brokerage firms. But while recognizing, as a Fund for the Republic report concluded, that "the underworld is an independent power, vying with other great classes and movements in America for wealth and influence in our culture," it is salutary to view the problem in its historical and sociological perspective.

New York's "Bowery Boys" and the "Dead Rabbits" of the eighteen-sixties, the gangs of the Far West in the eighteen-seventies and Chicago's "Mike McDonald Democrats" of the eighteen-eighties testify that organized crime has been an enduring, even a glamorized, element in American culture for 100 years. Racketeers flourish in catering to desires which Americans periodically declare illegal: drink, sex, gambling or security from economic competition. No government can outlaw these human appetites; to the degree that it tries to do so, the organized underworld will continue to find ready customers. In our refusal to tolerate human weakness, we have produced a legion of Lucky Lucianos and Frank Costellos.

Yet recent trends in America have led to a relative decline in the influence of such men. Once-illicit activities, like drinking, have returned to the domain of legitimate business. The economy is no longer as competitive as in the past. Labor unions have, by and large, won acceptance and there is little need for terrorism as a means of protecting workers in an era of surplus labor. All of these changes signal the passing of big-city, organized crime—at least in the form in which we have known it.

The means are also at hand to curb the racketeers even further, if the public conscience really demanded it. Robert Kennedy, as Attorney General, increased Justice Department prosecutions of organized crime from 17 in 1960 to 262 in 1963. The Los Angeles police, by internal house-cleaning and external vigilance, has almost eliminated the Mafia, reducing gang killings to an average of one a year. Even Chicago, under Chief O. W. Wilson, has tightened its laws, refurbished its police and begun to clean out the more poisonous elements. The answer to organized crime, therefore, lies in the effective pursuit of justice—and just possibly in the repeal of laws that take too little cognizance of mankind's foibles.

The third question the President put to the commission is, Why do one-third of parolees revert to crime?

According to the most authoritative research in this field (the recent studies of Prof. Daniel Glaser, who traced the histories of more than 1,000 men in the Illinois penal system), approximately one-third of parolees *do* return to a life of crime. But this rate of failure should not invite condemnation of present trends in penal reform. On the contrary, the evidence suggests that the spread of an enlightened approach to rehabilitation has markedly enhanced the effectiveness of the American prison.

In the nineteen-thirties, Sheldon and Eleanor Glueck of Harvard followed up hundreds of men who had been imprisoned in Massachusetts. They found that over 80 per cent reverted to crime, and the longer a man spent in prison, the greater were the chances of recidivism. Reform schools in the nineteen-thirties and nineteen-forties seemed equally ineffective. An evaluation of typical Eastern reformatories revealed that 85 per cent of inmates went on to commit crimes in adulthood.

Today, this rate of failure has been substantially reduced. Most states now practice "parole prediction," using statistical tables to forecast a man's performance on parole rather accurately. In Illinois, only 3 per cent of parolees with favorable predictions violated their trust, while 75 per cent of those regarded as bad risks reverted to crime. The State of Washington's parole predictions have so far proved 100 per cent accurate!

A second factor accounting for the decline in parole violations has been the modernization and humanization of the rehabilitation process. Federal prisons have introduced individual and group therapy; the relatively "open" prison system typified by Chino, Calif., has been widely adopted; new facilities for the criminally insane, like California's Vacaville, have been established; older prisons have tried such new techniques as San Quentin's group discussions for convicts and their families; and even conjugal visiting has been allowed in such an unlikely place as Mississippi.

Encouraged by the success of New Jersey's Highfields project and New York's Wiltwyck School, many of the nation's juvenile reformatories have also replaced the techniques of punishment with those of rehabilitation. This quiet, almost unreported revolution in the penal system demonstrates how the application of social science can benefit society.

Can the number of parole violations be even further reduced? Probably yes. Proven methods of treatment could be introduced in those states, particularly in the South, which have been almost untouched by prison reform.

The parole program itself could be further improved by an expansion of staff, the establishment of more counseling centers, and particularly by easing the task of parolees seeking a legal way to make a living. (The Glaser research showed that 90 per cent of convicts seek legitimate employment for a month after leaving prison, but that their initial income amounts to only $80 a month and one-third of them are still unemployed after three months.)

A more radical solution might also deserve consideration by the National Crime Commission: the introduction of more "indeterminate sentences" with an attendant revision in legal concepts of punishment and responsibility. The accuracy of parole prediction indicates that certain types of intractable offenders cannot benefit from the present penal system. A man like Albert Fish, who murdered, cooked and ate a young girl, had repeatedly served time in prison, yet, by contemporary law, had not been considered insane and consequently had been released each time he had been suitably "punished."

Might it not be wiser to declare such men not responsible for their actions and make them liable to an indefinite, nonpunitive sentence? In varying degrees, Britain, Sweden and Denmark already follow a policy of confining certain types of offenders to hospitals for an undetermined period.

Why does one man break the law and another living in the same circumstances does not? This was the fourth question, and one that the National Crime Commission will, I trust, dispose of expeditiously. The circumstances which lead one man to crime and another to good citizenship are, in reality, always quite different.

I am personally acquainted with cases where a child has, it would seem, miraculously escaped the influence of a highly criminal environment. In one Boston family, for example, the eldest son became a murderer and another boy committed violent sex crimes, but the youngest turned into a mild and harmless, if highly neurotic, bookkeeper.

Until recently, these variations were attributed to the mysterious workings of moral fiber or free will or chance but now criminology has reached the point where nearly all the differences in "circumstances" can be weighed and calculated.

Research by the Gluecks has most dramatically demonstrated that distinctive factors that lead to crime can be identified early in life, even at the time when a child enters school. From the findings of their "Unraveling Juvenile Delinquency"—an analysis of the differing environments of delinquents and nondelinquents—the Gluecks constructed a prediction table based on such influences as parental discipline, family cohesiveness and affection. Individual children can thus be graded on the risk of becoming delinquent. Even children in the same family can often receive a different score, since one child may be his mother's pet and the other treated as a black sheep, or one may have been born when his father was at home while another's arrival may have triggered the father's desertion.

The New York Youth Board used this scale to predict delinquency among boys starting school in one section of the city in 1952. Now they have reached adolescence, and preliminary reports indicate that the board's predictions have turned out to be 89 per cent accurate.

In a similar research project among boys who averaged 11 years of age in 1939, none of those raised in environments judged as the most "positive" had become criminal 25 years later while 91 per cent of those who suffered the most negative influences had criminal records.

Clearly, when an adult's behavior can be predicted from a knowledge of forces operating in childhood—influences which he could not conceivably control—society must begin to question the belief that a person acts from willful intent, that he should be held personally responsible for his actions and that he deserves punishment for behaving in an evil fashion.

On the other hand, such new procedures raise the delicate question of how society should utilize them. What limits should be imposed? We may soon be faced with a momentous choice between intervening in a child's family, perhaps forcibly—in defiance of our conception of parents' rights to raise their own children—and not intervening even though we *know* they are injuring a child to the point where he may one day threaten society.

The President's commission would do well to examine these issues, for they will soon become a matter of wide debate.

Why does juvenile delinquency know no economic or educational boundaries? Focusing on this fifth question may again deflect the Crime Commission from more basic issues. Every type of American boy does, in fact, commit crimes, but persistent delinquents needing help seldom emerge from the privileged educated segments of American society.

Admittedly, one can find drug addiction in Darien, rich teen-age robbers in Phoenix, "sex orgies" at Stanford, and sophisticated burglars among Harvard's student body. These wealthy, educated youths do not normally appear on police blotters; their prominence and connections insure that they will not be labeled as delinquents. (As a teen-ager, I myself committed a flagrant and dangerous traffic violation which, properly, resulted in arrest. My best friend's father, however, judged the case, and I was released with friendly admonitions.) This double standard is a disgrace that the commission, as other groups have done, should expose and condemn.

Yet, while recognizing the universality of delinquency and class distortions in the statistics, every social scientist knows that the most brutal crimes are confined to that segment of society which has been thoroughly dehumanized, that professional stealing is most prevalent where the American Dream has been least fulfilled, and that gang warfare breaks out where American ideals of courage, brotherhood and manliness are taken seriously but with the fewest rewards.

Despite the bias in criminal reporting, one can be reasonably certain that young Negroes commit 30 per cent more larcenies, 60 per cent more murders and 70 per cent more assaults than whites. But on the other hand, white urban slum delinquents commit twice as many assaults, three times as many larcenies and four times as many rapes as their fellow Caucasians in rural areas.

Discrepancies like these have been noted in America since 1800 and they cannot be explained in terms of the nature of Negroes or Puerto Ricans or working-class whites, or whoever else, at the moment, happens to have a reputation for delinquency. Urban Jews, Irish, Italians and Frenchmen have all previously been America's juvenile champions of crime—until they, in turn, found more useful and rewarding outlets in American life.

Boys who have to struggle up from the lowest social strata have traditionally been more prone to delinquency. Our society, in psychologist Kenneth Kenniston's words, offers working-class boys "few prospects as dignified, exciting and challenging as truancy, gang warfare, vandalism and theft." The middle-class boy, in contrast, soon outgrows his indiscretions as he finds more opportunities open to him for a happier or more productive or more profitable existence.

Until the preconditions of crime—ethnic discrimination, family disintegration and the rest of the characteristic malaise of industrial civilizations—are eliminated, we cannot uproot the cancer of delinquency at the center of American life.

To eradicate crime in America will take a revolution. The National Crime Commission cannot turn America back into a poor, rural, village-based society where the crime rate was so much lower. Nor can the commission change the American tradition that honors the violent cowboy-gangster here. And clearly, a Presidential group cannot fundamentally change an entire social structure—one that forces Negroes in Watts or Puerto Ricans in Harlem or K.K.K. murderers in Alabama to pursue their ways of tragic, brutal, purposeless violence.

But the commission can accomplish two tasks. It can sweep away false questions about a new wave in drug addiction and a supposed growth in organized crime, and myths about "the good boy gone wrong" that continue to confuse the public. And it can propose solutions to new questions that the public, let alone its intellectual leaders, has hardly examined:

What would be the impact of legalizing drug addiction?

Should America legalize gambling and prostitution (thus depriving organized crime of these particular sources of income)?

Should American lawyers abandon their concepts of "responsibility," "willful intent" and, in fact, the whole set of easily accepted but barely defensible assumptions about human nature that underlie contemporary law?

Should judges revise their sentencing procedures, so that men would be treated in terms of their nature rather than their illegal acts?

Should the state consider intervening in families that, with seeming inevitability, will produce criminals?

I have no pat answers to these questions and I am deeply worried about how they will affect our tradition of privacy, our belief in man's rationality and our conviction that some men (at least) have the power to choose freely. But I am sure that by confronting these complex, essentially philosophical problems, the National Crime Commission can best fulfill its duty.

DAVID E. LILIENTHAL

•

300,000,000 Americans Would Be Wrong[1]

By the year 2000, just one generation away, the population of the United States will probably be about 300 million—100 million higher than it is now and 200 million higher than it was in 1920. Yet, in comparison with many underdeveloped nations, population growth would not seem to be a serious problem in America.

Certainly this vastly increased population will not lack for food. While population growth in Latin America, for example, has brought per capita food production below pre-World War II levels, we in the U.S. worry about overweight, spend huge sums to restrict farm production and give away enough food to prevent famine in poor nations throughout the world. In contrast to less developed nations, we have enough space, too. Just fly over this country and see the huge, sparsely populated areas that could easily accommodate additional tens of millions.

Great differences in resources, technology and education help explain why Americans regard overpopulation as a menace only to other peoples. It can't happen here, they think. I used to think so, too; I don't any more.

During the past 10 years, much of it spent overseas, I came to the easy conclusion that if we succeeded in tripling or quadrupling food production in hungry nations—and in some areas in which I worked we did just that—the problem of overpopulation could be solved. But gradually I learned I was mistaken to believe that increased food production was the complete answer to the crisis of population abroad. Gradually, I also learned that America's overflowing cornucopia has obscured a deeper crisis developing here: a population of at least 300 million by 2000 will, I now believe, threaten the very quality of life of individual Americans.

[1] From *The New York Times Magazine,* January 9, 1966. © 1966 by The New York Times Company. Reprinted by permission of the author and The New York Times. Mr. Lilienthal has been Chairman of Development and Resources Corporation since he founded it in 1955.

An additional 100 million people will undermine our most cherished traditions, erode our public services and impose a rate of taxation that will make current taxes seem tame. The new masses, concentrated (as they will be) in the already strangling urban centers, cannot avoid creating conditions that will make city life almost unbearable. San Francisco, to take a still tolerable example, once was one of my favorite cities—cosmopolitan, comfortable, lovely. Now the high-rise buildings have sprouted like weeds and suburban blight is advancing on the Golden Gate. The value of real estate has increased while people's enjoyment of life declines.

Historically the United States owes much of its vigor and power to population growth. (Only 50 million people rattled around in America in 1880.) Large markets, skilled manpower, huge factories, a country able to spend billions on war, space and social welfare—all this, plus 75 million passenger cars—is surely a consequence of rising population. But no economy and no physical environment can sustain infinite population growth. There comes a point at which a change in quantity becomes a change in quality—when we can no longer speak of "more of the same." And another 100 million people will, I fear, make just that change in the joy of life in America.

It is probably true that as the population will grow, so will the dollar value of our output. U.S. wealth, measured by Gross National Product, is now $670 billion; barring a major economic setback, total output will be doubled in about two decades. With G.N.P. climbing at the rate of $40 billion a year, the U.S. probably can afford to build the schools, housing projects, roads and other necessities of life for 300 million Americans.

But if our resources are mainly spent merely to survive, to cope with life in a congested America, then where is the enjoyment of living? Our teeming cities are not pleasant places today; imagine them by the middle of the next century when the areas of some might be 100 times larger than they are now. This is the real possibility envisioned by Roger Revelle, director of the newly established Center for Population Studies at the Harvard School of Public Health. And it will be to the cities that tomorrow's millions will flock. Or consider the picture, drawn with characteristic wit, by economist John Kenneth Galbraith: "It is hard to suppose that penultimate Western man, stalled in the ultimate traffic jam and slowly succumbing to carbon monoxide will be especially enchanted to hear from the last survivor that in the preceding year Gross National Product went up by a record amount."

Nor does the nightmare consist only of traffic jams and a bumper-to-bumper way of life. As we have seen in the history of the last 25 years, public services only the Federal Government can provide will continue to expand. Moreover, state governments, until now unable (or unwilling) to pay their share of the bills, show signs of awakening to their responsibilities. But bigger government efforts do not produce better results for human beings; they are simply a way of getting a job done when no more feasible methods exist.

Even today, most of the nation's most serious problems are caused largely by the pressures of a too rapidly rising population. In the next generation, the problems may become unmanageable. Take four basic needs: education, water, air and power.

The quality of education is closely related to the problem of numbers. Within the next five years, we are told, the number of high school students will rise to 15 million (a 50 per cent increase over 1960), forcing hundreds of communities to consider imposing stiff new taxes. Many taxpayers will refuse to accept the added burden and their children will attend even more crowded classes. Farsighted citizens will approve new school bond issues, but the increased financial drain probably will not result in an improved education.

Our standard of democracy entitles everyone to free schooling through high school. But our educational standards are rising. Two-year junior colleges, many of them supported by cities and states, loom as the next step in our system of free, universal education. Along with the surge in enrollment at traditional four-year colleges and universities, higher education is expected to attract about 12 million students in 1980 (triple the 1960 figure).

Merely building the physical facilities for such huge increases is a formidable prospect. Creating a sympathetic atmosphere for education, and filling the need for qualified teachers is a much more staggering problem. Of course, we may argue for the radical reform of U.S. education. We may plead for overhauling the existing system of teacher training, as James B. Conant has eloquently done. But I see few signs we are about to undertake such vast changes in the machinery of U.S. education; nor does it seem possible, even if the mood for drastic reform was overwhelming, simply to order new procedures, new goals and new solutions and then put them into practice. Good teachers cannot be turned out by fiat. We do not live in a planner's paradise. Ask Robert Moses.

With increased urbanization and industrialization, demands on the water supply will be much greater than most Americans have remotely imagined. The drought in the northeast United States last summer was an indication of shortages even greater to come. And though engineers and scientists can, and will, tap new sources of water and devise ways to purify polluted rivers like the Hudson, the cost will be fantastic—hundreds of billions of dollars. Add to the current strain the pressure of a 50 per cent increase in population and the result may well be a chronic water shortage that can hardly be solved at any tolerable price.

Imaginative but impractical water schemes have been proposed, such as one to bring to the United States the almost limitless supply of far northern water, carrying it a thousand miles and more to our own boundaries. Assuming that Canada would agree to the politically prickly diversion of her waters, the cost is estimated in the neighborhood of $100-billion. But it has taken more than a generation of hot dispute and interminable litigation to decide priorities of water among our own sister states of the West. How much greater the difficulties of diverting Canada's water to care for U.S. needs?

As for nuclear-powered desalination plants, quite apart from the cost of constructing the huge installations we would need and the pipelines to carry the water inland, there is the additional problem of safety in disposing of radioactive waste. Technicians may solve the problem, but at what social cost? The conversion of precious open spaces into atomic garbage dumps?

Just as easily accessible water supplies dwindle, air pollution will increase. Air pollution is the result of congestion, industrialization and the multiplication of automobiles—factors in direct relation to population density in urban areas. Los Angeles is not an industrial city, yet at times its air is hardly fit to breathe. And with the spread of industry in the sprawling cities of the nation, more and more places will be Los Angelized.

We have long assumed that at least the air we breathe is free. It won't be for much longer as we expand our efforts to purify the atmosphere. In California, for example, an aroused public finally insisted that automobile manufacturers install exhaust filters to trap toxic chemicals. Keeping automobile fumes and industrial poisons out of the air we breathe is going to be an increasingly costly business. By the year 2000 the high cost of breathing will be a real issue, not just a phrase.

Packing too many people into an urban area increases the cost of providing still another essential of everyday living: electric power. Even more serious, such concentrations of people may make absolutely reliable electric service more and more difficult to maintain. I doubt if it was a mere coincidence, for example, that New York City needed 10 hours to restore electricity after the recent Northeast power failure while smaller communities were able to turn on their lights in a much shorter time. Growth is desirable up to a point; then the advantage of size diminishes and the multiplication of complexity multiplies the headaches. And by 1980 we can expect at least a 300 per cent increase in the nation's electrical energy needs. Most of this will flow into urban areas. The present difficulties of maintaining absolutely reliable service to such concentrations of people and industry, and holding down costs, will thus be magnified.

As chairman of T.V.A. and the Atomic Energy Commission, and in my present work in Asia and Latin America, I have become familiar with the problems of producing and distributing electricity on a large scale. Indeed, it was T.V.A. a generation ago that pioneered the concept that the greater the use of electricity the lower the cost per kilowatt hour. This is still generally true. But for great cities the exact contrary is coming to pass. To *distribute* electricity in a large, densely populated area such as New York is more costly than in smaller urban markets. Huge generating power plants produce ever lower generating costs; but to bring this power to the consumer in massive concentrations of population grows more and more expensive. Consequently, the price of this essential of modern life probably will go up in the great cities as population growth continues.

Without realizing it, we are fast approaching what may be called the population barrier beyond which lie unpredictability and, I fear, problems of unmanageable size. Consider, for example, the relationship between population growth and the poor.

The Federal Aid to Dependent Children program has doubled to more than four million cases during the last decade, while the costs have soared from about $600 million to more than $1.8 billion. Even more depressing than the numbers of families who cannot survive without welfare assistance is the phenomenon known as the "cycle of dependency."

More than 40 per cent of parents whose children receive A.D.C. funds themselves had parents who received relief checks. This cycle is sad but not surprising. Poor people tend to have more children than they want or can afford, and the children have less chance to receive the education and training they need to break the pattern. Thus, even the third generation appears on relief rolls in the U.S., the most socially mobile nation in the world. In America, reports the National Academy of Sciences in a recent study, "The Growth of U.S. Population," "the burden of unwanted children among impoverished and uneducated mothers . . . is much like that experienced by mothers in underdeveloped countries."

Since the poor cannot contribute their share of the mounting costs of education, medical care, public housing and similar necessary government enterprises, the money must be supplied by the rest of the population through taxation. But the most painful loss is not measured in dollars but in human resources. And one measure of the potential loss is the fact that one-fourth of America's children are the offspring of poor parents.

Belatedly, we are helping poor couples who need and want financial and medical help in family planning. The White House Conference on Health in November gave high priority to birth control as part of Federal efforts to halt the cycle of dependency and poverty. Tax-supported activities in 40 states, combined with such large-scale private efforts as Harvard's Center for Population Studies and the $14.5 million grant by the Ford Foundation for basic research by the Columbia-Presbyterian Medical Center and the Population Council, herald new progress in a long-neglected field.

We tend to patronize the poor by preaching to them about birth control; though poverty-stricken parents with four, five or six children are the most publicized aspect of population growth, they are by no means the most important numerical aspect of the problem. As a matter of simple arithmetic, the four-fifths of the nation's families who earn more than the poverty-line income of $3,000 a year—and who can afford two, three or four children—produce a greater total of children than the one poor couple out of five which may have six youngsters.

In fact, the latest census information reveals that though poor families may have more children than do better-off families, the difference is much smaller than many people believe. According to the National Academy of Sciences analysis, in 1960 married women 40 to 44 years old in families with incomes below $4,000 and above $4,000 differed in the average number of children by less than one. The postwar baby boom, for example, was more pronounced among middle- and upper-income families than among the poor.

Thus, these relatively well-off families are the ones mainly responsible for our rapidly rising population curve. They and their children are the ones who will account for most of the 100 million additional Americans by the end of the century.

How many children a couple should have is a decision only they should make; a government inducement or deterrent—a tax, for example—is morally repugnant and politically impossible. We cannot penalize the poor in order to limit the size of their families while we allow more prosperous parents to have as many children as they want. The large majority of middle- and upper-class parents need no birth-control help from government, nor will they welcome outside advice on so personal a matter. Yet it is this group of families who will want to have three, four or more children for the very natural reason that they like children and can afford to support them. The question is, can the *country* support them?

Any notion that The Pill or some other scientific device is the sole and complete answer is very dubious. At a symposium on birth control not long ago, Dr. Stephen J. Plank, a professor in the Harvard School of Public Health, cautioned against "the facile assumption . . . that we may be able to contracept our way to the Great Society." Birth control, he said, is a question of motivation rather than technology alone.

The neglected arithmetic of the population problem facing us is depressing. Look at this table showing the birth and death rates over the past quarter-century in the United States:

Year	*Births*	*Rate (per 1,000 pop.)*	*Deaths*	*Rate (per 1,000 pop.)*
1940	2,360,399	17.9	1,417,269	10.8
1945	2,735,456	19.5	1,401,719	10.6
1950	3,554,149	23.6	1,452,454	9.6
1955	4,047,295	24.6	1,528,717	9.3
1960	4,257,850	23.7	1,711,982	9.5
1964	4,027,490	21.0	1,798,051	9.4

Although the birth rate has been declining since the mid-50's, while the death rate has remained relatively stable, the drop in the birth rate is too little and too late to prevent an oversized population. The surge in the number of births over deaths continues (2.3 million were added to the population in 1964).

Or examine these low and high population projections prepared by the Census Bureau:

Year	*Low*	*High*
1970	206,000,000	211,000,000
1985	248,000,000	276,000,000
2010	322,000,000	438,000,000

The high figure would be reached if birth rates returned to the levels of the early 1950's. The low estimate—enormous as it is—is based on the possibility that the rates may decline by 1985 to the comparatively low levels of the early World War II years.

One theoretical way out of the dilemma would be to say that since America can no longer sustain complete "family freedom," some form of compulsory birth control is, regrettably, necessary. It would not be the first time in our history that government intervened to restrain individual impulse in the name of collective welfare. Yet, where children and parents are concerned, I do not believe we can yet advocate the sacrifice of one freedom for the sake of preserving another. Such a "solution" would make no sense at all, theorectically, practically or ethically.

Government policies and private programs must make plain the kind of life we all face if economically comfortable families reproduce at rates they personally can afford. With equal urgency we must make plain the dangers if poor families have children in numbers they cannot afford.

Obviously, a stationary population—one in which the birth rate matches the death rate—is out of the question for many years to come. It is probably not feasible, nor even desirable. All we can hope to achieve is a slower rise in the size of our population rather than the present steep increase. What is needed is a far more drastic cut in the birth rate—a voluntary curtailment of the right to breed. It is needed, but I have no great conviction that it will happen.

For though scientific ingenuity may be able to solve many of the technological problems we are only beginning to understand people always change more slowly than technology. It is easier, after all, to design a new industrial process than redesign a cultural tradition. Yet that is the order of change we face if we are to preserve life's dignity and quality. Confronted by the crisis of population growth, we must, at present, appeal to private conscience for the sake of the general good.

JOHN HOPE FRANKLIN

•

The Two Worlds of Race: A Historical View[1]

I

Measured by universal standards the history of the United States is indeed brief. But during the brief span of three and one-half centuries of colonial

[1] Reprinted by permission from *Daedalus,* published by the American Academy of Arts and Sciences, Boston, Massachusetts. Vol. 94, No. 4, *The Negro American.*

and national history Americans developed traditions and prejudices which created the two worlds of race in modern America. From the time that Africans were brought as indentured servants to the mainland of English America in 1619, the enormous task of rationalizing and justifying the forced labor of peoples on the basis of racial differences was begun; and even after legal slavery was ended, the notion of racial differences persisted as a basis for maintaining segregation and discrimination. At the same time, the effort to establish a more healthy basis for the new world social order was begun, thus launching the continuing battle between the two worlds of race, on the one hand, and the world of equality and complete human fellowship, on the other.

For a century before the American Revolution the status of Negroes in the English colonies had become fixed at a low point that distinguished them from all other persons who had been held in temporary bondage. By the middle of the eighteenth century, laws governing Negroes denied to them certain basic rights that were conceded to others. They were permitted no independence of thought, no opportunity to improve their minds or their talents or to worship freely, no right to marry and enjoy the conventional family relationships, no right to own or dispose of property, and no protection against miscarriages of justice or cruel and unreasonable punishments. They were outside the pale of the laws that protected ordinary humans. In most places they were to be governed, as the South Carolina code of 1712 expressed it, by special laws "as may restrain the disorders, rapines, and inhumanity to which they are naturally prone and inclined. . . ." A separate world for them had been established by law and custom. Its dimensions and the conduct of its inhabitants were determined by those living in a quite different world.

By the time that the colonists took up arms against their mother country in order to secure their independence, the world of Negro slavery had become deeply entrenched and the idea of Negro inferiority well established. But the dilemmas inherent in such a situation were a source of constant embarrassment. "It always appeared a most iniquitous scheme to me," Mrs. John Adams wrote her husband in 1774, "to fight ourselves for what we are daily robbing and plundering from those who have as good a right to freedom as we have." There were others who shared her views, but they were unable to wield much influence. When the fighting began General George Washington issued an order to recruiting officers that they were not to enlist "any deserter from the ministerial army, nor any stroller, negro, or vagabond, or person suspected of being an enemy to the liberty of America nor any under eighteen years of age." In classifying Negroes with the dregs of society, traitors, and children, Washington made it clear that Negroes, slave or free, were not to enjoy the high privilege of fighting for political independence. He would change that order later, but only after it became clear that Negroes were enlisting with the "ministerial army" in droves in order to secure their own freedom. In changing his policy if not his views, Washington availed himself of the services of more than 5,000 Negroes who took up arms against England.[2]

Many Americans besides Mrs. Adams were struck by the inconsistency of their stand during the War for Independence, and they were not averse to making moves to emancipate the slaves. Quakers and other religious groups organized antislavery societies, while numerous individuals manumitted their slaves. In the years following the close of the war most of the states of the East made provisions for the gradual emancipation of slaves. In the South, meanwhile, the antislavery societies were unable to effect programs of statewide emancipation. When the Southerners came to the Constitutional Convention in 1787 they succeeded in winning some representation on the basis of slavery, in securing federal support of the capture and rendition of fugitive slaves, and in preventing the closing of the slave trade before 1808.

Even where the sentiment favoring emancipation was pronounced, it was seldom accompanied by a view that Negroes were the equals of whites and should become a part of one family of Americans. Jefferson, for example, was opposed to slavery; and if he could have had his way, he would have condemned it in the Declaration of Independence. It did not follow, however, that he believed Negroes to be the equals of whites. He did not want to "degrade a whole race of men from the work in the scale of beings which their Creator may *perhaps* have given them. . . . I advance it therefore, as a suspicion only, that the blacks, whether originally a distinct race, or made distinct by time and circumstance, are inferior to the whites in the endowment both of body and mind." It is entirely possible that Jefferson's later association with the extraordinarily able Negro astronomer and mathematician, Benjamin Banneker, resulted in some modification of his views. After reading a copy of Banneker's almanac, Jefferson told him that it was "a document to which your whole race had a right for its justifications against the doubts which have been entertained of them."[3]

In communities such as Philadelphia and New York, where the climate was more favorably disposed to the idea of Negro equality than in Jefferson's Virginia, few concessions were made, except by a limited number of Quakers and their associates. Indeed, the white citizens in the City of Brotherly Love contributed substantially to the perpetuation of two distinct worlds of race. In the 1780's, the white Methodists permitted Negroes to worship with them, provided the Negroes sat in a designated place in the balcony. On one occasion, when the Negro worshippers occupied the front rows of the balcony, from which they had been excluded, the officials pulled them from their knees during prayer and evicted them from the church. Thus, in the early days of

[2] Benjamin Quarles, *The Negro in the American Revolution* (Chapel Hill: University of North Carolina Press, 1961), pp. 15–18.
[3] John Hope Franklin, *From Slavery to Freedom: A History of American Negroes* (New York: Alfed A. Knopf, 1956), pp. 156–157.

the Republic and in the place where the Republic was founded, Negroes had a definite "place" in which they were expected at all times to remain. The white Methodists of New York had much the same attitude toward their Negro fellows. Soon, there were separate Negro churches in these and other communities. Baptists were very much the same. In 1809 thirteen Negro members of a white Baptist church in Philadelphia were dismissed, and they formed a church of their own. Thus, the earliest Negro religious institutions emerged as the result of the rejection by white communicants of their darker fellow worshippers. Soon there would be other institutions—schools, newspapers, benevolent societies—to serve those who lived in a world apart.

Those Americans who conceded the importance of education for Negroes tended to favor some particular type of education that would be in keeping with their lowly station in life. In 1794, for example, the American Convention of Abolition Societies recommended that Negroes be instructed in "those mechanic arts which will keep them most constantly employed and, of course, which will less subject them to idleness and debauchery, and thus prepare them for becoming good citizens of the United States." When Anthony Benezet, a dedicated Pennsylvania abolitionist, died in 1784 his will provided that on the death of his wife the proceeds of his estate should be used to assist in the establishment of a school for Negroes. In 1787 the school of which Benezet had dreamed was opened in Philadelphia, where the pupils studied reading, writing, arithmetic, plain accounts, and sewing.

Americans who were at all interested in the education of Negroes regarded it as both natural and normal that Negroes should receive their training in separate schools. As early as 1773 Newport, Rhode Island, had a colored school, maintained by a society of benevolent clergymen of the Anglican Church. In 1798 a separate private school for Negro children was established in Boston; and two decades later the city opened its first public primary school for the education of Negro children. Meanwhile, New York had established separate schools, the first one opening its doors in 1790. By 1814 there were several such institutions that were generally designated as the New York African Free Schools.[4]

Thus, in the most liberal section of the country, the general view was that Negroes should be kept out of the main stream of American life. They were forced to establish and maintain their own religious institutions, which were frequently followed by the establishment of separate benevolent societies. Likewise, if Negroes were to receive any education, it should be special education provided in separate educational institutions. This principle prevailed in most places in the North throughout the period before the Civil War. In some Massachusetts towns, however, Negroes gained admission to schools that had been maintained for whites. But the School Committee of Boston refused to

[4] Carter G. Woodson, *The Education of the Negro Prior to 1861* (Washington, D. C.: Associated Publishers, 1919), pp. 93–97.

admit Negroes, arguing that the natural distinction of the races, which "no legislature, no social customs, can efface renders a promiscuous intermingling in the public schools disadvantageous both to them and to the whites." Separate schools remained in Boston until the Massachusetts legislature in 1855 enacted a law providing that in determining the qualifications of students to be admitted to any public school no distinction should be made on account of the race, color, or religious opinion of the applicant.

Meanwhile, in the Southern states, where the vast majority of the Negroes lived, there were no concessions suggesting equal treatment, even among the most liberal elements. One group that would doubtless have regarded itself as liberal on the race question advocated the deportation of Negroes to Africa, especially those who had become free. Since free Negroes "neither enjoyed the immunities of freemen, nor were they subject to the incapacities of slaves," their condition and "unconquerable prejudices" prevented amalgamation with whites, one colonization leader argued. There was, therefore, a "peculiar moral fitness" in restoring them to "the land of their fathers." Men like Henry Clay, Judge Bushrod Washington, and President James Monroe thought that separation—expatriation—was the best thing for Negroes who were or who would become free.[5]

While the colonization scheme was primarily for Negroes who were already free, it won, for a time, a considerable number of sincere enemies of slavery. From the beginning Negroes were bitterly opposed to it, and only infrequently did certain Negro leaders, such Dr. Martin Delany and the Reverend Henry M. Turner, support the idea. Colonization, however, retained considerable support in the most responsible quarters. As late as the Civil War, President Lincoln urged Congress to adopt a plan to colonize Negroes, as the only workable solution to the race problem in the United States. Whether the advocates of colonization wanted merely to prevent the contamination of slavery by free Negroes or whether they actually regarded it as the just and honorable thing to do, they represented an important element in the population that rejected the idea of the Negro's assimilation into the main stream of American life.

Thus, within fifty years after the Declaration of Independence was written, the institution of slavery, which received only a temporary reversal during the Revolutionary era, contributed greatly to the emergence of the two worlds of race in the United States. The natural rights philosophy appeared to have little effect on those who became committed, more and more, to seeking a rationalization for slavery. The search was apparently so successful that even in areas where slavery was declining, the support for maintaining two worlds of race was strong. Since the Negro church and school emerged in Northern communities where slavery was dying, it may be said that the free society believed almost as strongly in racial separation as it did in racial freedom.

[5] P. J. Staudenraus, *The African Colonization Movement, 1816–1865* (New York: Columbia University Press, 1961), pp. 22–32.

II

The generation preceding the outbreak of the Civil War witnessed the development of a set of defenses of slavery that became the basis for much of the racist doctrine to which some Americans have subscribed from then to the present time. The idea of the inferiority of the Negro enjoyed wide acceptance among Southerners of all classes and among many Northerners. It was an important ingredient in the theory of society promulgated by Southern thinkers and leaders. It was organized into a body of systematic thought by the scientists and social scientists of the South, out of which emerged a doctrine of racial superiority that justified any kind of control over the slave. In 1826 Dr. Thomas Cooper said that he had not the slightest doubt that Negroes were an "inferior variety of the human species; and not capable of the same improvement as the whites." Dr. S. C. Cartwright of the University of Louisiana insisted that the capacities of the Negro adult for learning were equal to those of a white infant; and the Negro could properly perform certain physiological functions only when under the control of white men. Because of the Negro's inferiority, liberty and republican institutions were not only unsuited to his temperament, but actually inimical to his well-being and happiness.

Like racists in other parts of the world, Southerners sought support for their ideology by developing a common bond with the less privileged. The obvious basis was race; and outside the white race there was to be found no favor from God, no honor or respect from man. By the time that Europeans were reading Gobineau's *Inequality of Races,* Southerners were reading Cartwright's *Slavery in the Light of Ethnology.* In admitting all whites into the pseudonobility of race, Cartwright won their enthusiastic support in the struggle to preserve the integrity and honor of *the* race. Professor Thomas R. Dew of the College of William and Mary comforted the lower-class whites by indicating that they could identify with the most privileged and affluent of the community. In the South, he said, "no white man feels such inferiority of rank as to be unworthy of association with those around him. Color alone is here the badge of distinction, the true mark of aristocracy, and all who are white are equal in spite of the variety of occupation."[6]

Many Northerners were not without their own racist views and policies in the turbulent decades before the Civil War. Some, as Professor Louis Filler has observed, displayed a hatred of Negroes that gave them a sense of superiority and an outlet for their frustrations. Others cared nothing one way or the other about Negroes and demanded only that they be kept separate.[7] Even some of the abolitionists themselves were ambivalent on the question of Negro equality. More than one antislavery society was agitated by the suggestion that

[6] John Hope Franklin, *The Militant South, 1800–1861* (Cambridge, Mass.: Harvard University Press, 1956), pp. 83–86.

[7] Louis Filler, *The Crusade Against Slavery, 1830–1860* (New York: Harper & Row, 1960), pp. 142–145.

Negroes be invited to join. Some members thought it reasonable for them to attend, but not to be put on an "equality with ourselves." The New York abolitionist, Lewis Tappan, admitted "that when the subject of acting out our profound principles in treating men irrespective of color is discussed heat is always produced."[8]

In the final years before the beginning of the Civil War, the view that the Negro was different, even inferior, was widely held in the United States. Leaders in both major parties subscribed to the view, while the more extreme racists deplored any suggestion that the Negro could ever prosper as a free man. At Peoria, Illinois, in October 1854, Abraham Lincoln asked what stand the opponents of slavery should take regarding Negroes. "Free them, and make them politically and socially, our equals? My own feelings will not admit of this; and if mine would, we well know that those of the great mass of white people will not. Whether this feeling accords with justice and sound judgment, is not the sole question, if indeed, it is any part of it. A universal feeling, whether well or ill founded, cannot be safely disregarded. We cannot, then, make them equals."

The Lincoln statement was forthright, and it doubtless represented the views of most Americans in the 1850's. Most of those who heard him or read his speech were of the same opinion as he. In later years, the Peoria pronouncement would be used by those who sought to detract from Lincoln's reputation as a champion of the rights of the Negro. In 1964, the White Citizens' Councils reprinted portions of the speech in large advertisements in the daily press and insisted that Lincoln shared their views on the desirability of maintaining two distinct worlds of race.

Lincoln could not have overcome the nation's strong predisposition toward racial separation if he had tried. And he did not try very hard. When he called for the enlistment of Negro troops, after issuing the Emancipation Proclamation, he was content not only to set Negroes apart in a unit called "U. S. Colored Troops," but also to have Negro privates receive $10 per month including clothing, while whites of the same rank received $13 per month plus clothing. Only the stubborn refusal of many Negro troops to accept discriminatory pay finally forced Congress to equalize compensation for white and Negro soldiers.[9] The fight for union that became also a fight for freedom never became a fight for equality or for the creation of one racial world.

The Lincoln and Johnson plans for settling the problems of peace and freedom never seriously touched on the concomitant problem of equality. To be sure, in 1864 President Lincoln privately raised with the governor of Louisiana the question of the franchise for a limited number of Negroes, but when the governor ignored the question the President let the matter drop.

[8] Leon F. Litwack, *North of Slavery; The Negro in the Free States, 1790–1860* (Chicago: University of Chicago Press, 1961), pp. 216–217.

[9] Benjamin Quarles, *The Negro in the Civil War* (Boston: Little, Brown, 1953), p. 200.

Johnson raised a similar question in 1866, but he admitted that it was merely to frustrate the design of radical reformers who sought a wider franchise for Negroes. During the two years following Appomattox Southern leaders gave not the slightest consideration to permitting any Negroes, regardless of their service to the Union or their education or their property, to share in the political life of their communities. Not only did every Southern state refuse to permit Negroes to vote, but they also refused to provide Negroes with any of the educational opportunities that they were providing for the whites.

The early practice of political disfranchisement and of exclusion from public educational facilities helped to determine subsequent policies that the South adopted regarding Negroes. While a few leaders raised their voices against these policies and practices, it was Negroes themselves who made the most eloquent attacks on such discriminations. As early as May 1865, a group of North Carolina Negroes told President Johnson that some of them had been soldiers and were doing everything possible to learn how to discharge the higher duties of citizenship. "It seems to us that men who are willing on the field of battle to carry the muskets of the Republic, in the days of peace ought to be permitted to carry the ballots; and certainly we cannot understand the justice of denying the elective franchise to men who have been fighting *for* the country, while it is freely given to men who have just returned from *four* years fighting against it." Such pleas fell on deaf ears, however; and it was not until 1867, when Congress was sufficiently outraged by the inhuman black codes, widespread discriminations in the South, and unspeakable forms of violence against Negroes, that new federal legislation sought to correct the evils of the first period of Reconstruction.

The period that we know as Radical Reconstruction had no significant or permanent effect on the status of the Negro in American life. For a period of time, varying from one year to fifteen or twenty years, some Negroes enjoyed the privileges of voting. They gained political ascendancy in a very few communities only temporarily, and they never even began to achieve the status of a ruling class. They made no meaningful steps toward economic independence or even stability; and in no time at all, because of the pressures of the local community and the neglect of the federal government, they were brought under the complete economic subservience of the old ruling class. Organizations such as the Ku Klux Klan were committed to violent action to keep Negroes "in their place" and, having gained respectability through sponsorship by Confederate generals and the like, they proceeded to wreak havoc in the name of white supremacy and protection of white womanhood.[10]

Meanwhile, various forms of segregation and discrimination, developed in the years before the Civil War in order to degrade the half million free Ne-

[10] John Hope Franklin, *Reconstruction After the Civil War* (Chicago: University of Chicago Press, 1961), pp. 154–158.

groes in the United States, were now applied to the four million Negroes who had become free in 1865. Already the churches and the military were completely segregated. For the most part the schools, even in the North, were separate. In the South segregated schools persisted, even in the places where the radicals made a half-hearted attempt to desegregate them. In 1875 Congress enacted a Civil Rights Act to guarantee the enjoyment of equal rights in carriers and all places of public accommodation and amusement. Even before it became law Northern philanthropists succeeded in forcing the deletion of the provision calling for desegregated schools. Soon, because of the massive resistance in the North as well as in the South and the indifferent manner in which the federal government enforced the law, it soon became a dead letter everywhere. When it was declared unconstitutional by the Supreme Court in 1883, there was universal rejoicing, except among the Negroes, one of whom declared that they had been "baptized in ice water."

Neither the Civil War nor the era of Reconstruction made any significant step toward the permanent elimination of racial barriers. The radicals of the post-Civil War years came no closer to the creation of one racial world than the patriots of the Revolutionary years. When Negroes were, for the first time, enrolled in the standing army of the United States, they were placed in separate Negro units. Most of the liberals of the Reconstruction era called for and worked for separate schools for Negroes. Nowhere was there any extensive effort to involve Negroes in the churches and other social institutions of the dominant group. Whatever remained of the old abolitionist fervor, which can hardly be described as unequivocal on the question of true racial equality, was rapidly disappearing. In its place were the sentiments of the business men who wanted peace at any price. Those having common railroad interests or crop-marketing interests or investment interests could and did extend their hands across sectional lines and joined in the task of working together for the common good. In such an atmosphere the practice was to accept the realities of two separate worlds of race. Some even subscribed to the view that there were significant economic advantages in maintaining the two worlds of race.

III

The post-Reconstruction years witnessed a steady deterioration in the status of Negro Americans. These were the years that Professor Rayford Logan has called the "nadir" of the Negro in American life and thought. They were the years when Americans, weary of the crusade that had, for the most part, ended with the outbreak of the Civil War, displayed almost no interest in helping the Negro to achieve equality. The social Darwinists decried the very notion of equality for Negroes, arguing that the lowly place they occupied was natural and normal. The leading literary journals vied with each other in describing Negroes as lazy, idle, improvident, immoral, and criminal.[11] Thomas Dixon's novels, *The Klansman* and *The Leopard's Spots,* and D. W. Griffith's motion picture, "The Birth of A Nation," helped to give Americans a view of the Negro's role in American history that "proved" that he was unfit for citizenship, to say nothing of equality. The dictum of William Graham Sumner and his followers that "stateways cannot change folkways" convinced many Americans that legislating equality and creating one great society where race was irrelevant was out of the question.

But many Americans believed that they *could* legislate inequality; and they proceeded to do precisely that. Beginning in 1890, one Southern state after another revised the suffrage provisions of its constitution in a manner that made it virtually impossible for Negroes to qualify to vote. The new literacy and "understanding" provisions permitted local registrars to disqualify Negroes while permitting white citizens to qualify. Several states, including Louisiana, North Carolina, and Oklahoma, inserted "grandfather clauses" in their constitutions in order to permit persons, who could not otherwise qualify, to vote if their fathers or grandfathers could vote in 1866. (This was such a flagrant discrimination against Negroes, whose ancestors could not vote in 1866, that the United States Supreme Court in 1915 declared the "grandfather clause" unconstitutional.) Then came the Democratic white primary in 1900 that made it impossible for Negroes to participate in local elections in the South, where, by this time, only the Democratic party had any appreciable strength. (After more than a generation of assaults on it, the white primary was finally declared unconstitutional in 1944.)

Inequality was legislated in still another way. Beginning in the 1880's, many states, especially but not exclusively in the South, enacted statutes designed to separate the races. After the Civil Rights Act was declared unconstitutional in 1883 state legislatures were emboldened to enact numerous segregation statutes. When the United States Supreme Court, in the case of Plessy *v.* Ferguson, set forth the "separate but equal" doctrine in 1896, the decision provided a new stimulus for laws to separate the races and, of course, to discriminate against Negroes. In time, Negroes and whites were separated in the use of schools, churches, cemeteries, drinking fountains, restaurants, and all places of public accommodation and amusement. One state enacted a law providing for the separate warehousing of books used by white and Negro children. Another required the telephone company to provide separate telephone booths for white and Negro customers. In most communities housing was racially separated by law or practice.[12]

Where there was no legislation requiring segregation, local practices filled the void. Contradictions and inconsistencies seemed not to disturb those who

[11] Rayford W. Logan, *The Negro in American Life and Thought: The Nadir, 1877–1901* (Princeton, N.J.: Van Nostrand, 1954), pp. 239–274.

[12] John Hope Franklin, "History of Racial Segregation in the United States," *Annals of the Academy of Political and Social Science,* Vol. 304 (March 1956), pp. 1–9.

sought to maintain racial distinctions at all costs. It mattered not that one drive-in snack bar served Negroes only on the inside, while its competitor across the street served Negroes only on the outside. Both were committed to making racial distinctions; and in communities where practices and mores had the force of law, the distinction was everything. Such practices were greatly strengthened when, in 1913, the federal government adopted policies that segregated the races in its offices as well as in its eating and rest-room facilities.

By the time of World War I, Negroes and whites in the South and in parts of the North lived in separate worlds, and the apparatus for keeping the worlds separate was elaborate and complex. Negroes were segregated by law in the public schools of the Southern states, while those in the Northern ghettos were sent to predominantly Negro schools, except where their numbers were insufficient. Scores of Negro newspapers sprang up to provide news of Negroes that the white press consistently ignored. Negroes were as unwanted in the white churches as they had been in the late eighteenth century; and Negro churches of virtually every denomination were the answer for a people who had accepted the white man's religion even as the white man rejected his religious fellowship.

Taking note of the fact that they had been omitted from any serious consideration by the white historians, Negroes began in earnest to write the history of their own experiences as Americans. There had been Negro historians before the Civil War, but none of them had challenged the white historians' efforts to relegate Negroes to a separate, degraded world. In 1882, however, George Washington Williams published his *History of the Negro Race in America* in order to "give the world more correct ideas about the colored people." He wrote, he said, not "as a partisan apologist, but from a love for the truth of history."[13] Soon there were other historical works by Negroes describing their progress and their contributions and arguing that they deserved to be received into the full fellowship of American citizens.

It was in these post-Reconstruction years that some of the most vigorous efforts were made to destroy the two worlds of race. The desperate pleas of Negro historians were merely the more articulate attempts of Negroes to gain complete acceptance in American life. Scores of Negro organizations joined in the struggle to gain protection and recognition of their rights and to eliminate the more sordid practices that characterized the treatment of the Negro world by the white world. Unhappily, the small number of whites who were committed to racial equality dwindled in the post-Reconstruction years, while government at every level showed no interest in eliminating racial separatism. It seemed that Negro voices were indeed crying in the wilderness, but they carried on their attempts to be heard. In 1890 Negroes from twenty-one

[13] George W. Williams, *History of the Negro Race in America from 1619 to 1880* (New York: Putnam's, 1882), p. x.

states and the District of Columbia met in Chicago and organized the Afro-American League of the United States. They called for more equitable distribution of school funds, fair and impartial trial for accused Negroes, resistance "by all legal and reasonable means" to mob and lynch law, and enjoyment of the franchise by all qualified voters. When a group of young Negro intellectuals, led by W. E. B. Du Bois, met at Niagara Falls, Ontario, in 1905, they made a similar call as they launched their Niagara Movement.

However eloquent their pleas, Negroes alone could make no successful assault on the two worlds of race. They needed help—a great deal of help. It was the bloody race riots in the early years of the twentieth century that shocked civic minded and socially conscious whites into answering the Negro's pleas for support. Some whites began to take the view that the existence of two societies whose distinction was based solely on race was inimical to the best interests of the entire nation. Soon, they were taking the initiative and in 1909 organized the National Association for the Advancement of Colored People. They assisted the following year in establishing the National Urban League. White attorneys began to stand with Negroes before the United States Supreme Court to challenge the "grandfather clause," local segregation ordinances, and flagrant miscarriages of justice in which Negroes were the victims. The patterns of attack developed during these years were to become invaluable later. Legal action was soon supplemented by picketing, demonstrating, and boycotting, with telling effect particularly in selected Northern communities.[14]

IV

The two world wars had a profound effect on the status of Negroes in the United States and did much to mount the attack on the two worlds of race. The decade of World War I witnessed a very significant migration of Negroes. They went in large numbers—perhaps a half million—from the rural areas of the South to the towns and cities of the South and North. They were especially attracted to the industrial centers of the North. By the thousands they poured into Pittsburgh, Cleveland, and Chicago. Although many were unable to secure employment, others were successful and achieved a standard of living they could not have imagined only a few years earlier. Northern communities were not altogether friendly and hospitable to the newcomers, but the opportunities for education and the enjoyment of political self-respect were the greatest they had ever seen. Many of them felt that they were entirely justified in their renewed hope that the war would bring about a complete merger of the two worlds of race.

Those who held such high hopes, however, were naive in the extreme. Already the Ku Klux Klan was being revived—this time in the North as well as in the South. Its leaders were determined to develop a broad program to

[14] Franklin, *From Slavery to Freedom,* pp. 437–443.

unite "native-born white Christians for concerted action in the preservation of American institutions and the supremacy of the white race." By the time that the war was over, the Klan was in a position to make capital of the racial animosities that had developed during the conflict itself. Racial conflicts had broken out in many places during the war; and before the conference at Versailles was over race riots in the United States had brought about what can accurately be described as the "long, hot summer" of 1919.

If anything, the military operations which aimed to save the world for democracy merely fixed more permanently the racial separation in the United States. Negro soldiers not only constituted entirely separate fighting units in the United States Army, but, once overseas, were assigned to fighting units with the French Army. Negroes who sought service with the United States Marines or the Air Force were rejected, while the Navy relegated them to menial duties. The reaction of many Negroes was bitter, but most of the leaders, including Du Bois, counseled patience and loyalty. They continued to hope that their show of patriotism would win for them a secure place of acceptance as Americans.

Few Negro Americans could have anticipated the wholesale rejection they experienced at the conclusion of World War I. Returning Negro soldiers were lynched by hanging and burning, even while still in their military uniforms. The Klan warned Negroes that they must respect the rights of the white race "in whose country they are permitted to reside." Racial conflicts swept the country, and neither federal nor state governments seemed interested in effective intervention. The worlds of race were growing further apart in the postwar decade. Nothing indicated this more clearly than the growth of the Universal Negro Improvement Association, led by Marcus Garvey. From a mere handful of members at the end of the war, the Garvey movement rapidly became the largest secular Negro group ever organized in the United States. Although few Negroes were interested in settling in Africa—the expressed aim of Garvey—they joined the movement by the hundreds of thousands to indicate their resentment of the racial duality that seemed to them to be the central feature of the American social order.[15]

More realisic and hardheaded were the Negroes who were more determined than ever to engage in the most desperate fight of their lives to destroy racism in the United States. As the editor of the *Crisis* said in 1919, "We return from fighting. We return fighting. Make way for Democracy! We saved it in France, and by the Great Jehovah, we will save it in the U.S.A., or know the reason why." This was the spirit of what Alain Locke called "The New Negro." He fought the Democratic white primary, made war on the whites who consigned him to the ghetto, attacked racial discrimination in employment, and pressed for legislation to protect his rights. If he was seldom successful during the

[15] Edmund David Cronon, *Black Moses, The Story of Marcus Garvey and the Universal Negro Improvement Association* (Madison, Wis.: University of Wisconsin Press, 1955), pp. 202–206.

postwar decade and the depression, he made it quite clear that he was unalterably opposed to the un-American character of the two worlds of race.

Hope for a new assault on racism was kindled by some of the New Deal policies of Franklin D. Roosevelt. As members of the economically disadvantaged group, Negroes benefited from relief and recovery legislation. Most of it, however, recognized the existence of the two worlds of race and accommodated itself to it. Frequently bread lines and soup kitchens were separated on the basis of race. There was segregation in the employment services, while many new agencies recognized and bowed to Jim Crow. Whenever agencies, such as the Farm Security Administration, fought segregation and sought to deal with people on the basis of their needs rather than race they came under the withering fire of the racist critics and seldom escaped alive. Winds of change, however slight, were discernible, and nowhere was this in greater evidence than in the new labor unions. Groups like the Congress of Industrial Organizations, encouraged by the support of the Wagner Labor Relations Act, began to look at manpower resources as a whole and to attack the old racial policies that viewed labor in terms of race.

As World War II approached, Negroes schooled in the experiences of the nineteen-twenties and thirties were unwilling to see the fight against Nazism carried on in the context of an American racist ideology. Some white Americans were likewise uncomfortable in the role of freeing Europe of a racism which still permeated the United States; but it was the Negroes who dramatized American inconsistency by demanding an end to discrimination in employment in defense industries. By threatening to march on Washington in 1941 they forced the President to issue an order forbidding such discrimination. The opposition was loud and strong. Some state governors denounced the order, and some manufacturers skillfully evaded it. But it was a significant step toward the elimination of the two worlds.

During World War II the assault on racism continued. Negroes, more than a million of whom were enlisted in the armed services, bitterly fought discrimination and segregation. The armed services were, for the most part, two quite distinct racial worlds. Some Negro units had white officers, and much of the officer training was desegregated. But it was not until the final months of the war that a deliberate experiment was undertaken to involve Negro and white enlisted men in the same fighting unit. With the success of the experiment and with the warm glow of victory over Nazism as a backdrop, there was greater inclination to recognize the absurdity of maintaining a racially separate military force to protect the freedoms of the country.[16]

During the war there began the greatest migration in the history of Negro Americans. Hundreds of thousands left the South for the industrial centers of the North and West. In those places they met hostility, but they also secured employment in aviation plants, automobile factories, steel mills, and

[16] Lee Nichols, *Breakthrough on the Color Front* (New York: Random House, 1954), pp. 221–226.

numerous other industries. Their difficulties persisted as they faced problems of housing and adjustment. But they continued to move out of the South in such large numbers that by 1965 one third of the twenty million Negroes in the United States lived in twelve metropolitan centers of the North and West. The ramifications of such large-scale migration were numerous. The concentration of Negroes in communities where they suffered no political disabilities placed in their hands an enormous amount of political power. Consequently, some of them went to the legislatures, to Congress, and to positions on the judiciary. In turn, this won for them political respect as well as legislation that greatly strengthened their position as citizens.

V

Following World War II there was a marked acceleration in the war against the two worlds of race in the United States. In 1944 the Supreme Court ruled against segregation in interstate transportation, and three years later it wrote the final chapter in the war against the Democratic white primary. In 1947 the President's Committee on Civil Rights called for the "elimination of segregation, based on race, color, creed, or national origin, from American life."[17] In the following year President Truman asked Congress to establish a permanent Fair Employment Practices Commission. At the same time he took steps to eliminate segregation in the armed services. These moves on the part of the judicial and executive branches of the federal government by no means destroyed the two worlds of race, but they created a more healthy climate in which the government and others could launch an attack on racial separatism.

The attack was greatly strengthened by the new position of world leadership that the United States assumed at the close of the war. Critics of the United States were quick to point to the inconsistencies of an American position that spoke against racism abroad and countenanced it at home. New nations, brown and black, seemed reluctant to follow the lead of a country that adhered to its policy of maintaining two worlds of race—the one identified with the old colonial ruling powers and the other with the colonies now emerging as independent nations. Responsible leaders in the United States saw the weakness of their position, and some of them made new moves to repair it.

Civic and religious groups, some labor organizations, and many individuals from the white community began to join in the effort to destroy segregation and discrimination in American life. There was no danger, after World War II, that Negroes would ever again stand alone in their fight. The older interracial organizations continued, but they were joined by new ones. In addition to the numerous groups that included racial equality in their over-all programs, there were others that made the creation of one racial world their principal objective. Among them were the Congress of Racial Equality, the

[17] *To Secure These Rights, The Report of the President's Committee on Civil Rights* (New York, 1947), p. 166.

Southern Christian Leadership Conference, and the Student Non-Violent Coordinating Committee. Those in existence in the 1950's supported the court action that brought about the decision against segregated schools. The more recent ones have taken the lead in pressing for new legislation and in developing new techniques to be used in the war on segregation.

VI

The most powerful direct force in the maintenance of the two worlds of race has been the state and its political subdivisions. In states and communities where racial separation and discrimination are basic to the way of life, the elected officials invariably pledge themselves to the perpetuation of the duality. Indeed, candidates frequently vie with one another in their effort to occupy the most extreme segregationist position possible on the race question. Appointed officials, including the constabulary and, not infrequently, the teachers and school administrators, become auxiliary guardians of the system of racial separation. In such communities Negroes occupy no policy-making positions, exercise no influence over the determination of policy, and are seldom even on the police force. State and local resources, including tax funds, are at the disposal of those who guard the system of segregation and discrimination; and such funds are used to enforce customs as well as laws and to disseminate information in support of the system.

The white community itself acts as a guardian of the segregated system. Schooled in the specious arguments that assert the supremacy of the white race and fearful that a destruction of the system would be harmful to their own position, they not only "go along" with it but, in many cases, enthusiastically support it. Community sanctions are so powerful, moreover, that the independent citizen who would defy the established order would find himself not only ostracized but, worse, the target of economic and political reprisals.

Within the community many self-appointed guardians of white supremacy have emerged at various times. After the Civil War and after World War I it was the Ku Klux Klan, which has shown surprising strength in recent years. After the desegregation decision of the Supreme Court in 1954 it was the White Citizens' Council, which one Southern editor has called the "uptown Ku Klux Klan." From time to time since 1865, it has been the political demagogue, who has not only made capital by urging his election as a sure way to maintain the system but has also encouraged the less responsible elements of the community to take the law into their own hands.

Violence, so much a part of American history and particularly of Southern history, has been an important factor in maintaining the two worlds of race. Intimidation, terror, lynchings, and riots have, in succession, been the handmaiden of political entities whose officials have been unwilling or unable to put an end to it. Violence drove Negroes from the polls in the 1870's and has kept them away in droves since that time. Lynchings, the spectacular rope and faggot kind or the quiet kind of merely "doing away" with some insubordinate Negro, have served their special purpose in terrorizing whole communities of Negroes. Riots, confined to no section of the country, have demonstrated how explosive the racial situation can be in urban communities burdened with the strain of racial strife.

The heavy hand of history has been a powerful force in the maintenance of a segregated society and, conversely, in the resistance to change. Americans, especially Southerners whose devotion to the past is unmatched by that of any others, have summoned history to support their arguments that age-old practices and institutions cannot be changed overnight, that social practices cannot be changed by legislation. Southerners have argued that desegregation would break down long-established customs and bring instability to a social order that, if left alone, would have no serious racial or social disorders. After all, Southern whites "know" Negroes; and their knowledge has come from many generations of intimate association and observation, they insist.

White Southerners have also summoned history to support them in their resistance to federal legislation designed to secure the civil rights of Negroes. At every level—in local groups, state governments, and in Congress—white Southerners have asserted that federal civil rights legislation is an attempt to turn back the clock to the Reconstruction era, when federal intervention, they claim, imposed a harsh and unjust peace.[18] To make effective their argument, they use such emotion-laden phrases as "military occupation," "Negro rule," and "black-out of honest government." Americans other than Southerners have been frightened by the Southerners' claim that civil rights for Negroes would cause a return to the "evils" of Reconstruction. Insecure in their own knowledge of history, they have accepted the erroneous assertions about the "disaster" of radical rule after the Civil War and the vengeful punishment meted out to the South by the Negro and his white allies. Regardless of the merits of these arguments that seem specious on the face of them—to say nothing of their historical inaccuracy—they have served as effective brakes on the drive to destroy the two worlds of race.

One suspects, however, that racial bigotry has become more expensive in recent years. It is not so easy now as it once was to make political capital out of the race problem, even in the deep South. Local citizens—farmers, laborers, manufacturers—have become a bit weary of the promises of the demagogue that he will preserve the integrity of the races if he is, at the same time, unable to persuade investors to build factories and bring capital to their communities. Some Southerners, dependent on tourists, are not certain that their vaunted racial pride is so dear, if it keeps visitors away and brings depression to their economy. The cities that see themselves bypassed by a prospective manufacturer because of their reputation in the field of race relations might have some sober second thoughts about the importance of maintaining their

18 John Hope Franklin, "As For Our History," in Charles G. Sellers (ed.), *The Southerner as American* (Chapel Hill, N. C.: University of North Carolina Press, 1960), pp. 1–18.

two worlds. In a word, the economics of segregation and discrimination is forcing, in some quarters, a reconsideration of the problem.

It must be added that the existence of the two worlds of race has created forces that cause some Negroes to seek its perpetuation. Some Negro institutions, the product of a dual society, have vested interests in the perpetuation of that society. And Negroes who fear the destruction of their own institutions by desegregation are encouraged by white racists to fight for their maintenance. Even where Negroes have a desire to maintain their institutions because of their honest commitment to the merits of cultural pluralism, the desire becomes a strident struggle for survival in the context of racist forces that seek with a vengeance to destroy such institutions. The firing of a few hundred Negro school teachers by a zealous, racially-oriented school board forces some second thoughts on the part of the Negroes regarding the merits of desegregation.

VII

The drive to destroy the two worlds of race has reached a new, dramatic, and somewhat explosive stage in recent years. The forces arrayed in behalf of maintaining these two worlds have been subjected to ceaseless and powerful attacks by the increasing numbers committed to the elimination of racism in American life. Through techniques of demonstrating, picketing, sitting-in, and boycotting they have not only harrassed their foes but marshaled their forces. Realizing that another ingredient was needed, they have pressed for new and better laws and the active support of government. At the local and state levels they began to secure legislation in the 1940's to guarantee the civil rights of all, eliminate discrimination in employment, and achieve decent public and private housing for all.

While it is not possible to measure the influence of public opinion in the drive for equality, it can hardly be denied that over the past five or six years public opinion has shown a marked shift toward vigorous support of the civil rights movement. This can be seen in the manner in which the mass-circulation magazines as well as influential newspapers, even in the South, have stepped up their support of specific measures that have as their objective the elimination of at least the worst features of racism. The discussion of the problem of race over radio and television and the use of these media in reporting newsworthy and dramatic events in the world of race undoubtedly have had some impact. If such activities have not brought about the enactment of civil rights legislation, they have doubtless stimulated the public discussion that culminated in such legislation.

The models of city ordinances and state laws and the increased political influence of civil rights advocates stimulated new action on the federal level. Civil rights acts were passed in 1957, 1960, and 1964—after almost complete federal inactivity in this sphere for more than three quarters of a century. Strong leadership on the part of the executive and favorable judicial interpretations of old as well as new laws have made it clear that the war against the two worlds of race now enjoys the sanction of the law and its interpreters. In many respects this constitutes the most significant development in the struggle against racism in the present century.

The reading of American history over the past two centuries impresses one with the fact that ambivalence on the crucial question of equality has persisted almost from the beginning. If the term "equal rights for all" has not always meant what it appeared to mean, the inconsistencies and the paradoxes have become increasingly apparent. This is not to say that the view that "equal rights for some" has disappeared or has even ceased to be a threat to the concept of real equality. It is to say, however, that the voices supporting inequality, while no less strident, have been significantly weakened by the very force of the numbers and elements now seeking to eliminate the two worlds of race.

Political Philosophy

THOMAS PAINE

•

The American Crisis, I[1]

These are the times that try men's souls: The summer soldier and the sunshine patriot will, in this crisis, shrink from the service of his country; but he that stands it NOW, deserves the love and thanks of man and woman. Tyranny, like hell, is not easily conquered; yet we have this consolation with us, that the harder the conflict, the more glorious the triumph. What we obtain too cheap, we esteem too lightly:—'Tis dearness only that gives everything its value. Heaven knows how to put a proper price upon its goods; and it would be strange indeed if so celestial an article as FREEDOM should not be highly rated. Britain, with an army to enforce her tyranny, has declared that she has a right (*not only to* TAX) but "to BIND us in ALL CASES WHATSOEVER"; and if being *bound in that manner* is not slavery, then is there not such a thing as slavery upon earth. Even the expression is impious; for so unlimited a power can belong only to GOD.

Whether the independence of the continent was declared too soon, or delayed too long, I will not now enter into as an argument; my own simple opinion is, that had it been eight months earlier, it would have been much better. We did not make a proper use of last winter; neither could we, while we were in a dependent state. However, the fault, if it were one, was all our own; we have none to blame but ourselves. But no great deal is lost yet. All that Howe has been doing for this month past is rather a ravage than a conquest, which the spirit of the Jerseys a year ago would have quickly repulsed, and which time and a little resolution will soon recover.

I have as little superstition in me as any man living; but my secret opinion has ever been, and still is, that God Almighty will not give up a people to military destruction, or leave them unsupportedly to perish, who have so earnestly and so repeatedly sought to avoid the calamities of war, by every decent method which wisdom could invent. Neither have I so much of the infidel in me as to suppose that he has relinquished the government of the world, and given us up to the care of devils; and as I do not, I cannot see on what grounds the king of Britain can look up to Heaven for help against us; a common murderer, a highwayman, or a house-breaker, has as good a pretense as he.

[1] First published December 19, 1776.

'Tis surprising to see how rapidly a panic will sometimes run through a country. All nations and ages have been subject to them: Britain has trembled like an ague at the report of a French fleet of flat-bottomed boats; and in the fourteenth century the whole English army, after ravaging the kingdom of France, was driven back like men petrified with fear; and this brave exploit was performed by a few broken forces collected and headed by a woman, Joan of Arc. Would that heaven might inspire some Jersey maid to spirit up her countrymen, and save her fair fellow sufferers from ravage and ravishment! Yet panics, in some cases, have their uses; they produce as much good as hurt. Their duration is always short; the mind soon grows through them, and acquires a firmer habit than before. But their peculiar advantage is, that they are the touchstones of sincerity and hypocrisy, and bring things and men to light, which might otherwise have lain forever undiscovered. In fact, they have the same effect on secret traitors which an imaginary apparition would have upon a private murderer. They sift out the hidden thoughts of man, and hold them up in public to the world. Many a disguised tory has lately shown his head, that shall penitentially solemnize with curses the day on which Howe arrived upon the Delaware.

As I was with the troops at Fort Lee, and marched with them to the edge of Pennsylvania, I am well acquainted with many circumstances which those who live at a distance know but little or nothing of. Our situation there was exceedingly cramped, the place being a narrow neck of land between the North River and Hackensack. Our force was inconsiderable, being not one-fourth so great as Howe could bring against us. We had no army at hand to have relieved the garrison, had we shut ourselves up and stood on our defence. Our ammunition, light artillery, and the best part of our stores, had been removed, on the apprehension that Howe would endeavor to penetrate the Jerseys, in which case Fort Lee could be of no use to us; for it must occur to every thinking man, whether in the army or not, that these kind of field forts are only for temporary purposes, and last in use no longer than the enemy directs his force against the particular object which such forts are raised to defend. Such was our situation and condition at Fort Lee on the morning of the 20th of November, when an officer arrived with information that the enemy with 200 boats had landed about seven miles above. Major General Green, who commanded the garrison, immediately ordered them under arms, and sent express to General Washington at the town of Hackensack, distant by the way of the ferry, six miles. Our first object was to secure the bridge over the Hackensack, which laid up the river between the enemy and us, about six miles from us, three from them. General Washington arrived in about three-quarters of an hour, and marched at the head of the troops towards the bridge, which place I expected we should have a brush for; however, they did not choose to dispute it with us, and the greatest part of our troops went over the bridge, the rest over the ferry except some which passed at a mill on a small creek between the bridge and the ferry, and made their way through some marshy grounds up to the town of Hackensack, and there passed the river. We brought off as much baggage as the wagons could contain, the rest was lost. The simple object was to bring off the garrison, and march them on till they could be strengthened by the Jersey or Pennsylvania militia, so as to be enabled to make a stand. We staid four days at Newark, collected our outposts with some of the Jersey militia, and marched out twice to meet the enemy on being informed that they were advancing, though our numbers were greatly inferior to theirs. Howe, in my opinion, committed a great error in generalship in not throwing a body of forces off from Staten Island through Amboy, by which means he might have seized all our stores at Brunswick and intercepted our march into Pennsylvania; but if we believe the power of hell to be limited, we must likewise believe that their agents are under some providential control.

I shall not now attempt to give all the particulars of our retreat to the Delaware; suffice it for the present to say that both officers and men, though greatly harassed and fatigued, frequently without rest, covering, or provision, the inevitable consequences of a long retreat, bore it with a manly and martial spirit. All their wishes centered in one; which was, that the country would turn out and help them to drive the enemy back. Voltaire has remarked that King William never appeared to full advantage but in difficulties and in action; the same remark may be made on General Washington, for the character fits him. There is a natural firmness in some minds which cannot be unlocked by trifles, but which, when unlocked, discovers a cabinet of fortitude; and I reckon it among those kinds of public blessings, which we do not immediately see, that GOD hath blessed him with uninterrupted health, and given him a mind that can even flourish upon care.

I shall conclude this paper with some miscellaneous remarks on the state of our affairs; and shall begin with asking the following question, Why is it that the enemy have left the New England provinces, and made these middle ones the seat of war. The answer is easy: New England is not infested with tories, and we are. I have been tender in raising the cry against these men, and used numberless arguments to show them their danger, but it will not do to sacrifice a world either to their folly or their baseness. The period is now arrived in which either they or we must change our sentiments, or one or both must fall. And what is a tory? Good GOD! What is he? I should not be afraid to go with a hundred whigs against a thousand tories, were they to attempt to get into arms. Every tory is a coward; for servile, slavish self-interested fear is the foundation of toryism; and a man under such influence, though he may be cruel, never can be brave.

But, before the line of irrecoverable separation be drawn between us, let us reason the matter together: Your conduct is an invitation to the enemy, yet not one in a thousand of you has heart enough to join him. Howe is as much deceived by you as the American cause is injured by you. He expects you will all take up arms and flock to his standard with muskets on your shoulders. Your opinions are of no use to him unless you support him personally, for 'tis soldiers, and not tories, that he wants.

I once felt all that kind of anger, which a man ought to feel, against the mean principles that are held by the tories: A noted one, who kept a tavern at Amboy, was standing at his door, with as pretty a child in his hand, about eight or nine years old, as I ever saw, and after speaking his mind as freely as he thought was prudent, finished with this unfatherly expression, *"Well! Give me peace in my day."* Not a man lives on the continent but fully believes that a separation must some time or other finally take place, and a generous parent should have said, *"If there must be trouble, let it be in my day, that my child may have peace";* and this single reflection, well applied, is sufficient to awaken every man to duty. Not a place upon earth might be so happy as America. Her situation is remote from all the wrangling world, and she has nothing to do but to trade with them. A man can distinguish himself between temper and principle, and I am as confident as I am that GOD governs the world, that America will never be happy till she gets clear of foreign dominion. Wars, without ceasing, will break out till that period arrives, and the continent must in the end be conqueror; for though the flame of liberty may sometimes cease to shine, the coal can never expire.

America did not, nor does not want force; but she wanted a proper application of that force. Wisdom is not the purchase of a day, and it is no wonder that we should err at the first setting off. From an excess of tenderness, we were unwilling to raise an army, and trusted our cause to the temporary defence of a well-meaning militia. A summer's experience has now taught us better; yet with those troops, while they were collected, we were able to set bounds to the progress of the enemy, and thank God! they are again assembling. I always considered militia as the best troops in the world for a sudden exertion, but they will not do for a long campaign. Howe, it is probable, will make an attempt on this city; should he fail on this side of the Delaware, he is ruined. If he succeeds, our cause is not ruined. He stakes all on his side against a part on ours; admitting he succeeds, the consequences will be, that armies from both ends of the continent will march to assist their suffering friends in the middle states; for he cannot go everywhere, it is impossible. I consider Howe as the greatest enemy the Tories have; he is bringing a war into their country, which, had it not been for him and partly for themselves, they had been clear of. Should he now be expelled, I wish with all the devotion of a Christian, that the names of Whig and Tory may never more be mentioned; but should the Tories give him encouragement to come, or assistance if he come, I as sincerely wish that our next year's arms may expel them from the continent, and the Congress appropriate their possessions to the relief of those who have suffered in well-doing. A single successful battle next year will settle the whole. America could carry on a two years' war by the confiscation of the property of disaffected persons, and be made happy by their expulsion. Say not that this is revenge; call it rather the soft resentment of a suffering people, who, having no object in view but the GOOD OF ALL, have staked their OWN ALL upon a seemingly doubtful event. Yet it is folly to argue against determined hardness; eloquence may strike the ear, and the language of sorrow draw forth the tear of compassion, but nothing can reach the heart that is steeled with prejudice.

Quitting this class of men, I turn with the warm ardor of a friend to those who have nobly stood, and are yet determined to stand the matter out: I call not upon a few, but upon all: not on THIS state or THAT state, but on EVERY state: up and help us; lay your shoulders to the wheel; better have too much force than too little, when so great an object is at stake. Let it be told to the future world, that in the depth of winter, when nothing but hope and virtue could survive, that the city and the country, alarmed at one common danger, came forth to meet and to repulse it. Say not that thousands are gone, turn out your tens of thousands; throw not the burden of the day upon Providence, but *"shew your faith by your works,"* that God may bless you. It matters not where you live, or what rank of life you hold, the evil or the blessing will reach you all. The far and the near, the home counties and the back, the rich and the poor, will suffer or rejoice alike. The heart that feels not now is dead; the blood of his children will curse his cowardice who shrinks back at a time when a little might have saved the whole and made *them* happy. I love the man that can smile in trouble, that can gather strength from distress and grow brave by reflection. 'Tis the business of little minds to shrink; but he whose heart is firm, and whose conscience approves his conduct, will pursue his principles unto death. My own line of reasoning is to myself as straight and clear as a ray of light. Not all the treasures of the world, so far as I believe, could have induced me to support an offensive war, for I think it murder; but if a thief breaks into my house, burns and destroys my property, and kills or threatens to kill me or those that are in it, and to *"bind me in all cases whatsoever"* to his absolute will, am I to suffer it? What signifies it to me whether he who does it is a king or a common man; my countryman or not my countryman; whether it be done by an individual villain, or an army of them? If we reason to the root of things we shall find no difference; neither can any just cause be assigned why we should punish in the one case and pardon in the other. Let them call me rebel and welcome, I feel no concern from it; but I should suffer the misery of devils, were I to make a whore of my soul by swearing allegiance to one whose character is that of a sottish, stupid, stubborn, worthless, brutish man. I conceive likewise a horrid idea in receiving mercy from a being, who at the last day shall be shrieking to the rocks and mountains to cover him, and fleeing with terror from the orphan, the widow, and the slain of America.

There are cases which cannot be overdone by language, and this is one.

There are persons, too, who see not the full extent of the evil which threatens them; they solace themselves with hopes that the enemy, if he succeed, will be merciful. It is the madness of folly, to expect mercy from those who have refused to do justice; and even mercy, where conquest is the object, is only a trick of war. The cunning of the fox is as murderous as the violence of the wolf, and we ought to guard equally against both. Howe's first object is, partly by threats and partly by promises, to terrify or seduce the people to deliver up their arms and receive mercy. The ministry recommended the same plan to Gage, and this is what the tories call making their peace, *"a peace which passeth all understanding,"* indeed! A peace which would be the immediate forerunner of a worse ruin than any we have yet thought of. Ye men of Pennsylvania, do reason upon these things! Were the back counties to give up their arms, they would fall an easy prey to the Indians, who are all armed: this perhaps is what some tories would not be sorry for. Were the home counties to deliver up their arms, they would be exposed to the resentment of the back counties, who would then have it in their power to chastise their defection at pleasure. And were any one state to give up its arms, THAT state must be garrisoned by all Howe's army of Britons and Hessians to preserve it from the anger of the rest. Mutual fear is the principal link in the chain of mutual love, and woe be to that state that breaks the compact. Howe is mercifully inviting you to barbarous destruction, and men must be either rogues or fools that will not see it. I dwell not upon the vapors of imagination; I bring reason to your ears, and, in language as plain as ABC, hold up truth to your eyes.

I thank GOD that I fear not. I see no real cause for fear. I know our situation well, and can see the way out of it. While our army was collected, Howe dared not risk a battle; and it is no credit to him that he decamped from the White Plains, and waited a mean opportunity to ravage the defenceless Jerseys; but it is great credit to us, that with a handful of men, we sustained an orderly retreat for near an hundred miles, brought off our ammunition, all our field pieces, the greatest part of our stores, and had four rivers to pass. None can say that our retreat was precipitate; for we were near three weeks in performing it, that the country might have time to come in. Twice we marched back to meet the enemy, and remained out till dark. The sign of fear was not seen in our camp, and had not some of the cowardly and disaffected inhabitants spread false alarms through the country, the Jerseys had never been ravaged. Once more we are again collected and collecting; our new army at both ends of the continent is recruiting fast, and we shall be able to open the next campaign with sixty thousand men, well armed and clothed. This is our situation, and who will may know it. By perseverance and fortitude we have the prospect of a glorious issue; by cowardice and submission, the sad choice of a variety of evils: a ravaged country—a depopulated city—habitations without safety, and slavery without hope—our homes turned into barracks and bawdy-houses for Hessians—and a future race to provide for, whose fathers we shall doubt of. Look on this picture and weep over it! and if there yet remains one thoughtless wretch who believes it not, let him suffer it unlamented.

THOMAS JEFFERSON

•

Declaration of Independence

The unanimous declaration of the thirteen United States of America, in Congress, July 4, 1776

When, in the course of human events, it becomes necessary for one people to dissolve the political bands which have connected them with another, and to assume among the powers of the earth the separate and equal station to which the laws of nature and of nature's God entitle them, a decent respect to the opinions of mankind requires that they should declare the causes which impel them to the separation.

We hold these truths to be self-evident: That all men are created equal; that they are endowed by their Creator with certain inalienable rights; that among these are life, liberty, and the pursuit of happiness. That, to secure these rights, governments are instituted among men, deriving their just powers from the consent of the governed; that, whenever any form of government becomes destructive of these ends, it is the right of the people to alter or to abolish it, and to institute a new government, laying its foundation on such principles, and organizing its powers in such form, as to them shall seem most likely to effect their safety and happiness. Prudence, indeed, will dictate that governments long established should not be changed for light and transient causes; and accordingly all experience hath shown that mankind are more disposed to suffer, while evils are sufferable, than to right themselves by abolishing the forms to which they are accustomed. But when a long train of abuses and usurpations, pursuing invariably the same object, evinces a design to reduce them under absolute despotism, it is their right, it is their duty, to throw off such government and to provide new guards for their future security. Such has been the patient suffering of these colonies, and such is now the necessity which constrains them to alter their former systems of government. The history of the present king of Great Britain is a history of repeated injuries and usurpations, all having in direct object the establishment of an absolute tyranny over these states. To prove this, let facts be submitted to a candid world.

He has refused his assent to laws the most wholesome and necessary for the public good.

He has forbidden his governors to pass laws of immediate and pressing importance, unless suspended in their operation till his assent should be obtained, and, when so suspended, he has utterly neglected to attend to them.

He has refused to pass other laws for the accommodation of large districts of people, unless those people would relinquish the right of representation in the legislature—a right inestimable to them and formidable to tyrants only.

He has called together legislative bodies, at places unusual, uncomfortable, and distant from the repository of their public records, for the sole purpose of fatiguing them into compliance with his measures.

He has dissolved representative houses repeatedly for opposing with manly firmness his invasions on the rights of the people.

He has refused for a long time after such dissolutions to cause others to be elected; whereby the legislative powers, incapable of annihilation, have returned to the people at large for their exercise: the state remaining, in the meantime, exposed to all the dangers of invasion from without and convulsions within.

He has endeavored to prevent the population of these states; for that purpose obstructing the laws for naturalization of foreigners; refusing to pass others to encourage their migration hither, and raising the conditions of new appropriations of lands.

He has obstructed the administration of justice by refusing his assent to laws for establishing his judiciary powers.

He has made judges dependent on his will alone for the tenure of their offices and the amount and payment of their salaries.

He has erected a multitude of new offices and sent hither swarms of officers to harass our people and eat out their substance.

He has kept among us, in times of peace, standing armies without the consent of our legislatures.

He has affected to render the military independent of and superior to the civil power.

He has combined with others to subject us to a jurisdiction foreign to our constitutions and unacknowledged by our laws, giving his assent to their acts of pretended legislation:

For quartering large bodies of armed troops among us;

For protecting them by a mock trial from punishment for any murders which they should commit on the inhabitants of these states;

For cutting off our trade with all parts of the world;

For imposing taxes on us without our consent;

For depriving us in many cases of the benefits of trial by jury;

For transporting us beyond seas to be tried for pretended offenses;

For abolishing the free system of English laws in a neighboring province, establishing therein an arbitrary government, and enlarging its boundaries so as to render it at once an example and fit instrument for introducing the same absolute rule into these colonies;

For taking away our charters, abolishing our most valuable laws, and altering fundamentally the forms of our government;

For suspending our own legislatures and declaring themselves invested with power to legislate for us in all cases whatsoever.

He has abdicated government here by declaring us out of his protection and waging war against us.

He has plundered our seas, ravaged our coasts, burnt our towns and destroyed the lives of our people.

He is at this time transporting large armies of foreign mercenaries to complete the work of death, desolation, and tyranny already begun, with circumstances of cruelty and perfidy scarcely parallelled in the most barbarous ages and totally unworthy the head of a civilized nation.

He has constrained our fellow citizens taken captive upon the high seas to bear arms against their country, to become the executioners of their friends and brethren, or to fall themselves by their hands.

He has excited domestic insurrection amongst us, and has endeavored to bring on the inhabitants of our frontiers the merciless Indian savages, whose known rule of warfare is an undistinguished destruction of all ages, sexes, and conditions.

In every stage of these oppressions we have petitioned for redress, in the most humble terms; our repeated petitions have been answered only by repeated injury. A prince whose character is thus marked by every act which may define a tyrant is unfit to be the ruler of a free people.

Nor have we been wanting in attention to our British brethren. We have warned them, from time to time, of attempts by their legislature to extend an unwarrantable jurisdiction over us. We have reminded them of the circumstances of our emigration and settlement here. We have appealed to their native justice and magnanimity; and we have conjured them by the ties of our common kindred, to disavow these usurpations, which would inevitably interrupt our connections and correspondence. They, too, have been deaf to the voice of justice and consanguinity. We must, therefore, acquiesce in the necessity which denounces our separation, and hold them, as we hold the rest of mankind, enemies in war; in peace, friends.

We, therefore, the representatives of the United States of America, in general congress assembled, appealing to the Supreme Judge of the World for the rectitude of our intentions, do, in the name and by the authority of the good people of these colonies, solemnly publish and declare that these united colonies are, and of right ought to be, free and independent states; that they are absolved from all allegiance to the British crown, and that all political connection between them and the state of Great Britain is, and ought to be, totally dissolved; and that as free and independent states they have full power to levy war, conclude peace, contract alliances, establish commerce, and to do all other acts and things which independent states may of right do. And for the support of this declaration, with a firm reliance on the protection of Divine Providence, we mutually pledge to each other our lives, our fortunes, and our sacred honor.

The Bill of Rights[1]

Article I

Congress shall make no law respecting an establishment of religion, or prohibiting the free exercise thereof; or abridging the freedom of speech, or of the press; or the right of the people peaceably to assemble, and to petition the government for a redress of grievances.

Article II

A well regulated militia being necessary to the security of a free State, the right of the people to keep and bear arms, shall not be infringed.

Article III

No soldier shall, in time of peace be quartered in any house, without the consent of the owner, nor in time of war, but in a manner to be prescribed by law.

Article IV

The right of the people to be secure in their persons, houses, papers, and effects, against unreasonable searches and seizures, shall not be violated, and no warrants shall issue, but upon probable cause, supported by oath or affirmation, and particularly describing the place to be searched, and the persons or things to be seized.

Article V

No person shall be held to answer for a capital, or otherwise infamous crime, unless on a presentment or indictment of a grand jury, except in cases arising in the land or naval forces, or in the militia, when in actual service in time of war or public danger; nor shall any person be subject for the same offense to be twice put in jeopardy of life or limb; nor shall be compelled in any criminal case to be a witness against himself, nor be deprived of life, liberty, or property, without due process of law; nor shall private property be taken for public use without just compensation.

[1] Passed by Congress, September 25, 1789; ratified by three-fourths of the states, December 15, 1791.

Article VI

In all criminal prosecutions, the accused shall enjoy the right to a speedy and public trial, by an impartial jury of the State and district wherein the crime shall have been committed, which district shall have been previously ascertained by law, and to be informed of the nature and cause of the accusation; to be confronted with the witnesses against him; to have compulsory process for obtaining witnesses in his favor, and to have the assistance of counsel for his defense.

Article VII

In suits at common law, where the value in controversy shall exceed twenty dollars, the right of trial by jury shall be preserved, and no fact tried by a jury shall be otherwise reexamined in any court of the United States, than according to the rules of the common law.

Article VIII

Excessive bail shall not be required, nor excessive fines imposed, nor cruel and unusual punishments inflicted.

Article IX

The enumeration in the Constitution of certain rights shall not be construed to deny or disparage others retained by the people.

Article X

The powers not delegated to the United States by the Constitution, nor prohibited by it to the States, are reserved to the States respectively, or to the people.

HENRY DAVID THOREAU

•

On the Duty of Civil Disobedience[1]

I heartily accept the motto—"That government is best which governs least"; and I should like to see it acted up to more rapidly and systematically. Carried out, it finally amounts to this, which also I believe,—"That government is best which governs not at all"; and when men are prepared for it, that will be the kind of government which they will have. Government is at best but an expedient; but most governments are usually, and all governments are sometimes,

[1] From *Aesthetic Papers,* edited by Elizabeth Peabody, 1849.

inexpedient. The objections which have been brought against a standing army, and they are many and weighty, and deserve to prevail, may also at last be brought against a standing government. The standing army is only an arm of the standing government. The government itself, which is only the mode which the people have chosen to execute their will, is equally liable to be abused and perverted before the people can act through it. Witness the present Mexican war, the work of comparatively a few individuals using the standing government as their tool; for, in the outset, the people would not have consented to this measure.

This American government—what is it but a tradition, though a recent one, endeavoring to transmit itself unimpaired to posterity, but each instant losing some of its integrity? It has not the vitality and force of a single living man; for a single man can bend it to his will. It is a sort of wooden gun to the people themselves. But it is not the less necessary for this; for the people must have some complicated machinery or other, and hear its din, to satisfy that idea of government which they have. Governments show us how successfully men can be imposed on, even impose on themselves, for their own advantage. It is excellent, we must all allow. Yet this government never of itself furthered any enterprise, but by the alacrity with which it got out of its way. *It* does not keep the country free. *It* does not settle the West. *It* does not educate. The character inherent in the American people has done all that has been accomplished; and it would have done somewhat more, if the government had not sometimes got in its way. For government is an expedient by which men would fain succeed in letting one another alone; and, as has been said, when it is most expedient, the governed are most let alone by it. Trade and commerce, if they were not made of India-rubber, would never manage to bounce over the obstacles which legislators are continually putting in their way; and, if one were to judge these men wholly by the effects of their actions and not partly by their intentions, they would deserve to be classed and punished with those mischievous persons who put obstructions on the railroads.

But, to speak practically and as a citizen, unlike those who call themselves no-government men, I ask for, not at once no government, but *at once* a better government. Let every man make known what kind of government would command his respect, and that will be one step toward obtaining it.

After all, the practical reason why, when the power is once in the hands of the people, a majority are permitted, and for a long period continue, to rule is not because they are most likely to be in the right, nor because this seems fairest to the minority, but because they are physically the strongest. But a government in which the majority rule in all cases cannot be based on justice, even as far as men understand it. Can there not be a government in which majorities do not virtually decide right and wrong, but conscience?—in which majorities decide only those questions to which the rule of expediency is applicable? Must the citizen ever for a moment, or in the least degree, resign his conscience to the legislator? Why has every man a conscience, then? I think that we should be men first, and subjects afterward. It is not desirable to cultivate a respect for the law, so much as for the right. The only obligation which I have a right to assume is to do at any time what I think right. It is truly enough said, that a corporation has no conscience; but a corporation of conscientious men is a corporation *with* a conscience. Law never made men a whit more just; and, by means of their respect for it, even the well-disposed are daily made the agents of injustice. A common and natural result of an undue respect for law is, that you may see a file of soldiers, colonel, captain, corporal, privates, powder-monkeys, and all, marching in admirable order over hill and dale to the wars, against their wills, ay, against their common sense and consciences, which makes it very steep marching indeed, and produces a palpitation of the heart. They have no doubt that it is a damnable business in which they are concerned; they are all peaceably inclined. Now, what are they? Men at all? or small movable forts and magazines, at the service of some unscrupulous man in power? Visit the Navy-Yard, and behold a marine, such a man as an American government can make, or such as it can make a man with its black arts,—a mere shadow and reminiscence of humanity, a man laid out alive and standing, and already, as one may say, buried under arms with funeral accompaniments, though it may be,—

> Not a drum was heard, not a funeral note,
> As his corpse to the rampart we hurried;
> Not a soldier discharged his farewell shot
> O'er the grave where our hero we buried.

The mass of men serve the state thus, not as men mainly, but as machines, with their bodies. They are the standing army, and the militia, jailors, constables, posse comitatus, etc. In most cases there is no free exercise whatever of the judgment or of the moral sense; but they put themselves on a level with wood and earth and stones; and wooden men can perhaps be manufactured that will serve the purpose as well. Such command no more respect than men of straw or a lump of dirt. They have the same sort of worth only as horses and dogs. Yet such as these even are commonly esteemed good citizens. Others—as most legislators, politicians, lawyers, ministers, and officeholders —serve the state chiefly with their heads; and as they rarely make any moral distinctions, they are as likely to serve the Devil, without *intending* it, as God. A very few, as heroes, patriots, martyrs, reformers in the great sense, and *men*, serve the state with their consciences also, and so necessarily resist it for the most part; and they are commonly treated as enemies by it. A wise man will only be useful as a man, and will not submit to be "clay," and "stop a hole to keep the wind away," but leave that office to his dust at least:—

> I am too high-born to be propertied,
> To be a secondary at control,
> Or useful serving-man and instrument
> To any sovereign state throughout the world.

He who gives himself entirely to his fellow-men appears to them useless and selfish; but he who gives himself partially to them is pronounced a benefactor and philanthropist.

How does it become a man to behave toward this American government to-day? I answer, that he cannot without disgrace be associated with it. I cannot for an instant recognize that political organization as *my* government which is the *slave's* government also.

All men recognize the right of revolution; that is, the right to refuse allegiance to, and to resist, the government, when its tyranny or its inefficiency are great and unendurable. But almost all say that such is not the case now. But such was the case, they think, in the Revolution of '75. If one were to tell me that this was a bad government because it taxed certain foreign commodities brought to its ports, it is most probable that I should not make an ado about it, for I can do without them. All machines have their friction; and possibly this does enough good to counterbalance the evil. At any rate, it is a great evil to make a stir about it. But when the friction comes to have its machine, and oppression and robbery are organized, I say, let us not have such a machine any longer. In other words, when a sixth of the population of a nation which has undertaken to be the refuge of liberty are slaves, and a whole country is unjustly overrun and conquered by a foreign army, and subjected to military law, I think that it is not too soon for honest men to rebel and revolutionize. What makes this duty the more urgent is the fact that the country so overrun is not our own, but ours is the invading army.

Paley, a common authority with many on moral questions, in his chapter on the "Duty of Submission to Civil Government," resolves all civil obligation into expediency; and he proceeds to say, "that so long as the interest of the whole society requires it, that is, so long as the established government cannot be resisted or changed without public inconveniency, it is the will of God that the established government be obeyed, and no longer. . . . This principle being admitted, the justice of every particular case of resistance is reduced to a computation of the quantity of the danger and grievance on the one side, and of the probability and expense of redressing it on the other." Of this, he says, every man shall judge for himself. But Paley appears never to have contemplated those cases to which the rule of expediency does not apply, in which a people, as well as an individual, must do justice, cost what it may. If I have unjustly wrested a plank from a drowning man, I must restore it to him though I drown myself. This, according to Paley, would be inconvenient. But he that would save his life, in such a case, shall lose it. This people must cease to hold slaves, and to make war on Mexico, though it cost them their existence as a people.

In their practice, nations agree with Paley; but does any one think that Massachusetts does exactly what is right at the present crisis?

> A drab of state, a cloth-o'-silver slut,
> To have her train borne up, and her soul trail in the dirt.

Practically speaking, the opponents to a reform in Massachusetts are not a hundred thousand politicians at the South, but a hundred thousand merchants and farmers here, who are more interested in commerce and agriculture than they are in humanity, and are not prepared to do justice to the slave and to Mexico, *cost what it may*. I quarrel not with far-off foes, but with those who, near at home, coöperate with, and do the bidding of, those far away, and without whom the latter would be harmless. We are accustomed to say, that the mass of men are unprepared; but improvement is slow, because the few are not materially wiser or better than the many. It is not so important that many should be as good as you, as that there be some absolute goodness somewhere; for that will leaven the whole lump. There are thousands who are *in opinion* opposed to slavery and to the war, who yet in effect do nothing to put an end to them; who, esteeming themselves children of Washington and Franklin, sit down with their hands in their pockets, and say that they know not what to do, and do nothing; who even postpone the question of freedom to the question of free-trade, and quietly read the prices-current along with the latest advices from Mexico, after dinner, and, it may be, fall asleep over them both. What is the price-current of an honest man and patriot to-day? They hesitate, and they regret, and sometimes they petition; but they do nothing in earnest and with effect. They will wait, well disposed, for others to remedy the evil, that they may no longer have it to regret. At most, they give only a cheap vote, and a feeble countenance and God-speed, to the right, as it goes by them. There are nine hundred and ninety-nine patrons of virtue to one virtuous man. But it is easier to deal with the real possessor of a thing than with the temporary guardian of it.

All voting is a sort of gaming, like checkers or backgammon, with a slight moral tinge to it, a playing with right and wrong, with moral questions; and betting naturally accompanies it. The character of the voters is not staked. I cast my vote, perchance, as I think right; but I am not vitally concerned that right should prevail. I am willing to leave it to the majority. Its obligation, therefore, never exceeds that of expediency. Even voting *for the right* is *doing* nothing for it. It is only expressing to men feebly your desire that it should prevail. A wise man will not leave the right to the mercy of chance, nor wish it to prevail through the power of the majority. There is but little virtue in the action of masses of men. When the majority shall at length vote for the abolition of slavery, it will be because they are indifferent to slavery, or because there is but little slavery left to be abolished by their vote. *They* will then be the only slaves. Only *his* vote can hasten the abolition of slavery who asserts his own freedom by his vote.

I hear of a convention to be held at Baltimore, or elsewhere, for the selection of a candidate for the Presidency, made up chiefly of editors, and men who are politicians by profession; but I think, what is it to any independent, intelligent, and respectable man what decision they may come to? Shall we not have the advantage of his wisdom and honesty, nevertheless? Can we not count upon some independent votes? Are there not many individuals in the country who do not attend conventions? But no: I find that the respectable man, so called, has immediately drifted from his position, and despairs of his country, when his country has more reason to despair of him. He forthwith adopts one of the candidates thus selected as the only *available* one, thus proving that he is himself *available* for any purposes of the demagogue. His vote is of no more worth than that of any unprincipled foreigner or hireling native, who may have been bought. O for a man who is a *man,* and, as my neighbor says, has a bone in his back which you cannot pass your hand through! Our statistics are at fault: the population has been returned too large. How many *men* are there to a square thousand miles in this country? Hardly one. Does not America offer any inducement for men to settle here? The American has dwindled into an Odd Fellow,—one who may be known by the development of his organ of gregariousness, and a manifest lack of intellect and cheerful self-reliance; whose first and chief concern, on coming into the world, is to see that the Almshouses are in good repair; and, before yet he has lawfully donned the virile garb, to collect a fund for the support of the widows and orphans that may be; who, in short, ventures to live only by the aid of the Mutual Insurance company, which has promised to bury him decently.

It is not a man's duty, as a matter of course, to devote himself to the eradication of any, even the most enormous wrong; he may still properly have other concerns to engage him; but it is his duty, at least, to wash his hands of it, and, if he gives it no thought longer, not to give it practically his support. If I devote myself to other pursuits and contemplations, I must first see, at least, that I do not pursue them sitting upon another man's shoulders. I must get off him first, that he may pursue his contemplations too. See what gross inconsistency is tolerated. I have heard some of my townsmen say, "I should like to have them order me out to help put down an insurrection of the slaves, or to march to Mexico;—see if I would go"; and yet these very men have each, directly by their allegiance, and so indirectly, at least, by their money, furnished a substitute. The soldier is applauded who refuses to serve in an unjust war by those who do not refuse to sustain the unjust government which makes the war; is applauded by those whose own act and authority he disregards and sets at naught; as if the state were penitent to that degree that it hired one to scourge it while it sinned, but not to that degree that it left off sinning for a moment. Thus, under the name of Order and Civil Government, we are all made at last to pay homage to and support our own meanness. After the first blush of sin comes its indifference; and from immoral it becomes, as it were, *un*moral, and not quite unnecessary to that life which we have made.

The broadest and most prevalent error requires the most disinterested virtue to sustain it. The slight reproach to which the virtue of patriotism is commonly liable, the noble are most likely to incur. Those who, while they disapprove of the character and measures of a government, yield to it their allegiance and support are undoubtedly its most conscientious supporters, and so frequently the most serious obstacles to reform. Some are petitioning the state to dissolve the Union, to disregard the requisitions of the President. Why do they not dissolve it themselves—the union between themselves and the state,—and refuse to pay their quota into its treasury? Do not they stand in the same relation to the state that the state does to the Union? And have not the same reasons prevented the state from resisting the Union which have prevented them from resisting the state?

How can a man be satisfied to entertain an opinion merely, and enjoy *it?* Is there any enjoyment in it, if his opinion is that he is aggrieved? If you are cheated out of a single dollar by your neighbor, you do not rest satisfied with knowing that you are cheated, or with saying that you are cheated, or even with petitioning him to pay you your due; but you take effectual steps at once to obtain the full amount, and see that you are never cheated again. Action from principle, the perception and the performance of right, changes things and relations; it is essentially revolutionary, and does not consist wholly with anything which was. It not only divides states and churches, it divides families; ay, it divides the *individual,* separating the diabolical in him from the divine.

Unjust laws exist: shall we be content to obey them, or shall we endeavor to amend them, and obey them until we have succeeded, or shall we transgress them at once? Men generally, under such a government as this, think that they ought to wait until they have persuaded the majority to alter them. They think that, if they should resist, the remedy would be worse than the evil. But it is the fault of the government itself that the remedy *is* worse than the evil. *It* makes it worse. Why is it not more apt to anticipate and provide for reform? Why does it not cherish its wise minority? Why does it cry and resist before it is hurt? Why does it not encourage its citizens to be on the alert to point out its faults, and *do* better than it would have them? Why does it always crucify Christ, and excommunicate Copernicus and Luther, and pronounce Washington and Franklin rebels?

One would think, that a deliberate and practical denial of its authority was the only offense never contemplated by government; else, why has it not assigned its definite, its suitable and proportionate penalty? If a man who has no property refuses but once to earn nine shillings for the state, he is put in prison for a period unlimited by any law that I know, and determined only by the discretion of those who placed him there; but if he should steal ninety times nine shillings from the state, he is soon permitted to go at large again.

If the injustice is part of the necessary friction of the machine of government, let it go, let it go: perchance it will wear smooth,—certainly the machine will wear out. If the injustice has a spring, or a pulley, or a rope, or a crank, exclusively for itself, then perhaps you may consider whether the remedy will not be worse than the evil; but if it is of such a nature that it requires you to be the agent of injustice to another, then, I say, break the law. Let your life be a counter friction to stop the machine. What I have to do is to see, at any rate, that I do not lend myself to the wrong which I condemn.

As for adopting the ways which the state has provided for remedying the evil, I know not of such ways. They take too much time, and a man's life will be gone. I have other affairs to attend to. I came into this world, not chiefly to make this a good place to live in, but to live in it, be it good or bad. A man has not everything to do, but something; and because he cannot do *everything,* it is not necessary that he should do *something* wrong. It is not my business to be petitioning the Governor or the Legislature any more than it is theirs to petition me; and if they should not hear my petition, what should I do then? But in this case the state has provided no way: its very Constitution is the evil. This may seem to be harsh and stubborn and unconciliatory; but it is to treat with the utmost kindness and consideration the only spirit that can appreciate or deserves it. So is all change for the better, like birth and death, which convulse the body.

I do not hesitate to say, that those who call themselves Abolitionists should at once effectually withdraw their support, both in person and property, from the government of Massachusetts and not wait till they constitute a majority of one, before they suffer the right to prevail through them. I think that it is enough if they have God on their side, without waiting for that other one. Moreover, any man more right than his neighbors constitutes a majority of one already.

I meet this American government, or its representative, the state government, directly, and face to face, once a year—no more—in the person of its tax-gatherer; this is the only mode in which a man situated as I am necessarily meets it; and it then says distinctly, Recognize me; and the simplest, most effectual, and, in the present posture of affairs, the indispensablest mode of treating with it on this head, of expressing your little satisfaction with and love for it, is to deny it then. My civil neighbor, the tax-gatherer, is the very man I have to deal with,—for it is, after all, with men and not with parchment that I quarrel,—and he has voluntarily chosen to be an agent of the government. How shall he ever know well what he is and does as an officer of the government, or as a man, until he is obliged to consider whether he shall treat me, his neighbor, for whom he has respect, as a neighbor and well-disposed man, or as a maniac and disturber of the peace, and see if he can get over this obstruction to his neighborliness without a ruder and more impetuous thought or speech corresponding with his action. I know this well, that if one thousand, if one hundred, if ten men whom I could name,—if ten *honest* men only,—ay, if *one* HONEST man, in this State of Massachusetts, *ceasing to hold slaves,* were actually to withdraw from this copartnership, and be locked up in the county jail therefor, it would be the abolition of slavery in America. For it matters not how small the beginning may seem to be: what is once well done is done forever. But we love better to talk about it: that we say is our mission. Reform keeps many scores of newspapers in its service, but not one man. If my esteemed neighbor, the State's ambassador, who will devote his days to the settlement of the question of human rights in the Council Chamber, instead of being threatened with the prisons of Carolina, were to sit down the prisoner of Massachusetts, that State which is so anxious to foist the sin of slavery upon her sister,—though at present she can discover only an act of inhospitality to be the ground of a quarrel with her,—the Legislature would not wholly waive the subject the following winter.

Under a government which imprisons any unjustly, the true place for a just man is also a prison. The proper place to-day, the only place which Massachusetts has provided for her freer and less desponding spirits, is in her prisons, to be put out and locked out of the State by her own act, as they have already put themselves out by their principles. It is there that the fugitive slave, and the Mexican prisoner on parole, and the Indian come to plead the wrongs of his race should find them; on that separate, but more free and honorable ground, where the State places those who are not *with* her, but *against* her,—the only house in a slave State in which a free man can abide with honor. If any think that their influence would be lost there, and their voices no longer afflict the ear of the State, that they would not be as an enemy within its walls, they do not know by how much truth is stronger than error, nor how much more eloquently and effectively he can combat injustice who has experienced a little in his own person. Cast your whole vote, not a strip of paper merely, but your whole influence. A minority is powerless while it conforms to the majority; it is not even a minority then; but it is irresistible when it clogs by its whole weight. If the alternative is to keep all just men in prison, or give up war and slavery, the State will not hesitate which to choose. If a thousand men were not to pay their tax-bills this year, that would not be a violent and bloody measure, as it would be to pay them, and enable the State to commit violence and shed innocent blood. This is, in fact, the definition of a peaceable revolution, if any such is possible. If the tax-gatherer, or any other public officer, asks me, as one has done, "But what shall I do?" my answer is, "If you really wish to do anything, resign your office." When the subject has refused allegiance, and the officer has resigned his office, then the revolution is accomplished. But even suppose blood should flow. Is there not a sort of blood shed when the conscience is wounded? Through this wound a man's real manhood and immortality flow out, and he bleeds to an everlasting death. I see this blood flowing now.

I have contemplated the imprisonment of the offender, rather than the seizure of his goods,—though both will serve the same purpose,—because they who assert the purest right, and consequently are most dangerous to a corrupt State, commonly have not spent much time in accumulating property. To such the State renders comparatively small service, and a slight tax is wont to appear exorbitant, particularly if they are obliged to earn it by special labor with their hands. If there were one who lived wholly without the use of money, the State itself would hesitate to demand it of him. But the rich man —not to make any invidious comparison—is always sold to the institution which makes him rich. Absolutely speaking, the more money, the less virtue;

for money comes between a man and his objects, and obtains them for him; and it was certainly no great virtue to obtain it. It puts to rest many questions which he would otherwise be taxed to answer; while the only new question which it puts is the hard but superfluous one, how to spend it. Thus his moral ground is taken from under his feet. The opportunities of living are diminished in proportion as what are called the "means" are increased. The best thing a man can do for his culture when he is rich is to endeavor to carry out those schemes which he entertained when he was poor. Christ answered the Herodians according to their condition. "Show me the tribute-money," said he;—and one took a penny out of his pocket;—if you use money which has the image of Cæsar on it and which he has made current and valuable, that is, *if you are men of the State,* and gladly enjoy the advantages of Cæsar's government, then pay him back some of his own when he demands it. "Render therefore to Cæsar that which is Cæsar's, and to God those things which are God's,"—leaving them no wiser than before as to which was which; for they did not wish to know.

When I converse with the freest of my neighbors, I perceive that, whatever they may say about the magnitude and seriousness of the question, and their regard for the public tranquillity, the long and the short of the matter is, that they cannot spare the protection of the existing government, and they dread the consequences to their property and families of disobedience to it. For my own part, I should not like to think that I ever rely on the protection of the State. But, if I deny the authority of the State when it presents its tax-bill, it will soon take and waste all my property, and so harass me and my children without end. This is hard. This makes it impossible for a man to live honestly, and at the same time comfortably, in outward respects. It will not be worth the while to accumulate property; that would be sure to go again. You must hire or squat somewhere, and raise but a small crop, and eat that soon. You must live within yourself, and depend upon yourself always tucked up and ready for a start; and not have many affairs. A man may grow rich in Turkey even, if he will be in all respects a good subject of the Turkish government. Confucius said: "If a state is governed by the principles of reason, poverty and misery are subjects of shame; if a state is not governed by the principles of reason, riches and honors are the subjects of shame." No: until I want the protection of Massachusetts to be extended to me in some distant Southern port, where my liberty is endangered, or until I am bent solely on building up an estate at home by peaceful enterprise, I can afford to refuse allegiance to Massachusetts, and her right to my property and life. It costs me less in every sense to incur the penalty of disobedience to the State than it would to obey. I should feel as if I were worth less in that case.

Some years ago, the State met me in behalf of the Church, and commanded me to pay a certain sum toward the support of a clergyman whose preaching my father attended, but never I myself. "Pay," it said, "or be locked up in the jail." I declined to pay. But, unfortunately, another man saw fit to pay it.

I did not see why the schoolmaster should be taxed to support the priest, and not the priest the schoolmaster; for I was not the State's schoolmaster, but I supported myself by voluntary subscription. I did not see why the lyceum should not present its tax-bill, and have the State to back its demand, as well as the Church. However, at the request of the selectmen, I condescended to make some such statement as this in writing:—"Know all men by these presents, that I, Henry Thoreau, do not wish to be regarded as a member of any incorporated society which I have not joined." This I gave to the town clerk; and he has it. The State, having thus learned that I did not wish to be regarded as a member of that church, has never made a like demand on me since; though it said that it must adhere to its original presumption that time. If I had known how to name them, I should then have signed off in detail from all the societies which I never signed on to; but I did not know where to find a complete list.

I have paid no poll-tax for six years. I was put into a jail once on this account, for one night; and, as I stood considering the walls of solid stone, two or three feet thick, the door of wood and iron, a foot thick, and the iron grating which strained the light, I could not help being struck with the foolishness of that institution which treated me as if I were mere flesh and blood and bones, to be locked up. I wondered that it should have concluded at length that this was the best use it could put me to, and had never thought to avail itself of my services in some way. I saw that, if there was a wall of stone between me and my townsmen, there was a still more difficult one to climb or break through before they could get to be as free as I was. I did not for a moment feel confined, and the walls seemed a great waste of stone and mortar. I felt as if I alone of all my townsmen had paid my tax. They plainly did not know how to treat me, but behaved like persons who are underbred. In every threat and in every compliment there was a blunder; for they thought that my chief desire was to stand the other side of that stone wall. I could not but smile to see how industriously they locked the door on my meditations, which followed them out again without let or hindrance, and *they* were really all that was dangerous. As they could not reach me, they had resolved to punish my body; just as boys, if they cannot come at some person against whom they have a spite, will abuse his dog. I saw that the State was half-witted, that it was timid as a lone woman with her silver spoons, and that it did not know its friends from its foes, and I lost all my remaining respect for it, and pitied it.

Thus the State never intentionally confronts a man's sense, intellectual or moral, but only his body, his senses. It is not armed with superior wit or honesty, but with superior physical strength. I was not born to be forced. I will breathe after my own fashion. Let us see who is the strongest. What force has a multitude? They only can force me who obey a higher law than I. They force me to become like themselves. I do not hear of *men* being *forced* to live this way or that by masses of men. What sort of life were that to live? When I meet a government which says to me, "Your money or your life," why should I be in haste to give it my money? It may be in a great strait, and not know what to do: I cannot help that. It must help itself; do as I do. It is not worth the while to snivel about it. I am not responsible for the successful working of the machinery of society. I am not the son of the engineer. I perceive that, when an acorn and a chestnut fall side by side, the one does not remain inert to make way for the other, but both obey their own laws, and spring and grow and flourish as best they can, till one, perchance, overshadows and destroys the other. If a plant cannot live according to its nature, it dies; and so a man.

The night in prison was novel and interesting enough. The prisoners in their shirt-sleeves were enjoying a chat and the evening air in the doorway, when I entered. But the jailer said, "Come, boys, it is time to lock up;" and so they dispersed, and I heard the sound of their steps returning into the hollow apartments. My roommate was introduced to me by the jailer as "a first-rate fellow and a clever man." When the door was locked, he showed me where to hang my hat, and how he managed matters there. The rooms were whitewashed once a month; and this one, at least, was the whitest, most simply furnished, and probably the neatest apartment in the town. He naturally wanted to know where I came from, and what brought me there; and, when I had told him, I asked him in my turn how he came there, presuming him to be an honest man, of course; and, as the world goes, I believe he was. "Why," said he, "they accuse me of burning a barn; but I never did it." As near as I could discover, he had probably gone to bed in a barn when drunk, and smoked his pipe there; and so a barn was burnt. He had the reputation of being a clever man, had been there some three months waiting for his trial to come on, and would have to wait as much longer; but he was quite domesticated and contented, since he got his board for nothing, and thought that he was well treated.

He occupied one window, and I the other; and I saw that if one stayed there long, his principal business would be to look out the window. I had soon read all the tracts that were left there, and examined where former prisoners had broken out, and where a grate had been sawed off, and heard the history of the various occupants of that room; for I found that even here there was a history and a gossip which never circulated beyond the walls of the jail. Probably this is the only house in the town where verses are composed, which are afterward printed in a circular form, but not published. I was shown quite a long list of verses which were composed by some young men who had been detected in an attempt to escape, who avenged themselves by singing them.

I pumped my fellow-prisoner as dry as I could, for fear I should never see him again; but at length he showed me which was my bed, and left me to blow out the lamp.

It was like traveling into a far country, such as I had never expected to behold, to lie there for one night. It seemed to me that I never had heard the town-clock strike before, nor the evening sounds of the village; for we slept with the windows open, which were inside the grating. It was to see my native village in the light of the Middle Ages, and our Concord was turned into a Rhine stream, and visions of knights and castles passed before me. They were the voices of old burghers that I heard in the streets. I was an involuntary spectator and auditor of whatever was done and said in the kitchen of the adjacent village-inn,—a wholly new and rare experience to me. It was a closer view of my native town. I was fairly inside of it. I never had seen its institutions before. This is one of its peculiar institutions; for it is a shire town. I began to comprehend what its inhabitants were about.

In the morning, our breakfasts were put through the hole in the door, in small oblong-square tin pans, made to fit, and holding a pint of chocolate, with brown bread, and an iron spoon. When they called for the vessels again, I was green enough to return what bread I had left; but my comrade seized it, and said that I should lay that up for lunch or dinner. Soon after he was let out to work at haying in a neighboring field, whither he went every day, and would not be back till noon; so he bade me good-day, saying that he doubted if he should see me again.

When I came out of prison,—for some one interfered, and paid that tax,—I did not perceive that great changes had taken place on the common, such as he observed who went in a youth and emerged a tottering and gray-headed man; and yet a change had to my eyes come over the scene,—the town, and State, and country—greater than any that mere time could effect. I saw yet more distinctly the State in which I lived. I saw to what extent the people among whom I lived could be trusted as good neighbors and friends; that their friendship was for summer weather only; that they did not greatly propose to do right; that they were a distinct race from me by their prejudices and superstitions, as the Chinamen and Malays are; that in their sacrifices to humanity they ran no risks, not even to their property; that after all they were not so noble but they treated the thief as he had treated them, and hoped, by a certain outward observance and a few prayers, and by walking in a particular straight though useless path from time to time, to save their souls. This may be to judge my neighbors harshly; for I believe that many of them are not aware that they have such an institution as the jail in their village.

It was formerly the custom in our village, when a poor debtor came out of jail, for his acquaintances to salute him, looking through their fingers, which were crossed to represent the grating of a jail window. "How do ye do?" My neighbors did not thus salute me, but first looked at me, and then at one another, as if I had returned from a long journey. I was put into jail as I was going to the shoemaker's to get a shoe which was mended. When I was let out the next morning, I proceeded to finish my errand, and, having put on my mended shoe, joined a huckleberry party, who were impatient to put themselves under my conduct; and in half an hour,—for the horse was soon tackled,—was in the midst of a huckleberry field, on one of our highest hills, two miles off, and then the State was nowhere to be seen.

This is the whole history of "My Prisons."

I have never declined paying the highway tax, because I am as desirous of being a good neighbor as I am of being a bad subject; and as for supporting schools, I am doing my part to educate my fellow-countrymen now. It is for no particular item in the tax-bill that I refuse to pay it. I simply wish to refuse allegiance to the State, to withdraw and stand aloof from it effectually. I do not care to trace the course of my dollar, if I could, till it buys a man or a musket to shoot with,—the dollar is innocent,—but I am concerned to trace the effects of my allegiance. In fact, I quietly declare war with the State, after my fashion, though I will still make what use and get what advantage of her I can, as is usual in such cases.

If others pay the tax which is demanded of me, from a sympathy with the State, they do but what they have already done in their own case, or rather they abet injustice to a greater extent than the State requires. If they pay the tax from a mistaken interest in the individual taxed, to save his property, or prevent his going to jail, it is because they have not considered wisely how far they let their private feelings interfere with the public good.

This, then, is my position at present. But one cannot be too much on his guard in such a case, lest his action be biased by obstinacy or an undue regard for the opinions of men. Let him see that he does only what belongs to himself and to the hour.

I think sometimes, Why, this people mean well, they are only ignorant; they would do better if they knew how: why give your neighbors this pain to treat you as they are not inclined to? But I think again, This is no reason why I should do as they do, or permit others to suffer much greater pain of a different kind. Again, I sometimes say to myself, When many millions of men, without heat, without ill will, without personal feeling of any kind, demand of you a few shillings only, without the possibility, such is their constitution, of retracting or altering their present demand, and without the possibility, on your side, of appeal to any other millions, why expose yourself to this overwhelming brute force? You do not resist cold and hunger, the winds and the waves, thus obstinately; you quietly submit to a thousand similar necessities. You do not put your head into the fire. But just in proportion as I regard this as not wholly a brute force, but partly a human force, and consider that I have relations to those millions as to so many millions of men, and not of mere brute or inanimate things, I see that appeal is possible, first and instantaneously, from them to the Maker of them, and, secondly, from them to themselves. But if I put my head deliberately into the fire, there is no appeal to fire or to the Maker of fire, and I have only myself to blame. If I could convince myself that I have any right to be satisfied with men as they are, and to treat them accordingly, and not according, in some respects, to my requisitions and expectations of what they and I ought to be, then, like a good Mussulman and fatalist, I should endeavor to be satisfied with things as they are, and say it is the will of God. And, above all, there is this difference between resisting this and a purely brute or natural force, that I can resist this with some effect;

but I cannot expect, like Orpheus, to change the nature of the rocks and trees and beasts.

I do not wish to quarrel with any man or nation. I do not wish to split hairs, to make fine distinctions, or set myself up as better than my neighbors. I seek rather, I may say, even an excuse for conforming to the laws of the land. I am but too ready to conform to them. Indeed, I have reason to suspect myself on this head; and each year, as the tax-gatherer comes round, I find myself disposed to review the acts and position of the general and State governments, and the spirit of the people, to discover a pretext for conformity.

> We must affect our country as our parents,
> And if at any time we alienate
> Our love or industry from doing it honor,
> We must respect effects and teach the soul
> Matter of conscience and religion,
> And not desire of rule or benefit.

I believe that the State will soon be able to take all my work of this sort out of my hands, and then I shall be no better a patriot than my fellow-countrymen. Seen from a lower point of view, the Constitution, with all its faults, is very good; the law and the courts are very respectable; even this State and this American government are, in many respects, very admirable, and rare things, to be thankful for, such as a great many have described them; but seen from a point of view a little higher, they are what I have described them; seen from a higher still, and the highest, who shall say what they are, or that they are worth looking at or thinking of at all?

However, the government does not concern me much, and I shall bestow the fewest possible thoughts on it. It is not many moments that I live under a government, even in this world. If a man is thought-free, fancy-free, imagination-free, that which *is not* never for a long time appearing *to be* to him, unwise rulers or reformers cannot fatally interrupt him.

I know that most men think differently from myself; but those whose lives are by profession devoted to the study of these or kindred subjects content me as little as any. Statesmen and legislators, standing so completely within the institution, never distinctly and nakedly behold it. They speak of moving society, but have no resting-place without it. They may be men of a certain experience and discrimination, and have no doubt invented ingenious and even useful systems, for which we sincerely thank them; but all their wit and usefulness lie within certain not very wide limits. They are wont to forget that the world is not governed by policy and expediency. Webster never goes behind government, and so cannot speak with authority about it. His words are wisdom to those legislators who contemplate no essential reform in the existing government; but for thinkers, and those who legislate for all time, he never once glances at the subject. I know of those whose serene and wise speculations on this theme would soon reveal the limits of his mind's range and hospitality. Yet, compared with the cheap professions of most reformers, and the still cheaper wisdom and eloquence of politicians in general, his are almost the only sensible and valuable words, and we thank Heaven for him. Comparatively, he is always strong, original, and, above all, practical. Still, his quality is not wisdom, but prudence. The lawyer's truth is not Truth, but consistency or a consistent expediency. Truth is always in harmony with herself, and is not concerned chiefly to reveal the justice that may consist with wrong-doing. He well deserves to be called, as he has been called, the Defender of the Constitution. There are really no blows to be given by him but defensive ones. He is not a leader, but a follower. His leaders are the men of '87. "I have never made an effort," he says, "and never propose to make an effort; I have never countenanced an effort, and never mean to countenance an effort, to disturb the arrangement as originally made, by which the various States came into the Union." Still thinking of the sanction which the Constitution gives to slavery, he says, "Because it was a part of the original compact,—let it stand." Notwithstanding his special acuteness and ability, he is unable to take a fact out of its merely political relations, and behold it as it lies absolutely to be disposed of by the intellect,—what, for instance, it behooves a man to do here in America to-day with regard to slavery,—but ventures, or is driven, to make some such desperate answer as the following while professing to speak absolutely, and as a private man,—from which what new and singular code of social duties might be inferred? "The manner," says he, "in which the governments of those States where slavery exists are to regulate it is for their own consideration, under their responsibility to their constituents, to the general laws of propriety, humanity, and justice, and to God. Associations formed elsewhere, springing from a feeling of humanity, or other cause, have nothing whatever to do with it. They have never received any encouragement from me, and they never will."

They who know of no purer sources of truth, who have traced up its stream no higher, stand, and wisely stand, by the Bible and the Constitution, and drink at it there with reverence and humility; but they who behold where it comes trickling into this lake or that pool, gird up their loins once more, and continue their pilgrimage toward its fountainhead.

No man with a genius for legislation has appeared in America. They are rare in the history of the world. There are orators, politicians, and eloquent men, by the thousand; but the speaker has not yet opened his mouth to speak who is capable of settling the much-vexed questions of the day. We love eloquence for its own sake, and not for any truth which it may utter, or any heroism it may inspire. Our legislators have not yet learned the comparative value of free-trade and of freedom, of union, and of rectitude, to a nation. They have no genius or talent for comparatively humble questions of taxation and finance, commerce and manufactures and agriculture. If we were left solely to the wordy wit of legislators in Congress for our guidance, uncorrected by the seasonable experience and the effectual complaints of the people, America would not long retain her rank among the nations. For eighteen hundred years, though perchance I have no right to say it, the New Testament has been written; yet where is the legislator who has wisdom and practical talent enough to avail himself of the light which it sheds on the science of legislation?

The authority of government, even such as I am willing to submit to,—for I will cheerfully obey those who know and can do better than I, and in many things even those who neither know nor can do so well,—is still an impure one: to be strictly just, it must have the sanction and consent of the governed. It can have no pure right over my person and property but what I concede to it. The progress from an absolute to a limited monarchy, from a limited monarchy to a democracy, is a progress toward a true respect for the individual. Even the Chinese philosopher was wise enough to regard the individual as the basis of the empire. Is a democracy, such as we know it, the last improvement possible in government? Is it not possible to take a step further towards recognizing and organizing the rights of man? There will never be a really free and enlightened State until the State comes to recognize the individual as a higher and independent power, from which all its own power and authority are derived, and treats him accordingly. I please myself with imagining a State at last which can afford to be just to all men, and to treat the individual with respect as a neighbor; which even would not think it inconsistent with its own repose if a few were to live aloof from it, not meddling with it, nor embraced by it, who fulfilled all the duties of neighbors and fellow-men. A State which bore this kind of fruit, and suffered it to drop off as fast as it ripened, would prepare the way for a still more perfect and glorious State, which also I have imagined, but not yet anywhere seen.

E. B. WHITE

•

Walden—1954[1]

In his journal for July 10-12, 1841, Thoreau wrote: "A slight sound at evening lifts me up by the ears, and makes life seem inexpressibly serene and grand. It may be in Uranus, or it may be in the shutter." The book into which he later managed to pack both Uranus and the shutter was published in 1854, and now, a hundred years having gone by, *Walden*, its serenity and grandeur unimpaired, still lifts us up by the ears, still translates for us that language we

[1] "A Slight Sound at Evening" (Allen Cove, Summer, 1954) from *The Points of My Compass* by E. B. White. Copyright 1954 by E. B. White. Originally published in *The Yale Review*, under the title "Walden—1954," and reprinted by permission of Harper & Row, Publishers.

are in danger of forgetting, "which all things and events speak without metaphor, which alone is copious and standard."

Walden is an oddity in American letters. It may very well be the oddest of our distinguished oddities. For many it is a great deal too odd, and for many it is a particular bore. I have not found it to be a well-liked book among my acquaintances, although usually spoken of with respect, and one literary critic for whom I have the highest regard can find no reason why anyone gives *Walden* a second thought. To admire the book is, in fact, something of an embarrassment, for the mass of men have an indistinct notion that its author was a sort of Nature Boy.

I think it is of some advantage to encounter the book at a period in one's life when the normal anxieties and enthusiasms and rebellions of youth closely resemble those of Thoreau in that spring of 1845 when he borrowed an axe, went out to the woods, and began to whack down some trees for timber. Received at such a juncture, the book is like an invitation to life's dance, assuring the troubled recipient that no matter what befalls him in the way of success or failure he will always be welcome at the party—that the music is played for him, too, if he will but listen and move his feet. In effect, that is what the book is—an invitation, unengraved; and it stirs one as a young girl is stirred by her first big party bid. Many think it a sermon; many set it down as an attempt to rearrange society; some think it an exercise in nature-loving; some find it a rather irritating collection of inspirational puffballs by an eccentric show-off. I think it none of these. It still seems to me the best youth's companion yet written by an American, for it carries a solemn warning against the loss of one's valuables, it advances a good argument for traveling light and trying new adventures, it rings with the power of positive adoration, it contains religious feeling without religious images, and it steadfastly refuses to record bad news. Even its pantheistic note is so pure as to be noncorrupting—pure as the flute-note blown across the pond on those faraway summer nights. If our colleges and universities were alert, they would present a cheap pocket edition of the book to every senior upon graduating, along with his sheepskin, or instead of it. Even if some senior were to take it literally and start felling trees, there could be worse mishaps: the axe is older than the Dictaphone and it is just as well for a young man to see what kind of chips he leaves before listening to the sound of his own voice. And even if some were to get no farther than the table of contents, they would learn how to name eighteen chapters by the use of only thirty-nine words and would see how sweet are the uses of brevity.

If Thoreau had merely left us an account of a man's life in the woods, or if he had simply retreated to the woods and there recorded his complaints about society, or even if he had contrived to include both records in one essay, *Walden* would probably not have lived a hundred years. As things turned out, Thoreau, very likely without knowing quite what he was up to, took man's relation to nature and man's dilemma in society and man's capacity for elevating his spirit and he beat all these matters together, in a wild free interval of self-justification and delight, and produced an original omelette from which people can draw nourishment in a hungry day. *Walden* is one of the first of the vitamin-enriched American dishes. If it were a little less good than it is, or even a little less queer, it would be an abominable book. Even as it is, it will continue to baffle and annoy the literal mind and all those who are unable to stomach its caprices and imbibe its theme. Certainly the plodding economist will continue to have rough going if he hopes to emerge from the book with a clear system of economic thought. Thoreau's assault on the Concord society of the mid-nineteenth century has the quality of a modern Western: he rides into the subject at top speed, shooting in all directions. Many of his shots ricochet and nick him on the rebound, and throughout the melee there is a horrendous cloud of inconsistencies and contradictions, and when the shooting dies down and the air clears, one is impressed chiefly by the courage of the rider and by how splendid it was that somebody should have ridden in there and raised all that ruckus.

When he went to the pond, Thoreau struck an attitude and did so deliberately, but his posturing was not to draw the attention of others to him but rather to draw his own attention more closely to himself. "I learned this at least by my experiment: that if one advances confidently in the direction of his dreams, and endeavors to live the life which he has imagined, he will meet with a success unexpected in common hours." The sentence has the power to resuscitate the youth drowning in his sea of doubt. I recall my exhilaration upon reading it, many years ago, in a time of hesitation and despair. It restored me to health. And now in 1954 when I salute Henry Thoreau on the hundredth birthday of his book, I am merely paying off an old score—or an installment on it.

In his journal for May 3-4, 1838—Boston to Portland—he wrote: "Midnight—head over the boat's side—between sleeping and waking—with glimpses of one or more lights in the vicinity of Cape Ann. Bright moonlight—the effect heightened by seasickness." The entry illuminates the man, as the moon the sea on that night in May. In Thoreau the natural scene was heightened, not depressed, by a disturbance of the stomach, and nausea met its match at last. There was a steadiness in at least one passenger if there was none in the boat. Such steadiness (which in some would be called intoxication) is at the heart of *Walden*—confidence, faith, the discipline of looking always at what is to be seen, undeviating gratitude for the life-everlasting that he found growing in his front yard. "There is nowhere recorded a simple and irrepressible satisfaction with the gift of life, any memorable praise of God." He worked to correct that deficiency. *Walden* is his acknowledgment of the gift of life. It is the testament of a man in a high state of indignation because (it seemed to him) so few ears heard the uninterrupted poem of creation, the morning wind that forever blows. If the man sometimes wrote as though all his readers were male, unmarried, and well-connected, it is because he gave his testimony during the callow years, and, for that matter, never really grew up. To reject the book because of the immaturity of the author and the bugs in the logic is to throw away a bottle of good wine because it contains bits of the cork.

Thoreau said he required of every writer, first and last, a simple and sincere account of his own life. Having delivered himself of this chesty dictum, he proceeded to ignore it. In his books and even in his enormous journal, he withheld or disguised most of the facts from which an understanding of his life could be drawn. *Walden,* subtitled "Life in the Woods," is not a simple and sincere account of a man's life, either in or out of the woods; it is an account of a man's journey into the mind, a toot on the trumpet to alert the neighbors. Thoreau was well aware that no one can alert his neighbors who is not wide awake himself, and he went to the woods (among other reasons) to make sure that he would stay awake during his broadcast. What actually took place during the years 1845-47 is largely unrecorded, and the reader is excluded from the private life of the author, who supplies almost no gossip about himself, a great deal about his neighbors and about the universe.

As for me, I cannot in this short ramble give a simple and sincere account of my own life, but I think Thoreau might find it instructive to know that this memorial essay is being written in a house that, through no intent on my part, is the same size and shape as his own domicile on the pond—about ten by fifteen, tight, plainly finished, and at a little distance from my Concord. The house in which I sit this morning was built to accommodate a boat, not a man, but by long experience I have learned that in most respects it shelters me better than the larger dwelling where my bed is, and which, by design, is a manhouse not a boathouse. Here in the boathouse I am a wilder and, it would appear, a healthier man, by a safe margin. I have a chair, a bench, a table, and I can walk into the water if I tire of the land. My house fronts a cove. Two fishermen have just arrived to spot fish from the air—an osprey and a man in a small yellow plane who works for the fish company. The man, I have noticed, is less well equipped than the hawk, who can dive directly on his fish and carry it away, without telephoning. A mouse and a squirrel share the house with me. The building is, in fact, a multiple dwelling, a semidetached affair. It is because I am semidetached while here that I find it possible to transact this private business with the fewest obstacles.

There is also a woodchuck here, living forty feet away under the wharf. When the wind is right, he can smell my house; and when the wind is contrary, I can smell his. We both use the wharf for sunning, taking turns, each adjusting his schedule to the other's convenience. Thoreau once ate a woodchuck. I think he felt he owed it to his readers, and that it was little enough, considering the indignities they were suffering at his hands and the dressing-down they were taking. (Parts of *Walden* are pure scold.) Or perhaps he ate the woodchuck because he believed every man should acquire strict business habits, and the woodchuck was destroying his market beans. I do not know.

Thoreau had a strong experimental streak in him. It is probably no harder to eat a woodchuck than to construct a sentence that lasts a hundred years. At any rate, Thoreau is the only writer I know who prepared himself for his great ordeal by eating a woodchuck; also the only one who got a hangover from drinking too much water. (He was drunk the whole time, though he seldom touched wine or coffee or tea.)

Here in this compact house where I would spend one day as deliberately as Nature if I were not being pressed by *The Yale Review,* and with a woodchuck (as yet uneaten) for neighbor, I can feel the companionship of the occupant of the pondside cabin in Walden woods, a mile from the village, near the Fitchburg right of way. Even my immediate business is no barrier between us: Thoreau occasionally batted out a magazine piece, but was always suspicious of any sort of purposeful work that cut into his time. A man, he said, should take care not to be thrown off the track by every nutshell and mosquito's wing that falls on the rails.

There has been much guessing as to why he went to the pond. To set it down to escapism is, of course, to misconstrue what happened. Henry went forth to battle when he took to the woods, and *Walden* is the report of a man torn by two powerful and opposing drives—the desire to enjoy the world (and not be derailed by a mosquito wing) and the urge to set the world straight. One cannot join these two successfully, but sometimes, in rare cases, something good or even great results from the attempt of the tormented spirit to reconcile them. Henry went forth to battle, and if he set the stage himself, if he fought on his own terms and with his own weapons, it was because it was his nature to do things differently from most men, and to act in a cocky fashion. If the pond and the woods seemed a more plausible site for a house than an intown location, it was because a cowbell made for him a sweeter sound than a churchbell. *Walden,* the book, makes the sound of a cowbell, more than a churchbell, and proves the point, although both sounds are in it, and both remarkably clear and sweet. He simply preferred his churchbell at a little distance.

I think one reason he went to the woods was a perfectly simple and commonplace one—and apparently he thought so, too. "At a certain season of our life," he wrote, "we are accustomed to consider every spot as the possible site of a house." There spoke the young man, a few years out of college, who had not yet broken away from home. He hadn't married, and he had found no job that measured up to his rigid standards of employment, and like any young man, or young animal, he felt uneasy and on the defensive until he had fixed himself a den. Most young men, of course, casting about for a site, are content merely to draw apart from their kinfolks. Thoreau, convinced that the greater part of what his neighbors called good was bad, withdrew from a great deal more than family: he pulled out of everything for a while, to serve everybody right for being so stuffy, and to try his own prejudices on the dog.

The house-hunting sentence above, which starts the Chapter called "Where

I Lived, and What I Lived For," is followed by another passage that is worth quoting here because it so beautifully illustrates the offbeat prose that Thoreau was master of, a prose at once strictly disciplined and wildly abandoned. "I have surveyed the country on every side within a dozen miles of where I live," continued this delirious young man. "In imagination I have bought all the farms in succession, for all were to be bought, and I knew their price. I walked over each farmer's premises, tasted his wild apples, discoursed on husbandry with him, took his farm at his price, at any price, mortgaging it to him in my mind; even put a higher price on it—took everything but a deed of it—took his word for his deed, for I dearly love to talk—cultivated it, and him too to some extent, I trust, and withdrew when I had enjoyed it long enough, leaving him to carry it on." A copydesk man could get a double hernia trying to clean up that sentence for the management, but the sentence needs no fixing, for it perfectly captures the meaning of the writer and the quality of the ramble.

"Wherever I sat, there I might live, and the landscape radiated from me accordingly." Thoreau, the home-seeker, sitting on his hummock with the entire State of Massachusetts radiating from him, is to me the most humorous of the New England figures, and *Walden* the most humorous of the books, though its humor is almost continuously subsurface and there is nothing funny anywhere, except a few weak jokes and bad puns that rise to the surface like the perch in the pond that rose to the sound of the maestro's flute. Thoreau tended to write in sentences, a feat not every writer is capable of, and *Walden* is, rhetorically speaking, a collection of certified sentences, some of them, it would now appear, as indestructible as they are errant. The book is distilled from the vast journals, and this accounts for its intensity: he picked out bright particles that pleased his eye, whirled them in the kaleidoscope of his content, and produced the pattern that has endured—the color, the form, the light.

On this its hundredth birthday, Thoreau's *Walden* is pertinent and timely. In our uneasy season, when all men unconsciously seek a retreat from a world that has got almost completely out of hand, his house in the Concord woods is a haven. In our culture of gadgetry and the multiplicity of convenience, his cry "Simplicity, simplicity, simplicity!" has the insistence of a fire alarm. In the brooding atmosphere of war and the gathering radioactive storm, the innocence and serenity of his summer afternoons are enough to burst the remembering heart, and one gazes back upon that pleasing interlude—its confidence, its purity, its deliberateness—with awe and wonder, as one would look upon the face of a child asleep.

"This small lake was of most value as a neighbor in the intervals of a gentle rain-storm in August, when, both air and water being perfectly still, but the sky overcast, midafternoon had all the serenity of evening, and the wood-thrush sang around, and was heard from shore to shore." Now, in the perpetual overcast in which our days are spent, we hear with extra perception and deep gratitude that song, tying century to century.

I sometimes amuse myself by bringing Henry Thoreau back to life and showing him the sights. I escort him into a phone booth and let him dial Weather. "This is a delicious evening," the girl's voice says, "when the whole body is one sense, and imbibes delight through every pore." I show him the spot in the Pacific where an island used to be, before some magician made it vanish. "We know not where we are," I murmur. "The light which puts out our eyes is darkness to us. Only that day dawns to which we are awake." I thumb through the latest copy of "Vogue" with him. "Of two patterns which differ only by a few threads more or less of a particular color," I read, "the one will be sold readily, the other lie on the shelf, though it frequently happens that, after the lapse of a season, the latter becomes the most fashionable." Together we go outboarding on the Assabet, looking for what we've lost—a hound, a bay horse, a turtledove. I show him a distracted farmer who is trying to repair a hay baler before the thunder shower breaks. "This farmer," I remark, "is endeavoring to solve the problem of a livelihood by a formula more complicated than the problem itself. To get his shoe strings he speculates in herds of cattle."

I take the celebrated author to Twenty-One for lunch, so the waiters may study his shoes. The proprietor welcomes us. "The gross feeder," remarks the proprietor, sweeping the room with his arm, "is a man in the larva stage." After lunch we visit a classroom in one of those schools conducted by big corporations to teach their superannuated executives how to retire from business without serious injury to their health. (The shock to men's systems these days when relieved of the exacting routine of amassing wealth is very great and must be cushioned.) "It is not necessary," says the teacher to his pupils, "that a man should earn his living by the sweat of his brow, unless he sweats easier than I do. We are determined to be starved before we are hungry."

I turn on the radio and let Thoreau hear Winchell beat the red hand around the clock. "Time is but the stream I go a-fishing in," shouts Mr. Winchell, rattling his telegraph key. "Hardly a man takes a half hour's nap after dinner, but when he wakes he holds up his head and asks, 'What's the news?' If we read of one man robbed, or murdered, or killed by accident, or one house burned, or one vessel wrecked, or one steamboat blown up, or one cow run over on the Western Railroad, or one mad dog killed, or one lot of grasshoppers in the winter—we need never read of another. One is enough."

I doubt that Thoreau would be thrown off balance by the fantastic sights and sounds of the twentieth century. "The Concord nights," he once wrote, "are stranger than the Arabian nights." A four-engined air liner would merely serve to confirm his early views on travel. Everywhere he would observe, in new shapes and sizes, the old predicaments and follies of men—the desperation, the impediments, the meanness—along with the visible capacity for elevation of the mind and soul. "This curious world which we inhabit is more wonderful than it is convenient; more beautiful than it is useful; it is more to be admired and enjoyed than used." He would see that today ten thousand engineers are busy making sure that the world shall be convenient if they bust doing it, and others are determined to increase its usefulness even though its beauty is lost somewhere along the way.

At any rate, I'd like to stroll about the countryside in Thoreau's company for a day, observing the modern scene, inspecting today's snowstorm, pointing out the sights, and offering belated apologies for my sins. Thoreau is unique among writers in that those who admire him find him uncomfortable to live with—a regular hairshirt of a man. A little band of dedicated Thoreauvians would be a sorry sight indeed: fellows who hate compromise and have compromised, fellows who love wildness and have lived tamely, and at their side, censuring them and chiding them, the ghostly figure of this upright man, who long ago gave corroboration to impulses they perceived were right and issued warnings against the things they instinctively knew to be their enemies. I should hate to be called a Thoreauvian, yet I wince every time I walk into the barn I'm pushing before me, seventy-five feet by forty, and the author of *Walden* has served as my conscience through the long stretches of my trivial days.

Hairshirt or no, he is a better companion than most, and I would not swap him for a soberer or more reasonable friend even if I could. I can reread his famous invitation with undiminished excitement. The sad thing is that not more acceptances have been received, that so many decline for one reason or another, pleading some previous engagement or ill health. But the invitation stands. It will beckon as long as this remarkable book stays in print—which will be as long as there are August afternoons in the intervals of a gentle rainstorm, as long as there are ears to catch the faint sounds of the orchestra. I find it agreeable to sit here this morning, in a house of correct proportions, and hear across a century of time his flute, his frogs, and his seductive summons to the wildest revels of them all.

LEARNED HAND

•

A Plea for the Freedom of Dissent[1]

What do we mean by "principles of civil liberties and human rights"? We cannot go far in that inquiry until we have achieved some notion of what we mean by Liberty; and that has always proved a hard concept to define. The natural, though naïve, opinion is that it means no more than that each individual shall be allowed to pursue his own desires without let or hindrance; and that, although it is true that this is practically impossible, still it does remain

[1] From *The New York Times Magazine* (February 6, 1955), pp. 11 ff. Copyright, 1955, by *The New York Times*. Reprinted by permission.

the goal, approach to which measures our success. Why, then, is not a beehive or an anthill a perfect example of a free society? Surely you have been a curious and amused watcher beside one of these.

In and out of their crowded pueblo the denizens pass in great number, each bent upon his own urgent mission, quite oblivious of all the rest except as he must bend his path to avoid them. It is a scene of strenuous, purposeful endeavor in which each appears to be, and no doubt in fact is, accomplishing his own purpose; and yet he is at the same time accomplishing the purpose of the group as a whole. As I have gazed at it, the sentence from the Collect of the Episcopal prayerbook has come to me: "Whose service is perfect freedom."

Why is it, then, that we so positively rebel against the hive and the hill as a specimen of a free society? Why is it that such prototypes of totalitarianisms arouse our deepest hostility? Unhappily it is not because they cannot be realized, or at least because they cannot be approached, for a substantial period. Who can be sure that such appalling forecasts as Aldous Huxley's *Brave New World* or Orwell's *1984* are not prophetic? Indeed, there have often been near approaches to such an order.

Germany at the end of 1940 was probably not far removed from one, and who of us knows that there are not countless persons today living within the boundaries of Russia and perhaps of China who are not willing partners, accepting as their personal aspirations the official definitions of the good, the true and the beautiful? Indeed, there have been, and still are, in our own United States large and powerful groups who, if we are to judge their purposes by their conduct, see treason in all dissidence and would welcome an era in which all of us should think, feel and live in consonance with duly prescribed patterns.

Human nature is malleable, especially if you can indoctrinate the disciple with indefectible principles before anyone else reaches him. (I fancy that the Janissaries were as fervent Mohammedans as the authentic Turks.) Indeed, we hear from those who are entitled to an opinion that at times the abject confessions made in Russia by victims who know that they are already marked for slaughter are not wrung from them by torture or threats against their families. Rather, they come from partisans, so obsessed with the faith that when they are told that the occasion calls for scapegoats and that they have been selected, recognize and assent to the propriety of the demand and cooperate in its satisfaction. It is as though, when the right time comes, the drones agreed to their extinction in the interest of the hive.

Nor need we be surprised that men so often embrace almost any doctrines, if they are proclaimed with a voice of absolute assurance. In a universe that we do not understand, but with which we must in one way or another somehow manage to deal, and aware of the conflicting desires that clamorously beset us, between which we must choose and which we must therefore manage to weigh, we turn in our bewilderment to those who tell us that they have found a path out of the thickets and possess the scales by which to appraise our needs.

Over and over again such prophets succeed in converting us to unquestioning acceptance; there is scarcely a monstrous belief that has not had its day and its passionate adherents, so eager are we for safe footholds in our dubious course. How certain is any one of us that he, too, might not be content to follow any fantastic creed, if he was satisfied that nothing would ever wake him from the dream? And, indeed, if there were nothing to wake him, how should he distinguish its articles from the authentic dictates of verity?

Remember, too, that it is by no means clear that we are happier in the faith we do profess than we should be under the spell of an orthodoxy that was sage against all heresy. Cruel and savage as orthodoxies have always proved to be, the faithful seem able to convince themselves that the heretics, as they continue to crop up, get nothing worse than their due, and to rest with an easy conscience.

In any event, my thesis is that the best answer to such systems is not so much in their immoral quality—immoral though they be—as in the fact that they are inherently unstable because they are at war with our only trustworthy way of living in accord with the facts. For I submit that it is only by trial and error, by insistent scrutiny and by readiness to re-examine presently accredited conclusions that we have risen, so far as in fact we have risen, from our brutish ancestors, and I believe that in our loyalty to these habits lies our only chance, not merely of progress, but even of survival.

They were not indeed a part of our aboriginal endowment: Man, as he emerged, was not prodigally equipped to master the infinite diversity of his environment. Obviously, enough of us did manage to get through; but it has been a statistical survival, for the individual's native powers of adjustment are by no means enough for his personal safety any more than are those of other creatures. The precipitate of our experience is far from absolute verity, and our exasperated resentment at all dissent is a sure index of our doubts. Take, for instance, our constant recourse to the word, "subversive," as a touchstone of impermissible deviation from accepted canons.

All discussion, all debate, all dissidence tends to question and in consequence to upset existing convictions: that is precisely its purpose and its justification. He is, indeed, a "subversive" who disputes those precepts that I most treasure and seeks to persuade me to substitute his own. He may have no shadow of desire to resort to anything but persuasion; he may be of those to whom any forcible sanction of conformity is anathema; yet it remains true that he is trying to bring about my apostasy, and I hate him just in proportion as I fear his success.

Contrast this protective resentment with the assumption that lies at the base of our whole system that the best chance for truth to emerge is a fair field for all ideas. Nothing, I submit, more completely betrays our latent disloyalty to this premise to all that we pretend to believe than the increasingly common resort to this and other question-begging words. Their imprecision comforts us by enabling us to suppress arguments that disturb our complacency and yet to continue to congratulate ourselves on keeping the faith as we have received it from the Founding Fathers.

Heretics have been hateful from the beginning of recorded time; they have been ostracized, exiled, tortured, maimed and butchered; but it has generally proved impossible to smother them, and when it has not, the society that has succeeded has always declined. Façades of authority, however imposing, do not survive after it has appeared that they rest upon the sands of human conjecture and compromise.

And so, if I am to say what are "the principles of civil liberties and human rights," I answer that they lie in habits, customs—conventions, if you will—that tolerate dissent and can live without irrefragable certainties; that are ready to overhaul existing assumptions; that recognize that we never see save through a glass, darkly, and that at long last we shall succeed only so far as we continue to undertake "the intolerable labor of thought"—that most distasteful of all our activities.

If such a habit and such a temper pervade a society, it will not need institutions to protect its "civil liberties and human rights"; so far as they do not, I venture to doubt how far anything else can protect them: whether it be Bills of Rights, or courts that must in the name of interpretation read their meaning into them.

This may seem to you a bleak and cheerless conclusion, too alien to our nature to be practical. "We must live from day to day"—you will say—"to live is to act, and to act is to choose and decide. How can we carry on at all without some principles, some patterns to meet the conflicts in which each day involves us?" Indeed, we cannot, nor am I suggesting that we should try; but I *am* suggesting that it makes a vital difference—*the* vital difference—whether we deem our principles and our patterns to be eternal verities, rather than the best postulates so far attainable.

Was it not Holmes who said: "The highest courage is to stake everything on a premise that you know tomorrow's evidence may disprove"? "Ah"—you will reply—"there's the rub. That may be the highest courage, but how many have it? You are hopelessly wrong if you assume the general prevalence of such a virtue; ordinary men must be given more than conjectures if they are to face grave dangers."

But do you really believe that? Do you not see about you every day and everywhere the precise opposite? Not alone on the battlefield but in the forest, the desert and the plain; in the mountains, at sea, on the playing field, even in the laboratory and the factory—yes (do not laugh), at the card table and the racetrack—men are forever putting it "upon the touch to win or lose it all." Without some smack of uncertainty and danger, to most of us the world would be a tepid, pallid show.

Surely, like me, you have all felt something of this when you have looked on those pathetic attempts to depict in paint or stone the delights of paradise. I own that the torments of hell never fail to horrify me; not even the glee of the demons in charge is an adequate relief, though the artist has generally been successful in giving a veracious impression of the gusto with which they discharge their duties.

But when I turn to the Congregation of the Blessed, I cannot avoid a sense of anticlimax; strive as I may, the social atmosphere seems a bit forced; and I recall those very irreverent verses of Lowes Dickinson:

> Burning at first no doubt would be worse,
> But time the impression would soften,
> While those who are bored with praising the Lord,
> Would be more bored with praising him often.

By some happy fortuity man is a projector, a designer, a builder, a craftsman; it is among his most dependable joys to impose upon the flux that passes before him some mark of himself, aware though he always must be of the odds against him. His reward is not so much in the work as in its making; not so much in the prize as in the race. We may win when we lose, if we have done what we can; for by so doing we have made real at least some part of that finished product in whose fabrication we are most concerned—ourselves.

And if at the end some friendly critic shall pass by and say, "My friend, how good a job do you really think you have made of it all?" we can answer, "I know as well as you that it is not of high quality, but I did put into it whatever I had, and that was the game I started out to play."

It is still in the lap of the gods whether a society can succeed, based on "civil liberties and human rights," conceived as I have tried to describe them; but of one thing at least we may be sure: the alternatives that have so far appeared have been immeasurably worse, and so, whatever the outcome, I submit to you that we must press along. Borrowing from Epictetus, let us say to ourselves: "Since we are men we will play the part of a Man," and how can I better end than by recalling to you the concluding passage of "Prometheus Unbound"?

> To suffer woes which Hope thinks infinite;
> To forgive wrongs darker than death or night;
> To defy Power, which seems omnipotent
> To love, and bear; to hope till Hope creates
> From its own wreck the thing it contemplates;
> Neither to change, nor falter, nor repent;
> This, like thy glory, Titan, is to be
> Good, great and joyous, beautiful and free;
> This is alone Life, Joy, Empire and Victory.

Social Analysis

SIGMUND FREUD

•

The Anatomy of the Mental Personality[1]

Ladies and Gentlemen—I am sure you all recognise in your dealings, whether with persons or things, the importance of your starting-point. It was the same with psycho-analysis: the course of development through which it has passed, and the reception which it has met with have not been unaffected by the fact that what it began working upon was the symptom, a thing which is more foreign to the ego than anything else in the mind. The symptom has its origin in the repressed, it is as it were the representative of the repressed in relation to the ego; the repressed is a foreign territory to the ego, an internal foreign territory, just as reality is—you must excuse the unusual expression—an external foreign territory. From the symptom the path of psycho-analysis led to the unconscious, to the life of the instincts, to sexuality, and it was then that psycho-analysis was met by illuminating criticisms to the effect that man is not merely a sexual being but has nobler and higher feelings. It might have been added that, supported by the consciousness of those higher feelings, he often allowed himself the right to think nonsense and to overlook facts.

You know better than that. From the very beginning our view was that men fall ill owing to the conflict between the demands of their instincts and the internal resistance which is set up against them; not for a moment did we forget this resisting, rejecting and repressing factor, which we believed to be furnished with its own special forces, the ego-instincts, and which corresponds to the ego of popular psychology. The difficulty was that, since the progress of all scientific work is necessarily laborious, psycho-analysis could not study every part of the field at once or make a pronouncement on every problem in one breath. At last we had got so far that we could turn our attention from the repressed to the repressing forces, and we came face to face with the ego, which seemed to need so little explanation, with the certain expectation that there, too, we should find things for which we could not have been prepared; but it was not easy to find a first method of approach. That is what I am going to talk to you about to-day.

Before I start, I may tell you that I have a suspicion that my account of the

[1] Reprinted from *New Introductory Lectures on Psychoanalysis* by Sigmund Freud. Translated by W. J. H. Sprott. By permission of W. W. Norton & Company, Inc. Copyright 1933 by Sigmund Freud. Copyright renewed 1961 by W. J. H. Sprott. By permission also of The Hogarth Press, Limited, London.

psychology of the ego will affect you differently than the introduction into the psychological underworld that preceded it. Why that should be the case, I cannot say for certain. My original explanation was that you would feel that, whereas hitherto I have been telling you in the main about facts, however strange and odd they might appear, this time you would be listening chiefly to theories, that is to say, speculations. But that is not quite true; when I weighed the matter more carefully I was obliged to conclude that the part played by intellectual manipulation of the facts is not much greater in our ego-psychology than it was in the psychology of the neuroses. Other explanations turned out to be equally untenable, and I now think that the character of the material itself is responsible, and the fact that we are not accustomed to dealing with it. Anyhow I shall not be surprised if you are more hesitant and careful in your judgment than you have been hitherto.

The situation in which we find ourselves at the beginning of our investigation will itself suggest the path we have to follow. We wish to make the ego the object of our study, our own ego. But how can we do that? The ego is the subject *par excellence,* how can it become the object? There is no doubt, however, that it can. The ego can take itself as object, it can treat itself like any other object, observe itself, criticise itself, and do Heaven knows what besides with itself. In such a case one part of the ego stands over against the other. The ego can, then, be split; it splits when it performs many of its functions, at least for the time being. The parts can afterwards join up again. After all that is saying nothing new; perhaps it is only underlining more than usual something that every one knows already. But on the other hand we are familiar with the view that pathology, with its magnification and exaggeration, can make us aware of normal phenomena which we should otherwise have missed. Where pathology displays a breach or a cleft, under normal conditions there may well be a link. If we throw a crystal to the ground, it breaks, but it does not break haphazard; in accordance with the lines of cleavage it falls into fragments, whose limits were already determined by the structure of the crystal, although they were invisible. Psychotics are fissured and splintered structures such as these. We cannot deny them a measure of that awe with which madmen were regarded by the peoples of ancient times. They have turned away from external reality, but for that very reason they know more of internal psychic reality and can tell us much that would otherwise be inaccessible to us. One group of them suffer what we call delusions of observation. They complain to us that they suffer continually, and in their most intimate actions, from the observation of unknown powers or persons, and they have hallucinations in which they hear these persons announcing the results of their observations: "now he is going to say this, now he is dressing himself to go out," and so on. Such observation is not the same thing as persecution, but it is not far removed from it. It implies that these persons distrust the patient, and expect to catch him doing something that is forbidden and for which he will be punished. How would it be if these mad people were right, if we all of us had an observing function in our egos threatening us with punishment, which, in their case, had merely become sharply separated from the ego and had been mistakenly projected into external reality?

I do not know whether it will appeal to you in the same way as it appeals to me. Under the strong impression of this clinical picture, I formed the idea that the separating off of an observing function from the rest of the ego might be a normal feature of the ego's structure; this idea has never left me, and I was driven to investigate the further characteristics and relations of the function which had been separated off in this way. The next step is soon taken. The actual content of the delusion of observation makes it probable that the observation is only a first step towards conviction and punishment, so that we may guess that another activity of this function must be what we call conscience. There is hardly anything that we separate off from our ego so regularly as our conscience and so easily set over against it. I feel a temptation to do something which promises to bring me pleasure, but I refrain from doing it on the ground that "my conscience will not allow it." Or I allow myself to be persuaded by the greatness of the expectation of pleasure into doing something against which the voice of my conscience has protested, and after I have done it my conscience punishes me with painful reproaches, and makes me feel remorse for it. I might say simply that the function which I am beginning to distinguish within the ego is the conscience; but it is more prudent to keep that function as a separate entity and assume that conscience is one of its activities, and that the self-observation which is necessary as a preliminary to the judicial aspect of conscience is another. And since the process of recognizing a thing as a separate entity involves giving it a name of its own, I will henceforward call this function in the ego the "super-ego."

At this point I am quite prepared for you to ask scornfully whether our ego-psychology amounts to no more than taking everyday abstractions literally, magnifying them, and turning them from concepts into things—which would not be of much assistance. My answer to that is, that in ego-psychology it will be difficult to avoid what is already familiar, and that it is more a question of arriving at new ways of looking at things and new groupings of the facts than of making new discoveries. I will not ask you, therefore, to abandon your critical attitude but merely to await further developments. The facts of pathology give our efforts a background for which you will look in vain in popular psychology. I will proceed. No sooner have we got used to the idea of this super-ego, as something which enjoys a certain independence, pursues its own ends, and is independent of the ego as regards the energy at its disposal, than we are faced with a clinical picture which throws into strong relief the severity, and even cruelty, of this function, and the vicissitudes through which its relations with the ego may pass. I refer to the condition of melancholia, or more accurately the melancholic attack, of which you must have heard often enough, even if you are not psychiatrists. In this disease, about whose causes and mechanism we know far too little, the most remarkable characteristic is the way in which the super-ego—you may call it, but in a whisper, the conscience—treats the ego. The melancholiac during periods of health can, like any one else, be more or less severe towards himself; but when he has a melancholic attack, his super-ego becomes over-severe, abuses, humiliates, and ill-treats his unfortunate ego, threatens it with the severest punishments, reproaches it for long forgotten actions which were at the time regarded quite lightly, and behaves as though it had spent the whole interval in amassing complaints and was only waiting for its present increase in strength to bring them forward, and to condemn the ego on their account. The super-ego has the ego at its mercy and applies the most severe moral standards to it; indeed it represents the whole demands of morality, and we see all at once that our moral sense of guilt is the expression of the tension between the ego and the super-ego. It is a very remarkable experience to observe morality, which was ostensibly conferred on us by God and planted deep in our hearts, functioning as a periodical phenomenon. For after a certain number of months the whole moral fuss is at an end, the critical voice of the super-ego is silent, the ego is reinstated, and enjoys once more all the rights of man until the next attack. Indeed in many forms of the malady something exactly the reverse takes place during the intervals; the ego finds itself in an ecstatic state of exaltation, it triumphs, as though the super-ego had lost all its power or had become merged with the ego, and this liberated, maniac ego gives itself up in a really uninhibited fashion, to the satisfaction of all its desires. Happenings rich in unsolved riddles!

You will expect me to do more than give a mere example in support of my statement that we have learnt a great deal about the formation of the super-ego, that is of the origin of conscience. The philosopher Kant once declared that nothing proved to him the greatness of God more convincingly than the starry heavens and the moral conscience within us. The stars are unquestionably superb, but where conscience is concerned God has been guilty of an uneven and careless piece of work, for a great many men have only a limited share of it or scarcely enough to be worth mentioning. This does not mean, however, that we are overlooking the fragment of psychological truth which is contained in the assertion that conscience is of divine origin! but the assertion needs interpretation. Conscience is no doubt something within us, but it has not been there from the beginning. In this sense it is the opposite of sexuality, which is certainly present from the very beginning of life, and is not a thing that only comes in later. But small children are notoriously a-moral. They have no internal inhibitions against their pleasure-seeking impulses. The rôle, which the super-ego undertakes later in life, is at first played by an external power, by parental authority. The influence of the parents dominates the child by granting proofs of affection and by threats of punishment, which, to the child, mean loss of love, and which must also be feared on their own account. This objective anxiety is the forerunner of the later moral anxiety; so long as the former is dominant one need not speak of super-ego or of conscience. It is only later that the secondary situation arises, which we are far too ready to regard as the normal state of affairs; the external restrictions are introjected, so that the super-ego takes the place of the parental function, and thenceforward observes, guides and threatens the ego in just the same way as the parents acted to the child before.

The super-ego, which in this way has taken over the power, the aims and even the methods of the parental function, is, however, not merely the legatee of parental authority, it is actually the heir of its body. It proceeds directly from it, and we shall soon learn in what way this comes about. First, however, we must pause to consider a point in which they differ. The super-ego seems to have made a one-sided selection, and to have chosen only the harshness and severity of the parents, their preventive and punitive functions, while their loving care is not taken up and continued by it. If the parents have really ruled with a rod of iron, we can easily understand the child developing a severe super-ego, but, contrary to our expectations, experience shows that the super-ego may reflect the same relentless harshness even when the up-bringing has been gentle and kind, and avoided threats and punishment as far as possible. We shall return to this contradiction later, when we are dealing with the transmutation of instincts in the formation of the super-ego.

I cannot tell you as much as I could wish about the change from the parental function to the super-ego, partly because that process is so complicated that a description of it does not fit into the framework of a set of introductory lectures such as these, and partly because we ourselves do not feel that we have fully understood it. You will have to be satisfied, therefore, with the following indications. The basis of the process is what we call an identification, that is to say, that one ego becomes like another, one which results in the first ego behaving itself in certain respects in the same way as the second; it imitates it, and as it were takes it into itself. This identification has been not inappropriately compared with the oral cannibalistic incorporation of another person. Identification is a very important kind of relationship with another person, probably the most primitive, and is not to be confused with object-choice. One can express the difference between them in this way: when a boy identifies himself with his father, he wants to *be like* his father; when he makes him the object of his choice, he wants to *have* him, to possess him; in the first case his ego is altered on the model of his father, in the second case that is not necessary. Identification and object-choice are broadly speaking independent of each other; but one can identify oneself with a person, and alter one's ego accordingly, and take the same person as one's sexual object. It is said that this influencing of the ego by the sexual object takes place very often with women, and is characteristic of femininity. With regard to what is by far the most instructive relation between identification and object-choice, I must have given you some information in my previous lectures. It can be as easily observed in children as in adults, in normal as in sick persons. If one has lost a love-object or has had to give it up, one often compensates oneself by identifying oneself with it; one sets it up again inside one's ego, so that in this case object-choice regresses, as it were, to identification.

I am myself not at all satisfied with this account of identification, but it will suffice if you will grant that the establishment of the super-ego can be described as a successful instance of identification with the parental function. The fact which is decisively in favour of this point of view is that this new creation of a superior function within the ego is extremely closely bound up with the fate of the Oedipus complex, so that the super-ego appears as the heir of that emotional tie, which is of such importance for childhood. When the Oedipus complex passes away the child must give up the intense object-cathexes which it has formed towards its parents, and to compensate for this loss of object, its identifications with its parents, which have probably long been present, become greatly intensified. Identifications of this kind, which may be looked on as precipitates of abandoned object-cathexes, will recur often enough in the later life of the child; but it is in keeping with the emotional importance of this first instance of such a transformation that its product should occupy a special position in the ego. Further investigation also reveals that the super-ego does not attain to full strength and development if the overcoming of the Oedipus complex has not been completely successful. During the course of its growth, the super-ego also takes over the influence of those persons who have taken the place of the parents, that is to say of persons who have been concerned in the child's upbringing, and whom it has regarded as ideal models. Normally the super-ego is constantly becoming more and more remote from the original parents, becoming, as it were, more impersonal. Another thing that we must not forget is that the child values its parents differently at different periods of its life. At the time at which the Oedipus complex makes way for the super-ego, they seem to be splendid figures, but later on they lose a good deal of their prestige. Identifications take place with these later editions of the parents as well, and regularly provide important contributions to the formation of character; but these only affect the ego, they have no influence on the super-ego, which has been determined by the earliest parental images.

I hope you will by now feel that in postulating the existence of a super-ego I have been describing a genuine structural entity, and have not been merely personifying an abstraction, such as conscience. We have now to mention another important activity which is to be ascribed to the super-ego. It is also the vehicle of the ego-ideal, by which the ego measures itself, towards which it strives, and whose demands for ever-increasing perfection it is always striving to fulfill. No doubt this ego-ideal is a precipitation of the old idea of the parents, an expression of the admiration which the child felt for the perfection which it at that time ascribed to them. I know you have heard a great deal about the sense of inferiority which is said to distinguish the neurotic subject. It crops up especially in the pages of works that have literary pretensions. A writer who brings in the expression "inferiority-complex" thinks he has satisfied all the demands of psycho-analysis and raised his work on to a higher psychological plane. As a matter of fact the phrase "inferiority-complex" is hardly ever used in psycho-analysis. It does not refer to anything which we regard as simple, let alone elementary. To trace it back to the perception in oneself of some organic disability or other, as the school of so-called Individual Psychologists like to do, seems to us a short-sighted error. The sense of inferiority has a strong erotic basis. The child feels itself inferior when it perceives that it is not loved, and so does the adult as well. The only organ that is really regarded as inferior is the stunted penis—the girl's clitoris. But the major part of the sense of inferiority springs from the relationship of the ego to its super-ego, and, like the sense of guilt, it is an expression of the tension between them. The sense of inferiority and the sense of guilt are exceedingly difficult to distinguish. Perhaps we should do better if we regarded the former as the erotic complement to the sense of moral inferiority. We have paid but little attention to such questions of conceptual differentiation in psycho-analysis.

Seeing that the inferiority-complex has become so popular, I shall venture to treat you to a short digression. A historical personage of our time, who is still living but who for the present has retired into the background, suffers from the mal-development of a limb caused by an injury at birth. A very well-known contemporary writer who has a predilection for writing the biographies of famous persons, has dealt with the life of the man to whom I am referring. Now if one is writing a biography, it is naturally very difficult to suppress the urge for psychological understanding. The author has therefore made an attempt to build up the whole development of his hero's character on the basis of a sense of inferiority, which was caused by his physical defect. While doing this he has overlooked a small but not unimportant fact. It is usual for mothers to whom fate has given a sickly or otherwise defective child to try to compensate for this unfair handicap with an extra amount of love. In the case we are speaking of, the proud mother behaved quite differently; she withdrew her love from the child on account of his disability. When the child grew up into a man of great power, he proved beyond all doubt by his behavior that he had never forgiven his mother. If you will bear in mind the importance of mother-love for the mental life of the child, you will be able to make the necessary corrections in the inferiority-theory of the biographer.

But let us get back to the super-ego. We have allocated to it the activities of self-observation, conscience, and the holding up of ideals. It follows from our account of its origin that it is based upon an overwhelmingly important biological fact no less than upon a momentous psychological fact, namely the lengthy dependence of the human child on its parents and the Oedipus complex; these two facts, moreover, are closely bound up with each other. For us the super-ego is the representative of all moral restrictions, the advocate of the impulse towards perfection, in short it is as much as we have been able to apprehend psychologically of what people call the "higher" things in human life. Since it itself can be traced back to the influence of parents, teachers, and so on, we shall learn more of its significance if we turn our attention to these sources. In general, parents and similar authorities follow the dictates of their own super-egos in the up-bringing of children. Whatever terms their ego may be on with their super-ego, in the education of the child they are severe and exacting. They have forgotten the difficulties of their own childhood, and are glad to be able to identify themselves fully at last with their own parents, who in their day subjected them to such severe restraints. The result is that the super-ego of the child is not really built up on the model of the parents, but on that of the parents' super-ego; it takes over the same content, it becomes the vehicle of tradition and of all the age-long values which have been handed down in this way from generation to generation. You may easily guess what great help is afforded by the recognition of the super-ego in understanding the social behaviour of man, in grasping the problem of delinquency, for example, and perhaps, too, in providing us with some practical hints upon education. It is probable that the so-called materialistic conceptions of history err in that they underestimate this factor. They brush it aside with the remark that the "ideologies" of mankind are nothing more than resultants of their economic situation at any given moment or superstructures built upon it. That is the truth, but very probably it is not the whole truth. Mankind never lives completely in the present; the ideologies of the super-ego perpetuate the past, the traditions of the race and the people, which yield but slowly to the influence of the present and to new developments, and, so long as they work through the super-ego, play an important part in man's life, quite independently of economic conditions.

In 1921 I tried to apply the distinction between the ego and the super-ego to the study of group psychology. I reached a formula, which ran like this: A psychological group is a collection of individuals, who have introduced the same person into their super-ego, and on the basis of this common factor have identified themselves with one another in their ego. This naturally only holds for groups who have a leader. If we could find more applications of this kind, the hypothesis of the super-ego would lose all its strangeness for us, and we should be entirely relieved of the embarrassment which we cannot help feeling when, used as we are to the atmosphere of the underworld, we make excursions into the more superficial and higher planes of the mental apparatus. Of course we do not for a moment think that the last word on ego-psychology has been spoken with the demarcation of the super-ego. It is rather the beginning of the subject, but in this case it is not only the first step that is difficult.

But now another task awaits us, as it were at the opposite end of the ego. This question is raised by an observation which is made during analytic work, an observation which is, indeed, an old one. As so often happens, it has taken a long time for its true value to be appreciated. As you are aware, the whole of psycho-analytic theory is in fact built up on the perception of the resistance exerted by the patient when we try to make him conscious of his unconscious.

The objective indication of resistance is that his associations stop short or wander far away from the theme that is being discussed. He may also become subjectively aware of the resistance by experiencing painful feelings when he approaches the theme. But this last indication may be absent. In such a case we say to the patient that we conclude from his behaviour that he is in a state of resistance, and he replies that he knows nothing about it and is only aware of a difficulty in associating. Experience shows that we were right, but, if so, his resistance too must have been unconscious, just as unconscious as the repressed material which we were trying to bring to the surface. Long ago we should have asked from which part of the mind such an unconscious resistance could operate. The beginner in psycho-analysis will be ready at once with the answer that it must be the resistance of the unconscious. An ambiguous and useless answer! If it means that the resistance operates from the repressed, then we must say: "Certainly not!" To the repressed we must rather ascribe a strong upward-driving force, an impulsion to get through to consciousness. The resistance can only be a manifestation of the ego, which carried through the repression at one time or other and is now endeavouring to keep it up. And that too was our earlier view. Now that we have posited a special function within the ego to represent the demand for restriction and rejection, *i.e.* the super-ego, we can say that repression is the work of the super-ego,—either that it does its work on its own account or else that the ego does it in obedience to its orders. If now we are faced with the case where the patient under analysis is not conscious of his resistance, then it must be either that the super-ego and the ego can operate unconsciously in quite important situations, or, which would be far more significant, that parts of both ego and super-ego themselves are unconscious. In both cases we should have to take account of the disturbing view that the ego (including the super-ego) does not by any means completely coincide with the conscious, nor the repressed with the unconscious.

Ladies and Gentlemen—I feel I must have a little breathing space, which I expect you will welcome with relief, and before I go on I must make an apology. Here am I giving you a supplement to the introduction to psycho-analysis which I started fifteen years ago, and I am behaving as though you yourselves had been doing nothing but psycho-analysis all that time. I know it is a monstrous supposition, but I am helpless, I have no alternative. The reason is that it is exceedingly difficult to give an insight into psycho-analysis to any one who is not himself a psycho-analyst. I assure you that we do not like to give the effect of being members of a secret society carrying on a secret science. And yet we have been obliged to recognise and state as our considered opinion that no one has a right to say in psycho-analysis unless he has been through certain experiences which he can only have by being analysed himself. When I delivered my lectures to you fifteen years ago I tried to let you off certain speculative parts of our theory, but it is with those very parts that are connected the new discoveries which I am going to speak of to-day.

Now let me return to my theme. With regard to the two alternatives—that the ego and the super-ego may themselves be unconscious, or that they may merely give rise to unconscious effects—we have for good reasons decided in favour of the former. Certainly, large portions of the ego and super-ego can remain unconscious, are, in fact, normally unconscious. That means to say that the individual knows nothing of their contents and that it requires an expenditure of effort to make him conscious of them. It is true, then, that ego and conscious, repressed and unconscious do not coincide. We are forced fundamentally to revise our attitude towards the problem of conscious and unconscious. At first we might be inclined to think very much less of the importance of consciousness as a criterion, since it has proved so untrustworthy. But if we did so, we should be wrong. It is the same with life: it is not worth much, but it is all that we have. Without the light shed by the quality of consciousness we should be lost in the darkness of depth-psychology. Nevertheless we must try to orientate ourselves anew.

What is meant by "conscious," we need not discuss; it is beyond all doubt. The oldest and best meaning of the word "unconscious" is the descriptive one; we call "unconscious" any mental process the existence of which we are obliged to assume—because, for instance, we infer it in some way from its effects—but of which we are not directly aware. We have the same relation to that mental process as we have to a mental process in another person, except that it belongs to ourselves. If we want to be more accurate, we should modify the statement by saying that we call a process "unconscious" when we have to assume that it was active *at a certain time,* although *at that time* we knew nothing about it. This restriction reminds us that most conscious processes are conscious only for a short period; quite soon they become *latent,* though they can easily become conscious again. We could also say that they had become unconscious, if we were certain that they were still something mental when they were in the latent condition. So far we should have learnt nothing, and not even have earned the right to introduce the notion of the unconscious into psychology. But now we come across a new fact which we can already observe in the case of errors. We find that, in order to explain a slip of the tongue, for instance, we are obliged to assume that an intention to say some particular thing had formed itself in the mind of the person who made the slip. We can infer it with certainty from the occurrence of the speech-disturbance, but it was not able to obtain expression; it was, that is to say, unconscious. If we subsequently bring the intention to the speaker's notice, he may recognise it as a familiar one, in which case it was only temporarily unconscious, or he may repudiate it as foreign to him, in which case it was permanently unconscious. Such an observation as this justifies us in also regarding what we have called "latent" as something "unconscious." The consideration of these dynamic relations puts us in a position to distinguish two kinds of unconscious: one which is transformed into conscious material easily and under conditions which frequently arise, and another in the case of which such a transformation is difficult, can only come about with a considerable expenditure of energy, or may never occur at all. In order to avoid any ambiguity as to whether we are referring to the one or the other unconscious, whether we are using the word in the descriptive or dynamic sense, we make use of a legitimate and simple expedient. We call the unconscious which is only latent, and so can easily become conscious, the "preconscious," and keep the name "unconscious" for the other. We have now three terms, "conscious," "preconscious," and "unconscious," to serve our purposes in describing mental phenomena. Once again, from a purely descriptive point of view, the "preconscious" is also unconscious, but we do not give it that name, except when we are speaking loosely, or when we have to defend in general the existence of unconscious processes in mental life.

You will, I hope, grant that so far things are not so bad and that the scheme is a convenient one. That is all very well; unfortunately our psycho-analytic work has compelled us to use the word "unconscious" in yet another, third, sense; and this may very well have given rise to confusion. Psycho-analysis has impressed us very strongly with the new idea that large and important regions of the mind are normally removed from the knowledge of the ego, so that the processes which occur in them must be recognised as unconscious in the true dynamic sense of the term. We have consequently also attributed to the word "unconscious" a topographical or systematic meaning; we have talked of *systems* of the preconscious and of the unconscious, and of a conflict between the ego and the Ucs. system; so that the word "unconscious" has more and more been made to mean a mental province rather than a quality which mental things have. At this point, the discovery, inconvenient at first sight, that parts of the ego and super-ego, too, are unconscious in the dynamic sense, has a facilitating effect and enables us to remove a complication. We evidently have no right to call that region of the mind which is neither ego nor super-ego the Ucs. system, since the character of unconsciousness is not exclusive to it. Very well; we will no longer use the word "unconscious" in the sense of a system, and to what we have hitherto called by that name we will give a better one, which will not give rise to misunderstandings. Borrowing, at G. Groddeck's suggestion, a term used by Nietzsche, we will call it henceforward the "id." This impersonal pronoun seems particularly suited to express the essential character of this province of the mind—the character of being foreign to the ego. Super-ego, ego and id, then, are the three realms, regions or provinces into which we divide the mental apparatus of the individual; and it is their mutual relations with which we shall be concerned in what follows.

But before we go on I must make a short digression. I have no doubt that you are dissatisfied with the fact that the three qualities of the mind in respect to consciousness and the three regions of the mental apparatus do not fall together into three harmonious pairs, and that you feel that the clarity of our conclusions is consequently impaired. My own view is that we ought not to deplore this fact but that we should say to ourselves that we had no right to expect any such neat arrangement. Let me give you an analogy; analogies prove nothing, that is quite true, but they can make one feel more at home. Let us picture a country with a great variety of geographical configurations, hills, plains and chains of lakes, and with mixed nationalities living in it, Germans, Magyars and Slovaks, who, moreover, are engaged upon a number of different occupations. Now the distribution might be such that the Germans lived in the hills and kept cattle, the Magyars on the plains and grew corn and vines, while the Slovaks lived by the lakes and caught fish and plaited reeds. If this distribution were neat and exact it would no doubt give great satisfaction to a President Wilson; it would also be convenient for giving a geography lesson. It is probable, however, that you would find a less orderly state of affairs if you visited the region. Germans, Magyars and Slovaks would be living everywhere mixed up together, and there would be cornfields too in the hills, and cattle would be kept on the plains as well. One or two things would be as you expected, for one cannot catch fish on the mountains, and wine does not grow in water. The picture of the region which you had brought with you might on the whole fit the facts, but in details you would have to put up with departures from it.

You must not expect me to tell you much that is new about the id, except its name. It is the obscure inaccessible part of our personality; the little we know about it we have learnt from the study of dream-work and the formation of neurotic symptoms, and most of that is of a negative character, and can only be described as being all that the ego is not. We can come nearer to the id with images, and call it a chaos, a cauldron of seething excitement. We suppose that it is somewhere in direct contact with somatic processes, and takes over from them instinctual needs and gives them mental impression, but we cannot say in what substratum this contact is made. These instincts fill it with energy, but it has no organisation and no unified will, only an impulsion to obtain satisfaction for the instinctual needs, in accordance with the pleasure-principle. The laws of logic—above all, the law of contradiction—do not hold for processes in the id. Contradictory impulses exist side by side without neutralising each other or drawing apart; at most they combine in compromise formations under the overpowering economic pressure towards discharging their energy. There is nothing in the id which can be compared to negation, and we are astonished to find in it an exception to the philosophers' assertion that space and time are necessary forms of our mental acts. In the id there is nothing corresponding to the idea of time, no recognition of the passage of time, and (a thing which is very remarkable and awaits adequate attention in philosophic thought) no alteration of mental processes by the passage of time. Conative impulses which have never got beyond the id, and even impressions which have been pushed down into the id by repression, are virtually immortal and are preserved for whole decades as though they had only recently occurred. They can only be recognised as belonging to the past, deprived of their significance, and robbed of their charge of energy, after they have been made conscious by the work of analysis, and no small part of the therapeutic effect of analytic treatment rests upon this fact.

It is constantly being borne in upon me that we have made far too little use of our theory of the indubitable fact that the repressed remains unaltered by the passage of time. This seems to offer us the possibility of an approach to some really profound truths. But I myself have made no further progress here.

Naturally, the id knows no values, no good and evil, no morality. The economic, or, if you prefer, the quantitative factor, which is so closely bound up with the pleasure-principle, dominates all its processes. Instinctual cathexes seeking discharge,—that, in our view, is all that the id contains. It seems, indeed, as if the energy of these instinctual impulses is in a different condition from that in which it is found in the other regions of the mind. It must be far more fluid and more capable of being discharged, for otherwise we should not have those displacements and condensations, which are so characteristic of the id and which are so completely independent of the qualities of what is cathected. (In the ego we should call it an idea.) What would one not give to understand these things better? You observe, in any case, that we can attribute to the id other characteristics than that of being unconscious, and you are aware of the possibility that parts of the ego and super-ego are unconscious without possessing the same primitive and irrational quality. As regards a characterisation of the ego, in so far as it is to be distinguished from the id and the super-ego, we shall get on better if we turn our attention to the relation between it and the most superficial portion of the mental apparatus; which we call the Pcpt-cs (perceptual-conscious) system. This system is directed on to the external world, it mediates perceptions of it, and in it is generated, while it is functioning, the phenomenon of consciousness. It is the sense-organ of the whole apparatus, receptive, moreover, not only of excitations from without but also of such as proceed from the interior of the mind. One can hardly go wrong in regarding the ego as that part of the id which had been modified by its proximity to the external world and the influence that the latter has had on it, and which serves the purpose of receiving stimuli and protecting the organism from them, like the cortical layer with which a particle of living substance surrounds itself. This relation to the external world is decisive for the ego. The ego has taken over the task of representing the external world for the id, and so of saving it; for the id, blindly striving to gratify its instincts in complete disregard of the superior strength of outside forces, could not otherwise escape annihilation. In the fulfilment of this function, the ego has to observe the external world and preserve a true picture of it in the memory traces left by its perceptions, and, by means of the reality-test, it has to eliminate any element in this picture of the external world which is a contribution from internal sources of excitation. On behalf of the id, the ego controls the path of access to motility, but it interpolates between desire and action the procrastinating factor of thought, during which it makes use of the residues of experience stored up in memory. In this way it dethrones the pleasure-principle, which exerts undisputed sway over the processes in the id, and substitutes for it the reality-principle, which promises greater security and greater success.

The relation to time, too, which is so hard to describe, is communicated to the ego by the perceptual system; indeed it can hardly be doubted that the mode in which this system works is the source of the idea of time. What, however, especially marks the ego out in contradistinction to the id, is a tendency to synthesise its contents, to bring together and unify its mental processes which is entirely absent from the id. When we come to deal presently with the instincts in mental life, I hope we shall succeed in tracing this fundamental characteristic of the ego to its source. It is this alone that produces that high degree of organisation which the ego needs for its highest achievements. The ego advances from the function of perceiving instincts to that of controlling them, but the latter is only achieved through the mental representative of the instinct becoming subordinated to a larger organisation, and finding its place in a coherent unity. In popular language, we may say that the ego stands for reason and circumspection, while the id stands for the untamed passions.

So far we have allowed ourselves to dwell on the enumeration of the merits and capabilities of the ego; it is time now to look at the other side of the picture. The ego is after all only a part of the id, a part purposively modified by its proximity to the dangers of reality. From a dynamic point of view it is weak; it borrows its energy from the id, and we are not entirely ignorant of the methods—one might almost call them "tricks"—by means of which it draws further amounts of energy from the id. Such a method, for example, is the process of identification, whether the object is retained or given up. The object-cathexes proceed from the instinctual demands of the id. The first business of the ego is to take note of them. But by identifying itself with the object, it recommends itself to the id in the place of the object and seeks to attract the libido of the id on to itself. We have already seen that, in the course of a person's life, the ego takes into itself a large number of such precipitates of former object-cathexes. On the whole the ego has to carry out the intentions of the id; it fulfils its duty if it succeeds in creating the conditions under which these intentions can best be fulfilled. One might compare the relation of the ego to the id with that between a rider and his horse. The horse provides the locomotive energy, and the rider has the prerogative of determining the goal and of guiding the movements of his powerful mount towards it. But all too often in the relations between the ego and the id we find a picture of the less ideal situation in which the rider is obliged to guide his horse in the direction in which it itself wants to go.

The ego has separated itself off from one part of the id by means of repression-resistances. But the barrier of repression does not extend into the id; so that the repressed material merges into the rest of the id.

The proverb tells us that one cannot serve two masters at once. The poor ego has a still harder time of it; it has to serve three harsh masters, and has to do its best to reconcile the claims and demands of all three. These demands are always divergent and often seem quite incompatible; no wonder that the ego so frequently gives way under its task. The three tyrants are the external world, the super-ego and the id. When one watches the efforts of the ego to satisfy them all, or rather, to obey them all simultaneously, one cannot regret having personified the ego, and established it as a separate being. It feels itself hemmed in on three sides and threatened by three kinds of danger, towards which it reacts by developing anxiety when it is too hard pressed. Having originated in the experiences of the perceptual system, it is designed to represent the demands of the external world, but it also wishes to be a loyal servant of the id, to remain upon good terms with the id, to recommend itself to the id as an object, and to draw the id's libido on to itself. In its attempt to mediate between the id and reality, it is often forced to clothe the Ucs. commands of the id with its own Pcs. rationalisations, to gloss over the conflicts between the id and reality, and with diplomatic dishonesty to display a pretended regard for reality, even when the id persists in being stubborn and uncompromising. On the other hand, its every movement is watched by the severe super-ego, which holds up certain norms of behaviour, without regard to any difficulties coming from the id and the external world; and if these norms are not acted up to, it punishes the ego with the feelings of tension which manifest themselves as a sense of inferiority and guilt. In this way, goaded on by the id, hemmed in by the super-ego, and rebuffed by reality, the ego struggles to cope with its economic task of reducing the forces and influences which work in it and upon it to some kind of harmony; and we may well understand how it is that we so often cannot repress the cry: "Life is not easy." When the ego is forced to acknowledge its weakness, it breaks out into anxiety: reality anxiety in face of the external world, normal anxiety in face of the super-ego, and neurotic anxiety in the face of the strength of the passions in the id.

I have represented the structural relations within the mental personality, as I have explained them to you, in a simple diagram, which I here reproduce.

You will observe how the super-ego goes down into the id; as the heir to the Oedipus complex it has, after all, intimate connections with the id. It lies further from the perceptual system than the ego. The id only deals with the external world through the medium of the ego, at least in this diagram. It is certainly still too early to say how far the drawing is correct; in one respect I know it is not. The space taken up by the unconscious id ought to be incomparably greater than that given to the ego or to the preconscious. You must, if you please, correct that in your imagination.

And now, in concluding this certainly rather exhausting and perhaps not very illuminating account, I must add a warning. When you think of this dividing up of the personality into ego, super-ego and id, you must not imagine sharp dividing lines such as are artificially drawn in the field of political geography. We cannot do justice to the characteristics of the mind by means of

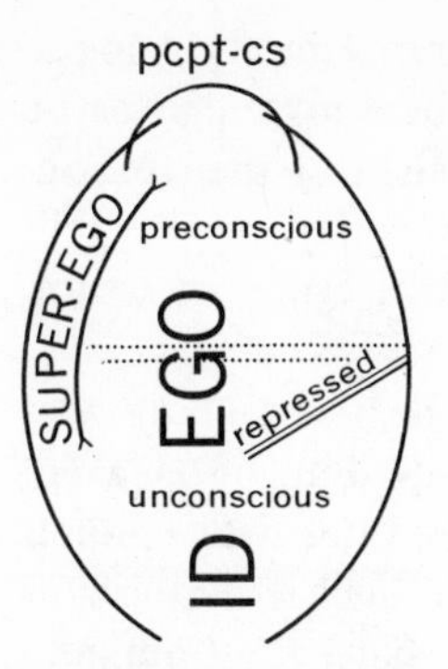

linear contours, such as occur in a drawing or in a primitive painting, but we need rather the areas of colour shading off into one another that are to be found in modern pictures. After we have made our separations, we must allow what we have separated to merge again. Do not judge too harshly of a first attempt at picturing a thing so elusive as the human mind. It is very probable that the extent of these differentiations varies very greatly from person to person; it is possible that their function itself may vary, and that they may at times undergo a process of involution. This seems to be particularly true of the most insecure and, from the phylogenetic point of view, the most recent of them, the differentiation between the ego and the super-ego. It is also incontestable that the same thing can come about as a result of mental disease. It can easily be imagined, too, that certain practices of mystics may succeed in upsetting the normal relations between the different regions of the mind, so that, for example, the perceptual system becomes able to grasp relations in the deeper layers of the ego and in the id which would otherwise be inaccessible to it. Whether such a procedure can put one in possession of ultimate truths, from which all good will flow, may be safely doubted. All the same, we must admit that the therapeutic efforts of psycho-analysis have chosen much the same method of approach. For their object is to strengthen the ego, to make it more independent of the super-ego, to widen its field of vision, and so to extend its organisation that it can take over new portions of the id. Where id was, there shall ego be.

It is reclamation work, like the draining of the Zuyder Zee.

PLATO

•

The Apology of Socrates[1]

SOCRATES' DEFENCE

What effect my accusers had upon you, Men of Athens, I know not. As for me, they well-nigh made me forget who I was, so telling were their speeches! And yet, so to say, not one atom of truth did they utter. But that which astonished me most among all their fabrications was this, that they said you must be on your guard, and not be deceived by me, as I was a masterly

[1] *Plato on the Trial and Death of Socrates,* Lane Cooper trans. (Ithaca, N. Y.: Cornell University Press, 1941), pp. 49–77. Reprinted by permission of the publishers.

speaker. That they should not be ashamed when they were promptly going to be caught by me in a lie, through the fact, since I shall show myself to be no orator at all, therein methought they reached the very height of their effrontery; unless perchance what they call masterly speaker means the one who tells the truth. If that is what they are saying, then I will admit I am an orator, though not of the sort they describe.

Well then, as I say, these men have uttered nothing, or next to nothing, that is true. From me, however, you shall hear the simple truth. But, by Heaven! fellow citizens, it will not be in language like theirs, decked out with epithets and phrases, nor beautifully ordered; rather you shall hear such utterances as come to me, in any words that offer, for of the justice of what I say I am convinced, and from me you need none of you expect aught else. No, Gentlemen! it would hardly befit a man of my age to come into your presence moulding phrases like a youngster. And nevertheless, my fellow citizens, and above all, I do request and beg of you this thing: if you should hear me pleading my cause with the same expressions I habitually have used in speaking, whether at the market by the counters, where many of you have heard me, or elsewhere, do not for that reason marvel and make a disturbance. The facts stand thus. At the age of seventy years I now for the first time have come up before a tribunal, and so I am an absolute stranger to the language of this place. Let it be as if I really were a foreigner here, since then you surely would excuse me if I used the accent and manner of speech in which I was reared. And so I now make this request of you, a matter of justice as it seems to me, that you let me use my way of speaking; it may be better, it may be worse, but the only thing you have to consider is this, and this is what you have to put your mind on, whether that which I say is right or not. That is the merit of a judge; the merit of a speaker is to tell the truth.

To begin with, fellow citizens, it is right for me to answer the earliest charges falsely brought against me, and my first accusers, and then I must answer the charges and accusers that come later.

Many, in fact, were they who formerly brought charges against me, yes many years ago, and spoke not a word of truth. And them I fear more than I do the group of Anytus, dangerous as these are too. No, Gentlemen, those others are more dangerous, for they have prejudiced the major part of you since your childhood, convincing you of an utterly false charge against me; to wit, 'There is a person, Socrates by name, a "wise man," who speculates about the heavens above, and also searches into everything below the earth, and in argument can make the worse case win.'[2] Those persons who have spread this charge abroad, they, fellow citizens, are my dangerous accusers; for people who listen to them think that men who make the said investigations do not believe in any gods. Add that these accusers are many in number, have brought their charges for a long time now, and, moreover, made them to you when you

[2] The proverbial translation is: 'To make the worse appear the better reason.'

most readily believed things, when some of you were children or striplings; sheer accusation of an absent person without anybody to defend him. And what is most baffling of all, it is impossible to identify and name them, unless perchance in the case of a certain comic poet. For the rest, for all who through jealousy and malice misled you, and those who, once they were misled, got others to believe the same—with all these it is impossible to deal. There is no means of bringing one of them here to court, or putting a single one to cross-examination. No, in making my defence I am simply forced to fight, as it were, with shadows, and to question with nobody to make reply. Accordingly, I ask you to assume with me that, as I say, my accusers fall into these two classes, one group who are accusing me at present, the other those who of old accused me as aforesaid; and understand that it is these I must reply to first, for it is they whom you heard bringing charges earlier, and far more than this group who now come after.

Well then, fellow citizens, I must now make my defence, and must try to clear away in this brief time that calumny which you have entertained so long. I would that this might come to pass, if so it should be better for both you and me, and if it profits me to plead. But I think the task to be a hard one, and what its nature is I am by no means unaware. Still, let the outcome be as it pleases God; the law must be obeyed, and the defence be made.

Let us, then, go back and look at the original accusation from which the slander arose, the slander that gave Meletus his ground for this indictment he has lodged against me. Let us see. Precisely what did the slanderers say when they slandered? We must read their complaint as if it were a legal accusation: 'Socrates is wicked; overdoes inquiry into what occurs below the earth and in the heavens; in arguing makes the worse case win; and teaches others to do the same as he.' Such is in substance the accusation—what you actually saw in the comedy [the *Clouds*] of Aristophanes, where a man called 'Socrates' is swung about, declaring that he treads the air, and sputtering a deal of other nonsense on matters of which I have not one bit of knowledge either great or small. And I do not say so in disparagement of any science such as that, if any one is learned in such matters; I should not wish to be attacked by Meletus upon so grave a charge. But actually, fellow citizens, to me these matters are of absolutely no concern. I call the greater part of you yourselves to witness, and beg all who ever heard me in discussion to tell one another and declare it; many of you are in a position to do this. Declare to one another, therefore, whether any of you ever heard me dealing with such matters either briefly or at length. In that way you will see what all the rest amounts to of what the generality of people say concerning me.

No, there is nothing in it whatsoever. And if you have heard anybody say that I profess to give instruction, and get money in that way, neither is that true; although to my mind it is very fine indeed if any one is able to instruct his fellows, as are Gorgias of Leontini, and Prodicus of Ceos, and Hippias of Elis. Each one of them is able, Gentlemen, to go to city after city and attract young men; youths who might without expense consort with any one they chose among their own fellow citizens, these they persuade to give up that fellowship, to consort with them, to pay them money, and to be grateful to them besides. And indeed there is another man of learning here, from Paros, who, I learned, was staying in the City, for I happened to be calling on a man, Callias son of Hipponicus, who has paid more money to the Sophists than have all the others put together. And so I questioned him, he having, in fact, two sons:

'Callias,' said I, 'if your two sons had been colts or calves, we should have no trouble in finding some one to look after them, who for pay would make them fine and good according to the standard of their kind. We should pick some trainer of horses, say, or farmer. But now that they are human beings, whom have you in mind to put in charge of them? Who is there with a knowledge of their proper quality, the excellence of a human being and a citizen? I fancy you have given thought to this since you have sons. Is there any one,' said I, 'or not?'

'Yes, certainly,' said he.

'Who?' said I. 'Whence comes he? What does he charge for teaching?'

'Socrates,' he said, 'it is Evenus; comes from Paros; charge, five minae.' So I thought Evenus was a lucky man if he really had this art, and would teach it at so reasonable a rate. For myself, I should be very proud and self-conceited if I knew all that. But the truth is, fellow citizens, I have no such knowledge.

Then perhaps some one of you may be inclined to ask: 'But Socrates, what *is* the matter with you? What is the origin of these charges that are made against you? Unless you acted very differently from everybody else, surely no such story and repute would have arisen—if you did not do something other than most people do. Tell us what it is, in order to keep us from rushing to our own conclusion about you.'

That, I take it, would be fairly spoken; and I shall try to show you what it is that has given me this name and ill repute. Pray listen. Some of you, perhaps, will take me to be joking, but be assured that I shall tell you the simple truth. The fact is, fellow citizens, that I have got this name through my possession of a certain wisdom. What sort of wisdom is it? A wisdom, doubtless, that appertains to man. With respect to this, perhaps, I actually am wise; whereas those others whom I just now mentioned may possibly be wise with a wisdom more than human, or else I do not know what to say of it; as for me, I certainly do not possess it, and whoever says I do is lying, and seeks to injure me.

And, fellow citizens, do not interrupt me even if I say what seems extravagant, for the statement I shall make is not my own; instead, I shall refer you to a witness whose word can be accepted. Your witness to my wisdom, if I have any, and to its nature, is the god at Delphi. You certainly knew Chaerephon. He was a friend of mine from our youth, and a friend of your popular party as well; he shared in your late exile, and accompanied you on your return. Now you know the temper of Chaerephon, how impulsive he was in everything he undertook. Well so it was when once he went to Delphi, and made bold to ask the oracle this question—and, Gentlemen, please do not make an uproar over what I say; he asked if there was any one more wise than I. Then the Pythian oracle made response that there was no one who was wiser. To this response his brother here will bear you witness, since Chaerephon himself is dead.

Now bear in mind the reason why I tell you this. It is because I am going on to show you whence this calumny of me has sprung; for when I heard about the oracle, I communed within myself: 'What can the god be saying, and what does the riddle mean? Well I know in my own heart that I am without wisdom great or small. What is it that he means, then, in declaring me to be most wise? It cannot be that he is lying; it is not in his nature.' For a long time I continued at a loss as to his meaning, then finally decided, much against my will, to seek it in the following way.

I went to one of those who pass for wise men, feeling sure that there if anywhere I could refute the answer, and explain to the oracle: 'Here is a man that is wiser than I, but you said I was the wisest.' The man I went to see was one of our statesmen; his name I need not mention. Him I thoroughly examined, and from him, as I studied him and conversed with him, I gathered, fellow citizens, this impression. This man appeared to me to seem to be wise to others, and above all to himself, but not to be so. And then I tried to show him that he thought that he was wise, but was not. The result was that I gained his enmity and the enmity as well of many of those who were present. So, as I went away, I reasoned with myself: 'At all events I am wiser than this man is. It is quite possible that neither one of us knows anything fine and good. But this man fancies that he knows when he does not, while I, whereas I do not know, just so I do not fancy that I know. In this small item, then, at least, I seem to be wiser than he, in that I do not fancy that I know what I do not.' Thereafter I went to another man, one of those who passed for wiser than the first, and I got the same impression. Whereupon I gained his enmity as well as that of many more.

Thereafter I went from one man to another, perceiving, with grief and apprehension, that I was getting hated, but it seemed imperative to put the service of the god above all else. In my search for the meaning of the oracle I must go to all who were supposed to have some knowledge. And, fellow citizens, by the Dog, since I have to tell you the truth, here is pretty much what I encountered. The persons with the greatest reputation seemed to me to be the ones who were well-nigh the most deficient, as I made my search in keeping with the god's intent; whereas others of inferior reputation I found to be men superior in regard to their possession of the truth. I needs must tell you all about my wandering course, a veritable round of toils heroic, which I underwent to prove that the oracle was not to be refuted.

After the statesmen, I went to the poets, tragic, dithyrambic, and the rest. There, I thought, my ignorance would be self-evident in comparison with them. So I took those poems of theirs which seemed to me to have been most carefully wrought by them, and asked the authors what they meant, in order that I might at the same time learn from them. Well, Gentlemen, I am ashamed to tell you the truth; and yet it must be done. The fact is, pretty nearly everybody, so to say, who was present could have spoken better than the authors did about the poems they themselves had written. So here again in a short time I learned this about the poets too, that not by wisdom do they make what they compose, but by a gift of nature and an inspiration similar to that of the diviners and the oracles. These also utter many beautiful things, but understand not one of them. And such, I saw, was the experience of the poets. At the same time I perceived that their poetic gift led them to fancy that in all else, too, they were the wisest of mankind, when they were not. So I went away from them as well, believing that I had the same advantage over them as over the statesmen.

To make an end, I went, then, to the artisans. Conscious that I did not, so to say, know anything myself, I was certain I should find that they knew many things and fine. Nor in that was I deceived; they did indeed know things which I did not, and in that they were wiser than I. But, fellow citizens, these excellent workmen seemed to me to have the same defect as the poets. Because they were successful in the practice of their art, each thought himself most wise about all other things of the highest import, and this mistake of theirs beclouded all that wisdom. So I asked myself the question, for the oracle, whether I preferred to be just what I was, neither wise as they were wise nor ignorant as they were ignorant, or to be both wise and ignorant like them. And my response to myself and the oracle was that it paid me to be as I was.

Such, fellow citizens, was the quest which brought me so much enmity, hatreds so utterly harsh and hard to bear, whence sprang so many calumnies, and this name that is given me of being 'wise'; for every time I caught another person in his ignorance, those present fancied that I knew what he did not. But, Gentlemen, in all likelihood it really is the god who is wise, and by that oracle he meant to say that human wisdom is of little worth, or none. And it appears that when he picked out 'Socrates,' he used my name to take me for an example; it was as if he said: 'O race of men, he is the wisest among you, who, like Socrates, knows that in truth his knowledge is worth nothing.' So even now I still go about in my search, and, in keeping with the god's intent, question anybody, citizen or stranger, whom I fancy to be wise. And when it seems to me that he is not, in defence of the god I show that he is not. And this activity has left me without leisure either to take any real part in civic affairs or to care for my own. Instead, I live in infinite poverty through my service to the god.

In addition, the young men who of their own accord are my companions, of the class who have most leisure, sons of the very rich—they listen with joy to the men who are examined; they often imitate me, and in turn attempt to test out others. And thereupon, I take it, they find a great abundance of men who imagine they have some knowledge, and yet know little or nothing. And then these men whom they examine get angry, not at them, but at me, and say there is one Socrates, a perfect blackguard, who corrupts the young. Yet when anybody asks them how he does it, and by teaching what, they have nothing to tell, nor do they know. But in order not to seem quite at a loss, they make the usual attacks that are leveled at philosophers, namely, about 'things occurring in the heavens and below the earth,' 'not believing in the gods,' and 'making the worse case win.' What they do not care to utter, I imagine, is the truth: that they have been shown up in their pretence to knowledge when they actually knew nothing. Accordingly, since they are proud, passionate, and numerous, and organized and effective in speaking about me, they have long since filled your ears with their violent calumnies.

From among them have come Meletus, Anytus, and Lycon to attack me; Meletus aggrieved on behalf of the poets, Anytus on behalf of the artists and the politicians, Lycon on behalf of the rhetoricians. Consequently, as I said at the beginning, I shall be surprised if I succeed, within so short a time, in ridding you of all this swollen mass of calumny.

There, fellow citizens, you have the truth. I hide nothing from you, either great or small, nor do I dissimulate. And yet I know that even by this I stir up hatred, which itself proves that I tell the truth, and that it is precisely this that constitutes the charge against me, and is the cause of it. And whether now or later you investigate the matter, you will find it to be so.

Therewith let me close my defence to you on the charges made against me by my first accusers. As for Meletus, that honest man and good friend of the City, as he styles himself, to him and my more recent foes I will now endeavour to reply.

Here again, since the present charges vary from the former, let us take the actual text of the complaint. It runs, in effect, as follows: 'Socrates,' it declares, 'offends against the law since he corrupts the young, does not believe in the gods the State believes in, and believes in novel deities [spirits, *daimonia*] instead.' Such is the accusation. Let us examine it point by point.

First, it holds that I offend by corrupting the young. But I, fellow citizens, I hold that Meletus offends in that he makes a jest of a serious matter, when he lightly brings men to trial on questions in which he pretends to be deeply interested and concerned, whereas he never took the slightest interest in any of them. That this is so, I will try to prove to you.

Your attention, Meletus! Answer! Do you not attach the utmost importance to the moral improvement of our youth?

[MELETUS] I do indeed.

Well then, tell the assembly here, who makes the young men better? You obviously know, for it is your special concern. You have discovered, so you state, who it is that corrupts them: I, whom you bring hither and accuse. Come now, tell who the person is who makes them better, and name him to these judges.

See, Meletus, you are silent. Have you nothing to say? Doesn't that seem shameful to you, and proof enough of my assertion that you have had no interest in the matter? But come, friend, say who makes them better?

[MELETUS] The laws.

No, my good fellow, that is not what I ask. I mean, what man? for, obviously, first of all he will have to know this very thing, the laws.

[MELETUS] These judges, Socrates.

What say you, Meletus? These judges here are competent to instruct the young, and make them better?

[MELETUS] Most certainly.

All are able? Or some are, and some are not?

[MELETUS] All of them!

By Hera, that is welcome news! We have an ample store of men who benefit their kind! What next? What about the audience here, do these too make them better?

[MELETUS] Yes, they too.

What about the Council?

[MELETUS] Yes, the Council also.

But, Meletus, what about the men in the Assembly, the members of it, do they corrupt the young, or do they one and all make young men better?

[MELETUS] Yes, they do it too.

So it seems that every one in Athens except me makes them fine and good, and I alone corrupt them. Is that your meaning?

[MELETUS] Precisely that.

You detect me in a most unlucky situation. Answer me, though. Does the same thing seem to you to hold for horses too? Do you think all other men make horses better, and only one man ruins them? Or is it just the opposite of this, that some one man, or a very few, the horsemen, can improve them, whereas most people, if they have to deal with horses, and to make use of them, will spoil them? Is that not so, Meletus, both with horses and all other animals? It surely is, whether Anytus and you deny it or admit it. And what wonderful luck it would be for the young people if there were only one who did them harm, and all others did them good! But no, Meletus, you give ample proof that you never cared at all about the young; and your indifference is clearly shown—that you had no interest whatever in the things for which you bring me into court.

Now, Meletus, another question. In the name of Zeus, tell us whether it is better to live with honest citizens or with bad ones. Answer, friend; I ask you nothing difficult. Don't the wicked always do some evil to their neighbours, and the good some good?

[MELETUS] Certainly.

Well, is there anybody who would rather be harmed than helped by those he lives with? Answer my friend; the law requires you to do so. Does anybody like to be injured?

[MELETUS] Certainly not.

Come now. When you bring me into court for corrupting the younger generation and making them worse, do you charge that I do so purposely or without design?

[MELETUS] Purposely, say I.

What's that, Meletus? Are you at your age so much wiser than I am at mine? And thus, while you know that the wicked always do some injury to their nearest neighbours, and the good some good, I, you think, am come to such a state of ignorance as not to know that if I make some one I live with bad, I run the risk of getting injured by him? So according to you I do myself all this harm on purpose! That, Meletus, you will not get me to believe, nor, I fancy, anybody else in all the world. No, either I do not corrupt them, or if I do corrupt them, it is not by design. So either way you lie. If I ruin them unwittingly, the case is that of an involuntary error which does not legally bring me before this court; the proper thing would be to take me privately, and to instruct and warn me; for obviously when I learn better I shall stop doing what I do unwittingly. But you avoided joining me in order to instruct me; you chose not to do it. You bring me to this court where it is legal to try those who stand in need of punishment, not of learning.

There, fellow citizens, you have evidence enough of what I said, that Meletus has not taken the slightest interest in these matters.

Yet tell us, Meletus: in what way do you say I corrupt the younger men? Or is it not clear from the text of your complaint that you mean I teach them not to believe in the gods the State believes in, but in other new divinities? Isn't that the way you mean I corrupt them by my teaching?

[MELETUS] Yes, that is just what I assert.

In that case, Meletus, in the name of those very gods we are discussing, explain your meaning still more clearly to these gentlemen here and me, for there is a point I am unable to make out. If you mean that I teach them to believe in the existence of certain gods, then I myself believe that there are gods, and so I am not out and out an atheist, and do not break the law in that respect. Or do you mean that they are not the gods the State believes in, but other gods instead, and is this the point of your complaint, that they are different? Or do you say that I myself do not believe in any gods at all, and that I teach this disbelief to others?

[MELETUS] Yes, that is what I maintain, that you do not believe in any gods at all.

You amaze me, Meletus. How can you say so? Do you mean that I do not, like other men, regard the sun and moon as gods?

[MELETUS] By Heaven, Gentlemen of the Jury, he does not; he holds that the sun is a stone, and the moon an earth.

You must think you are accusing Anaxagoras, my dear Meletus. Have you such a poor opinion of these men here, and do you think them so illiterate as not to know that the works of Anaxagoras of Clazomenae are full of these ideas? And so you think that the young men learn these things from me, when on occasion they could buy the books for a drachma at most in the orchestra, and then laugh at Socrates if he pretended that these theories were his—apart from the fact that they are so bizarre! But, by Heaven, is that the way you think of me, that I don't believe in any god whatever?

[MELETUS] No, by Heaven, not a single one.

Now that, Meletus, is incredible, and something that I take it you do not believe yourself. In my opinion, fellow citizens, this man is an utterly overweening and unbridled person, who has brought this accusation simply out of insolence, intemperance, and youthful rashness. It looks as if he had made up a riddle with which to try me out: 'See whether Socrates, the wise man, will know that I am jesting and self-contradictory, or whether I shall fool him and all the rest who listen'; for to me he clearly contradicts himself in the complaint, where in effect he says: 'Socrates offends by not believing in gods, but by believing in gods.' And that is simply joking.

Examine with me, Gentlemen, my way of showing that he says this. And, Meletus, you answer us. But, Gentlemen, remember the request I made at the outset, and do not interrupt if I pursue the argument in my customary fashion.

Is there any living man, Meletus, who believes that there are human things, but does not believe that there are human beings? Let him answer, Gentlemen, and not make noisy protests beside the point. Does any one believe in horsemanship, and not in horses? Or does any one believe there is an art of piping, but that there are no pipers? No, honorable sir, there isn't any one who does it. If you do not choose to answer, I will speak for you and these others here as well. But give the answer to this. Is there anybody who believes in the doings of spirits [*daimonia*], but thinks there are no spirits [*daimones*]?

[MELETUS] No.

How you oblige me by the grudging answer these gentlemen force you to make! Well then, you admit, I believe and teach that there are doings of spirits, whether recent or of old. At all events I do believe in them according to your statement; you have even sworn to this in your complaint. But if I believe in them, then quite necessarily, I suppose, I must believe in spirits. Isn't it so? It must be. I put you down as in agreement since you make no reply.

Now, must we not consider spirits as either gods or the offspring of gods? Say yes or no.

[MELETUS] Yes, certainly.

If, then, I think that there are spirits, as you assert, and if the spirits are in some way gods, am I not right in saying that you talk in riddles and are jesting? First you say that I do not believe in gods, and next that I do believe in them inasmuch as I believe in spirits. Or again: if the spirits [*daimones*] are illegitimate children of the gods, whether by nymphs or other mothers as report will have it, who on earth will ever think that there are children of the gods, but that there are no gods? It would be as queer as to think that mules were the offspring of horses and asses, but that horses and asses did not exist. No, Meletus, there is no way out of it; either you formulated this complaint in order to try us out, or else you could find no real crime with which to charge me. That you could get a living person with the least intelligence to admit that a given man believed in the doings of spirits but not of gods, and that the same man, again, believed in neither spirits, gods, nor heroes, is quite beyond the bounds of possibility.

No, fellow citizens, that I am guiltless with respect to Meletus' indictment seems to me to call for no long defence; rather, let this argument suffice. But what I have said before, that much antagonism has arisen against me in the minds of many, rest assured that it is true. And this it is that will undo me, if I am undone, not Meletus nor Anytus, but the slander of the many, and their malice. Many another man, and good ones, has it undone, and, methinks, it will yet undo. There is no danger that the thing may stop with me.

Perhaps some one will say: 'Well, Socrates, aren't you ashamed that you pursued a course from which you now are in danger of death?' To that it would be right for me to reply: Good sir, it is not well said if you think that a man of any worth at all ought to calculate his chances of living or dying, and not rather look to this alone, when he acts, to see if what he does is right or wrong, and if his are the deeds of a good man or a bad. By your account, the demigods who fell at Troy would be sorry fellows, all of them, and notably the son of Thetis, who so despised all danger in comparison with any disgrace awaiting him, and with what result? When his mother saw him eager to slay Hector, she, the goddess, addressed him, as I recall, approximately thus: "My child, if you avenge the death of your comrade Patroclus by slaying Hector, then you yourself will die. For you the lot of death," she said, "comes straightway after Hector's." But he, on hearing that, made light of death and danger, fearing far more to live a coward and not avenge his loved ones. "Straightway let me die," said he, "once I give the villain his reward, and not continue here, a laughing-stock, beside the hollow ships, a burden to the earth." Do you think that he took heed of death or danger?

That, fellow citizens, is the way things really stand. If any one is stationed where he thinks it is best for him to be, or where his commander has put him, there, as it seems to me, it is his duty to remain, no matter what the risk, heedless of death or any other peril in comparison with disgrace.

It would have been dreadful conduct, fellow citizens, had I acted otherwise. When the leaders you had chosen to command me assigned a post to me at Potidaea, at Amphipolis, and at Delium, in the face of death itself I was as steadfast as any one could be in holding the position where they placed me; and when the god, as I believed and understood, assigned to me as my duty that I should live the life of a philosopher, and examine myself and others, it would have been dreadful had I through fear of death, or of anything else whatever, deserted my post. Dreadful indeed would it be, and verily any one would then be justified in bringing me to trial for not believing in gods, when I had disobeyed the oracle, feared death, and thought that I was wise when I was not.

For, Gentlemen, to be afraid of death is nothing else than thinking that one is wise when one is not, since it means fancying that one knows what one does not. Nobody knows, in fact, what death is, nor whether to man it is not perchance the greatest of all blessings; yet people fear it as if they surely knew it to be the worst of evils. And what is this but the shameful ignorance of supposing that we know what we do not? It is there and in that perhaps that I differ, Gentlemen, from the majority of mankind; and if I might call myself more wise than another, it would be in this, that as I do not know enough about what goes on in Hades, so too I do not think that I know. But doing wrong, and disobeying the person who is better than myself, be it god or man, that I know is base and wicked. Therefore never for the sake of evils which I know to be such will I fear or flee from what for all I know may be a good.

Accordingly, suppose you were now to acquit me, and went against Anytus; he who says that either I ought not to have been summoned hither to begin with, or, once I appeared I must inevitably be put to death; for he tells you that, if I am freed, your sons, who already put in practice what Socrates teaches, will all be utterly ruined. Suppose with reference to that you were to say to me: 'Socrates, at present we shall not give Anytus our assent, but will acquit you, yet upon one condition, namely, that hereafter you shall not pass your time in this investigation nor pursue philosophy; if you are caught doing it again, you die.' Well, as I said, if you were ready to let me go upon these conditions, my reply to you would be:

'Fellow citizens, I respect and love you, but I must obey the god rather than you, and so long as I draw breath, and can pursue philosophy, I will not cease from it nor from exhorting you, and ever pointing out the way to any one of you I meet, saying to him as I have been wont: "Good friend, you are a citizen of Athens, the greatest of all cities and the most renowned for power and learning, and yet you feel no shame at giving your mind to money so that you may get as much as possible, and to your reputation and to honor; but for insight, for the truth, for your soul and how it shall be at its best, you do not care nor trouble." '

And if any one of you disputes it, and says that he does care, I shall not forthwith dismiss him and go away, but will question him, and sift him, and put him to the test; and if he seems to me to have no fund of virtue, while professing to have it, I shall reproach him with attaching little value to what has most importance, and taking paltry things for what is larger. So will I do with young and old, whatever he be that I meet with, foreigner or native, yet rather with you citizens since you are nearer to me by kin; for this, you may rest assured, is what the god demands of me. And I think that there never came to you a greater good in the City than the service I render the god.

All I do is to go about persuading you, both young and old, not to think first of your bodies or your property, nor to be so mightily concerned about them as about your souls, how the spirit shall be at its best; it is my task to tell you that virtue does not spring from wealth, but that wealth and every other good that comes to men in private life or in public proceed from virtue. If it is by saying this that I corrupt the young, then this must be injurious; but any one who holds that I say anything save this says nothing. On that head, fellow citizens, I may assure you that whether you trust Anytus or not, and whether you acquit me or do not acquit me, I shall not alter my course, no matter if I have to die a hundred times.

Now, fellow citizens, do not interrupt, but continue granting my request of you not to cry out at what I may say, but to listen; I do believe that you will profit if you listen. I am, in fact, about to tell you certain other things at which you might possibly protest. Yet please do not. No; for you may rest assured that if you condemn me to death, I being such a person as I say, you will do yourselves more harm than you do me. As for me, Meletus will no more hurt me than will Anytus. It does not lie in his power, for in my belief the eternal order does not permit a better man to be harmed by a worse. Oh yes! quite possibly he might kill or banish me, or rob me of my civil rights; and doubtless this man and the next will think that these are major evils. I do not think them such; no, I think it a far greater evil for a man to do what this man now is doing, namely trying to get a man condemned to death unjustly.

So, fellow citizens, at present I am far from making my defence upon my own account, as one might think; I make it for your sake, in order that you may not, by condemning me, do wrong about the gift of the god to you; for if you have me put to death, you will not easily find another of the sort, fastened upon the City by the god, for all the world (if I may use a rather ludicrous comparison) like a gadfly on a great and noble horse that is somewhat sluggish on account of his size and needs the fly to wake him up. So, it seems to me, the god has fastened me like that upon the City, to rouse, exhort, and rebuke each one of you, everywhere besetting you, and never once ceasing all day long. Another one like that, Gentlemen, you will not come by so easily; but if you listen to me, you will take good care of me. You may, however, quite possibly be annoyed, like people awakened from their slumbers, and, striking out at me, may listen readily to Anytus and condemn me to death. Then you would finish out the rest of your life in sleep, unless the god were in mercy to send you some one else to take my place. That it is the deity by whom I, such as I am, have been given to the City you may see from this: it is not like human nature for me to neglect all my own concerns, to put up with a neglected household all these years, and to attend to your affair, ever going to you individually in private, like a father or an elder brother, urging you to care for your moral welfare. And if I got any profit from it all, if these exhortations brought me any pay, there would seem to be some reason in my conduct. As it is, you see for yourselves that my accusers, who, unashamed, have brought so many other charges against me, have yet not had the effrontery to present a witness to allege that I ever took any sort of fee or sought one. Why not? Because, methinks, the witness I present to show that I speak the truth is quite enough—my poverty.

Possibly it may look odd that I should busily go about in private with my counsels, but in public dare not approach the mass of you with counsel for the City. The reason for that is something you have often heard me speak of in many a place; it is that there comes to me a thing divine and spiritual, what Meletus has mockingly referred to in his indictment. From childhood on, this sign has come to me; it is a voice, which, when it comes, always deters me from what I am about to do, but never urges me to act. It is this that fights against my entering political affairs; and the opposition strikes me as being altogether good; for, fellow citizens, you may rest assured that if I, long ago, had tried to take up politics, I should long ago have perished, and been of no service whatever either to you or to myself. And do not be aggrieved at me for telling the truth: there is not a man on earth that is safe if he nobly puts himself in opposition to you or to any other crowd, and strives to stop all sorts of wrong and lawlessness in the State. But if any one is really going to battle for the right, and to be safe for some short time in doing it, he must perforce remain a private citizen; he must not appear in public life.

Of that I will furnish you with telling evidence, not arguments, but what you value, facts. Listen to what happened in my case, and you will see that I am not a man to yield to any one unjustly for fear of death, not even if by my not yielding I were at once to perish. The tale I shall tell you is of the legal sort and uninspiring, but is true.

I never held any public office, fellow citizens, but one: I was a member of the Council. And it happened that our tribe, Antiochis, had the executive function [*prytany*] at the time you wished to sentence in a body the ten commanders who failed to pick up the survivors of the naval action [at Arginusae]. The procedure was illegal, as after a while you all admitted. But at the time I was the only one of the prytanes who stood out against your doing an illegal act and voted against you; and although the orators were ready to indict me and arrest me, while you urged them on and made an uproar, I thought that I ought to risk all danger on the side of law and justice rather than side with you in an unjust decree for fear of imprisonment or death.

This took place while Athens still was a democracy. But again, when the oligarchy was established, the Thirty had me and four others summoned to the Rotunda, and ordered us to go get Leon of Salamis, and bring him thence to have him put to death; they gave such orders frequently to many other persons in order to involve as many as they could in their crimes. But there again I showed, by deeds, and not by words, that death, if I may speak quite baldly, meant nothing at all to me, while not to do an unjust or an impious act, this meant everything; for that power, however huge its sway, did not terrify me into doing what was wrong. No, when we came out of the Rotunda, the other four went off to Salamis and brought back Leon, and as for me I went to my home. And for that I might well have paid with my life, had the government not promptly fallen. Of these facts many persons will bear witness to you.

Well then, do you think I could have survived through all these years if I had taken part in state affairs, and, acting properly as a good citizen, had fought for justice, making this perforce of paramount importance? Far from it, fellow citizens; nor could any other living man have done it. As for me, all my life long, if ever I did anything in an official way, I showed myself to be that sort of person, and in private just the same; never once did I yield to anyone in any point against the right, not even to one of those whom my slanderers declare to be my pupils.

But I never have been anybody's teacher. If anyone cares to listen to me as I speak and carry on my special function, be he young or old, I never have begrudged it. I am not one who will engage in discussion if he gets money, and if not refuses. No, rich and poor alike I am prepared to question, and whoever will may listen to what I say when I make reply. And for my part, if any of them turns out well or ill, I cannot rightly be held responsible when I never offered to give any one instruction, nor gave it. If any one asserts that he ever learned or heard a thing from me other than what all the others heard as well, rest assured that he who says so does not tell the truth.

Well then, why do certain persons like to spend so much of their time with me? I told you, fellow citizens, what the reason is. The truth of the matter is just what I said: they like to hear the sifting out of those who think that they are wise, but are not. The thing, in fact, is not unpleasant. But for me, as I aver, it is a task enjoined upon me by the deity, through oracles, through dreams, and in every single way that ever a divine injunction was laid upon a man to do a thing. These statements, fellow citizens, are true and are easily proved. Suppose I am at present ruining some of the young people, and already have perverted others; then necessarily, no doubt, a number of them, when they grew older, would have seen that on occasion, when they were young, I gave them evil advice, and would now appear in court to accuse and punish me. Or, if they themselves were unwilling to do it, then some of their relations, fathers, brothers, or others of their kin—if it were true that members of the family had received some injury from me—would now remember it, and have me punished. Certainly there are many of them present whom I see: first Crito here, a man of my own generation and my deme, father of yon Critobulus; next, Lysanias of Sphettus, father of yon Aeschines; add Antiphon here of Kephisia, father of Epigenes. Among others, men whose brothers have attended at the pastime, Nicostratus, son of Theozotides and brother of Theodotus—as for Theodotus, he is dead, and therefore could not plead for me against him; so also Paralus here whose father is Demodocus and whose brother is Theages, Adeimantus son of Ariston whose brother is Plato here, and Aiantodorus, whose brother is yon Apollodorus. And many others I could name to you, of whom Meletus surely ought to have offered somebody as witness in his accusation. If he forgot it then, let him present it now—I yield the point—and let him say if he has any evidence of the sort. But, Gentlemen, you will find the case to be the very opposite of that; will find them all prepared to help me, the ruiner, the man who has done injury to their kin, as Meletus and Anytus aver. The ruined themselves, of course, might have some reason for coming to my aid. But those who are not ruined, men already mature, the relatives of these, what other reason could they have for coming to my aid except the straight and just one, that they know that Meletus is lying, and that I am telling the truth?

There you have it, Gentlemen. That is pretty much what I might have to say in my defence, that with possibly some additions, to the like effect. Perhaps, however, one or another of you will be angry when he recalls his own experience, in some trial he was engaged in of less gravity than this; if he besought and with many tears implored the judges, and, in order to arouse the greatest pity, brought in his children along with others of his kin and many friends; while, as for me, I shall do nothing of the sort, although I am in danger, as I might suppose, to the last degree of peril. Perhaps, then, as he thinks of this, he will bear himself with the less remorse towards me, and, irritated by these very things, will cast his vote in anger. Now if any of you feels so, though for my part I do not impute it—but if anybody feels that way, then it seems to me the proper thing for me to say to him would be: 'Good friend, I too have friends and relatives; in fact, my case is just as Homer says. "I did not spring from either oak or rock," but from mankind, and so I have a family and sons; three sons, my fellow citizens, one a youth, and the other two are little boys.' Nevertheless not one of them will I bring hither imploring you to let me off. And why shall I do nothing of all that? Not, fellow citizens, out of hardihood, nor in disdain of you. And whether I fear death or not is another question; but for my own honor, and yours, and the honor of the entire City, it does not seem proper for me at my age, and with the name I have, to do any of these things. The opinion may be true, or may be false; at all events the view is held that Socrates is somehow different from the mass of men. Well, if those of you who are regarded as distinguished in point of wisdom, or of courage, or of any other quality, behaved like that, it would be shameful. And yet, often enough, I have seen persons of such sort, persons of some reputation, behaving in extraordinary fashion when they were to hear the verdict, as if they thought they must be going to suffer something terrible if they had to die—as if they thought that they would be immortal in case you did not condemn them. To my mind, they brought shame upon the City; anybody from another city would infer that the Athenians who were eminent for their virtue, those whom their fellows selected as their rulers and for other places of distinction, were in no way better than women. These things, fellow citizens, it behoves us not to do if we have any reputation whatsoever; and if we do them, you should not allow it. No; you should make this very thing quite clear, that you will far more readily give your vote against the person who drags in these tearful dramas, and makes the City ridiculous, than against the man who argues quietly.

But apart from the question of propriety, Gentlemen, it does not seem right to me to beg the judge for mercy, or, by doing it, to get away, when one ought rather to enlighten and convince him. He does not take his seat for this, the judge, to render justice as a favor, but to decide on what is just. Indeed he took an oath that he would not favor people according to his notion of them, but that he would give judgment in accordance with the laws. And so we should not get you into the habit of perjuring yourselves, nor should you get into it; neither of us should commit impiety. So do not ask me, fellow citizens, to treat you in a way which I take to be dishonorable, wrong, and impious; above all, by Zeus! when I am under accusation of impiety by this Meletus here present; for obviously, if I swayed you and by begging forced you to act against your oath, I would be teaching you not to believe that there are gods, and by my defence would simply accuse myself of not believing in them. But that be far from me! I do believe in them, my fellow citizens, as none of my accusers does; and to you I commend myself, and to the Deity, to judge concerning me what shall be best at once for me and for you.

AFTER THE VOTE AGAINST HIM

If I am not distressed, my fellow citizens, at what has happened in that you voted to convict me, there are many reasons for it, and in particular that the outcome was to me not unexpected. What is to me far more surprising is the actual division of the votes. I thought for my part that the vote would go not by this small majority, but by a large one. As it is, apparently, if only thirty votes had gone the other way, I should have been acquitted. Accordingly, so far as Meletus is concerned, it seems to me I do now stand acquitted, and not only that, but it must be clear to everyone that if Anytus and Lycon had not come hither to accuse me, he would have had to pay one thousand drachmas as a fine for not obtaining a fifth part of the votes.

Meanwhile the man proposes for me the penalty of death. So be it. What penalty, fellow citizens, am I to offer you instead? Evidently what I ought to get? What is it, then? What do I deserve to get or pay? I who, when I had learned a thing, did not lead my life in peace, but neglecting what the many care for—wealth, household matters, military leadership and civic and the other high positions, coalitions, factions that arise in the State—thought myself in fact too good a man to enter into these affairs with safety. I did not enter there where if I came I was not to be of any use either to you or to myself, but going to you one by one in private, I did you, I aver, the greatest service possible. There I went trying to persuade each one of you not to care first for his own possessions before caring for himself and how he might be at his best and wisest, nor to set the affairs of the City above the City itself, and to give attention to all other things in just that way. Being a man of that description, what ought I to get? Something good, my fellow citizens, if the award must truly square with the desert; and the good ought further to be something that fits my case. What, then, befits a poor man, a benefactor, who needs leisure for the office of exhorting you? Nothing is so proper as the maintenance of such a man in the Prytaneum, a reward far more befitting him than for any one of you who may have won a victory at Olympia with a horse or a pair of them or four. He makes you think that you are happy; I cause you to be so. He, moreover, has no need of maintenance; I stand in need of it. And so if I must get what I deserve, there is my proposal: maintenance in the Prytaneum.

Perhaps when I say that to you, you will think that I am talking with the same bravado as about the tears and supplications. It is not, fellow citizens, as you think; no, it is more like this. I am persuaded that I never willingly wronged any man, but I have not persuaded you, since we have had small time to reach an understanding; whereas if the law with you were what it is with others, if a case involving the penalty of death could not be settled in a day, but took a number, I believe I would have won you over. As matters stand, it is not easy in a limited time to refute a mass of slanders.

Persuaded that I do no wrong to any one, I am far from ready to do injustice to myself, and will not say of myself that I merit some evil, and should allot myself that sort of penalty. In fear of what? For fear that otherwise I shall suffer the thing which Meletus proposes, that of which I say I know not whether it is good or evil? Instead of that ought I to choose one of the things that I know for certain to be ills, and penalize myself with that? Imprisonment? Why should I live in prison, a slave to a recurrent board of governors, the Eleven? Or say a fine, and to be jailed until I pay it? But that would be no different for me from what I just now mentioned, since I have no money to pay with. Well, suppose I offered to go into exile. Perhaps you would accept that. But truly, fellow citizens, the love of life must have a powerful hold on me, and make me heedless, if I cannot reason thus: You who are my fellow citizens could not endure my doings and discussions; no, they were too much for you, and so irritating that now you seek to be rid of them. Well, will others bear them easily? Far from it, fellow citizens. And what a fine existence that would be, for a man of my age to go away and live a wanderer and a waif driven from city to city; for well I know that wherever I went the young would listen to me just as they do here. And if I drove them off, they would get the older men's permission, and themselves expel me. And if I did not, their fathers and relations would expel me on the sons' account.

Well, perhaps some one will say: 'Why can't you go away from us, and then keep quiet, Socrates, and live in peace?' But that is the thing that is hardest of all to make some of you see. If I say that this means disobedience to the god, and for that very reason I cannot keep still, you will not believe me, but will think I speak in irony. If, on the other hand, I say it is perhaps the greatest good that can befall a man, daily to argue about virtue, and to discuss the other subjects about which you have heard me debating and examining myself as well as others, if I add that for mankind the unexamined life is not worth living, still less will you believe me when I tell you that. These matters stand, however, Gentlemen, precisely as I say, only it is not easy to convince you. And meanwhile, for my part, I am not in the habit of thinking that I merit ill at all. If I had wealth, I would suggest a sum that I was in a position to pay, for in that case I should do myself no harm. But now the fact is that I haven't, unless you chose to set a fine for me at a rate that I could pay. Perhaps I could pay you a silver mina; so that is what I offer.

But Plato here, my fellow citizens, and Crito, Critobulus, and Apollodorus, bid me offer thirty minæ upon their security. Well then, I offer that; these men will be adequate security to you for the amount.

After He Is Condemned to Death

For no great thrift in time, my fellow citizens, you will have from those who wish to vilify the City the name and blame of having put to death the wise man, Socrates; for they will call me wise, even if I am not, they who would defame you. If only you had waited for a little while, the thing would have occurred for you in the course of nature; for you can see my age, that I am far along in life, and near to death. I say this, not to all of you, but only to those who voted for my death. And to them I have also to say this as well. It may be, Gentlemen, that you think I lost my cause for lack of arguments of the sort with which I might have won you over, if I had thought that I ought to say and do all things in order to escape the verdict. Far from it. I lost for a lack, but not of arguments; it was for lack of impudence and daring, and for not being ready to say to you the sort of thing it would have given you most pleasure to hear—me weeping and wailing, and doing and saying any and every sort of thing that I hold to be unworthy of me, but you are accustomed to hear from the rest. No, I did not then believe that, to avoid a danger, I ought to do anything unseemly in a freeman, nor do I now regret my manner of defence. No, far rather would I choose this manner of defence, and die, than follow that, and live. Whether in a court of justice or in war neither I nor any other man should seek by using every means conceivable to escape from death; for in battle you very often see that if you throw away your weapons and beg those who are pursuing you for mercy, you may get out of dying. Indeed, in every sort of danger there are various ways of winning through, if one is ready to do and say anything whatever. No, Gentlemen, that is not the hard thing, to escape from death; ah no, far harder is it to escape from sin, for sin is swifter than death. And so I, being old and slow, am overtaken by the slower enemy; while my accusers, who are strong and swift, have been caught by the swifter, namely wickedness. And so I now depart, by you condemned to pay the penalty of death; and they, by the truth convicted of a base injustice. And as I abide the payment, so do they. Who knows? Perhaps it had to be so, and I think that things are as they ought to be.

Touching the future, I desire to make for you who voted to condemn me, a prediction; for I am at the point where men foresee the future best—when they are soon to die. Let me tell you then, you men who have condemned me, that after I am gone there will straightway come upon you a chastisement far heavier, by Zeus, than the death you have set for me. You have now done this in the belief that you have freed yourselves from giving any reckoning for your life; but I tell you the result will be the very opposite for you. There will be more inquisitors to sift you, men whom I now hold in check without your knowing it. And they will be more critical as they are younger, and will annoy you more; for if you think that by putting men to death you will prevent the slur from being cast at you that you do not live aright, you are in error. This way of getting freedom is neither very sure nor fine; no, the finest and readiest way is this, not to interfere with other people, but to render oneself as good a man as possible. There is the prophecy I make for you who voted to condemn me. And of them I take my leave.

With those of you who voted to acquit me I should be glad to talk about this thing that has occurred, while the magistrates are busy and it is not time for me to go to the place where I must die. So, Gentlemen, please wait with me as long as that. There is nothing to keep us from talking to each other as long as it is allowed. To you as to friends I wish to explain the real meaning of what has just happened to me.

Justices, for when I call you that I am naming you aright, the thing that has come to me is wonderful.

My customary warning, by the spirit, in previous times has always, up to now, come to me very often to oppose me, even when a matter was quite important, if ever I was going to do something amiss. But to-day, as you yourselves have witnessed, that thing has happened to me which anybody might suppose, and which is considered, to be the uttermost of evils. Yet neither did the sign from god oppose me when I left my house this morning, nor at the point when I ascended here to the tribunal, nor in my speech at anything I was about to say; though often when I have been talking elsewhere it has stopped me in the middle of a speech. But to-day, with reference to the whole procedure, not once did it oppose me in a thing I did or said. What, then, do I take to be the cause of this? No doubt this thing that has happened to me is good, and it cannot be that our supposition is correct when any of us think that death is a misfortune. For me, the proof of this is telling: it cannot be but that the customary sign would have opposed me, if I had not been about to do a thing that was good.

Let us view in another way how ample are the grounds for our hope that death is good. To be dead is one of two things. Either it is a sort of non-existence, and the dead man has no feeling about anything whatever, or else, as people say, the soul experiences a shift and a migration from here into another place. Now if there is no feeling, if death is like a sleep in which one does not even dream, what a wonderful gain it would be! I believe if a man were to take that night in which he slept so deeply that he did not have a single dream, and compared it with the other nights and days of his life; if he had to say, upon reflection, how many days and nights, all told, in his life, he had passed better and more sweetly than that night; I believe that every one, not merely any private citizen, but the Great King himself, would find them easy to count up in comparison with all the others. So if death is a sleep like that, I say it is a gain; for thus all time appears to be no more than a single night. If, on the other hand, death is like a journey from here to another place, and if what they say is true, that everybody who has died is there, then, Justices, what greater good than this could there be? If, on arriving in Hades, one could be freed from those who here pretend that they are Justices, and there find those who by report deal real justice, Minos, Rhadamanthus, Aæcus, and Triptolemus, and all the rest of the demigods who were just in their lives here, what a small thing would that journey seem! Or, again, to be with Orpheus and Musæus, with Hesiod and Homer, what price would not any of you pay for that? I would gladly die repeatedly, if all that is true. To me it would be a wonderful way to pass my time, there where I could meet with Palamedes and with Ajax son of Telamon, and any one else among the ancients who died through an unjust decision. To compare my lot with theirs, methinks, would not be so unpleasant; and most important of all would be to go on sifting people there, as here, and finding out who is wise, and who thinks he is so, but is not. What would not anybody give to examine, Justices, the leader of that mighty expedition against Troy, or else Odysseus, or Sisyphus, or a myriad of others one might mention, men and women too? There to talk with them, consort with them, examine them, would be a happiness beyond compare! Surely there, I take it, they do not put a man to death for doing that; for, happy in all else, people are happier there than here in that henceforth they are immortal, at all events if what is said is true.

But, Justices, you also it behoves to have good hope with reference to death, and this one thing you must bear in mind as true, that, living or dead, to a good man there can come no evil, nor are his affairs a matter of indifference to the gods. Nor has my destiny now come about by chance; rather, it is clear to me that it was better for me now to die and to be released from my troubles. That is why the sign did not at any point deter me, and why I am not very bitter at those who voted to condemn me, or at my accusers. It is true they did not have this notion in condemning and accusing me; no, they thought to injure me, and therein they merit blame.

One thing, however, I do beg of them. When my sons grow up, then, Gentlemen, I ask you to punish them, you hurting them the same as I hurt you, if they seem to you to care for money, or aught else, more than they care for virtue. And if they pretend to be somewhat when they are nothing, do you upbraid them as I upbraided you, for not regarding as important what they ought to think so, and for thinking they have worth when they do not. If you do that, I shall have received just treatment from you, and my sons as well.

And now the time has come for our departure, I to die, and you to live. Which of us goes to meet the better lot is hidden from all unless it be known to God.

THUCYDIDES

•

The Funeral Oration of Pericles[1]

THE SETTING OF THE SPEECH

During the following winter the Athenians, in keeping with a time-honored custom, held a state funeral for those who were the first to fall in this war.[2] The ceremonies are as follows. First the bodies of the deceased lie in state for three days in a special pavilion; during this time the relatives bring whatever offerings they wish. In the procession to the grave cypress-wood coffins are carried on wagons, one for each tribe, and each containing the bodies of the dead from that tribe. One wagon carries an empty bier, fully decked, for the missing, those whose bodies could not be found for burial. Anyone who wishes, citizen or foreigner, may join in the procession, and the women of the family also attend and set up the cry of mourning at the grave.

The burial takes place at the state monument, which stands in the most beautiful suburb of the city. All the war dead of Athens have been buried there except the men of Marathon, whose valor was considered so pre-eminent that their tomb was built on the battlefield itself. After the interment is finished, a man chosen by the citizens, someone of high reputation for intelligence and prominent in the community, pronounces a fitting eulogy over the dead, and the gathering disperses. Such are the state funerals; and the custom was maintained throughout the war whenever there was occasion for it. At this first observance the chosen speaker was Pericles son of Xanthippus. When the proper moment came he stepped forward from the monument onto a high platform constructed so that he could be heard by as many of the throng as possible, and spoke more or less as follows:

DIFFICULTY OF THE SPEAKER'S TASK

"Most of the previous speakers on these occasions have praised the man who added this oration to the ceremonies; they considered it a fine and fitting thing that it should be delivered over our war dead. I on the contrary should think it would be sufficient for men who have shown their bravery in action to have their honors paid them in action also, as in fact you see has been done in this solemn ceremony under the auspices of the state, and that the reputation of so many men should not be made to depend on the chance of a single speaker's eloquence or lack of it. It is difficult, you know, to speak

[1] From Thucydides' *History*, transl. by Gerald F. Else, in *Classics in Translation,* ed. Paul L. MacKendrick and Herbert M. Howe (Madison: The University of Wisconsin Press, 1952), I, 239–243. Copyright, 1952, by the Regents of the University of Wisconsin. Reprinted by permission.

[2] Between Athens and Sparta—The Peloponnesian War, 431–404 B.C.

fittingly on a subject in which one can hardly hope to gain credit for telling the truth. The friends of the dead, who know something about the case, may well feel that the speaker falls short of their expectation and their knowledge, while the stranger, out of jealousy at any story that goes beyond his own powers, may suspect him of exaggeration. A man can usually tolerate praise of others only up to the point where he thinks that he could have done the same; anything that exceeds his own capacity arouses his jealousy and therefore his disbelief. However, since this custom was sanctioned by past generations as a fitting one, I too must abide by the law and try to satisfy the expectations and beliefs of each of you so far as I can.

Tribute to the Builders of the Athenian Empire

"I will begin first with our forefathers. It is both right and appropriate on an occasion like this to pay them this tribute of remembrance; for they were the same stock that has dwelt in the land from the beginning, and by their valor, in unbroken succession of generations, handed it down to us a free country. They deserve our praise and admiration, but our own fathers deserve it still more; it was they who added to their inheritance the great empire we now possess and, not without toil, left it to us of this generation. Finally, those of us who are still more or less in the prime of life have given the empire its further expansion and provided our city with all the resources needed to make it completely self-sufficient in war and peace.

The Way of Life That Has Made Athens Great

"The various wars and campaigns through which our conquests were made, the stout resistance that we or our fathers have offered against invasion by Greek or foreign invaders—all that you know and I do not want to dwell on it at length. Instead I will speak first of the way of life that is responsible for our achievements, the form of government and kind of character that have made Athens a great city. I am prefacing all this to my eulogy of the dead because I think it is not only suitable to the occasion but profitable for this whole gathering of citizens and foreigners to hear.

"Our form of government is not modelled on the constitutions of our neighbors; instead of imitating others we are actually an example to them. So far as the name goes we are called a democracy, because the power rests with the majority instead of a few. But though every citizen has equal rights under the law with respect to his private disputes, high standing, and honor in the community depend on a man's merits, his achievement in some pursuit, and no one is debarred by poverty and obscurity of birth from contributing what he can to the well-being of the city. We are a free people not only in our management of public affairs but in our personal tolerance of one another's everyday conduct. We do not get angry at our neighbors for doing as they please, or try to inflict on them the petty marks of disapproval which, though harmless, are so unpleasant to experience. While this spirit of tolerance prevails in our private lives, in our public affairs it is fear more than anything else that keeps us law-abiding, obedient to the magistrates of the moment and to the laws, especially those whose purpose is to help the victims of wrongdoing and those unwritten laws which men by common consent are ashamed to transgress.

"Not only that, but we have provided for our enjoyment a great variety of relaxations from the day's work: games, contests, festivals lasting through the year, and beautiful private homes and furnishings. To see all this around us every day cheers us and drives away fatigue. Also, thanks to the greatness of Athens, the wares of the whole world find their way to us; we are in a position to enjoy the products of the rest of mankind as easily and naturally as we do our own crops from our own land.

"We also hold an advantage over our opponents in our way of preparing for war. Our city is open to everybody; there are no periodical deportations to keep foreigners from learning or observing things that might be of use to an enemy if they were not concealed. We put our trust in our own inborn readiness for action rather than in armaments and military secrets. Their system of training involves the pursuit of courage through laborious discipline, beginning in their youth, while we allow ourselves some relaxation and yet are equally prepared to face any reasonable danger.

"The proof is that the Spartans have not invaded our country with their own forces alone but have brought along all their allies; we manage to attack our neighbors' territory without help and usually win, though fighting on foreign soil and against men who are defending their own homes and possessions. No enemy has ever yet encountered the full strength of our combined forces, since we have the maintenance of our navy to think about as well as the dispatch of armies by land to a number of places at once. If they do engage a small force of ours somewhere and defeat it, they boast that they have repelled us all, and when they are beaten, that they were defeated by us all. Now if we choose relaxation in the face of danger instead of endless drill, and rely on native courage rather than rules and regulations, the advantage is ours twice over: we do not wear ourselves out over future troubles, and when they do come we show as much venturesomeness as those who are forever moiling and toiling. Athens has a claim to men's admiration for all this, and for other things besides.

"We strive for distinction, but with economy, and for intelligence without loss of energy. Thus we use wealth to meet the needs of action, not the craving for display, and think it is no disgrace to admit poverty but a real disgrace not to act to escape it. Again, we combine the conduct of public and private affairs in the same persons and make it possible for others, though absorbed in their work, to gain some insight into politics; for unlike other peoples we judge the man who takes no part in this at all a useless, not just a 'quiet,' person. Hence also we arrive at sound decisions, or at least sound ideas, on policy, because we do not believe that action is spoiled by discussion, but by failure to be informed through debate before the necessary action is taken. In fact this is another point in our superiority: we are usually daring and also unusually disposed to weigh the pros and cons of a proposed undertaking, while with others ignorance brings boldness and second thought brings hesitation. One would not go wrong in saying that the bravest men are those who foresee most clearly the dangerous as well as the pleasurable possibilities and still are not deterred from taking the risk.

"Again, so far as generosity goes we are the opposite of most men: we try to win friends not by accepting kindness but by conferring it. We know that the man who does a favor is the firmer friend: he will keep the debt alive out of good will towards the recipient, while the debtor does not feel it so keenly, knowing that a good turn will be put down as payment on his debt, not as a real favor. Our fearless way of serving others rests on the confidence of freedom rather than on calculations of profit; and in this too we are unique.

"To sum it all up, I say not only that our city as a whole is a model of all Greece, but that, in my opinion, there is no other place where the individual can develop independence and self-reliance so easily, so gracefully, and in so many directions. That all this is not a matter of boastful talk for this occasion but of plain truth, is proved by the fact of our power, which we acquired because we possessed those qualities. Athens alone, in our time, is greater than her own fame when the test comes; she alone gives the invader no excuse for annoyance at the quality of the foe who handles him so roughly, and her subjects no ground for complaint that their masters do not deserve to rule them.

"Our power is surely not unsubstantiated; we have given weighty proofs of it that will earn us the admiration of our own time and of posterity. We have no need of a Homer to sing our praises, or anyone whose poetic language will please for the moment but whose mere guesses at the facts will be wrecked by the truth. We have assured our own fame by forcing every land and every sea to become a path for our adventuring spirit and by founding memorials of our enmity and favor in every part of the world. That is the kind of city for which these men died, facing battle with the high determination that she should not be taken from them; and it is only fitting that every man who is left should be willing to suffer for her.

The Dead Were Worthy of Such a City

"The reason why I have expatiated on Athens at such length is that I wanted to demonstrate to you how much greater is our stake in this struggle than theirs who do not share our advantages, and also to give force to my eulogy of the dead by citing real evidence. I have almost finished; for the glories of Athens, the theme of my hymn of praise, are the garland she owes to these men and others like them. Few Greeks can show so equal a balance as they between their deeds and what we say about them. I think that their recent death, still fresh in our minds, is both the first evidence and the final confirmation of their worth as men. If some of them fell short in other things, we have every right to put their brave defense of the fatherland in time of war first in the reckoning; the good has erased the bad from our memory, the benefits of their common service outweigh any harm they did in private life. Not one of these men turned soft because he preferred the continual enjoyment of his own wealth; not one was tempted by poverty to put off the danger, hoping that he might still escape it and grow rich. Welcoming vengeance on the enemy as a prize more to be coveted than these, and considering the present danger nobler than any other, they accepted it and chose vengeance for the one part, renunciation for the other. They left to hope the unforeseeable chances of future success, but were men enough to rely on themselves in action, where the issue was already clear; convinced that to fight hard and endure is in itself a better guarantee of survival than surrender, they shrank from the reproach of men's words but stood the brunt of action with their lives, and so passed away in that brief moment in the play of fortune when their glory and not their fear was at its prime.

"If they were brave, then, it was a bravery characteristic of Athenians, and those who are left behind should pray that their resolution towards the enemy may be less hazardous, but determine that it shall be no less valorous, than theirs. Do not weigh the benefits merely in words—an orator could remind you at length of what you know as well as he, reciting all the manifold blessings of a firm defense against the enemy—but fix your eyes on the power of Athens as you see it in action from day to day, make yourselves her lovers, and when you find her a great city remember that men won that greatness for her by their boldness, their ability to grasp what was required of them, and the sense of honor with which they carried it out. Even when one of their ventures failed they would not stoop to injure the city by denying her the best of their manhood, but showered it upon her as their finest offering.

"Through this common gift of their lives they won for themselves individually unfading glory and the most conspicuous of all monuments: not the one in which they lie here but the one in which their fame survives them, to be remembered afresh as each new occasion arises for speech or action. For the real tomb of famous men is the whole earth; they are marked out not merely by the inscription over a grave in their own country but in other lands also by an unwritten memory, recording their spirit more than their actions, which lives on in the minds of men. Emulate them, then, in your own lives; learn from them that the key to happiness is freedom, the key to freedom a stout heart, and do not set a false value on the dangers of war. It is not the unfortunate, those with no hope of anything better, who have most reason to sacrifice their lives freely, but those who face the danger of a change for the worse if they go on living and, if they come to disaster in any undertaking, risk the greatest loss. To a man of any spirit the suffering and humiliation that go with cowardice are more painful to endure than a quick death, coming unnoticed in the full flush of strength and common hopes.

Exhortation to the Bereaved Relatives

"And for the same reason I offer good courage instead of mourning to the parents of these dead, those of them who are present. You know that your lives have seen all kinds of fortune, good and bad, and that the luckiest are those who have been vouchsafed the most glorious end, like these—or grief, like you—whose lives were so measured that their allotment of happiness and of death came to an even balance. I know this will be hard for you to believe; you will be reminded of them again and again when you see others with the happiness that you once enjoyed yourselves. And it is true, we do not grieve at being deprived of blessings we have never tasted, but at losing what we had grown accustomed to.

"But you should bear up in the hope of having more children, those of you who are still of an age to do so. Not only will the new ones help many of you individually to forget those who are gone, but the city will profit doubly, by not being depopulated, and in her security; for a citizen cannot possibly weigh the issue fairly and impartially if he has no children to contribute and so does not share the danger equally.

"As for those of you who are past the prime, set down the longer and happier part of your lives as profit, remember that the rest will be short, and let your sons' glory lighten the burden. Only the craving for honor is ageless, and in a man's declining years it is not profit, as some say, but the sense of being honored that brings real joy.

"Again, for those of you who are sons or brothers of these men I see a great contest in the making; for people always tend to praise those who are gone, and you will find that it takes a supreme effort to be rated, not even equal, but nearly equal to them. Men envy the living because they are competitors; what does not stand in their way they honor freely, with a good will untouched by rivalry.

"Finally, if I must say something about womanly virtue, for those of you who will be widows henceforth, I will sum it all up in one brief exhortation. Great is your good name when you do not fall below the standards of your sex, and when you give men the least occasion to talk about you, whether it be by way of praise or blame.

"Thus, so far as words go, I too have complied with the law and said what I had to say. As for acts, part of the funeral honors have already been paid the dead, and the rest will be paid by the city in public maintenance of their children until they come of age. That is the garland, worth while to the survivors as well as the dead, which she awards for this kind of contest: for the best men serve that state where the best prizes for merit are offered. And now make your lamentations, each for your own relatives, and then depart."

JONATHAN SWIFT

•

A Modest Proposal[1]

For Preventing the Children of Poor People From Being A Burthen to Their Parents or Country, and for Making Them Beneficial to the Public.

It is a melancholy object to those who walk through this great town, or travel in the country, when they see the streets, the roads, and cabin-doors crowded with beggars of the female sex, followed by three, four, or six children, *all in rags,* and importuning every passenger for an alms. These mothers, instead of being able to work for their honest livelihood, are forced to employ all their time in strolling, to beg sustenance for their helpless infants, who, as they grow up, either turn thieves for want of work, or leave their dear Native Country to fight for the Pretender in Spain, or sell themselves to the Barbadoes.

I think it is agreed by all parties that this prodigious number of children, in the arms, or on the backs, or at the heels of their mothers, and frequently of their fathers, is in the present deplorable state of the kingdom a very great additional grievance; and therefore whoever could find out a fair, cheap, and easy method of making these children sound useful members of the commonwealth would deserve so well of the public as to have his statue set up for a preserver of the nation.

But my intention is very far from being confined to provide only for the children of professed beggars; it is of a much greater extent, and shall take in the whole number of infants at a certain age who are born of parents in effect as little able to support them as those who demand our charity in the streets.

As to my own part, having turned my thoughts, for many years, upon this important subject, and maturely weighed the several schemes of other projectors, I have always found them grossly mistaken in their computation. It is true a child, just dropped from its dam, may be supported by her milk for a solar year with little other nourishment, at most not above the value of two shillings, which the mother may certainly get, or the value in scraps, by her lawful occupation of begging, and it is exactly at one year old that I propose to provide for them, in such a manner as, instead of being a charge upon their parents, or the parish, or wanting food and raiment for the rest of their lives, they shall, on the contrary, contribute to the feeding and partly to the clothing of many thousands.

There is likewise another great advantage in my scheme, that it will pre-

[1] First published in 1729.

vent those voluntary abortions, and that horrid practice of women murdering their bastard children, alas, too frequent among us, sacrificing the poor innocent babes, I doubt, more to avoid the expense than the shame, which would move tears and pity in the most savage and inhuman breast.

The number of souls in this kingdom being usually reckoned one million and a half, of these I calculate there may be about two hundred thousand couple whose wives are breeders, from which number I subtract thirty thousand couple who are able to maintain their own children, although I apprehend there cannot be so many under the present distresses of the kingdom, but this being granted, there will remain an hundred and seventy thousand breeders. I again subtract fifty thousand for those women who miscarry, or whose children die by accident or disease within the year. There only remain an hundred and twenty thousand children of poor parents annually born: The question therefore is, how this number shall be reared, and provided for, which, as I have already said, under the present situation of affairs, is utterly impossible by all the methods hitherto proposed, for we can neither employ them in handicraft, or agriculture; we neither build houses (I mean in the country), nor cultivate land: they can very seldom pick up a livelihood by stealing till they arrive at six years old, except where they are of towardly parts, although I confess they learn the rudiments much earlier, during which time they can however be properly looked upon only as *probationers,* as I have been informed by a principal gentleman in the County of Cavan, who protested to me that he never knew above one or two instances under the age of six, even in a part of the kingdom so renowned for the quickest proficiency in that art.

I am assured by our merchants that a boy or a girl, before twelve years old, is no saleable commodity, and even when they come to this age, they will not yield above three pounds, or three pounds and half-a-crown at most on the Exchange, which cannot turn to account either to the parents of the kingdom, the charge of nutriment and rags having been at least four times that value.

I shall now therefore humbly propose my own thoughts, which I hope will not be liable to the least objection.

I have been assured by a very knowing American of my acquaintance in London, that a young healthy child well nursed is at a year old a most delicious, nourishing, and wholesome food, whether stewed, roasted, baked, or boiled, and I make no doubt that it will equally serve in a fricassee, or a ragout.

I do therefore humbly offer it to public consideration, that of the hundred and twenty thousand children already computed, twenty thousand may be reserved for breed, whereof only one fourth part to be males, which is more than we allow to sheep, black-cattle, or swine, and my reason is that these children are seldom the fruits of marriage, a circumstance not much regarded by our savages, therefore one male will be sufficient to serve four females.

That the remaining hundred thousand may at a year old be offered in sale to the persons of quality, and fortune, through the kingdom, always advising the mother to let them suck plentifully in the last month, so as to render them plump, and fat for a good table. A child will make two dishes at an entertainment for friends, and when the family dines alone, the fore or hind quarters will make a reasonable dish, and seasoned with a little pepper or salt will be very good boiled on the fourth day, especially in winter.

I have reckoned upon a medium, that a child just born will weigh 12 pounds, and in a solar year if tolerably nursed increaseth to 28 pounds.

I grant this food will be somewhat dear, and therefore very proper for landlords, who, as they have already devoured most of the parents, seem to have the best title to the children.

Infants' flesh will be in season throughout the year, but more plentiful in March, and a little before and after, for we are told by a grave author, an eminent French physician, that fish being a prolific diet, there are more children born in Roman Catholic countries about nine months after Lent than at any other season; therefore reckoning a year after Lent, the markets will be more glutted than usual, because the number of Popish infants is at least three to one in this kingdom, and therefore it will have one other collateral advantage by lessening the number of Papists among us.

I have already computed the charge of nursing a beggar's child (in which list I reckon all cottagers, labourers, and four-fifths of the farmers) to be about two shillings *per annum,* rags included, and I believe no gentleman would repine to give ten shillings for the carcass of a good fat child, which, as I have said, will make four dishes of excellent nutritive meat, when he hath only some particular friend or his own family to dine with him. Thus the Squire will learn to be a good landlord, and grow popular among his tenants, the mother will have eight shillings net profit, and be fit for work till she produces another child.

Those who are more thrifty (as I must confess the times require) may flay the carcass; the skin of which, artificially dressed, will make admirable gloves for ladies, and summer boots for fine gentlemen.

As to our City of Dublin, shambles may be appointed for this purpose, in the most convenient parts of it, and butchers we may be assured will not be wanting, although I rather recommend buying the children alive, and dressing them hot from the knife, as we do roasting pigs.

A very worthy person, a true lover of this country, and whose virtues I highly esteem, was lately pleased, in discoursing on this matter, to offer a refinement upon my scheme. He said that many gentlemen of this kingdom, having of late destroyed their deer, he conceived that the want of venison might be well supplied by the bodies of young lads and maidens, not exceeding fourteen years of age, nor under twelve, so great a number of both sexes in every country being now ready to starve, for want of work and service:

and these to be disposed of by their parents if alive, or otherwise by their nearest relations. But with due deference to so excellent a friend, and so deserving a patriot, I cannot be altogether in his sentiments; for as to the males, my American acquaintance assured me from frequent experience that their flesh was generally tough and lean, like that of our schoolboys, by continual exercise, and their taste disagreeable, and to fatten them would not answer the charge. Then as to the females, it would, I think with humble submission, be a loss to the public, because they soon would become breeders themselves: And besides, it is not improbable that some scrupulous people might be apt to censure such a practice (although indeed very unjustly) as a little bordering upon cruelty, which, I confess, hath always been with me the strongest objection against any project, however so well intended.

But in order to justify my friend, he confessed that this expedient was put into his head by the famous Psalmanazer, a native of the island Formosa, who came from thence to London, above twenty years ago, and in conversation told my friend that in his country when any young person happened to be put to death, the executioner sold the carcass to persons of quality, as a prime dainty, and that, in his time, the body of a plump girl of fifteen, who was crucified for an attempt to poison the emperor, was sold to his Imperial Majesty's Prime Minister of State, and other great Mandarins of the Court, in joints from the gibbet, at four hundred crowns. Neither indeed can I deny that if the same use were made of several plump young girls in this town, who, without one single groat to their fortunes, cannot stir abroad without a chair, and appear at the playhouse, and assemblies in foreign fineries, which they never will pay for, the kingdom would not be the worse.

Some persons of a desponding spirit are in great concern about that vast number of poor people, who are aged, diseased, or maimed, and I have been desired to employ my thoughts what course may be taken to ease the nation of so grievous an encumbrance. But I am not in the least pain upon that matter, because it is very well known that they are every day dying, and rotting, by cold, and famine, and filth, and vermin, as fast as can be reasonably expected. And as to the younger labourers they are now in almost as hopeful a condition. They cannot get work, and consequently pine away for want of nourishment, to a degree, that if at any time they are accidentally hired to common labour, they have not strength to perform it; and thus the country and themselves are happily delivered from the evils to come.

I have too long digressed, and therefore shall return to my subject. I think the advantages by the proposal which I have made are obvious and many, as well as of the highest importance.

For first, as I have already observed, it would greatly lessen the number of Papists, with whom we are yearly over-run, being the principal breeders of the nation, as well as our most dangerous enemies, and who stay at home on purpose with a design to deliver the kingdom to the Pretender, hoping to take their advantage by the absence of so many good Protestants, who have chosen rather to leave their country than stay at home, and pay tithes against their conscience to an Episcopal curate.

Secondly, the poorer tenants will have something valuable of their own, which by law be made liable to distress, and help to pay their landlord's rent, their corn and cattle being already seized and *money a thing unknown.*

Thirdly, Whereas the maintenance of an hundred thousand children, from two years old, and upwards, cannot be computed at less than ten shillings a piece *per annum,* the nation's stock will be thereby increased fifty thousand pounds *per annum,* besides the profit of a new dish, introduced to the tables of all gentlemen of fortune in the kingdom, who have any refinement in taste, and the money will circulate among ourselves, the goods being entirely of our own growth and manufacture.

Fourthly, The constant breeders, besides the gain of eight shillings sterling *per annum,* by the sale of their children, will be rid of the charge of maintaining them after the first year.

Fifthly, This food would likewise bring great custom to taverns, where the vintners will certainly be so prudent as to procure the best receipts for dressing it up to perfection, and consequently have their houses frequented by all the fine gentlemen, who justly value themselves upon their knowledge in good eating; and a skillful cook, who understands how to oblige his guests, will contrive to make it as expensive as they please.

Sixthly, This would be a great inducement to marriage, which all wise nations have either encouraged by rewards, or enforced by laws and penalties. It would increase the care and tenderness of mothers toward their children, when they were sure of a settlement for life, to the poor babes, provided in some sort by the public to their annual profit instead of expense. We should see an honest emulation among the married women, which of them could bring the fattest child to the market, men would become as fond of their wives, during the time of their pregnancy, as they are now of their mares in foal, their cows in calf, or sows when they are ready to farrow, nor offer to beat or kick them (as it is too frequent a practice) for fear of a miscarriage.

Many other advantages might be enumerated: For instance, the addition of some thousand carcasses in our exportation of barrelled beef; the propagation of swine's flesh, and improvement in the art of making good bacon, so much wanted among us by the great destruction of pigs, too frequent at our tables, which are no way comparable in taste or magnificence to a well-grown, fat yearling child, which roasted whole will make a considerable figure at a Lord Mayor's feast, or any other public entertainment. But this and many others I omit, being studious of brevity.

Supposing that one thousand families in this city would be constant customers for infants' flesh, besides others who might have it at merry-meetings, particularly weddings and christenings, I compute that Dublin would take off annually about twenty thousand carcasses, and the rest of the kingdom (where probably they will be sold somewhat cheaper) the remaining eighty thousand.

I can think of no one objection that will possibly be raised against this proposal, unless it should be urged that the number of people will be thereby much lessened in the kingdom. This I freely own, and it was indeed one principal design in offering it to the world. I desire the reader will observe, that I calculate my remedy for this one individual *Kingdom of Ireland, and for no other that ever was, is, or, I think, ever can be upon earth.* Therefore let no man talk to me of other expedients: *Of taxing our absentees at five shillings a pound: Of using neither clothes, nor household furniture, except what is of our own growth and manufacture: Of utterly rejecting the materials and instruments that promote foreign luxury: Of curing the expensiveness of pride, vanity, idleness, and gaming in our women: Of introducing a vein of parsimony, prudence, and temperance: Of learning to love our Country, wherein we differ even from* LAPLANDERS, *and the inhabitants of* TOPINAMBOO: *Of quitting our animosities and factions, nor act any longer like the Jews, who were murdering one another at the very moment their city was taken: Of being a little cautious not to sell our country and consciences for nothing: Of teaching landlords to have at least one degree of mercy toward their tenants. Lastly, of putting a spirit of honesty, industry, and skill into our shopkeepers, who, if a resolution could now be taken to buy only our native goods, would immediately unite to cheat and exact upon us in the price, the measure, and the goodness, nor could ever yet be brought to make one fair proposal of just dealing, though often and earnestly invited to it.*

Therefore I repeat, let no man talk to me of these and the like expedients, till he hath at least some glimpse of hope that there will ever be some hearty and sincere attempt to put them in practice.

But as to myself, having been wearied out for many years with offering vain, idle, visionary thoughts, and at length utterly despairing of success, I fortunately fell upon this proposal, which as it is wholly new, so it hath something solid and real, of no expense and little trouble, full in our own power, and whereby we can incur no danger in *disobliging* ENGLAND. For this kind of commodity will not bear exportation, the flesh being too tender a consistence to admit a long continuance in salt, *although perhaps I could name a country which would be glad to eat up our whole nation without it.*

After all I am not so violently bent upon my own opinion as to reject any offer, proposed by wise men, which shall be found equally innocent, cheap, easy, and effectual. But before something of that kind shall be advanced in contradiction to my scheme, and offering a better, I desire the author, or authors, will be pleased maturely to consider two points. First, as things now stand, how they will be able to find food and raiment for an hundred thousand useless mouths and backs. And secondly, there being a round million of creatures in human figure, throughout this kingdom, whose whole subsistence put into a common stock would leave them in debt two millions of pounds sterling; adding those, who are beggars by profession, to the bulk of farmers, cottagers, and labourers with their wives and children, who are beggars in effect. I desire those politicians, who dislike my overture, and may perhaps be so bold to attempt an answer, that they will first ask the parents of these mortals whether they would not at this day think it a great happiness to have been sold for food at a year old, in the manner I prescribe, and thereby have avoided such a perpetual scene of misfortunes as they have since gone through, by the oppression of landlords, the impossibility of paying rent without money or trade, the want of common sustenance, with neither house nor clothes to cover them from the inclemencies of the weather, and the most inevitable prospect of entailing the like, or greater miseries upon their breed for ever.

I profess in the sincerity of my heart that I have not the least personal interest in endeavoring to promote this necessary work, having no other motive than the *public good of my country, by advancing our trade, providing for infants, relieving the poor, and giving some pleasure to the rich.* I have no children by which I can propose to get a single penny; the youngest being nine years old, and my wife past child-bearing.

PART VII

PHILOSOPHY AND RELIGION

The Good Life

ARISTOTLE

•

Virtue[1]

But it may be asked what we mean by saying that people must become just by doing what is just and temperate by doing what is temperate. For if they do what is just and temperate, they are *ipso facto* proved, it will be said, to be just and temperate in the same way as, if they practise grammar and music, they are proved to be grammarians and musicians.

But is not the answer that the case of the arts is not the same? For a person may do something that is grammatical either by chance or at the suggestion of somebody else; hence he will not be a grammarian unless he not only does what is grammatical but does it in a grammatical manner, i.e. in virtue of the grammatical knowledge which he possesses.

There is another point too of difference between the arts and the virtues. The productions of art have their excellence in themselves. It is enough therefore that, when they are produced, they should be of a certain character. But actions in accordance with virtue are not e.g. justly or temperately performed because they are in themselves just or temperate. It is necessary that the agent at the time of performing them should satisfy certain conditions, i.e. in the first

[1] From *The Nichomachean Ethics of Aristotle, translated* by J. E. C. Weldon (London: Macmillan & Co., Ltd., 1920), Book II, with omissions. Reprinted by permission of Macmillan & Co., Ltd.

place that he should know what he is doing, secondly that he should deliberately choose to do it and to do it for its own sake, and thirdly that he should do it as an instance of a settled and immutable moral state. If it be a question whether a person possesses any art, these conditions, except indeed the condition of knowledge, are not taken into account; but if it be a question of possessing the virtues, the mere knowledge is of little or no avail, and it is the other conditions, which are the results of frequently performing just and temperate actions, that are not of slight but of absolute importance. Accordingly deeds are said to be just and temperate, when they are such as a just or temperate person would do, and a just and temperate person is not merely one who does these deeds but one who does them in the spirit of the just and the temperate.

It may fairly be said then that a just man becomes just by doing what is just and a temperate man becomes temperate by doing what is temperate, and if a man did not so act, he would not have so much as a chance of becoming good. But most people, instead of doing such actions, take refuge in theorizing; they imagine that they are philosophers and that philosophy will make them virtuous; in fact they behave like people who listen attentively to their doctors but never do anything that their doctors tell them. But it is as improbable that a healthy state of the soul will be produced by this kind of philosophizing as that a healthy state of the body will be produced by this kind of medical treatment.

We have next to consider the nature of virtue.

Now, as the qualities of the soul are three, viz. emotions, faculties and moral states, it follows that virtue must be one of the three. By the emotions I mean desire, anger, fear, courage, envy, joy, love, hatred, regret, emulation, pity, in a word whatever is attended by pleasure or pain. I call those faculties in respect of which we are said to be capable of experiencing these emotions, e.g. capable of getting angry or being pained or feeling pity. And I call those moral states in respect of which we are well or ill disposed towards the emotions, ill-disposed e.g. towards the passion of anger, if our anger be too violent or too feeble, and well-disposed, if it be duly moderated, and similarly towards the other emotions.

Now neither the virtues nor the vices are emotions; for we are not called good or evil in respect of our emotions but in respect of our virtues or vices. Again, we are not praised or blamed in respect of our emotions; a person is not praised for being afraid or being angry, nor blamed for being angry in an absolute sense, but only for being angry in a certain way; but we are praised or blamed in respect of our virtues or vices. Again, whereas we are angry or afraid without deliberate purpose, the virtues are in some sense deliberate purposes, or do not exist in the absence of deliberate purpose. It may be added that while we are said to be moved in respect of our emotions, in respect of our virtues or vices we are not said to be moved but to have a certain disposition.

These reasons also prove that the virtues are not faculties. For we are not called either good or bad, nor are we praised or blamed, as having an abstract capacity for emotion. Also while Nature gives us our faculties, it is not Nature that makes us good or bad, but this is a point which we have already discussed. If then the virtues are neither emotions nor faculties, it remains that they must be moral states.

The nature of virtue has been now generically described. But it is not enough to state merely that virtue is a moral state, we must also describe the character of that moral state.

It must be laid down then that every virtue or excellence has the effect of producing a good condition of that of which it is a virtue or excellence, and of enabling it to perform its function well, Thus the excellence of the eye makes the eye good and its function good, as it is by the excellence of the eye that we see well. Similarly, the excellence of the horse makes a horse excellent and good at racing, at carrying its rider and at facing the enemy.

If then this is universally true, the virtue or excellence of man will be such a moral state as makes a man good and able to perform his proper function well. We have already explained how this will be the case, but another way of making it clear will be to study the nature or character of this virtue.

Now in everything, whether it be continuous or discrete,[2] it is possible to take a greater, a smaller, or an equal amount, and this either absolutely or in relation to ourselves, the equal being a mean between excess and deficiency. By the mean in respect of the thing itself, or the absolute mean, I understand that which is equally distinct from both extremes; and this is one and the same thing for everybody. By the mean considered relatively to ourselves I understand that which is neither too much nor too little; but this is not one thing, nor is it the same for everybody. Thus if 10 be too much and 2 too little we take 6 as a mean in respect of the thing itself; for 6 is as much greater than 2 as it is less than 10, and this is a mean in arithmetical proportion. But the mean considered relatively to ourselves must not be ascertained in this way. It does not follow that if 10 pounds *of meat* be too much and 2 be too little for a man to eat, a trainer will order him 6 pounds, as this may itself be too much or too little for the person who is to take it; it will be too little e.g. for Milo,[3] but too much for a beginner in gymnastics. It will be the same with running and wrestling; *the right amount will vary with the individual.* This being so, everybody who understands his business avoids alike excess and deficiency; he seeks and chooses the mean, not the absolute mean, but the mean considered relatively to ourselves.

Every science then performs its function well, if it regards the mean and refers the works which it produces to the mean. This is the reason why it is usually said of successful works that it is impossible to take anything from them or to add anything to them, which implies that excess or deficiency is

[2] In Aristotelian language, as Mr. Peters says, a straight line is a "continuous quantity" but a rouleau of sovereigns a "discrete quantity."
[3] The famous Crotoniate wrestler.

fatal to excellence but that the mean state ensures it. Good artists too, as we say, have an eye to the mean in their works. But virtue, like Nature herself, is more accurate and better than any art; virtue therefore will aim at the mean; —I speak of moral virtue, as it is moral virtue which is concerned with emotions and actions, and it is these which admit of excess and deficiency and the mean. Thus it is possible to go too far, or not to go far enough, in respect of fear, courage, desire, anger, pity, and pleasure and pain generally, and the excess and the deficiency are alike wrong; but to experience these emotions at the right times and on the right occasions and towards the right persons and for the right causes and in the right manner is the mean or the supreme good, which is characteristic of virtue. Similarly there may be excess, deficiency, or the mean, in regard to actions. But virtue is concerned with emotions and actions, and here excess is an error and deficiency a fault, whereas the mean is successful and laudable, and success and merit are both characteristics of virtue.

It appears then that virtue is a mean state, so far at least as it aims at the mean.

Again, there are many different ways of going wrong; for evil is in its nature infinite, to use the Pythagorean[4] figure, but good is finite. But there is only one possible way of going right. Accordingly the former is easy and the latter difficult; it is easy to miss the mark but difficult to hit it. This again is a reason why excess and deficiency are characteristics of vice and the mean state a characteristic of virtue.

For good is simple, evil manifold.[5]

Virtue then is a state of deliberate moral purpose consisting in a mean that is relative to ourselves, the mean being determined by reason, or as a prudent man would determine it.

It is a mean state *firstly as lying* between two vices, the vice of excess on the one hand, and the vice of deficiency on the other, and secondly because, whereas the vices either fall short of or go beyond what is proper in the emotions and actions, virtue not only discovers but embraces the mean.

Accordingly, virtue, if regarded in its essence or theoretical conception, is a mean state, but, if regarded from the point of view of the highest good, or of excellence, it is an extreme.

But it is not every action or every emotion that admits of a mean state. There are some whose very name implies wickedness, as e.g. malice, shamelessness, and envy, among emotions, or adultery, theft, and murder, among actions. All these, and others like them, are censured as being intrinsically wicked, not merely the excess or deficiencies of them. It is never possible then to be right in respect of them; they are always sinful. Right or wrong in such

[4] The Pythagoreans, starting from the mystical significance of number, took the opposite principles of "the finite" (τὸ πέρασ or τὸ πεπερασμένου) and "the infinite" (τὸ απειρου) to represent good and evil.

[5] A line—perhaps Pythagorean—of unknown authorship.

actions as adultery does not depend on our committing them with the right person, at the right time or in the right manner; on the contrary it is sinful to do anything of the kind at all. It would be equally wrong then to suppose that there can be a mean state or an excess or deficiency in unjust, cowardly or licentious conduct; for, if it were so, there would be a mean state of an excess or of a deficiency, an excess of an excess and a deficiency of a deficiency. But as in temperance and courage there can be no excess or deficiency because the mean is, in a sense, an extreme, so too in these cases there cannot be a mean or an excess or deficiency, but, however the acts may be done, they are wrong. For it is a general rule that an excess or deficiency does not admit of a mean state, nor a mean state of an excess or deficiency.

But it is not enough to lay down this as a general rule; it is necessary to apply it to particular cases, as in reasonings upon actions, general statements, although they are broader, are less exact than particular statements. For all action refers to particulars, and it is essential that our theories should harmonize with the particular cases to which they apply.

We must take particular virtues then from the catalogue[6] of *virtues.*

In regard to feelings of fear and confidence, courage is a mean state. On the side of excess, he whose fearlessness is excessive has no name, as often happens, but he whose confidence is excessive is foolhardy, while he whose timidity is excessive and whose confidence is deficient is a coward.

In respect of pleasures, and pains, although not indeed of all pleasures and pains, and to a less extent in respect of pains than of pleasures, the mean state is temperance, the excess is licentiousness. We never find people who are deficient in regard to pleasures, accordingly such people again have not received a name, but we may call them insensible.

As regards the giving and taking of money, the mean state is liberality, the excess and deficiency are prodigality and illiberality. Here the excess and deficiency take opposite forms; for while the prodigal man is excessive in spending and deficient in taking, the illiberal man is excessive in taking and deficient in spending.

(For the present we are giving only a rough and summary account *of the virtues,* and that is sufficient for our purpose; we will hereafter determine their character more exactly.)

In respect of money there are other dispositions as well. There is the mean state which is magnificence; for the magnificent man, as having to do with large sums of money, differs from the liberal man who has to do only with small sums; and the excess *corresponding to it* is bad taste or vulgarity, the deficiency is meanness. These are different from the excess and deficiency of liberality; what the difference is will be explained hereafter.

In respect of honour and dishonour the mean state is highmindedness, the

[6] It would seem that a catalogue of virtues (διαγραφή or ὑπογραφή) must have been recognized in the Aristotelian school. Cp. *Eud. Eth.* ii, ch. 3.

excess is what is called vanity, the deficiency littlemindedness. Corresponding to liberality, which, as we said, differs from magnificence as having to do *not with great but* with small sums of money, there is a moral state which has to do with petty honour and is related to highmindedness which has to do with great honour; for it is possible to aspire to honour in the right way, or in a way which is excessive or insufficient, and if a person's aspirations are excessive, he is called ambitious, if they are deficient, he is called unambitious, while if they are between the two, he has no name.

Anger, like other emotions, has its excess, its deficiency, and its mean state. It may be said that they have no names, but as we call one who observes the mean gentle, we will call the mean state gentleness. Among the extremes, if a person errs on the side of excess, he may be called passionate and his vice passionateness, if on that of deficiency, he may be called impassive and his deficiency impassivity.

There are also three other mean states with a certain resemblance to each other, and yet with a difference. For while they are all concerned with intercourse in speech and action, they are different in that one of them is concerned with truth in such intercourse, and the others with pleasantness, one with pleasantness in amusement and the other with pleasantness in the various circumstances of life. We must therefore discuss these states in order to make it clear that in all cases it is the mean state which is an object of praise, and the extremes are neither right nor laudable but censurable. It is true that these mean and extreme states are generally nameless, but we must do our best here as elsewhere to give them a name, so that our argument may be clear and easy to follow.

In the matter of truth then, he who observes the mean may be called truthful, and the mean state truthfulness. Pretence, if it takes the form of exaggeration, is boastfulness, and one who is guilty of pretence is a boaster; but if it takes the form of depreciation it is irony, and he who is guilty of it is ironical.

There are also mean states in the emotions and in the expression of the emotions. For although modesty is not a virtue, yet a modest person is praised as if he were virtuous; for here too one person is said to observe the mean and another to exceed it, as e.g. the bashful man who is never anything but modest, whereas a person who has insufficient modesty or no modesty at all is called shameless, and one who observes the mean modest.

Righteous indignation, again, is a mean state between envy and malice. They are all concerned with the pain and pleasure which we feel at the fortunes of our neighbours. A person who is righteously indignant is pained at the prosperity of the undeserving; but the envious person goes further and is pained at anybody's prosperity, and the malicious person is so far from being pained that he actually rejoices *at misfortunes*. . . .

There are then three dispositions, two being vices, viz. one the vice of excess and the other that of deficiency, and one virtue, which is the mean state between them; and they are all in a sense mutually opposed. For the extremes are opposed both to the mean and to each other, and the mean is opposed to the extremes. For as the equal if compared with the less is greater but if compared with the greater is less, so the mean states, whether in the emotions or actions, if compared with the deficiencies, are excessive, but if compared with the excesses are deficient. Thus the courageous man appears foolhardy as compared with the coward, but cowardly as compared with the foolhardy. Similarly, the temperate man appears licentious as compared with the insensible but insensible as compared with the licentious, and the liberal man appears prodigal as compared with the illiberal, but illiberal as compared with the prodigal. The result is that the extremes mutually repel and reject the mean; the coward calls the courageous man foolhardy, but the foolhardy man calls him cowardly, and so on in the other cases.

But while there is this mutual opposition between the extremes and the mean, there is greater opposition between the two extremes than between either extreme and the mean; for they are further removed from each other than from the mean, as the great from the small and the small from the great than both from the equal. Again, while some extremes exhibit more or less similarity to the mean, as foolhardiness to courage and prodigality to liberality, there is the greatest possible dissimilarity between the extremes. But things which are furthest removed from each other are defined to be opposites; hence the further things are removed, the greater is the opposition between them.

It is in some cases the deficiency and in others the excess which is the more opposed to the mean. Thus it is not foolhardiness the excess, but cowardice the deficiency which is the more opposed to courage, nor is it insensibility the deficiency, but licentiousness the excess which is the more opposed to temperance. There are two reasons why this should be so. One lies in the nature of the thing itself; for as one of the two extremes is the nearer and more similar to the mean, it is not this extreme, but its opposite, that we chiefly set against the mean. For instance, as it appears that foolhardiness is more similar and nearer to courage than cowardice, it is cowardice that we chiefly set against courage; for things which are further removed from the mean seem to be more opposite to it. This being one reason which lies in the nature of the thing itself, there is a second which lies in our own nature. It is the things to which we ourselves are naturally more inclined that appear more opposed to the mean. Thus we are ourselves naturally more inclined to pleasures *than to their opposites,* and are more prone therefore to licentiousness than to decorum. Accordingly we speak of those things, in which we are more likely to run to great lengths, as being more opposed to the mean. Hence it follows that licentiousness which is an excess is more opposed to temperance than insensibility.

It has now been sufficiently shown that moral virtue is a mean state, and in what sense it is a mean state; it is a mean state as lying between two vices, a vice of excess on the one side and a vice of deficiency on the other, and as aiming at the mean in the emotions and actions.

The Sermon on the Mount[1]

And seeing the multitudes, he went up into a mountain; and when he was set, his disciples came unto him: and he opened his mouth, and taught them, saying, Blessed are the poor in spirit: for theirs is the kingdom of heaven. Blessed are they that mourn: for they shall be comforted. Blessed are the meek: for they shall inherit the earth. Blessed are they which do hunger and thirst after righteousness: for they shall be filled. Blessed are the merciful: for they shall obtain mercy. Blessed are the pure in heart: for they shall see God. Blessed are the peacemakers: for they shall be called the children of God. Blessed are they which are persecuted for righteousness' sake: for theirs is the kingdom of heaven. Blessed are ye, when men shall revile you, and persecute you, and shall say all manner of evil against you falsely, for my sake. Rejoice, and be exceeding glad: for great is your reward in heaven: for so persecuted they the prophets which were before you.

Ye are the salt of the earth: but if the salt have lost his savour, wherewith shall it be salted? it is thenceforth good for nothing, but to be cast out, and to be trodden under foot of men. Ye are the light of the world. A city that is set on an hill cannot be hid. Neither do men light a candle, and put it under a bushel, but on a candlestick; and it giveth light unto all that are in the house. Let your light so shine before men, that they may see your good works, and glorify your Father which is in heaven. Think not that I am come to destroy the law, or the prophets; I am not come to destroy, but to fulfil. For verily I say unto you, Till heaven and earth pass, one jot or one tittle shall in no wise pass from the law, till all be fulfilled. Whosoever therefore shall break one of these least commandments, and shall teach men so, he shall be called the least in the kingdom of heaven: but whosoever shall do and teach them, the same shall be called great in the kingdom of heaven. For I say unto you, That except your righteousness shall exceed the righteousness of the scribes and Pharisees, ye shall in no case enter into the kingdom of heaven.

Ye have heard that it was said by them of old time, Thou shalt not kill; and whosoever shall kill shall be in danger of the judgment: but I say unto you, That whosoever is angry with his brother without a cause shall be in danger of the judgment: and whosoever shall say to his brother, Raca, shall be in danger of the council: but whosoever shall say, Thou fool, shall be in danger of hell fire. Therefore if thou bring thy gift to the altar, and there rememberest that thy brother hath ought against thee; leave there thy gift before the altar, and go thy way; first be reconciled to thy brother, and then come and offer thy gift. Agree with thine adversary quickly, whiles thou art in the way with him; lest at any time the adversary deliver thee to the judge, and

[1] From *The Gospel According to Saint Matthew* (King James Version of the Bible), Chapters 5, 6, 7.

the judge deliver thee to the officer, and thou be cast into prison. Verily I say unto thee, Thou shalt by no means come out thence, till thou hast paid the uttermost farthing.

Ye have heard that it was said by them of old time, Thou shalt not commit adultery; but I say unto you, That whosoever looketh on a woman to lust after her hath committed adultery with her already in his heart. And if thy right eye offend thee, pluck it out, and cast it from thee: for it is profitable for thee that one of thy members should perish, and not that thy whole body should be cast into hell. And if thy right hand offend thee, cut it off, and cast it from thee: for it is profitable for thee that one of thy members should perish, and not that thy whole body should be cast into hell. It hath been said, Whosoever shall put away his wife, let him give her a writing of divorcement: but I say unto you, That whosover shall put away his wife, saving for the cause of fornication, causeth her to commit adultery: and whosoever shall marry her that is divorced committeth adultery.

Again, ye have heard that it hath been said by them of old time, Thou shalt not forswear thyself, but shalt perform to the Lord thine oaths: but I say unto you, Swear not at all; neither by heaven; for it is God's throne: nor by the earth; for it is his footstool: neither by Jerusalem; for it is the city of the great King. Neither shalt thou swear by thy head, because thou canst not make one hair white or black. But let your communication be, Yea, yea; Nay, nay: for whatsoever is more than these cometh of evil.

Ye have heard that it hath been said, An eye for an eye, and a tooth for a tooth: but I say unto you, That ye resist not evil: but whosoever shall smite thee on thy right cheek, turn to him the other also. And if any man will sue thee at the law, and take away thy coat, let him have thy cloke also. And whosoever shall compel thee to go a mile, go with him twain. Give to him that asketh thee, and from him that would borrow of thee turn not thou away.

Ye have heard that it hath been said, Thou shalt love thy neighbor, and hate thine enemy. But I say unto you, Love your enemies, bless them that curse you, do good to them that hate you, and pray for them which despitefully use you, and persecute you; that ye may be the children of your Father which is in heaven; for he maketh his sun to rise on the evil and on the good, and sendeth rain on the just and on the unjust. For if ye love them which love you, what reward have ye? do not even the publicans the same? And if ye salute your brethren only, what do ye more than others? do not even the publicans so? Be ye therefore perfect, even as your Father which is in heaven is perfect.

Take heed that ye do not your alms before men, to be seen of them: otherwise ye have no reward of your Father which is in heaven. Therefore when thou doest thine alms, do not sound a trumpet before thee, as the hypocrites do in the synagogues and in the streets, that they may have glory of men. Verily I say unto you, They have their reward. But when thou doest alms, let not thy left hand know what thy right hand doeth: that thine alms may be in secret: and thy Father which seeth in secret himself shall reward thee openly. And when thou prayest, thou shalt not be as the hypocrites are: for they love to pray standing in the synagogues and in the corners of the streets, that they may be seen of men. Verily I say unto you, They have their reward. But thou, when thou prayest, enter into thy closet, and when thou hast shut thy door, pray to thy Father, which is in secret; and thy Father which seeth in secret shall reward thee openly. But when ye pray, use not vain repetitions, as the heathen do: for they think that they shall be heard for their much speaking. Be not ye therefore like unto them: for your Father knoweth what things ye have need of, before ye ask him. After this manner therefore pray ye: Our Father which art in heaven, Hallowed by thy name. Thy kingdom come. Thy will be done in earth, as it is in heaven. Give us this day our daily bread. And forgive us our debts, as we forgive our debtors. And lead us not into temptation, but deliver us from evil: for thine is the kingdom, and the power, and the glory, for ever. Amen. For if ye forgive men their trespasses, your heavenly Father will also forgive you: but if ye forgive not men their trespasses, neither will your Father forgive your trespasses.

Moreover when ye fast, be not, as the hypocrites, of a sad countenance: for they disfigure their faces, that they may appear unto men to fast. Verily I say unto you, They have their reward. But thou, when thou fastest, anoint thine head, and wash thy face; that thou appear not unto men to fast, but unto thy Father which is in secret; and thy Father, which seeth in secret, shall reward thee openly.

Lay up not for yourselves treasures upon earth, where moth and rust doth corrupt, and where thieves break through and steal: but lay up for yourselves treasures in heaven, where neither moth nor rust doth corrupt, and where thieves do not break through nor steal: for where your treasure is, there will your heart be also. The light of the body is the eye: if therefore thine eye be single, thy whole body shall be full of light. But if thine eye be evil, thy whole body shall be full of darkness. If therefore the light that is in thee be darkness, how great is that darkness! No man can serve two masters: for either he will hate the one, and love the other; or else he will hold to the one, and despise the other. Ye cannot serve God and mammon. Therefore I say unto you, Take no thought for your life, what ye shall eat, or what ye shall drink; nor yet for your body, what ye shall put on. Is not the life more than meat, and the body than raiment? Behold the fowls of the air: for they sow not, neither do they reap, nor gather into barns; yet your heavenly Father feedeth them. Are ye not much better than they? Which of you by taking thought can add one cubit unto his stature? And why take ye thought for raiment? Consider the lilies of the field, how they grow; they toil not, neither do they spin: and yet I say unto you, That even Solomon in all his glory was not arrayed like one of these. Wherefore, if God so clothe the grass of the field, which to day is, and to morrow is cast into the oven, shall he not much more clothe you, O ye of little faith? Therefore take no thought, saying, What shall we eat? or, What shall we drink? or, Wherewithal shall we be clothed? (For after all these things do the Gentiles seek:) for your heavenly Father knoweth that ye have need of all these things. But seek ye first the kingdom of God, and his righteousness; and all these things shall be added unto you. Take therefore no thought for the morrow: for the morrow shall take thought for the things of itself. Sufficient unto the day is the evil thereof.

Judge not, that ye be not judged. For with what judgment ye judge, ye shall be judged: and with what measure ye mete, it shall be measured to you again. And why beholdest thou the mote that is in thy brother's eye, but considerest not the beam that is in thine own eye? Or how wilt thou say to thy brother, Let me pull out the mote out of thine eye; and, behold, a beam is in thine own eye? Thou hypocrite, first cast out the beam out of thine own eye; and then shalt thou see clearly to cast out the mote out of thy brother's eye.

Give not that which is holy unto the dogs, neither cast ye your pearls before swine, lest they trample them under their feet, and turn again and rend you. Ask, and it shall be given you; seek and ye shall find; knock, and it shall be opened unto you: for every one that asketh receiveth; and he that seeketh findeth; and to him that knocketh it shall be opened. Or what man is there of you, whom if his son ask bread, will he give him a stone? Or if he ask a fish, will he give him a serpent? If ye then, being evil, know how to give good gifts unto your children, how much more shall your Father which is in heaven give good things to them that ask him? Therefore all things whatsoever ye would that men should do to you, do ye even so to them: for this is the law and the prophets.

Enter ye in at the strait gate: for wide is the gate, and broad is the way, that leadeth to destruction, and many there be which go in thereat: because strait is the gate, and narrow is the way, which leadeth unto life, and few there be that find it. Beware of false prophets, which come to you in sheep's clothing, but inwardly they are ravening wolves. Ye shall know them by their fruits. Do men gather grapes of thorns, or figs of thistles? Even so every good tree bringeth forth good fruit; but a corrupt tree bringeth forth evil fruit. A good tree cannot bring forth evil fruit, neither can a corrupt tree bring forth good fruit. Every tree that bringeth not forth good fruit is hewn down, and cast into the fire. Wherefore by their fruits ye shall know them. Not every one that saith unto me, Lord, Lord, shall enter into the kingdom of heaven; but he that doeth the will of my Father which is in heaven. Many will say to me in that day, Lord, Lord, have we not prophesied in thy name? And in thy name have cast out devils? and in thy name done many wonderful works? And then will I profess unto them, I never knew you: depart from me, ye that work iniquity. Therefore whosoever heareth these sayings of mine, and doeth them, I will liken him unto a wise man, which built his house upon a rock: and the rain descended, and the floods came, and the winds blew, and beat upon that house; and it fell not: for it was founded upon a rock. And every one that heareth these sayings of mine, and doeth them not, shall be likened unto a foolish man, which built his house upon the sand: and the rain descended, and the floods came, and the winds blew, and beat upon that house; and it fell: and great was the fall of it. And it came to pass, when Jesus had ended these sayings, the people were astonished at his doctrine: For he taught them as one having authority, and not as the scribes.

MARCUS AURELIUS

•

The Stoic Code[1]

Begin the morning by saying to thyself, I shall meet with the busybody, the ungrateful, arrogant, deceitful, envious, unsocial. All these things happen to them by reason of their ignorance of what is good and evil. But I who have seen the nature of the good that it is beautiful, and of the bad that it is ugly, and the nature of him who does wrong, that it is akin to me, not [only] of the same blood or seed, but that it participates in [the same] intelligence and [the same] portion of the divinity, I can neither be injured by any of them, for no one can fix on me what is ugly, nor can I be angry with my kinsman, nor hate him. For we are made for co-operation, like feet, like hands, like eyelids, like the rows of the upper and lower teeth. To act against one another, then, is contrary to nature; and it is action against one another to be vexed and to turn away.

2. Whatever this is that I am, it is a little flesh and breath, and the ruling part. Throw away thy books; no longer distract thyself: it is not allowed; but as if thou wast now dying, despise the flesh; it is blood and bones and a network, a contexture of nerves, veins, and arteries. See the breath also, what kind of a thing it is; air, and not always the same, but every moment sent out and again sucked in. The third, then, is the ruling part; consider thus: Thou art an old man; no longer let this be a slave, no longer be pulled by the strings like a puppet to unsocial movements, no longer be either dissatisfied with thy present lot, or shrink from the future.

3. All that is from the gods is full of providence. That which is from fortune is not separated from nature or without an interweaving and involution with the things which are ordered by providence. From thence all things flow; and there is besides necessity, and that which is for the advantage of the whole universe, of which thou art a part. But that is good for every part of nature which the nature of the whole brings, and what serves to maintain this nature.

[1] From *The Thoughts of the Emperor Marcus Aurelius,* translated by George Long (Boston: Little, Brown & Company, 1897), Book II.

Now the universe is preserved, as by the changes of the elements so by the changes of things compounded of the elements. Let these principles be enough for thee; let them always be fixed opinions. But cast away the thirst after books, that thou mayest not die murmuring, but cheerfully, truly, and from thy heart thankful to the gods.

4. Remember how long thou hast been putting off these things, and how often thou hast received opportunity from the gods, and yet dost not use it. Thou must now at last perceive of what universe thou art a part, and of what administrator of the universe thy existence is an efflux, and that a limit of time is fixed for thee, which if thou dost not use for clearing away the clouds from thy mind, it will go and thou wilt go, and it will never return.

5. Every moment think steadily as a Roman and a man to do what thou hast in hand with perfect and simple dignity, and feeling of affection, and freedom, and justice, and to give thyself relief from all other thoughts. And thou wilt give thyself relief if thou doest every act of thy life as if it were the last, laying aside all carelessness and passionate aversion from the commands of reason, and all hypocrisy, and self-love, and discontent with the portion which has been given to thee. Thou seest how few the things are, the which if a man lays hold of, he is able to live a life which flows in quiet, and is like the existence of the gods; for the gods on their part will require nothing more from him who observes these things.

6. Do wrong to thyself, do wrong to thyself, my soul; but thou wilt no longer have the opportunity of honoring thyself. Every man's life is sufficient. But thine is nearly finished, though thy soul reverences not itself, but places thy felicity in the souls of others.

7. Do the things external which fall upon thee distract thee? Give thyself time to learn something new and good, and cease to be whirled around. But then thou must also avoid being carried about the other way; for those too are triflers who have wearied themselves in life by their activity, and yet have no object to which to direct every movement, and, in a word, all their thoughts.

8. Through not observing what is in the mind of another a man has seldom been seen to be unhappy; but those who do not observe the movements of their own minds must of necessity be unhappy.

9. This thou must always bear in mind, what is the nature of the whole, and what is my nature, and how this is related to that, and what kind of a part it is of what kind of a whole, and that there is no one who hinders thee from always doing and saying the things which are according to the nature of which thou art a part.

10. Theophrastus, in his comparison of bad acts—such a comparison as one would make in accordance with the common notions of mankind—says, like a true philosopher, that the offences which are committed through desire are more blamable than those which are committed through anger. For he who is excited by anger seems to turn away from reason with a certain pain and unconscious contraction; but he who offends through desire, being over-

powered by pleasure, seems to be in a manner more intemperate and more womanish in his offences. Rightly, then, and in a way worthy of philosophy, he said that the offence which is committed with pleasure is more blamable than that which is committed with pain; and on the whole the one is more like a person who has been first wronged and through pain is compelled to be angry; but the other is moved by his own impulse to do wrong, being carried towards doing something by desire.

11. Since it is possible that thou mayest depart from life this very moment, regulate every act and thought accordingly. But to go away from among men, if there are gods, is not a thing to be afraid of, for the gods will not involve thee in evil; but if indeed they do not exist, or if they have no concern about human affairs, what is it to me to live in a universe devoid of gods or devoid of providence? But in truth they do exist, and they do care for human things, and they have put all the means in man's power to enable him not to fall into real evils. And as to the rest, if there was anything evil, they would have provided for this also, that it should be altogether in a man's power not to fall into it. Now that which does not make a man worse, how can it make a man's life worse? But neither through ignorance, nor having the knowledge but not the power to guard against or correct these things, is it possible that the nature of the universe has overlooked them; nor is it possible that it has made so great a mistake, either through want of power or want of skill, that good and evil should happen indiscriminately to the good and the bad. But death certainly, and life, honor and dishonor, pain and pleasure,—all these things equally happen to good men and bad, being things which make us neither better nor worse. Therefore they are neither good nor evil.

12. How quickly all things disappear,—in the universe the bodies themselves, but in time the remembrance of them. What is the nature of all sensible things, and particularly those which attract with the bait of pleasure or terrify by pain, or are noised abroad by vapory fame; how worthless, and contemptible, and sordid, and perishable, and dead they are,—all this it is the part of the intellectual faculty to observe. To observe too who these are whose opinions and voices give reputation; what death is, and the fact that, if a man looks at it in itself, and by the abstractive power of reflection resolves into their parts all the things which present themselves to the imagination in it, he will then consider it to be nothing else than an operation of nature; and if any one is afraid of an operation of nature, he is a child. This, however, is not only an operation of nature, but it is also a thing which conduces to the purposes of nature. To observe too how man comes near to the Deity, and by what part of him, and when this part of man is so disposed.

13. Nothing is more wretched than a man who traverses everything in a round, and pries into the thing beneath the earth, as the poet says, and seeks by conjecture what is in the minds of his neighbors, without perceiving that it is sufficient to attend to the daemon within him, and to reverence it sincerely. And reverence of the daemon consists in keeping it pure from passion

and thoughtlessness, and dissatisfaction with what comes from gods and men. For the things from the gods merit veneration for their excellence; and the things from men should be dear to us by reason of kinship; and sometimes even, in a manner, they move our pity by reason of men's ignorance of good and bad; this defect being not less than that which deprives us of the power of distinguishing things that are white and black.

14. Though thou shouldest be going to live three thousand years, and as many times ten thousand years, still remember that no man loses any other life than this which he now lives, nor lives any other than this which he now loses. The longest and shortest are thus brought to the same. For the present is the same to all, though that which perishes is not the same; and so that which is lost appears to be a mere moment. For a man cannot lose either the past or the future: for what a man has not, how can any one take this from him? These two things then thou must bear in mind; the one, that all things from eternity are of like forms and come round in a circle, and that it makes no difference whether a man shall see the same things during a hundred years, or two hundred, or an infinite time; and the second, that the longest liver and he who will die soonest lose just the same. For the present is the only thing of which a man can be deprived, if it is true that this is the only thing which he has, and that a man cannot lose a thing if he has it not.

15. Remember that all is opinion. For what was said by the Cynic Monimus is manifest: and manifest too is the use of what was said, if a man receives what may be got out of it as far as it is true.

16. The soul of man does violence to itself, first of all, when it becomes an abscess, and, as it were, a tumor on the universe, so far as it can. For to be vexed at anything which happens is a separation of ourselves from nature, in some part of which the natures of all other things are contained. In the next place, the soul does violence to itself when it turns away from any man, or even moves towards him with the intention of injuring, such as are the souls of those who are angry. In the third place, the soul does violence to itself when it is overpowered by pleasure or by pain. Fourthly, when it plays a part, and does or says anything insincerely and untruly. Fifthly, when it allows any act of its own and any movement to be without an aim, and does anything thoughtlessly and without considering what it is, it being right that even the smallest things be done with reference to an end; and the end of rational animals is to follow the reason and the law of the most ancient city and polity.

17. Of human life the time is a point, and the substance is in a flux, and the perception dull, and the composition of the whole body subject to putrefaction, and the soul a whirl, and fortune hard to divine, and fame a thing devoid of judgment. And, to say all in a word, everything which belongs to the body is a stream, and what belongs to the soul is a dream and vapor, and life is a warfare and a stranger's sojourn, and after-fame is oblivion. What then is that which is able to conduct a man? One thing, and only one, philosophy. But this consists in keeping the daemon within a man free from vio-

lence and unharmed, superior to pains and pleasures, doing nothing without a purpose, nor yet falsely and with hypocrisy, not feeling the need of another man's doing or not doing anything; and beside, accepting all that happens, and all that is allotted, as coming from thence, wherever it is, from whence he himself came; and, finally, waiting for death with a cheerful mind, as being nothing else than a dissolution of the elements of which every living being is compounded. But if there is no harm to the elements themselves in each continually changing into another, why should a man have any apprehension about the change and dissolution of all the elements? For it is according to nature, and nothing is evil which is according to nature.

GAUTAMA BUDDHA

•

The Sermon at Benares[1]

On seeing their old teacher approach, the five bhikkhus agreed among themselves not to salute him, nor to address him as a master, but by his name only. "For," so they said, "he has broken his vow and has abandoned holiness. He is no bhikkhu but Gotama, and Gotama has become a man who lives in abundance and indulges in the pleasures of worldliness."

But when the Blessed One approached in a dignified manner, they involuntarily rose from their seats and greeted him in spite of their resolution. Still they called him by his name and addressed him as "friend Gotama."

When they had thus received the Blessed One, he said: "Do not call the Tathagata by his name nor address him as 'friend,' for he is the Buddha, the Holy One. The Buddha looks with a kind heart equally on all living beings, and they therefore call him 'Father.' To disrespect a father is wrong; to despise him, is wicked."

"The Tathagata," the Buddha continued, "does not seek salvation in austerities, but neither does he for that reason indulge in worldly pleasures, nor live in abundance. The Tathagata has found the middle path."

"There are two extremes, O Bhikkhus, which the man who has given up the world ought not to follow—the habitual practice, on the one hand, of self-indulgence which is unworthy, vain and fit only for the worldly-minded —and the habitual practice, on the other hand, of self-mortification, which is painful, useless and unprofitable.

"Neither abstinence from fish or flesh, nor going naked, nor shaving the head, nor wearing matted hair, nor dressing in a rough garment, nor covering

[1] From *The Gospel of Buddha* by Paul Carus (La Salle, Illinois, The Open Court Publishing Company, 1912).

oneself with dirt, nor sacrificing to Agni, will cleanse a man who is not free from delusions.

"Reading the Vedas, making offerings to priests, or sacrifices to the gods, self-mortification by heat or cold, and many such penances performed for the sake of immortality, these do not cleanse the man who is not free from delusions.

"Anger, drunkenness, obstinacy, bigotry, deception, envy, self-praise, disparaging others, superciliousness and evil intentions constitute uncleanness; not verily the eating of flesh.

"A middle path, O Bhikkhus, avoiding the two extremes, has been discovered by the Tathagata—a path which opens the eyes, and bestows understanding, which leads to peace of mind, to the higher wisdom, to full enlightenment, to Nirvana!

"What is that middle path, O Bhikkhus, avoiding these two extremes, discovered by the Tathagatha—that path which opens the eyes, and bestows understanding, which leads to peace of mind, to the higher wisdom, to full enlightenment, to Nirvana?

"Let me teach you, O Bhikkhus, the middle path, which keeps aloof from both extremes. By suffering, the emaciated devotee produces confusion and sickly thoughts in his mind. Mortification is not conducive even to worldly knowledge; how much less to a triumph over the senses!

"He who fills his lamp with water will not dispel the darkness, and he who tries to light a fire with rotten wood will fail. And how can anyone be free from self by leading a wretched life, if he does not succeed in quenching the fires of lust, if he still hankers after either worldly or heavenly pleasures. But he in whom self has become extinct is free from lust; he will desire neither worldly nor heavenly pleasures, and the satisfaction of his natural wants will not defile him. However, let him be moderate, let him eat and drink according to the needs of the body.

"Sensuality is enervating; the self-indulgent man is a slave to his passions, and pleasure-seeking is degrading and vulgar.

"But to satisfy the necessities of life is not evil. To keep the body in good health is a duty, for otherwise we shall not be able to trim the lamp of wisdom, and keep our mind strong and clear. Water surrounds the lotus-flower, but does not wet its petals.

"This is the middle path, O Bhikkhus, that keeps aloof from both extremes." . . .

Then the Buddha said:

"He who recognizes the existence of suffering, its cause, its remedy, and its cessation has fathomed the four Noble Truths. He will walk the right path.

"Right views will be the torch to light his way. Right aspirations will be his guide. Right speech will be his dwelling place on the road. His gait will be straight, for it is right behavior. His refreshments will be the right way of earning his livelihood. Right efforts will be his steps: right thoughts his breath; and right contemplation will give him the peace that follows in his footprints.

"Now, this, O Bhikkhu, is the noble truth concerning suffering.

"Birth is attended with pain, decay is painful, disease is painful, death is painful. Union with the unpleasant is painful, painful is separation from the pleasant; and any craving that is unsatisfied, that too is painful. In brief, bodily conditions which spring from attachments are painful.

"Now this, O Bhikkhus, is the noble truth concerning the origin. Verily, it is that craving which causes the renewal of existence, accompanied by sensual delight, seeking satisfaction now here, now there, the craving for the gratification of the passions, the craving for a future life, and the craving for happiness in this life.

"Now this is the noble truth concerning the destruction of suffering: Verily it is the destruction, in which no passion remains, of this very thirst: It is the laying aside of, the being free from, the dwelling no longer upon this thirst.

"Now this is the noble truth concerning the way which leads to the destruction of sorrow. Verily; it is this noble eightfold path; that is to say:

1. right views
2. right aspirations
3. right speech
4. right behavior
5. right livelihood
6. right effort
7. right thoughts
8. right contemplation

"This, then, is the noble truth concerning the destruction of sorrow. By the practice of loving kindness I have attained liberation of heart, and thus I am assured that I shall never return in renewed births. I have even now attained Nirvana."

And when the Blessed One had thus set the royal chariot wheel of truth rolling onward, a rapture thrilled through all the universes.

And when the doctrine was propounded, the venerable Kondanna, the oldest one among the five bhikkhus, discerned the truth with his mental eye, and he said: "Truly, O Buddha, our Lord, thou hast found the truth!" Then the other bhikkhus, too, joined him and exclaimed: "Truly, thou art the Buddha, thou hast found the truth."

And the Blessed One observed the ways of society and noticed how much misery came from malignity and foolish offenses done only to gratify vanity and self-seeking pride. And the Buddha said: "If a man foolishly does me wrong, I will return to him the protection of my ungrudging love; the more evil comes from him, the more good shall go from me; the fragrance of goodness always comes to me and the harmful air of evil goes to him."

A foolish man, learning that the Buddha observed the principle of great love which commends the return of good for evil, came and abused him. The Buddha was silent, pitying his folly.

When the man had finished his abuse, the Buddha asked him, saying: "Son, if a man declined to accept a present made to him, to whom would it belong?" And he answered: "In that case, it would belong to the man who offered it."

"My son," said the Buddha, "thou hast railed at me, but I decline to accept thy abuse, and request thee to keep it thyself. Will it not be a source of misery to thee? As the echo belongs to the sound, and the shadow to the substance, so misery will overtake the evil-doer without fail."

The abuser made no reply, and Buddha continued: "A wicked man who reproaches a virtuous one is like one who looks up and spits at heaven; the spittle soils not the heaven, but comes back and defiles his own person. The slanderer is like one who flings dust at another when the wind is contrary; the dust does but return on him who threw it. The virtuous man cannot be hurt and the misery that the other would inflict comes back on himself."

The abuser went away ashamed, but he came again and took refuge in the Buddha, the Dharma, and the Sangha.

And Buddha said: "All that we are is the result of what we have thought: it is founded on our thoughts, it is made up of our thoughts. If a man speaks or acts with an evil thought, pain follows him, as the wheel follows the foot of the ox that draws the carriage: If a man speaks or acts with a pure thought, happiness follows him, like a shadow that never leaves him.

"He abused me, he beat me, he defeated me, he robbed me"—in those who harbor such thoughts, hatred will never cease; in those who do not harbor such thoughts, hatred will cease. For hatred does not cease by hatred at any time: hatred ceases by love—that is an old rule.

He who lives looking for pleasures only, his senses uncontrolled, immoderate in his food, idle and weak, will certainly be overthrown by temptation, as the wind throws down a weak tree. He who lives without looking for pleasures, his senses well controlled, moderate in his food, faithful and strong, will certainly not be overthrown, any more than the wind throws down a rocky mountain. . . .

The thoughtless man, even if he can recite a large portion of the law, but is not a doer of it, has no share in the priesthood, but is like a cowherd counting the cows of others. The follower of the law, even if he can recite only a small portion of the law, but, having forsaken passion and hatred and foolishness, possesses true knowledge and serenity of mind, he, caring for nothing in this world or that to come, has indeed a share in the priesthood. . . .

As a fletcher makes straight his arrow, a wise man makes straight his trembling and unsteady thought, which is difficult to guard, difficult to hold back. It is good to tame the mind, which is difficult to hold in and flighty, rushing wherever it listeth; a tamed mind brings happiness. Let the wise man guard his thoughts, for they are difficult to perceive, very artful, and they rush wherever they list. . . .

Knowing that this body is fragile like a jar, and making his thought firm like a fortress, one should attack Mara, the tempter, with the weapon of knowledge, one should watch him when conquered, and should never rest. Before long, alas! this body will lie on the earth, despised, without understanding, like a useless log.

Kisa Gotami had an only son, and he died. In her grief she carried the dead child to all her neighbors, asking them for medicine, and the people said: "She has lost her senses. The boy is dead."

At length, Kisa Gotami met a man who replied to her request: "I cannot give thee medicine for thy child, but I know a physician who can."

And the girl said: "Pray tell me, sir; who is it?" And the man replied "Go to Sakyamuni, the Buddha."

Kisa Gotami repaired to the Buddha and cried: "Lord and Master, give me the medicine that will cure my boy."

The Buddha answered: "I want a handful of mustard-seed." And when the girl in her joy promised to procure it, the Buddha added: "The mustard-seed must be taken from a house where no one has lost a child, husband, parent, or friend."

Poor Kisa Gotami now went from house to house, and the people pitied her and said: "Here is mustard-seed; take it!" But when she asked, "Did a son or daughter, a father or mother, die in your family?" they answered her: "Alas! the living are few, but the dead are many. Do not remind us of our deepest grief." And there was no house but some beloved one had died in it.

Kisa Gotami became weary and hopeless, and sat down at the wayside, watching the lights of the city, as they flickered up and were extinguished again. At last the darkness of the night reigned everywhere. And she considered the fate of men, that their lives flicker up and are extinguished again. And she thought to herself: "How selfish am I in my grief! Death is common to all; yet in this valley of desolation there is a path that leads him to immortality who has surrendered all selfishness."

The Buddha said: "The life of mortals in this world is troubled and brief and combined with pain. For there is not any means by which those that have been born can avoid dying; after reaching old age there is death; of such a nature are living beings. As ripe fruits are early in danger of falling, so mortals when born are always in danger of death. As all earthen vessels made by the potter end in being broken, so is the life of mortals. Both young and adult, both those who are fools and those who are wise, all fall into the power of death; all are subject to death.

"Of those who, overcome by death, depart from life, a father cannot save his son, nor kinsmen their relations. Mark! while relatives are looking on and lamenting deeply, one by one mortals are carried off, like an ox that is led to the slaughter. So the world is afflicted with death and decay, therefore the wise do not grieve, knowing the terms of the world.

"Not from weeping nor from grieving will any one obtain peace of mind; on the contrary, his pain will be the greater and his body will suffer. He will make himself sick and pale, yet the dead are not saved by his lamentation. He who seeks peace should draw out the arrow of lamentation, and complaint, and grief. He who has drawn out the arrow and has become composed will obtain peace of mind; he who has overcome all sorrow will become free from sorrow, and be blessed."

And Punna, wishing to preach the path to enlightenment, sought the Buddha, and the Buddha said, "But, O Punna, the men of that country are violent, cruel and savage. When they become angry at you and do you harm, what will you think then?"

"I shall think them truly good and kind folk, for whilst they speak angry and insolent words, they refrain from striking or stoning me."

"They are very violent folk, Punna. What if they strike or stone you?"

"I shall think them kind and good not to smite me with their staff and sword."

"And what if they do so?"

"I shall think them kind and good indeed who free me from this vile body with so little pain."

"Well said, Punna, well said. With your gift of patience, you may indeed essay this task. Go, Punna, yourself saved, save others."

Religion

The Strength and Glory of Man[1]

O Lord our Lord, how excellent is thy name in all the earth! who hast set thy glory above the heavens.

Out of the mouth of babes and sucklings hast thou ordained strength because of thine enemies, that thou mightest still the enemy and the avenger.

When I consider thy heavens, the work of thy fingers, the moon and the stars, which thou hast ordained;

What is man, that thou art mindful of him? and the son of man, that thou visitest him?

For thou hast made him a little lower than the angels, and hast crowned him with glory and honour.

Thou madest him to have dominion over the works of thy hands; thou hast put all things under his feet:

All sheep and oxen, yea, and the beasts of the field;

The fowl of the air, and the fish of the sea, and whatsoever passeth through the paths of the seas.

O Lord our Lord, how excellent is thy name in all the earth!

The Folly of Man[2]

The fool hath said in his heart, There is no God. Corrupt are they, and have done abominable iniquity: there is none that doeth good.

God looked down from heaven upon the children of men, to see if there were any that did understand, that did seek God.

Every one of them is gone back: they are altogether become filthy; there is none that doeth good, no, not one.

Have the workers of iniquity no knowledge? who eat up my people as they eat bread: they have not called upon God.

There were they in great fear, where no fear was: for God hath scattered the bones of him that encampeth against thee: thou hast put them to shame, because God hath despised them.

Oh that the salvation of Israel were come out of Zion! When God bringeth back the captivity of his people, Jacob shall rejoice, and Israel shall be glad.

[1] From *The Book of Psalms* (King James Version of the Bible), Chapter 8.
[2] From *The Book of Psalms* (King James Version of the Bible), Chapter 53.

The Providence of God[1]

The Lord is my shepherd; I shall not want.

He maketh me to lie down in green pastures: he leadeth me beside the still waters.

He restoreth my soul: he leadeth me in the paths of righteousness for his name's sake.

Yea, though I walk through the valley of the shadow of death, I will fear no evil: for thou art with me; thy rod and thy staff they comfort me.

Thou preparest a table before me in the presence of mine enemies: thou anointest my head with oil; my cup runneth over.

Surely goodness and mercy shall follow me all the days of my life: and I will dwell in the house of the Lord for ever.

LORD, thou hast been our dwelling place in all generations.

Before the mountains were brought forth, or ever thou hadst formed the earth and the world, even from everlasting to everlasting, thou art God.

Thou turnest man to destruction; and sayest, Return, ye children of men.

For a thousand years in thy sight are but as yesterday when it is past, and as a watch in the night.

Thou carriest them away as with a flood; they are as a sleep: in the morning they are like grass which groweth up.

In the morning it flourisheth, and groweth up; in the evening it is cut down, and withereth.

For we are consumed by thine anger, and by thy wrath are we troubled.

Thou hast set our iniquities before thee, our secret sins in the light of thy countenance.

For all our days are passed away in thy wrath: we spend our years as a tale that is told.

The days of our years are threescore years and ten; and if by any reason of strength they be fourscore years, yet is their strength labour and sorrow; for it is soon cut off, and we fly away.

Who knoweth the power of thine anger? even according to thy fear, so is thy wrath.

So teach us to number our days, that we may apply our hearts unto wisdom.

Return, O LORD, how long? and let it repent thee concerning thy servants.

O satisfy us early with thy mercy; that we may rejoice and be glad all our days.

[1] From *The Book of Psalms* (King James Version of the Bible), Chapters 23 and 90.

Make us glad according to the days wherein thou hast afflicted us, and the years wherein we have seen evil.

Let thy work appear unto thy servants, and thy glory unto their children.

And let the beauty of the LORD our GOD be upon us: and establish thou the work of our hands upon us; yea, the work of our hands establish thou it.

The Upanishads: Svetasvatara[1]

OM . . .
With our ears may we hear what is good.
With our eyes may we behold thy righteousness.
Tranquil in body, may we who worship thee find rest.
OM . . . Peace—peace—peace.
OM . . . Hail to the supreme Self!

Disciples inquire within themselves:

What is the cause of this universe?—is it Brahman? Whence do we come? Why do we live? Where shall we at last find rest? Under whose command are we bound by the law of happiness and its opposite?

Time, space, law, chance, matter, primal energy, intelligence—none of these, nor a combination of these, can be the final cause of the universe, for they are effects, and exist to serve the soul. Nor can the individual self be the cause, for, being subject to the law of happiness and misery, it is not free.

The seers, absorbed in contemplation, saw within themselves the ultimate reality, the self-luminous being, the one God, who dwells as the self-conscious power in all creatures. He is One without a second. Deep within all beings he dwells, hidden from sight by the coverings of the gunas—*sattwa, rajas,* and *tamas*. He presides over time, space, and all apparent causes.

This vast universe is a wheel. Upon it are all creatures that are subject to birth, death, and rebirth. Round and round it turns, and never stops. It is the wheel of Brahman. As long as the individual self thinks it is separate from Brahman, it revolves upon the wheel in bondage to the laws of birth, death, and rebirth. But when through the grace of Brahman it realizes its identity with him, it revolves upon the wheel no longer. It achieves immortality.[2]

He who is realized by transcending the world of cause and effect, in deep contemplation, is expressly declared by the scriptures to be the Supreme Brahman. He is the substance, all else the shadow. He is the imperishable.

[1] From *The Upanishads:* The Principal Texts Selected and Translated from the Original Sanscrit by Swami Prabhavananda and Frederick Manchester (New York: The New American Library of World Literature, 1964). Copyright 1948, 1957 by The Vedanta Society of Southern California, Hollywood, California. Reprinted by permission.

[2] Here appears for the first time in extant Hindu literature the image of the wheel as applied to birth, death, and rebirth.

The knowers of Brahman know him as the one reality behind all that seems. For this reason they are devoted to him. Absorbed in him, they attain freedom from the wheel of birth, death, and rebirth.

The Lord supports this universe, which is made up of the perishable and the imperishable, the manifest and the unmanifest. The individual soul, forgetful of the Lord, attaches itself to pleasure and thus is bound. When it comes to the Lord, it is freed from all its fetters.

Mind and matter, master and servant—both have existed from beginningless time. The Maya which unites them has also existed from beginningless time. When all three—mind, matter, and Maya—are known as one with Brahman, then is it realized that the Self is infinite and has no part in action. Then is it revealed that the Self is all.

Matter is perishable. The Lord, the destroyer of ignorance, is imperishable, immortal. He is the one God, the Lord of the perishable and of all souls. By meditating on him, by uniting oneself with him, by identifying oneself with him, one ceases to be ignorant.

Know God, and all fetters will be loosed. Ignorance will vanish. Birth, death, and rebirth will be no more. Meditate upon him and transcend physical consciousness. Thus will you reach union with the lord of the universe. Thus will you become identified with him who is One without a second. In him all your desires will find fufillment.

The truth is that you are always united with the Lord. But you must *know* this. Nothing further is there to know. Meditate, and you will realize that mind, matter, and Maya (the power which unites mind and matter) are but three aspects of Brahman, the one reality.

Fire, though present in the firesticks, is not perceived until one stick is rubbed against another. The Self is like that fire: it is realized in the body by meditation on the sacred syllable OM.

Let your body be the stick that is rubbed, the sacred syllable OM the stick that is rubbed against it. Thus shall you realize God, who is hidden within the body as fire is hidden within the wood.

Like oil in sesame seeds, butter in cream, water in the river bed, fire in tinder, the Self dwells within the soul. Realize him through truthfulness and meditation.

Like butter in cream is the Self in everything. Knowledge of the Self is gained through meditation. The Self is Brahman. By Brahman is all ignorance destroyed.

To realize God, first control the outgoing senses and harness the mind. Then meditate upon the light in the heart of the fire—meditate, that is, upon pure consciousness as distinct from the ordinary consciousness of the intellect. Thus the Self, the Inner Reality, may be seen behind physical appearance.

Control your mind so that the Ultimate Reality, the self-luminous Lord, may be revealed. Strive earnestly for eternal bliss.

With the help of the mind and the intellect, keep the senses from attaching themselves to objects of pleasure. They will then be purified by the light of the Inner Reality, and that light will be revealed.

The wise control their minds, and unite their hearts with the infinite, the omniscient, the all-pervading Lord. Only discriminating souls practice spiritual disciplines. Great is the glory of the self-luminous being, the Inner Reality.

Hear, all ye children of immortal bliss, also ye gods who dwell in the high heavens: Follow only in the footsteps of the illumined ones, and by continuous meditation merge both mind and intellect in the eternal Brahman. The glorious Lord will be revealed to you.

Control the vital force. Set fire to the Self within by the practice of meditation. Be drunk with the wine of divine love. Thus shall you reach perfection.

Be devoted to the eternal Brahman. Unite the light within you with the light of Brahman. Thus will the source of ignorance be destroyed, and you will rise above karma.

Sit upright, holding the chest, throat, and head erect. Turn the senses and the mind inward to the lotus of the heart. Meditate on Brahman with the help of the syllable OM. Cross the fearful currents of the ocean of worldliness by means of the raft of Brahman—the sacred syllable OM.

With earnest effort hold the senses in check. Controlling the breath, regulate the vital activities. As a charioteer holds back his restive horses, so does a persevering aspirant hold back his mind.

Retire to a solitary place, such as a mountain cave or a sacred spot. The place must be protected from the wind and rain, and it must have a smooth, clean floor, free from pebbles and dust. It must not be damp, and it must be free from disturbing noises. It must be pleasing to the eye and quieting to the mind. Seated there, practice meditation and other spiritual exercises.

As you practice meditation, you may see in vision forms resembling snow, crystals, smoke, fire, lightning, fireflies, the sun, the moon. These are signs that you are on your way to the revelation of Brahman.

As you become absorbed in meditation, you will realize that the Self is separate from the body and for this reason will not be affected by disease, old age, or death.

The first signs of progress on the path of yoga are health, a sense of physical lightness, clearness of complexion, a beautiful voice, an agreeable odor of the person, and freedom from craving.

As a soiled piece of metal, when it has been cleaned, shines brightly, so the dweller in the body, when he has realized the truth of the Self, loses his sorrow and becomes radiant with bliss.

The yogi experiences directly the truth of Brahman by realizing the light of the Self within. He is freed from all impurities—he the pure, the birthless, the bright.

He is the one God, present in the north, the east, the south, and the west. He is the creator. He enters into all wombs. He alone is now born as all beings, and he alone is to be born as all beings in the future. He is within all persons as the Inner Self, facing in all directions.

Let us adore the Lord, the luminous one, who is in fire, who is in water, who is in plants and trees, who pervades the whole universe.

The one absolute, impersonal Existence, together with his inscrutable Maya, appears as the divine Lord, the personal God, endowed with manifold glories. By his divine power he holds dominion over all the worlds. At the periods of creation and dissolution of the universe, he alone exists. Those who realize him become immortal.

The Lord is One without a second. Within man he dwells, and within all other beings. He projects the universe, maintains it, and withdraws it into himself.

His eyes are everywhere; his face, his arms, his feet are in every place. Out of himself he has produced the heavens and the earth, and with his arms and his wings he holds them together.

He is the origin and support of the gods. He is the lord of all. He confers bliss and wisdom upon those who are devoted to him. He destroys their sins and their sorrows.

He punishes those who break his laws. He sees all and knows all. May he endow us with good thoughts!

O Lord, clothed in thy most holy form, which is calm and blissful, and which destroys all evil and ignorance, look upon us and make us glad.

O Lord, thou hast revealed thy sacred syllable OM, which is one with thee. In thy hands it is a weapon with which to destroy ignorance. O protector of thy devotees, do not conceal thy benign person.

Thou art the supreme Brahman. Thou art infinite. Thou hast assumed the forms of all creatures, remaining hidden in them. Thou pervadest all things. Thou art the one God of the universe. Those who realize thee become immortal.

Said the great seer Svetasvatara:

I have known, beyond all darkness, that great Person of golden effulgence. Only by knowing him does one conquer death. There is no other way of escaping the wheel of birth, death, and rebirth.

There is nothing superior to him, nothing different from him, nothing subtler or greater than he. Alone he stands, changeless, self-luminous; he, the Great One, fills this universe.

Though he fills the universe, he transcends it. He is untouched by its sorrow. He has no form. Those who know him become immortal. Others remain in the depths of misery.

The Lord God, all-pervading and omnipresent, dwells in the heart of all beings. Full of grace, he ultimately gives liberation to all creatures by turning their faces toward himself.

He is the innermost Self. He is the great Lord. He it is that reveals the purity within the heart by means of which he, who is pure being, may be reached. He is the ruler. He is the great Light, shining forever.

This great Being, assuming a form of the size of a thumb, forever dwells in the heart of all creatures as their innermost Self. He can be known directly by the purified mind through spiritual discrimination. Knowing him, men become immortal.

This great Being has a thousand heads, a thousand eyes, and a thousand feet. He envelops the universe. Though transcendent, he is to be meditated upon as residing in the lotus of the heart, at the center of the body, ten fingers above the navel.

He alone is *all this*—what has been done and what shall be. He has become the universe. Yet he remains forever changeless, and is the lord of immortality.

His hands and feet are everywhere; his eyes and mouths are everywhere. His ears are everywhere. He pervades everything in the universe.

Without organs of sense, yet reflecting the activities of the senses, he is the lord and ruler of all.

He is the friend and refuge of all.

He resides in the body, the city of nine gates. He sports in the world without in innumerable forms. He is the master, the ruler, of the whole world, animate and inanimate.

He moves fast, though without feet. He grasps everything, though without hands. He sees everything, though without eyes. He hears everything, though without ears. He knows all that is, but no one knows him. He is called the Supreme, the Great One.

Subtler than the subtlest, greater than the greatest, the Self is hidden in the heart of all creatures. Through his grace a man loses his cravings, transcends grief, and realizes him as Brahman Supreme.

O Brahman Supreme!
Formless art thou, and yet
(Though the reason none knows)
Thou bringest forth many forms;
Thou bringest them forth, and then
Withdrawest them to thyself.
Fill us with thoughts of thee!

Thou art the fire,
Thou art the sun,
Thou art the air,
Thou art the moon,
Thou art the starry firmament,
Thou art Brahman Supreme:
Thou art the waters—thou,
The creator of all!

Thou art woman, thou art man,
Thou art the youth, thou art the maiden,
Thou art the old man tottering with his staff;
Thou facest everywhere.

Thou art the dark butterfly,
Thou art the green parrot with red eyes,
Thou art the thunder cloud, the seasons, the seas.
Without beginning art thou,
Beyond time, beyond space.
Thou art he from whom sprang
The three worlds.

Maya is thy divine consort—
Wedded to thee.
Thou art her master, her ruler.
Red, white, and black is she,
Each color a guna.
Many are her children—
The rivers, the mountains,
Flower, stone, and tree,
Beast, bird, and man—
In every way like herself.
Thou, spirit in flesh,
Forgetting what thou art,
Unitest with Maya—
But only for a season.
Parting from her at last,
Thou regainest thyself.

Thou, Brahman Immortal,
And thou, woven of clay
(Two beings, yet one)—
Like two beautiful birds,
Golden of plumage,
Companions inseparable,
Perched high up on the branches
Of the selfsame tree—
As man thou tastest
The sweet fruits of the tree,
The sweet and bitter fruits;
But as Brahman, master of Maya,
Thou remainest unseen,
Immobile,
Calmly observing.

Forgetting his oneness with thee,
Bewildered by his weakness,
Full of sorrow is man;
But let him look close on thee,
Know thee as himself,
O Lord, most worshipful,
And behold thy glory—
Lo, all his heavy sorrow
Is turned to joy.

Changeless thou art,
Supreme, pure!
In thee dwell the gods.
The source of all scriptures thou art;
Yet what shall scriptures avail
If they be smooth on the lip
But absent from the heart?
To him who knows thee comes fullness—
To him alone!

Thou art lord and master of Maya,
Man is her slave.
With Maya uniting, thou hast brought forth the universe.
The source of all scriptures thou art,
And the source of all creeds.
The universe is thy Maya;
And thou, great God, her lord,
Wherever the eye falls,
There, within every form,
Thou dwellest.

One thou art, one only.
Born from many wombs,
Thou hast become many:
Unto thee all return.
Thou, Lord God, bestowest all blessings,
Thou the Light, thou the Adorable One.
Whoever finds thee
Finds infinite peace.

Thou art Lord God of all gods,
All the worlds rest in thee;
Thou art ruler of the beasts,
Two-footed, four-footed:
Our heart's worship be thine!

Thou art the blissful Lord,
Subtler than the subtlest.
In thee alone is there peace.

Thou, sole guardian of the universe,
Thou, lord of all,
In the hearts of thy creatures
Thou hidest thyself.
Gods and seers become one with thee.
Those who know thee die not.

Of all religions thou art the source.
The light of thy knowledge shining,
There is nor day nor night,
Nor being nor non-being—
Thou alone art.

Thou alone art—thou the Light
Imperishable, adorable;
Great Glory is thy name.
No one is there beside thee,
No one equal to thee.

Invisible is thy form,
Invisible to mortal eyes;
The seers alone,
In their purified hearts—
They alone see thee.
They alone are immortal.

Neither male nor female art thou,
Nor neuter;
Whatsoever form thou assumest,
That thou art.

Thou dost pervade the universe,
Thou art consciousness itself,
Thou art creator of time.
All-knowing art thou.

At thy bidding Maya,
Thy power divine,
Projects this visible universe,
Projects name and form.

Thou art the Primal Being.
Thou appearest as this universe
Of illusion and dream.
Thou art beyond time.
Indivisible, infinite, the Adorable One—
Let a man meditate on thee
Within his heart,
Let him consecrate himself to thee,
And thou, infinite Lord,
Wilt make thyself known to him.

Thou, womb and tomb of the universe,
And its abode;
Thou, source of all virtue,
Destroyer of all sins—
Thou art seated in the heart.
When thou art seen,
Time and form disappear.
Let a man feel thy presence,
Let him behold thee within,
And to him shall come peace,
Eternal peace—
To none else, to none else!

Thou art the eternal among non-eternals,
The consciousness of the conscious;
Though one, thou fulfillest
The desires of many.

Let a man devote himself
To knowledge of thee,
Let him follow thy path,
And he shall know thee:
All his fetters shall be loosed.

Can a man roll up the sky
Like a piece of skin?
Can he end his misery
And know not thee?

If the truths of these scriptures are meditated upon by a man in the highest degree devoted to God, and to his Guru as to his God, they will shine forth. They will shine forth indeed!

OM . . . Peace—peace—peace.

SAINT AUGUSTINE

•

The Confessions[1]

BOOK I

[I.] 1. *Great art Thou, O Lord, and greatly to be praised; great is Thy power, and Thy wisdom infinite.* And Thee would man praise; man, but a particle of Thy creation; man, that bears about him his mortality, the witness of his sin, the witness, that *Thou resisteth the proud:* yet would man praise Thee; he, but a particle of Thy creation. Thou awakest us to delight in Thy praise; for Thou madest us for Thyself, and our heart is restless, until it repose in Thee. Grant me, Lord, to know and understand which is first, to call on Thee or to praise Thee? and, again, to know Thee or to call on Thee? For who can call on Thee, not knowing Thee? For he that knoweth Thee not, may call on Thee as other than Thou art. Or, is it rather, that we call on Thee that we may know Thee? But *how shall they call on Him in whom they have not believed? or how shall they believe without a preacher?* And *they that seek the Lord shall praise Him.* For *they that seek shall find Him,* and they that find shall praise Him. I will seek Thee, Lord, by calling on Thee; and will call on Thee, believing in Thee; for to us hast Thou been preached. My faith, Lord, shall call on Thee, which Thou hast given me, wherewith Thou has inspired me, through the Incarnation of Thy Son, through the ministry of the Preacher.[2]

[II.] 2. And how shall I call upon my God, my God and Lord, since, when I call for Him, I shall be calling Him to myself? and what room is there within me, whither my God can come into me? Whither can God come into me, God who made heaven and earth? Is there, indeed, O Lord my God, aught in me that can contain Thee? Do then heaven and earth, which Thou hast made, and wherein Thou hast made me, contain Thee? or, because nothing which exists could exist without Thee, doth therefore whatever exists contain Thee? Since, then, I too exist, why do I seek that Thou shouldest enter into me, who were not, wert Thou not in me? Why? Because I am not gone down in hell, and yet Thou art there also. For *if I go down into hell, Thou art there.* I could not be then, O my God, could not be at all, wert Thou not in me; or, rather, unless I were in Thee, *of whom are all things, by whom are all*

[1] *The Confessions of Saint Augustine,* translated by E. B. Pusey, Everyman's Library Edition. Reprinted by permission of E. P. Dutton & Co., Inc. (New York: E. P. Dutton & Co., Inc., 1946), pp. 1–4.

[2] S. Ambrose; from whom were the beginnings of his conversion and by whom he was baptised.

things, in whom are all things? Even so, Lord, even so. Whither do I call Thee, since I am in Thee? or whence canst Thou enter into me? For whither can I go beyond heaven and earth, that thence My God should come into me, who hath said, *I fill the heaven and the earth?*

[III.] 3. Do[3] the heaven and earth then contain Thee, since Thou fillest them? or dost Thou fill them and yet overflow, since they do not contain Thee? And whither, when the heaven and the earth are filled, pourest Thou forth the remainder of thyself? Or hast Thou no need that aught contain Thee, who containest all things, since what Thou fillest Thou fillest by containing it? For the vessels which Thou fillest uphold Thee not, since, though they were broken, Thou wert not poured out. And when Thou art *poured out* on us, Thou art not cast down, but Thou upliftest us; Thou art not dissipated, but Thou gatherest us. But Thou who fillest all things, fillest Thou them with Thy whole self? or, since all things cannot contain Thee wholly, do they contain part of Thee? and all at once the same part? or each its own part, the greater more, the smaller less? And is, then, one part of Thee greater, another less? or, art Thou wholly every where, while nothing contains Thee wholly?

[IV.] 4. What art Thou then, my God? What, but the Lord God? *For who is Lord but the Lord? or who is God save our God?* Most highest, most good, most potent, most omnipotent; most merciful, yet most just; most hidden, yet most present; most beautiful, yet most strong; stable, yet incomprehensible; unchangeable, yet all-changing; never new, never old; all-renewing, and *bringing age upon the proud, and they know it not;* ever working, ever at rest; still gathering, yet nothing lacking; supporting, filling, and over-spreading; creating, nourishing, and maturing; seeking, yet having all things. Thou lovest, without passion; art jealous, without anxiety; repentest, yet grievest not; art angry, yet serene; changest Thy works, Thy purpose unchanged; receivest again what Thou findest, yet didst never lose; never in need, yet rejoicing in gains; never covetous, yet exacting usury. Thou receivest over and above, that Thou mayest owe; and who hath aught that is not Thine? Thou payest debts, owing nothing; remittest debts, losing nothing. And what have I now said, my God, my life, my holy joy? or what saith any man when he speaks of Thee? Yet woe to him that speaketh not, since mute are even the most eloquent.

[V.] 5. Oh! that I might repose on Thee! Oh! that Thou wouldest enter into my heart, and inebriate it, that I may forget my ills, and embrace Thee, my sole good? What art Thou to me? In Thy pity, teach me to utter it. Or what am I to Thee that Thou demandest my love, and, if I give it not, art wroth with me, and threatenest me with grievous woes? Is it then a slight woe to love Thee not? Oh! for Thy mercies' sake, tell me, O Lord my God, what Thou art unto me. *Say unto my soul, I am thy salvation.* So speak, that

[3] Against the Manichees.

I may hear. Behold, Lord, my heart is before Thee; open Thou the ears thereof, and *say unto my soul, I am thy salvation.* After this voice let me haste, and take hold on Thee. Hide not Thy face from me. Let me die[4]—lest I die—only let me see thy face.

[4] That is, let me see the face of God, though I die, (Ex. 33, 20.) since if I see it not, but it be turned away, I must needs die, and that "the second death."

JOHN DONNE

•

Meditation XVII[1]

Nunc lento sonitu dicunt, morieris[2]

Perchance he for whom this bell tolls may be so ill as that he knows not it tolls for him; and perchance I may think myself so much better than I am as that they who are about me and see my state may have caused it to toll for me, and I know not that. The church is catholic, universal, so are all her actions; all that she does belongs to all. When she baptizes a child, that action concerns me; for that child is thereby connected to that body which is my head too and ingrafted into that body whereof I am a member. And when she buries a man, that action concerns me. All mankind is of one author, and is one volume; when one man dies, one chapter is not torn out of the book, but translated into a better language; and every chapter must be so translated. God employs several translators; some pieces are translated by age, some by sickness, some by war, some by justice; but God's hand is in every translation, and his hand shall bind up all our scattered leaves again for that library where every book shall lie open to one another. As therefore the bell that rings to a sermon calls not upon the preacher only but upon the congregation to come, so this bell calls us all; but how much more me who am brought so near the door by this sickness! There was a contention as far as a suit—in which piety and dignity, religion and estimation, were mingled—which of the religious orders should ring to prayers first in the morning; and it was determined that they should ring first that rose earliest. If we understood aright the dignity of this bell that tolls for our evening prayer, we would be glad to make it ours by rising early, in that application, that it might be ours as well as his, whose indeed it is. The bell doth toll for him that thinks it doth; and though it intermit again, yet from that minute that that occasion wrought upon him he is united to God. Who casts not up his eye to the sun when it

[1] From *Devotions upon Emergent Occasions* by John Donne (London, 1624).
[2] Now this bell tolling softly says, you must die.

rises? but who takes off his eye for a comet when that breaks out? Who bends not his ear to any bell which upon any occasion rings? but who can remove it from that bell which is passing a piece of himself out of this world? No man is an island entire of itself; every man is a piece of the continent, a part of the main. If a clod be washed away by the sea, Europe is the less, as well as if a promontory were, as well as if a manor of thy friend's or of thine own were. Any man's death diminishes me, because I am involved in mankind, and therefore never send to know for whom the bell tolls; it tolls for thee. Neither can we call this a begging of misery or a borrowing of misery, as though we were not miserable enough of ourselves but must fetch in more from the next house, in taking upon us the misery of our neighbors. Truly it were an excusable covetousness if we did, for affliction is a treasure, and scarce any man hath enough of it. No man hath affliction enough that is not matured and ripened by it and made fit for God by that affliction. If a man carry treasure in bullion or in a wedge of gold and have none coined into current money, his treasure will not defray him as he travels. Tribulation is treasure in the nature of it, but it is not current money in the use of it, except we get nearer and nearer our home, heaven, by it. Another man may be sick, too, and sick to death, and this affliction may lie in his bowels as gold in a mine and be of no use to him; but this bell that tells me of his affliction digs out and applies that gold to me, if by this consideration of another's danger I take mine own into contemplation and so secure myself by making my recourse to my God, who is our only security.

JOHN WOOLMAN

•

In His Will Is Our Peace[1]

Twenty-sixth of eighth month [1772].—Being now at George Crosfield's, in the county of Westmoreland, I feel a concern to commit to writing the following uncommon circumstance.

In a time of sickness, a little more than two years and a half ago, I was brought so near the gates of death that I forgot my name. Being then desirous to know who I was, I saw a mass of matter of a dull gloomy color between the south and the east, and was informed that this mass was human beings in as great misery as they could be, and live, and that I was mixed with them, and that henceforth I might not consider myself as a distinct or separate being. In this state I remained several hours. I then heard a soft melodious voice, more pure and harmonious than any I had heard with my ears before; I believed it was the voice of an angel who spake to the other angels; the words were, "John Woolman is dead." I soon remembered that I was once John

[1] From the *Journal* of John Woolman. First printed in 1774.

Woolman, and being assured that I was alive in the body, I greatly wondered what that heavenly voice could mean. I believed beyond doubting that it was the voice of an holy angel, but as yet it was a mystery to me.

I was then carried in spirit to the mines where poor oppressed people were digging rich treasures for those called Christians, and heard them blaspheme the name of Christ, at which I was grieved, for his name to me was precious. I was then informed that these heathens were told that those who oppressed them were the followers of Christ, and they said among themselves, "If Christ directed them to use us in this sort, then Christ is a cruel tyrant."

All this time the song of the angel remained a mystery; and in the morning my dear wife and some others coming to my bedside, I asked them if they knew who I was, and they telling me I was John Woolman, thought I was lightheaded, for I told them not what the angel said, nor was I disposed to talk much to anyone, but was very desirous to get so deep that I might understand this mystery.

My tongue was often so dry that I could not speak till I had moved it about and gathered some moisture, and as I lay still for a time I at length felt a Divine power prepare my mouth that I could speak, and I then said, "I am crucified with Christ, nevertheless I live; yet not I, but Christ liveth in me. And the life which I now live in the flesh I live by the faith of the Son of God, who loved me and gave himself for me." Then the mystery was opened and I perceived there was joy in heaven over a sinner who had repented, and that the language "John Woolman is dead," meant no more than the death of my own will. . . .

After this sickness I spake not in public meetings for worship for nearly one year, but my mind was very often in company with the oppressed slaves as I sat in meetings; and though under his dispensation I was shut up from speaking, yet the spring of the gospel ministry was many times livingly opened in me, and the Divine gift operated by abundance of weeping, in feeling the oppression of this people. It being so long since I passed through this dispensation, and the matter remaining fresh and lively in my mind, I believe it safest for me to commit it to writing.

FRIEDRICH NIETZSCHE

•

God Is Dead[1]

The figs are falling from the trees; they are good and sweet; and, as they fall, their red skin bursts. I am a north wind to ripe figs.

[1] From *The Portable Nietzsche,* Edited and Trans. by Walter Kaufmann. Copyright 1954 by The Viking Press, Inc. Reprinted by permission of The Viking Press, Inc.

Thus, like figs, these teachings fall to you, my friends; now consume their juice and their sweet meat. It is autumn about us, and pure sky and afternoon. Behold what fullness there is about us! And out of such overflow it is beautiful to look out upon distant seas. Once one said God when one looked upon distant seas; but now I have taught you to say: overman.

God is a conjecture; but I desire that your conjectures should not reach beyond your creative will. Could you *create* a god? Then do not speak to me of any gods. But you could well create the overman. Perhaps not you yourselves, my brothers. But into fathers and forefathers of the overman you could re-create yourselves: and let this be your best creation.

God is a conjecture; but I desire that your conjectures should be limited by what is thinkable. Could you *think* a god? But this is what the will to truth should mean to you: that everything be changed into what is thinkable for man, visible for man, feelable by man. You should think through your own senses to their consequences.

And what you have called world, that shall be created only by you: your reason, your image, your will, your love shall thus be realized. And verily, for your own bliss, you lovers of knowledge.

And how would you bear life without this hope, you lovers of knowledge? You could not have been born either into the incomprehensible or into the irrational.

But let me reveal my heart to you entirely, my friends: *if* there were gods, how could I endure not to be a god! *Hence* there are no gods. Though I drew this conclusion, now it draws me.

God is a conjecture; but who could drain all the agony of this conjecture without dying? Shall his faith be taken away from the creator, and from the eagle, his soaring to eagle heights?

God is a thought that makes crooked all that is straight, and makes turn whatever stands. How? Should time be gone, and all that is impermanent a mere lie? To think this is a dizzy whirl for human bones, and a vomit for the stomach; verily, I call it the turning sickness to conjecture thus. Evil I call it, and misanthropic—all this teaching of the One and the Plenum and the Unmoved and the Sated and the Permanent. All the permanent—that is only a parable. And the poets lie too much.

It is of time and becoming that the best parables should speak: let them be a praise and a justification of all impermanence.

Creation—that is the great redemption from suffering, and life's growing light. But that the creator may be, suffering is needed and much change. Indeed, there must be much bitter dying in your life, you creators. Thus are you advocates and justifiers of all impermanence. To be the child who is newly born, the creator must also want to be the mother who gives birth and the pangs of the birth-giver.

Verily, through a hundred souls I have already passed on my way, and through a hundred cradles and birth pangs. Many a farewell have I taken; I know the heart-rending last hours. But thus my creative will, my destiny, wills it. Or, to say it more honestly: this very destiny—my will wills.

Whatever in me has feeling, suffers and is in prison; but my will always comes to me as my liberator and joy-bringer. Willing liberates: that is the true teaching of will and liberty—thus Zarathustra teaches it. Willing no more and esteeming no more and creating no more—oh, that this great weariness might always remain far from me! In knowledge too I feel only my will's joy in begetting and becoming; and if there is innocence in my knowledge, it is because the will to beget is in it. Away from God and gods this will has lured me; what could one create if gods existed?

But my fervent will to create impels me ever again toward man; thus is the hammer impelled toward the stone. O men, in the stone there sleeps an image, the image of my images. Alas, that it must sleep in the hardest, the ugliest stone! Now my hammer rages cruelly against its prison. Pieces of rock rain from the stone: what is that to me. I want to perfect it; for a shadow came to me—the stillest and lightest of all things once came to me. The beauty of the overman came to me as a shadow. O my brothers, what are the gods to me now?

Thus spoke Zarathustra. . . .

Not long, however, after Zarathustra had got away from the magician, he again saw somebody sitting by the side of his path: a tall man in black, with a gaunt pale face; and *this* man displeased him exceedingly. "Alas!" he said to his heart, "there sits muffled-up melancholy, looking like the tribe of priests: what do *they* want in my realm? How now? I have scarcely escaped that magician; must another black artist cross my way so soon—some wizard with laying-on of hands, some dark miracle worker by the grace of God, some anointed world-slanderer whom the devil should fetch? But the devil is never where he should be: he always comes too late, this damned dwarf and clubfoot!"

Thus cursed Zarathustra, impatient in his heart, and he wondered how he might sneak past the black man, looking the other way. But behold, it happened otherwise. For at the same moment the seated man had already spotted him; and not unlike one on whom unexpected good fortune has been thrust, he jumped up and walked toward Zarathustra.

"Whoever you may be, you wanderer," he said, "help one who has lost his way, a seeker, an old man who might easily come to grief here. This region is remote and strange to me, and I have heard wild animals howling; and he who might have offered me protection no longer exists himself. I sought the last pious man, a saint and hermit who, alone in his forest, had not yet heard what all the world knows today."

"What does all the world know today?" asked Zarathustra. "Perhaps this, that the old god in whom all the world once believed no longer lives?"

"As you say," replied the old man sadly. "And I served that old god until his last hour. But now I am retired, without a master, and yet not free, nor ever cheerful except in my memories. That is why I climbed these mountains, that I might again have a festival at last, as is fitting for an old pope and church father—for behold, I am the last pope—a festival of pious memories and divine services. But now he himself is dead, the most pious man, that saint in the forest who constantly praised his god with singing and humming. I did not find him when I found his cave; but there were two wolves inside, howling over his death, for all animals loved him. So I ran away. Had I then come to these woods and mountains in vain? Then my heart decided that I should seek another man, the most pious of all those who do not believe in God—that I should seek Zarathustra!"

Thus spoke the old man, and he looked with sharp eyes at the man standing before him; but Zarathustra seized the hand of the old pope and long contemplated it with admiration. "Behold, venerable one!" he said then; "what a beautiful long hand! That is the hand of one who has always dispensed blessings. But now it holds him whom you seek, me, Zarathustra. It is I, the godless Zarathustra, who speaks; who is more godless than I, that I may enjoy his instruction?"

Thus spoke Zarathustra, and with his glances he pierced the thoughts and the thoughts behind the thoughts of the old pope. At last the pope began, "He who loved and possessed him most has also lost him most now; behold, now I myself am probably the more godless of the two of us. But who could rejoice in that?"

"You served him to the last?" Zarathustra asked thoughtfully after a long silence. "You know *how* he died? Is it true what they say, that pity strangled him, that he saw how *man* hung on the cross and that he could not bear it, that love of man became his hell, and in the end his death?"

The old pope, however, did not answer but looked aside, shy, with a pained and gloomy expression. "Let him go!" Zarathustra said after prolonged reflection, still looking the old man straight in the eye. "Let him go! He is gone. And although it does you credit that you say only good things about him who is now dead, you know as well as I *who* he was, and that his ways were queer."

"Speaking in the confidence of three eyes," the old pope said cheerfully (for he was blind in one eye), "in what pertains to God, I am—and have the right to be—more enlightened than Zarathustra himself. My love served him many years, my will followed his will in everything. A good servant, however, knows everything, including even things that his master conceals from himself. He was a concealed god, addicted to secrecy. Verily, even a son he got himself in a sneaky way. At the door of his faith stands adultery.

"Whoever praises him as a god of love does not have a high enough opinion of love itself. Did this god not want to be a judge too? But the lover loves beyond reward and retribution.

"When he was young, this god out of the Orient, he was harsh and vengeful and he built himself a hell to amuse his favorites. Eventually, however, he became old and soft and mellow and pitying, more like a grandfather than a father, but most like a shaky old grandmother. Then he sat in his nook by the hearth, wilted, grieving over his weak legs, weary of the world, weary of willing, and one day he choked on his all-too-great pity."

"You old pope," Zarathustra interrupted at this point, "did you see that with your own eyes? Surely it might have happened that way—that way, and also in some other way. When gods die, they always die several kinds of death. But—well then! This way or that, this way and that—he is gone! He offended the taste of my ears and eyes; I do not want to say anything worse about him now that he is dead.

"I love all that looks bright and speaks honestly. But he—you know it, you old priest, there was something of your manner about him, of the priest's manner: he was equivocal. He was also indistinct. How angry he got with us, this wrath-snorter, because we understood him badly! But why did he not speak more cleanly? And if it was the fault of our ears, why did he give us ears that heard him badly? If there was mud in our ears—well, who put it there? He bungled too much, this potter who had never finished his apprenticeship. But that he wreaked revenge on his pots and creations for having bungled them himself, that was a sin against *good taste*. There is good taste in piety too; and it was this that said in the end, 'Away with *such* a god! Rather no god, rather make destiny on one's own, rather be a fool, rather be a god oneself!' "

"What is this I hear?" said the old pope at this point, pricking up his ears. "O Zarathustra, with such disbelief you are more pious than you believe. Some god in you must have converted you to your godlessness. Is it not your piety itself that no longer lets you believe in a god? And your overgreat honesty will yet lead you beyond good and evil too. Behold, what remains to you? You have eyes and hands and mouth, predestined for blessing from all eternity. One does not bless with the hand alone. Near you, although you want to be the most godless, I sent a secret, sacred, pleasant scent of long blessings: it gives me gladness and grief. Let me be your guest, O Zarathustra, for one single night! Nowhere on earth shall I now feel better than with you."

"Amen! So be it!" said Zarthustra in great astonishment. "Up there goes the way, there lies Zarathustra's cave. I should indeed like to accompany you there myself, you venerable one, for I love all who are pious. But now a cry of distress urgently calls me away from you. In my realm no one shall come to grief; my cave is a good haven. And I wish that I could put everyone who is sad back on firm land and firm legs.

"But who could take your melancholy off your shoulders? For that I am too weak. Verily, we might wait long before someone awakens your god again. For this old god lives no more: he is thoroughly dead."

Thus spoke Zarathustra.

MARTIN BUBER

•

God and the Spirit of Man[1]

This book discusses the relations between religion and philosophy in the history of the spirit, and deals with the part that philosophy has played in its late period in making God and all absoluteness appear unreal.

If philosophy is here set in contrast to religion, what is meant by religion is not the massive fullness of statements, concepts, and activities that one customarily describes by this name and that men sometimes long for more than for God. Religion is essentially the act of holding fast to God. And that does not mean holding fast to an image that one has made of God, nor even holding fast to the faith in God that one has conceived. It means holding fast to the existing God. The earth would not hold fast to its conception of the sun (if it had one), nor to its connections with it, but to the sun itself.

In contrast to religion so understood, philosophy is here regarded as the process, reaching from the time when reflection first became independent to its more contemporary crisis, the last stage of which is the intellectual letting go of God.

This process begins with man's no longer contenting himself, as did the pre-philosophical man, with picturing the living God, to whom one formerly only called—with a call of despair or rapture which occasionally became his first name—as a Something, a thing among things, a being among beings, an It.

The beginning of philosophizing means that this Something changes from an object of imagination, wishes, and feelings to one that is conceptually comprehensible, to an object of thought. It does not matter whether this object of thought is called "Speech" (*Logos*), because in all and each one hears it speak, answer, and directly address one; or "the Unlimited" (*Apeiron*), because it has already leapt over every limit that one may try to set for it; or simply "Being," or whatever. If the living quality of the conception of God refuses to enter into this conceptual image, it is tolerated alongside of it, usually in an unprecise form, as in the end identical with it or at least essentially dependent on it. Or it is depreciated as an unsatisfactory surrogate, helpful to men incapable of thought.

In the progress of its philosophizing, the human spirit is ever more inclined to fuse characteristically this conception, of the Absolute as an object of an adequate thought, with itself, the human spirit. In the course of this process,

[1] From *Eclipse of God: Studies in the Relation between Philosophy and Religion*, by Martin Buber, copyrighted 1952 by Harper & Row, Publishers, Inc. Used by permission. "God and the Spirit of Man" is the substance of a lecture delivered by Buber at a number of American universities in 1951.

the idea which was at first noetically contemplated finally becomes the potentiality of the spirit itself that thinks it, and it attains on the way of the spirit its actuality. The subject, which appeared to be attached to being in order to perform for it the service of contemplation, asserts that it itself produced and produces being. Until, finally, all that is over against us, everything that accosts us and takes possession of us, all partnership of existence, is dissolved in free-floating subjectivity.

The next step already takes us to the stage familiar to us, the stage that understands itself as the final one and plays with its finality: the human spirit, which adjudges to itself mastery over its work, annihilates conceptually the absoluteness of the absolute. It may yet imagine that it, the spirit, still remains there as bearer of all things and coiner of all values; in truth, it has also destroyed its own absoluteness along with absoluteness in general. The spirit can now no longer exist as an independent essence. There now exists only a product of human individuals called spirit, a product which they contain and secrete like mucus and urine.

In this stage, there first takes place the conceptual letting go of God because only now philosophy cuts off its own hands, the hands with which it was able to grasp and hold him.

But an analogous process takes place on the other side, in the development of religion itself (in the usual broad sense of the word).

From the earliest times, the reality of the relation of faith, man's standing before the face of God, world-happening as dialogue, has been threatened by the impulse to control the power yonder. Instead of understanding events as calls which make demands on one, one wishes oneself to demand without having to hearken. "I have," says man, "power over the powers I conjure." And that continues, with sundry modifications, wherever one celebrates rites without being turned to the Thou and without really meaning its Presence.

The other pseudo-religious counterpart of the relation of faith, not so elementally active as conjuration but acting with the mature power of the intellect, is unveiling. Here one takes the position of raising the veil of the manifest, which divides the revealed from the hidden, and leading forth the divine mysteries. "I am," says the man, "acquainted with the unknown, and I make it known." The supposedly divine It that the magician manipulates as the technician his dynamo, the gnostic lays bare—the whole divine apparatus. His heirs are not "theosophies" and their neighbors alone; in many theologies also, unveiling gestures are to be discovered behind the interpreting ones.

We find this replacement of I-Thou by an I-It in manifold forms in that new philosophy of religion which seeks to "save" religion. In it, the "I" of this relation steps ever more into the foreground as "subject" of "religious feeling," as profiter from a pragmatist decision to believe, and the like.

Much more important than all this, however, is an event penetrating to the innermost depth of the religious life, an event which may be described as the subjectivizing of the act of faith itself. Its essence can be grasped most clearly through the example of prayer.

We call prayer in the pregnant sense of the term that speech of man to God which, whatever else is asked, ultimately asks for the manifestation of the divine Presence, for this Presence becoming dialogically perceivable. The single presupposition of a genuine state of prayer is thus the readiness of the whole man for this Presence, simple-turned-towardness, unreserved spontaneity. This spontaneity, ascending from the roots, succeeds time and again in overcoming all that disturbs and diverts. But in this our stage of subjectivized reflection not only the concentration of the one who prays, but also his spontaneity, is assailed. The assailant is consciousness, the overconsciousness of this man here that he is praying, that he is *praying,* that *he* is praying. And the assailant appears to be invincible. The subjective knowledge of the one turning-toward about his turning-toward, this holding back of an I which does not enter into the action with the rest of the person, an I to which the action is an object—all this de-possesses the moment, takes away its spontaneity. The specifically modern man who has not yet let go of God knows what that means: he who is not present perceives no Presence.

One must understand this correctly: this is not a question of a special case of the known sickness of modern man, who must attend his own actions as spectator. It is the confession of the Absolute into which he brings his unfaithfulness to the Absolute, and it is the relation between the Absolute and him upon which this unfaithfulness works, in the midst of the statement of trust. And now he too who is seemingly holding fast to God becomes aware of the eclipsed Transcendence.

What is it that we mean when we speak of an eclipse of God which is even now taking place? Through this metaphor we make the tremendous assumption that we can glance up to God with our "mind's eye," or rather being's eye, as with our bodily eye to the sun, and that something can step between our existence and his as between the earth and the sun. That this glance of the being exists, wholly unillusory, yielding no images yet first making possible all images, no other court in the world attests than that of faith. It is not to be proved; it is only to be experienced; man has experienced it. And that other, that which steps in between, one also experiences, today. I have spoken of it since I have recognized it, and as exactly as my perception has allowed me.

The double nature of man, as the being that is both brought forth from "below" and sent from "above," results in the duality of his basic characteristics. These cannot be understood through the categories of the individual man existing-for-himself, but only through the categories of his existing as man-with-man. As a being who is sent, man exists over against the existing being before which he is placed. As a being who is brought forth, he finds himself beside all existing beings in the world, beside which he is set. The first of these categories has its living reality in the relation I-Thou, the second has its reality in the relation I-It. The second always brings us only to the aspects of an existing being, not to that being itself. Even the most intimate contact with another remains covered over by an aspect if the other has not become Thou for me. Only the first relation, that which establishes essential immediacy between me and an existing being, brings me precisely thereby not to an aspect of it, but to that being itself. To be sure, it brings me only to the existential meeting with it; it does not somehow put me in a position to view it objectively in its being. As soon as an objective viewing is established, we are given only an aspect and ever again only an aspect. But it is also only the relation I-Thou in which we can meet God at all, because of him, in absolute contrast to all other existing beings, no objective aspect can be attained. Even a vision yields no objective viewing, and he who strains to hold fast an afterimage after the cessation of the full I-Thou relation has already lost the vision.

It is not the case, however, that the I in both relations, I-Thou and I-It, is the same. Rather where and when the beings around one are seen and treated as objects of observation, reflection, use, perhaps also of solicitude or help, there and then another I is spoken, another I manifested, another I exists than where and when one stands with the whole of one's being over against another being and steps into an essential relation with him. Everyone who knows both in himself—and that is the life of man, that one comes to know both in himself and ever again both—knows whereof I speak. Both together build up human existence; it is only a question of which of the two is at any particular time the architect and which is his assistant. Rather, it is a question of whether the I-Thou relation remains the architect, for it is self-evident that it cannot be employed as assistant. If it does not command, then it is already disappearing.

In our age, the I-It relation, gigantically swollen, has usurped, practically uncontested, the mastery and the rule. The I of this relation, an I that possesses all, makes all, succeeds with all, this I that is unable to say Thou, unable to meet a being essentially, is the lord of the hour. This selfhood that has become omnipotent, with all the It around it, can naturally acknowledge neither God nor any genuine absolute which manifests itself to men as of nonhuman origin. It steps in beween and shuts off from us the light of heaven.

Such is the nature of this hour. But what of the next? It is a modern superstition that the character of an age acts as fate for the next. One lets it prescribe what is possible to do and hence what is permitted. One surely cannot swim against the stream, one says. But perhaps one can swim with a new stream whose source is still hidden? In another image, the I-Thou relation has gone into the catacombs—who can say with how much greater power it will step forth! Who can say when the I-It relation will be directed anew to its assisting place and activity!

The most important events in the history of that embodied possibility called man are the occasionally occurring beginnings of new epochs, determined by forces previously invisible or unregarded. Each age is, of course, a continuation of the preceding one, but a continuation can be confirmation and it can be refutation.

Something is taking place in the depths that as yet needs no name. Tomorrow even it may happen that it will be beckoned to from the heights, across the heads of the earthly archons. The eclipse of the light of God is no extinction; even tomorrow that which has stepped in between may give way.

JACQUES MARITAIN

•

Confession of Faith[1]

As a child I was brought up in "Liberal Protestantism." Later on I became acquainted with the different phases of secularistic thought. The scientist and phenomenist philosophy of my teachers at the Sorbonne at last made me despair of reason. At one time I thought I might be able to find complete certitude in the sciences, and Felix Le Dantec thought that my fiancée and I would become followers of his biological materialism. The best thing I owe to my studies at that time is that they let me meet, in the School of Sciences, the woman who since then has always, happily for me, been at my side in a perfect and blessed communion. Bergson was the first to answer our deep desire for metaphysical truth—he liberated in us the sense of the absolute.

Before being captured by St. Thomas Aquinas, I underwent some great influences, those of Charles Péguy, Bergson, and Leon Bloy. A year after we met Bloy, my wife and I were baptized Catholics, and we chose him as our godfather.

It was after my conversion to Catholicism that I came to know St. Thomas. I had voyaged passionately among all the doctrines of modern philosophers and had found in them nothing but deception and grandiose uncertainty. What I now experienced was like an illumination of reason. My vocation as philosopher became perfectly clear to me. *Woe to me if I do not thomisticize,* I wrote in one of my first books. And through thirty years of work and battles I have kept to this same path, with the feeling of sympathizing all the more profoundly with the researches, the discoveries and the agonies of modern thought, the more I tried to penetrate them with the light which comes to us from a wisdom worked out through the centuries, a wisdom resistant to the fluctuations of time.

[1] Reprinted with the permission of Charles Scribner's Sons from *The Social and Political Philosophy of Jacques Maritain,* pages 331-343, edited by J. W. Evans and L. R. Ward. Copyright 1955 Charles Scribner's Sons.

In order to advance in this path we are obliged constantly to bring together singularly distant extremes, for no solution of our problems is found ready-made in the heritage of the ancients. We are also obliged to make a difficult sifting of the pure substance of truths which many a modern rejects in his loathing of the trashy opinions of the past, from all the dross, the prejudices, the out-of-date images and arbitrary constructions which many a traditionalist confuses with what is really worthy of being venerated by intelligence.

I have spoken of the different experiences through which I passed, because they gave me the occasion to try personally the state of mind of the idealist freethinker, of the inexperienced convert, and of the Christian who becomes aware, in proportion as his faith takes root, of the purifications to which that faith must be subjected. I was also able to obtain some experimental idea of what the anti-religious camp and the straddlers' camp are worth. Neither of them is worth very much. And the worst disgrace of the second camp is that it runs the risk of compromising along with itself the innocent and persecuted Church, the Mystical Body of Christ, whose essential life, *sine macula sine ruga,* is in the Truth and in the saints, and which travels towards its fullness through the weaknesses of its own and the ferocity of the world. In my view, God educates us through our deceptions and mistakes, in order to make us understand at last that we ought to believe only in Him and not in men—which readily brings one to marvel at all the good which is in men despite everything and at all the good they do in spite of themselves.

I have decidedly come to the conclusion that in practice there are only two ways to know the depths of things, or, if one wishes, two "wisdoms," each of them a kind of folly, though in opposite manners. One is the way of sinners, who in order to drain things to the dregs embrace the nothingness of which all things are made and thereby have a full experience of this world, in the evil of the world more than in its good. The other way is the way of the saints, who adhere to subsisting Goodness, maker of all things, and receive in love a full experience of God and of creation, and who stand surety for all the world by their suffering and compassion. Well, it is normal to hope that the disciples of vain wisdom, if they are not hardened by pride and if they are loyal to their own experience, will finally be saved "through fire" by the lovers of true wisdom. And if they should live to be converted, they will perhaps be harsher than others in censuring any of their brothers still in darkness, so that, after having long tasted the delights of the world, they will taste for a moment the delights of their virtues and will continue vain till the last day, till they enter eternity.

This is not the place to give an exposition of theses in speculative philosophy. I will only say that I consider Thomistic philosophy to be a living and present philosophy, with all the greater power to make conquests in new fields of discovery just because its principles are so firm and so organically bound together. Confronted with the succession of scentific hypotheses, some minds are surprised that anyone could find inspiration today in metaphysical principles acknowledged by Aristotle and Thomas Aquinas and rooted in the oldest intellectual heritage of the race. My reply is that the telephone and the radio do not prevent man from still having two arms, two legs and two lungs, or from falling in love and seeking happiness as did his faraway ancestors. Besides, truth recognizes no chronological criteria, and the art of the philosopher is not to be confused with the art of the great dressmakers.

On a deeper level, we must explain that progress in the sciences of phenomena, where the "problem" aspect is so characteristic, takes place chiefly by *substitution* of one theory for another which saved less well the known facts and phenomena; but in metaphysics and philosophy, where the "mystery" aspect is predominant, progress takes place chiefly by *deeper penetration.* Besides, the different philosophical systems, however ill founded they may be, constitute in some way, in their totality, a virtual and fluent philosophy, overlapping contrary formulations and unfriendly doctrines and carried along by the elements of truth they all contain. If, therefore, there exists among men a doctrinal organism entirely supported by true principles, it will incorporate—more or less tardily, due to the laziness of its defenders—it will progressively realize within itself this virtual philosophy, and this will thereby, and in a proportionate degree, take on form and organic arrangement. Such is my idea of progress in philosophy.

If I say next that the metaphysics which I hold to be founded on truth may be described as a critical realism and as a philosophy of intelligence and of being, or still more precisely as a philosophy of the *act of existing* regarded as the act and perfection of all perfections, these formulas, of course, will be of interest only to specialists. A brief reflection on the historical significance of modern philosophy will no doubt be more appropriate.

In the Middle Ages, philosophy was in fact ordinarily treated as an instrument in the service of theology. Culturally, it was not in the state required by its nature. The coming of a philosophical or lay wisdom which had completed its own formation for itself and according to its own finalities was therefore a response to an historical necessity. But unfortunately this work was brought about under the aegis of division and of a sectarian rationalism; Descartes *separated* philosophy from any higher wisdom, from anything in man which comes from above man. I am convinced that what the world and civilization have lacked in the intellectual order for three centuries has been a philosophy which would develop its autonomous exigencies in a Christian climate, a wisdom of reason not closed but open to the wisdom of grace. Today reason must battle an irrational deification of elemental and instinctive forces that threatens to ruin all civilization. In this struggle, reason's task is one of integration; understanding that intelligence is not the enemy of mystery, but lives on it, reason must come to terms with the irrational world of affectivity and instinct, as well as with the world of the will, of freedom and of love, and the suprarational world of grace and of divine life.

The dynamic harmony of the degrees of knowledge will at the same time become manifest. From this point of view, the problem proper to the age we are entering will be, it seems, to reconcile *science* and *wisdom*. The sciences themselves seem to invite intelligence to this work. We see them stripping themselves of the remains of materialistic and mechanistic metaphysics which for a time hid their true features. They call for a philosophy of nature, and the wonderful progress in contemporary physics restores to the scientist the sense of the mystery stammered by the atom and by the universe. A critique of knowledge formed in a genuinely realist and metaphysical spirit has a chance henceforth to be heard when it affirms the existence of structures of knowledge specifically and hierarchically distinct—distinct, but not separated—and shows that they correspond to original types of explanation which cannot be substituted one for another.

The Greeks recognized the great truth that contemplation is in itself superior to action. But they at once transformed this truth into a great error: they believed that the human race exists for a few intellectuals. As they saw it, there was a category of specialists, the philosophers, who lived a superhuman life, and the properly human life, namely, civil or political life, existed to serve them. To serve civil or political life, in turn, there was the subhuman life of labor, which in final analysis was the life of the slave. The lofty truth of the superiority of the contemplative life was thus bound to a contempt for labor and to the evil of slavery.

Christianity transfigured all this. It taught men that love is of more value than intelligence. It transformed the notion of contemplation, which henceforth does not stop in the intellect, but only in the love of God, the contemplated object. It restored to action its human significance as a service to our neighbor, and rehabilitated work by disclosing in it a value of natural redemption, as it were, and even a natural prefiguration of the communications of charity. It called to the contemplation of the saints and to perfection, not a few specialists or privileged persons, but all men, who are all bound proportionately by the law of work. Man is at once "homo faber" and "homo sapiens," and he is "homo faber" before truly and actually being "homo sapiens" and in order to become the latter. In this way Christianity saved, but by transforming and delivering from the error which tainted it, the Greek idea of the superiority of the contemplative life.

The saints' contemplation completes and consummates a natural aspiration to contemplation consubstantial to man, of which the sages of India and Greece especially give testimony. It is through love that the knowledge of divine things becomes experimental and fruitful. And precisely because this knowledge is the work of love in act, it also passes into action by virtue of the very generosity and abundance of love, which is gift of self. Then action proceeds from the superabundance of contemplation, and that is why, far from suppressing action or being opposed to it, contemplation vivifies it. It is in this sense, which relates to the essential generosity of the contemplation of love, that we must recognize with Bergson, in the superabundance and excess of the giving of self shown by the Christian mystics, the sign of their success in reaching the heroic summit of human life.

The pursuit of the highest contemplation and the pursuit of the highest freedom are two aspects of the same pursuit. In the order of spiritual life, man aspires to a perfect and absolute freedom, and therefore to a superhuman condition; sages of all times give evidence of this. The function of law is a function of protection and education of freedom, the function of a pedagogue. At the conclusion of this tutelage the perfect spiritual man is freed from every servitude, even, St. Paul says, from the servitude of the law, because he does spontaneously what is of the law and is simply one spirit and one love with the Creator.

To my way of thinking, the pursuit of freedom is also at the base of the social and political problem. But in the order of temporal life, it is not a divine freedom which is the object of our desires, but rather a freedom proportionate to the human condition and to the natural possibilities of our earthly existence. It is important not to deceive ourselves on the nature of the good thus pursued. It is not simply the preservation of each one's *freedom of choice,* nor the social community's *freedom of power.* The good in question is the *freedom of expansion* of human persons making up a people and participating in its good. Political society has as an end to develop conditions of life in common which, while assuring first of all the good and peace of the whole, will positively aid each person in the progressive conquest of this freedom of expansion, a freedom which consists above all in the flowering of moral and rational life.

Thus justice and friendship are the very foundations of society's life; and it is to truly human goods that society ought to subordinate all material goods, technical progress and the implements of power which also make up part of society's common good.

I believe that historical conditions and the yet backward state of human development make it difficult for social life fully to reach its end, and that in regard to the possibilities and demands which the Gospel brings to us in the socio-temporal order, we are still in a prehistoric age. As we see today in the psychoses of the masses which adore Stalin or Hitler, or dream of exterminating certain groups that they judge to be diabolical, in particular the Jews, doubtless because they are the people of God, human collectivities bear such a burden of willingly diseased animality that it will still require many centuries for the life of personality to be able truly to take on among the masses the fullness to which it aspires. But it still remains that the end towards which social life of itself tends is to procure the common good of the multitude in such a way that the concrete person, not merely in a privileged class but in the entire mass, may truly reach that measure of independence which belongs to civilized life and which is assured alike by the economic guarantees of work and property, by political rights, civic virtues and the cultivation of the mind.

These ideas are tied up with wider views which seem to me most properly designated by the expression *integral humanism,* and which involve a whole philosophy of modern history. Such a humanism, considering man in the integral wholeness of his natural and supernatural being and setting no a priori limits to the descent of the divine into man, may also be called a humanism of the Incarnation.

In the socio-temporal order it does not ask men to sacrifice themselves to the imperialism of race, of class or of nation. It asks them to sacrifice themselves to a better life for their brothers and to the concrete good of the community of human persons. That is why it cannot be less than an heroic humanism.

It has often been remarked that "bourgeois" liberalism, which tries to base everything on the individual taken as a little god and on his good pleasure, on an absolute freedom of ownership, of business and the pleasures of life, ends up fatally in statism. The rule of numbers produces the omnipotence of the State, of a ruminant or plutocratic State. Communism may be regarded as a reaction against this individualism. It claims to be oriented towards the absolute emancipation of man, who would thus become the god of history, but in reality this emancipation, supposing it were accomplished, would then be that of collective man, not that of the human person. Society as economic community would enslave the whole life of the person, because the essential work of civil society would be made to consist in economic functions, instead of subordinating this work to the freedom of expansion of persons: what the Communists propose as the emancipation of collective man would be the enslavement of human persons.

What of the anti-communist and anti-individualistic reactions of a totalitarian or dictatorial type? It is not in the name of the social community and the freedom of collective man, it is in the name of the sovereign dignity of the State, a state of the carnivorous type, or in the name of the spirit of a people, in the name of race or of blood, that they would annex man in his entirety to a social whole where the person of the ruler is the only one, properly speaking, to enjoy the privileges of personality. This is why totalitarian states, needing for themselves the total devotion of the person and having no sense of or respect for the person, inevitably seek a principle of human exaltation in myths of external grandeur and in the never-ending struggle for power and prestige. By its nature this tends to war and the self-destruction of the civilized community. If there are people in the Church—and they are fewer and fewer—who count on dictatorships of this kind to promote the religion of Christ and Christian civilization, they forget that the totalitarian phenomenon is an aberrant religious phenomenon in which an earthly mysticism devours every other mysticism whatever it may be, and will tolerate none besides itself.

Confronted with "bourgeois" liberalism, communism and totalitarian statism, what we need, I do not cease to say, is a new solution, one that is at the same time personalist and communal, one that sees human society as an organization of freedoms. We are thus brought to a conception of democracy, the community of free men, very different from that of Jean-Jacques Rousseau. We may call it *pluralist,* because it requires that the body politic guarantee the organic freedoms of the different spiritual families and different social bodies assembled within it, beginning with the basic natural community, the society of the family. The drama of modern democracies is that, under the appearance of an error—the deification of a fictitious individual entirely closed up in himself—they have without knowing it pursued a good thing: the expansion of the real person open to higher realities and to the common service of justice and friendship.

Personalist democracy holds that each is called, by virtue of the common dignity of human nature, to participate actively in political life, and that those who hold authority—which is a vital function in society and a real right to direct people—should be freely designated by the people. This is why personalist democracy sees in universal suffrage the first practical token by which a democratic society becomes aware of itself and which it may not in any case renounce. It has no better or more meaningful motto than the republican motto, understood as indicating, not an established condition in which man has only to be installed, but an end to be reached, a difficult and lofty goal to which man must tend by force of courage, justice and virtue. For freedom must be conquered, by the progressive elimination of the several forms of servitude, and it is not enough to proclaim equality of the fundamental rights of human persons, whatever one's race, one's religion, one's condition. This equality ought to pass in a real way into custom and into social structures and ought to yield fruit in a larger and larger participation by all in the common good of civilization. Finally, fraternity in the body politic requires that the loftiest and most generous of virtues, the love to which the Gospel has called our ungrateful species, pass into the very order of political life. A personalist democracy is not really conceivable without the super-elevations which nature and temporal civilizations receive, each in its own order, from the energies of the Christian leaven.

I am convinced that the coming of such a democracy, which presupposes that class antagonism has been overcome, demands that, by a genuine renewal of life and of justice, we truly go beyond "capitalism" and beyond socialism, each of which is vitiated by a materialistic conception of life. Nothing is more opposed to personalist democracy than fascist totalitarianism—whether social-nationalist or national-socialist; for it goes beyond "capitalism" only through the paroxysm of the evils it begets.

Let me remark that Christians are confronted today, in the socio-temporal order, with problems quite similar to those their sixteenth- and seventeenth-century ancestors encountered in the area of the philosophy of nature. At that time modern physics and astronomy, then in their beginnings, were simply one with philosophies set against tradition. The defenders of tradition did not know how to make the necessary distinctions. They took sides against what was to become modern science, at the same time that they took sides against the philosophical errors which at the start were parasitic on science. It took three centuries to get rid of this misunderstanding, if indeed the world is yet rid of it. It would be a sad story if we should be guilty today, in the field of practical and social philosophy, of like errors.

In the words of Pope Pius XI, the great scandal of the nineteenth century was the divorce of the working classes from the Church of Christ. In the temporal order, the moral secession of the working masses from the political community was a comparable tragedy. The awakening in the working masses of what the socialist vocabulary calls "class consciousness" appears to us as a great gain, so far as we see in it man's becoming aware of an offended and humiliated human dignity and of a vocation. But it has been chained to an historic calamity, because this awakening has been spoiled by the gospel of despair and of social welfare which is at the bottom of the Marxist idea of class struggle and the dictatorship of the proletariat. And it was precisely into this *secessionist* conception, whose protagonist was Marx and whose demand is that proletarians of all countries should recognize no other common good than that of their class, that the blindiness of the possessing classes in the nineteenth century precipitated the working masses.

Whoever has pondered on these fundamental facts and on the history of the labor movement understands that the central problem of our times is the temporal and spiritual problem of the *reintegration of the masses*. In my view, it is only an artificial and illusory solution of this problem when the attempt is made, as in the case of German National Socialism, to manufacture happy slaves through violence linked with material ameliorations good in themselves but achieved in a spirit of domination, and with a psychotechnic solicitude vowed to satisfy and to benumb appetites. The fact is that one manufactures only unhappy slaves, robots of non-being.

However difficult, slow and painful it may be, the reintegration of the proletariat within the national community, not to exercise a class dictatorship in it, but to collaborate body and soul in the work of the community, will take place really, which means humanly, only by a recasting of social structures worked out in the spirit of justice. I am not naive enough to believe that this reintegration can be accomplished without knocks and sacrifices, on the one hand as regards the well-being of the privileged sons of fortune and on the other as regards the theories and the destructive instincts of fanatical revolutionaries. But I am persuaded that it requires above all else the free cooperation of the workers' leaders (elites) and of the masses who follow them, and this cooperation must go along with a better general understanding of historical realities and with an awareness, not wiped out but heightened, of the human being's dignity as worker and citizen. In like manner the return of the masses to Christianity will be brought about only through love, I mean love stronger than death, the fire of the Gospel.

We shall never give up hope of a new Christendom, a new temporal order of Christian inspiration. Now the means should correspond to the end, and already are the end itself as in the state of movement and preparation. If this is so, it is clear that in order to prepare a Christian social order we must use Christian means, that is to say true means, just means, and these are means animated, even when they are of necessity harsh, by a genuine spirit of love. In two books published in 1930 and 1933[2] I have insisted at length on these axiomatic truths. Nothing is more serious or scandalous than to see, as we have for some years seen in certain countries, iniquitous and barbarous means used by men in the name of Christian order and Christian civilizations. It is a truth embedded in the very nature of things that Christendom will be renewed through Christian means or it will be completely eclipsed.

The present state of nations obliges us to declare that never has the spirit been so profoundly humiliated in the world. And yet pessimism in the end always dupes itelf. It disregards the great law which may be called the law of the double movement involving the energy of history. While the wear and tear of time naturally dissipates and degrades the things of this world and the "energy of history," and this means the mass of human activity on which the movement of history depends, the creative forces which are characteristic of spirit and freedom and are a witness to them, forces which ordinarily find their point of application in the effort of the few—who are thereby bound to sacrifice—improve more and more the quality of this energy. This is exactly the work of the sons of God in history, it is the work of Christians if they do not belie their name.

People do not understand this work at all if they imagine that it aims at installing the world in a state from which all evil and all injustice would have disappeared. If this were the aim, it would be quite easy, considering the results, stupidly to condemn the Christian as utopian. The work the Christian has to do is to keep up and to increase in the world the internal tension and movement of slow and painful deliverance, a tension and movement due to the invisible powers of truth and justice, of goodness and love, acting on the mass which is opposed to them. This work cannot be in vain, it assuredly bears its fruit.

Woe to the world should Christians turn their back on it, should they fail

[2] *Religion et culture; Du regime temporel et de la liberté.* (*Religion and Culture; Freedom in the Modern World.*)

to do their work, which is to heighten here on earth the charge and tension of the spiritual; should they listen to blind leaders of the blind who seek the means to order and to good in things which of themselves lead to dissolution and death. We have no illusions about the misery of human nature and the malice of this world. But neither have we any illusions about the blindness and malfeasance of pseudo-realists who cultivate and exalt evil in order to fight evil, and who take the Gospel as a decorative myth which cannot be regarded seriously without wrecking the machinery of the world. They themselves, meantime, take it upon themselves to ruin, to distract, and to torment this unhappy world.

The ferment of the pharisees, against which Christ put us on our guard, is a permanent temptation for the religious conscience. Undoubtedly, this ferment will not be altogether driven out of the world till the end of history. Meantime, in the social as well as in the spiritual order, we must never let up the fight against it. However great may be the mass of evil which a mass of pharisaism means to oppose, the latter is always as great an evil, because the good it sets against that evil is a good which does not give life but kills, as does the letter without the spirit: it is a good which leaves God without resources in man.

One of the gravest lessons afforded us by the experience of life is that, in fact, in the practical conduct of most people, all those things which in themselves are good and very good—science, technical progress, culture, etc., and even the knowledge of moral laws, and religious faith itself, faith in the living God (which of itself demands the love of charity—all these things, *without love and good will,* serve to make men all the more evil and the more unhappy. So far as religious faith is concerned, this was demonstrated in the Spanish civil war by the inhuman feelings that surged up in the "crusaders" as well as in the "reds," but were confirmed in the former in the sanctuary of the soul. What happens is that, without love and charity, man turns the best in him into an evil that is yet greater.

When one has understood this, he no longer puts his hope on earth in anything less than that good will of which the Gospel speaks—it speaks of good will, not of good velleity; he puts his hope in these obscure energies of a little real goodness which persists in making life germinate and regerminate in the secret depths of things. There is nothing more destitute, nothing more hidden, nothing nearer to the weakness of the infant. And there is no wisdom more fundamental or more effective than that simple and tenacious confidence, not in the means of violence, deceit and malice, which certainly are capable of crushing men and of triumphing, but which a grain of sand is nevertheless enough to cause to be smashed one against the other—but simple and tenacious confidence in the resources of personal courage to give oneself, and of good will set to do as one ought the tasks of every day. Through this disinterested spirit flows the power of nature and the Author of nature.

DIETRICH BONHOEFFER

•

Letters From Prison[1]

April 30th 1944

Another month gone! Do you find time flies as I do here? It often amazes me—and when will the month come when we shall meet again? Such tremendous events are taking place in the world outside, events which will have a profound effect on the course of our lives. This makes me wish I could write to you more frequently, if partly because I don't know how much longer I shall be able to, but above all because I want to make the most of what opportunities I have of sharing everything with you. I am firmly convinced that by the time you get this letter great decisions will have been reached on all fronts. During the coming weeks we shall have to be very brave: we must keep our wits about us and be prepared for the worst. I am reminded of the biblical δεῖ and I feel as curious as the angels in I Peter 1.12 as to how God intends to resolve these apparently insoluble issues. I am sure God is about to do something which we can only accept with wonder and amazement. We shall, if we have eyes to see, realize the truth of Psalm 58.12b and Psalm 9.20f. And we shall have to repeat Jeremiah 45.5 to ourselves every day. It is harder for you to go through all this alone than it is for me, so I will think of you especially, as indeed I am already doing now.

How good it would be if we could go through this time together, standing side by side. But it is probably best for us to face it alone. I am so sorry I can't help you at all, except by thinking of you as I read the Bible every morning and evening, and often during the day. You really must not worry about me, for I'm getting on uncommonly well, and you would be astonished if you came to see me. They keep on telling me that I am "radiating so much peace around me," and that I am "ever so cheerful." Very flattering, no doubt, but I'm afraid I don't always feel like that myself. You would be surprised and perhaps disturbed if you knew how my ideas on theology are taking shape. This is where I miss you most of all, for there is no one else who could help me so much to clarify my own mind. The thing that keeps coming back to me is, what *is* Christianity, and indeed what *is* Christ, for us to-day? The time when men could be told everything by means of words, whether theological or simply pious, is over, and so is the time of inwardness and conscience, which is to say the time of religion as such. We are proceeding towards a time of no religion at all: men as they are now simply cannot be religious any more. Even those who honestly describe themselves as "reli-

[1] Reprinted with permission of the publisher from *Prisoner for God: Letters and Papers from Prison*, by Dietrich Bonhoeffer, edited by Eberhard Bethage, translated by Reginald H. Fuller; pp. 161–169; 174–178; 188–191. Copyright, 1953, The Macmillan Company.

gious" do not in the least act up to it, and so when they say "religious" they evidently mean something quite different. Our whole nineteen-hundred-year-old Christian preaching and theology rests upon the "religious premise" of man. What we call Christianity has always been a pattern—perhaps a true pattern—of religion. But if one day it becomes apparent that this *a priori* "premise" simply does not exist, but was an historical and temporary form of human self-expression, i.e. if we reach the stage of being radically without religion—and I think this is more or less the case already, else how is it, for instance, that this war, unlike any of those before it, is not calling forth any "religious" reaction?—what does that mean for "Christianity"?

It means that the linchpin is removed from the whole structure of our Christianity to date, and the only people left for us to light on in the way of "religion" are a few "last survivals of the age of chivalry," or else one or two who are intellectually dishonest. Would they be the chosen few? Is it on this dubious group and none other that we are to pounce, in fervour, pique, or indignation, in order to sell them the goods we have to offer? Are we to fall upon one or two unhappy people in their weakest moment and force upon them a sort of religious coercion?

If we do not want to do this, if we had finally to put down the western pattern of Christianity as a mere preliminary stage to doing without religion altogether, what situation would result for us, for the Church? How can Christ become the Lord even of those with no religion? If religion is no more than the garment of Christianity—and even that garment has had very different aspects at different periods—then what is a religionless Christianity? Barth, who is the only one to have started on this line of thought, has still not proceeded to its logical conclusion, but has arrived at a positivism of revelation which has nevertheless remained essentially a restoration. For the religionless working man, or indeed, man generally, nothing that makes any real difference is gained by that. The questions needing answers would surely be: What is the significance of a Church (church, parish, preaching, Christian life) in a religionless world? How do we speak of God without religion, i.e. without the temporally-influenced presuppositions of metaphysics, inwardness, and so on? How do we speak (but perhaps we are no longer capable of speaking of such things as we used to) in secular fashion of God? In what way are we in a religionless and secular sense Christians, in what way are we the *Ekklesia*, "those who are called forth," not conceiving of ourselves religiously as specially favoured, but as wholly belonging to the world? Then Christ is no longer an object of religion, but something quite different, indeed and in truth the Lord of the world. Yet what does that signify? What is the place of worship and prayer in an entire absence of religion? Does the secret discipline, or, as the case may be, the distinction (which you have met with me before) between penultimate and ultimate, at this point acquire fresh importance? I must break off for to-day, so that the letter can be posted straight away. In two days I will write to you further on the subject. I hope you have a rough idea what I'm getting at, and that it does not bore you. Good-bye for the present. It isn't easy to keep writing without any echo from you. You must excuse me if that makes it rather a monologue!

I find after all I can carry on writing.—The Pauline question whether circumcision is a condition of justification is to-day, I consider, the question whether religion is a condition of salvation. Freedom from circumcision is at the same time freedom from religion. I often ask myself why a Christian instinct frequently draws me more to the religionless than to the religious, by which I mean not with any intention of evangelizing them, but rather, I might almost say, in "brotherhood." While I often shrink with religious people from speaking of God by name—because that Name somehow seems to me here not to ring true, and I strike myself as rather dishonest (it is especially bad when others start talking in religious jargon: then I dry up completely and feel somehow oppressed and ill at ease)—with people who have no religion I am able on occasion to speak of God quite openly and as it were naturally. Religious people speak of God when human perception is (often just from laziness) at an end, or human resources fail: it is really always the *Deus ex machina* they call to their aid, either for the so-called solving of insoluble problems or as support in human failure—always, that is to say, helping out human weakness or on the borders of human existence. Of necessity, that can only go on until men can, by their own strength, push those borders a little further, so that God becomes superfluous as a *Deus ex machina.* I have come to be doubtful even about talking of "borders of human existence." Is even death to-day, since men are scarcely afraid of it any more, and sin, which they scarcely understand any more, still a genuine borderline? It always seems to me that in talking thus we are only seeking frantically to make room for God. I should like to speak of God not on the borders of life but at its centre, not in weakness but in strength, not, therefore, in man's suffering and death but in his life and prosperity. On the borders it seems to me better to hold our peace and leave the problem unsolved. Belief in the Resurrection is not the solution of the problem of death. The "beyond" of God is not the beyond of our perceptive faculties. The transcendence of theory based on perception has nothing to do with the transcendence of God. God is the "beyond" in the midst of our life. The Church stands not where human powers give out, on the borders, but in the centre of the village. That is the way it is in the Old Testament, and in this sense we still read the New Testament far too little on the basis of the Old. The outward aspect of this religionless Christianity, the form it takes, is something to which I am giving much thought, and I shall be writing to you about it again soon. It may be that on us in particular, midway between East and West, there will fall an important responsibility.

It would be grand to have a line from you on all this; indeed it would mean more to me than you can imagine, I'm sure. I suggest you should look at Proverbs 22.11, 12. There's something that will bar the way against any kind of pious escapism.

May 5th 1944

I imagine you must be on leave by now, and this letter will have to be sent on to you. Unfortunately that will mean it will be out of date by the time it reaches you, for life is so uncertain nowadays. Yet long experience suggests that everything remains as it is rather than suddenly changes, so I should like to write to you all the same. I'm getting along pretty well, and so is the case, though the date still hasn't been fixed. But all good things take us by surprise when they do come, so I'm waiting confidently for that.

A bit more about "religionlessness." I expect you remember Bultmann's paper on the demythologizing of the New Testament? My view of it to-day would be not that he went too far, as most people seem to think, but that he did not go far enough. It is not only the mythological conceptions, such as the miracles, the ascension and the like (which are not in principle separable from the conceptions of God, faith and so on) that are problematic, but the "religious" conceptions themselves. You cannot, as Bultmann imagines, separate God and miracles, but you do have to be able to interpret and proclaim both of them in a "non-religious" sense. Bultmann's approach is really at bottom the liberal one (i.e. abridging the Gospel), whereas I seek to think theologically.

What do I mean by "interpret in a religious sense"? In my view, that means to speak on the one hand metaphysically, and on the other individualistically. Neither of these is relevant to the Bible message or to the man of to-day. Is it not true to say that individualistic concern for personal salvation has almost completely left us all? Are we not really under the impression that there are more important things than bothering about such a matter? (Perhaps not more important than the matter itself, but more than bothering about it.) I know it sounds pretty monstrous to say that. But is it not, at bottom, even biblical? Is there any concern in the Old Testament about saving one's soul at all? Is not righteousness and the kingdom of God on earth the focus of everything, and is not Romans 3.14ff., too, the culmination of the view that in God alone is righteousness, and not in an individualistic doctrine of salvation? It is not with the next world that we are concerned, but with this world as created and preserved and set subject to laws and atoned for and made new. What is above the world is, in the Gospel, intended to exist *for* this world—I mean that not in the anthropocentric sense of liberal, pietistic, ethical theology, but in the Bible sense of the creation and of the incarnation, crucifixion, and resurrection of Jesus Christ.

Barth was the first theologian to begin the criticism of religion,—and that remains his really great merit—but he set in its place the positivist doctrine of revelation which says in effect, "Take it or leave it": Virgin Birth, Trinity or anything else, everything which is an equally significant and necessary part of the whole, which latter has to be swallowed as a whole or not at all. That is not in accordance with the Bible. There are degrees of perception and degrees of significance, i.e. a secret discipline must be re-established whereby the *mysteries* of the Christian faith are preserved from profanation. The positivist doctrine of revelation makes it too easy for itself, setting up, as in the ultimate analysis it does, a law of faith, and mutilating what is, by the incarnation of Christ, a gift for us. The place of religion is taken by the Church—that is, in itself, as the Bible teaches it should be—but the world is made to depend upon itself and left to its own devices, and that is all wrong.

I am thinking over the problem at present how we may reinterpret in the manner "of the world"—in the sense of the Old Testament and of John 1.14—the concepts of repentance, faith, justification, rebirth, sanctification and so on. I shall be writing to you again about that.

Forgive me for writing all this in German script—normally I only use it when making notes for myself. And perhaps my reason for writing all this is to clear my own mind, rather than for your edification. I don't really want to bother you with such problems, for I don't supose you will find time to come to grips with them, and there's no need to worry you unnecessarily. But I can't help sharing my thoughts with you, for the simple reason that that's the only way I can clarify my own mind. If this doesn't suit you, please say so.—To-morrow is Cantate [the Fourth Sunday after Easter], and I shall be thinking of you, and enjoying pleasant memories. Good-bye. Be patient like me, and take care of yourself.

May 18th 1944

I wanted to write something for the day of the baptism, and my chief reason for sending it is to show you that I'm thinking of you. . . . I hope this day will be a long-cherished memory, and that it will set the tone for your leave. That I'm afraid will be all too brief, but I hope you'll soon be home for good. Some memories are painful, others can be an inspiration: may the memory of this day be an inspiration to you when you are parted again. . . . Please don't harbour any regrets about me. Martin [Neimöller] has had nearly seven years of it—and that's very different. . . . I have just heard you are coming to see me to-morrow. How wonderful; I had given up all hope of it myself. So I'm spending this day getting ready for your visit. Who managed to arrange it? Whoever it was, I am most grateful.

May 19th 1944

I cannot tell you how much joy your visit has given me, and also your courage in coming, just the two of you together. It was marvellous. I was deeply moved to hear about your recent experiences. I'm in too great a hurry to go into detail to-day. Above all, I pray you may find that peace which you so badly need, both within and without, after all these upsets you've had lately. I was awfully sorry the alarm was on just when you came, and I breathed a sigh of relief when the commandant brought your telephone message. The meaning of things is often obscure. But don't you find it a relief to know that some things are unavoidable, and have just got to be endured, even though we can't see the purpose behind it all? That's something I have learnt more clearly here.

May 20th 1944

There is always a danger of intense love destroying what I might call the "polyphony" of life. What I mean is that God requires that we should love him eternally with our whole hearts, yet not so as to compromise or diminish our earthly affections, but as a kind of *cantus firmus* to which the other melodies of life provide the counterpoint. Earthly affection is one of these contrapuntal themes, a theme which enjoys an autonomy of its own. Even the Bible can find room for the Song of Songs, and one could hardly have a more passionate and sensual love than is there portrayed (see 7.6). It is a good thing that that book is included in the Bible as a protest against those who believe that Christianity stands for the restraint of passion (is there any example of such restraint anywhere in the Old Testament?). Where the ground bass is firm and clear, there is nothing to stop the counterpoint from being developed to the utmost of its limits. Both ground bass and counterpoint are "without confusion and yet distinct," in the words of the Chalcedonian formula, like Christ in his divine and human natures. Perhaps the importance of polyphony in music lies in the fact that it is a musical reflection of this Christological truth, and that it is therefore an essential element in the Christian life. All this occurred to me after you were here. Can you see what I'm driving at? I wanted to tell you that we must have a good, clear *cantus firmus*. Without it there can be no full or perfect sound, but with it the counterpoint has a firm support and cannot get out of tune or fade out, yet is always a perfect whole in its own right. Only a polyphony of this kind can give life a wholeness, and at the same time assure us that nothing can go wrong so long as the *cantus firmus* is kept going. Perhaps your leave and the separation which lies ahead will be easier for you to bear. Please do not fear or hate separation if it should come, with all its attendant perils, but pin your faith on the *cantus firmus*.—I don't know if I have made myself clear, but one speaks so seldom of such things. . . .

May 21st 1944

I have put the date at the head of this letter as my share in the christening and all the preparations for it. At the same moment the siren went off, and I'm now sitting in the guardroom and hoping you won't have an air raid on this day of all days. What times we live in! What a baptism! And how much we shall have to look back on in years to come! All that matters is that we should make proper use of these memories and turn them to spiritual account. That will make them harder, clearer and more defiant, which is a good thing. There is no place for sentimentality on a day like this. If in the middle of an air raid God sends forth the gospel summons into his Kingdom in Holy Baptism, that will be a clear sign of the nature and purpose of that Kingdom. For it is a Kingdom stronger than war and danger, a Kingdom of power and might, signifying to some eternal terror and judgement, to others eternal joy and righteousness, not a Kingdom of the heart, but one as wide as the earth, not transitory, but eternal, a Kingdom which makes a way for itself and summons men to itself to prepare its way, a Kingdom worthy of our life's devotion. The shooting is just starting, but it doesn't look as though it's going to be too bad to-day. How I should love to hear you preaching in a few hours' time! At eight this morning I heard a choral performance of *Was Gott tut, das ist wohlgetan*—a good beginning for the day. As I listened I thought of you. I hadn't heard an organ for a long time, and its clear tone was like a refuge in time of trouble.

I suppose you will be making an after-dinner speech, and thinking of me as you do so. I should love to hear you. The very fact that we so rarely say such words to one another makes one yearn for them from time to time. Do you understand that? Perhaps absence makes one feel it all the more strongly. I used to take such things for granted, and I do so still, in spite of everything.

The subject of polyphony is still pursuing me. I was thinking to-day how painful it is without you, and it occurred to me how pain and joy are also part of the polyphony of life, and that they can exist independently side by side.

All clear! I'm so glad for your sake. I have two sprigs of lilac on my desk: someone brought them for me to-day, touching of them, wasn't it? I have also put the photos you brought in front of me, and am gazing at the baby who is being baptized to-day. I think he's lovely, and if he takes after me in looks, I only hope he will be as free from toothache and headache as I am, and be blessed with my leg muscles and sensitive gums—though that can sometimes be a disadvantage. For other things he can do better elsewhere. . . . He has also inherited the best thing about me, my name. I have always been satisfied with it, and in my younger days I was actually proud of it. Believe me, I shall always be a good godfather to him and do all I can to help him. In fact, I don't believe he could have a better one!

If war seems to you to spell nothing else but death, you are certainly not doing justice to the manifold ways of God. We have all our appointed hour of death, and it will always find us wherever we go. And we must be ready for it. But

He knows ten thousand ways
To save us from death's power.

He gives us food and meat
A boon in famine's hour.

—that's something we must never forget. I am sending you a letter for you to give to Niebuhr, in case the worst comes true.[2] We must also fix a rendezvous. Later on I have no doubt we shall be able to keep in touch through N. and Uncle George.[3]

May 25th 1944

I hope that despite the alarms you are enjoying the peace and beauty of these warm, summer-like Whitsun days. Gradually one acquires an inner detachment from the dangers that beset us. Detachment however seems too negative, artificial and stoic a word to use. Rather, we assimilate these dangers into the wholeness of our life. I have repeatedly observed here how few there are who can make room for conflicting emotions at the same time. When the bombers come, they are all fear; when there is something good to eat, they are all greed; when they are disappointed they are all despair; when they are successful, they can think of nothing else. They miss the fullness of life and the wholeness of an independent existence. Everything subjective and objective is dissolved for them into fragments. By contrast, Christianity plunges us into many different dimensions of life simultaneously. We can make room in our hearts, to some extent at least, for God and the whole world. We weep with them that weep, and rejoice with them that do rejoice. We are afraid (I was again interrupted by the alarm, and am now sitting out of doors enjoying the sun) for our life, but at the same time we must think of things more important than life itself. When an alarm goes off, for example, we have other things to think about than anxiety for our own safety; we have, e.g., to help others around us to keep calm. The moment that happens, the whole picture is changed. Life is not compressed into a single dimension, but is kept multi-dimensional and polyphonous. What a deliverance it is to be able to *think,* and in thinking to preserve this multi-dimensionality. When people tremble at an impending air raid, I have almost made it a rule to tell them how much worse it would be for a small town. We have to keep men out of their one-track minds. That is a sort of preparation for faith, although it is only faith itself that can make possible a multi-dimensional life, and enable us to keep even this Whitsun despite the alarms.

At first I was disconcerted, and not a little grieved to have no letters this Whitsun. But I said to myself it was perhaps a sign that no one was worrying about me. It's strange how we like others to be anxious about us, a little bit at any rate.

Weizsäcker's book on the world view of physics is still keeping me busy. It has brought home to me how wrong it is to use God as a stop-gap for the

[2] In case the Editor should be taken prisoner of war.
[3] The Bishop of Chichester.

incompleteness of our knowledge. For the frontiers of knowledge are inevitably being pushed back further and further, which means that you only think of God as a stop-gap. He also is being pushed back further and further, and is in more or less continuous retreat. We should find God in what we do know, not in what we don't; not in outstanding problems, but in those we have already solved. This is true not only for the relation between Christianity and science, but also for wider human problems such as guilt, suffering and death. It is possible nowadays to find answers to these problems which leave God right out of the picture. It just isn't true to say that Christianity alone has the answers. In fact the Christian answers are no more conclusive or compelling than any of the others. Once more, God cannot be used as a stop-gap. We must not wait until we are at the end of our tether: he must be found at the centre of life: in life, and not only in death; in health and vigour, and not only in suffering; in activity, and not only in sin. The ground for this lies in the revelation of God in Christ. Christ is the centre of life, and in no sense did he come to answer our unsolved problems. From the centre of life certain questions are seen to be wholly irrelevant, and so are the answers commonly given to them—I am thinking for example of the judgement pronounced on the friends of Job. In Christ there are no Christian problems. Enough of this; I have just been disturbed again.

POPE JOHN XXIII

Pacem in Terris, April 10, 1963[1]

INTRODUCTION

ORDER IN THE UNIVERSE

Peace on earth, which men of every era have most eagerly yearned for, can be firmly established only if the order laid down by God be dutifully observed. The progress of learning and the inventions of technology clearly show that, both in living things and in the forces of nature, an astonishing order reigns, and they also bear witness to the greatness of man, who can understand that order and create suitable instruments to harness those forces of nature and use them to his benefit.

But the progress of science and the inventions of technology show above all the infinite greatness of God, who created the universe and man himself. He created all things out of nothing, pouring into them the abundance of His wisdom and goodness, so that the holy psalmist praises God in these words:

[1] From the encyclical *Pacem in Terris* by His Holiness, Pope John XXIII; the official English translation provided by the Vatican Press Office as published in *The New York Times* April 11, 1963. Reprinted with the permission of the Vatican Press Office.

"O Lord our master! The majesty of Thy name fills all the earth."[2] Elsewhere he says: "What diversity, Lord in thy creatures! What wisdom has designed them all![3] God also created man in his own image and likeness,[4] endowed him with intelligence and freedom, and made him lord of creation, as the same psalmist declares in the words: "Thou hast placed him only a little below the angels, crowning him with glory and honor and bidding him rule over the works of thy hands. Thou hast put all under his dominion."[5]

Order in Human Beings

How strongly does the turmoil of individual men and peoples contrast with the perfect order of the universe! It is as if the relationships which bind them together could be controlled only by force. But the creator of the world has imprinted in man's heart an order which his conscience reveals to him and enjoins him to obey: This shows that the obligations of the law are written in their hearts, their conscience utters its own testimony.[6] And how could it be otherwise? For whatever God has made shows forth His infinite wisdom, and it is manifested more clearly in the things which have greater perfection.[7]

But fickleness of opinion often produces this error, that many think that the relationships between men and states can be governed by the same laws as the forces and irrational elements of the universe, whereas the laws governing them are of quite a different kind and are to be sought elsewhere, namely, where the Father of all things wrote them, that is, in the nature of man. By these laws men are most admirably taught, first of all how they should conduct their mutual dealings among themselves, then how the relationships between the citizens and the public authorities of each state should be regulated, then how states should deal with one another, and finally how, on the one hand, individual men and states, and on the other hand, the community of all peoples, should act towards each other, the establishment of such a world community of peoples being urgently demanded today by the requirements of universal common good.

PART I

Order Between Men

Every Man Is a Person with Rights and Duties

First of all, it is necessary to speak of the order which should exist between men. Any human society, if it is to be well-ordered and productive,

[2] Psalms viii: 1.
[3] Psalms ciii: 24.
[4] Cf. Genesis i: 26.
[5] Psalms viii: 3–6.
[6] Romans ii: 15.
[7] Cf. Pslams xviii: 3–11.

must lay down as a foundation this principle, namely, that every human being is a person, that is, his nature is endowed with intelligence and free will. By virtue of this, he has rights and duties of his own, flowing directly and simultaneously from his very nature, which are therefore universal, inviolable and inalienable.[8]

If we look upon the dignity of the human person in the light of divinely revealed truth, we cannot help but esteem it far more highly. For men are redeemed by the blood of Jesus Christ, they are by grace the children and friends of God and heirs of eternal glory.

Rights

The Right to Life and a Worthy Standard of Living

Beginning our discussion of the rights of man, we see that every man has the right to life, to bodily integrity and to the means which are necessary and suitable for the proper development of life. These are primarily food, clothing, shelter, rest, medical care and, finally, the necessary social services. Therefore, a human being also has the right to security in cases of sickness, inability to work, widowhood, old age, unemployment, or in any other case in which he is deprived of the means of subsistence through no fault of his own.[9]

The Right Pertaining to Moral and Cultural Values

By the natural law every human being has the right to respect for his person, to his good reputation, the right to freedom in searching for truth and in expressing and communicating his opinions, and in pursuit of art, within the limits laid down by the moral order and the common good. And he has the right to be informed truthfully about public events.

The natural law also gives man the right to share in the benefits of culture, and therefore the right to a basic education and to technical and professional training in keeping with the stage of educational development in the country to which he belongs. Every effort should be made to insure that persons be enabled, on the basis of merit, to go on to higher studies, so that, as far as possible, they may occupy posts and take on responsibilities in human society in accordance with their natural gifts and the skills they have acquired.[10]

The Right to Worship God According to One's Conscience

Every human being has the right to honor God according to the dictates of an upright conscience, and therefore the right to worship God privately

[8] Cf. Pius XII's radio message on Christmas Eve, 1942. *Acta Apostolicae Sedis,* Vol. 35, pp. 9–24, and John XXIII's sermon Jan. 4, 1963. *Acta Apostolicae Sedis,* Vol. 55, pp. 89–91.

[9] Cf. Pius XI's encyclical letter "*Divini Redemptoris*" ("Of the Divine Redeemer"). *Acta Apostolicae Sedis,* Vol. 29, p. 78, and radio message by Pius XII on the Feast of Pentecost, 1941, *Acta Apostolicae Sedis,* Vol. 33, pp. 195–205.

[10] Cf. Pius XII's radio message on Christmas Eve, 1942, *op. cit.,* pp. 9–24.

and publicly. For, as Lactantius so clearly taught: We were created for the purpose of showing to the God who bore us the submission we owe Him, of recognizing Him alone, and of serving Him. We are obliged and bound by this duty to God. From this religion itself receives its name.[11] And on this point our predecessor of immortal memory, Leo XIII, declared: "This genuine, this honorable freedom of the sons of God, which most nobly protects the dignity of the human person, is greater than any violence or injustice. It has always been sought by the church, and always most dear to her. This was the freedom which the apologists claimed with intrepid constancy, which the apologists defended with their writings, and which the martyrs in such numbers consecrated with their blood."[12]

The Right to Choose Freely One's State of Life

Human beings have the right to choose freely the state of life which they prefer, and therefore the right to set up a family, with equal rights and duties for man and woman, and also the right to follow a vocation to the priesthood or the religious life.[13]

The family, grounded on marriage freely contracted, monogamous and indissoluble, is and must be considered the first and essential cell of human society. To it must be given every consideration of an economic, social, cultural and moral nature which will strengthen its stability and facilitate the fulfillment of its specific mission.

Parents, however, have a prior right in the support and education of their children.[14]

Economic Rights

Human beings have the natural right to free initiative in the economic field, and the right to work.[15]

Indissolubly linked with those rights is the right to working conditions in which physical health is not endangered, morals are safeguarded and young people's normal development is not impaired. Women have the right to working conditions in accordance with their requirements and their duties as wives and mothers.[16]

From the dignity of the human person, there also arises the right to carry on economic activities according to the degree of responsibility of which one

[11] Divinae Institutiones, Vol. 4, Chap. 28, Subheading 2, editions P. L. 6, 5:5.

[12] Encyclical letter "*Libertas praestantissimum*" ("freedom of the most excellent"), Acts of Leo XIII, Vol. 8, pp. 237–38.

[13] Cf. Pius XII's radio message on Christmas Eve, 1942, *loc. cit.*

[14] Cf. Pius XI's encyclical letter "Casti Connubii" ("Of Chaste Marriage") *Acta Apostolicae Sedis,* Vol. 22, pp. 539–92, and Pius XII's radio message on Christmas Eve, 1942, *loc. cit.*

[15] Cf. Pius XII's radio message on the Feast of Pentecost, 1941, *loc. cit.*, p. 201.

[16] Cf. Leo XIII's encyclical letter "Rerum Novarum" ("Of New Things"), Acts of Leo XIII, Vol. 11, pp. 128–29.

is capable.[17] Furthermore—and this must be specially emphasized—there is the right to a working wage, determined according to criterions of justice and sufficient, therefore, in proportion to the available resources to give the worker and his family a standard of living in keeping with the dignity of the human person. In this regard, our predecessor Pius XII said: "To the personal duty to work imposed by nature, there corresponds and follows the natural right of each individual to make of his work the means to provide for his own life and the lives of his children. So profoundly is the empire of nature ordained for the preservation of man."[18]

The right to private property, even of productive goods, also derives from the nature of man. This right, as we have elsewhere declared, is a suitable means for safeguarding the dignity of the human person and for the exercise of responsibility in all fields; it strengthens and gives serenity to family life, thereby increasing the peace and prosperity of the state.[19]

However, it is opportune to point out that there is a social duty essentially inherent in the right of private property.[20]

The Right of Meeting and Association

From the fact that human beings are by nature social, there arises the right of assembly and association. They have also the right to give the societies of which they are members the form they consider most suitable for the aim they have in view, and to act within such societies on their own initiative and on their own responsibility in order to achieve their desired objectives.[21]

We ourselves stated in the encyclical "Mater et Magistra" that, for the achievement of ends which individual human beings cannot attain except by association, it is necessary and indispensable to set up a great variety of such intermediate groups and societies in order to guarantee for the human person a sufficient sphere of freedom and responsibility.[22]

The Right to Emigrate and Immigrate

Every human being has the right to freedom of movement and of residence within the confines of his own country; and, when there are just reasons for it, the right to emigrate to other countries and take up residence there.[23]

[17] Cf. John XXIII's encyclical letter "Mater et Magistra" ("Mother and Teacher"), *Acta Apostolicae Sedis,* Vol. 53, p. 422.
[18] Cf. Pope Pius XII, *loc. cit.*
[19] "*Mater et Magistra,*" p. 428.
[20] Cf. *Ibid.,* p. 430.
[21] Cf. "*Rerum Novarum,*" pp. 134–42; Pius XI's encyclical "Quadragesimo Anno" ("in the fortieth year"), *Acta Apostolicae Sedis,* Vol. 23, pp. 199–200, and Pius XII's encyclical letter "*Sertum Laetitiae*" ("A Garland of Joy"), *Acta Apostolicae Sedis,* Vol. 31, pp. 635–44.
[22] Cf. *Acta Apostolicae Sedis,* Vol. 53, p. 430.
[23] Cf. Pius XII's radio message on Christmas Eve, 1942, *op. cit.,* pp. 33–46.

The fact that one is a citizen of a particular state does not detract in any way from his membership of the human family as a whole, nor from his citizenship of the world community.

Political Rights

The dignity of the human person involves the right to take an active part in public affairs and to contribute one's part to the common good of the citizenry. For, as our predecessor of happy memory, Pius XII, pointed out: The human individual, far from being an object and, as it were, a merely passive element in the social order, is in fact, must be and must continue to be, its subject, its foundation and its end.[24]

The human person is also entitled to a juridical protection of his rights, a protection that should be efficacious, impartial and inspired by the true norms of justice.

As our predecessor Pius XII teaches: That perpetual privilege proper to man, by which every individual has a claim to the protection of his rights, and by which there is assigned to each a definite and particular sphere of rights, immune from all arbitrary attacks, is the logical consequence of the order of justice willed by God.[25]

DUTIES

Rights and Duties Necessarily Linked in the One Person

The natural rights with which we have been dealing are, however, inseparably connected, in the very person who is their subject, with just as many respective duties; and rights as well as duties find their source, their sustenance and their inviolability in the natural law which grants or enjoins them.

For example, the right of every man to life is correlative with the duty to preserve it; his right to a decent standard of living with the duty of living it becomingly; and his right to investigate the truth freely, with the duty of seeking it and of possessing it ever more completely and profoundly.

Reciprocity of Rights and Duties between Persons

Once this is admitted, it is also clear that in human society to one man's right there corresponds a duty in all other persons: the duty, namely, of acknowledging and respecting the right in question. For every fundamental human right draws its indestructible moral force from the natural law, which, in granting it, imposes a corresponding obligation. Those, therefore, who claim their own rights, yet altogether forget or neglect to carry out their respective duties, are people who build with one hand and destroy with the other. . . .

[24] Cf. Pius XII's radio message on Christmas Eve, 1944, *Acta Apostolicae Sedis,* Vol. 37, p. 12.

[25] Cf. Pius XII's radio message on Christmas Eve, 1942, *op. cit.,* p. 21.

Social Life in Truth, Justice, Charity and Freedom

A political society is to be considered well-ordered, beneficial and in keeping with human dignity if it is grounded on truth. As the Apostle Paul exhorts us: "Away with falsehood then: let everyone speak out the truth to his neighbor; membership of the body binds us to one another."[26] This demands that reciprocal rights and duties be sincerely recognized. Furthermore, human society will be such as we have just described it, if the citizens, guided by justice, apply themselves seriously to respecting the rights of others and discharging their own duties; if they are moved by such fervor of charity as to make their own the needs of others and share with others their own goods: If, finally, they work for a progressively closer fellowship in the world of spiritual values. Human society is realized in freedom, that is to say, in ways and means in keeping with the dignity of its citizens, who accept the responsibility of their actions, precisely because they are by nature rational beings.

Human society, venerable brothers and beloved children, ought to be regarded above all as a spiritual reality: in which men communicate knowledge to each other in the light of truth; in which they can enjoy their rights and fulfil their duties, and are inspired to strive for moral good. Society should enable men to share in and enjoy every legitimate expression of beauty, and encourage them constantly to pass on to others all that is best in themselves, while they strive to make their own the spiritual achievements of others. These are the spiritual values which continually give life and basic orientation to cultural expressions, economic and social institutions, political movements and forms, laws, and all other structures by which society is outwardly established and constantly developed.

God and the Moral Order

The order which prevails in society is by nature moral. Grounded as it is in truth, it must function according to the norms of justice, it should be inspired and perfected by mutual love, and finally it should be brought to an ever more refined and human balance in freedom.

Now an order of this kind, whose principles are universal, absolute and unchangeable, has its ultimate source in the one true God, who is personal and transcends human nature. Inasmuch as God is the first truth and the highest good, He alone is that deepest source from which human society can draw its vitality, if that society is to be well-ordered, beneficial, and in keeping with human dignity.[27] As St. Thomas Aquinas says: "Human reason is the norm of the human will, according to which its goodness is measured, because reason derives from the eternal law which is the divine reason itself. It is

[26] Ephesians, iv: 25.

[27] Cf. Pius XII's 1942 radio message *op. cit.*, p. 14.

evident then that the goodness of the human will depends much more on the eternal law than on human reason."[28]

Characteristics of the Present

Our age has three distinctive characteristics. First of all, the working classes have gradually gained ground in economic and public affairs. They began by claiming their rights in the socio-economic sphere; they extended their action then to claims on the political level; and finally applied themselves to the acquisition of the benefits of a more refined culture. Today, therefore, workers all over the world refuse to be treated as if they were irrational objects without freedom, to be used at the arbitrary disposition of others. They insist that they be always regarded as men with a share in every sector of human society: in the social and economic sphere, in the fields of learning and culture, and in public life.

Secondly, it is obvious to everyone that women are now taking a part in public life. This is happening more rapidly, perhaps, in nations of Christian civilization, and, more slowly but broadly, among peoples who have inherited other traditions or cultures. Since women are becoming ever more conscious of their human dignity, they will not tolerate being treated as mere material instruments, but demand rights befitting a human person both in domestic and in public life.

Finally, the modern world, as compared with the recent past, has taken on an entirely new appearance in the field of social and political life. For since all nations have either achieved or are on the way to achieving independence, there will soon no longer exist a world divided into nations that rule others and nations that are subject to others.

Men all over the world have today—or will soon have—the rank of citizens in independent nations. No one wants to feel subject to political powers located outside his own country or ethnic group. Thus in very many human beings the inferiority complex which endured for hundreds and thousands of years is disappearing, while in others there is an attenuation and gradual fading of the corresponding superiority complex which had its roots in social-economic privileges, sex or political standing.

On the contrary, the conviction that all men are equal by reason of their natural dignity has been generally accepted. Hence racial discrimination can no longer be justified, at least doctrinally or in theory. And this is of fundamental importance and significance for the formation of human society according to those principles which we have outlined above. For, if a man becomes conscious of his rights, he must become equally aware of his duties. Thus he who possesses certain rights has likewise the duty to claim those

[28] St. Thomas Aquinas, "Summa Theologica," I/A-II/AE, quest. 19, para. 4, cf. para. 9.

rights as marks of his dignity, while all others have the obligation to acknowledge those rights and respect them.

When the relations of human society are expressed in terms of rights and duties, men become conscious of spiritual values, understand the meaning and significance of truth, justice, charity and freedom, and become deeply aware that they belong to this world of values. Moreover, when moved by such concerns, they are brought to a better knowledge of the true God who is personal and transcendent, and thus they make the ties that bind them to God the solid foundations and supreme criterion of their lives, both of that life which they live interiorly in the depths of their own souls and of that in which they are united to other men in society.

The Nature of Reality

PLATO

•

The Allegory of the Cave[1]

Next, said I, here is a parable to illustrate the degrees in which our nature may be enlightened or unenlightened. Imagine the condition of men living in a sort of cavernous chamber underground, with an entrance open to the light and a long passage all down the cave.[2] Here they have been from childhood, chained by the leg and also by the neck, so that they cannot move and can see only what is in front of them, because the chains will not let them turn their heads. At some distance higher up is the light of a fire burning behind them; and between the prisoners and the fire is a track[3] with a parapet built along it, like the screen at a puppet-show, which hides the performers while they show their puppets over the top.

I see, said he.

Now behind this parapet imagine persons carrying along various artificial objects, including figures of men and animals in wood or stone or other materials, which project above the parapet. Naturally, some of these persons will be talking, others silent.[4]

It is a strange picture, he said, and a strange sort of prisoners.

Like ourselves, I replied; for in the first place prisoners so confined would have seen nothing of themselves or of one another, except the shadows thrown by the fire-light on the wall of the Cave facing them, would they?

Not if all their lives they had been prevented from moving their heads.

[1] From *The Republic,* translated by Francis MacDonald Cornford (Oxford: The Clarendon Press, 1941), pp. 227–231. Reprinted by permission of The Clarendon Press.

[2] The *length* of the "way in" (*eisodos*) to the chamber where the prisoners sit is an essential feature, explaining why no daylight reaches them.

[3] The track crosses the passage into the cave at right angles, and is *above* the parapet built along it.

[4] A modern Plato would compare his Cave to an underground cinema, where the audience watch the play of shadows thrown by the film passing before a light at their backs. The film itself is only an image of "real" things and events in the world outside the cinema. For the film Plato has to substitute the clumsier apparatus of a procession of artificial objects carried on their heads by persons who are merely part of the machinery, providing for the movement of the objects and the sounds whose echo the prisoners hear. The parapet prevents these persons' shadows from being cast on the wall of the Cave.

And they would have seen as little of the objects carried past.

Of course.

Now, if they could talk to one another, would they not suppose that their words referred only to those passing shadows which they saw?[5]

Necessarily.

And suppose their prison had an echo from the wall facing them? When one of the people crossing behind them spoke, they could only suppose that the sound came from the shadow passing before their eyes.

No doubt.

In every way, then, such prisoners would recognize as reality nothing but the shadows of those artificial objects.[6]

Inevitably.

Now consider what would happen if their release from the chains and the healing of their unwisdom should come about in this way. Suppose one of them set free and forced suddenly to stand up, turn his head, and walk with eyes lifted to the light; all these movements would be painful, and he would be too dazzled to make out the objects whose shadows he had been used to see. What do you think he would say, if someone told him that what he had formerly seen was meaningless illusion, but now, being somewhat nearer to reality and turned towards more real objects, he was getting a truer view? Suppose further that he were shown the various objects being carried by and were made to say, in reply to questions, what each of them was. Would he not be perplexed and believe the objects now shown him to be not so real as what he formerly saw?

Yes, not nearly so real.

And if he were forced to look at the fire-light itself, would not his eyes ache, so that he would try to escape and turn back to the things which he could see distinctly, convinced that they really were clearer than these other objects now being shown to him?

Yes.

And suppose someone were to drag him away forcibly up the steep and rugged ascent and not let him go until he had hauled him out into the sunlight, would he not suffer pain and vexation at such treatment, and, when he had come out into the light, find his eyes so full of its radiance that he could not see a single one of the things that he was now told were real?

Certainly he would not see them all at once.

He would need, then, to grow accustomed before he could see things in that upper world. At first it would be easiest to make out shadows, and then the images of men and things reflected in water, and later on the things themselves. After that, it would be easier to watch the heavenly bodies and the sky

[5] Adam's text and interpretation. The prisoners, having seen nothing but shadows, cannot think their words refer to the objects carried past behind their backs. For them shadows (images) are the only realities.

[6] The state of mind called *eikasia* in the previous chapter.

itself by night, looking at the light of the moon and stars rather than the Sun and the Sun's light in the day-time.

Yes, surely.

Last of all, he would be able to look at the Sun and contemplate its nature, not as it appears when reflected in water or any alien medium, but as it is in itself in its own domain.

No doubt.

And now he would begin to draw the conclusion that it is the Sun that produces the seasons and the course of the year and controls everything in the visible world, and moreover is in a way the cause of all that he and his companions used to see.

Clearly he would come at last to that conclusion.

Then if he called to mind his fellow prisoners and what passed for wisdom in his former dwelling-place, he would surely think himself happy in the change and be sorry for them. They may have had a practice of honouring and commending one another, with prizes for the man who had the keenest eye for the passing shadows and the best memory for the order in which they followed or accompanied one another, so that he could make a good guess as to which was going to come next.[7] Would our released prisoner be likely to covet those prizes or to envy the men exalted to honour and power in the Cave? Would he not feel like Homer's Achilles, that he would far sooner "be on earth as a hired servant in the house of a landless man"[8] or endure anything rather than go back to his old beliefs and live in the old way?

Yes, he would prefer any fate to such a life.

Now imagine what would happen if he went down again to take his former seat in the Cave. Coming suddenly out of the sunlight, his eyes would be filled with darkness. He might be required once more to deliver his opinion on those shadows, in competition with the prisoners who had never been released, while his eyesight was still dim and unsteady; and it might take some time to become used to the darkness. They would laugh at him and say that he had gone up only to come back with his sight ruined; it was worth no one's while even to attempt the ascent. If they could lay hands on the man who was trying to set them free and lead them up, they would kill him.[9]

Yes, they would.

Every feature in this parable, my dear Glaucon, is meant to fit our earlier analysis. The prison dwelling corresponds to the region revealed to us through the sense of sight, and the fire-light within it to the power of the Sun. The ascent to see the things in the upper world you may take as standing for the

[7] The empirical politician, with no philosophic insight, but only a "knack of remembering what usually happens" (*Gorg.* 501 A). He has *eikasia* = conjecture as to what is likely (*eikos*).

[8] This verse, being spoken by the ghost of Achilles, suggests that the Cave is comparable with Hades.

[9] An allusion to the fate of Socrates.

upward journey of the soul into the region of the intelligible; then you will be in possession of what I surmise, since that is what you wish to be told. Heaven knows whether it is true; but this, at any rate, is how it appears to me. In the world of knowledge, the last thing to be perceived and only with great difficulty is the essential Form of Goodness. Once it is perceived, the conclusion must follow that, for all things, this is the cause of whatever is right and good; in the visible world it gives birth to light and to the lord of light, while it is itself sovereign in the intelligible world and the parent of intelligence and truth. Without having had a vision of this Form no one can act with wisdom, either in his own life or in matters of state.

RENÉ DESCARTES

•

A Discourse on Method[1]

I was then in Germany, attracted thither by the wars in that country, which have not yet been brought to a termination; and as I was returning to the army from the coronation of the emperor, the setting in of winter arrested me in a locality where, as I found no society to interest me, and was besides fortunately undisturbed by any cares or passions, I remained the whole day in seclusion, with full opportunity to occupy my attention with my own thoughts. Of these one of the very first that occurred to me was, that there is seldom so much perfection in works composed of many separate parts, upon which different hands had been employed, as in those completed by a single master. Thus it is observable that the buildings which a single architect has planned and executed, are generally more elegant and commodious than those which several have attempted to improve, by making old walls serve for purposes for which they were not originally built. Thus also, those ancient cities which, from being at first only villages, have become, in course of time, large towns, are usually but ill laid out compared with the regularly constructed towns which a professional architect has freely planned on an open plain; so that although the several buildings of the former may often equal or surpass in beauty those of the latter, yet when one observes their indiscriminate juxtaposition, there a large one and here a small, and the consequent crookedness and irregularity of the streets, one is disposed to allege that chance rather than any human will guided by reason must have led to such an arrangement. And if we consider that nevertheless there have been at all times certain

[1] From *A Discourse on Method* (1637), by René Descartes, in *The Method, Meditations, and Philosophy of Descartes,* translated by John Veitch (New York: Tudor Publishing Co., n.d.), pp. 155–172, omitting Ch. 3.

officers whose duty it was to see that private buildings contributed to public ornament, the difficulty of reaching high perfection with but the materials of others to operate on, will be readily acknowledged. In the same way I fancied that those nations which, starting from a semibarbarous state and advancing to civilization by slow degrees, have had their laws successively determined, and, as it were, forced upon them simply by experience of the hurtfulness of particular crimes and disputes, would by this process come to be possessed of less perfect institutions than those which, from the commencement of their association as communities, have followed the appointment of some wise legislator. It is thus quite certain that the constitution of the true religion, the ordinances of which are derived from God, must be incomparably superior to that of every other. And, to speak of human affairs, I believe that the past pre-eminence of Sparta was due not to the goodness of each of its laws in particular, for many of these were very strange, and even opposed to good morals, but to the circumstance that, originated by a single individual, they all tended to a single end. In the same way I thought that the sciences contained in books (such of them at least as are made up of probable reasonings, without demonstrations), composed as they are of the opinions of many different individuals massed together, are farther removed from truth than the simple inferences which a man of good sense using his natural and unprejudiced judgment draws respecting the matters of his experience. And because we have all to pass through a state of infancy to manhood, and have been of necessity, for a length of time, governed by our desires and preceptors (whose dictates were frequently conflicting, while neither perhaps always counselled us for the best), I farther concluded that it is almost impossible that our judgments can be so correct or solid as they would have been, had our reason been mature from the moment of our birth, and had we always been guided by it alone.

It is true, however, that it is not customary to pull down all the houses of a town with the single design of rebuilding them differently, and thereby rendering the streets more handsome; but it often happens that a private individual takes down his own with the view of erecting it anew, and that people are even sometimes constrained to this when their houses are in danger of falling from age, or when the foundations are insecure. With this before me by way of example, I was persuaded that it would indeed be preposterous for a private individual to think of reforming a state by fundamentally changing it throughout, and overturning it in order to set it up amended; and the same I thought was true of any similar project for reforming the body of the sciences, or the order of teaching them established in the schools: but as for the opinions which up to that time I had embraced, I thought that I could not do better than resolve at once to sweep them wholly away, that I might afterwards be in a position to admit either others more correct, or even perhaps the same when they had undergone the scrutiny of reason. I firmly believed that in this way I should much better succeed in the conduct of my life, than if I built only upon old foundations, and leaned upon principles which, in my youth, I had taken upon trust. For although I recognized various difficulties in this undertaking, these were not, however, without remedy, nor once to be compared with such as attend the slightest reformation in public affairs. Large bodies, if once overthrown, are with great difficulty set up again, or even kept erect when once seriously shaken, and the fall of such is always disastrous. Then if there are any imperfections in the constitutions of states (and that many such exist the diversity of constitutions is alone sufficient to assure us), custom has without doubt materially smoothed their inconveniences, and has even managed to steer altogether clear of, or insensibly corrected a number which sagacity could not have provided against with equal effect; and, in fine, the defects are almost more tolerable than the change necessary for their removal; in the same manner that highways which wind among mountains, by being much frequented, become gradually so smooth and commodious, that it is much better to follow them than to seek a straighter path by climbing over the tops of rocks and descending to the bottoms of precipices.

Hence it is that I cannot in any degree approve of those restless and busy meddlers who, called neither by birth no fortune to take part in the management of public affairs, are yet always projecting reforms; and if I thought that this tract contained aught which might justify the suspicion that I was a victim of such folly, I would by no means permit its publication. I have never contemplated anything higher than the reformation of my own opinions, and basing them on a foundation wholly my own. And although my own satisfaction with my work has led me to present here a draft of it, I do not by any means therefore recommend to everyone else to make a similar attempt. Those whom God has endowed with a larger measure of genius will entertain, perhaps, designs still more exalted; but for the many I am much afraid lest even the present undertaking be more than they can safely venture to imitate. The single design to strip one's self of all past beliefs is one that ought not to be taken by every one. The majority of men is composed of two classes, for neither of which would this be at all a befitting resolution: in the first place, of those who with more than a due confidence in their own powers, are precipitate in their judgments and want the patience requisite for orderly and circumspect thinking; whence it happens, that if men of this class once take the liberty to doubt of their accustomed opinions, and quit the beaten highway, they will never be able to thread the byway that would lead them by a shorter course, and will lose themselves and continue to wander for life; in the second place, of those who, possessed of sufficient sense or modesty to determine that there are others who excel them in the power of discriminating between truth and error, and by whom they may be instructed, ought rather to content themselves with the opinions of such than trust for more correct to their own reason.

For my own part, I should doubtless have belonged to the latter class, had I received instruction from but one master, or had I never known the diversities of opinion that from time immemorial have prevailed among men of the greatest learning. But I had become aware, even so early as during my college life, that no opinion, however absurd and incredible, can be imagined, which has not been maintained by some one of the philosophers; and afterwards in the course of my travels I remarked that all those whose opinions are decidedly repugnant to ours are not on that account barbarians and savages, but on the contrary that many of these nations make an equally good, if not a better, use of their reason than we do. I took into account also the very different character which a person brought up from infancy in France or Germany exhibits, from that which, with the same mind originally, this individual would have possessed had he lived always among the Chinese or with savages, and the circumstance that in dress itself the fashion which pleased us ten years ago, and which may again, perhaps, be received into favour before ten years have gone, appears to us at this moment extravagant and ridiculous. I was thus led to infer that the ground of our opinions is far more custom and example than any certain knowledge. And, finally, although such be the ground of our opinions, I remarked that a plurality of suffrages is no guarantee of truth where it is at all of difficult discovery, as in such cases it is much more likely that it will be found by one than by many. I could, however, select from the crowd no one whose opinions seemed worthy of preference, and thus I found myself constrained, as it were, to use my own reason in the conduct of my life.

But like one walking alone and in the dark, I resolved to proceed so slowly and with such circumspection, that if I did not advance far, I would at least guard against falling. I did not even choose to dismiss summarily any of the opinions that had crept in my belief without having been introduced by reason, but first of all took sufficient time carefully to satisfy myself of the general nature of the task I was setting myself, and ascertain the true method by which to arrive at the knowledge of whatever lay within the compass of my powers.

Among the branches of philosophy, I had, at an earlier period, given some attention to logic, and among those of the mathematics to geometrical analysis and algebra—three arts or sciences which ought, as I conceived, to contribute something to my design. But, on examination, I found that, as for logic, its syllogisms and the majority of its other precepts are of avail rather in the communication of what we already know, or even as the art of Tully, in speaking without judgment of things of which we are ignorant, than in the investigation of the unknown; and although this science contains indeed a number of correct and very excellent precepts, there are, nevertheless, so many others, and these either injurious or superfluous, mingled with the former, that it is almost quite as difficult to effect a severance of the true from the false as it is to extract a Diana or a Minerva from a rough block of marble. Then as to the analysis of the ancients and the algebra of the moderns, besides that they embrace only matters highly abstract, and, to appearance, of no use, the former is so exclusively restricted to the consideration of figures, that it can exercise the understanding only on condition of greatly fatiguing the imagination; and, in the latter, there is so complete a subjection to certain rules and formulas, that there results an art full of confusion and obscurity calculated to embarrass, instead of a science fitted to cultivate the mind. By these considerations I was induced to seek some other method which would comprise the advantages of the three and be exempt from their defects. And as a multitude of laws often only hampers justice, so that a state is best governed when, with few laws, these are rigidly administered; in like manner, instead of the great number of precepts of which logic is composed, I believed that the four following would prove perfectly sufficient for me, provided I took the firm and unwavering resolution never in a single instance to fail to observe them.

The first was never to accept anything for true which I did not clearly know to be such; that is to say, carefully to avoid precipitancy and prejudice, and to comprise nothing more in my judgment than was presented to my mind so clearly and distinctly as to exclude all ground of doubt.

The second, to divide each of the difficulties under examination into as many parts as possible, and as might be necessary for its adequate solution.

The third, to conduct my thoughts in such order that, by commencing with objects the simplest and easiest to know, I might ascend by little and little, and, as it were, step by step, to the knowledge of the more complex; assigning in thought a certain order even to those objects which in their own nature do not stand in a relation of antecedence and sequence.

And the last, in every case to make enumerations so complete, and reviews so general, that I might be assured that nothing was omitted.

The long chains of simple and easy reasonings by means of which geometers are accustomed to reach the conclusions of their most difficult demonstrations, had led me to imagine that all things, to the knowledge of which man is competent, are mutually connected in the same way, and that there is nothing so far removed from us as to be beyond our reach, or so hidden that we cannot discover it, provided only we abstain from accepting the false for the true, and always preserve in our thoughts the order necessary for the deduction of one truth from another. And I had little difficulty in determining the objects with which it was necessary to commence, for I was already persuaded that it must be with the simplest and easiest to know, and, considering that of all those who have hitherto sought truth in the sciences, the mathematicians alone have been able to find any demonstrations, that is, any certain and evident reasons, I did not doubt but that such must have been the rule of their investigations. I resolved to commence, therefore, with the examination of the simplest objects, not anticipating, however, from this any other advantage than that to be found in accustoming my mind to the love and nourishment of truth, and to a distaste for all such reasonings as were unsound. But I had no intention on that account of attempting to master all the particular sciences commonly denominated mathematics: but observing that, however different their objects, they all agree in considering only the various relations or proportions subsisting among those objects, I thought it best for my purpose to consider these proportions in the most general form possible, without referring them to any objects in particular, except such as would most facilitate the knowledge of them, and without by any means restricting them to these, that afterwards I might thus be the better able to apply them to every other class of objects to which they are legitimately applicable. Perceiving further, that in order to understand these relations I should sometimes have to consider them one by one, and sometimes only to bear them in mind, or embrace them in the aggregate, I thought that, in order the better to consider them individually, I should view them as subsisting between straight lines, than which I could find no objects more simple, or capable of being more distinctly represented to my imagination and senses; and on the other hand, that in order to retain them in the memory, or embrace an aggregate of many, I should express them by certain characters the briefest possible. In this way I believed that I could borrow all that was best both in geometrical analysis and in algebra, and correct all the defects of the one by help of the other.

And in point of fact, the accurate observance of these few precepts gave me, I take the liberty of saying, such ease in unravelling all the questions embraced in these two sciences, that in the two or three months I devoted to their examination, not only did I reach solutions of questions I had formerly deemed exceedingly difficult, but even as regards questions of the solution of which I continued ignorant, I was enabled, as it appeared to me, to determine the means whereby, and the extent to which, a solution was possible; results attributable to the circumstance that I commenced with the simplest and most general truths, and that thus each truth discovered was a rule available in the discovery of subsequent ones. Nor in this perhaps shall I appear too vain, if it be considered that, as the truth on any particular points is one, whoever apprehends the truth, knows all that on that point can be known. The child, for example, who has been instructed in the elements of arithmetic, and has made a particular addition, according to rule, may be assured that he has found, with respect to the sum of the numbers before him, all that in this instance is within the reach of human genius. Now, in conclusion, the method which teaches adherence to the true order, and an exact enumeration of all the conditions of the thing sought includes all that gives certitude to the rules of arithmetic.

But the chief ground of my satisfaction with this method, was the assurance I had of thereby exercising my reason in all matters, if not with absolute perfection, at least with the greatest attainable by me: besides, I was conscious that by its use my mind was becoming gradually habituated to clearer and more distinct conceptions of its objects; and I hoped also, from not having restricted this method to any particular matter, to apply it to the difficulties of the other sciences, with not less success than to those of algebra. I should not, however, on this account have ventured at once on the examination of all the difficulties of the sciences which presented themselves to me, for this would have been contrary to the order prescribed in the method, but observing that the knowledge of such is dependent on principles borrowed from philosophy, in which I found nothing certain, I thought it necessary first of all to endeavour to establish its principles. And because I observed, besides, that an inquiry of this kind was of all others of the greatest moment, and one in which precipitancy and anticipation in judgment were most to be dreaded, I thought that I ought not to approach it till I had reached a more mature age (being at that time but twenty-three), and had first of all employed much of my time in preparation for the work, as well by eradicating from my mind all the erroneous opinions I had up to that moment accepted, as by amassing variety of experience to afford materials for my reasonings, and by continually exercising myself in my chosen method with a view to increased skill in its application. . . .

I am in doubt as to the propriety of making my first meditations, in the place above mentioned, matter of discourse; for these are so metaphysical, and so uncommon, as not, perhaps, to be acceptable to every one. And yet, that it may be determined whether the foundations that I have laid are sufficiently secure, I find myself in a measure constrained to advert to them. I had long before remarked that, in relation to practice, it is sometimes necessary to adopt, as if above doubt, opinions which we discern to be highly uncertain, as has been already said; but as I then desired to give my attention solely to the search after truth, I thought that a procedure exactly the opposite was called for, and that I ought to reject as absolutely false all opinions in regard to which I could suppose the least ground for doubt, in order to ascertain whether after that there remained aught in my belief that was wholly indubitable. Accordingly, seeing that our senses sometimes deceived us, I was willing to suppose that there existed nothing really such as they presented to us; and because some men err in reasoning, and fall into paralogisms, even on the simplest matters of geometry, I, convinced that I was as open to error as any other, rejected as false all the reasonings I had hitherto taken for demonstrations; and finally, when I considered that the very same thoughts (presentations) which we experience when awake may also be experienced when we are asleep, while there is at that time not one of them true, I supposed that all the objects (presentations) that had ever entered into my mind when awake, had in them no more truth than the illusions of my dreams. But immediately upon this I observed that, whilst I thus wished to think that all was false, it was absolutely necessary that I, who thus thought, should be somewhat; and as I observed that this truth, I THINK, HENCE I AM, was so certain and of such evidence, that no ground of doubt, however extravagant, could be alleged by the sceptics capable of shaking it, I concluded that I might, without scruple, accept it as the first principle of the philosophy of which I was in search.

In the next place, I attentively examined what I was, and as I observed that I could suppose that I had no body, and that there was no world nor any place in which I might be; but that I could not therefore suppose that I was not; and that, on the contrary, from the very circumstance that I thought to doubt of the truth of other things, it most clearly and certainly followed that I was; while, on the other hand, if I had only ceased to think, although all the other objects which I had ever imagined had been in reality existent, I would have had no reason to believe that I existed; I thence concluded that I was a substance whose whole essence or nature consists only in thinking, and which, that it may exist, has need of no place, nor is dependent on any material thing, so that "I," that is to say, the mind by which I am what I am, is wholly distinct from the body, and is even more easily known than the latter, and is such, that although the latter were not, it would still continue to be all that it is.

After this I inquired in general into what is essential to the truth and certainty of a proposition; for since I had discovered one which I knew to be true, I thought that I must likewise be able to discover the ground of this certitude. And as I observed that in the words *I think, hence I am,* there is nothing at all which gives me assurance of their truth beyond this, that I see very clearly that in order to think it is necessary to exist, I concluded that I might take, as a general rule, the principle, that all the things which we very clearly and distinctly conceive are true, only observing, however, that there is some difficulty in rightly determining the objects which we distinctly conceive.

JOHN LOCKE

•

An Essay Concerning Human Understanding[1]

1. Every man being conscious to himself that he thinks; and that which his mind is applied about whilst thinking being the *ideas* that are there, it is past doubt that men have in their minds several ideas—such as are those expressed by the words *whiteness, hardness, sweetness, thinking, motion, man, elephant, army, drunkenness,* and others: it is in the first place then to be inquired, *How he comes by them?*

I know it is a received doctrine, that men have native ideas, and original characters, stamped upon their minds in their very first being. This opinion I have at large examined already; and, I suppose what I have said in the foregoing Book will be much more easily admitted, when I had shown whence the understanding may get all the ideas it has; and by what ways and degrees they may come into the mind;—for which I shall appeal to every one's own observation and experience.

2. Let us then suppose the mind to be, as we say, white paper, void of all

[1] *An Essay Concerning Human Understanding* (1690), ed., Alexander Campbell Fraser (Oxford: The Clarendon Press, 1894), Book II, Chap. I.

characters, without any ideas:—How comes it to be furnished? Whence comes it by that vast store which the busy and boundless fancy of man has painted on it with an almost endless variety? Whence has it all the *materials* of reason and knowledge? To this I answer, in one word, from EXPERIENCE. In that all our knowledge is founded; and from that it ultimately derives itself. Our observation employed either about external sensible objects, or about the internal operations of our minds perceived and reflected on by ourselves, is that which supplies our understandings with all the *materials* of thinking. These two are the fountains of knowledge, from whence all the ideas we have, or can naturally have, do spring.

3. First, our Senses, conversant about particular sensible objects, do convey into the mind several distinct perceptions of things, according to those various ways wherein those objects do affect them. And thus we come by those *ideas* we have of *yellow, white, heat, cold, soft, hard, bitter, sweet,* and all those which we call sensible qualities; which when I say the senses convey into the mind, I mean, they from external objects convey into the mind what produces there those perceptions. This great source of most of the ideas we have, depending wholly upon our senses, and derived by them to the understanding, I call SENSATION.

4. Secondly, the other fountain from which experience furnisheth the understanding with ideas is—the perception of the operations of our own mind within us, as it is employed about the ideas it has got;—which operations, when the soul comes to reflect on and consider, do furnish the understanding with another set of ideas, which could not be had from things without. And such are *perception, thinking, doubting, believing, reasoning, knowing, willing,* and all the different actings of our own minds;—which we being conscious of, and observing in ourselves, do from these receive into our understandings as distinct ideas as we do from bodies affecting our senses. This source of ideas every man has wholly in himself; and though it be not sense, as having nothing to do with external objects, yet it is very like it, and might properly enough be called *internal sense*. But as I call the other Sensation, so I call this REFLECTION, the ideas it affords being such only as the mind gets by reflecting on its own operations within itself. By reflection then, in the following part of this discourse, I would be understood to mean, that notice which the mind takes of its own operations, and the manner of them, by reason whereof there come to be ideas of these operations in the understanding. These two, I say, viz. external material things, as the objects of SENSATION, and the operations of our own minds within, as the objects of REFLECTION, are to me the only originals from whence all our ideas take their beginnings. The term *operations* here I use in a large sense, as comprehending not barely the actions of the mind about its ideas, but some sort of passions arising sometimes from them, such as is the satisfaction or uneasiness arising from any thought.

5. The understanding seems to me not to have the least glimmering of any ideas which it doth not receive from one of these two. *External objects* fur-

nish the mind with the ideas of sensible qualities, which are all those different perceptions they produce in us; and *the mind* furnishes the understanding with ideas of its own operations.

These, when we have taken a full survey of them, and their several modes, [combinations, and relations,] we shall find to contain all our whole stock of ideas; and that we have nothing in our minds which did not come in one of these two ways. Let any one examine his own thoughts, and thoroughly search into his understanding; and then let him tell me, whether all the original ideas he has there, are any other than of the objects of his senses, or of the operations of his mind, considered as objects of his reflection. And how great a mass of knowledge soever he imagines to be lodged there, he will, upon taking a strict view, see that he has not any idea in his mind but what one of these two have imprinted;—though perhaps, with infinite variety compounded and enlarged by the understanding, as we shall see hereafter.

6. He that attentively considers the state of a child, at his first coming into the world, will have little reason to think him stored with plenty of ideas, that are to be the matter of his future knowledge. It is *by degrees* he comes to be furnished with them. And though the ideas of obvious and familiar qualities imprint themselves before the memory begins to keep a register of time and order, yet it is often so late before some unusual qualities come in the way, that there are few men that cannot recollect the beginning of their acquaintance with them. And if it were worth while, no doubt a child might be so ordered as to have but a very few, even of the ordinary ideas, till he were grown up to a man. But all that are born into the world, being surrounded with bodies that perpetually and diversely affect them, variety of ideas, whether care be taken of it or not, are imprinted on the minds of children. Light and colours are busy at hand everywhere, when the eye is but open; sounds and some tangible qualities fail not to solicit their proper senses, and force an entrance to the mind;—but yet, I think, it will be granted easily, that if a child were kept in a place where he never saw any other but black and white till he were a man, he would have no more ideas of scarlet or green, than he that from his childhood never tasted an oyster, or a pineapple, has of those particular relishes.

7. Men then come to be furnished with fewer or more simple ideas from without, according as the objects they converse with afford greater or less variety; and from the operations of their minds within, according as they more or less reflect on them. For, though he that contemplates the operations of his mind cannot but have plain and clear ideas of them; yet, unless he turn his thoughts that way, and considers them *attentively,* he will no more have clear and distinct ideas of all the operations of his mind, and all that may be observed therein, than he will have all the particular ideas of any landscape, or of the parts and motions of a clock, who will not turn his eyes to it, and with attention heed all the parts of it. The picture, or clock may be so placed, that they may come in his way every day; but yet he will have but a confused

idea of all the parts they are made up of, till he applies himself with attention, to consider them each in particular.

8. And hence we see the reason why it is pretty late before most children get ideas of the operations of their own minds; and some have not any very clear or perfect ideas of the greatest part of them all their lives. Because, though they pass there continually, yet, like floating visions, they make not deep impressions enough to leave in their mind clear, distinct, lasting ideas, till the understanding turns inward upon itself, reflects on its own operations, and makes them the objects of its own contemplation. Children, when they come first into it, are surrounded with a world of new things, which, by a constant solicitation of their senses, draw the mind constantly to them; forward to take notice of new, and apt to be delighted with the variety of changing objects. Thus the first years are usually employed and diverted in looking abroad. Men's business in them is to acquaint themselves with what is to be found without; and so growing up in a constant attention to outward sensations, seldom make any considerable reflection on what passes within them, till they come to be of riper years; and some scarce ever at all.

WILLIAM JAMES

•

What Pragmatism Is[1]

Some years ago, being with a camping party in the mountains, I returned from a solitary ramble to find every one engaged in a ferocious metaphysical dispute. The *corpus* of the dispute was a squirrel—a live squirrel supposed to be clinging to one side of a tree-trunk; while over against the tree's opposite side a human being was imagined to stand. This human witness tries to get sight of the squirrel by moving rapidly round the tree, but no matter how fast he goes, the squirrel moves as fast in the opposite direction, and always keeps the tree between himself and the man, so that never a glimpse of him is caught. The resultant metaphysical problem now is this: *Does the man go round the squirrel or not?* He goes round the tree, sure enough, and the squirrel is on the tree; but does he go round the squirrel? In the unlimited leisure of the wilderness, discussion had been worn threadbare. Every one had taken sides and was obstinate; and the numbers on both sides were even. Each side, when I appeared, therefore appealed to me to make it a majority. Mindful of

[1] From William James, *Pragmatism.* Copyright 1907 by William James. Reprinted by permission of Paul R. Reynolds Inc., 599 Fifth Avenue, New York, N.Y., 10017.

the scholastic adage that whenever you meet a contradiction you must make a distinction, I immediately sought and found one, as follows: "Which party is right," I said, "depends on what you *practically mean* by 'going round' the squirrel. If you mean passing from the north of him to the east, then to the south, then to the west, and then to the north of him again, obviously the man does go round him, for he occupies these successive positions. But if on the contrary you mean being first in front of him, then on the right of him, then behind him, then on his left, and finally in front again, it is quite obvious that the man fails to go round him, for by compensating movements the squirrel makes, he keeps his belly turned towards the man all the time, and his back turned away. Make the distinction, and there is no occasion for any further dispute. You are both right and both wrong, according as you conceive the verb 'to go round' in one practical fashion or the other."

Although one or two of the hotter disputants called my speech a shuffling evasion, saying they wanted no quibbling or scholastic hair-splitting, but meant just plain honest English "round," the majority seemed to think that the distinction had assuaged the dispute.

I tell this trivial anecdote because it is a peculiarly simple example of what I wish now to speak of as *the pragmatic method.* The pragmatic method is primarily a method of settling metaphysical disputes that otherwise might be interminable. Is the world one or many?—fated or free?—material or spiritual?—here are notions either of which may or may not hold good of the world; and disputes over such notions are unending. The pragmatic method in such cases is to try to interpret each notion by tracing its respective practical consequences. What difference would it practically make to any one if this notion rather than that notion were true? If no practical difference whatever can be traced, then the alternatives mean practically the same thing, and all dispute is idle. Whenever a dispute is serious, we ought to be able to show some practical difference that must follow from one side or the other's being right.

A glance at the history of the idea will show you still better what pragmatism means. The term is derived from the same Greek word πραγμά, meaning action, from which our words "practice" and "practical" come. It was first introduced into philosophy by Mr. Charles Peirce in 1878. In an article entitled "How to Make Our Ideas Clear," in the *Popular Science Monthly* for January of that year, Mr. Peirce, after pointing out that our beliefs are really rules for action, said that, to develop a thought's meaning, we need only determine what conduct it is fitted to produce: that conduct is for us its sole significance. And the tangible fact at the root of all our thought-distinctions, however subtle, is that there is no one of them so fine as to consist in anything but a possible difference of practice. To attain perfect clearness in our thoughts of an object, then, we need only consider what conceivable effects of a practical kind the object may involve—what sensations we are to expect from it, and what reactions we must prepare. Our conception of these effects whether immediate or remote, is then for us the whole of our conception of the object, so far as that conception has positive significance at all.

This is the principle of Peirce, the principle of pragmatism. It lay entirely unnoticed by any one for twenty years, until I, in an address before Professor Howison's philosophical union at the University of California, brought it forward again and made a special application of it to religion. By that date (1898) the times seemed ripe for its reception. The word "pragmatism" spread, and at present it fairly spots the pages of the philosophic journals. On all hands we find the "pragmatic movement" spoken of, sometimes with respect, sometimes with contumely, seldom with clear understanding. It is evident that the term applies itself conveniently to a number of tendencies that hitherto have lacked a collective name, and that it has "come to stay."

To take in the importance of Peirce's principle, one must get accustomed to applying it to concrete cases. I found a few years ago that Ostwald, the illustrious Leipzig chemist, had been making perfectly distinct use of the principle of pragmatism in his lectures on the philosophy of science, though he had not called it by that name,

"All realities influence our practice," he wrote me, "and that influence is their meaning for us. I am accustomed to put questions to my classes in this way: In what respects would the world be different if this alternative or that were true? If I can find nothing that would become different, then the alternative has no sense."

That is, the rival views mean practically the same thing, and meaning, other than practical, there is for us none. Ostwald in a published lecture gives this example of what he means. Chemists have long wrangled over the inner constitution of certain bodies called "tautomerous." Their properties seemed equally consistent with the notion that an instable hydrogen atom oscillates inside of them, or that they are instable mixtures of two bodies. Controversy raged, but never was decided. "It would never have begun," says Ostwald, "if the combatants had asked themselves what particular experimental fact could have been made different by one or the other view being correct. For it would then have appeared that no difference of fact could possibly ensue; and the quarrel was as unreal as if, theorising in primitive times about the raising of dough by yeast, one party should have invoked a 'brownie,' while another insisted on an 'elf' as the true cause of the phenomenon."

It is astonishing to see how many philosophical disputes collapse into insignificance the moment you subject them to this simple test of tracing a concrete consequence. There can *be* no difference anywhere that doesn't *make* a difference elsewhere—no difference in abstract truth that doesn't express itself in a difference in concrete fact and in conduct consequent upon that fact, imposed on somebody, somehow, somewhere, and somewhen. The whole function of philosophy ought to be to find out what definite difference it will make to you and me, at definite instants of our life, if this world-formula or that world-formula be the true one.

There is absolutely nothing new in the pragmatic method. Socrates was an adept at it. Aristotle used it methodically. Locke, Berkeley, and Hume made momentous contributions to truth by its means. Shadworth Hodgson keeps insisting that realities are only what they are "known as." But these forerunners of pragmatism used it in fragments: they were a prelude only. Not until in our time has it generalized itself, become conscious of a universal mission, pretended to a conquering destiny. I believe in that destiny, and I hope I may end by inspiring you with my belief.

Pragmatism represents a perfectly familiar attitude in philosophy, the empiricist attitude, but it represents it, as it seems to me, both in a more radical and in a less objectionable form than it has ever yet assumed. A pragmatist turns his back resolutely and once for all upon a lot of inveterate habits dear to professional philosophers. He turns away from abstraction and insufficiency, from verbal solutions, from bad *a priori* reasons, from fixed principles, closed systems, and pretended absolutes and origins. He turns towards concreteness and adequacy, towards facts, towards action and towards power. That means the empiricist temper regnant and the rationalist temper sincerely given up. It means the open air and possibilities of nature, as against dogma, artificiality, and the pretence of finality in truth.

At the same time it does not stand for any special results. It is a method only. But the general triumph of that method would mean an enormous change in what I called in my last lecture the "temperament" of philosophy. Teachers of the ultra-rationalistic type would be frozen out, much as the courtier type is frozen out in republics, as the ultra-montane type of priest is frozen out in protestant lands. Science and metaphysics would come much nearer together, would in fact work absolutely hand in hand.

Metaphysics has usually followed a very primitive kind of quest. You know how men have always hankered after unlawful magic, and you know what a great part in magic *words* have always played. If you have his name, or the formula of incantation that binds him, you can control the spirit, genie, afrite, or whatever the power may be. Solomon knew the names of all the spirits, and having their names, he held them subject to his will. So the universe has always appeared to the natural mind as a kind of enigma, of which the key must be sought in the shape of some illuminating or power-bringing word or name. That word names the universe's *principle,* and to possess it is after a fashion to possess the universe itself. "God," "Matter," "Reason," "the Absolute," "Energy," are so many solving names. You can rest when you have them. You are at the end of your metaphysical quest.

But if you follow the pragmatic method you cannot look on any such word as closing your quest. You must bring out of each word its practical cash-value, set it at work within the stream of your experience. It appears less as a solution, then, than as a programme for more work, and more particularly as an indication of the ways in which existing realities may be *changed*.

Theories thus become instruments, not answers to enigmas, in which we can rest. We don't lie back upon them, we move forward, and, on occasion, make nature over again by their aid. Pragmatism unstiffens all our theories, limbers them up and sets each one at work. Being nothing essentially new, it harmonizes with many ancient philosophic tendencies. It agrees with nominalism, for instance, in always appealing to particulars; with utilitarianism in emphasizing practical aspects; with positivism in its disdain for verbal solutions, useless questions, and metaphysical abstractions.

All these, you see, are *anti-intellectualist* tendencies. Against rationalism as a pretension and a method pragmatism is fully armed and militant. But, at the outset, at least, it stands for no particular results. It has no dogmas, and no doctrines save its method. As the young Italian pragmatist Papini has well said, it lies in the midst of our theories like a corridor in a hotel. Innumerable chambers open out of it. In one you may find a man writing an atheistic volume; in the next some one on his knees praying for faith and strength; in a third a chemist investigating a body's properties; in a fourth a system of idealistic metaphysics is being excogitated; in a fifth the impossibility of metaphysics is being shown. But they all own the corridor, and all must pass through it if they want a practicable way of getting into or out of their respective rooms.

No particular results then, so far, but only an attitude of orientation, is what the pragmatic method means. *The attitude of looking away from first things, principles, "categories," supposed necessities; and of looking towards last things, fruits, consequences, facts.*

So much for the pragmatic method! You may say that I have been praising it rather than explaining it to you, but I shall presently explain it abundantly enough by showing how it works on some familiar problems. Meanwhile the word pragmatism has come to be used in a still wider sense, as meaning also a certain *theory of truth*. I mean to give a whole lecture to the statement of that theory, after first paving the way, so I can be very brief now. But brevity is hard to follow, so I ask for your redoubled attention for a quarter of an hour. If much remains obscure, I hope to make it clearer in the later lectures.

One of the most successfully cultivated branches of philosophy in our time is what is called inductive logic, the study of the conditions under which our sciences have evolved. Writers on this subject have begun to show a singular unanimity as to what the laws of nature and elements of fact mean when formulated by mathematicians, physicists, and chemists. When the first mathematical, logical, and natural uniformities, the first *laws,* were discovered, men were so carried away by the clearness, beauty, and simplification that resulted that they believed themselves to have deciphered authentically the eternal thoughts of the Almighty. His mind also thundered and reverberated in syllogisms. He also thought in conic sections, squares, and roots and ratios, and geometrized like Euclid. He made Kepler's laws for the planets to follow; he made velocity increase proportionally to the time in falling bodies; he made the law of the sines for light to obey when refracted; he established the classes, orders, families, and genera of plants and animals, and fixed the distances between them. He thought the archetypes of all things, and devised their variations; and when we rediscover any one of these his wondrous institutions, we seize his mind in its very literal intention.

But as the sciences have developed farther, the notion has gained ground that most, perhaps all, of our laws are only approximations. The laws themselves, moreover, have grown so numerous that there is no counting them; and so many rival formulations are proposed in all the branches of science that investigators have become accustomed to the notion that no theory is absolutely a transcript of reality, but that any one of them may from some point of view be useful. Their great use is to summarize old facts and to lead to new ones. They are only a man-made language, a conceptual shorthand, as some one calls them, in which we write our reports of nature; and languages, as is well known, tolerate much choice of expression and many dialects.

Thus human arbitrariness has driven divine necessity from scientific logic. If I mention the names of Sigwart, Mach, Ostwald, Pearson, Milhaud, Poincaré, Duhem, Heymans, those of you who are students will easily identify the tendency I speak of, and will think of additional names.

Riding now on the front of this wave of scientific logic, Messrs. Schiller and Dewey appear with their pragmatistic account of what truth everywhere signifies. Everywhere, these teachers say, "truth" in our ideas and beliefs means the same thing that it means in science. It means, they say, nothing but this, *that ideas (which themselves are but parts of our experience) become true just in so far as they help us to get into satisfactory relation with other parts of our experience,* to summarize them and get about among them by conceptual shortcuts instead of following the interminable succession of particular phenomena. Any idea upon which we can ride, so to speak; any idea that will carry us prosperously from any one part of our experience to any other part, linking things satisfactorily, working securely, simplifying, saving labour—is true for just so much, true in so far forth, true *instrumentally.* This is the "instrumental" view of truth taught so successfully at Chicago, the view that truth in our ideas means their power to "work," promulgated so brilliantly at Oxford.

Messrs. Dewey, Schiller, and their allies, in reaching this general conception of all truth, have only followed the example of geologists, biologists, and philologists. In the establishment of these other sciences, the successful stroke was always to take some simple process actually observable in operation—as denudation by weather, say, or variation from parental type, or change of dialect by incorporation of new words and pronunciations—and then to generalize it, making it apply to all times, and produce great results by summating its effects through the ages.

The observable process which Schiller and Dewey particularly singled out for generalization is the familiar one by which any individual settles into *new opinions*. The process here is always the same. The individual has a stock of old opinions already, but he meets a new experience that puts them to a strain. Somebody contradicts them; or in a reflective moment he discovers that they contradict each other; or he hears of facts with which they are incompatible; or desires arise in him which they cease to satisfy. The result is an inward trouble to which his mind till then had been a stranger, and from which he seeks to escape by modifying his previous mass of opinions. He saves as much of it as he can, for in this matter of belief we are all extreme conservatives. So he tries to change first this opinion, and then that (for they resist change very variously), until at last some new idea comes up which he can graft upon the ancient stock with a minimum of disturbance of the latter, some idea that mediates between the stock and the new experience and runs them into one another most felicitously and expediently.

This new idea is then adopted as the true one. It preserved the older stock of truths with a minimum of modification, stretching them just enough to make them admit the novelty, but conceiving that in ways as familiar as the case leaves possible. An *outrée* explanation, violating all our preconceptions, would never pass for a true account of a novelty. We should scratch round industriously till we found something less eccentric. The most violent revolutions in an individual's beliefs leave most of his old order standing. Time and space, cause and effect, nature and history, and one's own biography remain untouched. New truth is always a go-between, a smoother-over of transitions. It marries old opinion to new fact so as ever to show a minimum of jolt, a maximum of continuity. We hold a theory true just in proportion to its success in solving this "problem of maxima and minima." But success in solving this problem is eminently a matter of approximation. We say this theory solves it on the whole more satisfactorily than that theory; but that means more satisfactorily to ourselves, and individuals will emphasize their points of satisfaction differently. To a certain degree, therefore, everything here is plastic.

WILLIAM C. BARRETT

•

Existentialism as a Symptom of Man's Contemporary Crisis[1]

Nowadays we speak quite easily and naturally of the crisis through which our civilization is passing. Without questioning the assumption that we are in

[1] From *Spiritual Problems in Contemporary Literature*, edited by Stanley R. Hopper, copyrighted by Harper & Brothers. Used by permission.

the midst of a crisis, I should like to ask whether this feeling of crisis is not something inseparable from human life in any historical period. The more closely we examine the past, the more we find that it, too, is uneasy with its own sense of historical crisis and urgency. Sometimes, in retrospect, these crises look illusory, for mankind has survived some of its worst apprehensions; and then we have to remind ourselves that these men and women of the past felt that bygone crisis in their bones, with the same intimate uneasiness with which we feel ours. We begin to suspect that to live itself is to exist in crisis (more or less actual at any moment), and that only in periods of real historic somnolence and lethargy—real decadence, in short—has mankind been without a sense of crisis. No doubt, there are important differences of degree, and one age may be more plainly a period of breakdown than another; it would be folly to neglect such differences of degree, but the thought that crisis, or the sense of it is a permanent part of human life, does fortify us to see our own contemporary crisis in a much broader light—as a total human condition.

This thought will explain why I prefer to discuss existential philosophy as a symptom, rather than a solution, of our present crisis. For to the degree that we see our crisis as a total and concrete condition, to that degree we shall doubt that any philosophy, no matter how ambitious, can propose itself as the unique path of salvation. Anyone who has had any personal experience of a spiritual crisis will know that recovery does not come through the acquisition of any new abstract ideas. The progress from health to sickness is a change of being, rather than a change in thought. So, if we agree that our civilization is spiritually sick, we should also expect that the recovery will not come through any single set of ideas, or philosophy, but only through a transformation of our whole existence—thus requiring social, economic, and religious change. A new philosophy would be only a necessary *part* of this total change.

Moreover, it is the very characteristic of Existentialism as a philosophy that it must look with irony upon any system of thought that proposes itself as *the* solution for all of life's crises. Let us remember that Kierkegaard, the founder of Existentialism, began to philosophize with the purpose of discovering difficulties, rather than offering easy and readymade solutions. Existentialism as a philosophy attempts to make man aware of certain basic realities of his life. In this sense it seeks to increase, rather than minimize, our human difficulties. The business of finding solutions must come only after a man is aware of the whole depth, import, and, therefore, difficulty, of his human life.

I

This preliminary definition of existential philosophy will be understood better, if we contrast it with the usual kinds of philosophy now taught in our academies. The various schools of philosophy are distinguished from each other by different beliefs. Thus it comes about that a philosophy is understood as a set of beliefs, or propositions, to which a man gives intellectual assent. A man is said to have a philosophy, then, if he has a system of propositions which he holds to be true on purely intellectual or rational grounds. This is the understanding of philosophy that has prevailed particularly in our period of the departmentalization of all human knowledge. But Existentialism seeks to restore a much more primitive sense of the word, "philosophy," than this: namely, the ancient sense of philosophy as a concrete way of life, rather than an abstract set of propositions. Nietzsche, also an Existentialist, pointed out that for ancient man, and even the modern Oriental, the business of achieving a philosophy is one that engaged the whole man, his total being, and was not pursued simply as one specialized department of knowledge among others. Kierkegaard attacked the Hegelian professors of his time as being philosophers without any real philosophic existence: they had a system of propositions to teach, but the system itself was a means of forgetting the concrete realities of human life. For us in America today the philosopher is merely a "professional" savant among many others.

Existentialism, on the contrary, understands philosophy as a thing that is to be lived, and not merely a body of knowledge to be taught to pupils. I have said that Existentialism attempts to bring to human consciousness the basic, even banal, realities of human life: realities such as death, anxiety, choice, love, freedom, guilt, conscience, the willing acceptance of anxiety, etc., etc. In American academic philosophy today these are not the prevailing concepts: philosophers discuss concepts relating to science, knowledge, logic. Existential concepts are thought to belong to literature, perhaps to poetry. This rejection is an evidence of how far one particular tradition among the intellectual elite of our society has tended to set knowledge above life. If the philosopher exists professionally as a member of a department in a university, and if he accepts his role as one that deals with one special department of knowledge among others, then he is inevitably drawn to devote himself to those very special and technical problems that seem to be the peculiar province of the "expert." Our technological civilization has tended more and more to worship the expert and the philosopher, assimilated to his civilization, strives more and more to justify his own professional existence by a high technical competence in the special problems of logic and philosophical analysis. The result is that a great deal of modern philosophy has tended to become divorced from life. Hence it is only natural that Existentialism, which struggles against this tendency, is looked on somewhat askance by a great many American philosophers.

All this has been by way of explaining why it seemed preferable to discuss Existentialism as a symptom, rather than a solution, of our contemporary crisis. But there has also been in the background of my remarks another, and much more drastic point, which will be substantiated by my further discussion, but can be announced now: the point, quite simply, that there is never a solution to any of life's crises. This is one of the cardinal points in existential philosophy itself. The word, "solution," belongs to the vocabulary of science and engineering, suggesting some kind of blueprint that would immediately deliver us from the pain and muddle of suffering, when, in fact, we know that our really deep crises in life are precisely those that we have to live through. Our deepest personal problems do not in the least resemble any problem of engineering, and it is the same, we suggest, with the sickness of civilization, even though the "cure" of a sick civilization might require vast exploits of engineering.

II

That movement in thought should be a symptom of its time, is not in the least a condemnation of this movement as a wild or trivial aberration. I am using the word, "symptom," in its simple and unprejudiced sense of a sign—something that instructs us about the state of the organism from which it arises. Thus Existentialism has a great deal to teach us—which we might otherwise not know—about the condition of the Western civilization that has brought it to birth.

Most Americans connect Existentialism with the current French movement, and particularly with the name of its most brilliant publicist, Jean Paul Sartre. Sartre's is an agile and energetic mind, but his doctrine represents, I believe, a dilution of existential philosophy, and in any case does not take us back to its original sources. These lie in the nineteenth century, and the great innovators are Kierkegaard and Nietzsche—though the latter, unlike Kierkegaard, is not fully aware of his existential point of departure. Existential themes are treated in the fiction of Tolstoi and Dostoievski. In this century the two most important existential philosophers have been the German professors, Martin Heidegger and Karl Jaspers. To these names we might add the considerable figure of the Spanish philosopher, José Ortega y Gasset, who has described his philosophy as one of "vital reason," though it is fundamentally existential in its directions. These names should indicate that Existentialism is not a momentary intellectual fad, derived from the French, but a much wider and deeper movement in Western thought, having roots indeed in the profound upheavals of this civilization during the past two centuries. To see what these roots are, we may find it more convenient to turn, not to an abstruse text in philosophy, but to a work of literature that takes a simpler and more direct grasp of the issues involved: Tolstoi's great story, "The Death of Ivan Ilyich," which by this time has become something of a basic scripture for existential thought.

The plot of Tolstoi's story is slight and almost negligible. Ivan Ilyich is an amiable and undistinguished bourgeois, who has spent his whole life trying to be like everyone else in his social class: a successful and happy man, where happiness means only the absence of suffering. But one day Ivan Ilyich feels a pain in his side, which resists all treatment by doctors, and as his illness progresses, he suddenly realizes that he is going to die. For the first time in his life death becomes a reality for him. In the face of this awful presence, all his disguises fall away: confronting death for the first time in his life, he is also confronting himself for the first time. Hitherto in his life he had hid from himself amid the routine mechanisms of all his social, official, and familial functions. Now, as he is about to die, he asks himself the questions: Who am I? What has been the meaning of my life? In the end Ivan Ilyich dies content, because he has reached the point of knowing that the life he lived was empty, futile, and meaningless.

What Tolstoi is saying here, to put it now as a general thesis, is that modern life has alienated the individual from himself. The materialistic and rationalistic nineteenth century, with its emphasis upon all the bourgeois routines of life, has so externalized the individual that he has lost the feeling and the passion for his own personal existence. Modern man, Tolstoi is saying, has lost the meaning of life, and, as with Ivan Ilyich, it will take nothing less than the presence of death to restore this sense of life.

The sense of decadence haunts the nineteenth century, even at the moments of its most splendid optimism. There is a widespread uneasiness that life has lost its passion, intensity, and meaning; that there has been some secret decline in human vitality. Kierkegaard puts it as eloquently and compactly as one could wish:

> Let others complain that times are bad; I complain that they are petty because they lack passion. Men's thoughts are as flimsy as thin ice and men themselves as insignificant as the thin snow that covers it. Their thoughts are too petty to be sinful. A worm might consider such thoughts to be sinful, but not a man created in the image of God. Their pleasures are circumspect and boring; their passions, sleep; these materialistic souls fulfill their duties, but they collect their usury for it; they believe that although our Lord keeps His accounts in good order, they can hand Him counterfeit. Out with them! This is why my soul always hearkens back to Shakespeare and the Old Testament. There one feels that those who speak are men; there they hate; there they love; there they kill the enemy, curse their descendants for generations to come, there they sin.

This passage might almost have been written by Nietzsche, who launches his plea from the diametrically opposite anti-Christian pole. Modern man, says Nietzsche, lacks a goal, and his existence is, therefore, purposeless and nihilistic. Similar themes appear also in such diverse writers as Stendhal and Burckhardt.

The twentieth century has no reason to forget these fears. Our technological civilization has become even more involved with elaborate apparatus to catch and smother the individual. We have gone beyond the nineteenth century in the development of a fantastic mass culture—in radio, movies, and television—that stamps out all individual differences. Modern society has become more and more a mass society. Cities grow larger, crowds become more and more potent factors, and the individual threatened more than ever by anonymity in the mass. The image of modern man lies in T. S. Eliot's line: "Men and bits of paper, whirled by the cold wind."[2] These fears of the nineteenth century

[2] T. S. Eliot, "Burnt Norton," *Collected Poems of T. S. Eliot, 1909–1935* (New York: Harcourt, Brace & World, Inc., 1936), p. 217.

turn out to be prophetic for us: amid this general purposelessness of life, this mass drifting, we set ourselves the task of recapturing the sense and the meaning of life.

III

When Tolstoi speaks of a loss of the meaning of life, he is not referring to a loss of some rational explanation. Nor is the meaning that is to be restored an intellectual one, some new fact or discovery of the mind. On the contrary, the disorder in modern man that Tolstoi's story speaks of is a disorder in the more primitive and irrational, or non-rational, parts of man's being. Existentialism as a philosophy seeks to deal with these irrational parts of our existence in a way that philosophy has never done before, and by so doing gives reason itself a new place in the human hierarchy.

This is why existential philosophy has been frequently—and, I think, unjustly—criticized as anti-rational. One is not against reason, if one insists that the irrational is an inseparable part of life, and that it is precisely with the irrational parts of our being that modern civilization fails to deal adequately. This so-called "anti-rational" tendency in modern philosophy has now had a long history, from Rousseau to Bergson, Whitehead, and Heidegger in our century, and it embraces too many great names to be dismissed out of hand. Any future rationalism worth its salt will have to assimilate a great deal from these thinkers, and we ourselves would be less than rational, if we did not make an earnest effort to understand in detail how the irrational enters human life.

We gain some idea of the irrational character of life, if we turn back again to Tolstoi's "Ivan Ilyich." As death appears to Ivan Ilyich, it presents itself as something altogether unreasonable and incomprehensible. Immersed in the comfortable structure of his life, he sees this strange and dark intruder creep in to destroy everything. Yet, death is a banal fact, and we know that all men have to die; Ivan Ilyich knows all this with his head, but his heart cannot grasp the incomprehensible fact that he, Ivan Ilyich, should have to die. This bewilderment may strike us as childish, but it is Tolstoi's means of showing us how the irrational, like death, may fall upon us in the most incalculable and unpredictable way, upsetting all our plans for life.

Kierkegaard has expounded the presence of the irrational in another area of human life—in the act of choice or decision. We do not doubt that some decisions are more rational than others, and we may even speak of a decision as being the only rational choice under the circumstances. But is a rational choice one from which the irrational is ever completely excluded? Is any choice, however rational it be, free from the uncertain contingencies of risk and adventure? Of course, there are certain trivial choices that we make every day, and that we may reverse the next day, if we are proved wrong. But these are choices that do not commit us deeply, that leave us relatively disengaged from the consequences. As soon, however, as a choice cuts deeply; as soon as it commits our whole life in a certain direction; so soon, then, do the immense difficulties appear, the balance of probabilities becomes harder, and each alternative appears, however we may canvass its possibilities, as a leap into the unknown.

The choice that personally involved Kierkegaard happened to be the question whether or not to marry. Engaged to a young woman in Copenhagen, he desired marriage intensely, but he felt in himself also a certain religious mission that would prevent him from giving himself completely in marriage. The particular psychological facts involved here are important for an understanding of Kierkegaard's biography, but the peculiarly personal difficulties should not obscure for us the fact that the pathos of choice Kierkegaard faced is universal. There are, in short, choices in life that are irreversible. Kierkegaard could not have made an *experimental* choice of marriage, in the expectation that if it "did not work out"—to use the expression that has become common among us these days—he could return to his religious vocation and its tasks, for the vocation might have been lost through his marriage. On the other hand, if he renounced marriage experimentally, he could not hope to return to the young lady, should the other alternative not work out. She might not be there (as in fact she was not) when he returned. Love has to be seized at the moment it is offered; our indecision pollutes and destroys it.

All of this points to the fact that the situation of human choice is not at all a situation of scientific experiment. A situation is experimental in science when certain scientific controls have been established, so that through these controls we can repeat the experiment at any time and place we choose, and indeed repeat it indefinitely. The more precisely scientific the experiment becomes, the more its features of accidental particularity become refined away, and the easier it becomes to repeat it in all its detail. But our fundamental choices in life do not permit us this degree of control, because they do not permit us this degree of detachment. We have to choose here and now, and for the rest of our life, and the alternative we renounce is lost forever. We could be completely experimental about our own lives only if we were immortal, and so could repeat any situation or choice indefinitely.

But as death is real and our lives finite, every choice is also a renunciation, and this is why Kierkegaard speaks of the *pathos* of human choice. It was this sacrificial and pathetic aspect of choice that led Kierkegaard to his great polemic against the excessively rational philosophy of Hegel. The old adage puts the matter quite simply and adequately, "You cannot eat your cake and have it, too"; but Hegel devised a sophisticated dialectic by which it was possible to bring together two conflicting alternatives, thesis and antithesis, into a higher synthesis, so that the speculative philosopher, triumphing over life, could both have his cake and eat it, too. Such a reconciling of opposites is indeed possible in knowledge, where a more inclusive theory may embrace two conflicting alternatives; but it is not possible in life, where the suffering of renunciation cannot be altogether eliminated by reason. This opposition between knowledge and life has been one of the chief themes of Existentialism, as well as of a great deal of modern philosophy and literature.

IV

These two brief illustrations of the irrational—death and human choice—which cannot be altogether expunged from our existence, also illustrate that science, and scientific experiment, cannot take over the whole of life. The fear that science might devour the whole of human life has been a very powerful current of thought in the West, from William Blake onward. Indeed, from the Enlightenment in the eighteenth century to the present day, two deeply opposed attitudes toward science have dominated Western thinking: along with the great hope in science and its possibilities of human liberation, there has developed a great fear that science would somehow mechanize and impoverish human life. This fear of science cannot be dismissed simply as a crude popular superstition, for it embraces too many great names of our culture: Blake, Wordsworth, Kierkegaard, Nietzsche, Dostoievski, Tolstoi, Bergson. Our task, rather, should be to disengage the philosophical traits that characterize this fear of science at its deepest level.

One of the best expressions of the fear of science is found in the first part of Dostoievski's great novel, *Notes from Underground.* The hero is afraid of the scientific society of the future, in which human life can be rationally controlled and ordered, down to the very last detail. When human life is so scientifically precise and predictable, nobody would want to live it. Dostoievski's hero would prefer to smash this machine that would seek to contain him—out of sheer spite, as he puts it—to show that his human will in its liberty transcends the mathematically predictable, even if he has to show this in a destructive way. We come back thus to our principal point: what Dostoievski is saying, through his tormented and oppressed little hero, is that human life must be more than pure reason, and to attempt to reduce it to the latter is to destroy it, even if we make that reduction in the name of universal enlightenment.

It would be a mistake to consider the Underground Man as merely a sick and neurotic individual produced by the stresses of modern society. He is that, of course, but he is also a universal human character. We are all the Underground Man, to some degree or other. He is that dark side of our being, with which we must try to live in peace, and if we take lightly his fulminations against a human regime completely controlled by science and reason, we do so at our own risk.

As he is thus universal, the Underground Man reappears, and perhaps I may drive home my point by turning to the rather extraordinary position advanced in the nineteen hundred and twenties by I. A. Richards, the British critic and psychologist—a position that seems to me to express the extreme of hope that science will master life. (In justice to Richards, however, we must point out that at the time he was much more enamored of the possibilities of psychology than he is today.) Richards contended nothing less than this: that we can anticipate the time when psychological science will have advanced to the point where we can have, if we choose, whatever minds we desire. In the perfectly scientific utopia, in short, you could order your personality at a psychological laboratory the way you might order a prescription at a druggist's. Select your label, follow the prescription carefully, and you will have the personality, or the mind, that you want. Science which has performed so many miracles in the transformation of matter, and has found synthetic substitutes for almost everything, would here have found at last a substitute for life itself. In this psychological utopia it would be possible for a man to have a certain character without living through the risks, anxieties, and uncertain struggles that make it. We need not live to become a certain kind of being; science would provide it readymade.

We notice that this possibility that once inspired Richards with such hopes, is precisely the possibility against which Dostoievski's Underground Man rebels. Sick and resentful though he may be, the Underground Man at least insists upon having his own human life, rather than some mechanized substitute for it. The science of psychology has gone on developing since Richards's remark, but it is now further from maintaining any such utopian claims as once enchanted him. Among some circles in America, psychoanalysis may be regarded as a kind of magic, but not by the analysts themselves. Some people tend to think of psychoanalysis as a process in which the analyst, somewhat like a mechanic, overhauls the patient and gives him a new engine or set of works. But the serious analyst, while hoping to transform the neurotic patient's fundamental orientations toward life, insists that the patient can solve his problems only in actual life and not in the psychoanalytic session. Life has to be lived, there is no substitute for living—not even psychoanalysis.

Existential philosophy, in its insistence that the categories of life cannot be reduced to science, carries this point further. It may seem a rather trivial platitude to say that there can be no substitute for living, but the saying may not strike us as so platitudinous when we reflect upon the vast mechanized passivity that our civilization imposes upon so many of its members. In such circumstances the living rediscovery of certain banalities may represent an immense task and an immense triumph. Some of the greatest chapters in the history of philosophy are its discoveries of what lay obvious, but unnoticed, before every man's eyes. We may recall the great saying of Heraclitus, at the very dawn of philosophy in the sixth century B.C.: "Man is estranged from that with which he is most familiar, and he must continuously seek to rediscover it." This saying might serve as a very good motto for Existentialism. Among other things, it may make clear why the modern Existentialist, Heidegger, finds these early pre-Socratic Greeks his real forebears in the effort to confront human life and the whole life of nature with a primitive directness. The ancestry of existential philosophy thus turns out to be very ancient. I come back thus to a point made at the beginning, which should now be considerably clearer in its import: Existentialism, a modern movement in philosophy, is, in fact, an effort to recapture an old and very primitive sense of philosophy. Philosophy, here, is not the mere putting together of certain abstract propositions into a system; it is rather the concrete effort of the living individual to relate himself to his own life and the life of others around him. Quite literally, philosophy is a task that each individual has to perform for himself.

V

In this search for the primitive, Existentialism is in line with the most considerable movements in art and literature in this century. The word, "primitive," here is bound to arouse misunderstandings, if it is associated with the life of savages, barbarians, or big game hunters. Primitivism suggests to some the beat of tom-toms, Tahiti, maidens in sarongs, Gauguin; in short, an escape from modern civilization into the illusory simplicities of some South Sea island. These forms of primitivism have abounded, but they have always ended in a blind alley, because the desire for escape is itself a very nonprimitive state of being. I am using the word, "primitive," in a much more basic—I almost wrote primitive—sense: the primitive is the primary; and the valid search for the primitive is a search for the sources of our being which a too routinized civilization tends to obscure. In this sense, nearly all the art and literature that matter in the past half century have been primitive.

Modern painting and sculpture, for example, have really succeeded in creating a new kind of vision. In these works we stand in a new and more direct relation to colors, shapes, and forms. It is a vision of things at once simpler and more complex than the Western art of the past. In its distorting simplifications, bold arbitrary forms, it often resembles primitive art, from which indeed it has consciously drawn inspiration in certain cases, though it could not exist without the whole tradition of Western art. Moreover, the artist himself seems to stand in a new and direct relation to the very materials of his art: he seeks naïvely to assert the presence of his paint, stone, or metal, and his art is no longer a device to conceal or transcend this presence.

In literature, in writers such as D. H. Lawrence, James Joyce, and Thomas Mann, we find similar and diverging efforts to deal with the primitive. In his Joseph stories, Mann seeks to restore the primitive mythic consciousness to literature. James Joyce, in his last work, uses the most sophisticated literary technique, drawing upon the whole past of Western literature for its resources, in order to render the most unconscious, inarticulate, and primitive parts of human experience. Of these writers perhaps Lawrence is the most explicitly programmatic in his search for the primitive simplicities that he believes modern life to have lost. The organic unity of being that Lawrence seeks through sexual experience, is something that existential philosophers have sought in other directions. As T. S. Eliot reminds us, Lawrence was a man with an intense spiritual vocation, and his interest in sex was not at all a message of sex-for-sex's sake. Nevertheless, his proposed solution to the sickness of modern civilization seems to us today to be rather onesided. His perception of the sickness was real enough, but his prescription for cure represents a kind of impatient rush toward a solution. We are reminded, again, that when a sickness is total, the recovery can come only through development along many avenues of being at once.

This list could be swelled indefinitely to show that this struggle for rebirth is one of the great themes of modern culture. I have appended these brief indications to my main discussion only to point to the total historical context in which we must try to see the development of modern existential philosophy; and to suggest that this philosophy is not an eccentric movement, but lies in the main stream of modern culture. Existentialism makes clearer the human tasks that our epoch confronts. Unless we realize what the tasks are, we can hardly work significantly toward any solution at all.

Can Philosophy Save Civilization?

BERTRAND RUSSELL

•

The Value of Philosophy[1]

Having now come to the end of our brief and very incomplete review of the problems of philosophy, it will be well to consider, in conclusion, what is the value of philosophy and why it ought to be studied. It is the more necessary to consider this question, in view of the fact that many men, under the influence of science or of practical affairs, are inclined to doubt whether philosophy is anything better than innocent but useless trifling, hair-splitting distinctions, and controversies on matters concerning which knowledge is impossible.

This view of philosophy appears to result, partly from a wrong conception of the ends of life, partly from a wrong conception of the kind of goods which philosophy strives to achieve. Physical science, through the medium of inventions, is useful to innumerable people who are wholly ignorant of it; thus the study of physical science is to be recommended, not only, or primarily, because of the effect on the student, but rather because of the effect on mankind in general. This utility does not belong to philosophy. If the study of philosophy has any value at all for others than students of philosophy, it must be only indirectly, through its effects upon the lives of those who study it. It is in these effects, therefore, if anywhere, that the value of philosophy must be primarily sought.

But further, if we are not to fail in our endeavour to determine the value of philosophy, we must first free our minds from the prejudices of what are wrongly called "practical" men. The "practical" man, as this word is often used, is one who recognises only material needs, who realises that men must have food for the body, but is oblivious of the necessity of providing food for the mind. If all men were well off, if poverty and disease had been reduced to their lowest possible point, there would still remain much to be done to produce a valuable society; and even in the existing world the goods of the mind are at least as important as the goods of the body. It is exclusively among the goods of the mind that the value of philosophy is to be found; and only those who are not indifferent to these goods can be persuaded that the study of philosophy is not a waste of time.

[1] From *Problems of Philosophy* by Bertrand Russell. A Galaxy Book, 1959. Reprinted by permission of Oxford University Press, Inc.

Philosophy, like all other studies, aims primarily at knowledge. The knowledge it aims at is the kind of knowledge which gives unity and system to the body of the sciences, and the kind which results from a critical examination of the grounds of our convictions, prejudices, and beliefs. But it cannot be maintained that philosophy has had any very great measure of success in its attempts to provide definite answers to its questions. If you ask a mathematician, a mineralogist, a historian, or any other man of learning, what definite body of truths has been ascertained by his science, his answer will last as long as you are willing to listen. But if you put the same question to a philosopher, he will, if he is candid, have to confess that his study has not achieved positive results such as have been achieved by other sciences. It is true that this is partly accounted for by the fact that, as soon as definite knowledge concerning any subject becomes possible, this subject ceases to be called philosophy, and becomes a separate science. The whole study of the heavens, which now belongs to astronomy, was once included in philosophy; Newton's great work was called "the mathematical principles of natural philosophy." Similarly, the study of the human mind, which was, until very lately, a part of philosophy, has now been separated from philosophy and has become the science of psychology. Thus, to a great extent, the uncertainty of philosophy is more apparent than real: those questions which are already capable of definite answers are placed in the sciences, while those only to which, at present, no definite answer can be given, remain to form the residue which is called philosophy.

This is, however, only a part of the truth concerning the uncertainty of philosophy. There are many questions—and among them those that are of the profoundest interest to our spiritual life—which, so far as we can see, must remain insoluble to the human intellect unless its powers become of quite a different order from what they are now. Has the universe any unity of plan or purpose, or is it a fortuitous concourse of atoms? Is consciousness a permanent part of the universe, giving hope of indefinite growth in wisdom, or is it a transitory accident on a small planet on which life must ultimately become impossible? Are good and evil of importance to the universe or only to man? Such questions are asked by philosophy, and variously answered by various philosophers. But it would seem that, whether answers be otherwise discoverable or not, the answers suggested by philosophy are none of them demonstrably true. Yet, however slight may be the hope of discovering an answer, it is part of the business of philosophy to continue the consideration of such questions, to make us aware of their importance, to examine all the approaches to them, and to keep alive that speculative interest in the universe which is apt to be killed by confining ourselves to definitely ascertainable knowledge.

Many philosophers, it is true, have held that philosophy could establish the truth of certain answers to such fundamental questions. They have supposed that what is of most importance in religious beliefs could be proved by strict demonstration to be true. In order to judge of such attempts, it is necessary to take a survey of human knowledge, and to form an opinion as to its methods and its limitations. On such a subject it would be unwise to pronounce dogmatically; but if the investigations of our previous chapters have not led us astray, we shall be compelled to renounce the hope of finding philosophical proofs of religious beliefs. We cannot, therefore, include as part of the value of philosophy any definite set of answers to such questions. Hence, once more, the value of philosophy must not depend upon any supposed body of definitely ascertainable knowledge to be acquired by those who study it.

The value of philosophy is, in fact, to be sought largely in its very uncertainty. The man who has no tincture of philosophy goes through life imprisoned in the prejudices derived from common sense, from the habitual beliefs of his age or his nation, and from convictions which have grown up in his mind without the co-operation or consent of his deliberate reason. To such a man the world tends to become definite, finite, obvious; common objects rouse no questions, and unfamiliar possibilities are contemptuously rejected. As soon as we begin to philosophise, on the contrary, we find, as we saw in our opening chapters, that even the most everyday things lead to problems to which only very incomplete answers can be given. Philosophy, though unable to tell us with certainty what is the true answer to the doubts which it raises, is able to suggest many possibilities which enlarge our thoughts and free them from the tyranny of custom. Thus, while diminishing our feeling of certainty as to what things are, it greatly increases our knowledge as to what they may be; it removes the somewhat arrogant dogmatism of those who have never travelled into the region of liberating doubt, and it keeps alive our sense of wonder by showing familiar things in an unfamiliar aspect.

Apart from its utility in showing unsuspected possibilities, philosophy has a value—perhaps its chief value—through the greatness of the objects which it contemplates, and the freedom from narrow and personal aims resulting from this contemplation. The life of the instinctive man is shut up within the circle of his private interests: family and friends may be included, but the outer world is not regarded except as it may help or hinder what comes within the circle of instinctive wishes. In such a life there is something feverish and confined, in comparison with which the philosophic life is calm and free. The private world of instinctive interests is a small one, set in the midst of a great and powerful world which must, sooner or later, lay our private world in ruins. Unless we can so enlarge our interests as to include the whole outer world, we remain like a garrison in a beleaguered fortress, knowing that the enemy prevents escape and that ultimate surrender is inevitable. In such a life there is no peace, but a constant strife between the insistence of desire and the powerlessness of will. In one way or another, if our life is to be great and free, we must escape this prison and this strife.

One way of escape is by philosophic contemplation. Philosophic contemplation does not, in its widest survey, divide the universe into two hostile camps—friends and foes, helpful and hostile, good and bad—it views the whole impartially. Philosophic contemplation when it is unalloyed, does not aim at proving that the rest of the universe is akin to man. All acquisition of knowledge is an enlargement of the Self, but this enlargement is best attained when it is not directly sought. It is obtained when the desire for knowledge is alone operative, by a study which does not wish in advance that its objects should have this or that character, but adapts the Self to the characters which it finds in its objects. This enlargement of Self is not obtained when, taking the Self as it is, we try to show that the world is so similar to this Self that knowledge of it is possible without any admission of what seems alien. The desire to prove this is a form of self-assertion, and like all self-assertion, it is an obstacle to the growth of Self which it desires, and of which the Self knows that it is capable. Self-assertion, in philosophic speculation as elsewhere, views the world as a means to its own ends; thus it makes the world of less account than Self, and the Self sets bounds to the greatness of its goods. In contemplation, on the contrary, we start from the not-Self, and through its greatness the boundaries of Self are enlarged; through the infinity of the universe the mind which contemplates it achieves some share in infinity.

For this reason greatness of soul is not fostered by those philosophies which assimilate the universe to Man. Knowledge is a form of union of Self and not-Self; like all union, it is impaired by dominion, and therefore by any attempt to force the universe into conformity with what we find in ourselves. There is a widespread philosophical tendency towards the view which tells us that man is the measure of all things, that truth is man-made, that space and time and the world of universals are properties of the mind, and that, if there be anything not created by the mind, it is unknowable and of no account for us. This view, if our previous discussions were correct, is untrue; but in addition to being untrue, it has the effect of robbing philosophic contemplation of all that gives it value, since it fetters contemplation to Self. What it calls knowledge is not a union with the not-Self, but a set of prejudices, habits, and desires, making an impenetrable veil between us and the world beyond. The man who finds pleasure in such a theory of knowledge is like the man who never leaves the domestic circle for fear his word might not be law.

The true philosophic contemplation, on the contrary, finds its satisfaction in every enlargement of the not-Self, in everything that magnifies the objects contemplated, and thereby the subject contemplating. Everything, in contemplation, that is personal or private, everything that depends upon habit, self-interest, or desire, distorts the object, and hence impairs the union which the intellect seeks. By thus making a barrier between subject and object, such personal and private things become a prison to the intellect. The free intellect will see as God might see, without a *here* and *now,* without hopes and fears, without the trammels of customary beliefs and traditional prejudices, calmly, dispassionately, in the sole and exclusive desire of knowledge—knowledge as impersonal, as purely contemplative, as it is possible for man to attain. Hence also the free intellect will value more the abstract and universal knowledge into which the accidents of private history do not enter, than the knowledge brought by the senses, and dependent, as such knowledge must be, upon an exclusive and personal point of view and a body whose sense-organs distort as much as they reveal.

The mind which has become accustomed to the freedom and impartiality of philosophic contemplation will preserve something of the same freedom and impartiality in the world of action and emotion. It will view its purposes and desires as parts of the whole, with the absence of insistence that results from seeing them as infinitesimal fragments in a world of which all the rest is unaffected by any one man's deeds. The impartiality which, in contemplation, is the unalloyed desire for truth, is the very same quality of mind which, in action, is justice, and in emotion is that universal love which can be given to all, and not only to those who are judged useful or admirable. Thus contemplation enlarges not only the objects of our thoughts, but also the objects of our actions and our affections: it makes us citizens of the universe, not only of one walled city at war with all the rest. In this citizenship of the universe consists man's true freedom, and his liberation from the thraldom of narrow hopes and fears.

Thus, to sum up our discussion of the value of philosophy: Philosophy is to be studied, not for the sake of any definite answers to its questions, since no definite answers can, as a rule, be known to be true, but rather for the sake of the questions themselves; because these questions enlarge our conception of what is possible, enrich our intellectual imagination, and diminish the dogmatic assurance which closes the mind against speculation; but above all because, through the greatness of the universe which philosophy contemplates, the mind also is rendered great, and becomes capable of that union with the universe which constitutes its highest good.

ERICH FROMM

•

The Present Human Condition[1]

At the close of the middle ages, Western man seemed to be headed for the final fulfillment of his keenest dreams and visions. He freed himself from the authority of a totalitarian church, the weight of traditional thought, the geographical limitations of our but half-discovered globe. He built a new science which eventually has led to the release of hitherto unheard-of productive

[1] From *The American Scholar,* XXV (Winter, 1955–56), 29–35. Copyright 1956 by Erich Fromm and reprinted with his permission.

powers, and to the complete transformation of the material world. He created political systems which seem to guarantee the free and productive development of the individual; he reduced the time of work to such a level that man was free to enjoy hours of leisure to an extent his forefathers had hardly dreamed of.

YET WHERE ARE WE TODAY?

The danger of an all-destructive war hangs over the head of humanity, a danger which is by no means overcome by the spirit of Geneva prevalent at the time of this writing. But even if man's political representatives have enough sanity left to avoid a war, man's condition is far from the fulfillment of the hopes of the sixteenth, seventeenth and eighteenth centuries.

Man's character has been molded by the demands of the world he has built with his own hands. In the eighteenth and nineteenth centuries, man's character orientation was essentially exploitative and hoarding. His course through life was determined by the desire to exploit others and to save his earnings to make further profit from them. In the twentieth century, man's character orientation is essentially a receptive and a marketing one. He is receptive in most of his leisure time. He is the eternal consumer; he "takes in" drink, food, cigarettes, lectures, sights, books, movies—all are consumed, swallowed. The world is one great object for his appetite, a big bottle, a big apple, a big breast. Man has become the suckler, the eternally expectant—and the eternally disappointed one.

If "privately," individually, modern man is a consumer, he is "publicly," in his active participation in his society, a trader. Our economic system is centered around the function of the market as determining the value of all commodities, and as the regulator of each one's share in the social product. Neither force nor tradition, as in previous periods of history, nor fraud or trickery govern man's economic activities. He is free to produce and to sell; market day is judgment day for the success of his efforts. Not only are commodities offered and sold on the market; labor itself has become a commodity, sold on the labor market under the same conditions of fair competition. But the market system has reached out farther than the economic sphere of commodities and labor. Man has transformed *himself* into a commodity, experiences his life as capital to be invested profitably; if he succeeds in this, he is "successful," and his life has meaning; if not, "he is a failure." His "value" lies in his salability, not in his human qualities of love and reason or in his artistic capacities. Hence his sense of his own value depends on extraneous factors, his success, the judgment of others. Hence he is dependent on these others, and his security lies in conformity, in never being more than two feet away from the herd.

However, it is not only the market which determines modern man's "public" character. Another factor, though one closely related to the market function, is the mode of industrial production. Enterprises become bigger and bigger; the number of people employed by these enterprises as workers or clerks grows incessantly; ownership is separated from management, and the industrial giants are governed by a professional bureaucracy which is mainly interested in the smooth functioning and in the expansion of their enterprise, rather than in profit per se.

What kind of man, then, does our society need in order to function smoothly? It needs men who co-operate smoothly in large groups; who want to consume more and more, and whose tastes are standardized and can be easily influenced and anticipated. It needs men who feel free and independent, who do not feel subject to any authority or principle or conscience, yet are willing to be commanded, to do what is expected, to fit unto the social machine without friction—men who can be guided without force, led without leaders, be prompted without any aim except the one to be on the move, to function, to go ahead. Modern capitalism has succeeded in producing this kind of man; he is the automaton, the alienated man. He is alienated in the sense that his acts and forces have become estranged from him; they stand above and against him, and rule him rather than being ruled by him. His life forces have flowed into things and institutions, and these things, having become idols, are not experienced as the result of his own efforts, but as something apart from him which he worships and to which he submits. Alienated man bows down before the works of his own hands. His idols represent his own life forces in an alienated form. Man does not experience himself as the active bearer of his own forces and riches, but as an impoverished "thing," dependent on other things—things outside himself, into which he has projected his living substance.

Man's social feelings are projected into the state. Just because he has made the state the embodiment of his own social feelings, he worships it and its symbols. He projects his sense of power, wisdom and courage into his leaders, and he worships them as his idols. As a worker, clerk or manager, modern man is alienated from his work. The worker has become an economic atom that dances to the tune of automatized management. He has no part in planning the work process, in its outcome; he is hardly ever in touch with the whole product. The manager, on the other hand, is in touch with the whole product, but he is alienated from it as something concrete and useful. His aim is to employ profitably the capital invested by others; the commodity is the abstractified embodiment of capital, not something which, as a concrete entity, matters to him. The manager has become a bureaucrat who handles things, figures and human beings as mere objects of his activity. Their manipulation is considered to be a concern with human relations, when actually one deals with the most inhuman relations—those between abstractified automatons.

Our consumption is equally alienated. It is determined by the advertising slogans, rather than by our palates, eyes or ears.

As a citizen, then, modern man is willing even to give his life for his fellow men; as a private individual, he is filled with an egotistical concern for himself. The meaninglessness and alienation of work result in a longing for complete laziness. Man hates his working life because it makes him feel a prisoner and a fraud. His ideal becomes absolute laziness, in which he will not have to make a move, where everything goes according to the Kodak slogan: "You press the button; we do the rest." This tendency is reinforced by the type of consumption necessary for the expansion of the inner market, leading to a principle which Huxley has very succinctly expressed in his *Brave New World.* One might epitomize the way many of us today have been conditioned from childhood with: "Never put off till tomorrow the fun you can have today." If I do not postpone the satisfaction of my wish (and I am conditioned only to wish for what I can get), I have no conflicts, no doubts; no decision has to be made; I am never alone with myself because I am always busy—either working or having fun. I have no need to be aware of myself as myself because I am constantly absorbed with consuming. I am a system of desires and satisfactions; I have to work in order to fulfill my desires, and these very desires are constantly stimulated and directed by the economic machine.

We claim that we pursue the aims of the Judaeo-Christian tradition, the love of God and of our neighbor. We are even told that we are going through a period of a promising religious renaissance. Nothing could be further from the truth. We use symbols belonging to a genuinely religious tradition, and transform them into formulas serving the purposes of alienated man. Religion becomes a self-help device for increasing one's own powers for success. God becomes a partner in business. The "Power of Positive Thinking" is the successor of "How to Make Friends and Influence People."

Love of man is a rare phenomenon too. Automatons do not love; alienated men do not care. What is praised by love experts and marriage counselors is a team relationship between two people who manipulate each other with the right techniques, and whose love is essentially a haven from an otherwise unbearable aloneness, an egotism *à deux.*

What, then, can be expected from the future? If one ignores those thoughts produced by our wishes, one has to admit, I am afraid, that the most likely possibility is still that the discrepancy between technical intelligence and reason will lead the world into an atomic war. The most likely outcome of such a war is the destruction of industrial civilization and the regression of the world to a primitive agrarian level. Or, if the destruction should not prove to be as thorough as many specialists in the field believe, the result will be the necessity for the victor to organize and dominate the whole world. This could be realized only by a centralized state based on force, and it would make little difference whether Moscow or Washington would be the seat of government.

But, unfortunately, even the avoidance of war does not in itself promise a bright future. In the development of both capitalism and communism as we can visualize them in the next fifty or a hundred years, the process of automatization and alienation will proceed. Both these systems are developing managerial societies in which inhabitants are well fed and well clad, having their wishes satisfied, and not having wishes that cannot be satisfied; automatons, who follow without force, who are guided without leaders, who make machines that act like men and produce men who act like machines; men whose reason deteriorates while their intelligence rises, thus creating the dangerous situation of equipping man with the greatest material power without the wisdom to use it.

In spite of increasing production and comfort, man loses more and more the sense of self, feels that his life is meaningless, even though such feeling is largely unconscious. In the nineteenth century the problem was that *God is dead;* in the twentieth century the problem is that *man is dead.* In the nineteenth century inhumanity meant cruelty; in the twentieth century it means schizoid self-alienation. The danger of the past was that men became slaves. The danger of the future is that men may become robots. True enough, robots do not rebel. But given man's nature, robots cannot live and remain sane. They become "golems"; they will destroy their world and themselves because they cannot stand any longer the boredom of a meaningless life.

What is the alternative to war and robotism? Most fundamentally, perhaps, the answer could be given by reversing Emerson's phrase: "Things are in the saddle and ride mankind," and saying: "Put mankind in the saddle so that it rides things." This is another way of saying that man must overcome the alienation which makes him an impotent and irrational worshiper of idols. This means, if we remain in the psychological sphere, that he must overcome the marketing and receptive orientation which dominates him now, and emerge into the mature, productive orientation. He must acquire again a sense of self, he must be capable of loving, and of making his work a meaningful and concrete activity. He must emerge from a materialistic orientation and arrive at a level where spiritual values, love, truth and justice truly become of ultimate concern to him. But any attempt to change only one section of life, the human or spiritual one, is doomed to failure. In fact, any progress which occurs only in one sphere is destructive of progress in all spheres. The gospel concerned only with spiritual salvation led to the establishment of the Roman Catholic Church; the French Revolution, with its exclusive concern with political reform, led to Robespierre and Napoleon; socialism, insofar as it was only concerned with economic change, led to Stalinism.

Applying this principle of simultaneous change to all spheres of life, we must think of those economic and political changes which are necessary in order to overcome the psychological fact of alienation. We must retain the industrial method. But we must decentralize work and the state so as to give them *human* proportions, and permit centralization only to an optimal point which is necessary because of the requirements of industry. In the economic sphere we need co-management of all who work in an enterprise to permit their active and responsible participation. The new forms for such participation can be found. In the political sphere, we must return to the town meeting by creating thousands of small face-to-face groups which are well informed, which discuss, and whose decisions are integrated in a new "lower house." A cultural renaissance must combine work education for the young, adult education, and a new system of popular art and secular ritual throughout the whole nation.

Just as primitive man was helpless before the natural forces, modern man is helpless before the social and economic forces created by himself. He worships the works of his own hands, bowing to the new idols, yet swearing by the name of the God who commanded him to destroy all idols. Man can protect himself from the consequences of his own madness only by creating a sane society which conforms with the needs of man, needs which are rooted in the very conditions of his existence: a society in which man relates to man lovingly, in which he is rooted in bonds of brotherliness and solidarity, rather than in the ties of blood and soil; a society which gives him the possibility of transcending nature by creating rather than by destroying; one in which everyone gains a sense of self by experiencing himself as the subject of his powers rather than by conformity; one in which a system of orientation and devotion exists without man's needing to distort reality and to worship idols.

Building such a society means taking the next step; it means the end of "humanoid" history, the phase in which man has not become fully human. It does not mean the "end of days," the "completion," the state of perfect harmony in which no conflicts or problems confront man. On the contrary, it is man's fate that his existence is beset by contradictions which he is impelled to solve without ever solving them. When he has overcome the primitive state of human sacrifice, be it in the ritualistic form of the Aztecs or in the secular form of war; when he has been able to regulate his relationship with nature reasonably instead of blindly; when things have truly become his servants rather than his idols—he will be confronted with the truly human conflicts and problems. He will have to be adventuresome, courageous, imaginative, capable of suffering and of joy, but his powers will be in the service of life, and not in the service of death. The new phase of human history, if it comes to pass, will be a beginning, not an end.

Biographical Notes

ARISTOTLE (384–322 B.C.), versatile Greek philosopher, was a student of Plato. He was appointed by Philip of Macedon to tutor his son, Alexander the Great. Later he returned to Athens where he lectured to many disciples and wrote his numerous works on poetry, logic, natural science, politics, rhetoric, philosophy, and metaphysics. His influence, particularly great during the Middle Ages, continues to this day.

SAINT AUGUSTINE (354–430), one of the Fathers of the Church, was bishop of Hippo in northern Africa after 395. His *Confessions* (*c.* 400) is a classic of Christian devotion. In *The City of God* (c. 412), St. Augustine gives his views of a Christian society. He is also author of *On the Trinity* and forty other theological treatises controverting Manichaens and other heretics.

FRANCIS BACON (1561–1626), scientist, philosopher, and man of letters, became Lord Chancellor of England. His works, which have influenced the development of human thought and progress, include *The Advancement of Learning* (1605), *Instauratio Magna,* and *Novum Organum* (1627).

WILLIAM C. BARRETT (1913–), formerly editor of *Pa tisan Review,* is a member of the Department of Philosophy at New York University. He has taught at the University of Illinois and at Brown University. Besides contributing to the periodicals, he has written *What is Existentialism?* (1947). *Irrational Man* (1958), and *Philosophy in the Twentieth Century* (1961).

WALTER JACKSON BATE (1918–) is Abbot Lawrence Lowell professor of humanities at Harvard. His *John Keats* (1963), one of several books he has written on Keats, received the Pulitzer Prize. Among his other books are *From Classic to Romantic* (1946) and *The Achievement of Samuel Johnson* (1955).

GEORGE BEADLE (1903–) was educated at the University of Nebraska and Cornell, where he took his Ph.D. His distinguished career as a professor of biology includes teaching at Cornell, California Institute of Technology, Harvard, Stanford, and Oxford. He is now Chancellor of the University of Chicago. In 1958 he received the Nobel Prize in medicine and physiology. He has been honored with many other degrees and awards. He is author of *An Introduction to Genetics* (1939) and of many scientific papers. In 1953 he married Muriel Barnett, with whom he wrote *The Language of Life* (1966).

DANIEL BELL (1919–), chairman of the Department of Sociology at Columbia University, was born in New York City and educated at City College and Columbia. He has also taught at the University of Chicago. He has written for *The New Leader, Common Sense,* and *Fortune* and has contributed to the learned journals. He is author of *Work and Its Discontents* (1956), *The New American Right* (1955), *The End of Ideology* (1960), *The Radical Right* (1963), and *The Reforming of General Education* (1966). He is one of the editors of *Daedalus* and *The American Scholar* and is a Fellow of the American Academy of Arts and Sciences.

CLAUDE BERNARD (1813–1878), French physiologist and opponent of "vitalism," carried out experimental investigation on nerves and chemical research. He discovered the function of the vasomotor nerves. His theory of the "interior environment" has been of major importance. Two of his books are *An Introduction to Experimental Medicine* (1865) and *General Physiology* (1872).

MORRIS GILBERT BISHOP (1893–), scholar and former teacher of Romance Languages at Cornell University, is also known as a satirist and humorist. He has published biographical and critical works on Cabeza de Vaca, Pascal, and Ronsard, and a number of volumes of humorous poems and sketches, as well as *A History of Cornell* (1962).

DIETRICH BONHOEFFER (1906–1945), German theologian, was educated at the University of Berlin. After a brief pastorate in Barcelona and study at Union Theological Seminary in New York, he became a professor at Berlin, and taught there until forbidden to do so by the Nazis. Returning from America to Germany at the beginning of World War II, he became involved in the Resistance Movement. He was arrested by the Nazis in 1943 and executed two years later.

WAYNE C. BOOTH (1921–) received his graduate training at the University of Chicago, where he is now Pullman professor of English and dean of the college. He has been a Ford Fellow and a Guggenheim Fellow. He is the author of *The Rhetoric of Fiction* (1961) and of many articles on literature, rhetoric, and the teaching of English.

CLEANTH BROOKS (1906–) is Gray professor of Rhetoric at Yale. Probably he has been the most influential of the New Critics in contemporary letters. In addition to collaborating on a group of distinguished college textbooks, he has written *Modern Poetry and the Tradition* (1939), (with W. K. Wimsatt, Jr.) *Literary Criticism: A Short History* (1957), and *The Hidden God: Studies in Hemingway, Faulkner, Yeats, Eliot, and Warren* (1963) among others.

ROLLO WALTER BROWN (1880–), author and teacher, was born in Ohio. He has taught English at Carleton College and Harvard, lectured, contributed to magazines, and written a number of books, among which are *Next Door to a Poet* (1937), *The Writer's Art* (1921), *Harvard Yard in the Golden Age* (1948), and *Dr. Howe and the Forsyth Infirmary* (1952).

ART BUCHWALD (1925–), newspaper columnist, was born in New York and educated at the University of Southern California. During the Second World War he served as a sergeant in the Marines. He began writing in 1948 for the Paris edition of the New York *Herald Tribune*. He is also author of a number of books, among which are *Paris After Dark* (1950), *Art Buchwald's Paris* (1954), *Is It Safe to Drink the Water?* (1962).

MARTIN BUBER (1878–1965), Jewish theologian and philosopher, was a native of Vienna. He did much to interpret Judaism to contemporary America. The present selection is substantially a lecture which he delivered in 1951 at a number of American universities. Among his books are *I and Thou* (1923), *Israel and the World* (1948), *Good and Evil* (1952), *Pointing the Way* (1957), *I And Thou* (1958), *Hasidism and Modern Man* (1958), *and The Origin and Meaning of Hasidism* (1960).

GAUTAMA BUDDHA (c. 563–c. 483), born an Indian prince, renounced his royal state about 533 B.C. and spent the remainder of his life teaching throughout Northern India. Tradition holds that spiritual emancipation and enlightenment came to him at Buddh Gaya, from which his name (the enlightened one) derives.

INGRAM BYWATER (1841–1914) was an English Hellenist and translator of Aristotle.

AARON COPLAND (1900–) has composed numerous symphonies, sonatas, concertos, film scores, and opera. Among his more recent works are *Tender Land* (opera, 1954), *Piano Fantasy* (1957), and *Music for a Great City* (1964).

RONALD S. CRANE (1886–) was for many years chairman of the English Department at the University of Chicago, where he is now Distinguished Service Professor Emeritus. In 1952 he edited *Critics and Criticism, Ancient and Modern. The Language of Criticism and the Structure of Poetry* (1953) is another of his books.

ROBERT GORHAM DAVIS (1908–), a graduate of Harvard, is professor of English at Columbia University. The author of many critical essays and reviews, he has also published short stories. He has written *Ten Modern Masters* (1959) and *John Dos Passos* (1962).

CARL N. DEGLER (1921–), professor of history at Vassar College, took his Ph.D. at Columbia. He has written *Out of Our Past: the Forces That Shaped Modern America* (1959) and has contributed to periodicals.

RENÉ DESCARTES (1596–1650) was the French philosopher whose system did much to sweep aside the subtleties of medieval thinkers and thus to influence greatly the formation of the modern mind. A mathematician as well as a philosopher, Descartes aimed at the ideal of mathematical certitude in metaphysical problems. His principal works are *Discours de la Methode, Meditationes de Prima Philosophia,* and *Principia Philosophiae.*

JOHN DONNE (1573–1631), the famous Dean of St. Paul's and metaphysical poet, was born a Roman Catholic. After his conversion to the Anglican Church he took holy orders at the suggestion of King James I, who was pleased to grant him several preferments in the Church, culminating in the Deanship of St. Paul's. Though Donne in early youth was worldly, and wrote some of the most passionate love poetry in English literature, he became fervent in spirit and zealous for the Lord. His sermons, many of them preached before Charles I, are among the most eloquent in all English pulpit oratory. His *Devotions,* occasioned by a grave illness, were written in 1623. Donne is considered one of the greatest of English prose writers by many critics.

HUBERT L. DREYFUS, associate professor of philosophy at Massachusetts Institute of Technology, received his Ph.D. from Harvard University. His published works include articles and reviews on Heidegger, Sartre, and Merleau-Ponty, and a Rand Corporation paper entitled "Alchemy and Artificial Intelligence."

THOMAS STEARNS ELIOT (1888–1965), born in St. Louis and graduated from Harvard, became a British subject in 1927. He is famous as a poet, critic, and playwright (*Complete Poems and Plays,* 1952, and *Selected Essays,* 1950).

SIR ARTHUR STANLEY EDDINGTON (1882–1944), English physicist and astronomer, made distinguished contributions to astrophysics and the theory of relativity with such books as *Space, Time and Gravitation* (1920), *The Internal Constitution of the Stars* (1926), and *The Expanding Universe* (1933).

FRANCIS FERGUSSON (1904–), professor of comparative literature at Rutgers University, is a literary critic with a special interest in the theater. His translations of Greek plays include Sophocles' *Electra.* Among his writings are *The Idea of a Theatre* (1949), *The Human Image in Dramatic Literature* (1957), *Poems 1929–1961* (1962), and *Dante* (1966).

HENRI FRANKFORT (1897–1954) was a native of Holland. He was educated at the Universities of Amsterdam, Leiden, and London, and at the British School of Archeology at Athens. From 1929 to 1937 he was Field Director in Iraq for the Oriental Institute of the University of Chicago. Later he taught at the University of Chicago and, from 1949 until his death, at the University of London, where he was Director of the Warburg Institute and professor of the History of Preclassical Antiquity. Among his books are *Ancient Egyptian Religion, An Interpretation* (1948), *Before Philosophy, The Intellectual Adventure of Ancient Man* (1951), *The Art and Architecture of the Ancient Orient* (1955), and *The Birth of Civilization in the Near East* (1956).

MRS. H. A. FRANKFORT, also a native of Holland and her husband's collaborator, took her degree in philosophy at the University of Amsterdam, and was a member of Professor Frankfort's archeological expeditions.

BENJAMIN FRANKLIN (1706–1790) was printer and publisher, public servant and diplomat, man of letters, and philosopher. He is best known for his *Autobiography.* The current edition of his writings from Yale best shows his breadth and versatility.

JOHN HOPE FRANKLIN (1915–), historian, was educated at Fisk University and Harvard. He has taught at Harvard, Cambridge, and the University of Chicago, where he is professor of American history. Among other works, he has written *From Slavery to Freedom: A History of American Negroes* (2d edition, 1957), *Reconstruction After the Civil War* (1961), and *The Emancipation Proclamation* (1963).

SIGMUND FREUD (1856–1939), Viennese neurologist and psychologist and the founder of psychoanalysis, has exerted a profound influence on modern art, literature, and philosophy as well as on psychology and medicine. He is best known for such writings as *The Interpretation of Dreams* (1913) and *A General Introduction to Psychoanalysis* (1920).

ERICH FROMM (1900–) was born in Frankfurt, Germany. Trained in psychoanalysis in Munich and at the Psychoanalytic Institute in Berlin, he has devoted his time since 1925 to work as a clinical psychologist and partly to theoretical work especially in the field of the application of psychoanalytic theory to problems of culture and society. A naturalized American citizen, he now teaches at the National University of Mexico and at New York University. Among his books are *Escape from Freedom* (1941), *Man for Himself* (1947), *The Forgotten Language* (1951), *The Sane Society* (1955), and *The Heart of Man* (1964).

CLEMENT GREENBERG (1909–), art critic and consultant, has written books on Joan Miro, Henri Matisse, and Jackson Pollock. *Art and Culture* (1961) is a collection of critical essays by him.

LEARNED HAND (1872–1961) was born at Albany and educated at Harvard and the Harvard Law School. He was Judge of the United States Circuit Court, Second Circuit, from 1924 to 1951. Because of the probity and wisdom of his decisions, other lawyers, as well as the public, revere him as the dean of the American bar.

WILLIAM HARVEY (1578–1657), English physiologist and physician to Charles I, was educated at Cambridge and Padua. A series of experiments, now regarded as classic, led to his discovery and description of the circulation of the blood. *On the Motion of the Heart and Blood in Animals* was published under a Latin title in 1628.

ERNEST HEMINGWAY (1899–1961) began his career as a newspaper reporter in the Middle West. Few contemporary writers have been more influential, from his first book, *In Our Time* (1925), a collection of short stories, through novels like *A Farewell to Arms* (1929), to the posthumous volume of reminiscences of Paris, *A Moveable Feast* (1964).

GILBERT HIGHET (1906–), born in Scotland and a graduate of Glasgow and Oxford, came to the United States in 1937. A professor of Latin at Columbia, he is widely known for his radio and television talks. Among his books are *The Classical Tradition* (1949), *Poets in a Landscape* (1957), *The Powers of Poetry* (1960), and *The Anatomy of Satire* (1962).

ALFRED EDWARD HOUSMAN (1859–1936), distinguished English poet and classical scholar, was educated at Oxford, where he failed to receive honors and took a pass degree. In 1892 he became professor of Latin at University College, London, and in 1911, professor of Latin at Cambridge. His "Introductory Lecture" was delivered on the occasion of his becoming professor of Latin at University College. He edited Manilius, Juvenal, and Lucan. He ranks among the greatest classical scholars England has produced. But he is more highly esteemed by most readers for his three slender volumes of poems: *A Shropshire Lad* (1896), *Last Poems* (1922), and *More Poems* (1936).

ROBERT MAYNARD HUTCHINS (1899–), formerly president of the University of Chicago and now president of the Fund for the Republic, was educated at Oberlin and Yale. A controversial figure in American education, he has published many articles and books, among them *No Friendly Voice* (1936), *Education for Freedom* (1943), *The University of Utopia* (1953), and *Some Observations on American Education* (1956).

WILLIAM JAMES (1842–1910), educated in Europe and at the Harvard Medical School, became an internationally famous psychologist and philosopher. He founded at Harvard the first American psychology laboratory. He was the author of *Principles of Psychology, Pragmatism,* and *The Meaning of Truth.* With Charles S. Peirce, he founded the pragmatic school of philosophy.

THOMAS JEFFERSON (1743–1826) composed his own epitaph: "Here was buried Thomas Jefferson, Author of the Declaration of Independence, of the Statute of Virginia for Religious Freedom, and Father of the University of Virginia."

POPE JOHN XXIII (1881–1963), the 262d Supreme Pontiff of the Roman Catholic Church, was born Angelo Guiseppe Roncalli, eldest of thirteen children in a peasant family. Much of his life was spent outside Italy in the diplomatic service of the Church. In 1953 he was made Cardinal and Patriarch of Venice, and in 1958 he became Pope.

JOHN M. KEYNES (1883–1946), British economist, was educated at Eton and Cambridge. He served in the highest advisory posts of the British government and was a director of the Bank of England and a governor of the International Bank for Reconstruction and Development. *His Treatise on Money* (2 vols., 1930), has changed the economic thinking of the world. He also wrote *The End of Laissez-Faire* (1926) and *The General Theory of Employment, Interest, and Money* (1936).

ARTHUR KOESTLER (1905–), born in Hungary, has been a correspondent and a soldier in the French and British armies. Among his books are *Darkness at Noon*

(1941), *The Lotos and the Robot* (1960), *The Act of Creation* (1964), and *Janus, or the Ambiguity of Man* (1966).

SUSANNE LANGER (1895–), a graduate of Radcliffe (A.B., A.M., Ph.D.), is professor emerita of philosophy at Connecticut College. Her best known works are *Philosophy in a New Key* (1942) and its sequel *Feeling and Form* (1953). Recently she has written *Philosophical Sketches* (1962).

CLIVE STAPLES LEWIS (1898–1963), English novelist and essayist, was a fellow of Magdalen College, Oxford, where he lectured on English literature. He won acclaim for *The Screwtape Letters* (1942). He wrote parables, such as *Perelandra* (1943), fantasies, such as *That Hideous Strength* (1945), and a widely read series of children's books.

DAVID E. LILIENTHAL (1899–), businessman and government administrator, was educated at DePauw University and the Harvard Law School. Formerly director of TVA and chairman of the U.S. Atomic Energy Commission, since 1955 he has been chairman of Developmental Resources Corporation. Among his books are *TVA: Democracy on the March* (1944), *This I Do Believe* (1949), *Big Business, A New Era* (1953), and *The Multi-national Corporation* (1960).

SEYMOUR M. LIPSET (1922–), sociologist, was educated at the City College of New York and at Columbia, where he took his Ph.D. in 1949. He is professor of sociology at the University of California at Berkeley and director of the Institute of International Studies. He is author of many books, among which are *Social Mobility in Industrial Society* (1959), *Political Man* (1960), and *The First New Nation* (1963).

JOHN LOCKE (1632–1704) was an English philosopher whose writings turned from the subtleties of Aristotle and the Schoolmen and helped point the modern world toward experimental science. Locke has been called the father of English empiricism, and his influence on the development of psychology, philosophy, education, and political science has been tremendous. His principal philosophical work is *An Essay Concerning Human Understanding*. His two *Treatises of Government* denied the divine right of kings and justified the Revolution of 1688, thus indirectly providing justification for the American Revolution. He was probably the most influential English thinker of the seventeenth century, and his influence is still felt in Western democracies.

F. L. LUCAS (1894–), fellow and lecturer of King's College, Cambridge, is the author of poems, criticism, fiction, and plays. Two of his books are *The Decline and Fall of the Romantic Ideal* (1936) and *The Art of Living: Four Eighteenth-Century Minds* (1959).

MARCUS AURELIUS ANTONINUS (121–180), Roman emperor and philosopher, was one of the greatest Stoics. His *Meditations,* written in Greek, consist of twelve books of sage advice on conduct and living. Learned and gentle, he nevertheless opposed Christianity, even to the extent of persecuting Christians.

JACQUES MARITAIN (1882–), Catholic philosopher, was born in Paris and educated at the University of Paris and at Rome. In 1906, he was converted to Roman Catholicism, and since then he has been widely regarded as one of the most influential Catholic spokesmen in the world. For many years he has specialized in the scholastic philosophy of St. Thomas Aquinas, on which subject he has lectured at many of the great universities of the world. From 1948–1953 he was professor of philosophy at Princeton, and since 1953 he has been professor emeritus. Some of the most important of his many books are *The Person and the Common Good* (1947), *Existence and the Existent* (1948), *Man and the State* (1950), *The Range of Reason* (1952), *Creative Intuition in Art and Poetry* (1953), *Ap-*

proaches to God (1954), *The Responsibility of the Artist* (1960), and *Moral Philosophy* (1964).

SAINT MATTHEW (*fl.* 70 A.D.) was one of the twelve disciples of Christ and author of the Gospel of St. Matthew.

HENRY F. MAY (1915–), historian, was educated at the University of California and at Harvard, where he took the Ph.D. A professor at Berkeley, he has written *Protestant Churches and Industrial America* (1949), *The End of American Innocence* (1959), and *The Discontent of the Intellectuals* (1963).

WILLIAM M. MCCORD (1930–), sociologist, teaches at Rice University. He was educated at Stanford and Harvard, and has taught at Stanford and Stanford-in-France. He has been director of the mental health project of the National Institute of Mental Health and consultant to the Office of Scientific Research, U.S. Air Force. He is author of *Psychopathy and Delinqency* (1956), *Origins of Crime* (1959), *Origins of Alcoholism* (1960), *The Psychopath* (1964), and *The Springtime of Freedom: Evolution of Developing Societies* (1965).

VED MEHTA (1934–) is a young Indian writer, blind since the age of three, who was educated in England and the United States. He has written *Face to Face* (1957), autobiography, *Walking the Indian Streets* (1960), and *The New Theologian* (1966).

H. L. MENCKEN (1880–1956), critic, editor, and philologist, edited *The American Mercury* from 1924 until 1933, and long was associated with the *Baltimore Evening Sun.* His six series of *Prejudices* (1919–1927) exemplify his work as a critic, and *The American Language* (1918, with later revisions) is his philological masterpiece.

OGDEN NASH (1902–) has established himself as a leading humorous poet since *Hard Lines* appeared in 1931. Other titles are *The Face Is Familiar* (1940) and *The Christmas That Almost Wasn't* (1957). Recent collections are *Verses from 1929 On* (1959) and *Everyone But Thee and Me* (1962).

FRIEDRICH WILHELM NIETZSCHE (1844–1900), German philosopher and moralist, studied at Bonn and Leipsig, and taught at the University of Basel (1869–1879). Because of nervous disorders he gave up his professorship and lived in various places in Switzerland and Italy. In 1899 he became hopelessly insane, and spent the remainder of his life at Weimar under the care of his mother and his sister. Among his books are *The Birth of Tragedy* (1872), *Thus Spake Zarathustra* (1883–1884), and *Beyond Good and Evil* (1886).

ROBERT OPPENHEIMER (1904–), physicist, was Director of the Institute for Advanced Study at Princeton from 1947 to 1966. Born in New York City, he graduated from Harvard and did graduate work at Cambridge University and Göttingen, where he received the Ph.D. in 1927. After a distinguished teaching career at the University of California and the California Institute of Technology, he became Director of the Los Alamos Scientific Laboratory (1943–1945), where he guided the development and production of the first atomic bomb.

GEORGE ORWELL is the pseudonym of Eric Blair (1903–1950), British essayist and novelist. Among his best known books are *Animal Farm* (1954) and *1984* (1949).

THOMAS PAINE (1737–1809), American political philosopher, encouraged the American Revolution by publishing *Common Sense,* which called for an immediate declaration of independence (January 10, 1776), and *The Crisis,* twelve issues of which appeared during the course of the war. He is also the author of *The Rights of Man* and *The Age of Reason.*

ERWIN PANOFSKY (1899–) received his Ph.D. from the University of Freiburg in 1914. Recipient of many honorary degrees and awards, he has been a professor at the Institute for Advanced Study at Princeton since 1935. Among his books are *Studies in Iconology* (1939), *Early Netherlandish Painting* (1953), and *Tomb Sculpture* (1964).

C. NORTHCOTE PARKINSON (1909–), educated at Cambridge, was Raffles Professor of History at the University of Malaya from 1950 to 1958. Among his books are *Parkinson's Law* (1957), *Law and the Profits* (1960), *Inlaws and Outlaws* (1962), and *East and West* (1963). He has also taught at Harvard, Illinois, and Berkeley.

DONALD CULROSS PEATTIE (1898–) worked in the Department of Agriculture from 1922 to 1925. Since then, writing in the tradition of Agassiz and Thoreau, he has published many books on the natural scene in America, including *Audubon's America* (1940), *Lives of Destiny* (1954), and *Parade with Banners* (1957).

CHARLES S. PEIRCE (1839–1914), first outlined pragmatic philosophy in an essay in *Popular Science Monthly* in 1878. He lectured at Johns Hopkins and Harvard on logic and other philosophical subjects. Also a physicist and a mathematician, Peirce was perhaps the foremost logician of his age. He greatly influenced William James.

PLATO (428–347 B.C.), the Greek philosopher, was a pupil and admirer of Socrates. Most of his adult life was spent in teaching at Athens, his native city, and in the composition of his *Dialogues,* all of which are extant. The *Dialogues* are based on the teachings of Socrates, who figures largely in them as the conductor of the discussions.

DAVID M. RIESMAN (1909–), Henry Ford professor of social science at Harvard, was educated at Harvard College and Harvard Law School. After legal practice, he became a professor of the social science department at the University of Chicago in 1946. His most influential book is *The Lonely Crowd* (1950). Author of many articles, he has also written *Individualism Reconsidered and Other Essays* (1954), *Constraint and Variety in American Education* (1956), and *Abundance for What? and Other Essays* (1963).

PAUL ROBERTS (1917–), professor of English linguistics at Cornell University, has written *Understanding Grammar* (1954) and *Patterns of English* (1956). He has taught abroad, as *Cornflakes and Beaujolais* (1958) attests, and is expert in the teaching of English as a foreign language.

LEONARD Q. ROSS is the pseudonym of Leo Calvin Rosten (1908–), who, after beginning an academic career as English teacher and student in the social sciences, has been largely associated with motion-picture projects (since 1937). From this latter part of his career has come *Hollywood: the Movie Colony—the Movie Makers* (1941). He has edited *The Religions of America* (1955), and has written *The Return of H*y*m*a*n K*a*p*l*a*n* (1959), and *The Many Worlds of Leo Rosten* (1964).

BERTRAND RUSSELL (1872–), philosopher and mathematician, was educated at Cambridge. He has taught mathematics and philosophy at Cambridge, Harvard, the University of Chicago, and the University of California at Los Angeles. He is co-author with Alfred North Whitehead of *Principia Mathematica* (1910–1913). Among his other books are *Introduction to Mathematical Philosophy* (1919), *The Analysis of Matter, Philosophical Essays, Marriage and Morals, Education and the Social Order*. He has recently published *The Wisdom of the West* (1959), *Has Man a Future?* (1961), and *Unarmed Victory* (1963). His views on marriage and pacifism have at times involved him in controversies. Though he is an English nobleman, he refuses to use his title.

NATHANIEL SOUTHGATE SHALER (1841–1906), a Kentuckian by birth, was a distinguished American geologist. During most of his life he was identified with Harvard, and it was there that he studied with the great Louis Agassiz. He was graduated from Lawrence School of Science, Harvard, in 1862. After serving two years as an artillery officer in the Union Army, he taught at Harvard successively zoology, geology, and paleontology, becoming professor of geology in 1888, a position he held until his death. He was director of the Kentucky Geologic Survey. He wrote *A First Book in Geology, Aspects of the Earth, The Interpretation of Nature,* and *Man and Death.*

HARLOW SHAPLEY (1885–), distinguished American scientist, is Paine professor emeritus of astronomy at Harvard. He was educated at the University of Missouri and at Princeton, where he took his Ph.D. in 1913. Professor Shapley was director of the Harvard Observatory from 1921 to 1952. He is past president of the American Association for the Advancement of Science. Among his books are *Of Stars and Men* (1958) and *The View from a Distant Star* (1964).

ALAN SIMPSON (1912–), a graduate of Oxford University, is President of Vassar College. Formerly he was Dean of the College of the University of Chicago, where he was Thomas E. Donnelly professor of history. He has written *Puritanism in Old and New England* (1955) and *Wealth of the Gentry, 1540–1650* (1961).

ADLAI E. STEVENSON (1900–1965), twice Democratic candidate for President of the United States and later U.S. representative to the U.N., was educated at Princeton and Oxford. Lawyer, newspaper owner and editor, and holder of various Federal appointments, he was Governor of Illinois 1949–1953. Widely honored with degrees and awards, he achieved an affectionate place in the hearts of Americans as our most literate and sophisticated statesman.

FRANK SULLIVAN (1892–), a graduate of Cornell, is the author of humorous sketches collected under such titles as *A Pearl in Every Oyster* (1938), *A Rock in Every Snowball* (1946), *The Night the Old Nostalgia Burned Down* (1953), and *A Moose in the House* (1959).

JONATHAN SWIFT (1667–1745), greatest English prose satirist, was born in Dublin and educated at Trinity College. In addition to his masterpiece, *Travels into Several Remote Nations of the World,* commonly known as *Gulliver's Travels,* he is also the author of *A Tale of a Tub,* a brilliant satire on the divisions of the Christian Church, *The Battle of the Books, A Modest Proposal,* a masterpiece of irony, and *The Journal to Stella,* as well as a number of poems, most of which are humorous.

HAROLD TAYLOR (1914–), a graduate of the universities of Toronto and London, served as president of Sarah Lawrence College from 1945 to 1959. Two of his books are *On Education and Freedom* (1954) and *Art and the Intellect* (1960).

DYLAN THOMAS (1914–1953), Welsh poet, was the leader in neoromantic writing of the 1940s and a superb oral interpreter of his own and other poets' poetry. His first volume appeared in 1934; later books were *In Country Sleep* (1952) and *Under Milk Wood* (1954).

HENRY DAVID THOREAU (1817–1862) called himself "a mystic, a transcendental philosopher, and a natural philosopher to boot." His dominant individualism is evident in his most famous book, *Walden* (1854). It also appears, but tempered by a belief in acting collectively "according to the spirit of our institutions," in the three John Brown speeches (1859–1860) and *Life Without Principle* (1863) as well as in the essay printed here.

THUCYDIDES (c. 471–c. 400 B.C.), greatest of the ancient historians, wrote *The*

History of the Peloponnesian War. He served his native Athens as a commander in the Peloponnesian War.

JAMES THURBER (1894–1961), one of the best contemporary humorists and cartoonists, was educated at Ohio State University. After working on several newspapers, he joined the staff of *The New Yorker,* where he was for a time managing editor. Later he wrote the "Talk of the Town" for the same magazine. Until his death he was a frequent contributor to *The New Yorker.* He wrote *My Life and Hard Times* (1933), *Let Your Mind Alone* (1937), *The Male Animal* (1940), *Fables for Our Times* (1941), *My World—and Welcome to It!* (1944), and others.

LIONEL TRILLING (1905–) is the author of a novel, *The Middle of the Journey* (1947), and of short stories that have frequently been anthologized. Critical volumes by him include *E. M. Forster* (1943), *The Liberal Imagination* (1950), and *Beyond Culture: Essays on Learning and Literature* (1965). He has been a professor of English at Columbia University since 1948.

ROBERT PENN WARREN (1905–), a graduate of Vanderbilt and California and a Rhodes Scholar at Oxford, is a poet, critic, and novelist. Among his works are *Brother to Dragons* (1953), *Flood* (1964), and *Who Speaks for the Negro?* (1965). His major teaching appointments have been at Minnesota and Yale, where he has been professor of English since 1961.

RENÉ WELLEK (1903–) received his Ph.D. from Charles University, Prague, in 1926. Sterling professor of comparative literature at Yale and chairman of the department, he is the author (with Austin Warren) of the influential *Theory of Literature* (1949). Four volumes of *A History of Modern Criticism* have appeared since 1955, and the work will be completed with a fifth volume on critics of the twentieth century.

E. B. WHITE (1899–), essayist, lives at North Brooklyn, Maine. Born in Mt. Vernon, New York, he was educated at Cornell. He began his career as a reporter. Formerly a contributor to *Harper's,* he has been for a number of years a contributing editor of *The New Yorker.* In addition to his frequent contributions to magazines, he has written many books: *Is Sex Necessary?* (in collaboration with James Thurber), *One Man's Meat* (1944), *Stuart Little* (1945), *Charlotte's Web* (1952), *The Second Tree from the Corner* (1953), and *The Points of My Compass* (1962).

JOHN WOOLMAN (1720–1772), Quaker preacher and author, was born in New Jersey, where he was apprenticed to a tailor. He traveled widely throughout the Colonies, visiting meetings of the Friends and denouncing slavery. His most famous work is his *Journal,* which gives an account of these activities. It has been frequently reprinted and is much praised for its style. Charles Lamb once suggested that aspiring writers "get Woolman's writings by heart."

FRANK LLOYD WRIGHT (1869–1959) began his illustrious career in 1893 at Chicago. *An Autobiography—Frank Lloyd Wright* (1932, rev. 1943) tells the long story of his struggle in establishing modern architecture.

Index

Allegory of the Cave, The, 697
American Crisis, I, The, 538
American Language, The, 118
Anatomy of the Mental Personality, The, 576
Apology of Socrates, The, 591
Aristotle, 301
ARISTOTLE, 307, 625
Art and Neurosis, 332
AUGUSTINE, SAINT, 657
AURELIUS, MARCUS, 636
Autobiography of Benjamin Franklin, The, 95

BACON, FRANCIS, 68, 201
BARRETT, WILLIAM C., 716
BATE, WALTER JACKSON, 301
BEADLE, GEORGE AND MURIEL, 404
BELL, DANIEL, 476
BERNARD, CLAUDE, 401
BISHOP, MORRIS, 92
BONHOEFFER, DIETRICH, 680
BOOTH, WAYNE C., 135
BROOKS, CLEANTH, 277
BROWN, ROLLO WALTER, 22
BUBER, MARTIN, 666
BUCHWALD, ART, 42
BUDDHA, GAUTAMA, 640
Burnt Norton, 97
BYWATER, INGRAM, 307

Carbon Monoxide Poisoning, 401
Case for Abstract Art, The, 218
Changing American Character?, A, 419
Changing Place of Women in America, The, 491
Chlorophyll: The Sun Trap, 396
Cliché Expert Reveals Himself in His True Colors, The, 115
Confessions, The, 657
Confession of Faith, 670
COPLAND, AARON, 253
CRANE, R. S., 290
Crime in America, 506
Cultural Importance of the Arts, The, 210
Cultural Snobbery, 258

DAVIS, ROBERT GORHAM, 193
Declaration of Independence, 544
DEGLER, CARL, N., 491
DESCARTES, RENÉ, 700
Discourse on Method, A, 700
Do Computers Think?, 185
DONNE, JOHN, 659
DREYFUS, HUBERT L., 185

EDDINGTON, ARTHUR STANLEY, 375
ELIOT, T. S., 97, 349
Emancipation of Thought from Myth, The, 144
Essay Concerning Human Understanding, An, 707
Et in Arcadia ego: Poussin and The Elegiac Tradition, 225
Evolution of the Physical World, The, 375
Existentialism as a Symptom of Man's Contemporary Crisis, 716

FERGUSSON, FRANCIS, 295
Folly of Man, The, 646
For Want of a Teacher, 42
Formation of Character, The, 450
FRANKFORT, H. and H. A., 144
FRANKLIN, BENJAMIN, 95
FRANKLIN, JOHN HOPE, 519
FREUD, SIGMUND, 576
From an Interview, 99
FROMM, ERICH, 731
Funeral Oration of Pericles, The, 612

God and the Spirit of Man, 666
God Is Dead, 661
GREENBERG, CLEMENT, 218

HAND, LEARNED, 571
HARVEY, WILLIAM, 394
HEMINGWAY, ERNEST, 99
HIGHET, GILBERT, 154
HOUSMAN, A. E., 64
How Agassiz Taught Shaler, 19
How to Make Our Ideas Clear, 358
How We Listen, 253
HUTCHINS, ROBERT M., 56, 169

Idols of the Mind, 201
In His Will Is Our Peace, 660
In My Craft or Sullen Art, 98
Injelititis, or Palsied Paralysis, 163
Introductory Lecture, 64

JAMES, WILLIAM, 710
JEFFERSON, THOMAS, 544
JOHN XXIII, POPE, 688

KEYNES, JOHN MAYNARD, 378
Kittredge of Harvard, 22
KOESTLER, ARTHUR, 258

Laments for a Dying Language, 113
LANGER, SUSANNE K., 173, 210
Language and Thought, 173
Language of Life: The Structure of DNA, The, 404
Lesson Read in American Books, A, 346
Letters from Prison, 680
LEWIS, C. S., 86
LILIENTHAL, DAVID E., 513
LIPSET, SEYMOUR M., 419
LOCKE, JOHN, 707
Logical Fallacies, 193
LUCAS, F. L., 100

Macbeth as the Imitation of an Action, 295
Main Trends of Twentieth-Century Criticism, The, 264
Man's Fourth Adjustment, 390
MARCUS AURELIUS, 636
MARITAIN, JACQUES, 670
Marks of an Educated Man, The, 44
MATTHEW, SAINT, 632

MAY, HENRY F., 32
MC CORD, WILLIAM M., 506
Meaning and Significance of Academic Freedom, The, 56
Meditation XVII, 659
MEHTA, VED, 177
MENCKEN, H. L., 118
Mr. K*a*p*l*a*n and Shakespeare, 81
Modern Architecture: The Cardboard House, 243
Modernity and Mass Society: On the Varieties of Cultural Experience, 476
Modest Proposal, A, 618

Naked Babe and the Cloak of Manliness, The, 277
NASH, OGDEN, 113
Newton the Man, 378
NIETZSCHE, FRIEDRICH, 661

Of the Quantity of Blood Passing through the Heart, 394
Of Studies, 68
On Albert Einstein, 385
On the Duty of Civil Disobedience, 548
On Misreading By the Literary, 86
On Teaching the Appreciation of Poetry, 349
OPPENHEIMER, ROBERT, 385
ORWELL, GEORGE, 125

Pacem in Terris, 688
PAINE, THOMAS, 538
PANOFSKY, ERWIN, 225
PARKINSON, C. NORTHCOTE, 163
PEATTIE, DONALD CULROSS, 396
PEIRCE, CHARLES, 358
PLATO, 591, 697
Plea for the Freedom of Dissent, A, 571
Poetics, 307
Politics and the English Language, 125
POPE JOHN, XXIII, 688
Postscript, 1965, 16
Present Human Condition, The, 731
Private World of the Man with a Book, The, 69
Providence of God, The, 647

Reading, 75
Reading Machine, The, 92
Review of Riesman's *The Lonely Crowd,* 471
Revival of Rhetoric, The, 135
RIESMAN, DAVID, 5, 16, 450
ROBERTS, PAUL, 107
ROSS, LEONARD Q., 81
RUSSELL, BERTRAND, 727

SAINT AUGUSTINE, 657
SAINT MATTHEW, 632
Sermon at Benares, The, 640
Sermon on the Mount, The, 632
SHALER, NATHANIEL SOUTHGATE, 19
SHAPLEY, HARLOW, 390
SIMPSON, ALAN, 44
STEVENSON, ADLAI E., 49
Stoic Code, The, 636
Strength and Glory of Man, The, 646
Structure of *Macbeth,* The, 290
Student Movement, Some Impressions at Berkeley, The, 32
SULLIVAN, FRANK, 115
SWIFT, JONATHAN, 618

TAYLOR, HAROLD, 69
That Candles May Be Brought, 169
[Thinker: Wittgenstein, A], 177
THOMAS, DYLAN, 98
THOREAU, HENRY DAVID, 75, 548
300,000,000 Americans Would Be Wrong, 513

THUCYDIDES, 612
THURBER, JAMES, 1
Trained Intelligence—The Nation's Greatest Weapon, 49
Transformational Grammar, 107
TRILLING, LIONEL, 332, 471
Two Worlds of Race: A Historical View, The, 519

University Days, 1
Unpredictable Intellect, The, 154
Upanishads: Svetasvatara, 648

Value of Philosophy, The, 727
Virtue, 625

Walden—1954, 564
WARREN, ROBERT PENN, 346
WELLEK, RENÉ, 264
What is Style?, 100
What Pragmatism Is, 710
Where is the College Generation Headed?, 5
WHITE, E. B., 564
WOOLMAN, JOHN, 660
WRIGHT, FRANK LLOYD, 243